ESSENTIAL KNOWLEDGE

Readings in Epistemology

* * *

Edited by

STEVEN LUPER

Trinity University

PEARSON
Longman

New York   San Francisco   Boston
London   Toronto   Sydney   Tokyo   Singapore   Madrid
Mexico City   Munich   Paris   Cape Town   Hong Kong   Montreal

⟡

*I dedicate this volume to the memories of Robert Nozick,
W. V. O. Quine, and Roderick Firth, my honored teachers.*

⟡

Vice President and Publisher: Priscilla McGeehon
Marketing Manager: Wendy Albert
Production Manager: Douglas Bell
Project Coordination and Electronic Page Makeup: Elm Street Publishing Services, Inc.
Cover Design Manager: John Callahan
Cover Designer: Maria Ilardi
Manufacturing Buyer: Lucy Hebard
Printer and Binder: Hamilton Printing Co.
Cover Printer: Phoenix Color Corporation

For permission to use copyrighted material, grateful acknowledgement is made to the copyright
holders on page 504 which is hereby made part of this copyright page.

Library of Congress Cataloging-in-Publication Data

Essential knowledge : readings in epistemology / edited by Steven Luper.
    p. cm.
  ISBN 0-321-10641-5 (alk. paper)
  1. Knowledge, Theory of. I. Luper, Steven.
BD161.E75 2003
121–dc21

                                  2003044739

Please visit our website at http://www.ablongman.com

ISBN 0-321-10641-5

1 2 3 4 5 6 7 8 9 10—HT—06 05 04 03

✧ CONTENTS ✧

PART I. HISTORICAL READINGS

PART II. CONTEMPORARY READINGS

✧ PREFACE ✧

Essential Knowledge is designed to introduce students and general readers to the theory of knowledge. Part I includes selections from historically influential writers, such as Plato, Sextus, Descartes, the British empiricists, Kant, and the pragmatists; while Part II provides selections from the best of contemporary epistemology, organized topically. A general introduction to the field appears at the beginning of the volume. It orients the newcomer to the issues discussed in the selections. Each chapter begins with a brief introduction that places the essays in context and discusses their significance. Readers will also find a set of Questions for Reflection at the end of each chapter, and suggested Further Readings at the end of the book.

While I have tried to provide a broad range of materials, I have also tried to keep the overall length of the volume within manageable bounds. All too often introductory texts include far more material than can be covered in a semester, and given the high costs of reprinting materials, texts have grown more and more expensive.

Several selections were written or revised especially for the volume. New essays were written by Stewart Cohen, Richard Foley, and Peter Klein. Richard Feldman and Earl Conee contributed a revised version of their essay "Evidentialism." In addition, Louise Antony provided an abridged version of her essay, "Quine as Feminist," and John Greco provided a condensed version of his essay, "Virtues in Epistemology."

Not all instructors will want to use the materials gathered here in the same order. There are many ways to recombine the selections. For instance, some instructors will combine the materials in Part I with the selections in Part II. The selections from Plato's *Meno* and *Republic* and from Locke's *Essay* go well with readings in Chapter 3, on the analysis of knowledge; the excerpts from Plato's *Theaetetus* go naturally with Chapter 9, on relativism and subjectivism. The Sextus, Berkeley, and Descartes selections go well with Chapter 5, on skepticism. Peirce can easily be read in connection with Chapter 4, on justification, and Kant in connection with Chapter 8, on a priori knowledge. There are good reasons, moreover, to cover the chapters of Part II in the following order: 9 (because most of the selections in other chapters presuppose that there is objective, nonrelative truth), 3, 4, then 6 and 7 (since these cover topics that bear on the analysis of knowledge and justification), 8, and 5.

Many of the essays discuss views taken in other chapters; a great deal of cross-chapter dialogue occurs; this will lead some instructors to want to rearrange readings around issues in which they have special interest. For example, the theme of reliabilism, as an account of knowledge or justification, is touched on in Chapter 3 by Klein, Goldman and Nozick, in Chapter 4 by Goldman, in 5 by Dretske, Lewis, and Luper, and in 6 by Armstrong, Conee and Feldman, and Goldman. The theme of externalism comes up repeatedly: it is discussed in Chapter 3 by Goldman and Nozick, in 4 by

Goldman, Feldman and Conee, and Greco, in 5 by Dretske, in 6 by all the essays, and in 7 by most of the essays. Similar points hold for the topics of skepticism and many other topics.

In editing *Essential Knowledge*, I have incurred many debts. I am especially grateful to the colleagues who wrote essays for the volume. I also thank Priscilla McGeehon of Longman for suggesting the project, Cathy Schultz for her expertise in editing it, and the following reviewers who provided helpful advice about the contents of the volume:

Robert Almeder, Georgia State University; Murat Bac, Dalhousie University; John W. Bender, Ohio University; Andrew Botterell, Sonoma State University; Joseph Cruz, Williams College; Bruce Hauptli, Florida International University; Deborah Heikes, University of Alabama in Huntsville; Stephen Phillips, University of Texas; Saul Traiger, Occidental College; Bruce Umbaugh, Webster University; and Michael Wreen, Marquette University.

Finally, I thank Jennifer Westrick and Rosemary O'Connor for their help in putting together the manuscript and in seeking reprint permissions.

Steven Luper

The Main Project

The subject of this book is epistemology. Epistemology is the theory of knowledge, the study of the nature, sources, and limitations of knowledge and justification. In studying the nature of knowledge and justification, theorists typically try to delineate the conditions that must be met for a given person to know, or justifiably believe, that a given proposition is true. That is, they offer analyses of knowledge and justification. In this introduction, we will briefly describe the task of analysis, and review some of the ways people have understood knowledge and justification. We will also outline some of the difficulties theorists have confronted while working out what may be known.

The Analysis of Knowledge

Sometimes when people speak of knowledge, they mean to refer to various skills or abilities, such as are displayed when we know *how* to perform some task (Ryle, 1949). For example, I know *how* to ride a bicycle. This type of knowledge we might refer to as *ability* knowledge. A different sort of knowledge is involved in knowing *that* something is the case. For example, I know that snow is white. This we might call *propositional* knowledge. Epistemologists are interested primarily in propositional knowledge as opposed to ability knowledge.

As usually understood, a *proposition* is an abstract object; it is that which a declarative sentence expresses. For example, the words *Snow is white* express the proposition that snow is white, and the same proposition is expressed by the German equivalent of these words, namely, *Schnee ist weiss*. Propositions purport to describe the world, and true propositions do so accurately. Moreover, when you and I accept the same belief, we are linked to the same proposition through the relationship or belief.

Knowledge (and justified belief) can be classified in terms of the types of propositions believed. For example, there is knowledge of *necessary truths*, such as 2 + 2 + 4, which are propositions that cannot fail to be true, and knowledge of *contingent truths*, such as Bush is President, which are propositions that, while true, might have been false. Philosophers sometimes express the distinction between necessity and contingency in terms of possible worlds. A necessary truth is a proposition that holds in all possible worlds. A contingent truth is a proposition that holds in only some possible worlds. What is a possible world? Well, one example is the actual world. Imagine setting out a complete description of the world, a set of statements that lay out, in a completely accurate way, everything that was, is, and will be the case. This complex description says everything there is to say about the actual world. It also characterizes a possible world, in that none of the statements in the description is inconsistent with the others. But the actual world is not the only possible world. We can arrive at other possible worlds by starting with our description of the actual world and altering some of the statements in its description, being careful not to introduce contradictions. For example, there is a possible world that differs from the actual world in that you did not read this book.

Knowledge can also be classified in terms of its sources. A *posteriori* or *empirical* knowledge is based on experience. The source of a priori or *nonempirical* knowledge is thought or reason. Your knowledge that you are reading this book is *a posteriori* because it is based on experience. By contrast, it seems possible to know that 2 + 2 = 4 with out consulting experience. Unaided reason informs us that 2 + 2 = 4, so we know it a priori.

Epistemologists, like mathematicians, often use symbols to make their ideas clear. Most of us recall letting the letter 'c' stand for the longest length of a right triangle, and 'a' and 'b' for the lengths of the other two sides, so that we can express the formula, $a^2 + b^2 = c^2$, which holds for any right triangle, regardless of its size. Epistemologists do something similar when they use 'p' (or 'P') to stand for an arbitrary proposition, and the symbol 'S' to stand for a person or subject. When we want to distinguish among propositions, we can use 'p' for one and 'q' or 'r' and so forth for the other. Accordingly,

S believes p

means that an arbitrary person S believes that an arbitrary proposition p is true.

When theorists attempt to clarify the conditions under which knowledge and justification exist, they are trying to set forth the essential ingredients in knowledge and justification. They are offering ways of completing the blanks in the following two schemata:

S knows p if and only if _____ is the case.

S's belief p is justified if and only if _____ is the case.

Let's break these schemata down a bit more by clarifying the phrase 'if and only if'.

Saying something of the form,

p if and only if q

is simply another way of asserting that both

p if q

and

p only if q

are true. By way of illustration, consider the following two claims, which are true:

a. I am a bachelor if I am an unmarried male.
b. I am a bachelor only if I am an unmarried male.

Claim (a) means the same thing as

If I am an unmarried male, then I am a bachelor.

Claim (b), on the other hand, means the same thing as

If I am a bachelor, then I am an unmarried male.[1]

So it follows from (a) and (b) together that I am a bachelor if and only if I am an unmarried male.

In discussing analyses of knowledge, it is useful to use another bit of terminology: the terms *necessary* and *sufficient* condition. To say proposition p is a necessary condition for proposition q is to say that if p is false then so is q. For example, being over 5 feet tall is a necessary condition for being 6 feet tall. And to say that proposition p is a sufficient condition for proposition q is to say that if p is true then so is q. An example: being 6 feet tall is a *sufficient condition* for being over 5 feet tall. When theorists fill in the blank of the schema

S knows p if and only if _____ is the case,

they are trying to supply conditions that are individually necessary and jointly sufficient for S to know p.

To better familiarize ourselves with the task of analysis, let us consider some proposed conditions for knowledge—some proposals for filling in the above blank.

The Standard Conditions for Knowledge

What conditions must be met for knowledge to exist? Three suggestions come to mind: the truth condition, the belief condition, and the justification condition. Let us discuss each in turn.

The Truth Condition   Almost everyone will grant that if we know a proposition is true, then it *is* true. That is, the following is a necessary condition for S to know p:

p is true.

Call this the truth condition.

But what is truth? The matter is quite controversial, but there are three main views. First, the *correspondence theory* (Moore 1953, Russell 1910) says that truth is a relationship between a proposition (or sentence) and the world whereby elements of the former in some way correlate to elements of the latter, in much the same way that objects and their features correlate to their reflections in mirrors. Unfortunately, it has proven difficult to state clearly what sort of correspondence constitutes truth. Some theorists try to make do with a principle suggested by Alfred Tarski (1944). Tarski pointed out that however truth is defined, it must be consistent with the following condition: the statement, "Snow is white" is true if and only if snow is white; the statement, "Coal is black" is true if and only if coal is black; and so on, for all statements. Notice that when "Snow is white" is placed within quotation marks, it refers to a statement; otherwise, it refers to the state of affairs of snow being white. Thus Tarski's principle suggests to some theorists that what makes statements true is a corresponding state of affairs, but the matter is controversial.

A second view called the *coherence theory* of truth (Blandshard 1939) says that statements are made true by cohering with others to form a comprehensive worldview. However, advocates have had a great deal of trouble in clarifying the notion of coherence without drawing on the notion of truth, which would make their account ultimately *circular*. An analysis or definition is circular when it uses the very term it purports to analyze or define. If, when asked to define the term '*ixapitl*,' I say it refers to anything that has the property of ixapitlness, my account is unhelpful because it is circular. If coherentists were to draw on the idea of truth when they clarified "truth," no one without a prior acquaintance with the idea of truth could understand the account that is supposed to clarify the idea of truth. Coherentists have also been plagued by the charge that there are too many coherent schemes of claims, each mutually inconsistent. If two or more schemes are mutually inconsistent, they cannot all be true.

A third account, the *pragmatic theory*, comes in at least two versions. The first, developed by Charles Peirce (1877b), says that "the opinion which is fated to be ultimately agreed to by all who investigate, is what we mean by the truth." A second, defended by William James (1896), says statements are made true when accepting them helps us to accomplish useful goals, such as the aim of making sense of experience. Many charge that such pragmatic criteria for truth are too weak: can't we imagine false claims that would be accepted by inquirers even in the long run? Aren't there false claims that would serve all sorts of useful goals?

While the nature of truth is very controversial, there is widespread agreement that truth is necessary for knowledge. The truth condition implies that we can never know a claim is true if in fact it is false. And this seems plausible. If the earth is *not* flat, then I do not know that it *is* flat.

If we object to the truth condition, the chances are we are confused about its implications. Consider, for example, the worry that the truth condition makes it impossible to decide whether we know something, since, in order to know it, we must first establish that it is true, which is tantamount to establishing that we know it! To see where this objection goes wrong, we must distinguish between the conditions under which a claim is true, and a practical procedure for verifying that the claim is true. Consider, as an example, the claim that I am an alien—an extraterrestrial life form, not a citizen of a different country—who looks and acts just like a human being. As a condition for my being an alien, we might use this: I am a member of a life form that evolved outside the earth. Meeting this condition seems to be a necessary and a sufficient condition for my being an alien. But it does not supply a practical way for you to verify that I am an alien if I have clever ways of hiding my origins. Similarly, there can be conditions for knowing *p* that are difficult in practice to verify. In analyzing knowledge, we are not attempting to set out a practical test for knowledge.

Related points are these: first, truth is not a condition that *we* must meet in order to know that a proposition is true. Rather, it is a condition that the *proposition we believe* must meet. Second, in a certain way, *I know my name is Steve* is like *I killed Fred*: the logic of success applies to the concepts of knowledge and killing. No matter what I do to Fred, I have not *killed* him unless he really is dead; similarly, no matter what I do, I do not know that something is true unless I get it right.

The Belief Condition If we know *p*, then we believe *p*. That is, S knows *p* only if the following condition is met:

S believes *p*.

The belief condition is widely accepted, but is a bit more controversial than the truth condition. Some have argued that knowledge entails states of mind that are very similar to, but not quite the same as, belief. Some of the proposed substitutes are states of psychological certainty (Ayer 1956), conviction (Lehrer 1974), and acceptance (Lehrer 1989). And some challenge the belief condition on the grounds that knowing and believing are incompatible (Plato, Duncan-Jones 1938) or at least separable (Radford 1966). Duncan-Jones points out that we say things like, "I don't believe the trade center towers were destroyed, I *know* it!," which might suggest that 'belief' applies only when an opinion is held on weak grounds, so that a belief state is not compatible with knowledge. But examples like this hardly show that believing excludes knowing. It is still possible that knowing involves believing plus something else, such as good evidence.

So far we have mentioned two conditions, each *necessary* for knowledge. Let us pause a moment and ask the following question: are the truth and belief conditions jointly *sufficient* for knowledge? If we say that these two conditions jointly suffice for knowledge, we would be making an assertion of the following sort:

If *p* is true *and* S believes *p*, then S knows *p*.

Is this assertion correct? No, we can easily see that it is not. Imagine that we are lost in a desert and we decide whether there is water just beyond a hill to the north by tossing a coin, telling ourselves that if the coin comes up heads then there is water beyond the hill, and otherwise there is not. We toss the coin; it comes up heads, so we believe that there is water. By dumb luck, it turns out there *is* water beyond the hill. But it is clear that we do not know there is water over the hill. Our belief is true, but only by sheer coincidence. For a belief to count as knowledge, it is not enough that it be true.

The Justification Condition   What more is required? The matter is controversial. But a preliminary answer is this: Our belief *p* must be *justified*. We must have substantial grounds for believing *p*. Admittedly, a person who predicts the presence of water on the basis of a coin toss can be said to have 'grounds' for believing what they do. However, these grounds are poor indeed, and it takes substantial grounds to position ourselves for knowing things.

Justification

Justification is clearly an ingredient of knowledge, but the notion of justification is itself the subject of much debate in epistemology. At the heart of the controversy are two questions: What makes something justification? What is the structure of justification?

What Makes For Justification?

One way to answer the question, What constitutes justification? is to relate it back to the analysis of knowledge. Whatever else justification is, it seems clear that it is something that helps convert a true belief into knowledge. So what must be added to a true belief if it is to count as knowledge?

A great many people (for example, Feldman and Conee 1985, 2003) think of justification as evidence that a proposition is true. This longstanding view is sometimes called *evidentialism*. The notion of evidence is sometimes cashed out in terms of entailment, for generally we will say that *e* is evidence for *p* when *e entails p*; that is, when *p* cannot possibly be false if *e* holds. But we rarely have this kind of evidence for our beliefs. An alternative is that *e* is evidence for *p* when *e* is the *best explanation* that *p* is true. For example, if the best explanation of facts about the crime scene (shoe prints left outside the broken window, a written will involving lots of money, and so on) is that Jeeves the butler murdered Mrs. Bigbucks, we are justified in believing that Jeeves did it. Following up on this idea, theorists (for example, Quine and Ullian 1970) have tried to clarify the conditions under which one explanation is superior to another. In doing so they help us to understand the notion of evidence.

Some theorists try to elucidate the idea of justification by emphasizing its normative or evaluative dimension (Alston 1985). Perhaps, for example, we are justified in believing *p* when it is epistemically permissible (permissible insofar as we adopt the role of knowers) for us to believe *p*, which means roughly that we violate no epistemic rules when we believe *p*. Here justification is treated as a *deontological* concept, a concept concerned with duty. Or perhaps we are justified in believing *p* when believing *p* facilitates our achieving some suitable epistemic aim, such as the goal of constructing an accurate view of reality, or the goal of maximizing our true beliefs while minimizing our false beliefs. Here justification is treated as a *teleological* concept, a concept concerned with goal attainment.

Finally, some theorists (Goldman 1976b) attempt to explain justification in terms of reliable methods or processes that generate or support beliefs. The main idea is that a method of belief formation is reliable when it tends to produce mostly true beliefs rather than false ones, and a belief is justified when it is generated by a reliable method of belief formation. This is known as the *reliabilist theory of justification*.

The Structure of Justification

However we understand its *ingredients*, we face questions about the *structure* of justification. Chief among these is the question of whether epistemically viable beliefs rest on a foundation. Theorists called *foundationalists* say respectable beliefs must have a foundation, while others called *coherentists* say they need not.

Foundationalism Traditionally, philosophers have held that epistemically respectable beliefs are arranged in a hierarchy in which higher beliefs depend for their justification on lower beliefs (Descartes 1641, Quinton 1973, Chisholm 1966, 1982, Alston 1976, Audi 1993). (For example, your belief that you are reading a book seems to rest on more fundamental beliefs, such as your seeming to see a book, your seeming to see words on its pages, and so forth.) The exception is the beliefs at the base of the hierarchy: they are justified, but not in terms of any other beliefs. (Your belief that you *seem* to see a book might be an example of a basic belief.) The beliefs forming the base of the hierarchy are called *basic*, or *foundational* beliefs, and the kind of justification they possess is called *noninferential* justification (or *basic* or *foundational* or *self* justification). Derivative beliefs are called *nonbasic* (or *nonfoundational*) and the form of justification a belief acquires from other beliefs is called *inferential* justification (or *nonbasic* or *nonfoundational* justification).

The traditional, foundationalist, view is that some of our beliefs have sufficient noninferential support to qualify as adequately justified, and that the justification of basic beliefs can be transferred to nonbasic beliefs, making adequate inferential justification

possible. The first foundationalists, such as René Descartes, insisted that basic beliefs are *incorrigible*: we cannot be wrong when we believe them. Contemporary foundationalists rarely defend incorrigibilism; they are more likely to be *fallibilists* who say that basic beliefs have enough justification to support other claims but not enough to completely rule out the possibility of error. But for both incorrigibilists and fallibilists, justification is linear, since each belief is supported by the beliefs on which it rests and ultimately by basic beliefs.

Foundationalists face the task of clarifying how basic justification is possible, and how (and which) nonbasic beliefs can be justified in terms of basic beliefs. Often, foundationalists try to explain basic justification in terms of the relationship between beliefs and certain (other) psychological states. For example, my *seeming to see a table*, which is a psychological state, could be said to support my belief that a table is before me. But critics attempt to impale this explanation on the horns of a dilemma, as follows: either the relationship between a psychological state and the belief it 'supports' is inferential (I infer there is a table on the basis of being in the psychological state of seemingly seeing a table) or it is causal (seemingly seeing a table causes me to believe there is a table). If the former, then foundationalists have not really given us an account of *basic* justification, for an inferred belief is not basic. But if the relationship is causal, then the foundationalist's explanation fails, since the causal relationship is not a justificatory relationship. After all, a certain sort of blow to the head might cause me to believe there are tables in front of me (or stars before my eyes), but undergoing such a blow does not justify me in believing anything about tables.

Foundationalists have also offered the *reliabilist* account of basic justification, according to which the justified status of basic beliefs derives from the reliability of their source. A basic belief is said to be justified by the reliability of its source, not by the further belief that the belief source is reliable. So a belief can be justified by the reliability of its source even if we are wholly unaware of the source's reliability. But critics question the view that justification can derive from aspects of the world of which we are unaware. For example, it seems possible to imagine that Claire the Clairvoyant truly has a reliable source for beliefs of a certain sort—say beliefs about her dog. If people like Claire existed, the reliabilist would have to say that their (dog) beliefs are justified. But unless she has grounds for thinking that she has such a reliable source, it is worrisome to say that her beliefs really are justified. And, of course, if she does have grounds, her beliefs would then be inferential, not basic.

Coherentism   Many (perhaps most) epistemologists are unhappy with the idea of basic justification. According to the *coherentist* theory (Bosanquet 1920, Sellars 1973, BonJour 1985), justification is structured not as an edifice but rather as a web or mesh. The whole web is justified because of many justificatory interconnections among the beliefs constituting the web, and individual beliefs are justified because they are part of such a web. The tighter the justificatory interconnections among the component beliefs, the more *coherent* the web as a whole is said to be. On this view, the justification of individual beliefs is circular rather than linear. For while belief 1 might receive support from belief 2, and 2 from 3, belief 3 might also receive support from belief 1. But coherentists maintain that circular justification can be proper, so long as a set of beliefs forms a substantial and tightly woven system, like the threads of a web, or, like Haack (1997) suggests, like the pieces of a complex puzzle. The task for coherentists is to clarify which sorts of interrelationships constitute coherence, and to make it clear why such interrelationships constitute support. While coherentism is a work in progress, there is agreement that coherence is enhanced by the relations of entailment and explanation: coherence is enhanced, that is, to the extent that the beliefs in a web are mutually explanatory, or mutually entailing. Still, critics charge that a great many sets of beliefs are, individually, highly coherent; collectively, these sets of beliefs are mutually incompatible, and hence not all of them can be rationally acceptable.

Typically, coherentists say that a belief is justi-fied only if there are positive grounds (derived from other beliefs in the web) for thinking it is true; that is, only if holding it makes the web significantly more coherent. This view might be called *positive co-herentism*. But some theorists (Peirce 1877, Harman 1986) say that a belief is justified (or rational) so long as there are not positive grounds for thinking it is false; that is, a belief is justified unless holding it makes the web significantly less coherent. This posi-tion can be called *negative coherentism*.

Structural Contextualism   Some theorists (Wittgenstein 1969, Annis 1978) claim that some groundless beliefs (ones that lack any justification, whether basic or nonbasic), which are selected by the context, can justify other beliefs. Thus, for example, given the context of home construction, carpenters take it for granted that wood will continue to be rigid and will not suddenly become as weak as cotton candy; they do not need to justify their beliefs about the fundamental properties of wood for these beliefs to serve as justifying grounds for other beliefs, such as the belief that a certain configuration of two-by-fours will support a roof. This view might be called *structural contextualism*.

Structural contextualism is not the view that, in the modern philosophical literature, most com-monly bears the name 'contextualism'. As we shall see in Chapter 4, the name 'contextualism' gener-ally refers to one version of the view that the stan-dards which a given person S's beliefs must meet in order to qualify as justified or known vary from con-text to context. For ordinary purposes, such as my efforts to landscape my house, relatively weak stan-dards must be met if I am to know such things as that the plant outside my window is a persimmon tree, but in the context of a scientific investigation, tighter standards are appropriate. Some theorists, whom we might call *agent-centered* contextualists, say that the applicable standards vary depending on the context of the person (say, S) whose belief is as-sessed. Other theorists (Lewis 1979, 1996; Cohen 1988, 1998; DeRose 1995), whom we may call *speaker-centered* contextualists, say that the applica-ble standards vary depending on the context of the *speaker*, the person who assesses the epistemic status of S's beliefs. That is, whether it is correct for you to say that I know there is a persimmon tree outside my window depends on facts about your situation, rather than mine. If you are a fastidious scientist, perhaps it would be false for you to say that I know I own a persimmon, but for me, a layperson, it is cor-rect to say that I know I own a persimmon. Almost all theorists now accept agent-centered contextualism, and say that our epistemic apparatus must be more versatile in some circumstances than others in order to produce knowledge. But the term 'contextualism' is usually associated with *speaker-centered* contextualism. Speaker-centered contextualism remains highly controversial.

Analyses of Knowledge

Do the truth, belief, and justification conditions constitute necessary and sufficient conditions for knowledge? That is, can we accept the following analysis of knowledge:

S knows p if and only if the following conditions are met:

1. p is true
2. S believes p
3. S's belief p is justified?

It is a versatile account—so powerful, in fact, that it is known as the *standard analysis* of knowledge. However, it faces substantial difficulties. Chief among these is the charge that so-called *Gettier cases* show that the standard analysis is too weak. Gettier cases seem to show it is possible to believe a true proposition on eminently good grounds yet fail to know the proposition is true. In response to Gettier cases, we will want to adopt an account of knowledge that is more demanding than the standard analysis. But when we strengthen our account, we must try to avoid a second difficulty: if we adopt conditions for knowledge that are very difficult to meet, we will find it harder to resist certain powerful *skeptical arguments* that support the idea that we truly know, or even justifiably believe, little if anything.

Gettier Cases

It was Edmund Gettier (1963) who drove home the point that the standard analysis is too weak (although his reasoning was hinted at by others, such as Bertrand Russell 1912). Using examples, Gettier was able to show that we can have substantial grounds for believing something yet still be correct only by accident (Unger 1968). Consider the following situation

(the example is Keith Lehrer's (1965) modification of Gettier's own illustration):

The Ford Case: suppose I were in my office, along with a fellow named Mr. Nogot, who has just shown me a document certifying that he owns a Ford. I would have excellent grounds for believing the following proposition:

1. Mr. Nogot is in my office and he owns a Ford.

Suppose, further, that I notice that (1) entails the following:

2. Someone in my office owns a Ford.

Because it follows from (1), I come to believe (2), and have excellent grounds for doing so. So according to the standard analysis, I would know that (2) is true—I would know someone in my office owns a Ford. Now let us embellish the case a bit: suppose that, as it turns out, the car Nogot used to own has been stolen and completely destroyed.

So Nogot does not own a Ford; (1) is false. Yet I would still have good reason for thinking that (1) is true, and hence that (2) is true. According to the standard analysis, I would still know that (2) is true. Yet it is obvious that I would know no such thing. Apparently, the conditions that make up the standard analysis are not sufficient for knowledge.

Internalism Versus Externalism

Contemporary epistemologists have attempted to strengthen the standard analysis in such a way as to render it adequate to handle cases like Gettier's. In doing so, however, they have found it tempting to abandon old ways of thinking about the discriminatory powers we need to achieve knowledge or justified belief. Traditionally, our discriminatory powers were understood in terms of evidence that is directly accessible; that is, the evidence which allows us to select among a belief p and the alternatives to p was assumed to be available through introspective access. This traditional view is *internalist*: the conditions that determine whether we are justified in believing something are accessible from the inside, from within our cognitive perspective, accessible in the (presumptively error-resistant) way that pains, beliefs, and desires are accessible. This view may be called *justification internalism*. The corresponding doctrine as applied to knowledge is *knowledge internalism*: the factors that determine whether we know something are accessible from within our cognitive perspective.

Gettier's challenge has led many theorists to abandon knowledge internalism. Some abandon both knowledge and justification internalism. Contemporary theorists have given *externalist* accounts of the discriminatory powers that make knowledge or justified belief possible. They say that the relevant powers depend on features of belief-formation processes (and the circumstances of their use) that are external to the epistemic agent's internal perspective. For example, externalists will insist, primitive people who saw a tiger would have known there was a tiger in front of them so long as their visual apparatus was functioning properly, and so long as it was used in the sort of circumstances appropriate to the identification of large animals. Yet early human beings had little grasp of the factors that allow the visual process to work and little idea about the circumstances under which it provides accurate information. Knowledge and perhaps even justified belief are made possible by the reception of information about the world even if we have no good perspective on how that reception is possible.

The four leading responses to Gettier all abandon knowledge internalism. These are the causal theory, the defeasibility theory, the true lemmas view, and the reliabilist theory. (The injunctions against defeaters and against false lemmas are externalist conditions.) Let us discuss each of these theories.

The Causal Theory

When confronted with the Ford case, and asked why I would fail to know that someone in my office owns a Ford, causal theorists (Grice 1961, Goldman 1967) say that my belief lacks the appropriate sort of *cause*. The appropriate cause involves a chain of events, a series in which each event causes the next, like a row of dropping dominos. For example, the event of my hearing a certain sound was caused by the event of sound waves moving through the air, which was

in turn caused by rocks falling down the face of a cliff, and so on. Our coming to believe something is itself an event brought about by a previous chain of occurrences. According to causal theorists, if I am to know p, my belief p must be brought about by a causal chain that includes the fact p, where the fact p is the state of affairs that makes the proposition p true. I know there is a table in front of me because the fact that there is a table in front of me causes light with certain characteristics to stimulate my visual receptors, resulting ultimately in my belief that there is a table in front of me. Thus, simplifying the view somewhat, the causal theory is this:

S knows p if and only if the following conditions are met:

1. p is true
2. S believes p
3. The fact p (is part of a causal chain that) causes S to believe p.

Consider how the causal theory would handle the Ford case. What makes p true is the fact that Mr. Havit, who is in my office, owns a Ford. But this is not the cause of my belief p. Instead, my belief is caused by facts about Mr. Nogot, who does not own a Ford. Hence the causal account gives the right verdict about the Ford case. My belief does not count as knowledge.

Is the causal theory adequate? Apparently not, as a new case will show.

The Papier-Mâché Barns Case: Suppose I am driving down the road and see a barn. I come to believe that there is a barn to my left. However, unknown to me, I am looking at the only real barn in the area. I have wandered into a region in which a crazy artist (Christo's dumber younger brother) has set out hundreds of papier-mâché barns that, visually, cannot be distinguished from the real thing.

So far as the causal theory is concerned, I would know that there is a barn to my left. Intuitively, however, this result is incorrect; in an area filled with fake barns, I would not know I am seeing a barn even if am; I am correct about the barn, but only by accident.

The Defeasibility Theory

Proponents of the defeasibility theory (Lehrer and Paxson 1969, Sosa 1969, Klein 1971) suggest that in Gettier cases evidence that normally would count as adequate justification for believing a proposition *p* is undermined or defeated by some proposition about our situation. They then specify what is involved when a proposition defeats a justification. According to one simple version of the view, a proposition *d defeats* person S's justification *e* for believing *p* if and only if

a. *d* is true, and

b. the conjunction of *e* and *d* does not completely justify S in believing *p*.

Knowledge is analyzed in terms of defeasibility, as follows:

S knows *p* if and only if the following conditions are met:

1. S believes *p*
2. S is justified in believing *p*
3. S's justification *e* is not (capable of being) defeated.

Notice that *not-p*, if true, automatically defeats our justification for believing *p*, no matter what that justification might be. So condition 3 entails that *p* is true, which renders a truth condition redundant.

The defeasibility account has no difficulty dealing with the Ford case. In that case, S's belief that someone in S's office owns a Ford was inferred from S's belief that Mr. Nogot has a Ford. But Mr. Nogot doesn't own a Ford, and this fact defeats the evidence S has for believing that someone in S's office owns a Ford. The defeasibility theory can also handle the papier-mâché barns case; there the defeating proposition is the fact that the region I am in is filled with fake barns that cannot easily be distinguished from the real thing.

So the defeasibility theory is not without virtues. Unfortunately, it is not without flaws as well. The problem with the account as we have stated it so far is that it is implausible to claim that *any* true statement can be allowed to defeat the justification we might have for our known beliefs. Some truths are misleading, and they ruin a justification without undermining

S's knowledge. Lehrer and Paxson (1969) provide a straightforward example.

> *The Tom Grabit Case:* Suppose I see Tom Grabit make off with a library book and am therefore justified in believing *p*: Tom Grabit has stolen a library book. Across town and out of earshot, however, Tom's mother, Bernice Grabit, has claimed that Tom was not in the library at all; rather, Tom's twin brother, Tim, was there. But Bernice is a compulsive liar!

Because Tom's mother is a compulsive liar and Tom has no brother at all, we would be inclined to say that I know *p*. But the fact that Bernice has claimed that Tom was not in the library defeats my justification for believing *p*. It, conjoined with the evidence that was good grounds for accepting *p*, does not justify me in believing *p*.

Dutifully, defeasibilists suggest revisions of their view to accommodate the Tom Grabit case, but we shall put these aside and turn to a third analysis of knowledge.

The True Lemmas View

According to some theorists (Clark 1963, Harman 1968), the key to handling Gettier cases is to supplement the truth condition we discussed earlier with a second truth condition. Let us use the term 'lemma' to refer to claims on which we rely in the course of arriving at a conclusion. For example, in the Ford case, in concluding that someone in my office owns a Ford, my reasoning depended on the claim that Mr. Nogot owns a Ford; the latter is therefore a lemma. And it is a false lemma, which suggests that the proper way to analyze knowledge is to insist that our lemmas be true, as in the following analysis, called the *true lemmas view:*

S knows *p* if and only if the following conditions are met:

1. *p* is true
2. S believes *p*
3. S's belief *p* is justified.
4. All claims essential to S's justification for believing *p* (all lemmas) are true.

But does the true lemmas view handle the papier-mâché barns case? It does if we stipulate that, on the way to my belief in the reality of the barn before me, I assumed (perhaps implicitly, that is, without spelling it out to myself) that my circumstances were ones in which barn appearances were reliable indicators of the presence of barns, for that assumption was false.

How does the view fare with the Tom Grabit case? Arguably, it performs well, given that no assumptions about Bernice G. were part of my reasoning.

The Reliabilist Theory

A fourth account of knowledge is called the *reliabilist theory* (or *reliabilism*). Reliabilists, such as Armstrong (1973), develop the observation that knowledge is produced by methods of belief formation or sustenance that are in some sense *reliable*. They focus on methods or processes of forming or sustaining beliefs. The visual process, for example, might be a method of forming a belief (as when I come to believe my puppy is at the door by seeing it), or a method of sustaining a belief (as when I continue to believe my dog is staying put by keeping an eye on it). Exploiting this insight, reliability theorists offer roughly the following analysis of knowledge:

S knows *p* if and only if the following conditions are met:

1. *p* is true
2. S believes *p* via method M
3. M is reliable.

Notice that the true lemmas view entails reliabilism given that, as the true lemmas theorist will say, we always assume, either implicitly or explicitly, that the method by which we arrive at a belief is reliable, and given that our belief's source must truly be reliable if our belief is to count as knowledge. Defeasibilism also entails reliabilism, given that the evidence we might have for a belief is defeated by the fact that we have arrived at our belief through an unreliable method.

The reliability theory gets complicated when its proponents try to clarify what they mean by 'reliable'. At this point it becomes clear that many versions of reliabilism are possible. One idea of reliability centers on the fact that after producing (or sustaining) many beliefs, some methods come to have good track records for guiding us to the truth. In fact, over the course of their entire performance in the past, present and future, they will have produced substantially more true beliefs than false beliefs. This we might term *track record reliability*.

Unfortunately, knowledge cannot be analyzed in terms of track record reliability. The main problem involves ways of arriving at beliefs that are rarely used, as in the following illustration.

The Dirty Prediction Case: Suppose that I base my belief that the winning numbers for the next state lottery are 3, 18, 63, 33, 41, and 24 on the fact that a certain patch of dirt has some specific bizarre configuration. Suppose, too, that this configuration will occur just once in all of time—I'm seeing it the one and only time it presents itself. Finally, suppose that my belief is correct: these *are* the winning numbers.

So this method produces just one belief in its entire history, and that belief is correct. Its track record is therefore excellent: the proportion of true beliefs versus false beliefs is as high as it could be! Yet it is obvious that I cannot know the winning state lottery numbers on the basis of some unique and unrepeated configuration of dirt.

In response to the dirty prediction case, let us consider a different type of reliability. Note that even though the dirt-based method of belief formation will in fact be used only once, it might have been used any number of times. Hence we can ask about the track record it *would have* if, contrary to fact, it *were* used over and over again. That is, we can ask what goes into the blank in the following counterfactual conditional:

If the dirt-based method were used many times, its track record would be _____.

(A proposition is said to be a *conditional* when it is of the form *if p then q*. For example, *if pigs had wings they could fly* is a conditional. A conditional is said to be *counterfactual* when the 'if' clause—the proposition substituted for *p*—is in fact false. For more on counterfactual and subjunctive conditionals, see Lewis 1973.)

So what is the answer to our question about the dirt-based method? Clearly, its track record would have been dismal. That is, if, after observing the same configuration of dirt, I were to predict that the winning numbers for the next state lottery will be 3, 18, 63, 33, 41, and 24, I would almost always, if not always, be misled. Let us use the term *propensity reliability* to refer to the property a method of belief formation M has when the following counterfactual conditional is met:

> If M were used repeatedly, it would produce substantially more true beliefs than false beliefs.

Can knowledge be defined in terms of propensity reliability?

No, the resulting account is still too weak. In the papier-mâché barns case my method of believing that there is a barn to the left—namely the visual process—is reliable in the sense that it would produce mostly true beliefs if used repeatedly, yet it does not position me to know there is a barn to the left. But perhaps we are on the right track anyway. Perhaps what we need to see between a method and the beliefs that it produces is a counterfactual dependence that is strong enough to count as a kind of infallibility within a limited set of circumstances. Perhaps a method M that enables a person S to know *p* must meet something like the following condition, as several theorists (Dretske 1970 and 1971, Carrier 1971, Goldman 1976a, Nozick 1981) have suggested—or perhaps some version of its contraposition, as others (Luper 1984; Sosa 1999, 2003) have suggested:

> if *p* were false, M would not (in S's circumstances and in others much like them) lead S to believe that *p* was true.[2]

When this condition is met, let us say (using Nozick's helpful terminology) that S's belief *tracks the truth* of *p* via M. Accordingly, tracking theorists analyze knowledge in roughly the following way:

1. Method M led S to believe *p*
2. if *p* were false, M would not (in S's circumstances and in others much like them) have led S to believe *p*.

(The combination of these two conditions implies that *p* is true, so the truth condition is redundant.)

If we adopt the form of reliabilism developed by tracking theorists, we can handle the papier-mâché barns case. In the situation described, the visual process is my method for believing that there is a barn to my left. Yet I do not track the truth via this method: if there had not been a barn to my left, the

visual process still might have led me to believe there was, since I was surrounded by fake barns, and could easily have been misled by one of them. Tracking theorists can also handle the Grabit case, where my method is: seeming to see Tom G. steal a book. Notwithstanding Bernice G.'s lies, if it had been false that Tom stole the book, this method would not have led me to believe it was true, given the circumstances as described in the case.

The Relevant Alternatives Theory

This last account of knowledge is closely related to a view of knowledge that has been called the *relevant alternatives theory*, defended by Gail Stine (1976) and attributable to J.L. Austin (1961b). On this view, to know *p* we must be able to rule out all of the possible alternatives to *p* that are relevant. Now, not *all* of the ways in which *p* might be false are relevant. If I am looking right at a crow in Texas, I can know I see a crow even if I cannot distinguish crows from some sort of black bird that only lives in the Amazon jungle, and even if I cannot tell the difference between crows and the robot birds assembled by the inhabitants of the far planet Crouton, for, in my situation, the possibility that I am seeing the bird from the Amazon or from Crouton is not relevant. But when a possibility is relevant, and inconsistent with *p*'s truth, then we must be able to rule it out, according to the relevant alternatives view. If, for example, I cannot distinguish crows from grackles, then I do not know that the crow I see really is a crow, for grackles are common in central Texas, and the possibility that I am seeing one is relevant.

The chief weakness of the relevant alternatives theory is that it is not obvious what makes an alternative relevant. Still, by combining the relevant alternatives view with a clearer account, such as the tracking theory, this weakness can be overcome (Nozick 1981). For example, we can say that A is a relevant alternative to *p* if and only if the following counterfactual condition is met: if, in circumstances like S's, *p* were false, A would (or might) hold. Even if the bird in front of me were not a crow, it would not be a robot bird, so the robot bird possibility is irrelevant. However, if the bird in front of me were not a crow, it might well be a grackle, so the grackle possibility is relevant.

This concludes our sketch of the leading analyses of knowledge. Now let us turn to the topic of skepticism.

Skepticism

One of the most puzzling challenges facing epistemologists is how to respond to skeptical arguments that suggest that we know little if anything (*knowledge skepticism*) or that we justifiably believe little or nothing (*justification* skepticism). *Global* (or *radical*) skepticism challenges the epistemic credentials of *all* beliefs, saying that no one knows anything, or no belief is justified. More *local* skepticism challenges the beliefs of some domain. For example, some skeptics challenge our claim to know about the existence and contents of minds other than our own, and do not deny that we know other sorts of things.

Defenses of Skepticism

To defend their views, skeptics presuppose or defend requirements for knowledge or justified belief, and try to show that these requirements are not met—or cannot be met. Two requirements in particular have seemed necessary to both skeptics and many of their adversaries. To know p, or even to be justified in believing p,

1. We must have *grounds* for accepting p, and
2. These grounds must be *discriminating*: they must make p more likely than competing alternatives to p, where an alternative to p entails that p is false.

Regress skeptics try to show that neither condition is met. *Indiscernability* (or Cartesian) skeptics try to show that we lack discriminating grounds for our beliefs. Let us briefly discuss each form of skepticism.

Regress Skepticism Starting with the followers of the ancient philosopher Pyrrho of Elis (c.365–270B.C.), some skeptics assume that to be justified or known a proposition must be supported on the basis of another proposition or chain of propositions, and then argue that no such support is ever possible. For a chain of putative support must (a) begin with propositions that are based on nothing, or (b) circle back on itself, or (c) go on endlessly. However, endless chains of justification are impossible for human beings to grasp or construct, so we can rule out (c). Circular chains, on the other hand, do not provide justification, and neither do chains that begin with arbitrary assumptions; either way—whether we choose possibility (a) or (b)—our beliefs are ultimately groundless, and hence not justified. This defense of skepticism might be called the *belief regress argument*. It is one form of regress skepticism. We will consider another form in a later chapter.

Indiscernability Skepticism Other skeptics base their doubts on our inability to rule out certain possibilities we might call *skeptical scenarios*. A skeptical scenario has the following peculiarity: whether the scenario holds or not, everything appears the same—either way, we have the same beliefs and perceptual states. For example, consider the possibility that I am in my bed in the midst of a brightly vivid (and wholly boring!) dream that mirrors the events of a normal day in the life of a philosopher. Assuming, as the skeptic does, that evidence or justification is entirely a matter of the ways things appear to us, then no evidence that I possess enables me to distinguish between the skeptic's possibility (vividly dreaming) and the situation in which I am awake. My evidence is compatible with both possibilities. So I do not know, and am not justified in believing, that I am not dreaming, and it seems to follow that I do not know, and am not justified in believing, a great many of the common sense things I believe, such as that I am awake, in my office, typing, and so forth. This defense of skepticism can be called *indiscernability skepticism*. It might also be called Cartesian skepticism, after the philosopher René Descartes, who discussed it in his *Meditations* (1641).

But does my inability to completely rule out the skeptic's possibilities really undermine the epistemic status of my common sense beliefs? It certainly seems to, for, as some contemporary theorists have pointed out, the following *principle of closure* (or *principle of entailment*) appears to be true:

We know things when we believe them upon seeing that they are entailed by other things we know.

Using this principle, the skeptic can offer the following *skeptical argument from closure*, which uses skeptical possibilities to undermine the epistemic status of commonsense beliefs:

1. If a person S knows one thing, *p*, and believes something else, *q*, on the basis of the accurate realization that *p* entails *q*, then S knows *q* (this is the principle of closure).
2. Being at work in my office at school entails that I am not in my bedroom across town dreaming; I am at work in my office (it also entails that I am not a brain in a vat on a distant planet, and that various other skeptical scenarios fail to hold).
3. So if I knew I was at work in my office, I would know I was not in my bedroom dreaming (and, similarly, that various other skeptical scenarios fail to hold).
4. But I don't know that I am not in bed dreaming (since if I were I would still think I am not).
5. So I don't know I am at work in my office, and for similar reasons I know none of the commonsense claims that are incompatible with my being in bed dreaming.

Responses to Skepticism

Critics of skepticism can take three main approaches. They can target global skepticism and try to show that the skeptic's thesis is incoherent in some way. This tactic might be called an *incoherence response* to skepticism. If successful, an incoherence response would allow us to bypass the skeptics' arguments and reject their conclusion on the grounds that it makes no sense. A second tactic is an *indefensibility response*, which draws our attention to the tension between the global skeptic's thesis, which is the denial that any claim is defensible, and its defense. On this approach we say that any attempt to defend global skepticism is condemned from the start by the skeptical thesis itself. A third strategy is

to focus on the skeptics' arguments themselves and offer *counterdefense responses*. This sort of response targets the skeptic who argues that the requirements for knowledge or justified belief are not satisfied. A counterdefense tries to establish that the requirements *are* met, or that the skeptics' arguments do not show that the requirements are not met. For example, the skeptical argument from closure is sometime criticized (Dretske 1970, Nozick 1981) on the grounds that it relies on a false premise, namely the assumption that the principle of closure is true.

While skepticism has been attacked in all of these ways, it remains one of the most highly contested issues in philosophy. In part this is because the term 'skepticism' is not limited to any one argument or claim, and those who defeat one skeptical argument or claim will encounter critics who consider skepticism unscathed because other skeptical arguments have not been overcome.

Notes

1. But wait! Aren't the words 'only if' synonymous with the word 'if'? No. Suppose that Fred wants his mother to buy him a motorcycle. She is reluctant; and she says she will buy it if he does various things but she also says she is not yet ready to list all of the things he will have to do before she will buy the bike (she'll get back to him later). But she can list several things that he must do if he is to get the bike. She will buy the bike *only if* he washes her car every week, and does the dishes every night, and takes several safety classes, and wears a helmet. That is, she will buy the bike *only if* he washes the car weekly, and she will buy the bike *only if* he does the dishes nightly, and so forth. Notice that no one item she lists—washing the car weekly, doing the dishes daily, and so forth—is enough to get the bike. It is false that she will buy Fred the bike *if* he washes the car every week; it is false that she will buy the bike *if* he does the dishes nightly—and so on. Yet it is true that she will buy Fred the bike *only if* he washes the car every week, and true that she will buy it *only if* he does the dishes daily, and so forth.
2. Alternatively: (2') if *p* were false, M would not have indicated that *p* was true. The contraposition of (2'), namely, If M indicated that *p* is true, *p* would be true, is also worth considering.

❖ CHAPTER 1 ANCIENT ORIGINS ❖

INTRODUCTION

Two ancient Greek figures made especially important contributions to the development of epistemology: Plato and Pyrrho of Elis. Plato shaped the epistemic views of theorists for generations. He defended a position called *rationalism*, which says that knowledge derives from thought or reason. Pyrrho is important, not because of his ideas about what knowledge is, but rather because of his strategies for arguing that it is not possible. Pyrrho was the consummate skeptic, and his arguments have been taken up, sharpened, and criticized again and again.

Plato (427–347 B.C.)

Plato was born into an aristocratic Athenian family. Inspired by his mentor Socrates (c.470–399 B.C.) from an early age, Plato founded the Academy, an early research institution, whose alumni included Aristotle (384–322 B.C.). In his *Republic*, Plato develops views about knowledge that are in some ways related to the standard account (the justified true belief analysis). The main point of similarity is the sharp distinction Plato draws between knowledge and mere belief. For Plato, knowledge requires an element of explanation or justification, unlike mere belief. He also says that the object of knowledge—that which is known—is reality, which commits him to something like the truth condition. However, it is awkward to attribute the belief condition to Plato, since he claims that the objects of (the faculty of) belief and of (the faculty of) knowledge are wholly distinct kinds of things. The object of mere belief or opinion is the appearances, but the object of knowledge is a changeless reality that does not include mutable objects such as rivers and fish that are part of the perceivable realm of appearance. Instead, knowable reality includes certain immutable abstract entities that Plato called forms or ideas. As to what forms are, there is considerable disagreement among scholars. Roughly, forms are essences; they determine what things are; and yet they do not depend, for their existence, on particular things. For example, the form or essence of justice is that which all just things have in common, and it would exist even if no particular thing were just.

According to Plato, forms are not perceivable, so we cannot learn about them through experience. Consequently, it becomes incumbent upon Plato to explain how we are able to know the forms. He says they are accessible through thought, even though they exist independently of the mind. In the *Meno*, Plato offers a view called the doctrine of recollection: our present knowledge of the forms is limited to what we can recollect about them after having access to them in an earlier life.

In his *Theatetus*, Plato returns to the topic of knowledge. In our selection, he considers the claim that knowledge is perception, which he equates with the Protagorean thesis that knowledge and truth are relative—that what *seems* true to a given person *is* in fact true for, and known to, that person. Socrates criticizes the Protagorean view on the grounds that its proponents cannot defend it. (Relativism is discussed in more depth in the final chapter of this volume.) Plato also considers, and rejects, the suggestion that knowledge is true belief. The view he takes to be most plausible is the position that knowledge is not mere true belief. Instead, knowing a fact requires being able to explain it.

Pyrrhonism

Our next selection is from *Outlines of Pyrrhonism*, by Sextus Empiricus, a relatively obscure figure who lived sometime in the second century A.D. Sextus's writings are the main source of our knowledge of the form of skepticism associated with the ancient Greek philosopher Pyrrho of Elis, who lived roughly from 360 B.C. to 270 B.C. Pyrrho himself wrote nothing, and little is known about how he developed his ideas, although it is possible that Indian ascetics influenced him when he accompanied Alexander the Great to Asia. Pyrrho inspired a group of physicians led by Herophilus in the third century B.C.; Sextus seems to have been a member of this school.

Sextus is at pains to emphasize that Pyrrhonian skepticism is not a positive thesis. It does not, for example, say that we can know nothing. Instead, it is a state of mind in which we have suspended belief about virtually all matters. According to Sextus, the purpose of Pyrrhonism is to enable us to achieve happiness, or tranquility of mind. Tranquility is achieved by matching up each claim we are tempted to accept with another, opposing, claim that is equally likely to be true. After doing so, we will not believe either claim. Through this technique, we give up our beliefs about the world, and we come to resemble a tranquil tree, that "neither shuns nor pursues anything eagerly; and, in consequence . . . is unperturbed" (Cp. XII).

The skeptic does not suspend belief about all things. Instead, the skeptic withholds belief about "the nonevident objects of scientific inquiry" (Cp. VII). Unfortunately, the terms *evident* and *nonevident* are not entirely clear. At one point Sextus says that skeptics "assent to the feelings which are the necessary results of sense impressions" (VII). And at another he says, "we do not overthrow the affective sense impressions which induce our assent involuntarily; and these impressions are 'the appearances'" (X). When, for example, we taste honey, we cannot help believing that it tastes sweet. That honey *appears* sweet is a claim we can make without going beyond the appearances themselves, and Sextus says that skeptics do not doubt such claims. Instead, their doubts concern our beliefs about the real nature of things.

To help us suspend belief, Sextus points out that the appearance of things varies depending on various circumstances. When we judge the real nature of something in one set of circumstances, we come to a different conclusion than when we judge the nature of that thing in a different set of circumstances. Moreover, we lack good reason to believe that our judgment in one set of circumstances is more accurate than our judgment in other circumstances. For example, water that appears cold after my hand is heated will appear hot after it is cooled, and I do not have good reason for thinking the water is truly hot or that it is truly cold. So I must suspend belief about the actual temperature of the water.

In Chapter XIII Sextus sketches 'modes' for setting things in opposition so as to eliminate belief. In the next chapter he gathers ten different sorts of circumstances that generate conflicting appearances. Thus, for example, the first mode deals with ways animals differ, and provides pairs of statements of the form,

x appears F to animals of type T.

Our selection from Chapter XIV focuses on the fourth mode, which deals with differences in the physical states of observers, opposing claims of the form

x appears F to an observer in state S.

For example, the statement,

I appear to be a teacher at work when I am awake

can be paired off as against

I appear to be lost at sea (or whatever) when I am asleep dreaming.

These statements about contrary appearances generate the following skeptical argument:

1. I appear to be a teacher at work when I am awake.

2. I appear to be lost at sea when I am asleep dreaming.

3. I lack grounds for saying that my actual features are ones I appear to have while awake rather than the ones I appear to have while I am asleep, or vice versa.

4. So I can rationally believe neither that I am really a teacher at work nor that I am lost at sea.

The weakest link in the argument is the third premise. Two further arguments are provided in its defense. The first is the belief regress argument (as described in the introduction to this volume). The second is the argument from bias, which says that preferring waking to sleeping appearances (or vice versa) shows illegitimate bias: when we are in a state of wakefulness, we will simply accept the accuracy of waking appearances, but when we are in a state of sleep, we will accept the accuracy of sleeping appearances. So it is irrational to assume that waking appearances are more accurate than sleeping appearances.

Chapter XIV refers to the "older" skeptics; it is probably our best characterization of the views of Pyrrho. These older skeptics spoke of ten modes for suspending belief, depending on differences in: (1) animals, (2) people, (3) sense organs, (4) circumstances, (5) locations, (6) admixtures, (7) composition, (8) relativity, (9) frequency, and (10) customs. This classification scheme is obscure in many ways. Chapter XV is a bit clearer. It speaks of "later" skeptics who speak of five modes. According to the later skeptics, we should suspend belief about a matter when: (1) it is highly controversial; (2) our beliefs about it fall victim to the belief regress argument; (3) we judge the matter differently relative to varying factors; (4) our beliefs about it ultimately are based on arbitrary assumptions; and (5) our beliefs about it are based on chains of reasoning that are circular.

QUESTIONS FOR REFLECTION

1. Does Plato think that only the immutable is real? If so, why? Is he correct?

2. Is knowledge limited to immutable reality, as Plato thought?

3. Does Plato accept the standard account of knowledge as justified true belief? If not, which part of the standard account does he reject?

4. Is Sextus's belief regress argument plausible? Presumably beliefs are rational if based on plausible grounds, but do the grounds themselves need support to be plausible?

5. According to Sextus's argument from bias, we automatically trust dreaming appearances when we are dreaming. But is this true? If not, what are the consequences for the argument?

6. According to the third premise of the skeptic's dream argument, there are no grounds for the contention that waking appearances are more reliable indicators of reality than dreamt appearances. Is this correct? If not, is there any way to repair the dream argument?

7. How might Plato answer the Pyrrhonian skeptic? Would his response be convincing?

✧ ANCIENT RATIONALISM ✧

1. MENO

Plato

SOCRATES. What, according to you and your friend, is the definition of virtue?

MENO. O Socrates; I used to be told, before I knew you, that you are always puzzling yourself and others; and now you are casting your spells over me, and I am simply getting bewitched and enchanted, and am at my wits' end. And if I may venture to make a jest upon you, you seem to me both in your appearance and in your power over others to be very like the flat torpedo fish, who torpifies those who come near him with the touch, as you have now torpified me, I think. For my soul and my tongue are really torpid, and I do not know how to answer you.

SOCRATES. As to my being a torpedo, if the torpedo is torpid as well as the cause of torpidity in others, then indeed I am a torpedo, but not otherwise; for I perplex others, not because I am clear, but because I am utterly perplexed myself. And now I know not what virtue is, and you seem to be in the same case, although you did once know before you touched me. However, I have no objection to joining with you in the inquiry.

MENO. And how will you inquire, Socrates, into that which you know not? What will you put forth as the subject of inquiry? And if you find what you want, how will you ever know that this is what you did not know?

SOCRATES. I know, Meno, what you mean; but just see what a tiresome dispute you are introducing. You argue that a man cannot inquire either about that which he knows, or about that which he does not know; for he knows, and therefore has no need to inquire about that—nor about that which he does not know; for he does not know that about which he is to inquire.

MENO. Well, Socrates, and is not the argument sound?

SOCRATES. I think not.

MENO. Why not?

SOCRATES. I will tell you why. I have heard from certain wise men and women who spoke of a glorious truth, as I conceive.

MENO. What was that? and who were they?

SOCRATES. Some of them were priests and priestesses, who had studied how they might be able to give a reason of their profession: there have been poets also, such as the poet Pindar and other inspired men. And what they say is—mark, now, and see whether their words are true—they say that the soul of man is immortal, and at one time has an end, which is termed dying, and at another time is born again, but is never destroyed. And the moral is, that a man ought to live always in perfect holiness. For in the ninth year Persephone sends the souls of those from whom she has received the penalty of ancient crime back again into the light of this world, and these are they who become noble kings and mighty men and great in wisdom, and are called saintly heroes in after ages. The soul, then, as being immortal, and having been born again many times, and having seen all things that there are, whether in this world or in the world below, has knowledge of them all; and it is no

wonder that she should be able to call to remembrance all that she ever knew about virtue, and about everything; for as all nature is akin, and the soul has learned all things, there is no difficulty in her eliciting, or as men say learning, all out of a single recollection, if a man is strenuous and does not faint; for all inquiry and all learning is but recollection. And therefore we ought not to listen to this sophistical argument about the impossibility of inquiry: that is a saying which will make us idle, and is sweet only to the sluggard; but the other saying will make us active and enterprising. In that confiding, I will gladly inquire with you into the nature of virtue.

MENO. Yes, Socrates; but what do you mean by saying that we do not learn, and that what we call learning is only a process of recollection? Can you teach me that?

SOCRATES. Meno, you are a rogue, and now you ask whether I can teach you, when I am saying that there is no teaching, but only recollection; and thus you imagine that you will involve me in a contradiction.

MENO. Indeed, Socrates, I protest that I had no such intention. I only asked the question from habit; but if you can prove to me that what you say is true, I wish that you would.

SOCRATES. That is no easy matter, but I will try to please you to the utmost of my power. Suppose that you call one of your numerous attendants, that I may demonstrate on him.

MENO. Certainly. Come hither, boy.

SOCRATES. He is Greek, and speaks Greek, does he not?

MENO. Yes; he was born in the house.

SOCRATES. Attend now to the questions which I ask him, and observe whether he learns of me or only remembers.

MENO. I will.

SOCRATES. Tell me, boy, do you know that a figure like this is a square?

BOY. I do.

SOCRATES. And you know that a square figure has these four lines equal?

BOY. Certainly.

SOCRATES. And these lines which I have drawn through the middle of the square are also equal?

BOY. Yes.

SOCRATES. A square may be of any size?

BOY. Certainly.

SOCRATES. And if one side of the figure be of two feet, and the other side be of two feet, how much will the whole be? Let me explain: if in one direction the space was of two feet, and in the other direction of one foot, the whole would be of two feet taken once?

BOY. Yes.

SOCRATES. But since this side is also of two feet, there are twice two feet?

BOY. There are.

SOCRATES. Then the square is of twice two feet?

BOY. Yes.

SOCRATES. And how many are twice two feet? Count and tell me.

BOY. Four, Socrates.

SOCRATES. And might there not be another square twice as large as this, and having like this equal lines?

BOY. Yes.

SOCRATES. And of how many feet will that be?

BOY. Of eight feet.

SOCRATES. And now try and tell me the length of the line which forms the side of that double square: this is two feet—what will that be?

BOY. Clearly, Socrates, that will be double.

SOCRATES. Do you observe, Meno, that I am not teaching the boy anything, but only asking him questions; and now he fancies that he knows how long a line is necessary in order to produce a figure of eight square feet; does he not?

MENO. Yes.

SOCRATES. And does he really know?

MENO. Certainly not.

SOCRATES. He only guesses that because the square is double, the line is double.

MENO. True.

SOCRATES. Observe him while he recalls the steps in regular order. (*To the Boy.*) Tell me, boy, do you assert that a double space comes from a double line? Remember that I am not speaking of an oblong, but of a square, and of a square twice the size of this one—that is to say of eight feet; and I want to know whether you still say that a double square comes from a double line?

BOY. Yes.

SOCRATES. But does not this line become doubled if we add another such line here?

BOY. Certainly.

SOCRATES. And four such lines will make a space containing eight feet?

BOY. Yes.

SOCRATES. Let us describe such a figure: is not that what you would say is the figure of eight feet?

BOY. Yes.

SOCRATES. And are there not these four divisions in the figure, each of which is equal to the figure of four feet?

BOY. True.

SOCRATES. And is not that four times four?

BOY. Certainly.

SOCRATES. And four times is not double?

BOY. No, indeed.

SOCRATES. But how much?

BOY. Four times as much.

SOCRATES. Therefore the double line, boy, has formed a space, not twice, but four times as much.

BOY. True.

SOCRATES. And four times four are sixteen—are they not?

BOY. Yes.

SOCRATES. What line would give you a space of eight feet, as this gives one of sixteen feet; do you see?

BOY. Yes.

SOCRATES. And the space of four feet is made from this half line?

BOY. Yes.

SOCRATES. Good; and is not a space of eight feet twice the size of this, and half the size of the other?

BOY. Certainly.

SOCRATES. Such a space, then, will be made out of a line greater than this one, and less than that one.

BOY. Yes; that is what I think.

SOCRATES. Very good; I like to hear you say what you think. And now tell me, is not this a line of two feet and that of four?

BOY. Yes.

SOCRATES. Then the line which forms the side of eight feet ought to be more than this line of two feet, and less than the other of four feet?

BOY. It ought.

SOCRATES. Try and see if you can tell me how much it will be.

BOY. Three feet.

SOC. Then if we add a half to this line of two, that will be the line of three. Here are two and there is one; and on the other side, here are two also and there is one: and that makes the figure of which you speak?

BOY. Yes.

SOCRATES. But if there are three feet this way and three feet that way, the whole space will be three times three feet?

BOY. That is evident.

SOCRATES. And how much are three times three feet?

BOY. Nine.

SOCRATES. And how much is the double of four?

BOY. Eight.

SOCRATES. Then the figure of eight is not made out of a line of three?

BOY. No.

SOCRATES. But from what line?—tell me exactly; and if you would rather not reckon, try and show me the line.

BOY. Indeed, Socrates, I do not know.

SOCRATES. Do you see, Meno, what advances he has made in his power of recollection? He did not know at first, and he does not know now, what is the side of a figure of eight feet; but then he thought that he knew, and answered confidently as if he knew, and had no difficulty; but now he has a difficulty, and neither knows nor fancies that he knows.

MENO. True.

SOCRATES. Is he not better off in knowing his ignorance?

MENO. I think that he is.

SOCRATES. If we have made him doubt, and given him the "torpedo's shock," have we done him any harm?

MENO. I think not.

SOCRATES. We have certainly done something that may assist him in finding out the truth of the matter; and now he will wish to remedy his ignorance, but then he would have been ready to tell all the world that the double space should have a double side.

MENO. True.

SOCRATES. But do you suppose that he would ever have inquired or learned what he fancied that he knew and did not know, until he had fallen into perplexity under the idea that he did not know, and had desired to know?

MENO. I think not, Socrates.

SOCRATES. Then he was the better for the torpedo's touch?

MENO. I think that he was.

SOCRATES. Mark now the farther development. I shall only ask him, and not teach him, and he shall share the inquiry with me: and do you watch and see if you find me telling or explaining anything to him, instead of eliciting his opinion. Tell me, boy, is not this a square of four feet which I have drawn?

BOY. Yes.

SOCRATES. And now I add another square equal to the former one.

BOY. Yes.

SOCRATES. And a third, which is equal to either of them?

BOY. Yes.

SOCRATES. Suppose that we fill up the vacant corner.

BOY. Very good.

SOCRATES. Here, then, there are four equal spaces?

BOY. Yes.

SOCRATES. And how many times is this space larger than this?

BOY. Four times.

SOCRATES. But it ought to have been twice only, as you will remember.

BOY. True.

SOCRATES. And does not this line, reaching from corner to corner bisect each of these spaces?

BOY. Yes.

SOCRATES. And are there not here four equal lines which contain this space?

BOY. There are.

SOCRATES. Look and see how much this space is.

BOY. I do not understand.

SOCRATES. Has not each interior line cut off half of the four spaces?

BOY. Yes.

SOCRATES. And how many such spaces are there in this division?

BOY. Four.

SOCRATES. And how many in this?

BOY. Two.

SOCRATES. And four is how many times two?

BOY. Twice.

SOCRATES. And this space is how many feet?

BOY. Of eight feet.

SOCRATES. And from what line do you get this figure?

BOY. From this.

SOCRATES. That is, from the line which extends from corner to corner?

BOY. Yes.

SOCRATES. And that is the line which the learned call the diagonal. And if this is the proper name, then you, Meno's slave, are prepared to affirm that the double space is the square of the diagonal?

BOY. Certainly, Socrates.

SOCRATES. What do you say of him, Meno? Were not all these answers given out of his own head?

MENO. Yes, they were all his own.

SOCRATES. And yet, as we were just now saying, he did not know?

MENO. True.

SOCRATES. And yet he had those notions in him?

MENO. Yes.

SOCRATES. Then he who does not know still has true notions of that which he does not know?

MENO. He has.

SOCRATES. And at present these notions are just wakening up in him, as in a dream; but if he were frequently asked the same questions, in different forms, he would know as well as any one at last?

MENO. I dare say.

SOCRATES. Without any one teaching him he will recover his knowledge for himself, if he is only asked questions?

MENO. Yes.

SOCRATES. And this spontaneous recovery in him is recollection?

MENO. True.

SOCRATES. And this knowledge which he now has must he not either have acquired or always possessed?

MENO. Yes.

SOCRATES. But if he always possessed this knowledge he would always have known; or if he has acquired the knowledge he could not have acquired it in this life, unless he has been taught geometry; for he may be made to do the same with all geometry and every other branch of knowledge. Now, has any one ever taught him? You must know that, if, as you say, he was born and bred in your house.

MENO. And I am certain that no one ever did teach him.

SOCRATES. And yet has he not the knowledge?

MENO. That, Socrates, is most certain.

SOCRATES. But if he did not acquire this knowledge in this life, then clearly he must have had and learned it at some other time?

MENO. That is evident.

SOCRATES. And that must have been the time when he was not a man?

MENO. Yes.

SOCRATES. And if there have been always true thoughts in him, both at the time when he was and was not a man, which only need to be awakened into knowledge by putting questions to him, his soul must have always possessed this knowledge, for he always either was or was not a man?

MENO. That is clear.

SOCRATES. And if the truth of all things always existed in the soul, then the soul is immortal. Wherefore be of good cheer, and try to recollect what you do not know, or rather do not remember.

MENO. I feel, somehow, that I like what you are saying.

SOCRATES. And I, Meno, like what I am saying. Some things I have said of which I am not altogether confident. But that we shall be better and braver and less helpless if we think that we ought to inquire, than we should have been if we indulged in the idle fancy that there was no knowing and no use in searching after what we know not: that is a theme upon which I am ready to fight, in word and deed, to the utmost of my power.

◈ ANCIENT RATIONALISM ◈

2. THE REPUBLIC

Plato

[In the following passages from Books V, VI, and VII of Plato's *Republic*, Socrates and Glaucon discuss philosophy and go on to talk about knowledge and its relationship to belief. Socrates speaks first.]

Book V

When we describe a man as longing for something, do we say that he wants all that pertains to it, or only one part, to the exclusion of another?

He wants the whole.

Then shall we not maintain that the philosopher loves all wisdom and not just parts of it?

True.

So that if a person is reluctant to study, especially while he is young and unable to discriminate between what is profitable and what is not, we shall pronounce him to be no lover of learning or of wisdom; just as when a man is dainty about his food, we deny that he is hungry, or fond of eating.

Yes, and we shall be right in doing so.

On the other hand, when a man is ready and willing to taste every kind of knowledge, and applies himself to his studies with gusto, we shall justly call such a person a philosopher, shall we not?

To which Glaucon replied, You will find your description includes a peculiar group of people. All the lovers of sights, I suppose, will be philosophers, because they take pleasure in acquiring knowledge; and those who delight in hearing novel things are a very odd bunch to count among philosophers—those, I mean, who will never, if they can help it, be present at a philosophical discussion, or any similar entertainment, but are unfailing attendants at every Dionysian festival. Are we then to give the title of philosophers to all these people, as well as to others who have a taste for any similar studies, and to the practitioners of small arts?

Certainly not, I replied, though they do resemble philosophers.

And whom, he asked, do you call genuine philosophers?

Those who love to see truth, I answered.

In that, he said, you cannot be wrong: but will you explain what you mean?

That would not be easy with a different questioner, but you, I imagine, will grant the assumption I require.

What is it?

That since beauty is the opposite of ugliness, they are two things.

Of course they are.

Then since they are two, each of them taken separately is one thing.

That is also true.

The same thing may be said likewise of justice and injustice, good and bad, and all other forms. Each of them in itself is one thing, but by the intermixture with actions and bodies and with one another, through which they are everywhere made visible, each appears to be many things.

You are right.

By the help of this principle, then, I draw a distinction between those whom you described just now as lovers of sights, lovers of arts, and practical persons, on the one hand, and on the other, those about whom we are now inquiring, to whom alone we can rightly give the name of philosopher.

Explain what you mean.

Well, those who love sights and sounds admire beautiful sounds and colors and shapes, and all artistic products that art creates from them; but beauty itself their understanding is unable to recognize and appreciate. Therefore if a man recognizes the existence of beautiful things, but does not believe in beauty itself, and lacks the power to follow should another lead the way to the knowledge of it, is his life a dreaming or a waking one? Is it not dreaming when a person, whether asleep or awake, mistakes the likeness of anything for the real thing of which it is a likeness?

I should say that a person in that predicament was dreaming.

Take again the opposite case, of one who acknowledges the existence of beauty itself, and has the power to discern both this essence and the objects into which it enters, and who never confuses the one with the other: does such a person live a dreaming or a waking life?

A waking life, undoubtedly.

So, shall we not say that the latter knows, and has knowledge, while the former merely has belief in appearances?

Yes, that is perfectly right.

Well then, if this person, whom we describe as believing but not knowing, should grow angry with us, and contend that what we say is not true, is there a way to convince him without telling him that he is not in his right mind?

That certainly would be desirable.

Come then, consider what we are to say to him. Answer us this question, we shall say: When a man knows, does he know something or nothing? Be so good, Glaucon, as to answer for him.

My answer will be, that he knows something.

Something that exists, or not?

Something that exists, for how could a thing that does not exist be known?

Are we then quite sure that what entirely exists is entirely knowable, whereas that which has no existence at all must be wholly unknowable?

We are perfectly sure of it.

Good. Now, if there be anything so constituted as at the same time to be and not to be, must it not lie somewhere between the purely existent and the absolutely nonexistent?

It must.

Well then, knowledge corresponds to the existent, and the absence of knowledge necessarily to the nonexistent. So if there is something between the existent and the nonexistent, we must try to find something intermediate between knowledge and ignorance.

Yes, by all means.

Do we speak of something called belief or opinion?

Undoubtedly we do.

Is it distinct from knowledge or identical with it?

Distinct from it.

Therefore belief concerns one thing and knowledge another, each according to its own peculiar power.

Just so.

Hence knowledge concerns what exists; it is able to know what is and how it is. But before we go on, there is a distinction which I think it necessary to establish.

What is that?

We shall use the term 'faculties' for the features whereby we, and every other thing, are able to do whatever we can do—for example, I call sight and hearing faculties, if you happen to understand the special conception which I wish to describe.

I do understand it.

Then let me tell you what view I take of them. In a faculty I do not find either color, or shape, or any of those qualities which, in the case of many other things, allow me to distinguish between one thing and another. No, in a faculty I look only to its effects and its function, and this allows me to identify the faculties. Those faculties are identical whose effects and functions are identical, and those whose effects and functions are diverse are distinct faculties. Is this how you see things?

Yes.

Now then, my friend, would you call knowledge a faculty?

Yes I would; it is of all the faculties the most powerful.

Well, is belief a faculty?

Yes, since it enables us to believe.

Well, earlier you admitted that knowledge and belief are not identical.

Right; how could a sensible man identify the fallible with the infallible?

Very good. So we agree that belief is distinct from knowledge. And so each of them has by its nature different functions and different effects.

The inference is inevitable.

The function of knowledge is to know nature of the existent.

Yes.

And the function of belief is, we say, to believe. Can the object of belief be the same as the object of knowledge?

Not if different faculties have different functions, and belief and knowledge are distinct faculties—all which we affirm. Given these assumptions, the same things cannot be objects of both.

Then if the object of knowledge is the existent, that of belief must be something other than the existent?

It must.

Well then, is the object of belief the nonexistent, or is that an impossible object even for belief? Consider—if we have a belief, isn't there something before the mind? We cannot have a belief about nothing, right?

It is impossible.

Then the person who believes has a belief about something; yet the nonexistent could not be called something; instead, it must be called nothing at all.

Just so.

But to the nonexistent we were constrained to assign ignorance, and to the existent, knowledge. So neither the existent nor the nonexistent is the object of belief.

No.

Therefore belief cannot be either ignorance or knowledge.

Apparently not.

Then does it lie beyond these, so as to surpass either knowledge in certainty or ignorance in uncertainty?

It does neither.

Then tell me, do you look upon belief as something more obscure than knowledge, but more luminous than ignorance? Does it lie within these extremes?

Yes.

Now a little while back, did we not say, that if anything could at the same time be and not be, it must lie between the purely existent and the nonexistent, and must be the object neither of knowledge nor of ignorance, but of a third faculty, which should be similarly discovered in the interval between knowledge and ignorance?

We did.

But now what we have discovered between these two is the faculty we call belief. It remains for us to find what it is that both is and is not. If we can find it, we may justly proclaim it to be the object of belief.

Right.

These positions being laid down, I shall interrogate that man who denies the existence of beauty, or the enduring form of beauty, though he acknowledges a variety of beautiful objects—that the lover of sights, who cannot bear to be told that beauty is one, and justice one, and so on of the rest: My good sir, I shall say, of all these beautiful things, is there one which will never appear ugly? Of all these just things, is there one which will never appear unjust?

No, answered Glaucon, they must inevitably appear both beautiful and ugly, both just and unjust.

Again, the many double things may be considered halves just as well as doubles. And the things which we describe as large, small, light, and heavy, may as well be described as small, large, and light.

They will always be equally entitled to either description.

Yes, and however we describe one of these many objects, can we say absolutely that it *is* that way, and not that it is the opposite?

You remind me of the riddles told at parties, and of the children's riddle* about what a eunuch threw at a bat and what the bat perched on. These things have the same ambiguous character, and one cannot positively conceive of them as either being or not being, as both being and not being, or as neither.

Can you tell me where they may be better put than in the space between being and not being? For I presume they will not appear either more obscure, and hence less real, than the nonexistent, or clearer, and therefore more real, than the existent.

You are perfectly right.

Hence we have discovered that the mass of notions, current among the mass of people, about beauty, justice, and the rest, drift about between pure existence and pure nonexistence.

We have.

And earlier we agreed that if anything of this kind should be brought to light, it ought to be described as the object of belief or opinion, and not of knowledge—these intermediate rovers being seized by the intermediate faculty.

We did make this admission.

Therefore, when people have an eye for a multitude of beautiful objects, but can neither see beauty in itself, nor follow those who would lead them to it—when they behold a number of just things, but not justice in itself, and so forth, we shall say they have an opinion or belief, but no real knowledge of the things about which they have beliefs.

It follows.

But what, on the other hand, must we say of those who contemplate things as they are, eternal and unchanging? Shall we not speak of them as knowing, not merely believing?

That also follows.

Then shall we not assert that such persons love the objects of knowledge, and the others, the objects of opinion? For we have not forgotten, have we, that these latter love beautiful sounds and colors and the like, while they will not hear of the existence of beauty itself?

We have not forgotten it.

So is it fair to call these people philodoxical rather than philosophical, that is to say, lovers of opinion rather than lovers of wisdom? Will they be offended by this description?

No, not if they will take my advice: it is wrong to be offended with the truth.

Those therefore that set their affections on that which in each case really exists, we must call not philodoxical, but philosophical?

Yes, by all means.

Book VI

What is the highest kind of knowledge, and what does it deal with?

Assuredly you have heard the answer many times, but at this moment either you have forgotten it, or else you intend to raise objections. For you have often been told that the form of the good is the highest object of knowledge, and that this essence, by blending with just things and all other created objects, renders them useful and advantageous. If we know nothing of the good, our knowledge of everything else will be useless. How can we gain from possessing everything except what is good, or from apprehending everything else, without apprehending what is good?

We cannot, But Socrates, do you assert the chief good to be knowledge or pleasure or something different from either?

Ho, ho, my friend! I saw long ago that you would not put up with the opinions of other people on these subjects. But I distrust my own powers, and I feel afraid that my awkward zeal will expose me to ridicule. No, let us put aside all inquiry into the real nature of the chief good. It is beyond the scope of our inquiry. But I am willing to talk to you about that which appears to be the offspring of the chief good, and which bears the strongest resemblance to it.

Tell us about it, he replied.

I will do so, as soon as we have come to an understanding, and you have been reminded of certain statements made in a previous part of our conversation. We have distinguished between the multiplicity of things that are beautiful, and good, on the one hand, and beauty and goodness themselves, on the other. Corresponding to each group of multiple things we suppose that there is a single form.

Just so.

And we assert that the former can be seen, but are not objects of pure reason, whereas the forms are objects of reason, but are not visible.

Certainly.

Now with what part of ourselves do we see visible objects?

With the eyesight.

In the same way we hear sounds with the hearing, and perceive everything sensible with the other senses, do we not?

Certainly.

Then have you noticed that the designer of the senses has used exceptionally lavish materials to enable the eyes to see?

Not exactly, he replied.

Well then, look at it in this light. Hearing and sound do not require a third thing for the ear to hear or a sound to be heard. The same is true of most, if not all, of the other senses. But a third thing is needed in the case of sight and visible things. Without a third thing, especially constituted for this purpose, eyesight will see nothing, and colors will be invisible. Of course I refer to what you call light.

You are right.

Hence it appears that of all the pairs mentioned before, the sense of sight, and the power of being visible, are joined by the noblest link, given the great value of light.

Yes, it is very far from being ignoble.

And whose light is it that enables our sight to see so excellently well, and makes objects visible?

There can be but one opinion on the subject; you evidently allude to the sun.

Then neither sight, nor the eye which is the seat of sight, can be identified with the sun, and yet, of all the organs of sensation, the eye bears the closest resemblance to the sun. Also, the eye's power is derived from the sun, and while the sun is not identical with sight, it is nevertheless the cause of sight, and is moreover seen by its aid.

Yes, quite true.

Well then, I continued, I meant the sun when I spoke of the offspring of the chief good, begotten by it in a certain resemblance to itself—that is to say, bearing the same relation in the visible world to sight and its objects, which the chief good bears in the intellectual world to pure reason and its objects.

Please explain.

You know that when you see things that are illuminated by the sun, the eyes see clearly, and it is evident that they have the power of vision. But in darkness vision is lost.

Unquestionably it is so.

The soul is like the eye: when it considers something illuminated by truth and reality, the soul understands and knows it, and possesses intelligence. But when it considers the dark world of things that come into existence and cease to be, its sight dims, and it can only form beliefs and opinions. It seems bereft of intelligence.

True.

Now, this power, which gives to the objects of real knowledge their truth, and to knowers the power of knowing, is the form or essence of the good, and it is the cause of knowledge, and truth, insofar as truth is knowable. As beautiful as truth and knowledge are, the good is more so. And just as knowledge and truth are like but different from the sun, so they are like but different from the good, which is more precious. Again like the sun and the things it illuminates and nourishes, the good gives things not only their knowability, but also their very being, and while the good is distinct from being, it is greater than being in dignity and power.

Hereupon Glaucon exclaimed with a very amusing air, good heavens, what a miraculous superiority!

Well, I said, you are the person to blame, because you compel me to state my opinions on the subject.

No, let me entreat you not to stop, till you have at least elaborated on your metaphor of the sun, if you are leaving anything out.

Now understand that, according to us, two powers reign: the good over all that is intelligible, and the sun over what is visible, or the "firmament" I might say. Well then, do you grasp these two orders of things—the visible, and the intelligible?

Yes, I do.

Suppose you take a line divided into unequal parts, one to represent the visible realm, the other the intelligible realm. Divide each part again in the same proportion. Let the lengths of the segments represent degrees of clarity or obscurity. One of the two segments of the part which stands for the visible world will represent all images—meaning by images, shadows, and reflections, if you understand me.

Yes, I do understand.

Let the other segment stand for the real objects corresponding to these images, namely, animals and everything produced by nature or human hands.

Very good.

Would you agree that the ratio of the subdivisions represents the degree of reality in each, and that it is the very same ratio as found between belief and knowledge?

Certainly I should.

Then let us consider how we must divide that part of the line which represents the intelligible world.

How must we do it?

Thus: the lower segment will represent what the soul is compelled to investigate by reducing things to images, starting from assumptions, and traveling not to first principles, but to conclusions. The higher segment will represent what the soul investigates by making its way from hypotheses to first principles, unaided by images, and relying entirely on forms.

I have not understood your description so well as I could wish.

Then we will try again. Students of subjects like geometry and arithmetic take for granted odd and even numbers, figures, the three kinds of angles, and other things.

Having adopted them as assumptions, they decline to give any account of them, either to themselves or to others, on the assumption that they are self-evident; and, making these their starting point, they arrive at last, with perfect consistency, at the conclusions they sought to verify.

I am perfectly aware of the fact, he replied.

Then you also know that they use visible shapes, and analyze them, though they understand these to be images of the originals—the real square or diagonal and so forth. They use figures and diagrams, which are real since they leave reflections and shadows, but these aids to thought convert the real into images. What is sought is a reality the mind alone can perceive.

True.

This, then, was the class of things I called intelligible, but with qualifications, since the mind must employ hypotheses in investigating them, and cannot transcend these, so as to come to first principles. Also, it uses as images real things that have their own images in the realm below, and these real things are much clearer and tangible, and valued accordingly.

I understand you to be speaking of the subject-matter of geometry and the kindred arts.

Again, by the second segment of the intelligible world understand me to mean all that unaided reason apprehends by the power of dialectic, when it treats assumptions not as first principles, but as genuine hypotheses, that is to say, as stepping-stones whereby it may rise to a level that requires nothing hypothetical, the first principle of all. Having grasped this, it may turn, and, retaining consequences which depend on it, come down to a conclusion, using no sensible object whatever, but forms alone, and ending with forms.

I do not understand you so well as I could wish, for I believe you to be describing an arduous task, but at any rate I understand that you wish to say that the field of intelligible reality contemplated by dialectic is more certain than the field investigated by what are called the arts, which proceed from hypotheses. The students of the arts are compelled, it is true, to use the understanding and not the senses, but because they do not come back, in the course of inquiry, to a first principle, but start with hypotheses, you think that they do not exercise higher reason on the questions that engage them, although their subject matter is intelligible if associated with a first principle. And I believe you apply the term understanding, not reason, to the mental habit dealing with geometry and like sciences, since you regard understanding as something intermediate between opinion and reason.

You have taken in my meaning most satisfactorily. Please accept these four kinds of cognition as corresponding to the four divisions in our line—namely, reason or intellect, corresponding to the highest, understanding to the second, belief or opinion to the third, and conjecture or imagining to the last. Arrange these in gradation so that the kinds of cognition are clear in the same degree that their objects are true.

Book VII

An allegory illustrates how education or its absence affects our nature. Imagine a number of men living in an underground chamber, with an entrance open to light, extending along the entire length of the cavern, in which they have been confined, from their childhood, with their legs and necks so shackled, that they are obliged to sit still and look directly forwards, because their chains prevent them from turning their heads. And imagine a bright fire burning some way off, above and behind them, and an elevated roadway passing between the fire and the prisoners, with a low wall built along it, like the screens concealing puppeteers, above which they show their puppets.

I have it, he replied.

Also visualize a number of persons walking behind this wall, and carrying with them statues of men, and images of other animals, wrought in wood and stone

and all kinds of materials, together with various other articles, which overtop the wall. As you might expect, some of the passersby will be talking, and others silent.

You describe a strange scene, and strange prisoners.

They resemble us, I replied. Would persons so confined have seen anything of themselves or of each other, beyond the shadows thrown by the fire upon the part of the cave facing them?

Certainly not, if they could never move their heads their entire lives.

And is not their knowledge of the things carried past them equally limited?

Unquestionably it is.

And if they were able to converse with one another, wouldn't they speak of the shadows as reality?

Doubtless they would.

Again, if their prison-house returned an echo from the wall facing them, whenever one of the passersby spoke, wouldn't the prisoners believe the sound came from the passing shadows?

Unquestionably they would.

Then surely such persons would hold the shadows of those manufactured articles to be the only reality.

Without a doubt they would.

Now consider how they might be freed of bondage and error in the following manner. One of them is released, compelled to stand up, turn, and walk with open eyes towards the light. How would he respond, if someone told him that the things he saw before were illusion, but now he is nearer to reality, seeing real things and so seeing more truly? What if someone asked him what the objects above the wall are? Should you not expect him to be puzzled, and to regard the shadows he once saw as truer than the objects now forced to his attention?

Yes, much truer.

And if he were forced to gaze at the light itself, would not his eyes hurt, and would he not flee and turn back to the things which he could see distinctly, and consider them to be really clearer than the things pointed out to him?

Just so.

And if some one were to drag him out of the cave, and force him into the light of the sun, would he not feel pain and resentment, and on reaching the light, would he not find his eyes so dazzled by the glare as to be incapable of seeing any of what are now called realities?

Yes, he would find it so at first.

Hence, habituation will be necessary to enable him to perceive objects in that upper world. At first he will see shadows best. Then he will see the reflections of men and other things in water, and afterwards the things themselves. After this he will see heavenly things—more easily examining the moon and stars by night than the sun by day.

Doubtless.

Last of all, I imagine, he will be able to observe and contemplate the sun, not as reflected in water or fleeting images, but as it is in itself in its own domain.

Of course.

Then he will conclude that the sun causes the seasons and the years, and governs all things in the visible world, and also causes all those things which he and his companions used to see.

Obviously, this will be his next step.

What then? When he recalls his original home, his old fellow-prisoners, and what passes for wisdom among them, do you not think he will pity them and congratulate himself on the change in his circumstances?

Assuredly he will.

And if it was their practice to receive honor and commendations one from another, and to give prizes to him who had the keenest eye, do you fancy that he will covet these prizes? Do you not rather imagine that he would say with Homer that it is "better to be the poor servant of a poor master," and to go through anything, rather than believe those things, and live that way?

I believe he would do anything rather than live that way.

And now consider what would happen if he returned to the cave. Would he not be blinded by the gloom?

Certainly, he would.

And if forced to compete with the others in watching shadows, before becoming habituated to the dim light, would he not be laughed at? Would it not be said of him, that he had gone up only to come back again with his eyesight destroyed, and that it was not worthwhile even to attempt the ascent? And if any one tried to set them free and carry them to the light, would they not kill him, if they got their hands on him?

Yes, they would.

Now, my dear Glaucon, you must apply our allegory to what we have said. The cave is like the visible world, and the light relates to the sun, and if, by the ascent and the contemplation of the upper world, you understand the ascent of the soul into the intelligible order, you will grasp my views, since you desire to be told what they are; though, indeed, God only knows whether they are correct. But, be that as it may, this is the way I see things. In the intelligible world, the essential form of the good is the last thing to be seen, and then very dimly; but, when perceived, we cannot help concluding that it is the cause of all that is right and beautiful, that in the visible world it gives birth to light and its source, that in the intelligible world it is the author of truth and reason, and that whosoever would act wisely, either in private or in public life, must fix his eyes upon the good.

I quite agree with you.

Well, would it be surprising if a person just returning from the contemplation of divine things should appear awkward? What if he were required to answer questions involving arbitrary suppositions made by those who have never yet had a glimpse of justice itself?

No, it would not be surprising if he seemed awkward.

Right, for a sensible man will recollect that the eyes may be confused by sudden transitions either from light to darkness, or from darkness to light. And, believing the soul goes through the same experience, he will not laugh when he sees a case in which the mind is unable to comprehend something, but will ask whether it has just passed from a brighter life to unaccustomed darkness, or from the darkness of ignorance to dazzling light, and not till then will he congratulate the one, and pity the other.

You speak with great judgment.

Hence, education is not what certain professors say, namely those who claim to transfer the power of knowledge into a soul with none. Our present argument shows us that the power of knowledge is already in the soul of each person. Just as it is impossible to turn the eye from darkness to light without turning the whole body, so it is with the power of knowledge. One must turn the whole soul away from the transient world, until we learn to endure the contemplation of the real world and the brightest part thereof, which, according to us, is goodness itself. Am I not right?

You are.

What is needed is an art that would change the soul, not by giving it sight, but by directing its gaze in the proper direction.

So it would appear.

Hence, while, on the one hand, the other so-called virtues of the soul seem to resemble those of the body, inasmuch as they really do not preexist in the soul, but are formed in it in the course of time by habit and exercise, the virtue of wisdom is divine. Its power is constant. But depending on how it is directed, it can be benign or malevolent. If from earliest childhood our characters had been shorn and stripped of those leaden, earthborn weights, which grow and cling to the pleasures of eating and gluttonous enjoyments of a similar nature, and keep the eye of the soul turned upon the things below—if, I repeat, they had been released from these snares, and turned round to look at objects that are true, then these very same souls of these very same men would have had as keen an eye for such pursuits as they actually have for those in which they are now engaged.

Notes

* The riddle is thus given by the Scholiast: "A tale is told, that a man and not a man, seeing and not seeing a bird and not a bird, seated on wood and not on wood, hit it and did not hit it with a stone and not a stone."

⋄ ANCIENT RATIONALISM ⋄

3. THEAETETUS

Plato

SOCRATES. Theaetetus, start again and try to explain what knowledge is.

THEAETETUS. ... It seems to me that one who knows something is perceiving the thing he knows, and, so far as I can see at present, knowledge is nothing but perception.

SOCRATES. The account you give of the nature of knowledge is not, by any means, to be despised. It is the same that was given by Protagoras, though he stated it in a somewhat different way. He says, you will remember, that 'man is the measure of all things—alike of the being of things that are and of the not-being of things that are not.' No doubt you have read that.

THEAETETUS. Yes, often.

SOCRATES. He puts it in this sort of way, doesn't he, that any given thing 'is to me such as it appears to me, and is to you such as it appears to you,' you and I being men?

THEAETETUS. Yes, that is how he puts it.

SOCRATES. Well, what a wise man says is not likely to be nonsense. So let us follow up his meaning. Sometimes, when the same wind is blowing, one of us feels chilly, the other does not, or one may feel slightly chilly, the other quite cold.

THEAETETUS. Certainly.

SOCRATES. Well, in that case are we to say that the wind in itself is cold or not cold? Or shall we agree with Protagoras that it is cold to the one who feels chilly, and not to the other?

THEAETETUS. That seems reasonable.

SOCRATES. And further that it so 'appears' to each of us?

THEAETETUS. Yes.

SOCRATES. And 'appears' means that he 'perceives' it so?

THEAETETUS. True.

SOCRATES. 'Appearing,' then, is the same thing as 'perceiving' in the case of what is hot or anything of that kind. They *are* to each man such as he *perceives* them.

THEAETETUS. So it seems.

SOCRATES. Perception, then, is always of something that *is*, and, as being knowledge, it is infallible.

THEAETETUS. That is clear ...

SOCRATES. And now, perhaps, you may wonder what argument Protagoras will find to defend his position. Shall we try to put it into words?

THEAETETUS. By all means.

SOCRATES. No doubt, then, Protagoras will make all the points we have put forward in our attempt to defend him, and at the same time will come to close quarters with the assailant, dismissing us with contempt. Your admirable Socrates, he will say, finds a little boy who is scared at being asked whether one and the same person can remember and at the same time not know one and the same thing. When the child is frightened into saying no, because he cannot foresee the consequence, Socrates turns the conversation so as to make a figure of fun of my unfortunate self. . . .

I do indeed assert that the truth is as I have written. Each one of us is a measure of what is and of what is not, but there is all the difference in the world between one man and another just in the very fact that what is and appears to one is different from what is and appears to the other. And as for wisdom and the wise man, I am very far from saying they do not exist. By a wise man I mean precisely a man who can change any one of us, when what is bad appears and is to him, and make what is good appear and be to him. In this statement, again, don't set off in chase of words, but let me explain still more clearly what I mean. Remember how it was put earlier in the conversation. To the sick man his food appears sour and is so; to the healthy man it is and appears the opposite. Now there is no call to represent either of the two as wiser—that cannot be—nor is the sick man to be pronounced unwise because he thinks as he does, or the healthy man wise because he thinks differently. What is wanted is a change to the opposite condition, because the other state is better.

And so too in education a change has to be effected from the worse condition to the better; only, whereas the physician produces a change by means of drugs, the Sophist does it by discourse. It is not that a man makes someone who previously thought what is false think what is true, for it is not possible either to think the thing that is not or to think anything but what one experiences, and all experiences are true. Rather, I should say, when someone by reason of a depraved condition of mind has thoughts of a like character, one makes him, by reason of a sound condition, think other and sound thoughts, which some people ignorantly call true, whereas I should say that one set of thoughts is better than the other, but not in any way truer . . . In this way it is true both that some men are wiser than

others and that no one thinks falsely, and you, whether you like it or not, must put up with being a measure, since by these considerations my doctrine is saved from shipwreck. . . .

SOCRATES. Well now, Protagoras, we are expressing what seems true to a man, or rather to all men, when we say that everyone without exception holds that in some respects he is wiser than his neighbors and in others they are wiser than he. For instance, in moments of great danger and distress, whether in war or in sickness or at sea, men regard as a god anyone who can take control of the situation and look to him as a savior, when his only point of superiority is his knowledge. Indeed, the world is full of people looking for those who can instruct and govern men and animals and direct their doings, and on the other hand of people who think themselves quite competent to undertake the teaching and governing. In all these cases what can we say, if not that men do hold that wisdom and ignorance exist among them?

THEODORUS [SPEAKING FOR PROTAGORAS]: We must say that.

SOCRATES. And they hold that wisdom lies in thinking truly, and ignorance in false belief?

THEODORUS. Of course.

SOCRATES. In that case, Protagoras, what are we to make of your doctrine? Are we to say that what men think is always true, or that it is sometimes true and sometimes false? From either supposition it results that their thoughts are not always true, but both true and false. For consider, Theodorus. Are you, or is any Protagorean, prepared to maintain that no one regards anyone else as ignorant or as making false judgments?

THEODORUS. That is incredible, Socrates.

SOCRATES. That, however, is the inevitable consequence of the doctrine which makes man the measure of all things.

THEODORUS. How so?

SOCRATES. When you have formed a judgment on some matter in your own mind and express an opinion about it to me, let us grant that, as Protagoras's theory says, it is true for you, but are we to understand that it is impossible for us, the rest of the company, to pronounce any judgment upon your judgment, or, if we can, that we always pronounce your opinion to be true? Do you not rather find thousands of opponents who set their opinion against yours on every occasion and hold that your judgment and belief are false?

THEODORUS. I should just think so, Socrates—thousands and tens of thousands, as Homer says, and they give me all the trouble in the world.

SOCRATES. And what then? Would you have us say that in such a case the opinion you hold is true for yourself and false for these tens of thousands?

THEODORUS. The doctrine certainly seems to imply that.

SOCRATES. And what is the consequence for Protagoras himself? Is it not this? Supposing that not even he believed in man being the measure and the world in general did not believe it either—as in fact it doesn't—then this *Truth* which he wrote would not be true for anyone. If, on the other hand, he did believe it, but the mass of mankind does not agree with him, then, you see, it is more false than true by just so much as the unbelievers outnumber the believers.

THEODORUS. That follows, if its truth or falsity varies with each individual opinion.

SOCRATES. Yes, and besides that it involves a really exquisite conclusion. Protagoras, for his part, admitting as he does that everybody's opinion is true, must acknowledge the truth of his opponents belief about his own belief, where they think he is wrong.

THEODORUS. Certainly.

SOCRATES. That is to say, he would acknowledge his own belief to be false, if he admits that the belief of those who think him wrong is true?

THEODORUS. Necessarily.

SOCRATES. But the others, on their side, do not admit to themselves that they are wrong.

THEODORUS. No.

SOCRATES. Whereas Protagoras, once more, according to what he has written, admits that this opinion of theirs is as true as any other.

THEODORUS. Evidently.

SOCRATES. On all hands, then, Protagoras included, his opinion will be disputed, or rather Protagoras will join in the general consent—when he admits to an opponent the truth of his contrary opinion, from that moment Protagoras himself will be admitting that a dog or the man in the street is not a measure of anything whatever that he does not understand. Isn't that so?

THEODORUS. Yes.

SOCRATES. Then, since it is disputed by everyone, the *Truth* of Protagoras is true to nobody—to himself no more than to anyone else.

. . .

SOCRATES. To start all over again, then, what is one to say that knowledge is? For surely we are not going to give up yet.

THEAETETUS. Not unless you do so.

SOCRATES. Then tell me, what definition can we give with the least risk of contradicting ourselves?

THEAETETUS. The one we tried before, Socrates. I have nothing else to suggest.

SOCRATES. What was that?

THEAETETUS. That true belief is knowledge. Surely there can at least be no mistake in believing what is true and the consequences are always satisfactory.

SOCRATES. Try, and you will see, Theaetetus, as the man said when he was asked if the river was too deep to ford. So here, if we go forward on our search, we may stumble upon something that will reveal the thing we are looking for. We shall make nothing out, if we stay where we are.

THEAETETUS. True. Let us go forward and see.

SOCRATES. Well, we need not go far to see this much. You will find a whole profession to prove that true belief is not knowledge.

THEAETETUS. How so? What profession?

SOCRATES. The profession of those paragons of intellect known as orators and lawyers. There you have men who use their skill to produce conviction, not by instruction, but by making people believe whatever they want them to believe. You can hardly imagine teachers so clever as to be able, in the short time allowed by the clock, to instruct their hearers thoroughly in the true facts of a case of robbery or other violence which those hearers had not witnessed.

THEAETETUS. No, I cannot imagine that, but they can convince them.

SOCRATES. And by convincing you mean making them believe something.

THEAETETUS. Of course.

SOCRATES. And when a jury is rightly convinced of facts which can be known only by an eyewitness, then, judging by hearsay and accepting a true belief, they are judging without knowledge, although, if they find the right verdict, their conviction is correct?

THEAETETUS. Certainly.

SOCRATES. But if true belief and knowledge were the same thing, the best of jurymen could never have a correct belief without knowledge. It now appears that they must be different things.

THEAETETUS. Yes, Socrates, I have heard someone make the distinction. I had forgotten, but now it comes back to me. He said that true belief with the addition of an account (λόγος) was knowledge, while belief without an account was outside its range. Where no account could be given of a thing, it was not 'knowable'—that was the word he used—where it could, it was knowable.

SOCRATES. A good suggestion. But tell me how he distinguished these knowable things from the unknowable. It may turn out that what you were told tallies with something I have heard said.

THEAETETUS. I am not sure if I can recall that, but I think I should recognize it if I heard it stated.

SOCRATES. If you have had a dream, let me tell you mine in return. I seem to have heard some people say that what might be called the first elements of which we and all other things consist are such that no account can be given of them. Each of them just by itself can only be named; we cannot attribute to it anything further or say that it exists or does not exist, for we should at once be attaching to it existence or nonexistence, whereas we ought to add nothing if we are to express just it alone. We ought not even to add 'just' or 'it' or 'each' or 'alone' or 'this,' or any other of a host of such terms. These terms, running loose about the place, are attached to everything, and they are distinct from the things to which they are applied. If it were possible for an element to be expressed in any formula exclusively belonging to it, no other terms ought to enter into that expression. But in fact there is no formula in which any element can be expressed; it can only be named, for a name is all there is that belongs to it. But when we come to things composed of these elements, then, just as these things are complex, so the names are combined to make a description (λόγος), a description being precisely a combination of names. Accordingly, elements are inexplicable and unknowable, but they can be perceived, while complexes ('syllables') are knowable and explicable, and you can have a true notion of them. So when a man gets hold of the true notion of something without an

account, his mind does think truly of it, but he does not know it, for if one cannot give and receive an account of a thing, one has no knowledge of that thing. But when he has also got hold of an account, all this becomes possible to him and he is fully equipped with knowledge.

Does that version represent the dream as you heard it, or not?

THEAETETUS. Perfectly.

SOCRATES. So this dream finds favor and you hold that a true notion with the addition of an account is knowledge?

THEAETETUS. Precisely.

. . .

SOCRATES. Well then, what is this term 'account' intended to convey to us? . . . If, on the one hand, it means adding the notion of how a thing differs from other things; such an injunction is simply absurd.

THEAETETUS. How so?

SOCRATES. When we have a correct notion of the way in which certain things differ from other things, it tells us to add a correct notion of the way in which they differ from other things. On this showing, the most vicious of circles would be nothing to this injunction. It might better deserve to be called the sort of direction a blind man might give. To tell us to get hold of something we already have, in order to get to know something we are already thinking of, suggests a state of the most absolute darkness.

THEAETETUS. Whereas, if . . . ? The supposition you made just now implied that you would state some alternative. What was it?

SOCRATES. If the direction to add an 'account' means that we are to get to *know* the differentness, as opposed to merely having a notion of it, this most admirable of all definitions of knowledge will be a pretty business, because 'getting to know' means acquiring knowledge, doesn't it?

THEAETETUS. Yes.

SOCRATES. So, apparently, to the question, 'What is knowledge?' our definition will reply, 'Correct belief together with knowledge of a differentness,' for, according to it, 'adding an account' will come to that.

THEAETETUS. So it seems.

SOCRATES. Yes, and when we are inquiring after the nature of knowledge, nothing could be sillier than to say that it is correct belief together with a *knowledge* of differentness or of anything whatever.

So, Theaetetus, neither perception, nor true belief, nor the addition of an 'account' to true belief can be knowledge.

THEAETETUS. Apparently not.

SOCRATES. Are we in labor, then, with any further child, my friend, or have we brought to birth all we have to say about knowledge?

THEAETETUS. Indeed we have, and for my part I have already, thanks to you, given utterance to more than I had in me.

✧ ANCIENT SKEPTICISM ✧

4. OUTLINES OF PYRRHONISM

Sextus Empiricus

Book One

Chapter I: The Basic Difference Between Philosophies

It is a fair presumption that when people search for a thing the result will be either its discovery, a confession of non-discovery and of its non-apprehensibility, or perseverance in the search. Perhaps this is the reason why in matters of philosophical research some claim to have discovered the truth, while others declare that finding it is an impossibility, and others are still seeking it. There are some who think they have found the truth, such as Aristotle, Epicurus, the Stoics, and certain others. These are, in a special sense of the term, the so-called dogmatists. Clitomachus and Carneades, on the other hand, and other Academics, claim it is a search for inapprehensibles. But the Sceptics go on searching. It is, therefore, a reasonable inference that basically there are three philosophies, the dogmatic, the Academic, and the Sceptic. For the present our task will be to present an outline of the Sceptic discipline, leaving it to such others as it befits to treat of the former two. We declare at the outset that we do not make any positive assertion that anything we shall say is wholly as we affirm it to be. We merely report accurately on each thing as our impressions of it are at the moment.

Chapter II: The Arguments of Scepticism

The Sceptic philosophy comprises two types of argument, the general and the special. In the first we undertake an exposition of the character of Scepticism by stating its notion, the principles and methods of reasoning involved, and its criterion and end. We set forth also the various modes of suspension of judgement, the manner in which we use the Sceptic formulae, and the distinction between Scepticism and those philosophies which closely approach it. The special argument is that in which we dispute the validity of so-called philosophy in all its parts. Let us, then, first treat of the general argument and begin our sketch with the various appellations of the Sceptic discipline.

Chapter III: The Names of Scepticism

Now, the Sceptic discipline is called the "zetetic" (searching) from its activity of searching and examining. It is also called the "ephectic" (suspending) from the experience which the inquirer feels after the search. "Aporetic" (doubting) is another name for it, either from the fact that their doubting and searching extends to everything (the opinion of some), or from their inability to give final assent or denial. It is also called "Pyrrhonean," because Pyrrho appears to us to have applied himself to Scepticism more thoroughly and with more distinction than his predecessors.

Chapter IV: The Meaning of Scepticism

Scepticism is an ability to place in antithesis, in any manner whatever, appearances and judgements, and thus—because of the equality of force in the objects and arguments opposed—to come first of all to a suspension of judgement and then to mental tranquillity. Now, we call it an "ability" not in any peculiar sense of the word, but simply as it denotes a "being able." "Appearances" we take as meaning the objects of sense-perception, hence we set over against them the objects of thought. The phrase "in any manner whatever" may attach itself to "ability," so that we may understand that word (as we have said) in its simple sense, or it may be understood as modifying the phrase "to place in antithesis appearances and judgements." For since the antitheses we make take various forms, appearances opposed to appearances, judgements to judgements, or appearances to judgements, we say "in any manner whatever" in order to include all the antitheses. Or, we may understand it as "any manner of appearances and judgements whatever," in order to relieve ourselves of the inquiry into how appearances appear or how judgements are formed, and thus take them at their face value. When we speak of arguments which are "opposed," we do not at all mean denial and affirmation, but use this word in the sense of "conflicting." By "equality of force" we mean equality in respect of credibility and incredibility, since we do not admit that any of the conflicting arguments can take precedence over another on grounds of its being more credible. "Suspension of judgement" is a cessation of the thought processes in consequence of which we neither deny nor affirm anything. "Mental tranquillity" is an undisturbed and calm state of soul.

Chapter V: The Sceptic

The definition of the Pyrrhonean philosopher is also virtually included in the concept of the Sceptic discipline. It is, of course, he who shares in the "ability" we have spoken of.

Chapter VI: The Principles of Scepticism

Scepticism has its inception and cause, we say, in the hope of attaining mental tranquillity. Men of noble nature had been disturbed at the irregularity in things, and puzzled as to where they should place

their belief. Thus they were led on to investigate both truth and falsehood in things, in order that, when truth and falsehood were determined, they might attain tranquillity of mind. Now, the principle fundamental to the existence of Scepticism is the proposition, "To every argument an equal argument is opposed," for we believe that it is in consequence of this principle that we are brought to a point where we cease to dogmatize.

Chapter VII: Does the Sceptic Dogmatize?

We say that the Sceptic does not dogmatize. But in saying this we do not understand the word "dogma" as some do, in the more general sense of "approval of a thing." The Sceptic, of course, assents to feelings which derive necessarily from sense-impressions; he would not, for example, when feeling warm (or cold), say, "I believe I am not warm (or cold)." But some say that "dogma" is "the assent given to one of the non-evident things which form the object of scientific research." It is this meaning of "dogma" that we have in view when we say that the Sceptic does not dogmatize, for concerning non-evident things the Pyrrhonean philosopher holds no opinion. In fact, he does not even dogmatize when he is uttering the Sceptic formulae in regard to non-evident things (these formulae, the "No more," the "I determine nothing," and the others, we shall speak of later). No—for the dogmatizer affirms the real existence of that thing about which he is said to be dogmatizing, whereas the Sceptic does not take the real existence of these formulae wholly for granted. As he understands them, the formula "All things are false," for example, asserts its own falsity together with that of all other things, and the formula "Nothing is true" likewise. Thus also the formula "No more" asserts not only of other things but of itself also that it is "no more" existent than anything else, and hence cancels itself together with the other things. We say the same about the other Sceptic formulae also. However, if the dogmatizer affirms the real existence of the thing about which he is dogmatizing, while the Sceptic, uttering his own formulae, does so in such a way that they virtually cancel themselves, he can hardly be said to be dogmatizing when he pronounces them. The greatest indication of this is that in the enunciation of these formulae he is saying what appears to him and is reporting his own feeling, without indulging in opinion or making positive statements about the reality of things outside himself.

Chapter VIII: Does the Sceptic Have a System?

Our attitude is the same when we are asked whether the Sceptic has a system. For if one defines "system" as "an adherence to a set of numerous dogmas which are consistent both with one another and with appearances," and if "dogma" is defined as "assent to a non-evident thing," then we shall say that we have no system. But if one means by "system" a "discipline which, in accordance with appearance, follows a certain line of reasoning, that line of reasoning indicating how it is possible to seem to live rightly ('rightly' understood not only with reference to virtue, but more simply), and extending also to the ability to suspend judgement," then we say that we do have a system. For we follow a certain line of reasoning which indicates to us, in a manner consistent with appearances, how to live in accordance with the customs, the laws, and the institutions of our country, and with our own natural feelings.

Chapter X: Do the Sceptics Deny Appearances?

Those who say that the Sceptics deny appearances seem to me to be ignorant of what we say. As we said above, we do not deny those things which, in accordance with the passivity of our sense-impressions, lead us involuntarily to give our assent to them; and these are the appearances. And when we inquire whether an object is such as it appears, we grant the fact of its appearance. Our inquiry is thus not directed at the appearance itself. Rather, it is a question of what is predicated of it, and this is a different thing from investigating the fact of the appearance itself. For example, honey appears to us to have a sweetening quality. This much we concede, because it affects us with a sensation of sweetness. The question, however, is whether it is sweet in an absolute sense. Hence not the appearance is questioned, but that which is predicated of the appearance. Whenever we do expound arguments directly against appearances, we do so not with the intention of denying them, but in order to point out the hasty

judgement of the dogmatists. For if reason is such a rogue as to all but snatch even the appearances from under our very eyes, should we not by all means be wary of it, at least not be hasty to follow it, in the case of things non-evident?

Chapter XI: The Criterion of Scepticism

That we pay attention to appearances is clear from what we say about the criterion of the Sceptic discipline. Now, the word "criterion" is used in two senses. First, it is the standard one takes for belief in reality or non-reality. This we shall discuss in our refutation. Second, it is the standard of action the observance of which regulates our actions in life. It is this latter about which we now speak. Now, we say that the criterion of the Sceptic discipline is the appearance, and it is virtually the sense-presentation to which we give this name, for this is dependent on feeling and involuntary affection and hence is not subject to question. Therefore no one, probably, will dispute that an object has this or that appearance; the question is whether it is in reality as it appears to be. Now, we cannot be entirely inactive when it comes to the observances of everyday life. Therefore, while living undogmatically, we pay due regard to appearances. This observance of the requirements of daily life seems to be fourfold, with the following particular heads: the guidance of nature, the compulsion of the feelings, the tradition of laws and customs, and the instruction of the arts. It is by the guidance of nature that we are naturally capable of sensation and thought. It is by the compulsion of the feelings that hunger leads us to food and thirst leads us to drink. It is by virtue of the tradition of laws and customs that in everyday life we accept piety as good and impiety as evil. And it is by virtue of the instruction of the arts that we are not inactive in those arts which we employ. All these statements, however, we make without prejudice.

Chapter XII: The End of Scepticism

The next point to go through would be the end of Scepticism. An end is "that at which all actions or thoughts are directed, and which is itself directed at nothing, in other words, the ultimate of desirable things." Our assertion up to now is that the Sceptic's end, where matters of opinion are concerned, is mental tranquillity; in the realm of things unavoidable, moderation of feeling is the end. His initial purpose in philosophizing was to pronounce judgement on appearances. He wished to find out which are true and which false, so as to attain mental tranquillity. In doing so, he met with contradicting alternatives of equal force. Since he could not decide between them, he withheld judgement. Upon his suspension of judgement there followed, by chance, mental tranquillity in matters of opinion. For the person who entertains the opinion that anything is by nature good or bad is continually disturbed. When he lacks those things which seem to him to be good, he believes he is being pursued, as if by the Furies, by those things which are by nature bad, and pursues what he believes to be the good things. But when he has acquired them, he encounters further perturbations. This is because his elation at the acquisition is unreasonable and immoderate, and also because in his fear of a reversal all his exertions go to prevent the loss of the things which to him seem good. On the other side there is the man who leaves undetermined the question what things are good and bad by nature. He does not exert himself to avoid anything or to seek after anything, and hence he is in a tranquil state.

The Sceptic, in fact, had the same experience as that related in the story about Apelles the artist. They say that when Apelles was painting a horse, he wished to represent the horse's foam in the painting. His attempt was so unsuccessful that he gave it up and at the same time flung at the picture his sponge, with which he had wiped the paints off his brush. As it struck the picture, the sponge produced an image of horse's foam. So it was with the Sceptics. They were in hopes of attaining mental tranquillity, thinking that they could do this by arriving at some rational judgement which would dispel the inconsistencies involved in both appearances and thoughts. When they found this impossible, they withheld judgement. While they were in this state, they made a chance discovery. They found that they were attended by mental tranquillity as surely as a body by its shadow.

Nevertheless, we do not suppose the Sceptic to be altogether free from disturbance, rather, we say that when he is disturbed, it is by things which are

unavoidable. Certainly we concede that he is sometimes cold and thirsty, and that he suffers in other such ways. But even here there is a difference. Two circumstances combine to the detriment of the ordinary man: he is hindered both by the feelings themselves and not less by the fact that he believes these conditions to be evil by nature. The Sceptic, on the other hand, rejects this additional notion that each of these things is evil by nature, and thus he gets off more easily. These, then, are our reasons for saying that the Sceptic's end is mental tranquillity where matters of opinion are concerned, and moderate feeling in the realm of things unavoidable. Some notable Sceptics have, however, added to these a third: suspension of judgement in investigations.

Chapter XIII: General Introduction to the Modes of Suspension of Judgment

We were saying that mental tranquillity follows on suspension of judgement in regard to all things. Next, it would be proper for us to state how we attain suspension of judgement. As a general rule, this suspension of judgement is effected by our setting things in opposition. We oppose appearances to appearances, or thoughts to thoughts, or appearances to thoughts. For example, when we say, "The same tower appears round from a distance, but square from close by," we are opposing appearances to appearances. When a person is trying to prove the existence of providence from the order of the celestial bodies, and we counter him with the observation that the good often fare ill while the evil prosper and then conclude from this that there is no providence, we are opposing thoughts to thoughts. And then appearances may be opposed to thoughts. Anaxagoras, for instance, could oppose to the fact that snow is white his reasoning that "Snow is frozen water, and water is black, snow therefore is black also." And sometimes, from the point of view of a different concept, we oppose present things to present things, as in the foregoing, and sometimes present things to past or future things. An example of this is the following. Whenever someone propounds an argument that we are not able to dispose of, we make this reply: "Before the birth of the founder of the school to which you belong, this argument of your school was not yet seen to be a sound argument. From the point of view of nature, however, it existed all the while as such. In like manner it is possible, as far as nature is concerned, that an argument antithetical to the one now set forth by you is in existence, though as yet unknown to us. This being so, the fact that an argument seems valid to us now is not yet a sufficient reason why we must assent to it."

But for a better understanding of these antitheses, I shall now present also the modes by which suspension of judgement is induced. I cannot, however, vouch for their number or validity, since it is possible that they are unsound, and that there are more of them than the ones to be discussed.

Chapter XIV: The Ten Modes

With the older Sceptics the usual teaching is that the modes by which suspension of judgement seems to be brought about are ten in number, which they also term synonymously "arguments" and "forms." These are as follows. First is that in which suspension is caused by the variation in animals. In the second it is caused by the differences in human beings. Third, by the differences in the construction of the organs of sense. Fourth, by the circumstances. Fifth, by the positions, distances, and places involved. Sixth, by the admixtures present. Seventh, by the quantities and compoundings of the underlying objects. Eighth, by the relativity of things. Ninth, by the frequency or rarity of occurrence. Tenth, by the institutions, customs, laws, mythical beliefs, and dogmatic notions. This order, however, is merely arbitrary.

Transcending these are three modes: the argument from the subject judging, the argument from the object judged, and that from both. The first four modes above are subordinate to the argument from the subject judging (for that which judges is either an animal or a human being or a sense, and is in some circumstance or other). The seventh and the tenth are referred to the argument from the object judged. The fifth, sixth, eighth, and ninth are referred to the argument from both combined. These three modes are in turn referred to the mode of relativity, so that the mode of relativity is the *summum genus*, while the three are its species, and the ten are subordinate.

The Fourth Mode   But we can also reach suspension by basing our argument on each sense separately, or even by disregarding the senses. To this end we employ the fourth mode of suspension, which we call

the mode based on the circumstances. We understand by "circumstances" the states in which we are. This mode, we say, is seen in cases of natural or unnatural states, in states of waking or sleeping, in cases where age, motion or rest, hating or loving are involved; or where the determining factor is a state of want or satiety, drunkenness or soberness; in cases of predispositions, or when it is a question of confidence or fear, or grief or joy. For example, things appear dissimilar according to whether we are in a natural or unnatural state; delirious people, and those who are possessed by a god, think that they hear divine voices, while we do not. Often they claim that they perceive, among a number of other things, the odour of storax or frankincense, or something of that sort, where we perceive nothing. And the same water that seems hot to a person when poured on inflamed parts seems lukewarm to us. The coat which appears yellowish-orange to men with bloodshot eyes does not appear so to me, yet it is the same coat. And the same honey that appears sweet to me appears bitter to those suffering from jaundice.

Now, one might object that in those whose condition is unnatural it is the intermingling of certain humours that causes them to get unnatural impressions from the external objects. Our reply to this would be that it is possible that the external objects actually are in reality such as they appear to those who are said to be in an unnatural state; and that since persons in a state of good health also have mixed humours, it may be that it is these humours that make the objects appear different to them. For it would be a fabrication to attribute to the humours of sick people a power to to change external objects, and to deny this power to the humours of the healthy. After all, it is natural for the healthy to be in a healthy state, and unnatural for them to be in a sick state. By the same token it is unnatural for the sick to be in a healthy state, but natural for them to be in a sick state. Consequently, the sick warrant credence also, since they too are in some respect in a natural state. Whether one is in a sleeping or a waking state also makes a difference in the sense-impressions, since our manner of perception while awake differs from the perception we have in sleep; and our manner of perception in sleep is not like our waking perception. As a result, the existence or non-existence of our sense-impressions is not absolute but relative, since they bear a relation to our sleeping or waking state. It is probable, therefore, that although our dream-images are unreal in our waking state, they are nevertheless not absolutely unreal, for they do exist in our dreams. In the same manner the realities of the waking state, even if they do not exist in dreams, nevertheless exist. Age also makes a difference. Old men, for example, may think the air is cold, but the same air seems mild to those who are in the prime of life. The same colour appears dim to older persons but full to those in their prime. And a sound, likewise the same, seems faint to the former but quite audible to the latter.

Now, considering the fact that so much discrepancy is due to the states we are in, and that men are in different states at different times, it is easy, perhaps, to state the nature of each object as it appears to this or that person, but difficult to say further what its real nature is. This is because the discrepancy does not lend itself to judgement. In fact, whoever attempts to resolve this discrepancy will find himself either in one or the other of the aforesaid states or else in no state at all. But now to say that he is in no state at all, that he is neither healthy nor sick, neither in motion nor at rest, that he is not of any particular age, and that he is free from the other states, is perfectly absurd. On the other hand, the fact of his being in some state or other while attempting to pass judgement will make him a party to the controversy. And moreover, he will be confused by the states in which he finds himself, and this will prevent him from being an absolute judge in the matter. A person, therefore, who is in the waking state cannot compare the impressions of a sleeping person with those of waking persons, and a healthy person cannot compare the impressions of sick people with those of the healthy. We do, after all, tend to give our assent to those things which are present and have a present influence over us rather than to things which are not present.

The discrepancy between such impressions is irresolvable on other grounds also, for if a person prefers one sense-impression to another, and one circumstance to another, he does so either without judging and without proof or by judging and offering proof. But he cannot do so without judgement and proof, for then he will be discredited. Nor can he do so even with judgement and proof, for if he judges the impressions, he must at all events use a criterion in judging them. And this criterion he will declare to be either true or false. If false, he will not be worthy of belief; but if he claims it is true, then his statement that the criterion is true will be offered either without proof or with proof. If without proof, again he will not be worthy of belief; but if he offers proof for his statement, the proof must in any case be a true one, otherwise he will not be worthy of belief. Now, if he says that the proof employed for the confirmation of his criterion is true, will he say this after having passed judgement on the proof, or without having judged it? If he has not judged it, he will not be worthy of belief, but if he has, obviously he will say he has used a criterion in his judgement. We shall ask for a proof for this criterion, and for this proof another criterion. For the proof always needs a criterion to confirm it, and the criterion needs a proof to show that it is true. A proof cannot be sound without the pre-existence of a true criterion, and a criterion cannot be true either without prior confirmation of the proof. And so both the criterion and the proof fall into circular argument, in which both are found to be untrustworthy. The fact that each expects confirmation from the other makes both of them equally untrustworthy. It is impossible, then, for a person to give the preference to one sense-impression over another. This being so, such differences in sense-impressions as arise from a disparity of states will be irresolvable. As a result, this mode also serves to introduce suspension of judgement with regard to the nature of external objects.

Chapter XV: The Five Modes

The later Sceptics, however, teach five modes of suspension. These are the following. The first is based on disagreement. The second is that which produces to infinity. Third, that based on relativity. Fourth, that from assumption. And fifth, the argument in a circle.

That based on disagreement is the one in which we find that in regard to a proposed matter there has arisen in the opinions both of people at large and of the philosophers an unresolved dissension. Because of this dissension we are unable either to choose or to reject anything, and thus we end with suspension of judgement. The mode based on the extension to infinity is the one in which we say that the proof offered for the verification of a proposed matter requires a further verification, and this one another, and so on to infinity, so that since we lack a point of departure for our reasoning, the consequence is suspension of judgement. That based on relativity is that in which, just as we have already said, the object appears thus or thus in relation to the thing judging and the things perceived along with it, while as to its true nature we suspend judgement. The mode from assumption exists when the dogmatists, in their *regressus ad infinitum*, take as their point of departure a proposition which they do not establish by reasoning, but simply and without proof assume as conceded to them. The mode of argument in a circle arises when that which ought itself to be confirmatory of the matter under investigation requires verification from the thing being investigated; at that point, being unable to take either of them to establish the other, we suspend judgement about both.

That it is possible to refer every question to these modes we shall show briefly as follows. The object proposed is either an object of sense or an object of thought; but no matter which it is, it is a disputed point. For some say that the objects of sense alone are true, some say only the objects of thought are true, while others say that some objects of sense and some objects of thought are true. Now, will they assert that the disagreement is resolvable, or irresolvable? If irresolvable, then we have the necessity of suspension pension granted; for it is not possible to pronounce on things when the dispute about them is irresolvable. But if the dispute is resolvable, then we ask from what quarter the decision is to come. Taking, for example, the object of sense (to fix our argument on this one first), is it to be judged by an object of sense or by an object of thought? If by an object of sense, then, seeing that our inquiry is about objects of sense, that object too will need another as confirmation. And if that other is an object of sense, again it will itself need another to confirm it, and so on to infinity. But if the object of sense will have to be judged by an object of thought, then, since objects of thought also are a matter of dispute, this object, being an object of thought, will require judgement and

confirmation. Where, then, is the confirmation to come from? If it is to be confirmed by an object of thought, we shall likewise have an extension *ad infinitum*; but if by an object of sense, the mode of circular reasoning is introduced, because an object of thought was employed for the confirmation of the object of sense and an object of sense for the confirmation of the object of thought.

If, however, our interlocutor should try to escape from these conclusions and claim the right to assume, as a concession without proof, some proposition serving to prove the rest of his argument, then the mode of assumption will be brought in, which leaves him no way out. For if a person is worthy of credence when he makes an assumption, then we shall in each case also be not less worthy of credence if we make the opposite assumption. And if the person making the assumption assumes something which is true, he renders it suspicious by taking it on assumption instead of proving it. But if what he assumes is false, the foundation of what he is trying to prove will be unsound. Moreover, if assumption conduces at all towards proof, let the thing in question itself be assumed and not something else by means of which he will then prove the thing under discussion. But if it is absurd to assume the thing in question, it will also be absurd to assume what transcends it.

But it is evident that all objects of sense are also relative, for they exist as such in relation to those who perceive them. It is clear, then, that whatever sensible object is set before us, it can easily be referred to the five modes. Our reasoning concerning the intelligible object is similar. For if it should be said that it is the subject of an irresolvable disagreement, the necessity of suspending judgement on this matter will be granted us. But in the case of a resolution of the disagreement, if the resolution is reached by means of an object of thought, we shall have recourse to the extension *ad infinitum*; if by means of an object of sense, we shall have recourse to the mode of circular reasoning. For as the sensible again is an object of disagreement, and incapable, because of the extension to infinity, of being decided by means of itself, it will stand in need of the intelligible just as the intelligible also requires the sensible. For these reasons, whoever accepts anything on assumption will again be in an absurd position. But intelligibles are also relative, for they are relative to the intellect in which they appear, whence their name. And if they really were in nature such as they are said to be, there would be no disagreement about them. Thus the intelligible too has been referred to the five modes, so that in any case we must suspend judgement with regard to the object presented.

Such are the five modes taught by the later Sceptics. Their purpose in setting them forth is not to repudiate the ten modes, but to provide for a more diversified exposure of the rashness of the dogmatists by combining these modes with the others.

Chapter XVI: The Two Modes

They also teach two other modes of suspension. Since everything apprehended seems to be apprehended either through itself or through something else, they show us that nothing is apprehended either through itself or through another thing, thus introducing, as they think, doubt about all things. That nothing is apprehended through itself is clear, they say, from the disagreement existing amongst the physicists regarding, I believe, all sensibles and intelligibles. Since we are not able to take either an object of sense or an object of thought as a criterion (any criterion we take, if there is disagreement about it, is unreliable), the disagreement is of course irresolvable. Because of this they do not concede that anything can be apprehended through another thing either. For if that through which something is apprehended must itself always be apprehended through another thing, we fall into the mode of circular reasoning or into the mode of infinity. But if a person should wish to assume a thing (through which another thing is apprehended) as being apprehended through itself, an objection arises in the fact that, by reason of what we have said above, nothing is apprehended through itself. And we are uncertain as to how that which conflicts with itself can be apprehended either through itself or through something else, since no criterion of truth or of apprehension appears, and since even signs apart from proof are rejected, as we shall recognize in the next book. So much, then, for the modes of suspension. What we have said will be sufficient for the present.

✧ CHAPTER 2 MODERN READINGS ✧

INTRODUCTION

The scholastic tradition inspired by Plato and Aristotle dominated the Middle Ages and was still powerful during the seventeenth century, when the French philosopher René Descartes lived. By breaking in important ways with the scholasticism of his peers, Descartes initiated the period known as the modern era, and earned the title of father of modern philosophy. Inspired by his successes in mathematics, Descartes believed that human inquiry should be conducted in accordance with principles that would guarantee truth. By employing the proper methodology, in principle any individual could come to see the truth for him- or herself. Inquiry, for Descartes, makes the truth evident to any individual whose faculties are intact, so long as that person is willing to make the careful effort required. Hence all of us can rely on our own careful judgment to decide what to believe. In this way Descartes combated one of the most prominent features of scholasticism and Platonism, namely, deference to authority, or the idea that the vast majority of us should simply go along with what authorities tell us, since their intellectual resources are superior to ours. In many other ways, however, Descartes' perspective was a product of his times. Like Plato, he was a rationalist; he thought that true knowledge derives from reason and thought, and was skeptical about basing belief on experience. Nonetheless, Descartes helped lend credence to the empiricist view that sensation is a source of knowledge by suggesting that first-person experience reports, such as "I am in pain," like other introspective reports, such as "I am thinking," are indubitable, and thus suitable as partial grounds for further knowledge claims.

Many of Descartes's successors were heavily influenced by his (and Plato's) rationalism; it is traditional to rank Spinoza and Leibniz alongside of Descartes as the 'Continental rationalists,' to distinguish from them a second group called the 'British empiricists' that includes John Locke, George Berkeley, and David Hume, and to view Immanuel Kant as a bridge figure who attempted to synthesize rationalism and empiricism. This framework is useful, but instead of drawing a sharp line between the two camps, it might be best to say that the empiricists gradually narrowed the role that reason plays in knowledge, and gradually widened the role that experience plays. The rationalists and the empiricists disagreed about the relative extensiveness of the contributions of experience and reason to knowledge.

The earliest indigenous philosophical movement in the United States was itself an offshoot of empiricism. Called *pragmatism*, it was initiated by Charles Peirce and William James in the latter part of the nineteenth century. Pragmatists offered theories about a range of issues, including the nature of truth and of the meanings of elements of language, which have been widely influential, both in the United States and abroad. For our purposes its most significant legacy may have been the abandonment of the profoundly anti-conservative Cartesian presupposition that to be epistemically respectable each of our beliefs must be substantiated. Descartes was aware that this presupposition fostered skeptical doubts; he had thought that these doubts could be usefully applied to reveal the structure of knowledge and then eliminated. But it became increasingly clear to Descartes's successors that unrestricted doubt destroys all belief, and that to meet a doubt about one thing, we must take other things for granted. Peirce's theory about justification was as conservative as Descartes's was anti-conservative. Peirce took the view that belief is a default state and does not automatically require corroboration; rather, it is doubt that must be eliminated through inquiry. By contrast, James's view was roughly that a belief is justified so long as maintaining it has good results in practice.

René Descartes (1596–1650)

In his *Meditations,* the first three chapters of which are reprinted here, René Descartes set out to rid himself of false beliefs using the method of doubt, a technique for identifying beliefs about which he could be absolutely certain, or impervious to error. His method was to test his beliefs using skeptical scenarios. If we can imagine a situation in which a given belief *p* is false, then *p* is not certain, unless we can somehow rule out the possibility that that situation holds. By dropping all beliefs except those that are certain, Descartes hoped to clear his mind of all error.

Using the method of doubt, Descartes cast a shadow on the deliverances of the senses. Using his senses, he could not eliminate the possibility that he was asleep dreaming a vivid and realistic dream. Nor could he, on the basis of sensation, eliminate the possibility that he was being deceived by a powerful evil demon. And if either scenario held, his senses would be prompting him to accept a wholly inaccurate picture of the world. Nonetheless, he believed he could overcome his doubts, reasoning as follows: first, he noted that he was certain that he existed, since he had to exist to think, and could not be mistaken about thinking even if he was being deceived by a powerful demon. (The Latin version of Descartes's famous reasoning—I think therefore I am—is *cogito ergo sum.*) Second, since he was certain that he existed, he had to be aware of a *criterion* of certainty. He decided it was clarity and distinctness: any clear and distinct belief must be true. The third step was to deal with a possibility he termed a "metaphysical" doubt: mightn't the demon make a *false* belief clear and distinct? To prove otherwise, Descartes tried to show that God's existence eliminates the metaphysical doubt. However, at this stage Descartes seemed to rely on circular reasoning, as follows:

1. I have an idea of a perfect being, God.
2. It is clear and distinct to me that this idea could only be caused by God.
3. What is clear and distinct to me must be true.
4. So God exists.
5. Being perfect, God would not allow me to be wrong about things that are clear and distinct to me.
6. So what is clear and distinct to me must be true.

Not all scholars think that Descartes's reasoning was circular in this way. However, the 'Cartesian circle' is unconvincing as a way to underwrite the clarity and distinctness criterion, since it relies on that criterion (at step 3) in the course of defending it.

John Locke (1632–1704)

In his *Essay Concerning Human Understanding* (1690), John Locke inquires into "the original, certainty, and extent of human knowledge, together with the grounds and degrees of belief, opinion and assent." Because he assumes that what can be known is limited by what can be expressed in words, he sets out a theory about the meanings of words. The view he defends is now called the *ideational theory of meaning.* It says that the meaning of strings of words consists in associated ideas. For example, in my mind the words 'red dot' are associated with certain ideas of a vividly colored spot, which are, therefore, the meaning of my words 'red dot.' Locke adds, as an empiricist, that ultimately all ideas are derived from experience, whether sensation (the outer sense), or reflection (the inner sense). Prior to experience, the mind is a *tabula rasa,* a blank tablet. In this way Locke rejects the rationalist view that some ideas are innate. Locke's ideas about language also support an influential doctrine of meaningfulness: if, when we trace back to their source the ideas for which words seem to stand, no originative experiences can be found, there is no such idea. If no derivative ideas attach to a string, it is meaningless.

In formulating his theory of meaning, Locke uses the term 'idea' to refer only to things in the mind. But he is not always consistent in this practice. Confusingly, he defines 'idea' as "whatsoever is the object of the understanding when a man thinks," which makes the distinction between ideas and other things no distinction at all. Given his broad definition, anything we think of is an idea, whether it is in the mind or not.

Locke may have been using 'idea' in this broad sense when, in Book IV, he turns his attention to knowledge. Initially, he says that "knowledge . . . [is] nothing but the perception of the connection and agreement, or disagreement and repugnancy of any of our ideas." He speaks of four types of "agreement"—namely, identity or diversity; relation; co-existence, or necessary connection; and real existence—that yield four kinds of knowledge:

1. *identity*, which is direct, introspective knowledge that an idea is not different from another;
2. *relation*, also direct and introspective, which is knowledge of the relations that hold among geometrical figures;
3. *co-existence*, which *would* be knowledge that various qualities, such as the yellowness and hardness of gold, always go together, but such knowledge is not available; and
4. *real existence*, or knowledge that there really are objects outside of the mind.

But, perhaps because he notices that the last of these—real existence—is not reducible to a relation of ideas, if all ideas are mental entities, Locke modifies his initial conception of knowledge. He offers the *representational theory of perception*, which says that "the mind knows not things immediately, but only by the intervention of the *ideas* it has of them. *Our knowledge* therefore is *real*, only so far as there is a conformity between our *ideas* and the reality of things." Here Locke juxtaposes ideas in the mind with things in the world, not ideas with ideas. On his view, we acquire information and hence knowledge about the world via the conformity between things in the world and the ideas those things produce in us. Locke adds that our knowledge of real existence extends to three things:

1. *ourselves:* we know we exist by intuition, which is "the mind('s) per(ception of) the agreement or disagreement of two ideas immediately by

themselves, without the intervention of any other";
2. *God:* God's existence is demonstrable since we know intuitively that we exist, and (given certain scholastic assumptions) the only explanation of our existence is God's existence;
3. *other things:* Locke offers a causal theory of our knowledge of "other things"; we know that things like tables and fish exist by virtue of the fact that, through sensation, such things cause ideas in us that correspond to (or represent) the things themselves.

George Berkeley (1685–1753)

In his *Treatise Concerning the Principles of Human Knowledge* (1710), George Berkeley rejects Locke's materialism. Locke had distinguished between substances (or objects) and their qualities, and said that a substance is something, "we know not what," in which qualities inhere. Taking advantage of Locke's confusion over the notion of substance, Berkeley defends a view he called *immaterialism*, the doctrine that reality is exhausted by minds and their contents. To exist is either to be a perceiver or else to be perceived: *Esse est percipi.* Immaterialism is a version of a view that is now called *idealism*, the position that reality is mind-dependent. Berkeley defends immaterialism by arguing that the qualities that normally are attributed to things in the world are actually ideas in the mind, and that the only intelligible conception of substances is as collections of qualities, so that substances are collections of ideas, which puts them in the mind.

Berkeley also attacks Locke's representational theory of perception, on the grounds that (1) ideas cannot resemble physical objects, since ideas and objects have nothing in common, and (2) even if there were a resemblance between ideas and objects we could never verify its existence.

Despite his immaterialism, Berkeley portrays himself as a proponent of common sense, for he thought he had undercut skepticism (if material things don't exist, there is no problem of getting to the truth about them) and retained the ordinary distinction between reality, understood in terms of involuntary, coherent, and vivid ideas, and appearance or illusion, understood in terms of voluntary, incoherent, and faint ideas. If we make an *objective* distinction between reality and appearance, whereby reality is that which does not depend for its existence on mind, and appearance is that which is dependent, then Berkeley is saying that all is appearance. However, Berkeley's view is that our ordinary reality-appearance distinction is actually *subjective*; it is made entirely within the world of things that, seen objectively, are appearance.

David Hume (1711–1776)

David Hume's *Enquiry concerning Human Understanding* (1748) is usually combined with his *Enquiry concerning the Principles of Morals* (1751) and called the *Enquiries*. It is a revised, briefer version of the *Treatise of Human Nature* (1739), which he wrote when he was only twenty-six. Hume sets out to describe the nature of the mind and the sorts of things the mind is suited to understand. He uses the term *perceptions* to refer to the contents of the mind, and divides perceptions into two sorts: impressions and ideas. He says that the distinction is made entirely in terms of force and vivacity: ideas are less forceful and vivid than corresponding impressions. Still, the two are ordered temporally—impressions are prior to ideas—and related through resemblance: ideas are copies of impressions.

In Section IV of *Enquiries*, Hume divides the objects of inquiry into *relations of ideas*, our knowledge of which is unproblematic, a priori (that is, knowable independently of experience), and demonstrative, and *matters of fact*, our knowledge of which is a posteriori (that is, knowable on the basis of experience). Some knowledge of matters of fact is straightforward, he thought. Through immediate perception we know what our impressions are, and through memory we know what we immediately perceived in the past. But knowledge of other matters of fact is deeply problematic. If we know of them, we arrive at our knowledge through *causal inference* (or "*moral reasoning*"). That is, in taking some state of affairs (such as our seeming to see an aardvark) to be grounds for thinking that a fact holds (such as there being an aardvark), we take it that the one caused the other (the presence of an aardvark initiated a chain of events that ultimately caused us to have a visual impression of an aardvark). Hence causal inference depends on our knowing when an event is the cause of another. Our knowledge of causation, in turn, is arrived at through the application of *enumerative induction*, whereby a series of observations of the form,

This A is B,

together with the fact that no observed A has failed to be B, authorizes a conclusion of the form,

All As are Bs (or: The next A will be B).

For example, if I note a white swan, then another, and another, and so on, and conclude that all swans are white, I am relying on enumerative induction. However, Hume says, our confidence about the reliability of enumerative induction is entirely baseless. To support the view that induction is reliable, we would have to rely on induction, which would be circular and hence useless. And since all causal inferences, and the beliefs supported thereby, are based on enumerative induction, these inferences, too, are ultimately baseless.

As Hume realizes, it is puzzling that we rely on enumerative induction even though, as he claims, we have no grounds whatever for thinking that it is reliable. (We also lack grounds for thinking that configurations of tea leaves in cups serve as the basis for accurate predictions; why do we rely on induction but not on tea leaves?) In Section V he confronts this puzzle and offers an explanation that he calls a "skeptical solution" to his skeptical doubts. He notes that we infer that one event, call it C, is the cause of another, say E, only after we observe that events of the same type as E are always preceded by events of the same sort as C. Anytime green wood is ignited, smoke is generated, for example. When we observe lots of C-type events followed by E-type events, we develop a *habit of mind* whereby the thought of a C-type event starts us thinking of an E-type event, and noticing a C-type event automatically prompts us to anticipate the occurrence of an E-type event. Nature has wired inductive belief into us.

Immanuel Kant (1724–1804)

After publishing his *Critique of Pure Reason* (1781), and before revising it in the 'B' edition in 1787, Kant published a briefer review, the *Prolegomena to Any Future Metaphysics* (1783). In these works Immanuel Kant resists skepticism by defending *direct realism*, according to which we have direct knowledge of the world, unmediated by sensation. Realizing that knowledge that is not mediated by sensation is possible only if the world is mind-dependent, he is forced to accept a kind of idealism. But Kant also wants to say that there is a world external to perceivers. In order to reconcile this with the idealism he needs for direct knowledge, he distinguishes between two senses in which the world can be "external": we can make the internal-external distinction subjectively, or we can make it objectively. The world is objectively external if it is in no sense mental. By contrast, the world can be subjectively external even if it, and everything that is part of it, including perceivers, is mental. To this array of items that are ultimately mental, Kant attaches the label *phenomenal*. The subjective distinction between internal and external is made out entirely within the phenomenal realm: "inner objects" are things that depend on perceivers while "outer objects" are things that do not. According to Kant, we directly know the things that are external and internal to us in the subjective sense. Kant calls his brand of idealism *transcendental idealism*.

On the basis of transcendental idealism, Kant tries to explain how metaphysics, which deals with that which goes beyond experience, is possible. He distinguishes between two classes of judgments: analytic and synthetic. *Analytic judgments,* such as 'all bachelors are unmarried males,' are those wherein the concept of the predicate is included in the concept of the subject (the concept of an unmarried male is part of the concept of a bachelors). They are true in virtue of the law of contradiction. By contrast, the concept of the predicate of a *synthetic judgment* goes beyond what is contained in the concept of the subject. Synthetic judgments are not tautologies; their denials of are not contradictions. According to Kant, viable metaphysics consists in synthetic a priori judgments, which go beyond experience in that no particular experience implies them. Included among such judgments are truths of mathematics and geometry, which are both necessary as well as knowable a priori because they are true by virtue of the spatial and temporal structure that the mind imposes. Space and time are forms of sensibility; they are part of the way mind structures things in experiencing the world, so that all possible sensory experience is shaped spatially and temporally. Kant admits that Humean skepticism concerning substantive matters such as our views about cause and effect would be inevitable if we had to establish that our picture of reality conforms to the way things are in themselves. Kant says his explanation of how we know synthetic principles a priori and with certainty amounts to a "Copernican revolution": we know them not by establishing that our representations conform to things, but rather by establishing that things must conform to our representations.

Kant downplays the importance of the objectively external world, which he calls the *noumenal world*; he does not deny that it exists, but says it is wholly unknowable. Metaphysics is limited, Kant says, to the preconditions of experience, to that which is imposed on all experience, and therefore to the phenomenal realm.

Charles Saunders Peirce (1839–1914)

Charles Peirce, a mathematician and physicist as well as a philosopher, developed distinctive ideas of knowledge, meaning, and truth that he dubbed 'pragmatism.' He sets forth the heart of his philosophy in "The Fixation of Belief" and "How to Make Our Ideas Clear."

From Alexander Bain, a fellow member of the Metaphysics Club, which was a group of intellectuals who met in Cambridge, Massachusetts to discuss philosophy, Peirce borrowed the view that belief is " 'an attitude or disposition of preparedness to act' when occasion offers," and the view that doubt is distinct from disbelief. The chief mark of belief is contentedness, while the mark of doubt is discomfort and discontent. Belief is our default psychological attitude, and doubt is introduced only when some event disrupts belief. Belief is also a habit of behavior enabling people to meet their needs, and thus to get on with life. On the basis of these views, Peirce attacked Descartes's view of doubt, according to which the absence of belief is the default, and each belief requires special justification. According to Peirce, it is doubt, not belief, that requires special justification, and when doubt is eliminated, the default state of belief is restored. Moreover, claims that evade doubt are perfectly acceptable as premises in arguments. Inquiry, Peirce says, is the attempt to overcome doubt so as to restore belief. It is prompted by doubt and ends when doubt is overcome. The point of inquiry is the fixation of belief—the settling of opinion. As for meaning, Peirce provides a *pragmatic formulation*: the meaning of an item such as a thought is solely the practical effects that item might conceivably have. Truth Peirce understood in practical terms as well: a belief is true if, in the long run, scientific investigators would agree to it were they to conduct inquiry indefinitely.

QUESTIONS FOR REFLECTION

1. In *Meditations* 1, Descartes raises the possibility that he is mad, and then dismisses it with the joke that he'd have to be mad to take the possibility seriously. He never tries to eliminate it the way he tries to eliminate other skeptical scenarios such as the evil demon possibility. Is there reasoning he could use to establish he is not mad? Does madness make any reasoning of mad people unreliable? Must he establish that he is not mad before it is rational for him to do any reasoning?

2. Is there a way to eliminate "metaphysical doubt" without relying on a circular argument? Was Descartes's own argument really circular?

3. Would Descartes's way of answering skeptical doubt help him to deal with Pyrrho's regress argument?

4. Locke adopts a causal theory of the knowledge of things. Why, then, does he add that sensitive knowledge extends no further than to objects present to the senses?

5. Berkeley thinks we cannot know of the existence of physical objects outside the mind. Yet we can know that other minds exist. Is Berkeley consistent? How is the one possible if the other is not?

6. Berkeley tries to establish his immaterialism by assuming that we cannot think of anything existing unconceived. Is this argument convincing?

7. Hume does not consider it problematic to rely on reason. He does, however, consider it problematic to rely on induction. What is the relationship between reason and induction? Why is the one problematic but not the other? Or are both problematic?

8. Kant takes himself to be offering a kind of idealism that differs in important ways from Berkeley's. But does he? Compare and contrast the two versions of idealism.

9. As Israel Scheffler (1974, p. 67) pointed out, a peculiarity of Peirce's work is that it is not clear whether it is supposed to be psychology (a descriptive discipline) or epistemology (a prescriptive discipline). Is Peirce describing how we do operate, or is he prescribing how we ought to operate?

10. Is it really true, as Peirce usually says, that scientific inquiry must begin with real and living doubt, a breakdown in prior habits? What view about this matter does Peirce express in footnote 4, where he says doubt is "the power of making believe we hesitate"? Given the position Peirce takes in this footnote, what should we say about Peirce's criticism that Descartes's method is not based on real and living doubt?

✧ INDISCERNABLLILITY ✧
SKEPTICISM

5. MEDITATIONS ON FIRST PHILOSOPHY

René Descartes

Meditation I

Of the Things of Which We May Doubt

Several years have now elapsed since I first became aware that I had accepted, even from my youth, many false opinions for true, and that consequently what I afterwards based on such principles was highly doubtful; and from that time I was convinced of the necessity of undertaking once in my life to rid myself of all the opinions I had adopted, and of commencing anew the work of building from the foundation, if I desired to establish a firm and abiding superstructure in the sciences. But as this enterprise appeared to me to be one of great magnitude, I waited until I had attained an age so mature as to leave me no hope that at any stage of life more advanced I should be better able to execute my design. On this account, I have delayed so long that I should henceforth consider I was doing wrong were I still to consume in deliberation any of the time that now remains for action. Today, then, since I have opportunely freed my mind from all cares, [and am happily disturbed by no passions], and since I am in the secure possession of leisure in a peaceable retirement, I will at length apply myself earnestly and freely to the general overthrow of all my former opinions. But, to this end, it will not be necessary for me to show that the whole of these are false—a point, perhaps, which I shall never reach; but as even now my reason convinces me that I ought not the less carefully to withhold belief from what is not entirely certain and indubitable, than from what is manifestly false, it will be sufficient to justify the rejection of the whole if I shall find in each some ground for doubt. Nor for this purpose will it be necessary even to deal with each belief individually, which would be truly an endless labour; but, as the removal from below of the foundation necessarily involves the downfall of the whole edifice, I will at once approach the criticism of the principles on which all my former beliefs rested.

All that I have, up to this moment, accepted as possessed of the highest truth and certainty, I received either from or through the senses. I observed, however, that these sometimes misled us; and it is the part of prudence not to place absolute confidence in that by which we have even once been deceived.

But it may be said, perhaps, that, although the senses occasionally mislead us respecting minute objects, and such as are so far removed from us as to be beyond the reach of close observation, there are yet many other of their representations, of the truth of which it is manifestly impossible to doubt; as for example, that I am in this place, seated by the fire, clothed in a winter dressing-gown, that I hold in my hands this piece of paper, with other intimations of the same nature. But how could I deny that I possess these hands and this body, and escape being classed with persons in a state of insanity, whose brains are so disordered and clouded by dark bilious vapours as to cause them pertinaciously to assert that they are monarchs when they are in the greatest poverty; or clothed [in gold] and purple when destitute of any covering; or that their head is made of clay, their body of glass, or that they are gourds? I should certainly be not less insane than they, were I to regulate my procedure according to examples so extravagant.

Though this be true, I must nevertheless here consider that I am a man, and that, consequently, I am in the habit of sleeping, and representing to myself in dreams those same things, or even sometimes others less probable, which the insane think are presented to them in their waking moments. How often have I dreamt that I was in these familiar circumstances,—that I was dressed, and occupied this place by the fire, when I was lying undressed in bed? At the present moment, however, I certainly look upon this paper with eyes wide awake; the head which I now move is not asleep; I extend this hand consciously and with express purpose, and I perceive it; the occurrences in sleep are not so distinct as all this. But I cannot forget that, at other times, I have been deceived in sleep by similar illusions; and, attentively considering those cases, I perceive so clearly that there exist no certain marks by which the state of waking can ever be distinguished from sleep, that I feel greatly astonished; and in amazement I almost persuade myself that I am now dreaming.

Let us suppose, then, that we are dreaming, and that all these particulars—namely, the opening of the eyes, the motion of the head, the forth-putting of the hands—are merely illusions; and even that we really possess neither an entire body nor hands such as we see. Nevertheless, it must be admitted at least that the objects which appear to us in sleep are, as it were, painted representations which could not have been formed unless in the likeness of realities; and, therefore, that

those general objects, at all events,—namely, eyes, a head, hands, and an entire body—are not simply imaginary, but really existent. For, in truth, painters themselves, even when they study to represent sirens and satyrs by forms the most fantastic and extraordinary, cannot bestow upon them natures absolutely new, but can only make a certain medley of the members of different animals; or if they chance to imagine something so novel that nothing at all similar has ever been seen before, and such as is, therefore, purely fictitious and absolutely false, it is at least certain that the colours of which this is composed are real.

And on the same principle, although these general objects, viz. [a body], eyes, a head, hands, and the like, be imaginary, we nevertheless absolutely must admit the reality at least of some other objects still more simple and universal than these, of which, just as of certain real colours, all those images of things, whether true and real, or false and fantastic, that are found in our consciousness (*cogitatio*), are formed.

To this class of objects seem to belong corporeal nature in general and its extension; the shape of extended things, their quantity or magnitude, and their number, as also the place in, and the time during, which they exist, and other things of the same sort. We will not, therefore, perhaps reason illegitimately if we conclude from this that Physics, Astronomy, Medicine, and all the other sciences that have for their end the consideration of composite objects, are indeed of a doubtful character; but that Arithmetic, Geometry, and the other sciences of the same class, which regard merely the simplest and most general objects, and scarcely inquire whether or not these are really existent, contain somewhat that is certain and indubitable: for whether I am awake or dreaming, it remains true that two and three make five, and that a square has but four sides; nor does it seem possible that truths so apparent can ever fall under a suspicion of falsity or uncertainty.

Nevertheless, the belief that there is a God who is all-powerful, and who created me, such as I am, has, for a long time, obtained steady possession of my mind. How, then, do I know that he has not arranged that there should be neither earth, nor sky, nor any extended thing, nor figure, nor magnitude, nor place, providing at the same time, however, for [the rise in me of the perceptions of all these objects, and] the persuasion that these do not exist otherwise than as I perceive them? And further, as I sometimes think that others are in error respecting matters of which they believe themselves to possess a perfect knowledge, how do I know that I am not also deceived each time I add together two and three, or number the sides of a square, or form some judgment still more simple, if more simple indeed can be imagined? But perhaps Deity has not been willing that I should be thus deceived, for He is said to be supremely good. If, however, it were repugnant to the goodness of Deity to have created me subject to constant deception, it would seem likewise to be contrary to his goodness to allow me to be occasionally deceived; and yet it is clear that this is permitted. Some, indeed, might perhaps be found who would be disposed rather to deny the existence of a Being so powerful than to believe that there is nothing certain. But let us for the present refrain from opposing this opinion, and grant that all which is here said of a Deity is fabulous: nevertheless in whatever way it be supposed that I reached the state in which I exist, whether by fate, or chance, or by an endless series of antecedents and consequents, or by any other means, it is clear (since to be deceived and to err is a certain defect) that the probability of my being so imperfect as to be the constant victim of deception, will be increased exactly in proportion as the power possessed by the cause, to which they assign my origin, is lessened. To these reasonings I have assuredly nothing to reply, but am constrained at last to avow that there is nothing of all that I formerly believed to be true of which it is impossible to doubt, and that not through thoughtlessness or levity, but from cogent and maturely considered reasons; so that henceforward, if I desire to discover anything certain, I ought not the less carefully to refrain from assenting to those same opinions than to what might be shown to be manifestly false.

But it is not sufficient to have made these observations; care must be taken likewise to keep them in remembrance. For those old and customary opinions perpetually recur—long and familiar usage giving them the right of occupying my mind, even almost against my will, and subduing my belief; nor will I lose the habit of deferring to them and confiding in them so long as I shall consider them to be what in truth they are, viz., opinions to some extent doubtful, as I have already shown, but still highly probable, and such as it is much more reasonable to believe than deny. It is for this reason I am persuaded that I shall not be doing wrong, if, taking an opposite judgment of deliberate design, I become my own deceiver, by supposing, for a time, that all those opinions are entirely false and imaginary, until at length, having thus balanced my old by my new prejudices, my judgment shall no longer be turned aside by perverted usage from the path that may conduct to the perception of truth. For I am assured that, meanwhile, there will arise neither peril nor error from this course, and that I cannot for the present yield too much to distrust, since the end I now seek is not action but knowledge.

I will suppose, then, not that Deity, who is sovereignly good and the fountain of truth, but that some evil demon, who is at once exceedingly potent and deceitful, has employed all his artifice to deceive me; I will suppose that the sky, the air, the earth, colours, figures, sounds, and all external things, are nothing better than the illusions of dreams, by means of which this being has laid snares for my credulity; I will consider myself as without hands, eyes, flesh, blood, or any of the senses, and as falsely believing that I am possessed of these; I will continue resolutely fixed in this belief, and if indeed by this means it be not in my power to arrive at the knowledge of truth, I shall at least do what is in my power, viz., [suspend my judgment], and guard with settled purpose against giving my assent to what is false, and being imposed upon by this deceiver, whatever be his power and artifice.

But this undertaking is arduous, and a certain indolence insensibly leads me back to my ordinary course of life; and just as the captive, who, perchance, was enjoying in his dreams an imaginary liberty, when he begins to suspect that it is but a vision, dreads awakening, and conspires with the agreeable illusions that the deception may be prolonged; so I, of my own accord, fall back into the train of my former beliefs, and fear to arouse myself from my slumber, lest the time of laborious wakefulness that would succeed this quiet rest, in place of bringing any light of day, should prove inadequate to dispel the darkness that will arise from the difficulties that have now been raised.

Meditation II

Of the Nature of the Human Mind; and That It Is More Easily Known Than the Body

The Meditation of yesterday has filled my mind with so many doubts, that it is no longer in my power to forget them. Nor do I see, meanwhile, any principle on which they can be resolved; and, just as if I had fallen all of a sudden into very deep water, I am so greatly disconcerted as to be unable either to plant my feet firmly on the bottom or sustain myself by swimming on the surface. I will, nevertheless, make an effort, and try anew the same path on which I had entered yesterday, that is, proceed by casting aside all that admits of the slightest doubt, not less than if I had discovered it to be absolutely false; and I will continue always in this track until I shall find something that is certain, or at least, if I can do nothing more, until I shall know with certainty that there is nothing certain. Archimedes, that he might transport the entire globe from the place it occupied to another, demanded only a point that was firm and immoveable; so also, I shall be entitled to entertain the highest expectations, if I am fortunate enough to discover only one thing that is certain and indubitable.

I suppose, accordingly, that all the things which I see are false (fictitious); I believe that none of those objects which my fallacious memory represents ever existed; I suppose that I possess no senses; I believe that body, figure, extension, motion, and place are merely fictions of my mind. What is there, then, that can be esteemed true? Perhaps this only, that there is absolutely nothing certain.

But how do I know that there is not something different altogether from the objects I have now enumerated, of which it is impossible to entertain the slightest doubt? Is there not a God, or some being, by whatever name I may designate him, who causes these thoughts to arise in my mind? But why suppose such a being, for it may be I myself am capable of producing them? Am I, then, at least not something? But I before denied that I possessed senses or a body; I hesitate, however, for what follows from that? Am I so dependent on the body and the senses that without these I cannot exist? But I had the persuasion that there was absolutely nothing in the world, that there was no sky and no earth, neither minds nor bodies; was I not, therefore, at the same time, persuaded that I did not exist? Far from it; I assuredly existed, since I was persuaded. But there is I know not what being, who is possessed at once of the highest power and the deepest cunning, who is constantly employing all his ingenuity in deceiving me. Doubtless, then, I exist, since I am deceived; and, let him deceive me as he may, he can never bring it about that I am nothing, so long as I shall be conscious that I am something. So that it must, in short, be maintained, all things being maturely and carefully considered, that this proposition I am, I exist, is necessarily true each time it is expressed by me, or conceived in my mind.

But I do not yet know with sufficient clearness what I am, though assured that I am; and hence, in the next place, I must take care, lest perchance I inconsiderately substitute some other object in room of what is properly myself, and thus wander from truth, even in that knowledge which I hold to be of all others the most certain and evident. For this reason, I will now consider anew what I formerly believed myself to be, before I entered on the present train of thought; and of my previous opinion I will subtract all that can in the least be invalidated by the grounds of doubt I have adduced, in order that there may at length remain nothing but what is certain and indubitable. What then did I formerly think I was? Undoubtedly I judged that I was a man. But what is a man? Shall I say a rational animal? Assuredly not; for it would be necessary forthwith to inquire into what is meant by animal, and what by rational, and thus, from a single question, I should insensibly glide into others, and these more difficult than the first; nor do I now possess enough of leisure to warrant me in wasting my time amid subtleties of this sort. I prefer here to attend to the thoughts that sprung up of themselves in my mind, and were inspired by my own nature alone, when I applied myself to the consideration of what I was. In the first place, then, I thought that I possessed a countenance, hands, arms, and all the fabric of members that appears in a corpse, and which I called by the name of body. It further occurred to me that I was nourished, that I walked, perceived, and thought, and all those actions I referred to the soul; but what the soul itself was I either did not stay to consider, or, if I did, I imagined that it was something extremely rare and subtle, like wind, or flame, or ether, spread through my grosser parts. As regarded the body, I did not even doubt of its nature, but thought I distinctly knew it, and if I had wished to describe it according to the notions I then entertained, I should have explained myself in this manner: By body I understand all that can be bounded by a certain shape; that can be comprised in a certain place, and so fill a certain space as therefrom to exclude every other body; that can be perceived either by touch, sight, hearing, taste, or smell; that can be moved in different ways, not indeed of itself, but by something foreign to it by which it is touched [and from which it receives the impression]; for the power of self-motion, as likewise that of perceiving and thinking, I held as by no means pertaining to the nature of body; on the contrary, I was somewhat astonished to find such faculties existing in some bodies.

But [as to myself, what can I now say that I am], since I suppose there exists an extremely powerful, and, if I may so speak, evil being, whose whole endeavours are directed towards deceiving me? Can I affirm that I possess any one of all those attributes of which I have lately spoken as belonging to the nature of body? After attentively considering them in my own mind, I find none of them that can properly be said to belong to myself. To recount them were idle and tedious. Let us pass, then, to the attributes of the soul. The first mentioned were the powers of nutrition and walking; but, if it be true that I have no body, it is true likewise that I am capable neither of walking nor of being nourished. Perception is another attribute of the soul; but perception too is impossible without the body: besides, I have frequently, during sleep, believed that I perceived objects which I afterwards observed I did not in reality perceive. Thinking is another attribute of the soul; and here I discover what properly belongs to myself. This alone is inseparable from me. I am—I exist: this is certain; but how often? As often as I think; for perhaps it would even happen, if I should wholly cease to think, that I should at the same time altogether cease to be. I now admit nothing that is not necessarily true: I am therefore speaking precisely, only a thinking thing, that is, a mind, understanding, or reason,—terms whose signification was before unknown to me. I am, however, a real thing, and really existent; but what thing? The answer was, a thinking thing. The question now arises, am I anything else? I will stimulate my imagination with a view to discover whether I am not still something more than a thinking being. Now it is plain I am

not the assemblage of members called the human body; I am not a thin and penetrating air diffused through all these members, or wind, or flame, or vapour, or breath, or any of all the things I can imagine; for I supposed that all these were not, and, without changing the supposition, I find that I still feel assured of my existence.

But it is true, perhaps, that those very things which I suppose to be non-existent, because they are unknown to me, are not in truth different from myself whom I know. This is a point I cannot determine, and do not now enter into any dispute regarding it. I can only judge of things that are known to me: I am conscious that I exist, and I who know that I exist inquire into what I am. It is, however, perfectly certain that the knowledge of my existence, thus precisely taken, is not dependent on things, the existence of which is as yet unknown to me: and consequently it is not dependent on any of the things I can feign in imagination. Moreover, the phrase itself, I frame an image, reminds me of my error; for I should in truth frame one if I were to imagine myself to be anything, since to imagine is nothing more than to contemplate the shape or image of a corporeal thing; but I already know that I exist, and that it is possible at the same time that all those images, and in general all that relates to the nature of body, are merely dreams [or chimeras]. From this I discover that it is not more reasonable to say, I will excite my imagination that I may know more distinctly what I am, than to express myself as follows: I am now awake, and perceive something real; but because my perception is not sufficiently clear, I will of express purpose go to sleep that my dreams may represent to me the object of my perception with more truth and clearness. And, therefore, I know that nothing of all that I can embrace in imagination belongs to the knowledge which I have of myself, and that there is need to recall with the utmost care the mind from this mode of thinking, that it may be able to know its own nature with perfect distinctness.

But what, then, am I? A thinking thing, it has been said. But what is a thinking thing? It is a thing that doubts, understands, [conceives], affirms, denies, wills, refuses, that imagines also, and perceives. Assuredly it is not little, if all these properties belong to my nature. But why should they not belong to it? Am I not that very being who now doubts of almost everything; who, for all that, understands and conceives certain things; who affirms one alone as true, and denies the others; who desires to know more of them, and does not wish to be deceived; who imagines many things, sometimes even despite his will; and is likewise percipient of many, as if through the medium of the senses. Is there nothing of all this as true as that I am, even although I should be always dreaming, and although he who gave me being employed all his ingenuity to deceive me? Is there also any one of these attributes that can be properly distinguished from my thought, or that can be said to be separate from myself? For it is of itself so evident that it is I who doubt, I who understand, and I who desire, that it is here unnecessary to add anything by way of rendering it more clear. And I am as certainly the same being who imagines; for, although it may be (as I before supposed) that nothing I imagine is true, still the power of imagination does not cease really to exist in me and to form part of my thought. In fine, I am the same being who perceives, that is, who apprehends certain objects as by the organs of sense, since, in truth, I see light, hear a noise, and feel heat. But it will be said that these representations are false, and that I am dreaming. Let it be so. At all events it is certain that I seem to see light, hear a noise, and feel heat; this cannot be false, and this is what in me is properly called perceiving, which is nothing else than thinking. From this I begin to know what I am with somewhat greater clearness and distinctness than heretofore.

But, nevertheless, it still seems to me, and I cannot help believing, that corporeal things, whose images are formed by thought, and which the senses examine, are known with much greater distinctness than the 'I', this thing that I know not what, which is not imaginable; although, in truth, it may seem strange to say that I know and comprehend with greater distinctness things whose existence appears to me doubtful, that are unknown, and do not belong to me, than others of whose reality I am persuaded, that are known to me, and appertain to my proper nature; in a word, than myself. But I see clearly what is the state of the case. My mind is apt to wander, and will not yet submit to be restrained within the limits of truth. Let us therefore give it free rein, so that later it will be more easily controlled.

Let us now accordingly consider the objects that are commonly thought to be [the most easily, and likewise] the most distinctly known, viz., the bodies we touch and see; not, indeed, bodies in general, for these general notions are usually somewhat more confused, but one body in particular. Take, for example, this piece of wax; it is quite fresh, having been but recently taken from the bee-hive; it has not yet lost the sweetness of the honey it contained; it still retains some of the odour of the flowers from which it was gathered; its colour, figure, size, are apparent (to the sight); it is hard, cold, easily handled; and sounds when struck upon with the finger. In short, all that contributes to make a body as distinctly known as possible, is found in the one before us. But, while I am speaking, let it be placed near the fire—what remained of the taste disappears, the smell evaporates, the colour changes, its shape is destroyed, its size increases, it becomes liquid, it grows hot, it can hardly be handled, and, although struck, it emits no sound. Does the same wax still remain after this change? It must be admitted that it does remain; no one doubts it, or judges otherwise. What, then, was it I knew with so much distinctness in the piece of wax? Assuredly, it could be nothing of all that I observed by means of the senses, since all the things that fell under taste, smell, sight, touch, and hearing are changed, and yet the same wax remains. It was perhaps what I now think, viz., that this wax was neither the sweetness of honey, the pleasant odour of flowers, the whiteness, the shape, nor the sound, but only a body that a little before appeared to me conspicuous under these forms, and which is now perceived under others. But, to speak precisely, what is it that I imagine when I think of it in this way? Let it be attentively considered, and, removing all that does not belong to the wax, let us see what remains. There certainly remains nothing, except something extended, flexible, and movable. But what is meant by flexible and movable? Is it not that I imagine that the piece of wax, being round, is capable of becoming square, or of passing from a square into a triangular figure? Assuredly such is not the case, because I conceive that it admits of an infinity of similar changes; and I am, moreover, unable to capture this infinity by imagination, and consequently this conception which I have of the wax is not the product of the faculty of imagination. But what now is this extension? Is it not also unknown? for it becomes greater when the wax is melted, greater when it is boiled, and greater still when the heat increases; and I should not conceive [clearly and] according to truth, the wax as it is, if I did not suppose that the piece we are considering admitted even of a wider variety of extension than I ever imagined. I must, therefore, admit that I cannot even comprehend by imagination what the piece of wax is, and that it is the mind alone which perceives it. I speak of one piece in particular; for, as to wax in general, this is still more evident. But what is this wax that can be perceived only by the [understanding or] mind? It is certainly the same wax which I see, touch, imagine; and, in short, it is the same which, from the beginning, I believed it to be. But (and this it is important to observe) the perception of it is neither an act of sight, of touch, nor of imagination, and never was either of these, though it might formerly seem so, but is simply an intuition of the mind, which may be imperfect and confused, as it formerly was, or very clear and distinct, as it is at present, according as the attention is more or less directed to the elements which it contains, and of which it is composed.

But, meanwhile, I feel greatly astonished when I observe [the weakness of my mind, and] its proneness to error. For although, without at all giving expression to what I think, I consider all this in my own mind, words yet occasionally impede my progress, and I am almost led into error by the terms of ordinary language. We say, for example, that we see the same wax when it is before us, and not that we judge it to be the same from its retaining the same colour and figure: whence I should forthwith be disposed to conclude that the wax is known by the act of sight, and not by the intuition of the mind alone, were it not for the analogous instance of human beings passing on in the street below, as observed from a window. In this case I do not fail to say that I see the men themselves, just as I say that I see the wax; and yet what do I see from the window beyond hats and cloaks that might cover artificial machines, whose motions might be determined by springs? But I judge that there are human beings from these appearances, and thus I comprehend, by the faculty of judgment alone which is in the mind, what I believed I saw with my eyes.

The man who makes it his aim to rise to knowledge superior to the common, ought to be ashamed to seek occasions of doubting from the vulgar forms of speech: instead, therefore, of doing this, I shall proceed with the matter in hand, and inquire whether I had a clearer and more perfect perception of the piece of wax when I first saw it, and when I thought I knew it by means of the external sense itself, or, at all events, by the common sense, as it is called, that is, by the imaginative faculty; or whether I rather apprehend it more clearly at present, after having examined with greater care, both what it is, and in what way it can be known. It would certainly be ridiculous to entertain any doubt on this point. For what, in that first perception, was there distinct? What did I perceive which any animal might not have perceived? But when I distinguish the wax from its exterior forms, and when, as if I had stripped it of its vestments, I consider it quite naked, it is certain, although some error may still be found in my judgment, that I cannot, nevertheless, thus apprehend it without possessing a human mind.

But, finally, what shall I say of the mind itself, that is, of myself? for as yet I do not admit that I am anything but mind. What, then! I who seem to possess so distinct an apprehension of the piece of wax,—do I not know myself, both with greater truth and certitude, and also much more distinctly and clearly? For if I judge that the wax exists because I see it, it assuredly follows, much more evidently, that I myself am or exist, for the same reason: for it is possible that what I see may not in truth be wax, and that I do not even possess eyes with which to see anything; but it cannot be that when I see, or, which comes to the same thing, when I think I see, I myself who think am nothing. So likewise, if I judge that the wax exists because I touch it, it will still also follow that I am; and if I determine that my imagination, or any other cause, whatever it be, persuades me of the existence of the wax, I will still draw the same conclusion. And what is here remarked of the piece of wax, is applicable to all the other things that are external to me. And further, if the [notion or] perception of wax appeared to me more precise and distinct, after that not only sight and touch, but many other causes besides, rendered it manifest to my apprehension, with how much greater distinctness must I now know myself, since all the reasons that contribute to the knowledge of the nature of wax, or of any body whatever, manifest still better the nature of my mind? And there are besides so many other things in the mind itself that contribute to the illustration of its nature, that those dependent on the body, to which I have here referred, scarcely merit to be taken into account.

But, in conclusion, I find I have insensibly reverted to the point I desired; for, since it is now manifest to me that bodies themselves are not properly perceived by the senses nor by the faculty of imagination, but by the intellect alone; and since they are not perceived because they are seen and touched, but only because they are understood [or rightly comprehended by thought], I readily discover that there is nothing more easily or clearly apprehended than my own mind. But because it is difficult to rid one's self so promptly of an opinion to which one has been long accustomed, it will be desirable to tarry for some time at this stage, that, by long continued meditation, I may more deeply impress upon my memory this new knowledge.

Meditation III

Of God: That He Exists

I will now close my eyes, I will stop my ears, I will turn away my senses from their objects, I will even efface from my consciousness all the images of corporeal things; or at least, because this can hardly be accomplished, I will consider them as empty and illusory; and thus, discoursing only with myself, and closely examining my nature, I will endeavour to obtain by degrees a more intimate and familiar knowledge of myself. I am a thinking (conscious) thing, that is, a being who doubts, affirms, denies, knows a few objects, and is ignorant of many,—[who loves, hates], wills, refuses,—who imagines likewise, and perceives; for, as I before remarked, although the things which I perceive or imagine are perhaps nothing at all apart from me [and in themselves], I am nevertheless assured that those modes of consciousness which I call perceptions and imaginations, in as far only as they are modes of consciousness, exist in me. And in the little I have said I think I have summed up all that I really know, or at least all that up to this time I was aware I knew. Now, as I am endeavouring to extend my knowledge more widely, I will use circumspection, and consider with care whether I can still discover in myself anything further which I have not yet hitherto observed. I am certain that I am a thinking thing; but do I not therefore likewise know what is required to render me certain of a truth? In this first knowledge, doubtless, there is

nothing that gives me assurance of its truth except the clear and distinct perception of what I affirm, which would not indeed be sufficient to give me the assurance that what I say is true, if it could ever happen that anything I thus clearly and distinctly perceived should prove false; and accordingly it seems to me that I may now take as a general rule, that all that is very clearly and distinctly perceived is true.

Nevertheless I before received and admitted many things as wholly certain and manifest, which yet I afterwards found to be doubtful. What, then, were those? They were the earth, the sky, the stars, and all the other objects which I was in the habit of perceiving by the senses. But what was it that I clearly [and distinctly] perceived in them? Nothing more than that the ideas and the thoughts of those objects were presented to my mind. And even now I do not deny that these ideas are found in my mind. But there was yet another thing which I affirmed, and which, from having been accustomed to believe it, I thought I clearly perceived, although, in truth, I did not perceive it at all; I mean the existence of objects external to me, from which those ideas proceeded, and to which they had a perfect resemblance; and it was here I was mistaken, or if I judged correctly, this assuredly was not to be traced to any knowledge I possessed.

But when I considered any matter in arithmetic and geometry, that was very simple and easy, as, for example, that two and three added together make five, and things of this sort, did I not view them with at least sufficient clearness to warrant me in affirming their truth? Indeed, if I afterwards judged that we ought to doubt of these things, it was for no other reason than because it occurred to me that a God might perhaps have given me such a nature as that I should be deceived, even respecting the matters that appeared to me the most evidently true. But as often as this preconceived opinion of the sovereign power of a God presents itself to my mind, I am constrained to admit that it is easy for him, if he wishes it, to cause me to err, even in matters where I think I possess the highest evidence; and, on the other hand, as often as I direct my attention to things which I think I apprehend with great clearness, I am so persuaded of their truth that I naturally break out into expressions such as these: Deceive me who may, no one will yet ever be able to bring it about that I am not, so long as I shall be conscious that I am, or at any future time cause it to be true that I have never been, it being now true that I am, or make two and three more or less than five, in supposing which, and other like absurdities, I discover a manifest contradiction.

And in truth, as I have no ground for believing that Deity is deceitful, and as, indeed, I have not even considered the reasons by which the existence of a Deity of any kind is established, the ground of doubt that rests only on this supposition is very slight, and, so to speak, metaphysical. But, that I may be able wholly to remove it, I must inquire whether there is a God, as soon as an opportunity of doing so shall present itself; and if I find that there is a God, I must examine likewise whether he can be a deceiver; for, without the knowledge of these two truths, I do not see that I can ever be certain of anything. And that I may be enabled to examine this without interrupting the order of meditation I have proposed to myself [which is, to pass by degrees from the notions that I shall find first in my mind to those I shall afterwards discover in it], it is necessary at this stage to divide all my thoughts into certain classes, and to consider in which of these classes truth and error are, strictly speaking, to be found.

Of my thoughts some are, as it were, images of things, and to these alone properly belongs the name *idea*; as when I think [represent to my mind] a man, a chimera, the sky, an angel, or God. Others, again, have certain other forms; as when I will, fear, affirm, or deny, I always, indeed, apprehend something as the object of my thought, but I also embrace in thought something more than the representation of the object; and of this class of thoughts some are called volitions or affections, and others judgments.

Now, with respect to ideas, if these are considered only in themselves, and are not referred to any object beyond them, they cannot, properly speaking, be false; for, whether I imagine a goat or a chimera, it is not less true that I imagine the one than the other. Nor need we fear that falsity may exist in the will or affections; for, although I may desire objects that are wrong, and even that never existed, it is still true that I desire them. There thus only remain our judgments, in which we must take diligent heed that we be not deceived. But the chief and most ordinary error that arises in them consists in judging that the ideas which are in us are like or conformed to the things that are external to

us; for assuredly, if we but considered the ideas themselves as certain modes of our thought (consciousness), without referring them to anything beyond, they would hardly afford any occasion of error.

But, among these ideas, some appear to me to be innate, others adventitious, and others to be made by myself (factitious); for, as I have the power of conceiving what is called a thing, or a truth, or a thought, it seems to me that I hold this power from no other source than my own nature; but if I now hear a noise, if I see the sun, or if I feel heat, I have all along judged that these sensations proceeded from certain objects existing out of myself; and, in fine, it appears to me that sirens, hippogryphs, and the like, are inventions of my own mind. But I may even perhaps come to be of opinion that all my ideas are of the class which I call adventitious, or that they are all innate, or that they are all factitious, for I have not yet clearly discovered their true origin; and what I have here principally to do is to consider, with reference to those that appear to come from certain objects without me, what grounds there are for thinking them like these objects.

The first of these grounds is that it seems to me I am so taught by nature; and the second that I am conscious that those ideas are not dependent on my will, and therefore not on myself, for they are frequently presented to me against my will,—as at present, whether I will or not, I feel heat; and I am thus persuaded that this sensation or idea of heat is produced in me by something different from myself, viz., by the heat of the fire by which I sit. And it is very reasonable to suppose that this object impresses me with its own likeness rather than any other thing.

But I must consider whether these reasons are sufficiently strong and convincing. When I speak of being taught by nature in this matter, I understand by the word nature only a certain spontaneous impetus that impels me to believe in a resemblance between ideas and their objects, and not a natural light that affords a knowledge of its truth. But these two things are widely different; for what the natural light shows to be true can be in no degree doubtful, as, for example, that I am because I doubt, and other truths of the like kind: inasmuch as I possess no other faculty whereby to distinguish truth from error, which can teach me the falsity of what the natural light declares to be true, and which is equally trustworthy; but with respect to [seemingly] natural impulses, I have observed, when the question related to the choice of right or wrong in action, that they frequently led me to take the worse part; nor do I see that I have any better ground for following them in what relates to truth and error. Then, with respect to the other reason, which is that because these ideas do not depend on my will, they must arise from objects existing without me, I do not find it more convincing than the former; for, just as those natural impulses, of which I have lately spoken, are found in me, notwithstanding that they are not always in harmony with my will, so likewise it may be that I possess some power not sufficiently known to myself capable of producing ideas without the aid of external objects, and, indeed, it has always hitherto appeared to me that they are formed during sleep, by some power of this nature, without the aid of anything external. And, in short, although I should grant that they proceeded from those objects, it is not a necessary consequence that they must be like them. On the contrary, I have observed, in a number of instances, that there was a great difference between the object and its idea. Thus, for example, I find in my mind two wholly diverse ideas of the sun; the one, by which it appears to me extremely small, draws its origin from the senses, and should be placed in the class of adventitious ideas; the other, by which it seems to be many times larger than the whole earth, is taken up on astronomical grounds, that is, elicited from certain notions born with me, or is framed by myself in some other manner. These two ideas cannot certainly both resemble the same sun; and reason teaches me that the one which seems to have immediately emanated from it is the most unlike. And these things sufficiently prove that hitherto it has not been from a certain and deliberate judgment, but only from a sort of blind impulse, that I believed in the existence of certain things different from myself, which, by the organs of sense, or by whatever other means it might be, conveyed their ideas or images into my mind [and impressed it with their likenesses].

But there is still another way of inquiring whether, of the objects whose ideas are in my mind, there are any that exist out of me. If ideas are taken in so far only as they are certain modes of consciousness, I do not notice any difference or inequality among them, and all seem, in the same manner, to proceed from myself; but, considering them as images, of which one represents

one thing and another a different, it is evident that a great diversity obtains among them. For, without doubt, those that represent substances are something more, and contain in themselves, so to speak, more objective reality [that is, participate by representation in higher degrees of being or perfection] than those that represent only modes or accidents; and again, the idea by which I conceive a God [sovereign], eternal, infinite, [immutable], all-knowing, all-powerful, and the creator of all things that are out of himself,—this, I say, has certainly in it more objective reality than those ideas by which finite substances are represented.

Now, it is manifest by the natural light that there must at least be as much reality in the efficient and total cause as in its effect; for whence can the effect draw its reality if not from its cause? and how could the cause communicate to it this reality unless it possessed it in itself? And hence it follows, not only that what is cannot be produced by what is not, but likewise that the more perfect,—in other words, that which contains in itself more reality,—cannot be the effect of the less perfect: and this is not only evidently true of those effects, whose reality is actual or formal, but likewise of ideas, whose reality is only considered as objective.

And in proportion to the time and care with which I examine all those matters, the conviction of their truth brightens and becomes distinct. But, to sum up, what conclusion shall I draw from it all? It is this;— if the objective reality [or perfection] of any one of my ideas be such as clearly to convince me, that this same reality exists in me neither formally nor eminently, and if, as follows from this, I myself cannot be the cause of it, it is a necessary consequence that I am not alone in the world, but that there is besides myself some other being who exists as the cause of that idea; while, on the contrary, if no such idea be found in my mind, I shall have no sufficient ground of assurance of the existence of any other being besides myself; for, after a most careful search, I have, up to this moment, been unable to discover any other ground.

But, among these my ideas, besides that which represents myself, respecting which there can be here no difficulty, there is one that represents a God.

By the name God, I understand a substance infinite, [eternal, immutable], independent, all-knowing, all-powerful, and by which I myself, and every other thing that exists, if any such there be, were created. But these properties are so great and excellent, that the more attentively I consider them the less I feel persuaded that the idea I have of them owes its origin to myself alone. And thus it is absolutely necessary to conclude, from all that I have before said, that God exists: for though the idea of substance be in my mind owing to this, that I myself am a substance, I should not, however, have the idea of an infinite substance, seeing I am a finite being, unless it were given me by some substance in reality infinite.

The idea, I say, of a being supremely perfect, and infinite, is in the highest degree true; for although, perhaps, we may imagine that such a being does not exist, we cannot, nevertheless, suppose that his idea represents nothing real, as I have already said of the idea of cold. It is likewise clear and distinct in the highest degree, since whatever the mind clearly and distinctly conceives as real or true, and as implying any perfection, is contained entire in this idea.

There remains only the inquiry as to the way in which I received this idea from God; for I have not drawn it from the senses, nor is it even presented to me unexpectedly, as is usual with the ideas of sensible objects, when these are presented or appear to be presented to the external organs of the senses; it is not even a pure production or fiction of my mind, for it is not in my power to take from or add to it; and consequently there but remains the alternative that it is innate, in the same way as is the idea of myself. And, in truth, it is not to be wondered at that God, at my creation, implanted this idea in me, that it might serve, as it were, for the mark of the workman impressed on his work; and it is not also necessary that the mark should be something different from the work itself; but considering only that God is my creator, it is highly probable that he in some way fashioned me after his own image and likeness, and that I perceive this likeness, in which is contained the idea of God, by the same faculty by which I apprehend myself,—in other words, when I make myself the object of reflection, I not only find that I am an incomplete, [imperfect] and dependent being, and one who unceasingly aspires after something better and greater than he is; but, at the same time, I am assured likewise that he upon whom I am dependent possesses in himself all the goods after which I aspire, [and the ideas of which I find in my mind], and that not merely indefinitely

and potentially, but infinitely and actually, and that he is thus God. And the whole force of the argument of which I have here availed myself to establish the existence of God, consists in this, that I perceive I could not possibly be of such a nature as I am, and yet have in my mind the idea of a God, if God did not in reality exist,—this same God, I say, whose idea is in my mind—that is, a being who possesses all those lofty perfections, of which the mind may have some slight conception, without, however, being able fully to comprehend them—and who is wholly superior to all defect; [and has nothing that marks imperfection]: whence it is sufficiently manifest that he cannot be a deceiver, since it is a dictate of the natural light that all fraud and deception spring from some defect.

Meditation IV

Of Truth and Error

And now I seem to discover a path that will conduct us from the contemplation of the true God, in whom are contained all the treasures of science and wisdom, to the knowledge of the other things in the universe.

For, in the first place, I discover that it is impossible for him ever to deceive me, for in all fraud and deceit there is a certain imperfection: and although it may seem that the ability to deceive is a mark of subtlety or power, yet the will testifies without doubt of malice and weakness; and such, accordingly, cannot be found in God. In the next place, I am conscious that I possess a certain faculty of judging [or discerning truth from error], which I doubtless received from God, along with whatever else is mine; and since it is impossible that he should will to deceive me, it is likewise certain that he has not given me a faculty that will ever lead me into error, provided I use it aright.

And there would remain no doubt on this head, did it not seem to follow from this, that I can never therefore be deceived; for if all I possess be from God, and if he planted in me no faculty that is deceitful, it seems to follow that I can never fall into error.

And assuredly there is no doubt that God could have created me such as that I should never be deceived; it is certain, likewise, that he always wills what is best; is it better, then, that I should be capable of being deceived than that I should not?

Whence, then, spring my errors? They arise from this cause alone, that I do not restrain the will, which is of much wider range than the understanding, within the same limits, but extend it even to things I do not understand, and as the will is of itself indifferent to such, it readily falls into error and sin by choosing the false in room of the true, and evil instead of good.

If I abstain from judging of a thing when I do not conceive it with sufficient clearness and distinctness, it is plain that I act rightly, and am not deceived; but if I resolve to deny or affirm, I then do not make a right use of my free will; and if I affirm what is false, it is evident that I am deceived: moreover, even although I judge according to truth, I stumble upon it by chance, and do not therefore escape the imputation of a wrong use of my freedom; for it is a dictate of the natural light, that the knowledge of the understanding ought always to precede the determination of the will.

As often as I so restrain my will within the limits of my knowledge, that it forms no judgment except regarding objects which are clearly and distinctly represented to it by the understanding, I can never be deceived; because every clear and distinct conception is doubtless something, and as such cannot owe its origin to nothing, but must of necessity have God for its author—God, I say, who, as supremely perfect, cannot, without a contradiction, be the cause of any error; and consequently it is necessary to conclude that every such conception [or judgment] is true. Nor have I merely learned to-day what I must avoid to escape error, but also what I must do to arrive at the knowledge of truth; for I will assuredly reach truth if I only fix my attention sufficiently on all the things I conceive perfectly, and separate these from others which I conceive more confusedly and obscurely: to which for the future I shall give diligent heed.

◇ THE REPRESENTATIONAL THEORY OF PERCEPTION ◇
6. ESSAY CONCERNING HUMAN UNDERSTANDING
John Locke

Book II

Chapter I: Of Ideas in General, and Their Original

1. Every man being conscious to himself that he thinks, and that which his mind is employed about whilst thinking, being the ideas that are there, 'tis past doubt that men have in their minds several ideas, such as are those expressed by the words, whiteness, hardness, sweetness, thinking, motion, man, elephant, army, and drunkenness, and others: it is in the first place then to be enquired, how he comes by them? I know it is a received doctrine, that men have native ideas and original characters stamped upon their minds, in their very first being. This opinion I have at large examined already: and, I suppose, what I have said in the foregoing book will be much more easily admitted, when I have showed

whence the understanding may get all the ideas it has, and by what ways and degrees they may come into the mind; for which I shall appeal to everyone's own observation and experience.

2. Let us then suppose the mind to be, as we say, white paper, void of all characters, without any ideas; how comes it to be furnished? Whence comes it by that vast store, which the busy and boundless fancy of man has painted on it, with an almost endless variety? Whence has it all the materials of reason and knowledge? To this I answer, in one word, from experience: in that, all our knowledge is founded; and from that it ultimately derives itself. Our observation employed either about external, sensible objects; or about the internal operations of our minds, perceived and reflected on by our selves, is that which supplies our understandings with all the materials of thinking. These two are the fountains of knowledge, from whence all the ideas we have, or can naturally have, do spring.

3. First, our senses, conversant about particular, sensible objects, do convey into the mind several distinct perceptions of things, according to those various ways wherein those objects do affect them: and thus we come by those ideas we have, of yellow, white, heat, cold, soft, hard, bitter, sweet, and all those which we call sensible qualities. This great source, of most of the ideas we have, depending wholly upon our senses, and derived by them to our understanding, I call *sensation*.

4. Secondly, the other fountain, from which experience furnishes the understanding with ideas, is the perception of the operations of our own minds within us, as it is employed about the ideas it has got; which operations, when the soul comes to reflect on, and consider, do furnish the understanding with another set of ideas, which could not be had from things without. . . . As I call the other sensation, so I call this *reflection*, the ideas it affords being such only as the mind gets by reflecting on its own operations within itself. By reflection then, in the following part of this discourse, I would be understood to mean that notice which the mind takes of its own operations, and the manner of them, by reason whereof, there come to be ideas of these operations in the understanding. These two, I say, *viz* external, material things, as the objects of sensation; and the operations of our own minds within, as the objects of reflection, are, to me, the only originals, from whence all our ideas take their beginnings. The term *operations*, here, I use in a large sense, as comprehending not barely the actions of the mind about its ideas, but some sort of passions arising sometimes from them, such as is the satisfaction of uneasiness arising from any thought.

23. If it shall be demanded then, when a man begins to have any ideas? I think the true answer is, when he first has any sensation. For since there appear not to be any ideas in the mind before the senses have conveyed any in, I conceive that ideas in the understanding are coeval with sensation; which is such an impression or motion, made in some part of the body, as makes it be taken notice of in the understanding.

24. The impressions, then, that are made on our senses by outward objects, that are extrinsical to the mind and its own operations, about these impressions reflected on by itself, as proper objects to be contemplated by it, are, I conceive, the original

of all knowledge; and the first capacity of human intellect is that the mind is fitted to receive the impressions made on it; either through the senses, by outward objects; or by its own operations, when it reflects on them.

Chapter II: Of Simple Ideas

1. The better to understand the nature, manner, and extent of our knowledge, one thing is carefully to be observed, concerning the ideas we have; and that is, that some of them are simple, and some complex.

Though the qualities that affect our senses are, in the things themselves, so united and blended that there is no separation, no distance between them; yet 'tis plain, the ideas they produce in the mind enter by the senses simple and unmixed. For though the sight and touch often take in from the same object, at the same time, different ideas; as a man sees at once motion and color, the hand feels softness and warmth in the same piece of wax: yet the simple ideas thus united in the same subject are as perfectly distinct as those that come in by different senses.

2. These simple ideas, the materials of all our knowledge, are suggested and furnished to the mind only by those two ways above mentioned, *viz.* sensation and reflection. When the understanding is once stored with these simple ideas, it has the power to repeat, compare, and unite them even to an almost infinite variety, and so can make at pleasure new complex ideas. But it is not in the power of the most exalted wit, or enlarged understanding, by any quickness or variety of thought, to invent or frame one new simple idea in the mind, not taken in by the ways before mentioned: nor can any force of understanding destroy those that are there.

Chapter VIII: Some Further Considerations Concerning Our Simple Ideas

1. Concerning the simple ideas of sensation, 'tis to be considered that, whatsoever is so constituted in nature as to be able, by affecting our senses, to cause any perception in the mind, does thereby produce in the understanding a simple idea; which, whatever be the external cause of it, when it comes to be taken notice of by our discerning faculty, it is by the mind looked on and considered there to be a real positive idea in the understanding, as much as any other

whatsoever; though, perhaps, the cause of it be but a privation in the subject.

7. To discover the nature of our ideas the better, and to discourse of them intelligibly, it will be convenient to distinguish them, as they are ideas or perceptions in our minds; and as they are in the bodies that cause such perceptions in us: that so we may not think (as perhaps usually is done) that they are exactly the images and resemblances of something inherent in the subject; most of those of sensation being in the mind no more the likeness of something existing without us than the names that stand for them are the likeness of our ideas, which yet, upon hearing, they are apt to excite in us.

8. Whatsoever the mind perceives in itself, or is the immediate object of perception, thought, or understanding, that I call *idea;* and the power to produce any idea in our mind, I call *quality* of the subject wherein that power is. Thus a snowball having the power to produce in us the ideas of white, cold, and round, the powers to produce those ideas in us, as they are in the snowball, I call qualities; and as they are sensations, or perceptions, in our understandings, I call them ideas: which ideas, if I speak of sometimes, as in the things themselves, I would be understood to mean those qualities in the objects which produce them in us.

9. Concerning these qualities, we may, I think, observe these *primary* ones in bodies, that produce simple ideas in us, *viz.* solidity, extension, motion or rest, number and figure.

10. These, which I call original or primary qualities of body, are wholly inseparable from it; and such as in all the alterations and changes it suffers, all the force can be used upon it, it constantly keeps; and such as sense constantly finds in every particle of matter, which has bulk enough to be perceived, and the mind finds inseparable from every particle of matter, though less than to make itself singly be perceived by our senses. *e.g.* Take a grain of wheat, divide it into two parts, each part has still solidity, extension, figure, and mobility; divide it again, and it retains still the same qualities. . . .

11. The next thing to be considered is how bodies operate one upon another, and that is manifestly by impulse, and nothing else. It being impossible to conceive, that body should operate on what it does not

touch (which is all one as to imagine it can operate where it is not) or when it does touch, operate any other way than by motion.

12. If then bodies cannot operate at a distance; if external objects be not united to our minds, when they produce ideas in it; and yet we perceive these original qualities in such of them as singly fall under our senses, 'tis evident that some motion must be then continued by our nerves, or animal spirits, by some parts of our bodies, to the brains, the seat of sensation, there to produce in our minds the particular ideas we have of them. And since the extension, figure, number, and motion of bodies of an observable bigness may be perceived at a distance by the sight, 'tis evident some singly imperceptible bodies must come from them to the eyes, and thereby convey to the brain some motion, which produces these ideas we have of them in us.

13. After the same manner, that the ideas of these original qualities are produced in us, we may conceive that the ideas of secondary qualities are also produced, *viz.* by the operation of insensible particles on our senses. . . . Let us suppose, at present, that the different motions and figures, bulk, and number of such particles, affecting the several organs of our senses, produce in us those different sensations which we have from the colors and smells of bodies, *e.g.* a violet, by which impulse of those insensible particles of matter of different figures and bulks, and in a different degree and modification, we may have the ideas of the blue color and sweet scent of a violet produced in our minds. It being no more conceived impossible, to conceive that God should annex such ideas to such motions, with which they have no similitude; than that he should annex the idea of pain to the motion of a piece of steel dividing our flesh, with which that idea has no resemblance.

14. What I have said, concerning colors and smells, may be understood also of tastes and sounds, and other like sensible qualities; which, whatever reality we by mistake attribute to them, are in truth nothing in the objects themselves but powers to produce various sensations in us, and depend on those primary qualities of bodies, *viz.* bulk, figure, texture, and motion of parts; and therefore I call them secondary qualities.

15. From whence, I think, it is easy to draw this observation, that the ideas of primary qualities of bodies are resemblances of them, and their patterns do really exist in the bodies themselves; but the ideas, produced in us by these secondary qualities, have no resemblance of them at all. There is nothing like our ideas existing in the bodies themselves. They are in the bodies, we denominate from them only a power to produce those sensations in us: and what is sweet, blue, or warm in idea, is but the certain bulk, figure, and motion of the insensible parts, in the bodies themselves we call so.

16. Flame is denominated, hot and light; snow, white and cold; and manna, white and sweet, from the ideas they produce in us. Which qualities are commonly thought to be the same in those bodies, that those ideas are in us, the one the perfect resemblance of the other, as they are in a mirror; and it would by most men be judged very extravagant if one should say otherwise. And yet he that will consider, that the same fire that at one distance produces in us the sensation of warmth, does at a nearer approach produce in us the far different sensation of pain, ought to bethink himself, what reason he has to say that his idea of warmth, which was produced in him by the fire, is actually in the fire; and his idea of pain, which the same fire produced in him the same way, is not in the fire. Why is whiteness and coldness in snow, and pain not when it produces the one and the other idea in us; and can do neither, but by the bulk, figure, number, and motion of its solid parts.

17. The particular bulk, number, figure, and motion of the parts of fire, or snow, are really in them, whether anyone's senses perceive them or no: and therefore they may be called *real qualities*, they really exist in those bodies. But light, heat, whiteness, or coldness are no more really in them, than sickness or pain is in manna. Take away the sensation of them, let not the eyes see the light, or colors, nor the ears hear sounds; let the palate not taste, nor the nose smell, and all colors, tastes, odors, and sounds, as they are such particular ideas, vanish and cease, and are reduced to their causes, i.e. bulk, figure, and motion of parts.

23. The qualities then that are in bodies rightly considered are of three sorts:

First, the bulk, figure, number, situation, and motion, or rest of their solid parts; these are in them, whether we perceive them or no; and when they are of that size that we can discover them, we have by these an idea of the thing, as it is in itself, as is plain in artificial things. These I call *primary qualities*.

Secondly, the power that is in any body, by reason of its insensible primary qualities, to operate after a peculiar manner on any of our senses, and thereby produce in us the different ideas of several colors, sounds, smells, tastes, etc. These are usually called sensible qualities.

Thirdly, the power that is in any body, by reason of the particular constitution of its primary qualities, to make such a change in the bulk, figure, texture, and motion of another body, as to make it operate on our senses differently from what it did before. Thus the sun has a power to make wax white, and fire to make lead fluid.

The first of these, as has been said, I think, may be properly called real, original, or primary qualities, because they are in the things themselves, whether they are perceived or no: and upon their different modifications it is, that the secondary qualities depend.

The other two are only powers to act differently upon other things, which powers result from the different modifications of those primary qualities.

26. To conclude, beside those before mentioned primary qualities in bodies, *viz.* bulk, figure, extension, number, and motion of their solid parts; all the rest, whereby we take notice of bodies, and distinguish them one from another, are nothing else but several powers in them, depending on those primary qualities; whereby they are fitted, either by immediately operating on our bodies to produce several different ideas in us, different from what before they did. The former of these, I think, may be called secondary qualities, immediately perceivable; the latter, secondary qualities, mediately perceivable.

Chapter IX: Of Perception

1. *Perception*, as it is the first faculty of the mind, exercised about our ideas, so it is the first and simplest idea we have from reflection, and it is, by some, called thinking in general. Though thinking, in the propriety of the English tongue, signifies that sort of operation of the mind about its ideas, wherein the mind is active; where it with some degree of voluntary attention, considers anything. For in bare naked perception, the mind is, for the most part, only passive; and what it perceives, it cannot avoid perceiving.

2. What perception is, everyone will know better, by reflecting on what he does himself, when he sees, hears, feels, etc., or thinks, than by any discourse of mine. Whoever reflects on what passes in himself in his own mind, cannot miss it: and if he does not reflect, all the words in the world cannot make him have any notion of it.

3. This is certain, that whatever alterations are made in the body, if they reach not the mind; whatever impressions are made on the outward parts, if they are not taken notice of within, there is not perception.

8. We are further to consider, concerning perception, that the ideas we receive by sensation are often in grown people altered by the judgment, without our taking notice of it. When we set before our eyes a round globe of any uniform color, *e.g.* gold, alabaster, or jet, 'tis certain that the idea thereby imprinted in our mind is of a flat circle, variously shadowed with several degrees of light and brightness coming to our eyes. But we having by use been accustomed to perceive what kind of appearance convex bodies are wont to make in us; what alterations are made in the reflections of light by the difference of the sensible figures of bodies, the judgment presently, by an habitual custom, alters the appearances into their causes: so that from that, which truly is variety of shadow or color, collecting the figure, it makes it pass for a mark of figure, and frames to itself the perception of a convex figure and a uniform color; when the idea we receive from thence, is only a plane variously colored, as is evident in painting.

9. But this is not, I think, usual in any of our ideas, but those received by sight: because sight, the most comprehensive of all our senses, conveying to our minds the far different ideas of light and colors, which are peculiar only to that sense; and also of space, figure, and motion, the several varieties whereof, change the appearances of its proper objects, *viz.* light and colors, it accustoms itself by use to judge of the one by the other. This in many cases, by a settled habit, in things whereof we have frequent experience, is performed so constantly, and so quick, that we take that for the perception of our sensation, which is but an idea formed by our judgment; so that one, *viz.* that of sensation, serves only to excite the other, and is scarce taken notice of itself; as a man who reads and hears with attention and understanding takes little notice of the characters or sounds, but of the ideas that are excited in him by them.

Perception then being the first step and degree towards knowledge, and the inlet of all the materials of it, the fewer senses any man, as well as any other creature, has; and the fewer and duller the impressions are that are made by them; and the duller the faculties are that are employed about them, the more remote are they from that knowledge which is to be found in some men.

Chapter X: Of Retention

1. The next faculty of the mind, whereby it makes a farther progress towards knowledge, is that I call *retention*; or the keeping of those simple ideas, which from sensation or reflection it has received, which is done two ways; first, either by keeping the idea, which is brought into it, for some time actually in view, which is called *contemplation*.

2. The other is the power to revive again in our minds those ideas, which after imprinting have disappeared, or have been, as it were, laid aside out of sight: and thus we do, when we conceive heat or light, yellow or sweet, the object being removed; and this is *memory*, which is, as it were, the storehouse of our ideas. . . .

Chapter XII: Of Complex Ideas

1. We have hitherto considered those ideas, in the reception whereof, the mind is only passive, which are those simple ones received from sensation and reflection before-mentioned, whereof the mind cannot make anyone to itself, nor have any idea which does not wholly consist of them. But as these simple ideas are observed to exist in several combinations united together, so the mind has a power to consider several of them united together, as one idea; and that not only as they are united in external objects, but as itself has joined them. Ideas thus made up of several simple ones put together, I call *complex*. . . .

3. Complex ideas, however compounded and decompounded, though their number be infinite, and the variety endless, wherewith they fill and entertain

the thoughts of men; yet, I think, they may be all reduced under these three heads: (1) modes (2) substances (3) relations. . . .

Chapter XXIII: Of Our Complex Ideas of Substances

1. The mind being furnished with a great number of the simple ideas, conveyed in by the senses, as they are found in exterior things, or by reflection on its own operations, takes notice also, that a certain number of these simple ideas go constantly together; which being presumed to belong to one thing, and, words being suited to common apprehensions, and made use of for quick dispatch, are called, so united in one subject, by one name; which by inadvertency we are apt afterward to talk of and consider as one single idea, which indeed is a complication of many ideas together: because, as I have said, not imagining how these simple ideas can subsist by themselves, we accustom ourselves, to suppose some substratum, wherein they do subsist, and from which they do result, which therefore we call *substance*.

2. So that if anyone will examine himself concerning his notion of pure substance in general, he will find he has no other idea of it at all, but only a supposition of he knows not what support of such qualities, which are capable of producing simple ideas in us; which qualities are commonly called accidents: and if anyone should be asked, what is the subject wherein color or weight inheres, he would have nothing to say, but the solid extended parts: and if he were demanded, what is it, that that solidity and extension inhere in, he would not be in a much better case than the Indian before mentioned; who saying that the world was supported by a great elephant, was asked what the elephant rested on; to which his answer was, A great tortoise: but being again pressed to know what gave support to the broad-backed tortoise, replied, something, he knew not what. And thus here, as in all other cases, where we use words without having clear and distinct ideas, we talk like children; who being questioned what such a thing is, which they know not; readily give this satisfactory answer, That is something; which in truth signifies no more when so used, whether by children or men, but that they knew not what; and that the thing they pretend to know, and talk of, is what they have no distinct idea of at all, and so are perfectly ignorant of it and in the dark. The idea then we have, to which we give the general name substance, being nothing but the supposed, but unknown, support of those qualities we find existing, which we imagine cannot subsist, *sine he substante*, without something to support them, we call that support *substantia*; which according to the true import of the word is, plain English, *standing under*, or *upholding*.

3. An obscure and relative idea of substance in general being thus made, we come to have the ideas of particular sorts of substances, by collecting such combinations of simple ideas as are by experience and observation of men's senses taken notice of to exist together, and are therefore supposed to flow from the particular internal constitution, or unknown essence, of that substance. Thus we come to have the ideas of a man, horse, gold, water, etc. . . . Only we must take notice that our complex ideas of substances, besides all these simple ideas they are made up of, have always confused the idea of something to which they belong, and in which they subsist: and therefore when we speak of any sort of substance, we say it is a thing having such or such qualities, as body is a thing that is extended, figured, and capable of motion; a spirit a thing capable of thinking: and so hardness, friability, and power to draw iron, we say, are qualities to be found in a loadstone. These and the like fashions of speaking intimate, that the substance is supposed always something besides the extension, figure, solidity, motion, thinking, or other observable ideas, though we know not what it is.

4. Hence when we talk or think of any particular sort of corporeal substances as horse, stone, etc., though the idea we have of either of them be but the complication, or collection, of those several simple ideas of sensible qualities which we use to find united in the thing called horse or stone, yet because we cannot conceive how they should subsist alone, nor one in another, we suppose them to exist in, and supported by, some common subject; which support we denote by the name substance, though it be certain we have no clear or distinct idea of that thing, we suppose a support.

5. The same happens concerning the operations of the mind, *viz.* thinking, reasoning, fearing, etc., which we concluding not to subsist of themselves, nor apprehending how they can belong to body, or be produced by it, we are apt to think these the actions of

some other substance, which we call spirit; whereby yet it is evident that having no other idea or notion of matter, but something wherein those many sensible qualities which affect our senses do subsist; by supposing a substance wherein thinking, knowing, doubting, and a power of moving, etc., do subsist, we have as clear a notion of the nature, or substance, of spirit as we have of body; the one being supposed to be (without knowing what it is) the substratum to those simple ideas we have from without; and the other supposed (with a like ignorance of what it is) to be the substratum to those operations, which we experiment in ourselves within. . . .

Chapter XXVI: Of Cause and Effect, and Other Relations

1. In the notice that our senses take of the constant vicissitude of things, we cannot but observe that several particular, both qualities and substances, begin to exist; and that they receive this their existence from the due application and operation of some other being. From this observation, we get our ideas of cause and effect. That which produces any simple or complex idea, we denote by the general name *cause*; and that which is produced, *effect*. Thus, finding that in that substance which we call wax, fluidity, which is a simple idea that was not in it before, is constantly produced by the application of a certain degree of heat, we call the simple idea of heat, in relation to fluidity in wax, the cause of it; and fluidity the effect. So also finding that the substance, wood, which is a certain collection of simple ideas, so called, will, by the application of fire, be turned into another substance called ashes; i.e. another complex idea, consisting of a collection of simple ideas, quite different from that complex idea, which we call wood; we consider fire, in relation to ashes, as cause, and the ashes, as effect.

Chapter XXXI: Of True and False Ideas

1. Though truth and falsehood belong, in propriety of speech, only to propositions; yet ideas are oftentimes termed true or false (as what words are there that are not used with great latitude, and with some deviation from their strict and proper significations), though I think that when ideas themselves are termed true or false, there is still some secret or tacit proposition which is the foundation of that denomination: as we shall see, if we examine the particular occasions wherein they come to be called true or false. In all which, we shall find some kind of affirmation or negation, which is the reason of that denomination. For our ideas, being nothing but bare appearances or perceptions in our minds, cannot properly and simply in themselves be said to be true or false, no more than a single name of anything can be said to be true or false. . . .

4. Whenever the mind refers any of its ideas to anything extraneous to them, they are then capable to be called true or false. Because the mind, in such a reference, makes a tacit supposition of their conformity to that thing: which supposition, as it happens to be true or false; so the ideas themselves come to be denominated. . . .

Book III

Chapter II: Of the Significance of Words

Words in their primary and immediate signification stand for nothing, but the ideas in the mind of him that uses them, how imperfectly whatsoever, or carelessly those ideas are collected from the things, which they are supposed to represent. When a man speaks to another, it is, that he may be understood; and the end of the speech is that those sounds, as marks, may make known his ideas to the hearer. . . .

4. But though words, as they are used by men, can properly and immediately signify nothing but the ideas that are in their minds; yet they, in their thoughts, give them a secret reference to two other things.

First, they suppose their words to be marks of the ideas in the minds also of other men, with whom they communicate: for else they should talk in vain, and could not be understood, if the sounds they applied to one idea, were such, as by the hearer, were applied to another, which is to speak two languages. But in this, men stand not usually to examine, whether the idea they, and he they discourse with, be the same: but think it enough, that they use the word, as they imagine, in the common acceptation of that language; in which case, they suppose that the idea, they make it a sign of, is precisely the same, to which the understanding men of that country apply that name.

5. Secondly, because men would not be thought to talk barely of their own imaginations, but of things as really they are; therefore they often suppose their words to stand also for the reality of things.

Chapter III: Of General Terms

1. All things that exist, being particulars, it may perhaps be thought reasonable that words, which ought to be conformed to things, should be so too, I mean in their signification: but yet we find the quite contrary. The far greatest part of words, that make all languages, are general terms: which has not been the effect of neglect, or chance, but of reason, and necessity. . . .

7. It will not, perhaps, be amiss to trace our notions and names from their beginning, and observe by what degrees we proceed, and by what steps we enlarge our ideas from our first infancy. There is nothing more evident than that the ideas of the persons children converse with (to instance in them alone), are like the persons themselves, only particular. The ideas of the nurse and the mother are well-framed in their minds; and, like pictures of them there, represent only those individuals. The names they first give to them, are confined to these individuals; and the names of Nurse and Mamma, the child uses, determine themselves to those persons. Afterwards, when time and a larger acquaintance, has made them observe, that there are a great many other things in the world that, in some common agreements of shape, and several other qualities, resemble their father and mother: and those persons they have been used to, they frame an idea, which they find those many particulars do partake in; and to that they give, with others, the name *man*, for example. And thus they come to have a general name and a general idea. Wherein they make nothing new, but only leave out of the complex idea they had of Peter and James, Mary and Jane, that which is particular to each, and retain only what is common to them all. . . .

11. It is plain, by what has been said, that general and universal belong not to the real existence of things, but are the inventions and creatures of the understanding, made by it for its own use, and concern only signs, whether words or ideas. Words are general, as has been said, when used for signs of general ideas; and so are applicable indifferently to many particular

things: and ideas are general, when they are set up as the representatives of many particular things: but universality belongs not to things themselves.

12. The next thing therefore to be considered is what kind of signification it is that general words have. For, as it is evident that they do not signify barely one particular thing, for then they would not be general terms, but proper names; so on the other side, 'tis as evident, they do not signify a plurality, for man and men would then signify the same, and the distinction of numbers (as grammarians call them) would be superfluous and useless. That, then, which general words signify, is a sort of things; and that each of them does, by being a sign of an abstract idea in the mind, to which idea, as things existing are found to agree, so they come to be ranked under that name; or, which is all one, be of that sort. Whereby it is evident, that the essences of the sorts, or (if the Latin word pleases better) species of things, are nothing else but these abstract ideas. For the having the essence of any species, being that which makes any thing to be of that species, and the conformity to the idea, to which the name is annexed, being that which gives a right to that name, the having the essence, and the having that conformity, must needs be the same thing: since to be of any species, and to have a right to the name of that species, is all one. As for example, to be a man, or of the species *man*, and to have a right to the name *man*, is the same thing. Again, to be a man, or of the species *man*, and have the essence of a man, is the same thing. Now since nothing can be a man, or have a right to be of the species *man*, but what has the essence of that species, it follows, that the abstract idea, for which the name stands, and the essence of the species, is one and the same. From whence it is easy to observe that the essences of the sorts of things, and consequently the sorting of things, is the workmanship of the understanding, since it is the understanding that abstracts and makes those general ideas.

15. But since the essences of things are thought, by some (and not without reason) to be wholly unknown; it may not be amiss to consider the several significations of the word *essence*.

First, essence may be taken for the very being of anything, whereby it is what it is. And thus the real internal but, generally in substances, unknown constitution of things, whereon their discoverable qualities depend, may be called their essence. This is the proper original signification of the word, as is evident from the formation of it; *essentia*, in its primary notation signifying properly being. And in this sense it is still used, when we speak of the essence of particular things, without giving them any name.

Secondly, the learning and disputes of the schools, having been much busied about genus and species, the word *essence* has almost lost its primary signification; and instead of the real constitution of things, has been almost wholly applied to the artificial constitution of genus and species. 'Tis true, there is ordinarily supposed a real constitution, of the sorts of things; and 'tis past doubt, there must be some real constitution, on which any collection of simple ideas coexisting, must depend. But it being evident, that things are ranked under names into sorts or species, only as they agree to certain abstract ideas, to which we have annexed those names, the essence of each genus, or sort, comes to be nothing but that abstract idea, which the general, or sortal (if I may have leave so to call it from sort, as I do general from genus) name stands for. And this we shall find to be that which the word essence imports, in its most familiar use. These two sorts of essence, I suppose, may not unfitly be termed, the one the *real*, the other the *nominal* essence.

18. Essences thus distinguished into nominal and real, we may observe that in the species of simple ideas and modes, they are always the same, but in substances, always quite different. Thus a figure including a space between three lines is the real as well as nominal essence of a triangle; it being not only the abstract idea to which the general name is annexed, but the very *essentia*, or being, of the thing itself, that foundation from which all its properties flow, and to which they are all inseparably annexed. But it is far otherwise concerning that parcel of matter which makes the ring on my finger, wherein these two essences are apparently different. For it is the real constitution of its insensible parts, on which depend all those properties of color, weight, fusibility, fixedness, etc., which are to be found in it. Which constitution we know not; and so having no particular idea of, have no name that is the sign of it. But yet it is its color, weight, fusibility, and fixedness, etc., which makes it to be gold, or gives it a right to that name, which is therefore its nominal essence. Since nothing can be called gold, but what has a conformity of qualities to that abstract complex idea, to which that name is annexed.

Chapter VI: Of the Names of Substances

35. This then, in short, is the case: nature makes many particular things, which do agree, one with another, in many sensible qualities, and probably too, in their internal frame and constitution: but 'tis not this real essence that distinguishes them into species; 'tis men, who, taking occasion from the qualities they find united in them, and wherein they observe often several individuals to agree, range them into sorts, in order to their naming, for the convenience of comprehensive signs; under which particular individuals, according to their conformity to this or that abstract idea, come to be ranked, as under ensigns: so that this is of the blue, that the red regiment; this is a man, that a drill: and in this, I think, consists the whole business of genus and species.

Book IV

Chapter I: Of Knowledge in General

1. Since the mind, in all its thoughts and reasonings, hath no other immediate object but its own ideas, which it alone does or can contemplate, it is evident that our knowledge is only conversant about them.

2. Knowledge then seems to me to be nothing but the perception of the connection and agreement, or disagreement and repugnancy of any of our ideas.

3. But to understand a little more distinctly, wherein this agreement or disagreement consists, I think we may reduce it all to these four sorts: (1) identity, or diversity, (2) relation, (3) coexistence, or necessary connection, (4) real existence.

4. First, as to the first sort of agreement or disagreement, *viz.* identity or diversity. 'Tis the first act of the mind, when it has any sentiments, or ideas at all, to perceive its ideas, and so far as it perceives them, to know each what it is, and thereby also to perceive their difference, and that one is not another. This is so absolutely necessary that without it there could be no knowledge, no reasoning, no imagination, no distinct

thoughts at all. By this the mind clearly and infallibly perceives each idea to agree with itself, and to be what it is; and all distinct ideas to disagree, i.e. the one not to be the other: and this it does without any pains, labor, or deduction; but though men of art have reduced this into those general rules, what is, is; and it is impossible for the same thing to be, and not to be, for ready application in all cases, wherein there may be occasion to reflect on it; yet it is certain, that the first exercise of this faculty, is about particular ideas. A man infallibly knows, as soon as ever he has them in his mind, that the ideas he calls white and round are the very ideas they are, and that they are not other ideas which he calls red or square. Nor can any maxim or proposition in the world make him know it clearer or surer than he did before, or without any such general rule. This then is the first agreement, or disagreement, which the mind perceives in its ideas; which it always perceives at first sight: And if there ever happen any doubt about it, 'twill always be found to be about the names, and not the ideas themselves, whose identity and diversity will always be perceived, as soon and as clearly as the ideas themselves are, nor can it possibly be otherwise.

5. Secondly, the next sort of agreement or disagreement the mind perceives in any of its ideas, may, I think, be called relative, and is nothing but the perception of the relation between any two ideas, of what kind whatsoever, whether substances, modes, or any other. For since all distinct ideas must eternally be known not to be the same, and so be universally and constantly denied one of another, there could be no room for any positive knowledge at all, if we could not perceive any relation between our ideas, and find out the agreement or disagreement they have one with another, in several ways the mind takes of comparing them.

6. Thirdly, the third sort of agreement or disagreement to be found in our ideas, which the perception of the mind is employed about, is coexistence, or non-coexistence in the same subject; and this belongs particularly to substances. Thus when we pronounce concerning gold, that it is fixed, our knowledge of this truth amounts to no more but this, that fixedness, or a power to remain in the fire unconsumed, is an idea, that always accompanies, and is joined with that particular sort of yellowness, weight, fusibility, malleableness, and solubility in *aq. regia*, which make our complex idea, signified by the word *gold*.

7. Fourthly, the fourth and last sort is that of actual real existence agreeing to any idea. Within these four sorts of agreement or disagreement is, I suppose, contained all the knowledge we have, or are capable of: for all the enquiries that we can make, concerning them, is that it is, or is not, the same with some other; that it does, or does not always coexist with some other idea in the same subject; that it has this or that relation to some other idea; or that it has a real existence without the mind. Thus *blue is not yellow*, is of identity. *Two triangles upon equal basis, between two parallels, are equal*, is of relation. *Iron is susceptible of magnetical impressions*, is of coexistence. *God is*, is of real existence.

Chapter II: Of the Degrees of Our Knowledge

1. The different clearness of our knowledge seems to me to lie in the different way of perception the mind has of the agreement or disagreement of any of its ideas. For if we will reflect on our own ways of thinking, we shall find that sometimes the mind perceives the agreement or disagreement of two ideas immediately by themselves, without the intervention of any other: and this, I think, we may call *intuitive* knowledge. For in this, the mind is at no pains of proving or examining, but perceives the truth, as the eyes doth light, only by being directed toward it. Thus the mind perceives that white is not black, that a circle is not a triangle, that three are more than two, and equal to one and two. . . . 'Tis on this intuition that depends all the certainty and evidence of all our knowledge, which certainty everyone finds to be so great that he cannot imagine, and therefore not require, a greater: for a man cannot conceive himself capable of a greater certainty, than to know that any idea in his mind is such, as he perceives it to be; and that two ideas, wherein he perceives a difference, are different, and not precisely the same. He that demands a greater certainty than this, demands he knows not what; and shows only that he has a mind to be a skeptic, without being able to be so. Certainty depends so wholly on this intuition that in the next degree of knowledge, which I call demonstrative, this intuition is necessary in all the connections of the intermediate ideas, without which we cannot attain knowledge and certainty.

2. The next degree of knowledge is where the mind perceives the agreement or disagreement of any ideas, but not immediately. Though wherever the mind

perceives the agreement or disagreement of any of its ideas, there be certain knowledge: yet it does not always happen, that the mind sees that agreement or disagreement which there is between them, even where it is discoverable; and in that case, remains in ignorance, or at most, gets no farther than a probable conjecture. The reason why the mind cannot always perceive presently the agreement or disagreement of two ideas is because those ideas, concerning whose agreement or disagreement the enquiry is made, cannot by the mind be so put together, as to show it. In this case . . . it is required, by the intervention of other ideas (one or more, as it happens), to discover the agreement or disagreement, which it searches; and this is that which we call reasoning. Thus the mind being willing to know the agreement or disagreement in bigness, between the three angles of a triangle, and two right ones, cannot by an immediate view and comparing them, do it: because the three angles of a triangle cannot be brought at once, and be compared with any other one or two angles; and so of this the mind has no immediate, no intuitive knowledge. In this case the mind is fain to find out some other angles, to which the three angles of a triangle have an equality; and finding those equal to two right ones, comes to know their equality to two right ones.

3. Those intervening ideas, which serve to show the agreement of any two others, are called proofs; and where the agreement or disagreement is by this means plainly and clearly perceived, it is called demonstration, it being shown to the understanding, and the mind made see that it is so.

Chapter III: Of the Extent of Human Knowledge

1. Knowledge, as has been said, lying in the perception of the agreement, or disagreement, of any of our ideas, it follows from hence that,

First, we can have knowledge no farther than we have ideas.

2. Secondly, that we can have no knowledge farther than we can have perception of that agreement or disagreement: which perception being, (1) either by intuition, or the immediate comparing any two ideas; or (2) by reason, examining the agreement, or disagreement of two ideas, by the intervention of some others: or (3) by sensation, perceiving the existence of particular things. Hence it also follows,

3. Thirdly, that we cannot have an intuitive knowledge that shall extend itself to all our ideas, and all that we would know about them; because we cannot examine and perceive all the relations they have one to another, by juxtaposition or an immediate comparison one with another. . . .

4. Fourthly, it follows also, from what is above observed, that our rational knowledge cannot reach to the whole extent of our ideas. Because between two different ideas we would examine, we cannot always find such mediums, as we can connect one to another with an intuitive knowledge in all the parts of the deduction; and wherever that fails, we come short of knowledge and demonstration.

5. Fifthly, sensitive knowledge reaching no farther than the existence of things actually present to our senses, is yet much narrower than either of the former.

6. From all which it is evident, that the extent of our knowledge comes not only short of the reality of things, but even of the extent of our own ideas. . . .

7. The affirmations or negations we make concerning the ideas we have may, as I have before intimated in general, be reduced to these four sorts, *viz.* identity, coexistence, relation, and real existence. I shall examine how far our knowledge extends in each of these:

8. First, as to identity and diversity in this way, of the agreement or disagreement of our ideas, our intuitive knowledge is as far extended as our ideas themselves: and there can be no idea in the mind which it does not presently, by an intuitive knowledge, perceive to be what it is, and to be different from any other.

9. Secondly, as to the second sort, which is the agreement or disagreement of our ideas in coexistence, in this our knowledge is very short, though in this consists the greatest and most material part of our knowledge concerning substances. For our ideas of the species of substances being, as I have showed, nothing but certain collections of simple ideas united in one subject, and so coexisting together: *e.g.* our idea of flame is a body hot, luminous, and moving upward; of gold, a body heavy to a certain degree, yellow, malleable, and fusible: for these, or some such complex ideas as these in men's minds, do these two names of different substances, flame and gold, stand for. When we would know anything farther concerning these, or any other sort of substances, what do we

enquire but what other qualities, or powers, these substances have, or have not; which is nothing else but to know, whether simple ideas do or do not coexist with those that make up that complex idea.

10. This, how weighty and considerable a part whatsoever of human science, is yet very narrow, and scarce any at all. The reason whereof is that the simple ideas whereof our complex ideas of substances are made up are, for the most part, such as carry with them, in their own nature, no visible necessary connection or inconsistency with any other simple ideas, whose coexistence with them, we would inform ourselves about.

11. The ideas that our complex ones of substances are made up of, and about which our knowledge concerning substances is most employed, are those of their secondary qualities; which depending all (as has been showed) upon the primary qualities of their minute and insensible parts; or if not upon them, upon something yet more remote from our comprehension, 'tis impossible we should know, which have a necessary union or inconsistency one with another: For not knowing the root they spring from, not knowing what size, figure, and texture of parts they are, on which depend, and from which result those qualities which make our complex idea of gold, 'tis impossible we should know what other qualities result from the same constitution of the insensible parts of gold; and so consequently must always coexist with that complex idea we have of it, or else are inconsistent with it.

12. Besides this ignorance of the primary qualities of the insensible parts of bodies, on which depend all their secondary qualities, there is yet another and more incurable part of ignorance, which sets us more remote from a certain knowledge of the coexistence, or incoexistence (if I may so say) of different ideas in the same subject; and that is, that there is no discoverable connection between any secondary quality and those primary qualities that it depends on. . . .

14. In vain therefore shall we endeavor to discover by our ideas (the only true way of certain and universal knowledge), what other ideas are to be found constantly joined with that of our complex idea of any substance. . . . Thus though we see the yellow color, and upon trial find the weight, malleableness, fusibility, and fixedness that are united in a piece of gold; yet because no one of these ideas has any evident dependence or necessary connection with the other, we cannot certainly know that where any four of these are, the fifth will be there also, how highly probable soever it may be: because the highest probability amounts not to certainty; without which, there can be no true knowledge. For this coexistence can be no farther known, than it is perceived; and it cannot be perceived, but either in particular subjects, by the observation of our senses, or in general, by the necessary connection of the ideas themselves. . . .

18. As to the third sort of our knowledge, *viz.* the agreement or disagreement of any of our ideas in any other relation: this, as it is the largest field of our knowledge, so it is hard to determine how far it may extend: because the advances that are to be made in this part of knowledge, depending on our sagacity in finding intermediate ideas, that may show the relations and habitudes of ideas whose coexistence is not considered, 'tis a hard matter to tell, when we are at an end of such discoveries; and when reason has all the help it is capable of, for the finding of proofs, and examining the agreement or disagreement of remote ideas. . . .

21. As to the fourth sort of our knowledge, *viz.* of the real, actual existence of things without us, we have an intuitive knowledge of our own existence; a demonstrative knowledge of the existence of a God; of the existence of anything else, we have no other but a sensitive knowledge, which extends not beyond the objects present to our senses.

Chapter IX: Of Our Knowledge of Existence

3. As for our own existence, we perceive it so plainly and so certainly that it neither needs, nor is capable of, any proof. For nothing can be more evident to us than our own existence. I think, I reason, I feel pleasure and pain; can any of these be more evident to me than my own existence? If I doubt of all other things, that very doubt makes me perceive my own existence, and will not suffer me to doubt of that. Experience then convinces us that we have an intuitive knowledge of our own existence, and an internal infallible perception that we are. In every act

of sensation, reasoning, or thinking, we are conscious to ourselves of our own being; and, in this matter, come not short of the highest degree of certainty.

Chapter XI: Of Our Knowledge of the Existence of Other Things

1. The knowledge of our own being, we have by intuition. The existence of a God, reason clearly makes known to us.

The knowledge of the existence of any other thing, we can have only by sensation: for there being no necessary connection of real existence, with any idea a man has in his memory, nor of any other existence but that of God, with the existence of any particular man, no particular man can know the existence of any other being, but only when by actual operating upon him, it makes itself perceived by him. For the having the idea of anything in our mind no more proves the existence of that thing, than the picture of a man evidences his being in the world, or the visions of a dream make thereby a true history.

2. 'Tis therefore the actual receiving of ideas from without, that gives us notice of the existence of other things, and makes us know that something doth exist at that time without us, which causes that idea in us, though perhaps we neither know nor consider how it does it: for it takes not from the certainty of our senses, and the ideas we receive by them, that we know not the manner wherein they are produced: *e.g.* while I write this, I have, by the paper affecting my eyes, that idea produced in my mind; which whatever object causes, I call white; by which I know that that quality or accident (i.e. whose appearance before my eyes, always causes that idea) does really exist, and has a being without me. And of this, the greatest assurance I can possibly have, and to which my faculties can attain, is the testimony of my eyes, which are the proper and sole judges of this thing, and whose testimony I have reason to rely on as so certain that I can no more doubt, while I write this, that I see white and black, and that something really exists that causes that sensation in me, than that I write or move my hand; which is a certainty as great as human nature is capable of, concerning the existence of anything but a man's self alone, and of God.

3. The notice we have by our senses of the existing of things without us, though it be not altogether so certain as our intuitive knowledge, or the deductions of our reason, employed about the clear abstract ideas of our own minds; yet it is an assurance that deserves the name of knowledge, if we persuade ourselves that our faculties act and inform us right, concerning the existence of those objects that affect them, it cannot pass for an ill-grounded confidence. For I think nobody can, in earnest, be so skeptical as to be uncertain of the existence of those things he sees and feels. This is certain, the confidence that our faculties do not herein deceive us is the greatest assurance we are capable of, concerning the existence of material beings. For we cannot act anything but by our faculties; nor talk of knowledge itself, but by the help of those faculties which are fitted to apprehend even what knowledge is. But besides the assurance our senses themselves give us, that they do not err in the information they give us of the existence of things without us, when they are affected by them, we are farther confirmed in this assurance by other concurrent reasons.

4. First, 'tis plain, those perceptions are produced in us by exterior causes affecting our senses: because those that want the organs of any sense never can have the ideas belonging to that sense produced in their minds. This is too evident to be doubted: and therefore we cannot but be assured that they come in by the organs of that sense, and no other way. The organs themselves, 'tis plain, do not produce them: for then the eyes of a man in the dark would produce colors, and his nose smell roses in the winter: but we see nobody gets the relish of a pineapple until he goes to the Indies where it is, and tastes it.

5. Secondly, because sometimes I find that I cannot avoid those ideas produced in my mind. For though when my eyes are shut, or windows fast, I can at pleasure recall to my mind the ideas of light, or the sun, which former experience had lodged in my memory; so I can at pleasure lay by that idea, and take into my view that of the smell of a rose, or taste of sugar. But if I turn my eyes at noon towards the sun, I cannot avoid the ideas, which the light, or sun, then produces in me. So that there is a manifest difference between the ideas laid up in my memory (over which, if they were there only, I should have constantly the same

power to dispose of them, and lay them by at pleasure), and those which force themselves upon me, and I cannot avoid having. And therefore it must needs be some exterior cause, and the brisk acting of some objects without me, whose efficacy I cannot resist, that produces those ideas in my mind, whether I will or no. Besides, there is nobody who does not perceive the difference in himself, between contemplating the sun, as he has the idea of it in his memory, and actually looking upon it: of which two, his perception is so distinct, that few of his ideas are more distinguishable one from another. And therefore he has certain knowledge that they are not both memory, or the actions of his mind, and fancies only within him; but that actual seeing has a cause without.

6. Thirdly, add to this that many of those ideas are produced in us with pain, which afterward we remember without the least offense. Thus the pain of heat or cold, when the idea of it is revived in our minds, gives us no disturbance; which, when felt, was very troublesome, and is again, when actually repeated: which is occasioned by the disorder the external object causes in our bodies when applied to it: and we remember the pain of hunger, thirst, or the headache, without any pain at all; which would either never disturb us, or else constantly do it, as often as we thought of it, were there nothing more but ideas floating in our minds, and appearances entertaining our fancies, without the real existence of things affecting us from abroad.

7. Fourthly, our senses, in many cases, bear witness to the truth of each other's report, concerning the existence of sensible things without us. He that sees a fire may, if he doubt whether it be anything more than a bare fancy, feel it too; and be convinced, by putting his hand in it. Which certainly could never be put into such exquisite pain, by a bare idea or phantom, unless that the pain be a fancy too: which yet he cannot when the burn is well, by raising the idea of it, bring upon himself again.

Thus I see, while I write this, I can change the appearance of the paper; and by designing the letters, tell beforehand what new idea it shall exhibit the very next moment, barely by my drawing the pen over it: which will neither appear (let me fancy as much as I will) if my hand stand still; or though I move my pen, if my eyes be shut: nor when those characters are once made on the paper, can I choose afterwards but see them as they are; that is, have the ideas of such letters as I have made. Whence it is manifest, that they are not barely the sport and play of my own imagination, when I find that the characters that were made at the pleasure of my own thoughts do not obey them; nor yet cease to be, whenever I shall fancy it, but continue to affect my senses constantly and regularly, according to the figures I made them. To which if we will add, that the sight of those shall, from another man, draw such sounds as I beforehand design they shall stand for, there will be little reason left to doubt that those words I write do really exist without me, when they cause a long series of regular sounds to affect my ears which could not be the effect of my imagination, nor could my memory retain them in that order.

8. But yet, if after all this anyone will be so skeptical as to distrust his senses, and to affirm that all we see and hear, feel and taste, think and do, during our whole being, is but the series and deluding appearances of a long dream, whereof there is no reality; and therefore will question the existence of all things, or our knowledge of anything: I must desire him to consider that if all be a dream, then he doth but dream that he makes the question; and so it is not much matter that a man should answer. But yet, if he please, he may dream that I make this answer, that the certainty of things existing *in rerum naturá*, when we have the testimony of our senses for it, is not only as great as our frame can attain to, but as our condition needs. For our faculties being suited not to the full extent of being, nor to a perfect, clear, comprehensive knowledge of things, free from all doubt and scruple; but to the preservation of us in whom they are; and accommodated to the use of life: they serve to our purpose well enough, if they will but give us certain notice of those things which are convenient or inconvenient to us.

9. In fine then, when our senses do actually convey into our understandings any idea, we are well assured that there does something at that time really exist without us, which does affect our senses, and actually produce that idea which we then perceive; and we cannot so far distrust their testimony, as to doubt that such collections of simple ideas, as we have observed by our senses to be united together, do really exist together. But this knowledge extends as far as the present testimony of our senses, employed about particular objects that do then affect them, and no

farther. For if I saw such a collection of simple ideas, as is wont to be called man, existing together one minute since, and am now alone, I cannot be sure that the same man exists now, since there is no necessary connection of his existence a minute since, with his existence now: by a thousand ways he may cease to be, since I had the testimony of my senses for his existence. And if I cannot be sure, that the man I saw last today, is now in being, I can be less sure that he is so, who has been longer removed from my senses, and I have not seen since yesterday, or since the last year, and much less can I be certain of the existence of men that I never saw. And therefore though it be highly probable that millions of men do now exist, yet while I am alone writing of this, I have no unquestionable knowledge of it; though the great likelihood of it puts me past doubt, and it be reasonable for me to do several things upon the confidence that there are men (and men also of my acquaintance, with whom I have to do) now in the world: but this is but probability, not knowledge.

10. Whereby yet we may observe how foolish and vain a thing it is, for a man of narrow knowledge, who having reason given him to judge of the different evidence and probability of things, and to be swayed accordingly; how vain, I say, it is to expect demonstration and certainty in things not capable of it; and refuse assent to very rational propositions, and act contrary to very plain and clear truths, because they cannot be made out so evident, as to surmount every the least (I will not say reason, but) pretense of doubting.

✧ IDEALISM ✧

7. TREATISE CONCERNING THE PRINCIPLES OF HUMAN KNOWLEDGE

George Berkeley

Part I

1. It is evident to any one who takes a survey of the objects of humane knowledge, that they are either ideas actually imprinted on the senses, or else such as are perceived by attending to the passions and operations of the mind, or lastly ideas formed by help of memory and imagination, either compounding, dividing, or barely representing those originally perceived in the aforesaid ways. By sight I have the ideas of light and colours with their several degrees and variations. By touch I perceive, for example, hard and soft, heat and cold, motion and resistance, and of all these more and less either as to quantity or degree. Smelling furnishes me with odors; the palate with tastes, and hearing conveys sounds to the mind in all their variety of Tone and Composition. And as several of these are observed to accompany each other, they come to be marked by one name, and so to be reputed as one thing. Thus, for example, a certain colour, taste, smell, figure and consistence having been observed to go together, are accounted one distinct thing, signified by the name *Apple*. Other collections of ideas constitute a stone, a tree, a book, and the like sensible things; which, as they are pleasing or disagreeable, excite the passions of love, hatred, joy, grief, and so forth.

2. But besides all that endless variety of Ideas or objects of knowledge, there is likewise something which knows or perceives them, and exercises divers operations, as willing, imagining, remembering about them. This perceiving, active being is what I call *Mind, Spirit, Soul* or *my Self*. By which words I do not denote any one of my Ideas, but a thing entirely distinct from them, wherein they exist, or, which is the same thing, whereby they are perceived; for the existence of an Idea consists in being perceived.

3. That neither our thoughts, nor passions, nor ideas formed by the imagination exist without the

mind, is what everybody will allow. And it seems no less evident that the various sensations or ideas imprinted on the sense, however blended or combined together (that is, whatever objects they compose) cannot exist otherwise than in a mind perceiving them. I think an intuitive knowledge may be obtained of this, by any one that shall attend to what is meant by the term *exist* when applied to sensible things. The table I write on, I say, exists, that is, I see and feel it; and if I were out of my study I should say it existed, meaning thereby that if I was in my study I might perceive it, or that some other spirit actually does perceive it. There was an odor, that is, it was smelled; there was a sound, that is to say, it was heard; a colour or figure, and it was perceived by sight or touch. This is all that I can understand by these and the like expressions. For as to what is said of the absolute existence of unthinking things without any relation to their being perceived, that seems perfectly unintelligible. Their *esse* is *percipi*, nor is it possible they should have any existence, out of the minds or thinking things which perceive them.

4. It is indeed an opinion strangely prevailing amongst men, that houses, mountains, rivers, and in a word all sensible objects have an existence natural or real, distinct from their being perceived by the understanding. But with how great an assurance and acquiescence soever this principle may be entertained in the world; yet whoever shall find in his heart to call it in question, may, if I mistake not, perceive it to involve a manifest contradiction. For what are the forementioned objects but the things we perceive by sense, and what do we perceive besides our own ideas or sensations; and is it not plainly repugnant that any one of these or any combination of them should exist unperceived?

5. If we throughly examine this tenet, it will, perhaps be found at bottom to depend on the doctrine of *abstract ideas*. For can there be a nicer strain of abstraction than to distinguish the existence of sensible objects from their being perceived, so as to conceive them existing unperceived? Light and colours, heat and cold, extension and figures, in a word the things we see and feel, what are they but so many sensations, notions, ideas or impressions on the sense; and is it possible to separate, even in thought, any of these from perception? For my part I might as easily divide a thing from itself. I may indeed divide in my

thoughts or conceive apart from each other those things which, perhaps, I never perceived by sense so divided. Thus I imagine the trunk of a human body without the limbs, or conceive the smell of a rose without thinking on the rose itself. So far I will not deny I can abstract, if that may properly be called *abstraction*, which extends only to the conceiving separately such objects, as it is possible may really exist or be actually perceived asunder. But my conceiving or imagining power does not extend beyond the possibility of real existence or perception. Hence as it is impossible for me to see or feel any thing without an actual sensation of that thing, so is it impossible for me to conceive in my thoughts any sensible thing or object distinct from the sensation or perception of it.

6. Some truths there are so near and obvious to the mind, that a man need only open his eyes to see them. Such I take this important one to be, to wit, that all the choir of heaven and furniture of the earth, in a word all those bodies which compose the mighty frame of the world, have not any subsistence without a mind, that their being is to be perceived or known; that consequently so long as they are not actually perceived by me, or do not exist in my mind or that of any other created spirit, they must either have no existence at all, or else subsist in the mind of some eternal Spirit; It being perfectly unintelligible and involving all the absurdity of abstraction, to attribute to any single part of them an existence independent of a spirit. To be convinced of which, the reader need only reflect and try to separate in his own thoughts the being of a sensible thing from its being perceived.

7. From what has been said, it follows, there is not any other substance than *spirit*, or that which perceives. But for the fuller proof of this point, let it be considered, the sensible qualities are colour, figure, motion, smell, taste, and such like, that is, the ideas perceived by sense. Now for an idea to exist in an unperceiving thing, is a manifest contradiction; for to have an idea is all one as to perceive: that therefore wherein colour, figure, and the like qualities exist, must perceive them; hence it is clear there can be no unthinking substance or *substratum* of those ideas.

8. But say you, though the ideas themselves do not exist without the mind, yet there may be things like them whereof they are copies or resemblances, which things exist without the mind, in an unthink-

ing substance. I answer, an idea can be like nothing but an idea; a colour or figure can be like nothing but another colour or figure. If we look but ever so little into our thoughts, we shall find it impossible for us to conceive a likeness except only between our ideas. Again, I ask whether those supposed originals or external things, of which our ideas are the pictures or representations, be themselves, perceivable or no? If they are, then they are ideas, and we have gained our point; but if you say they are not, I appeal to any one whether it be sense, to assert a colour is like something which is invisible; hard or soft, like something which is intangible; and so of the rest.

9. Some there are who make a distinction betwixt *primary* and *secondary* qualities: By the former, they mean extension, figure, motion, rest, solidity of impenetrability and number: By the latter they denote all other sensible qualities, as colours, sounds, tastes, and so forth. The ideas we have of these they acknowledge not to be the resemblances of any thing existing without the mind or unperceived; but they will have our ideas of the primary qualities to be patterns or images of things which exist without the mind, in an unthinking substance which they call *matter*. By matter therefore we are to understand an inert, senseless substance, in which extension, figure, and motion, do actually subsist. But it is evident from what we have already shewn, that extension, figure and motion are only ideas existing in the mind, and that an idea can be like nothing but another idea, and that consequently neither they nor their archetypes can exist in an unperceiving substance. Hence it is plain, that the very notion of what is called *matter* or *corporeal substance*, involves a contradiction in it.

10. They who assert that figure, motion, and the rest of the primary or original qualities do exist without the mind, in unthinking substances, do at the same time acknowledge that colours, sounds, heat, cold, and such like secondary qualities, do not, which they tell us are sensations existing in the mind alone, that depend on and are occasioned by the different size, texture and motion of the minute particles of matter. This they take for an undoubted truth, which they can demonstrate beyond all exception. Now if it be certain, that those original qualities are inseparably united with the other sensible qualities, and not, even in thought, capable of being abstracted from them, it plainly follows

that they exist only in the mind. But I desire any one to reflect and try, whether he can by any abstraction of thought, conceive the extension and motion of a body, without all other sensible qualities. For my own part, I see evidently that it is not in my power to frame an idea of a body extended and moved, but I must withal give it some colour or other sensible quality which is acknowledged to exist only in the mind. In short, extension, figure, and motion, abstracted from all other qualities, are inconceivable. Where therefore the other sensible qualities are, there must these be also, to wit, in the Mind and no where else.

11. Again, *great and small, swift* and *slow,* are allowed to exist no where without the mind, being entirely relative, and changing as the frame or position of the organs of sense varies. The extension therefore which exists without the mind, is neither great nor small, the motion neither swift nor flow, that is, they are nothing at all. But say you, they are extension in general, and motion in general. Thus we see how much the tenet of extended, moveable substances existing without the mind, depends on that strange doctrine of *abstract ideas.* And here I cannot but remark, how nearly the vague and indeterminate description of matter or corporeal substance, which the modern philosophers are run into by their own principles, resembles that antiquated and so much ridiculed notion of *materia prima,* to be met with in *Aristotle* and his followers. Without extension solidity cannot be conceived; since therefore it has been shewn that extension exists not in an unthinking substance, the same must also be true of solidity.

12. That number is entirely the creature of the mind, even though the other qualities be allowed to exist without, will be evident to whoever considers, that the same thing bears a different denomination of number, as the mind views it with different respects. Thus, the same extension is one or three or thirty six, according as the mind considers it with reference to a yard, a foot, or an inch. Number is so visibly relative, and dependent on men's understanding, that it is strange to think how any one should give it an absolute existence without the mind. We say one book, one page, one line; all these are equally unit, though some contain several of the others. And in each instance it is plain, the unit relates to some particular combination of ideas arbitrarily put together by the mind.

13. Unity I know some will have to be a simple or uncompounded idea, accompanying all other ideas into the mind. That I have any such idea answering the word *unity*, I do not find; and if I had, methinks I could not miss finding it; on the contrary it should be the most familiar to my understanding, since it is said to accompany all other ideas, and to be perceived by all the ways of sensation and reflexion. To say no more, it is an *abstract idea*.

14. I shall farther add, that after the same manner, as modern philosophers prove certain sensible qualities to have no existence in matter, or without the mind, the same thing may be likewise proved of all other sensible qualities whatsoever. Thus, for instance, it is said that heat and cold are affections only of the mind, and not at all patterns of real beings, existing in the corporeal substances which excite them, for that the same body which appears cold to one hand, seems warm to another. Now why may we not as well argue that figure and extension are not patterns or resemblances of qualities existing in matter, because to the same eye at different stations, or eyes of a different texture at the same station, they appear various, and cannot therefore be the images of any thing settled and determinate without the mind? Again, it is proved that sweetness is not really in the sapid thing, because the thing remaining unaltered the sweetness is changed into Bitter, as in case of a fever or otherwise vitiated palate. Is it not as reasonable to say, that motion is not without the mind, since if the succession of ideas in the mind become swifter, the motion, it is acknowledged, shall appear flower without any alteration in any external object.

15. In short, let any one consider those arguments, which are thought manifestly to prove that colours and tastes exist only in the mind, and he shall find they may with equal force, be brought to prove the same thing of extension, figure, and motion. Though it must be confessed this method of arguing doth not so much prove that there is no extension or colour in an outward object, as that we do not know by sense which is the true extension or colour of the object. But the arguments foregoing plainly shew it to be impossible that any colour or extension at all, or other sensible quality whatsoever should exist in an unthinking subject without the mind, or in truth, that there should be any such thing as an outward object.

16. But let us examine a little the received opinion. It is said extension is a mode or accident of matter, and that matter is the substratum that supports it. Now I desire that you would explain what is meant by matter's *supporting* extension: Say you, I have no idea of matter, and therefore cannot explain it. I answer, though you have no positive, yet if you have any meaning at all, you must at least have a relative idea of matter; though you know not what it is, yet you must be supposed to know what relation it bears to accidents, and what is meant by its supporting them. It is evident *support* cannot here be taken in its usual or literal sense, as when we say that pillars support a building: In what sense therefore must it be taken?

17. If we inquire into what the most accurate philosophers declare themselves to mean by *material substance*; we shall find them acknowledge, they have no other meaning annexed to those sounds, but the idea of being in general, together with the relative notion of its supporting accidents. The general idea of being appeareth to me the most abstract and incomprehensible of all other; and as for its supporting accidents, this, as we have just now observed, cannot be understood in the common sense of those words; it must therefore be taken in some other sense, but what that is they do not explain. So that when I consider the two parts or branches which make the signification of the words *material substance*, I am convinced there is no distinct meaning annexed to them. But why should we trouble ourselves any farther, in discussing this material *substratum* or support of figure and motion, and other sensible qualities? Does it not suppose they have an existence without the mind? And is not this a direct repugnancy, and altogether inconceivable?

18. But though it were possible that solid, figured, moveable substances may exist without the mind, corresponding to the ideas we have of bodies, yet how is it possible for us to know this? Either we must know it by sense, or by reason. As for our senses, by them we have the knowledge only of our sensations, ideas, or those things that are immediately perceived by sense, call them what you will: But they do not inform us that things exist without the mind, or unperceived, like to those which are perceived. This the materialists themselves acknowledge. It remains therefore that if we have any knowledge at all of external things, it must be by reason,

inferring their existence from what is immediately perceived by sense. But what reason can induce us to believe the existence of bodies without the mind, from what we perceive, since the very patrons of matter themselves do not pretend, there is any necessary connexion betwixt them and our ideas? I say it is granted on all hands (and what happens in dreams, phrensies, and the like, puts it beyond dispute) that it is possible we might be affected with all the ideas we have now, though no bodies existed without, resembling them. Hence it is evident the supposition of external bodies is not necessary for the producing our ideas: Since it is granted they are produced sometimes, and might possibly be produced always in the same order we see them in at present, without their concurrence.

19. But though we might possibly have all our sensations without them, yet perhaps it may be thought easier to conceive and explain the manner of their production, by supposing external bodies in their likeness rather than otherwise; and so it might be at least probable there are such things as Bodies that excite their ideas in our minds. But neither can this be said; for though we give the materialists their external bodies, they by their own consession are never the nearer knowing how our ideas are produced: Since they own themselves unable to comprehend in what manner body can act upon spirit, or how it is possible it should imprint any idea in the mind. Hence it is evident the production of ideas or sensations in our minds, can be no reason why we should suppose matter or corporeal substances, since that is acknowledged to remain equally inexplicable with, or without this supposition. If therefore it were possible for bodies to exist without the mind, yet to hold they do so, must needs be a very precarious opinion; since it is to suppose, without any reason at all, that God has created innumerable beings that are entirely useless, and serve to no manner of purpose.

20. In short, if there were external bodies, it is impossible we should ever come to know it; and if there were not, we might have the very same reasons to think there were that we have now. Suppose, what no one can deny possible, an intelligence, without the help of external bodies, to be affected with the same train of sensations or ideas that you are, imprinted in the same order and with like vividness in his mind. I ask whether that intelligence hath not all the reason to believe the existence of corporeal substances, represented by his Ideas, and exciting them in his mind, that you can possibly have for believing the same thing? Of this there can be no question; which one consideration is enough to make any reasonable person suspect the strength of whatever arguments he may think himself to have, for the existence of bodies without the mind.

22. I am afraid I have given cause to think me needlessly prolix in handling this subject. For to what purpose is it to dilate on that which may be demonstrated with the utmost evidence in a line or two, to any one that is capable of the least reflexion? It is but looking into your own thoughts, and so trying whether you can conceive it possible for a sound, or figure, or motion, or colour, to exist without the mind, or unperceived. This easy trial may make you see, that what you contend for, is a downright contradiction. Insomuch that I am content to put the whole upon this issue; if you can but conceive it possible for one extended moveable substance, or in general, for any one idea or any thing like an idea, to exist otherwise than in a mind perceiving it, I shall readily give up the cause: And as for all that *compages* of external bodies which you contend for, I shall grant you its existence, though you cannot either give me any reason why you believe it exists, or assign any use to it when it is supposed to exist. I say, the bare possibility of your opinion's being true, shall pass for an argument that it is so.

23. But say you, surely there is nothing easier than to imagine trees, for instance, in a park, or books existing in a closet, and no body by to perceive them, I answer, you may so, there is no difficulty in it: But what is all this, I beseech you, more than framing in your mind certain ideas which you call *Books* and *Trees*, and at the same time omitting to frame the idea of any one that may perceive them? But do not you your self perceive or think of them all the while? This therefore is nothing to the purpose: It only shows you have the power of imagining or forming ideas in your mind; but it doth not show that you can conceive it possible, the objects of your thought may exist without the mind: To make out this, it is necessary that you conceive them existing unconceived or unthought of, which is a manifest repugnancy. When we do our utmost to conceive the existence of external bodies, we are all the while only contemplating our own Ideas. But the mind taking no notice of itself, is deluded to think it can and

doth conceive bodies existing unthought of or without the mind; though at the same time they are apprehended by or exist in itself. A little attention will discover to any one the truth and evidence of what is here said, and make it unnecessary to insist on any other proofs against the existence of material substance.

24. It is very obvious, upon the least inquiry into our own thoughts, to know whether it be possible for us to understand what is meant, by the *absolute existence of sensible objects in themselves, or without the mind*. To me it is evident those words mark out either a direct contradiction, or else nothing at all. And to convince others of this, I know no readier or fairer way, than to entreat they would calmly attend to their own thoughts: And if by this attention, the emptiness or repugnancy of those expressions does appear, surely nothing more is requisite for their conviction. It is on this therefore that I insist, to wit, that the absolute existence of unthinking things are words without a meaning, or which include a contradiction. This is what I repeat and inculcate, and earnestly recommend to the attentive thoughts of the reader.

25. All our ideas, sensations, or the things which we perceive, by whatsoever names they may be distinguished, are visibly inactive, there is nothing of power or agency included in them. So that one idea or object of thought cannot produce, or make any Alteration in another. To be satisfied of the truth of this, there is nothing else requisite but a bare observation of our ideas. For since they and every part of them exist only in the mind, it follows that there is nothing in them but what is perceived. But whoever shall attend to his ideas, whether of sense or reflexion, will not perceive in them any power or activity; there is therefore no such thing contained in them. A little attention will discover to us that the very being of an idea implies passiveness and inertness in it insomuch that it is impossible for an idea to do any thing, or, strictly speaking, to be the cause of any thing; neither can it be the resemblance or pattern of any active being, as is evident from *sect.* 8. Whence it plainly follows that extension, figure and motion, cannot be the cause of our sensations. To say therefore, that these are the effects of powers resulting from the configuration, number, motion, and size of corpuscies, must certainly be false.

26. We perceive a continual succession of ideas, some are anew excited, others are changed or totally disappear. There is therefore some cause of these ideas whereon they depend, and which produces and changes them. That this cause cannot be any quality or idea or combination of ideas, is clear from the preceding section. It must therefore be a substance; but it has been shown that there is no corporeal or material substance: It remains therefore that the cause of ideas is an incorporeal active substance or spirit.

27. A spirit is one simple, undivided, active being: as it perceives ideas, it is called the *understanding*, and as it produces or otherwise operates about them, it is called the *will*. Hence there can be no idea formed of a soul or spirit: For all ideas whatever, being passive and inert, *vide sect.* 25, they cannot represent unto us, by way of image or likeness, that which acts. A little attention will make it plain to any one, that to have an idea which shall be like that active principle of motion and change of ideas, is absolutely impossible. Such is the nature of *spirit* or that which acts, that it cannot be of itself perceived, but only by the effects which it produceth. If any man shall doubt of the truth of what is here delivered, let him but reflect and try if he can frame the idea of any power or active being; and whether he hath ideas of two principal powers, marked by the names *will* and *understanding*, distinct from each other as well as from a third idea of substance or being in general, with a relative notion of its supporting or being the subject of the aforesaid powers, which is signified by the name *soul* or *spirit*. This is what some hold; but so far as I can see, the words *will, soul, spirit*, do not stand for different ideas, or in truth, for any idea at all, but for something which is very different from ideas, and which being an agent cannot be like unto, or represented by, any idea whatsoever. Though it must be owned at the same time, that we have some notion of soul, spirit, and the operations of the mind, such as willing, loving, hating, in as much as we know or understand the meaning of those words.

28. I find I can excite ideas in my mind at pleasure, and vary and shift the Scene as ost as I think sit. It is no more than willing, and straightway this or that idea arises in my fancy: And by the same power it is obliterated, and makes way for another. This making and unmaking of ideas doth very properly denominate the mind active. Thus much is certain, and grounded on experience: But when we talk of unthinking agents, or of exciting ideas exclusive of volition, we only amuse ourselves with words.

29. But whatever power I may have over my own thoughts, I find the ideas actually perceived by sense have not a like dependence on my will. When in broad day-light I open my eyes, it is not in my power to choose whether I shall see or no, or to determine what particular objects shall present themselves to my view; and so likewise as to the hearing and other senses, the ideas imprinted on them are not creatures of my will. There is therefore some other will or spirit that produces them.

30. The ideas of sense are more strong, lively, and distinct than those of the imagination; they have likewise a steddiness, order, and coherence, and are not excited at random, as those which are the effects of humane wills often are, but in a regular train or series, the admirable connexion whereof sufficiently testifies the wisdom and benevolence of its author. Now the set rules or established methods, wherein the mind we depend on excites in us the ideas of sense, are called the *laws of nature:* And these we learn by experience, which teaches us that such and such ideas are attended with such and such other ideas, in the ordinary course of things.

31. This gives us a sort of foresight, which enables us to regulate our actions for the benefit of life. And without this we should be eternally at a loss: We could not know how to act any thing that might procure us the least pleasure, or remove the least pain of sense. That food nourishes, sleep refreshes, and fire warms us; that to sow in the seed-time is the way to reap in the harvest, and, in general, that to obtain such or such ends, such or such means are conducive, all this we know, not by discovering any necessary connexion between our ideas, but only by the observation of the settled laws of nature, without which we should be all in uncertainty and confusion, and a grown man no more know how to manage himself in the affairs of life, than an infant just born.

32. And yet this consistent uniform working, which so evidently displays the goodness and wisdom of that governing spirit whose will constitutes the laws of nature, is so far from leading our thoughts to him, that it rather sends them a wandering after second causes. For when we perceive certain ideas of sense constantly followed by other ideas, and we know this is not of our own doing, we forthwith attribute power and agency to the ideas themselves, and make one the cause of another, than which nothing can be more absurd and unintelligible. Thus, for example, having observed that when we perceive by sight a certain round luminous figure, we at the same time perceive by touch the idea or sensation called *heat*, we do from thence conclude the sun to be the cause of heat. And in like manner perceiving the motion and collision of bodies to be attended with sound, we are inclined to think the latter an effect of the former.

33. The Ideas imprinted on the senses by the author of nature are called *real things:* And those excited in the imagination being less regular, vivid and constant, are more properly termed *ideas,* or *images of things,* which they copy and represent. But then our sensations, be they never so vivid and distinct, are nevertheless *ideas,* that is, they exist in the mind, or are perceived by it, as truly as the ideas of its own framing. The ideas of sense are allowed to have more reality in them, that is, to be more strong, orderly, and coherent than the creatures of the mind; but this is no argument that they exist without the mind. They are also less dependent on the spirit, or thinking substance which perceives them, in that they are excited by the will of another and more powerful spirit: yet still they are *ideas,* and certainly no *idea,* whether faint or strong, can exist otherwise than in a Mind perceiving it.

35. I do not argue against the existence of any one thing that we can apprehend, either by sense or reflexion. that the things I see with mine eyes and touch with my hands do exist, really exist, I make not the least question. The only thing whose existence we deny, is that which philosophers call matter or corporeal substance. And in doing of this, there is no damage done to the rest of mankind, who, I dare say, will never miss it. The atheist indeed will want the colour of an empty name to support his impiety; and the philosophers may possibly find, they have lost a great handle for trifling and disputation.

36. If any man thinks this detracts from the existence or reality of things, he is very far from understanding what hath been premised in the plainest terms I could think of. Take here an abstract of what has been said. There are spiritual substances, minds, or human souls, which will or excite Ideas in themselves at pleasure: but these are faint, weak, and unsteady in respect of others they perceive by sense, which being impressed upon them according to certain rules or laws

of nature, speak themselves the effects of a mind more powerful and wise than human spirits. These latter are said to have more *reality* in them than the former: by which is meant that they are more affecting, orderly, and distinct, and that they are not fictions of the mind perceiving them. And in this sense, the Sun that I see by day is the real sun, and that which I imagine by night is the idea of the former. In the sense here given of *reality*, it is evident that every vegetable, star, mineral, and in general each part of the mundane system, is as much a *real being* by our principles as by any other. Whether others mean any thing by the term *reality* different from what I do, I entreat them to look into their own thoughts and see.

✧ EMPIRICISM ✧

8. AN INQUIRY CONCERNING HUMAN UNDERSTANDING

David Hume

Section II: Of the Origin of Ideas

Everyone will readily allow that there is a considerable difference between the perceptions of the mind when a man feels the pain of excessive heat or the pleasure of moderate warmth, and when he afterwards recalls to his memory this sensation or anticipates it by his imagination. These faculties may mimic or copy the perceptions of the senses, but they never can entirely reach the force and vivacity of the original sentiment.

Here, therefore, we may divide all the perceptions of the mind into two classes or species, which are distinguished by their different degrees of force and vivacity. The less forcible and lively are commonly denominated "thoughts" or "ideas." The other species want a name in our language, and in most others; I suppose, because it was not requisite for any but philosophical purposes to rank them under a general term or appellation. Let us, therefore, use a little freedom and call them "impressions," employing that word in a sense somewhat different from the usual. By the term "impression," then, I mean all our more lively perceptions, when we hear, or see, or feel, or love, or hate, or desire, or will. And impressions are distinguished from ideas, which are the less lively perceptions of which we are conscious when we reflect on any of those sensations or movements above mentioned.

Nothing, at first view, may seem more unbounded than the thought of man, which not only escapes all human power and authority, but is not even restrained within the limits of nature and reality. To form monsters and join incongruous shapes and appearances costs the imagination no more trouble than to conceive the most natural and familiar objects.

But though our thought seems to possess this unbounded liberty, we shall find upon a nearer examination that it is really confined within very narrow limits, and that all this creative power of the mind amounts to no more than the faculty of compounding, transposing, augmenting, or diminishing the materials afforded us by the senses and experience. When we think of a golden mountain, we only join two consistent ideas, "gold" and "mountain," with which we were formerly acquainted. A virtuous horse we can conceive, because, from our own feeling, we can conceive virtue; and this we may unite to the figure and shape of a horse, which is an animal familiar to us. In short, all the materials of thinking are derived either from our outward or inward sentiment; the mixture and composition of these belongs alone to the mind and will, or, to express myself in philosophical language, all our ideas or more feeble perceptions are copies of our impressions or more lively ones.

To prove this, the two following arguments will, I hope, be sufficient. *First,* when we analyze our thoughts or ideas, however compounded or sublime, we always find that they resolve themselves into such simple ideas as were copied from a precedent feeling or sentiment. Even those ideas which at first view seem the most wide of this origin are found, upon a nearer scrutiny, to be derived from it. The idea of God, as meaning an infinitely intelligent, wise, and good Being, arises from reflecting on the operations of our own mind and augmenting, without limit, those qualities of goodness and wisdom.

Secondly, if it happen, from a defect of the organ, that a man is not susceptible of any species of sensation, we always find that he is as little susceptible of the correspondent idea. A blind man can form no notion of colors, a deaf man of sounds.

There is, however, one contradictory phenomenon which may prove that it is not absolutely impossible for ideas to arise independent of their correspondent impressions. Suppose a person to have enjoyed his sight for thirty years and to have become perfectly acquainted with colors of all kinds, except one particular shade of blue, for instance, which it never has been his fortune to meet with; let all the different shades of that color, except that single one, be placed before him, descending gradually from the deepest to the lightest, it is plain that he will perceive a blank where that shade is wanting, and will be sensible that there is a greater distance in that place between the contiguous colors than in any other. Now I ask whether it be possible for him, from his own imagination, to supply this deficiency and raise up to himself the idea of that particular shade, though it had never been conveyed to him by his senses? I believe there are few but will be of opinion that he can; and this may serve as a proof that the simple ideas are not always, in every instance, derived from the correspondent impressions.

Here, therefore, is a proposition which not only seems in itself simple and intelligible, but, if a proper use were made of it, might render every dispute equally intelligible, and banish all that jargon which has so long taken possession of metaphysical reasonings and drawn disgrace upon them. All ideas, especially abstract ones, are naturally faint and obscure. On the contrary, all impressions, that is, all sensations either outward or inward, are strong and vivid. The limits between them are more exactly determined, nor is it easy to fall into any error or mistake with regard to them. When we entertain, therefore, any suspicion that a philosophical term is employed without any meaning or idea (as is but too frequent), we need but inquire, *from what impression is that supposed idea derived?* And if it be impossible to assign any, this will serve to confirm our suspicion. By bringing ideas in so clear a light, we may reasonably hope to remove all dispute which may arise concerning their nature and reality.

Section III: Of the Association of Ideas

It is evident that there is a principle of connection between the different thoughts or ideas of the mind, and that, in their appearance to the memory or imagination, they introduce each other with a certain degree of method and regularity. In our more serious thinking or discourse this is so observable that any particular thought which breaks in upon the regular tract or chain of ideas is immediately remarked and rejected. And even in our wildest and most wandering reveries, nay, in our very dreams, we shall find, if we reflect, that the imagination ran not altogether at adventures, but that there was still a connection upheld among the different ideas which succeeded each other. Were the loosest and freest conversation to be transcribed, there would immediately be observed something which connected it in all its transitions. Or where this is wanting, the person who broke the thread of discourse might still inform you that there had secretly revolved in his mind a succession of thought which had gradually led him from the subject of conversation. Among different languages, even when we cannot suspect the least connection or communication, it is found that the words expressive of ideas the most compounded do yet nearly correspond to each other—a certain proof that the simple ideas comprehended in the compound ones were bound together by some universal principle which had an equal influence on all mankind.

Though it be too obvious to escape observation that different ideas are connected together, I do not find that any philosopher has attempted to enumerate or class all the principles of association—a subject, however, that seems worthy of curiosity. To me there appear to be only three principles of connection among ideas, namely, *Resemblance, Contiguity* in time or place, and *Cause or Effect.*

That these principles serve to connect ideas will not, I believe, be much doubted. A picture naturally leads our thoughts to the original. The mention of one apartment in a building naturally introduces an inquiry or discourse concerning the others; and if we think of a wound, we can scarcely forbear reflecting on the pain which follows it.

Section IV: Skeptical Doubts Concerning the Operations of the Understanding

Part I

All the objects of human reason or inquiry may naturally be divided into two kinds, to wit, "Relations of Ideas," and "Matters of Fact." Of the first kind are the sciences of Geometry, Algebra, and Arithmetic, and, in short, every affirmation which is either intuitively or demonstratively certain. *That the square of the hypotenuse is equal to the square of the two sides* is a proposition which expresses a relation between these figures. *That three times five is equal to the half of thirty* expresses a relation between these numbers. Propositions of this kind are discoverable by the mere operation of thought, without dependence on what is anywhere existent in the universe. Though there never were a circle or triangle in nature, the truths demonstrated by Euclid would forever retain their certainty and evidence.

Matters of fact, which are the second objects of human reason, are not ascertained in the same manner, nor is our evidence of their truth, however great, of a like nature with the foregoing. The contrary of every matter of fact is still possible, because it can never imply a contradiction and is conceived by the mind with the same facility and distinctness as if ever

so conformable to reality. *That the sun will not rise tomorrow* is no less intelligible a proposition and implies no more contradiction than the affirmation *that it will rise.* We should in vain, therefore, attempt to demonstrate its falsehood. Were it demonstratively false, it would imply a contradiction and could never be distinctly conceived by the mind.

It may, therefore, be a subject worthy of curiosity to inquire what is the nature of that evidence which assures us of any real existence and matter of fact beyond the present testimony of our senses or the records of our memory.

All reasonings concerning matter of fact seem to be founded on the relation of *cause* and *effect.* By means of that relation alone we can go beyond the evidence of our memory and senses. If you were to ask a man why he believes any matter of fact which is absent, for instance, that his friend is in the country or in France, he would give you a reason, and this reason would be some other fact: as a letter received from him or the knowledge of his former resolutions and promises. A man finding a watch or any other machine in a desert island would conclude that there had once been men in that island. All our reasonings concerning fact are of the same nature. And here it is constantly supposed that there is a connection between the present fact and that which is inferred from it. Were there nothing to bind them together, the inference would be entirely precarious. The hearing of an articulate voice and rational discourse in the dark assures us of the presence of some person. Why? Because these are the effects of the human make and fabric, and closely connected with it. If we anatomize all the other reasonings of this nature, we shall find that they are founded on the relation of cause and effect, and that this relation is either near or remote, direct or collateral. Heat and light are collateral effects of fire, and the one effect may justly be inferred from the other.

If we would satisfy ourselves, therefore, concerning the nature of that evidence which assures us of matters of fact, we must inquire how we arrive at the knowledge of cause and effect.

I shall venture to affirm, as a general proposition which admits of no exception, that the knowledge of this relation is not, in any instance, attained by reasonings a priori, but arises entirely from experience, when we find that any particular objects are constantly conjoined with each other. Let an object be presented to a man of ever so strong natural reason and abilities—if that object be entirely new to him, he will not be able, by the most accurate examination of its sensible qualities, to discover any of its causes or effects. Adam, though his rational faculties be supposed, at the very first, entirely perfect, could not have inferred from the fluidity and transparency of water that it would suffocate him, or from the light and warmth of fire that it would consume him. No object ever discovers, by the qualities which appear to the senses, either the causes which produced it or the effects which will arise from it; nor can our reason, unassisted by experience, ever draw any inference concerning real existence and matter of fact.

This proposition, *that causes and effects are discoverable, not by reason, but by experience,* will readily be admitted with regard to such objects as we remember to have once been altogether unknown to us, since we must be conscious of the utter inability which we then lay under of foretelling what would arise from them. Present two smooth pieces of marble to a man who has no tincture of natural philosophy; he will never discover that they will adhere together in such a manner as to require great force to separate them in a direct line, while they make so small a resistance to a lateral pressure. Such events as bear little analogy to the common course of nature are also readily confessed to be known only by experience, nor does any man imagine that the explosion of gunpowder or the attraction of a loadstone could ever be discovered by arguments a priori. In like manner, when an effect is supposed to depend upon an intricate machinery or secret structure of parts, we make no difficulty in attributing all our knowledge of it to experience. Who will assert that he can give the ultimate reason why milk or bread is proper nourishment for a man, not for a lion or tiger?

But the same truth may not appear at first sight to have the same evidence with regard to events which have become familiar to us from our first appearance in the world, which bear a close analogy to the whole course of nature, and which are supposed to depend on the simple qualities of objects without any secret structure of parts. We are apt to imagine that we could discover these effects by the mere operation of our reason without experience. We fancy that, were we brought on a sudden into this world, we could at first have inferred that one billiard ball would communicate motion to another upon impulse, and that we needed not to have waited for the event in order to pronounce with certainty concerning it. Such is the influence of custom that where it is strongest it not only covers our natural ignorance but even conceals itself, and seems not to take place, merely because it is found in the highest degree.

But to convince us that all the laws of nature and all the operations of bodies without exception are known only by experience, the following reflections may perhaps suffice. Were any object presented to us, and were we required to pronounce concerning the effect which will result from it without consulting past observation, after what manner, I beseech you, must the mind proceed in this operation? It must invent or imagine some event which it ascribes to the object as its effect; and it is plain that this invention must be entirely arbitrary. The mind can never possibly find the effect in the supposed cause by the most accurate scrutiny and examination. For the effect is totally different from the cause, and consequently can never be discovered in it. Motion in the second billiard ball is a quite distinct event from motion in the first, nor is there anything in the one to suggest the smallest hint of the other. A stone or piece of metal raised into the air and left without any support immediately falls. But to consider the matter a priori, is there anything we discover in this situation which can beget the idea of a downward rather than an upward or any other motion in the stone or metal?

And as the first imagination or invention of a particular effect in all natural operations is arbitrary where we consult not experience, so must we also esteem the supposed tie or connection between the cause and effect which binds them together and renders it impossible that any other effect could result from the operation of that cause. When I see, for instance, a billiard ball moving in a straight line toward another, even suppose motion in the second ball should by accident be suggested to me as the result of their contact or impulse, may I not conceive that a hundred different events might as well follow from that cause? May not both these balls remain at absolute rest? May not the first ball return in a straight line or leap off from the second in any line or direction? All these suppositions are consistent and conceivable. Why, then, should we give the preference to one which is no more consistent or conceivable than the rest? All our reasonings a priori will never be able to show us any foundation for this preference.

In a word, then, every effect is a distinct event from its cause. It could not, therefore be discovered in the cause, and the first invention or conception of it, a priori must be entirely arbitrary. And even after it is suggested, the conjunction of it with the cause must appear equally arbitrary, since there are always many other effects which, to reason, must seem fully as consistent and natural. In vain, therefore, should we pretend to determine any single event or infer any cause or effect without the assistance of observation and experience.

Hence we may discover the reason why no philosopher who is rational and modest has ever pretended to assign the ultimate cause of any natural operation, or to show distinctly the action of that power which produces any single effect in the universe. It is confessed that the utmost effort of human reason is to reduce the principles productive of natural phenomena to a greater simplicity, and to resolve the many particular effects into a few general causes, by means of reasonings from analogy, experience, and observation. But as to the causes of these general causes, we should in vain attempt their discovery, nor shall we ever be able to satisfy ourselves by any particular explication of them. These ultimate springs and principles are totally shut up from human curiosity and inquiry.

Part II

But we have not yet attained any tolerable satisfaction with regard to the question first proposed. Each solution still gives rise to a new question as difficult as the foregoing and leads us on to further inquiries. When it is asked, *What is the nature of all our reasonings concerning matter of fact?* the proper answer seems to be, That they are founded on the relation of cause and effect. When again it is asked, *What is the foundation of all our reasonings and conclusions concerning that relation?* it may be replied in one word, *experience*. But if we still carry on our sifting humor and ask, *What is the foundation of all conclusions from experience?* this implies a new question which may be of more difficult solution and explication.

I shall content myself in this section with an easy task and shall pretend only to give a negative answer to the question here proposed. I say, then, that even

after we have experience of the operations of cause and effect, our conclusions from that experience are *not* founded on reasoning or any process of the understanding. This answer we must endeavor both to explain and to defend.

All reasonings may be divided into two kinds, namely, demonstrative reasoning, or that concerning relations of ideas, and moral reasoning, or that concerning matter of fact and existence. That there are no demonstrative arguments in the case seems evident, since it implies no contradiction that the course of nature may change and that an object, seemingly like those which we have experienced, may be attended with different or contrary effects. May I not clearly and distinctly conceive that a body, falling from the clouds and which in all other respects resembles snow, has yet the taste of salt or feeling of fire? Is there any more intelligible proposition than to affirm that all the trees will flourish in December and January, and will decay in May and June? Now, whatever is intelligible and can be distinctly conceived implies no contradiction and can never be proved false by any demonstrative argument or abstract reasoning a priori.

If we be, therefore, engaged by arguments to put trust in past experience and make it the standard of our future judgment, these arguments must be probable only, or such as regard matter of fact and real existence, according to the division above mentioned. But that there is no argument of this kind must appear if our explication of that species of reasoning be admitted as solid and satisfactory. We have said that all arguments concerning existence are founded on the relation of cause and effect, that our knowledge of that relation is derived entirely from experience, and that all our experimental conclusions proceed upon the supposition that the future will be conformable to the past. To endeavor, therefore, the proof of this last supposition by probable arguments, or arguments regarding existence, must be evidently going in a circle and taking that for granted which is the very point in question.

In reality, all arguments from experience are founded on the similarity which we discover among natural objects, and by which we are induced to expect effects similar to those which we have found to follow from such objects. And though none but a fool or madman will ever pretend to dispute the authority of experience or to reject that great guide of human life, it may surely be allowed a philosopher to have so much curiosity at least as to examine the principle of human nature which gives this mighty authority to experience and makes us draw advantage from that similarity which nature has placed among different objects. From causes which appear similar, we expect similar effects. This is the sum of all our experimental conclusions. Now it seems evident that, if this conclusion were formed by reason, it would be as perfect at first, and upon one instance, as after ever so long a course of experience; but the case is far otherwise. Nothing so like as eggs, yet no one, on account of this appearing similarity, expects the same taste and relish in all of them. It is only after a long course of uniform experiments in any kind that we attain a firm reliance and security with regard to a particular event. Now, where is that process of reasoning which, from one instance, draws a conclusion so different from that which it infers from a hundred instances that are nowise different from that single one? This question I propose as much for the sake of information as with an intention of raising difficulties. I cannot find, I cannot imagine any such reasoning. But I keep my mind still open to instruction if anyone will vouchsafe to bestow it on me.

Should it be said that, from a number of uniform experiments, we *infer* a connection between the sensible qualities and the secret powers, this, I must confess, seems the same difficulty, couched in different terms. The question still occurs, On what process of argument is this *inference* founded? Where is the medium, the interposing ideas which join propositions so very wide of each other? It is confessed that the color, consistency, and other sensible qualities of bread appear not of themselves to have any connection with the secret powers of nourishment and support; for otherwise we could infer these secret powers from the first appearance of these sensible qualities without the aid of experience, contrary to the sentiment of all philosophers, and contrary to plain matter of fact. Here, then, is our natural state of ignorance with regard to the powers and influence of all objects. How is this remedied by experience? It only shows us a number of uniform effects resulting from certain objects, and teaches us that those particular objects, at that particular time, were endowed with such powers and forces. When a new object endowed with similar sensible qualities is produced, we expect similar powers and forces, and look for a like effect. From a body of like color and consistency with bread, we expect like nourishment

and support. But this surely is a step or progress of the mind which wants to be explained. When a man says, *I have found, in all past instances, such sensible qualities, conjoined with such secret powers,* and when he says, *similar sensible qualities will always be conjoined with similar secret powers,* he is not guilty of a tautology, nor are these propositions in any respect the same. You say that the one proposition is an inference from the other; but you must confess that the inference is not intuitive, neither is it demonstrative. Of what nature is it then? To say it is experimental is begging the question. For all inferences from experience suppose, as their foundation, that the future will resemble the past and that similar powers will be conjoined with similar sensible qualities. If there be any suspicion that the course of nature may change, and that the past may be no rule for the future, all experience becomes useless and can give rise to no inference or conclusion. It is impossible, therefore, that any arguments from experience can prove this resemblance of the past to the future, since all these arguments are founded on the supposition of that resemblance. Let the course of things be allowed hitherto ever so regular, that alone, without some new argument or inference, proves not that for the future it will continue so. In vain do you pretend to have learned the nature of bodies from your past experience. Their secret nature, and consequently all their effects and influence, may change without any change in their sensible qualities. This happens sometimes, and with regard to some objects. Why may it not happen always, and with regard to all objects? What logic, what process of argument secures you against this supposition? My practice, you say, refutes my doubts. But you mistake the purport of my question. As an agent, I am quite satisfied in the point; but as a philosopher who has some share of curiosity, I will not say skepticism, I want to learn the foundation of this inference. No reading, no inquiry has yet been able to remove my difficulty or give me satisfaction in a matter of such importance. Can I do better than propose the difficulty to the public, even though, perhaps, I have small hopes of obtaining a solution? We shall at least, by this means, be sensible of our ignorance, if we do not augment our knowledge.

I must confess that a man is guilty of unpardonable arrogance who concludes, because an argument has escaped his own investigation, that therefore it does not really exist. I must also confess that, though all the learned, for several ages, should have employed themselves in fruitless search upon any subject, it may still, perhaps, be rash to conclude positively that the subject must therefore pass all human comprehension. Even though we examine all the sources of our knowledge and conclude them unfit for such a subject, there may still remain a suspicion that the enumeration is not complete or the examination not accurate. But with regard to the present subject, there are some considerations which seem to remove all this accusation of arrogance or suspicion of mistake.

It is certain that the most ignorant and stupid peasants, nay infants, nay even brute beasts, improve by experience and learn the qualities of natural objects by observing the effects which result from them. When a child has felt the sensation of pain from touching the flame of a candle, he will be careful not to put his hand near any candle, but will expect a similar effect from a cause which is similar in its sensible qualities and appearance. If you assert, therefore, that the understanding of the child is led into this conclusion by any process of argument or ratiocination, I may justly require you to produce that argument, nor have you any pretense to refuse so equitable a demand. You cannot say that the argument is abstruse and may possible escape your inquiry, since you confess that it is obvious to the capacity of a mere infant. If you hesitate, therefore, a moment or if, after reflection, you produce an intricate or profound argument, you, in a manner, give up the question and confess that it is not reasoning which engages us to suppose the past resembling the future, and to expect similar effects from causes which are to appearance similar. This is the proposition which I intended to enforce in the present section. If I be right, I pretend not to have made any mighty discovery. And if I be wrong, I must acknowledge myself to be indeed a very backward scholar, since I cannot now discover an argument which, it seems, was perfectly familiar to me long before I was out of my cradle.

Section V: Skeptical Solution of These Doubts

Though we should conclude, for instance, as in the foregoing section, that in all reasonings from experience there is a step taken by the mind which is not supported by any argument or process of the understanding, there is no danger that these reasonings, on which almost all knowledge depends, will ever be affected by such a discovery. If the mind be not engaged by argument to make this step, it must be induced by some other principle of equal weight and authority; and that principle will preserve its influence as long as human nature remains the same. What that principle is may well be worth the pains of inquiry.

Suppose a person, though endowed with the strongest faculties of reason and reflection, to be brought on a sudden into this world; he would, indeed, immediately observe a continual succession of objects and one event following another, but he would not be able to discover anything further. He would not at first, by any reasoning, be able to reach the idea of cause and effect, since the particular powers by which all natural operations are performed never appear to the senses; nor is it reasonable to conclude, merely because one event in one instance precedes another, that therefore the one is the cause, the other the effect. The conjunction may be arbitrary and casual. There may be no reason to infer the existence of one from the appearance of the other: and, in a word, such a person without more experience could never employ his conjecture or reasoning concerning any matter of fact or be assured of anything beyond what was immediately present to his memory or senses.

Suppose again that he has acquired more experience and has lived so long in the world as to have observed similar objects or events to be constantly conjoined together—what is the consequence of this experience? He immediately infers the existence of one object from the appearance of the other, yet he has not, by all his experience, acquired any idea or knowledge of the secret power by which the one object produces the other, nor is it by any process of reasoning he is engaged to draw this inference; but still he finds himself determined to draw it, and though he should be convinced that his understanding has no part in the operation, he would nevertheless continue in the same course of thinking. There is some other principle which determines him to form such a conclusion.

This principle is *custom* or *habit*. For wherever the repetition of any particular act or operation produces a propensity to renew the same act or operation without being impelled by any reasoning or process of the understanding, we always say that this propensity is the effect of *custom*. By employing that word we pretend not to have given the ultimate reason of such a propensity. We only point out a principle of human nature which is universally acknowledged, and which is well known by its effects. Perhaps we can push our inquiries no further or pretend to give the cause of this cause, but must rest contented with it as the ultimate principle which we can assign of all our conclusions from experience. It is sufficient satisfaction that we can go so far without repining at the narrowness of our faculties, because they will carry us no further. And it is certain we here advance a very intelligible proposition at least, if not a true one, when we assert that after the constant conjunction of two objects, heat and flame, for instance, weight and solidity, we are determined by custom alone to expect the one from the appearance of the other. This hypothesis seems even the only one which explains the difficulty why we draw from a thousand instances an inference which we are not able to draw from one instances that is in no respect different from them. Reason is incapable of any such variation. The conclusions which it draws from considering one circle are the same which it would form upon surveying all the circles in the universe. But no man, having seen only one body move after being impelled by another, could infer that every other body will move after a like impulse. All inferences from experience, therefore, are effects of custom, not of reasoning.

Custom, then, is the great guide of human life. It is that principle alone which renders our experience useful to us and makes us expect, for the future, a similar train of events with those which have appeared in the past. Without the influence of custom we should be entirely ignorant of every matter of fact beyond what is immediately present to the memory and senses. We should never know how to adjust means to ends or to employ our natural powers in the production of any effect. There would be an end at once of all action as well as of the chief part of speculation.

But here it may be proper to remark that though our conclusions from experience carry us beyond our memory and senses and assure us of matters of fact which happened in the most distant places and most remote ages, yet some fact must always be present to the senses or memory from which

we may first proceed in drawing these conclusions. A man who should find in a desert country the remains of pompous buildings would conclude that the country had, in ancient times, been cultivated by civilized inhabitants; but did nothing of this nature occur to him, he could never form such an inference. We learn the events of former ages from history, but then we must peruse the volume in which this instruction is contained, and thence carry up our inferences from one testimony to another, till we arrive at the eyewitnesses and spectators of these distant events. In a word, if we proceed not upon some fact present to the memory or senses, our reasonings would be merely hypothetical; and however the particular links might be connected with each other, the whole chain of inferences would have nothing to support it, nor could we ever, by its means, arrive at the knowledge of any real existence. If I ask why you believe any particular matter of fact which you relate, you must tell me some reason; and this reason will be some other fact connected with it. But as you cannot proceed after this manner *in infinitum*, you must at last terminate in some fact which is present to your memory or senses or must allow that your belief is entirely without foundation.

What, then, is the conclusion of the whole matter? A simple one, though, it must be confessed, pretty remote from the common theories of philosophy. All belief of matter of fact or real existence is derived merely from some object present to the memory or senses and a customary conjunction between that and some other object; or, in other words, having found, in many instances, that any two kinds of objects, flame and heat, snow and cold, have always been conjoined together: if flame or snow be presented anew to the senses, the mind is carried by custom to expect heat or cold, and to *believe that such a quality does exist* and will discover itself upon a nearer approach. This belief is the necessary result of placing the mind in such circumstances. It is an operation of the soul, when we are so situated, as unavoidable as to feel the passion of love, when we receive benefits; or hatred, when we meet with injuries. All these operations are a species of natural instincts, which no reasoning or process of the thought and understanding is able either to produce or to prevent.

Section VII: Of the Idea of Necessary Connection

To be fully acquainted with the idea of power or necessary connexion, let us examine its impression; and in order to find the impression with greater certainty, let us search for it in all the sources, from which it may possibly be derived.

When we look about us towards external objects, and consider the operation of causes, we are never able, in a single instance, to discover any power or necessary connexion; any quality, which binds the effect to the cause, and renders the one an infallible consequence of the other. We only find, that the one does actually, in fact, follow the other. The impulse of one billiard-ball is attended with motion in the second. This is the whole that appears to the *outward* senses. The mind feels no sentiment or *inward* impression from this succession of objects: Consequently, there is not, in any single, particular instance of cause and effect, any thing which can suggest the idea of power or necessary connexion.

From the first appearance of an object, we never can conjecture what effect will result from it. But were the power or energy of any cause discoverable by the mind, we could foresee the effect, even without experience; and might, at first, pronounce with certainty concerning it, by the mere dint of thought and reasoning.

In reality, there is no part of matter, that does ever, by its sensible qualities, discover any power or energy, or give us ground to imagine, that it could produce any thing, or be followed by any other object, which we could denominate its effect.

Since, therefore, external objects as they appear to the senses, give us no idea of power or necessary connexion, by their operation in particular instances, let us see, whether this idea be derived from reflection on the operations of our own minds, and be copied from any internal impression. It may be said, that we are every moment conscious of internal power; while we feel, that, by the simple command of our will, we can move the organs of our body, or direct the faculties of our mind. An act of volition produces motion in our limbs, or raises a new idea in our imagination. This influence of the will we know by consciousness. Hence we acquire the idea of power or energy; and are certain, that we ourselves and all other intelligent beings are possessed of power. This idea, then, is an idea of reflection, since it arises from reflecting on the operations of our own mind, and on the command which is exercised by will, both over the organs of the body and faculties of the soul.

Part II

We have sought in vain for an idea of power or necessary connexion in all the sources from which we could suppose it to be derived. It appears that, in single instances of the operation of bodies, we never can, by our utmost scrutiny, discover any thing but one event following another; without being able to comprehend any force or power by which the cause operates, or any connexion between it and its supposed effect. One event follows another; but we never can observe any tie between them. They seem *conjoined*, but never *connected*. And as we can have no idea of any thing which never appeared to our outward sense or inward sentiment, the necessary conclusion *seems* to be that we have no idea of connexion or power at all, and that these words are absolutely without any meaning, when employed either in philosophical reasonings or common life.

But there still remains one method of avoiding this conclusion, and one source which we have not yet examined. When one particular species of event has always, in all instances, been conjoined with another, we make no longer any scruple of foretelling one upon the appearance of the other, and of employing that reasoning, which can alone assure us of any matter of fact or existence. We then call the one object, *Cause*; the other, *Effect*. We suppose that there is some connexion between them; some power in the one, by which it infallibly produces the other, and operates with the greatest certainty and strongest necessity.

It appears, then, that this idea of a necessary connexion among events arises from a number of similar instances which occur of the constant conjunction of these events; nor can that idea ever be suggested by any one of these instances, surveyed in all possible lights and positions. But there is nothing in a number of instances, different from every single instance, which is supposed to be exactly similar; except only, that after a repetition of similar instances, the mind is carried by habit, upon the appearance of one event, to expect its usual attendant, and to believe that it will exist. This connexion, therefore, which we *feel* in the mind, this customary transition of the imagination from one object to its usual attendant, is the sentiment or impression from which we form the idea of power or necessary connexion. Nothing farther is in the case.

Similar objects are always conjoined with similar. Of this we have experience. Suitably to this experience, therefore, we may define a cause to be *an object followed by another, and where all the objects similar to the first are followed by objects similar to the second.* Or in other words *where, if the first object had not been, the* second *never had existed.* The appearance of a cause always conveys the mind, by a customary transition, to the idea of the effect. Of this also we have experience. We may, therefore, suitably to this experience, form another definition of cause, and call it, *an object followed by another, and whose appearance always conveys the thought to that other.* But though both these definitions be drawn from circumstances foreign to the cause, we cannot remedy this inconvenience, or attain any more perfect definition, which may point out that circumstance in the cause, which gives it a connexion with its effect.

◈ TRANSCENDENTAL IDEALISM ◈

9. PROLEGOMENA TO ANY FUTURE METAPHYSICS

Immanuel Kant

Introduction

My purpose is to propose the question "Whether such a thing as metaphysics be even possible at all?"

Since the first rise of metaphysics as far as its history will reach, no event has occurred that in view of the fortunes of the science could be more decisive than the attack made upon it by David Hume.

Hume took for his starting-point, mainly, a single but important conception of metaphysics, namely, that of the *connection of Cause and Effect* (together with the derivative conceptions of Force and Action, etc., and required of Reason which professes to have given it birth a rigid justification of its right to think that something is so constructed that on its being posited something else is therewith necessarily also posited; for so much is contained in the conception of Cause. He proved irrefutably that it is quite impossible for Reason *à priori*, using mere concept, to grasp this connection, since it involves necessity; but the problem nevertheless was not to be overlooked, how that, because something exists, something else must necessarily also exist, and thus how the concept of such a connection can be

regarded as à priori, Hence he concluded that Reason completely deceived itself with this concept, that it falsely claimed it as its own child, while it was nothing more than a bastard of the imagination, which, impregnated by experience, had brought certain presentations under the law of association, and had substituted a subjective necessity arising thence, i.e., from habit, for an objective one founded on insight. From this he concluded that Reason possessed no power to think such connections even in general, because its concepts would then be mere inventions, and all its pretended à priori cognitions nothing but common experiences mislabelled; which is as much as to say, no such thing as metaphysics exists at all, and there is no possibility of its ever existing.

I readily confess, the reminder of David Hume was what many years ago first broke my dogmatic slumber, and gave my researches in the field of speculative philosophy quite a different direction.

First of all, I tried whether Hume's observation could not be made general, and soon found that the concept of the connection of cause and effect was not the only one by which the understanding thinks à priori the connections of things, but that metaphysics consists entirely of such. I endeavoured to ascertain their number, and as I succeeded in doing this to my satisfaction, starting from a single principle, I proceeded to the deduction of these concepts, which I was now assured could not, as Hume had pretended, be derived from experience but must have originated in pure understanding. This deduction, that seemed impossible to my acute predecessor, that had not even occurred to any one except him, although every one unconcernedly used the concept (without asking on what its objective validity rested); this, I say, was the most difficult problem that could ever be undertaken in the interests of metaphysics, and the worst of it was, that metaphysics, so far as it anywhere exists at present, could not afford me the least help, because the above deduction had in the first place to make metaphysics possible. Having now succeeded in the solution of Hume's problem, not in one particular case only, but in respect of the whole capacity of pure Reason, I could at least more surely, though still only by slow steps, determine the whole range of pure Reason, in its limits as well as in its content, completely and from universal principles, which was what metaphysics required, in order to construct its system on an assured plan.

The above work, which presents the capacity of pure Reason in its whole range and boundaries, always remains the foundation to which the Prolegomena are only preparatory; for the Critique must, as science, stand complete and systematic even down to the smallest detail, before we can so much as think of the rise of metaphysics, or even allow ourselves the most distant hope in this direction.

Introductory Remarks on the Speciality of All Metaphysical Knowledge

Of the Source of Metaphysics

IN presenting a branch of knowledge as *science*, it is necessary to be able to define with precision its distinguishing characteristic, that which it possesses in common with no other branch, and which is therefore *special* to itself: when this is not the case the boundaries of all sciences run into one another, and no one of them can be thoroughly treated of, according to its own nature.

Now this speciality may consist in the distinction of its *object*, of its *sources of cognition*, of its *mode of cognition*, or lastly, of several if not all these points taken together, on which the idea of a possible science and of its territory primarily rests.

Firstly, as regards the *sources* of metaphysical knowledge, the very concept of the latter shows that these cannot be empirical. Its principles (under which not merely its axioms, but also its fundamental concept are included) must consequently never be derived from experience; since it is not *physical* but *metaphysical* knowledge, i.e., knowledge beyond experience, that is wanted. Thus neither external experience, the source of physical science proper, nor internal experience, the groundwork of empirical psychology, will suffice for its foundation. It consists, then, in knowledge à priori, that is, knowledge derived from pure understanding and pure reason.

Of the Mode of Cognition That Can Alone Be Termed Metaphysical

a. Of the distinction between synthetic and analytic judgments generally. Metaphysical knowledge must contain simply judgments à priori, so much is demanded by the peculiarity of its sources. But judgments, let them have what origin they may, or let them even as regards logical form be constituted as they may, possess a distinction according to their content, by virtue of which they are either simply *explanatory* and contribute nothing to the content of a cognition, or they are ampliative, and enlarge the given cognition; the first may be termed *analytic*, and the second *synthetic* judgments.

Analytic judgments say nothing in the predicate, but what was already thought in the concept of the subject, though perhaps not so clearly, or with the same degree of consciousness. When I say, all bodies are extended, I do not thereby enlarge my concept of a body in the least, but simply analyse it, inasmuch as extension, although not expressly stated, was already thought in that concept; the judgment is, in other words, analytic. On the other hand, the proposition, some bodies are heavy, contains something in the predicate which was not already thought in the general concept of a body; it enlarges, that is to say, my knowledge, in so far as it adds something to my concept; and must therefore be termed a synthetic judgment.

b. The common principle of all analytic judgments is the principle of contradiction. All analytic judgments are based entirely on the principle of contradiction, and are by their nature cognitions à priori, whether the concept serving as their matter be empirical or not. For inasmuch as the predicate of an affirmative analytic judgment is already thought in the concept of the subject, it cannot without contradiction be denied of it; in the same way, its contrary, in a negative analytic judgment, must necessarily be denied of the subject, likewise in accordance with the principle of contradiction. It is thus with the propositions—every body is extended; no body is unextended (simple). For this reason all analytic propositions are judgments à priori, although their concepts may be empirical. Let us take as an instance the proposition, gold is a yellow metal. Now, to know this, I require no further experience beyond my concept of gold, which contains the propositions that this body is yellow and a metal; for this constitutes precisely my concept, and therefore I have only to dissect it, without needing to look around for anything elsewhere.

c. Synthetic judgments demand a principle other than that of contradiction. There are synthetic judgments à *posteriori* whose origin is empirical; but there are also others of an à priori certainty, that spring from the Understanding and Reason. But both are alike in this, that they can never have their source solely in the principle of analysis, viz., the principle of contradiction; they require an altogether different principle, notwithstanding that whatever principle they may be deduced from, they must always *conform to the principle of contradiction*, for nothing can be opposed to this principle, although not everything can be deduced from it. I will first of all classify synthetic judgments.

1. *Judgments of experience* are always synthetic. It would be absurd to found an analytic judgment on experience, as it is unnecessary to go beyond my own concept in order to construct the judgment, and therefore the confirmation of experience is unnecessary to it. That a body is extended is a proposition possessing à priori certainty, and is not a judgment of experience. For before I go to experience I have all the conditions of my judgment already present in the concept, out of which I simply draw the predicate in accordance with the principle of contradiction, and thereby at the same time the *necessity* of the judgment may be known, a point which experience could never teach me.

2. *Mathematical judgments* are in their entirety synthetic. This truth seems hitherto to have altogether escaped the analysts of human Reason; indeed, to be directly opposed to all their suppositions, although it is indisputably certain and very important in its consequences. For, because it was found that the conclusions of mathematicians all proceed according to the principle of contradiction (which the nature of every apodeictic certainty demands), it was concluded that the axioms were also known through the principle of contradiction, which was a great error; for though a synthetic proposition can be viewed in the light of the above principle, it can only be so by presupposing another synthetic proposition from which it is derived, but never by itself.

It must be first of all remarked that genuinely mathematical propositions are always à priori, and never empirical, because they involve necessity, which cannot be inferred from experience. Should any one be unwilling to admit this, I will limit my assertion to *pure mathematics*, the very concept of which itself brings with it the fact that it contains nothing empirical, but simply pure knowledge à priori.

At first sight, one might be disposed to think the proposition $7 + 5 = 12$ merely analytic, resulting from the concept of a sum of seven and five, according to the principle of contradiction. But more closely considered it will be found that the concept of the sum of 7 and 5 comprises nothing beyond their union in a single number, and that therein nothing whatever is thought as to what this single number is, that comprehends both the others. The concept of twelve is by no means already thought, when I think merely of the union of seven and five, and I may dissect my concept of such a possible sum as long as I please, without discovering therein the number twelve. One must leave these concepts, and call to one's aid an intuition corresponding to one or other of them, as for instance one's five fingers (or, like Segner in his Arithmetic, five points), and so gradually add the units of the five given in intuition to the concept of the seven. One's concept is therefore really enlarged by the proposition $7 + 5 = 12$; to the first a new one being added, that was in nowise thought in the former; in other words, arithmetical propositions are always synthetic, a truth which is more apparent when we take rather larger numbers, for we must then be clearly convinced, that turn and twist our concepts as we may, without calling intuition to our aid, we shall never find the sum required, by the mere dissection of them.

Just as little is any principle of pure geometry analytic. That a *straight* line is the shortest between two points, is a synthetic proposition. For my concept of *straight*, has no reference to size, but only to quality. The concept of the "shortest" therefore is quite additional, and cannot be drawn from any analysis of the concept of a straight line. Intuition must therefore again be taken to our aid, by means of which alone the synthesis is possible.

Certain other principles postulated by geometricians, are indeed really analytic and rest on the principle of contradiction, but they only serve, like identical propositions, as links in the chain of method, and not themselves as principles; as for instance $a = a$, the whole is equal to itself, or $(a + b) > a$, i.e., the whole is greater than its part. But even these, although their validity is recognized from mere concepts, are only admitted in mathematics because they can be presented in intuition. What produces the common belief that the predicate of such apodeictic judgments lies already in our concept, and that the judgment is therefore analytic, is merely the ambiguity of expression. We must think of a certain predicate, as contained in a given concept, and this necessity inheres in the concepts themselves. But the question is not what we must but what we actually *do*, although obscurely, join in thought to a concept; this shows us that the predicate belongs to those concepts necessarily, but indirectly, by means of an added intuition.

The General Question of the Prolegomena

Is Metaphysics Possible at All?

The essential feature distinguishing pure mathematical knowledge from all other knowledge à priori, is that it does not proceed from concepts themselves, but always through the construction of concepts. (Critique, p.

435) Since, therefore, in its propositions it must pass out of the conception to that containing the corresponding intuition, these can and ought never to arise from the dissection of concepts, that is, analytically; in other words, they are, in their entirety, synthetic.

I cannot refrain from remarking on the disadvantage resulting to philosophy from a neglect of this simple and apparently insignificant observation. Hume, indeed, feeling it a task worthy of a philosopher, cast his eye over the whole field of pure knowledge à priori in which the human understanding claims such extensive possession. He, however, inconsiderately severed from it an entire, and indeed the most important, province, namely, that of pure mathematics, under the impression that its nature, and, so to speak, its constitution, rested on totally different principles, that is, solely on the principle of contradiction; and although he did not make such a formal and universal division of propositions as is here done by me, or under the same name, yet it was as good as saying, pure mathematics contains simply analytic judgments, but metaphysics, synthetic judgments à priori. Now in this he made a great mistake, and this mistake had decidedly injurious consequences on his whole conception. For if he had not made it, he would have extended his question respecting the origin of our synthetic judgments far beyond his metaphysical conception of causality, and comprehended therein the possibility of mathematics à priori; for he must have regarded this as equally synthetic. But in the latter case he could, under no circumstances, have based his metaphysical propositions on mere experience, as he would then have been obliged to have subordinated the axioms of pure mathematics themselves to experience, a proceeding for which he was much too penetrating.

The good company into which metaphysics would then have been brought must have ensured it against contemptuous treatment; for the strokes aimed at the latter must have also hit the former, and this neither was nor could have been his intention. The result must have been to lead the acute man to considerations similar to those with which we are now occupied, but which must have gained infinitely by his inimitable style.

Essentially metaphysical judgments are, in their entirety, synthetic. We must distinguish between judgments belonging to metaphysics from metaphysical judgments proper. Among the former are comprised many that are analytic, but they only furnish the means for metaphysical judgments, these forming the entire purpose of the science, and being all synthetic. For when concepts belong to metaphysics, as, for instance, that of substance, the judgments arising from their dissection belong also to metaphysics; e.g., substance is that which only exists as subject etc., and many more similar analytic judgments, by means of which an endeavour is made to approach the definition of the concept. Since, however, the analysis of a pure concept of the understanding (such as those metaphysics contains) cannot proceed differently from the analysis of any other concept (even an empirical one) not belonging to metaphysics (e.g., air is an elastic fluid, the elasticity of which is not destroyed by any known degree of cold), it follows that the concept but not the analytic judgment, is properly metaphysical. The science in question has something special and peculiar in the production of its cognitions à priori, which must be distinguished from what it has in common with all other cognitions of the understanding; so, for instance, the proposition, "all that is substance in things is permanent," is a synthetic and properly metaphysical judgment.

The conclusion drawn in this section is then, that metaphysics is properly concerned with synthetic propositions à priori, and that these alone constitute its purpose, but that, in addition to this, it requires frequent dissections of its conceptions, or analytic judgments, the procedure in this respect being only the same as in other departments of knowledge, where conceptions are sought to be made plain by analysis. But the *generation* of knowledge à priori, as much in intuition as in concepts, in fine, synthetic propositions à priori in philosophical cognitions, make up the essential content of metaphysics.

Wearied, then, of the dogmatism that teaches us nothing, as well as of the scepticism that promises us nothing, not even the rest of a permissible ignorance, led on by the importance of the knowledge we need, rendered mistrustful by a long experience, of all we believe ourselves to possess, or that offers itself in the name of pure Reason, there only remains one critical question, the answer to which must regulate our future procedure—*Is metaphysics possible at all?* But this question must not be answered by sceptical objections to particular assertions of any actual system of metaphysics (for we do not admit any at present), but

from the, as yet, only problematical conception of such a science.

In the 'Critique of Pure Reason,' I went synthetically to work in respect of this question, in instituting researches into the pure Reason itself, and in this source endeavoured to determine the elements, as well as the laws of its pure use, according to principles. The task is difficult, and demands a resolute reader, gradually to think out a system, having no datum other than Reason itself, and which, therefore, without supporting itself on any fact, seeks to unfold knowledge from its original germs. Prolegomena should, on the contrary, be preparatory exercises, designed more to show what has to be done, to realise a science as far as is possible, than to expound one. They must, therefore, rely on something known as trustworthy, from which we may with confidence proceed, and ascend to its sources, as yet unknown to us, and the discovery of which will not only explain what we already knew, but at the same time exhibit to us a range of many cognitions, all arising from these same sources. The methodical procedure of Prolegomena, especially of those destined to prepare a future system of metaphysics, will therefore be analytic.

Now it fortunately happens that, although we cannot accept metaphysics as a real science, we may assert with confidence that certain pure synthetic cognitions are really given à priori, namely, pure mathematics and pure natural science, for both contain propositions, partly apodictically certain through mere Reason, and partly recognised by universal consent as coming from experience, and yet as completely independent of it.

We have, then, at least some uncontested, synthetic knowledge à priori, and do not require to ask whether this is possible, since it is actual, but only— *How it is possible,* in order to be able to deduce from the principle, rendering possible what is already given, the possibility of all the rest.

General Question

How Is Knowledge Possible from Pure Reason?

We have already seen the important distinction between analytic and synthetic judgments. The possibility of analytic propositions can be very easily conceived, for they are based simply on the principle of contradiction. The possibility of synthetic propositions *à posteriori*, i.e., of such as are derived from experience, requires no particular explanation, for experience is nothing more than a continual adding together (synthesis) of perceptions. There remains, then, only synthetic propositions à priori, the possibility of which has yet to be sought for, or examined, because it must rest on other principles than that of contradiction.

But we do not require to search out the possibility of such propositions, that is, to ask whether they are possible, for there are enough of them, actually given, and with unquestionable certainty; and as the method we are here following is analytic, we shall assume at the outset that such synthetic but pure knowledge from the Reason, is real; but thereupon we must investigate the ground of this possibility and proceed to ask—How is this knowledge possible?

It may be said that the whole transcendental philosophy which necessarily precedes all metaphysics is itself nothing more than the full solution in systematic order and completeness of the question here propounded, and that therefore as yet we have no transcendental philosophy. For what bears its name is properly a part of metaphysics, but the former science must first constitute the possibility of the latter, and must therefore precede all metaphysics.

As we now proceed to this solution according to analytio method, in which we presuppose that such cognitions from pure Reason are real, we can only call to our aid two sciences of theoretic knowledge (with which alone we are here concerned), namely, *pure mathematics* and *pure natural science*, for only these can present to us objects in intuition, and therefore (if a cognition à priori should occur in them) show their truth or agreement with the object *in concreto*, i.e., their reality; from which to the ground of their possibility we can proceed on the analytic road. This facilitates the matter very much, as the universal considerations are not merely applied to facts but even start from them, rather than as in synthetic procedure, being obliged to be derived, wholly *in abstracto*, from conceptions.

But from these real and at the same time well-grounded pure cognitions à priori, to rise to a possible one such as we are seeking, namely, to metaphysics as a science, we must needs embrace under our main question that which occasions it, to wit, the naturally given, though as regards its truth not unsuspicious, knowledge à priori lying at its foundation, and the working out of which, without any critical examination of its possibility, is now usually called metaphysics—in a word, the natural tendency to such a science; and thus the transcendental main question, divided into four other questions, will be answered step by step:—

1. *How is pure mathematics possible?*
2. *How is pure natural science possible?*
3. *How is metaphysics in general possible?*
4. *How is metaphysics as a science possible?*

It will be seen, that although the solution of these problems is chiefly meant to illustrate the essential contents of the Critique, it has nevertheless something special, which is of itself worthy of attention, namely, to seek the sources of given sciences in Reason, in order to investigate and measure this, their faculty of knowing something à priori, by means of the act itself. In this way the particular science itself must gain, if not in respect of its content, at least as regards its right employment, and while it throws light on the higher question of its common origin, at the same time give occasion to better elucidating its own nature.

The Transcendental Main Question—First Part

How Is Pure Mathematics Possible?

But we find that all mathematical knowledge has this peculiarity, that it must present its concept previously in *intuition*, and indeed à priori, that is, in an intuition that is not empirical but pure, without which means it cannot make a single step; its judgments therefore are always intuitive, whereas philosophy must be satisfied with *discursive* judgments out of mere concepts; for though it can explain its apodeictic doctrines by intuition, these can never be derived from such a source. This observation respecting the nature of mathematics, itself furnishes us with a guide as to the first and foremost condition of its possibility, namely, that *some pure intuition* must be at its foundation, wherein it can present all its concepts *in concreto* and à priori at the same time, or as it is termed, *construct* them. If we can find out this pure intuition together with its possibility, it will be readily explicable how synthetic propositions à priori are possible in pure mathematics, and therefore, also, how this science is itself possible. For just as empirical intuition enables us, without difficulty, to extend synthetically in experience the concept we form of an object of intuition, by new predicates, themselves afforded us by intuition, so will the pure intuition, only with this difference: that in the last case the synthetic judgment à priori is certain and apodeictic, while in the first case it is no more than *à posteriori* and empirically certain, because the latter only contains what is met with in chance empirical intuition, but the former what is necessarily met with in the pure intuition, inasmuch as being intuition à priori, it is indissolubly bound up with the concept before all experience or perception of individual things.

8. But the difficulty seems rather to increase than to diminish by this step. For the question is now: How is it possible to intuite anything à priori? Intuition is a presentation, as it would immediately depend on the presence of the object. It seems therefore impossible to intuite originally à priori, because the intuition must then take place without either a previous or present object to which it could refer, and hence could not be intuition. Concepts are indeed of a nature that some of them, namely, those containing only the thought of an object in general, may be very well formed à priori, without our being in immediate relation to the object (e.g., the conceptions of quantity, of cause, etc.), but even these require a certain use *in concreto*, i.e., an application to some intuition, if they are to acquire sense and meaning, whereby an object of them is to be given us. But how can intuition of an object precede the object itself?

9. Were our intuition of such a nature as to present *things as they are in themselves*, no intuition à priori would take place at all, but it would always be empirical. For what is contained in the object in itself, I can only know when it is given and present to me. It is surely then inconceivable how the intuition of a present thing should enable me to know it as it is in itself,

seeing that its properties cannot pass over into my presentative faculty. But granting the possibility of this, the said intuition would not take place à priori, that is, before the object was presented to me, for without it no ground of connection between my presentation and the object could be imagined: in which case it must rest on inspiration (*Eingebung*). Hence there is only one way possible, by which my intuition can precede the reality of the object and take place as knowledge à priori, and that is, if it contain nothing else but that form of sensibility which precedes in my subject all real impressions, by which I am affected by objects. For, that objects of sense can only be intuited in accordance with this form of sensibility, is a fact I can know à priori. From this it follows, that propositions merely concerning the form of sensible intuition, will be valid and possible for all objects of sense; and conversely, that intuitions possible à priori, can never concern other things than objects of our sense.

10. Hence, it is only by means of the form of sensuous intuition that we can intuite things à priori, but in this way we intuite the objects only as they appear to our senses, not as they may be in themselves; an assumption absolutely necessary if synthetic propositions à priori are to be admitted as possible, or in the event of their being actually met with, if their possibility is to be conceived and defined beforehand.

Now, such intuitions are space and time, and these lie at the basis of all the cognitions and judgments of pure mathematics, exhibiting themselves at once as apodeictic and necessary. For mathematics must present all its concepts primarily in intuition, and pure mathematics in pure intuition, i.e., it must construct them. The pure intuition of space constitutes the basis of geometry—even arithmetic brings about its numerical concepts by the successive addition of units in time: but above all, pure mechanics can evolve its conception of motion solely with the aid of the presentation of time. Both presentations, however, are mere intuitions; for when all that is empirical, namely, that belongs to feeling, is left out of the empirical intuitions of bodies and their changes (motion), space and time still remain over, and are therefore pure intuitions, lying à priori at the foundation of the former. For this reason, they can never be left out, but being pure intuitions à priori, prove that they are the bare forms of our sensibility, which must precede all empirical intuition, i.e., the perception of real objects, and in accordance with which objects can be known à priori, though only as they appear to us.

11. The problem of the present section is therefore solved. Pure mathematics is only possible as synthetic knowledge à priori, in so far as it refers simply to objects of sense, whose empirical intuition has for its foundation a pure intuition à priori (that of time and space), which intuition is able to serve as a foundation, because it is nothing more than the pure form of sensibility itself, that precedes the real appearance of objects, in that it makes them in the first place possible. Yet this faculty of intuiting à priori does not concern the matter of the phenomenon, i.e., that which is feeling (*Empfindung*) in the latter, for this constitutes the empirical element therein; but only its form, space and time. Should anybody cast the least doubt on the fact that neither of them are conditions of things in themselves, but only dependent on their relation to sensibility, I should be glad to be informed how he deems it possible to know à priori, and therefore before all acquaintance with the things, that is, before they are given us, how their intuition must be constructed, as is here the case with space and time. Yet this is quite conceivable, as soon as they both count for nothing more than formal determinations of our sensibility, and the objects merely as phenomena, for in that case the form of the phenomenon, that is, the pure intuition, can be conceived as coming from ourselves, in other words, as à priori.

Remark

All that is given us as object, must be given us in intuition. But all our intuition takes place by means of the senses alone; the understanding intuites nothing, but only reflects. Inasmuch as the senses, according to what is above observed, never enable us to know things in themselves, but only their appearances, which are mere representations of sensibility, then "all bodies, together with the space in which they are found, must be held to be nothing but mere "presentations, existing nowhere but in our thoughts." Now is this not the plainest idealism?

Idealism consists in the assertion that there exist none but thinking entities; the other things we think we perceive in intuition, being only presentations of the thinking entity, to which no object outside the latter can be found to correspond. I say, on the contrary, things are given as objects of our senses, external to us, but of what they may be in themselves we know nothing; we know only their appearances, i.e., the representations they produce in us as they affect our senses. I therefore certainly admit that there are bodies outside us, that is, things, which although they are wholly unknown to us, as to what they may be in themselves, we know through representations, obtained by means of their influence on our sensibility. To these we give the designation of body, a word signifying merely the appearance of that to us unknown, but not the less real, object. Can this be termed idealism? It is indeed rather the contrary thereof.

That without calling in question the existence of external things, it may be said of a number of their predicates that they do not belong to the things in themselves, but only to their appearances, and have no genuine existence outside our representation, is what has been generally accepted and admitted long before Locke's time, but more than ever since then. To these belong heat, colour, taste, etc. No one can adduce the least ground for saying that it is inadmissible on my part, to rank as mere appearances also the remaining qualities of bodies called primary, such as extension, place, and in general space, together with what is dependent thereon (impenetrability or materiality, shape. And just as little as the man who will not admit colours to be properties of the object in itself, but only to pertain as modifications to the sense of sight, is on that account called an idealist, so little can my concept be termed idealistic because I find in addition that *all properties which make up the intuition of a body* belong merely to its appearance. For the existence of a thing, which appears, is not thereby abolished as with real idealism, but it is only shown that we cannot know it, as it is in itself, through the senses.

10. THE FIXATION OF BELIEF and HOW TO MAKE OUR IDEAS CLEAR

C. S. Peirce

The Fixation of Belief

The object of reasoning is to find out, from the consideration of what we already know, something else which we do not know. Consequently, reasoning is good if it be such as to give a true conclusion from true premises, and not otherwise. Thus, the question of its validity is purely one of fact and not of thinking. A being the premises and B the conclusion, the question is, whether these facts are really so related that if A is B is. If so, the inference is valid; if not, not. It is not in the least the question whether, when the premises are accepted by the mind, we feel an impulse to accept the conclusion also. It is true that we do generally reason correctly by nature. But that is an accident; the true conclusion would remain true if we had no impulse to accept it; and the false one would remain false, though we could not resist the tendency to believe in it. . . .

That which determines us, from given premises, to draw one inference rather than another, is some habit of mind, whether it be constitutional or acquired. The habit is good or otherwise, according as it produces true conclusions from true premises or not; and an inference is regarded as valid or not, without reference to the truth or falsity of its conclusion specially, but according as the habit which determines it is such as to produce true conclusions in general or not. The particular habit of mind which governs this or that inference may be formulated in a proposition whose truth depends on the validity of the inferences which the habit determines; and such a formula is called a *guiding principle* of inference. Suppose, for example, that we observe that a rotating disk of copper quickly comes to rest when placed between the poles of a magnet, and we infer that this will happen with every disk of copper. The guiding principle is, that what is true of one piece of copper is true of another. Such a guiding principle with regard to copper would be much safer than with regard to many other substances—brass, for example. . . .

Almost any fact may serve as a guiding principle. But it so happens that there exists a division among facts, such that in one class are all those which are absolutely essential as guiding principles, while in the others are all which have any other interest as objects of research. This division is between those which are necessarily taken for granted in asking whether a certain conclusion follows from certain premises, and those which are not implied in that question. A moment's thought will show that a variety of facts are already assumed when the logical question is first asked. It is implied, for instance, that there are such states of mind as doubt and belief—that a passage from one to the other is possible, the object of thought remaining the same, and that this transition is subject to some rules which all minds are alike bound by. As these are facts which we must already know before we can have any clear conception of reasoning at all, it cannot be supposed to be any longer of much interest to inquire into their truth or falsity. On the other hand, it is easy to believe that those rules of reasoning which are deduced from the very idea of the process are the ones which are the most essential; and, indeed, that so long as it conforms to these it will, at least, not lead to false conclusions from true premises. In point of fact, the importance of what may be deduced from the assumptions involved in the logical question turns out to be greater than might be supposed, and this for reasons which it is difficult to exhibit at the outset. The only one which I shall here mention is, that conceptions which are really products of logical reflection, without being readily seen to be so, mingle with our ordinary thoughts, and are frequently the causes of great confusion. This is the case, for example, with the conception of quality. A quality as such is never an object of observation. We can see that a thing is blue or green, but the quality of being blue and the quality of being green are not things which we see; they are products of logical reflection. The truth is, that common-sense, or thought as it first emerges above the level of the narrowly practical, is deeply imbued with that bad logical quality to which the epithet *metaphysical* is commonly applied; and nothing can clear it up but a severe course of logic.

We generally know when we wish to ask a question and when we wish to pronounce a judgment, for there is a dissimilarity between the sensation of doubting and that of believing.

But this is not all which distinguishes doubt from belief. There is a practical difference. Our beliefs guide our desires and shape our actions. The Assassins, or followers of the Old Man of the Mountain, used to rush into death at his least command, because they believed that obedience to him would insure everlasting felicity. Had they doubted this, they would not have acted as they did. So it is with every belief, according to its degree. The feeling of believing is a more or less sure indication of there being established in our nature some habit which will determine our actions. Doubt never has such an effect.

Nor must we overlook a third point of difference. Doubt is an uneasy and dissatisfied state from which we struggle to free ourselves and pass into the state of belief; while the latter is a calm and satisfactory state which we do not wish to avoid, or to change to a belief in anything else.[1] On the contrary, we cling tenaciously, not merely to believing, but to believing just what we do believe.

Thus, both doubt and belief have positive effects upon us, though very different ones. Belief does not make us act at once, but puts us into such a condition that we shall behave in a certain way, when the occasion arises. Doubt has not the least effect of this sort, but stimulates us to action until it is destroyed. This reminds us of the irritation of a nerve and the reflex action produced thereby; while for the analogue of belief, in the nervous system, we must look to what are called nervous association—for example, to that habit of the nerves in consequence of which the smell of a peach will make the mouth water.

The irritation of doubt causes a struggle to attain a state of belief. I shall term this struggle *inquiry*, though it must be admitted that this is sometimes not a very apt designation.

The irritation of doubt is the only immediate motive for the struggle to attain belief. It is certainly best for us that our beliefs should be such as may truly guide our actions so as to satisfy our desires; and this reflection will make us reject any belief which does not seem to have been so formed as to insure this result. But it will only do so by creating a doubt in the place of that belief. With the doubt, therefore, the struggle begins, and with the cessation of doubt it ends. Hence, the sole object of inquiry is the settlement of opinion. We may fancy that this is not enough for us, and that we seek, not merely an opinion, but a true opinion. But put this fancy to the test, and it proves groundless; for as soon as a firm belief is reached we are entirely satisfied, whether the belief be true or false. And it is clear that nothing out of the sphere of our knowledge can be our object, for nothing which does not affect the mind can be the motive for a mental effort. The most that can be maintained is, that we seek for a belief that we shall *think* to be true. But we think each one of our beliefs to be true, and, indeed, it is mere tautology to say so.

That the settlement of opinion is the sole end of inquiry is a very important proposition. It sweeps away, at once, various vague and erroneous conceptions of proof. A few of these may be noticed here.

1. Some philosophers have imagined that to start an inquiry it was only necessary to utter a question or set it down upon paper; and have even recommended us to begin our studies with questioning everything! But the mere putting of a proposition into the interrogative form does not stimulate the mind to any struggle after belief. There must be a real and living doubt, and without this all discussion is idle.

2. It is a very common idea that a demonstration must rest on some ultimate and absolutely indubitable propositions. These, according to one school, are first principles of a general nature; according to another, are first sensations. But, in point of fact, an inquiry, to have that completely satisfactory result called demonstration, has only to start with propositions perfectly free from all actual doubt. If the premises are not in fact doubted at all, they cannot be more satisfactory than they are.

3. Some people seem to love to argue a point after all the world is fully convinced of it. But no further advance can be made. When doubt ceases, mental action on the subject comes to an end; and, if it did go on, it would be without a purpose.

If the settlement of opinion is the sole object of inquiry, and if belief is of the nature of a habit, why should we not attain the desired end, by taking any answer to a question which we may fancy, and constantly reiterating it to ourselves, dwelling on all which may conduce to that belief, and learning to turn with contempt and hatred from anything which might disturb it? . . .

But this method of fixing belief, which may be called the method of tenacity, will be unable to hold its ground in practice. The social impulse is against it. The man who adopts it will find that other men think differently from him, and it will be apt to occur to him, in some saner moment, that their opinions are quite as good as his own, and this will shake his confidence in his belief. This conception, that another man's thought or sentiment may be equivalent to one's own, is a distinctly new step, and a highly important one. It arises from an impulse too strong in man to be suppressed, without danger of destroying the human species. Unless we make ourselves hermits, we shall necessarily influence each other's opinions; so that the problem becomes how to fix belief, not in the individual merely, but in the community.

Let the will of the state act, then, instead of that of the individual. Let an institution be created which shall have for its object to keep correct doctrines before the attention of the people, to reiterate them perpetually, and to teach them to the young; having at the same time power to prevent contrary doctrines from being taught, advocated, or expressed. Let all possible causes of a change of mind be removed from men's apprehensions. Let them be kept ignorant, lest they should learn of some reason to think otherwise than they do. Let their passions be enlisted, so that they may regard private and unusual opinions with hatred and horror. Then, let all men who reject the established belief be terrified into silence. . . .

In judging this method of fixing belief, which may be called the method of authority, we must, in the first place, allow its immeasurable mental and moral superiority to the method of tenacity. Its success is proportionately greater; and, in fact, it has over and over again worked the most majestic results. The mere structures of stone which it has caused to be put together—in Siam, for example, in Egypt, and in Europe—have many of them a sublimity hardly more than rivaled by the greatest works of Nature. And, except the geological epochs, there are no periods of time so vast as those which are measured by some of these organized faiths. If we scrutinize the matter closely, we shall find that there has not been one of their creeds which has remained always the same; yet the change is so slow as to be imperceptible during one person's life,

so that individual belief remains sensibly fixed. For the mass of mankind, then, there is perhaps no better method than this. If it is their highest impulse to be intellectual slaves, then slaves they ought to remain.

But no institution can undertake to regulate opinions upon every subject. Only the most important ones can be attended to, and on the rest men's minds must be left to the action of natural causes. This imperfection will be no source of weakness so long as men are in such a state of culture that one opinion does not influence another—that is, so long as they cannot put two and two together. But in the most priestridden states some individuals will be found who are raised above that condition. These men possess a wider sort of social feeling; they see that men in other countries and in other ages have held to very different doctrines from those which they themselves have been brought up to believe; and they cannot help seeing that it is the mere accident of their having been taught as they have, and of their having been surrounded with the manners and associations they have, that has caused them to believe as they do and not far differently. And their candor cannot resist the reflection that there is no reason to rate their own views at a higher value than those of other nations and other centuries; and this gives rise to doubts in their minds.

They will further perceive that such doubts as these must exist in their minds with reference to every belief which seems to be determined by the caprice either of themselves or of those who originated the popular opinions. The willful adherence to a belief, and the arbitrary forcing of it upon others, must, therefore, both be given up, and a new method of settling opinions must be adopted, which shall not only produce an impulse to believe, but shall also decide what proposition it is which is to be believed. Let the action of natural preferences be unimpeded, then, and under their influence let men, conversing together and regarding matters in different lights, gradually develop beliefs in harmony with natural causes. This method resembles that by which conceptions of art have been brought to maturity. The most perfect example of it is to be found in the history of metaphysical philosophy. Systems of this sort have not usually rested upon any observed facts, at least not in any great degree. They have been chiefly adopted because their fundamental propositions seemed "agreeable to reason." This is an apt expression; it does not mean that which agrees with experience, but that which we find ourselves inclined to believe. Plato, for example, finds it agreeable to reason that the distances of the celestial spheres from one another should be proportional to the different lengths of strings which produce harmonious chords. Many philosophers have been led to their main conclusions by considerations like this; but this is the lowest and least developed form which the method takes, for it is clear that another man might find Kepler's theory, that the celestial spheres are proportional to the inscribed and circumscribed spheres of the different regular solids, more agreeable to *his* reason. But the shock of opinions will soon lead men to rest on preferences of a far more universal nature. Take, for example, the doctrine that man only acts selfishly—that is, from the consideration that acting in one way will afford him more pleasure than acting in another. This rests on no fact in the world, but it has had a wide acceptance as being the only reasonable theory.

This method is far more intellectual and respectable from the point of view of reason than either of the others which we have noticed. But its failure has been the most manifest. It makes of inquiry something similar to the development of taste; but taste, unfortunately, is always more or less a matter of fashion, and accordingly metaphysicians have never come to any fixed agreement, but the pendulum has swung backward and forward between a more material and a more spiritual philosophy, from the earliest times to the latest. And so from this, which has been called the a priori method, we are driven, in Lord Bacon's phrase, to a true induction. We have examined into this a priori method as something which promised to deliver our opinions from their accidental and capricious element. But development, while it is a process which eliminates the effect of some casual circumstances, only magnifies that of others. This method, therefore, does not differ in a very essential way from that of authority. The government may not have lifted its finger to influence my convictions; I may have been left outwardly quite free to choose, we will say, between monogamy and polygamy, and, appealing to my conscience only, I may have concluded that the latter practice is in itself licentious. But when I come to see that the chief obstacle to the spread of Christianity among a people of as high culture as the Hindoos has been a conviction of the immorality of our way of treating women, I cannot help seeing that, though governments do not interfere, sentiments in their development will be very greatly

determined by accidental causes. Now, there are some people, among whom I must suppose that my reader is to be found, who, when they see that any belief of theirs is determined by any circumstance extraneous to the facts, will from that moment not merely admit in words that that belief is doubtful, but will experience a real doubt of it, so that it ceases to be a belief.

To satisfy our doubts, therefore, it is necessary that a method should be found by which our beliefs may be caused by nothing human, but by some external permanency—by something upon which our thinking has no effect. Some mystics imagine that they have such a method in a private inspiration from on high. But that is only a form of the method of tenacity, in which the conception of truth as something public is not yet developed. Our external permanency would not be external, in our sense, if it was restricted in its influence to one individual. It must be something which affects, or might affect, every man. And, though these affections are necessarily as various as are individual conditions, yet the method must be such that the ultimate conclusion of every man shall be the same. Such is the method of science. Its fundamental hypothesis, restated in more familiar language, is this: There are real things, whose characters are entirely independent of our opinions about them; those realities affect our senses according to regular laws, and, though our sensations are as different as our relations to the objects, yet, by taking advantage of the laws of perception, we can ascertain by reasoning how things really are, and any man, if he have sufficient experience and reason enough about it, will be led to the one true conclusion. The new conception here involved is that of reality. It may be asked how I know that there are any realities. If this hypothesis is the sole support of my method of inquiry, my method of inquiry must not be used to support my hypothesis. The reply is this: 1. If investigation cannot be regarded as proving that there are real things, it at least does not lead to a contrary conclusion; but the method and the conception on which it is based remain ever in harmony. No doubts of the method, therefore, necessarily arise from its practice, as is the case with all the others. 2. The feeling which gives rise to any method of fixing belief is a dissatisfaction at two repugnant propositions. But here already is a vague concession that there is some *one* thing to which a proposition should conform. Nobody, therefore, can really doubt that there are realities, or, if he did, doubt would not be a source of dissatisfaction. The hypothesis, therefore, is one which every mind admits. So that the social impulse does not cause me to doubt it. 3. Everybody uses the scientific method about a great many things, and only ceases to use it when he does not know how to apply it. 4. Experience of the method has not led me to doubt it, but, on the contrary, scientific investigation has had the most wonderful triumphs in the way of settling opinion. These afford the explanation of my not doubting the method or the hypothesis which it supposes; and not having any doubt, nor believing that anybody else whom I could influence has, it would be the merest babble for me to say more about it. If there be anybody with a living doubt upon the subject, let him consider it.

To describe the method of scientific investigation is the object of this series of papers. At present I have only room to notice some points of contrast between it and other methods of fixing belief.

This is the only one of the four methods which presents any distinction of a right and a wrong way. If I adopt the method of tenacity and shut myself out from all influences, whatever I think necessary to doing this is necessary according to that method. So with the method of authority: the state may try to put down heresy by means which, from a scientific point of view, seem very ill-calculated to accomplish its purposes; but the only test *on that method* is what the state thinks, so that it cannot pursue the method wrongly. So with the a priori method. The very essence of it is to think as one is inclined to think. All metaphysicians will be sure to do that, however they may be inclined to judge each other to be perversely wrong. The Hegelian system recognizes every natural tendency of thought as logical, although it be certain to be abolished by counter-tendencies. Hegel thinks there is a regular system in the succession of these tendencies, in consequence of which, after drifting one way and the other for a long time, opinion will at last go right. And it is true that metaphysicians get the right ideas at last; Hegel's system of Nature represents tolerably the science of that day; and one may be sure that whatever scientific investigation has put out of doubt will presently receive a priori demonstration on the part of the metaphysicians. But with the scientific method the case is different. I may start with known and observed facts to proceed to the unknown; and yet the rules which I follow in doing so may not be such as investigation would approve. The test of whether I am truly following the method is not an immediate appeal to my feelings and purposes, but, on the contrary, itself involves the application of the method. Hence it is that bad reasoning as well as good reasoning is possible; and this fact is the foundation of the practical side of logic.

How to Make Our Ideas Clear

The whole function of thought is to produce habits of action; and whatever there is connected with a thought, but irrelevant to its purpose, is an accretion to it, but no part of it. If there be a unity among our sensations which has no reference to how we shall act on a given occasion, as when we listen to a piece of music, why we do not call that thinking. To develop its meaning, we have, therefore, simply to determine what habits it produces, for what a thing means is simply what habits it involves. Now, the identity of a habit depends on how it might lead us to act, not merely under such circumstances as are likely to arise, but under such as might possibly occur, no matter how improbable they may be. What the habit is depends on *when* and *how* it causes us to act. As for the *when*, every stimulus to action is derived from perception; as for the *how*, every purpose of action is to produce some sensible result. Thus, we come down to what is tangible and practical, as the root of every real distinction of thought, no matter how subtle it may be; and there is no distinction of meaning so fine as to consist in anything but a possible difference of practice.

To see what this principle leads to, consider in the light of it such a doctrine as that of transubstantiation. The Protestant churches generally hold that the elements of the sacrament are flesh and blood only in a tropical sense; they nourish our souls as meat and the juice of it would our bodies. But the Catholics maintain that they are literally just that; although they possess all the sensible qualities of wafer-cakes and diluted wine. But we can have no conception of wine except what may enter into a belief, either—

1. That this, that, or the other, is wine; or,
2. That wine possesses certain properties.

Such beliefs are nothing but self-notifications that we should, upon; occasion, act in regard to such things as we believe to be wine according to the qualities which we believe wine to possess. The occasion of such action would be some sensible perception, the motive of it to produce some sensible result. Thus our action has exclusive reference to what affects the senses, our habit has the same bearing as our action, our belief the same as our habit, our conception the same as our belief; and we can consequently mean nothing by wine but what has certain effects, direct or indirect, upon our senses; and to talk of something as having all the sensible characters of wine, yet being in reality blood, is senseless jargon. Now, it is not my object to pursue the theological question; and having used it as a logical example I drop it, without caring to anticipate the theologian's reply. I only desire to point out how impossible it is that we should have an idea in our minds which relates to anything but conceived sensible effects of things. Our idea of anything *is* our idea of its sensible effects; and if we fancy that we have any other we deceive ourselves, and mistake a mere sensation accompanying the thought for a part of the thought itself. It is absurd to say that thought has any meaning unrelated to its only function. It is foolish for Catholics and Protestants to fancy themselves in disagreement about the elements of the sacrament, if they agree in regard to all their sensible effects, here or hereafter.

It appears, then, that the rule for attaining the third grade of clearness of apprehension is as follows: Consider what effects, which might conceivably have practical bearings, we conceive the object of our conception to have. Then, our conception of these effects is the whole of our conception of the object.

Let us illustrate this rule by some examples; and, to begin with the simplest one possible, let us ask what we mean by calling a thing *hard*. Evidently that it will not be scratched by many other substances. The whole conception of this quality, as of every other, lies in its conceived effects. There is absolutely no difference between a hard thing and a soft thing so long as they are not brought to the test. Suppose, then, that a diamond could be crystallized in the midst of a cushion of soft cotton, and should remain there until it was finally burned up. Would it be false to say that that diamond was soft? This seems a foolish question, and would be so, in fact, except in the realm of logic. There such questions are often of the greatest utility as serving to bring logical principles into sharper relief than real discussions ever could. In studying logic we must not put them aside with hasty answers, but must consider them with attentive care, in order to make out the principles involved. We may, in the present case, modify our question, and ask what prevents us from saying that all hard

bodies remain perfectly soft until they are touched, when their hardness increases with the pressure until they are scratched. Reflection will show that the reply is this: there would be no *falsity* in such modes of speech. They would involve a modification of our present usage of speech with regard to the words hard and soft, but not of their meanings. For they represent no fact to be different from what it is; only they involve arrangements of facts which would be exceedingly maladroit. This leads us to remark that the question of what would occur under circumstances which do not actually arise is not a question of fact, but only of the most perspicuous arrangement of them. For example, the question of free-will and fate in its simplest form, stripped of verbiage, is something like this: I have done something of which I am ashamed; could I, by an effort of the will, have resisted the temptation, and done otherwise? The philosophical reply is, that this is not a question of fact, but only of the arrangement of facts. Arranging them so as to exhibit what is particularly pertinent to my question—namely, that I ought to blame myself for having done wrong—it is perfectly true to say that, if I had willed to do otherwise than I did, I should have done otherwise. On the other hand, arranging the facts so as to exhibit another important consideration, it is equally true that, when a temptation has once been allowed to work, it will, if it has a certain force, produce its effect, let me struggle how I may. There is no objection to a contradiction in what would result from a false supposition. The *reductio ad absurdum* consists in showing that contradictory results would follow from a hypothesis which is consequently judged to be false. Many questions are involved in the free-will discussion, and I am far from desiring to say that both sides are equally right. On the contrary, I am of opinion that one side denies important facts, and that the other does not. But what I do say is, that the above single question was the origin of the whole doubt; that, had it not been for this question, the controversy would never have arisen; and that this question is perfectly solved in the manner which I have indicated. . . .

Let us now approach the subject of logic, and consider a conception which particularly concerns it, that of *reality*. Taking clearness in the sense of familiarity, no idea could be clearer than this. Every child uses it with perfect confidence, never dreaming that he does not understand it. As for clearness in its second grade, however, it would probably puzzle most men, even among those of a reflective turn of mind, to give an abstract definition of the real. Yet such a definition may perhaps be reached by considering the points of difference between reality and its opposite, fiction. A figment is a product of somebody's imagination; it has such characters as his thought impresses upon it. That whose characters are independent of how you or I think is an external reality. There are, however, phenomena within our own minds, dependent upon our thought, which are at the same time real in the sense that we really think them. But though their characters depend on how we think, they do not depend on what we think those characters to be. Thus, a dream has a real existence as a mental phenomenon, if somebody has really dreamt it; that he dreamt so and so, does not depend on what anybody thinks was dreamt, but is completely independent of all opinion on the subject. On the other hand, considering, not the fact of dreaming, but the thing dreamt, it retains its peculiarities by virtue of no other fact than that it was dreamt to possess them. Thus we may define the real as that whose characters are independent of what anybody may think them to be.

But, however satisfactory such a definition may be found, it would be a great mistake to suppose that it makes the idea of reality perfectly clear. Here, then, let us apply our rules. According to them, reality, like every other quality, consists in the peculiar sensible effects which things partaking of it produce. The only effect which real things have is to cause belief, for all the sensations which they excite emerge into consciousness in the form of beliefs. The question therefore is, how is true belief (or belief in the real) distinguished from false belief (or belief in fiction). Now, as we have seen in the former paper, the ideas of truth and falsehood, in their full development, appertain exclusively to the scientific method of settling opinion. All the followers of science are fully persuaded that the processes of investigation, if only pushed far enough, will give one certain solution to every question to which they can be applied. One man may investigate the velocity of light by studying the transits of Venus and the aberration of the stars; another by the oppositions of Mars and the eclipses of Jupiter's satellites; a third by the method of Fizeau; a fourth by that of Foucault; a fifth by the motions of the curves of Lissajoux; a sixth, a seventh, an eighth, and a ninth, may follow the different methods of comparing the measures of statical and dynamical electricity. They may at first obtain different results, but, as each perfects

his method and his processes, the results will move steadily together toward a destined centre. So with all scientific research. Different minds may set out with the most antagonistic views, but the progress of investigation carries them by a force outside of themselves to one and the same conclusion. This activity of thought by which we are carried, not where we wish, but to a foreordained goal, is like the operation of destiny. No modification of the point of view taken, no selection of other facts for study no natural bent of mind even, can enable a man to escape the predestinate opinion. This great law is embodied in the conception of truth and reality. The opinion which is fated to be ultimately agreed to by all who investigate, is what we mean by the truth, and the object represented in this opinion is the real. That is the way I would explain reality.

But it may be said that this view is directly opposed to the abstract definition which we have given of reality, inasmuch as it makes the characters of the real to depend on what is ultimately thought about them. But the answer to this is that, on the one hand, reality is independent, not necessarily of thought in general, but only of what you or I or any finite number of men may think about it; and that, on the other hand, though the object of the final opinion depends on what that opinion is, yet what that opinion is does not depend on what you or I or any man thinks. Our perversity and that of others may indefinitely postpone the settlement of opinion; it might even conceivably cause an arbitrary proposition to be universally accepted as long as the human race should last. Yet even that would not change the nature of the belief, which alone could be the result of investigation carried sufficiently far; and if, after the extinction of our race, another should arise with faculties and disposition for investigation, that true opinion must be the one which they would ultimately come to. "Truth crushed to earth shall rise again," and the opinion which would finally result from investigation does not depend on how anybody may actually think. But the reality of that which is real does depend on the real fact that investigation is destined to lead, at last, if continued long enough, to a belief in it.

Notes

1. I am not speaking of secondary effects occasionally produced by the interference of other impulses.

INTRODUCTION

In 1963 Edmund Gettier published a brief essay called "Is Justified True Belief Knowledge?" in which he argued that the standard analysis of knowledge is too weak. The impact of his essay was wholly out of proportion to its length; the literature that discusses Gettier's piece is enormous. Most theorists agreed with Gettier; many have tried to devise conditions for knowledge strong enough to handle Gettier-style cases. But the ill that Gettier detected has proven hard to cure, and while several versatile theories are available, none has formed a consensus behind it. The most influential of these new theories are the true lemmas view, the causal theory, the defeasibility theory, and reliabilist analyses such as the tracking account. This chapter offers defenses of each of these main accounts.

Harman and the True Lemmas View

Gilbert Harman claims that inductive inference is best understood as inference to the best explanation, and that the key to responding to Gettier is the idea that we know a proposition p only when the reasoning essential to our justifiably believing p avoids false assumptions or lemmas. In "Knowledge, Inference, and Explanation" (1968), Harman gives a preliminary version of his theory of knowledge. He develops it more thoroughly in his book *Thought* (1973). Clark (1963) defended an early version of the true lemmas approach, but Harman is the philosopher most commonly credited with the true lemmas view due to the sophistication of the defense he gives it.

Goldman and the Causal Theory

The view Goldman develops in his essay "A Causal Theory of Knowing" is no longer defended but it provides many insights that were appropriated by later theorists. Echoing Hume, Goldman maintains that we know an empirical fact only when that fact causes us to believe that it holds. Goldman divides empirical knowledge into inferential and noninferential, depending on whether the belief at hand is inferential or not. A person S's belief is noninferential if the causal chain that led to it does not include another belief of S's. S's belief is inferential if the chain does. Noninferential knowledge is the sort of knowledge we acquire through perception and memory. Goldman analyzes it roughly as follows:

1. p is true
2. S believes p
3. The fact that p (is part of a causal chain that) causes S to believe p.

Inferential knowledge is more complicated. First Goldman stipulates that S knows p if and only if:

1. the fact that p is causally connected in an "appropriate" way to S's believing p, and
2. S has correctly reconstructed the important links of the chain linking belief to fact using inferences that are justified.

Then Goldman tells us which sorts of causal connections are appropriate:

1. perception,
2. memory,
3. causal chains of two sorts: ones in which the fact that p (is part of a causal chain that) causes S to believe p (a pattern 1 chain), or ones in which the fact that p and S's belief p have a common cause (a pattern 2 chain), and
4. combinations of perception, memory, and patterns 1 and 2 chains.

Klein and the Defeasibility Theory

Several authors, including Keith Lehrer and Thomas Paxson, Jr. (1969), Ernest Sosa (1969), and Peter Klein (1971), were involved in the introduction of the defeasibility theory of knowledge. In "Knowledge is True, Non-Defeated, Justified Belief," a revised and updated version of his 1971 essay, Peter Klein states a preliminary version of the defeasibility theory, discusses some of its weaknesses, and then provides an improved version. According to the preliminary version, inferential knowledge is true belief with undefeated justification, where the justification e for a belief p is *defeated* if there is some true proposition that, combined with e, constitutes insufficient grounds for believing p. After noting that this preliminary account cannot handle the Tom Grabit case (discussed in the general introduction), Klein points out that some defeaters of justification are misleading, in that they support false claims that can undermine perfectly respectable grounds for a belief. Hence the key to repairing the defeasibility theory is to distinguish between *genuine* defeaters, whose power to defeat derives from their being true, and *misleading* defeaters, whose power to defeat derives from their support for falsehoods. Then we can understand knowledge to be true belief whose justification is not undermined by a *genuine* defeater.

Nozick, and the Tracking Theory

In "Knowledge," our selection from *Philosophical Explanations* (1981), the late Robert Nozick (1938-2002) develops a version of reliabilism that he calls the tracking theory of knowledge. The tracking theory is, roughly, that knowing p entails that we would not believe p if p were false. An earlier version of the tracking analysis was defended by Fred Dretske (b. 1932) in 1970 and 1971, and in "Skepticism: What Perception Teaches," reprinted in chapter 5. Another version was defended by Alvin Goldman (b. 1938) in 1976. The tracking account is also closely related to the "thermometer" analysis which D.M. Armstrong (b. 1926) set out in *Belief, Truth, and Knowledge* (1973), a selection from which is included in chapter 7, and to the relevant alternatives theory, associated with Gail Stine (1976) but anticipated by others, including J. L.

Austin (1911-1960) in 1961, according to which a person S knows p if and only if S can eliminate all of the relevant alternatives to p.

The idea of tracking can be explained using an example introduced by Goldman in his 1976 essay "Discrimination and Perceptual Knowledge." In Goldman's example, a person, Sam, believes that he recognizes Judy. But suppose that Judy has a twin Trudy. According to Goldman, Sam knows Judy when he sees her only if he has some way of distinguishing her from her twin. According to Nozick, Sam knows he sees Judy only if he would not believe he does see Judy if it were false that he sees her.

QUESTIONS FOR REFLECTION

1. Does Gettier really show that the standard analysis of knowledge is inadequate? Why shouldn't we respond to Gettier by saying that in his cases the people actually fail to have knowledge because they have inadequate justification?

2. The relevant alternatives theory says that we know p when we can rule out the alternatives to p that are relevant. Is this theory compatible with defeasibilism and with the true lemmas view? Under what conditions is an alternative to p relevant given defeasibilism and given the true lemmas view?

3. Defeasibilists generally say that the standard justified true belief analysis is adequate for *non*inferential knowledge. Their defeasibilism is an account of inferential knowledge only. But *is* the standard account adequate for noninferential knowledge? Can we devise Gettieresque cases involving noninferential belief?

4. Several authors, including Klein, point out that the following account of inferential knowledge is too weak: S know p if and only if (a) p is true, (b) S is justified in believing p on the basis of e, and (c) S's justification e does not include any falsehoods. Examples like the papier-mâché barns case (or Klein's modification of the Tom Grabit case), in which my justification does not explicitly include a falsehood, show it is too weak. But do these examples also count against the true lemmas view, which requires that the reasoning *essential* to our justifiably believing p avoids false assumptions? (In

the papier-mâché barns case is there a false assumption I must make, perhaps implicitly, if I am to justifiably believe that I see a real barn?)

5. Consider the following proposition *b:* I do not believe everything. Do you know that *b* is true? Given the tracking theory would you know that *b* is true? If not, how might the tracking theory be modified to handle this concern?

6. Recall the papier-mâché barn case, discussed in the introduction. In terms of this case, what are the relative merits of defeasibilism, the true lemmas view, and the tracking theory?

7. Recall the Tom Grabit case, discussed in the introduction. In terms of this case, what are the relative merits of defeasibilism and the true lemmas view?

8. Consider a necessary truth, such as 2 + 2 = 4. Can we analyze our knowledge of such truths using the causal theory? Are any of the other analyses better able to account for such knowledge?

✦ (AGAINST) THE "STANDARD" THEORY ✦

11. IS JUSTIFIED TRUE BELIEF KNOWLEDGE?

Edmund L. Gettier

Various attempts have been made in recent years to state necessary and sufficient conditions for someone's knowing a given proposition. The attempts have often been such that they can be stated in a form similar to the following:[1]

    a. S knows that P   *IFF*

    (i) P is true,

    (ii) S believes that P, and

    (iii) S is justified in believing that P.

For example, Chisholm has held that the following gives the necessary and sufficient conditions for knowledge:[2]

    b. S knows that P   *IFF*

    (i) S accepts P,

    (ii) S has adequate evidence for P, and

    (iii) P is true.

Ayer has stated the necessary and sufficient conditions for knowledge as follows:[3]

    c. S knows that P   *IFF*

    (i) P is true,

    (ii) S is sure that P is true, and

    (iii) S has the right to be sure that P is true.

I shall argue that (a) is false in that the conditions stated therein do not constitute a *sufficient* condition for the truth of the proposition that S knows that P. The same argument will show that (b) and (c) fail if 'has adequate evidence for' or 'has the right to be sure that' is substituted for 'is justified in believing that' throughout.

I shall begin by noting two points. First, in that sense of 'justified' in which S's being justified in believing P is a necessary condition of S's knowing that P, it is possible for a person to be justified in believing a proposition that is in fact false. Secondly, for any proposition P, if S is justified in believing P, and P entails Q, and S deduces Q from P and accepts Q as a result of this deduction, then S is justified in believing Q. Keeping these two points in mind, I shall now present two cases in which the conditions stated in (a) are true for some proposition, though it is at the same time false that the person in question knows that proposition.

Case I:

Suppose that Smith and Jones have applied for a certain job. And suppose that Smith has strong evidence for the following conjunctive proposition:

> d. Jones is the man who will get the job, and Jones has ten coins in his pocket.

Smith's evidence for (d) might be that the president of the company assured him that Jones would in the end be selected, and that he, Smith, had counted the coins in Jones's pocket ten minutes ago. Proposition (d) entails:

> e. The man who will get the job has ten coins in his pocket.

Let us suppose that Smith sees the entailment from (d) to (e), and accepts (e) on the grounds of (d), for which he has strong evidence. In this case, Smith is clearly justified in believing that (e) is true.

But imagine, further, that unknown to Smith, he himself, not Jones, will get the job. And, also, unknown to Smith, he himself has ten coins in his pocket. Proposition (e) is then true, though proposition (d), from which Smith inferred (e), is false. In our example, then, all of the following are true: (*i*) (e) is true, (*ii*) Smith believes that (e) is true, and (*iii*) Smith is justified in believing that (e) is true. But it is equally clear that Smith does not *know* that (e) is true; for (e) is true in virtue of the number of coins in Smith's pocket, while Smith does not know how many coins are in Smith's pocket, and bases his belief in (e) on a count of the coins in Jones's pocket, whom he falsely believes to be the man who will get the job.

Case II:

Let us suppose that Smith has strong evidence for the following proposition:

> f. Jones owns a Ford.

Smith's evidence might be that Jones has at all times in the past within Smith's memory owned a car, and always a Ford, and that Jones has just offered Smith a ride while driving a Ford. Let us imagine, now, that Smith has another friend, Brown, of whose whereabouts he is totally ignorant. Smith selects three place-names quite at random, and constructs the following three propositions:

> g. Either Jones owns a Ford, or Brown is in Boston;
>
> h. Either Jones owns a Ford, or Brown is in Barcelona;
>
> i. Either Jones owns a Ford, or Brown is in Brest-Litovsk.

Each of these propositions is entailed by (f). Imagine that Smith realizes the entailment of each of these propositions he has constructed by (f), and proceeds to accept (g), (h), and (i) on the basis of (f). Smith has correctly inferred (g), (h), and (i) from a proposition for which he has strong evidence. Smith is therefore completely justified in believing each of these three propositions. Smith, of course, has no idea where Brown is.

But imagine now that two further conditions hold. First, Jones does *not* own a Ford, but is at present driving a rented car. And secondly, by the sheerest coincidence, and entirely unknown to Smith, the place mentioned in proposition (h) happens really to be the place where Brown is. If these two conditions hold then Smith does *not* know that (h) is true, even though (*i*) (h) *is* true, (*ii*) Smith does believe that (h) is true, and (*iii*) Smith is justified in believing that (h) is true.

These two examples show that definition (a) does not state a *sufficient* condition for someone's knowing a given proposition. The same cases, with appropriate changes, will suffice to show that neither definition (b) nor definition (c) do so either.

Notes

1. Plato seems to be considering some such definition at *Theaetetus* 201, and perhaps accepting one at *Meno* 98.
2. Roderick M. Chisholm, *Perceiving: A Philosophical Study*, Cornell University Press (Ithaca, New York, 1957), p. 16.
3. A. J. Ayer, *The Problem of Knowledge*, Macmillan (London, 1956), p. 34.

12. KNOWLEDGE, INFERENCE, AND EXPLANATION

Gilbert Harman*

I: Introduction

This paper examines applications of an *empiricist analysis of knowledge*. Without attempting to defend the analysis, I shall assume that it is roughly correct and shall draw some consequences. I shall argue in particular that it suggests solutions of problems in inductive logic and statistical explanation. These applications support the analysis; but I shall also show that the analysis is not completely adequate, since it does not provide for a "social aspect" of knowledge.

II: How Belief Is Based on Inference

In this paper I often use the expression "based on inference," and similar expressions. I do not say that, strictly speaking, the knower actually reasons (although I say this when I am speaking loosely). I say rather that, strictly speaking, his belief is based on reasoning. What a belief is based on depends upon how the belief came about; but belief can be based on reasoning even if the belief is not the result of conscious reasoning.

Consider how people talk about computers. Computers are said to add, multiply, compute, reason, and make use of data, even though no one means by this that some person literally does these things. When we talk about computers, we use words like "reasoning," "inference," "data," etc., in a wider sense than when we talk about people. I suggest that empiricists use the wider sense of these terms when they describe knowledge as based on reasoning from data in immediate experience. Thus psychologists have come more and more to explain human behavior by thinking of people as if they were in part computers. They speak of psychological mechanisms and psychological models. Many psychologists have said that the first step in any good psychological explanation is a description of a mechanism that can duplicate the behavior to be

explained.[1] If we think of a person (or his brain) as a mechanism like a computer, then we can ascribe inference and reasoning to that person, in the sense in which computers infer and reason. The conscious inferences a person makes are in the extended sense of the term only some of the inferences he makes. We can in this way make sense of the notion that (loosely speaking) a person is not always aware of the inferences he makes.

Psychological explanation typically describes a mechanism by means of a program or flow chart rather than its psychological realization. The same automaton can be constructed in various ways, with either tubes or transistors for example. Two computers, made of different materials but programmed in the same way, may be said to be in the same state when they carry out the same part of the program. Putnam and Fodor have persuasively argued that psychological states are more like being at a particular place in the program than like having something or other happening in your transistors.[2]

I now want to describe two principles that an empiricist must accept if he is to offer a plausible account of knowledge. The first is that all inductive inference infers the truth of an explanation. The second is the condition that the lemmas be true. I shall begin with a brief account of each of these principles.

III: Explanations and Lemmas

The first principle is illustrated whenever a person infers from certain evidence to an explanation of that evidence. The detective infers that the butler did it, since that's the only way to explain the fingerprints on the gun. A scientist infers something about unit charges in order to account for the behavior of oil drops in an experiment he has done. Since the reasoner must infer that one explanation is better than competing explanations, I say he makes an *inference to the best explanation*. In my view, all inductive inference takes this form. Even when a person infers a generalization of the evidence, his inference is good only to the extent that the generalization offers (or is entailed by) a better explanation of the evidence than competing hypotheses. (But note, I do not say that the explanation must be the best of *alternative* explanations; I say rather that it must be the best of *competing* explanations.)

The connection between explanation and induction is implicit in recent work in inductive logic and the theory of explanation. Goodman has shown that one can ordinarily infer a generalization of the evidence only if the generalization is lawlike, and Hempel and Oppenheim have pointed out that only lawlike generalizations can explain their instances.[3] This provides confirmation of the claim that all inductive inference is inference to the best explanation. More confirmation will be provided later.

The second principle an empiricist must accept, the condition that the lemmas be true, says that a person cannot come to know something by inferring it from something false. In Keith Lehrer's example,[4] suppose Mary has strong evidence that Mr. Nogot, who is in her office, owns a Ford; but suppose that Mr. Nogot does not in fact own a Ford. Perhaps someone else in her office, Mr. Havit, does own a Ford. Still, Mary cannot come to *know* that someone in her office owns a Ford by inferring this from the false premiss that Mr. Nogot, who is in her office, owns a Ford.

I speak of "lemmas" because the relevant propositions need not be included in Mary's initial premiss. Her initial premisses may be that she has seen Mr. Nogot driving a new Ford, that she has heard him say he owns a Ford, etc., where all of these initial premisses are true. It is false that Mr. Nogot owns a Ford; but that is not one of her initial premisses. It is, rather, a provisional conclusion reached on the way to the final conclusion. Such a provisional conclusion, that is a premiss for later steps of the argument, is a lemma. The condition that the lemmas be true says that, if Mary is to know something by virtue of an inference on which her belief is based, every premiss and lemma of that inference must be true.

Mary's belief will often be based on several inferences, only one of which needs to satisfy the condition that the lemmas be true. For example, she might also possess evidence that Mr. Havit owns a Ford and infer from that that someone in her office owns a Ford. That

one of her inferences fails to satisfy the condition that the lemmas be true does not prevent Mary from obtaining knowledge from her other inference. Furthermore, even when Mary explicitly reasons in one particular way, we may want to say her belief is also based on other unexpressed reasoning. If Mary has evidence that Mr. Havit owns a Ford, we may also want to ascribe the second of the above inferences to her even though she consciously formulated only the first. Sect. VI, below, describes how the inferences we shall want to ascribe to a person will depend upon our intuitive judgments about when people know things.

So, inferential knowledge requires two things: inference to the best explanation and the condition that the lemmas be true. I shall now illustrate and support these requirements with some examples.[5]

I shall describe two cases, the *testimony case* and the *lottery case*, and appeal to your natural nonphilosophical judgments about these cases. In the testimony case a person comes to know something when he is told about it by an eyewitness or when he reads about it in the newspaper. In the lottery case, a person fails to come to know he will lose a fair lottery, even though he reasons as follows: "Since there are N tickets, the probability of losing is $(N - 1)/N$. This probability is very close to one. Therefore, I shall lose the lottery." A person can know in the testimony case but not in the lottery case, or so we would ordinarily and naturally judge. In the lottery case a person cannot know he will lose no matter how probable this is. The contrast between the two cases may seem paradoxical, since witnesses are sometimes mistaken and newspapers often print things that are false. For some N, the likelihood that a person will lose the lottery is higher than the likelihood that the witness has told the truth or that the newspaper is right. Our ordinary, natural judgments thus seem almost contradictory. How could a person know in the testimony case but not in the lottery case?

At this point many philosophers would reject one of the ordinary judgments no matter how natural the judgment may be. But such rejection would be premature. My strategy is to ask how beliefs are based on reasoning in the two cases. The only relevant reasoning in the lottery case seems to be deductive. From the premiss that the lottery is fair and that there are N tickets, it follows that the probability of any ticket being a loser is $(N - 1)/N$. One can only deduce the probability statement. No deductive inference permits one to detach the probability qualification from the statement that the ticket will lose. I claim moreover that there is no inductive way to detach this qualification, since inductive inference must take the form of inference to the best explanation and no explanation is involved in the lottery case.

The testimony case is different. No obvious deductive inference leads to a probabilistic conclusion in this case; and acceptance of the testimony can be based on two consecutive inferences to the best explanation. To see this, consider how we would ordinarily explain our evidence, the testimony. First, we would infer that the speaker so testifies because he believes what he says (and not because he has something to gain by so testifying, or because he has gotten confused and has said the opposite of what he means, etc.). Second, we would infer that he believes as he does because in fact he witnessed what he described (and not because he suffered an hallucination, or because his memory deceives him, etc.).

There is, then, an important divergence between the two cases. In the testimony case, the relevant conclusion can be reached by inference to the best explanation. This is not true in the lottery case. It is the appeal to explanation, over and above any appeal to probability, that is important when a person comes to know a nonprobabilistic conclusion.

A person who believes testimony rarely is conscious of reasoning as I have suggested. But, in the ordinary case, such reasoning must be warranted. For suppose that the hearer had good reason to doubt that the speaker has said what be believes, so that the hearer would not be warranted in reasoning in the required way. Then, even if he accepted what the speaker has said and the speaker has spoken truly, the hearer could not be said to know this. The hearer would also fail to gain knowledge if he had good reason to doubt that the speaker's belief is the result of what the speaker witnessed, since again the hearer could not reason in the required way. My analysis of the testimony case would explain why this reason must be warranted if the hearer is to come to know the truth of what he hears. According to that analysis, the hearer's belief is based on the suggested reasoning; and if his belief is to be knowledge, reasoning must be warranted. Therefore, that the this

reasoning must be warranted provides some confirmation of my analysis of the testimony case.

Stronger confirmation arises from an application of the condition that the lemmas be true. Suppose that a person who has no reason not to believe a witness does believe him. The hearer cannot thereby come to know unless *in fact* the testimony was an expression of what the witness believes and unless *in fact* the witness's belief was the result of what he witnessed. If the witness were to say the opposite of what he believes, a listener could not come to know, even if the witness inadvertently spoke the truth. Nor could he come to know if the witness said what is true as a result of remembering the wrong occasion. The witness's knowledge requires the truth of two explanatory claims. We can understand this if we assume that knowledge in the testimony case is based on the reasoning I have already mentioned and if we apply the condition that the lemmas be true. The two explanatory claims appear as lemmas in that reasoning. These lemmas must be true if the hearer is to gain knowledge from the testimony. The empiricist analysis thus permits us to explain things we might not otherwise be able to explain.

We have, then, a rough analysis of knowledge that involves two principles. If we take the analysis as a working hypothesis, we can apply the two principles in order to learn something about knowledge, inference, explanation, and perception. The discussion of the lottery case *versus* the testimony case has provided one example of such an application. I shall now describe other examples.

Notice that to take the analysis as a working hypothesis in this way is to render it immune to a certain sort of counterexample. According to the analysis, knowledge is based on inference to the best explanation; but in order to determine when belief is based on inference and in order to discover what constitutes good inference to the best explanation, one must appeal to the analysis plus intuitions about when people know things. Therefore, the test of the resulting theory cannot be whether or not it conflicts with one's intuitions about when people know things. (This is only partially correct; see the final section of this paper.) Instead, the theory must be judged by whether it can be developed without appeal to *ad hoc* assumptions in a way that sheds light on epistemological and psychological subjects and whether it does this better than competing alternatives. The next three sections of this paper are meant to suggest some of the range and power of this theory.

IV: Application to Inductive Logic

We can use the analysis in finding criteria of good inductive inference. Instead of asking directly whether a particular inference is warranted, we can ask whether a person could come to know by virtue of that inference. If we identify what can be known with what can be inferred, we can discover something important about "detachment" in inductive logic. A principle of detachment would let us "detach" the probability qualification from our conclusion. If there were no rule of detachment, induction would never permit anything more than probabilistic conclusions. But, as inductive logicians have found, it is difficult to state a rule of detachment that does not lead to inconsistency.

Suppose, for example, that detachment were permitted whenever the evidence made a conclusion highly probable. Thus suppose that we could detach a probability qualification whenever our conclusion had a probability (on our total evidence) of at least $(N-1)/N$. Since any ticket in a fair lottery among N tickets has a probability of $(N-1)/N$ of being a loser, the suggested principle of detachment would permit us to conclude for each ticket that it will lose. But we also know that one of these tickets will win, so use of high probability to warrant detachment had led us to inconsistency. Some logicians take this result to show that there should be no principle of detachment in inductive logic.[6]

We can avoid this extreme position if we identify the possibility of detachment with the possibility of knowing a nonprobabilistic conclusion. The testimony case tells us that induction sometimes allows nonprobabilistic conclusions, since in that case a person comes to know such a conclusion. The lottery case shows that the inference to such a conclusion is not determined by the high probability one's premises give his conclusion, since in the lottery

case one can only come to know a probability statement. Detachment is possible in the testimony case but not in the lottery case. I have argued that explanation marks the difference between these cases. In the testimony case a person infers the truth of certain explanations. Not so in the lottery case. The problem of detachment arises through failure to notice the role of explanation in inductive inference. Such inference is not just a matter of probability; one must infer the truth of an explanation. Detachment can and must be justified by inference to the best explanation.

This is not to say that probability, or degree of confirmation, is irrelevant to inductive inference. We can, in fact, use the empiricist analysis again to discover how induction involves probability. Suppose that John and Sam have tossed a fair coin to determine who will have a new hundred-dollar bill. The new hundreds are easily recognizable, being pink, an innovation of the Treasury Department. An hour later, Peter, who knows about the toss, sees John with a new hundred-dollar bill. Peter realizes that John could have received such a bill in only two ways, the most likely being that he won the toss with Sam. There is also an extremely unlikely way, hardly even worth considering. That morning, as a result of a *Consumer Digest* promotion scheme, some person, chosen at random from the population of the United States, has received the only other pink hundred now in general circulation. The odds are two-hundred million to one that John did not receive the *Digest's* bill. So Peter infers that John won the toss with Sam. He infers that the explanation of John's having the bill is that he won the toss and not that he received the *Digest's* bill. If the explanation is right, an ordinary, natural judgment about the *coin toss case* would be that Peter knows John won the toss.

If this is correct, it suggests one way in which probability can serve as a guide to the best of several competing explanations. Other things equal, the best one will be the most probable one. If it is sufficiently more probable than the others, then a person may infer the truth of that explanation. If *Consumer Digest* had sent pink hundred-dollar bills to every third person, randomly selected, then Peter could not know John has won the coin toss, since that explanation of John's having the bill would no longer be sufficiently more probable than a competing hypothesis. An important issue is how much more probable the one hypothesis must be if it is to provide knowledge. This question may be pursued by further application of the empiricist analysis; but I shall not do so. I shall instead turn to a different aspect of inductive inference.

A complication must be added to what has been said. The best explanation is more than just a highly probable explanation. It must also make what is to be explained considerably more probable than would the denial of that explanation. That is, a weak maximum likelihood principle must be satisfied.[7]

To see this, consider the following case. Terry has received a special certificate if he has won a fair lottery among 1000 people. If Terry hasn't won, then George has given him a duplicate of the winning certificate, since George wants Terry to have such a certificate no matter what. Arthur, knowing all this, sees Terry with a certificate. Why cannot Arthur infer that George gave Terry the certificate? That explanation of Terry's having the certificate is very probable; but Arthur cannot make such an inference, because he cannot come to know by virtue of that inference that Terry didn't win the lottery. The most probable explanation does not make what is to be explained any more probable than the denial of that explanation does. That George has given Terry the certificate would make it certain that Terry has a certificate; but this is just as certain if George has not given it to him, because Terry has then won the lottery. Since Terry would have a certificate in any event, Arthur cannot infer that it came from George, even though this explanation is the most probable.

So two things are necessary if an explanation is to be inferable. First, it must be much more probable on the evidence than its denial. Second, it must make what is to be explained more probable than its denial does. This amounts to a synthesis of two apparently conflicting approaches to statistical inference. The Bayesian approach is reflected in the requirement that the best explanation be more probable on the evidence than its denial. The maximum likelihood approach is reflected in the requirement that the explanation make what is to be explained more probable than its denial does.[8]

More needs to be said about this since even these two conditions are not sufficient; but further investigation would place us in the middle of the theory of confirmation. Enough has been said to show how the analysis may be used to study induction from an unusual point of view.

V: Application to the Theory of Explanation

If we exploit the connection between explanations and projectible (or inferable) hypotheses, we may use the analysis to study explanation. An hypothesis is directly confirmed by evidence only if it explains the evidence. So, an hypothesis is a potential explanation if it is the sort of thing that can be directly inferred; and the legitimacy of an inference can again be determined by the possibility of obtaining knowledge by virtue of that inference.

One can show, for example, that a conjunction does not always explain its conjuncts. Let one conjunct be that this is a ticket in a fair lottery among N tickets. Let the other conjunct be that this ticket loses. It is easy to show that the conjunction (that this is a ticket in a fair lottery among N tickets and will lose) cannot explain its first conjunct (that this is a ticket in a fair lottery among N tickets). The result is perfectly obvious, of course, but I want to show how to use the empiricist analysis to demonstrate such a result.

The argument is simple. If the conjunction provides an explanation, then it sometimes provides the best explanation. But then we ought to be able to know something we cannot know. We ought to be able to know in the lottery case that we have a losing ticket; and we cannot know this. If the conjunction provided the best explanation of our evidence, a person in the lottery case could infer the truth of the conjunction from this evidence. In that way he could come to know that his ticket will lose. Since he can't come to know this, the conjunction does not explain its conjunct.

To prove that the conjunction, if an explanation, sometimes satisfies the requirements on the best explanation, notice that it always satisfies the first requirement. The evidence makes the conjunction more probable than not, since the conjunction has a probability on the evidence of $(N - 1)/N$. Furthermore, there will be situations in which the weak maximum likelihood principle is satisfied. Typically, in fact, the falsity of the conjunction would make it very improbable that this is a ticket in an N ticket lottery. So, if the conjunction can explain, it can be the best explanation.

This result is trivial and obvious, but the same method can be applied to less trivial cases. It is especially useful in the study of statistical explanation. Consider, for example, the most basic question, whether there can be such a thing as statistical explanation at all. Use of the empiricist analysis shows there can be and also shows what sort of explanation it is.

Consider cases in which a person comes to know something by means of statistical sampling methods. Suppose, for example, that there are two batches of widgets such that about 70 percent of the widgets in one batch are defective and only about 1 percent of the widgets in the other batch are defective. Confronted with one of the batches, David must decide whether it is the largely defective batch or the good batch. He randomly selects ten widgets from the batch and discovers that seven out of the ten are defective. He infers correctly that this is the defective batch. In this way he comes to know that this is the defective batch, or so we would naturally judge. To apply the empiricist analysis requires assuming his inference is to the best explanation; and to assume this is to assume that there can be statistical explanation. David must choose between two explanations of the makeup of his sample. Both are statistical. Each explains the sample as the result of a random selection from among the items of one of the batches. The explanation David accepts is much more probable than its denial, given the sample he has drawn and assuming that before he had the sample either batch was equally likely. The same explanation makes David's having drawn such a sample more likely than this is made by the explanation he rejects. Therefore, the explanation he accepts is the best explanation of his evidence, and he can come to know the truth of that explanation. He could not, on the empiricist analysis, make his inference if there were no such thing as statistical explanation.

This kind of statistical explanation does not always make what it explains very probable. It is possible, given David's evidence, that the explanation of the makeup of his sample is that he drew randomly from the good batch and this was one of those times when the unlikely thing happens. Such a possibility contradicts the Hempelian account of statistical explanation,[9] so I shall elaborate.

I can make my point clearer if I change the example. Suppose Sidney selects one of two similar looking coins, a fair one and a weighted one such that the probability of getting heads on a toss of the fair coin is 1/2 and the probability of getting heads on a toss of the weighted coin is 9/10. To discover which coin he has, Sidney tosses it ten times. The coin comes up heads three times and tails seven times. Sidney correctly concludes the coin must be the fair one. We would ordinarily think that Sidney could in this way come to know he has the fair coin. On the empiricist analysis, this means he has inferred the best explanation of that distribution of heads and tails. But the explanation, that these were random tosses of a fair coin, does not make it probable that the coin comes up heads three times and tails seven times. The probability of this happening with a fair coin is considerably less than 1/2. If we want to accept the empiricist analysis, we must agree that statistical explanation sometimes makes what is to be explained less probable than its denial. This means one has not explained why three heads have come up rather than some other number of heads. The explanation is of a different sort. One explains, as it were, how it happened that three heads came up, what led to this happening. One does not explain why this happened rather than something else, since the same thing could have led to something else.

Suppose Stuart walks into the casino and sees the roulette wheel stop at red fifty times in a row. The explanation of this may be that the wheel is fixed. It may also be that the wheel is fair and this is one of those times when fifty reds are going to come up. Given a fair wheel one expects that to happen sometime (although not very often). But, if the explanation is that the wheel is fair and this is just one of those times, it says what the sequence of reds is the result of, the "outcome" of. It does not say why fifty reds in a row occurred this time rather than some other time, nor why that particular series occurred rather than any of the $2^{50}-1$ other possible series.

I am inclined to suppose that this is the only sort of statistical explanation. But that is another story. I do not want to pursue the theory of explanation in detail. My point has been that the empiricist analysis can be used in the study of explanation and that it results in conclusions different from those generally accepted.

VI: Discovering Inferences Belief Is Based On

Another way to use the analysis exploits the condition that the lemmas be true in order to discover what reasoning knowledge is based on. I begin with a simple example. Normally, if a hearer is to gain knowledge of what a witness reports, the witness must say what he does because he believes it; and he must believe as he does because of what he saw. Two conditions must thus be satisfied if the hearer is to know. If we wanted to discover the hearer's reasoning, we could use the fact that there are these conditions. We could explain these conditions if we were to assume that they represent lemmas in the hearer's reasoning, since that would make the conditions special cases of the condition that the lemmas be true. Thus we can often account for conditions on knowledge, if we assume that the knowledge is based on relevant reasoning and if we apply the condition that the lemmas be true.

One example worth pursuing, although I shall not say much about it, is knowledge one gets from reading the newspaper. Suppose a misprint changes a false statement into a true one (by, perhaps, substituting the word "not" for the word "now"). In any ordinary case, one cannot come to know by reading that sentence even though the sentence is true. Our method tells us to assume that this fact about misprints represents a lemma in our inference. And it does seem reasonable to assume we infer that the sentence we read is there as a result of the printer correctly forming the sentence that appears in the manuscript. What else do we infer? We ordinarily do not make detailed assumptions about how the reporter got his story, nor about whether the story comes from wire services or from the paper's own reporters. If we are to discover just what we do infer, we must make extensive use of the condition that the lemmas be true. We must discover what has to be true about the way the story gets from reporters to the printer and what has to be true about the way the reporter got his story. We must then associate these conditions with the condition that the lemmas be true, in order to discover what we infer when we come to know by reading the paper. But I shall say nothing more about this problem.

Now consider a case of perceptual knowledge in which a person, as we say, *just sees* that something is true. It is obvious that there are conditions to be satisfied if a case of seeing is to be a case of seeing that something is true. We can account for some of these conditions if we assume that direct perceptual knowledge is based on reasoning. Suppose that Gregory sees a table in the room. As many philosophers have noted, ordinarily, if he is to see *that* there is a table in the room, it must look to him as if there is a table in the room. Furthermore, there must be some causal relationship between the table and its looking to Gregory as if there is a table in the room. It will not do if there is a mirror between Gregory and the table such that he is really seeing the reflection of a different table in a different room. Nor could Gregory see that there is a table if he was hallucinating, even if, by some coincidence he hallucinated a scene exactly like the one in fact before him.

Applying the analysis, we assume that such direct perceptual knowledge is based on inference and attempt to apply the condition that the lemmas be true. This leads us to say that perceptual knowledge is based on inference from data in immediate experience, where such data include how things look, sound, feel, smell, taste, etc. The relevant reasoning infers an explanation of some aspect of immediate experience. In the example, Gregory reasons that it looks as if there is a table because there is a table there and he is looking at it. If he is to reach the conclusion that there is a table, he needs the explanatory statement as a lemma. That is why the truth of the explanatory statement is required if Gregory is to see that there is a table in the room. A similar analysis applies to other cases of direct perceptual knowledge.

I have been purposefully vague about immediate experience, because the empiricist analysis can probably be adapted to any conception. It can apply even if one denies there is any such thing as immediate experience, for one can speak about stimulations of sense organs instead. If Gregory is to see that there is a table in the room, then his eye must be stimulated in a way that depends in part on the table in the room. I can imagine an empiricist who holds that perceptual knowledge is based on inference from immediate stimulation.

Two things must always be remembered. First, an empiricist analysis is not necessarily an analysis of meaning. It is merely an interesting set of necessary and sufficient conditions. It is irrelevant to an empiricist analysis whether the meaning of knowledge claims implies anything about stimulation of sense organs. Second, knowledge can be based on reasoning even when no one actually reasons.

Usually the relevant reasoning will be reasoning only in the sense in which computers reason. The computer analogy is particularly useful if perceptual knowledge is analyzed in terms of stimulations rather than immediate experience, since stimulations are data only in the sense in which a computer can be supplied with data. One might think here of a computer used to aim antiaircraft missiles in the light of data obtained by radar.

VII: Knowledge of the External World?

Philosophers have wanted to avoid this conception of perceptual knowledge, because they have thought it leads to scepticism. If a person has only his immediate experience to go on, how can he know there is a world of objects surrounding him? How does he know it is not a dream? How does he know it is not the creation of an evil demon?

The problem, if there is one, is not just how one comes to know there is a world of objects, for it arises in any instance of perceptual knowledge. I can see that there is a table in the room only if I can infer an explanation of my immediate experience. How can I legitimately make this inference? How can I rule out the possibility that I may be dreaming? How do I know that a demon psychologist has not attached my brain to a computer that stimulates me as if I were seeing a table? If veridical perception is to provide the best explanation of my experience, that explanation must be more probable than the others. But how can I assume that it is more probable without begging the question? How can I know I have not had many dreams just like this?

How can I know I have not had many experiments played on me by the demon psychologist?

Notice that we have no independent way to discover the likelihoods of the various explanations. If one applies the empiricist method for dealing with problems in inductive logic, he may take the fact of perceptual knowledge to show that the hypothesis of veridical perception is highly probable on a person's evidence. The empiricist can in this way avoid the problem of our knowledge of the external world, indeed he can exploit the problem for his own ends in order to argue that there is a predilection for veridical perception built into our confirmation function.

I have tried to show how the empiricist analysis can be used to study induction and explanation and to account for certain requirements on knowledge as special cases of the condition that the lemmas be true. I have described how the analysis can lead one to say that even direct perceptual knowledge is based on inference. In my opinion, the applications of the empiricist analysis show that there must be something to that analysis. I shall now show that the analysis does not provide the whole story and that it leaves out a "social aspect" of knowledge.

VIII: The "Social Aspect" of Knowledge

An empiricist assumes that whether a person knows depends only on the data that person has and not on the data someone else has. There are qualifications, of course. One person may rely indirectly on another's data if he relies on the other person's testimony. The validity of someone else's data may thus be relevant by virtue of the condition that the lemmas be true. But if this condition is satisfied, empiricists assume that the *sufficiency* of a person's data is not affected by information someone else has. In making this assumption, empiricists overlook the social aspect of knowledge.

Suppose that Tom enters a room in which many people are talking excitedly although he cannot understand what they are saying. He sees a copy of the morning paper on a table. The headline and main story reveal that a famous civil-rights leader has been assassinated. On reading the story he comes to believe it; it is true; and the condition that the lemmas be true has been satisfied since a reporter who witnessed the assassination wrote the story that appears under his by-line. According to an empiricist analysis, Tom ought to know the assassination had occurred. It ought to be irrelevant what information other people have, since Tom has no reason to think they have information that would contradict the story in the paper.

But this is a mistake. For, suppose that the assassination has been denied, even by eyewitnesses, the point of the denial being to avoid a racial explosion. The assassinated leader is reported in good health; the bullets are said, falsely, to have missed him and hit someone else. The denials occurred too late to prevent the original and true story from appearing in the paper that Tom has seen; but everyone else in the room has heard about the denials. None of them know what to believe. They all have information that Tom lacks. Would we judge Tom to be the only one who knows that the assassination has actually happened? Could we say that he knows this because he does not yet have the information everyone else has? I do not think so. I believe we would ordinarily judge that Tom does not know.

This reveals the social aspect of knowledge. The evidence that a person has is not always all the evidence relevant to whether he knows. Someone else's information may also be relevant.[10] But how, exactly, ought the empiricist analysis be changed? Should we count information that any person at all has? Should we combine information possessed in part by several people, even if the information each has does not appear significant taken by itself? Must we take all the information one of these others has, or can we select bits and pieces that may give a misleading impression? And what is it that makes another person's information relevant?

The last question seems easiest to answer. Another person's information is relevant if the original person could not have properly reasoned as he did had he known about this information. If Tom had known about the denials as everyone else in the room knows, then Tom could not properly infer that the newspaper story is true. The other questions I have mentioned are not as easily answered, if we are to avoid the consequence that people rarely know anything. For example, if one could select bits and pieces of someone's information in a misleading way, he might be able to undermine almost any claim to knowledge. A similar result would follow if he could combine the information that several people hold separately, since he might choose people such that their

information combined to give a misleading result. On the other hand, it is not required that one combine the information everyone has, in order to see whether that prevents Tom's inference. That information would support Tom's inference, since it includes the fact that the explanations Tom originally inferred are correct.

The hardest problem is who may have the information that undermines Tom's reasoning. I doubt that we can allow his reasoning to be faulted by *any* one person's information. Otherwise, I would prevent many people from knowing things if I were to fake evidence about various things and show it to you. But I do not know how many people or what sort of people must be taken into account. Perhaps we must even consider people living at a different time, since we think our predecessors were sometimes right for the wrong reasons. It isn't just a matter of numbers. There can be evidence known only to a few that contradicts what the majority believe. This is certainly a subject worth pursuing; but I shall follow it no farther at this time.

In this paper I have tried to show two things. One is that there is something importantly right about the empiricist analysis. The other is that the analysis is not enough.[11]

Notes

* I have discussed the subject of this paper with a great many people. I am especially grateful to Paul Benacerraf, John Earman, Richard Jeffrey, and Saul Kripke. Earman suggested several of the examples. The form of the argument is my own, as is the responsibility for errors.

1. E.g., J. A. Deutsch, *The Structural Basis of Behavior* (Chicago, University of Chicago Press, 1960).

2. Hilary Putnam, "Minds and Machines" in Sidney Hook (ed.), *Dimensions of Mind* (New York, New York University Press, 1960); "Robots: Machines or Artificially Created Life?" *The Journal of Philosophy*, vol. 61 (1964), pp. 668–691. Jerry A. Fodor, "Explanations in Psychology" in Max Black (ed.), *Philosophy in America* (New York, Ithaca, Cornell University Press, 1965).

3. Nelson Goodman, *Fact, Fiction, and Forecast* (Cambridge, Mass., Harvard University Press, 1955). C. G. Hempel and Paul Oppenheim, "Studies in the Logic of Explanation," *Philosophy of Science*, vol. 15 (1948), pp. 135–175.

4. Keith Lehrer, "Knowledge, Truth, and Evidence," *Analysis*, vol. 25 (1965), pp. 168–175.

5. See also Gilbert H. Harman, "The Inference to the Best Explanation," *The Philosophical Review*, vol. 74 (1965), pp. 88–95.

6. Cf. Henry E. Kyburg, "Probability, Rationality, and a Rule of Detachment" in Brouwer *et. al.* (eds.), *Proceedings of the 1964 Congress on Logic, Methodology, and the Philosophy of Science* (Amsterdam, North Holland Publishing Co., 1965), and references therein. I shall not discuss Kyburg's own solution, since he retains inductive detachment at the expense of deduction. For him one cannot in general infer deductive consequences of what one accepts.

7. An explanation of the maximum likelihood principle with further references appears in Ian Hacking, *Logic of Statistical Inference* (Cambridge, Cambridge University Press, 1965).

8. The Bayesian position is forcefully presented in Richard Jeffrey, *The Logic of Decision* (New York, McGraw Hill, 1965). The maximum likelihood principle is defended against the Bayesians in Hacking, *op. cit.*

9. C. G. Hempel, "Aspects of Scientific Explanation" in his *Aspects of Scientific Explanation and Other Essays in the Philosophy of Science* (New York, The Free Press, 1965), esp. pp. 376–412.

10. Why "social"? Can there be relevant evidence no one knows, has know n, or will know about? I doubt it. In the example it is important that people have heard the denials. If they had been spoken into a dead microphone, I believe Tom would not be deprived of knowledge in the way he is by everyone's knowing about the denials.

11. Apparently the social aspect of knowledge fails to provide a counter-example to the empiricist analysis of knowledge. Suppose we represent that aspect by the claim that the following condition is necessary for knowledge, where the condition is stated quite roughly and where we agree that there are serious problems in giving a precise formulation of the condition.

(1) No further evidence exists that would, if known, cast doubt on one's conclusion. Ernest Sosa mentions a similar condition in his article, "The Analysis of 'Knowledge That P'," *Analysis* 25.1 (1964), pp. 1–8 (see condition (oj_3). Sosa also mentions another condition (sj_5) which I would express as follows:

(2) One must be justified in not believing that (1) is false.

To account for (2) we need only assume that the inference on which belief is based (if nondeductive) requires (1) as premiss or lemma. Furthermore the social aspect of knowledge then becomes a special case of the condition that the lemmas be true. Therefore, the social aspect of knowledge does not provide a counter-example to the empiricist analysis, indeed it is even to be explained in terms of that analysis along with (2).

✧ THE CAUSAL THEORY ✧

13. A CAUSAL THEORY OF KNOWING*

Alvin Goldman

Since Edmund L. Gettier reminded us recently of a certain important inadequacy of the traditional analysis of "S knows that *p*," several attempts have been made to correct that analysis.[1] In this paper I shall offer still another analysis (or a sketch of an analysis) of "S knows that *p*," one which will avert Gettier's problem. My concern will be with knowledge of empirical propositions only, since I think that the traditional analysis is adequate for knowledge of nonempirical truths.

Consider an abbreviated version of Gettier's second counterexample to the traditional analysis. Smith believes

q. Jones owns a Ford

and has very strong evidence for it. Smith's evidence might be that Jones has owned a Ford for many years and that Jones has just offered Smith a ride while driving a Ford. Smith has another friend, Brown, of whose whereabouts he is totally ignorant. Choosing a town quite at random, however, Smith constructs the proposition

p. Either Jones owns a Ford or Brown is in Barcelona.

Seeing that *q* entails *p*, Smith infers that *p* is true. Since he has adequate evidence for *q*, he also has adequate evidence for *p*. But now suppose that Jones does *not* own a Ford (he was driving a rented car when he offered Smith a ride), but, quite by coincidence,

Brown happens to be in Barcelona. This means that *p* is true, that Smith believes *p*, and that Smith has adequate evidence for *p*. But Smith not know *p*.

A variety of hypotheses might be made to account for Smith's not knowing *p*. Michael Clark, for example, points to the fact that *q* is false, and suggests this as the reason why Smith cannot be said to know *p*. Generalizing from this case, Clark argues that, for *S* to know a proposition, each of *S*'s grounds for it must be *true*, as well as his grounds for his grounds, etc.[2] I shall make another hypothesis to account for the fact that Smith cannot be said to know *p*, and I shall generalize this into a new analysis of "*S* knows that *p*."

Notice that what *makes p* true is the fact that Brown is in Barcelona, but that this fact has nothing to do with Smith's believing *p*. That is, there is no *causal* connection between the fact that Brown is in Barcelona and Smith's believing *p*. If Smith had come to believe *p* by reading a letter from Brown postmarked in Barcelona, then we might say that Smith knew *p*. Alternatively, if Jones did own a Ford, and his owning the Ford was manifested by his offer of a ride to Smith, and this in turn resulted in Smith's believing *p*, then we would say that Smith knew *p*. Thus, one thing that seems to be missing in this example is a causal connection between the fact that makes *p* true [or simply: the fact that *p*] and Smith's belief of *p*. The requirement of such a *causal connection* is what I wish to add to the traditional analysis.

To see that this requirement is satisfied in all cases of (empirical) knowledge, we must examine a variety of such causal connections. Clearly, only a sketch of the important kinds of cases is possible here.

Perhaps the simplest case of a causal chain connecting some fact *p* with someone's belief of *p* is that of *perception*. I wish to espouse a version of the causal theory of perception, in essence that defended by H. P. Grice.[3] Suppose that *S* sees that there is a vase in front of him. How is this to be analyzed? I shall not attempt a complete analysis of this, but a necessary condition of *S*'s seeing that there is a vase in front of him is that there be a certain kind of causal connection between the presence of the vase and *S*'s believing that a vase is present. I shall not attempt to describe this causal process in detail. Indeed, to a large extent, a description of this process

must be regarded as a problem for the special sciences, not for philosophy. But a certain causal process—viz. that which standardly takes place when we say that so-and-so *sees* such-and-such—must occur. That our ordinary concept of sight (i.e., knowledge acquired by sight) includes a causal requirement is shown by the fact that if the relevant causal process is absent we would withhold the assertion that so-and-so *saw* such-and-such. Suppose that, although a vase is directly in front of *S*, a laser photograph[4] is interposed between it and *S*, thereby blocking it from *S*'s view. The photograph, however, is one of a vase (a different vase), and when it is illuminated by light waves from a laser, it looks to *S* exactly like a real vase. When the photograph is illuminated, *S* forms the belief that there is a vase in front of him. Here we would deny that *S* sees that there is a vase in front of him, for his view of the real vase is completely blocked, so that it has no causal role in the formation of his belief. Of course, *S* might *know* that there was a vase in front of him even if the photograph is blocking his view. Someone else, in a position to see the vase, might tell *S* that there is a vase in front of him. Here the presence of the vase might be a causal ancestor of *S*'s belief, but the causal process would not be a (purely) *perceptual* one. *S* could not be said to *see* that there is a vase in front of him. For this to be true, there must be a causal process, but one of a very special sort, connecting the presence of the vase with *S*'s belief.

I shall here assume that perceptual knowledge of facts is noninferential. This is merely a simplifying procedure, and not essential to my account. Certainly a percipient does not *infer* facts about physical objects from the state of his brain or from the stimulation of his sense organs. He need not know about these goings-on at all. But some epistemologists maintain that we directly perceive only sense data and that we infer physical-object facts from them. This view could be accommodated within my analysis. I could say that physical-object facts cause sense data, that people directly perceive sense data, and that they infer the physical object facts from the sense data. This kind of process would be fully accredited by my analysis, which will allow for knowledge based on inference. But for purposes of exposition it will be convenient to regard perceptual knowledge of external facts as independent of any inference.

Here the question arises about the *scope* of perceptual knowledge. By perception I can know noninferentially that there is a vase in front of me. But can I know noninferentially that the painting I am viewing is a Picasso? It is unnecessary to settle such issues here. Whether the knowledge of such facts is to be classed as inferential or noninferential, my analysis can account for it. So the scope of noninferential knowledge may be left indeterminate.

I turn next to memory, i.e., knowledge that is based, in part, on memory. Remembering, like perceiving, must be regarded as a causal process. S remembers p at time t only if S's believing p at an earlier time is a cause of his believing p at t. Of course, not every causal connection between an earlier belief and a later one is a case of remembering. As in the case of perception, however, I shall not try to describe this process in detail. This is a job mainly for the scientist. Instead, the kind of causal process in question is to be identified simply by example, by "pointing" to paradigm cases of remembering. Whenever causal processes are of that kind—whatever that kind is, precisely—they are cases of remembering.[5]

A causal connection between earlier belief (or knowledge) of p and later belief (knowledge) of p is certainly a necessary ingredient in memory.[6] To remember a fact is not simply to believe it at t_0 and also to believe it at t_1. Nor does someone's knowing a fact at t_0 and his knowing it at t_1 entail that he remembers it at t_1. He may have perceived the fact at t_0, forgotten it, and then relearned it at t_1 by someone's telling it to him. Nor does the inclusion of a memory "impression"—a feeling of remembering—ensure that one really remembers. Suppose S perceives p at t_0, but forgets it at t_1. At t_2 he begins to believe p again because someone tells him p, but at t_2 he has no memory impression of p. At t_3 we artificially stimulate in S a memory impression of p. It does not follow that S remembers p at t_3. The description of the case suggests that his believing p at t_0 has no causal effect whatever on his believing p at t_3; and if we accepted this fact, we would deny that he remembers p at t_3.

Knowledge can be acquired by a combination of perception and memory. At t_0, the fact p causes S to believe p, by perception. S's believing p at t_0 results, via memory, in S's believing p at t_1. Thus, the fact p is a cause of S's believing p at t_1, and S can be said to know

p at t_1. But not all knowledge results from perception and memory alone. In particular, much knowledge is based on *inference*.

As I shall use the term 'inference', to say that S knows p by "inference" does not entail that S went through an explicit, conscious process of reasoning. It is not necessary that he have "talked to himself," saying something like "Since such-and-such is true, p must also be true." My belief that there is a fire in the neighborhood is based on, or inferred from, my belief that I hear a fire engine. But I have not gone through a process of explicit reasoning, saying "There's a fire engine; therefore there must be a fire." Perhaps the word 'inference' is ordinarily used only where explicit reasoning occurs; if so, my use of the term will be somewhat broader than its ordinary use.

Suppose S perceives that there is solidified lava in various parts of the countryside. On the basis of this belief, plus various "background" beliefs about the production of lava, S concludes that a nearby mountain erupted many centuries ago. Let us assume that this is a highly warranted inductive inference, one which gives S adequate evidence for believing that the mountain did erupt many centuries ago. Assuming this proposition is true, does S know it? This depends on the nature of the causal process that induced his belief. If there is a continuous causal chain of the sort he envisages connecting the fact that the mountain erupted with his belief of this fact, then S knows it. If there is no such causal chain, however, S does not know that proposition.

Suppose that the mountain erupts, leaving lava around the countryside. The lava remains there until S perceives it and infers that the mountain erupted. Then S does know that the mountain erupted. But now suppose that, after the mountain has erupted, a man somehow removes all the lava. A century later, a different man (not knowing of the real volcano) decides to make it look as if there had been a volcano, and therefore puts lava in appropriate places. Still later, S comes across this lava and concludes that the mountain erupted centuries ago. In this case, S cannot be said to know the proposition. This is because the fact that the mountain did erupt is not a cause of S's believing that it erupted. A necessary condition of S's knowing p is that his believing p be connected with p by a causal chain.

In the first case, where S knows p, the causal connection may be diagrammed as in Figure 1. (p) is the

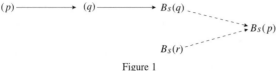

Figure 1

fact that the mountain erupted at such-and-such a time. (q) is the fact that lava is (now) present around the countryside. 'B' stands for a belief, the expression in parentheses indicating the proposition believed, and the subscript designating the believer. (r) is a "background" proposition, describing the ways in which lava is produced and how it solidifies. Solid arrows in the diagram represent causal connections; dotted arrows represent inferences. Notice that, in Figure 1, there is not only an arrow connecting (q) with S's belief of (q), but also an arrow connecting (p) with (q). In the suggested variant of the lava case, the latter arrow would be missing, showing that there is no continuous causal chain connecting (p) with S's belief of (p). Therefore, in that variant case, S could not be said to know (p).

I have said that p is causally connected to S's belief of p, in the case diagrammed in Figure 1. This raises the question, however, of whether the inferential part of the chain is itself a causal chain. In other words, is S's belief of q a cause of his believing p? This is a question to which I shall not try to give a definitive answer here. I am inclined to say that inference *is* a causal process, that is, that when someone *bases* his belief of one proposition on his belief of a set of other propositions, then his belief of the latter propositions can be considered a cause of his belief of the former proposition. But I do not wish to rest my thesis on this claim. All I do claim is that, if a chain of inferences is "added" to a causal chain, then the entire chain is causal. In terms of our diagram, a chain consisting of solid arrows plus dotted arrows is to be considered a causal chain, though I shall not take a position on the question of whether the dotted arrows represent causal connections. Thus, in Figure 1, p is a cause of S's belief of p, whether or not we regard S's belief of q a cause of his belief of p.[7]

Consider next a case of knowledge based on "testimony." This too can be analyzed causally. p causes a person T to believe p, by perception. T's belief of p gives rise to (causes) his asserting p. T's asserting p causes S, by auditory perception, to believe that T is

asserting p. S infers that T believes p, and from this, in turn, he infers that p is a fact. There is a continuous causal chain from p to S's believing p, and thus, assuming that each of S's inferences is warranted, S can be said to know p.

This causal chain is represented in Figure 2. 'A' refers to an act of asserting a proposition, the expression in parentheses indicating the proposition asserted and the subscript designating the agent. (q), (r), (u), and (v) are background propositions. (q) and (r), for example, pertain to T's sincerity; they help S conclude, from the fact that T asserted p, that T really believes p.

In this case, as in the lava case, S knows p because he has correctly reconstructed the causal chain leading from p to the evidence for p that S perceives, in this case, T's asserting (p). This correct reconstruction is shown in the diagram by S's inference "mirroring" the rest of the causal chain. Such a correct reconstruction is a necessary condition of knowledge based on inference. To see this, consider the following example. A newspaper reporter observes p and reports it to his newspaper. When printed, however, the story contains a typographical error so that it asserts not-p. When reading the paper, however, S fails to see the word 'not', and takes the paper to have asserted p. Trusting the newspaper, he infers that p is true. Here we have a continuous causal chain leading from p to S's believing p; yet S does not know p S thinks that p resulted in a report to the newspaper about p and that this report resulted in its printing the statement p. Thus, his reconstruction of the causal chain is mistaken. But, if he is to know p, his reconstruction must contain no mistakes. Though he need not reconstruct *every* detail of the causal chain, he must reconstruct all the important links.[8] An additional requirement for knowledge based on inference is that the knower's inferences be warranted. That is, the propositions on which he bases his belief of p must genuinely confirm p very highly,

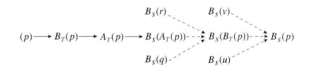

Figure 2

whether deductively or inductively. Reconstructing a causal chain merely by lucky guesses does not yield knowledge.

With the help of our diagrams, we can contrast the traditional analysis of knowing with Clark's analysis (*op. cit.*) and contrast each of these with my own analysis. The traditional analysis makes reference to just three features of the diagrams. First, it requires that p be true; i.e., that (p) appear in the diagram. Secondly, it requires that S believe p; i.e., that S's belief of p appear in the diagram. Thirdly, it requires that S's inferences, if any, be warranted; i.e., that the sets of beliefs that are at the tail of a dotted arrow must jointly highly confirm the belief at the head of these arrows. Clark proposes a further requirement for knowledge. He requires that *each* of the beliefs in S's chain of inference be *true*. In other words, whereas the traditional analysis requires a fact to correspond to S's belief of p, Clark requires that a fact correspond to *each* of S's beliefs on which he based his belief of p. Thus, corresponding to each belief on the right side of the diagram there must be a fact on the left side. (My diagrams omit facts corresponding to the "background" beliefs.)

As Clark's analysis stands, it seems to omit an element of the diagrams that my analysis requires, viz., the arrows indicating causal connections. Now Clark might reformulate his analysis so as to make implicit reference to these causal connections. If he required that the knower's beliefs include *causal beliefs* (of the relevant sort), then his requirement that these beliefs be true would amount to the requirement that there *be* causal chains of the sort I require. This interpretation of Clark's analysis would make it almost equivalent to mine, and would enable him to avoid some objections that have been raised against him. But he has not explicitly formulated his analysis this way, and it therefore remains deficient in this respect.

Before turning to the problems facing Clark's analysis, more must be said about my own analysis. So far, my examples may have suggested that, if S knows p, the fact that p is a cause of his belief of p. This would clearly be wrong, however. Let us grant that I can know facts about the future. Then, if we required that the known fact cause the knower's belief, we would have to countenance "backward" causation. My analysis, however, does not face this dilemma. The analysis requires

that there be a causal *connection* between p and S's belief, not necessarily that p be a *cause* of S's belief. p and S's belief of p can also be causally connected in a way that yields knowledge if both p and S's belief of p have a *common* cause. This can be illustrated as follows.

T intends to go downtown on Monday. On Sunday, T tells S of his intention. Hearing T say he will go downtown, S infers that T really does intend to go downtown. And from this S concludes that T *will* go downtown on Monday. Now suppose that T fulfills his intention by going downtown on Monday. Can S be said to know that he would go downtown? If we ever can be said to have knowledge of the future, this is a reasonable candidate for it. So let us say S did know that proposition. How can my analysis account for S's knowledge? T's going downtown on Monday clearly cannot be a cause of S's believing, on Sunday, that he would go downtown. But there is a fact that is the *common* cause of T's going downtown and of S's belief that he would go downtown, viz., T's intending (on Sunday) to go downtown. This intention resulted in his going downtown and also resulted in S's believing that he would go downtown. This causal connection between S's belief and the fact believed allows us to say that S *knew* that T would go downtown.

The example is diagrammed in Figure 3. (p) = T's going downtown on Monday. (q) = T's intending (on Sunday) to go downtown on Monday. (r) = T's telling S (on Sunday) that he will go downtown on Monday. (u) and (v) are relevant background propositions pertaining to T's honesty, resoluteness, etc. The diagram reveals that q is a cause both of p and of S's belief of p. Cases of

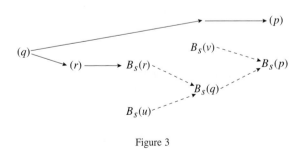

Figure 3

this kind I shall call *Pattern 2* cases of knowledge. Figures 1 and 2 exemplify *Pattern 1* cases of knowledge.

Notice that the causal connection between q and p is an essential part of S's knowing p. Suppose, for example, that T's intending (on Sunday) to go downtown does not result in, or cause, T's going downtown on Monday. Suppose that T, after telling S that he would go downtown, changes his mind. Nevertheless, on Monday he is kidnapped and forced, at the point of a gun, to go downtown. Here both q and p actually occur, but they are not causally related. The diagram in Figure 3 would have to be amended by deleting the arrow connecting (q) with (p). But if the rest of the facts of the original case remain the same, S could not be said to know p. It would be false to say that S knew, on Sunday, that T would go downtown on Monday.

Pattern 2 cases of knowledge are not restricted to knowledge of the future. I know that smoke was coming out of my chimney last night. I know this because I remember perceiving a fire in my fireplace last night, and I infer that the fire caused smoke to rise out of the chimney. This case exemplifies Pattern 2. The smoke's rising out of the chimney is not a causal factor of my belief. But the fact that there was a fire in the fireplace was a cause both of my belief that smoke was coming out of the chimney and of the fact that smoke was coming out of the chimney. If we supplement this case slightly, we can make my knowledge exemplify *both* Pattern 1 and Pattern 2. Suppose that a friend tells me today that he perceived smoke coming out of my chimney last night and I base my continued belief of this fact on his testimony. Then the fact was a cause of my current belief of it, as well as an *effect* of another fact that caused my belief. In general, numerous and diverse kinds of causal connections can obtain between a given fact and a given person's belief of that fact.

Let us now examine some objections to Clark's analysis and see how the analysis presented here fares against them. John Turk Saunders and Narayan Champawat have raised the following counterexample to Clark's analysis:[10]

Suppose that Smith believes (p) Jones owns a Ford because his friend Brown whom he knows to be generally reliable and honest yesterday told Smith that Jones had always owned a Ford.

Brown's information was correct, but today Jones sells his Ford and replaces it with a Volkswagen. An hour later Jones is pleased to find that he is the proud owner of two cars: he has been lucky enough to win a Ford in a raffle. Smith's belief in p is not only justified and true, but is fully grounded, e.g., we suppose that each link in the . . . chain of Smith's grounds is true (8).

Clearly Smith does not know p; yet he seems to satisfy Clark's analysis of knowing.

Smith's lack of knowledge can be accounted for in terms of my analysis. Smith does not know p because his believing p is not causally related to p, Jones's owning a Ford *now*. This can be seen by examining Figure 4. In the diagram, (p) = Jones's owning a Ford now; (q) = Jones's having always owned a Ford (until yesterday); (r) = Jones's winning a Ford in a raffle today. (t), (u), and (v) are background propositions. (v), for example, deals with the likelihood of someone's continuing to own the same car today that he owned yesterday. The subscript 'B' designates Brown, and the subscript 'S' designates Smith. Notice the absence of an arrow connecting (p) with (q). The absence of this arrow represents the absence of a causal relation between (q) and (p). Jones's owning a Ford in the past (until yesterday) is not a cause of his owning one now. Had he continued owning the same Ford today that he owned yesterday, there would be a causal connection between q and p and, therefore, a causal connection between p and Smith's believing p. This causal connection would exemplify Pattern 2. But, as it happened, it is purely a coincidence that Jones owns a Ford today as well as yesterday. Thus, Smith's belief of p is not connected with p by Pattern 2, nor is there any Pattern 1 connection between them. Hence, Smith does not know p.

If we supplement Clark's analysis as suggested above, it can be saved from this counterexample. Though Saunders and Champawat fail to mention this explicitly, presumably it is one of Smith's be-

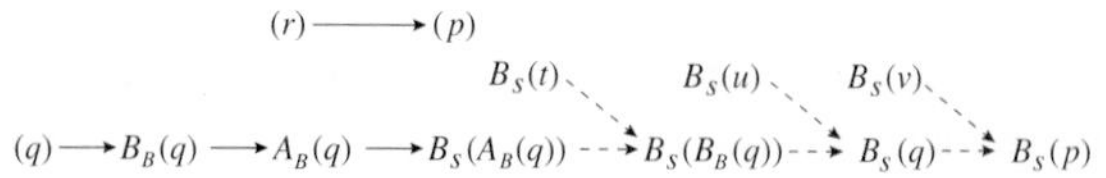

$$(r) \longrightarrow (p)$$
$$B_S(t) \quad\quad B_S(u) \quad\quad B_S(v)$$
$$(q) \longrightarrow B_B(q) \longrightarrow A_B(q) \longrightarrow B_S(A_B(q)) \dashrightarrow B_S(B_B(q)) \dashrightarrow B_S(q) \dashrightarrow B_S(p)$$

Figure 4

liefs that Jones's owning a Ford yesterday would *result* in Jones's owning a Ford now. This was undoubtedly one of his grounds for believing that Jones owns a Ford now. (A complete diagram of S's beliefs relevant to *p* would include this belief.) Since this belief is false, however, Clark's analysis would yield the correct consequence that Smith does not know *p*. Unfortunately, Clark himself seems not to have noticed this point, since Saunders and Champawat's putative counterexample has been allowed to stand.

Another sort of counterexample to Clark's analysis has been given by Saunders and Champawat and also by Keith Lehrer. This is a counterexample from which his analysis cannot escape. I shall give Lehrer's example (*op. cit.*) of this sort of difficulty. Suppose Smith bases his belief of

p. Someone in his office owns a Ford on his belief of four propositions

q. Jones owns a Ford

r. Jones works in his office

s. Brown owns a Ford

t. Brown works in his office

In fact, Smith knows *q*, *r*, and *t*, but he does not know *s* because *s* is false. Since *s* is false, not *all* of Smith's grounds for *p* are true, and, therefore, on Clark's analysis, Smith does not know *p*. Yet clearly Smith does know *p*. Thus, Clark's analysis is *too strong*.

Having seen the importance of a causal chain for knowing, it is fairly obvious how to amend Clark's requirements without making them too weak. We need not require, as Clark does, that *all* of S's grounds be true. What is required is that enough of them be true to ensure the existence of at least *one* causal connection between *p* and S's belief of *p*. In Lehrer's example, Smith thinks that there are two ways in which he knows *p*: via his knowledge of the conjunction of *q* and *r*, and via his knowledge of the conjunction of *s* and *t*. He does not know *p* via the conjunction of *s* and *t*, since *s* is false. But there is a causal connection, via *q* and *r*, between *p* and Smith's belief of *p*. And this connection is enough.

Another sort of case in which one of S's grounds for *p* may be false without preventing him from knowing *p* is where the false proposition is a dispensable background assumption. Suppose S bases his belief of *p* on 17 background assumptions, but only 16 of these are true. If these 16 are strong enough to confirm *p*, then the 17th is dispensable. S can be said to know *p* though one of his grounds is false.

Our discussion of Lehrer's example calls attention to the necessity of a further clarification of the notion of a "causal chain." I said earlier that causal chains with admixtures of inferences are causal chains. Now I wish to add that causal chains with admixtures of logical connections are causal chains. Unless we allow this interpretation, it is hard to see how facts like "Someone in the office owns a Ford" or "All men are mortal" could be *causally* connected with beliefs thereof.

The following principle will be useful: *If x is logically related to y and if y is a cause of x, then x is a cause of x.* Thus, suppose that *q* causes S's belief of *q* and that *r* causes S's belief of *r*. Next suppose that S infers *q & r* from his belief of *q* and of *r*. Then the facts *q* and *r* are causes of S's believing *q & r*. But the fact *q & r* is logically related to the fact *q* and to the fact *r*. Therefore, using the principle enunciated above, the fact *q & r* is a cause of S's believing *q & r*.

In Lehrer's case another logical connection is involved: a connection between an existential fact and an instance thereof. Lehrer's case is diagrammed in Figure 5. In addition to the usual conventions, logical relationships are represented by double solid lines. As the diagram shows, the fact *p*—someone in Smith's office owning a Ford—is logically related to the fact *q & r*—Jones's owning a Ford and Jones's working in Smith's office. The fact *q & r* is, in turn, logically related to the fact *q* and to the fact *r*, *q* causes S's belief of *q* and, by inference, his belief of *q & r* and of *p*. Similarly, *r* is a cause of S's belief of *p*. Hence, by the above principle, *p* is a cause of S's belief of *p*. Since Smith's in-

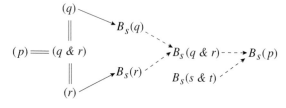

Figure 5

ferences are warranted, even setting aside his belief of *s & t*, he knows *p*.

In a similar way, universal facts may be causes of beliefs thereof. The fact that all men are mortal is logically related to its instances: John's being mortal, George's being mortal, Oscar's being mortal, etc. Now suppose that *S* perceives George, John, Oscar, etc. to be mortal (by seeing them die). He infers from these facts that all men are mortal, an inference which, I assume, is warranted. Since each of the facts, John is mortal, George is mortal, Oscar is mortal, etc., is a cause of *S*'s believing that fact, each is also a cause of *S*'s believing that all men are mortal. Moreover, since the universal fact that all men are mortal is logically related to each of these particular facts, this universal fact is a cause of *S*'s belief of it. Hence, *S* can be said to know that all men are mortal. In analogous fashions, *S* can know various other logically compound propositions.

We can now formulate the analysis of knowing as follows:

S knows that p if and only if *the fact p is causally connected in an "appropriate" way with S's believing p*.

"Appropriate," knowledge-producing causal processes include the following:

1. perception
2. memory
3. a causal chain, exemplifying either Pattern 1 or 2, which is correctly reconstructed by inferences, each of which is warranted (background propositions help warrant an inference only if they are true)[11]
4. combinations of (1), (2), and (3)

We have seen that this analysis is *stronger* than the traditional analysis in certain respects: the causal requirement and the correct reconstruction requirement are absent from the older analysis. These additional requirements enable my analysis to circumvent Gettier's counterexamples to the traditional one. But my analysis is *weaker* than the traditional analysis in another respect. In at least one popular interpretation of the traditional analysis, a knower must be able to justify or give evidence for

any proposition he knows. For *S* to know *p* at *t*, *S* must be able, at *t*, to *state* his justification for believing *p*, or his grounds for *p*. My analysis makes no such requirement, and the absence of this requirement enables me to account for cases of knowledge that would wrongly be excluded by the traditional analysis.

I know now, for example, that Abraham Lincoln was born in 1809.[12] I originally came to know this fact, let us suppose, by reading an encyclopedia article. I believed that this encyclopedia was trustworthy and that its saying Lincoln was born in 1809 must have resulted from the fact that Lincoln was indeed born in 1809. Thus, my original knowledge of this fact was founded on a warranted inference. But now I no longer remember this inference. I remember that Lincoln was born in 1809, but not that this is stated in a certain encyclopedia. I no longer have any pertinent beliefs that highly confirm the proposition that Lincoln was born in 1809. Nevertheless, I know this proposition now. My original knowledge of it was preserved until now by the causal process of memory.

Defenders of the traditional analysis would doubtlessly deny that I really do know Lincoln's birth year. This denial, however, stems from a desire to protect their analysis. It seems clear that many things we know were originally learned in a way that we no longer remember. The range of our knowledge would be drastically reduced if these items were denied the status of knowledge.

Other species of knowledge without explicit evidence could also be admitted by my analysis. Notice that I have not closed the list of "appropriate" causal processes. Leaving the list open is desirable, because there may be some presently controversial causal processes that we may later deem "appropriate" and, therefore, knowledge-producing. Many people now doubt the legitimacy of claims to extrasensory perception. But if conclusive evidence were to establish the existence of causal processes connecting physical facts with certain persons' beliefs without the help of standard perceptual processes, we might decide to call such beliefs items of knowledge. This would be another species of knowledge in which the knower might be unable to justify or defend his belief. My analysis allows for the possibility of such knowledge, though it doesn't commit one to it.

Special comments are in order about knowledge of our own mental states. This is a very difficult and controversial topic, so I hesitate to discuss it, but something must be said about it. Probably there are some mental states that are clearly distinct from the subject's belief that he is in such a state. If so, then there is presumably a causal process connecting the existence of such states with the subject's belief thereof. We may add this kind of process to the list of "appropriate" causal processes. The more difficult cases are those in which the state is hardly distinguishable from the subject's believing that he is in that state. My being in pain and my believing that I am in pain are hardly distinct states of affairs. If there is no distinction here between the believing and the believed, how can there be a causal connection between them? For the purposes of the present analysis, we may regard identity as a "limiting" or "degenerate" case of a causal connection, just as zero may be regarded as a "limiting" or "degenerate" case of a number. It is not surprising that knowledge of one's own mental state should turn out to be a limiting or degenerate case of knowledge. Philosophers have long recognized its peculiar status. While some philosophers have regarded it as a paradigm case of knowledge, others have claimed that we have no "knowledge" of our mental states at all. A theory of knowledge that makes knowledge of one's own mental states rather different from garden-variety species of knowledge is, in so far forth, acceptable and even welcome.

In conclusion, let me answer some possible objections to my analysis. It might be doubted whether a causal analysis adequately provides the meaning of the word 'knows' or of the sentence (-schema) "S knows p." But I am not interested in giving the *meaning* of "S knows p"; only its *truth conditions*. I claim to have given one correct set of truth conditions for "S knows p." Truth conditions of a sentence do not always provide its meaning. Consider, for example, the following truth-conditions statement: "The sentence 'Team T wins the baseball game' is true if and only if team T has more runs at the end of the game than the opposing team." This statement fails to provide the meaning of the sentence 'Team T wins the baseball game'; for it fails to indicate an essential part of the meaning of that sentence, viz.,

that to win a game is to achieve the presumed goal of playing it. Someone might fully understand the truth conditions given above and yet fail to understand the meaning of the sentence because he has no understanding of the notion of "winning" in general.

Truth conditions should not be confused with verification conditions. My analysis of "S knows p" does not purport to give procedures for *finding out* whether a person (including oneself) knows a given proposition. No doubt, we sometimes do know that people know certain propositions, for we sometimes know that their beliefs are causally connected (in appropriate ways) with the facts believed. On the other hand, it may often be difficult or even impossible to find out whether this condition holds for a given proposition and a given person. For example, it may be difficult for me to find out whether I really do remember a certain fact that I seem to remember. The difficulties that exist for *finding out* whether someone knows a given proposition do not constitute difficulties for my analysis, however.

In the same vein it should be noted that I have made no attempt to answer skeptical problems. My analysis gives no answer to the skeptic who asks that I start from the content of my own experience and then prove that I know there is a material world, a past, etc. I do not take this to be one of the jobs of giving truth conditions for "S knows that p."

The analysis presented here flies in the face of a well-established tradition in epistemology, the view that epistemological questions are questions of logic or justification, not causal or genetic questions. This traditional view, however, must not go unquestioned. Indeed, I think my analysis shows that the question of whether someone knows a certain proposition is, in part, a causal question, although, of course, the question of what the correct analysis is of "S knows that p" is not a causal question.

Notes

* I wish to thank members of the University of Michigan Philosophy Department, several of whom made helpful comments on earlier versions of this paper.
1. "Is True Justified Belief Knowledge?" *Analysis*, XXIII.6, ns 96 (June 1963): 121–123. I say "reminded" because

essentially the same point was made by Russell in 1912. Cf. *The Problems of Philosophy* (Oxford, 1912), ch. XIII, pp. 132 ff. New analyses have been proposed by Michael Clark, "Knowledge and Grounds: A Comment on Mr. Gettier's Paper," *Analysis*, XXIV.2, ns 98 (December 1963): 46–48; Ernest Sosa, "The Analysis of 'Knowledge that *p*'," *ibid.*, XXV.1, ns 103 (October 1964): 1–3; and Keith Lehrer, "Knowledge, Truth, and Evidence," *ibid.*, XXV.5, ns 105 (April 1965): 168–175.

2. *Op. cit.* Criticisms of Clark's analysis will be discussed below.

3. "The Causal Theory of Perception," *Proceedings of the Aristotelian Society* supp. vol. XXXV (1961).

4. If a laser photograph (hologram) is illuminated by light waves, especially waves from a laser, the effect of the hologram on the viewer is exactly as if the object were being seen. It preserves three-dimensionality completely, and even gives appropriate parallax effects as the viewer moves relative to it. Cf. E. N. Leith and J. Upatnieks, "Photography by Laser," *Scientific American*, CCXII, 6 (June 1965): 24.

5. For further defense of this kind of procedure, with attention to perception, cf. Grice, *op. cit.*

6. Causal connections can hold between states of affairs, such as believings, as well as between events. If a given event or state, in conjunction with other events or states, "leads to" or "results in" another event or state (or the same state obtaining at a later time), it will be called a "cause" of the latter. I shall also speak of "facts" being causes.

7. A fact can be a cause of a belief even if it does not *initiate* the belief. Suppose I believe that there is a lake in a certain locale, this belief having started in a manner quite unconnected with the existence of the lake. Continuing to have the belief, I go to the locale and perceive the lake. At this juncture, the existence of the lake becomes a cause of my believing that there is a lake there. This is analogous to a table top that is supported by four legs. When a fifth leg is inserted flush beneath the table top, it too becomes a cause of the table top's not falling. It has a causal role in the support of the table top even though, before it was inserted, the table top was adequately supported.

8. Clearly we cannot require someone to reconstruct every detail, since this would involve knowledge of minute physical phenomena, for example, of which ordinary people are unaware. On the other hand, it is difficult to give criteria to identify which details, in general, are "important." This will vary substantially from case to case.

10. "Mr. Clark's Definition of 'Knowledge'," *Analysis*, XXV.1, ns 103 (October 1964): 8–9.

11. Perhaps background propositions that help warrant S's inference must be *known* by S, as well as true. This requirement could be added without making our analysis of "S knows that *p*" circular. For these propositions would not include *p*. In other words, the analysis of knowledge could be regarded as recursive.

12. This kind of case is drawn from an unpublished manuscript of Gilbert Harman.

✧ THE DEFEASIBILITY THEORY ✧

14. KNOWLEDGE IS TRUE, NON-DEFEATED, JUSTIFIED BELIEF*

Peter Klein

The development of a satisfactory definition of propositional knowledge (i.e., knowledge of facts) is essential if an adequate comprehensive theory of knowledge is to become possible. Propositional knowledge is knowing that p, where "p" stands for any proposition whatsoever, e.g., knowing *that* there is a computer screen in front of me, knowing *that* there once were dinosaurs, knowing *that* the sun will rise tomorrow.

Finding a satisfactory definition of propositional knowledge becomes all the more urgent because Edmund Gettier has shown that the attempt to develop such a definition of propositional knowledge within the traditional threefold conditions (true, justified, belief) is not possible and subsequent attempts to solve the "Gettier Problem" have not produced a widely accepted solution.[1]

In this paper, I will put forth a definition of propositional knowledge and defend it. I think this definition makes a satisfactory epistemology possible because it satisfies the two *desiderata* of a successful definition, namely, it captures the essential intuitions that inform our concept of knowledge, and it remains neutral in the conflict between various rival epistemological theories. The first *desideratum* requires no defense. The second one, however, might not be so obvious. Neutrality is a highly desirable feature, for if one theory were to claim that a certain type of proposition is not a proper object of knowledge, and another theory were to argue that such a proposition is a proper object of knowledge, both theories must mean the same thing by propositional knowledge if their disagreement is to be genuine. For example, if knowledge were defined in such a way that a proposition is known only if it is *entailed* by propositions expressing only the content of how things appear to us, a fruitful dialogue between a skeptic and non-skeptic would not be possible because the definition cuts so heavily in favor of the skeptic. Most, if not all, of our knowledge of the world (if, indeed there really is such knowledge) is not based upon exclusively deductive reasoning from propositions expressing the content of our sense-experience. On the other hand, if knowledge were defined as mere true belief, then skepticism would not have a foothold in the debate with the non-skeptic because mere true belief is so easy to stumble upon.

The relevant use of "knowledge" that I am seeking to define occurs in the following paragraph quoted from *Theory of Knowledge* by Chisholm:

> In Plato's dialogue the *Meno* Socrates remarks: "That there is a difference between right opinion and knowledge is not at all a conjecture with me but something I would particularly assert that I know. There are not many things of which I would say that, but this one, at any rate, I will include

among those that I know." [97C] The distinction would seem to be obvious. If one has knowledge, then one also has right or true opinion. But the converse is not true: one may have right or true opinion without having knowledge. Thus, we may guess correctly today, and therefore, have true opinion, but not know until tomorrow. Or we may have true opinion *and* never know at all.[2]

Ernest Sosa quotes Russell as saying:

> It is very easy . . . to give examples of true beliefs that are not knowledge. There is the man who looks at a clock which is not going though he thinks it is and who happens to look at it at the moment when it is right; this man acquires a true belief about the time of the day but cannot be said to have knowledge.[3]

I cite these examples not only to illustrate the relevant use of 'S knows that p,' but also to underscore the point that propositional knowledge must not be equated with accidentally correct belief. In addition to the passage already cited from the *Meno* Plato appeals to the intuition that knowledge cannot result from mere cognitive good luck in the *Theaetetus*.[4] Descartes proposes methods for acquiring beliefs that would (he thinks) necessarily lead to truth,[5] Locke suggests that even if persons arrive at a true belief by accident, they are not thereby free from criticism.[6]

The traditional way of attempting to eliminate epistemic luck was to require that the true belief be acquired through a satisfactory process of reasoning. If my reasoning was good and I arrived at the truth, then it was not a matter of luck—or so it was thought. The traditional definition of propositional knowledge was this:

A person, S, knows that p if and only if:

1. p is true;
2. S believes p (to a sufficiently strong degree);
3. S is justified in believing that p on the basis of adequately good reasoning.[7]

As Gettier demonstrated, there are clear and convincing counterexamples to the traditional definition that show that this account of knowledge is inadequate to eliminate important kinds of epistemic luck, but before discussing them it would be useful to make a few comments on the second and third conditions of the traditional definition of knowledge.

How strongly must a person believe something before they can truly be said to know it? Some have argued that it is not even necessary for the person to consciously endorse the proposition at all. Suppose that on a multiple choice test I am asked when Queen Victoria died and I claim that I have no inkling when she died, but I circle the correct answer. Suppose further that I circle the correct answers to many questions about the dates of many events in her lifetime. Some would claim that I know the answers although I mistakenly believe that I am just guessing.[8] Others have claimed that knowledge entails absolutely settled belief—belief such that no belief could be stronger.[9] Who is right? How strongly do I have to endorse a proposition, p, in order to know that p?

I do not think that there is a clear answer here because of the varied and wide applications of "know." But that should not bother us here anymore than it should bother us that in order to define a good automobile we would have to include a requirement that it is powerful—to a sufficiently strong degree. Let the circumstances dictate what degree of power is required. If we will be driving only in Flatsville, an engine that is not sufficiently powerful in Mountainsville could suffice. There is no problem in leaving the belief-condition flexible enough to handle varying requirements on the strength of belief required in order to have knowledge.

Now to the third condition. As I mentioned above, the prevailing traditional approach relied on the quality of the reasoning to insure that knowledge is not merely true belief resulting from epistemic good luck.[10] The third condition requires that S's reasoning be sufficiently good so that the belief is justified. Just as philosophers differed on the required strength of belief, they have also differed on the required probative force of the reasoning. Some have required that the reasoning must absolutely settle whether p is true. They have required that the propositions that serve as the reasons be self-evident or beyond doubt and that the inferences from those propositions to p be deductive.[11] Others have been less stringent.[12] Let us take the same approach we used

with regard to the second condition: There is probably no one, correct standard of rigor that encompasses all cases of knowledge. In math, for example, deductive reasoning is the norm. But it seems that in "ordinary life" we can come to know something on less than certain evidence and on reasoning that is less than absolutely truth preserving. For example, it seems that I can come to know that my car will stop when I step on the brakes on less than self-evident truths and on less than exclusively deductively valid reasoning. Of course, as mentioned above, if we are to leave room for skepticism, our definition must leave open the possibility that knowledge can only be gained through deduction. We should grant that standards vary and that on some occasions it seems that I can come to know something on the basis of reasoning that is less than absolutely truth preserving. Indeed, we can grant that there are contextual constraints on the amount of evidence required for a proposition to be known. For example, in "ordinary life" citing various encyclopedia articles seems to suffice as good enough evidence for the claim that there are black holes, whereas at the World Astronomical Meeting such evidence will not suffice. Just as condition (2) was written in such a way as to permit the appropriate flexibility, condition (3) is able to accommodate various degrees of stringency. If it didn't, the *desideratum* of neutrality could not be obtained.

So let us stipulate that there are contextually sensitive standards that determine when a proposition has sufficiently good evidence for it to be counted, *ceteris paribus*, as an instance of knowledge. The crucial thing to note here is that p can be justified by some evidence, say e, but that there could be some further evidence that when combined with e defeats the justification. For example, I could justifiably believe that Mr. Seeming Guilty committed the crime on the basis of very good evidence, but later learn that he didn't commit the crime because there is some further evidence that exonerates him. Let us say that a proposition, p, is justified for S on the basis of some evidence, e, just in case the reasoning from e to p satisfies the contextually determined criteria for good reasoning and S has no sufficiently strong countervailing reason which is such that added to e would not satisfy the contextually deter-mined criteria. For example, S would be justified in believing that it was 5 P.M. whenever he believed his watch indicated that time, he believed that it had been reliable in the past, he remembered winding it recently and it appeared to be running.[13]

But because e defeasibly warrants the proposition that it is 5 p.m. and does not strictly imply p (e could be true and p false) there could be a highly unlikely, felici-tous coincidence such that both e is true and p is true, but S's belief is still too much a matter of epistemic luck for it to be counted as knowledge. Suppose that it is 5 p.m., but also that the watch had not worked for 24 hours (the second hand moved when S turned his wrist to look at the watch); S would not know that it was 5 P.M. even though that belief is true and justified.[14]

This is a telling counterexample to the traditional definition of knowledge because it shows that such an account cannot sufficiently rule out epistemic luck. It is merely a felicitous coincidence that S's belief is correct that it is 5 p.m. *Normally*, the evidence that S has would be sufficient to certify his belief as knowledge (if it is 5 P.M.). What is important here is that in these *special* circumstances it is merely a felicitous coinci-dence that his belief is correct.

This could be formulated in terms of a general principle which I will call the *Felicitous Coincidence Principle*.

Felicitous Coincidence Principle: Even if S's evi-dence for p is sufficient to justify the belief that p, it is not sufficient to generate knowledge whenev-er there is some true proposition which, if S were to conjoin it with the evidence for p, would no longer justify S in believing that p.

It may be thought that felicitous coincidences could be avoided by requiring that the set of proposi-tions which justifies p may neither contain a false proposition nor justify any false proposition.[15] This surely is an improvement. It would dispose of many counterexamples to the traditional definition including the one presented above because that set does justify the false proposition that the watch has been running since it was last wound.

There are, however, additional counterexamples to this proposed, strengthened definition that reveal

that the restrictions remain too weak. Ernest Sosa de-velops one which I will modify.[16]

Suppose that S has been working in an office next to Tom Grabit's office for many years and has often spoken informally with Tom, but does not know anything at all about Tom's personal life. One day he sees what he takes to be Tom stealing a library book. S would be justified in believing that Tom did steal the book. Further, let us suppose that Tom did, in fact, steal the book. But unbeknown to S, Tom has an identical twin, John, who was in town in the library on the day in question. Further, Tom has never before stolen a book from the library but John is a klep-tomaniac who steals library books quite often.

In this case, although S has a true, justified belief that Tom stole the book, it can hardly be certified as knowledge, because S's evidence points more towards John being the thief than Tom being the thief. The Fe-licitous-Coincidence Principle is at work here; and this is a counterexample to the improved traditional defini-tion, because in this case there is no false proposition that either plays a role in the justification or is rendered justified by S's evidence. S has no reason to believe anything at all about John since he knows nothing about Tom's personal life.[17]

The improved definition remains too weak be-cause it is concerned only with the defeat of the justi-fication by the negation of those false propositions justified for S; whereas there are occasions when S's true, justified belief fails to be knowledge for reasons that S had no way of anticipating. To return to the Felicitous Coincidence Principle, if there is *any* cir-cumstance such that, given S's evidence for p, it is not reasonable to expect that p is true (given S's evi-dence), even if p is true, S does not know that p. The circumstances mentioned in the principle need not be circumstances about which S has any beliefs or any justified beliefs. To put the principle in a slightly dif-ferent manner: If there is any true proposition, d, such that when d is combined with S's evidence, e, for p would make p no longer sufficiently justified accord-ing to the appropriate contextually governed criteria, then S does not know p.

Based upon these considerations, the following definition seems to initially suggest itself:

S knows that p at some time, t, if and only if:

i.   p is true;
ii. S believes p at t on the basis of some evidence, e;
iii. e justifies S in believing that p at t;
iv. there is no true proposition, d, such that when combined with e is such that S would no longer be justified in believing p at t.

We will see that a slight amendment is needed in the fourth condition. But for the moment let us look at the merits of this initial proposal. The first three conditions (i)–(iii) have been called the "traditional" conditions, and I will continue so to refer to them. In what follows I will assume that they are necessary conditions of knowledge. The primary question before us is whether condition (iv) correctly captures the Felicitous Coincidence Principle without being too strong, i.e. ruling out genuine cases of knowledge. For the sake of simplicity I will refer to a true proposition such that when combined with the evidence, e, for p is such that the conjunction (e & d) does not justify p as a *defeating proposition*.[18]

There is an important point about the proposed definition that becomes immediately obvious, namely that condition (i) follows from condition (iv). For if p were false, ~p is true. And ~p is a defeater because p could not be justified on the basis of (e & ~p). Hence, if condition (iv) is fulfilled, condition (i) is fulfilled. Thus if S's evidence, e, is such that there is no defeating proposition, it *could not* be a lucky break that his/her evidence is directly connected with the truth of p. In other words, this definition captures the sought-after connection between justification and truth that motivated the traditional definition. That speaks strongly in favor of condition (iv) since it is sufficient to block the Gettier-type counterexamples that showed the traditional definition was too weak.[19]

But what of counterexamples generally? Is the account too weak? Is the account too strong?

Let us begin by considering whether it is too weak. That is, are there cases in which S does not have knowledge but all of the proposed conditions are satisfied? I have just given a general argument for the claim that the proposed account of knowledge is powerful enough to block the Gettier-type counterexamples. In those Gettier-type cases in which a false proposition, f, plays an essential role in the justification, its denial, ~f, would be a defeater because ~f is true and such that the conjunction of it with S's evidence would no longer justify p. For S's evidence would then include both f and ~f.[20] In the Gettier-type cases in which there is no false proposition in the evidence, for example Russell's case of the stopped watch and Sosa's Tom Grabit Case, there are defeaters: 'The watch is not working now' and 'Tom, who has never before stolen a book, has an identical kleptomaniac twin, John, who was in the library on the day in question.'[21] In other words, what shows that S does not have knowledge in these cases is a true proposition describing the circumstances mentioned in the Felicitous Coincidence Principle.

But, perhaps, there are other potential counterexamples in addition to the Gettier-type that show that the definition is too weak. Perhaps something else is needed in order for S to obtain knowledge.

Now is the appropriate time to briefly mention an alternative approach to accounting for the felicitous coincidences because it is relevant to the issue at hand. As I have suggested above, the prevailing traditional approach hoped to capture the intuition that epistemic luck could generate knowledge by requiring that the true belief be justified. The reasoning had to meet certain relatively high, but contextually variant, normative standards. Gettier showed that hope could not be fulfilled. The defeasibility solution to the Gettier-type counterexamples remains within the spirit of the traditional, normative approach by requiring that the justification be of a certain type, namely, a non-defeated type. The defeasibility solution blocks the felicitous coincidence between the *justification* condition and *truth* condition by requiring that the justification be non-defeated, and hence, if a proposition were so justified, it had to be true. [Recall that condition (iv) entailed condition (i).]

But there is another approach to blocking epistemic luck which eschews the traditional, normative approach. It sees the felicitous coincidence as obtaining not between the justification and truth conditions, but rather as obtaining between the *belief* and the *truth* conditions. It seeks to rule out epistemic luck *not* by requiring that S's reasons be of a certain sort, but rather by requiring that the causal conditions responsible for S's belief be such that it is not causally accidental that S's belief is true. Roughly, a true belief is certifiable as knowledge just in case it is produced by a reliable psychological process, that is, a process that results in a sufficiently high proportion of true beliefs.[22] That view goes under the general name "reliabilism" since its defenders hold that knowledge is at least true, *reliably* produced belief. Reliabilism comes in many varieties and it is not the purpose of this paper to discuss this approach in any detail. But what is relevant here is that is could be thought that by ignoring the importance of the causal genesis of belief, the defeasibility theory has left out an important necessary condition of knowledge and, consequently, that the proposed definition is too weak. If this were correct, the neutrality of the defeasibility theory would be seriously threatened.

Let us take a typical case in which reliabilist intuitions come to bear. Suppose I am looking at what appears to be a red spot on a white table, and as a (causal) result of my perceptual experiences and some internal cognitive processes I come to believe that the spot is red. Suppose, further, that it is. Nevertheless, if I were in a circumstance in which most of the white tables around me were being illuminated by a red light making it appear that there is a red spot on them, it could be thought that the process that brought my belief about would not be sufficiently reliable in *those* circumstances because in *those* circumstances the process would not bring about true beliefs sufficiently often.[23]

The defeasibility theory can accommodate those intuitions. There is a defeating proposition, namely, *most of the tables around me are being illuminated by a red light making it appear that there is a red spot*. Adding that true proposition to my evidence would lower the degree of justification below the needed threshold for knowledge. More generally, whenever the reliabilist thinks that S fails to know because the belief was not produced by a sufficiently reliable process, there will be a defeating proposition — one which describes the circumstance in a way that shows that S's belief acquisition process was not reliable. S would no longer be justified in believing the proposition once that defeating proposition was added to his/her reasons.[24] Thus, even

were the reliabilists right in requiring that the belief be reliably produced, that provides no basis for thinking that the defeasibility account is too weak because if the belief forming process was not reliable, there will be a defeater. Hence there will be no cases in which S satisfies conditions (i)–(iv) but fails to know because the belief was not reliably produced.

Thus, it appears the initial account is not too weak. But is it too strong? I think the answer is "yes" and two modifications in the account are needed. The *first* required modification results from recognizing that the account presupposes that all knowledge is based upon reasoning. Many reliabilists and many foundationalists think some knowledge — knowledge of so-called basic propositions — does not result from reasoning. If we are to preserve the neutrality of our definition, we must allow for that position. So, some modification is called for.

There are only two options: (1) develop an account of basic knowledge (knowledge that does not require evidence or reasoning) within the parameters of the defeasibility theory and append it to the definition given above or (2) restrict the definition to non-basic knowledge (knowledge that does require reasoning). Although, for the reasons given below, I opt for (2), it is important to show that the defeasibility definition of knowledge could be employed to develop an account of basic knowledge in order to indicate that the theory can maintain the desired neutrality between those who believe that there is basic knowledge and those who do not. The defeasibility theory could define basic knowledge as follows:

S *basically* knows that p at t if and only if:

   a. p is true;
   b. S believes p at t;
   c. S is entitled to believe that p at t but not on the basis of any evidence;
   d. there is no true proposition, d, such that when combined with S's beliefs is such that S would no longer be entitled to believe p at t.

Obviously, there are some difficult issues to work out here. For example, what is the type of entitlement referred to in (c) and (d)? And how is it related to justification?

Those issues could be worked out, but I choose option (2) for two reasons. First, I do not think that there is any basic knowledge and although developing a full-blown account of what *could* be basic knowledge would be an interesting exercise, it strikes me as an extravagance not to be indulged in this essay.[25] Second, and more importantly, I take it that the primary issues surrounding the Gettier problem are related to determining what makes our reasoning sufficiently good to yield knowledge, *ceteris paribus*. So, let us simply amend the definition so that the *definiendum* is inferential knowledge. That is, we will be restricting the definition to knowledge that requires having reasons.

The *second* required modification results from noting that there are cases in which some philosophers would hold both that (1) there is a true proposition such that were it added to S's evidence, e, for p makes it such that S is no longer justified in believing that p and that (2) S knows that p. Consider this variation on the Grabit case discussed earlier that was first presented, I believe, by Paxson and Lehrer:

> Suppose I see a man walk into the library and remove a book from the library by concealing it beneath his coat. Since I am sure the man is Tom Grabit, whom I have often seen before when he attended my classes, I report that I know that Tom Grabit has removed the book. However, suppose further that Mrs. Grabit, the mother of Tom, has averred that on the day in question Tom was not in the library, indeed, was thousands of miles away, and that Tom's identical twin brother, John Grabit, was in the library. Imagine, moreover, that I am entirely ignorant of the fact that Mrs. Grabit has said these things. The statement that she has said these things would defeat any justification I have for believing that Tom Grabit removed the book, according to our present definition of defeasibility. Thus, I could not be said to have nonbasic knowledge that Tom Grabit removed the book.[26]

Do I know that Tom stole the book? I think most will say that I do, but there is a defeating proposition, namely, *Mrs. Grabit said that Tom was not in the library etc.* It is true that she said those things and adding that true proposition to my evidence would

have the effect of defeating my justification. So, condition (iv), as presented thus far, is too strong. It rules out cases of knowledge.

I think there is a rather easy way to modify condition (iv) within the spirit of the initial definition. The general idea was to block fortuitously obtained true belief by requiring that the justification be *immune to truths* that defeat it. In this case, what actually defeats the justification is not that Mrs. Grabit uttered the words she did, but rather that what she said renders it at least plausible that it was John who stole the book. If we knew that she was demented, her statement would have no defeating effect. So, it is not her statement, *per se*, that is doing the defeating. It is that her statement renders plausible another proposition which does the defeating. And her statement is misleading since that other statement is false. Tom was not out of town and there is no kleptomaniac twin.

Put another way: The true proposition that Mrs. Grabit said that it wasn't Tom defeats only because it renders plausible another proposition that is *false*.[27] The dirty work, so to speak, is being done by a *falsehood*. Condition (iv) was designed to insure that the justification would not be defeated by the truth. Here it is actually being defeated by a *falsehood* that was rendered plausible by the truth. So, we should distinguish between those defeaters that defeat in virtue of being true (and rendering other propositions true) from those defeaters that defeat *only* by rendering a false proposition at least plausible. *Genuine* defeaters defeat through the truth. *Misleading* defeaters defeat only through falsehoods. True beliefs based upon adequate justifications that are defeated only by misleading defeaters are instances of knowledge. True beliefs whose adequate justifications are defeated by genuine defeaters are not instances of knowledge. So we should amend the definition as follows:

S *inferentially* knows that p at t if and only if:

i. p is true;
ii. S believes p at t on the basis of some evidence, e;
iii. e justifies S in believing that p at t;
iv. There is no genuine defeater of the justification of p by e.

To see how this modified account works and to return to one of the initial *desiderata*, i.e., neutrality, let us consider another case.[28]

Jones, who goes to the house of an acquaintance, Mr. Magic, for the first time sees what he takes to be some flowers on the mantelpiece, and throughout the evening the various guests and Magic comment on the flowers. Their comments cohere. Everything seems normal. However, later Mr. Jones discovers that Magic is a magician and delights in fooling his guests by creating some extremely cleverly devised illusions of flowers on a mantel. Presumably, at that point, if Jones did not check further, he would not be justified in believing that there were flowers on the mantel. But, suppose further that on the night in question Magic was not up to his old tricks.

Did Mr. Jones know that there were flowers on the mantel before he discovered that Magic was a magician? I think some people would say that he did. After all, Magic was not up to his old tricks and everything is "normal" — there are no bogus flowers or illusions of flowers. Others might say that Jones did not know because this is the house of a magician and that alone makes it such that Jones' evidence is not good enough *in this circumstance*. Intuitions will differ here. How does our revised definition fare?

Those who believe that Jones does know that there are flowers on the mantel can appeal to the revised definition and claim that the true proposition, *Jones is in the house of a magician who often delights in fooling his guests*, though true, defeats only because it renders plausible the proposition, *Magic is up to his old tricks*, and that proposition is false. Hence, they could claim that there is no genuine defeater. On the other hand, those who thought that Jones did not know that there are flowers on the mantel could claim that the true proposition, *Jones is in the house of a magician who often delights in fooling his guests*, defeats on its own and does not need to rely on a false proposition being rendered plausible. In other words, our revised definition can accommodate both intuitions. That both those who think Jones knows and those who think that Jones fails to know can employ the same definition,

provides good evidence that the definition is correct and indicates that the *desideratum* of neutrality is being satisfied. A discussion between both parties is possible because they can agree on the definition of knowledge.

The disagreement about the status of Jones' knowledge is merely one instance of a general disagreement about the extent of our knowledge and some might think that condition (iv) is so strong that it prejudices the issue in favor of one or another form of skepticism. Some may believe that the definition is so strong that:

i. The definition implies that S could never know that p, because S could never know that the fourth condition is fulfilled.

ii. The definition implies that S could never know that p, because the fourth condition could not be fulfilled.

iii. The definition implies that S could never be justified in asserting that he/she knew that p, because S would never be justified in asserting that the fourth condition holds.

iv. The definition implies that S could never know that he/she knows that p because S could never know that the fourth condition held.

Now if any one of these forms of skepticism were *implied* by the definition, it would lose its neutrality and, hence, would not be acceptable. The definition must allow for the various forms of skepticism, but it ought not to imply them.[29] Let me take them one at a time, leaving (II) for last.

In reply to (I), let me simply point out that the fourth condition is *not* "S knows that there is no genuine defeater of the justification of p by e." According to the definition, S can know that p without knowing or, for that matter, without even considering whether there are any defeating propositions. The condition merely asserts that his/her evidence must be such that there are no genuine defeating propositions.

In reply to (III), it should be pointed out that S would be justified in asserting or believing that he/she knew that p, whenever S is justified in believing that conditions (i)–(iv) obtained. That is, no doubt, not an easy task. For one thing, S would have to be justified in believing that he/she was justified in believing that p, and that requires having carefully thought about what makes a proposition justified. In addition, it requires having thought carefully about how likely it is that there are genuine defeaters of the particular justification in question. But however difficult that might be, the proposed definition does not make it impossible. The skeptic will have to produce an argument — and perhaps there is one — with the conclusion that those second order beliefs cannot be justified. The anti-skeptic will have to show — and perhaps he/she can — that such second order beliefs can be justified. The point here is that the definition can be accepted by both parties and they can employ it along with other propositions to demonstrate their respective positions. The definition itself is neutral.

In response to (IV), applying the proposed definition of propositional knowledge and substituting 'S knows that p' for 'p,' we would obtain the result that 'S knows that he/she knows that p' would be true just in case the following are true:

1. 'S knows that p' is true;
2. S believes that he/she knows that p on the basis of some evidence, e. (i.e., there is some evidence, e, on the basis of which S believes that he/she knows that p.)
3. S is justified in believing that S knows that p on the basis of e.
4. There is no genuine defeater of the justification of the proposition, S knows that p, by e.

If S can know that p, it seems possible that conditions (2)–(4) could be fulfilled. Conditions (2) and (3) have already been handled in response to (III) and condition (4) would seem to present no insurmountable obstacle unless there were an all-purpose defeater of all of the justifications of what we ordinarily think we know. And if there were such an all-purpose defeater, S could never know that p.

That leads directly to a consideration of (II). The question is whether condition (iv) is ever fulfilled. I believe that the definition remains neutral on that question. To see that, consider a Cartesian skeptic and the critics of that form of skepticism. These two camps hold views about as far apart as possible and if I can show that condition (iv) should be acceptable to both parties to the dispute, that would be good evidence for the claim that the definition satisfies the neutrality *desideratum*.

Cartesian skeptics think that it is possible to legitimately question what we ordinarily take to be knowledge, for example, that there is now a computer screen in front of me, that there once were dinosaurs and that the sun will rise tomorrow. They would say that these propositions are beyond our ken, not because we have some evidence against any particular claim, but because there is an all-purpose defeater that applies in each case. In other words, they would claim that condition (iv) cannot be fulfilled no matter how strong our justifications are.

Employing our definition, the issue, then, can be put as follows: Is there a genuine defeating proposition for all those propositions which we ordinarily take to be beyond doubt true? Will, for example, any of the following serve as a genuine defeating proposition:

1. Possibly I am dreaming now.
2. I have been deceived before, so possibly I am being deceived now.
3. Possibly something other than material objects is causing our experience, for example, an evil genius.
4. Possibly I am mad.
5. Possibly my epistemic equipment is not reliable (because its creator was not sufficiently perfect).[30]

I do not propose to attempt to determine which, if any, of the above propositions is true or whether, if true, it would be a *genuine* defeater.[31] What I wish to point out is that the proposed definition of propositional knowledge does not prejudge the issue in favor of either the Cartesian skeptics or the anti-skeptics. Indeed, the definition can provide a basis for clarifying the dispute by focusing attention on the considerations surrounding the possibility of the existence of such an all purpose genuine defeating proposition.

Conclusion

The definition of propositional knowledge that I have proposed seems to meet the *desiderata* of any such attempt and, in addition, seems to provide a procedure for evaluating various epistemological theories. It provides an intuitively appealing response to the Gettier Problem, it remains neutral between rival epistemological theories, and it furnishes a basis for clarifying and perhaps even resolving the dispute between the Cartesian Skeptics and their opponents. I doubt if much more could be required of a definition.

Notes

* I want to thank Anne Ashbaugh for her help with this paper. It is a significantly revised version of my paper, "A Proposed Definition of Propositional Knowledge," *Journal of Philosophy*, 67, no. 16, 1971, 47–82. There are additional changes to the original paper that should have been made if the task had been to present the present state of the defeasibility theory. But I took the task here to be to present the theory in its fundamental form and to remain within the general spirit of the earlier paper. The defeasibility theory has gone through many revisions because of the many criticisms of it. The best place to find a full discussion of those criticisms is Robert Shope's *The Analysis of Knowing* (Princeton, NJ: Princeton University Press, 1983). That book also contains a full discussion of all the then-current proposed solutions to the Gettier Problem. (See fn. 1.) My, no doubt, biased view is that the best presentation of the theory is in my own book, *Certainty: A Refutation of Scepticism* (Minneapolis: University of Minnesota Press, 1981), especially pp. 137–71.

1. Edmund Gettier, "Is Justified True Belief Knowledge?" *Analysis* 23, no. 6, 1963, 121–23. The catalog of attempts to solve the "Gettier Problem" is legion. I refer the reader to the entry "Gettier Problems" by Robert Shope in the *Encyclopedia of Philosophy* (London: Routledge Press, 1998).

2. Roderick Chisholm, *Theory of Knowledge* (Englewoods Cliff, N.J.: Prentice Hall, 1966), p.5.

3. Ernest Sosa, "Propositional Knowledge," *Philosophical Studies* 20, no. 3, 1969, p. 33–43

4. Plato, *Theaetetus*, 201b–201c.

5. Descartes, *Rules for the Direction of the Mind*. Also see Descartes, *Meditations on First Philosophy* in *The Philosophical Works of Descartes* (Mineola, N.Y.: Dover Publications, 1955), vol. 1, eds. E. Haldane and G.R.T. Ross, especially "Mediation IV" in which Descartes employs the notion of knowledge requiring nonaccidentally true beliefs, p. 176.

6. John Locke, *An Essay Concerning Human Understanding*. Book XI, chapter 23, section 28.

7. This is the way that Gettier characterized the traditional definition, *op, cit*.

8. See Colin Radford, "Knowledge—by examples," *Analysis* 27, no. 1, 1966, 1–11.

9. See Peter Unger, *Ignorance* (New York: Oxford University Press, 1975).

10. I say "prevailing" traditional approach because another view also played a role in the tradition, albeit not as great. That alternative approach attempts to eliminate epistemic luck by imposing various constraints on the causal process that led to the true belief. This tradition can be traced as far as back as Aristotle's *Posterior Analytics* in which he suggests that there are noninferential cognitive mechanisms responsible for the transition from ignorance to knowledge of first principles in science. We will discuss this approach briefly later.

11. Many think that Descartes is an exponent of that view. But see his "Sixth Meditation" in the *Meditations on First Philosophy* where he seems to allow that knowledge of facts of the world can be based upon what we would call "inference to the best explanation."

12. Many philosophers have advocated fallibilism. Perhaps the clearest defense of the view is given by Charles Peirce in his "Principles of Philosophy" in *Collected Papers of C.S. Peirce* (Cambridge, Mass.: Harvard University Press, 1931), eds. C. Hartshorne and P. Weiss, Vol. 1, especially section 1.120.

13. Thus, Russell could have used his Watch Case to show that knowledge is not mere true, justified belief, but he didn't.

14. If S believed that the watch had not been running for 24 hours, then even though he believed e, he would not be justified in believing that it was 5 P.M.

15. Many philosophers suggested that improvement. Two such examples are: Sosa *op. cit*, Keith Lehrer and Thomas Paxson, "Knowledge: Undefeated Justified True Belief," *Journal of Philosophy* 66, no. 8, 1969, 225–37.

16. Sosa, *op. cit*.

17. It may be thought that there is one false proposition that is justified by the propositions that justify that Tom Grabit stole the book, i.e., S knows that Tom stole the book. But that proposition is not justified by that evidence since the evidence does not contain any evidence regarding what knowledge is or whether S fulfills those conditions.

18. In the original paper, I called these propositions "disqualifying propositions." But the generally used term now is "defeating propositions" or more simply "defeaters."

19. Even though condition (iv) implies condition (i), for the sake of the argument in this paper, I will continue to use (i) as a separate condition of propositional knowledge because it is condition (iv) that is probably

the most controversial, and in defending it I should not assume what follows from it.

20. Although a contradiction strictly implies every proposition, it cannot serve to justify any proposition. This is important to note since it shows that even when e entails p, the justification can be defeated by ~e or ~p. Hence, the defeasibility theory can account for knowledge based on deductive inferences.

21. I say there need be none because in Russell's case, S could employ as evidence the false proposition that the watch has been running in the past 24 hours, and in Sosa's case S could believe that there is no Tom-look-alike in the library. But in neither case would S have to use those propositions as evidence.

22. This is a very non-nuanced statement of the reliabilist position but it does capture the central idea that motivates the position and is sufficient for my purpose here. For a full discussion of reliabilism see Alvin Goldman, *Epistemology and Cognition* (Cambridge, Mass.: Harvard University Press, 1986): *Liaisons: Philosophy Meets the Cognitive and Social Sciences* (Cambridge, Mass.: MIT Press. 1992). Also see Fred Dretske, *Knowledge and the Flow of Information*. (Cambridge, Mass. MIT Press, 1981).

23. I say that it "could be thought" that the process was not sufficiently reliable rather than the less qualified claim that process was not sufficiently reliable. This case strikes me as one in which there might be a legitimate difference of opinion concerning the extent of my knowledge. The defeasibility theory can accommodate the divergent intuitions by appealing to the distinction between genuine and misleading defeaters presented below.

24. I should point out that although the defeasibility theory will come to the same judgement about whether S has knowledge in cases in which the process was unreliable, it will not inherit a main objection to reliabilism, namely the so-called "generality problem" (For a discussion of that problem see Richard Feldman, "Reliability and Justification," *Monist* 68, no. 2, 1985, 159–74.) The reason is simply that the defeasibility theory need not have a general account of what makes a belief reliably produced since the defeater in each case that shows that the process is not reliable will be specific to the particular circumstances in which the belief is produced. No general account of *reliably* formed or of *unreliably* formed beliefs is necessary.

25. I have given some reasons for thinking that foundationalism is not able to solve the regress problem in "Foundationalism and the Infinite Regress of Reasons," *Philosophy and Phenomenological Research* 58, no. 4, 1998, 919–25; "Human Knowledge and the Infinite Regress of Reasons," *Philosophical Perspectives* 13, J.

Tomberlin (ed.), 1999, 297–325; "Why Not Infinitism?" in *Epistemology Proceedings of the Twentieth World Congress in Philosophy*, Richard Cobb-Stevens (ed.), 2000, vol 5, 199–208.

25. Keith Lehrer and Thomas Paxson, *op. cit.* p. 228.

27. I say that the true proposition *renders plausible* the false proposition rather than *justifies* it because the true proposition need not be such that it raises the false one to the level of being justified. That is a relatively high level of epistemic warrant. Plausibility seems sufficient here. Roughly, I take it that a proposition is plausible if and only if it is one that must be taken into account when determining what we are justified in believing.

28. Cases similar to this one were suggested to me in conversation by A. J. Ayer and Marc Cohen.

29. For my take on the various forms of skepticism, see my "Skepticism and Closure: Why the Evil Genius Argument Fails," *Philosophical Topics* 23, no. 1, 1995, 213–36; "Skepticism," *Stanford Encyclopedia of Philosophy* at http://plato.stanford.edu/entries/skepticism/: "Skepticism" to appear in *The Oxford Handbook of Epistemology* edited by Paul Moser (Oxford: Oxford University Press, forthcoming).

30. I think Descartes holds that 5 is the "all-purpose" defeater. Near the end of the "First Meditation" he proposes a ground for doubt about which he says that he "certainly has no reply." He has "replied" to each of the preceding grounds. He puts it this way:

> . . . In whatever way [it is supposed] that I have arrived at the state of being that I have reached—whether [it is attributed] to fate or to accident, or [made] out that it is by a continual succession of antecedents, or by some other method—since to err and deceive oneself is a defect, it is clear that the greater will be the probability of my being so imperfect as to deceive myself ever, as is the Author of my being to whom [is assigned] my origin the less powerful. [*Meditations on First Philosophy* in *Philosophical Works of Descartes* eds. Elizabeth Haldane and G.R.T. Ross (Dover Publications, 1931), vol. I,p. 147.]

In contemporary parlance, he is claiming (at this point in the *Meditations*) that possibly his epistemic equipment is not reliable. Of course, one of the central arguments in the *Meditations* is designed to show that our epistemic equipment is, indeed, reliable. If that argument is a good one, someone armed with it has a way to reject the "all-purpose" defeater.

31. The situation is a bit more complex than might be suggested by the text because the five sentences are multiply ambiguous. The 'Possibly' in 'Possibly I am dreaming now' (and in all the other sentences)

could mean epistemic possibility, nomic possibility, logical possibility, or some other notion of possibility. Hence, an assessment of Cartesian skepticism would have to begin by disambiguating the various senses of possibility and determining whether there is a sense in which the proposition expressed is true and whether in that sense it is also a genuine defeater.

✦ THE TRACKING THEORY ✦

15. KNOWLEDGE

Robert Nozick

Conditions for Knowledge

Our task is to formulate further conditions to go alongside

1. *p* is true
2. S believes that *p*.

The causal condition on knowledge, provides an inhospitable environment for mathematical and ethical knowledge; also there are well-known difficulties in specifying the type of causal connection. If someone floating in a tank oblivious to everything around him is given (by direct electrical and chemical stimulation of the brain) the belief that he is floating in a tank with his brain being stimulated, then even though that fact is part of the cause of his belief, still he does not know that it is true.

Let us consider a different third condition:

3. If *p* weren't true, S wouldn't believe that *p*.

Throughout this work, let us write the subjunctive 'if-then' by an arrow, and the negation of a sentence by prefacing "not-" to it. The above condition thus is rewritten as:

3. not-*p* → not-(S believes that *p*).

This subjunctive condition is not unrelated to the causal condition. Often when the fact that *p* (partially) causes someone to believe that *p*, the fact also will be causally necessary for his having the belief—without the cause, the effect would not occur. In that case, the subjunctive condition 3 also will be satisfied. Yet this condition is not equivalent to the causal condition. For the causal condition will be satisfied in cases of causal overdetermination, where either two sufficient causes of the effect actually operate, or a back-up cause (of the same effect) would operate if the first one didn't; whereas the subjunctive condition need not hold for these cases. When the two conditions do agree, causality indicates knowledge because it acts in a manner that makes the subjunctive 3 true.

The subjunctive condition 3 serves to exclude cases of the sort first described by Edward Gettier, such as the following. Two other people are in my office and

I am justified on the basis of much evidence in believing the first owns a Ford car; though he (now) does not, the second person (a stranger to me) owns one. I believe truly and justifiably that someone (or other) in my office owns a Ford car, but I do not know someone does. Concluded Gettier, knowledge is not simply justified true belief.

The following subjunctive, which specifies condition 3 for this Gettier case, is not satisfied: if no one in my office owned a Ford car, I wouldn't believe that someone did. The situation that would obtain if no one in my office owned a Ford is one where the stranger does not (or where he is not in the office); and in that situation I still would believe, as before, that someone in my office does own a Ford, namely, the first person. So the subjunctive condition 3 excludes this Gettier case as a case of knowledge.

The subjunctive condition is powerful and intuitive, not so easy to satisfy, yet not so powerful as to rule out everything as an instance of knowledge. A subjunctive conditional "if p were true, q would be true", $p \rightarrow q$, does not say that p entails q or that it is logically impossible that p yet not-q. It says that in the situation that would obtain if p were true, q also would be true. This point is brought out especially clearly in recent 'possible-worlds' accounts of subjunctives: the subjunctive is true when (roughly) in all those worlds in which p holds true that are closest to the actual world, q also is true. (Examine those worlds in which p holds true closest to the actual world, and see if q holds true in all these.) Whether or not q is true in p worlds that are still farther away from the actual world is irrelevant to the truth of the subjunctive.

The subjunctive condition 3 also handles nicely cases that cause difficulties for the view that you know that p when you can rule out the relevant alternatives to p in the context. For, as Gail Stine writes, "what makes an alternative relevant in one context and not another? . . . If on the basis of visual appearances obtained under optimum conditions while driving through the countryside Henry identifies an object as a barn, normally we say that Henry knows that it is a barn. Let us suppose, however, that unknown to Henry, the region is full of expertly made papier-mâché facsimiles of barns. In that case, we would not say that Henry knows that the object

is a barn, unless he has evidence against it being a papier-mâché facsimile, which is now a relevant alternative. So much is clear, but what if no such facsimiles exist in Henry's surroundings, although they once did? Are either of these circumstances sufficient to make the hypothesis (that it's a papier-mâché object) relevant? Probably not, but the situation is not so clear." Let p be the statement that the object in the field is a (real) barn, and q the one that the object in the field is a papier-mâché barn. When papier-mâché barns are scattered through the area, if p were false, q would be true or might be. Since in this case (we are supposing) the person still would believe p, the subjunctive

3. not-$p \rightarrow$ not-(S believes that p)

is not satisfied, and so he doesn't know that p. However, when papier-mâché barns are or were scattered around another country, even if p were false q wouldn't be true, and so (for all we have been told) the person may well know that p. A hypothesis q contrary to p clearly is relevant when if p weren't true, q would be true; when not-$p \rightarrow q$. It clearly is irrelevant when if p weren't true, q also would not be true; when not-$p \rightarrow$ not-q. The remaining possibility is that neither of these opposed subjunctives holds; q might (or might not) be true if p weren't true. In this case, q also will be relevant, according to an account of knowledge incorporating condition 3 and treating subjunctives along the lines sketched above. Thus, condition 3 handles cases that befuddle the "relevant alternatives" account; though that account can adopt the above subjunctive criterion for when an alternative is relevant, it then becomes merely an alternate and longer way of stating condition 3.

Despite the power and intuitive force of the condition that if p weren't true the person would not believe it, this condition does not (in conjunction with the first two conditions) rule out every problem case. There remains, for example, the case of the person in the tank who is brought to believe, by direct electrical and chemical stimulation of his brain, that he is in the tank and is being brought to believe things in this way; he does not know this is true. However, the subjunctive condition is satisfied: if he weren't floating in the tank, he wouldn't believe he was.

The person in the tank does not know he is there, because his belief is not sensitive to the truth. Although it is caused by the fact that is its content, it is not sensitive to that fact. The operators of the tank could have produced any belief, including the false belief that he wasn't in the tank; if they had, he would have believed that. Perfect sensitivity would involve beliefs and facts varying together. We already have one portion of that variation, subjunctively at least; if p were false he wouldn't believe it. This sensitivity as specified by a subjunctive does not have the belief vary with the truth or falsity of p in all possible situations, merely in the ones that would or might obtain if p were false.

The subjunctive condition

3. not-p → not-(S believes that p)

tells us only half the story about how his belief is sensitive to the truth-value of p. It tells us how his belief state is sensitive to p's falsity, but not how it is sensitive to p's truth; it tells us what his belief state would be if p were false, but not what it would be if p were true.

To be sure, conditions 1 and 2 tell us that p is true and he does believe it, but it does not follow that his believing p is sensitive to p's being true. This additional sensitivity is given to us by a further subjunctive; if p were true, he would believe it.

4. p → S believes that p.

Not only is p true and S believes it, but if it were true he would believe it. Compare: not only was the photon emitted and did it go to the left, but (it was then true that): if it were emitted it would go to the left. The truth of antecedent and consequent is not alone sufficient for the truth of a subjunctive; 4 says more than 1 and 2. Thus, we presuppose some (or another) suitable account of subjunctives. According to the suggestion tentatively made above, 4 holds true if not only does he actually truly believe p, but in the "close" worlds where p is true, he also believes it. He believes that p for some distance out in the p neighborhood of the actual world; similarly, condition 3 speaks not of the whole not-p neighborhood of the actual world, but only of the first portion of it. (If, as is likely, these explanations do not help, please use your own intuitive understanding of the subjunctives 3 and 4.)

The person in the tank does not satisfy the subjunctive condition 4. Imagine as actual a world in which he is in the tank and is stimulated to believe he is, and consider what subjunctives are true in that world. It is not true of him there that if he were in the tank he would believe it; for in the close world (or situation) to his own where he is in the tank but they don't give him the belief that he is (much less instill the belief that he isn't) he doesn't believe he is in the tank. Of the person actually in the tank and believing it, it is not true to make the further statement that if he were in the tank he would believe it—so he does not know he is in the tank.

The subjunctive condition 4 also handles a case presented by Gilbert Harman. The dictator of a country is killed; in their first edition, newspapers print the story, but later all the country's newspapers and other media deny the story, falsely. Everyone who encounters the denial believes it (or does not know what to believe and so suspends judgment). Only one person in the country fails to hear any denial and he continues to believe the truth. He satisfies conditions 1 through 3 (and the causal condition about belief) yet we are reluctant to say he knows the truth. The reason is that if he had heard the denials, he too would have believed them, just like everyone else. His belief is not sensitively tuned to the truth, he doesn't satisfy the condition that if it were true he would believe it. Condition 4 is not satisfied.

There is a pleasing symmetry about how this account of knowledge relates conditions 3 and 4, and connects them to the first two conditions. The account has the following form.

1. (1)
2. (2)
3. not-1 → not-2
4. 1 → 2

I am not inclined, however, to make too much of this symmetry, for I found also that with other conditions experimented with as a possible fourth condition there was some way to construe the resulting third and fourth conditions as symmetrical answers to some symmetrical looking questions, so that they appeared to arise in parallel fashion from similar questions about the components of true belief.

Symmetry, it seems, is a feature of a mode of presentation, not of the contents presented. A uniform transformation of symmetrical statements can leave the results nonsymmetrical. But if symmetry attaches to mode of presentation, how can it possibly be a deep feature of, for instance, laws of nature that they exhibit symmetry? (One of my favorite examples of symmetry is due to Groucho Marx. On his radio program he spoofed a commercial, and ended, "And if you are not completely satisfied, return the unused portion of our product and we will return the unused portion of your money.") Still, represent our subject symmetrically makes the connection of knowledge to true belief especially perspicuous. It seems to me that a symmetrical formulation is a sign of our understanding, rather than a mark of truth. If we cannot understand an asymmetry as arising from an underlying symmetry through the operation of a particular factor,

we will not understand why that asymmetry exists in that direction. (But do we also need to understand why the underlying asymmetrical factor holds instead of the opposite?)

A person knows that p when he not only does truly believe it, but also would truly believe it and wouldn't falsely believe it. He not only actually has a true belief, he subjunctively has one. It is true that p and he believes it; if it weren't true he wouldn't believe it, and if it were true he would believe it. To know that p is to be someone who would believe it if it were true, and who wouldn't believe it if it were false.

It will be useful to have a term for this situation when a person's belief is thus subjunctively connected to the fact. Let us say of a person who believes that p, which is true, that when 3 and 4 hold, his belief *tracks* the truth that p. To know is to have a belief that tracks the truth. Knowledge is a particular way of being connected to the world, having a specific real factual connection to the world: tracking it.

CHAPTER 4 JUSTIFICATION

INTRODUCTION

The essays in this chapter present leading views of the structure and nature of justification. That is, some of the essays discuss the requirements for justification, while others discuss the way groups of beliefs must be structured if they are to be justified: to count as justified, must beliefs be structured hierarchically, which is the position of most early philosophers, or are circular configurations acceptable, as many contemporary theorists maintain?

The leading views concerning the structure of justification are foundationalism (Descartes 1641; Quinton 1973; Chisholm 1966, 1982; Alston 1976; Audi 1993) and coherentism (Bosanquet 1920, Sellars 1973, BonJour 1985). In recent years some philosophers, such as Susan Haack (1999 and this volume), have proposed ways of bringing these two positions closer together by combining elements of each.

As for the nature of justification, some theorists have proposed new ways of understanding the conditions under which justified belief is possible, while others continue to defend traditional accounts. Among the latter are Richard Feldman and Earl Conee, who defend the ordinary view that justification hinges on evidence. They label this view evidentialism (Feldman and Conee 1985, 2003). Other approaches suggested in recent years include reliabilism (Goldman 1976), contextualism (Wittgenstein 1969, Annis 1978, Cohen 1988, 1998; Lewis 1996; DeRose 1995), and the virtue ethics approach (Sosa 1991; Greco 1993, 2003).

BonJour and Foundationalism (Versus Coherentism)

In "Foundationalism and Coherentism," Laurence BonJour introduces, and discusses the strengths and weaknesses of, the two leading accounts of the structure of justification. By foundationalism he means the view that justification derives from "a set of basic or foundational elements whose justification does not depend in turn on that of anything else." Coherentism, by contrast, sees justification as the property that a system of beliefs has when the component beliefs are tightly bound by inferential relations such as deduction and explanation.

In earlier work (1985) BonJour was enthusiastic about the prospects of coherentism, and critical of foundationalism, but in recent work (1999) he suggests that foundationalism is more plausible than coherentism. This new allegiance is evident in "Foundationalism and Coherentism," where he rejects coherentism and offers a partial defense of foundationalism. In this defense, he attempts to explain how basic, or foundational, beliefs can be justified. As he acknowledges, a more complete defense of foundationalism would take on a second task: explaining how commonsense beliefs about the world can be justified through the support of basic beliefs.

Haack and Foundherentism

In "Foundherentism," Susan Haack tries to provide an account of justification that is neither entirely foundationalist nor solely coherentist, but that combines elements of the two. She suggests that her hybrid view is more plausible than the traditional alternatives.

Harman and Negative Coherentism

In Chapters 4 and 5 of his *Change in View* (1986), reproduced here under the title "Negative Coherentism," Gilbert Harman distinguishes between views he calls the foundations theory and the coherence theory. The foundations theory says that justifying beliefs are more fundamental than justifi*ed* beliefs, that justification cannot involve circularity or infinite regresses, so justification chains come to an end with beliefs that are 'intrinsically' justified (justified but not on the basis of other beliefs), and that if all of my justification for a belief is lost and not replaced, then I should abandon my belief. By contrast, Harman defends a negative version of the coherence theory that is closely allied with Peirce's (1877) view of justification. It says that our beliefs *are* justified unless we have a special reason to change them; the only changes allowed increase the overall coherence of our scheme of beliefs. Beliefs are justified simply in virtue of being believed. Thus "all of one's beliefs are, in a sense, equally fundamental." In a later essay called "Skepticism and Foundations" (2003) Harman makes a similar claim concerning methods of justification such as experience: "one is justified in continuing to believe as one believes and to continue to use whatever epistemic methods one uses in the absence of any special reason not to."

According to Harman, (a) the foundations theory of rational belief seems to be more in line with our intuitions about how people *ought* to revise their beliefs than is the coherence theory, while (b) the coherence theory is more in line with what people *actually do* in cases of belief revision, but (c) the coherence theory is in the end preferable. Coherentism can incorporate the *principle of positive undermining*: one should stop believing *p* whenever one positively believes that one's reasons for believing *p* are no good, which contrasts with the *principle of negative undermining* associated with the foundations theory: one should stop believing *p* whenever one does not associate one's belief in *p* with an adequate justification.

Goldman and Reliabilism

In "What Is Justified Belief?" Alvin Goldman tries to set out "substantive conditions" for justified belief. That is, he wants his conditions to avoid epistemic terms such as 'justify', 'know,' and so forth. His view, roughly, is that a belief is justified if and only if it has a reliable source, and a source is reliable when it tends to produce beliefs that are true rather than false. The detailed analysis depends on a distinction between belief-*dependent* and belief-*independent* processes, where the former have beliefs as inputs, and the latter do not. Each has its own kind of reliability:

1. belief-independent processes are *unconditionally reliable* when they generate mostly true beliefs, while

2. belief-dependent processes are *conditionally reliable* when they generate mostly true beliefs given that their input beliefs are true.

Then Goldman offers a two-part account of justification:

1. If generated by a belief-independent process that is unconditionally reliable, then S's belief is justified.

2. If generated by a belief-dependent process that is conditionally reliable, and the beliefs on which the process operates are justified, then S's belief is justified.

Feldman, Conee, and Evidentialism

"Evidentialism" is a slightly revised version of an earlier essay by the same name, first published in *Philosophical Studies* 48 (1985): 15–34. In their essay, Richard Feldman and Earl Conee defend evidentialism, the view that justification turns entirely on evidence, against criticisms. Contrary to critics, for example, they claim that "doxastic attitudes" (belief states and their kin) are appropriate targets of epistemic appraisal whether they are voluntary or not. (Even if you cannot help believing that you are reading this sentence, it is appropriate to say you are justified in believing it.) They also defend evidentialism against alternative accounts that imply that we can be epistemically obligated to believe things that do not fit our evidence. For instance, Roderick Chisholm argues that we are epistemically obligated to believe all and only the true propositions we consider. Yet Chisholm's claim seems to imply that we are justified in believing things for which we have no evidence, since believing them helps us reach the goal of truth. They also resist the charge that evidentialism is refuted by examples of justifying evidence a person does not use properly. To do so, they develop a concept of well-foundedness. A belief is well-founded when it is not only justified but also it is arrived at in the right way. Finally, they defend evidentialism against charges based on reliabilism.

Cohen and Contextualism

In "Contextualism" Stewart Cohen clarifies the view called contextualism, and describes some of its strengths. As he notes, the theorists who call themselves contextualists say that whether it is correct for a speaker to attribute knowledge to a given agent depends on features of the *speaker's* context. In the general introduction, we called this position *speaker-centered* contextualism, and contrasted it with *agent-centered* contextualism, which claims that whether it is correct to attribute knowledge to a given agent S depends on features of *agent S's* context (as opposed to the context of the speaker who is evaluating the epistemic status of S's beliefs). According to (speaker-centered) contextualism, whether I, the speaker, am right when I say that Mary, the agent, knows *p*, depends on my context, as opposed to Mary's. The truth conditions for knowledge attributions vary with speakers' contexts. Thus speaker-centered contextualists say something that typically is denied by theorists who accept agent-centered contextualism, namely, that the *truth conditions* of knowledge attributions vary with speakers' contexts, and when I say that Mary knows *p*, and you say that Mary does not know *p*, we can both be correct.

Greco and Virtue Epistemology

In "Virtues in Epistemology," John Greco describes a view called virtue epistemology which he traces to the work of Ernest Sosa (see, for example, Sosa's essay in Chapter 7). He comments on various attempts to develop a virtue epistemology; in particular, he assesses the work of theorists such as Zagzebski (1996) who wish to model the intellectual virtues on moral virtues. Then he lays out a virtue epistemology that is also a form of reliabilism, and defends it by showing how it can be used to address certain persistent problems in epistemology, such as Gettier cases.

QUESTIONS FOR REFLECTION

1. What criticisms does BonJour wield against coherentism? Do these criticisms succeed? How might Harman respond to them?

2. Does Haack succeed in bringing the best of foundationalism and of coherentism together into one plausible view?

3. How would Goldman respond to the claim that processes that do not generate justified beliefs might nonetheless be reliable in various other possible worlds; for example, wishful thinking might be reliable in a world controlled by a wish-fulfilling demon? Would Goldman's response be adequate?

4. Suppose that Sal's belief is caused by a reliable process, but Sal has no grounds for thinking this is so, or worse: Sal has grounds for thinking her belief is caused by an unreliable process. Would Goldman say that Sal's belief is justified? If not, how does he avoid this conclusion?

5. Are there rational beliefs whose sources would be unreliable in imaginable situations (e.g., brain in vat scenarios)? In those situations, would the resulting beliefs be irrational? How would Goldman respond?

6. Do the truth conditions of knowledge attributions vary with speakers' contexts? Suppose that my standards for knowledge are higher than yours. Does this fact affect the truth of 'you know such and such' as uttered by me?

7. Suppose that no one has good evidence for or against claim *p*, but I want to believe it. Suppose, too, that I successfully believe *p*, realizing that there is no evidence for or against it. Does Harman's view imply that I am now justified in believing *p*, because beliefs carry intrinsic justification? If so, is this consequence acceptable?

8. Critically assess the following principle: If S is justified in believing *p*, and S believes *q* because *q* follows from *p*, then S is justified in believing *q*.

9. In "Evidentialism," Feldman and Conee criticize the reliabilist account of justification. How might a reliabilist respond to these criticisms? Would the responses succeed?

◇ FOUNDATIONALISM (VERSUS COHERENTISM) ◇

16. FOUNDATIONALISM AND COHERENTISM

Laurence BonJour

Descartes's basic epistemological approach is *foundationalist* in character: it views justification and knowledge as ultimately derivative from a set of basic or foundational elements whose justification does not depend in turn on that of anything else. For Descartes, as for many foundationalists, the foundation for knowledge and justification consists of (i) a person's immediate awarenesses of his or her own conscious states of mind, together with (ii) his or her a priori grasp of self-evidently true propositions. Beliefs deriving from these two sources require no further justification, whereas beliefs about most or all other matters, and especially beliefs concerning objects and occurrences in the material world, require justification or reasons that ultimately appeal whether directly or indirectly, to immediate experience and a priori insight.[1] As the term "foundation" itself suggests, the underlying metaphor is an architectural one: think of a building or structure, perhaps a very tall one with many different levels, but all of them resting on a bottom level that does not rest in the same way on anything else.

Most historical epistemological views have been broadly foundationalist in character (though they have not always agreed with Descartes about the specific composition of the foundation). But in recent times a fairly widespread apparent consensus has developed to the effect that the whole foundationalist approach is deeply flawed and ultimately untenable.

In the present chapter, we explore this issue. We begin by considering a basic problem pertaining to the structure of justified belief or knowledge, one that is usually taken to provide the most telling argument in favor of foundationalism and that will also help to clarify the foundationalist view. Next we consider some of the main objections that have been advanced against foundationalism. This will lead to a consideration and assessment of the main contemporary alternative to foundationalism, namely *coherentism*.[2] Doubts about the tenability of this alternative will

then motivate a reconsideration of foundationalism in the final part of the chapter.

The Epistemic Regress Problem and the Foundationalist Argument

I will formulate the general problem abstractly, since it is the structure and not the particular beliefs that matters. Suppose that there is a belief, which we will refer to as B_1, that is allegedly justified for a particular person at a particular time, and consider what specific from this justification might take. One obvious possibility is the following: B_1 might be justified because the person holds some other justified belief B_2 (which might of course be a conjunction of simpler beliefs) from which B_1 follows by some rationally acceptable kind of *inference*, whether deductive, inductive, abductive (inference to the best explanation), or whatever. I am not suggesting that the mere existence of this other belief and of the inferential relation is by itself sufficient for B_1 to be justified. Clearly if the person in question is not at all inclined to appeal to B_2 as a reason for B_1 or has no idea that any inferential relation holds between the two or has a mistaken conception of this inferential relation, B_1 will not be justified in this way for him or her. For the moment, however, I will simply assume that whatever further conditions are required for B_1 to be justified for this person by virtue of its inferential relation to B_2 are in fact satisfied.[3]

But whatever these further conditions may turn out to be, it is clear at least that, as already stipulated, B_2 must itself be somehow justified if it is to confer justification, via a suitable inferential relation, upon B_1. If the person in question has no good reason to think that B_2 is true, then the fact that B_1 follows from B_2 cannot constitute a good reason to think that B_1 is true. Thus we need to ask how B_2 might in turn be justified. Here again one possibility, the only one that we have identified so far, is that the justification of B_2 derives, via a suitable inferential or argumentative relation, from some further justified belief B_3. And now if the question regarding the justification of B_3 is answered in the same way by appeal to another justified belief B_4, and so on, we seem to be faced with a potential *infinite regress* in which each answer to an issue of justification simply raises a new issue of the same kind, thus seemingly never reaching any settled result and leaving it uncertain whether any of the beliefs in question is genuinely justified.

To think more carefully about this issue, we need to ask what the alternatives are as to the eventual outcome of this regress. What, that is, might eventually happen if we continue to ask for the justification of each new belief that is cited as a reason for an earlier belief in the sequence? (You should think about this issue carefully for yourself before reading further. For the moment try to consider all apparent possibilities, no matter how bizarre or implausible they may seem and no matter whether or not they seem initially to be compatible with the alleged justification of the original belief B_1.)

In fact, there seem to be only four possible outcomes of the regress.[4] First, we might eventually arrive at a belief, say B_6, upon which the justification of the previous belief in the series rests, but which is itself simply *unjustified*. This, however, would surely mean that the belief whose justification rests directly on B_6 is also not really justified, and so on up the line, so that the original belief B_1 turns out not to be justified either— contrary to our original supposition. There can be no doubt that some alleged justificatory chains do in fact end in this way, but if this were true in general, and if there were no other sort of justification available that does not rely in this way on inference from other beliefs, then we would have the skeptical result that no belief is ever justified, that we never have a good reason to think that anything is true. This would obviously be a very implausible result, at least from a commonsense standpoint.

Second, it *seems* to be at least logically possible that the regress might continue *infinitely*, with new beliefs being appealed to at each stage that are sufficient to justify the preceding belief but are themselves in need of justification from yet another new belief. This is perhaps the alternative that it is most difficult to get a clear focus on. Is it really even a logical possibility? And if it is logically possible, is there any serious chance that it might turn out to actually be realized, either in a particular case or in general?

It is tempting to argue that no finite person could have an infinite number of independent beliefs, but this does not seem to be strictly correct. As I gaze at my bare desk, can't I believe, all at once, that there is not an armadillo sitting on it, that there are not two armadillos sitting on it, that there are not three armadillos sitting on it, and so on for all of the infinitely many natural numbers (positive whole numbers), thus resulting in an infinite set of beliefs? Moreover, the members of such an infinite set of beliefs might even stand in the right inferential relations to yield a justificatory chain, as is indeed true with the present example: that there is not even one armadillo is a good, indeed conclusive reason for thinking that there are not two; that there are not even two is a conclusive reason for thinking that there are not three; and so on.

But though the actual infinite regress alternative is interesting to think about, it still seems clear that it could not play a role in an account of how beliefs are actually justified. One reason is that it is difficult or impossible to see how this picture could be applied to most actual cases of apparently justified belief, where no plausible infinite chain of this sort seems to be forthcoming. A deeper reason is that it is clear on reflection that merely having an infinite chain of beliefs related in the right way is not in fact sufficient for justification. Suppose that instead of believing that there are no armadillos on my desk, I am crazy enough to have the infinite set of beliefs to the effect that for each natural number n, there are at least n armadillos on my desk. You may doubt that I could really be this crazy (I hope you do!). If I were, however, then I could construct an infinite justificatory chain: that there are at least two armadillos is a conclusive reason for believing that there is at least one, that there are at least three is a conclusive reason for believing that there are at least two, and so on. But it still seems clear that none of these beliefs would really be justified. The reason is that in such a justificatory chain, the justification conferred at each step is only *provisional*, dependent on whether the beliefs further along in the chain are justified. But then if the regress continues infinitely, *all* of the alleged justification remains merely provisional: we never can say more than that the beliefs up to a particular stage *would* be justified *if* all of the others that come further back in the sequence are justified. And if this is all that we can ever say in such a case, and if all chains of inferential justification were infinite in this way, and if there were no other account of how beliefs are justified that does not rely on inference from other beliefs, then we again would have the unpalatable skeptical result that no belief is ever genuinely justified.

The third apparent possibility is that the chain of inferential justification, if pursued far enough, would eventually circle back upon itself: that is, that some belief that has already appeared in the sequence (or perhaps a conjunction of such beliefs) would be appealed to again. The belief that has this status might be the original belief B_1, or it might be some later belief in the sequence; suppose again that it is B_6 and that the belief for which it is supposed to provide the justification on this second occurrence is B_{10}. The obvious problem with a justificatory chain having this structure is that the overall reasoning that it reflects appears to be circular or question-begging in a way that deprives it of any justificatory force: Dropping out some of the intermediate stages (and assuming that the inferences are all correct), B_1 is justified if B_6 is, and B_6 is justified if B_{10} is, and B_{10} is justified if B_6 is. But then B_6 is justified just in case B_6 is justified, which is obviously true, but provides no reason at all to think that B_6 is in fact justified; and since the justification of B_1 depends on that of B_6, such a chain of justification also provides again no real justification for B_1. Once again we have an apparently skeptical result: if all inferential justification were ultimately circular in this way, and if there were no noninferential way in which beliefs are justified, then no belief would ever be genuinely justified.[5]

The fourth and final alternative is the one advocated by the foundationalist. It holds, first, that there is a way (or perhaps more than one way) in which beliefs can be justified that does not rely on inferential relations to other beliefs and so does not generate a regress of the sort we have been considering; and, second, that any chain of alleged inferential justifications that genuinely yields justification must terminate with beliefs that are justified in this other, noninferential way.

These noninferentially justified or *basic* beliefs are thus the *foundation* upon which the justification of all other beliefs ultimately rests.

The main argument for foundationalism is that this last alternative must be the correct one, since all of the other alternatives lead, in the ways we have seen, to the implausible skeptical result that no belief is ever justified. This may not be a conclusive argument for foundationalism, since it is hard to see any very clear basis for asserting that total skepticism could not possibly be correct (think about whether you agree with this), but it is surely a very powerful one, both intuitively and dialectically. Moreover, the most standard version of foundationalism, which is at least approximately the one reflected in part one of this book, has also a good deal of independent plausibility from a commonsense or intuitive standpoint: it certainly seems as though we have many beliefs that are justified, not via inference from other beliefs, but rather by sensory or introspective *experience* (and also by a priori insight). Thus the case for foundationalism appears initially to be quite strong.

Objections to Foundationalism

Nonetheless, as already remarked, there are many recent philosophers who hold that foundationalism is in fact seriously and irredeemably mistaken,[6] and we must try to understand the objections to foundationalism that they advance in support of this claim. These objections fall into two main categories, the first pertaining to the alleged relation of justification between the supposed foundational beliefs and the other, nonbasic beliefs that are supposed be justified by appeal to them and the second pertaining to the nature and justification of the foundational beliefs themselves.

The first kind of objection has to do with whether it is in fact possible on the basis of the foundation specified by a particular foundationalist position to provide an adequate justification for the other beliefs that we ordinarily regard as justified (which might be referred to as "superstructure" beliefs), or at least for a reasonably high proportion of such beliefs. For the Cartesian version of foundationalism we have been considering, the core of this issue is essentially: is it possible to justify beliefs concerning the external world of material objects on the basis of beliefs about immediately experienced states of mind (together with a priori justified beliefs in self-evident propositions)?

A foundationalist view that cannot justify giving an affirmative answer to this question, one for which a significant proportion of the beliefs that common sense regards as justified cannot be satisfactorily shown to be justifiable by appeal to its chosen foundation, will itself amount to a fairly severe version of skepticism, with the severity depending on just how thoroughgoing this failure turns out to be. Such a skeptical result obviously tends to seriously undercut the foundationalist argument from the regress problem, discussed above, which advocates foundationalism as the only way to *avoid* an implausible skepticism (though the skeptical consequences of any foundationalist view will never be as total as those that apparently result from the other possible outcomes of the regress, since at least the foundational beliefs themselves will still be justified).

In fact, the shape and seriousness of this first general sort of problem varies widely among foundationalist views, depending mainly on just how much is included in the specified set of basic or foundational beliefs.[7] There are versions of foundationalism according to which at least some perceptual beliefs about physical objects count as basic or foundational, and views of this sort have substantially less difficulty in giving a reasonably plausible account of the overall scope of nonfoundational knowledge than does the Cartesian view that restricts the empirical foundation to beliefs about subjective states of mind. In fact, however, as we will see toward the end of the present chapter, it is the Cartesian view that turns out to provide the most defensible response, indeed in my judgment the *only* defensible response, to the second main sort of objection to foundationalism, that concerning the justification of the foundational beliefs themselves. If this is right, then a defensible version of foundationalism will have to meet this first problem, not by expanding the foundation, but rather by arguing that the more restricted Cartesian foundation is indeed adequate to avoid unacceptably skeptical results.

Here, however, we will focus mainly on the second and seemingly more fundamental kind of objection to foundationalism, that which challenges the foundationalist to explain how the supposedly foundational or basic beliefs themselves are justified. In considering this issue, we will focus primarily on the empirical part of the foundation: the part that is not justified a priori and that thus consists of contingent beliefs, beliefs that are true in some possible worlds and false in others.[8] Most foundationalists follow the general line taken by the Cartesian view and hold that foundational beliefs of this kind are justified by appeal to sensory and introspective *experience*. But despite the apparent obviousness of this answer, it turns out to be more difficult than might be thought to give a clear account of how it is supposed to work.

There are in fact at least two ways of developing the problem that arises here, though they are perhaps in the end just different ways of getting at the same underlying point. The first version questions whether the whole idea of *sensory experience* justifying *beliefs* really makes intelligible sense,[9] and the starting point of the argument is the view that the distinctive content of a sensory experience is itself *nonpropositional* and *nonconceptual* in character.

Think here of an actual sensory experience, such as the one that I am presently having as I look out my window. (You should supply your own firsthand example.) There are many trees of different kinds at least partially in my field of view, and what I experience is a variegated field of mostly green with small patches of brown and gray and other colors, with many, many different shades and shapes, all changing in complicated and subtle ways as the wind blows or clouds move by. Given some time and close attention, I could apparently make many, many propositional and conceptual judgments about what I am experiencing: that one patch is larger than another, that one shape is similar to or different from another, that a particular patch is brighter than the one that was there a moment earlier, that various specific colors for which I have learned names are present, etc.[10] But my most fundamental experience of the sensory content itself is not propositional or conceptual in this way. It is not general or classificatory in character, not a consciousness *that* the experiential content falls under certain general categories or universals. The experienced sensory content itself is what these general or classificatory judgments are about, what makes them true or false, but this content is different from and vastly more specific than the various conceptual classifications, in a way that makes it extremely doubtful that it could ever be *fully* described in such conceptual terms.

Remember that the issue we are presently concerned with is whether sensory experience can *justify* beliefs. But if sensory experience is in this way nonconceptual, and given that beliefs are obviously formulated in propositional and conceptual terms, it becomes hard to see how there can be an intelligible justificatory relation between the two. How can something that is not even formulated in conceptual terms be a reason for thinking that something that is thus formulated is true? The present argument concludes that there can be no such justificatory relation—and hence, as the only apparent alternative, that the relation between sensory experience and beliefs must be merely *causal*. As the contemporary American philosopher Donald Davidson puts it:

> The relation between a sensation and a belief cannot be logical, since sensations are not beliefs or other propositional attitudes [that is, are not formulated in conceptual terms]. What then is the relation? The answer is, I think, obvious: the relation is causal. Sensations cause some beliefs and in *this* sense are the basis or ground of those beliefs. But a causal explanation of a belief does not show how or why the belief is justified.[11]

And if this is correct, then we have the extremely surprising result that the nonconceptual content of sensory experience, even though it undeniably exists, is apparently incapable of playing any justificatory role, and thus cannot provide the justification for foundational beliefs. Sensory experience in itself would thus turn out to have no very important epistemological significance.

The second, closely related antifoundationalist argument focuses on the person's *awareness* or *apprehension* of the experiential content.[12] Clearly (setting the previous argument aside for a moment) the experience that supposedly justifies a particular basic belief must have a correlative specific character that *somehow* makes it likely that that specific belief is true. Moreover, the person must somehow apprehend or be aware of the specific character of this experience if it is to provide him or her with justification (of an internalist sort) for his or her belief. But what is the nature of this apprehension or awareness of the character of the experience? There seem to be

two and only two possibilities here, neither of them apparently compatible with the foundationalist view. (Thus the argument takes the form standardly referred to by logicians as a *dilemma*.)

One possibility is that the specific character of the sensory experience is apprehended via a reflective *conceptual* awareness, that is, another *belief*: the belief that I have such-and-such a specific sort of experience. Here it is important to keep the whole picture in mind. We started with one supposedly foundational belief, which was presumably about some feature of the experience. In order to explain how that first belief is justified by the experience we needed to invoke an independent apprehension or awareness of the experience, and the suggestion is now that this apprehension or awareness takes the form of another belief. But now there are two problems. First, the original, supposedly basic belief that the experience was supposed to justify appears to have lost that status, since its justification now depends on this further belief, presumably via an inferential relation. Second and more importantly, there is now also a new issue as to how this further reflective belief is *itself* justified. Since this reflective belief is supposed to constitute the person's most basic apprehension or awareness of the experiential content (that was the whole point of introducing it), there is no apparent way for it to be justified by appeal to that content, since there is no further awareness of the content to appeal to.[13] And to invoke a further conceptual awareness of that same content, that is, yet another belief, only pushes this issue one step further back. In the process of trying to avoid the original regress, we seem to have generated a new one.

But the only apparent alternative is that the most fundamental apprehension or awareness of the specific character of the sensory content does not take the form of a conceptual belief *that* the experience is of a certain specific sort, but instead is not formulated in conceptual or classificatory terms at all. If so, then any further issue of justification is apparently avoided, since there is simply no further claim or assertion to be justified. But the problem now is that it becomes difficult to see how such an apprehension or awareness can provide a basis for the justification of the original, supposedly basic belief: If the apprehension of the experiential content is not in any way belief-like or propositional in character, then there is apparently no way to infer from that awareness to the truth (or likely truth) of the supposedly basic belief. And in the absence of such an inference, it is obscure how either the experience or the apprehension thereof constitutes any sort of reason for thinking that the supposedly basic belief is true.

These two objections are in effect two ways of getting at the fundamental issue of what the alleged justificatory relation between sensory experience and propositional, conceptual beliefs is supposed to amount to, how it is supposed to work. The relation cannot be logical or inferential, both because logical or inferential relations exist only between propositional or conceptual items, and sensory experience itself is not propositional or conceptual in character, and because an appeal to something that can stand in logical or inferential relations could not provide a genuine solution to the epistemic regress problem. But what then is the nature of this relation?

You may well think that these arguments must be somehow mistaken, that there must be some way in which the right sort of sensory experience can justify a belief. But then how exactly does this work? We will return to this issue at the end of the chapter, after we have had a look at the coherentist alternative.

In Search of Coherentism

The first problem we face in a discussion of coherentism is trying to get a clear idea of what a coherentist view really amounts to. The central idea is that epistemic justification depends on the *coherence* of a set of beliefs, rather than on inferential derivability from basic or foundational beliefs. But elaborating this initial idea into a developed position turns out to be extremely difficult. And while there are many specific positions, both historical and contemporary, that are fairly standardly identified as versions of coherentism,[14] it is unclear exactly what, if anything, they have in common beyond this central idea—or even that they all are entirely consistent in their adherence to it. Thus it is more than a little uncertain whether there is any clearly defined general view that can be identified as coherentism.

The best way to handle this problem is to consider some of the key issues that any coherentist view that is to be a genuine dialectical alternative to foundationalism must apparently face, attempting to figure out what a genuinely coherentist response might look like. Having done this, and having examined the problems and difficulties that arise along the way, we will then be in a position to attempt a further evaluation of coherentism.

The Nature of Coherence

The first and perhaps most obvious issue is the nature of coherence itself. It is clear that coherence is supposed to be primarily a property of a *group* or *system* of beliefs (though presumably a sufficiently complicated individual belief could be incoherent within itself). Proponents of coherence[15] speak of beliefs agreeing with each other or fitting together or "dovetailing" with each other. Part of what is required here is logical consistency: beliefs that are inconsistent with each other, that could not all be true at the same time in any possible world (for example, the belief that the earth is spherical and the belief that the earth is flat), plainly do not fit together or agree to any extent at all. But contrary to what opponents and even a few proponents of coherence sometimes seem to suggest, mere consistency is not by itself enough for any serious degree of coherence. Consider a set of entirely unrelated beliefs: the belief that grass is green, the belief that today is Tuesday, the belief that Caesar crossed the Rubicon in 49 B.C., and the belief that Matisse was a great painter. The set of beliefs is obviously consistent, simply because its members make no contact with each other at all and so could not possibly conflict, but it would be odd and misleading to describe it as coherent and perhaps still odder to suggest that this mere lack of conflict provides any real *justification* for these beliefs, any positive reason for thinking that they are true. And the same thing could obviously be true for a much larger set of beliefs.

In fact, it is clear that most of those loosely identified as coherentists have had a much stronger and more demanding relation among beliefs in mind, a relation in virtue of which a coherent set of beliefs will be tightly unified and structured, not merely an assemblage of unrelated items. Here it seems likely that all of the aspects or ingredients of this relation can be viewed as *inferential* relations of one sort or another among the component beliefs—with any sort of relation between two beliefs (or sets of beliefs) in virtue of which one would, if accepted, provide a good reason for thinking that the other is true counting as an inferential relation. The idea is thus that the members of a coherent system of beliefs are so related as to provide inferential support for each other, with the degree of coherence depending on the degree to which this is so, that is, on the number and strength of these inferential connections.

Although it is impossible to give a very good example of a coherent system of beliefs in the space reasonably available here, the following may help you to get a little better hold on the idea. Suppose that you are watching four birds in your back yard and form a set of ten beliefs about them, consisting of the beliefs with regard to each of the four (a) that the bird in question is a crow and (b) that the bird in question is black, together with the general beliefs (1) all crows are black and (2) that all black birds are crows. This set of ten beliefs is too small to be highly coherent, but it is far more coherent than the set of unrelated beliefs described earlier. The eight specific beliefs provide inductive support (one sort of inferential relation) for each of the two general beliefs, each member of the four pairs of specific beliefs provides deductive support (another sort of inferential relation) for the other when taken together with one of the general beliefs, and there are also inferential relations of an inductive sort between any seven of the specific beliefs and the eighth.[16] Thus this set of beliefs is about as closely unified as a set this small could be (though some mathematical examples might be even better in this respect) and provides an initial model of what a coherent set of beliefs might look like.

One general class of relations among beliefs that has received a great deal of emphasis in recent discussions of coherence is relations having to do with *explanation*. We have already seen in our earlier consideration of theoretical or explanatory reasoning how the fact that a hypothesis provides the best explanation for a set of justified claims might provide a reason for thinking that the hypothesis is true. But it is equally true that an explanatory hypothesis can, if accepted, help to provide inferential support for some of the claims that it could explain, though other premises will also be required. (The example in the previous paragraph provides a rough example of this sort of situation, though it is debatable to what extent, if at all, an inductive generalization really explains its instances.) Thus explanatory relations provide a basis

for inference and so constitute one ingredient of the general idea of coherence, one that goes beyond deductive and inductive relations. It seems excessive, however, to hold, as is sometimes done, that explanatory relations are all there is to coherence.

But while the foregoing discussion may suffice to give you some initial grasp of the concept of coherence, it is very far from an adequate account, especially one that would provide the basis for *comparative* assessments of the relative degrees of coherence possessed by different and perhaps conflicting systems of beliefs. And it is comparative assessments of coherence that seem to be needed if coherence is to be the sole basis that determines which beliefs are justified or even to play a significant role in such issues. There are somewhat fuller accounts of coherence available in the recent literature[17] but none that come at all close to achieving this goal. Thus practical assessments of coherence must be made on a rather ill-defined intuitive basis, making the whole idea of a coherentist epistemology more of a promissory note than a fully specified alternative.

A Response to the Epistemic Regress Problem: Nonlinear Justification

A second, equally urgent issue is how coherentism might respond to the epistemic regress problem. Of the four alternatives with regard to the outcome of the epistemic regress that were outlined above, the coherentist must apparently opt for the third, the idea that chains of inferential justification circle or loop back upon themselves, rather than ending in unjustified beliefs, going on infinitely, or terminating with foundational beliefs. Advocates of coherentism have occasionally claimed that such a view is acceptable as long as the circles and loops are large and complicated enough. But this response seems simply irrelevant to the objection discussed above: that such a picture involves circular reasoning and hence that the supposed chains of justification have in fact no genuine justificatory force. A large and complicated circle is still after all a circle. Is there anything better that the coherentist can say here?

Perhaps the best hope for a viable coherentist response to the regress problem is an idea offered originally by the nineteenth-century British idealist Bernard Bosanquet.[18] It amounts to the claim that the very formulation of this problem depends on a basic mistake concerning the structure of inferential justification: the mistaken idea that relations of inferential justification fundamentally involve a one-dimensional, asymmetrical, *linear* order of dependence among the beliefs in question. Once this linear picture is accepted, it is argued, the regress of justification is unavoidable and can be solved only in the (allegedly untenable) foundationalist way. Bosanquet's contrary suggestion is that inferential justification, when properly understood, is ultimately nonlinear or *holistic* in character, with all of the beliefs involved standing in relations of *mutual* support, but none being justificationally prior to the others. In this way, it is alleged, any objectionable circularity is avoided.

Such a view seems to amount to making the *group* or *system* of beliefs, rather than its individual members, the primary unit of justification, with the component beliefs being justified only derivatively, by virtue of their membership in such an adequately interrelated system. And the general property of such a system, in virtue of which it is justified, is of course identified as coherence.[19]

A further claim often made by proponents of nonlinear justification and by coherentist views generally is that the relevant "system" in relation to which issues of coherence and so of justification are to be decided is the entire set of beliefs held by the believer in question. Indeed, this is frequently taken completely for granted with little discussion. But such an extreme *holism* is in fact not required in any very clear way by the logic of the nonlinear view, and it moreover poses serious problems that the coherentist might be better advised to avoid. The already rather fuzzy idea of coherence becomes even more so when applied to comprehensive systems of beliefs, which will inevitably contain many beliefs having no discernible connection with each other. Moreover, even the minimal requirement of consistency is in fact rather unlikely to be satisfied by such a system. Thus it seems to be a mistake for the coherentist to take his holism this far (though this admittedly raises the far from easy issue of just what the relevant group or system is in relation to a particular belief).

Coherentism and Sense Perception

A third crucial issue facing the would-be coherentist is what to say about the epistemic role of sensory perception or observation.[20] Here the coherentist seems to

be faced with a stark choice. One alternative would be to simply deny that sensory perception plays any genuine justificatory role—deny, that is, that the fact that a belief is a result of perception contributes in any way to a reason for thinking that it is true. A coherentist who adopts this line need not deny the seemingly obvious fact that many of our beliefs are in fact *caused* by sensory experience. But he must insist that being produced in this way gives them no special justificatory status, so that their justification has to be assessed on the same basis as that of any other belief, namely by how well they fit into a coherent system of beliefs. Thus, according to this sort of view, a belief that is a mere hunch or is a product of wishful thinking or even is just arbitrarily made up but that coheres with a set of other beliefs (perhaps arrived at in the same ways!) will be justified, while a perceptual belief that is not related in this way to other beliefs will not be.

Such an extreme repudiation of the justificatory relevance of sensory perception or observation is both quite implausible from a commonsense standpoint and also greatly aggravates the issue, to be considered next, of why the fact that a belief satisfies the test of coherence is any reason for thinking that it is true. For these reasons, few coherentists have been willing to go this far.[21] But the alternative is to try to somehow accommodate an important justificatory role for sense perception or observation within the coherentist framework, something that it is not at all easy to see how to do, since at least the most straightforward ways of doing so seem to amount to a return to foundationalism.

Perhaps the best that the coherentist can do on this issue is to continue to insist that sensory experience in itself merely causes beliefs but cannot justify them, while adding that the fact that a belief was caused in this way rather than some other can play a crucial role in a special kind of coherentist justification. The idea is that the justification of these perceptual or observational beliefs, rather than merely appealing to the coherence of their propositional contents with the contents of other beliefs (so that the way that the belief was produced would be justificationally irrelevant), appeals instead to a general belief that beliefs caused in this specific way (and perhaps satisfying further conditions as well) are generally true, where this belief is in turn supported by inductive inference from many apparently true instances of beliefs of this kind, with the apparent truth of these instances being in turn justified by various inferences falling under the general heading of coherence. Such perceptual beliefs would obviously not be *arrived at* via inference, but they would still be inferentially *justified* in a way that allegedly depends ultimately on coherence: the coherence of the general belief about the reliability of beliefs caused in this way with the rest of the relevant system of beliefs.

In this way, it has been claimed, sense perception or observation can after all play a role in coherentist justification. Moreover, beliefs justified in this way, since their justification does not depend on their specific content but only on the way that they are caused, could either agree with or conflict with other beliefs that the person holds, thus providing the sort of independent check or test of one's beliefs that sensory observation is often claimed to provide. And a coherentist view could seemingly *require* (not merely allow) that beliefs justified in this way play a substantial justificatory role, while still retaining its coherentist character.[22]

Does the foregoing picture really succeed in accommodating the epistemic role of sense perception or observation within a coherentist framework? Like virtually everything about coherentism, the details are sketchy, and in fact there are very serious problems that lurk not far beneath the surface, some but not all of which will be addressed below.

Coherence and Truth

We come now to the most fundamental and obvious issue of all: Why should the fact that a belief satisfies the standards of a coherentist account be taken to show that it is justified in the sense of there being a good reason for thinking that it is *true*? What does coherence even have to do with truth or likelihood of truth (assuming, as we will here, that a coherence theory of truth is unacceptable).[23]

We may approach this issue by considering first how a coherentist might respond to two related, but more specific issues. The first of these is what is usually referred to as the *input* or *isolation* problem. If we assume, first, that there is much more to reality than a person's system of beliefs and, second, that most of those beliefs purport to describe that larger reality, then the obvious question is why the fact that those beliefs are coherent with each other constitutes any reason to think that what they say about the reality external to them is true or correct. Why couldn't a system of beliefs be perfectly coherent while nonetheless entirely impervious to any sort of influence or input from external reality, thus being completely isolated from it? But if this were so, it could seemingly be only an unlikely accident or coincidence if the beliefs in question happened to be true. Thus, it is argued, coherence is irrelevant to truth and so provides no basis for justification.

It is at this point that the defensibility of the coherentist account of sensory observation, briefly sketched above, becomes critical. For *if* that account can be fleshed out and defended, then (and, I would suggest, only then) the coherentist will have a response to this objection: that the observational beliefs justified in the way indicated are after all *caused* by external reality and so represent a kind of external input to the system of beliefs that can solve the isolation problem. Note that even the initial plausibility of this response depends on the fact that the way that observational beliefs are caused plays a role in their justification (and also on the admittedly vague requirement that beliefs justified in this way play a substantial justificatory role); if they were caused in this way but justified solely on the basis of the coherence of their contents with those of other beliefs, thus being on a par with hunches, products of wishful thinking, beliefs resulting from mere dogmatism, and so on (or if such observational beliefs were simply too rare to have much impact), then the influence of the world on the system of beliefs would be too minimal to make truth likely.

A second problem is raised by the apparent possibility of *alternative coherent systems*. Since coherence is a purely internal property of a group or system of beliefs, it seems possible to invent indefinitely many alternative systems of belief in a purely arbitrary way and yet make each of them entirely coherent, with *any* possible belief that is internally consistent and coherent being a member of some of these systems. But since the beliefs in one such system will conflict with those in others, they obviously cannot all be justified. Thus there must be some basis other than coherence for choosing among these systems and the beliefs they contain, so that coherence is not by itself an adequate basis for justification.

Here again the best response available to the coherentist seems to depend on the suggested coherentist account of observation. For *if* that account can be made to work, then the coherentist can seemingly require that any system whose coherence is to be a basis for genuine justification (i) must include such an observational ingredient and (ii) must *remain* coherent as new observational beliefs are added. There is no apparent reason to think that just any arbitrarily invented system of beliefs will satisfy these further requirements. Indeed, though the issues are very complicated, there is no very clear reason for thinking that more than one system will do so in the long run.

The responses to these two problems point toward a coherentist response to the general problem of truth. *If* (and this is still a very big if) the coherentist account of observational input can be successfully elaborated and defended, then the coherentist can attempt to argue that the best *explanation* for the long-run coherence of a system of beliefs in the face of continued observational input is that the beliefs in the system are being systematically caused by an external reality that they accurately depict, and hence that they are likely to be true.[24] Even apart from the worries about the account of observation itself, there is much more that would have to be done to spell out and elaborate this argument,[25] but for now, this initial outline of how an argument linking coherence with truth might go will have to do.

Further Objections to Coherentism

Coherentism emerges from the foregoing discussion as a shaky and problematic position at best, on the defensive from the beginning and afflicted with a multitude of problems and objections that are not answerable in any conclusive way. But there are many further objections as well. Here I will consider only two of them, both having to do in different ways with the general issue of the accessibility of coherentist justification to the believer.

First, if coherence is to be the basis for empirical justification,[26] then an *internalist* coherence theory must require that the believer have an adequate grasp or representation of the relevant system of beliefs, since it is in relation to this system that coherence and so justification are determined. Such a grasp would presumably take the form of a set of reflective beliefs (or one comprehensive reflective belief) specifying the contents of the relevant system. And the seemingly

glaring difficulty is that the coherentist view also seemingly precludes there being any way in which such reflective beliefs are themselves justified. Such beliefs are obviously contingent and presumably empirical in character; and yet any appeal to coherence for their justification would seem to be plainly circular or question-begging, since what is at issue is in part the specification of the very system of beliefs in relation to which coherence is to be assessed. Until I have a *justified* grasp of the contents of the relevant system, I can't tell which reflective beliefs of this kind are justified; but a justified grasp of the contents of that system depends on a prior answer to just this question.

Here it is hard to avoid suspecting that would-be coherentists have failed to adequately purge themselves of an intuitive outlook that is really compatible only with foundationalism. From a traditional foundationalist standpoint, there is no real problem about one's grasp of one's own beliefs, since this is a matter of immediate experience for occurrent beliefs and can be made so for dispositional beliefs. But coherentists reject any such appeal to immediate experience, and so cannot legitimately appeal to this sort of access.

Second, a less obvious but equally serious objection pertains to the coherentist's attempted account of observational input and the accompanying answer to the alternative coherent systems objection and argument for the connection between coherence and truth. An essential component of all of this is the idea that the observational status of a belief can be recognized *in a justified way* from within the person's system of beliefs, for only then could this status be used as a partial basis for the justification of such a belief, which then in turn would allow such observational beliefs to be appealed to for these various further purposes. Here again, recognizing that a belief is a result of sensory observation rather than arbitrary invention is at least reasonably unproblematic from a foundationalist standpoint that can invoke immediate experience. But for a coherentist, the basis for such a recognition can only be the further *belief*, itself supposedly justified by coherence, that a given belief has this status. And then there is no apparent reason why the various alternative coherent systems cannot include within themselves beliefs about the occurrence of various allegedly observational beliefs that would support the other beliefs in such a system, with these supposed observations being justified within each system in the way indicated above. Of course, such beliefs will not in general *really* be observational in character, but the coherentist has no way to appeal to this fact that is compatible with his coherentist framework. Thus there is no way consistent with coherentism to distinguish genuine observational input from this counterfeit variety, nor any way on the basis of the only sort of "observation" that is internally recognizable to answer the isolation and alternative coherent systems objections or to argue from coherence to likelihood of truth.

These last two objections appear in fact to be completely devastating to coherentism. I note in passing that it might be possible to avoid or at least mitigate them by adopting an *externalist* version of coherentism. But externalism, as we will see in the next chapter, faces serious problems of its own; and in any case, an externalist version of coherentism would have no dialectical point, since if externalism were otherwise acceptable, a foundationalist version would be much more straightforward and easier to defend.

Foundationalism Revisited

The sort of view that is often regarded as the main contemporary alternative to foundationalism has been examined and found wanting, but that is not enough, of course, to answer the antifoundationalist arguments, in particular the arguments purporting to show that sensory experience is incapable of justifying conceptual beliefs and thus incapable of providing a foundation of the sort that the foundationalist is seeking. We thus need to return to those arguments and see whether they are really as powerful as they have often been taken to be.

It will be useful to begin with the second of the two arguments that were presented earlier in this chapter. This argument, as we saw, takes the form of a *dilemma* concerning the apprehension of the character of the experience, mainly sensory experience, to which the foundationalist wants to appeal for the justification of foundational beliefs: if the character of such experience is apprehended in a conceptual or propositional state, a belief, then it seems capable of providing a reason for thinking that further beliefs are true, but is also itself in need of justification; whereas if the apprehension of the character of experience is not in conceptual

or propositional terms, if it does not involve any apprehension *that* the experience in question has one sort of general or classificatory character rather than another, the need for justification is avoided, but at the cost of rendering the apprehension seemingly incapable of providing justification for any further belief.

The suggestion that I want to offer here will be at least a bit easier to see if we focus initially on a somewhat different case, the case where the (alleged) basic belief in question is the reflective belief that I have some other specific occurrent belief. The natural place to look for justification for such a reflective belief is to the *experience* of having the other belief in question. And here the crucial fact that, I will suggest, allows an escape between the horns of the dilemma just mentioned is that my most fundamental experience or awareness of one of my own occurrent beliefs is *neither* a separate reflective belief or belief-like state that would itself require justification *nor* a noncognitive awareness of some sort that fails to reflect the specific character of the apprehended state, that is, in this case, the propositional content of the belief. Instead, I suggest, to have a conscious occurrent belief just *is*, in part, to have a conscious awareness of the content of that belief (and also of one's accepting attitude toward that content), an awareness that is not reflective (or "second order") in nature, but is instead partly *constitutive* of the first-level occurrent belief state itself. My further suggestion is then that it is by appeal to this nonreflective, constitutive awareness that a reflective, second-order belief can be justified—though we now see that it is this constituent, nonreflective awareness rather than the reflective belief that ultimately deserves to be called "basic."

The ideas in the previous paragraph are perhaps more difficult and philosophically sophisticated than anything that you have encountered so far in this book, so I want to pause a bit to make sure that you have them in clear focus. The main distinction is between (a) a belief that is about *another*, distinct belief (and thus reflective or "second-order") and (b) the conscious awareness of a belief's *own* content that is, I am claiming, a constitutive or intrinsic feature of any conscious, occurrent belief, without the need for a second, independent belief. To take a specific example, suppose that I have the first-order, conscious or occurrent belief that the sun is shining. Then the relevant second-order or reflective belief, which might or might not actually be present, would have the content *I (presently) believe that the sun is shining*; whereas the intrinsic or constitutive awareness of the content of the first-order belief, an awareness that *always* occurs when I have such a belief, would just be the conscious thought *the sun is shining*, with no reference to me as the thinker. The crucial point is simply that an occurrent belief is, after all, a *conscious state*, and that what one is primarily conscious of in having such a belief is precisely its propositional content (together with the fact that this content is being accepted rather than, say, doubted or wondered about).

If this is right, then this constitutive awareness of content can seemingly provide a justifying reason for the reflective belief that I have an occurrent belief with that very content. Indeed, in the normal case, it is precisely because I am aware in the constitutive way of the content of my belief that I am led, when and if I reflect, to form the reflective belief that I have such-and-such a first-order belief. But, at the same time, there is no apparent way in which the nonreflective, constituent awareness of content itself requires any sort of justification: an issue of justification can, of course, be raised about the belief as a whole (do I have any reason to think that the sun is shining?), but not about my non-reflective awareness of the content of the belief. Because of its nonreflective, constituent character, this "built-in" awareness, as it might be described, thus neither requires any justification, nor for that matter even admits of any. Indeed, this constituent awareness of content might be said to be strictly *infallible* in something like the way that many foundationalist views historically have claimed: because it is this constitutive or "built-in" awareness of content that *gives* the belief its specific content, that *makes* it the particular belief that it is with the content that it has (rather than some other belief or some nonbelief state), there is apparently no way in which this awareness could be mistaken, simply because there is no relevant fact independent of the awareness itself for it to be mistaken about.[271]

This infallibility does not, however, extend to a reflective, second-order belief: though such a belief can, I am claiming, be justified by appeal to the awareness that is a constitutive feature of the first-order belief that is its object, it would still apparently be possible to reflectively misapprehend the content of one's own belief, to have a reflective belief that does not accurately reflect the content contained in the constitutive or "built-in" awareness. Such a mistake might be due to mere inattention, or it might result from the complexity or obscurity of the belief content itself or from some further problem or disorder. But unless there is some reason in a particular case to think that the chance of such a misapprehension is large, this mere possibility of error does not seem enough to prevent the reflective belief from being justifiable by appeal to the constituent awareness.

The foregoing provides an outline of how a certain specific sort of belief, namely a reflective, second-order belief about the existence and content of one of my own conscious, occurrent beliefs, can be basic or foundational in the sense of there being an internally available reason why it is likely to be true without that reason depending on any further belief or other cognitive state that is itself in need of justification—though, as we have seen, it is really the constitutive awareness of content rather than the reflective belief that ultimately turns out to be foundational. But though my immediate awareness of my own occurrent beliefs is a part of my overall immediate experience and plays some role in justification, the most important part of that experience for issues of justification is my immediate awareness of sensory content. My suggestion is that an essentially parallel account can be given of how this awareness too can justify foundational beliefs.

Consider then a state of, for example, visual experience, such as the one that I am presently having as I look out of the window in my study (see the rough description offered earlier in this chapter). Like an occurrent belief, such an experience is of course a conscious state. This means, I suggest, that in a way that parallels the account of occurrent belief offered above, it automatically involves a constitutive or "built-in," nonreflective awareness of its own distinctive sort of content, in this case sensory or "phenomenal" content. And, again in parallel fashion, such an awareness is in no need of justification and is indeed in a sense infallible in that there is no sort of mistake that is even relevant to it. Thus this awareness of sensory content is also apparently able to justify reflective beliefs that are about that content. For example, the reflective belief that I am experiencing a patch of bright green in the middle of my visual field can be justified by appeal to the constitutive or built-in awareness that is what makes that experience the specific experience that it is. (If, that is, I am in fact having that experience—here, as with belief, mistakes are possible, even if unlikely.)

But does this really answer the antifoundationalist arguments offered above? Even if it is correct that the constitutive or built-in awareness raises no further issue of justification, is there really an intelligible justificatory relation between it and a basic belief about the character of the experience? Perhaps this relation of justification is plausible enough in the case considered earlier, where the constitutive awareness is an awareness of the content of an occurrent belief, for there the awareness of content is in conceptual terms that connect in an obvious way with the conceptual content of the reflective belief, even if the constitutive awareness involves no conceptual *judgment* about that content that could demand justification. (Think again about the example described earlier.) But does this really work in the present and ultimately more important case, in which the content of the constitutive awareness is, as we saw earlier, not at all in conceptual terms (so that some, indeed, would refuse even to describe it as "content")? Aren't the earlier arguments still correct that there can be no intelligible justificatory relationship between the constitutive awareness of content of *this* sort and a conceptual belief that purports to describe it?

In fact, we are now in a position to see that these arguments rest on too simple a view of the alternatives for the relation between a sensory experience and a conceptual belief. If we grant (and indeed insist) that the specific content of such an experience is itself nonpropositional and nonconceptual in character, then it is quite correct that there can be no strictly *logical* or *inferential* relation between (a) this content (or the constitutive awareness thereof) and (b) a reflective, conceptual belief about that content: since the awareness of nonconceptual content is neither true nor false (because it makes no conceptual claim), it cannot be the case (as an inference would require) that its truth guarantees the truth of the belief. But such an experience, like other kinds of nonconceptual phenomena, can of course still be conceptually *described* with various degrees of detail and precision. The relation between the nonconceptual

content and such a conceptual description of it is not logical or inferential, but it is also obviously not merely causal. Rather it is a *descriptive* relation, one in which the thing described does or does not fit or conform to the description. And where such a relation of description exists, the actual character of the nonconceptual object can obviously constitute a kind of reason or basis for thinking that the description is true or correct (or equally, of course, untrue or incorrect).

Thus suppose that I have a specific conscious state of sensory experience (an experience that includes a round, green patch in the middle of my visual field), and am, as already argued, consciously but nonconceptually aware of the specific sensory content of that state simply by virtue of having that experience. Suppose that at the same time I entertain a reflective belief that purports to describe or conceptually characterize that perceptual content, albeit no doubt incompletely (the reflective belief that I have a round, green patch in the middle of my visual field). If I *understand* the descriptive content of that belief, that is, understand what sort of experience it would take to fit or satisfy the conceptual description, then I seem to be in a good, indeed an ideal, position to judge whether the conceptual description is accurate as far as it goes, whether it fits the nonconceptual experience I am actually having, and if so, to be thereby justified in accepting the belief. Here again there is no reason to think that mistake is impossible and thus no reason to think that such a reflective belief is infallible. But as long as there is no special reason for suspecting that a mistake has occurred, the fact that such a belief seems to me on the basis of direct comparison to accurately characterize the conscious experience that it purports to describe seems to be an entirely adequate reason for thinking that the description is correct and hence an adequate basis for justification.

Such a reason is, of course, only available to one who has some sort of independent cognitive access to the character of the nonconceptual item, that is, an access that does not depend on the conceptual description itself. In most other cases, such as where it is some physical object or situation that is being described, one could have an access that is independent of the description in question only by having a second conceptual state embodying a second, perhaps more specific description, and this second description would of course itself equally require justification, so that no genuinely foundational justification would result. But in the very special case we are concerned with, where the nonconceptual item being described is *itself* a conscious state, one can, I am suggesting, be aware of its character via the constitutive or "built-in" awareness that any conscious state involves, without the need for a further conceptual description—and thereby be in a position to recognize that a reflective belief about that state is (or is not) correct.

Here we seem indeed to be in a position to make a direct comparison between a conceptual description and the nonconceptual chunk of reality that it purports to describe—something that seems intuitively to be essential if our conceptual descriptions are ever to make contact with reality in a verifiable way.[28] Such a comparison is only possible, to be sure, where the reality in question is itself a conscious state and where the description in question pertains to the conscious content of that very state, but in that specific case it seems to be entirely unproblematic.

Thus at least the most standard version of foundationalism seems to have an adequate response to the second general sort of objection to foundationalism distinguished earlier: the one that pertains to the nature and justification of the foundational beliefs themselves. As already suggested, however, this response seriously aggravates the first kind of objection, the one that challenges whether the rest of what common sense regards as knowledge can be justified on the basis of the foundation thus arrived at.

Notes

1. The formulation just given is probably more or less the way that Descartes would have put the point, if he had spoken explicitly in these terms. More recent versions of foundationalism have tended to say instead that the foundation consists of the *beliefs* about immediately experienced conscious states of mind together with the *beliefs* deriving from the a priori grasp of self-evident propositions, rather than the immediate awarenesses or a priori insights themselves. The significance of this difference will be considered further in the text.

2. The contextualist view is also, in a way, an alternative to foundationalism.

3. It turns out to be surprisingly difficult to say just what these conditions are. Having the argument explicitly in mind at the time in question is surely not necessary. Indeed it is doubtful if the person need *ever* have thought in a fully explicit way about the inferential relation in question. Our lives are very busy, and explicit formulation and consideration of arguments is something we do only rarely and usually where the need is in some way urgent. (See if you can think of examples, perhaps ones where you are the person involved, of a person apparently being justified in holding a belief by virtue of an inferential relation that he or she has never explicitly considered up to the time in question.) At the same time, it seems also clear that the availability of the justifying argument must be at least part of the reason that the person holds the belief if it is to be justified on that basis; merely the fact that the argument would have occurred to the person if the belief had been challenged is not enough.

4. Though a given case might realize more than one of these on different branches of the justificatory chain. In the text, I ignore for simplicity the possibility and indeed likelihood that the chain would branch over and over as two or more beliefs are appealed to in justifying a previous one.

5. The coherentist alternative to foundationalism is sometimes characterized as a realization of this third alternative. But while there is some point to saying this, it is also, as we will see, rather seriously misleading. Whatever the merits of coherentism may turn out to be, it will in fact give us no reason to question the objection to the third possibility just formulated.

6. Including an earlier incarnation of the present author. See my book *The Structure of Empirical Knowledge* (Cambridge, Mass.: Harvard University Press, 1985) (hereafter referred to as *SEK*).

7. Which will depend in turn on the specific account given of how those beliefs are justified—see below. As the discussion in the text suggests, the main divergences in this area pertain to the empirical part of the foundation.

8. This assumes, of course, that an adequate foundation could not consist entirely of beliefs justified a priori, and you should think about whether this is correct and how it might be argued for. You should also ask yourself to what extent there are problems with the a priori part of the foundation that parallel those that pertain to the contingent, empirical part—and indeed whether an a priori part is really required at all.

9. See for example Donald Davidson, "A Coherence Theory of Truth and Knowledge," in *Kant oder Hegel*, ed. Dieter Henrich (Stuttgart: Klett-Cotta, 1983), pp. 423–38.

10. According to the view considered and tentatively adopted in chapter 6, these judgements are either about my sense-data or about my adverbial contents.

11. Davidson, "A Coherence Theory of Truth and Knowledge," p. 428.

12. This objection was first advanced by Wilfrid Sellars. See Sellars, "Empiricism and the Philosophy of Mind," reprinted in his *Science, Perception and Reality* (London: Routledge & Kegan Paul, 1963); and "The Structure of Knowledge," his Matchette lectures at the University of Texas, in *Action, Knowledge, and Reality*, ed. Hector-Neri Castañeda (Indianapolis, Ind.: Bobbs-Merrill, 1975), pp. 295–347, especially Lecture III.

13. Might such a belief be *self-evident?* Not at least in the sense that applies to a priori claims: the contingent content of such a belief is not in itself a reason for thinking that it is true, since that content is true in some possible worlds or situations and not in others, and there is seemingly nothing else about the belief to appeal to.

14. Some of the main ones are the absolute idealist views of F. H. Bradley, Bernard Bosanquet, and Brand Blanshard; the views of some of the logical positivists, mainly Otto Neurath and a relatively early incarnation of Carl Hempel; the epistemological views of the contemporary philosophers Wilfrid Sellars, Keith Lehrer, Nicholas Rescher, and Donald Davidson; and the view held by the present author in *SEK*. The epistemological position of W. V. O. Quine is also sometimes regarded as a version of coherentism, though this is much more debatable. For some discussion of some of these views and specific references, see *SEK*.

15. Who are not always coherentists, since coherence can play less central but still important roles in foundationalist views. See, for example, C. I. Lewis, *An Analysis of Knowledge and Valuation*, chapter 11 (who appeals to what he calls "congruence"); and Roderick M. Chisholm, *Theory of Knowledge*, 2nd ed. (Englewood Cliffs, N.J.: Prentice-Hall, 1977), chapter 4 (who appeals to what he calls "concurrence").

16. In thinking about this example, it is important to put aside your background knowledge that there are other black birds besides crows, as well as any justification that might be thought to result from your perception of the birds. We are concerned only with the *internal* coherence of the set of beliefs, and for that purpose anything outside that set of beliefs is irrelevant. (Thinking about this point may, however, suggest one of the main problems with the idea that coherence is the sole basis for justification.)

17. See *SEK*, chapter 5 and appendix B.

18. See Bernard Bosanquet, *Implication and Linear Inference* (London: Macmillan, 1920).

19. For more development of this idea, see *SEK*, pp. 89–93.

20. There are also closely related issues concerned with introspection, which is often regarded as a kind of inner, nonsensory perception or observation, but I will not consider these explicitly here.

21. Two that at least seem to do so are Donald Davidson and Keith Lehrer. See the paper by Davidson referred to in note 11; and Keith Lehrer, *Knowledge* (Oxford: Oxford University Press, 1974).

22. Or at least its nonfoundationalist character. Such a view would not be a *pure* coherentist view, since the rationale for this further requirement is not in any clear way a product of coherence. But since the main dialectical rationale for coherentism is just the avoidance of foundationalism, this impurity does not seem to matter. For further discussion of all these matters, see *SEK*, chapters 6 and 7. (Though I should make clear that I no longer regard the view defended in that book as tenable.)

23. See the discussion in chapter 3. In fact, the adoption of coherentist views of justification constitutes the main historical motive for coherence theories of truth (though often enough the two were not very clearly distinguished).

24. For a somewhat fuller but still pretty schematic version, see *SEK*, chapter 8.

25. I will assume (and indeed have been assuming all along) that the coherentist view attempts to account only for empirical justification: the justification of contingent, nona priori beliefs. Since an a priori appeal is needed to establish some or all of the very ingredients of the concept of coherence (at least deductive inference relations and logical consistency, but arguably inductive and abductive inference relations as well), a coherentist account of a priori justification appears to be viciously circular in a way that the suggested coherentist response to the general concern about circularity cannot overcome.

26. Of course, this also means that there is no independent fact that it is correct about either, which is an important qualification on the sort of infallibility in question.

27. Doubts about the possibility of such a confrontation have sometimes been advanced as an additional argument against the correspondence theory of truth.

28. It is plausible to suppose that it is this sort of nonreflective, constituent awareness of the content of a conscious state that earlier epistemologists and some more recent ones have had at least primarily in mind in their use of the notions of "immediate awareness" or "direct acquaintance." (See the discussion in chapter 6) But if this is right, then many discussions of immediate experience or direct acquaintance have been needlessly obscure, suggesting as they do some sort of mysteriously authoritative or infallible apprehension of an *independent* cognitive object, rather than an

awareness that is simply constitutive of the conscious state itself. And the occasional suggestions that one might possibly be immediately aware of or directly acquainted with material objects simply make no sense on the present account of what immediate awareness amounts to. This is the fundamental reason why, in my judgment, a defensible version of foundationalism cannot avoid the problem of the external world by including perceptual beliefs about physical objects in the foundation (as the most straightforward version of direct realism in effect tries to do).

✧ FOUNDHERENTISM ✧

17. A FOUNDHERENTIST THEORY OF EMPIRICAL JUSTIFICATION[1]

Susan Haack

Let us remember how common the folly is, of going from one faulty extreme into the opposite.[2]

Does the evidence presented establish beyond a reasonable doubt that the defendant did it? Given the evidence recently discovered by space scientists, am I justified in believing there was once bacterial life on Mars? Is scientific evidence especially authoritative, and if so, why? Should we take those advertisements claiming that the Holocaust never happened seriously, and if not, why not? . . . Questions about what makes evidence better or worse, about what makes inquiry better or worse conducted, about disinterestedness and partiality, are of real, daily—and sometimes of life-and-death—consequence.

Of late, however, cynicism about the very legitimacy of such questions has become the familiar philosophical theme of a whole chorus of voices, from enthusiasts of the latest developments in neuroscience, to radical self-styled neo-pragmatists, radical feminists and multiculturalists, and followers of (by now somewhat dated) Paris fashions.

This cynicism is unwarranted; but dealing with it requires something a bit more radical than epistemological business-as-usual. Evidence is often messy, ambiguous, misleading; inquiry is often untidy, inconclusive, biased by the inquirers' interests; but it doesn't follow, as the cynics apparently suppose, that standards of good evidence and well-conducted inquiry are local, conventional, or mythical. And an even half-way adequate understanding of the complexities of real-life evidence and the untidiness of real-life inquiry requires a re-examination of some of those comfortably familiar dichotomies on which recent epistemology has relied—the logical versus the causal, internalism versus externalism, apriorism versus naturalism, foundationalism versus coherentism.

Though the other dichotomies will also come under scrutiny, the main theme here will be that foundationalism and coherentism—the traditionally rival theories of justified belief—do not exhaust the options, and that an intermediate theory is more plausible than either. I call it "foundherentism."

The Case for Foundherentism

Foundationalist theories of empirical justification hold that an empirical belief is justified if and only if it is either a basic belief justified by the subject's experience,[3] or else a derived belief justified, directly or indirectly, by the support of basic beliefs. Coherentist theories of empirical justification hold that a belief is justified if and only if it belongs to a coherent set of beliefs. In short, foundationalism requires a distinction of basic versus derived beliefs and an essentially one-directional notion of evidential support, while coherentism holds that beliefs can be justified only by mutual support among themselves.

The merit of foundationalism is that it acknowledges that a person's experience—what he sees, hears, etc.—is relevant to how justified he is in his beliefs about the world; its drawback is that it requires a privileged class of basic beliefs justified by experience alone but capable of supporting the rest of our justified beliefs, and ignores the pervasive interdependence among a person's beliefs. The merit of coherentism is that it acknowledges that pervasive interdependence, and requires no distinction of basic and derived beliefs; its drawback is that it allows no role for the subject's experience.

Foundationalists, naturally, are keenly aware of the problems with coherentism. How could one possibly be justified in believing there's a dog in the yard, they ask, if what one sees, hears, smells, etc., plays no role? And isn't the coherentist's talk of mutual support among beliefs just a euphemism for what is really a vicious circle in which what supposedly justifies the belief that p is the belief that q, and what justifies the belief that q the belief that r, . . . and what justifies the belief that z is the belief that p?

Coherentists, naturally, are no less keenly aware of the problems with foundationalism. What sense does it make to suppose that someone could have a justified belief that there's a dog in the yard, they ask, except in the context of the rest of his beliefs about dogs, etc.? Besides, why should we suppose that there *are* any beliefs both justified by experience alone and capable of supporting the rest of our justified beliefs? After all, foundationalists can't even agree among themselves whether the basic beliefs are about observable physical objects, along the lines of "there's a dog," or are about the subject's experience, along the lines of "it now seems to me that I see what looks like a dog" or "I am appeared to brownly." And anyway, only propositions, not events, can stand in logical relations to other propositions; so how *could* a subject's experience justify those supposedly basic beliefs?

As the two styles of theory have evolved, with each party trying to overcome the difficulties the other thinks insuperable, they have come closer together.

Strong foundationalism requires that basic beliefs be fully justified by the subject's experience; pure foundationalism requires that derived beliefs be justified exclusively by the support, direct or indirect, of basic beliefs. But weak foundationalism requires only that basic beliefs be justified to some degree by experience; and impure foundationalism, though requiring all derived beliefs to get some support from basic beliefs, allows mutual support among derived beliefs to raise their degree of justification.

Uncompromisingly egalitarian forms of coherentism hold that only overall coherence matters, so that every belief in a coherent set is equally justified. But moderated, inegalitarian forms of coherentism give a subject's beliefs about his present experience a distinguished initial status, or give a special standing to beliefs which are spontaneous rather than inferential in origin.

In a way, these moderated forms of foundationalism and coherentism lean in the right direction. But the leaning destabilizes them.

Weak foundationalism concedes that basic beliefs need not be fully justified by experience alone; but then what reason remains to deny that they could get more (or less) justified by virtue of their relations to other beliefs? Impure foundationalism concedes that there can be mutual support among derived beliefs; but then what reason remains to insist that more pervasive mutual support is unacceptable? And weak, impure foundationalism allows both that basic beliefs are less than fully justified by experience, and that derived beliefs may be mutually supportive; but now the insistence that derived beliefs can give no support to basic beliefs looks arbitrary, and the distinction of basic and derived beliefs pointless.[4]

Moderated, inegalitarian coherentism concedes that some beliefs are distinguished by their perceptual content or "spontaneous" origin; but isn't this implicitly to concede that justification is not after all a relation exclusively among beliefs, that input from experience is essential?

Not surprisingly, these fancier forms of foundationalism and compromising kinds of coherentism, though more sophisticated than their simpler ancestors, tend to be ambiguous and unstable. On the foundationalist side, for example, under pressure of just the kinds of difficulty my analysis identifies, C. I. Lewis moves from a pure to an impure foundationalism and then, briefly, to a kind of proto-foundherentism.[5] And on the coherentist side, under pressure of just the kind of difficulty my analysis identifies, BonJour tries to guarantee experiential input by adding an "Observation Requirement"—which, however, is ambiguous; on one interpretation it is genuinely coherentist, but doesn't allow the relevance of experience, and on the other it allows the relevance of experience, but isn't genuinely coherentist.[6] (BonJour now acknowledges that, after all, coherentism won't do.)[7]

Neither of the traditionally rival theories can be made satisfactory without sacrificing its distinctive character. The obvious conclusion—though those still wedded to the old dichotomy will doubtless continue to resist it—is that we need a new approach which allows the relevance of experience to empirical justification, but without postulating any privileged class of basic beliefs or requiring that relations of support be essentially one-directional: in other words, a foundherentist theory.

Explication of Foundherentism

The details get complicated, but the main ideas are simple.

A foundherentist account will acknowledge (like foundationalism) that how justified a person is in an empirical belief must depend in part on his experience—my version will give a role both to sensory experience, and to introspective awareness of one's own mental states. As coherentists point out, though experience can stand in causal relations to beliefs, it can't stand in logical relations to propositions. But what this shows is not that experience is irrelevant to empirical justification, but that justification is a double-aspect concept, partly causal as well as partly logical in character.

A foundherentist account will acknowledge (like coherentism) that there is pervasive mutual support among a person's justified beliefs. As foundationalists point out, a belief can't be justified by a vicious circle of reasons. But what this shows is not that mutual support is illegitimate, but that we need a better understanding of the difference between legitimate mutual support and vicious circularity—my version will rely on an analogy between the structure of evidence and a crossword puzzle.

Of course, the viability of the foundherentist approach doesn't depend on my being completely successful in articulating it. No doubt there could be other versions of foundherentism falling within these general contours but differing in their details.

I take as my starting point the following vague, but very plausible, formulation: "A is more/less justified, at t, in believing that p, depending on how good his evidence is."

By starting from here I take for granted, first, that justification comes in degrees: a person may be more or less justified in believing something. (I also assume that a person may be more justified in believing some things than he is in believing others.)

I also take for granted, second, that the concepts of evidence and justification are internally connected: how justified a person is in believing something depends on the quality of his evidence with respect to that belief.

I assume, third, that justification is personal: one person may be more justified in believing something than another is in believing the same thing—because one person's evidence may be better than another's. (But though justification is personal, it is not subjective. How justified A is in believing that p depends on how good *his*, A's, evidence is. But how justified A is in believing that p doesn't depend on how good A *thinks* his evidence is; and anyone who believed the same thing on the same evidence would be justified to the same degree.)

And I assume, fourth, that justification is relative to a time: a person may be more justified in believing something at one time than at another—because his evidence at one time may be better than his evidence at another.

"A is more/less justified, at t, in believing that p, depending on how good his evidence is." The main tasks, obviously, are to explain "his evidence" and "how good." The double-aspect character of the concept of justification is already in play; for "his," in "his evidence," is a causal notion, while "how good" is logical, or quasi-logical, in character.

The concept of justification is causal as well as logical across the board[8]—its causal aspect is not restricted to experiential evidence alone. Quite generally, how justified someone is in believing something depends not only on *what* he believes, but on *why* he believes it.

For example: if two people both believe the accused is innocent, one because he has evidence that she was a hundred miles from the scene of the crime at the relevant time, the other because he thinks she has an honest face, the former is more justified than the latter. In short, degree of justification depends on the quality of the evidence that actually causes the belief in question.

The word "belief" is ambiguous: sometimes it refers to a mental state, someone's believing something [an S-belief];[9] sometimes it refers to the content of what is believed, a proposition [a C-belief]. "A's evidence" needs to be tied somehow to what causes A's S-belief, but must also be capable of standing in logical or quasi-logical relations to the C-belief, the proposition believed.

The idea is to begin by characterizing A's S-evidence with respect to p—this will be a set of states of A causally related to his S-belief that p; and then to use this as the starting point of a characterization of A's C-evidence with respect to p—this will be a set of propositions capable of standing in logical or quasi-logical relations to the C-belief that p.

If A initially came to believe that the rock-rabbit is the closest surviving relative of the elephant because a fellow-tourist told him he read this somewhere, and later still believes it, but now because he has learned all the relevant biological details, he is more justified at the later time than at the earlier. So, if they are different, "A's S-evidence with respect to p" should relate to the causes of A's S-belief that p at the time in question rather than to what prompted it in the first place.

What goes on in people's heads is very complicated. There will likely be some factors inclining A towards believing that p, and others pulling against it. Perhaps, e.g., A believes that Tom Grabit stole the book because his seeing Grabit leave the library with a shifty expression and an suspicious bulge under his sweater exerts a stronger positive pull than his belief that it is possible that Tom Grabit has a light-fingered identical twin exerts in the opposite direction. Both sustaining and inhibiting factors are relevant to degree of justification, so both will included in A's S-evidence.

In this vector of forces [the causal nexus of A's S-belief that p], besides A's present experience and present memory traces of his past experience, and other S-beliefs of his, such factors as his wishes, hopes, and fears will often play a role. But A's desire not to believe ill of his students, say, or his being under the influence of alcohol, though they may affect whether or with what degree of confidence he believes that Grabit stole the book, aren't themselves part of his evidence with respect to that proposition.

So "A's S-evidence with respect to p" will refer to those experiential and belief-states of A's which belong, at the time in question, to the causal nexus of A's S-belief that p. The phrase "with respect to" signals the inclusion of both positive, sustaining, and negative, inhibiting, evidence [respectively, A's S-evidence for p, and A's S-evidence against p]. A's S-evidence with respect to p will include other beliefs of his [A's S-reasons with respect to p]; and his perceptions, his introspective awareness of his own mental goings-on, and memory traces of his earlier perceptual and introspective states [A's experiential S-evidence with respect to p].

The part about memory needs amplifying. A's experiential S-evidence may include present memory traces of past experience—such as his remembering seeing his car-keys on the dresser. This corresponds to the way we talk of A's remembering seeing, hearing, reading, etc., ... We also talk of A's remembering that p, meaning that he earlier came to believe that p and has not forgotten it. How justified A is in such persisting beliefs will depend on how good his evidence is—his evidence at the time in question, that is. A person's evidence for persisting beliefs will normally include memory traces of past perceptual experience; my belief that my high-school English teacher's name was "Miss Wright," for instance, is now sustained by my remembering hearing and seeing the name used by myself and others.

Testimonial evidence, in a broad sense—what a person reads, what others tell him—enters the picture by way of his hearing or seeing, or remembering hearing or seeing, what someone else says or writes. Of course, A's hearing B say that p won't contribute to his, A's, believing that p, unless A understands B's language. But if A believes that p in part because B told him that p, how justified A is in believing that p will depend in part on how justified A is in thinking B honest and reliable. But I anticipate.

A's S-evidence with respect to p is a set of states of A causally related to his S-belief that p. But in the part of the theory that explains what makes evidence better or worse, "evidence" will have to mean "C-evidence," and refer to a set of propositions. The two aspects interlock: A's C-evidence with respect to p will be a set of propositions, and how good it is will depend on those propositions' logical or quasi-logical relations to p; but *which* propositions A's C-evidence with respect to p consists of depends on which of A's S-beliefs and perceptual, etc., states belong to the causal nexus of the S-belief in question.

A's C-reasons with respect to p, obviously enough, should be the C-beliefs, i.e., the propositions, which are the contents of his S-reasons. For example, if one of A's S-reasons with respect to p is his S-belief that female cardinal birds are brown, the corresponding C-reason will be the proposition that female cardinal birds are brown.

But what about A's experiential C-evidence? My proposal is that "A's experiential C-evidence with respect to p" refer to propositions to the effect that A is in the perceptual/introspective/memory states which constitute his experiential S-evidence with respect to p. Since a perceptual, etc., state can't be part of the causal nexus of A's S-belief that p unless A is *in* that state, these propositions are all true. But they need not be propositions that A believes.[10]

So A's experiential C-evidence has a distinctive status. A's C-reasons may be true or may be false, and A may be more or less justified, or not justified at all, in believing them. But A's experiential C-evidence consists of propositions all of which are, *ex hypothesi*, true, and with respect to which the question of justification doesn't arise. (This is the foundherentist way of acknowledging that the ultimate evidence for empirical beliefs is experience—very different from the forced and unnatural way in which foundationalism tries to acknowledge it, by requiring basic *beliefs* justified by experience alone.)

In line with the way we ordinarily talk about the evidence of the senses—"Why do I think there's a cardinal in the oak tree? Well, I can see the thing; that distinctive profile is clear, though the light's not too good, and it's quite far away, so I can't really see the color"—I suggest a characterization of A's experiential C-evidence in terms of propositions to the effect that A is in the sort of perceptual state a normal subject would be in when seeing this or that in these or those circumstances. For example, if A's experiential S-evidence with respect to p is his perceptual state, its looking to him as it would to a normal observer seeing a female cardinal bird at a distance of forty feet in poor light, the corresponding experiential C-evidence will be a proposition to the effect that A is in the kind of perceptual state a normal observer would be in when looking at a female cardinal bird in those circumstances.

Built into my account of experiential evidence is a conception of perception as, in a certain sense, direct. This is not to deny that perception involves complicated neurophysiological goings-on. Nor is it to deny that the judgments causally sustained by the subject's experience are interpretative, that they depend on his background beliefs as well—which, on the contrary, is a key foundherentist thought. It is only to assert that in normal perception we interact with physical things and events around us, which look a certain way to all normal observers under the same circumstances.

You may be wondering why I include the subject's sensory and introspective experience as evidence, but not, say, his extrasensory perceptual experience. Well, the task here is descriptive—to articulate explicitly what is implicit when we say that A has excellent reasons for believing that p, that B is guilty of wishful thinking, that C has jumped to an unjustified conclusion, and so on. As those phrases "excellent reasons," and "guilty of wishful thinking," indicate, his other beliefs should be included as part of a subject's evidence, but his wishes should not. Actually, I think it most unlikely there is such a thing as ESP; but it is excluded because—unlike sensory experience, for which we even have the phrase, "the evidence of the senses"—it has no role in the implicit conception of evidence I am trying to make explicit.

The concepts of better and worse evidence, of more and less justified belief, are evaluative; so, after the descriptive task of explication, there will be the ratificatory question, whether our standards of better and worse evidence really are, as we hope and believe they are, indicative of truth. But that comes later.

The present task is to explicate "how good" in "how good A's C-evidence is." What factors raise, and what lower, degree of justification?

Foundationalists often think of the structure of evidence on the model of a mathematical proof—a model which, understandably, makes them leery of the idea of mutual support. My approach will be informed by the analogy of a crossword puzzle—where, undeniably, there is pervasive mutual support among entries, but, equally undeniably, no vicious circle. The clues are the analogue of experiential evidence, already-completed intersecting entries the analogue of reasons. As how reasonable a crossword entry is depends both on the clues and on other intersecting entries, the idea is, so how justified an empirical belief is depends on experiential evidence and reasons working together.

Perhaps needless to say, an analogy is only an analogy, not an argument. Its role is only to suggest ideas, which then have to stand on their own feet. And there are always disanalogies; there will be nothing in my theory analogous to the solution to today's crossword which appears in tomorrow's newspaper, for instance, nor any analogue of the designer of a crossword.

But the analogy does suggests a very plausible multi-dimensional answer to the question, what makes a belief more or less justified? How reasonable a crossword entry is depends on how well it is supported by the clue and any already-completed intersecting entries; how reasonable those other entries are, independent of the entry in question; and how much of the crossword has been completed. How justified A is in believing that p, analogously, depends on how well the belief in question is supported by his experiential evidence and reasons [supportiveness]; how justified his reasons are, independent of the belief in question [independent security]; and how much of the relevant evidence his evidence includes [comprehensiveness].

On the first dimension, A's C-evidence may be conclusive for p, conclusive against p, supportive-but-not-conclusive of p, undermining-but-not-conclusive against p, or indifferent with respect to p/with respect to not-p.

Foundationalists often take for granted that evidence is conclusive just in case it deductively implies the proposition in question; but this isn't quite right. Inconsistent premises deductively imply any proposition whatever; but inconsistent evidence isn't conclusive evidence for anything—let alone conclusive evidence for everything! Think, for example, of a detective whose evidence is: the murder was committed by a left-handed person; either Smith or Brown did it; Smith is left-handed; Brown is right-handed. Though this deductively implies that Smith did it, it certainly isn't conclusive evidence for that belief (let

alone conclusive evidence for the belief that Smith did it *and* conclusive evidence for the belief that Brown did it *and* conclusive evidence for the belief that extra-terrestrials did it!).

Deductive implication is necessary but not sufficient for conclusiveness. Evidence E is conclusive for p just in case the result of adding p to E [the p-extrapolation of E] is consistent, and the result of adding not-p to E [the not-p-extrapolation of E] is inconsistent. E is conclusive against p just in case its p-extrapolation is inconsistent and its not-p-extrapolation consistent. But if E itself is inconsistent, both its p-extrapolation and its not-p-extrapolation are also inconsistent, so E is indifferent with respect to p.

Often, though, evidence is not conclusive either way, nor yet inconsistent and hence indifferent, but supports the belief in question, or its negation, to some degree. Suppose the detective's evidence is: the murder was committed by a left-handed person; either Smith or Brown did it; Smith is left-handed; Brown is left-handed; Smith recently saw the victim, Mrs. Smith, in a romantic restaurant holding hands with Brown. Though not conclusive, this evidence is supportive to some degree of the belief that Smith did it—for, if he did, we have some explanation of why.

The example suggests that supportiveness depends on whether and how much adding p to E makes a better explanatory story. But a better explanatory story than what? Conclusiveness is a matter of the superiority of p over its negation with respect to consistency. But if p is potentially explanatory of E or some component of E, it is not to be expected that not-p will be too. So I construe supportiveness as depending on the superiority of p over its rivals with respect to explanatory integration; where a rival of p is any proposition adding which to E improves its explanatory integration to some degree, and which, given E, is incompatible with p.

The word "integration" was chosen to indicate that E may support p either because p explains E or some component of E, or vice versa—that there is "mutual reinforcement between an explanation and what it explains."[11] (So the concept of explanatory integration is closer kin to the coherentist concept of explanatory coherence than to the foundationalist concept of inference to the best explanation.)

Usually, as conclusiveness of evidence is taken to be the province of deductive logic, supportiveness of evidence is taken to be the province of inductive logic. But at least if "logic" is taken in its now-usual narrow sense, as depending on form alone, this looks to be a mistake. Explanation requires generality, kinds, laws—a motive for the murder, a mechanism whereby smoking causes cancer, and so forth. If so, explanatoriness, and hence supportiveness, requires a vocabulary which classifies things into real kinds; and hence depends on content, not on form alone. (Hempel *almost* drew the moral, many years ago now, from the "grue" paradox.)[12] But there is supportive-but-not-conclusive evidence, even if there is no formal inductive logic.

Supportiveness alone does not determine degree of justification, which also depends on independent security and comprehensiveness. Suppose our detective's evidence is: the murder was committed by a left-handed person; either Smith or Brown did it; Smith is right-handed, but Brown left-handed. The detective's evidence is conclusive that Brown did it; nevertheless, he is not well-justified in believing this unless, among other things, he is justified in believing that the murder was committed by a left-handed person, that either Smith or Brown did it, etc.

The idea of independent security is easiest to grasp in the context of the crossword analogy. In a crossword, how reasonable an entry is depends in part on its fit with intersecting entries, and hence on how reasonable those entries are, independently of the entry in question. Similarly, how justified a person is in believing something depends in part on how well it is supported by his other beliefs, and hence on how justified he is in believing those reasons, independently of the belief in question.

It is that last phrase—in my theory as with a crossword puzzle—that averts the danger of a vicious circle. The reasonableness of the entry for 3 down may depend in part on the reasonableness of the intersecting entry for 5 across—independent of the support given to the entry for 5 across by the entry for 3 down. Similarly, how justified A is in believing that p may depend in part on how justified he is in believing that q—independent of the support given his belief that q by his belief that p.

And, though "justified" appears on the right-hand side of the independent security clause, there is no danger of an infinite regress—any more than with a crossword puzzle. As in the case of a crossword eventually we reach the clues, so with empirical justification eventually we reach experiential evidence. And experiential C-evidence does not consist of other C-beliefs of the subject, but of propositions all of which are, *ex hypothesi*, true, and with respect to which the question of justification doesn't arise. This is not to deny that, as crossword clues may be cryptic, experiential evidence may be ambiguous or misleading; on the contrary, my account of experiential C-evidence is intended to recognize that it often is. It is only to say that the question of justification arises with respect to a person's beliefs, but not with respect to his experiences.

As how reasonable a crossword entry is depends not only on how well it is supported by the clue and other intersecting entries, and on how reasonable those other entries are, but also on how much of the crossword has been completed, so degree of justification depends not only on supportiveness and independent security, but also on comprehensiveness—on how much of the relevant evidence the subject's evidence includes.

Comprehensiveness promises to be even tougher to spell out than supportiveness and independent security; the crossword analogy isn't much help here, and neither is the nearest analogue in the literature, the total evidence requirement on inductions, which refers, not to the totality of relevant evidence, but to the totality of relevant available evidence—and then there is the further problem that relevance itself comes in degrees.

I am assuming, however, that (degree of) relevance is an objective matter. Naturally, whether I think your handwriting is relevant to your trustworthiness depends on whether I believe in graphology; but whether it *is* relevant depends on whether graphology is *true*.

As this reveals, though relevance, and hence comprehensiveness, is objective, judgments of relevance, and hence judgments of comprehensiveness, are perspectival, i.e., they depend on the background beliefs of the person making them. The same goes for judgments of supportiveness and independent security. How supportive you or I judge E to be with respect to p, for example, will depend on what rivals of p we happen to be able to think of; but how supportive E *is* of p does not. Quality of evidence is objective, but judgments of quality of evidence are perspectival.

Because quality of evidence is multi-dimensional, we should not necessarily expect a linear ordering of degrees of justification; e.g., A's evidence with respect to p might be strongly supportive but weak on comprehensiveness, while his evidence with respect to q might be strong on comprehensiveness but only weakly supportive. Nor, *a fortiori*, does it look realistic to aspire to anything as ambitious as a numerical scale of degrees of justification. But something can be said about what is required for A to be justified to *any* degree in believing that p.

One necessary condition is that there *be* such a thing as A's C-evidence with respect to p. If A's S-belief that p is caused simply by a blow to the head, or by one of those belief-inducing pills philosophers are fond of imagining, A isn't justified to any degree in believing that p. Since it is the justification of empirical beliefs that is at issue, another necessary condition is that A's C-evidence should include some experiential C-evidence—present experiential evidence, or memory traces of what he earlier saw, heard, read, etc. This is my analogue of BonJour's Observation requirement, obviously much more at home in foundherentism than his requirement was in his coherentist theory. (It is not meant to rule out the possibility that some of a person's beliefs may not be sustained directly by experiential evidence, not even by memory traces, but rely on other beliefs and their experiential evidence—as in an unconventional crossword some entries might have no clues of their own but rely on other entries and their clues.)[13] A third necessary condition is that A's C-evidence with respect to p should meet minimal conditions of supportiveness, independent security, and comprehensiveness; e.g., it should be better than indifferent in terms of supportiveness. Jointly, these necessary conditions look to be sufficient.

What about the upper end of the scale? Our ordinary use of phrases like "A is completely justified in believing that p" is vague and context-dependent, depending *inter alia* on whether it is A's particular business to know whether p, and how important it is to be right about whether p; perhaps it also runs together strictly epistemological with ethical concerns. This vague concept [*complete* justification] is useful for practical purposes—and for the statement of Gettier-type paradoxes. In other philosophical contexts, however, "A is completely justified in believing that p" is used in a context-neutralized, optimizing way, requiring conclusiveness, maximal independent security, and full comprehensiveness of evidence [COMPLETE justification].

The account sketched here has been personal, i.e., focused firmly on our friend A. But this is not to deny that in even the most ordinary of our everyday beliefs we rely extensively on testimonial evidence. And where the sciences are concerned, reliance on others' evidence—and hence on the interpretation of others' words and judgments of others' reliability—is absolutely pervasive. (This reveals that not only the social sciences but also the natural sciences presuppose the possibility of interpreting others' utterances: think, e.g., of an astronomer's reliance on others' reports of observations.)

Anyhow, thinking about evidence in the sciences prompts me to ask whether it is possible to extrapolate from my account of "A is more/less justified in believing that p" to a concept of justification applicable to groups of people. It might be feasible to do this by starting with the degree of justification of a hypothetical subject whose evidence includes all the evidence of each member of the group, and then discount this by some measure of the degree to which each member of the group is justified in believing that other members are competent and honest.

The Ratification of Foundherentism

Thus far the task has been to articulate our standards of better and worse evidence, of more and less justified belief. But what do I mean by "our"? And what assurance can I give that a belief's being justified, by those standards, is any indication that it is true?

When I speak of "our" standards of better and worse evidence, I emphatically do not mean to suggest that these standards are local or parochial, accepted in "our," as opposed to "their," community. Rather, I see these standards—essentially, how well a belief is anchored in experience and how tightly it is woven into an explanatory mesh of beliefs—as rooted in human nature, in the cognitive capacities and limitations of all normal human beings.

It is sure to be objected that the evidential standards of different times, cultures, communities, or scientific paradigms differ radically. But I think this supposed variability is at least an exaggeration, and quite possibly altogether an illusion, the result of mistaking the perspectival character of judgments of evidential quality for radical divergence in standards of better and worse evidence.

Because judgments of the quality of evidence are perspectival, people with radically different background beliefs can be expected to differ significantly in their judgments of degree of justification. It doesn't follow that there are no shared standards of evidence. If we think of the constraints of experiential anchoring and explanatory integration rather than of specific judgments of the relevance, supportiveness, etc., of this or that evidence, I believe we will find commonality rather than divergence.

Again, the point is easier to see in the context of the crossword analogy. Suppose you and I are both doing the same crossword puzzle, and have filled in some long central entry differently. You think, given your solution to that long central entry, that the fact that 14 down ends in a "T" is evidence in its favor; I think, given my solution to that long central entry, that the fact that it ends in a "D" is evidence in its favor. Nevertheless, we are both trying to fit the entry to its clue and to other already-completed entries. Now suppose you and I are both on an appointments committee. You think the way this candidate writes his "g"s indicates that he is not to be trusted; I think graphology is bunk and scoff at your "evidence." Because of a disagreement in background beliefs, we disagree about what evidence is relevant. Nevertheless, we are both trying to assess the supportiveness, independent security, and comprehensiveness of the evidence with respect to the proposition that the candidate is trustworthy.

But even if I am wrong about this, even if there really are radically divergent standards of evidential quality, it wouldn't follow that there are no objective indications of truth; *variability* of standards does not, in and of itself, imply *relativity* of standards.[14] So those epistemic relativists who have inferred that, since judgments of justification vary from community to community, there can be no objectively correct standards of better and worse evidence, have committed a *non sequitur* as well as relying on a dubious premiss.

As for those who have succumbed to epistemic relativism because they have given up on the concept of truth, I have room here only to say that theirs seems to me an entirely factitious despair.[15] In any case, all that will be required of the concept of truth in what follows is that a proposition or statement is true just in case things are as it says.

Supposing—as I believe, and so do you—that we humans are fallible, limited but inquiring creatures who live in a world which is largely independent of us and what we believe about it, but in which there are kinds, laws, regularities; and supposing—as I believe, and so do you—that our senses are a source, though by no means an infallible source, of information about things and events in the world around us, and introspection a source, though by no means an infallible source, of information about our own mental goings-on; then, if any indication of how things are is possible for us, how well our beliefs are anchored in our experience and knit into an explanatory mesh is such an indication. (And supposing—as I believe, and so, probably, do you—we have no other sources of information about the world and ourselves, no ESP or clairvoyance or etc., then this is the only indication we can have of how things are.)

That last paragraph was nothing like an a priori ratification of foundherentism; for those "supposing" clauses are empirical in character. Assumptions about human cognitive capacities and limitations are *built into* our standards of evidential quality; so the truth-indicativeness of those standards depends on the truth of those empirical assumptions. But neither was that last paragraph much like the appeals to psychology or cognitive science on which some epistemological naturalists of a more extreme stripe than mine propose to rely; for the assumptions referred to in my "supposing" clauses, though empirical, are of such generality as to be rather philosophical than scientific in character.

Those assumptions would surely be presupposed by any conceivable scientific experiment. But they are well integrated with what the sciences of cognition have to tell us about the mechanisms of perception and introspection, and of when and why they are more or less reliable, and with what the theory of evolution suggests about how we came to have the sort of information-detecting apparatus we do. As one would hope, the epistemological part of my crossword—the part where the entries are themselves about crosswords—interlocks snugly with other parts.

But what am I to say to those readers familiar with Descartes' failed attempt to prove "what I clearly and distinctly perceive is true," who are bound to suspect that I must be arguing in a circle? After pointing out that I have not offered a ratificatory argument in which some premiss turns out to be identical with the conclusion, nor an argument relying on a certain mode of inference to arrive at the conclusion that this very mode of inference is a good one—only that, to borrow Peirce's words, by now "the reader will, I trust, be too well-grounded in logic to mistake mutual support for a vicious circle of reasoning."[16]

And what am I to say to readers worried about the Evil Demon, who are bound to object that I have not ruled out the possibility that our senses are not a source of information about the external world at all? After pointing out that since, *ex hypothesi*, his machinations would be absolutely undetectable, if there were an Evil Demon *no* truth-indication would be possible for us—only that my claim is a conditional one: that, if any truth-indication is possible for us, the foundherentist criteria are truth-indicative. (I could discharge the antecedent, and arrive at a categorical conclusion, by adopting a definition of truth along Peircean lines, as the opinion that would survive all possible experiential evidence and the fullest logical scrutiny; but I prefer the more cautious, and more realist, strategy.)

Determined skeptics won't be persuaded; but determined skeptics never are! And the rest of you may notice that foundherentism enables us to sidestep another dichotomy which has—if you'll pardon the pun—bedeviled recent epistemology: *either* a hopeless obsession with hyperbolic skepticism, *or* a hopeless relativism or tribalism preoccupied with "our (local, parochial) epistemic practices." Foundherentism, I believe, provides a more realistic picture of our epistemic condition—a robustly fallibilist picture which,

without sacrificing objectivity, acknowledges something of how complex and confusing evidence can be.

Notes

1. This brief statement of foundherentism is based primarily on my *Evidence and Inquiry: Towards Reconstruction in Epistemology*, Blackwell, Oxford, 1993, especially chapters 1, 4, and 10. I have also drawn on material from earlier articles of mine, especially "Theories of Knowledge: An Analytic Framework," *Proceedings of the Aristotelian Society*, LXXXIII, 1982–83, 143–57 (where foundherentism was first introduced); "C. I. Lewis," in *American Philosophy*, ed. Marcus Singer, Royal Institute of Philosophy Lecture Series, 19, Cambridge University Press, Cambridge, 1985, 215–39; and "Rebuilding the Ship While Sailing on the Water," in *Perspectives on Quine*, eds Barrett, R. and Gibson, R., Blackwell, Oxford, 1990, 111–27 (where some of the key ideas of foundherentism were developed). I have drawn as well on material from the symposium on *Evidence and Inquiry* published in *Philosophy and Phenomenological Research*, LVI. 3, 1996, 611–57, and from my "Reply to BonJour," *Synthese*, volume 112, no. 1, July 1997, 25–35.

2. Thomas Reid, *Essays on the Intellectual Powers* (1785), in Beanblossom, R. E. and Lehrer, K., eds, *Thomas Reid: Inquiry and Essays*, Hackett, Indianapolis, IN, 1983, VI. 4.

3. I restrict my attention here to experientialist forms of foundationalism, ignoring, e.g., foundationalist theories of a priori knowledge.

4. My characterization of foundationalism is quite standard; cf. for example, Alston's in Sosa, E. and Dancy, J., eds, *Companion to Epistemology*, Blackwell, Oxford, 1992, p. 144; or Sosa's in "The Raft and the Pyramid," *Midwest Studies in Philosophy*, V, 1980, pp. 23–24. But matters have been confused because, in "Can Empirical Knowledge Have a Foundation?," *American Philosophical Quarterly*, 15, 1978, 1–13, and *The Structure of Empirical Knowledge*, Harvard University Press, Cambridge, MA, 1986, p. 28, BonJour uses "weak foundationalism" to refer a style of theory which is both weak *and* impure, in my sense, and in addition allows mutual support among basic beliefs and—apparently—allows "basic" beliefs to get support from "derived" beliefs. As my scare quotes indicate, once one-directionality has been so completely abandoned it is unclear that the theory really qualifies as foundationalist at all; certainly the basic/derived distinction has become purely *pro forma*. See also Haack, "Reply to BonJour," *Synthese*, volume 112, no. 1, July 1997, 25–35.

5. See *Evidence and Inquiry*, chapter 2, for details.

6. See *Evidence and Inquiry*, chapter 3, for details.

7. Laurence BonJour, "Haack on Justification and Experience," *Synthese*, volume 112, no. 1, July 1997, pp. 13–15.

8. An idea I first began to work out in "Epistemology With a Knowing Subject," *Review of Metaphysics*, XXXIII.2, 1979, 309–36.

9. Expressions introduced in square brackets are my new, technical terms, or special, technical uses of familiar terms.

10. So my theory is not straightforwardly externalist, since A's S-evidence must consist of states of A—states, furthermore, of which A can be aware; but neither is it straightforwardly internalist, since A's experiential C-evidence consists of propositions A need not believe or even conceive.

11. Quine, V. V. and Ullian, J., *The Web of Belief*, Random House, New York, 1970, p. 79.

12. Goodman, N., "The New Riddle of Induction" (1953), in *Fact, Fiction and Forecast*, Bobbs-Merrill, Indianapolis, IN, second edition, 1965, 59–83; Hempel, C. G., "Postscript on Confirmation" (1964), in *Aspects of Scientific Explanation*, Free Press, New York, 1965, 47–52.

13. In case a desperate foundationalist is tempted to try seizing on this in hopes of salvaging the derived/basic distinction, let me point out that beliefs without direct experiential evidence could contribute to the support of beliefs with direct experiential evidence; and that this maneuver would identify no plausible *kind* of belief as basic/as derived—think, e.g., of a scientist whose belief that electrons are composed thus and so is sustained by what he sees in the bubble chamber.

14. See also, Haack, "Reflections on Relativism: From Momentous Tautology to Seductive Contradiction," *Noûs*, Supplement, 1996, 297–315; also in Tomberlin, James E., ed., *Philosophical Perspectives, 10: Metaphysics*, Blackwell, Oxford, 1996, 297–315; reprinted in Haack, *Manifesto of a Passionate Moderate: Unfashionable Essays*, University of Chicago Press, Chicago, 1998, 149–66.

15. I have more to say in "Confessions of an Old-Fashioned Prig," in *Manifesto of a Passionate Moderate: Unfashionable Essays*, University of Chicago Press, Chicago, 1998, 7–30.

16. C. S. Peirce, *Collected Papers*, eds., Hartshorne, C., Weiss, P., and Burks, A., Harvard University Press, Cambridge, MA, 1931–58, 6.315.

◇ NEGATIVE COHERENTISM ◇

18. CHANGE IN VIEW
Gilbert Harman

Positive Versus Negative Undermining

I now want to compare two competing theories of reasoned belief revision, which I will call the foundations theory and the coherence theory since they are similar to certain philosophical theories of justification sometimes called foundations and coherence theories (Sosa 1980; Pollock 1979). But the theories I am concerned with are not precisely the same as the corresponding philosophical theories of justification, which are not normally presented as theories of belief revision. Actually, I am not sure what these philosophical theories of "justification" are supposed to be concerned with. So, although I will be using the *term* "justification" in what follows, as well as the terms "coherence" and "foundations," I do not claim that my use of any of these terms is the same as its use in these theories of justification. I mean to be raising a new issue, not discussing an old one.

The key issue is whether one needs to keep track of one's original justifications for beliefs. What I am calling the *foundations* theory says yes; what I am calling the *coherence* theory says no.

The foundations theory holds that some of one's beliefs "depend on" others for their current justification; these other beliefs may depend on still others, until one gets to foundational beliefs that do not depend on any further beliefs for their justification. In this view reasoning or belief revision should consist, first, in subtracting any of one's beliefs that do not now have a satisfactory justification and, second, in adding new beliefs that either need no justification or are justified on the basis of other justified beliefs one has.

On the other hand, according to the coherence theory, it is not true that one's ongoing beliefs have or ought to have the sort of justificational structure

From Gilbert Harmon, "Positive vs. Negative Undermining" and Implict Commitments." In *Change in View: Principles of Reasoning* © 1968 by The Massachusetts Institute of Technology Press: pps. 29-48. Reprinted with the permission of the publisher.

required by the foundations theory. In this view ongoing beliefs do not usually require any justification. Justification is taken to be required only if one has a special reason to doubt a particular belief. Such a reason might consist in a conflicting belief or in the observation that one's beliefs could be made more "coherent," that is, more organized or simpler or less ad hoc, if the given belief were abandoned (and perhaps if certain other changes were made). According to the coherence theory, belief revision should involve minimal changes in one's beliefs in a way that sufficiently increases overall coherence.

In this chapter I elaborate these two theories in order to compare them with actual reasoning and intuitive judgments about such reasoning. It turns out that the theories are most easily distinguished by the conflicting advice they occasionally give concerning whether one should *give up* a belief P from which many other of one's beliefs have been inferred, when P's original justification has to be abandoned. Here a surprising contrast seems to emerge—"is" and "ought" seem to come apart. The foundations theory seems, at least at first, to be more in line with our intuitions about how people *ought* to revise their beliefs; the coherence theory is more in line with what people *actually do* in such situations. Intuition seems strongly to support the foundations theory over the coherence theory as an account of what one is *justified* in doing in such cases; but *in fact* one will tend to act as the coherence theory advises.

After I explain this I consider how this apparent discrepancy can be resolved. I conclude that the coherence theory is normatively correct after all, despite initial appearances.

The Foundations Theory of Belief Revision

The basic principle of the foundations theory, as I will interpret it, is that one must keep track of one's original reasons for one's beliefs, so that one's ongoing beliefs have a justificational structure, some beliefs serving as reasons or justifications for others. These justifying beliefs are more basic or fundamental for justification than the beliefs they justify.

The foundations theory rejects any principle of *conservatism*. In this view a proposition cannot acquire justification simply by being believed. The justification of a given belief cannot be, either in whole or in part, that one has that belief. For example, one's justification

for believing something cannot be that one already believes it and that one's beliefs in this area are reliable.

Justifications are *prima facie* or defeasible. The foundations theory allows, indeed insists, that one can be justified in believing something P and then come to believe something else that undermines one's justification for believing P. In that case one should stop believing P, unless one has some further justification that is not undermined.

I say "unless one has some further justification," because in this view a belief can have more than one justification. To be justified, a belief must have *at least* one justification. That is, if a belief in P is to be justified, it is required either that P be a foundational belief whose intrinsic justification is not defeated or that there be at least one undefeated justification of P from other beliefs one is justified in believing. If one believes P and it happens that all one's justifications for believing P come to be defeated, one is no longer justified in continuing to believe P, and one should subtract P from one's beliefs.

Furthermore, and this is important, if one comes not to be justified in continuing to believe P in this way, then not only is it true that one must abandon belief in P but justifications one has for other beliefs are also affected if these justifications appeal to one's belief in P. Justifications appealing to P must be abandoned when P is abandoned. If that means further beliefs are left without justification, then these beliefs too must be dropped along with any justifications appealing to them. So there will be a chain reaction when one loses justification for a belief on which other beliefs depend for their justification. (This is worked out in more detail for an artificial intelligence system by Doyle (1979, 1980).)

Now, it is an important aspect of the foundations theory of reasoning that justifications cannot legitimately be circular. P cannot be part of the justification for Q while Q is part of the justification for P (unless one of these beliefs has a different justification that does not appeal to the other belief).

The foundations theory also disallows infinite justifications. It does not allow P to be justified by appeal to Q, which is justified by appeal to R, and so on forever. Since justification cannot be circular, justification must eventually end in beliefs that either need no justification or are justified but not by appeal to other beliefs. Let us say that such basic or foundational beliefs are intrinsically justified.

For my purposes it does not matter exactly which beliefs are taken to be intrinsically justified in this sense. Furthermore, I emphasize that the foundations theory allows for situations in which a basic belief has its intrinsic justification defeated by one or more other beliefs, just as it allows for situations in which the justification of one belief in terms of other beliefs is defeated by still other beliefs. As I am interpreting it, foundationalism is not committed to the *incorrigibility* of basic beliefs.

A belief is a basic belief if it has an intrinsic justification which does not appeal to other beliefs. A basic belief can also have one or more nonintrinsic justifications which do appeal to other beliefs. So, a basic belief can have its intrinsic justification defeated and still remain justified as long as it retains at least one justification that is not defeated.

The existence of basic beliefs follows from the restrictions against circular and infinite justifications. Infinite justifications are to be ruled out because a finite creature can have only a finite number of beliefs, or at least only a finite number of *explicit beliefs*, whose content is explicitly represented in the brain. What one is justified in believing either implicitly or explicitly depends entirely one what one is justified in believing explicitly. To consider whether one's implicit beliefs are justified is to consider whether one is justified in believing the explicit beliefs on which the implicit beliefs depend. A justification for a belief that appeals to other beliefs must always appeal to things one believes explicitly. Since one has only finitely many explicit beliefs, there are only finitely many beliefs that can be appealed to for purposes of justification, and so infinite justifications are ruled out.

The Coherence Theory of Belief Revision

The coherence theory is *conservative* in a way the foundations theory is not. The coherence theory supposes one's present beliefs are justified just as they are in the absence of special reasons to change them, where changes are allowed only to the extent that they yield sufficient increases in coherence. This is a striking difference from the foundations theory. The foundations theory says one is justified in continuing to believe something only if one has a special reason to continue to accept that belief, whereas the coherence theory says one is justified in continuing to believe something as long as one has no special reason to stop believing it.

According to the coherence theory, if one's beliefs are incoherent in some way, because of outright inconsistency or simple *ad hocness*, then one should try to make minimal changes in those beliefs in order to eliminate the incoherence. More generally, small changes in one's beliefs are justified to the extent these changes add to the coherence of one's beliefs.

For present purposes, I do not need to be too specific as to exactly what coherence involves, except to say it includes not only consistency but also a network of relations among one's beliefs, especially relations of implication and explanation.

It is important that coherence competes with conservatism. It is as if there were two aims or tendencies of reasoned revision, to maximize coherence and to minimize change. Both tendencies are important. Without conservatism a person would be led to reduce his or her beliefs to the single Parmenidean thought that all is one. Without the tendency toward coherence we would have what Peirce (1877) called the method of tenacity, in which one holds to one's initial convictions no matter what evidence may accumulate against them.

According to the coherence theory, the assessment of a challenged belief is always holistic. Whether such a belief is justified depends on how well it fits together with everything else one believes. If one's beliefs are coherent, they are mutually supporting. All one's beliefs are, in a sense, equally fundamental. In the coherence theory there are not the asymmetrical justification relations among one's ongoing beliefs that there are in the foundations theory. It can happen in the coherence theory that P is justified because of the way it coheres with Q and Q is justified because of the way it coheres with P. In the foundations theory, such a pattern of justification is ruled out by the restriction against circular justification. But there is nothing wrong with circular justification in the coherence theory, especially if the circle is a large one!

I turn now to testing the foundations and coherence theories against our intuitions about cases. This raises an apparent problem for the coherence theory.

An Objection to the Coherence Theory: Karen's Aptitude Test

Sometimes there clearly are asymmetrical justification relations among one's beliefs.

Consider Karen, who has taken an aptitude test and has just been told her results show she has a considerable aptitude for science and music but little aptitude for history and philosophy. This news does not correlate perfectly with her previous grades. She had previously done well not only in physics, for which her aptitude scores are reported to be high, but also in history, for which her aptitude scores are reported to be low. Furthermore, she had previously done poorly not only in philosophy, for which her aptitude scores are reported to be low, but also in music, for which her aptitude scores are reported to be high.

After carefully thinking over these discrepancies, Karen concludes that her reported aptitude scores accurately reflect and are explained by her actual aptitudes; so she has an aptitude for science and music and no aptitude for history and philosophy; therefore her history course must have been an easy one, and also she did not work hard enough in the music course. She decides to take another music course and not to take any more history.

It seems quite clear that, in reaching these conclusions, Karen bases some of her beliefs on others. Her belief that the history course was easy depends for its justification on her belief that she has no aptitude for history, a belief which depends in turn for its justification on her belief that she got a low score in history on her aptitude test. There is no dependence in the other direction. For example, her belief about her aptitude test score in history is not based on her belief that she has no aptitude for history or on her belief that the history course was an easy one.

According to the coherence theory, the relevant relations here are merely *temporal* or *causal* relations. The coherence theory can agree that Karen's belief about the outcome of her aptitude test precedes and is an important cause of her belief that the history course she took was an easy one. But the coherence theory denies that a relation of dependence or justification holds or ought to hold between these two beliefs as time goes by, once the new belief has been firmly accepted.

In order to test this, let me tell more of Karen's story. Some days later she is informed that the report about her aptitude scores was incorrect! The scores reported were those of someone else whose name was confused with hers. Unfortunately, her own scores have now been lost. How should Karen revise her views, given this new information?

The foundations theory says she should abandon all beliefs whose justifications depend in part on her prior belief about her aptitude test scores. The only exception is for beliefs for which she can now find another and independent justification which does not depend on her belief about her aptitude test scores. She should continue to believe only those things she would have been justified in believing if she had never been given the false information about those scores. The foundations theory says this because it does not accept a principle of conservatism. The foundations theory does not allow that a belief can acquire justification simply by being believed.

Let us assume that, if Karen had not been given the false information about her aptitude test scores, she could not have reasonably reached any of the conclusions she did reach about her aptitudes for physics, history, philosophy, and music; and let us also assume that without those beliefs Karen could not have reached any of her further conclusions about the courses she has already taken. Then, according to the foundations theory, Karen should abandon her beliefs about her relative aptitudes for these subjects, and she should give up her belief that the history course she took was easy as well as her belief that she did not work hard enough in the music course. She should also reconsider her decisions to take another course in music and not to take any more history courses.

The coherence theory does not automatically yield the same advice that the foundations theory gives about this case. Karen's new information does produce a loss of overall coherence in her beliefs, since she can no longer coherently suppose that her aptitudes for science, music, philosophy, and history are in any way responsible for the original report she received about the results of her aptitude test. She must abandon that particular supposition about the explanation of the original report of her scores. Still, there is considerable coherence among the beliefs she inferred from this false report. For example, there is a connection between her belief that she has little aptitude for history, her belief that her high grade in the history course was the result of the course's being an easy one, and her belief that she will not take any more courses in history. There are similar connections between her beliefs about her aptitudes for other subjects, how well she did in courses in those subjects, and her plans for the future in those areas. Let us suppose that from the original report Karen inferred a great many other things that I haven't mentioned; so there are many beliefs involved here. Abandoning all these beliefs is costly from the point of view of conservatism, which says to minimize change. Suppose that there are so many of these beliefs and that they are so connected with each other and with other things Karen believes that the coherence theory implies Karen should retain all these new beliefs even though she must give up her beliefs about the explanation of the report of her aptitude scores. (In fact, we do not really need to suppose these beliefs are intricately connected with each other or even that there are many of them, since in the coherence theory a belief *does* acquire justification simply by being believed.)

The foundations theory says Karen should give up all these beliefs, whereas the coherence theory says Karen should retain them. Which theory is right about what Karen ought to do? Almost everyone who has considered this issue sides with the foundations theory: Karen should not retain any beliefs she inferred from the false report of her aptitude test scores that she would not have been justified in believing in the absence of that false report. That does seem to be the intuitively right answer. The foundations theory is in accordance with our intuitions about what Karen *ought* to do in a case like this. The coherence theory is not.

Belief Perseverance

In fact, Karen would almost certainly keep her new beliefs! That is what people actually do in situations like this. Although the foundations theory seems to give intuitively satisfying advice about what Karen *ought* to do in such a situation, the coherence theory is more in accord with what people actually do.

To document the rather surprising facts here, let me quote at some length from a recent survey article (Ross and Anderson 1982, pp. 147–149), which speaks of

the dilemma of the social psychologist who has made use of deception in the course of an experiment and then seeks to debrief the subjects who had been the target of such deception. The psychologist reveals the totally contrived and inauthentic nature of the information presented presuming that this debriefing will thereby eliminate any effects such information might have exerted upon the subjects' feelings or

beliefs. Many professionals, however, have expressed public concern that such experimental deception may do great harm that is not fully undone by conventional debriefing procedures. . . .

Ross and Anderson go on to describe experiments designed to "explore" what they call "the phenomenon of belief perseverance in the face of evidential discrediting." In one experiment,

Subjects first received continuous false feedback as they performed a novel discrimination task (i.e., distinguishing authentic suicide notes from fictitious ones). . . . [Then each subject] received a standard debriefing session in which he learned that his putative outcome had been predetermined and that his feedback had been totally unrelated to actual performance. . . . [E]very subject was led to explicitly acknowledge his understanding of the nature and purpose of the experimental deception.

Following this total discrediting of the original information, the subjects completed a dependent variable questionnaire dealing with [their] performance and abilities. The evidence for postdebriefing impression perseverance was unmistakable. . . . On virtually every measure . . . the totally discredited initial outcome manipulation produced significant "residual" effects upon [subjects'] . . . assessments. . . .

Follow-up experiments have since shown that a variety of unfounded personal impressions, once induced by experimental procedures, can survive a variety of total discrediting procedures. For example, Jennings, Lepper, and Ross . . . have demonstrated that subjects' impressions of their ability at interpersonal persuasion (having them succeed or fail to convince a confederate to donate blood) can persist after they have learned that the initial outcome was totally inauthentic. Similarly, . . . two related experiments have shown that students' erroneous impressions of their "logical problem solving abilities" (and their academic choices in a follow-up measure two months later) persevered even after they had learned that good or poor teaching procedures provided a totally sufficient explanation for the successes or failures that were the basis for such impressions.

. . . [Other] studies first manipulated and then attempted to undermine subjects' theories about the functional relationship between two measured variables: the adequacy of firefighters' professional performances and their prior scores on a paper and pencil test of risk performance. . . . [S]uch theories survived the revelations that the cases in question had been totally fictitious and the different subjects had, in fact, received opposite pairings of riskiness scores and job outcomes. . . . [O]ver 50% of the initial effect of the "case history" information remained after debriefing.

In summary, it is clear that beliefs can survive . . . the total destruction of their original evidential bases.

It is therefore quite likely that Karen will continue to believe many of the things she inferred from the false report of her aptitude test scores. She will continue to believe these things even after learning that the report was false.

The Habit Theory of Belief

Why is it so hard for subjects to be debriefed? Why do people retain conclusions they have drawn from evidence that is now discredited? One possibility is that belief is a kind of habit. This is an implication of behaviorism, the view that beliefs and other mental attitudes are habits of behavior. But the suggestion that beliefs are habits might be correct even apart from behaviorism. The relevant habits need not be overt behavioral habits. They might be habits of thought. Perhaps, to believe that *P* is to be disposed to *think* that *P* under certain conditions, to be disposed to use this thought as a premise or assumption in reasoning and in deciding what to do. Then, once a belief has become established, considerable effort might be needed to get rid of it, even if the believer should come to see that he or she ought to get rid of it, just as it is hard to get rid of other bad habits. One can't simply decide to get rid of a bad habit; one must take active steps to ensure that the habit does not reassert itself. Perhaps it is just as difficult to get rid of a bad belief.

Goldman (1978) mentions a related possibility, observing that Anderson and Bower (1973) treat coming to believe something as the establishing of connections, or "associative links," between relevant conceptual representations in the brain. Now, it may be that, once set up, such connections or links cannot easily be broken unless competing connections are set up that overwhelm the original ones. The easiest case might be that in which one starts by believing *P* and then comes to believe *not P* by setting up stronger connections involving *not P* than those involved in believing *P*. It might be much harder simply to give up one's belief in *P* without substituting a contrary belief. According to this model of belief, in order to stop believing *P*, it would not be enough simply to notice passively that one's evidence for *P* had been discredited. One would have to take positive steps to counteract the associations that constitute one's belief in *P*. The difficulties in giving up a discredited belief would be similar in this view to the difficulties envisioned in the habit theory of belief.

But this explanation does not give a plausible account of the phenomenon of belief perseverance. Of course, there are cases in which one has to struggle in order to abandon a belief one takes to be discredited. One finds oneself coming back to thoughts one realizes one should no longer accept. There are such habits of thought, but this is not what is happening in the debriefing studies. Subjects in these studies are not struggling to abandon beliefs they see are discredited. On the contrary, the subjects do not see that the beliefs they have acquired have been discredited. They come up with all sorts of "rationalizations" (as we say) appealing to connections with other beliefs of a sort that the coherence theory, but not the foundations theory, might approve. So the correct explanation of belief perseverance in these studies is not that beliefs which have lost their evidential grounding are like bad habits.

Positive Versus Negative Undermining

In fact, what the debriefing studies show is that people simply do not keep track of the justification relations among their beliefs. They continue to believe things after the evidence for them has been discredited because they do not realize what they are doing. They do not understand that the discredited evidence was the *sole* reason why they believe as they do. They do not see they would not have been justified in forming those beliefs in the absence of the now discredited evidence. They do not realize these beliefs have been undermined. It is this, rather than the difficulty of giving up bad habits, that is responsible for belief perseverance.

The foundations theory says people should keep track of their reasons for believing as they do and should stop believing anything that is not associated with adequate evidence. So the foundations theory implies that, if Karen has not kept track of her reason for believing her history course was an easy one, she should have abandoned her belief even before she was told about the mix-up with her aptitude test scores. This seems clearly wrong.

Furthermore, since people rarely keep track of their reasons, the theory implies that people are unjustified in almost all their beliefs. This is an absurd result! The foundations theory turns out not to be a plausible normative theory after all. So let us see whether we cannot defend the coherence theory as a normative theory.

We have already seen how the coherence theory can appeal to a nonholistic *causal* notion of local justification by means of a limited number of one's prior beliefs, namely, those prior beliefs that are most crucial to one's justification for adding the new belief. The coherence theory does not suppose there are *continuing* links of justification dependency that can be consulted when revising one's beliefs. But the theory can admit that Karen's coming to believe certain things depended on certain of her prior beliefs in a way that it did not depend on others, where this dependence represents a kind of local justification, even though in another respect whether Karen was justified in coming to believe those things depended on everything she then believed.

Given this point, I suggest the coherence theory can suppose it is incoherent to believe both P and also that all one's reasons for believing P relied crucially on false assumptions. Within the coherence theory, this implies, roughly, the following:

Principle of Positive Undermining. One should stop believing P whenever one positively believes one's reasons for believing P are no good.

This is only roughly right, since there is also the possibility that one should instead stop believing that one's reasons for P are no good, as well as the possibility that one cannot decide between that belief and P. In any event, I want to compare this rough statement of the principle with the corresponding principle in a foundations theory:

Principle of Negative Undermining. One should stop believing P whenever one does not associate one's belief in P with an adequate justification (either intrinsic or extrinsic).

The Principle of Positive Undermining is much more plausible than the Principle of Negative Undermining. The Principle of Negative Undermining implies that, as one loses track of the justifications of one's beliefs, one should give up those beliefs. But, if one does not keep track of one's justifications for most of one's beliefs, as seems to be the case, then the Principle of Negative Undermining says that one should stop believing almost everything one believes, which is absurd On the other hand the Principle of Positive Undermining does no have this absurd implication. The Principle of Positive Undermining does not suppose that the absence of a justification is a reason to stop believing something. It only supposes that one's belief in P is undermined by the *positive* belief that one's reasons for P are no good.

It is relevant that subjects *can* be successfully debriefed after experiments involving deception if they are made vividly aware of the phenomenon of belief perseverance, that is, if they are made vividly aware of the tendency for people to retain false beliefs after the evidence for them has been undercut, and if they are also made vividly aware of how this phenomenon has acted in their own case (Nisbett and Ross 1980, p. 177). It might be suggested that this shows that under ideal conditions people really do act in accordance with the foundations theory after all, so that the foundations theory *is* normatively correct as an account of how one ideally ought to revise one's beliefs. But in fact this further phenomenon seems clearly to support the coherence theory, with its Principle of Positive Undermining, and not the foundations theory, with its Principle of Negative Undermining. The so-called process debriefing cannot merely undermine the evidence for the conclusions subjects have reached but must also directly attack each of these conclusions themselves. Process debriefing works not just by getting subjects to give up beliefs that originally served as evidence for the conclusions they have reached but by getting them to accept certain further positive beliefs about their lack of good reasons for each of these conclusions.

What About Our Intuitions?

It may seem to fly in the face of common sense to suppose that the coherence theory is normatively correct in cases like this. Remember that, after carefully considering Karen's situation, almost everyone agrees she should give up all beliefs inferred from the original false report, except those beliefs which would have been justified apart from any appeal to evidence tainted by that false information. Almost everyone's judgment about what Karen ought to do coincides with what the foundations theory says she ought to do. Indeed, psychologists who have studied the phenomenon of belief perseverance in the face of debriefing consider it to be a paradigm of irrationality. How can these strong normative intuitions possibly be taken to be mistaken, as they must be if the coherence theory is to be accepted as normatively correct?

The answer is that, when people think about Karen's situation, they ignore the possibility that she may have failed to keep track of the justifications of her beliefs. They imagine Karen is or ought to be aware that she no longer has any good reasons for the beliefs she inferred from the false report. And, of course, this is to imagine that Karen is violating the Principle of Positive Undermining. It is hard to allow for the possibility that she may be violating not that principle but only the foundationalist's Principle of Negative Undermining.

Keeping Track of Justification

People do not seem to keep track of the justifications of their beliefs. If we try to suppose that people do keep track of their justifications, we would have to suppose that either they fail to notice when their justifications are undermined or they do notice but have great difficulty in abandoning the unjustified beliefs in the way a person has difficulty abandoning a bad habit. Neither possibility offers a plausible account of the phenomenon of belief perseverance.

It stretches credulity to suppose people always keep track of the sources of their beliefs but often fail to notice when these sources are undermined. That is like supposing people always remember everything that has ever happened to them but cannot always retrieve the stored information from memory. To say one remembers something is to say one has stored it in a way that normally allows it to be retrieved at will. Similarly, to say people keep track of the sources of their beliefs must be to say they can normally use this information when it is appropriate to do so.

I have already remarked that the other possibility seems equally incredible, namely, that people have trouble abandoning the undermined beliefs in the way they have trouble getting rid of bad habits. To repeat, participants in belief perseverance studies show no signs of knowing their beliefs are ungrounded. They do

not act like people struggling with their beliefs as with bad habits. Again, I agree it sometimes happens that one keeps returning to thoughts after one has seen there can be no reason to accept those thoughts. There are habits of thought that can be hard to get rid of. But that is not what is going on in the cases psychologists study under the name of belief perseverance.

This leaves the issue of whether one should *try* always to keep track of the local justifications of one's beliefs, even if, in fact, people do not seem to do this. I want to consider the possibility that there is a good reason for not keeping track of these justifications.

Clutter Avoidance Again

We have seen there is a practical reason to avoid too much clutter in one's beliefs. There is a limit to what one can remember, a limit to the number of things one can put into long-term storage, and a limit to what one can retrieve. It is important to save room for important things and not clutter one's mind with a lot of unimportant matters. This is an important reason why one does not try to believe all sorts of logical consequences of one's beliefs. One should not try to infer all one can from one's beliefs. One should try not to retain too much trivial information. Furthermore, one should try to store in long-term memory only the key matters that one will later need to recall. When one reaches a significant conclusion from one's other beliefs, one needs to remember the conclusion but does not normally need to remember all the intermediate steps involved in reaching that conclusion. Indeed, one should not try to remember those intermediate steps; one should try to avoid too much clutter in one's mind.

Similarly, even if much of one's knowledge of the world is inferred ultimately from what one believes oneself to be immediately perceiving at one or another time, one does not normally need to remember these original perceptual beliefs or many of the various intermediate conclusions drawn from them. It is enough to recall the more important of one's conclusions. This means one should not be disposed to try to keep track of the local justifications of one's beliefs. One could keep track of these justifications only by remembering an incredible number of mostly perceptual original premises, along with many, many intermediate steps which one does not want and has little need to remember. One will not want to link one's beliefs to such justifications because one will not in general want to try to retain the prior beliefs from which one reached one's current beliefs.

The practical reason for not keeping track of the justifications of one's beliefs is not as severe as the reason that prevents one from trying to operate purely probabilistically, using generalized conditionalization as one's only principle of reasoned revision. The problem is not that there would be a combinatorial explosion. Still, there are important practical constraints. It is more efficient not to try to retain these justifications and the accompanying justifying beliefs. This leaves more room in memory for important matters.

Implicit Commitments
More on Positive Undermining

I stated the Principle of Positive Undermining somewhat roughly: "One should stop believing P whenever one positively believes one's reasons for believing P are no good." Let us now try to be more specific about the content of the undermining belief that one's reasons are "no good."

One suggestion would be that the relevant undermining belief is simply the belief that one is not now justified in believing P. But this cannot be right. Sometimes, thinking one's reasons for believing P are "no good" in the relevant sense, one follows the Principle of Positive Undermining and concludes that one is not justified in believing P. In such a case one's belief that one's reasons are "no good" has to be different from the belief that one is "not justified." Otherwise, one could not get started. One could not reach the conclusion that one's belief in P is unjustified without first having already reached that conclusion!

This may suggest the relevant belief is that one's reasons are "no good" in the sense that one was not *originally* justified in believing P when one first formed that belief. One could first believe *that* and then use the Principle of Positive Undermining to conclude that one is still not justified in believing P. But this is not right either. Karen was originally justified in reaching the various conclusions she reached on the basis of the initial report about her aptitude test scores. Later, given a full process debriefing that makes her vividly aware of what has happened in her case, she may come to see that her reasons are "no good," but that is not the same as coming to see she was originally unjustified, since she was justified originally.

At one point I stated the general principle like this: "It is incoherent to believe both P and also that all one's reasons for believing P relied crucially on false assumptions." This accounts for Karen's situation after a process debriefing. At that point she realizes she had been justified in accepting various conclusions only because of her belief in the accuracy of the original report of her aptitude test scores, a belief that she now sees is false.

I think this covers all the relevant cases. Although there may seem to be cases in which one comes to think one's original reasons are "no good," where this does not involve having relied on false beliefs, in all such cases I think there is a relevant *implicit* false belief.

Reliability Commitment

Consider this example. William looks out the window and, on the basis of what he sees, forms the belief that the girl his daughter is playing with in the backyard is the girl he met yesterday, named Connie. Later he learns Connie has an identical twin, Laura, whom he cannot distinguish from Connie. This leads him to realize that his reasons for his belief about the identity of the girl he saw playing with his daughter in the backyard are "no good." The Principle of Positive Undermining should apply here. It may seem that, in applying this Principle, William does not have to suppose that his original justification relied on any false beliefs. In particular, he needn't have explicitly considered whether Connie might have an identical twin.

But in such a case William at least implicitly relied on the belief that the perceptual appearances were an objectively reliable indicator of the identity of the girl he saw with his daughter. On learning that Connie has an identical twin, he now thinks appearances were not an objectively reliable indicator, so he thinks he was (subjectively) justified only because he relied on a false belief. The relevant belief here, that the appearances are an objectively reliable indicator, is, to repeat, ordinarily implicit rather than explicit. It is something William is committed to in coming to believe that the girl he sees is the same girl as the one he spoke to earlier, whether or not he explicitly notes this commitment.

Karen has a similar implicit belief. When she reaches her conclusions about her aptitudes and related matters, she assumes, at least implicitly, that the reports of her scores are an objectively reliable indicator of her scores. More generally, whenever one infers something new, one supposes one's grounds are an objectively reliable indicator of the truth of one's conclusion.

The existence of such commitments helps to account for a tendency some people have to think S does not know that P even if it is true that P and S is justified in believing that P, if S's grounds are not a reliable indicator of the truth of S's conclusion (Goldman 1976). For we might refuse to credit S with knowing that P if S's belief that P involves a commitment that is false (Harman 1980). Objective reliability is a kind of objective likelihood or probability. To say that evidence is a reliable indicator of a conclusion on a particular occasion is to say that on that occasion, given the evidence, there is no significant likelihood that the conclusion is false.

The following example indicates how objective likelihood can differ from "epistemic" likelihood. Suppose George has a bag of marbles, some red, some white, and George randomly selects a marble from the bag. It may be that, although George does not know this, a quarter of the marbles are white, the rest red. Then the objective likelihood that the marble George selects is white is 1/4, whereas the epistemic likelihood may be 1/2 (if it has any definite value at all).

Similarly, William's reasons for believing Connie is in the backyard are "no good" because, given his reasons, here is a significant objective likelihood that his belief is false, even if there is no significant epistemic likelihood of this for him until he learns about Connie's sister.

Objective likelihood is a relative notion. Something can be likely in relation to certain facts and unlikely in relation to others. There is a significant likelihood that a girl William takes to be Connie is really her sister, Laura. There is no significant likelihood that a girl whom William takes to be Connie and who parts her hair in the middle of her head is Laura, since Laura always parts her hair on the left. In other words, in relation to the fact that William takes it to be Connie in the backyard, there is a significant likelihood that it is not Connie; but, in relation to the fact that William takes her to be Connie and she parts her pair in the middle, there is no significant likelihood that it is not Connie.

Now, notice that William's reasons for believing that it is Connie in the backyard might well mention incidently that the girl in the backyard parts her hair in the middle. Then there is no significant likelihood that his belief is false, given a full statement of reasons. But his reasons are still "no good," since he does not know this distinguishes Connie from Laura.

Later, after William becomes familiar with the two twins, he might come to believe he is seeing Connie in the backyard on the basis of a similar presentation, again noticing the fact that her hair is parted in the middle. At this point his reasons are not "no good," since he now knows that this is what distinguishes Connie from Laura.

At first, William assumes that a certain general appearance is a reliable indicator of Connie's presence. Later he does not assume this and assumes only that such an appearance including hair parted in the middle is a reliable indicator of Connie's presence. This shows that the precise assumptions one makes about reliability depend on one's actual reasoning.

Conservatism: Tentative Versus Full Acceptance

[Earlier] I argued that beliefs and intentions are subject to the following:

> *Principle of Conservatism* One is justified in continuing fully to accept something in the absence of a special reason not to.

The Principle applies to what one fully accepts, what one fully believes or fully intends. It does not apply to the things one accepts as working hypotheses or tentative plans. In order to help bring out some of the force of this Principle, I now want to contrast these two sorts of acceptance, full acceptance and the more tentative acceptance of something as a working hypothesis. (I will discuss accepting something as a working hypothesis and will not say anything explicitly about accepting something as a working plan, although much that is true of working hypotheses is also true of working plans.)

To accept something as a working hypothesis is to "try it out," to see where one gets by accepting it, to see what further things such acceptance leads to. Accepting a particular working hypothesis is fruitful if it allows one to make sense of various phenomena; if it leads to solutions of problems, particularly when there are independent checks on these solutions; and if it leads naturally to other similarly fruitful hypotheses.

If a working hypothesis is sufficiently fruitful, one may become justified in fully accepting it. One's reason for such full acceptance or belief will not be the same as one's reason for having first accepted the hypothesis as a working hypothesis. One's original reason for having tentatively accepted a working hypothesis was that such acceptance promised to be fruitful. One's later reason for coming fully to accept or believe the hypothesis is that it has indeed proved fruitful in a way that suggests it is true.

This is not to say there is a sharp line between full beliefs and working hypotheses. One's acceptance of a working hypothesis can gradually become more than tentative, so that eventually one is no longer investigating that hypothesis but has fully accepted it. Things can go the other way, too. If "anomalies" arise with respect to a view, one can pass from fully accepting it to accepting it more tentatively and merely as a working hypothesis.

One is justified in continuing to accept something as a working hypothesis only as long as such acceptance promises to pay off. If something has been tentatively accepted already for some time, one is normally justified in continuing one's tentative acceptance of it only if such acceptance has already proved fruitful. It is not enough merely to be able to rebut objections in the sense that one can develop auxiliary hypotheses that keep one from being refuted. One also needs a positive payoff. One should avoid "degenerating research programs" (Lakatos 1970).

The Principle of Conservatism does not apply to such tentative acceptance. It is not true that one is justified in continuing to accept a working hypothesis in the absence of a special reason not to. One needs a special positive reason to keep on accepting something as a working hypothesis. (However, a looser strategic principle may be relevant. Perhaps, one should not too quickly abandon what one tentatively accepts simply because there is no immediate payoff. One should not get discouraged too quickly.)

Tentative acceptance is not easy. It takes a certain amount of sophistication and practice to be able to investigate an issue by tentatively accepting various hypotheses. Ordinary people, and even most scientists, are quick to convert tentative acceptance to full acceptance in a way that seems overly hasty to critical reflection (Nisbett and Ross 1980, chap. 8).

Full Acceptance Ends Inquiry

Belief in or full acceptance of P involves two things. First, one allows oneself to use P as part of one's starting point in further theoretical and practical thinking. Second, one takes the issue to be closed in the sense that, when one fully accepts P, one is no longer investigating whether P is true. Granted, one may continue investigating in order to get evidence that will stand up in court or for some other reason, but one is no longer investigating in order to find out whether P is true. In fully accepting P, one takes oneself to *know* that P is true.

Accepting something as a working hypothesis has the first of these features. If one accepts something as a working hypothesis, one can then use it as part of one's starting point in further thinking. But this sort of acceptance does not have the second feature. In accepting something as a working hypothesis, one is not ending inquiry into that matter. On the contrary, one is pursuing the inquiry in a particular way.

Since full acceptance does end inquiry in this way, one is *justified* in fully accepting P only if one is justified in ending one's investigation into whether P is true. This means one has to be justified in implicitly supposing that further investigation would not be sufficiently worthwhile, for example, by uncovering relevant evidence of a sort not yet considered. Popper (1959) stresses the point: It is not enough to look for positive evidence in favor of a hypothesis; one must also try to find evidence against the hypothesis. A hypothesis is "corroborated" only to the extent that it survives one's best attempts to refute it. Only then can one suppose further investigation would not be worthwhile. That is why it is important to check a variety of instances before accepting a generalization; it is not enough that one has checked many instances and found they are in accordance with the generalization if all the instances checked are of the same sort and if there are other sorts one has not checked (Hempel 1966).

Popper also argues against fully accepting any scientific hypothesis, but we can appreciate his methodological point without agreeing with that. Perhaps

Popper believes with Malcolm (1963) and Unger (1975) that full acceptance can only end inquiry if it involves a dogmatic commitment to disregard future negative evidence. But that is not true. Having ended inquiry at one time, one may always reopen it later. The point is merely that a special reason is needed to justify reopening an inquiry. The Principle of Conservatism applies.

Full acceptance ends inquiry into *P* in the sense that, having accepted *P*, one is justified in continuing to accept *P* in the absence of a special reason to doubt *P* or at least a special reason to reopen one's inquiry. Having accepted *P*, one is no longer actively looking for evidence as to whether *P* is true. One will now pass up opportunities to find such evidence, opportunities one would be pursuing if one had not ended one's investigation into *P*.

References

Anderson, J. R., and Bower, G.H. (1973) *Human Associative Memory* (Washington, D.C.: Winston).

Doyle, Jon (1979) "A Truth Maintenance System," *Artificial Intelligence* 12:231-272.

——(1980) *A Model for Deliberation, Action, and Introspection*, MIT Artificial Intelligence Laborator Technical Report 581.

Harman, Gilbert (1980) "Reasoning and Evidence One Does Not Posess," *Midwest Studies in Philosophy* 5: 163-182.

Lakatos, Imre (1970) "Falsification and the Methodology of Scientific Research Programmes," in *Criticism and the Growth of Knowledge,* Imre Lakatos and Alan Musgrave, eds. (Cambridge University Press), 91-196.

Malcom, Norman (1963) "Knowledge and Belief," in *Knowledge and Certainty* (Ithaca: Cornell University Press), 58-72.

Nisbett, Rhichard and Ross, Lee (1980) *Human Inference* (Englewood Cliffs: Prentice Hall).

Pierce, Charles (1877) "The Fixation of Belief," *Popular Science Monthly* 12: 1-15. Reprinted in this volume.

Poppler, Karl (1959) *Logic of Scientific Discovery* (New York: Basic Books).

Pollock, John (1979) "A Plethora of Epistemological Theories," in *Justification and Knowledge,* George Pappas, ed. (Dordrecht: Reidl), 93-114.

Ross, Lee, and Anderson, Craig (1982) "Shortcomings in the Attribution Process," in *Judgement Under Certainty,* Daniel Kahneman, Paul Slovic, and Amos Tversky, eds. (Cambridge: Cambridge University Press, 129-152.

Sosa, Ernest (1980) "The Raft and the Pyramid," *Midwest Studies in Philosophy* 5: 3-25.

✧ RELIABILISM ✧

19. WHAT IS JUSTIFIED BELIEF?

Alvin I. Goldman

The aim of this paper is to sketch a theory of justified belief. What I have in mind is an explanatory theory, one that explains in a general way why certain beliefs are counted as justified and others as unjustified. Unlike some traditional approaches, I do not try to prescribe standards for justification that differ from, or improve upon, our ordinary standards. I merely try to explicate the ordinary standards, which are, I believe, quite different from those of many classical, e.g., 'Cartesian', accounts.

Many epistemologists have been interested in justification because of its presumed close relationship to knowledge. This relationship is intended to be preserved in the conception of justified belief presented here. In previous papers on knowledge,[1] I have denied that justification is necessary for knowing, but there I had in mind 'Cartesian' accounts of justification. On the account of justified belief suggested here, it *is* necessary for knowing, and closely related to it.

The term 'justified', I presume, is an evaluative term, a term of appraisal. Any correct definition or synonym of it would also feature evaluative terms. I assume that such definitions or synonyms might be given, but I am not interested in them. I want a set of *substantive* conditions that specify when a belief is justified. Compare the moral term 'right'. This might be defined in other ethical terms or phrases, a task appropriate to meta-ethics. The task of normative ethics, by contrast, is to state substantive conditions for the rightness of actions. Normative ethics tries to specify non-ethical conditions that determine when an action is right. A familiar example is act-utilitarianism, which says an action is right if and only if it produces, or would produce, at least as much net happiness as any alternative open to the agent. These necessary and sufficient conditions clearly involve no ethical notions. Analogously, I want a theory of justified belief to specify in non-epistemic terms when a belief is justified. This is not the only kind of theory of justifiedness one might seek, but it is one important kind of theory and the kind sought here.

In order to avoid epistemic terms in our theory, we must know which terms are epistemic. Obviously, an exhaustive list cannot be given, but here are some examples: 'justified', 'warranted', 'has (good) grounds', 'has reason (to believe)', 'knows that', 'sees that', 'apprehends that', 'is probable' (in an epistemic or inductive sense), 'shows that', 'establishes that', and 'ascertains that'. By contrast, here are some sample non-epistemic expressions: 'believes that', 'is true', 'causes', 'it is necessary that', 'implies', 'is deducible from', and 'is probable' (either in the frequency sense or the propensity sense). In general, (purely) doxastic, metaphysical, modal, semantic, or syntactic expressions are not epistemic.

There is another constraint I wish to place on a theory of justified belief, in addition to the constraint that it be couched in non-epistemic language. Since I seek an explanatory theory, i.e., one that clarifies the underlying source of justificational status, it is not enough for a theory to state 'correct' necessary and sufficient conditions. Its conditions must also be appropriately deep or revelatory. Suppose, for example, that the following sufficient condition of justified belief is offered: 'If S senses redly at t and S believes at t that he is sensing redly, then S's belief at t that he is sensing redly is justified.' This is not the kind of principle I seek; for, even if it is correct, it leaves unexplained *why* a person who senses redly and believes that he does, believes this justifiably. Not every state is such that if one is in it and believes one is in it, this belief is justified. What is distinctive about the state of sensing redly, or 'phenomenal' states in general? A theory of justified belief of the kind I seek must answer this question, and hence it must be couched at a suitably deep, general, or abstract level.

A few introductory words about my *explicandum* are appropriate at this juncture. It is often assumed that whenever a person has a justified belief, he knows that it is justified and knows what the justification is. It is further assumed that the person can state or explain what his justification is. On this view, a justification is an argument, defense, or set of reasons that can be given in support of a belief. Thus, one studies the nature of justified belief by considering what a person might *say* if asked to defend, or justify, his belief. I make none of these sorts of assumptions here. I leave it an open question whether, when a belief *is* justified, the believer *knows* it is justified. I also leave it an open question whether, when a belief is justified, the believer can *state* or *give* a justification for it. I do not even assume that when a belief is justified there is something 'possessed' by the believer which can be called a 'justification'. I do assume that a justified belief gets its status of being justified from some processes or properties that make it justified. In short, there must be some justification-conferring processes or properties. But this does not imply that there must be an argument, or reason, or anything else, 'possessed' at the time of belief by the believer.

I

A theory of justified belief will be a set of principles that specify truth-conditions for the schema S's belief in p at time t is justified, i.e., conditions for the satisfaction of this schema in all possible cases. It will be convenient to formulate candidate theories in a recursive or inductive format, which would include (A) one or more base clauses, (B) a set of recursive clauses (possibly null), and (C) a closure clause. In such a format, it is permissible for the predicate 'is a justified belief' to appear in recursive clauses. But neither this predicate, nor any other epistemic predicate, may appear in (the antecedent of) any base clause.[2]

Before turning to my own theory, I want to survey some other possible approaches to justified belief. Identification of problems associated with other attempts will provide some motivation for the theory I shall offer. Obviously, I cannot examine all, or even very many, alternative attempts. But a few sample attempts will be instructive.

Let us concentrate on the attempt to formulate one or more adequate base-clause principles.[3] Here is a classical candidate:

(1) If S believes p at t, and p is indubitable for S (at t), then S's belief in p at t is justified.

To evaluate this principle, we need to know what 'indubitable' means. It can be understood in at least two ways. First, 'p is indubitable for S' might mean: 'S has no *grounds* for doubting p'. Since 'ground' is an epistemic term, however, principle (1) would be inadmissible on this reading, for epistemic terms may not legitimately appear in the antecedent of a base-clause. A second interpretation would avoid this difficulty. One might interpret 'p is indubitable for S' psychologically, i.e., as meaning 'S is psychologically incapable of doubting p'. This would make principle (1) admissible, but would it be correct? Surely not. A religious fanatic may be psychologically incapable of doubting the tenets of his faith, but that doesn't make his belief in them justified. Similarly, during the Watergate affair, someone may have been so blinded by the aura of the Presidency that even after the most damaging evidence against Nixon had emerged he was still incapable of doubting Nixon's veracity. It doesn't follow that his belief in Nixon's veracity was justified.

A second candidate base-clause principle is this:

(2) If S believes p at t, and p is self-evident, then S's belief in p at t is justified.

To evaluate this principle, we again need an interpretation of its crucial term, in this case 'self-evident'. On one standard reading, 'evident' is a synonym for 'justified'. 'Self-evident' would therefore mean something like 'directly justified', 'intuitively justified', or 'nonderivatively justified'. On this reading 'self-evident' is an epistemic phrase, and principle (2) would be disqualified as a base-clause principle.

However, there are other possible readings of 'p is self-evident' on which it isn't an epistemic phrase. One such reading is: 'It is impossible to understand p without believing it'.[4] According to this interpretation, trivial analytic and logical truths might turn out to be self-evident. Hence, any belief in such a truth would be a justified belief, according to (2).

What does 'it is *impossible* to understand p without believing it' mean? Does it mean '*humanly* impossible'? That reading would probably make (2) an unacceptable principle. There may well be propositions which humans have an innate and irrepressible disposition to believe, e.g., 'Some events have causes'. But it seems unlikely that people's inability to refrain from believing such a proposition makes every belief in it justified.

Should we then understand 'impossible' to mean 'impossible in principle', or 'logically impossible'? If that is the reading given, I suspect that (2) is a vacuous principle. I doubt that even trivial logical or analytic truths will satisfy this definition of 'self-evident'. Any proposition, we may assume, has two or more components that are somehow organized or juxtaposed. To understand the proposition one must 'grasp' the components and their juxtaposition. Now in the case of *complex* logical truths, there are (human) psychological operations that suffice to grasp the components and their juxtaposition but do not suffice to produce a belief that the proposition is true. But can't we at least *conceive* of an analogous set of psychological operations even for simple logical truths, operations which perhaps are not in the repertoire of human cognizers but which might be in the repertoire of some conceivable beings? That is, can't we conceive of psychological operations that would suffice to grasp the components and componential-juxtaposition of these simple propositions but do not suffice to produce *belief* in the propositions? I think we can conceive of such operations. Hence, for any proposition you choose, it will be possible for it to be understood without being believed.

Finally, even if we set these two objections aside, we must note that self-evidence can at best confer justificational status on relatively few beliefs, and the only plausible group are beliefs in necessary truths. Thus, other base-clause principles will be needed to explain the justificational status of beliefs in contingent propositions.

The notion of a base-clause principle is naturally associated with the idea of 'direct' justifiedness, and in the realm of contingent propositions first-person-current-mental-state propositions have often been assigned this role. In Chisholm's terminology, this conception is expressed by the notion of a '*self-presenting*' state or proposition. The sentence 'I am thinking', for example, expresses a self-presenting proposition. (At least I shall *call* this sort of content a 'proposition', though it only has a truth value given some assignment of a subject who utters or entertains the content and a time of entertaining.) When such a proposition is true for person S at time t, S is justified in believing it at t: in Chisholm's terminology, the proposition is 'evident' for S at t. This suggests the following base-clause principle.

(3) If p is a self-presenting proposition, and p is true for S at t, and S believes p at t, then S's belief in p at t is justified.

What, exactly, does 'self-presenting' mean? In the second edition of *Theory of Knowledge*, Chisholm offers this definition: "*h* is self-presenting for S at t = df. *h* is true at *t*; and necessarily, if *h* is true at *t*, then *h* is evident for S at *t*."[5] Unfortunately, since 'evident' is an epistemic term, 'self-presenting' also becomes an epistemic term on this definition, thereby disqualifying (3) as a legitimate base-clause. Some other definition of self-presentingness must be offered if (3) is to be a suitable base-clause principle.

Another definition of self-presentation readily comes to mind. 'Self-presentation' is an approximate synonym of 'self-intimation', and a proposition may be said to be self-intimating if and only if whenever it is true of a person that person believes it. More precisely, we may give the following definition.

(SP) Proposition p is self-presenting if and only if: necessarily, for any S and any t, if p is true for S at t, then S believes p at t.

On this definition, 'self-presenting' is clearly not an epistemic predicate, so (3) would be an admissible principle. Moreover, there is initial plausibility in the suggestion that it is *this* feature of first-person-current-mental-state propositions—viz., their truth guarantees their being believed—that makes beliefs in them justified.

Employing this definition of self-presentation, is principle (3) correct? This cannot be decided until we define self-presentation more precisely. Since the operator 'necessarily' can be read in different ways, there are different forms of self-presentation and correspondingly different versions of principle (3). Let us focus on two of these readings: a '*nomological*' reading and a '*logical*' reading. Consider first the nomological reading. On

this definition a proposition is self-presenting just in case it is nomologically necessary that if p is true for S at t, then S believes p at t.[6]

Is the nomological version of principle (3)—call it '(3_N)'—correct? Not at all. We can imagine cases in which the antecedent of (3_N) is satisfied but we would not say that the belief is justified. Suppose, for example, that p is the proposition expressed by the sentence 'I am in brain-state B', where 'B' is shorthand for a certain highly specific neural state description. Further suppose it is a nomological truth that anyone in brain-state B will ipso facto *believe* he is in brain-state B. In other words, imagine that an occurrent belief with the content 'I am in brain-state B' is realized whenever one is in brain-state B.[7] According to (3_N), any such belief is justified. But that is clearly false. We can readily imagine circumstances in which a person goes into brain-state B and therefore has the belief in question, though this belief is by no means justified. For example, we can imagine that a brain-surgeon operating on S artificially induces brain-state B. This results, phenomenologically, in S's suddenly believing—out of the blue—that he is in brain-state B, without any relevant antecedent beliefs. We would hardly say, in such a case, that S's belief that he is in brain-state B is justified.

Let us turn next to the logical version of (3)—call it '(3_L)'—in which a proposition is defined as self-presenting just in case it is logically necessary that if p is true for S at t, then S believes p at t. This stronger version of principle (3) might seem more promising. In fact, however, it is no more successful than (3_N). Let p be the proposition 'I am awake' and assume that it is logically necessary that if this proposition is true for some person S and time t, then S believes p at t. This assumption is consistent with the further assumption that S frequently believes p when it is false, e.g., when he is dreaming. Under these circumstances, we would hardly accept the contention that S's belief in this proposition is always justified. But nor should we accept the contention that the belief is justified when it is *true*. The truth of the proposition logically guarantees that the belief is *held*, but why should it guarantee that the belief is *justified*?

The foregoing criticism suggests that we have things backwards. The idea of self-presentation is that truth guarantees belief. This fails to confer justification because it is compatible with there being belief without truth. So what seems necessary—or at least sufficient—for justification is that belief should guarantee truth. Such a notion has usually gone under the label of 'infallibility', or 'incorrigibility'. It may be defined as follows.

(INC) Proposition p is incorrigible if and only if: necessarily, for any S and any t, if S believes p at t, then p is true for S at t.

Using the notion of incorrigibility, we may propose principle (4).

(4) If p is an incorrigible proposition, and S believes p at t, then S's belief in p at t is justified.

As was true of self-presentation, there are different varieties of incorrigibility, corresponding to different interpretations of 'necessarily'. Accordingly, we have different versions of principle (4). Once again, let us concentrate on a nomological and a logical version, (4_N) and (4_L) respectively.

We can easily construct a counterexample to (4_N) along the lines of the belief-state/brain-state counterexample that refuted (3_N). Suppose it is nomologically necessary that if anyone believes he is in brain-state B then it is true that he is in brain-state B, for the only way this belief-state is realized is through brain-state B itself. It follows that 'I am in brain-state B' is a nomologically incorrigible proposition. Therefore, according to (4_N), whenever anyone believes this proposition at any time, that belief is justified. But we may again construct a brain-surgeon example in which someone comes to have such a belief but the belief isn't justified.

Apart from this counterexample, the general point is this. Why should the fact that S's believing p guarantees the truth of p imply that S's belief is justified? The nature of the guarantee might be wholly fortuitous, as the belief-state/brain-state example is intended to illustrate. To appreciate the point, consider the following related possibility. A person's mental structure might be such that whenever he believes that p will be true (of him) a split second later, then p is true (of him) a split second later. This is because, we may suppose, his believing it brings it about. But surely we would not be compelled in such a circumstance to say that a belief of this sort is justified. So why should the fact that S's believing p guarantees the truth of p *precisely at the time of belief* imply that the belief is justified? There is no intuitive plausibility in this supposition.

The notion of *logical* incorrigibility has a more honored place in the history of conceptions of justification. But even principle (4_L), I believe, suffers from defects similar to those of (4_N). The mere fact that belief in p logically guarantees its truth does not confer justificational status on such a belief.

The first difficulty with (4_L) arises from logical or mathematical truths. Any true proposition of logic or mathematics is logically necessary. Hence, any such proposition p is logically incorrigible, since it is logically necessary that, for any S and any t, if S believes p at t then p is true (for S at t). Now assume that Nelson believes a certain very complex mathematical truth at time t. Since such a proposition is logically incorrigible, (4_L) implies that Nelson's belief in this truth at t is justified. But we may easily suppose that this belief of Nelson is not at all the result of proper mathematical reasoning, or even the result of appeal to trustworthy authority. Perhaps Nelson believes this complex truth because of utterly confused reasoning, or because of hasty and ill-founded conjecture. Then his belief is not justified, contrary to what (4_L) implies.

The case of logical or mathematical truths is admittedly peculiar, since the truth of these propositions is assured independently of any beliefs. It might seem, therefore, that we can better capture the idea of 'belief logically guaranteeing truth' in cases where the propositions in question are *contingent*. With this in mind, we might restrict (4_L) to *contingent* incorrigible propositions. Even this amendment cannot save (4_L), however, since there are counterexamples to it involving purely contingent propositions.

Suppose that Humperdink has been studying logic—or, rather, pseudo-logic—from Elmer Fraud, whom Humperdink has no reason to trust as a logician. Fraud has enunciated the principle that any disjunctive proposition consisting of at least 40 distinct disjuncts is very probably true. Humperdink now encounters the proposition p, a contingent proposition with 40 disjuncts, the 7th disjunct being 'I exist'. Although Humperdink grasps the proposition fully, he doesn't notice that it is entailed by 'I exist'. Rather, he is struck by the fact that it falls under the disjunction rule Fraud has enunciated (a rule I assume Humperdink is not *justified* in believing). Bearing this rule in mind, Humperdink forms a belief in p. Now notice that p is logically incorrigible. It is logically necessary that if anyone believes p, then p is true (of him at that time). This simply follows from the fact that, first, a person's believing anything entails that he exists, and second, 'I exist' entails p. Since p is logically incorrigible, principle (4_L) implies that Humperdink's belief in p is justified. But surely, given our example, that conclusion is false. Humperdink's belief in p is not at all justified.

One thing that goes wrong in this example is that while Humperdink's belief in p logically implies its truth, Humperdink doesn't *recognize* that his believing it implies its truth. This might move a theorist to revise (4_L) by adding the requirement that S 'recognize' that p is logically incorrigible. But this, of course, won't do. The term 'recognize' is obviously an epistemic term, so the suggested revision of (4_L) would result in an inadmissible base-clause.

II

Let us try to diagnose what has gone wrong with these attempts to produce an acceptable base-clause principle. Notice that each of the foregoing attempts confers the status of 'justified' on a belief without restriction on *why* the belief is held, i.e., on what *causally initiates* the belief or *causally sustains* it. The logical versions of principles (3) and (4), for example, clearly place no restriction on causes of belief. The same is true of the nomological versions of (3) and (4), since nomological requirements can be satisfied by simultaneity or cross-sectional laws, as illustrated by our brain-state/belief-state examples. I suggest that the absence of causal requirements accounts for the failure of the foregoing principles. Many of our counterexamples are ones in which the belief is caused in some strange or unacceptable way, e.g., by the accidental movement of a brain-surgeon's hand, by reliance on an illicit, pseudo-logical principle, or by the blinding aura of the Presidency. In general, a strategy for defeating a noncausal principle of justifiedness is to find a case in which the principle's antecedent is satisfied but the belief is caused by some faulty belief-forming process. The faultiness of the belief-forming process will incline us, intuitively, to regard the belief as unjustified.

Thus, correct principles of justified belief must be principles that make causal requirements, where 'cause' is construed broadly to include sustainers as well as initiators of belief (i.e., processes that determine, or help to overdetermine, a belief's continuing to be held.)[8]

The need for causal requirements is not restricted to base-clause principles. Recursive principles will also need a causal component. One might initially suppose that the following is a good recursive principle: 'If S justifiably believes q at t, and q entails p, and S believes p at t, then S's belief in p at t is justified'. But this principle is unacceptable. S's belief in p doesn't receive justificational status simply from the fact that p is entailed by q and S justifiably believes q. If what causes S to believe p at t is entirely different, S's belief in p may well not be justified. Nor can the situation be remedied by adding to the antecedent the condition that S justifiably believes that q entails p. Even if he believes this, and believes q as well, he might not put these beliefs together. He might believe p as a result of some other wholly extraneous, considerations. So once again, conditions that fail to require appropriate causes of a belief don't guarantee justifiedness.

Granted that principles of justified belief must make reference to causes of belief, what kinds of causes confer justifiedness? We can gain insight into this problem by reviewing some faulty processes of belief-formation, i.e., processes whose belief-outputs would be classed as unjustified. Here are some examples: confused reasoning, wishful thinking, reliance on emotional attachment, mere hunch or guesswork, and hasty generalization. What do these faulty processes have in common? They share the feature of *unreliability*: they tend to produce *error* a large proportion of the time. By contrast, which species of belief-forming (or belief-sustaining) processes are intuitively justification-conferring? They include standard perceptual processes, remembering, good reasoning, and introspection. What these processes seem to have in common is *reliability*: the beliefs they produce are generally true. My positive proposal, then, is this. The justificational status of a belief is a function of the reliability of the process or processes that cause it, where (as a first approximation) reliability consists in the tendency of a process to produce beliefs that are true rather than false.

To test this thesis further, notice that justifiedness is not a purely categorical concept, although I treat it here as categorical in the interest of simplicity. We can and do regard certain beliefs as more justified than others. Furthermore, our intuitions of comparative justifiedness go along with our beliefs about the comparative reliability of the belief-causing processes.

Consider perceptual beliefs. Suppose Jones believes he has just seen a mountain-goat. Our assessment of the belief's justifiedness is determined by whether he caught a brief glimpse of the creature at a great distance, or whether he had a good look at the thing only 30 yards away. His belief in the latter sort of case is (*ceteris paribus*) more justified than in the former sort of case. And, if his belief is true, we are more prepared to say he *knows* in the latter case than in the former. The difference between the two cases seems to be this. Visual beliefs formed from brief and hasty scanning, or where the perceptual object is a long distance off, tend to be wrong more often than visual beliefs formed from detailed and leisurely scanning, or where the object is in reasonable proximity. In short, the visual processes in the former category are less reliable than those in the latter category. A similar point holds for memory beliefs. A belief that results from a hazy and indistinct memory impression is counted as less justified than a belief that arises from a distinct memory impression, and our inclination to classify those beliefs as '*knowledge*' varies in the same way. Again, the reason is associated with the comparative reliability of the processes. Hazy and indistinct memory impressions are generally less reliable indicators of what actually happened; so beliefs formed from such impressions are less likely to be true than beliefs formed from distinct impressions. Further, consider beliefs based on inference from observed samples. A belief about a population that is based on random sampling, or on instances that exhibit great variety, is intuitively more justified than a belief based on biased sampling, or on instances from a narrow sector of the population. Again, the degree of justifiedness seems to be a function of reliability. Inferences based on random or varied samples will tend to produce less error or inaccuracy than inferences based on non-random or non-varied samples.

Returning to a categorical concept of justifiedness, we might ask just *how* reliable a belief-forming process must be in order that its resultant beliefs be justified. A precise answer to this question should not be expected. Our conception of justification is *vague* in this respect. It does seem clear, however, that *perfect* reliability isn't required. Belief-forming processes that *sometimes* produce error still confer justification. It follows that there can be justified beliefs that are false.

I have characterized justification-conferring processes as ones that have a 'tendency' to produce beliefs that are true rather than false. The term 'tendency' could refer either to *actual* long-run frequency, or to a 'propensity', i.e., outcomes that would occur in merely *possible* realizations of the process. Which of these is intended? Unfortunately, I think our ordinary conception of justifiedness is vague on this dimension too. For the most part, we simply assume that the 'observed' frequency of truth versus error would be approximately replicated in the actual long-run, and also in relevant counterfactual situations, i.e., ones that are highly 'realistic', or conform closely to the circumstances of the actual world. Since we ordinarily assume these frequencies to be roughly the same, we make no concerted effort to distinguish them. Since the purpose of my present theorizing is to capture our ordinary conception of justifiedness, and since our ordinary conception is vague on this matter, it is appropriate to leave the theory vague in the same respect.

We need to say more about the notion of a belief-forming '*process*'. Let us mean by a 'process' a *functional operation* or procedure, i.e., something that generates a *mapping* from certain states—'inputs'—into other states—'outputs'. The outputs in the present case are states of believing this or that proposition at a given moment. On this interpretation, a process is a *type* as opposed to a *token*. This is fully appropriate, since it is only types that have statistical properties such as producing truth 80% of the time; and it is precisely such statistical properties that determine the reliability of a process. Of course, we also want to speak of a process as *causing* a belief, and it looks as if types are incapable of being causes. But when we say that a belief is caused by a given process, understood as a functional procedure, we may interpret this to mean that it is caused by the particular *inputs* to the process (and by the intervening events 'through which' the functional procedure carries the inputs into the output) on the occasion in question.

What are some examples of belief-forming 'processes' construed as functional operations? One example is reasoning processes, where the inputs include antecedent beliefs and entertained hypotheses. Another example is functional procedures whose inputs include desires, hopes, or emotional states of various sorts (together with antecedent beliefs). A third example is a memory process, which takes as input beliefs or experiences at an earlier time and generates as output beliefs at a later time. For example, a memory process might take as input a belief *at* t_1 that Lincoln was born in 1809 and generate as output a belief *at* t_n that Lincoln was born in 1809. A fourth example is perceptual processes. Here it isn't clear whether inputs should include states of the environment, such as the distance of the stimulus from the cognizer, or only events within or on the surface of the organism, e.g., receptor stimulations. I shall return to this point in a moment.

A critical problem concerning our analysis is the degree of generality of the process-types in question. Input–output relations can be specified very broadly or very narrowly, and the degree of generality will partly determine the degree of reliability. A process-type might be selected so narrowly that only one instance of it ever occurs, and hence the type is either completely reliable or completely unreliable. (This assumes that reliability is a function of *actual* frequency only.) If such narrow process-types were selected, beliefs that are intuitively unjustified might be said to result from perfectly reliable processes; and beliefs that are intuitively justified might be said result from perfectly unreliable processes.

It is clear that our ordinary thought about process-types slices them broadly, but I cannot at present give a precise explication of our intuitive principles. One plausible suggestion, though, is that the relevant processes are *content-neutral*. It might be argued, for example, that the process of *inferring p whenever the Pope asserts p* could pose problems for our theory. If the Pope is infallible, this process will be perfectly reliable; yet we would not regard the belief-outputs of this process as justified. The content-neutral restriction would avert this difficulty. If relevant processes are required to admit as input beliefs (or other states) with *any* content, the aforementioned process will not count, for its input beliefs have a restricted propositional content, viz., 'the Pope asserts *p*'.

In addition to the problem of 'generality' or 'abstractness' there is the previously mentioned problem of the '*extent*' of belief-forming processes. Clearly, the causal ancestry of beliefs often includes events outside the organism. Are such events to be included among the 'inputs' of belief-forming processes? Or should we restrict the extent of belief-forming processes to '*cognitive*' events, i.e., events within the organism's nervous system? I shall choose the latter course, though with some hesitation. My general grounds for this decision are roughly as follows. Justifiedness seems to be a function of how a cognizer deals with his environmental input, i.e., with the goodness or badness of the operations that register and transform the stimulation that reaches him. ('Deal with', of course, does not mean *purposeful* action; nor is it restricted to *conscious* activity.) A justified belief is, roughly speaking, one that results from cognitive operations that are, generally speaking, good or successful. But '*cognitive*' operations are most plausibly construed as operations of the cognitive faculties, i.e., 'information-processing' equipment *internal* to the organism.

With these points in mind, we may now advance the following base-clause principle for justified belief.

(5) If *S*'s believing *p* at *t* results from a reliable cognitive belief-forming process (or set of processes), then *S*'s belief in *p* at *t* is justified.

Since 'reliable belief-forming process' has been defined in terms of such notions as belief, truth, statistical frequency, and the like, it is not an epistemic term. Hence, (5) is an admissible base-clause.

It might seem as if (5) promises to be not only a successful base clause, but the only principle needed whatever, apart from a closure clause. In other words, it might seem as if it is a necessary as well as a sufficient condition of justifiedness that a belief be produced by reliable cognitive belief-forming processes. But this is not quite correct, give our provisional definition of 'reliability'.

Our provisional definition implies that a reasoning process is reliable only if it generally produces beliefs that are true, and similarly, that a memory process is reliable only if it generally yields beliefs that are true. But these requirements are too strong. A reasoning procedure cannot be expected to produce true belief if it is is applied to false premises. And memory cannot be expected to yield a true belief if the original belief it attempts to retain is false. What we need for reasoning and memory, then, is a notion of *'conditional reliability'*. A process is conditionally reliable when a sufficient proportion of its output-beliefs are true *given that its input-beliefs are true*.

With this point in mind, let us distinguish *belief-dependent* and *belief-independent* cognitive processes. The former are processes *some* of whose inputs are belief-states.[9] The latter are processes *none* of whose inputs are belief-states. We may then replace principle (5) with the following two principles, the first a base-clause principle and the second a recursive-clause principle.

> (6$_A$) If S's belief in p at t results ('immediately') from a belief-independent process that is (unconditionally) reliable, then S's belief in p at t is justified.

> (6$_B$) If S's belief in p at t results ("immediately") from a belief-dependent process that is (at least) conditionally reliable, and if the beliefs (if any) on which this process operates in producing S's belief in p at t are themselves justified, then S's belief in p at t is justified.[10]

If we add to (6$_A$) and (6$_B$) the standard closure clause, we have a complete theory of justified belief. The theory says, in effect, that a belief is justified if and only it is *'well-formed'*, i.e., it has an ancestry of reliable and/or conditionally reliable cognitive operations. (Since a dated belief may be over-determined, it may have a number of distinct ancestral trees. These need not all be full of reliable or conditionally reliable processes. But at least one ancestral tree must have reliable or conditionally reliable processes throughout.)

The theory of justified belief proposed here, then, is an *Historical* or *Genetic* theory. It contrasts with the dominant approach to justified belief, an approach that generates what we may call (borrowing a phrase from Robert Nozick) *'Current Time-Slice'* theories. A Current Time-Slice theory makes the justificational status of a belief wholly a function of what is true of the cognizer *at the time* of belief. An Historical theory makes the justificational status of a belief depend on its prior history.

Since my Historical theory emphasizes the reliability of the belief-generating processes, it may be called *'Historical Reliabilism'*.

The most obvious examples of Current Time-Slice theories are 'Cartesian' Foundationalist theories, which trace all justificational status (at least of contingent propositions) to current mental states. The usual varieties of Coherence theories, however, are equally Current Time-Slice views, since they too make the justificational status of a belief wholly a function of *current* states of affairs. For Coherence theories, however, these current states include all other beliefs of the cognizer, which would not be considered relevant by Cartesian Foundationalism. Have there been other Historical theories of justified belief? Among contemporary writers, Quine and Popper have Historical epistemologies, though the notion of 'justification' is not their avowed *explicandum*. Among historical writers, it might seem that Locke and Hume had Genetic theories of sorts. But I think that their Genetic theories were only theories of ideas, not of knowledge or justification. Plato's theory of recollection, however, is a good example of a Genetic theory of knowing.[11] And it might be argued that Hegel and Dewey had Genetic epistemologies (if Hegel can be said to have had a clear epistemology at all).

The theory articulated by (6$_A$) and (6$_B$) might be viewed as a kind of 'Foundationalism,' because of its recursive structure. I have no objection to this label, as long as one keeps in mind how different this 'diachronic' form of Foundationalism is from Cartesian, or other 'synchronic' varieties of, Foundationalism.

Current Time-Slice theories characteristically assume that the justificational status of a belief is something which the cognizer is able to know or determine at the time of belief. This is made explicit, for example, by Chisholm.[12] The Historical theory I endorse makes no such assumption. There are many facts about a cognizer to which he lacks 'privileged access', and I regard the justificational status of his beliefs as one of those things. This is not to say that a cognizer is necessarily ignorant, at any given moment, of the justificational status of his current beliefs. It is only to deny that he necessarily has, or can get, knowledge or true belief about this status. Just as a person can know without knowing that he knows, so he can have justified belief without knowing that it is justified (or believing justifiably that it is justified.)

A characteristic case in which a belief is justified though the cognizer doesn't know that it's justified is where the original evidence for the belief has long since been forgotten. If the original evidence was compelling, the cognizer's original belief may have been justified; and this justificational status may have been preserved through memory. But since the cognizer no longer remembers how or why he came to believe, he may not know that the belief is justified. If asked now to justify his belief, he may be at a loss. Still, the belief *is* justified, though the cognizer can't demonstrate or establish this.

The Historical theory of justified belief I advocate is connected in spirit with the causal theory of knowing I have presented elsewhere.[13] I had this in mind when I remarked near the outset of the paper that my theory of justified belief makes justifiedness come out closely related to knowledge. Justified beliefs, like pieces of knowledge, have appropriate histories; but they may fail to be knowledge either because they are false or because they founder on some other requirement for knowing of the kind discussed in the post-Gettier knowledge-trade.

There is a variant of the Historical conception of justified belief that is worth mentioning in this context. It may be introduced as follows. Suppose S has a set B of beliefs at time t_0, and some of these beliefs are *unjustified*. Between t_0 and t_1 he reasons from the entire set B to the conclusion p, which he then accepts at t_1. The reasoning procedure he uses is a very sound one, i.e., one that is conditionally reliable. There is a sense or respect in which we are tempted to say that S's belief in p at t_1 is 'justified'. At any rate, it is tempting to say that the *person* is justified in believing p at t. Relative to his antecedent cognitive state, he did as well as could be expected: the *transition* from his cognitive state at t_0 to his cognitive state at t_1 was entirely sound. Although we may acknowledge this brand of justifiedness—it might be called '*Terminal-Phase Reliabilism*'—it is not a kind of justifiedness so closely related to knowing. For a person to know proposition p, it is not enough that the *final phase* of the process that leads to his belief in p be sound. It is also necessary that some entire history of the process be sound (i.e., reliable or conditionally reliable).

Let us return now to the Historical theory. In the next section of the paper, I shall adduce reasons for strengthening it a bit. Before looking at these reasons, however, I wish to review two quite different objections to the theory.

First, a critic might argue that *some* justified beliefs do not derive their justificational status from their causal ancestry. In particular, it might be argued that beliefs about one's current phenomenal states and intuitive beliefs about elementary logical or conceptual relationships do not derive their justificational status in this way. I am not persuaded by either of these examples. Introspection, I believe, should be regarded as a form of retrospection. Thus, a justified belief that I am 'now' in pain gets its justificational status from a relevant, though brief, causal history.[14] The apprehension of logical or conceptual relationships is also a cognitive process that occupies time. The psychological process of 'seeing' or 'intuiting' a simple logical truth is very fast, and we cannot introspectively dissect it into constituent parts. Nonetheless, there are mental operations going on, just as there are mental operations that occur in *idiots savants*, who are unable to report the computational processes they in fact employ.

A second objection to Historical Reliabilism focuses on the reliability element rather than the causal or historical element. Since the theory is intended to cover all possible cases, it seems to imply that for any cognitive process C, if C is reliable in possible world W, then any belief in W that results from C is justified. But doesn't this permit easy counterexamples? Surely we can imagine a possible world in which wishful thinking is reliable. We can imagine a possible world where a benevolent demon so arranges things that beliefs formed by wishful thinking usually come true. This would make wishful thinking a reliable process in that possible world, but surely we don't want to regard beliefs that result from wishful thinking as justified.

There are several possible ways to respond to this case and I am unsure which response is best, partly because my own intuitions (and those of other people I have consulted) are not entirely clear. One possibility is to say that in the possible world imagined, beliefs that result from wishful thinking *are* justified. In other words we reject the claim that wishful thinking could never, intuitively, confer justifiedness.[15]

However, for those who feel that wishful thinking couldn't confer justifiedness, even in the world imagined, there are two ways out. First, it may be suggested that the proper criterion of justifiedness is the propensity of a process to generate beliefs that are true *in a non-manipulated environment*, i.e., an environment in which there is no purposeful arrangement of the world either to accord or conflict with the beliefs that are formed. In other words, the suitability of a belief-forming process is only a function of its success in 'natural' situations, not situations of the sort involving benevolent or malevolent demons, or any other such manipulative creatures. If we reformulate the theory to include this qualification, the counterexample in question will be averted.

Alternatively, we may reformulate our theory, or reinterpret it, as follows. Instead of construing the theory as saying that a belief in possible world *W* is justified if and only if it results from a cognitive process that is reliable in *W*, we may construe it as saying that a belief in possible world *W* is justified if and only if it results from a cognitive process that is reliable *in our world*. In short, our conception of justifiedness is derived as follows. We note certain cognitive processes in the actual world, and form beliefs about which of these are reliable. The ones we believe to be reliable are then regarded as justification-conferring processes. In reflecting on hypothetical beliefs, we deem them justified if and only if they result from processes already picked out as justification-conferring, or processes very similar to those. Since wishful thinking is not among these processes, a belief formed in a possible world *W* by wishful thinking would not be deemed justified, even if wishful thinking is reliable *in W*. I am not sure that this is a correct reconstruction of our intuitive conceptual scheme, but it would accommodate the benevolent demon case, at least if the proper thing to say in that case is that the wishful-thinking-caused beliefs are unjustified.

Even if we adopt this strategy, however, a problem still remains. Suppose that wishful thinking turns out to be reliable *in the actual world!*[16] This might be because, unbeknownst to us at present, there is a benevolent demon who, lazy until now, will shortly start arranging things so that our wishes come true. The long-run performance of wishful thinking will be very good, and hence even the new construal of the theory will imply that beliefs resulting from wishful thinking (in *our* world) are justified. Yet this surely contravenes our intuitive judgment on the matter.

Perhaps the moral of the case is that the standard format of a 'conceptual analysis' has its shortcomings. Let me depart from that format and try to give a better rendering of our aim and the theory that tries to achieve that aim. What we really want is an *explanation* of why we count, or would count, certain beliefs as justified and others as unjustified. Such an explanation must refer to our *beliefs* about reliability, not to the actual *facts*. The reason we *count* beliefs as justified is that they are formed by what we *believe* to be reliable belief-forming processes. Our beliefs about which belief-forming processes are reliable may be erroneous, but that does not affect the adequacy of the explanation. Since we *believe* that wishful thinking is an unreliable belief-forming process, we regard beliefs formed by wishful thinking as unjustified. What matters, then, is what we *believe* about wishful thinking, not what is *true* (in the long run) about wishful thinking. I am not sure how to express this point in the standard format of conceptual analysis, but it identifies an important point in understanding our theory.

III

Let us return, however, to the standard format of conceptual analysis, and let us consider a new objection that will require some revisions in the theory advanced until now. According to our theory, a belief is justified in case it is caused by a process that is in fact reliable, or by one we generally believe to be reliable. But suppose that although one of *S*'s beliefs satisfies this condition, *S* has no reason to believe that it does. Worse yet, suppose *S* has reason to believe that his belief is caused by an *unreliable* process (although *in fact* its causal ancestry is fully reliable). Wouldn't we deny in such circumstances that *S*'s belief is justified? This seems to show that our analysis, as presently formulated, is mistaken.

Suppose that Jones is told on fully reliable authority that a certain class of his memory beliefs are almost all mistaken. His parents fabricate a wholly false story that Jones suffered from amnesia when he was seven but later developed *pseudo*-memories of that period. Though Jones listens to what his parents say and has excellent reason to trust them, he persists in believing the ostensible memories from his seven-year-old past. Are these memory beliefs justified? Intuitively, they are not justified. But since these beliefs result from genuine memory and original perceptions, which are adequately reliable processes, our theory says that these beliefs are justified.

Can the theory be revised to meet this difficulty? One natural suggestion is that the actual reliability of a belief's ancestry is not enough for justifiedness; in addition, the cognizer must be *justified in believing* that the ancestry of his belief is reliable. Thus one might think of replacing (6 A), for example, with (7). (For simplicity, I neglect some of the details of the earlier analysis.)

> (7) If S's belief in *p* at *t* is caused by a reliable cognitive process, and S justifiably believes at *t* that his *p*-belief is so caused, then S's belief in *p* at *t* is justified.

It is evident, however, that (7) will not do as a base clause, for it contains the epistemic term 'justifiably' in its antecedent.

A slightly weaker revision, without this problematic feature, might next be suggested, viz.,

> (8) If S's belief in *p* at *t* is caused by a reliable cognitive process, and S believes at *t* that his *p*-belief is so caused, then S's belief in *p* at *t* is justified.

But this won't do the job. Suppose that Jones believes that his memory beliefs are reliably caused despite all the (trustworthy) contrary testimony of his parents. Principle (8) would be satisfied, yet we wouldn't say that these beliefs are justified.

Next, we might try (9), which is stronger than (8) and, unlike (7), formally admissible as a base clause.

> (9) If S's belief in *p* at *t* is caused by a reliable cognitive process, and S believes at *t* that his *p*-belief is so caused, and this meta-belief is caused by a reliable cognitive process, than S's belief in *p* at *t* is justified.

A first objection to (9) is that it wrongly precludes unreflective creatures—creatures like animals or young children, who have no beliefs about the genesis of their beliefs—from having justified beliefs. If one shares my view that justified belief is, at least roughly, *well-formed* belief, surely animals and young children can have justified beliefs.

A second problem with (9) concerns its underlying rationale. Since (9) is proposed as a substitute for (6A), it is implied that the reliability of a belief's own cognitive ancestry does not make it justified. But, the suggestion seems to be, the reliability of a *meta-belief*'s ancestry confers justifiedness on the first-order belief. Why should that be so? Perhaps one is attracted by the idea of a 'trickle-down' effect: if an n+1-level belief is justified, its justification trickles down to an n-level belief. But even if the trickle-down theory is correct, it doesn't help here. There is no assurance from the satisfaction of (9)'s antecedent that the meta-belief itself is *justified*.

To obtain a better revision of our theory, let us re-examine the Jones case. Jones has strong evidence against certain propositions concerning his past. He doesn't *use* this evidence, but if he *were* to use it properly, he would stop believing these propositions. Now the proper use of evidence would be an instance of a (conditionally) reliable process. So what we can say about Jones is that he *fails* to use a certain (conditionally) reliable process that he could and should have used. Admittedly, had he used this process, he would have 'worsened' his doxastic states: he would have replaced some true beliefs with suspension of judgment. Still, he couldn't have known this in the case in question. So, he failed to do something which, epistemically, he should have done. This diagnosis suggests a fundamental change in our theory. The justificational status of a belief is not only a function of the cognitive processes *actually* employed in producing it; it is also a function of processes that could and should be employed.

With these points in mind, we may tentatively propose the following revision of our theory, where we again focus on a base-clause principle but omit certain details in the interest of clarity.

> (10) If S's belief in *p* at *t* results from a reliable cognitive process, and there is no reliable or conditionally reliable process available to S which,

had it been used by S in addition to the process actually used, would have resulted in S's not believing p at t, then S's belief in p at t is justified.

There are several problems with this proposal. First, there is a technical problem. One cannot use an additional belief-forming (or doxastic-state-forming) process *as well as* the original process if the additional one would result in a different doxastic state. One wouldn't be using the original process at all. So we need a slightly different formulation of the relevant counterfactual. Since the basic idea is reasonably clear, however, I won't try to improve on the formulation here. A second problem concerns the notion of 'available' belief-forming (or doxastic-state-forming) processes. What is it for a process to be 'available' to a cognizer? Were scientific procedures 'available' to people who lived in pre-scientific ages? Furthermore, it seems implausible to say that all 'available' processes ought to be used, at least if we include such processes as gathering *new* evidence. Surely a belief can sometimes be justified even if additional evidence-gathering would yield a different doxastic attitude. What I think we should have in mind here are such additional processes as calling previously acquired evidence to mind, assessing the implications of that evidence, etc. This is admittedly somewhat vague, but here again our ordinary notion of justifiedness is vague, so it is appropriate for our analysans to display the same sort of vagueness.

This completes the sketch of my account of justified belief. Before concluding, however, it is essential to point out that there is an important use of 'justified' which is not captured by this account but can be captured by a closely related one.

There is a use of 'justified' in which it is not implied or presupposed that there is a *belief* that is justified. For example, if S is trying to decide whether to believe p and asks our advice, we may tell him that he is 'justified' in believing it. We do not thereby imply that he *has* a justified *belief*, since we know he is still suspending judgement. What we mean, roughly, is that he *would* or *could* be justified if he were to believe p. The justificational status we ascribe here cannot be a function of the causes of S's believing p, for there is no belief by S in p. Thus, the account of justifiedness we have given thus far cannot explicate *this* use of 'justified'. (It

doesn't follow that this use of 'justified' has no connection with causal ancestries. Its proper use may depend on the causal ancestry of the cognizer's cognitive state, though not on the causal ancestry of his believing p.)

Let us distinguish two uses of 'justified': an *ex post* use and an *ex ante* use. The *ex post* use occurs when there exists a belief, and we say *of that belief* that it is (or isn't) justified. The *ex ante* use occurs when no such belief exists, or when we wish to ignore the question of whether such a belief exists. Here we say of the *person*, independent of his doxastic state vis-à-vis p, that p is (or isn't) suitable for him to believe.[17]

Since we have given an account of *ex post* justifiedness, it will suffice if we can analyze *ex ante* justifiedness in terms of it. Such an analysis, I believe, is ready at hand. S is *ex ante* justified in believing p at t just in case his total cognitive state at t is such that from that state he could come to believe p in such a way that this belief would be *ex post* justified. More precisely, he is *ex ante* justified in believing p at t just in case a reliable belief-forming operation is available to him such that the application of that operation to his total cognitive state at t would result, more or less immediately, in his believing p and this belief would be *ex post* justified. Stated formally, we have the following:

(11) Person S is *ex ante* justified in believing p at t if and only if there is a reliable belief-forming operation available to S which is such that if S applied that operation to his total cognitive state at t, S would believe p at t-plus-delta (for a suitably small delta) and that belief would be *ex post* justified.

For the analysans of (11) to be satisfied, the total cognitive state at t must have a suitable causal ancestry. Hence, (11) is implicitly an Historical account of *ex ante* justifiedness.

As indicated, the bulk of this paper was addressed to *ex post* justifiedness This is the appropriate analysandum if one is interested in the connection between justifiedness and knowledge, since what is crucial to whether a person *knows* a proposition is whether he has an actual *belief* in the proposition that is justified. However, since many epistemologists are interested in *ex ante* justifiedness, it is proper for a general theory of justification to try to provide an account of that concept as well. Our theory does this quite naturally, for the account of *ex ante* justifiedness falls out directly from our account of *ex post* justifiedness.[18]

Notes

1. 'A Causal Theory of Knowing,' *The Journal of Philosophy* 64, 12 (June 22, 1967): 357–372; 'Innate Knowledge,' in S. P. Stich, ed., *Innate Ideas* (Berkeley: University of California Press, 1975); and 'Discrimination and Perceptual Knowledge,' *The Journal of Philosophy* 73, 20 (November 18, 1976), 771–791.
2. Notice that the choice of a recursive format does not prejudice the case for or against any particular theory. A recursive format is perfectly general. Specifically, an explicit set of necessary and sufficient conditions is just a special case of a recursive format, i.e. one in which there is no recursive clause.
3. Many of the attempts I shall consider are suggested by material in William P. Alston, 'Varieties of Privileged Access,' *American Philosophical Quarterly* 8 (1971), 223–241.
4. Such a definition (though without the modal term) is given, for example, by W. V. Quine and J. S. Ullian in *The Web of Belief* (New York: Random House, 1970), p. 21. Statements are said to be self-evident just in case "to understand them, is to believe them".
5. Englewood Cliffs, N.J.: Prentice-Hall, Inc., 1977, p. 22.
6. I assume, of course, that 'nomologically necessary' is *de re* with respect to 'S' and 't' in this construction. I shall not focus on problems that may arise in this regard, since my primary concerns are with different issues.
7. This assumption violates the thesis that Davidson calls 'The Anomalism of the Mental'. Cf. 'Mental Events,' in L. Foster and J. W. Swanson, eds., *Experience and Theory* (Amherst: University of Massachusetts Press, 1970). But it is unclear that this thesis is a necessary truth. Thus, it seems fair to assume its falsity in order to produce a counterexample. The example neither entails nor precludes the mental–physical identity theory.
8. Keith Lehrer's example of the gypsy lawyer is intended to show the inappropriateness of a causal requirement. (See *Knowledge*, Oxford: University Press, 1974, pp. 124–125.) But I find this example unconvincing. To the extent that I clearly imagine that the lawyer fixes his belief solely as a result of the cards, it seems intuitively wrong to say that he *knows*—or has a *justified belief*—that his client is innocent.
9. This definition is not exactly what we need for the purposes at hand. As Ernest Sosa points out, introspection will turn out to be a belief–dependent process since sometimes the input into the process will be a belief (when the introspected content is a belief). Intuitively, however, introspection is not the sort of process which may be merely conditionally reliable. I do not know how to refine the definition so as to avoid this difficulty, but it is a small and isolated point.
10. It may be objected that principles (6A) and (6B) are jointly open to analogues of the lottery paradox. A series of processes composed of reliable but less-than-perfectly-reliable processes may be extremely unreliable. Yet applications of (6A) and (6B) would confer justifiedness on a belief that is caused by such a series. In reply to this objection, we might simply indicate that the theory is intended to capture our ordinary notion of justifiedness, and this ordinary notion has been formed without recognition of this kind of problem. The theory is not wrong *as* a theory of the ordinary (naive) conception of justifiedness. On the other hand, if we want a theory to do more than capture the ordinary conception of justifiedness, it might be possible to strengthen the principles to avoid lottery-paradox analogues.
11. I am indebted to Mark Pastin for this point.
12. Cf. *Theory of Knowledge*, Second Edition, pp. 17, 114–116.
13. Cf. 'A Causal Theory of Knowing,' *op. cit.* The reliability aspect of my theory also has its precursors in earlier papers of mine on knowing: 'Innate Knowledge,' *op. cit.* and 'Discrimination and Perceptual Knowledge,' *op. cit.*
14. The view that introspection is retrospection was taken by Ryle, and before him (as Charles Hartshorne points out to me) by Hobbes, Whitehead, and possibly Husserl.
15. Of course, if people in world *W* learn *inductively* that wishful thinking is reliable, and regularly base their beliefs on this inductive inference, it is quite unproblematic and straightforward that their beliefs are justified. The only interesting case is where their beliefs are formed *purely* by wishful thinking, without using inductive inference. The suggestion contemplated in this paragraph of the text is that, in the world imagined, even pure wishful thinking would confer justifiedness.
16. I am indebted here to Mark Kaplan.
17. The distinction between *ex post* and *ex ante* justifiedness is similar to Roderick Firth's distinction between *doxastic* and *propositional* warrant. See his 'Are Epistemic Concepts Reducible to Ethical Concepts?', in Alvin I. Goldman and Jaegwon Kim, eds., *Values and Morals, Essays in Honor of William Frankena, Charles Stevenson, and Richard Brandt* (Dordrecht: D. Reidel, 1978).
18. Research on this paper was begun while the author was a fellow of the John Simon Guggenheim Memorial Foundation and of the Center for Advanced Study in the Behavioral Sciences. I am grateful for their support. I have received helpful comments and criticism from Holly S. Goldman, Mark Kaplan, Fred Schmitt, Stephen P. Stich, and many others at several universities where earlier drafts of the paper were read.

20. EVIDENTIALISM

Richard Feldman and Earl Conee

I

We advocate evidentialism in epistemology. What we call evidentialism is the view that the epistemic justification of a belief is determined by the quality of the believer's evidence for the belief. Disbelief and suspension of judgment also can be epistemically justified. The one of these doxastic attitudes that a person is justified in having toward any given thought is the one that fits the person's evidence. More precisely:

> EJ Doxastic attitude D toward proposition p is epistemically justified for S at t if and only if having D toward p fits the evidence S has at t.[1]

The doxastic attitude of belief fits one's evidence when the evidence overall supports the proposition believed. Suspension of judgment is fitting when one has no evidence about the proposition or one's evidence, pro and con, is equibalanced. Disbelief is fitting when one's evidence overall supports the denial of the proposition.

We do not offer EJ as a definition of the word "justified." Rather EJ serves to indicate the kind of justification that we take to be characteristically epistemic. This is a sort of justification that is necessary for factual knowledge. We hold that this justification turns entirely on evidence.

Here are three examples that illustrate how attitudes can be justified by fitting one's evidence. First, when a physiologically normal man under ordinary circumstances looks at a plush green lawn that is directly in front of him in broad daylight, believing that there is something green before him is the attitude toward this proposition that fits his evidence. That is why the belief is epistemically justified. Second, suspension of judgment is the fitting attitude for each of us toward the proposition that an even number of ducks exists, since our evidence makes it equally likely that the number is odd. And third, when it comes to the proposition that sugar is sour, our recollection of some of our gustatory experiences makes disbelief the fitting attitude. Remembering the sweet taste of sugar epistemically justifies disbelief.[2]

We believe that EJ identifies the sort of justification that is illustrated in these examples. We find no adequate grounds for accepting recently discussed proposals about justification that may seem to cast doubt on EJ. In the remainder of this paper we defend evidentialism. Our purpose is to show that it continues to be the best view of epistemic justification.

II

In this section we consider two objections to EJ. Each is based on a claim about human limits and a claim about the conditions under which an attitude can be justified. One objection depends on the claim that an attitude can be justified only if it is voluntarily adopted; the other depends on the claim that an attitude toward a proposition or propositions can be justified for a person only if the ability to have that attitude toward the proposition or those propositions is within normal human limits.

Doxastic Voluntarism

EJ says that a doxastic attitude is justified for a person when that attitude fits the person's evidence. It is clear that there are cases in which a certain attitude toward a proposition fits a person's evidence, yet the person has no control over whether he forms that attitude toward that proposition. So some involuntarily adopted attitudes are justified according to EJ. John Heil finds this feature of the evidentialist position questionable. He says that the fact we "speak of a person's beliefs as being warranted, justified, or rational . . . makes it appear that . . . believing something can, at least sometimes, be under the voluntary control of the believer."[3] Hilary Kornblith claims that it seems "unfair" to evaluate beliefs if they "are not subject" to direct voluntary control.[4] Both Heil and Kornblith conclude that although beliefs are not under *direct* voluntary control, it is still appropriate to evaluate them because "they are not entirely out of our control either."[5] "One does have a say in the procedures one undertakes that lead to" the formation of beliefs.[6]

A doxastic attitude need not be under any sort of voluntary control for it to be suitable for epistemic evaluation. Examples confirm that beliefs may be both involuntary and subject to epistemic evaluation. Suppose that a person spontaneously and involuntarily believes that the lights are on in the room, as a result of visually experiencing the normal look of a well-lighted room. This belief is clearly justified, whether or not the person can voluntarily acquire, lose, or modify the cognitive process that led to the belief. Unjustified beliefs can also be involuntary. A paranoid man might believe without any supporting evidence that he is being spied on. This belief might be the result of an uncontrollable desire to be a recipient of special attention. In such case, the belief is clearly epistemically unjustified even if the belief is involuntary and the person cannot alter the process leading to it.

The contrary view that only voluntary beliefs are justified or unjustified may seem plausible if one confuses the topic of EJ with an assessment of the *person*.[7] A person deserves praise or blame for being in a doxastic state only if that state is under the person's control.[8] The person who involuntarily believes in the presence of overwhelming evidence that the lights are on does not deserve praise for this belief. The belief is nevertheless justified. It is supported by the person's evidence. The person who believes that he is being spied on as a result of an uncontrollable desire does not deserve to be blamed for that belief. But there is a fact about the belief's epistemic merit. It is epistemically defective—it is held in the presence of insufficient evidence and is therefore unjustified.

Doxastic Limits

It is sometimes claimed that it is inappropriate to set epistemic standards that are beyond normal human limits. Alvin Goldman recommends that epistemologists seek epistemic principles that can serve as practical guides to belief formation. Such principles, he contends, must take into account the limited cognitive capacities of people. For instance, each proposition logically implies infinitely many others. The proposition that snow is white logically implies the disjunctive propositions that snow is white or one is less than two, that snow is white or one is less than three, etc. Goldman is led to deny a principle instructing people to believe all the logical consequences of their beliefs, since they are unable to have the infinite number of beliefs that following such a principle would require. Goldman's view does not conflict with EJ, since EJ does not instruct anyone to believe anything. It simply states a necessary and sufficient condition for epistemic justification. Nor does Goldman think this view conflicts with EJ, since he makes it clear that the principles he is discussing are guides to action and not principles that apply the traditional concept of epistemic justification.

Although Goldman does not use facts about normal cognitive limits to argue against EJ, such an argument has been suggested by Kornblith and by Paul Thagard. Kornblith cites Goldman's work as an inspiration for his view that "having justified beliefs is simply doing the best one can in the light of the innate endowment one starts from . . .".[10] Thagard contends that rational or justified principles of inference "should not demand of a reasoner inferential performance which exceeds the general psychological abilities of human beings."[11] Neither Thagard nor Kornblith argues against EJ, but it is easy to see how such an argument would go: A doxastic attitude toward a proposition is justified for a person only if having that attitude toward that proposition is within the normal doxastic capabilities of people. Some doxastic attitudes that fit a person's evidence are not within those capabilities. Yet EJ classifies them as justified. Hence, EJ is false.[12]

We see no good reason here to deny EJ. The argument has as a premise the claim that some attitudes beyond normal limits do fit someone's evidence. The fact that we are limited to a finite number of beliefs is used to support this claim. But this fact does not establish the premise. There is no reason to think that an infinite number of beliefs fit any body of evidence that anyone ever has. The evidence that people have under ordinary circumstances never makes it evident, concerning every one of an infinite number of logical consequences of that evidence, that it is a consequence.

Thus, believing each consequence will not fit any ordinary evidence. Furthermore, even if there are circumstances in which more beliefs fit a person's evidence than he is able to have, all that follows is that he cannot have at one time all the beliefs that fit. It does not follow that there is any particular fitting belief which is unattainable. Hence, the premise of the argument that says that EJ classifies as justified some normally unattainable beliefs is not established by means of this example. There does not seem to be any sort of plausible evidence that would establish this premise. While some empirical evidence may show that people typically do not form fitting attitudes in certain contexts, or that some fitting attitudes are beyond some individual's abilities, such evidence fails to show that any fitting attitudes are beyond normal limits.

There is a more fundamental objection to this argument against EJ. The premise that restricts what is epistemically justified to feasible doxastic alternatives is doubtful. It can be a worthwhile thing to help people to choose among the epistemic alternatives open to them. But suppose that there were some situation in which forming the attitude that best fits a person's evidence was beyond normal cognitive limits. This would still be the attitude *justified* by the person's evidence. If the person has normal abilities, then he would be in the unfortunate position of being unable to do what is justified according to the standard for justification asserted by EJ. This is not a flaw in the account of justification. Some standards are met only by going beyond normal human limits. Standards that some teachers set for an "A" in a course are unattainable by most students. There are standards of artistic excellence that most people cannot meet in any available circumstance. Similarly, epistemic justification might have been normally unattainable.

We conclude that neither considerations of doxastic voluntarism nor of doxastic limits provide any good reason to abandon EJ as an account of epistemic justification.

III

EJ sets an epistemic standard for evaluating doxastic conduct. In any case of a standard for conduct, whether it is voluntary or not, it is appropriate to speak of "requirements" or "obligations" that the standard imposes. Thus, in the case of epistemic standards, it is natural to say: "The person who has overwhelming perceptual evidence for the proposition that the lights are on, epistemically ought to believe that proposition." "The paranoid person epistemically ought not believe that he is being spied upon when he has no evidence supporting this proposition." Using the language of obligation, then, we are defending the general view that one epistemically ought to have the doxastic attitudes that fit one's evidence. We think that being epistemically obligatory is equivalent to being epistemically justified.

There are in the literature two other sorts of view about epistemic obligations. What is epistemically obligatory, according to these other views, does not always fit with one's evidence. Thus, each of these views of epistemic obligation, when combined with our further thesis that being epistemically obligatory is equivalent to being epistemically justified, yields results incompatible with evidentialism. We shall consider how these proposals affect EJ.

Justification and the Obligation to Believe Truths

Roderick Chisholm holds that one has an "intellectual requirement" to try one's best to bring it about that, of the proposition one considers, one believes all and only the truths.[13] This theory of what our epistemic obligations are, in conjunction with our view that the justified attitudes are the one we have an epistemic obligation to hold, implies the following principle:

> CJ Doxastic attitude D toward proposition p is justified for person S at time t if and only if S considers p at t and S's having D toward p at t would result from S's trying his best to bring it about that S believes p at t iff p is true.

Evaluation of CJ is complicated by an ambiguity in "trying one's best." It might mean "trying in that way which will in fact have the best results." Since the goal is to believe all and only the truths one considers, the best results would be obtained by believing each truth one considers and not believing any falsehood one considers. On this interpretation,

CJ implies that believing each truth and not believing any falsehood one considers is justified whenever this outcome would result from something one could try to do.

On this interpretation CJ is plainly false. We are not justified in believing every proposition we consider that happens to be true and which we could believe by trying for the truth. It is possible to believe some unsubstantiated proposition in a reckless endeavor to believe a truth, and happen to be right. This would not be an epistemically justified belief.[14]

It might be contended that trying one's best to believe truths and not falsehoods really amounts to trying to believe in accordance with one's evidence. This is close to our view. We would agree that gaining the doxastic attitudes that fit one's evidence is the epistemically best way to use one's evidence in trying to believe all and only the truths one considers. This interpretation of CJ makes it nearly equivalent to EJ. There are two relevant differences. First, CJ implies that one can have justified attitudes only toward propositions one actually considers. EJ does not have this implication. CJ is also unlike EJ in implying that an attitude is justified if it would result from *trying* to form the attitude that fits one's evidence. The attitude that is justified according to EJ is the one that as a matter of fact does fit one's evidence. This seems more plausible. What would happen if one tried to have a fitting attitude seems irrelevant—one might try but fail to form the fitting attitude.

We conclude that the doxastic attitudes that would result from carrying out the intellectual requirement that Chisholm identifies are not the epistemically justified attitudes.

Justification and Epistemically Responsible Action

Another view about epistemic obligations, proposed by Hilary Kornblith, is that we are obligated to seek the truth and gather evidence in a responsible way. Kornblith also maintains that the justification of a belief depends on how responsibly one carried out the inquiry that led to the belief.[15] We shall now examine how the considerations leading to this view affect EJ.

Kornblith describes a case of what he regards as "epistemically culpable ignorance." It is an example in which a man's belief seems to fit his evidence, and

thus it seems to be justified because it results from epistemically irresponsible behavior. His example concerns a headstrong young physicist who is unable to tolerate criticism. After presenting a paper to his colleagues, the physicist, obsessed with his own success, fails even to hear the objection, which consequently has no impact on his beliefs. Kornblith says that after this, the physicist's belief in his own theory is unjustified. He suggests that evidentialist theories cannot account for this fact.

Crucial details of this example are left unspecified, but in no case does it provide a refutation of evidentialism. If the young physicist is aware of the fact that his senior colleague is making an objection, then this fact is evidence he has against his theory, although from just this much detail it is unclear how decisive that evidence would be. So, believing his theory may no longer be justified for him according to a purely evidentialist view. On the other hand, perhaps he remains entirely ignorant of the fact that a senior colleague is objecting to his theory. He might be "lost in thought"—for instance, suppose that he is privately engrossed in proud admiration of the paper he has just given. He does not even understand that an objection is being given by someone in the audience. If this happens, and his evidence supporting his theory is just as it was prior to his presentation of the paper, then believing the theory does remain justified for him (assuming that it was justified previously). There is no reason to doubt EJ in the light of this example. It may be that the young physicist is an unpleasant fellow, and that he lacks intellectual integrity. These evaluations concern the character of the physicist. They are supported by the fact that in this case he is not engaged in an impartial quest for the truth. But the physicist's character is not the topic of EJ. The topic is the epistemic justification of attitudes.

Responsible evidence-gathering obviously has some epistemic significance. One serious epistemological question is that of how to engage in a thoroughgoing rational pursuit of the truth. Such a pursuit may require gathering evidence in responsible ways. It may also be necessary to be open to new ideas, to think about a variety of important issues, and to consider a variety of opinions about such issues. Perhaps it requires, as Lawrence Bonjour suggests, that one "reflect critically upon one's beliefs."[16] But everyone has some justified beliefs, even though virtually no one is fully engaged in a rational pursuit of the truth. EJ has no implication about the actions one must take in a rational pursuit of the truth. It is about the epistemic evaluation of attitudes in any given situation, including whatever evidence one does have, however one came to possess that evidence.

Examples like that of the headstrong physicist show no defect in the evidentialist view. Justified beliefs can result from epistemically irresponsible actions.

Other Sorts of Obligations

Having acknowledged at the beginning of this section that justified attitudes are in a sense obligatory, we wish to forestall confusions involving other notions of obligations. It is not the case that there is always a *moral* obligation to believe in accordance with one's evidence. Having a fitting attitude can bring about disastrous personal or social consequences. Vicious beliefs that lead to vicious acts can be epistemically justified. These facts rule out any moral obligation to have the epistemically justified attitude.[17]

It is also false that there is always a *prudential* obligation to have each epistemically justified attitude. John Heil discusses the following example.[18] Sally has fairly good evidence that her husband Burt has been seeing another woman. Their marriage is in a precarious condition. It would be best for Sally if their marriage were preserved. Sally foresees that, were she to believe that Burt has been seeing another woman, her resulting behavior would lead to their divorce. Given these assumptions, EJ counts as justified at least some measure of belief by Sally in the proposition that Burt has been seeing another woman. But Sally would be better off if she did not have this belief, in light of the stipulated fact that she would be best served by continued marriage to Burt. Heil raises the question of what Sally's prudential duty is in this case. Sally's *epistemic* obligation is to believe that her husband is unfaithful. But that gives no reason to deny what seems obvious here. Sally prudentially ought to refrain from believing her husband to be unfaithful. It can be prudent not to have a doxastic attitude that is correctly said by EJ to be justified, just as it can be moral not to have such an attitude.

More generally, the causal consequences of having an unjustified attitude can be more beneficial in *any* sort of way than the consequences of having its justified alternative. We have seen that it can be morally and prudentially best not to have attitudes that are intuitively justified, and justified according to EJ. Failing to have these attitudes can also have the best results for the sake of *epistemic* goals such as the acquisition of knowledge. Roderick Firth points out that a scientist's believing against his evidence that he will recover from an illness may help to effect a recovery and so contribute to the growth of knowledge by enabling the scientist to continue his research.[19] William James's case for exercising "the will to believe" suggests that some evidence concerning the existence of God is available only after one believes in God in the absence of justifying evidence. EJ does not counsel against adopting such beliefs for the sake of these epistemic ends. EJ implies that the beliefs would be unjustified when adopted. This is not to say that having the beliefs would do no epistemic good. EJ allows that they are epistemically overall best. Thus, it is a mistake to think that what is epistemically obligatory, i.e., epistemically justified, is also morally or prudentially obligatory, or that it has the overall best epistemic consequences.

IV

Another argument that is intended to refute the evidentialist approach to justification concerns the ways in which a person can come to have an attitude that fits his evidence. Both Kornblith and Goldman propose examples designed to show that merely *having* good evidence for a proposition is not sufficient to make believing that proposition justified.[20] We shall work with Kornblith's formulation of the argument, since it is more detailed. Suppose Alfred is justified in believing p and justified in believing if p then q. Alfred also believes q. EJ seems to imply that believing q is justified for Alfred, since that belief does seem to fit this evidence. Kornblith argues that Alfred's belief in q may still not be justified. It is not justified, according to Kornblith, if Alfred has a strong distrust of this form of inference, *modus ponens*, and believes q because he likes the sound of the sentence expressing it rather than on the basis of the formal argument. Similarly, Goldman says that a person's belief in q is not justified unless the belief is *caused* in some appropriate way under such circumstances.

Whether EJ implies that Alfred's belief in q is justified depends in part on an unspecified detail—Alfred's evidence concerning *modus ponens*. It is possible that Alfred has evidence against *modus ponens*. Perhaps Alfred has been told by an apparently trustworthy source that a great logician has discovered a subtle hidden flaw in *modus ponens*. In the unlikely event that Alfred has such evidence, EJ implies that believing q is not justified for him. If rather, as we shall assume, his overall evidence supports *modus ponens* and q, then EJ does imply that believing q is justified for him.

When Alfred has strong evidence for q, his believing q is epistemically justified. This is the sense of "justified" that EJ is about. However, if Alfred's basis for believing q is not evidence for q, but rather the sound of the sentence expressing q, then it seems equally clear that the there is some sense in which this state of believing is epistemically "defective"—he did not arrive at the belief in the right way. The term "well-founded" is sometimes used to characterize an attitude that is both well-supported and properly arrived at. As we see it, well-foundedness is a second evidentialist notion used to evaluate doxastic attitudes. It is an evidentialist notion because its application depends on two matters of evidence—the evidence one *has*, and the evidence one *uses* in forming the attitude. More precisely:

WF S's doxastic attitude D at t toward proposition p is well-founded if

1. having D toward p is justified for S at t; and
2. S has D toward p on the basis of some *body* of evidence e, such that
   a. S has e as evidence at t;
   b. having D toward p fits e; and
   c. there is no more inclusive body of evidence e' had by S at t such that having D toward p does not fit e'.[21]

Cases in which a person has justifying evidence but does not use it do not refute evidentialism. The evidentialist can appeal to this notion of well-foundedness. Kornblith and Goldman's intuitions about such cases can be accommodated. A person in Alfred's position *is* in an epistemically defective state—his belief in q is not well-founded. Having said this, it is reasonable

also to affirm the other evidentialist judgment that believing q is the justified attitude for Alfred.[22]

V

Roughly speaking, reliabilism is the theory of justification asserting that epistemically justified beliefs are the ones that result from belief-forming processes that reliably lead to true beliefs.[23] In this section we consider whether reliabilism casts doubt on evidentialism.

Although reliabilists generally formulate their view as an account of epistemic justification, it is clear that in its simplest form it is better regarded as an account of well-foundedness. In order for a proposition to be favorably evaluated by the simple sort or reliabilism that we have just sketched, the proposition must be believed. Well-founded belief also requires belief. In contrast, believing can be the justified attitude to take without its being the attitude that is actually taken. And just as is the case with well-founded belief, a belief favorably evaluated by reliabilism must be "grounded" in the proper way. Reliabilism *appears* to differ with WF over the conditions under which a belief is properly grounded. According to WF, this occurs when the belief is based on fitting evidence. According to reliabilism, a belief is properly grounded if it results from a belief-forming process that reliably leads to true beliefs. These certainly are *conceptually* different accounts of the grounds of well-founded beliefs.

In spite of this conceptual difference, reliabilism and WF may be the same in their evaluations of all possible cases. This question of equivalence depends on the resolution of two unclarities in reliabilism. One pertains to the notion of a belief-forming process and the other to the notion of reliability.

An unclarity about belief-forming process arises because every belief results from a sequence of particular events which is an instance of many types of causal processes. Suppose that one evening Jones looks out of his window and sees a bright, shining, disk-shaped object. The object is in fact a glowing toy disk, and Jones clearly remembers having given one of these to his daughter. But Jones is attracted to the idea that extraterrestrials are visiting the earth. He manages to believe that he is seeing a saucer-shaped alien spacecraft flying by his window. Is the process that caused his belief reliable? Since the sequence of events leading to his belief is an instance of many types of process, the answer depends upon which of these many types is the relevant one. The sequence falls into highly general categories, such as perceptually-based belief formation and visually-based belief formation. It seems that if these are the relevant categories, then his belief is indeed reliably formed, since these are plausibly thought to be generally reliable sorts of belief forming processes. The sequence of events leading to Jones's belief also falls into many relatively specific categories such as night-vision-of-a-nearby-object object and vision-in-Jones's-precise-environmental-circumstances. These are not clearly reliable types. The sequence is also an instance of this contrived kind: process-leading-from-obviously-flimsy-evidence-to-the-belief-that-one-sees-a-flying-saucer. This, presumably, is an unreliable kind of process. Finally, there is the maximally specific process that occurs only when physiological events occur that are in every way exactly like those that led to Jones's belief that he saw a flying saucer. In all likelihood this kind of process occurred only once. Processes of these various types are of differing degrees of reliability, no matter how reliability is determined. The implications of reliabilism in this example are rendered definite only when the reliabilists specify the kind of process whose reliability is relevant. Reliabilists have given insufficient attention to this matter, and those that have specified relevant kinds have not done so in a way that gives their theory an intuitively acceptable extension.[24]

The second unclarity in reliabilism concerns the notion of reliability itself. Reliability is fundamentally a property of *kinds* of belief-forming processes, not of sequences of particular events. But we can say that a sequence of events leading to a belief is reliable provided its relevant type is reliable. The problem just raised concerns the specification of relevant types. The current problem is that of specifying the conditions under which a kind of process is *reliable*. Among possible accounts is one according to which a kind of process is reliable provided that most instances of the kind until now have led to true beliefs. Alternative accounts measure the reliability of a kind of process by the frequency with which instances of it produce true beliefs in the future as well as the past, or by the frequency with which its instances produce true beliefs in possible worlds that

are similar to the world of evaluation in some designated respect, or by the frequency with which its instances produce true beliefs in all possible worlds.[25]

Because there are such drastically different ways of filling in the details of reliabilism, the application of the theory is far from clear. The possible versions of reliabilism might even include one that is equivalent to WF. It might be held that all beliefs are formed by one of two relevant kinds of belief-forming process. One kind has as instances all and only those sequences of events leading to a belief that is based on fitting evidence; the other is a kind of process that has as instances all and only those sequences leading to a belief that is not based on fitting evidence. If a notion of reliability can be found on which the former sort of process is reliable and the latter is not, the resulting version of reliabilism would be very nearly equivalent to WF.[26] We do not claim that reliabilists would favor this version of reliabilism. Rather, our point is that the existence of this version of reliabilism shows that reliabilism is so open to further specification that it need not even be a rival to WF.[27]

Evaluation of reliabilism is further complicated by the fact that reliabilists seem to differ about whether they *want* their theory to make the same evaluations of examples that WF makes. The credibility of reliabilism and its relevance to WF depend in part on the concept of reliabilists are really attempting to analyze. An example first described by BonJour helps to bring out two alternatives.[28] BonJour's example is of a man who is clairvoyant. As a result of his clairvoyance, he comes to believe that the President of the U.S. is in New York City. The man has no evidence showing that he is clairvoyant and no other evidence supporting his belief about the president. BonJour claims that the example is a counterexample to reliabilism, since the clairvoyant's belief is not justified (we would add: and therefore ill-founded), although the process that caused it is reliable—the person really is clairvoyant.

The general sort of response to this example that seems to be most commonly adopted by reliabilists is in effect to agree that such beliefs are not well-founded. They interpret or revise reliabilism with the aim of avoiding the counterexample.[29] An alternative response is to argue that the reliability of clairvoyance shows that the belief *is* well-founded, and thus that the example does not refute reliabilism.[30]

We are tempted to respond to the second alternative—beliefs such as that of the clairvoyant in BonJour's example really are well-founded—that this is so clear an instance of an ill-founded belief that anyone who denies this must have in mind a different concept from the one we are discussing. The clairvoyant has no reason for holding his belief about the President. The fact that the belief was caused by a process of a reliable kind—clairvoyance—is a significant fact about it. Such a belief may merit some favorable term of epistemic appraisal. Perhaps it is "objectively probable." But the belief is not well-founded.

There are, however, two lines of reasoning that could lead philosophers to think that we must reconcile ourselves to the clairvoyant's belief turning out to be well-founded. According to one of these arguments, examples such as that of Alfred (discussed in section 4 above) show that the evidentialist account of epistemic merit is unsatisfactory and that epistemic merit must be understood in terms of the reliability of belief-forming processes.[31] Since the clairvoyant's belief is reliably formed, our initial inclination to regard it as ill-founded must be mistaken.

This argument is unsound. The most that the example about Alfred shows is that there is a concept of favorable epistemic appraisal other than justification, and that this other concept involves the notion of the *basis* of a belief. We believe that WF satisfactorily captures this other concept. There is no need to move to a reliabilist account, according to which some sort of causal reliability is sufficient for epistemic justification. The Alfred example does not establish that some version of reliabilism is correct.

The second argument for the conclusion that the clairvoyant's belief is well-founded makes use of the strong similarity between clairvoyance in BonJour's example and normal perception. We claim that BonJour's clairvoyant is not justified in his belief about the President because that belief does not fit his evidence. Simply having a spontaneous uninferred belief about the whereabouts of the President does not provide evidence for its truth. But, it might be asked, what better evidence is there for any ordinary belief, say, that one sees a book? If there is no relevant epistemological difference between ordinary

perceptual beliefs and the clairvoyant's belief, then they should be evaluated alike. The argument continues with the point that reliabilism provides an explanation of the crucial similarity between ordinary perceptual beliefs and the clairvoyant's belief. The reliabilist can point out that both perception and clairvoyance *work*, in the sense that both are reliable (given the stipulation of the example that the person is genuinely clairvoyant). So on a reliabilist account, beliefs caused by each process are well-founded. The fact that reliabilism satisfactorily explains this is to theory's credit. On the other hand, in advocating evidentialism we have claimed that perceptual beliefs are typically well-founded and that the clairvoyant's belief is not. But there appears to be no relevant evidential difference between these beliefs. Thus, if the evidentialist view of the matter cannot be defended, then reliabilism is the superior theory and we should accept its consequence—the clairvoyant's belief is well-founded.

One problem with this argument is that reliabilism has no satisfactory explanation of *anything* until the unclarities discussed above are removed in an acceptable way: What shows that perception and clairvoyance are relevant types of processes, or that they are reliable? In any event, there is an adequate evidentialist explanation of the difference between ordinary perceptual beliefs and the clairvoyant's belief. On one interpretation of clairvoyance, it is a process whereby one is caused by objects hidden from ordinary view to have beliefs about those objects, without any conscious state having a role in the causal process. The clairvoyant does not have the conscious experience of, say, seeming to see the President in some characteristic New York City setting, and on that basis form the belief that the President is in New York. In this respect, the current vision of clairvoyance is unlike ordinary perception, which does include conscious perceptual states. Because of this difference, ordinary perceptual beliefs are based on evidence—the evidence of the perceptual states—whereas the clairvoyant beliefs are not based on evidence. WF requires that well-founded beliefs be based on fitting evidence. Typical clairvoyant beliefs, on the current interpretation, are not based on any evidence at all. So the clairvoyant beliefs do not satisfy WF.

Suppose instead that clairvoyance does include visual experiences, though of remote objects that cannot stimulate the visual system in any normal way. Even if there are such visual experiences that could serve as a basis for a clairvoyant's beliefs, still there is a relevant epistemological difference between beliefs based on normal perceptual experience and the clairvoyant's belief in BonJour's example. We have collateral evidence to the effect that when we have perceptual experience of certain kinds, external conditions of the corresponding kinds normally obtain. For example, we have evidence supporting the proposition that when we have the usual sort of evidence of seeming to see a book, we usually do in fact see a book. This includes evidence from the coherence of these beliefs with beliefs arising from other perceptual sources, and it also includes testimonial evidence. This latter point is easily overlooked. One reason that the belief that one sees a book fits even a child's evidence, when it seems to her that she sees a book, is that children are taught, when they have the normal sort of visual experiences, that they are seeing a physical object of the relevant kind. This testimony, typically from people whom the child has reason to trust, provides evidence for the child. And of course testimony from others during adult life also gives evidence for the veridicality of normal visual experience. On the other hand, as BonJour describes his example, the clairvoyant has no confirmation at all of his clairvoyant beliefs. Indeed, he has evidence against these beliefs, since the clairvoyant perceptual experiences do not cohere with his other experiences. We conclude, therefore, that evidentialists can satisfactorily explain why ordinary perceptual beliefs are typically well-founded and unconfirmed clairvoyant beliefs, even if reliably caused, are not. There is no good reason to abandon our initial intuition that the beliefs such as those of the clairvoyant in BonJour's example are not well-founded.

Again, reliabilists could respond to BonJour's example either by claiming that the clairvoyant's belief is in fact well-founded or by arguing that reliabilism does not imply that it is well-founded. We turn now to the second of these alternatives, the one most commonly adopted by reliabilists. This view can be defended either by arguing that reliabilism can be reformulated so that it lacks this implication, or by arguing that as currently formulated it lacks this implication. We pointed out above that as a general approach reliabilism is sufficiently indefinite to allow interpretations under which it does lack the implication in question. The only otherwise satisfactory way to achieve this result that we know of requires the introduction of evidentialist concepts. The technique is to specify the relevant types of belief-forming processes in evidentialist terms. It is possible to hold that the relevant types of belief-forming process are believing something on the basis of fitting evidence and believing not as a result of fitting evidence. This sort of "reliabilism" is a roundabout approximation of the straightforward evidentialist thesis, WF. We see no reason to couch the approximated evidentialist theory in reliabilist terms. Moreover, the reliabilist approximation is not exactly equivalent to WF, and where it differs it appears to go wrong. The difference is this: it seems possible for the process of believing on the basis of fitting evidence to be unreliable. Finding a suitable sort of reliability makes all the difference here. In various possible worlds where our evidence is mostly misleading, the frequency with which fitting evidence causes true belief is low. Thus, this type of belief-forming process is not "reliable" in such worlds in any straightforward way that depends on actual frequencies of true beliefs. Perhaps a notion of reliability that avoids this result can be found. We know of no such notion which does not create trouble elsewhere for the theory. So the reliabilist view under consideration has the consequences that in such worlds beliefs based on fitting evidence are not well-founded. This is counterintuitive.[32]

In this section we have compared reliabilism and evidentialism. The indefiniteness of reliabilism makes it difficult to determine what implications the theory has. It is not entirely clear what implications reliabilists want their theory to have. If reliabilists want their theory to have approximately the same extension as WF, we see no better way to accomplish this than one which makes the theory an unnecessarily complex and relatively implausible approximation to evidentialism. If, on the other hand, reliabilists want their theory to have an extension that is substantially different from that of WF, and yet some familiar notion of "a reliable kind of process" is to be decisive for their notion of well-foundedness, then it becomes clear that the concept they are discussing is not one evidentialists seek to characterize. This follows from the fact that on this alternative they count as a well-founded attitudes that plainly fail to be based on justifying reasons. That is the concept that WF is about. In neither case, then, does reliabilism pose a threat to evidentialism.

VI

Summary and Conclusion

We have defended evidentialism. Some opposition to evidentialism rests on the view that a doxastic attitude can be justified for a person only if forming the attitude is an action under person's voluntary control. EJ is incompatible with the conjunction of this sort of doxastic voluntarism and the plain fact that some doxastic states that fit a person's evidence are out of that person's control. We have argued that no good reason has been given for thinking that an attitude is epistemically justified only if having it is under voluntary control.

A second thesis contrary to EJ is that a doxastic attitude can be justified only if having that attitude is within the normal doxastic limits of humans. We have held that the attitudes that are epistemically justified according to EJ are within these limits, and that even if they were not, that fact would not refute EJ.

Some philosophers have contended that believing a proposition, *p*, is justified for S only when S has gone about gathering evidence about *p* in a responsible way, or has come to believe *p* as a result of seeking a meritorious epistemic goal such as the discovery truth. This thesis conflicts with EJ, since believing *p* may fit one's evidence no matter how irresponsible one may have been in seeking evidence about *p* and no matter what were the goals that led to the belief. We agree that there is some epistemic merit is responsibly gathering evidence and in seeking the truth. But we see no reason to think that the epistemic justification of doxastic attitudes turns on such matters.

Another argument against EJ is that merely having evidence is not sufficient to justify belief, since the believer might not make proper use of the evidence in forming the belief. The sort of example that inspires this reasoning led us to identify a second evidentialist notion, well-foundedness. The reasoning does not, however, provide any good reason to think that EJ is false. Nor did we find reason to abandon evidentialism in favor of reliabilism. Evidentialism remains the most plausible view of epistemic justification.

Notes

1. EJ is compatible with the existence of varying strengths of belief and disbelief. If there is such variation, then the greater the preponderance of evidence, the stronger the doxastic attitude that fits the evidence.
2. There are difficult questions about the concept of fit, as well as about what it is for someone to *have* something as evidence, and of what kind of thing constitutes evidence. As a result, there are some cases in which it is difficult to apply EJ. For example, it is unclear whether a person has as evidence propositions he is not currently thinking of, but could readily recall. As to what constitutes evidence, it seems clear that this includes actively recalled memories and sensory states such as feeling very warm and having the visual experience of seeing blue. These problems of detail do not prevent the application of EJ from being clear enough to do the work that we intend here—a defense of the general evidentialist position.
3. John Heil, "Doxastic Agency," *Philosophical Studies* 43 (1983): 335–64. The quotation is from p. 355.
4. Hilary Kornblith, "The Psychological Turn," *Australasian Journal of Philosophy* 60 (1982): 238–53. The quotation is from p. 252.
5. Ibid., p. 253.
6. Heil, "Doxastic Agency," p. 363.
7. Kornblith may be guilty of this confusion. He writes, "If person has an unjustified belief, that person is epistemically culpable." "The Psychological Turn," p. 243.
8. Nothing we say here should be taken to imply that any doxastic states are in fact voluntarily entered.
9. Alvin Goldman, "Epistemics: The Regulative Theory of Cognition," *The Journal of Philosophy* 75 (1978): 509–23., esp. pp. 510 and 514.
10. Hilary Kornblith, "Justified Belief and Epistemically Responsible Action," *The Philosophical Review* 92 (1983): 33–48. The quotation is from p. 34.
11. Paul Thagard, "From the Descriptive to the Normative in Psychology and Logic," *The Philosophical of Science* 49 (1982): 24–42. The quotation is from p. 34.
12. Another version of this argument is that EJ is false because it classifies as justified for a person attitudes that are beyond *that person's* limits. This version is subject to similar criticism.

13. Roderick Chisholm, *Theory of Knowledge*, 2nd ed. (Englewood Cliffs, NJ: Prentice-Hall, 1977), especially pp. 12–15.

14. Roderick Firth makes a similar point against a similar view in "Are Epistemic Concepts Reducible to Ethical Concepts?" in *Values and Morals*, A.I. Goldman and J. Kim, eds. (Dordrecht, Netherlands: D. Riedel Publishing Co., 1978), pp. 215–19.

15. Kornblith defends his view in "Justified Belief and Epistemically Responsible Action," Some passages suggest that he intends to introduce a new notion of justification, one to be understood in terms of epistemically responsible action. But some passages, especially in section 2, suggest that the traditional analysis of justification is being found to be objectionable and inferior to the one he proposes.

16. BonJour, op. cit., p. 63.

17. This is contrary to the view of Richard Gale, defended in "William James and the Ethics of Belief," *American Philosophical Quarterly* 17 (1980): 1–14, and of W. K. Clifford, who said, "It is wrong always, everywhere, and for everyone, to believe anything upon insufficient evidence," quoted by William James in in "The Will to Believe," reprinted in *Reason and Responsibility*, J. Feinberg, ed. (Belmont, Calif.: Wadsworth Publishing Co., 1981), p. 100.

18. See John Heil, "Believing What One Ought," pp. 752ff.

19. See "Epistemic Merit, Intrinsic and Instrumental," *Proceedings and Addresses of the American Philosophical Association* 55 (1981): 5–6.

20. See Kornblith's "Beyond Foundationalism and the Coherence Theory," *The Journal of Philosophy* 77 (1980): 597–612, esp. pp. 601f., and Goldman's "What is Justified Belief?" in *Justification and Knowledge*, George S. Pappas, ed. (Dordrecht, Netherlands: D. Reidel Publishing Co., 1979), pp. 1–24.

21. Clause (ii) of WF is intended to accommodate the fact that a well-founded attitude need not be based upon the whole of a person's evidence, but she must not ignore any evidence she has that defeats the justifying power of the evidence she does base her attitude on. It might be that this defeating evidence is itself defeated by a still wider body of her evidence. In such a case, the person's attitude is well-founded only if she takes that wider body into account.

    WF uses our last main primitive concept—that of *basing* an attitude on a body of evidence. This notion is reasonably clear, though an analysis would be useful. See note 22 below for one difficult question about what is entailed.

22. Goldman uses this sort of example only to show that there is a causal element in the concept of justification. We acknowledge that there is an epistemic concept—well-foundedness—that appeals to the notion of basing an attitude on evidence, and this may be a causal notion. What seems to confer epistemic merit on basing one's belief on the evidence is that in doing

so one *appreciates* the evidence. It is unclear whether one can appreciate the evidence without being caused to have the belief by the evidence. But in any event we see no such causal requirement in the case of justification.

23. The clearest and most influential discussion of reliabilism is in Goldman's "What is Justified Belief?" One of the first statements of a broadly reliabilist theory appears in David Armstrong's *Belief, Truth and Knowledge* (London: Cambridge University Press, 1973). For extensive bibliographies on reliabilism, see Frederick Schmitt's "Reliability, Objectivity, and the Background of Justification," *Australasian Journal of Philosophy* 62 (1984): 1015; and Richard Feldman's "Reliability and Justification," *The Monist* 68 (April 1985): 159–74.

24. For discussion of the problem of determining relevant kinds of belief-forming processes, see Goldman, "What Is Justified Belief?"; Schmitt, "Reliability, Objectivity, and the Background of Justification"; Feldman, "Reliability and Justification"; and Feldman, "Schmitt on Reliability, Objectivity, and Justification," *Australasian Journal of Philosophy* 63 (1985): 354–60.

25. In "Reliability and Justified Belief," *Canadian Journal of Philosophy* 14 (1984): 103–15, John Pollock argues that there is no account of reliability suitable for reliabilists.

26. This version of reliabilism will not be exactly equivalent to WF because it ignores the factors introduced by clause (ii) of WF.

27. It is also possible that versions of reliabilism making use only of natural psychological kinds of belief-forming processes are equivalent to WF. Goldman seeks to avoid evaluative epistemic concepts in his theory of epistemic justification, so he would not find an account of justification satisfaction unless it appealed only to such natural kinds. See "What is Justified Belief?" p.6.

28. See Lawrence BonJour, "Externalist Theories of Empirical Justification," p. 62.

29. See Goldman, "What is Justified Belief?" pp. 18–20; Kornblith, "Beyond Foundationalism and the Coherence Theory," pp. 609–11; and Schmitt, "Reliability, Objectivity, and the Background of Justification."

30. We know of no one who has explicitly taken this approach. It seems to fit most closely with the view defended by David Armstrong in *Belief, Truth and Knowledge*.

31. We know of no one who explicitly defends this inference. In "The Psychological Turn," pp. 241f., Kornblith argues that these examples show that justification depends upon "psychological connections" and "the workings of the appropriate belief-forming process." But he clearly denies there that reliabilism is directly implied.

32. Stewart Cohen has made this point in "Justification and Truth," *Philosophical Studies* 46 (1984): 279–95. Cohen makes the point in the course of developing a dilemma. He argues that reliabilism has the sort of flaw that we describe above when we appeal to worlds

where evidence is mostly misleading. Cohen also contends that reliabilism has the virtue of providing a clear explanation of how the epistemic notion of justification is connected with the notion of truth. A theory that renders this truth connection inexplicable is caught on the second horn of Cohen's dilemma.

Although Cohen does not take up evidentialism as we characterize it, the second horn of his dilemma affects EJ and WF. They do not explain how having an epistemically justified or well-founded belief is connected to the truth of that belief. Evidentialists can safely say this much about the truth connection: evidence that makes believing p justified is evidence on which it is *epistemically* probable that p is true. Although there is this connection between justification and truth, we acknowledge that there may be no analysis of epistemic probability that makes the connection to truth as close, or as clear, as might have been hoped.

Cohen argues that there must be a truth connection. This shows no flaw in EJ or WF, unless they are incompatible with the existence of such a connection. Cohen does not argue for this incompatibility and we know of no reason to believe that it exists. So at most Cohen's dilemma shows that evidentialists have work left to do.

◆ CONTEXTUALISM ◆

21. CONTEXTUALISM

Stewart Cohen

The Basic Outline

Contextualism is the view that ascriptions of knowledge are context sensitive. According to this view, the truth value of sentences containing the word "know" and its cognates will depend on contextually determined standards. Because of this, such a sentence can have different truth-values in different contexts. To understand exactly what this means, we need to distinguish between the ascriber or speaker who makes a knowledge ascription, and the subject of the ascription to whom the speaker is ascribing knowledge. So consider a sentence "Smith knows it is raining", said by a particular speaker Jones. The truth value of this knowledge ascription will depend on factors pertaining to the Smith's situation—whether Smith has sufficient evidence, whether Smith's cognitive processes are reliable in the circumstance, whether in fact it is raining, etc. But this uncontroversial fact is not what is meant by the contextualist claim that the truth-value of a knowledge ascription depends on the context. What Contextualism claims is that the truth value of a knowledge ascription depends on the situation of the ascriber or speaker, Jones. In particular, the truth value of a knowledge ascription can vary depending on things like Jones' purposes, intentions, expectations, presuppositions, etc. This view has the consequence that, given a fixed subject S, and a fixed proposition p, two speakers may at the same time say "S knows p", and only one of them thereby say something true. For the same reason, one speaker may say "S knows p", and another say "S does not know p", and both speakers thereby say something true.

Why have some philosophers thought that ascriptions of knowledge are context sensitive in the sense just indicated? The simple answer is that various epistemological phenomena seem best describable on the assumption that Contextualism is true. Moreover, as certain philosophers, have argued, Contextualism allows us to solve, or at least make some headway against, some stubborn epistemological problems.[1]

Contextualism and Fallibilism

Fallibilism is accepted by nearly all epistemologists. Fallibilism denies what we can call "the entailment principle".

S knows P on the basis of (reason or evidence) R only if R entails P.

As we know the entailment principle leads to a skeptical result. The motivation for fallibilism stems from the widely held view that what we seek in constructing a theory of knowledge is an account that squares with our strong intuition that we know many things. It is not that skepticism is to be avoided at all costs. But while the entailent principle may look attractive in the abstract, it does not command the kind of assent sufficient to withstand the overwhelming case against it provided by our intuitions concerning what we know. Most philosophers find the entailment principle to be implausible once they see its skeptical consequences.

We can give a more precise statement of Fallibilism. First, let an alternative to P be any proposition incompatible with P. Then we can define Fallibilism:

S can know P on the basis of R even if there is some alternative to P, compatible with R.

So Fallibism allows that we can know on the basis of non-entailing reasons. But how good do the reasons have to be? This turns out to be a difficult question to answer. Let us consider a case[2]:

Mary and John are at the L.A. airport contemplating taking a certain flight to New York. They want to know whether the flight has a layover in Chicago. They overhear someone ask a passenger Smith if he knows whether the flight stops in Chicago. Smith looks at the flight itinerary he got from the travel agent and responds," Yes I know, it does stop in Chicago." It turns out that Mary and John have a very important business contact they have to make at the Chicago airport. Mary says, "How reliable is that itinerary? It could contain a misprint. They could have changed the schedule at the last minute." Mary and John agree that Smith doesn't really *know* that the plane will stop in Chicago on the basis of the itinerary. They decide to check with the airline agent.

What should we say about this case? Smith claims to know that the flight stops in Chicago Mary and John

deny that Smith knows this. In some sense, Mary and John are using a stricter standard than Smith for when one is in a position to know. Whose standard is the correct one? We can consider several answers:

1) Mary and John's stricter standard is too strong, i.e., Smith's standard is correct and so Smith knows the flight stops in Chicago (on the basis of consulting the itinerary).

Is this a good answer? If we say that contrary to what both Mary and John presuppose, the weaker standard is correct, we would have to say that their use of the word "know" is incorrect. But then it is hard to see how Mary and John should describe their situation. Certainly they are not being unreasonable in not relying on the itinerary. After all, it is very important that they make that meeting in Chicago. Yet if it is true that Smith knows the flight stops in Chicago, what should they have said? "Okay, Smith knows that the flight stops in Chicago, but that's not good enough, we need to check it out." That strikes me as a very strange way to talk. Moreover if the itinerary is good enough for Smith to know given the correct standard, then it is good enough for John and Mary to know. Thus John and Mary should have said, "Okay, *we* know the plane stops in Chicago, but that's not good enough. We need to check it out." Again, that strikes me as a very strange way to talk.

Let's consider then an alternative answer:

2) John and Mary are right and so Smith's standard is too weak. (Smith does not know, but John and Mary do know—after checking further with the agent.)

One natural response to this case is to think Mary and John are right and that Smith does not know. But notice that this contrasts with the standard we typically use for knowledge ascriptions. In many ordinary contexts, we readily attribute knowledge to someone on the basis of written information contained in things like flight itineraries. If we deny that Smith knows, then we have to deny that we know in many of the everyday cases in which we claim to know. We would have to say that a considerable amount of the time, we speak falsely in our everyday lives when we claim to know.

Moreover, there is a further difficulty with saying John and Mary's stronger standard is the correct one. We could describe a case where even Mary and John's standard does not seem strict enough: If someone's life were at stake, we might not even be willing to ascribe knowledge on the basis of the testimony of the airline agent. We might insist on checking with the pilot. So it does not look promising to say that Smith's standard is too weak.

This suggest a third option, viz., all of these standards are too weak. This option leads, of course, to skepticism. Presumably this is a result we want to avoid. We will return to this option when we talk about skepticism.

So far we have examined three different answers to the question of whose standard is correct: (1) Smith's is correct and so John and Mary's standard is too strong. (2) John and Mary's standard is correct and so Smith's standard is too weak. (3) Neither standard is correct—both are too weak. As we have seen none of these answers seems satisfactory. Here is where Contextualism enters the picture. According to the Contextualist, neither standard is simply correct or simply incorrect. Rather, which standard is correct depends on the context. The standards for knowledge ascriptions can vary across contexts so each claim (Smith's as well as Mary and John's) can be correct. When Smith says, "I know . . .", what he says is true given the weaker standard operating in that context. When Mary and John say "Smith does not know . . .", what they say is true given the stricter standard operating in their context. *And there is no context independent correct standard.* Not that John and Mary are somehow constrained to use that standard or that Smith is constrained to use his. Were any of them to have different purposes, intentions, etc., then a different standard could have been in effect.

Ways to Construe Context Sensitivity

We can think of the context sensitivity of knowledge ascriptions in this way: For each context of ascription, there is a standard for how strong a subject's epistemic position with respect to a proposition P must be in order for that subject to know P. There are various ways one might construe this notion of the strength of a subject's epistemic position. One could think of it as determined, at least in part, by the strength of one's reasons or justification for believing P. On this view, the context sensitivity of knowledge ascriptions derives from the context sensitivity of standards for justification.

Consider an analogy with flatness ascriptions. We can think of a surface as being flat to varying degrees and we can also think of a surface as being flat *simpliciter*. What is the standard for how flat a surface must be to count as flat *simpliciter*? In different contexts, there can be different standards. Typically, when the topic of conversation is, e.g., roads, there will be a much stricter standard in contexts where the speaker and hearers are Kansans than when the speaker and hearers are Coloradans. So a group of Kansans may truly say a road is not flat while a group of Coloradans truly say that the same road is flat. Each claim is true relative to the standard of the context in which it is made. In order to be flat *simpliciter*, a road has to be flatter in the Kansans context than in the Coloradans context.

Analogously, we can think of a belief as being justified to various degrees and we can think of a belief as being justified *simpliciter*. On many views, being justified *simpliciter* is a necessary condition for a belief to be an instance of knowledge. What is the standard for how justified a belief must be to count as justified *simpliciter*? For the contextualist view, in different contexts, there can be different standards. So in order to know that plane has to leave on time, one has to be more justified in John and Mary's context, than in Smith's context.[3]

But there are other ways of construing the context-sensitivity of knowledge ascriptions. Consider another analogy with flatness ascriptions. We could view flatness ascriptions as involving a kind of implicit quantification: X is flat iff X has no bumps. We could then view the context as restricting the domain of quantification. In the Coloradans context, small hills do not count as bumps whereas in the Kansans context, they do.

By analogy we can think of knowledge ascriptions as involving a kind of implicit quantification.

Suppose that S knows P iff S's evidence eliminates every alternative to P (Lewis, Unger). Then we can view the context as determining the domain of 'every', i.e., as determining which alternatives count in the context. So in Smith's context, the alternative that the itinerary is mistaken does not count whereas in John and Mary's it does.

Some epistemological theories do not analyze knowledge in terms of the strength of one's evidence or justification. Instead they employ some kind of so-called "externalist" criterion. One such criterion is the tracking condition[4].

> S knows P iff (S would not believe P, if P were false and S would believe P if P were true.)

The idea here is that S knows P just in case S's belief in P matches the fact as to whether P in near worlds. So in near worlds where P is true, S believes P, and in near worlds where P is false, S does not believe P.

But this raises the question of how near to the actual world a world must be in order to be relevant to whether S knows. According to a contextualist construal of this view, that will depend on context.[5] So in Smith's context, the world at which the itinerary is mistaken and Smith believes the plane stops in Chicago is too distant to undermine Smith's knowledge that the plane stops in Chicago. In John and Mary's context however, that very same world is close enough to undermine Smith's knowledge.

How do the standards for these predicates get set in a particular context of ascription? This is a very difficult matter which involves some complicated function of speaker intentions, listener expectations, presuppositions of the conversation, salience relations, etc., what David Lewis calls the conversational score. In the case of knowledge ascriptions, Contextualists generally agree that salience relations are particularly important. In particular, aspects of the context can make the chance of error salient. And when the chance of error is salient in a context, the standards tend to rise to the point that knowledge ascriptions are false. In the case of John and Mary, it was the importance of arriving on time that made the chance of error salient.

Skepticism

Proponents of Contextualism argue that the view can resolve certain skeptical paradoxes. We saw earlier that in order to avoid skepticism, we had to reject the entailment principle. Instead, the Fallibilist holds that one can know even when there are alternatives consistent with our evidence.

Unfortunately skepticism is not so easily dispatched. For there is another principle, weaker than the entailment principle, that is very difficult to reject. And this principle threatens to reinstate skepticism even for fallibilist theories. Rather than simply noting the existence of alternatives and then appealing to the entailment principle, the skeptical argument based on the weaker principle begins by arguing, quite plausibly, that whatever else we say about the significance of certain alternatives, we do not know they are false. We might think that we have some reason to believe that we are not deceived in the ways the skeptic suggests, but it is very hard to hold that we *know* we are not so deceived.

To use a famous example of Dretske's, suppose you are at the zoo looking at the Zebra exhibit.[6] Consider the possibility that what you see is not a zebra but rather a cleverly disguised mule. Though you may have some reason to deny you are looking at a cleverly disguised mule, it seems wrong to say you *know* you are not looking at a cleverly disguised mule. After all, that's just how it would look if it were a cleverly-disguised mule.

The skeptic then appeals to a principle with considerable intuitive appeal—a principle weaker than the entailment principle. This principle says that the set of known (by S) propositions is closed under known (by S) entailment:

> If S knows P and S knows that P entails Q, then S knows (or is in a position to know) Q.

Let P be some proposition I claim to know and let h be a skeptical alternative to P. Then from this closure principle, we can derive

> (1) If we know P, then we know not-h

Put this together with

(2) We do not know not-h

and it follows that

(3) We know P.

is false.

There are two kinds of fallibilist responses to this argument, those that deny (1) and those that deny (2). One way to deny (1) is to argue that our strong intuitions supporting (2) and (3) just show that (1), and therefore the closure principle, are false. This is one way to construe the relevant alternatives approach to knowledge. On this view, skeptical alternatives are simply not relevant to our everyday knowledge ascriptions, i.e., we can know mundane truths about the world without knowing that skeptical alternatives are false.[7]

The second fallibilist response to the skeptical argument agrees with the skeptic against the relevant alternatives theorist that the closure principle is true. But against the skeptic, they use the closure principle and the claim that we do know lots of things to reject the claim that we do not know skeptical alternatives are false. We can call this view "*modus ponens* fallibilism".[8]

It is not clear how to assess this situation. Are some of these views begging the question against the others? What we are confronting here is a paradox: (1), (2), and (3) constitute a set of inconsistent propositions each of which has considerable independent plausibility. Each view attempt to exploit intuitions favorable to it. The skeptic appeals to (1) and (2) to deny (3). The relevant alternatives theorist appeals to (2) and (3) to deny (1). And the *modus ponens* fallibilist appeals to (1) and (3) to deny (2). Because each member of set has independent plausibility, it looks arbitrary and therefore unsatisfying to appeal to any two against the third. Such a strategy does not provide what any successful resolution of a paradox should provide, viz., an explanation of how the paradox arises in the first place.

Presumably, none of us is a skeptic. In some sense skepticism is crazy. So what we want is a resolution of the paradox that preserves our belief that we know things. Any such resolution must explain

the undeniable appeal of skeptical arguments. For this is what gives rise to the paradox. Initially we claim to know many things, but under skeptical pressure we begin to worry. Often when we consider skeptical arguments, we find ourselves vacillating between thinking we know and worrying we don't. Any successful response to paradox must explain how we end up in this situation. After all, the paradox arises within our own thinking about knowledge. This is what makes the skeptical paradox interesting—the premises of skeptical argument are premises we are inclined to accept. In effect we have to explain, or explain away, the skeptic within ourselves. And that is what neither of these two fallibilist responses does.

Contextualists claim that by supporting that the truth-value of a knowledge ascription is relative to contextually determined standards, we can derive a satisfactory resolution of the skeptical paradox. That is, we can preserve the truth of our everyday knowledge attributions while explaining the appeal of skeptical arguments.

As we saw in the case of Mary and John at the L.A. airport, how good one's reasons have to be in order for one to know, depends on the context of ascription. So the truth-value of the knowledge ascription will depend on whether the subject of the ascription has strong enough reasons relative to the standard of the context. Thus the truth-value of a knowledge ascription will vary as we vary either the strength of the subject's reasons or as we vary the context that determines the standard. In everyday contexts, the standard is such that our mundane knowledge ascriptions can be true. This explains our confidence in the truth of our everyday knowledge ascriptions. When confronted with skeptical arguments however, the chance of error becomes salient and we can be lead to shift our standards. Skeptical arguments are forceful precisely because they can have this effect on us. In this new context, the standards are stricter and ascriptions true in everyday contexts are false. But we are not constrained to use skeptical standards. Upon further reflection we may shift the standard again, thereby treating skeptical alternatives as too remote to threaten our knowledge claims. Again sometimes we vacillate.

By supposing that knowledge ascriptions are context-sensitive in this way, we can do justice both to our strong inclination to say we know and to the undeniable appeal of skeptical arguments.

Closure

Let's return to the skeptical paradox. On the contextualist approach, which proposition of the paradox gets denied? Recall that the relevant alternatives theory denies (1) and so denies the closure principle. Although there may be an appearance of closure failure, to many it seems crazy to actually deny the principle. A better response is available from the contextualist theory. On the contextualist view, the appearance of closure failure results from our evaluating the antecedent and the consequent of the principle, relative to different standards. When we say we fail to know not-h, we're using stricter standards than when we say, in everyday contexts that we know P. Again, this is because thinking about skeptical alternatives can get us to raise the standards. But if we evaluate the closure principle relative to a fixed context, so the standard is fixed, it comes out true

Consider again the zebra case. Since our reason for believing we see a zebra can be no better than our reason for believing we do not see a cleverly disguised mule, relative to fixed standards, we know we see a zebra only if we know we see a cleverly disguised mule. So, in contexts where the standard is such that we know we see a zebra, we also know we do not see a cleverly disguised mule. Our reason for denying we see a cleverly disguised mule, e.g., the infrequency of such deceptions, is sufficient, relative to everyday standards, for us to know we do not see a cleverly disguised mule. But when we start thinking about cleverly disguised mules, the standards rise. Relative to these higher standards, our reasons are insufficient for us to know we do not see a cleverly disguised mule. But in this stricter context, we also fail to know we see a zebra. So on the contextualist view, the paradox arises because of our failure to pay attention to contextual shifts.

So which of the three propositions does the contextualist deny. This will depend on the context. We have just seen that the closure principle will be true in every context. In everyday contexts, (3) will be true as well and (2) will be false. And in skeptical contexts, (2) will be true and (3) will be false.[9]

Lotteries

Suppose S holds a ticket in a fair lottery with n tickets, where the probability $n-1/n$ of S losing is very high. If in fact S's ticket loses, can S know that it loses on the basis of the $n-1/n$ probability? Although S has very good reason to believe he will lose, most people balk at saying S knows he will lose. This remains true no matter how many tickets are in the lottery and so no matter how great $n-1/n$ is.

Now suppose S learns that the person running the lottery intends to fix the lottery so S's ticket will lose. Or suppose S reads in the paper that another ticket has won. In both of these cases we are inclined to say that S can know that he loses.

This set of intuitions presents us with a puzzle. In the first case, it seemed, contrary to fallibilist assumptions, that as long as there is a chance that S wins, no matter how small, he does not know that he loses. But the other two cases indicate otherwise. There we said that S can know, on the basis of his reasons, that he will lose. But surely his reasons do not entail that he loses. Generally reliable sources lie, have their intentions thwarted, make mistakes, etc. The probability that S loses conditional on these reasons is less than 1. Why do we ascribe knowledge to S in these cases but not in the first case? In each case, his reasons make his conclusion highly probable. And by increasing the number of tickets in the lottery in the first case, we can make it more probable that S loses in the first case where we do not ascribe knowledge than in the latter two cases where we do ascribe knowledge.[10]

Consider a related puzzle. S does not know that Smith loses the lottery if S's reason is simply that the probability that he loses is $n-1/n$. But if S knows Smith is generally reliable and Smith announces his intention to go to New York tomorrow, S can thereby come to know that Smith will be in New York tomorrow, even thought S knows that this entails that Smith loses the lottery (since if he were to win, he would be in New Jersey accepting the prize). So, S knowing that Smith will be in New York entails, by the closure principle, that S knows Smith loses the lottery. But, though we are willing to ascribe knowledge to S that Smith will be in New York, we are reluctant to ascribe knowledge to S that Smith loses the lottery (on the basis of the probabilities alone). So, as was true in the skeptical puzzle, there appears to be a failure of the closure principle.[11]

Some contextualists argue that Contextualism can provide a satisfactory treatment of these puzzles concerning the lottery. In the cases where S believes he will lose the lottery on the basis of a newspaper report or testimony that it will be fixed, the chance of error is not salient. When, e.g., we read a newspaper report about a mundane matter, we do not normally start thinking about the possibility of a misprint, or otherwise false report. So normal standards are in effect relative to which S can know that he loses. In the case where S bases his belief that he will lose on the probability alone, the chance or error is salient. One cannot think about the $n-1/n$ probability that S will lose without thinking about the $1/n$ probability that he will win. Since the chance of error is salient, the standards rise and relative to those stricter standards S fails to know. This explains why we are willing to ascribe knowledge in the newspaper case but not in the pure probability case.

Contextualism handles the apparent closure failure in the lottery case in the same way it handles it in the skeptical case. When S is focused on Smith's testimony that he will be in New York, the chance of error is not salient and so the standards are relatively low. In that context, S can know Smith will be in New York. And by those same standards, S can know that Smith will lose the lottery. When, however, S focuses on the reasons for believing he lose the lottery, viz the $n-1/n$ probability, the chance of error is salient and so the standards are higher. In this stricter context, S fails to

know that S loses the lottery. And by those same standards, S fails to know that Smith will be in New York. So again, if we hold the context fixed, closure is preserved.[12]

Can Contextualism Be Used to Support Skepticism?

The skeptic holds that all of our everyday knowledge ascriptions are false. We reject skepticism because we find it intuitively compelling that we know things. But just as we use contextualism to explain away the appeal of skeptical arguments, the skeptic could use contextualism to explain away the appeal of our everyday knowledge ascriptions. Why not say that what is governed by context is not when one can truly say that someone knows but rather when one can appropriately say that one knows? On this pragmatic view, though all knowledge ascriptions are false, it can serve a useful function, in everyday contexts, to assert that we know certain things. This explains the appeal of our everyday knowledge ascriptions. Such a view could usurp the entire contextualist machinery, interpreting context as governing merely the appropriateness-conditions for knowledge ascriptions rather than their truth-conditions.[13]

Is there any argument that favors the semantic version of contextualism over the skeptical pragmatic view? Perhaps the strongest argument against the skeptical pragmatic view is precisely that it is a skeptical view. The advantage of the semantic version of contextualism is that it enables us to avoid skepticism (about everyday contexts).

Does this argument beg the question against skepticism? Certainly it does—but again, no more than the skeptical pragmatic interpretation begs the question against common sense. Presumably neither side of this dispute can demonstrate the correctness of its view to the other side. But if we are antecedently convinced of the falsity of skepticism, the semantic version of Contextualism allows us to explain away our own skeptical inclinations—inclinations that give rise to the skeptical paradox. And that is enough to recommend it.

Does Contextualism Address Our Epistemological Concerns?

When we do epistemology, we are concerned with questions about the extent of human knowledge. The Contextualist in answering this question, claims that our knowledge ascriptions are true *relative to everyday standards*.

But what is the relevance of this claim to the original question? For by the Contextualist's own account, in everyday contexts, the standards are weaker standards than in contexts where we do epistemology and think about skeptical alternatives. This means that much less is required for the truth of a knowledge ascription in everyday contexts than is required in contexts where we do epistemology. So how is the truth of those ascriptions in everyday contexts relevant to our original epistemological concerns?[14]

Now it is true that in many contexts where we do epistemology, the standards for knowledge ascriptions are higher than the standards for knowledge ascriptions in everyday contexts. And, the Contextualist's claim that knowledge ascriptions are true in everyday contexts does not make contact with what we say about knowledge in those stricter philosophical contexts. But this the contextualist readily concedes—though crucially, the contextualist puts the emphasis in the other direction. For the point of Contextualism is that what we say about knowledge in skeptical contexts does not make contact with our everyday knowledge ascriptions. Our inclination in skeptical contexts to deny that we know does not conflict with our claims to know in everyday contexts.

According to the Contextualist, what is troubling and unacceptable about skepticism is the claim that all along in our everyday discourse, when we have been claiming to know, we have been speaking falsely. Contextualism attempts to show how the skeptical paradox can be resolved in a way that allows us to preserve the truth or our everyday knowledge ascriptions. This is not to say that a stricter knowledge of the sort that comes into play when we are thinking about skepticism is of no interest. It's just that according to contextualism, we fail to have it. To this extent, contextualism is a skeptical view. The point of contextualism is to give skepticism its due, while blocking the troubling and unacceptable consequence that our everyday knowledge ascriptions are false.

Notes

1. Strictly speaking, Contextualism should be expressed metalinguistically. Thus, we should say that sentences of the form "S knows P" are context sensitive. If we say, in the object language, that knowledge ascriptions are context sensitive, then the current context will determine what "Knowledge", as we just used it, expresses.
2. Cohen [2].
3. Cohen [2].
4. Dretske [4]; Nozick [9].
5. DeRose [3].
6. Dretske [4].
7. Dretske [4].
8. Versions of this view have been held by Moore [8]; Klein [6]; and Pryor [10].
9. Cohen [1], [2]; DeRose [3] Lewis [7].
10. Cohen [1].
11. Harman [5].
12. Cohen [1]; Lewis [7].
13. Unger [12].
14. Sosa [11].

References

Cohen, Stewart, "How to be a Fallibilist." In *Philosophical Perspectives, 2, Epistemology* (Tomberlin, James, ed.). 1988.

Cohen, Stewart, "Contextualism, Skepticism, and the Structure of Reasons." In *Philosophical Perspectives, 13, Epistemology* (Tomberlin, James, ed.). 1999.

DeRose, Keith, "Solving the Skeptical Problem." *Philosophical Review*, 1995:(104:1).

Dretske, Fred, "Epistemic Operators." *Journal of Philosophy* (Dec, 1970).

Harman, Gilbert, *Change in View* (MIT, 1986).

Klein, Peter, *Certainty*, 1981.

Lewis, David, "Elusive Knowledge." *Australasian Journal of Philosophy*, 1996:74(4).

Moore, G.E. "Proof of an External World." *Philosophical Papers*, 1959.

Nozick, Robert, *Philosophical Explanations* (Harvard, 1981).

Pryor, James, "The Skeptic and the Dogmatist." *Nous* 34, 2000.

Sosa, Ernest, "Contextualism and Skepticism." *Philosophical Issues*.

Unger, Peter, *Philosophical Relativity* (1984).

22. VIRTUES IN EPISTEMOLOGY

John Greco

What is a virtue in epistemology? In the broadest sense, a virtue is an excellence of some kind. In epistemology, the relevant kind of excellence will be "intellectual." But then what is an intellectual virtue? Some philosophers have understood intellectual virtues to be broad cognitive abilities or powers. On this view, intellectual virtues are innate faculties or acquired habits that enable a person to arrive at truth and avoid error in some relevant field. For example, Aristotle defined "intuitive reason" as the ability to grasp first principles, and he defined "science" as the ability to demonstrate further truths from these.[1] Some contemporary authors add accurate perception, reliable memory, and various kinds of good reasoning to the list of intellectual virtues. These authors follow Aristotle in the notion that intellectual virtues are cognitive abilities or powers, but they loosen the requirements for what count as such.[2]

Other authors have understood the intellectual virtues quite differently, however. On their view intellectual virtues are more like personality traits than cognitive abilities or powers. For example, intellectual courage is a trait of mind that allows one to persevere in one's ideas. Intellectual open-mindedness is a trait of mind that allows one to be receptive to the ideas of others. Among these authors, however, there is disagreement about why such personality traits count as virtues. Some think it is because they are truth-conducive, increasing one's chances of arriving at true beliefs while avoiding false beliefs.[3] Others think that such traits are virtues independently of their connection to truth—they would be virtues even if they were not truth-conducive at all.[4]

Who is right about the nature of the intellectual virtues? One might think that this is a matter of semantics—that different authors have simply decided to use the term "intellectual virtue" in different ways. In the essay that follows I will argue that there is some truth to this analysis. However, it is not the whole

truth. This is because epistemologists invoke the notion of an intellectual virtue for specific reasons, in the context of addressing specific problems in epistemology. In effect, they make claims that understanding the intellectual virtues in a certain way allows us to solve those problems. And of course claims like that are substantive, not merely terminological. In Part One of this essay I will review some recent history of epistemology, focusing on ways in which the intellectual virtues have been invoked to solve specific epistemological problems. The purpose of this part is to give a sense of the contemporary landscape that has emerged, and to clarify some of the disagreements among those who invoke the virtues in epistemology. In Part Two, I will explore some epistemological problems in greater detail. The purpose of this part is to defend a particular approach in virtue epistemology by displaying its power in addressing these problems.

Part One: History and Landscape

Sosa's Virtue Perspectivism

The intellectual virtues made their contemporary debut in a series of papers by Ernest Sosa.[5] In those papers Sosa is primarily concerned with two problems in the theory of knowledge. The first is the debate between foundationalism and coherentism. The second is a series of objections that have been raised against reliabilism.

Foundationalism and Coherentism Foundationalism and coherentism are positions regarding the structure of knowledge. According to foundationalism, knowledge is like a pyramid: a solid foundation of knowledge grounds the entire structure, providing the support required by knowledge at the higher levels. According to coherentism, knowledge is like a raft: different parts of the structure are tied together via relations of mutual support, with no part of the whole playing a more fundamental role than do others. Let us use the term "epistemic justification" to name whatever property it is that turns mere true belief into knowledge. We may then define "pure coherentism" as holding that only coherence contributes to epistemic justification, and we may define "pure foundationalism" as holding that coherence does not contribute to epistemic justification at all. In the papers that introduce the notion of an intellectual virtue, Sosa argues that neither pure coherentism nor pure foundationalism can be right.

Against pure coherentism is the well-known objection that there can be highly coherent belief-systems that are nevertheless largely divorced from reality. But then coherence cannot be the only thing that matters for epistemic justification. Sosa presses this basic point in various ways. For one, consider the victim of Descartes' evil demon. By hypothesis, the victim's beliefs are as coherent as our own. That is, they are members of a coherent system of beliefs, tied together by a great number and variety of logical and quasi-logical relations. Suppose that by chance some few of those beliefs are also true. Surely they do not amount to knowledge, although both true and coherent.

Another way that Sosa argues the point is to highlight the importance of experience for epistemic justification. Consider that any human being will have perceptual beliefs with few connections to other beliefs in her total belief system. For example, my perceptual belief that there is a bird outside my window has few logical relations to other beliefs that I have. But then one can generate counterexamples to pure coherentism by means of the following recipe. First, replace my belief that there is a bird outside my window with the belief that there is squirrel outside my window. Second, make whatever few other changes are necessary to preserve coherence. For example, replace my belief that I seem to see a bird with the belief that I seem to see a squirrel. Clearly, the overall coherence of the new belief system will be about the same as that of the first. This is because coherence is entirely a function of relations among beliefs, and those relations are about the same in the two systems. But it seems wrong that the new belief about the squirrel is as well justified as the old belief about the bird, for my sensory experience is still such

that I seem to see a bird, and do not seem to see a squirrel. Again, coherence cannot be the only thing that contributes to epistemic justification.

However, there is an equally daunting problem for pure foundationalism, although the way to see it is less direct. Consider how foundationalism might account for my knowledge that there is a bird outside the window. Since the knowledge in question is perceptual, it is plausible to say that it is grounded in sensory experience. Specifically, it is plausible to say that my belief that there is a bird outside the window is epistemically justified because it is grounded in a visual experience of a particular phenomenal quality. What is more, this explains the difference in epistemic status between my belief about the bird and the belief about the squirrel above. In the latter case, there is no grounding in sensory experience of a relevant sort. But here a problem lurks. Consider the foundationalist epistemic principle invoked above, i.e., that a particular sort of sensory experience, with a particular phenomenal quality, justifies the belief that there is a bird outside the window. Is this to be understood as a fundamental principle about epistemic justification, or is it to be understood as an instance of some more general principle? If we say the former, then there would seem to be an infinite number of such principles, with no hope for unity among them. In effect, we would be committed to saying that such principles, in all their number and variety, merely state brute facts about epistemic justification. This is hardly a satisfying position. The more attractive view is that such principles are derived. But then there is more work to be done. Something more fundamental about epistemic justification remains to be explained.

This is where the notion of an intellectual virtue is useful, Sosa argues. Virtues in general are excellences of some kind; more specifically, they are innate or acquired dispositions to achieve some end. Intellectual virtues, Sosa argues, will be dispositions to achieve the intellectual ends of grasping truths and avoiding falsehoods. This notion of an intellectual virtue can be used to give a general account of epistemic justification as follows:

> A belief B(p) is epistemically justified for a person S (i.e., justified in the sense required for knowledge) if and only if B(p) is produced by one or more intellectual virtues of S.

This account of justification, Sosa argues, allows us to explain the unifying ground of the foundationalist's epistemic principles regarding perceptual beliefs. Specifically, such principles describe various intellectually virtuous dispositions. Thus human beings are gifted with perceptual powers or abilities; i.e., dispositions to reliably form beliefs about the environment on the basis of sensory inputs of various modalities. Such abilities are relative to circumstances and environment, but they are abilities nonetheless. The foundationalist's epistemic principles relating perceptual beliefs to their experiential grounds can now be understood as describing or explicating these various abilities.

And the payoff does not end there. For it is possible to give similar accounts of other sources of justification traditionally recognized by foundationalism. Because they are reliable, such faculties as memory, introspection, and logical intuition count as intellectual virtues, and therefore give rise to epistemic justification for their respective products. In a similar fashion, various kinds of deductive and inductive reasoning reliably take one from true belief to further true belief, and hence count as virtues in their own right. By defining epistemic justification in terms of intellectual virtue, Sosa argues, we get a unified account of all the sources of justification traditionally recognized by foundationalism.

Once the foundationalist makes this move, however, pure foundationalism becomes untenable. We said that perception, memory, and the like are sources of epistemic justification because they are intellectual virtues. But now coherence has an equal claim to be an intellectual virtue, and hence an equal claim to be a source of epistemic justification. The intellectual virtues were characterized as cognitive abilities or powers; as dispositions that reliably give rise to true belief under relevant circumstances and in a relevant environment. We may now think of coherence—or more exactly, coherence-seeking reason—as just such a power. In our world, in normal circumstances, coherence-seeking reason is also a reliable source of true belief and hence a source of epistemic justification.

Finally, Sosa argues, we are now in a position to recognize two kinds of knowledge. First, there is "animal knowledge," enjoyed by any being whose true beliefs are the products of intellectual virtue. But second,

there is "reflective knowledge," which further requires a coherent perspective on one's beliefs and their source in intellectual virtue. We may also label the latter kind of knowledge "human knowledge," recognizing that the relevant sort of reflective coherence is a distinctively human virtue. More exactly,

S has animal knowledge regarding p only if

1. p is true, and
2. S's belief B(p) is produced by one or more intellectual virtues of S.

S has reflective knowledge regarding p only if

1. p is true,
2. S's belief B(p) is produced by one or more intellectual virtues of S, and
3. S has a true perspective on B(p) as being produced by one or more intellectual virtues, where such perspective is itself produced by an intellectual virtue of S.[6]

Reliabilism Let us define generic reliabilism as follows.

A belief B(p) is epistemically justified for S if and only if B(p) is the outcome of a sufficiently reliable cognitive process, i.e. a process that is sufficiently truth-conductive.

Generic reliabilism is a powerful view. For one, it accounts for a wide range of our pre-theoretical intuitions regarding which beliefs have epistemic justification. Thus reliabilism explains why beliefs caused by perception, memory, introspection, logical intuition, and sound reasoning are epistemically justified, and it explains why beliefs caused by hallucination, wishful thinking, hasty generalization, and other unreliable processes are not. The view also provides a powerful resource against well-known skeptical arguments. For example, a variety of skeptical arguments trade on the assumption that our cognitive faculties must be vindicated as reliable in order to count as sources of epistemic justification. Because it seems impossible to provide such vindication in a non-circular way, a broad skeptical conclusion threatens. Generic reliabilism cuts off this kind of skeptical reasoning at its roots, with the idea that epistemic justification requires *de facto* reliability rather than vindicated reliability: the difference between knowledge and mere opinion is that the former is grounded in cognitive processes that are in fact reliable in this world.[7]

The view is powerful, but subject to a variety of problems. One of these is that reliability seems insufficient for epistemic justification. To see why, consider the following case. Suppose that S suffers from a rare sort of brain lesion, one effect of which is to cause the victim to believe that he has a brain lesion. However, S has no evidence that he has such a condition, and even has evidence against it. We can imagine, for example, that he has just been given a clean bill of health by competent neurologists. It seems clear that S's belief that he has a brain lesion is unjustified, although (by hypothesis) it has been caused by a highly reliable cognitive process.[8]

The foregoing case seems to show that reliability is not sufficient for epistemic justification. A second case seems to show that reliability is not necessary for epistemic justification. Consider again Descartes' victim of an evil demon. We said that, by hypothesis, the victim's belief system is as coherent as our own. We may now add that the victim bases her beliefs on her experience as we do, and reasons to new beliefs as we do. Clearly, the victim's beliefs cannot amount to knowledge, since she is the victim of massive deception. But still, it seems wrong to say that her beliefs are not justified at all. Let us follow Sosa and call this "the new evil demon problem" for reliabilism. According to simple reliabilism, epistemic justification is entirely a matter of reliability. But the demon victim's beliefs are not reliably formed. The problem for reliabilism is to explain why the victim's beliefs are nevertheless justified.[9]

Sosa argues that both of the above problems can be solved by invoking the notion of an intellectual virtue. Consider the case of the epistemically serendipitous brain lesion. What the case shows is that not all reliable cognitive processes give rise to epistemic justification. On the contrary, the reliabilist must place some kind of restriction on the kind of processes that do so. Sosa's suggestion is that the relevant processes are those which are grounded in the knower's intellectual virtues; i.e., her cognitive abilities or powers. Since the belief about the brain lesion does not arise in this way, making this move allows the reliabilist to deny that the belief is epistemically justified.[10]

Now consider the new evil demon problem. Clearly the beliefs of the demon victim are not reliably formed, and therefore lack something important for knowledge. But notice that there are two ways that a belief can fail by way of reliability. One way is that something goes wrong "from the skin inward." For example, the subject might fail to respond appropriately to her sensory experience, or might fail to reason appropriately from her beliefs. Another way to go wrong, however, is "from the skin outward." Perhaps there is no flaw to be found downstream from experience and belief, but one's cognitive faculties are simply not fitted for one's environment. It is this second way that the demon victim fails. Internally speaking, she is in as good working order as we are. Externally speaking, however, her epistemic condition is a disaster. But then there is a straightforward sense in which even the victim's beliefs are internally justified, Sosa argues. Namely, they are beliefs that result from intellectual virtues.

We saw earlier that Sosa endorses the following account of epistemic justification.

> A belief B(p) is epistemically justified for a person S if and only if B(p) is produced by one or more intellectual virtues of S.

According to Sosa, we need only add that whether a cognitive faculty counts as a virtue is relative to an environment. The victim's perception and reasoning powers are not reliable in her demon environment, and hence are not virtues relative to her world. But those same faculties are reliable, and therefore do count as virtues, relative to the actual world. Accordingly, we have a sense in which the demon victim's beliefs are internally justified although not reliably formed. In fact, Sosa argues, they are internally justified in every respect relevant for animal knowledge.

Finally, it is possible to define a further kind of internal justification associated with reflective knowledge. Remember that reflective knowledge requires a perspective on one's beliefs and their sources in intellectual virtue. The victim of a deceiving demon might also enjoy such a perspective, together with the broad coherence that this entails. This perspective and coherence provides the basis for a further kind of internal justification, Sosa argues.

Moral Models of Intellectual Virtue

According to Sosa, an intellectual virtue is a reliable cognitive ability or power. Coherence-seeking reason is thus an intellectual virtue if reliable, but so are perception, memory, and introspection. Other philosophers have argued against this characterization of the intellectual virtues, however. For example, James Montmarquet's account differs from Sosa's in at least three major respects.

First, cognitive powers such as perception and reason do not count as intellectual virtues at all according to Montmarquet. Rather, on his view the virtues are conceived as personality traits, or qualities of character, such as intellectual courage and intellectual carefulness. In this way the intellectual virtues are analogous to the moral virtues, such as moral temperance and moral courage.

Second, Montmarquet argues that it is a mistake to characterize the intellectual virtues as reliable, or truth-conducive. This is because we can conceive of possible worlds, such as Descartes' demon world, where the beliefs of intellectually virtuous persons are almost entirely false. But traits such as intellectual courage and intellectual carefulness would remain virtues even in such a world, Montmarquet argues. Likewise, we can conceive of worlds where intellectual laziness and carelessness reliably produce true beliefs. But again, traits like laziness and carelessness would remain vices even in such worlds. Therefore, Montmarquet concludes, the intellectual virtues can not be defined in terms of their reliability. Montmarquet's alternative is to define the virtues in terms of a desire for truth. According to this model, the intellectual virtues are those personality traits that a person who desires the truth would want to have.

Finally, on Montmarquet's view the exercise and non-exercise of the intellectual virtues are under our control, and are therefore appropriate objects of praise and blame. When one faces a truck approaching at high speed, one cannot help but perceive accordingly. However, one can control whether one takes a new

idea seriously, or considers a line of argument carefully. Hence we have a third way in which Montmarquet's account of the intellectual virtues departs from Sosa's.

It is clear that Montmarquet's account of the intellectual virtues has affinities with Aristotle's account of the moral virtues. Hence Montmarquet thinks of the intellectual virtues as personality traits or qualities, he emphasizes the importance of proper motivation, and he holds that the exercise of the virtues is under our control. A philosopher who follows Aristotle's model of the moral virtues even more closely is Linda Zagzebski. In fact, Zagzebski criticizes Aristotle for maintaining a strong distinction between the intellectual and moral virtues, arguing that the former are best understood as a subset of the latter.

According to Zagzebski, all virtues are acquired traits of character that involve both a motivational component and a reliable success component. Hence, all moral virtues involve a general motivation to achieve the good, and are reliably successful in doing so. All intellectual virtues involve a general motivation to achieve true belief, and are reliably successful in doing so. But since the true is a component of the good, Zagzebski argues, intellectual virtues can be understood as a subset of the moral virtues. In addition to their general motivation and reliability, each virtue can be defined in terms of its specific or characteristic motivational structure. For example, moral courage is the virtue according to which a person is motivated to risk danger when something of value is at stake, and is reliably successful at doing so. Benevolence is the virtue according to which a person is motivated to bring about the well-being of others, and is reliably successful at doing so. Likewise, intellectual courage is the virtue according to which a person is motivated to be persevering in her own ideas, and is reliably successful at doing so.

One advantage of understanding the intellectual virtues this way, Zagzebski argues, is that it allows the following account of knowledge. First, Zagzebski defines an "act of intellectual virtue."

An act of intellectual virtue A is an act that arises from the motivational component of A, is something a person with virtue A would (probably) do in the circumstances, is successful in achieving the end of the A motivation, and is such that the agent acquires a true belief through these features of the act.[11]

We may then define knowledge as follows:

S has knowledge regarding p if and only if

1. p is true, and
2. S's true belief B(p) arises out of acts of intellectual virtue.

Since the truth condition is redundant in the above definition, we may say alternatively:

S has knowledge regarding p if and only if S's believing p arises out of acts of intellectual virtue.

Even more so than Montmarquet, Zagzebski adopts Aristotle's account of the moral virtues as her model for understanding the intellectual virtues. Thus on her account (a) the intellectual virtues are understood as acquired traits of character, (b) their acquisition is partly under our control, (c) both their possession and exercise are appropriate objects of moral praise, and (d) both their lack and non-exercise can be appropriate objects of moral blame. It is noteworthy that Zagzebski's account departs from Sosa's on all of these points. Thus for Sosa the intellectual virtues are cognitive abilities rather than character traits; they need not be acquired, and their acquisition and use need not be under one's control. On Sosa's account, the possession and exercise of the intellectual virtues are grounds for praise, but this need not be praise of a moral sort. Hence we praise people for their keen perception and sound reasoning, but this is more like praise for an athlete's prowess than like praise for a hero's courage.

On the face of things, therefore, there would seem to be a significant disagreement over the nature of the intellectual virtues. But at this point it might be suggested that the issue is merely terminological. What Zagzebski means by a virtue is something close to what Aristotle means by a moral virtue, and therefore natural cognitive powers such as perception and memory do not count as virtues on her meaning of the term. Sosa has adopted a different sense of the term, however, according to which anything that has a function has virtues. In this sense, a virtue is a characteristic excellence of some sort, and reliable perception and reliable memory qualify as intellectual excellences. But to see this as a terminological dispute obscures a substantive one. This comes out if we recall that both Sosa and Zagzebski offer accounts of knowledge in terms of their respective notions of intellectual virtue. The substantive question is now this: Which account of the intellectual virtues better serves this purpose? Sosa also invokes the intellectual virtues to address the dispute between foundationalism and coherentism over the structure of knowledge. Here we may ask again: Which notion of the intellectual virtues is best suited for this purpose?

Once the question regarding the nature of the intellectual virtues is framed this way, however, it seems clear that Zagzebski's account is too strong. Consider first the idea that knowledge arises out of acts of intellectual virtue. On Zagzebski's account, this means that knowledge must manifest dispositions that both (a) involve a certain motivational structure, and (b) involve relevant kinds of voluntary control. But neither of these requirements seems necessary for knowledge.

Consider a case of simple perceptual knowledge: You are crossing the street in good light, you look to your left, and you see that a large truck is moving quickly toward you. It would seem that you know that there is a truck moving toward you independently of any control, either over the ability to perceive such things in general, or over this particular exercise of that ability. Neither is it required that one have a motivation to be open-minded, careful, or the like. On the contrary, it would seem that you know that there is a truck coming toward you even if you are motivated *not* to be open-minded, careful, or the like.

In reply to this sort of objection, one might suggest that Zagzebski's conditions for perceptual knowledge do not require either the relevant kind of control or the relevant kind of motivation. This is because her definition of knowledge does not require that one actually possess intellectual virtues in her sense. Rather, knowledge requires only an *act* of intellectual virtue, and that is defined in terms of what an intellectually virtuous person *would* do in similar circumstances. Since intellectually virtuous persons form their perceptual beliefs without voluntarily control and without Zagzebski-type motivations, Zagzebski's account of knowledge does not require either of these.[12]

The appropriate reply to this objection depends on how we are to interpret the locution "something a person with virtue A would (probably) do in the circumstances" in Zagzebski's definition of an act of intellectual virtue. If we interpret this locution strongly, so that it implies intellectually virtuous control and motivation, then Zagzebski's definition of knowledge does require these. This is the natural interpretation, since Zagzebski thinks that moral credit requires these, and that knowers deserve moral credit for their knowledge. But suppose we interpret the locution so that acts of intellectual virtue do not require virtuous control or motivation. In that case, it may be true that someone with perceptual knowledge does "something a person with virtue would do" in the circumstances. But now that "something a person with virtue would do" will not be something the virtuous person does *qua* virtuous person. In other words, Zagzebki-type intellectual virtues will be doing no work in the resulting definition of knowledge, and so knowledge will no longer be defined in terms of Zagzebski-type intellectual virtues.

Similar considerations show that Zagzebski's account of the intellectual virtues is ill suited for addressing the dispute between foundationalism and coherentism. In that context, Sosa invoked the notion of an intellectual virtue to (a) give a unified account of traditional foundationalist sources of epistemic justification, and (b) explain how coherence can be a source of epistemic justification as well. We have already seen that Zagzebski's notion of an intellectual virtue is too strong to yield an adequate account of perceptual knowledge. For the same reasons, it is also too strong to yield an adequate account of other sources of foundational knowledge, such as memory, introspection, and logical intuition.

We may conclude that the accounts of intellectual virtue defended by Zagzebski and Montmarquet are ill suited to address either the nature of knowledge or the dispute between foundationalism and coherentism over the structure of knowledge. An account of the intellectual virtues modeled on Aristotle's account of the moral virtues is too strong for these purposes. That is not to say, however, that the moral model is not apt for other purposes. Montmarquet sees this clearly when he rejects the idea that he is giving an account of epistemic justification, or the kind of justification required

for knowledge. Rather, he uses the notion of an intellectual virtue to give an account of "doxastic responsibility," or the kind of responsibility for belief that can ground moral responsibility for actions. Often enough, the morally outrageous actions of tyrants, racists, and terrorists seem perfectly reasonable, even necessary, in the context of their distorted belief system. In order to find their actions blameworthy, it would seem that we have to find their beliefs blameworthy as well. An account of the intellectual virtues based on a moral model provides what we are looking for, Montmarquet argues. Such an account allows a plausible sense in which justified (and unjustified) beliefs are under a person's control, and therefore allows a way to view such beliefs as appropriate objects of moral blame and praise.

We have seen that Montmarquet's notion of an intellectual virtue is not intended to address traditional epistemological concerns about the nature and structure of knowledge. In fact, a number of authors who adopt a moral model for the intellectual virtues indicate that they are interested in problems that fall outside the scope of traditional epistemological inquiry. For example, Lorraine Code sets out to explore our "responsibility as knowers," and is concerned to emphasize the social, moral and political importance of our cognitive practices. A major focus of Code's inquiry is the ways in which our intellectual and moral responsibilities are intertwined and interdependent. It is no surprise, therefore, that Code adopts a notion of intellectual virtue that emphasizes agency and that can ground evaluations in terms of intellectual responsibility.[13] Vrinda Dalmiya is another author who adopts a moral model of intellectual virtue that is well suited for her purposes. Dalmiya argues that knowledge of other selves requires intellectual virtues centered on the activity of caring. In effect, to know another self requires a morally significant relationship—an interactive process that involves empathy and trust, as well as important moral choices. Here again, a notion of intellectual virtue that allows relevant kinds of agency and responsibility is appropriate for the purposes at hand.[14]

It seems clear that an account of the intellectual virtues modeled on Aristotle's account of the moral virtues is apt for addressing a variety of epistemological concerns. It is a mistake, however, to generalize from such concerns to an account of knowledge per se. As we have seen, the moral model is ill suited for that purpose, since it will result in an account of knowledge that is too strong.

Wisdom and Understanding

Perhaps another place where the moral model is useful is in accounts of "higher grade" epistemic achievements such as wisdom and understanding. According to Zagzebski, wisdom has clear moral dimensions. Thus wisdom unifies the knowledge of the wise person, but also her desires and values. This is why it is impossible for wisdom to be misused, she argues, and why it is incoherent to talk of a person that is wise but immoral. Also, wisdom is achieved only through extensive life experience, and hence takes time to acquire. Therefore, Zagzebski argues, wisdom is best understood on a moral model of the intellectual virtues, either because it is such a virtue itself, or because it is the product of such virtues. This seems plausible, especially if we mean wisdom to include practical wisdom, or wisdom regarding how one ought to live. But again, it would be a mistake to generalize from an account of wisdom to an account of knowledge per se. I suggest that Zabzebski's account of wisdom is plausible precisely because we think that wisdom is harder to achieve than knowledge. The stronger conditions implied by Zagzebski's account therefore seem more appropriate here than in a general account of knowledge.

I have argued that Zagzebski's position benefits from a distinction between knowledge and wisdom. By maintaining this distinction, it is possible to resist putting conditions on knowledge per se that are appropriate only for knowledge of a higher grade. In a similar fashion, Sosa's position benefits from a distinction between knowledge and understanding.[15] To see how this is so, it is useful to notice a tension in Sosa's thinking.

Recall that Sosa makes a distinction between animal knowledge and reflective knowledge. One has animal knowledge so long as one's true belief has its source in a reliable cognitive faculty. One has reflective knowledge only if one's first-order belief also fits into a coherent perspective, which perspective must include a belief that one's first-order belief has its reliable source. Sometimes Sosa writes as if animal knowledge is real knowledge, while reflective knowledge amounts to a higher achievement still. In other places Sosa's evaluation of animal knowledge is less enthusiastic. Hence he calls it

"servomechanic" and "mere animal" knowledge, and in one place suggests that the label is "metaphorical."[16] Either way, however, it is clear that Sosa thinks animal knowledge is of a lesser kind than reflective knowledge.

The tension is now this: As we saw above, Sosa holds that the virtue of coherence is its reliability. Like perception, memory, and introspection, reason-seeking coherence makes its contribution to epistemic justification and knowledge because it is reliable. But then why should reflective knowledge be of a higher kind than animal knowledge? If the difference between animal and reflective knowledge is a coherent perspective, and if the value of coherence is its reliability, it would seem that the distinction between animal knowledge and reflective knowledge is at most a difference in degree rather than in kind. Moreover, we have no good reason to think that a person with reflective knowledge will always be more reliable than a person with only animal knowledge. It seems clearly possible, that is, that the cognitive virtues of a person without an epistemic perspective could be more reliable than the cognitive virtues of a person with it. But then reflective knowledge is not necessarily higher than animal knowledge, even in degree.

Here is a different problem for Sosa's view. Suppose we take what seems to be Sosa's considered position, which is that human knowledge is reflective knowledge. On this view a broad skepticism threatens, because it seems clear that in the typical case most people lack the required epistemic perspective. That is, in the typical case most people lack beliefs about the source of their first-order belief, and whether that source is reliable. For example, in most cases where I have a belief that there is a bird outside my window, I do not have further beliefs about the source of that belief, or about the reliability of that source. Therefore, Sosa's position seems to result in skepticism regarding reflective knowledge.

In the preceding paragraphs we have identified two problems for Sosa's position. First, Sosa's distinction between animal and reflective knowledge seems unmotivated, given his claim that the virtue of coherence is its reliability. If that claim is correct, then there is no good reason for thinking that reflective knowledge is of a higher kind than animal knowledge, or that the two belong to significantly different kinds at all. Second, if we do maintain the distinction, then the result seems to be a broad skepticism with respect to reflective (or human) knowledge. This is because most human beings fail to have the required epistemic perspective. Both these problems can be solved, however, if we recognize two plausible claims: (a) that there is a distinction in kind between knowledge and understanding, and (b) that coherence has a distinctive value through its contribution to understanding. The first problem is solved because this allows us to make a principled distinction between non-reflective knowledge and reflective knowledge: in virtue of its greater coherence through an epistemic perspective, reflective knowledge involves a kind of understanding that non-reflective knowledge lacks. The second problem is solved because this allows us to drop the requirement of an epistemic perspective for human knowledge: non-reflective knowledge is real knowledge, and even real human knowledge. Reflective knowledge is of a higher grade and of a rarer sort, involving a special kind of understanding. On this view we still get a skeptical conclusion regarding reflective knowledge, since it will still be the case that few human beings have the kind of perspective that reflective knowledge requires. But the sting is taken out of this conclusion if we recognize that it is a special kind of understanding, rather than knowledge per se, that people so often lack. We never thought that such understanding was widespread in the first place, and so a skeptical conclusion in this regard is just what we would expect.[17]

In effect, I am making the same diagnosis of Sosa's account of knowledge as I did of Zagzebski's, and I am suggesting the same solution. In both cases I have argued that the requirements they put on knowledge are too strong, and that therefore their accounts have unattractive skeptical results. And in both cases the solution is to distinguish between knowledge per se and some epistemic value of a higher grade. This allows us to weaken the requirements on knowledge so as to make it generally attainable, and at the same time recognize the intellectual virtues that Zagzebski and Sosa want to emphasize.

However, one question remains: Why should the special kind of understanding involved in an epistemic perspective constitute a distinctive epistemic value? Granting that understanding is a distinctive epistemic value over and above knowledge per se, and granting that coherence contributes to that distinctive value, why should the particular sort of understanding involved in an epistemic perspective constitute a distinctive epistemic value all of its own? It seems to me that there is no good answer to this question. On the contrary, the above considerations show that reflective knowledge is not a distinctive epistemic kind at all. The important distinction is not between animal knowledge and reflective knowledge, but between knowledge per se and understanding per se.

Part Two: A Virtue Account of Knowledge

In Part One, we saw that different virtue theorists defend different, seemingly incompatible accounts of the intellectual virtues. In this context I argued for an irenic conclusion: that different kinds of intellectual virtue or excellence are best suited to address different issues in epistemology. In particular, I argued (1) that a minimalist notion of the intellectual virtues, in which the virtues are conceived as reliable cognitive abilities or powers, is best suited for an account of knowledge; and (2) that stronger notions of the intellectual virtues are best suited to address a range of other issues.

In Part Two, I will pursue the idea that a minimalist, reliabilist notion of the intellectual virtues is useful for constructing an account of knowledge. I begin with some general comments about virtue, epistemic justification, and knowledge. After that, I argue that a virtue account has good resources for addressing Gettier problems.

Agent Reliabilism

Recall generic reliabilism and the conditions it lays down for epistemic justification:

> A belief B(p) is epistemically justified if and only if B(p) is the outcome of a sufficiently reliable cognitive process.

We saw that these conditions are too weak, as is demonstrated by the case of the epistemically serendipitous brain lesion. The lesson to be learned from that case is that not all reliable cognitive processes give rise to epistemic justification and knowledge. Such considerations gave rise to an account in terms of intellectual virtue.

A belief B(p) is epistemically justified for a person S if and only if B(p) is produced by one or more intellectual virtues of S; i.e. by one or more of S's cognitive abilities or powers.

Here the key is to make the cognitive agent the seat of reliability, thereby moving from generic reliabilism to agent reliabilism. By restricting the relevant processes to those grounded in the knower's abilities or powers, we effectively disallow strange and fleeting processes, including brain lesions and the like, from giving rise to epistemic justification.

Recall also that this way of thinking allows an account of internal justification, or the kind of justification enjoyed even by the victim of Descartes's evil demon. Thus Sosa suggested:

A belief B(p) is epistemically justified for S relative to environment E if and only if B(p) is produced by one or more cognitive dispositions that are intellectual virtues in E.

Notice that on this account the beliefs of the demon's victim are as justified as ours, so long as we relativize to the same environment. This kind of justification is "internal" because it is entirely a function of factors "from the skin inward," or better, "from the mind inward." This is insured by relativizing justification to external environments.

Finally, it is possible to define a sense of subjective justification, or a sense in which a belief is justified from the knower's own point of view. We have already seen that knowledge must be reliably formed. Many have had the intuition that, in addition to this, a knower must be aware that her belief is reliably formed. One way to cash out such awareness is to require an epistemic perspective on the relevant belief, but I have argued that an account in these terms is too strong for a requirement on knowledge. Nevertheless, a kind of awareness of reliability is manifested in the very dispositions that constitute one's cognitive abilities: the fact that a person interprets experience one way rather than another, or draws one inference rather than another, manifests an awareness of sorts that some relevant evidence is a reliable indication of some relevant truth. Or at least this is so if the person is trying to form her beliefs accurately in the first place—if the person is in the normal mode of trying to believe

what is true, as opposed to what is convenient, or comforting, or politically correct. We may use these considerations to define a sense of subjective justification that is not too strong to be a requirement on knowledge.

A belief B(p) is subjectively justified for S if and only if B(p) is produced by cognitive dispositions that S manifests when S is motivated to believe what is true.

In cases of knowledge such dispositions will also be virtues, since they will be objectively reliable in addition to being well motivated. But even in cases where S is not reliable, she may nevertheless have justified beliefs in this sense, since her believing may nevertheless manifest well-motivated dispositions.

Since the notion of intellectual virtue employed in the above definitions is relatively weak, the account of epistemic justification and knowledge that results is relatively weak as well: there is no strong motivation condition, no control condition, and no condition requiring an epistemic perspective. In the section that follows, I will argue that this minimalist approach is just what is needed in a theory of knowledge.

Gettier Problems[18]

In 1963, Edmund Gettier wrote a short paper purporting to show that knowledge is not true justified belief. His argument proceeded by way of two counterexamples, each of which seemed to show that a belief could be both true and justified and yet not amount to knowledge. Here are two examples that are in the spirit of Gettier's originals.

Case 1. On the basis of excellent reasons, S believes that her co-worker Mr. Nogot owns a Ford: Nogot testifies that he owns a Ford, and this is confirmed by S's own relevant observations. From this S infers that someone in her office owns a Ford. As it turns out, S's evidence is misleading and Nogot does not in fact own a Ford. However, another person in S's office, Mr. Havit, does own a Ford, although S has no reason for believing this.[19]

Case 2. Walking down the road, S seems to see a sheep in the field and on this basis believes that there is a sheep in the field. However, due to an unusual trick of light, S has mistaken a dog for a sheep, and so what she sees is not a sheep at all. Nevertheless, unsuspected by S, there *is* a sheep in another part of the field.[20]

In both of these cases the relevant belief seems justified, at least in senses of justification that emphasize the internal or the subjective, and in both cases the relevant belief is true. Yet in neither case would we be inclined to judge that the person in question has knowledge.

These examples show that internal and/or subjective justification is not sufficient for knowledge. Put another way, they show that knowledge requires some stronger relation between belief and truth. From the perspective of a virtue theory, there is a natural way to think of this stronger relation. For it is natural to distinguish between (a) achieving some end by luck or accident, and (b) achieving the end through the exercise of one's abilities (or virtues). This suggests the following difference between Gettier cases and cases of knowledge. In Gettier cases, S believes the truth, but it is only by accident that she does so. In cases of knowledge, however, it is no accident that S believes the truth. Rather, in cases of knowledge S believes the truth as the result of her own cognitive abilities—her believing the truth can be credited to her, as opposed to dumb luck or blind chance.

These considerations suggest the following account of knowledge.

S has knowledge regarding p if and only if

1. S's belief B(p) is *subjectively* justified in the following sense: B(p) is produced by cognitive dispositions that S manifests when S is motivated to believe what is true,
2. S's belief B(p) is *objectively* justified in the following sense: B(p) is produced by one or more intellectual virtues of S; i.e. by one or more of S's cognitive abilities or powers, and
3. S believes the truth regarding p *because* S believes p out of intellectual virtue. Alternatively: The intellectual virtues that result in S's believing the truth regarding p are an important necessary part of the total set of causal factors that give rise to S's believing the truth regarding p.

If we stipulate that intellectual virtues involve a motivation to believe the truth, we may collapse the above account as follows.

S has knowledge regarding p if and only if S believes the truth regarding p *because* S believes p out of intellectual virtue.[21]

Notes

1. Aristotle, *Nicomachean Ethics*, Book VI.
2. For example, see Ernest Sosa, *Knowledge in Perspective* (Cambridge: Cambridge University Press, 1991); Alvin Goldman, "Epistemic Folkways and Scientific Epistemology," in his *Liaisons: Philosophy Meets the Cognitive and Social Sciences* (Cambridge, MA: MIT Press, 1992); and John Greco, "Virtues and Vices of Virtue Epistemology," *Canadian Journal of Philosophy* 23 (1993).
3. For example, see Linda Zagzebski, *Virtues of the Mind* (Cambridge: Cambridge University Press, 1996).
4. For example, see James Montmarquet, "Epistemic Virtue," Mind 96 (1987); and James Montmarquet, *Epistemic Virtue and Doxastic Responsibility* (Lanham, MD: Rowman and Littlefield, 1993).
5. See especially "The Raft and the Pyramid: Coherence versus Foundations in the Theory of Knowledge," Midwest Studies in Philosophy V (1980); "Epistemology Today: A Perspective in Retrospect," *Philosophical Studies* 40 (1981); "The Coherence of Virtue and the Virtue of Coherence: Justification in Epistemology," *Synthese* 64 (1985); and "Knowledge and Intellectual Virtue," *The Monist* 68 (1985), all reprinted in *Knowledge in Perspective*. See also "Reliabilism and Intellectual Virtue" and "Intellectual Virtue in Perspective," both *in Knowledge in Perspective*.
6. See especially "Knowledge and Intellectual Virtue" and "Intellectual Virtue in Perspective." At present I characterize the two kinds of knowledge in terms of necessary conditions only. This is because Sosa thinks that other conditions are necessary to make the set sufficient. I discuss further conditions on knowledge in Part Two of this essay, in the section on Gettier problems.
7. For more on the relation between skepticism and reliabilism, see my *Putting Skeptics in Their Place* (New York: Cambridge University Press, 2000); and "Agent Reliabilism," *Philosophical Perspectives*, 13, *Epistemology* (1999).
8. This example is due to Alvin Plantinga, *Warrant: The Current Debate* (Oxford: Oxford University Press, 1993), p. 199.
9. This problem is due to Keith Lehrer and Stewart Cohen, "Justification, Truth and Coherence," *Synthese* 55 (1983).

10. See "Proper Functionalism and Virtue Epistemology," *Nous* 27 (1993). Relevant sections of this paper are reprinted as "Three Forms of Virtue Epistemology," in Guy Axtell, ed., *Knowledge, Belief and Character* (Lanham, MD: Rowman and Littlefield, 2000).

11. *Virtues of the Mind*, p. 270.

12. A suggesstion along these lines can be found in *Virtues of the Mind*, pp. 273–83.

13. See Lorraine Code, "Toward a 'Responsibilist' Epistemology," *Philosophy and Phenomenological Research* XVL (1984); and *Epistemic Responsibility* (Hanover: University Press of New England and Brown University Press, 1987).

14. See Vrinda Dalmiya, "Knowing People," in Matthias Steup, ed., *Knowledge, Truth and Duty: Essays on Epistemic Justification, Responsibility and Virtue* (New York: Oxford University Press, 2001).

15. So argues Stephen Grimm in "Ernest Sosa, Knowledge and Understanding," forthcoming in *Philosophical Studies*. In the next two paragraphs I am indebted to Grimm's paper.

16. See "Intellectual Virtue in Perspective," pp. 274–75.

17. Richard Fumerton makes a similar point in "Achieving Epistemic Ascent," in John Greco, ed., *Sosa and his Critics* (Oxford: Blackwell Publishers, 2003).

18. In this section I draw on material from "Knowledge as Credit for True Belief," in Michael DePaul and Linda Zagzebski, eds., *Intellectual Virtue: Perspectives from Ethics and Epistemology* (Oxford: Oxford University Press, 2002).

19. The example is from Keith Lehrer, "Knowledge, Truth and Evidence," *Analysis* 25 (1965).

20. The example is slightly revised from Roderick Chisholm, *Theory of Knowledge*, 2nd edition (Englewood Cliffs, NJ: Prentice-Hall, Inc., 1977), p. 105.

21. A number of authors have defended the idea that, in cases of knowledge, one believes the truth because one believes out of intellectual virtue. See Ernest Sosa, "Beyond Skepticism, to the Best of our Knowledge," *Mind* 97 (1988), and *Knowledge in Perspective*; Linda Zagzebski, *Virtues of the Mind*, and "What is Knowledge?" in John Greco and Ernest Sosa, eds. *The Blackwell Guide to Epistemology* (Oxford: Blackwell Publishers, 1999); and Wayne Riggs, "Reliability and the Value of Knowledge," *Philosophy and Phenomenological Research*, forthcoming. I am indebted to many people for their comments on earlier versions of this material, including Robert Audi, Stephen Grimm, and Wayne Riggs. I would especially like to thank Ernest Sosa and Linda Zagzebski for many discussions on relevant topics.

✦ CHAPTER 5 SKEPTICISM ABOUT KNOWLEDGE ✦

INTRODUCTION

Skeptical challenges to our claims to knowledge or justification can be radical and global in the sense that they target all such claims, or moderate and local in that they target only claims within a limited domain (such as perceptual knowledge or knowledge about other minds). Skepticism is defended by regress arguments designed to show that our beliefs are ultimately groundless, and indiscernability arguments that challenge the epistemic credentials of our beliefs on the grounds that we cannot distinguish between our real situation and scenarios in which we would have the same experiences and beliefs as in real life yet our view of the world would be radically mistaken.

Some of the critics of global skepticism have argued that if the skeptic's thesis is correct, skeptics are in no position to defend it (the *indefensibility response*). If we lack reason to believe anything, we cannot have grounds to accept any argument for a skeptical conclusion. Other critics of global skepticism say that the skeptic's thesis is nonsense (the *incoherence response*). Less radical forms of skepticism are harder to criticize. Here opponents criticize local skeptics' own attempts to show that the requirements for knowledge or justified belief are not satisfied (*counterdefense responses*).

The incoherence response comes in two main varieties. The first claims that skeptical hypotheses are unverifiable nonsense. Logical positivists, such as Rudolph Carnap, whose work is included in this chapter, take this approach. The second variety (Putnam 1981) claims that radical skepticism can be shown false using facts about the nature of thought and language.

Those who offer counterdefense responses try to show that the requirements for knowledge or justified belief are met, or, at least, that skeptics do not show that these requirements cannot be met. Most of the selections in this chapter take this approach to skepticism.

While considering counterdefense responses, eventually we must confront the issue of who bears the *burden of proof*: to defend our claims to knowledge against skeptics in a way that is successful from the standpoint of reason(ableness), is it enough for antiskeptics to defeat skeptics' arguments for the claim that epistemic requirements cannot be met? Or does that merely create a standoff between skeptics and their opponents? Or is a third possibility correct: do skeptics win the day unless antiskeptics can show, using premises that are neutral vis-à-vis the truth of skepticism, that the skeptic's thesis is false? This third possibility is the most damaging, since antiskeptics cannot argue at all if they must grant skeptics a 'neutrality' veto against the premises of the antiskeptics' arguments. But this third possibility is also the least acceptable of the three, assuming that any premise that is plausible and not undermined by counterevidence should be suitable grounds for conclusions, even if the premise clashes with skepticism. In fact, it seems reasonable to make a stronger claim: that skeptics bear the burden of proof, for their thesis is, on its face, not plausible. It is up to them to convince us they are correct.

Moore (1873–1958) and the Common Sense Response

In "Proof of an External World," George Edward Moore attempts to respond to the skeptic by appealing to commonsense. In an earlier essay called "A Defence of Common Sense" Moore claimed that he is absolutely certain that various claims of commonsense are true, such as that he has a living human body that came into existence at a particular time and has existed continuously ever since, that he has had many kinds of experiences, that other people have also had various experiences, and so forth. Moore suggests that claims like these—claims of commonsense—are more obvious than the premises of any argument that can be leveled against them. In "Proof," he suggests that he is entitled to conclude that there is an external world because it follows from the fact that he has hands, which are physical objects in the external world. This claim about his hands is both an item of commonsense and something about which he cannot be wrong: it is certain, unlike the premises of arguments that suggest that he lacks hands.

Wittgenstein(1889–1951) and Certainty

In various work, Ludwig Wittgenstein tries to clarify the things we do with words by thinking of these activities as elements of "language games." In *On Certainty* (1969), written just before his death, he focuses on epistemic terms. According to him, we may reach important conclusions about 'knowledge' by considering how doubt functions in our language game. One point is that doubts cannot even be expressed if we question whether we have mastered a language and whether we live in a world in which the mastery of language occurs. "If you are not certain of any fact, you cannot be certain of the meaning of your words either." (sect. 114) Another point is that doubting and overcoming doubts are activities that presuppose a backdrop of presuppositions about which we are certain, or where mistakes are impossible. In fact, these presuppositions amount to an entire Weltanschauung, or worldview, which includes Moore-style propositions such as "here is a hand." They are "the inherited background against which I distinguish between true and false." They are the system in which "all testing, all confirmation and disconfirmation of a hypothesis takes place" (105). But Wittgenstein's view does not seem to be coherentist, since he seems to think that our fundamental worldview rests on nothing and is not rationally defensible.

Although our worldview stands firm for us, and is in that sense certain, Wittgenstein thinks it cannot be known, or justified. For given the rules of our

game, it is permissible and hence sensible to claim to know something only if it is sensible to raise real doubts about that thing. The words, 'I know such and such' are used to offer assurances that I can rule out the relevant doubts, and lose their moorings in practice if no possibility of doubt arises. But doubts about our worldview cannot be raised or settled precisely because doubting and settling doubts is possible only against the backdrop of our worldview. Hence it is nonsense—it is contrary to the rules of the game—for Moore to claim to know facts such as "here is a hand."

Carnap (1891–1970) and the Verificationist Response

Rudolph Carnap was one of the most important proponents of logical positivism, a movement that grew out of the discussions of the Vienna Circle, a group of philosophers and scientists who met in the second decade of the twentieth century. Like other positivists, Carnap was deeply influenced by the work of Ludwig Wittgenstein, especially his *Tractatus Logico-Philosophicus* (1921), and Bertrand Russell's (1910–13, 1919) contributions to mathematical logic. All three of these figures owed a great deal to the work of Gottlob Frege (1848–1925), especially 1879 and 1884. The positivists were united in their admiration for (then) recent developments in mathematical logic and the natural sciences, and in their determination to draw a sharp line separating these valuable paradigms of successful inquiry from the metaphysical excesses of G.W.F. Hegel (1770–1831) and philosophers influenced by him. Positivists attempted to specify a criterion of meaningfulness that would allow them to dismiss the whole of metaphysical inquiry as nonsense, a criterion that would uphold their view that a proposition is meaningful only if it is 'analytical' (like truths of mathematics and logic) or empirically verifiable (like the propositions of natural science). However, they were unable to specify a clear criterion that ruled out subject matter they called metaphysics and only that subject matter. They also found it difficult to resist the criticism that their verification principle was itself nonsense, being neither analytic nor empirically verifiable.

In "Empiricism, Semantics, and Ontology," Carnap claims that all legitimate inquiry must take place relative to a linguistic framework. A linguistic framework determines the observations that would verify or falsify the claims that can be formulated using the resources of that framework. Like Wittgenstein, Carnap was inclined to reinterpret some 'metaphysical' claims as assertions about language—about the framework—rather than the external world. For example, 'seven is a number' looks to be an assertion about what is real, but in fact is an assertion about the way we use words. Many apparent disputes about reality are actually disputes about the nature of grammar, and grammar varies from framework to framework. According to Carnap, genuine questions about what is real can be settled decisively using the resources of a linguistic framework, by making the observations that, according to the framework, resolve the matter. But if we try to raise a question about reality independently of any framework, as radical skeptics do, we will end up asking an "external" question that is a meaningless pseudoquestion. Such "external" questions as 'do things really exist?' are at best questions about grammar, questions about whether or not we should accept a certain sort of language, in this case the "thing language." And disputes about grammar are not to be settled on the basis of empirical observation. Instead, such disputes are settled on pragmatic grounds, on the basis of considerations about the usefulness of the framework. Thus the radical skeptic's question, "Is there a world of things beyond our experiences?" is either meaningless, or it is a question about how we should frame our language, to be resolved on pragmatic grounds.

Dretske (b.1932) and the Tracking Theorist Response

Tracking theorists like Fred Dretske try to meet indiscernability skeptics half way. They acknowledge that (a) we do not know that skeptical scenarios fail to hold (for example, we do not know we are not brains in vats), but resist the skeptic's claim that (b) we cannot know commonsense claims that are incompatible with being in skeptical scenarios. The fact that the tracking account supports (a) they take to be one of its main strengths. For knowing some proposition p entails tracking the fact that p: it is to arrive at the belief p via a method that would not lead us to believe p if p were false. And yet if we were brains in vats, we would still think we were not. So we do not track the fact that we are not brains in vats or the fact that some other skeptical scenario does not hold.

But if (a) is true, isn't it possible to defend (b), by relying on the principle of closure (we know things when we believe them upon seeing that they are entailed by other things we know)? So it would seem, but Dretske denies the principle of closure. Given the tracking account, the closure principle is false, for we can track a commonsense claim, such as I am working in my office, yet fail to track claims that follow from it, such as the claim that I am not in bed dreaming.

Stine and a Relevant Alternatives Response

In her essay "Skepticism, Relevant Alternatives, and Deductive Closure," Gail Stine draws on a relevant alternatives analysis of knowledge in order to respond to skepticism. Her essay is also an early defense of contextualism (preceding David Lewis's 1979 essay "Scorekeeping in a Language Game" by three years), and due to her influence, both speaker-centered contextualists (Lewis and Cohen, for example) and agent-centered contextualists (Nozick, for instance) have incorporated the notion of relevant alternatives. She says that it is our context that "determines what is taken to be a relevant alternative," and "it is an essential characteristic of our concept of knowledge that tighter criteria are appropriate in different contexts." Stine also argued, contrary to Dretske, that we should retain the closure principle, noting that if we hold "the set of relevant alternatives constant from beginning to end of the deductive closure argument" then the closure principle is true.

As for skepticism, she argues that (a) in ordinary contexts (in "normal circumstances") skeptical possibilities (such as that I am a brain in a vat) are not relevant, (b) if a possibility is irrelevant, we know it does not hold, so (c) in ordinary contexts we know that skeptical possibilities do not hold.

Lewis (1941–2002) and the Contextualist's Response

The late David Lewis, whose essay "Elusive Knowledge" is reproduced here, tries to meet the skeptic half way *without* rejecting the principle of closure. Lewis claims the skeptic is correct in saying that in contexts where we are investigating the nature of knowledge it is a mistake to attribute knowledge to people. But skeptics go wrong when they say that attributions of knowledge are incorrect in other, more ordinary contexts, where skeptical possibilities are not at issue. The main error skeptics make is the assumption that what goes in one context goes in others, so that by showing no one knows things in the epistemic context, they can conclude that no one knows anything in any context.

Lewis' contextualist account, an earlier version of which appeared in Lewis 1979, is a theory about when it is appropriate for a speaker to attribute knowledge to an agent. He says that it is correct for speaker A to say that subject S knows *p* if and only if S can eliminate every possibility in which not-*p*—except for those possibilities that speaker A is properly ignoring. It is A's context that determines which possibilities are properly ignored.

Klein and Infinitism

Theorists who respond to regress skepticism typically defend some form of foundationalism, saying the regress stops with self-justified beliefs, or some form of coherentism, saying that circular justification is acceptable. More rarely, theorists defend the arbitrary reasons view, suggesting that the regress stops with beliefs that are themselves not justified but that serve to justify other beliefs. In his work, Peter Klein (2000, 2003) rejects all three approaches in favor of a fourth response to regress skepticism: *infinitism*, which says that (a) infinitely regressing chains of distinct reasons are required for *fully* justified belief, and (b) accepting *provisionally* justified beliefs—beliefs that are more rational to hold than the alternatives given the reasoning so far—is the only rational and realistic practice. In "There is No Good Reason to be An Academic Skeptic," Klein defends a view that is closely associated with infinitism, namely the Pyrrhonian position

that, with respect to claims that require defense, withholding judgment is always appropriate. Against Pyrrhonians, he contrasts "academic skeptics," who claim to defend the position that knowledge and justified belief are out of reach. Relying on a Pyrrhonian perspective, Klein attempts to defeat arguments for academic skepticism.

Luper and Neo-Mooreanism

Various theorists, including Ernest Sosa (1999, 2003) and Luper (1984, 1987a, 2003), have developed a view of knowledge and a response to skepticism that is built around the following modification of the tracking account: S knows that *p* if and only if S believes *p* on the basis of a reason that would indicate that *p* is true only if *p* were true. When this condition is met, S's belief *p* has a property that Sosa calls *safety*, and that Luper calls *infallible indication*. In "Indiscernability Skepticism" Luper points out that knowledge as infallible indication supports the principle of closure, for an infallible indicator of the truth of S's belief *p* is also an infallible indicator of the truth of *p*'s logical consequences. Another implication of this view of knowledge is that, as Moore said, we know that skeptical hypotheses do not hold. As for the appeal of skepticism, it can be explained—or explained away—if we consider how easy it is to conflate the tracking condition with the modified indicator condition. Sometimes we apply the tracking condition and side with the skeptic, saying that we do not know that skeptical scenarios fail to hold. We overlook the way the tracking condition undermines the principle of entailment the skeptic needs. At other times we appeal to the modified condition, and side with Moore-style commonsense, saying that the principle of entailment is correct. At such times we may or may not notice the consequence that we know skeptical hypotheses do not hold.

QUESTIONS FOR REFLECTION

1. Moore claims he can prove, as against skeptics, that there is an external world, on the basis of the fact that he has hands. Why does Wittgenstein claim that skepticism cannot be refuted this way? Is he correct? How might Moore respond?

2. Simply insisting that I know I have a hand is not a satisfying response to skepticism. But isn't it still *true* that I know I have a hand, and thus that I know that there is an external world? Must I refute skepticism, using an argument whose premises skeptics would accept, before I can know I have a hand?

3. Wittgenstein says we cannot be mistaken about our worldview, but it is nonsense to say we know it is true. Are these claims consistent? If "I know my worldview is true" is nonsense, can we say the same about "I cannot be mistaken about the truth of my worldview?"

4. Consider the positivist's criterion of meaningfulness, which says that the only meaningful statements are those which are analytic or empirically verifiable. Is this statement meaningful? Is it analytic or empirically verifiable? Is the positivist criterion self-refuting?

5. Might the positivists refute the charge that their criterion of meaningfulness is self-refuting by treating it as a convention scientists adopt? Is there good reason to adopt such a convention?

6. Dretske says we do not know we are brains in vats on the far planet Crouton being deceived and so forth. Stine and Luper say we do. Who is correct, and why?

7. Suppose Fred knows, right now, that *b:* Fred is in Bonaire. Consider the further claim *not-c:* Fred is not a brain in a vat on fair Crouton being deceived into thinking he is in Bonaire. According to Lewis, Fred's claim 'I know *b*,' is true. But that claim would be false if it occurred to Fred that *b* entails *not-c*. Is this position plausible? Why or why not?

8. Are we ever really justified in believing something, according to Klein? If so, when? Is his position plausible?

◇ A COMMON SENSE RESPONSE ◇

23. PROOF OF AN EXTERNAL WORLD

G. E. *Moore*

In the preface to the second edition of Kant's *Critique of Pure Reason* some words occur, which, in Professor Kemp Smith's translation, are rendered as follows:

> It still remains a scandal to philosophy ... that the existence of things outside of us ... must be accepted merely on *faith*, and that, if anyone thinks good to doubt their existence, we are unable to counter his doubts by any satisfactory proof.[1]

It seems clear from these words that Kant thought it a matter of some importance to give a proof of 'the existence of things outside of us' or perhaps rather (for it seems to me possible that the force of the German words is better rendered in this way) of 'the existence of *the* things outside of us'; for had he not thought it important that a proof should be given, he would scarcely have called it a 'scandal' that no proof had been given. And it seems clear also that he thought that the giving of such a proof was a task which fell properly within the province of philosophy; for, if it did not, the fact that no proof had been given could not possibly be a scandal to *philosophy*.

Now, even if Kant was mistaken in both of these two opinions, there seems to me to be no doubt whatever that it is a matter of some importance and also a matter which falls properly within the province of philosophy, to discuss the question what sort of proof, if any, can be given of 'the existence of things outside of us'. And to discuss this question was my object when I began to write the present lecture. But I may say at once that, as you will find, I have only, at most, succeeded in saying a very small part of what ought to be said about it.

The words 'it . . . remains a scandal to philosophy . . . that we are unable . . .' would, taken strictly, imply that, at the moment at which he wrote them, Kant himself was unable to produce a satisfactory proof of the point in question. But I think it is unquestionable that Kant himself did not think that he personally was at the time unable to produce such a proof. On the contrary, in the immediately preceding sentence, he has declared that he has, in the second edition of his *Critique,* to which he is now writing the Preface, given a 'rigorous proof' of this very thing; and has added that he believes this proof of his to be 'the only possible proof'. It is true that in this preceding sentence he does not describe the proof which he has given as a proof of 'the existence of things outside of us' or of 'the existence of the things outside of us', but describes it instead as a proof of 'the objective reality of outer intuition'. But the context leaves no doubt that he is using these two phrases, 'the objective reality of outer intuition' and 'the existence of things (*or* 'the things') outside of us', in such a way that whatever is a proof of the first is also necessarily a proof of the second. We must, therefore, suppose that when he speaks as if *we* are unable to give a satisfactory proof, he does not mean to say that he himself, as well as others, is *at the moment* unable; but rather that, until he discovered the proof which he has given, both he himself and everybody else *were* unable. Of course, if he is right in thinking that he has given a satisfactory proof, the state of things which he describes came to an end as soon as his proof was published. As soon as that happened, anyone who read it was able to give a satisfactory proof by simply repeating that which Kant had given, and the 'scandal' to philosophy had been removed once for all.

If, therefore, it were certain that the proof of the point in question given by Kant in the second edition is a satisfactory proof, it would be certain that at least one satisfactory proof can be given; and all that would remain of the question which I said I proposed to discuss would be, firstly, the question as to what *sort* of a proof this of Kant's is, and secondly the question whether (contrary to Kant's own opinion) there may not perhaps be other proofs, of the same or of a different sort, which are also satisfactory. But I think it is by no means certain that Kant's proof is satisfactory. I think it is by no means certain that he did succeed in removing once for all the state of affairs which he

considered to be a scandal to philosophy. And I think, therefore, that the question whether it is possible to give *any* satisfactory proof of the point in question still deserves discussion.

But what is the point in question? I think it must be owned that the expression 'things outside of us' is rather an odd expression, and an expression the meaning of which is certainly not perfectly clear. It would have sounded less odd if, instead of 'things outside of us' I had said 'external things', and perhaps also the meaning of this expression would have seemed to be clearer; and I think we make the meaning of 'external things' clearer still if we explain that this phrase has been regularly used by philosophers as short for 'things external to *our minds*'. The fact is that there has been a long philosophical tradition, in accordance with which the three expressions 'external things', 'things external to *us*', and 'things external to *our minds*' have been used as equivalent to one another, and have, each of them, been used as if they needed no explanation. The origin of this usage I do not know. It occurs already in Descartes; and since he uses the expressions as if they needed no explanation, they had presumably been used with the same meaning before. Of the three, it seems to me that the expression 'external to *our minds*' is the clearest, since it at least makes clear that what is meant is not 'external to *our bodies*'; whereas both the other expressions might be taken to mean this: and indeed there has been a good deal of confusion, even among philosophers, as to the relation of the two conceptions 'external things' and 'things external to *our bodies*'. But even the expression 'things external to our minds' seems to me to be far from perfectly clear; and if I am to make really clear what I mean by 'proof of the existence of things outside of us', I cannot do it by merely saying that by 'outside of us' I mean 'external to our minds'.

There is a passage (*K.d.r.V.,* A 373) in which Kant himself says that the expression 'outside of us' 'carries with it an unavoidable ambiguity'. He says that 'sometimes it means something which exists as *a thing in itself* distinct from us, and sometimes something which merely belongs to external *appearance*'; he calls things which are 'outside of us' in the first of these two senses 'objects which might be called external in the transcendental sense', and things which are so in the second '*empirically external* objects'; and he says finally that, in order to remove all uncertainty as to the latter conception, he will distinguish empirically external objects from objects which might be called 'external' in the transcendental sense, 'by calling them outright things which are *to be met with in space*'.

I think that this last phrase of Kant's 'things which are to be met with in space', does indicate fairly clearly what sort of things it is with regard to which I wish to inquire what sort of proof, if any, can be given that there are any things of that sort. My body, the bodies of other men, the bodies of animals, plants of all sorts, stones, mountains, the sun, the moon, stars, and planets, houses and other buildings, manufactured articles of all sorts—chairs, tables, pieces of paper, etc., are all of them 'things which are to be met with in space'. In short, all things of the sort that philosophers have been used to call 'physical objects', 'material things', or 'bodies' obviously come under this head. But the phrase 'things that are to be met with in space' can be naturally understood as applying also in cases where the names 'physical object', 'material thing', or 'body' can hardly be applied. For instance, shadows are sometimes to be met with in space, although they could hardly be properly called 'physical objects', 'material things', or 'bodies'; and although in one usage of the term 'thing' it would not be proper to call a shadow a 'thing', yet the phrase 'things which are to be met with in space' can be naturally understood as synonymous with 'whatever can be met with in space', and this is an expression which can quite properly be understood to include shadows. I wish the phrase 'things which are to be met with in space' to be understood in this wide sense; so that if a proof can be found that there ever have been as many as two different shadows it will follow at once that there have been at least two 'things which were to be met with in space', and this proof will be as good a proof of the point in question as would be a proof that there have been at least two 'physical objects' of no matter what sort.

The phrase 'things which are to be met with in space' can, therefore, be naturally understood as having a very wide meaning—a meaning even wider than that of 'physical object' or 'body', wide as is the meaning of these latter expressions. But wide as is its meaning, it is not, in one respect, so wide as that of another phrase which Kant uses as if it were equivalent to this one; and a comparison between the two will, I think, serve to make still clearer what sort of things it is with regard to which I wish to ask what proof, if any, can be given that there are such things.

The other phrase which Kant uses as if it were equivalent to 'things which are to be met with in space' is used by him in the sentence immediately preceding that previously quoted in which he declares that the expression 'things outside of us' 'carries with it an unavoidable ambiguity' (A 373). In this preceding sentence he says that an 'empirical object' 'is called *external*, if it is presented (*vorgestellt*) in space'. He treats, therefore, the phrase 'presented in space' as if it were equivalent to 'to be met with in space'. But it is easy to find examples of 'things', of which it can hardly be denied that they are 'presented in space', but of which it could, quite naturally, be emphatically denied that they are 'to be met with in space'. Consider, for instance, the following description of one set of circumstances under which what some psychologists have called a 'negative after-image' and others a 'negative after-sensation' can be obtained. 'If, after looking steadfastly at a white patch on a black ground, the eye be turned to a white ground, a grey patch is seen for some little time.' (Foster's *Text-book of Physiology*, IV, iii, 3, page 1266; quoted in Stout's *Manual of Psychology*, 3rd edition, page 280.) Upon reading these words recently, I took the trouble to cut out of a piece of white paper a four-pointed star, to place it on a black ground, to 'look steadfastly' at it, and then to turn my eyes to a white sheet of paper: and I did find that I saw a grey patch for some little time—I not only saw a grey patch, but I saw it *on* the white ground, and also this grey patch was of roughly the same shape as the white four-pointed star at which I had 'looked steadfastly' just before—it also was a four-pointed star. I repeated this simple experiment successfully several times. Now each of those grey four-pointed stars, one of which I saw in each experiment, was what is called an 'after-image' or 'after-sensation'; and can anybody deny that each of these after-images can be quite properly said to have been 'presented in space'? I saw each of them on a real white background, and, if so, each of them was 'presented' on a real white background. But though they were 'presented in space' everybody, I think, would feel that it was gravely misleading to say that they were 'to be met with in space'.

The white star at which I 'looked steadfastly', the black ground on which I saw it, and the white ground on which I saw the after-images, were, of course, 'to be met with in space': they were, in fact, 'physical objects' or surfaces of physical objects. But one important difference between them, on the one hand, and the grey after-images, on the other, can be quite naturally expressed by saying that the latter were *not* 'to be met with in space'. And one reason why this is so is, I think, plain. To say that so and so was at a given time 'to be met with in space' naturally suggests that there are conditions such that *any one* who fulfilled them might, conceivably, have 'perceived' the 'thing' in question—might have seen it, if it was a visible object, have felt it, if it was a tangible one, have heard it, if it was a sound, have smelt it, if it was a smell. When I say that the white four-pointed paper star, at which I looked steadfastly, was a 'physical object' and was 'to be met with in space', I am implying that *anyone,* who had been in the room at the time, and who had normal eyesight and a normal sense of touch, might have seen and felt it. But, in the case of those grey after-images which I saw, it is not conceivable that anyone besides myself should have seen any one of them. It is, of course, quite conceivable that other people, if they had been in the room with me at the time, and had carried out the same experiment which I carried out, would have seen grey after-images *very like* one of those which I saw: there is no absurdity in supposing even that they might have seen after-images *exactly* like one of those which I saw. But there is an absurdity in supposing that any one of the after-images which I saw could also have been seen by anyone else: in supposing that two different people can ever see the *very same* after-image. One reason, then, why we should say that none of those grey after-images which I saw was 'to be met with in space', although each of them was certainly 'presented in space' to me, is simply that none of them could conceivably have been seen by anyone else. It is natural so to understand the phrase 'to be met with in space', that to say of anything which a man perceived that it was to be met with in space is to say that it might have been perceived by *others* as well as by the man in question.

Negative after-images of the kind described are, therefore, one example of 'things' which, though they must be allowed to be 'presented in space', are

nevertheless *not* 'to be met with in space', and are *not* 'external to our minds' in the sense with which we shall be concerned. And two other important examples may be given.

The first is this. It is well known that people sometimes see things double, an occurrence which has also been described by psychologists by saying that they have a 'double image', or two 'images', of some object at which they are looking. In such cases it would certainly be quite natural to say that each of the two 'images' is 'presented in space': they are seen, one in one place, and the other in another, in just the same sense in which each of those grey after-images which I saw was seen at a particular place on the white background at which I was looking. But it would be utterly unnatural to say that, when I have a double image, each of the two images is 'to be met with in space'. On the contrary it is quite certain that *both* of them are not 'to be met with in space'. If both were, it would follow that somebody else might see the *very same* two images which I see; and, though there is no absurdity in supposing that another person might see a pair of images exactly similar to a pair which I see, there is an absurdity in supposing that anyone else might see the *same identical pair.* In every case, then, in which anyone sees anything double, we have an example of at least one 'thing' which, though 'presented in space' is certainly not 'to be met with in space'.

And the second important example is this. Bodily pains can, in general, be quite properly said to be 'presented in space'. When I have a toothache, I feel it *in* a particular region of my jaw or *in* a particular tooth; when I make a cut on my finger smart by putting iodine on it, I feel the pain in a particular place in my finger; and a man whose leg has been amputated may feel a pain *in* a place where his foot might have been if he had not lost it. It is certainly perfectly natural to understand the phrase 'presented in space' in such a way that if, in the sense illustrated, a pain is felt *in* a particular place, that pain is 'presented in space'. And yet of pains it would be quite unnatural to say that they are 'to be met with in space', for the same reason as in the case of after-images or double images. It is quite conceivable that another person should feel a pain exactly like one which I feel, but there is an absurdity in supposing that he could feel *numerically the same* pain which I feel. And pains are in fact a typical example of the sort of 'things' of which philosophers say that they are *not* 'external' to our minds, but 'within' them. Of any pain which *I* feel they would say that it is necessarily *not* external to my mind but *in* it.

And finally it is, I think, worthwhile to mention one other class of 'things', which are certainly not 'external' objects and certainly not 'to be met with in space', in the sense with which I am concerned, but which yet some philosophers would be inclined to say are 'presented in space', though they are not 'presented in space' in quite the same sense in which pains, double images, and negative after-images of the sort I described are so. If you look at an electric light and then close your eyes, it sometimes happens that you see, for some little time, against the dark background which you usually see when your eyes are shut, a bright patch similar in shape to the light at which you have just been looking. Such a bright patch, if you see one, is another example of what some psychologists have called 'after-images' and others 'after-sensations'; but, unlike the negative after-images of which I spoke before, it is seen when your eyes are shut. Of such an after-image, seen with closed eyes, some philosophers might be inclined to say that this image too was 'presented in space', although it is certainly not 'to be met with in space'. They would be inclined to say that it is 'presented in space', because it certainly is presented as at some little distance from the person who is seeing it: and how can a thing be presented as at some little distance from me, without being 'presented in space'? Yet there is an important difference between such after-images, seen with closed eyes, and after-images of the sort I previously described—a difference which might lead other philosophers to deny that these after-images, seen with closed eyes, are 'presented in space' at all. It is a difference which can be expressed by saying that when your eyes are shut, you are not seeing any part of *physical* space at all—of the space which is referred to when we talk of 'things which are to be met with in *space*'. An after-image seen with closed eyes certainly is presented in *a* space, but it may be questioned whether it is proper to say that it is presented in *space*.

It is clear, then, I think, that by no means everything which can naturally be said to be 'presented in space' can also be naturally said to be 'a thing which is to be met with in space'. Some of the 'things', which

are presented in space, are very emphatically *not* to be met with in space: or, to use another phrase, which may be used to convey the same notion, they are emphatically *not* 'physical realities' at all. The conception 'presented in space' is therefore, in one respect, much wider than the conception 'to be met with in space': many 'things' fall under the first conception which do not fall under the second—many after-images, one at least of the pair of 'images' seen whenever anyone sees double, and most bodily pains, are 'presented in space', though none of them are to be met with in space. From the fact that a 'thing' is presented in space, it by no means follows that it is to be met with in space. But just as the first conception is, in one respect, wider than the second, so, in another, the second is wider than the first. For there are many 'things' to be met with in space, of which it is not true that they are presented in space. From the fact that a 'thing' is to be met with in space, it by no means follows that it is presented in space. I have taken 'to be met with in space' to imply, as I think it naturally may, that a 'thing' *might be* perceived; but from the fact that a thing *might be* perceived, it does not follow that it *is* perceived; and if it is not actually perceived, then it will not be presented in space. It is characteristic of the sorts of 'things', including shadows, which I have described as 'to be met with in space', that there is no absurdity in supposing with regard to any one of them which *is*, at a given time, perceived, both (I) that it might have existed at that very time, without being perceived; (2) that it might have existed at another time, without being perceived at that other time; and (3) that during the whole period of its existence, it need not have been perceived at any time at all. There is, therefore, no absurdity in supposing that many things, which were at one time to be met with in space, never were 'presented' at any time at all, and that many things which *are* to be met with in space now, are not now 'presented' and also never were and never will be. To use a Kantian phrase, the conception of 'things which are to be met with in space' embraces not only objects of actual experience, but also objects of *possible* experience; and from the fact that a thing is or was an object of *possible* experience, it by no means follows that it either was or is or will be 'presented' at all.

I hope that what I have now said may have served to make clear enough what sorts of 'things' I was originally referring to as 'things outside us' or 'things external to our minds'. I said that I thought that Kant's phrase 'things that are to be met with in space' indicated fairly clearly the sorts of 'things' in question; and I have tried to make the range clearer still, by pointing out that this phrase only serves the purpose, if (a) you understand it in a sense, in which many 'things', e.g. after-images, double images, bodily pains, which might be said to be 'presented in space', are nevertheless *not* to be reckoned as 'things that are to be met with in space', and (b) you realize clearly that there is no contradiction in supposing that there have been and are 'to be met with in space' things which never have been, are not now, and never will be perceived, nor in supposing that among those of them which have at some time been perceived many existed at times at which they were not being perceived. I think it will now be clear to everyone that, since I do not reckon as 'external things' after-images, double images, and bodily pains, I also should not reckon as 'external things', any of the 'images' which we often 'see with the mind's eye' when we are awake, nor any of those which we see when we are asleep and dreaming; and also that I was so using the expression 'external' that from the fact that a man was at a given time having a visual hallucination, it will follow that he was seeing at that time something which was *not* 'external' to his mind, and from the fact that he was at a given time having an auditory hallucination, it will follow that he was at the time hearing a sound which was *not* 'external' to his mind. But I certainly have not made my use of these phrases, 'external to our minds' and 'to be met with in space', so clear that in the case of every kind of 'thing' which might be suggested, you would be able to tell at once whether I should or should not reckon it as 'external to our minds' and 'to be met with in space'. For instance, I have said nothing which makes it quite clear whether a reflection which I see in a looking-glass is or is not to be regarded as 'a thing that is to be met with in space' and 'external to our minds', nor have I said anything which makes it quite clear whether the sky is or is not to be so regarded. In the case of the sky, everyone, I think, would feel that it was quite inappropriate to talk of it as 'a thing that is to be met with in space'; and most people, I think, would feel a strong reluctance to affirm, without qualification, that reflections which people see in looking-glasses are 'to be met

with in space'. And yet neither the sky nor reflections seen in mirrors are in the same position as bodily pains or after-images in the respect which I have emphasized as a reason for saying of these latter that they are *not* to be met with in space—namely that there is an absurdity in supposing that *the very same* pain which I feel could be felt by someone else or that *the very same* after-image which I see could be seen by someone else. In the case of reflections in mirrors we should quite naturally, in certain circumstances, use language which implies that another person may see the same reflection which we see. We might quite naturally say to a friend: 'Do you see that reddish reflection in the water there? I can't make out what it's a reflection of', just as we might say, pointing to a distant hill-side: 'Do you see that white speck on the hill over there? I can't make out what it is.' And in the case of the sky, it is quite obviously *not* absurd to say that other people see it as well as I.

It must, therefore, be admitted that I have not made my use of the phrase 'things to be met with in space', nor therefore that of 'external to our minds', which the former was used to explain, so clear that in the case of every kind of 'thing' which may be mentioned, there will be no doubt whatever as to whether things of that kind are or are not 'to be met with in space' or 'external to our minds'. But this lack of a clear-cut definition of the expression 'things that are to be met with in space', does not, so far as I can see, matter for my present purpose. For my present purpose it is, I think, sufficient if I make clear, in the case of many kinds of things, that I am so using the phrase 'things that are to be met with in space', that, in the case of each of these kinds, from the proposition that there are things of that kind it *follows* that there are things to be met with in space. And I have, in fact, given a list (though by no means an exhaustive one) of kinds of things which are related to my use of the expression 'things that are to be met with in space' in this way. I mentioned among others the bodies of men and of animals, plants, stars, houses, chairs, and shadows; and I want now to emphasize that I am so using 'things to be met with in space' that, in the case of each of these kinds of 'things', from the proposition that there are 'things' of that kind it *follows* that there are things to be met with in space: e.g. from the proposition that there are plants or that plants exist it *follows* that there are things to be met with in space, from the proposition that shadows exist, it *follows* that there are things to be met with in space, and so on, in the case of all the kinds of 'things' which I mentioned in my first list. That this should be clear is sufficient for my purpose, because, if it is clear, then it will also be clear that, as I implied before, if you have proved that two plants exist, or that a plant and a dog exist, or that a dog and a shadow exist, etc. etc., you will *ipso facto* have proved that there are things to be met with in space: you will not require *also* to give a separate proof that from the proposition that there are plants it *does* follow that there are things to be met with in space.

Now with regard to the expression 'things that are to be met with in space' I think it will readily be believed that I may be using it in a sense such that no proof is required that from 'plants exist' there follows 'there are things to be met with in space'; but with regard to the phrase 'things external to our minds' I think the case is different. People may be inclined to say: 'I can see quite clearly that from the proposition "At least two dogs exist at the present moment" there *follows* the proposition "At least two things are to be met with in space at the present moment", so that if you can prove that there are two dogs in existence at the present moment you will *ipso facto* have proved that two things at least are to be met with in space at the present moment. I can see that you do not also require a separate proof that from "Two dogs exist" "Two things are to be met with in space" *does* follow; it is quite obvious that there couldn't be a dog which wasn't to be met with in space. But it is not by any means so clear to me that if you can prove that there are two dogs or two shadows, you will *ipso facto* have proved that there are two things *external to our minds*. Isn't it possible that a dog, though it certainly must be "to be met with in space", might *not* be an external object—an object external to our minds? Isn't a separate proof required that anything that is to be met with in space must be external to our minds? Of course, if you are using "external" as a mere synonym for "to be met with in space", no proof will be required that dogs are external objects: in that case, if you can prove that two dogs exist, you will *ipso facto* have proved that there are some external things. But I find it difficult to believe that you, or anybody else, do really use "external" as a mere synonym for "to be met with in space"; and if you don't, isn't some proof

required that whatever is to be met with in space must be external to our minds?'

Now Kant, as we saw, asserts that the phrases 'outside of us' or 'external' are in fact used in two very different senses; and with regard to one of these two senses, that which he calls the 'transcendental' sense, and which he tries to explain by saying that it is a sense in which 'external' means 'existing *as a thing in itself* distinct from us', it is notorious that he himself held that things which are to be met with in space are *not* 'external' in that sense. There is, therefore, according to him, *a* sense of 'external', a sense in which the word has been commonly used by philosophers—such that, if 'external' be used in that sense, then from the proposition 'Two dogs exist' it will *not* follow that there are some external things. What this supposed sense is I do not think that Kant himself ever succeeded in explaining clearly; nor do I know of any reason for supposing that philosophers ever have used 'external' in a sense, such that in *that* sense things that are to be met with in space are *not* external. But how about the other sense, in which, according to Kant, the word 'external' has been commonly used—that which he calls 'empirically external'? How is this conception related to the conception 'to be met with in space'? It may be noticed that, in the passages which I quoted (A 373), Kant himself does not tell us at all clearly what he takes to be the proper answer to this question. He only makes the rather odd statement that, in order to remove all uncertainty as to the conception 'empirically external', he will distinguish objects to which it applies from those which might be called 'external' in the transcendental sense, by 'calling them outright things which are *to be met with in space*'. These odd words certainly suggest, as one possible interpretation of them, that in Kant's opinion the conception 'empirically external' is *identical* with the conception 'to be met with in space'—that he does think that 'external', when used in this second sense, is a mere synonym for 'to be met with in space'. But, if this is his meaning, I do find it very difficult to believe that he is right. Have philosophers, in fact, ever used 'external' as a mere synonym for 'to be met with in space'? Does he himself do so?

I do not think they have, nor that he does himself; and, in order to explain how they have used it, and how the two conceptions 'external to our minds' and 'to be met with in space' are related to one another, I think it is important expressly to call attention to a fact which hitherto I have only referred to incidentally: namely the fact that those who talk of certain things as 'external to' our minds, do, in general, as we should naturally expect, talk of other 'things', with which they wish to contrast the first, as 'in' our minds. It has, of course, been often pointed out that when 'in' is thus used, followed by 'my mind', 'your mind', 'his mind', etc., 'in' is being used metaphorically. And there are some metaphorical uses of 'in', followed by such expressions, which occur in common speech, and which we all understand quite well. For instance, we all understand such expressions as 'I had you in mind, when I made that arrangement' or 'I had you in mind, when I said that there are some people who can't bear to touch a spider'. In these cases 'I was thinking of you' can be used to mean the same as 'I had you in mind'. But it is quite certain that this particular metaphorical use of 'in' is not the one in which philosophers are using it when they contrast what is 'in' my mind with what is 'external' to it. On the contrary, in their use of 'external', you will be external to my mind even at a moment when I have you in mind. If we want to discover what this peculiar metaphorical use of '*in* my mind' is, which is such that nothing, which is, in the sense we are now concerned with, 'external' to my mind, can ever be 'in' it, we need, I think, to consider instances of the sort of 'things' which they would say are 'in' my mind in this special sense. I have already mentioned three such instances, which are, I think, sufficient for my present purpose: any bodily pain which I feel, any after-image which I see with my eyes shut, and any image which I 'see' when I am asleep and dreaming, are typical examples of the sort of 'thing' of which philosophers have spoken as '*in* my mind'. And there is no doubt, I think, that when they have spoken of such things as my body, a sheet of paper, a star—in short 'physical objects' generally—as 'external', they have meant to emphasize some important difference which they feel to exist between such things as these and such 'things' as a pain, an after-image seen with closed eyes, and a dream-image. But *what* difference? What difference do they feel to exist between a bodily pain which I feel or an after-image which I see with closed eyes, on the one hand, and my body itself, on the other—what difference which leads them to say that whereas the bodily pain and the after-image are 'in' my mind, my body itself is

not 'in' my mind—not even when I am feeling it and seeing it or thinking of it? I have already said that one difference which there is between the two, is that my body is to be met with in space, whereas the bodily pain and the after-image are not. But I think it would be quite wrong to say that this is *the* difference which has led philosophers to speak of the two latter as 'in' my mind, and of my body as *not* 'in' my mind.

The question what the difference is which has led them to speak in this way, is not, I think, at all an easy question to answer; but I am going to try to give, in brief outline, what I *think* is a right answer.

It should, I think, be noted, first of all, that the use of the word 'mind', which is being adopted when it is said that any bodily pains which I feel are 'in my mind', is one which is not quite in accordance with any usage common in ordinary speech, although we are very familiar with it in philosophy. Nobody, I think, would say that bodily pains (which I feel) are 'in my mind', unless he was also prepared to say that it is *with* my mind that I feel bodily pains; and to say this latter is, I think, not quite in accordance with common non-philosophic usage. It is natural enough to say that it is with my mind that I remember, and think, and imagine, and feel *mental* pains—e.g. disappointment, but not, I think, quite so natural to say that it is with my mind that I feel *bodily* pains, e.g. a severe headache; and perhaps even less natural to say that it is with my mind that I see and hear and smell and taste. There is, however, a well-established philosophical usage according to which seeing, hearing, smelling, tasting, and having a bodily pain are just as much *mental* occurrences or processes as are remembering, or thinking, or imagining. This usage was, I think, adopted by philosophers, because they saw a real resemblance between such statements as 'I saw a cat', 'I heard a clap of thunder', 'I smelt a strong smell of onions', 'My finger smarted horribly', on the one hand, and such statements as 'I remembered having seen him', 'I was thinking out a plan of action', 'I pictured the scene to myself', 'I felt bitterly disappointed', on the other—a resemblance which puts all these statements in one class together, as contrasted with other statements in which 'I' or 'my' is used, such as, e.g., 'I was less than four feet high', 'I was lying on my back', 'My hair was very long'. What is the resemblance in question? It is a resemblance which might be expressed by saying that all the first eight statements are the sort of statements which furnish data for psychology, while the three latter are not. It is also a resemblance which may be expressed, in a way now common among philosophers, by saying that in the case of all the first eight statements, if we make the statement more specific by adding a date, we get a statement such that, if it is true, then it *follows* that I was 'having an experience' at the date in question, whereas this does not hold for the three last statements. For instance, if it is true that I saw a cat between 12 noon and 5 minutes past, today, it *follows* that I was 'having some experience' between 12 noon and 5 minutes past, today; whereas from the proposition that I was less than four feet high in December 1877, it does not *follow* that I had any experiences in December 1877. But this philosophic use of 'having an experience' is one which itself needs explanation, since it is not identical with any use of the expression that is established in common speech. An explanation, however, which is, I think, adequate for the purpose, can be given by saying that a philosopher, who was following this usage, would say that I was at a given time 'having an experience' if and only if either (1) I was conscious at the time or (2) I was dreaming at the time or (3) something else was true of me at the time, which resembled what is true of me when I am conscious and when I am dreaming, in a certain very obvious respect in which what is true of me when I am dreaming resembles what is true of me when I am conscious, and in which what would be true of me, if at any time, for instance, I had a vision, would resemble both. This explanation is, of course, in some degree vague; but I think it is clear enough for our purpose. It amounts to saying that, in this philosophic usage of 'having an experience', it would be said of me that I was, at a given time, having *no* experience, if I was at the time neither conscious nor dreaming nor having a vision nor *anything else of the sort;* and, of course, this is vague in so far as it has not been specified what else would be *of the sort:* this is left to be gathered from the instances given. But I think this is sufficient: often at night when I am asleep, I am neither conscious nor dreaming nor having a vision nor *anything else of the sort*—that is to say, I am having no experiences. If this explanation of this philosophic usage of 'having an experience' is clear enough, then I think that what has been meant by saying that any pain which I feel or any after-image which I see with my eyes closed is 'in my

mind', can be explained by saying that what is meant is neither more nor less than that there would be a contradiction in supposing *that very same pain* or *that very same after-image* to have existed at a time at which I was having no experience; or, in other words, that from the proposition, with regard to any time, that *that* pain or *that* after-image existed at that time, it *follows* that I was having some experience at the time in question. And if so, then we can say that the felt difference between bodily pains which I feel and after-images which I see, on the one hand, and my body on the other, which has led philosophers to say that any such pain or after-image is 'in my mind', whereas my body *never* is but is always 'outside of' or 'external to' my mind, is just this, that whereas there is a contradiction in supposing a pain which I feel or an after-image which I see to exist at a time when I am having no experience, there is no contradiction in supposing my body to exist at a time when I am having no experience; and we can even say, I think, that just this and nothing more is what they have meant by these puzzling and misleading phrases 'in my mind' and 'external to my mind'.

But now, if to say of anything, e.g. my body, that it is external to *my* mind, means merely that from a proposition to the effect that it existed at a specified time, there in no case follows the further proposition that *I* was having an experience at the time in question, then to say of anything that it is external to *our* minds, will mean similarly that from a proposition to the effect that it existed at a specified time, it in no case follows that any of *us* were having experiences at the time in question. And if by *our* minds be meant, as is, I think, usually meant, the minds of human beings living on the earth, then it will follow that any pains which animals may feel, any after-images they may see, any experiences they may have, though not external to *their* minds, yet are external to *ours*. And this at once makes plain how different is the conception 'external to our minds' from the conception 'to be met with in space'; for, of course, pains which animals feel or after-images which they see are no more to be met with in space than are pains which *we* feel or after-images which *we* see. From the proposition that there are external objects—objects that are not in any of *our* minds, it does *not* follow that there are things to be met with in space; and hence 'external to our minds' is not a mere synonym for 'to be met with in space': that is to say, 'external to our minds' and 'to be met with in space' are two different conceptions. And the true relation between these conceptions seems to me to be this. We have already seen that there are ever so many kinds of 'things', such that, in the case of each of these kinds, from the proposition that there is at least one thing of that kind there *follows* the proposition that there is at least one thing to be met with in space: e.g. this follows from 'There is at least one star', from 'There is at least one human body', from 'There is at least one shadow', etc. And I think we can say that of every kind of thing of which this is true, it is also true that from the proposition that there is at least one 'thing' of that kind there *follows* the proposition that there is at least one thing external to our minds: e.g. from 'There is at least one star' there follows not only 'There is at least one thing to be met with in space' but also 'There is at least one external thing', and similarly in all other cases. My reason for saying this is as follows. Consider any kind of thing, such that anything of that kind, if there is anything of it, must be 'to be met with in space': e.g. consider the kind 'soap-bubble'. If I say of anything which I am perceiving, 'That is a soap-bubble', I am, it seems to me, certainly implying that there would be no contradiction in asserting that it existed before I perceived it and that it will continue to exist, even if I cease to perceive it. This seems to me to be part of what is meant by saying that it is a real soap-bubble, as distinguished, for instance, from an hallucination of a soap-bubble. Of course, it by no means follows, that if it really is a soap-bubble, it did in fact exist before I perceived it or will continue to exist after I cease to perceive it: soap-bubbles are an example of a kind of 'physical object' and 'thing to be met with in space', in the case of which it is notorious that particular specimens of the kind often do exist only so long as they are perceived by a particular person. But a thing which I perceive would not be a soap-bubble unless its existence at any given time were *logically independent* of my perception of it at that time; unless that is to say, from the proposition, with regard to a particular time, that it existed at that time, it *never* follows that I perceived it at that time. But, if it is true that it would not be a soap-bubble, unless it *could* have existed at any given time without being perceived by me at that time, it is certainly also true that it would not be a soap-bubble, unless it *could* have existed at any given time, without its being true that I was having any

experience of any kind at the time in question: it would not be a soap-bubble, unless, whatever time you take, from the proposition that it existed at that time it does *not* follow that I was having any experience at that time. That is to say, from the proposition with regard to anything which I am perceiving that it is a soap-bubble, there *follows* the proposition that it is external to *my* mind. But if, when I say that anything which I perceive is a soap-bubble, I am implying that it is external to *my* mind, I am, I think, certainly also implying that it is also external to all other minds: I am implying that it is not a thing of a sort such that things of that sort *can* only exist at a time when somebody is having an experience. I think, therefore, that from any proposition of the form 'There's a soap-bubble!' there does really *follow* the proposition 'There's an external object!' 'There's an object external to *all* our minds!' And, if this is true of the kind 'soap-bubble', it is certainly also true of any other kind (including the kind 'unicorn') which is such that, if there are any things of that kind, it follows that there are *some* things to be met with in space.

I think, therefore, that in the case of all kinds of 'things', which are such that if there is a pair of things, both of which are of one of these kinds, or a pair of things one of which is of one of them and one of them of another, then it will follow at once that there are some things to be met with in space, it is true also that if I can prove that there are a pair of things, one of which is of one of these kinds and another of another, or a pair both of which are of one of them, then I shall have proved *ipso facto* that there are at least two 'things outside of us'. That is to say, if I can prove that there exist now both a sheet of paper and a human hand, I shall have proved that there are now 'things outside of us'; if I can prove that there exist now both a shoe and sock, I shall have proved that there are now 'things outside of us'; etc.; and similarly I shall have proved it, if I can prove that there exist now two sheets of paper, or two human hands, or two shoes, or two socks, etc. Obviously, then, there are thousands of different things such that, if, at any time, I can prove any one of them, I shall have proved the existence of things outside of us. Cannot I prove any of these things?

It seems to me that, so far from its being true, as Kant declares to be his opinion, that there is only one possible proof of the existence of things outside of us, namely the one which he has given, I can now give a large number of different proofs, each of which is a perfectly rigorous proof; and that at many other times I have been in a position to give many others. I can prove now, for instance, that two human hands exist. How? By holding up my two hands, and saying, as I make a certain gesture with the right hand, 'Here is one hand', and adding, as I make a certain gesture with the left, 'and here is another'. And if, by doing this, I have proved *ipso facto* the existence of external things, you will all see that I can also do it now in numbers of other ways: there is no need to multiply examples.

But did I prove just now that two human hands were then in existence? I do want to insist that I did; that the proof which I gave was a perfectly rigorous one; and that it is perhaps impossible to give a better or more rigorous proof of anything whatever. Of course, it would not have been a proof unless three conditions were satisfied; namely (1) unless the premiss which I adduced as proof of the conclusion was different from the conclusion I adduced it to prove; (2) unless the premiss which I adduced was something which I *knew* to be the case, and not merely something which I believed but which was by no means certain, or something which, though in fact true, I did not know to be so; and (3) unless the conclusion did really follow from the premiss. But all these three conditions were in fact satisfied by my proof. (1) The premiss which I adduced in proof was quite certainly different from the conclusion, for the conclusion was merely 'Two human hands exist at this moment'; but the premiss was something far more specific than this—something which I expressed by showing you my hands, making certain gestures, and saying the words 'Here is one hand, and here is another'. It is quite obvious that the two were different, because it is quite obvious that the conclusion might have been true, even if the premiss had been false. In asserting the premiss I was asserting much more than I was asserting in asserting the conclusion. (2) I certainly did at the moment *know* that which I expressed by the combination of certain gestures with saying the words 'There is one hand and here is another'. I *knew* that there was one hand in the place indicated by combining a certain gesture with my first utterance of 'here' and that there was another in the different place indicated by combining a certain gesture with my second utterance of 'here'. How absurd it would be to suggest

that I did not know it, but only believed it, and that perhaps it was not the case! You might as well suggest that I do not know that I am now standing up and talking—that perhaps after all I'm not, and that it's not quite certain that I am! And finally (3) it is quite certain that the conclusion did follow from the premiss. This is as certain as it is that if there is one hand here and another here *now*, then it follows that there are two hands in existence *now*.

My proof, then, of the existence of things outside of us did satisfy three of the conditions necessary for a rigorous proof. Are there any other conditions necessary for a rigorous proof, such that perhaps it did not satisfy one of them? Perhaps there may be; I do not know; but I do want to emphasize that, so far as I can see, we all of us do constantly take proofs of this sort as absolutely conclusive proofs of certain conclusions—as finally settling certain questions, as to which we were previously in doubt. Suppose, for instance, it were a question whether there were as many as three misprints on a certain page in a certain book. A says there are, B is inclined to doubt it. How could A prove that he is right? Surely he *could* prove it by taking the book, turning to the page, and pointing to three separate places on it, saying 'There's one misprint here, another here, and another here': surely that is a method by which it *might* be proved! Of course, A would not have proved, by doing this, that there were at least three misprints on the page in question, unless it was certain that there was a misprint in each of the places to which he pointed. But to say that he *might* prove it in this way, is to say that it *might* be certain that there was. And if such a thing as that could ever be certain, then assuredly it was certain just now that there was one hand in one of the two places I indicated and another in the other.

I did, then, just now, give a proof that there were *then* external objects; and obviously, if I did, I could *then* have given many other proofs of the same sort that there were external objects *then*, and could now give many proofs of the same sort that there are external objects *now*.

But, if what I am asked to do is to prove that external objects have existed *in the past*, then I can give many different proofs of this also, but proofs which are in important respects of a different *sort* from those just given. And I want to emphasize that, when Kant says it is a scandal not to be able to give a proof of the existence of external objects, a proof of their existence in the past would certainly *help* to remove the scandal of which he is speaking. He says that, if it occurs to anyone to question their existence, we ought to be able to confront him with a satisfactory proof. But by a person who questions their existence, he certainly means not merely a person who questions whether any exist at the moment of speaking, but a person who questions whether any have *ever* existed; and a proof that some have existed in the past would certainly therefore be relevant to *part* of what such a person is questioning. How then can I prove that there have been external objects in the past? Here is one proof. I can say: 'I held up two hands above this desk not very long ago; therefore two hands existed not very long ago; therefore at least two external objects have existed at some time in the past, Q.E.D.' This is a perfectly good proof, provided I *know* what is asserted in the premiss. But I *do* know that I held up two hands above this desk not very long ago. As a matter of fact, in this case you all know it too. There's no doubt whatever that I did. Therefore I have given a perfectly conclusive proof that external objects have existed in the past; and you will all see at once that, if this is a conclusive proof, I could have given many others of the same sort, and could now give many others. But it is also quite obvious that this sort of proof differs in important respects from the sort of proof I gave just now that there were two hands existing *then*.

I have, then, given two conclusive proofs of the existence of external objects. The first was a proof that two human hands existed at the time when I gave the proof; the second was a proof that two human hands had existed at a time previous to that at which I gave the proof. These proofs were of a different sort in important respects. And I pointed out that I could have given, then, many other conclusive proofs of both sorts. It is also obvious that I could give many others of both sorts now. So that, if these are the sort of proof that is wanted, nothing is easier than to prove the existence of external objects.

But now I am perfectly well aware that, in spite of all that I have said, many philosophers will still feel that I have not given any satisfactory proof of the point in question. And I want briefly, in conclusion, to say something as to why this dissatisfaction with my proofs should be felt.

One reason why, is, I think, this. Some people understand 'proof of an external world' as including a proof of things which I haven't attempted to prove and haven't proved. It is not quite easy to say *what* it is that they want proved—*what* it is that is such that unless they got a proof of it, they would not say that they had a proof of the existence of external things; but I can make an approach to explaining what they want by saying that if I had proved the propositions which I used as *premisses* in my two proofs, then they would perhaps admit that I had proved the existence of external things, but, in the absence of such a proof (which, of course, I have neither given nor attempted to give), they will say that I have not given what they mean by a proof of the existence of external things. In other words, they want a proof of what I assert *now* when I hold up my hands and say 'Here's one hand and here's another'; and, in the other case, they want a proof of what I assert *now* when I say 'I did hold up two hands above this desk just now'. Of course, what they really want is not merely a proof of these two propositions, but something like a general statement as to how *any* propositions of this sort may be proved. This, of course, I haven't given; and I do not believe it can be given: if this is what is meant by proof of the existence of external things, I do not believe that any proof of the existence of external things is possible. Of course, in some cases what might be called a proof of propositions which seem like these can be got. If one of you suspected that one of my hands was artificial he might be said to get a proof of my proposition 'Here's one hand, and here's another', by coming up and examining the suspected hand close up, perhaps touching and pressing it, and so establishing that it really was a human hand. But I do not believe that any proof is possible in nearly all cases. How am I to prove now that 'Here's one hand, and here's another'? I do not believe I can do it. In order to do it, I should need to prove for one thing, as Descartes pointed out, that I am not now dreaming. But how can I prove that I am not? I have, no doubt, conclusive reasons for asserting that I am not now dreaming; I have conclusive evidence that I am awake: but that is a very different thing from being able to prove it. I could not tell you what all my evidence is; and I should require to do this at least, in order to give you a proof.

But another reason why some people would feel dissatisfied with my proofs is, I think, not merely that they want a proof of something which I haven't proved, but that they think that, if I cannot give such extra proofs, then the proofs that I have given are not conclusive proofs at all. And this, I think, is a definite mistake. They would say: 'If you cannot prove your premiss that here is one hand and here is another, then you do not know it. But you yourself have admitted that, if you did not know it, then your proof was not conclusive. Therefore your proof was not, as you say it was, a conclusive proof.' This view that, if I cannot prove such things as these, I do not know them, is, I think, the view that Kant was expressing in the sentence which I quoted at the beginning of this lecture, when he implies that so long as we have no proof of the existence of external things, their existence must be accepted merely on *faith*. He means to say, I think, that if I cannot prove that there is a hand here, I must accept it merely as a matter of faith—I cannot know it. Such a

view, though it has been very common among philosophers, can, I think, be shown to be wrong—though shown only by the use of premisses which are not known to be true, unless we do know of the existence of external things. I can know things, which I cannot prove; and among things which I certainly did know, even if (as I think) I could not prove them, were the premisses of my two proofs. I should say, therefore, that those, if any, who are dissatisfied with these proofs merely on the ground that I did not know their premisses, have no good reason for their dissatisfaction.

Notes

1. B xxxix, note: Kemp Smith, p. 34. The German words are 'so bleibt es immer ein Skandal der Philosophie . . . , das Dasein der Dinge ausser uns . . . bloss auf *Glauben* annehmen zu müssen, und wenn es jemand einfällt es zu bezweifeln, ihm keinen genugtuenden Beweis entgegenstellen zu können'.

◈ A VERIFICATIONIST RESPONSE ◈
24. EMPIRICISM, SEMANTICS, AND ONTOLOGY
Rudolf Carnap

The Problem of Abstract Entities

Empiricists are in general rather suspicious with respect to any kind of abstract entities like properties, classes, relations, numbers, propositions, etc. They usually feel much more in sympathy with nominalists than with realists (in the medieval sense). As far as possible they try to avoid any reference to abstract entities and to restrict themselves to what is sometimes called a nominalistic language, i.e., one not containing such references. However, within certain scientific contexts it seems hardly possible to avoid them. In the case of mathematics, some empiricists try to find a way out by treating the whole of mathematics as a mere calculus, a formal system for which no interpretation is given or can be given.

Accordingly, the mathematician is said to speak not about numbers, functions, and infinite classes, but merely about meaningless symbols and formulas manipulated according to given formal rules. In physics it is more difficult to shun the suspected entities, because the language of physics serves for the communication of reports and predictions and hence cannot be taken as a mere calculus. A physicist who is suspicious of abstract entities may perhaps try to declare a certain part of the language of physics as uninterpreted and uninterpretable, that part which refers to real numbers as space-time coordinates or as values of physical magnitudes, to functions, limits, etc. More probably he will just speak about all these things like anybody else but with an uneasy conscience, like a man who in his everyday life does with qualms many things which are not in accord with the high moral principles he professes on Sundays. Recently the problem of abstract entities has arisen again in connection with semantics, the theory of meaning and truth. Some semanticists say that certain expressions designate certain entities, and among these designated entities they include not only concrete material things but also abstract entities, e.g., properties as designated by predicates and propositions as designated by sentences.[1] Others object strongly to this procedure as violating the basic principles of empiricism and leading back to a metaphysical ontology of the Platonic kind.

It is the purpose of this article to clarify this controversial issue. The nature and implications of the acceptance of a language referring to abstract entities will first be discussed in general; it will be shown that using such a language does not imply embracing a Platonic ontology but is perfectly compatible with empiricism and strictly scientific thinking. Then the special question of the role of abstract entities in semantics will be discussed. It is hoped that the clarification of the issue will be useful to those who would like to accept abstract entities in their work in mathematics, physics, semantics, or any other field; it may help them to overcome nominalistic scruples.

Frameworks of Entities

Are there properties, classes, numbers, propositions? In order to understand more clearly the nature of these and related problems, it is above all necessary to recognize a fundamental distinction between two kinds of questions concerning the existence or reality of entities. If someone wishes to speak in his language about a new kind of entities, he has to introduce a system of new ways of speaking, subject to new rules; we shall call this procedure the construction of a *framework* for the new entities in question. And now we must distinguish two kinds of questions of existence: first, questions of the existence of certain entities of the new kind *within the framework*; we call them *internal questions*; and second, questions concerning the existence or reality *of the framework itself*, called *external questions*. Internal questions and possible answers to them are formulated with the help of the new

forms of expressions. The answers may be found either by purely logical methods or by empirical methods, depending upon whether the framework is a logical or a factual one. An external question is of a problematic character which is in need of closer examination.

The world of things. Let us consider as an example the simplest framework dealt with in the everyday language: the spatio-temporally ordered system of observable things and events. Once we have accepted this thing-language and thereby the framework of things, we can raise and answer internal questions, e. g., "Is there a white piece of paper on my desk?", "Did King Arthur actually live?", "Are unicorns and centaurs real or merely imaginary?", and the like. These questions are to be answered by empirical investigations. Results of observations are evaluated according to certain rules as confirming or disconfirming evidence for possible answers. (This evaluation is usually carried out, of course, as a matter of habit rather than a deliberate, rational procedure. But it is possible, in a rational reconstruction, to lay down explicit rules for the evaluation. This is one of the main tasks of a pure, as distinguished from a psychological epistemology.) The concept of reality occurring in these internal questions is an empirical, scientific, non-metaphysical concept. To recognize something as a real thing or event means to succeed in incorporating it into the framework of things at a particular space-time position so that it fits together with the other things recognized as real, according to the rules of the framework.

From these questions we must distinguish the external question of the reality of the thing world itself. In contrast to the former questions, this question is raised neither by the man in the street nor by scientists, but only by philosophers. Realists give an affirmative answer, subjective idealists a negative one, and the controversy goes on for centuries without ever being solved. And it cannot be solved because it is framed in a wrong way. To be real in the scientific sense means to be an element of the framework; hence this concept cannot be meaningfully applied to the framework itself. Those who raise the question of the reality of the thing world itself have perhaps in mind not a theoretical question as their formulation seems to suggest, but rather a practical question, a matter of a practical decision concerning the structure of our language. We have to make the choice whether or not to accept and use the forms of expression for the framework in question.

In the case of this particular example, there is usually no deliberate choice because we all have accepted the thing language early in our lives as a matter of course. Nevertheless, we may regard it as a matter of decision in this sense: we are free to choose to continue using the thing language or not; in the latter case we could restrict ourselves to a language of sense-data and other "phenomenal" entities, or construct an alternative to the customary thing language with another structure, or, finally, we could refrain from speaking. If someone decides to accept the thing language, there is no objection against saying that he has accepted the world of things. But this must not be interpreted as if it meant his acceptance of a *belief* in the reality of the thing world; there is no such belief or assertion or assumption, because it is not a theoretical question. To accept the thing world means nothing more than to accept a certain form of language, in other words, to accept rules for forming statements and for testing, accepting, or rejecting them. Thus the acceptance of the thing language leads, on the basis of observations made, also to the acceptance, belief, and assertion of certain statements. But the thesis of the reality of the thing world cannot be among these statements, because it cannot be formulated in the thing language or, it seems, in any other theoretical language.

The decision of accepting the thing language, although itself not of a cognitive nature, will nevertheless usually be influenced by theoretical knowledge, just like any other deliberate decision concerning the acceptance of linguistic or other rules. The purposes for which the language is intended to be used, for instance, the purpose of communicating factual knowledge, will determine which factors are relevant for the decision. The efficiency, fruitfulness, and simplicity of the use of the thing language may be among the decisive factors. And the questions concerning these qualities are indeed of a theoretical nature. But these questions cannot be identified with the question of realism. They are not yes-no questions but questions of degree. The thing language in the customary form works indeed with a high degree of efficiency for most purposes of everyday life. This is a matter of fact, based upon the content of our experiences. However, it would be wrong to describe this situation by saying: "The fact of the efficiency of the thing language is confirming evidence for the reality of the thing world"; we should rather say instead: "This fact makes it advisable to accept the thing language".

The system of numbers. As an example of a framework which is of a logical rather than a factual nature let us take the system of natural numbers. This system is established by introducing into the language new expressions with suitable rules: (1) numerals like "five" and sentence forms like "there are five books on the table"; (2) the general term "number" for the new entities, and sentence forms like "five is a number"; (3) expressions for properties of numbers (e. g., "odd", "prime"), relations (e. g., "greater than"), and functions (e. g., "plus"), and sentence forms like "two plus three is five"; (4) numerical variables ("m", "n", etc.) and quantifiers for universal sentences ("for every n, . . .") and existential sentences ("there is an n such that . . .") with the customary deductive rules.

Here again there are internal questions, e.g., "Is there a prime number greater than hundred?" Here, however, the answers are found, not by empirical investigation based on observations, but by logical analysis based on the rules for the new expressions. Therefore the answers are here analytic, i.e., logically true.

What is now the nature of the philosophical question concerning the existence or reality of numbers? To begin with, there is the internal question which, together with the affirmative answer, can be formulated in the new terms, say, by "There are numbers" or, more explicitly, "There is an n such that n is a number". This statement follows from the analytic statement "five is a number" and is therefore itself analytic. Moreover, it is rather trivial (in contradistinction to a statement like "There is a prime number greater than a million", which is likewise analytic but far from trivial), because it does not say more than that the new system is not empty; but this is immediately seen from the rule which states that words like "five" are substitutable for the new variables. Therefore nobody who meant the question "Are there numbers?" in the internal sense would either assert or even seriously consider a negative answer. This makes it plausible to assume that those philosophers who treat the question of the existence of numbers as a serious philosophical problem and offer lengthy arguments on either side, do not have in mind the internal question. And, indeed, if we were to ask them: "Do you mean the question as to whether the system of numbers, *if* we were to accept it, would be found to be empty or not?", they would probably reply: "Not at all; we mean a question *prior* to the acceptance of the new framework". They might try to explain what they mean by saying that it is a question of the ontological status of numbers; the question whether or not numbers have a certain metaphysical characteristic called reality (but a kind of ideal reality, different from the material reality of the thing world) or subsistence or status of "independent entities". Unfortunately, these philosophers have so far not given a formulation of their question in terms of the common scientific language. Therefore our judgement must be that they have not succeeded in giving to the external question and to the possible answers any cognitive content. Unless and until they supply a clear cognitive interpretation, we are justified in our suspicion that their question is a pseudo-question, that is, one disguised in the form of a theoretical question while in fact it is non-theoretical; in the present case it is the practical problem whether or not to incorporate into the language the new linguistic forms which represent the framework of numbers.

The framework of propositions. New variables, "*p*", "*q*", etc., are introduced with a rule to the effect that any (declarative) sentence may be substituted for a variable of this kind; this includes, in addition to the sentences of the original thing language, also all general sentences with variables of any kind which may have been introduced into the language. Further, the general term "proposition" is introduced. "*p* is a proposition" may be defined by "*p* or not *p*" (or by any other sentence form yielding only analytic sentences). Therefore, every sentence of the form ". . . is a proposition" (where any sentence may stand in the place of the dots) is analytic. This holds, for example, for the sentence:

a. "Chicago is large is a proposition".

(We disregard here the fact that the rules of English grammar require not a sentence but a that-clause as the subject of another sentence; accordingly, instead of (*a*) we should have to say "That Chicago is large is a proposition".) Predicates may be admitted whose argument expressions are sentences; these predicates may be either extensional (e. g., the customary truth-functional connectives) or not (e. g., modal predicates like "possible", "necessary", etc.). With the help of the new variables, general sentences may be formed, e. g.

b. "For every *p*, either *p* or not-*p*".

c. "There is a *p* such that *p* is not necessary and not-*p* is not necessary".

d. "There is a *p* such that *p* is a proposition".

e. and (d) assert internal existence. The statement "There are propositions" may be meant in the sense of (*d*); in this case it is analytic (since it follows from (*a*)) and even trivial. If, however, the statement is meant in an external sense, then it is non-cognitive.

It is important to notice that the system of rules for the linguistic expressions of the propositional framework (of which only a few rules have here been briefly indicated) is sufficient for the introduction of the framework. Any further explanations as to the nature of the propositions (i.e., the elements of the framework indicated, the values of the variables "*p*", "*q*", etc.) are theoretically unnecessary because, if correct, they follow from the rules. For example, are propositions mental events (as in Russell's theory)? A look at the rules shows us that they are not, because otherwise existential statements would be of the form: "If the mental state of the person in question fulfils such and such conditions, then there is a *p* such that . . . ". The fact that no references to mental conditions occur in existential statements (like (*c*), (*d*), etc.) shows that propositions are not mental entities. Further, a statement of the existence of linguistic entities (e.g., expressions, classes of expressions, etc.) must contain a reference to a language. The fact that no such reference occurs in the existential statements here, shows that propositions are not linguistic entities. The fact that in these statements no reference to a subject (an observer or knower) occurs (nothing like: "There is a *p* which is necessary for Mr. X"), shows that the propositions (and their properties, like necessity, etc.) are not subjective. Although characterizations of these or similar kinds are, strictly speaking, unnecessary, they may nevertheless be practically useful. If they are given, they should be understood, not as ingredient parts of the system, but merely as marginal notes with the purpose of supplying to the reader helpful hints or convenient pictorial associations which may make his learning of the use of the expressions easier than the bare system of the rules would do. Such a characterization is analogous to an extra-systematic explanation which a physicist sometimes gives to the beginner. He might, for example, tell him to imagine the atoms of a gas as small balls rushing around with great speed, or the electromagnetic field and its oscillations as quasi-elastic tensions and vibrations in an ether. In fact, however, all that can accurately be said about atoms or the field is implicitly contained in the physical laws of the theories in question.[2]

The framework of thing properties. The thing language contains words like "red", "hard", "stone", "house", etc., which are used for describing what things are like. Now we may introduce new variables, say "*f*", "*g*", etc., for which those words are substitutable and furthermore the general term "property". New rules are laid down which admit sentences like "Red is a property", "Red is a color", "These two pieces of paper have at least one color in common" (i. e., "There is an *f* such that *f* is a color, and . . . "). The last sentence is an internal asertion. It is of an empirical, factual nature. However, the external statement, the philosophical statement of the reality of properties—a special case of the thesis of the reality of universals—is devoid of cognitive content.

The frameworks of integers and rational numbers. Into a language containing the framework of natural numbers we may introduce first the (positive and negative) integers as relations among natural numbers and then the rational numbers as relations among integers. This involves introducing new types of variables, expressions substitutable for them and the general terms "integer" and "rational number".

The framework of real numbers. On the basis of the rational numbers, the real numbers may be introduced as classes of a special kind (segments) of rational numbers (according to the method developed by Dedekind and Frege). Here again a new type of variables is introduced, expressions substitutable for them (e. g., "$\sqrt{2}$"), and the general term "real number".

The framework of a spatio-temporal coordinate system for physics. The new entities are the space-time points. Each is an ordered quadruple of four real numbers, called its coordinates, consisting of three spatial and one temporal coordinates. The physical state of a spatio-temporal point or region is described either with the help of qualitative predicates (e.g., "hot") or by ascribing numbers as values of a physical magnitude (e.g., mass, temperature, and the like). The step from the framework of things (which does not contain space-time points but only extended objects with spatial and temporal relations between them) to the physical coordinate system is again a matter of decision. Our choice of certain features, although itself not theoretical, is suggested by theoretical knowledge, either logical or factual. For example, the choice of real numbers rather than rational numbers or integers as coordinates is not much influenced by the facts of experience but mainly due to considerations of mathematical simplicity. The restriction to rational coordinates would not be in conflict with any experimental knowledge we have, because the result of any measurement is a rational number. However, it would prevent the use of ordinary geometry (which says, e. g., that the diagonal of a square with the side 1 has the irrational value $\sqrt{2}$) and thus lead to great complications. On the other hand, the decision to use three rather than two or four spatial coordinates is strongly suggested, but still not forced upon us, by the result of common observations. If certain events allegedly observed in spiritualistic séances, e. g., a ball moving out of a sealed box, were confirmed beyond any reasonable doubt, it might seem advisable to use four spatial coordinates. Internal questions are here, in general, empirical questions to be answered by empirical investigations. On the other hand, the external questions of the reality of physical space and physical time are pseudo-questions. A question like "Are there (really) space-time points?" is ambiguous. It may be meant as an internal question; then the affirmative answer is, of course, analytic and trivial. Or it may be meant in the external sense: "Shall we introduce such and such forms into our language?"; in this case it is not a theoretical but a practical question, a matter of decision rather than assertion, and hence the proposed formulation would be misleading. Or finally, it may be meant in the following sense: "Are our experiences such that the use of the linguistic forms in question will be expedient and fruitful?" This is a theoretical question of a factual, empirical nature. But it concerns a matter of degree; therefore a formulation in the form "real or not?" would be inadequate.

What Does Acceptance of a Framework Mean?

Let us now summarize the essential characteristics of situations involving the introduction of a new framework of entities, characterictics which are common to the various examples outlined above.

The acceptance of a framework of new entities is represented in the language by introduction of new forms of expressions to be used according to a new set of rules. There may be new names for particular entities of the kind in question; but some such names may already occur in the language before the introduction of the new framework. (Thus, for example, the thing language contains certainly words of the type of "blue" and "house" before the framework of properties is introduced; and it may contain words like "ten" in sentences of the form "I have ten fingers" before the framework of numbers is introduced.) The latter fact shows that the occurrence of constants of the type in question—regarded as names of entities of the new kind after the new framework is introduced—is not a sure sign of the acceptance of the framework. Therefore the introduction of such constants is not to be regarded as an essential step in the introduction of the framework. The two essential steps are rather the following. First, the introduction of a general term, a predicate of higher level, for the new kind of entities, permitting us to say of any particular entity that it belongs to this kind (e. g., "Red is a *property*", "Five is a *number*"). Second, the introduction of variables of the new type. The new entities are values of these variables; the constants (and the closed compound expressions, if any) are substitutable for the variables.[3] With the help of the variables, general sentences concerning the new entities can be formulated.

After the new forms are introduced into the language, it is possible to formulate with their help internal questions and possible answers to them. A question of this kind may be either empirical or logical; accordingly a true answer is either factually true or analytic.

From the internal questions we must clearly distinguish external questions, i.e., philosophical questions concerning the existence or reality of the framework itself. Many philosophers regard a question of this kind as an ontological question which must be raised and answered *before* the introduction of the new language forms. The latter introduction, they believe, is legitimate only if it can be justified by an ontological insight supplying an affirmative answer to the question of reality. In contrast to this view, we take the position that the introduction of the new ways of speaking does not

need any theoretical justification because it does not imply any assertion of reality. We may still speak (and have done so) of "the acceptance of the framework" or "the acceptance of the new entities" since this form of speech is customary; but one must keep in mind that these phrases do not mean for us anything more than acceptance of the new linguistic forms. Above all, they must not be interpreted as referring to an assumption, belief, or assertion of "the reality of the entities". There is no such assertion. An alleged statement of the reality of the framework of entities is a pseudo-statement without cognitive content. To be sure, we have to face at this point an important question; but it is a practical, not a theoretical question; it is the question of whether or not to accept the new linguistic forms. The acceptance cannot be judged as being either true or false because it is not an assertion. It can only be judged as being more or less expedient, fruitful, conducive to the aim for which the language is intended. Judgments of this kind supply the motivation for the decision of accepting or rejecting the framework.[4]

Thus it is clear that the acceptance of a framework must not be regarded as implying a metaphysical doctrine concerning the reality of the entities in question. It seems to me due to a neglect of this important distinction that some contemporary nominalists label the admission of variables of abstract types as "platonism".[5] This is, to say the least, an extremely misleading terminology. It leads to the absurd consequence, that the position of everybody who accepts the language of physics with its real number variables (as a language of communication, not merely as a calculus) would be called platonistic, even if he is a strict empiricist who rejects platonic metaphysics.

A brief historical remark may here be inserted. The non-cognitive character of the questions which we have called here external questions was recognized and emphasized already by the Vienna Circle under the leadership of Moritz Schlick, the group from which the movement of logical empiricism originated. Influenced by ideas of Ludwig Wittgenstein, the Circle rejected both the thesis of the reality of the external world and the thesis of its irreality as pseudo-statements;[6] the same was the case for both the thesis of the reality of universals (abstract entities, in our present terminology) and the nominalistic thesis that they are not real and that their alleged names are not names of anything but merely *flatus vocis*. (It is obvious that the apparent negation of a pseudo-statement must also be a pseudo-statement.) It is therefore not correct to classify the members of the Vienna Circle as nominalists, as is sometimes done. However, if we look at the basic anti-metaphysical and proscientific attitude of most nominalists (and the same holds for many materialists and realists in the modern sense), disregarding their occasional pseudo-theoretical formulations, then it is, of course, true to say that the Vienna Circle was much closer to those philosophers than to their opponents.

Abstract Entities in Semantics

The problem of the legitimacy and the status of abstract entities has recently again led to controversial discussions in connection with semantics. In a semantical meaning analysis certain expressions in a language are often said to designate (or name or denote or signify or refer to) certain extralinguistic entities.[7] As long as physical things or events (e.g., Chicago or Caesar's death) are taken as designata (entities designated), no serious doubts arise. But strong objections have been raised, especially by some empiricists, against abstract entities as designata, e.g., against semantical statements of the following kind:

1. "The word 'red' designates a property of things;"
2. "The word 'color' designates a property of properties of things;"
3. "The word 'five' designates a number;"
4. "The word 'odd' designates a property of numbers;"
5. "The sentence 'Chicago is large' designates a proposition."

Those who criticize these statements do not, of course, reject the use of the expressions in question, like "red" or "five"; nor would they deny that these expressions are meaningful. But to be meaningful, they would say, is not the same as having a meaning in the sense of an entity designated. They reject the belief, which they regard as implicitly presupposed by those semantical statements, that to each expression of the types in question (adjectives like "red", numerals like

"five", etc.) there is a particular real entity to which the expression stands in the relation of designation. This belief is rejected as incompatible with the basic principles of empiricism or of scientific thinking. Derogatory labels like "Platonic realism", "hypostatization", or "'Fido'-Fido principle" are attached to it. The latter is the name given by Gilbert Ryle[8] to the criticized belief, which, in his view, arises by a naive inference of analogy: just as there is an entity well known to me, viz. my dog Fido, which is designated by the name "Fido", thus there must be for every meaningful expression a particular entity to which it stands in the relation of designation or naming, i. e., the relation exemplified by "Fido"-Fido. The belief criticized is thus a case of hypostatization, i.e., of treating as names expressions which are not names. While "Fido" is a name, expressions like "red", "five", etc. are said not to be names, not to designate anything.

Our previous discussions concerning the acceptance of frameworks enables us now to clarify the situation with respect to abstract entities as designata. Let us take as an example the statement:

a. "'Five' designates a number."

The formulation of this statement presupposes that our language L contains the forms of expressions corresponding to what we have called the framework of numbers, in particular, numerical variables and the general term "number". If L contains these forms, the following is an analytic statement in L:

b. "Five is a number."

Further, to make the statement (*a*) possible, L must contain an expression like "designates" or "is a name of" for the semantic relation of designation. If suitable rules for this term are laid down, the following is likewise analytic:

c. "'Five' designates five."

(Generally speaking, any expression of the form "'. . .' designates . . ." is an analytic statement provided the term ". . ." is a constant in an accepted framework. If the latter condition is not fulfilled, the expression is not a statement.) Since (*a*) follows from (*c*) and (*b*), (*a*) is likewise analytic.

Thus it is clear that *if* someone accepts the framework of numbers, then he must acknowledge (*c*) and (*b*) and hence (*a*) as true statements. Generally speaking, if someone accepts a framework of entities, then he is bound to admit its entities as possible designata. Thus the question of the admissibility of entities of a certain type or of abstract entities in general as designata is reduced to the question of the acceptability of those entities. Both the nominalistic critics, who refuse the status of designators or names to expressions like "red", "five", etc., because they deny the existence of abstract entities, and the skeptics, who express doubts concerning the existence and demand evidence for it, treat the question of existence as a theoretical question. They do, of course, not mean the internal question; the affirmative answer to *this* question is analytic and trivial and too obvious for doubt or denial, as we have seen. Their doubts refer rather to the framework itself; hence they mean the external question. They believe that only after making sure that there really are entities of the kinds in question are we justified in accepting the framework by incorporating the linguistic forms into our language. However, we have seen that the external question is not a theoretical question but rather the practical question whether or not to accept those linguistic forms. This acceptance is not in need of a theoretical justification (except with respect to expediency and fruitfulness), because it does not imply a belief or assertion. Ryle says that the "Fido"-Fido principle is "a grotesque theory". Grotesque or not, Ryle is wrong in calling it a theory. It is rather the practical decision to accept certain frameworks. Maybe Ryle is historically right with respect to those whom he mentions as previous representatives of the principle, viz. John Stuart Mill, Frege, and Russell. If these philosophers regarded the acceptance of a framework of entities as a theory, an assertion, they were victims of the same old, metaphysical confusion. But it is certainly wrong to regard *my* semantical method as involving a belief in the reality of abstract entities, since I reject a thesis of this kind as a metaphysical pseudo-statement.

The critics of the use of abstract entities in semantics overlook the fundamental difference between the acceptance of a framework of entities and an internal assertion, e.g., an assertion that there are elephants or electrons or prime numbers greater than a million. Whoever makes an internal assertion is certainly obliged to justify it by providing evidence, empirical evidence in the case of electrons, logical proof in the case of the prime numbers. The demand for a theoretical justification, correct in the case of internal assertions, is sometimes wrongly applied to the acceptance of a framework of entities. Thus, for example, Ernest Nagel[9] asks for "evidence relevant for affirming with warrant that there are such entities as infinitesimals or propositions". He characterizes the evidence required in these cases—in distinction to the empirical evidence in the case of electrons—as "in the broad sense logical and dialectical". Beyond this no hint is given as to what might be regarded as relevant evidence. Some nominalists regard the acceptance of abstract entities as a kind of superstition or myth, populating the world with fictitious or at least dubious entities, analogous to the belief in centaurs or demons. This shows again the confusion mentioned, because a superstition or myth is a false (or dubious) internal statement.

Let us take as example the natural numbers as cardinal numbers, i. e., in contexts like "Here are three books". The linguistic forms of the framework of numbers, including variables and the general term "number" are generally used in our common language of communication; and it is easy to formulate explicit rules for their use. Thus the logical characteristics of this framework are sufficiently clear (while many internal questions, i. e., arithmetical questions, are, of course, still open). In spite of this, the controversy concerning the external question of the ontological reality of numbers continues. Suppose that one philosopher says: "I believe that there are numbers as real entities. This gives me the right to use the linguistic forms of the numerical framework and to make semantical statements about numbers as designata of numerals". His nominalistic opponent replies: "You are wrong; there are no numbers. The numerals may still be used as meaningful expressions. But they are not names, there are no entities designated by them. Therefore the word "number" and numerical variables must not be used (unless a way were found to introduce them as merely abbreviating devices, a way of translating them into the nominalistic thing language)." I cannot think of any possible evidence that would be regarded as relevant by both philosophers, and therefore, if actually found, would decide the controversy or at least make one of the opposite theses more probable than the other. (To construe the numbers as classes or properties of the second level, according to the Frege-Russell method does, of course, not solve the controversy, because the first philosopher would affirm and the second deny the existence of classes or properties of the second level.) Therefore I feel compelled to regard the external question as a pseudo-question, until both parties to the controversy offer a common interpretation of the question as a cognitive question; this would involve an indication of possible evidence regarded as relevant by both sides.

There is a particular kind of misinterpretation of the importance of abstract entities in various fields of science and of semantics, that needs to be cleared up. Certain early British empiricists (e. g., Berkeley and Hume) denied the existence of abstract entities on the ground that immediate experience presents us only with particulars, not with universals, e. g., with this red patch, but not with Redness or Color-in-General; with this scalene triangle, but not with Scalene Triangularity or Triangularity-in-General. Only entities belonging to a type of which examples were to be found within immediate experience could be accepted as ultimate constituents of reality. Thus, according to this way of thinking, the existence of abstract entities could be asserted only if one could show either that some abstract entities fall within the given, or that abstract entities can be defined in terms of the types of entity which are given. Since these empiricists found no abstract entities within the realm of sense-data, they either denied their existence, or else made a futile attempt to define universals in terms of particulars. Some contemporary philosophers, especially English philosophers following Bertrand Russell, think in basically similar terms. They emphasize a distinction between the data (that which is immediately given in consciousness, e. g. sense-data, immediately past experiences, etc.) and the constructs based on the data. Existence or reality is ascribed only to the data; the constructs are not real entities; the corresponding linguistic expressions are merely ways of speech not actually designating anything (reminiscent of the nominalists' *flatus vocis*). We shall not criticize here this

general conception. (As far as it is a principle of accepting certain entities and not accepting others, leaving aside any ontological, phenomenalistic and nominalistic pseudo-statements, there cannot be any theoretical objection to it.) But if this conception leads to the view that other philosophers or scientists who accept abstract entities thereby assert or imply their occurrence as immediate data, then such a view must be rejected as a misinterpretation. References to space-time points, the electromagnetic field, or electrons in physics, to real or complex numbers and their functions in mathematics, to the excitatory potential or unconscious complexes in psychology, to an inflationary trend in economics, and the like, do not imply the assertion that entities of these kinds occur as immediate data. And the same holds for references to abstract entities as designata in semantics. Some of the criticisms by English philosophers against such references give the impression that, probably due to the misinterpretation just indicated, they accuse the semanticist not so much of bad metaphysics (as some nominalists would do) but of bad psychology. The fact that they regard a semantical method involving abstract entities not merely as doubtful and perhaps wrong, but as manifestly absurd, preposterous and grotesque, and that they show a deep horror and indignation against this method, is perhaps to be explained by a misinterpretation of the kind described. In fact, of course, the semanticist does not in the least assert or imply that the abstract entities to which he refers can be experienced as immediately given either by sensation or by a kind of rational intuition. An assertion of this kind would indeed be very dubious psychology. The psychological question as to which kinds of entities do and which do not occur as immediate data is entirely irrelevant for semantics, just as it is for physics, mathematics, economics, etc., with respect to the examples mentioned above.[10]

Conclusion

For those who want to develop or use semantical methods, the decisive question is not the alleged ontological question of the existence of abstract entities but rather the question whether the use of abstract linguistic forms or, in technical terms, the use of variables beyond those for things (or phenomenal data), is expedient and fruitful for the purposes for which semantical analyses are made, viz. the analysis, interpretation, clarification, or construction of languages of communication, especially languages of science. This question is here neither decided nor even discussed. It is not a question simply of yes or no, but a matter of degree. Among those philosophers who have carried out semantical analyses and thought about suitable tools for this work, beginning with Plato and Aristotle and, in a more technical way on the basis of modern logic, with C. S. Pierce and Frege, a great majority accepted abstract entities. This does, of course, not prove the case. After all, semantics in the technical sense is still in the initial phases of its development, and we must be prepared for possible fundamental changes in methods. Let us therefore admit that the nominalistic critics may possibly be right. But if so, they will have to offer better arguments than they did so far. Appeal to ontological insight will not carry much weight. The critics will have to show that it is possible to construct a semantical method which avoids all references to abstract entities and achieves by simpler means essentially the same results as the other methods.

The acceptance or rejection of abstract linguistic forms, just as the acceptance or rejection of any other linguistic forms in any branch of science, will finally be decided by their efficiency as instruments, the ratio of the results achieved to the amount and complexity of the efforts required. To decree dogmatic prohibitions of certain linguistic forms instead of testing them by their success or failure in practical use, is worse than futile; it is positively harmful because it may obstruct scientific progress. The history of science shows examples of such prohibitions based on prejudices deriving from religious, mythological, metaphysical, or other irrational sources, which slowed up the developments for shorter or longer periods of time. Let us learn from the lessons of history. Let us grant to those who work in any special field of investigation the freedom to use any form of expression which seems useful to them; the work in the field will sooner or later lead to the elimination of those forms which have no useful function. *Let us be cautious in making assertions and critical in examining them, but tolerant in permitting linguistic forms.*

Notes

1. The terms "sentence" and "statement" are here used synonymously for declarative (indicative, propositional) sentences.

2. In my book *Meaning and Necessity* (Chicago, 1947) I have developed a semantical method which takes propositions as entities designated by sentences (more specifically, as intensions of sentences). In order to facilitate the understanding of the systematic development, I added some informal, extra-systematic explanations concerning the nature of propositions. I said that the term "proposition" "is used neither for a linguistic expression nor for a subjective, mental occurrence, but rather for something objective that may or may not be exemplified in nature . . . . We apply the term 'proposition' to any entities of a certain logical type, namely, those that may be expressed by (declarative) sentences in a language" (p. 27). After some more detailed discussions concerning the relation between propositions and facts, and the nature of false propositions, I added: "It has been the purpose of the preceding remarks to facilitate the understanding of our conception of propositions. If, however, a reader should find these explanations more puzzling than clarifying, or even unacceptable, he may disregard them" (p. 31) (that is, disregard these extra-systematic explanations, not the whole theory of the propositions as intensions of sentences, as one reviewer understood). In spite of this warning, it seems that some of those readers who were puzzled by the explanations, did not disregard them but thought that by raising objections against them they could refute the theory. This is analogous to the procedure of some laymen who by (correctly) criticizing the other picture or other visualizations of physical theories, thought they had refuted those theories. Perhaps the discussions in the present paper will help in clarifying the role of the system of linguistic rules for the introduction of a framework of entities on the one hand, and that of extra-systematic explanations concerning the nature of the entities on the other.

3. W. V. O. Quine was the first to recognize the importance of the introduction of variables as indicating the acceptance of entities. "The ontology to which one's use of language commits him comprises simply the objects that he treats as falling . . . within the range of values of his variables" ("Notes on Existence and Necessity",

Journal of Philos., 40 (1943), pp. 113–127, see p. 118; compare also his "Designation and Existence", *ibid.*, 36 (1939), pp. 701–9, and "On Universals", *Journal of Symbolic Logic*, 12 (1947), pp. 74–84).

4. For a closely related point of view on these questions see the detailed discussions in Herbert FEIGL, *Existential Hypotheses*, forthcoming in *Philosophy of Science*, 1950.

5. Paul BERNAYS, *Sur le platonisme dans les mathématiques* (*L'Enseignement math.*, 34 (1935), pp. 52–69). W. V. Quine, see footnote p. 65, and a recent paper *On What There Is*, (*Review of Metaphysics*, 2 (1948), pp. 21–38). Quine does not acknowledge the distinction which I emphasize above, because according to his general conception there are no sharp boundary lines between logical and factual truth, between questions of meaning and questions of fact, between the acceptance of a language structure ant the acceptance of an assertion formulated in the language. This conception, which seems to deviate considerably from customary ways of thinking, will be explained in his forthcoming book. *Foundations of Logic*. When Quine in the article mentioned above classifies my logicistic conception of mathematics (derived from Frege and Russell) as "platonic realism" (p. 33), this is meant (according to a personal communication from him) not as ascribing to me agreement with Plato's metaphysical doctrine of universals, but merely as referring to the fact that I accept a language of mathematics containing variables of higher levels. With respect to the basic attitude to take in choosing a language form (an "ontology" in Quine's terminology, which seems to me misleading), there appears now to be agreement between us: "the obvious counsel is tolerance and an experimental spirit" (*op. cit.*, p. 38).

6. See CARNAP, *Scheinprobleme in der Philosophie: das Fremdpsychische und der Realismusstreit*. Berlin, 1928. Moritz Schlick, *Positivismus und Realismus*, reprinted in *Gesammelte Aujsäize*, Wien 1938.

7. *See Introduction to Semantics*, Cambridge Mass., 1942; *Meaning and Necessity*, Chicago, 1947. The distinction I have drawn in the latter book between the method of the name-relation and the method of intension and extension is not essential for our present discussion. The term "designation" is here used in a neutral way; it may be understood as referring to the name-relation or to the intension-relation or to the extension-relation or to any similar relations used in other semantical methods.

8. G. RYLE, *Meaning and Necessity* (*Philosophy*, 24 (1949), pp. 69–76).

9. E. NAGEL., Review of Carnap *Meaning and Necessity* (*Journal of Philos.*, 45 (1948), pp. 467–72).

10. Wilfrid Sellars (*Acquaintance and Description Again, in Journal of Philos.* 46 (1949), pp. 496–504, see pp. 502 f.) analyzes clearly the roots of the mistake "of taking the designation relation of semantic theory to be a reconstruction of *being present to an experience*".

✦ A STRUCTURAL CONTEXTUALIST RESPONSE ✦

25. ON CERTAINTY

Ludwig Wittgenstein

1. If you do know that *here is one hand*,[1] we'll grant you all the rest.

When one says that such and such a proposition can't be proved, of course that does not mean that it can't be derived from other propositions; any proposition can be derived from other ones. But they may be *no more* certain than it is itself. (On this a curious remark by H. Newman.)

2. From its *seeming* to me—or to everyone—to be so, it doesn't follow that it *is* so.

What we can ask is whether it can make sense to doubt it.

3. If e.g. someone says "I don't know if there's a hand here" he might be told "Look closer".—This possibility of satisfying oneself is part of the language-game. Is one of its essential features.

4. "I know that I am a human being." In order to see how unclear the sense of this proposition is, consider its negation. At most it might be taken to mean "I know I have the organs of a human". (E.g. a brain which, after all, no one has ever yet seen.) But what about such a proposition as "I know I have a brain"? Can I doubt it? Grounds for *doubt* are lacking! Everything speaks in its favour, nothing against

it. Nevertheless it is *imaginable* that my skull should turn out empty when it was operated on.

6. Now, can one enumerate what one knows (like Moore)? Straight off like that, I believe not.—For otherwise the expression "I know" gets misused. And through this misuse a queer and extremely important mental state seems to be revealed.

9. Now do I, in the course of my life, make sure I know that here is a hand—my own hand, that is?

10. I know that a sick man is lying here? Nonsense! I am sitting at his bedside, I am looking attentively into his face.—So I don't know, then, that there is a sick man lying here? *Neither* the question nor the assertion makes sense. Any more than the assertion "I am here", which I might yet use at any moment, if suitable occasion presented itself.—Then is "2 x 2 = 4" nonsense in the same way, and not a proposition of arithmetic, apart from particular occasions? "2 x 2 = 4" is a true proposition of arithmetic—not "on particular occasions" nor "always"—but the spoken or written sentence "2 x 2 = 4" in Chinese might have a different meaning or be out and out nonsense, and from this is seen that it is only in use that the proposition has its sense. And "I know that there's a sick man lying here", used in an *unsuitable* situation, seems not to be nonsense but rather seems matter-of-course, only because one can fairly easily imagine a situation to fit it, and one thinks that the words "I know that . . . " are always in place where there is no doubt, and hence even where the expression of doubt would be unintelligible.

20. "Doubting the existence of the external world" does not mean for example doubting the existence of a planet, which later observations proved to exist.—Or does Moore want to say that knowing that here is his hand is different in kind from knowing the existence of the planet Saturn? Otherwise it would be possible to point out the discovery of the planet Saturn to the doubters and say that its existence has been proved, and hence the existence of the external world as well.

23. If I don't know whether someone has two hands (say, whether they have been amputated or not) I shall believe his assurance that he has two hands, if he is trustworthy. And if he says he *knows* it, that can only signify to me that he has been able to make sure, and

hence that his arms are e.g. not still concealed by coverings and bandages, etc. etc. My believing the trustworthy man stems from my admitting that it is possible for him to make sure. But someone who says that perhaps there are no physical objects makes no such admission.

24. The idealist's question would be something like: "What right have I not to doubt the existence of my hands?" (And to that the answer can't be: I *know* that they exist.) But someone who asks such a question is overlooking the fact that a doubt about existence only works in a language-game. Hence, that we should first have to ask: what would such a doubt be like?, and don't understand this straight off.

36. "A is a physical object" is a piece of instruction which we give only to someone who doesn't yet understand either what "A" means, or what "physical object" means. Thus it is instruction about the use of words, and "physical object" is a logical concept. (Like colour, quantity, . . .) And that is why no such proposition as: "There are physical objects" can be formulated.
Yet we encounter such unsuccessful shots at every turn.

37. But is it an adequate answer to the scepticism of the idealist, or the assurances of the realist, to say that "There are physical objects" is nonsense? For them after all it is not nonsense. It would, however, be an answer to say: this assertion, or its opposite is a misfiring attempt to express what can't be expressed like that. And that it does misfire can be shewn; but that isn't the end of the matter. We need to realize that what presents itself to us as the first expression of a difficulty, or of its solution, may as yet not be correctly expressed at all. Just as one who has a just censure of a picture to make will often at first offer the censure where it does not belong, and an *investigation* is needed in order to find the right point of attack for the critic.

51. What sort of proposition is: "What could a mistake here be like!"? It would have to be a logical proposition. But it is a logic that is not used, because what it tells us is not learned through propositions.—It is a logical proposition; for it does describe the conceptual (linguistic) situation.

52. This situation is thus not the same for a proposition like "At this distance from the sun there is a planet" and "Here is a hand" (namely my own hand). The second can't be called a hypothesis. But there isn't a sharp boundary line between them.

53. So one might grant that Moore was right, if he is interpreted like this: a proposition saying that here is a physical object may have the same logical status as one saying that here is a red patch.

54. For it is not true that a mistake merely gets more and more improbable as we pass from the planet to my own hand. No: at some point it has ceased to be conceivable.
This is already suggested by the following: if it were not so, it would also be conceivable that we should be wrong in *every* statement about physical objects; that any we ever make are mistaken.

55. So is the *hypothesis* possible, that all the things around us don't exist? Would that not be like the hypothesis of our having miscalculated in all our calculations?

56. When one says: "Perhaps this planet doesn't exist and the light-phenomenon arises in some other way", then after all one needs an example of an object which does exist. This doesn't exist,—as *for example* does. . . .
Or are we to say that *certainty* is merely a constructed point to which some things approximate more, some less closely? No. Doubt gradually loses its sense. This language-game just *is* like that.
And everything descriptive of a language-game is part of logic.

58. If "I know etc." is conceived as a grammatical proposition, of course the "I" cannot be important. And it properly means "There is no such thing as a doubt in this case" or "The expression 'I do not know' makes no sense in this case". And of course it follows from this that "I *know*" makes no sense either.

59. "I know" is here a *logical* insight. Only realism can't be proved by means of it.

92. However, we can ask: May someone have telling grounds for believing that the earth has only existed for a short time, say since his own birth?— Suppose he had always been told that,—would he have any good reason to doubt it? Men have believed that they could make rain; why should not a king be brought up in the belief that the world began with him? And if Moore and this king were to meet and discuss, could Moore really prove his belief to be the right one? I do not say that Moore could not convert the king to his view, but it would be a conversion of a special kind; the king would be brought to look at the world in a different way.

94. But I did not get my picture of the world by satisfying myself of its correctness; nor do I have it because I am satisfied of its correctness. No: it is the inherited background against which I distinguish between true and false.

105. All testing, all confirmation and disconfirmation of a hypothesis takes place already within a system. And this system is not a more or less arbitrary and doubtful point of departure for all our arguments: no, it belongs to the essence of what we call an argument. The system is not so much the point of departure, as the element in which arguments have their life.

109. "An empirical proposition can be *tested*" (we say). But how? and through what?

110. What *counts* as its test?—"But is this an adequate test? And, if so, must it not be recognizable as such in logic?"—As if giving grounds did not come to an end sometime. But the end is not an ungrounded presupposition: it is an ungrounded way of acting.

115. If you tried to doubt everything you would not get as far as doubting anything. The game of doubting itself presupposes certainty.

121. Can one say: "Where there is no doubt there is no knowledge either"?

122. Doesn't one need grounds for doubt?

125. If a blind man were to ask me "Have you got two hands?" I should not make sure by looking. If I were to have any doubt of it, then I don't know why I should trust my eyes. For why shouldn't I test my *eyes* by looking to find out whether I see my two hands? *What* is to be tested by *what*? (Who decides *what* stands fast?)
And what does it mean to say that such and such stands fast?

136. When Moore says he *knows* such and such, he is really enumerating a lot of empirical propositions which we affirm without special testing; propositions, that is, which have a peculiar logical role in the system of our empirical propositions.

137. Even if the most trustworthy of men assures me that he *knows* things are thus and so, this by itself cannot satisfy me that he does know. Only that he

believes he knows. That is why Moore's assurance that he knows . . . does not interest us. The propositions, however, which Moore retails as examples of such known truths are indeed interesting. Not because anyone knows their truth, or believes he knows them, but because they all have a *similar* role in the system of our empirical judgments.

140. We do not learn the practice of making empirical judgments by learning rules: we are taught *judgments* and their connexion with other judgments. A *totality* of judgments is made plausible to us.

141. When we first begin to *believe* anything, what we believe is not a single proposition, it is a whole system of propositions. (Light dawns gradually over the whole.)

144. The child learns to believe a host of things. I.e. it learns to act according to these beliefs. Bit by bit there forms a system of what is believed, and in that system some things stand unshakeably fast and some are more or less liable to shift. What stands fast does so, not because it is intrinsically obvious or convincing; it is rather held fast by what lies around it.

151. I should like to say: Moore does not *know* what he asserts he knows, but it stands fast for him, as also for me; regarding it as absolutely solid is part of our *method* of doubt and enquiry.

155. In certain circumstances a man cannot make a *mistake*. ("Can" is here used logically, and the proposition does not mean that a man cannot say anything false in those circumstances.) If Moore were to pronounce the opposite of those propositions which he declares certain, we should not just not share his opinion: we should regard him as demented.

163. Does anyone ever test whether this table remains in existence when no one is paying attention to it?
We check the story of Napoleon, but not whether all the reports about him are based on sense-deception, forgery and the like. For whenever we test anything, we are already presupposing something that is not tested. Now am I to say that the experiment which perhaps I make in order to test the truth of a proposition presupposes the truth of the proposition that the apparatus I believe I see is really there (and the like)?

164. Doesn't testing come to an end?

165. One child might say to another: "I know that the earth is already hundreds of years old" and that would mean: I have learnt it.

166. The difficulty is to realize the groundlessness of our believing.

193. What does this mean: the truth of a proposition is *certain*?

194. With the word "certain" we express complete *conviction*, the total absence of doubt, and thereby we seek to convince other people. That is *subjective* certainty.
But when is something objectively certain? When a mistake is not possible. But what kind of possibility is that? Mustn't mistake be *logically* excluded?

195. If I believe that I am sitting in my room when I am not, then I shall not be said to have *made a mistake*. But what is the essential difference between this case and a mistake?

204. Giving grounds, however, justifying the evidence, comes to an end;—but the end is not certain propositions' striking us immediately as true, i.e. it is not a kind of *seeing* on our part; it is our *acting*, which lies at the bottom of the language-game.

243. One says "I know" when one is ready to give compelling grounds. "I know" relates to a possibility of demonstrating the truth. Whether someone knows something can come to light, assuming that he is convinced of it.
But if what he believes is of such a kind that the grounds that he can give are no surer than his assertion, then he cannot say that he knows what he believes.

341. That is to say, the *questions* that we raise and our *doubts* depend on the fact that some propositions are exempt from doubt, are as it were like hinges on which those turn.

342. That is to say, it belongs to the logic of our scientific investigations that certain things are *in deed* not doubted.

343. But it isn't that the situation is like this: We just *can't* investigate everything, and for that reason we are forced to rest content with assumption. If I want the door to turn, the hinges must stay put.

512. Isn't the question this: "What if you had to change your opinion even on these most fundamental things?" And to that the answer seems to me to be: "You don't *have* to change it. That is just what their being 'fundamental' is."

516. If something happened (such as someone telling me something) calculated to make me doubtful of my own name, there would certainly also be something that made the grounds of these doubts themselves

seem doubtful, and I could therefore decide to retain my old belief.

651. I cannot be making a mistake about 12 3 12 being 144. And now one cannot contrast *mathematical* certainty with the relative uncertainty of empirical propositions. For the mathematical proposition has been obtained by a series of actions that are in no way different from the actions of the rest of our lives, and are in the same degree liable to forgetfulness, oversight and illusion.

652. Now can I prophesy that men will never throw over the present arithmetical propositions, never say that now at last they know how the matter stands? Yet would that justify a doubt on our part?

653. If the proposition 12 x 12 = 144 is exempt from doubt, then so too must non-mathematical propositions be.

662. If I were to say "I have never been on the moon—but I may be mistaken", that would be idiotic. For even the thought that I might have been transported there, by unknown means, in my sleep, *would not give me any right* to speak of a possible mistake here. I play the game *wrong* if I do.

663. I have a right to say "I can't be making a mistake about this" even if I am in error.

Notes

1. See G.E. Moore, "Proof of an External World", *Proceedings of the British Academy*, Vol. XXV, 1939; also "A Defence of Common Sense" in *Contemporary British Philosophy, 2nd Series*, Ed. J.H. Muirhead, 1925. Both papers are in Moore's *Philosophical Papers*, London, George Allen and Unwin, 1959. *Editors*.

✧ A TRACKING THEORIST RESPONSE ✧

26. SKEPTICISM
WHAT PERCEPTION TEACHES
Fred Dretske

My views about knowledge and, perforce, skepticism have been shaped by my work on visual perception. Very early (c. 1966) I became convinced that if I know anything about the world—that my wife is on the sofa for instance—then one of the ways of knowing this is by seeing her there. If that doesn't qualify as a way of knowing, nothing does. If that doesn't count as a way of knowing she is on the sofa, skepticism (about the external world) is true.

In *Seeing and Knowing* (1969) I tried to describe the conditions that convert seeing a person or an object (for example my wife on the sofa) into knowledge—that, for example, my wife is on the sofa.[1] In developing the theory I became convinced of two things. I am still convinced of them. They have, for me, acquired the status of epistemological axioms. They are what my study of perception taught me

about knowledge and, therefore, the possibilities for answering the skeptic.

The first thing it taught me is that perceptual knowledge, if we have it, derives from the circumstances in which one comes to believe, not one's justification for the belief. To put it in currently fashionable jargon, I learned:

1. *Externalism: if skepticism is false, externalism is true.*

If, as a result of seeing her there, I know my wife is on the sofa, this knowledge cannot depend on my justification for thinking she is there—at least not if justification is understood (as most internalists understand it) as evidence I have, things I know to be true, that support—to a degree sufficient for knowing—that my wife is on the sofa. My seeing her there does not give me that kind of justification. What seeing my wife on the sofa provides is an experience, E, of a kind that is compatible with her not being there. There is always something (usually a lot of things) that can make E occur (make me have those reasons for believing she is on the sofa) without my belief being true. The fact, therefore, that none of these things did make E occur without her being there is something that must be true for my perceptual belief to be true and, hence, for me to know she is there. This is a fact, though, that seeing her there does not justify. The fact that the person on the sofa looks like my wife, the fact that causes me to believe she is on the sofa, is not evidence that the person on the sofa isn't an imposter put there to deceive me. So seeing her there doesn't provide me with evidence that my perceptual belief isn't false in this particular way. Additional evidence—evidence, for example, that deception of this sort is most improbable—is of no help. The skeptic merely enlarges the scope of the imagined deception until one's evidence is, once again, neutralized. As long as the evidence is (as in perception it always is) logically inconclusive, we can always find facts on which the truth of our belief (hence, our knowledge) depends which the totality of our evidence is powerless to justify.

Bertrand Russell's skeptical hypothesis about the past—how do we know the entire world, complete with fossils, memory traces, history books and so on, was not created minutes ago?—neatly illustrates this point. It provides a fact, the fact that a certain possibility did not materialize, that our knowledge of the past depends on (if things did occur in the way Russell imagines, then all our beliefs about the past are false) but which our evidence (for the past) is incapable of justifying. If my knowledge that I had granola for breakfast this morning requires me to have evidence that the world was not created (complete with records, memories and so on) a few minutes ago, then I am incapable of knowing, incapable (therefore) of remembering, what I had for breakfast. So if I do remember that I had granola for breakfast, knowing this does not require me to have a justification for things that must be true for me to know.

The same is true for perception. There are always things my knowledge depends on, facts without which my beliefs would be false, that I cannot justify. So the knowledge, if I have it, must be the product of things I

need not know or be justified in believing, facts that skeptical possibilities (targeted at what I can justify) do not undermine. This is externalism. In the case of Russell's hypothesis about the past, externalism in epistemology is the view that one doesn't have to be justified in thinking that the world was not created in the way Russell imagines in order to remember—hence, know—facts about the past. It is the fact that Russell's hypothesis is false, not one's justification for thinking it false, that enables one to remember what one had for breakfast. Externalism in epistemology requires that all mistakes in fact be avoided; it doesn't require you to be able to show, or be justified in believing, that they have been avoided. In the case of perception, I can see (hence, know) my wife is on the sofa not because I can justify my belief that she is there—I can't—but because I am connected to a state of affairs—her being on the sofa—in a way that gives me knowledge of her whereabouts. It is the fact that I am suitably connected to the world, not my awareness of, or justification for, this fact, that underlies my knowledge of the world.

So, as I see it, it isn't a question of *whether* a non-skeptic accepts externalism, but *when*. At the beginning—before insisting on justification, reasons, warrant, and the host of other internal resources—or at the end, after these resources (and their potential for quieting the skeptic) have been exhausted. Taking perception as one's guide, one accepts externalism at the very beginning. If lighting is normal I do not have to know or be justified in believing it to be normal in order to see, in normal light, what colour your tie is. Seeing your tie in this light 'connects' me (externally, as it were) to your tie and its colour in such a way as to give me, with or without a justification, knowledge of its colour.

That was my first conclusion. There are several immediate, more or less obvious, corollaries:

1a. Contextualism: *If skepticism is false, contextualism is true: whether S knows that p depends on circumstances of context that are (or may be) completely beyond S's ken.*

Whether or not I see (hence, know) that my wife is on the sofa depends on circumstances that are, or may be, subjectively speaking, inaccessible to me. In the case of my own form of externalism (in Dretske 1969), for instance, it depends on whether or not there are other women (or men or robots, for that matter) that might be on the couch who look (from where I am standing) exactly like my wife. If, unknown to me, there are, then despite seeing my wife on the sofa (it really is her), I can't see that it is. Since things would look the same to me if it was one of these twins (and it really might be one of these twins; this is not, by hypothesis, simply an abstract logical possibility) it is not true that things would not look this way to me unless my wife were on the sofa. So, despite a fully justified true belief (I may be fully justified in believing there are no people who look, from this distance and angle, like my wife), I do not, despite seeing her on the sofa, know my wife is on the sofa. Change the circumstances—by, say, eliminating the existence (or relevance) of twins—and I do know she is on the sofa. I can now, in this different context, see that she is on the sofa. My visual evidence is now, quite unknown to me, enough to eliminate relevant alternatives (alternatives that might actually be true if my wife were not on the sofa). So now I know. This means I can't tell whether or not I know that p when I see that p. Whether or not I know she is on the sofa when I see her on the sofa depends on the context in which I see her there, on the circumstances (of which I may be totally ignorant) in which I am caused (by my experience of her) to believe she is there. This is one accredited sense of *contextualism* in epistemology.[2]

1b. Non-supervenience: *If skepticism is false, facts about knowledge do not supervene on the knower.*

The failure of supervenience is obvious quite aside from externalism since on most standard accounts knowledge requires (besides belief and justification) truth, and the truth—the fact that my wife is on the sofa—does not supervene on facts about me, the person who knows she is on the sofa. Two people (or the same person at different times) could be the same in all physical and (if this is something more) mental respects (both have the same beliefs, justifications and so on) but differ in what they know because in one case, but not the other, the person's wife is on the sofa.

1c. Failure of KK (and JK): *If externalism is true, you don't have to know you know (KK)—or even be justified in believing you know (JK)—in order to know.*

Once again, the failure of KK (or JK) is not unique to externalism. Given the obvious fact that animals and young children (creatures who lack the concept of

knowledge) know things (without believing they know them), most philosophers reject KK and JK. I mention these doctrines here not because externalists are unique in rejecting them, but because externalism is unique in requiring their rejection. If you are an externalist, 1b and 1c are not optional: you have to reject supervenience and KK.

The type of externalism I developed in *Seeing and Knowing* was expressed by using counterfactuals: I see that (hence, know that[3]) she is on the sofa only if things would not look the way they do to me were she not there. I generalized this account to all factual knowledge in 'Conclusive Reasons' (1971). If the sofa wouldn't look the way it does to me if my wife were not on it, then its looking that way to me (that is, my experience of her) is (what I called) a *conclusive reason* for believing she is on the sofa. I would not be having that experience if what this experience causes me to believe were false. Later, in *Knowledge and the Flow of Information* (1981a), I described this connection in informational terms: a belief that my wife is on the sofa qualifies as knowledge only if it is caused by the information that she is on the sofa. Given the way I conceive of information, these formulae come down to pretty much the same thing; an event or condition (a 'signal') that carries the information that p turns out (because it requires a contextualized probability of 1) to be a conclusive reason for believing p. (I skip over technical details about differences in these accounts and why I felt changes were necessary.) Both formulae are versions of what is now called reliabilism—a species of externalism. They both imply (1a), (1b) and (1c). Whether one has conclusive reason (or information) depends on context, and you don't have to know you have a conclusive reason (or information) to have it. You do not, therefore, have to be justified in believing p in order to know that p.

So far, though, everything is conditional on the falsity of skepticism. Externalism (contextualism and so on) is true if skepticism is false. For all we have so far learned, though, we may not know anything. Skepticism may be true. I may not be able to see whether my wife is on the sofa. To know she is there I may need the kind of justification for my belief that I can never actually obtain.

Perception, though, teaches us something else, something unconditional in nature. Our ability to find out, discover or learn that something is so by seeing (hearing, smelling and so on) is not (as it is now expressed) *closed* under known implication. Knowledge itself may be closed (call this K-closure)—a controversial thesis to which I shall return—but perceptual knowledge (call this p-closure) clearly isn't.

> 2. Lack of p-closure: *From the fact that you know p implies q, it does not follow that if you can see (smell, feel and so on) that p, you can see (smell, feel and so on) that q.*

There are many things implied by what we perceive to be so that we are unable to perceive to be so. Despite knowing that cookies are physical (mind-independent) objects, I can see that there are cookies in the jar without seeing, without even being able to see, that there are physical objects. My claim to have found out, by seeing, that there are cookies in the jar is not a claim to have found out, by seeing, that there are mind-independent objects. Maybe one has to know there are physical objects in order to see that there are cookies in the jar (we'll come back to that), but one surely isn't claiming to see that there are physical objects in saying one can see that there are cookies in the jar. From the fact that anger is, and you know that it is, a state of mind, it does not follow that you can see that the waitress has a mind (is not, for example, a mindless robot) from the fact that you can see that she is getting angry. Visual perception is not an answer—nor, in claiming to see that a waitress is getting angry, do you represent it to be an answer—to the problem of other minds. Nor is a claim to have discovered, by visual means, that there is still some wine left in the bottle ('Just look; you can see that there is') a claim to have discovered, by visual means, what you know to be a consequence of this—that it is not merely coloured water in the bottle.

In *Seeing and Knowing* I described this phenomenon—lack of closure for perceptual knowledge—by speaking of 'protoknowledge'. Protoknowledge was a word I made up to describe the 'knowledge' (it might just be a belief[4]) that your perceptual report implies that you have but which you are not reporting having acquired by perceptual means. Perceptual reports, I said, were progress reports. They describe the way the claimant purports to have got from one place, his protoknowledge, to another

place—the fact he claims to have seen. In the case of seeing that there is wine in the bottle, it is a report on how one got from:

> a. the bottle is either empty or it has some wine left in it

to

> b. it has some wine left in it.

In the case of seeing that the waitress is getting angry, it is a report on how one got from:

> c. she is a waitress, that is a normal human being like you and me,

to

> d. she is angry.

In the case of seeing that there are cookies in the jar, it is a report on how one got from:

> e. the jar is either empty or has some cookies in it

to

> f. there are cookies in the jar.

They are not claims about how the speaker arrived at his starting points (a), (c) and (e). It is often unclear whether the starting point is knowledge or mere assumption (more of this in a moment). S's claim to have seen that there are cookies in the jar does not say how S knows there are physical objects. It certainly doesn't describe (or imply) that this is something S can determine by vision—by just looking. All a person who says she can see that there are cookies in the jar is claiming for her discriminatory powers is that she can distinguish, on visual grounds, empty cookie jars from ones with cookies in them. One can do this (and, thus, see that there are cookies in the jar) without being able to discriminate, visually, real cookies in real jars from hallucinatory 'cookies' in hallucinatory 'jars' or real cookies from expertly made fakes.

The failure of perceptual closure is a significant result. It means that there can be no valid skeptical objection—at least none of a general sort—to perceptual claims. If perceptual claims to have seen (smelled, tasted) that p are really epistemic progress reports, reports on how the speaker got from one (generally unspecified) place to another (the fact that p), then the magnitude of what has been done, and thus the possibility of doing it, depends on where (what fact?) the speaker came from in reaching his perceptual conclusion. Trying to find, as the skeptic purports to find, objections to the possibility of seeing (hearing, tasting and so on) that p would be like trying to find objections to the possibility of walking, say, to New York City. Whether a person can walk to New York City depends on where he walked from in getting there. Was it Boston? Paris? Hackensack, New Jersey? Maybe he couldn't have walked to New York City from *Paris*. Maybe he could have walked there from Hackensack. The claim to have walked to New York City, being, as it were, a progress report, doesn't specify where the speaker came from in getting to New York. It could have been a difficult, maybe even impossible, feat or a leisurely stroll across a Hudson River bridge. You can't tell. It would be silly, therefore, to object to the possibility of walking to New York City on the grounds that no one can walk on water. Maybe the impossibility of walking on water means one can't walk to New York from Paris, but that doesn't mean a person (even a Parisian) cannot walk to New York City. They can walk there from Hackensack. No trick at all.

Exactly the same is true of perceptual reports. Whether I can see that my wife is on the sofa depends on where I came from in reaching that conclusion. If all I am claiming to have done (and there are many conversational contexts in which this is all I am claiming to have done) is to distinguish, on visual grounds, my wife being on the sofa from your wife being on the sofa or (depending on contrastive intent) my wife being on the sofa from my wife somewhere else, that is no trick at all. The possibility of hallucinations, dreams and illusions—the usual bag of skeptical tricks—is totally irrelevant to these modest perceptual claims. What the possibility of hallucination and deception demonstrates is that one cannot arrive where one says one arrived—knowledge that one's wife is on the sofa—from a state of total ignorance. It shows that one cannot distinguish, at least not on purely visual grounds, veridical from illusory visual experiences. It shows that one cannot, as it were, walk on epistemological water. In saying that one sees that one's wife is on the sofa, though, one is not claiming to walk on water. All one is saying is that one

can successfully tell (visually) the difference between one's wife being on the sofa and her being wherever else she might be if she were not on the sofa. Epistemically speaking, *that* discrimination is a piece of cake—the epistemological equivalent of an easy stroll across a bridge.

A determined skeptic will not, of course, be silenced by the fact that p-closure fails. He is more interested in k-closure and (to take the analogy one more step) what it implies about the possibility of getting to a place, for example Hackensack, from which one can walk to New York City. The skeptic might grudgingly concede that if all we are claiming to have done when we report seeing that p is to have visually distinguished p from a relevant set of contextually understood alternatives (cookies in the jar from, say, an empty jar, my wife on the sofa from my wife being somewhere else in the room), then there is no objection—at least none of a general nature—to our having done what we said we did. The possibility of deception by Cartesian demons, for instance, certainly doesn't show that empty cookie jars look the same as jars with cookies in them or that the sofa looks the same to me whether or not my wife is on it. But to have reached the conclusion that p, to know that there are cookies in the jar, requires more than the ability to tell the difference between an empty jar and one with cookies in it. It requires more than completing the last *stage* of this cognitive journey. It requires that that final stage be undertaken from a state of knowledge. There's the rub. In visually distinguishing an empty cookie jar from one with cookies in it, a discrimination most people (or, indeed, animals) are perfectly able to make, one (with the help of a little background information) arrives at knowledge that there are cookies in the jar (that is sees that there are cookies in the jar) only if one makes this discrimination with the knowledge that those (an empty jar or one with cookies in it) are the only two remaining options. One sees that there are cookies in the jar only if one starts with knowledge that that (the thing one sees) is a real cookie jar (not just a figment of one's imagination) that is either empty or has cookies in it. Clever imitation cookies in real jars and hallucinatory cookies in hallucinatory jars are not options one is called upon to rule out on strictly visual grounds. If they are, if one can't exclude these other possibilities on other grounds, one can't see that there are cookies in the jar. If one doesn't start with knowledge of this sort, knowledge of a restricted set of competitors, the discriminatory powers that are supposed to take you to your destination—knowledge that there are cookies in the jar—are powerless to get you there. Yes, one can walk to New York City from Hackensack. In epistemology, though, there is no way to get to Hackensack—or, indeed, any place from which you can walk to New York City. That, the skeptic concludes, is what his arguments show.

So the skeptic's position comes down to this: although a way of discovering p need not be a way of discovering q, even when you know that p implies q, one cannot discover p in any way unless you know q. As a concession to ordinary language, the skeptic may be willing to concede that perceptual claims are progress reports: seeing that p is true may be just a way of going, by visual means, from some unspecified q (which p implies) to p. You need not, as a result, be able to see that q is true in order to see that p is true (even when you know that p implies q). Nonetheless, you have to know that q is true in order to see that p is true. Perceptual knowledge may not be closed under known logical implication, but knowledge is. That is why it is impossible for anyone, ever, to see whether there are cookies in the jar or who is on the sofa.

Is this true? Is it true that I cannot see that my wife is on the sofa unless I know that the woman on the sofa is not an expertly disguised imposter? In Dretske (1970) I asked the same question about my ability to see that an animal is a zebra and not a cleverly disguised mule. It seemed to me then, as it still seems to me today, that if this is true, if knowledge is closed under logical implication, if, in order to see that there are cookies in the jar (that my wife is on the sofa, that the waitress is getting angry) I have to know that the 'appearances' are not misleading, that I am not being fooled by a clever deception, then skepticism is true. I never see (to be true) what I think and say I do.[5] So I am tempted to add to my list of things perception teaches that K-closure is false. We don't have to know all the things we know to be implied by what we see (hence, know) to be so. Some of these things, yes. Maybe, most of the things. But not everything. There are some things—call them *limiting propositions*—that we know are implied by what we know that we needn't know. Or, if we really do have to know them, knowledge of them is a completely different animal, reached in a completely different way, than everyday meat and potatoes knowledge.

Is the denial of K-closure an acceptable option for dealing with skepticism? Can we retain knowledge of ordinary affairs and give up on knowledge of limiting propositions? It isn't a step one should take lightly. Many philosophers, indeed most philosophers, find it 'one of the least plausible ideas to gain currency in epistemology in recent years' (Feldman 1999). They find it 'intuitively bizzare' or 'abominable' (DeRose 1995). They take the failure of K-closure to be a 'devastating objection' (Fumerton 1987) or a *reductio ad absurdum* to any theory that implies or embraces it (BonJour 1987). Most philosophers, of course, are anxious to reject skepticism. Rejecting K-closure as a way around skepticism, though, is quite another thing. As the above reactions indicate, many philosophers are not willing to do it. So this leaves us with the question: aside from its usefulness in answering a skeptic, are there any reasons to abandon K-closure?

One possible reason to abandon K-closure is that its denial is not just *a* way to avoid skepticism, but the *only* way. This reason won't appeal to the skeptic, of course, but, if we could make a case for it, it might carry weight with those who find skepticism as 'bizarre' or 'abominable' as the rejection of K-closure. Many philosophers, though, have figured out a way to reject skepticism without abandoning K-closure. According to these theories, I get to know (such things as) that there are cookies in the jar (so skepticism is false) and (since I know the relevant implications) that all skeptical alternatives (to there being cookies in the jar) are false (so K-closure still holds). As a result, when I see there are cookies in the jar I know (at least I am evidentially positioned to know[6]) that I am not being tricked by cunning demons or meddlesome neighbours. Some of these theories come precariously close to the bizarreness they seek to avoid. Does the perception of cookies in a jar really give one all the evidence one needs to know that the experience is not illusory?

I won't, however, press the point. What I propose to do, instead, is say why, despite qualms, the denial of K-closure remains, for me, an attractive anti-skeptical option.

There is the fact that a 'relevant alternatives' analysis of knowledge—an analysis to which I am partial—leads so naturally (not inevitably,[7] but naturally) to a failure of K-closure. If knowledge that p requires one (or one's evidence) to exclude not all, but only all relevant, alternatives to p, then, it seems, one is committed to a failure of K-closure. The evidence that (by excluding all relevant alternatives) enables me to know my wife is on the sofa does not enable me to know that it is not a cleverly disguised imposter since, in most circumstances at least, this is not a relevant alternative. So my evidence for thinking it is my wife on the sofa doesn't have to be evidence that it is not a cleverly disguised imposter. So I end up knowing p (at least having good evidence to believe p) but not knowing (at least having no evidence to believe) $not\text{-}q$ even though I know that p implies $not\text{-}q$.

Although this is, as I say, a natural line of reasoning, it isn't very effective against the skeptic—not if the only reason one can give for embracing a relevant alternative analysis of knowledge is that it captures commonsense (basically anti-skeptical) intuitions about when and what we know. If, that is, one's reasons for accepting a relevant alternatives analysis of knowledge is that it accords with our ordinary practice of claiming to know something (that there are cookies in the jar) without having specific evidence against possible mistakes (that, for example, we are not being deceived by cunning demons), then the argument against K-closure is too tightly circular to be effective against a skeptic. One uses premises–basically what kind of evidence is good enough to know—that no self-respecting skeptic would concede.

A dialectically more effective strategy is to provide an independent (of skepticism) analysis of knowledge that yields the result that only certain alternatives (to what is known) are evidentially relevant.[8] If conclusive reasons of the sort I described earlier were, in fact, necessary for knowledge, then K-closure fails. Things turn out this way because

(C) I would not be having this experience if my wife weren't on the sofa

can be true—thus making my experience of my wife a conclusive reason for believing she is on the sofa—while

(C*) I would not be having this experience if the person on the sofa were someone who (merely) looked like my wife

is false—thus preventing the experience from being a conclusive reason for believing what I know to be implied by my wife's being on the sofa.

I have learned, though, that not many people agree that this is a necessary condition on knowledge. Nonetheless, I think many of the arguments for the necessity of this condition are good arguments. I have yet to see effective counterarguments.[9] I won't, however, bother with these arguments here. You don't make reasons better by repeating them. Instead, I close by mentioning two other considerations that point, suggestively, in the same direction.

Consider, first, the fact that not only is p-closure false, none of our non-perceptual ways of coming to know, none of our ways of preserving knowledge, and none of our ways of extending it are closed under known implication. Consider the following small sample:

1. Testimony, an important source of knowledge, isn't closed. We all know that tires are material objects. Yet I can learn, by being told, that I have a flat tire without learning, at least not by being told, that there is a material world. No one, in fact, ever told me there was a material world and, even if someone did (for example a philosophy teacher), that would not be the way I came to know there was one. Yet, being told is the way I come to know things that (I know) imply there is a material world. Testimony is not a way of coming to know a limiting proposition.

2. Proof, an important way of extending knowledge, isn't closed. I can prove that the square root of 5 is larger than the square root of 4 (the proof is quite simple) without being able to prove that 5 has a square root. A proof that 5 has a square root requires knowledge of the real number system of which one may be ignorant.

3. Memory, an important way of preserving knowledge, isn't closed under known implication. I can remember that I went to the bank before I stopped at the bakery without remembering what I know to be implied by this—that time, the succession of events (and, in particular, the past) is real. That the past is real, I suspect, is not something I can remember. That does not prevent me from remembering things that require there to be a past. That the past is real is, for memory, a limiting proposition. You don't have to be able to remember what has to be true for what you remember to be true.

If all this is so, if none of our ways of knowing, extending knowledge or preserving knowledge are closed, it seems odd to suppose that knowledge itself is closed. How is one supposed to get closure on something when every way of getting, extending and preserving it is open? Isn't this some kind of regress?

Skeptics, no doubt, will be quick to point out that it is a regress—exactly the one they have been harping about all along. Recognizing it is just another way of appreciating why knowledge is impossible. I prefer to think of it differently, as semantic evidence for the openness of all epistemic terms. Knowledge is what you get when you reduce some pre-existing, contextually understood, set of possibilities—the relevant alternatives—to one. You can do that, and thus have knowledge, without supposing that this pre-existing set can itself be reached from the universal set (all possibilities) by the same, or, indeed, by any, method. That would be like inferring that there must be a finite number of (whole) numbers because every (whole) number is finite.

Not only are all our ways of knowing open, the knowledge enabling relations we all depend on are open. They, too, stop short of limiting propositions. Consider *indication*. We come to know that there are deer in the woods by seeing the tracks that indicate this. Yet, tracks in the snow indicate that there are deer in the woods without indicating that there is a physical world. Tracks in the snow are *part* of the physical world, not something that indicates there is a physical world. Tree rings indicate the age of the tree and we use this fact to find out how old the tree is by counting the rings. Yet, the rings indicate the age of the tree without indicating what we know to be a necessary consequence of this—that the past is real. We cannot answer Russell's skeptical query about the past by looking for tree stumps with at least one ring in them. If there is a past, if that limiting proposition is true, tree rings will indicate how much of a past a tree has had, but they will not indicate that the tree has had a past.

In a sense, then, indication is an epistemologically stronger relation than logical implication. If I know that A indicates B, then, by learning that A is true, I can come to know that B is true. But if I know that A implies B, it does not follow that I can come to know that B is true by learning that A is true. If B

is one of our limiting propositions—that the past is real, that there is an external world, that there are other minds—then A, something I know to be true, can imply it without indicating it. So I cannot learn that these propositions are true by discovering that they are logically implied by what I already know. To know they are true I would need something to indicate that they are true. Skepticism gets its foothold in the fact that nothing we are aware of indicates that these propositions are true although their truth is assured by the things we know

Much the same can be said for another important epistemic relation: *information*. As it is ordinarily understood, information is that stuff out there—whatever, exactly, that stuff is—that one needs to have, or needs to get, in order to know. If you don't have it, you don't know. In order to get it we go to the library, surf the web, consult experts, go back to school or read the newspaper. It is significant, then, that information, like indication, is not closed. You can get information p—from measuring instruments, letters, books, informants—without getting information q even though you know p implies q.

To appreciate this, think about an ordinary measuring instrument. The speedometer in your car carries information about the speed of the car. It tells you ('informs' you) how fast you are going—60 mph. That is what enables you, by consulting the meter, to know that you are going 60 mph. When the instrument provides this information, does it also tell you that nothing is causing it to register '60' when the car, in fact, is going 70? I am not, mind you, asking whether you know you are not going 70 mph with a defective speedometer. Maybe you do. Maybe you had the instrument checked for accuracy and now know that it is performing flawlessly. No, what I am asking is whether the speedometer itself tells you it is not broken, that it is functioning properly, that it is not misrepresenting a speed of 70 as 60. You know, of course, that if the car is going 60 mph, it is not going 70 mph—hence, not being made to register '60' (by, say, a broken spring) while the car is going 70. Yet, though you know this, you depend on the speedometer to provide the first piece of information, not the second. No measuring instrument carries information that what it is providing is real information and not—because of faulty assembly, defective installation, or miscalibration—misinformation.

What this means, of course, is that all measuring instruments (and this includes the human senses) provide information without providing information known to be implied by the information they provide. Information, our most important epistemic commodity, is not closed under known implication.[10] Information, too, has its limiting propositions.

This is not a proof that K-closure fails anymore than the fact that p-closure is false is a proof that K-closure is false. It is, however, suggestive. Why should knowledge be closed when everything we depend on to give us knowledge isn't?

Notes

1. I say this is an 'example' because, of course, this is only one of the many things I might come to know by seeing my wife on the sofa. I might (because her back is turned to me) only see that someone is on the sofa or that a woman is on the sofa or (because a table blocks my view of what she is sitting on) that my wife is sitting on something. When I do see that my wife is on the sofa, there is also (because of differences in contrastive focusing) the difference between seeing who is on the sofa (that it is my wife) and seeing where my wife is (that she is on the sofa). These are different perceptual judgements, quite different cognitive acts. There are circumstances in which you can do the one without being able to do the other. See Dretske (1972) for a discussion of the epistemological relevance of contrastive focusing.

2. It corresponds to the kind of contextualism in Annis (1978). There is another version of contextualism (see Cohen 1999) that makes the truth of a knowledge claim depend on the context of the claimant—the person (this may be S herself) who says S knows that p. So, for instance, in this second form of contextualism, my claim that S knows that p depends on the circumstances in which I, the speaker, say that S knows that p, not (not necessarily anyway) the context of S, the person who is said to know that p. Contextualism of this sort makes compatible (because of possibly different contexts in which the claims occur) my claim that S knows that p and your denial that S knows that p. See the exchange between Cohen and myself in McLaughlin (1991). I have, since 1966 anyway, always been a contextualist of the first sort, never one of the second sort.

3. I assume that, generally speaking, when a perceptual verb is followed by a factive nominal (that so-and-so) or question word clause (who he is, where she went

and so on) knowledge is implied. This has been questioned, and there certainly are exceptions to the general rule (for example 'I heard that p' does not imply 'I know that p'; it doesn't even imply 'p'), but in most contexts there is this implication.

4. It might not even be a belief for third person (de re) perceptual reports. My statement that Clyde saw that your house was burning down does not only not imply that Clyde knew it was your house, it doesn't even imply that Clyde thought it was your house. All it implies (and this is only a conversational implicature) is that I, the speaker, believe it was your house. What I say here about proto-knowledge is intended to be for first person perceptual claims. Things get a lot messier in third person and/or past tensed statement—when I describe what you (or I) saw to be the case.

5. The parenthetical qualifier is necessary since skepticism is irrelevant to what objects (events, conditions and so on) I see—whether, for instance, I see my wife on the sofa, cookies in the jar or an angry waitress. That is, skepticism can be true, I can be completely ignorant of what it is I see, and still see things (people on sofas, cookies in jars, angry waitresses and so on). What I don't see if skepticism is true is that my wife (or anyone, for that matter) is on the sofa, that anything (much less cookies) are in the jar and so on.

6. This qualification is necessary because some of these theories embrace a form of contextualism according to which if the possibility of hallucination, being fooled by cunning demons and so on actually arises (thus changing the context in which the knowledge claim is advanced) you cease to know there are cookies in the jar since you cannot evidentially exclude these (now relevant) skeptical possibilities. You only know you aren't being fooled when the possibility of being fooled does not arise—when, in other words, you don't think about it.

7. It doesn't necessitate a rejection of K-closure because there are versions of a relevant alternatives analysis of knowledge that keep closure. Klein (1981, 1995), for instance, argues that despite having nothing to show in the way of specific evidence for thinking the zoo authorities have not put a disguised mule in the zebra pen, one can nonetheless know they didn't do it because one can see that it is a zebra and one knows that if it's a zebra the zoo authorities didn't do that. Knowing that not-q is implied by what one knows is good enough to know not-q even if one has no particular evidence bearing on whether or not q. Stine (1976), Cohen (1988) and Lewis (1996), while adopting a relevant alternative account of knowledge, retain closure by embracing a fairly radical form of contextualism. DeRose (1995) gives an externalist form of contextualism and argues that it retains closure while

permitting knowledge. For a general survey and discussion of options, see Brueckner (1985b).

8. This is Nozick's (1981) strategy.

9. An oft-mentioned criticism is that the theory is subject to the sort of counter examples (unpublished) Saul Kripke gave of Robert Nozick's (1981) theory. I do not think these examples work against my own theory even though there is a superficial similarity between Nozick's and my account (we both use counterfactuals to express the required relations between knower and known). I haven't the space to discuss this fully here, but for the cognoscenti it may suffice to say this much. When there are, in the relevant neighbourhood, fake barns but no fake *red* barns (so that something might look like a barn without being a barn, but nothing would look like a red barn without being a red barn), it turns out that on Nozick's theory you can track (Nozick's term) red barns (you wouldn't believe it was a red barn unless it was a red barn) without tracking barns. Thus, you can know of a red barn you see that it is a red barn but not that it is a barn. This is an embarrassment–even for someone (like Nozick) who denies closure. The example is not effective against a 'conclusive reason' (or 'informational') style analysis, though, since these theories are formulated not in terms of a *belief* tracking a condition, but one's reasons or evidence (the condition causing you to believe) tracking the condition. S knows it is a barn if that feature of the evidence causing S to believe it is a barn would not exist if it were not a barn. In the case of perception, if its looking like a red barn is what is causing S to believe it is a barn, then S has a conclusive reason to believe it is a barn: it would not look that way (like a red barn) unless it was a barn, and its looking like a red barn is what is causing S to believe it is a barn. Hence, he knows it is a barn. If, on the other hand, it is merely the building looking like a barn that is causing S to believe it is a barn (its colour being irrelevant to the causing of the belief) then S does not know it is a barn. His experience carries the information that it is a barn (since it looks like a red barn to him and its looking like a red barn carries the information that it is a barn), but that isn't the aspect of experience that is causing him to believe. Knowledge is *information caused belief* and in this second case the information isn't causing the belief.

All this should be evident to anyone who has thought about an example Alvin Goldman (1975) introduced years ago. Even if I mistakenly take wolves to be dogs so that my belief that x is a dog does not 'track' dogs in my environment I can nonetheless know of a dachshund, seen at close range in broad daylight, that it is a dog. What is crucial to knowing the dachshund is a dog is that it has a distinctive look (it is, in this respect, like a red barn), a look that only (dachshund) dogs have. If it is this distinctive look that causes me to believe it is a dog, I know it is a dog no matter how confused I am about wolves—no matter how much my beliefs about dogs fail to 'track' dogs.

10. I only dimly appreciated this when I wrote *Knowledge and the Flow of Information*. I understood (and said) that signals did not carry information about (what I called) the information channel, the stable set of conditions in which signals covary with, and carry information about, a variable source. No measuring instrument, for instance, carries the information that it, the instrument, is not broken. I should have more clearly realized, therefore, that a signal can carry information *p* but not carry information implied by *p*–that, for example, the signal has not arrived from a *not-p* source over a 'broken' channel of communication. As a result, I endorsed the idea (I called it the xerox principle) that if signal S carries information *p*, S carries all the information that condition *p* carries. Since condition *p* carries information about all the conditions implied by '*p*' (given *p*, the probability of all the conditions *p* implies is 1), the xerox principle was, in effect, an endorsement of closure for information. That was a mistake. The xerox principle must be restricted in the same way closure is restricted, namely to certain consequences.

References

Annis, David (1978) "A Contextualist Theory of Epistemic Justification," *American Philosophical Quaterley* 15: 213-19.

BonJour, Laurence (1987) "Nozick, Externalism, and Skepticism," in Luper, S., Ed., *The Possibility of Knowledge*. Totowa: Rowman and Littlefield.

Cohen, Stewart (1999) "Contextualism, Skepticism, and the Structure of Reasons," *Pholosophical Perspectives* 13: 57-89.

Dretske, Fred (1969) *Seeing and Knowing*. Chicago: University of Chicago Press. —— (1972) "Contrastive Statements," *Philosophical Review* 81: 411-30.

DeRose, Keith (1995) "Solving the Skeptical Problem," *Philosophical Review* 104: 1-52.

Feldman, Fred (1999) "Contextualism and Skepticism," in Tomberlin, J. (ed) *Philosophical Perspectives* 13: 91-114.

Goldman, Alvin (1975) "Discrimination and Perceptual Knowledge," *Journal of Philosophy* 73: 771-91.

Klein, Peter (1981) *Certainty*. Oxford: Clarendon Press.

—— (1995) "Skepticism and Closure," *Philosophical Topics* 23: 213-36.

McLaughlin, B., ed. (1991) *Dretske and his Critics*. Oxford: Basil Blackwell.

27. SKEPTICISM, RELEVANT ALTERNATIVES, AND DEDUCTIVE CLOSURE

G. C. *Stine*

Discussions of skepticism, defined with varying degrees of precision, are of course perennial in philosophy. Some recent discussions of the issue[1] give prominence to the notion of 'relevant alternatives', according to which a claim to know that p is properly made in the context of a limited number of competing alternatives to p; to be justified in claiming to know p (or simply to know p) it is sufficient to be able to rule out alternatives relevant to that context. This seems to me to be a correct and heartening development. Recent epistemological discussions have also brought up a relatively new subject, which is the validity of the general form of argument:

> a. *a* knows that p
> <u>*a* knows that p entails q</u>
> ∴ *a* knows that q

I shall call this the principle of epistemic deductive closure, or simply, in this paper, deductive closure.[2] What is interesting about recent comments on this principle is that it is perceived to have something to do with skepticism—in fact to lead to it—and hence is currently of very bad repute. And 'relevant alternatives' views of knowledge vis-à-vis skepticism are supposed to show us the falsity of the principle.

In this paper I propose to do three things. First, to give a qualified argument for deductive closure. Second, to give a qualified argument against skepticism which will make use of the relevant alternatives idea. It will be similar to others in leaving rather indeterminate the way in which the context determines what is taken to be a relevant alternative, although I shall distinguish different sources of this indeterminateness and draw some further conclusions. Third, I shall give an unqualified argument to the effect that the questions of the validity of the principle of epistemic deductive closure

and skepticism are completely *irrelevant* to one another, and that in fact proper attention to the idea of relevant alternatives tends to confirm the principle. This, of course, puts me in direct conflict with the recent trend I have mentioned.

Epistemic Deductive Closure

I am in principle suspicious of all principles of epistemic logic on the general grounds that while the logic of a knower who is in some way simplified and idealized may be useful for limited purposes, what we are ultimately interested in are actual knowers who can be pretty obtuse and idiosyncratic, yet still lay claim to knowledge. For this, among other reasons, I have elsewhere been concerned with epistemic logic which eschews possible worlds semantics imposing strong constraints on knowers.[3] Certainly, I would reject the pattern which goes:

> b. *a* knows that p
> <u>p entails q</u>
> ∴ *a* knows that q

However, the pattern which I have labeled epistemic deductive closure does seem to represent a certain bare minimum. One looks naturally for counterinstances involving failure of belief where p and q are very complicated, but any such case I can imagine turns out to be apparent only because it invariably raises doubts about the truth of the second premise which are as strong as the doubts about the truth of the conclusion. The principle seems to be on a par with epistemic conjunction, to wit:

> c. *a* knows p
> <u>*a* knows q</u>
> ∴ *a* knows p and q

There have, of course, been problems in reconciling this principle with commitments to rational belief in terms of degrees of confirmation and knowledge in terms of rational belief,[4] but one feels strongly inclined to the view that the adjustment must be made in the area of these commitments and not in the principle of conjunction.

In addition to failure of belief, one may look for counter-examples to the principle of epistemic deductive closure in the area of failure of evidence or warrant. One's initial reaction to this idea is that if one's evidence is not sufficient for knowing q, it is not sufficient for knowing p, either, where p is known to entail q. I shall be returning to this subject later, for some philosophers to whom I have referred deny this point which seems, initially, fairly obvious and I shall argue that their reasons are mistaken.

Actually, if instead of (A) we adopt the stronger epistemic deductive closure principle:

> d. a knows p
> a knows q
> a knows ($p \cdot q$ entails r)
> ∴ a knows r

(A) and (C) may be seen as instances of a common principle, provided we allow 'a knows ($p \cdot q$ entails $p \cdot q$)' as an uncontroversial instance of the third premise.[5] (D) is, ultimately, what we need, anyway to capture the idea of knowing the known logical consequences of what one knows, for (A) covers only the known consequences of the things one knows taken individually, not the known consequences of one's whole body of knowledge. And although (D) is stronger than (A), the arguments for (A) work just as strongly for (D), and, so far as I can see, there are no arguments that anyone might seriously offer against (D) which do not also apply to (A). However, for the sake of simplicity and conformity to other discussions in the literature, I shall continue to discuss deductive closure in the form of (A).

In summary, I am not absolutely convinced of the validity of the principle of epistemic deductive closure, as I am not absolutely convinced of the validity of the principle of epistemic conjunction, but in neither case can I think of an objection, and in both cases, apparent problems they lead to (skepticism, inconsistency) are either apparent only or are better handled by giving up other less obvious principles.

Skepticism

In *Belief, Truth and Knowledge*, D. M. Armstrong argues:

> It is not a conclusive objection to a thermometer that it is only reliable in a certain sort of environment. In the same way, reliability of belief, but only within a certain sort of environment, would seem to be sufficient for the believer to earn the accolade of knowledge if that sort of environment is part of his boundary-conditions.[6]

For example, I know that the striped animal I see in the zoo is a zebra.[7] I know this despite the fact that I have no particular evidence that it is not a mule painted to look like a zebra (I have not looked for a paint can, tried paint remover on the animal, etc.) In this context—under normal circumstances, in zoos of integrity, etc.—that an animal on display has been deliberately disguised to fool trusting zoo-goers is just not a relevant hypothesis, one that I need trouble myself about rejecting. If the skeptic tries to persuade me to his position by stressing my lack of evidence against such an hypothesis, my proper response is to turn a deaf ear. He has ensnared me by improper means and is more than halfway to (illegitimately) winning his point if he gets me to agree that I must argue with him, go look for further evidence, etc.

This view, which I call the relevant alternative view, seems to me fundamentally correct. It does leave a lot of things unsaid. What are normal circumstances? What makes an alternative relevant in one context and not in another? However, in ordinary life, we do exhibit rather strong agreement about what is relevant and what is not. But there are grey areas. Alvin Goldman makes this point nicely with the following example which he attributes to Carl Ginet: if on the basis of visual appearances obtained under optimum conditions while driving through the countryside Henry identifies an object as a barn, normally we say that Henry knows that it is a barn. Let us suppose, however, that unknown to Henry, the region is full of expertly made papier-maché facsimiles of barns. In this case, we would not say Henry knows that the object is a barn, unless he has evidence against it being a papier-maché facsimile, which is now a relevant alternative. So much is clear, but what if no such facsimiles exist in Henry's surroundings, although they do in Sweden? What if they do not now exist in Sweden, but they once did? Are either of these circumstances sufficient to make the hypothesis relevant? Probably not, but the situation is not so clear.

Another area of obscurity resides not in the nature of the case but in the formulation of the view in question. Goldman seems to hold what I regard as the correct version of it, which is that:

1. an alternative is relevant only if there is some reason to think that it is true.

But there is also the view that:

2. an alternative is relevant only if there is some reason to think it *could* be true.

Clearly, the force of the 'could' cannot be mere logical possibility, or the relevant alternative view would lose its distinguishing feature. However, if the 'could' is read in some stronger way, we could still have a version of the relevant alternative view. Dretske's 'Conclusive Reasons'[8] paper, espousing a view according to which if one knows, then given one's evidence, one could not be wrong (he reads 'could' as 'physically possible') suggests that we should consider an hypothesis a live one unless it *could not* be true, given one's evidence. Hence any alternative would be relevant, in the sense of blocking knowledge, if one has not the evidence to rule it out, so long as it is physically possible, given one's evidence. Also, the passage in 'Epistemic Operators' where Dretske says: "A relevant alternative is an alternative that *might* have been realized in the existing circumstances if the actual state of affairs had not materialized",[9] is more akin to (2) than (1), although so taking it depends on the force of his 'might'. This, I think, is the wrong way to take the relevant alternative view. First of all, however unclear it may be as to when there is some reason to think an alternative is true, it is much more unclear as to when there is reason to think it could be true.

Certainly, if there is a difference between (1) and (2), (2) is weaker, allows more to count as a relative alternative. So possibly Descartes thought there was some reason to think that there *could*, in some sense stronger than logical possibility, be an evil genius. But it seems safe to say he was wrong if he thought that there was some reason to think that there *was* an evil genius. That is, the evil genius hypothesis is not a relevant alternative according to (1) but may be according to (2) (although I shall qualify this). But the whole thrust of the relevant alternative position, as I conceive it, is that such an hypothesis is not relevant. To allow it as relevant seems to me to preclude the kind of answer to the skeptic which I sketched in the opening paragraph of this section.

In truth, Dretske does combine a relevant alternative view with an answer to skepticism. But his account is tied in with a view of knowledge, which, although it does defeat skepticism, does so in a way which gives small confort. On his account, we do know many things, i.e., there are many things about which given our evidence, we could not be wrong. However, he does not merely reject the view that knowing entails knowing that one knows.[10] He also seems committed to the view that one rarely, if ever, knows that one knows, for it is well high impossible on his account to defend the claim that one *knows*, given one's evidence, that one *could not* be wrong, in his sense of 'could'. Perhaps this is preferable to skepticism, but at best it is going from the fire into the frying pan.

Here some qualifications of this position that the relevant alternative view provides an answer to the skeptic are in order. In truth, *in some sense* skepticism is unanswerable. This rather supports the relevant alternative view, for the uncertainty which infects (1) as to when there is some reason to think an alternative true explains why this is so. The relevant alternative view does provide a kind of answer to the skeptic—the only kind of answer which can be given. But the skeptic has an entering wedge, and rightly so. It is an essential characteristic of our concept of knowledge that tighter criteria are appropriate in different contexts.[11] It is one thing in a street encounter, another in a classroom, another in a law court—and who is to say it cannot be another in a philosophical discussion? And this is directly mirrored by the fact we have different standards for judging that there is some reason to think an alternative is true, i.e., relevant. We can point out that some philosophers are very perverse in their standards (by *some* extreme standard, there is some reason to think there is an evil genius, after all)—but we cannot legitimately go so far as to say that their perversity has stretched the concept of knowledge out of all recognition—in fact they have played on an essential feature of the concept. On the other hand, a skeptical philosopher is wrong if he holds that *others* are wrong in any way–i.e., are sloppy, speaking only loosely, or whatever—when they say we know a great deal. And the relevant alternative view gives the correct account of why a skeptic is wrong if he makes such accusations.

Deductive Closure and Skepticism

Proponents of the relevant alternative view have tended to think that it provides grounds for rejecting deductive closure. Although many philosophers have recently taken this position, Dretske has provided the fullest published argument to this effect. He writes:

> To know that X is A is to know that X is A within a framework of relevant alternatives, B, C, and D. This set of contrasts together with the fact X is A, serve to define what it is that is known when one knows that X is A. One cannot change this set of contrasts without changing what a person is said to know when he is said to know that X is A. We have subtle ways of shifting these contrasts and, hence, changing what a person is said to know *without changing the sentence that we use to express what he knows.*[12]

Consider the following instance of (A):

e. John knows that the animal is a zebra
   John knows that [*the animal is a zebra* entails *the animal is not a mule painted to look like a zebra*]
   ∴ John knows that the animal is not a mule painted to look like a zebra

In Dretske's zoo example, the animal's being a mule painted to look like a zebra is not a relevant alternative. So what one means when one says that John knows the animal is a zebra, is that he knows it is a zebra, as opposed to a gazelle, an antelope, or other animals one would normally expect to find in a zoo. If, however, being a mule painted to look like a zebra became a relevant alternative, then one would literally mean something different in saying that John knows that the animal is a zebra from what one meant originally and that something else may well be false. Now, normally, in saying that one knows that p, one presupposes (in some sense) that not-p is a relevant alternative; hence one does not know p unless one has evidence to rule out not-p. This is in fact Dretske's view, for he holds that one does *not* know that the animal is not a mule painted to look like a zebra because one has no evidence to rule out the possibility that it is. However, according to Dretske, so long as the animal's being a mule painted to look like a zebra is not a relevant alternative, the fact that John does not know that it is not does not count against John's knowing that it is a zebra. Hence, deductive closure fails (we are assuming that John's knowing an animal's being a zebra entails his knowing that it is not a mule); i.e., (E) and hence (A), are invalid.

I submit that there is another account of this example on the relevant alternative view which does not entail giving up deductive closure. On this account, to say that John knows that p does normally presuppose that not-p is a relevant alternative. This is, however, a pragmatic, not a semantic presupposition.[13] That is, it is the speaker, not the sentence (or proposition) itself, who does the presupposing. Thus, the presupposition falls in the category of those which Grice labels 'cancellable'.[14] It is possible for 'John knows that p' to be true even though a pragmatic presupposition, that not-p is a relevant alternative, is false. I would say that we may create some sort of special circumstance which cancels the normal presupposition when we utter the sentence in the course of making a deductive closure argument. After all, the utterance has got to be an odd case where we are given that not-p is not a relevant alternative to begin with—we can expect something unusual to happen, other than being forced to admit that it is a relevant alternative, after all. For even if we would not normally *affirm* 'John knows that *p*' in such a situation, we would not normally *say* that John does *not* know that *p*, either. Or it may happen that stating a deductive closure argument affects normal presuppositions in another way. If we hesitate to say "John knows that the animal is not a mule painted to look like a zebra", we *may* well hesitate to affirm "John knows the animal is a zebra". If this is so, not being a mule painted to look like a zebra will have become a relevant alternative—we will have decided there is some reason to think it true—with respect to the latter sentence as well. Perhaps the mere utterance of the former sentence is enough to make us loosen up our notion of what counts as a relevant alternative.

Either way, my account holds the set of relevant alternatives constant from beginning to end of the deductive closure argument. This is as it should be; to do otherwise would be to commit some logical sin akin to equivocation. If the relevant alternatives, which have after all to do with the truth or falsity of the premises and conclusion, cannot be held fixed, it is hard so see on what basis one can decide whether the argument form is valid or not. And if the set of relevant alternatives is one thing for the first premise and another for the conclusion, how do we determine what it is for the second premise, and how does this affect the truth of the second premise? There is no reason for my account of the matter to make skeptics of us all. The skeptical argument goes: If you know it is a zebra, and you know its being a zebra entails its not being a painted mule, then you know it is not a mule painted to look like a zebra. But you do not know the last, so you do not know the first—i.e., you do not know it is a zebra. With our account in hand, let us see how the skeptic is to be treated. There are two possibilities. First, the skeptic may be up to something legitimate. He is beginning by suggesting that being a mule painted to look like a zebra is a relevant alternative—i.e., that there is some reason to think it is true. We point out to the skeptic that under normal circumstances, given what we know of people and zoos, etc., this is not the case. The skeptic may, however, persevere, playing on the looseness of 'some reason to think true'. At this point, while we cannot argue the

skeptic out of his position, we are perfectly within our rights in refusing to adopt the skeptic's standards and can comfort ourselves by feeling that the skeptic, if not flatly wrong, is at least very peculiar. On the other hand, the skeptic may be up to something illegitimate. He may be trying to get us to doubt that we know it is a zebra without going through the hard work of convincing us that being a mule painted to look like a zebra is a relevant alternative. The skeptic seeks to persuade us of his conclusion by getting us to admit that we do not know it is not a mule painted to look like a zebra because we do not have evidence to rule out the possibility that it is. This is what Dretske believes and this is why he believes we must give up deductive closure to defeat the skeptic. I think this a wrong move. We do know it is not a mule painted to look like a zebra. Let us grant temporarily for the sake of this argument we do not have evidence. But Dretske is deluded by the fact that many knowledge claims require evidence on the part of the knower into thinking that all knowledge claims require evidence. Normally, as I have admitted, saying '*a* knows that *p*' presupposes that not-*p* is a relevant alternative. And it does sound odd to say that we know it is not a mule painted to look like a zebra when its being one is not a relevant alternative. But the fact that it sounds odd - is indeed perhaps misleading or even improper to say—does not mean as we have seen that the presupposition is not cancellable, and that the proposition in question is not true. We often get results which sound odd to *say* when we draw valid conclusions from true premises the utterance of which does not sound odd. 'John knows that it is raining may be true and quite in order to say to convey its literal meaning. But on the assumption of minimal logical competence on John's part and deductive closure, it entails 'John knows that it is either raining or not raining'. But this sentence, if uttered at all, is most likely to be used to suggest the negation of the first sentence. We might, in fact, say that the speaker presupposes it. Given knowledge of the first sentence, the latter is too obviously true to bother uttering at all, except for purposes of sarcasm, ironic effect, or some purpose other than conveying the information expressed by the literal meaning of the words. Yet, for all that, it is literally true. Or take a case with per-haps more analogies to our example. This is an ex-ample from Grice.[15] 'My wife is in the kitchen' im-plies 'My wife is in the kitchen or in the bedroom'. Yet, the utterance of the latter, in normal circum-stances, presupposes the speaker's ignorance of the former and is thus an improper or at best misleading thing for him to say if he knows the former. But for all that, the latter is true if the former is, and the presupposition is cancellable.

The logical consequences of knowledge claims which the skeptic draws by deductive closure of the sort Dretske discusses, are the sorts of propositions which, in normal circumstances, are such that their negations are not relevant alternatives. Thus they sound odd to say and often have the effect of sug-gesting that the circumstances are abnormal. It is in-deed improper to utter them in normal circum-stances unless one explicitly cancels the relevant alternative presupposition which they carry, because one misleads. Nevertheless, they are literally true in normal circumstances. I endorse here a view which I believe to be Austin's.[16] This view is adumbrated in the following passage:

> If, for instance, someone remarks in casual con-versation, 'As a matter of fact I live in Oxford', the other party to the conversation may, if he finds it worth doing, verify this assertion; but the *speaker*, of course, has no need to do this—he knows it to be true (or, if he is lying, false). . . . Nor need it be true that he is in this position by virtue of having verified his assertion at some previous stage; for of how many people really, who know quite well where they live, could it be said that they have at any time *verified* that they live there? When could they be supposed to have done this? In what way? And why? What we have here, in fact, is an erroneous doctrine . . . about evidence.[17]

The point is that one does know what one takes for granted in normal circumstances. I do know that it is not a mule painted to look like a zebra. I do not need evidence for such a proposition. The evidence picture of knowledge has been carried too far. I would say

that I do not have evidence that it is a zebra, either. I simply *see* that it is one. But that is perhaps another matter. The point I want to make here is simply that if the negation of a proposition is not a relevant alter-native, then I know it obviously, without needing to provide evidence - and so obviously that it is odd, misleading even, to give utterance to my knowledge. And it is a virtue of the relevant alternative view that it helps explain why it is odd.

There is another way in which (E) could be de-fended. This line could be to claim that John does, after all, in his general knowledge of the ways of zoos and people, etc., have evidence that the animal is not a mule painted to look like a zebra. The same would hold for other consequences of knowledge claims which the skeptic draws by deductive clo-sure. This would involve a notion of evidence ac-cording to which having evidence is not just limited to cases in which one has a specific datum to which to point. Malcolm expresses this point of view when he says:

> . . . The reason is obvious for saying that my copy of James's book does not have the charac-teristic that its print undergoes spontaneous changes. I have read millions of printed words on many thousands of printed pages. I have not encountered a single instance of a printed word vanishing from a page or being replaced by another printed word, suddenly and without external cause. Nor have I heard of any other person who had such an encounter. There is *over whelming evidence* that printed words do not behave in that way. It is just as conclusive as the evidence that houses do not turn into flowers. That is to say, *absolutely conclusive evidence*[18] (underscore mine).

It is true that in the last sentence of this passage Malcolm talks about evidence for a universal propo-sition to the effect that printed words do not be-have in a certain way, but the thrust of his argu-ment is such that he commits himself to the view that he also (thereby) has evidence that the printed words on his particular copy of James's book will not behave that way. I am not inclined towards such a view of what it is to have adequate evidence for the proposition that the print of my own particular copy of James's book did not undergo a spontaneous change. I am inclined to reject Malcolm's view, and others akin, in favor of the Austinian sort of one previously discussed—that is, that in such a case, evidence is not required to support a knowledge claim. I mention the view only as a possible alternative view of defending epistemic deductive closure in a way consonant with the relevant alternative riew.

Summary

My view is that the relevant alternative position should be conceived of as in two parts:

1. With respect to many propositions, to establish a knowledge claim is to be able to support it as opposed to a limited number of alternatives—i.e., only those which are relevant in the context.
2. With respect to many propositions—in particular those which are such that their negations are not relevant alternatives in the context in question— we simply know them to be true and do not need evidence, in the normal sense, that they, rather than their negations, are true.

So conceived, the relevant alternative view neither supports the abandonment of deductive closure, nor is such abandonment in any way needed to provide the relevant alternative view with an answer to the skeptic, insofar as he can be answered.[19]

Notes

1. I am partial to J. L. Austin's approach in 'Other Minds' (*Philosophical Papers*, Oxford, 1961), and Chapter X of *Sense and Sensibilia* (Oxford, 1962). Other more recent and more explicitly developed accounts include those of Fred Dretske, most importantly in 'Epistemic Operators', *Journal of Philosophy*, LXVII (1970), 1007–1023, but also in 'Contrastive Statements', *Philosophical Review* LXXXI (1972), 411–430; D. M. Armstrong, *Belief, Truth and Knowledge* (Cambridge, 1973); Alvin Goldman 'Discrimination and Perceptual Knowledge', presented at the Annual Philosophy Colloquium, University of

Cincinnati, 1973; James Cargile, 'Knowledge and Deracination', presented at the Annual Philosophy Colloquium, University of Cincinnati, 1973; Norman Malcolm in 'The Verification Argument' in *Knowledge and Certainty* (Prentice-Hall, 1963) is more concerned with certainty than knowledge but his discussion of when a proposition is 'possible' is very much in accord with considerations which go towards making a proposition a 'relevant alternative'.

2. Dretske, 'Epistemic Operators', *Op. cit.*; Cargile, *Loc, cit*; Goldman, *Loc. cit.*

3. Cf. 'Quantified Logic for Knowledge Statements', *Journal of Philosophy* LXXI (1974), and 'Essentialism, Possible Worlds, and Propositional Attitudes', *Philosophical Review* LXXXII (1973), 471–482.

4. Cf. discussions of the place of a principle of conjunction in an account of rational belief in, for example, Isaac Levi, *Gambling With Truth*, Knopf (1967); and in *Induction, Acceptance, and Rational Belief*, ed. by Swain, Reidel (1970) the following papers: Marshall Swain, 'The Consistency of Rational Belief', Henry Kyburg, 'Conjunctivitis', and Keith Lehrer, 'Justification, Explanation, and Induction'. This case for conjunction holding for rational belief is, of course, more problematic than the case for knowledge.

5. I owe this point to David Kaplan.

6. Armstrong, *Op. cit*, p. 174.

7. The example is Dretske's in 'Epistemic Operators' *Loc. cit.*

8. In *Australasian Journal of Philosophy* **49** (1971), 1–22.

9. 'Epistemic Operators', *loc. cit.*, p. 1021.

10. This view has been criticized, for example, by Ronald DeSousa in 'Knowledge Consistent Belief, and Self-Consciousness', *Journal of Philosophy* (1970), against defenders of it such as Jaakko Hintikka in *Knowledge and Belief* (Cornell, 1962) and Keith Lehrer in 'Belief and Knowledge', *Philosophical Review* (1968). The view is also rejected by Armstrong, *Op. cit.* (p. 146), and at least implicitly rejected on such accounts of knowledge as, for example, those of Alvin Goldman, 'A Causal Theory of Knowing', *Journal of Philosophy* **64** (1967), 357–372; Brian Skyrms, 'The Explication of 'X Knows that P'', *Journal of Philosophy* **64** (1967), 373–389; and Peter Unger, 'An Analysis of Factual Knowledge,' *Journal of Philosophy* **65** (1968), 157–170.

11. Here I take a view directly opposed to that of Peter Unger, 'A Defense of Skepticism', *Philosophical Review* (1971), according to which knowledge is an 'absolute' concept, like the flatness of geometers.

12. 'Epistemic Operators', *Loc. cit.*, p. 1022.

13. Here I distinguish pragmatic from semantic presuppositions in the manner of Robert Stalnaker, 'Pragmatics', in *Semantics of Natural Language*, ed. by Davidson

and Harman (Reidel, 1972), 380–397. Attributing the notion of a semantic presupposition to Bas van Fraassen ('Singular Terms, Truth Value Gaps, and Free Logic', *Journal of Philosophy* **63** (1966), 481–495, and 'Presupposition, Implication, and Self Reference', *Journal of Philosophy* **65** (1968), 136–151, Stalnaker says (p. 387):

According to the *semantic* concept, a proposition P presupposes a proposition Q if and only if Q is necessitated both by P and by *not*-P. That is, in every model in which P is either true or false, Q is true. According to the *pragmatic* conception, presupposition is a propositional attitude, not a semantic relation. People, rather than sentences or propositions are said to have, or make, presuppositions in this sense.

. . . In general, any semantic presupposition of a proposition expressed in a given context will be a pragmatic presupposition of the people in that context, but the converse clearly does not hold.

To presuppose a proposition in the pragmatic sense is to take its truth for granted, and to assume that others involved in the context do the same.

14. H. P. Grice, 'The Causal Theory of Perception', *Proceedings of the Aristotelian Society*, Suppl. Vol. XXXV (1961).

15. *Ibid.*

16. In 'Other Minds', *Loc. cit.*, and Chapter X of *Sense and Sensibilia*, Oxford (1962).

17. *Sense and Sensibilia*, pp. 117–118.

18. 'The Verification Argument', *Loc. cit.*, p. 38.

19. A slightly different and shorter version of this paper was read at the Eastern Division meetings of the American Philosophical Association, December 1974.

✧ A SPEAKER–CENTERED ✧
CONTEXTUALIST RESPONSE

28. ELUSIVE KNOWLEDGE*

David Lewis

We know a lot. I know what food penguins eat. I know that phones used to ring, but nowadays squeal, when someone calls up. I know that Essendon won the 1993 Grand Final. I know that here is a hand, and here is another.

We have all sorts of everyday knowledge, and we have it in abundance. To doubt that would be absurd. At any rate, to doubt it in any serious and lasting way would be absurd; and even philosophical and temporary doubt, under the influence of argument, is more than a little peculiar. It is a Moorean fact that we know a lot. It is one of those things that we know better than we know the premises of any philosophical argument to the contrary.

Besides knowing a lot that is everyday and trite, I myself think that we know a lot that is interesting and esoteric and controversial. We know a lot about things unseen: tiny particles and pervasive fields, not to mention one another's underwear. Sometimes we even know what an author meant by his writings. But on these questions, let us agree to disagree peacefully with the champions of 'post-knowledgeism'. The most trite and ordinary parts of our knowledge will be problem enough.

For no sooner do we engage in epistemology—the systematic philosophical examination of knowledge—than we meet a compelling argument that we know next to nothing. The sceptical argument is nothing new or fancy. It is just this: it seems as if knowledge must be by definition infallible. If you claim that S knows that P, and yet you grant that S cannot eliminate a certain possibility in which not-P, it certainly seems as if you have granted that S does not after all know that P. To speak of fallible knowledge, of knowledge despite uneliminated possibilities of error, just *sounds* contradictory.

Blind Freddy can see where this will lead. Let your paranoid fantasies rip—CIA plots, hallucinogens in the tap water, conspiracies to deceive, old Nick himself—and soon you find that uneliminated possibilities of error are everywhere. Those possibilities of error are far-fetched, of course, but possibilities all the same. They bite into even our most everyday knowledge. We never have infallible knowledge.

Never—well, hardly ever. Some say we have infallible knowledge of a few simple, axiomatic necessary truths; and of our own present experience. They say that I simply cannot be wrong that a part of a part of something is itself a part of that thing; or that it seems to me now (as I sit here at the keyboard) exactly as if I am hearing clicking noises on top of a steady whirring. Some say so. Others deny it. No matter; let it be granted, at least for the sake of the argument. It is not nearly enough. If we have only that much infallible knowledge, yet knowledge is by definition infallible, then we have very little knowledge indeed—not the abundant everyday knowledge we thought we had. That is still absurd.

So we know a lot; knowledge must be infallible; yet we have fallible knowledge or none (or next to none). We are caught between the rock of fallibilism and the whirlpool of scepticism. Both are mad!

Yet fallibilism is the less intrusive madness. It demands less frequent corrections of what we want to say. So, if forced to choose, I choose fallibilism. (And so say all of us.) We can get used to it, and some of us have done. No joy there—we know that people can get used to the most crazy philosophical sayings imaginable. If you are a contented fallibilist, I implore you to be honest, be naive, hear it afresh.

'He knows, yet he has not eliminated all possibilities of error.' Even if you've numbed your ears, doesn't this overt, explicit fallibilism *still* sound wrong?

Better fallibilism than scepticism; but it would be better still to dodge the choice. I think we can. We will be alarmingly close to the rock, and also alarmingly close to the whirlpool, but if we steer with care, we can—just barely—escape them both.

Maybe epistemology is the culprit. Maybe this extraordinary pastime robs us of our knowledge. Maybe we do know a lot in daily life; but maybe when we look hard at our knowledge, it goes away. But only when we look at it harder than the sane ever do in daily life; only when we let our paranoid fantasies rip. That is when we are forced to admit that there always are uneliminated possibilities of error, so that we have fallible knowledge or none.

Much that we say is context-dependent, in simple ways or subtle ways. Simple: 'it's evening' is truly said when, and only when, it is said in the evening. Subtle: it could well be true, and not just by luck, that Essendon played rottenly, the Easybeats played brilliantly, yet Essendon won. Different contexts evoke different standards of evaluation. Talking about the Easybeats we apply lax standards, else we could scarcely distinguish their better days from their worse ones. In talking about Essendon, no such laxity is required. Essendon won because play that is rotten by demanding standards suffices to beat play that is brilliant by lax standards.

Maybe ascriptions of knowledge are subtly context-dependent, and maybe epistemology is a context that makes them go false. Then epistemology would be an investigation that destroys its own subject matter. If so, the sceptical argument might be flawless, when we engage in epistemology—and only then![1]

If you start from the ancient idea that justification is the mark that distinguishes knowledge from mere opinion (even true opinion), then you well might conclude that ascriptions of knowledge are context-dependent because standards for adequate justification are context-dependent. As follows: opinion, even if true, deserves the name of knowledge only if it is adequately supported by reasons; to deserve that name in the especially demanding context of epistemology, the arguments from supporting reasons must be especially watertight; but the special standards of justification that this special context demands never can be met (well, hardly ever). In the strict context of epistemology we know nothing, yet in laxer contexts we know a lot.

But I myself cannot subscribe to this account of the context-dependence of knowledge, because I question its starting point. I don't agree that the mark of knowledge is justification.[2] First, because justification is not sufficient: your true opinion that you will lose the lottery isn't knowledge, whatever the odds. Suppose you know that it is a fair lottery with one winning ticket and many losing tickets, and you know how many losing tickets there are. The greater the number of losing tickets, the better is your justification for believing you will lose. Yet there is no number great enough to transform your fallible opinion into knowledge—after all, you just might win. No justification is good enough—or none short of a watertight deductive argument, and all but the sceptics will agree that this is too much to demand.[3]

Second, because justification is not always necessary. What (non-circular) argument supports our reliance on perception, on memory, and on testimony?[4] And yet we do gain knowledge by these means. And sometimes, far from having supporting arguments, we don't even know how we know. We once had evidence, drew conclusions, and thereby gained knowledge; now we have forgotten our reasons, yet still we retain our knowledge. Or we know the name that goes with the face, or the sex of the chicken, by relying on subtle visual cues, without knowing what those cues may be.

The link between knowledge and justification must be broken. But if we break that link, then it is not—or not entirely, or not exactly—by raising the standards of justification that epistemology destroys knowledge. I need some different story.

To that end, I propose to take the infallibility of knowledge as my starting point.[5] Must infallibilist epistemology end in scepticism? Not quite. Wait and see. Anyway, here is the definition. Subject S *knows* proposition P iff P holds in every possibility left uneliminated by S's evidence; equivalently, iff S's evidence eliminates every possibility in which not-P.

The definition is short, the commentary upon it is longer. In the first place, there is the proposition, P. What I choose to call 'propositions' are individuated coarsely, by necessary equivalence. For instance, there is only one necessary proposition. It holds in every possibility; hence in every possibility left uneliminated by S's evidence, no matter who S may be and no matter what his evidence may be. So the necessary proposition is known always and everywhere. Yet this known proposition may go unrecognised when presented in impenetrable linguistic disguise, say as the proposition that every even number is the sum of two primes. Likewise, the known proposition that I have two hands may go unrecognised when presented as the proposition that the number of my hands is the least number n such that every even number is the sum of n primes. (Or if you doubt the necessary existence of numbers, switch to an example involving equivalence by logic alone.) These problems of disguise shall not concern us here. Our topic is modal, not hyperintensional, epistemology.[6]

Next, there are the possibilities. We needn't enter here into the question whether these are concreta, abstract constructions, or abstract simples. Further, we needn't decide whether they must always be maximally specific possibilities, or whether they need only be specific enough for the purpose at hand. A possibility will be specific enough if it cannot be split into subcases in such a way that anything we have said about possibilities, or anything we are going to say before we are done, applies to some subcases and not to others. For instance, it should never happen that proposition P holds in some but not all subcases; or that some but not all sub-cases are eliminated by S's evidence.

But we do need to stipulate that they are not just possibilities as to how the whole world is; they also include possibilities as to which part of the world is oneself, and as to when it now is. We need these possibilities *de se et nunc* because the propositions that may be known include propositions *de se et nunc*.[7] Not only do I know that there are hands in this world somewhere and somewhen. I know that I have hands, or anyway I have them *now*. Such propositions aren't just made true or made false by the whole world once and for all. They are true for some of us and not for others, or true at some times and not others, or both.

Further, we cannot limit ourselves to 'real' possibilities that conform to the actual laws of nature, and maybe also to actual past history. For propositions about laws and history are contingent, and may or may not be known.

Neither can we limit ourselves to 'epistemic' possibilities for S—possibilities that S does not know not to obtain. That would drain our definition of content. Assume only that knowledge is closed under strict implication. (We shall consider the merits of this assumption later.) Remember that we are not distinguishing between equivalent propositions. Then knowledge of a conjunction is equivalent to knowledge of every conjunct. P is the conjunction of all propositions not-W, where W is a possibility in which not-P. That suffices to yield an equivalence: S knows that P iff, for every possibility W in which not-P, S knows that not-W. Contraposing and cancelling a double negation: iff every possibility which S does not know not to obtain is one in which P. For short: iff P holds throughout S's epistemic possibilities. Yet to get this far, we need no substantive definition of knowledge at all! To turn this into a substantive definition, in fact the very definition we gave before, we need to say one more thing: S's epistemic possibilities are just those possibilities that are uneliminated by S's evidence.

So, next, we need to say what it means for a possibility to be eliminated or not. Here I say that the uneliminated possibilities are those in which the subject's entire perceptual experience and memory are just as they actually are. There is one possibility that actually obtains (for the subject and at the time in question); call it *actuality*. Then a possibility W is *uneliminated* iff the subject's perceptual experience and memory in W exactly match his perceptual experience and memory in actuality. (If you want to include other alleged forms of basic evidence, such as the evidence of our extrasensory faculties, or an innate disposition to believe in God, be my guest. If they exist, they should be included. If not, no harm done if we have included them conditionally.)

Note well that we do not need the 'pure sense-datum language' and the 'incorrigible protocol statements' that for so long bedevilled foundationalist epistemology. It matters not at all whether there are words to capture the subject's perceptual and memory evidence, nothing more and nothing less. If there are such words, it matters not at all whether the subject can hit upon them. The given does not consist of basic axioms to serve as premises in subsequent arguments. Rather, it consists of a match between possibilities.

When perceptual experience E (or memory) eliminates a possibility W, that is not because the propositional content of the experience conflicts with W. (Not even if it is the narrow content.) The propositional content of our experience could, after all, be false. Rather, it is the existence of the experience that conflicts with W: W is a possibility in which the subject is not having experience E. Else we would need to tell some fishy story of how the experience has some sort of infallible, ineffable, purely phenomenal propositional content . . . Who needs that? Let E have propositional content P. Suppose even—something I take to be an open question—that E is, in some sense, fully characterized by P. Then I say that E eliminates W iff W is a possibility in which the subject's experience or memory has content different from P. I do *not* say that E eliminates W iff W is a possibility in which P is false.

Maybe not every kind of sense perception yields experience; maybe, for instance, the kinaesthetic sense yields not its own distinctive sort of sense-experience but only spontaneous judgements about the position of one's limbs. If this is true, then the thing to say is that kinaesthetic evidence eliminates all possibilities except those that exactly resemble actuality with respect to the subject's spontaneous kinaesthetic judgements. In saying this, we would treat kinaesthetic evidence more on the model of memory than on the model of more typical senses.

Finally, we must attend to the word 'every'. What does it mean to say that every possibility in which not-P is eliminated? An idiom of quantification, like 'every', is normally restricted to some limited domain. If I say that every glass is empty, so it's time for another round, doubtless I and my audience are ignoring most of all the glasses there are in the whole wide world throughout all of time. They are outside the domain. They are irrelevant to the truth of what was said.

Likewise, if I say that every uneliminated possibility is one in which P, or words to that effect, I am doubtless ignoring some of all the uneliminated alternative possibilities that there are. They are outside the domain, they are irrelevant to the truth of what was said.

But, of course, I am not entitled to ignore just any possibility I please. Else true ascriptions of knowledge, whether to myself or to others, would be cheap indeed. I may properly ignore some uneliminated possibilities; I may not properly ignore others. Our definition of knowledge requires a *sotto voce* proviso. *S knows that P iff S's* evidence eliminates every possibility in which not-*P*—Psst!—except for those possibilities that we are properly ignoring.

Unger suggests an instructive parallel.[8] Just as *P* is known iff there are no uneliminated possibilities of error, so likewise a surface is flat iff there are no bumps on it. We must add the proviso: Psst!—except for those bumps that we are properly ignoring. Else we will conclude, absurdly, that nothing is flat. (Simplify by ignoring departures from flatness that consist of gentle curvature.)

We can restate the definition. Say that we *presuppose* proposition *Q* iff we ignore all possibilities in which not-*Q*. To close the circle: we *ignore* just those possibilities that falsify our presuppositions. *Proper* presupposition corresponds, of course, to proper ignoring. Then *S* knows that *P* iff *S's* evidence eliminates every possibility in which not-*P*—Psst!—except for those possibilities that conflict with our proper presuppositions.[9]

The rest of (modal) epistemology examines the *sotto voce* proviso. It asks: what may we properly presuppose in our ascriptions of knowledge? Which of all the uneliminated alternative possibilities may not properly be ignored? Which ones are the 'relevant alternatives'?—relevant, that is, to what the subject does and doesn't know?[10] In reply, we can list several rules.[11] We begin with three prohibitions: rules to tell us what possibilities we may not properly ignore.

First, there is the *Rule of Actuality*. The possibility that actually obtains is never properly ignored; actuality is always a relevant alternative; nothing false may

properly be presupposed. It follows that only what is true is known, wherefore we did not have to include truth in our definition of knowledge. The rule is 'externalist'—the subject himself may not be able to tell what is properly ignored. In judging which of his ignorings are proper, hence what he knows, we judge his success in knowing–not how well he tried.

When the Rule of Actuality tells us that actuality may never be properly ignored, we can ask: *whose* actuality? Ours, when we ascribe knowledge or ignorance to others? Or the subject's? In simple cases, the question is silly. (In fact, it sounds like the sort of pernicious nonsense we would expect from someone who mixes up what is true with what is believed.) There is just one actual world, we the ascribers live in that world, the subject lives there too, so the subject's actuality is the same as ours.

The definition restated in terms of presupposition resembles the treatment of knowledge in Kenneth S. Ferguson, *Philosophical Scepticism* (Cornell University doctoral dissertation, 1980).

But there are other cases, less simple, in which the question makes perfect sense and needs an answer. Someone may or may not know who he is; someone may or may not know what time it is. Therefore I insisted that the propositions that may be known must include propositions *de se et nunc*; and likewise that the possibilities that may be eliminated or ignored must include possibilities *de se et nunc*. Now we have a good sense in which the subject's actuality may be different from ours. I ask today what Fred knew yesterday. In particular, did he then know who he was? Did he know what day it was? Fred's actuality is the possibility *de se et nunc* of being Fred on September 19th at such-and-such possible world; whereas my actuality is the possibility *de se et nunc* of being David on September 20th at such-and-such world. So far as the world goes, there is no difference: Fred and I are worldmates, his actual world is the same as mine. But when we build subject and time into the possibilities *de se et nunc*, then his actuality yesterday does indeed differ from mine today.

What is more, we sometimes have occasion to ascribe knowledge to those who are off at other possible worlds. I didn't read the newspaper yesterday.

What would I have known if I had read it? More than I do in fact know. (More and less: I do in fact know that I left the newspaper unread, but if I had read it, I would not have known that I had left it unread.) I-who-did-not-read-the-newspaper am here at this world, ascribing knowledge and ignorance. The subject to whom I am ascribing that knowledge and ignorance, namely I-as-I-would-have-been-if-I-had-read-the-newspaper, is at a different world. The worlds differ in respect at least of a reading of the newspaper. Thus the ascriber's actual world is not the same as the subject's. (I myself think that the ascriber and the subject are two different people: the subject is the ascriber's otherworldly counterpart. But even if you think the subject and the ascriber are the same identical person, you must still grant that this person's actuality *qua* subject differs from his actuality *qua* ascriber.)

Or suppose we ask modal questions about the subject: what must he have known, what might he have known? Again we are considering the subject as he is not here, but off at other possible worlds. Likewise if we ask questions about knowledge of knowledge: what does he (or what do we) know that he knows?

So the question 'whose actuality?' is not a silly question after all. And when the question matters, as it does in the cases just considered, the right answer is that it is the subject's actuality, not the ascriber's, that never can be properly ignored.

Next, there is the *Rule of Belief*. A possibility that the subject believes to obtain is not properly ignored, whether or not he is right to so believe. Neither is one that he ought to believe to obtain—one that evidence and arguments justify him in believing—whether or not he does so believe.

That is rough. Since belief admits of degree, and since some possibilities are more specific than others, we ought to reformulate the rule in terms of degree of belief, compared to a standard set by the unspecificity of the possibility in question. A possibility may not be properly ignored if the subject gives it, or ought to give it, a degree of belief that is sufficiently high, and high not just because the possibility in question is unspecific.

How high is 'sufficiently high'? That may depend on how much is at stake. When error would be

especially disastrous, few possibilities may be properly ignored. Then even quite a low degree of belief may be 'sufficiently high' to bring the Rule of Belief into play. The jurors know that the accused is guilty only if his guilt has been proved beyond reasonable doubt.[12]

Yet even when the stakes are high, some possibilities still may be properly ignored. Disastrous though it would be to convict an innocent man, still the jurors may properly ignore the possibility that it was the dog, marvellously well-trained, that fired the fatal shot. And, unless they are ignoring other alternatives more relevant than that, they may rightly be said to know that the accused is guilty as charged. Yet if there had been reason to give the dog hypothesis a slightly less negligible degree of belief—if the world's greatest dog-trainer had been the victim's mortal enemy—then the alternative would be relevant after all.

This is the only place where belief and justification enter my story. As already noted, I allow justified true belief without knowledge, as in the case of your belief that you will lose the lottery. I allow knowledge without justification, in the cases of face recognition and chicken sexing. I even allow knowledge without belief, as in the case of the timid student who knows the answer but has no confidence that he has it right, and so does not believe what he knows.[13] Therefore any proposed converse to the Rule of Belief should be rejected. A possibility that the subject does not believe to a sufficient degree, and ought not to believe to a sufficient degree, may nevertheless be a relevant alternative and not properly ignored.

Next, there is the *Rule of Resemblance*. Suppose one possibility saliently resembles another. Then if one of them may not be properly ignored, neither may the other. (Or rather, we should say that if one of them may not properly be ignored *in virtue of rules other than this rule*, then neither may the other. Else nothing could be properly ignored; because enough little steps of resemblance can take us from anywhere to anywhere.) Or suppose one possibility saliently resembles two or more others, one in one respect and another in another, and suppose that each of these may not properly be ignored (in virtue of rules other than this rule). Then these resemblances may have an additive effect, doing more together than any one of them would separately.

We must apply the Rule of Resemblance with care. Actuality is a possibility uneliminated by the subject's evidence. Any other possibility W that is likewise uneliminated by the subject's evidence thereby resembles actuality in one salient respect: namely, in respect of the subject's evidence. That will be so even if W is in other respects very dissimilar to actuality—even if, for instance, it is a possibility in which the subject is radically deceived by a demon. Plainly, we dare not apply the Rules of Actuality and Resemblance to conclude that any such W is a relevant alternative—that would be capitulation to scepticism. The Rule of Resemblance was never meant to apply to *this* resemblance! We seem to have an *ad hoc* exception to the Rule, though one that makes good sense in view of the function of attributions of knowledge. What would be better, though, would be to find a way to reformulate the Rule so as to get the needed exception without *ad hocery*. I do not know how to do this.

It is the Rule of Resemblance that explains why you do not know that you will lose the lottery, no matter what the odds are against you and no matter how sure you should therefore be that you will lose. For every ticket, there is the possibility that it will win. These possibilities are saliently similar to one another: so either every one of them may be properly ignored, or else none may. But one of them may not properly be ignored: the one that actually obtains.

The Rule of Resemblance also is the rule that solves the Gettier problems: other cases of justified true belief that are not knowledge.[14]

1. I think that Nogot owns a Ford, because I have seen him driving one; but unbeknownst to me he does not own the Ford he drives, or any other Ford. Unbeknownst to me, Havit does own a Ford, though I have no reason to think so because he never drives it, and in fact I have often seen him taking the tram. My justified true belief is that one of the two owns a Ford. But I do not know it; I am right by accident. Diagnosis: I do not know, because I have not eliminated the possibility that Nogot drives a Ford he does not own whereas Havit neither-drives nor owns

a car. This possibility may not properly be ignored. Because, first, actuality may not properly be ignored; and, second, this possibility saliently resembles actuality. It resembles actuality perfectly so far as Nogot is concerned; and it resembles actuality well so far as Havit is concerned, since it matches actuality both with respect to Havit's carless habits and with respect to the general correlation between carless habits and carlessness. In addition, this possibility saliently resembles a third possibility: one in which Nogot drives a Ford he owns while Havit neither drives nor owns a car. This third possibility may not properly be ignored, because of the degree to which it is believed. This time, the resemblance is perfect so far as Havit is concerned, rather good so far as Nogot is concerned.

2. The stopped clock is right twice a day. It says 4:39, as it has done for weeks. I look at it at 4:39; by luck I pick up a true belief. I have ignored the uneliminated possibility that I looked at it at 4:22 while it was stopped saying 4:39. That possibility was not properly ignored. It resembles actuality perfectly so far as the stopped clock goes.

3. Unbeknownst to me, I am travelling in the land of the bogus barns; but my eye falls on one of the few real ones. I don't know that I am seeing a barn, because I may not properly ignore the possibility that I am seeing yet another of the abundant bogus barns. This possibility saliently resembles actuality in respect of the abundance of bogus barns, and the scarcity of real ones, hereabouts.

4. Donald is in San Francisco, just as I have every reason to think he is. But, bent on deception, he is writing me letters and having them posted to me by his accomplice in Italy. If I had seen the phoney letters, with their Italian stamps and postmarks, I would have concluded that Donald was in Italy. Luckily, I have not yet seen any of them. I ignore the uneliminated possibility that Donald has gone to Italy and is sending me letters from there. But this possibility is not properly ignored, because it resembles actuality both with respect to the fact that the letters are coming to me from Italy and with respect to the fact that those letters come, ultimately, from Donald. So I don't know that Donald is in San Francisco.

Next, there is the *Rule of Reliability*. This time, we have a presumptive rule about what *may* be properly ignored; and it is by means of this rule that we capture what is right about causal or reliabilist theories of knowing. Consider processes whereby information is transmitted to us: perception, memory, and testimony. These processes are fairly reliable.[15] Within limits, we are entitled to take them for granted. We may properly presuppose that they work without a glitch in the case under consideration. Defeasibly—*very* defeasibly!—a possibility in which they fail may properly be ignored.

My visual experience, for instance, depends causally on the scene before my eyes, and what I believe about the scene before my eyes depends in turn on my visual experience. Each dependence covers a wide and varied range of alternatives.[16] Of course, it is possible to hallucinate—even to hallucinate in such a way that all my perceptual experience and memory would be just as they actually are. That possibility never can be eliminated. But it can be ignored. And if it is properly ignored—as it mostly is—then vision gives me knowledge. Sometimes, though, the possibility of hallucination is not properly ignored; for sometimes we really do hallucinate. The Rule of Reliability may be defeated by the Rule of Actuality. Or it may be defeated by the Rules of Actuality and of Resemblance working together, in a Gettier problem: if I am not hallucinating, but unbeknownst to me I live in a world where people mostly do hallucinate and I myself have only narrowly escaped, then the uneliminated possibility of hallucination is too close to actuality to be properly ignored.

We do not, of course, presuppose that nowhere ever is there a failure of, say, vision. The general presupposition that vision is reliable consists, rather, of a standing disposition to presuppose, concerning whatever particular case may be under consideration, that we have no failure in that case.

In similar fashion, we have two permissive *Rules of Method*. We are entitled to presuppose—again, very defeasibly—that a sample is representative; and that the best explanation of our evidence is the true explanation. That is, we are entitled properly to ignore possible failures in these two standard

methods of non-deductive inference. Again, the general rule consists of a standing disposition to presuppose reliability in whatever particular case may come before us.

Yet another permissive rule is the *Rule of Conservatism*. Suppose that those around us normally do ignore certain possibilities, and it is common knowledge that they do. (They do, they expect each other to, they expect each other to expect each other to, ...) Then—again, very defeasibly!—these generally ignored possibilities may properly be ignored. We are permitted, defeasibly, to adopt the usual and mutually expected presuppositions of those around us.

(It is unclear whether we need all four of these permissive rules. Some might be subsumed under others. Perhaps our habits of treating samples as representative, and of inferring to the best explanation, might count as normally reliable processes of transmission of information. Or perhaps we might subsume the Rule of Reliability under the Rule of Conservatism, on the ground that the reliable processes whereby we gain knowledge are familiar, are generally relied upon, and so are generally presupposed to be normally reliable. Then the only extra work done by the Rule of Reliability would be to cover less familiar—and merely hypothetical?—reliable processes, such as processes that relied on extrasensory faculties. Likewise, *mutatis mutandis*, we might subsume the Rules of Method under the Rule of Conservatism. Or we might instead think to subsume the Rule of Conservatism under the Rule of Reliability, on the ground that what is generally presupposed tends for the most part to be true, and the reliable processes whereby this is so are covered already by the Rule of Reliability. Better redundancy than incompleteness, though. So, leaving the question of redundancy open, I list all four rules.)

Our final rule is the *Rule of Attention*. But it is more a triviality than a rule. When we say that a possibility *is* properly ignored, we mean exactly that; we do not mean that it *could have been* properly ignored. Accordingly, a possibility not ignored at all is *ipso facto* not properly ignored. What is and what is not being ignored is a feature of the particular conversational context. No matter how farfetched a certain possibility may be, no matter how properly we might have ignored it in some other context, if in *this* context we are not in fact ignoring it but attending to it, then for us now it is a relevant alternative. It is in the contextually determined domain. If it is an unelimated possibility in which not-P, then it will do as a counter-example to the claim that P holds in every possibility left unelimated by S's evidence. That is, it will do as a counter-example to the claim that S knows that P.

Do some epistemology. Let your fantasies rip. Find unelimated possibilities of error everywhere. Now that you are attending to them, just as I told you to, you are no longer ignoring them, properly or otherwise. So you have landed in a context with an enormously rich domain of potential counter-examples to ascriptions of knowledge. In such an extraordinary context, with such a rich domain, it never can happen (well, hardly ever) that an ascription of knowledge is true. Not an ascription of knowledge to yourself (either to your present self or to your earlier self, untainted by epistemology); and not an ascription of knowledge to others. That is how epistemology destroys knowledge. But it does so only temporarily. The pastime of epistemology does not plunge us forevermore into its special context. We can still do a lot of proper ignoring, a lot of knowing, and a lot of true ascribing of knowledge to ourselves and others, the rest of the time.

What is epistemology all about? The epistemology we've just been doing, at any rate, soon became an investigation of the ignoring of possibilities. But to investigate the ignoring of them was *ipso facto* not to ignore them. Unless this investigation of ours was an altogether atypical sample of epistemology, it will be inevitable that epistemology must destroy knowledge. That is how knowledge is elusive. Examine it, and straightway it vanishes.

Is resistance useless? If you bring some hitherto ignored possibility to our attention, then straightway we are not ignoring it at all, so *a fortiori* we are not properly ignoring it. How can this alteration of our conversational state be undone? If you are persistent, perhaps it cannot be undone—at least not so long as you are around. Even if we go off and play backgammon, and afterward start our conversation afresh, you might turn up and call our attention to it all over again.

But maybe you called attention to the hitherto ignored possibility by mistake. You only suggested that we ought to suspect the butler because you mistakenly thought him to have a criminal record. Now that you know he does not—that was the *previous* butler—you wish you had not mentioned him at all. You know as well as we do that continued attention to the possibility you brought up impedes our shared conversational purposes. Indeed, it may be common knowledge between you and us that we would all prefer it if this possibility could be dismissed from our attention. In that case we might quickly strike a tacit agreement to speak just as if we were ignoring it; and after just a little of that, doubtless it really would be ignored.

Sometimes our conversational purposes are not altogether shared, and it is a matter of conflict whether attention to some far-fetched possibility would advance them or impede them. What if some far-fetched possibility is called to our attention not by a sceptical philosopher, but by counsel for the defence? We of the jury may wish to ignore it, and wish it had not been mentioned. If we ignored it now, we would bend the rules of cooperative conversation; but we may have good reason to do exactly that. (After all, what matters most to us as jurors is not whether we can truly be said to know; what really matters is what we should believe to what degree, and whether or not we should vote to convict.) We would ignore the far-fetched possibility if we could—but can we? Perhaps at first our attempted ignoring would be make-believe ignoring, or self-deceptive ignoring; later, perhaps, it might ripen into genuine ignoring. But in the meantime, do we know? There may be no definite answer. We are bending the rules, and our practices of context-dependent attributions of knowledge were made for contexts with the rules unbent.

If you are still a contented fallibilist, despite my plea to hear the sceptical argument afresh, you will probably be discontented with the Rule of Attention. You will begrudge the sceptic even his very temporary victory. You will claim the right to resist his argument not only in everyday contexts, but even in those peculiar contexts in which he (or some other epistemologist) busily calls your attention to far-fetched possibilities of error. Further, you will claim the right to resist without having to bend any rules of cooperative conversation. I said that the Rule of Attention was a triviality: that which is not ignored at all is not properly ignored. But the Rule was trivial only because of how I had already chosen to state the *sotto voce* proviso. So you, the contented fallibilist, will think it ought to have been stated differently. Thus, perhaps: 'Psst!—except for those possibilities we *could* properly have ignored'. And then you will insist that those far-fetched possibilities of error that we attend to at the behest of the sceptic are nevertheless possibilities we could properly have ignored. You will say that no amount of attention can, by itself, turn them into relevant alternatives.

If you say this, we have reached a standoff. I started with a puzzle: how can it be, when his conclusion is so silly, that the sceptic's argument is so irresistible? My Rule of Attention, and the version of the proviso that made that Rule trivial, were built to explain how the sceptic manages to sway us— why his argument seems irresistible, however temporarily. If you continue to find it eminently resistible in all contexts, you have no need of any such explanation. We just disagree about the explanandum phenomenon.

I say S knows that P iff P holds in every possibility left uneliminated by S's evidence—Psst!—except for those possibilities that *we* are properly ignoring. 'We' means: the speaker and hearers of a given context; that is, those of us who are discussing S's knowledge together. It is our ignorings, not S's own ignorings, that matter to what we can truly say about S's knowledge. When we are talking about our own knowledge or ignorance, as epistemologists so often do, this is a distinction without a difference. But what if we are talking about someone else?

Suppose we are detectives; the crucial question for our solution of the crime is whether S already *knew*, when he bought the gun, that he was vulnerable to blackmail. We conclude that he did. We ignore various far-fetched possibilities, as hard-headed detectives should. But S does not ignore them. S is by profession a sceptical epistemologist.

He never ignores much of anything. If it is our own ignorings that matter to the truth of our conclusion, we may well be right that S already knew. But if it is S's ignorings that matter, then we are wrong, because S never knew much of anything. I say we may well be right; so it is our own ignorings that matter, not S's.

But suppose instead that we are epistemologists considering what S knows. If we are well-informed about S (or if we are considering a well-enough specified hypothetical case), then if S attends to a certain possibility, we attend to S's attending to it. But to attend to S's attending to it is *ipso facto* to attend to it ourselves. In that case, unlike the case of the detectives, the possibilities we are properly ignoring must be among the possibilities that S himself ignores. We may ignore fewer possibilities than S does, but not more.

Even if S himself is neither sceptical nor an epistemologist, he may yet be clever at thinking up far-fetched possibilities that are uneliminated by his evidence. Then again, we well-informed epistemologists who ask what S knows will have to attend to the possibilities that S thinks up. Even if S's idle cleverness does not lead S himself to draw sceptical conclusions, it nevertheless limits the knowledge that we can truly ascribe to him when attentive to his state of mind. More simply: his cleverness limits his knowledge. He would have known more, had he been less imaginative.[17]

Do I claim you can know P just by presupposing it?! Do I claim you can know that a possibility W does not obtain just by ignoring it? Is that not what my analysis implies, provided that the presupposing and the ignoring are proper? Well, yes. And yet I do not claim it. Or rather, I do not claim it for any specified P or W. I have to grant, in general, that knowledge just by presupposing and ignoring *is* knowledge; but it is an *especially* elusive sort of knowledge, and consequently it is an unclaimable sort of knowledge. You do not even have to practise epistemology to make it vanish. Simply *mentioning* any particular case of this knowledge, aloud or even in silent thought, is a way to attend to the hitherto ignored possibility, and thereby render it no longer ignored, and thereby create a context in which it is no longer true to ascribe the knowledge in question to yourself or others. So, just as we should think, presuppositions alone are not a basis on which to *claim* knowledge.

In general, when S knows that P some of the possibilities in which not-P are eliminated by S's evidence and others of them are properly ignored. There are some that can be eliminated, but cannot properly be ignored. For instance, when I look around the study without seeing Possum the cat, I thereby eliminate various possibilities in which Possum is in the study; but had those possibilities not been eliminated, they could not properly have been ignored. And there are other possibilities that never can be eliminated, but can properly be ignored. For instance, the possibility that Possum is on the desk but has been made invisible by a deceiving demon falls normally into this class (though not when I attend to it in the special context of epistemology).

There is a third class: not-P possibilities that might either be eliminated or ignored. Take the far-fetched possibility that Possum has somehow managed to get into a closed drawer of the desk—maybe he jumped in when it was open, then I closed it without noticing him. That possibility could be eliminated by opening the drawer and making a thorough examination. But if uneliminated, it may nevertheless be ignored, and in many contexts that ignoring would be proper. If I look all around the study, but without checking the closed drawers of the desk, I may truly be said to know that Possum is not in the study—or at any rate, there are many contexts in which that may truly be said. But if I did check all the closed drawers, then I would know *better* that Possum is not in the study. My knowledge would be better in the second case because it would rest more on the elimination of not-P possibilities, less on the ignoring of them.[18],[19]

Better knowledge is more stable knowledge: it stands more chance of surviving a shift of attention in which we begin to attend to some of the possibilities formerly ignored. If, in our new shifted context, we ask what knowledge we may truly ascribe to our earlier selves, we may find that only the better knowledge of our earlier selves still deserves the name. And yet, if our former ignorings were proper at the time, even the worse knowledge of our earlier selves could truly have been called knowledge in the former context.

Never—well, hardly ever—does our knowledge rest entirely on elimination and not at all on ignoring. So hardly ever is it quite as good as we might wish. To that extent, the lesson of scepticism is right—and right permanently, not just in the temporary and special context of epistemology.[20]

What is it all for? Why have a notion of knowledge that works in the way I described? (Not a compulsory question. Enough to observe that we do have it.) But I venture the guess that it is one of the messy short-cuts—like satisficing, like having indeterminate degrees of belief—that we resort to because we are not smart enough to live up to really high, perfectly Bayesian, standards of rationality. You cannot maintain a record of exactly which possibilities you have eliminated so far, much as you might like to. It is easier to keep track of which possibilities you have eliminated if you—Psst!—ignore many of all the possibilities there are. And besides, it is easier to list some of the propositions that are true in *all* the uneliminated, unignored possibilities than it is to find propositions that are true in *all and only* the uneliminated, unignored possibilities.

If you doubt that the word 'know' bears any real load in science or in metaphysics, I partly agree. The serious business of science has to do not with knowledge *per se*; but rather, with the elimination of possibilities through the evidence of perception, memory, etc., and with the changes that one's belief system would (or might or should) undergo under the impact of such eliminations. Ascriptions of knowledge to yourself or others are a very sloppy way of conveying very incomplete information about the elimination of possibilities. It is as if you had said:

The possibilities eliminated, whatever else they may also include, at least include all the not-P possibilities; or anyway, all of those except for some we are presumably prepared to ignore just at the moment.

The only excuse for giving information about what really matters in such a sloppy way is that at least it is easy and quick! But it *is* easy and quick; whereas giving full and precise information about which possibilities have been eliminated seems to be extremely difficult, as witness the futile search for a 'pure observation language'. If I am right about how ascriptions of knowledge work, they are a handy but humble approximation. They may yet be indispensable in practice, in the same way that other handy and humble approximations are.

If we analyse knowledge as a modality, as we have done, we cannot escape the conclusion that knowledge is closed under (strict) implication.[21] Dretske has denied that knowledge is closed under implication; further, he has diagnosed closure as the fallacy that drives arguments for scepticism. As follows: the proposition that I have hands implies that I am not a handless being, and *a fortiori* that I am not a handless being deceived by a demon into thinking that I have hands. So, by the closure principle, the proposition that I know I have hands implies that I know that I am not handless and deceived. But I don't know that I am not handless and deceived—for how can I eliminate that possibility? So, by *modus tollens*, I don't know that I have hands. Dretske's advice is to resist scepticism by denying closure. He says that although having hands *does* imply not being handless and deceived, yet knowing that I have hands *does not* imply knowing that I am not handless and deceived. I do know the former, I do not know the latter.[22]

What Dretske says is close to right, but not quite. Knowledge *is* closed under implication. Knowing that I have hands *does* imply knowing that I am not handless and deceived. Implication preserves truth—that is, it preserves truth in any given, fixed context. But if we switch contexts midway, all bets are off. I say (1) pigs fly; (2) what I just said had fewer than three syllables (true); (3) what I just said had fewer than four syllables (false). So 'less than three' does not imply 'less than four'? No! The context switched midway, the semantic value of the context-dependent phrase 'what I just said' switched with it. Likewise in the sceptical argument the context switched midway, and the semantic

value of the context-dependent word 'know' switched with it. The premise 'I know that I have hands' was true in its everyday context, where the possibility of deceiving demons was properly ignored. The mention of that very possibility switched the context midway. The conclusion 'I know that I am not handless and deceived' was false in *its* context, because that was a context in which the possibility of deceiving demons was being mentioned, hence was not being ignored, hence was not being properly ignored. Dretske gets the phenomenon right, and I think he gets the diagnosis of scepticism right; it is just that he misclassifies what he sees. He thinks it is a phenomenon of logic, when really it is a phenomenon of pragmatics. Closure, rightly understood, survives the test. If we evaluate the conclusion for truth not with respect to the context in which it was uttered, but instead with respect to the different context in which the premise was uttered, then truth is preserved. And if, *per impossibile*, the conclusion could have been said in the same unchanged context as the premise, truth would have been preserved.

A problem due to Saul Kripke turns upon the closure of knowledge under implication. *P* implies that any evidence against *P* is misleading. So, by closure, whenever you know that *P*, you know that any evidence against *P* is misleading. And if you know that evidence is misleading, you should pay it no heed. Whenever we know—and we know a lot, remember—we should not heed any evidence tending to suggest that we are wrong. But that is absurd. Shall we dodge the conclusion by denying closure? I think not. Again, I diagnose a change of context. At first, it was stipulated that *S* knew, whence it followed that *S* was properly ignoring all possibilities of error. But as the story continues, it turns out that there is evidence on offer that points to some particular possibility of error. Then, by the Rule of Attention, that possibility is no longer properly ignored, either by *S* himself or by we who are telling the story of *S*. The advent of that evidence destroys *S*'s knowledge, and thereby destroys *S*'s licence to ignore the evidence lest he be misled.

There is another reason, different from Dretske's, why we might doubt closure. Suppose two or more premises jointly imply a conclusion. Might not someone who is compartmentalized in his thinking—as we all are?—know each of the premises but fail to bring them together in a single compartment? Then might he not fail to know the conclusion? Yes; and I would not like to plead idealization-of-rationality as an excuse for ignoring such cases. But I suggest that we might take not the whole compartmentalized thinker, but rather each of his several overlapping compartments, as our 'subjects'. That would be the obvious remedy if his compartmentalization amounted to a case of multiple personality disorder; but maybe it is right for milder cases as well.[23]

A compartmentalized thinker who indulges in epistemology can destroy his knowledge, yet retain it as well. Imagine two epistemologists on a bushwalk. As they walk, they talk. They mention all manner of far-fetched possibilities of error. By attending to these normally ignored possibilities they destroy the knowledge they normally possess. Yet all the while they know where they are and where they are going! How so? The compartment in charge of philosophical talk attends to far-fetched possibilities of error. The compartment in charge of navigation does not. One compartment loses its knowledge, the other retains its knowledge. And what does the entire compartmentalized thinker know? Not an altogether felicitous question. But if we need an answer, I suppose the best thing to say is that S knows that P iff any one of S's compartments knows that P. Then we can say what we would offhand want to say: yes, our philosophical bushwalkers still know their whereabouts.

Context-dependence is not limited to the ignoring and non-ignoring of far-fetched possibilities. Here is another case. Pity poor Bill! He squanders all his spare cash on the pokies, the races, and the lottery. He will be a wage slave all his days. We know he will never be rich. But if he wins the lottery (if he wins big), then he will be rich. Contrapositively: his never being rich, plus other things we know, imply that he will lose. So, by closure, if we know that he will never be rich, we know that he will lose. But when we discussed the case before, we concluded that we cannot know that he will

lose. All the possibilities in which Bill loses and someone else wins saliently resemble the possibility in which Bill wins and the others lose; one of those possibilities is actual; so by the Rules of Actuality and of Resemblance, we may not properly ignore the possibility that Bill wins. But there is a loophole: the resemblance was required to be salient. Salience, as well as ignoring, may vary between contexts. Before, when I was explaining how the Rule of Resemblance applied to lotteries, I saw to it that the resemblance between the many possibilities associated with the many tickets was sufficiently salient. But this time, when we were busy pitying poor Bill for his habits and not for his luck, the resemblance of the many possibilities was not so salient. At that point, the possibility of Bill's winning was properly ignored; so then it was true to say that we knew he would never be rich. Afterward I switched the context. I mentioned the possibility that Bill might win, wherefore that possibility was no longer properly ignored. (Maybe there were two separate reasons why it was no longer properly ignored, because maybe I also made the resemblance between the many possibilities more salient.) It was true at first that we knew that Bill would never be rich. And at that point it was also true that we knew he would lose—but that was only true so long as it remained unsaid! (And maybe unthought as well.) Later, after the change in context, it was no longer true that we knew he would lose. At that point, it was also no longer true that we knew he would never be rich.

But wait. Don't you smell a rat? Haven't I, by my own lights, been saying what cannot be said? (Or whistled either.) If the story I told was true, how have I managed to tell it? In trendyspeak, is there not a problem of reflexivity? Does not my story deconstruct itself?

I said: S knows that P iff S's evidence eliminates every possibility in which not-P—Psst!—except for those possibilities that we are properly ignoring. That 'psst' marks an attempt to do the impossible—to mention that which remains unmentioned. I am sure you managed to make believe that I had succeeded. But I could not have done.

And I said that when we do epistemology, and we attend to the proper ignoring of possibilities, we make knowledge vanish. First we do know, then we do not. But I had been doing epistemology when I said that. The uneliminated possibilities were *not* being ignored—not just then. So by what right did I say even that we used to know?[24]

In trying to thread a course between the rock of fallibilism and the whirlpool of scepticism, it may well seem as if I have fallen victim to both at once. For do I not say that there are all those uneliminated possibilities of error? Yet do I not claim that we know a lot? Yet do I not claim that knowledge is, by definition, infallible knowledge?

I did claim all three things. But not all at once! Or if I did claim them all at once, that was an expository shortcut, to be taken with a pinch of salt. To get my message across, I bent the rules. If I tried to whistle what cannot be said, what of it? I relied on the cardinal principle of pragmatics, which overrides every one of the rules I mentioned: interpret the message to make it make sense—to make it consistent, and sensible to say.

When you have context-dependence, ineffability can be trite and unmysterious. Hush! [moment of silence] I might have liked to say, just then, 'All of us are silent'. It was true. But I could not have said it truly, or whistled it either. For by saying it aloud, or by whistling, I would have rendered it false.

I could have said my say fair and square, bending no rules. It would have been tiresome, but it could have been done. The secret would have been to resort to 'semantic ascent'. I could have taken great care to distinguish between (1) the language I use when I talk about knowledge, or whatever, and (2) the second language that I use to talk about the semantic and pragmatic workings of the first language. If you want to hear my story told that way, you probably know enough to do the job for yourself. If you can, then my informal presentation has been good enough.

Notes

* Thanks to many for valuable discussions of this material. Thanks above all to Peter Unger; and to Stewart Cohen, Michael Devitt, Alan Hajek, Stephen Hetherington, Denis Robinson, Ernest Sosa, Robert Stalnaker, Jonathan Vogel, and a referee for this Journal. Thanks also to the Boyce Gibson Memorial Library and to Ormond College.

1. The suggestion that ascriptions of knowledge go false in the context of epistemology is to be found in Barry Stroud, 'Understanding Human Knowledge in General' in Marjorie Clay and Keith Lehrer (eds.), *Knowledge and Skepticism* (Boulder: Westview Press, 1989); and in Stephen Hetherington, 'Lacking Knowledge and Justification by Theorising About Them' (lecture at the University of New South Wales, August 1992). Neither of them tells the story just as I do, however it may be that their versions do not conflict with mine.

2. Unless, like some, we simply define 'justification' as 'whatever it takes to turn true opinion into knowledge' regardless of whether what it takes turns out to involve argument from supporting reasons.

3. The problem of the lottery was introduced in Henry Kyburg, *Probability and the Logic of Rational Belief* (Middletown, CT: Wesleyan University Press, 1961), and in Carl Hempel, 'Deductive-Nomological vs. Statistical Explanation' in Herbert Feigl and Grover Maxwell (eds.), *Minnesota Studies in the Philosophy of Science*, Vol. II (Minneapolis: University of Minnesota Press, 1962). It has been much discussed since, as a problem both about knowledge and about our everyday, non-quantitative concept of belief.

4. The case of testimony is less discussed than the others; but see C.A.J. Coady, *Testimony: A Philosophical Study* (Oxford: Clarendon Press, 1992) pp. 79–129.

5. I follow Peter Unger, *Ignorance: A Case for Skepticism* (New York: Oxford University Press, 1975). But I shall not let him lead me into scepticism.

6. See Robert Stalnaker, *Inquiry* (Cambridge, MA: MIT Press, 1984) pp. 59–99.

7. See my 'Attitudes *De Dicto* and *De Se*', *The Philosophical Review* 88 (1979) pp. 513–543; and R. M. Chisholm, 'The Indirect Reflexive' in C. Diamond and J. Teichman (eds.), *Intention and Intentionality: Essays in Honour of G.E.M. Anscombe* (Brighton: Harvester, 1979).

8. Peter Unger, *Ignorance*, chapter II. I discuss the case, and briefly foreshadow the present paper, in my 'Scorekeeping in a Language Game', *Journal of Philosophical Logic* 8 (1979) pp. 339–359, esp. pp. 353–355.

9. See Robert Stalnaker, 'Presuppositions', *Journal of Philosophical Logic* 2 (1973) pp. 447–457; and 'Pragmatic Presuppositions' in Milton Munitz and Peter Unger (eds.), *Semantics and Philosophy* (New York:

New York University Press, 1974). See also my 'Score-keeping in a Language Game'.

10. See Fred Dretske, 'Epistemic Operators', *The Journal of Philosophy* 67 (1970) pp. 1007–1022, and 'The Pragmatic Dimension of Knowledge', *Philosophical Studies* 40 (1981) pp. 363–378; Alvin Goldman, 'Discrimination and Perceptual Knowledge', *The Journal of Philosophy* 73 (1976) pp. 771–791; G.C. Stine, 'Skepticism, Relevant Alternatives, and Deductive Closure', *Philosophical Studies* 29 (1976) pp. 249–261; and Stewart Cohen, 'How to be A Fallibilist', *Philosophical Perspectives* 2 (1988) pp. 91–123.

11. Some of them, but only some, taken from the authors just cited.

12. Instead of complicating the Rule of Belief as I have just done, I might equivalently have introduced a separate Rule of High Stakes saying that when error would be especially disastrous, few possibilities are properly ignored.

13. A.D. Woozley, 'Knowing and Not Knowing', *Proceedings of the Aristotelian Society* 53 (1953) pp. 151–172; Colin Radford, 'Knowledge—By Examples', *Analysis* 27 (1966) pp. 1–11.

14. See Edmund Gettier, 'Is Justified True Belief Knowledge?', *Analysis* 23 (1963) pp. 121–123. Diagnoses have varied widely. The four examples below come from: (1) Keith Lehrer and Thomas Paxson Jr., 'Knowledge: Undefeated True Belief', *The Journal of Philosophy* 66 (1969) pp. 225–237; (2) Bertrand Russell, *Human Knowledge: Its Scope and Limits* (London: Allen and Unwin, 1948) p. 154; (3) Alvin Goldman, 'Discrimination and Perceptual Knowledge', op. cit.; (4) Gilbert Harman, *Thought* (Princeton, NJ: Princeton University Press, 1973) p. 143.
    Though the lottery problem is another case of justified true belief without knowledge, it is not normally counted among the Gettier problems. It is interesting to find that it yields to the same remedy.

15. See Alvin Goldman, 'A Causal Theory of Knowing', *The Journal of Philosophy* 64 (1967) pp. 357–372; D.M. Armstrong, *Belief, Truth and Knowledge* (Cambridge: Cambridge University Press, 1973).

16. See my 'Veridical Hallucination and Prosthetic Vision', *Australasian Journal of Philosophy* 58 (1980) pp. 239–249. John Bigelow has proposed to model knowledge-delivering processes generally on those found in vision.

17. See Catherine Elgin, 'The Epistemic Efficacy of Stupidity', *Synthese* 74 (1988) pp. 297–311. The 'efficacy' takes many forms; some to do with knowledge (under various rival analyses), some to do with justified belief. See also Michael Williams, *Unnatural Doubts: Epistemological Realism and the Basis of Scepticism* (Oxford:

Blackwell, 1991) pp. 352–355, on the instability of knowledge under reflection.

18. Mixed cases are possible: Fred properly ignores the possibility W_1 which Ted eliminates; however Ted properly ignores the possibility W_2 which Fred eliminates. Ted has looked in all the desk drawers but not the file drawers, whereas Fred has checked the file drawers but not the desk. Fred's knowledge that Possum is not in the study is better in one way, Ted's is better in another.

19. To say truly that X is known, I must be properly ignoring any uneliminated possibilities in which not-X; whereas to say truly that Y is better known than X, I must be attending to some such possibilities. So I cannot say both in a single context. If I say 'X is known, but Y is better known', the context changes in midsentence: some previously ignored possibilities must stop being ignored. That can happen easily. Saying it the other way around—'Y is better known than X, but even X is known'—is harder, because we must suddenly start to ignore previously unignored possibilities. That cannot be done, really; but we could bend the rules and make believe we had done it, and no doubt we would be understood well enough. Saying 'X is flat, but Y is flatter' (that is, 'X has no bumps at all, but Y has even fewer or smaller bumps') is a parallel case. And again, 'Y is flatter, but even X is flat' sounds clearly worse—but not altogether hopeless.

20. Thanks here to Stephen Hetherington. While his own views about better and worse knowledge are situated within an analysis of knowledge quite unlike mine, they withstand transplantation.

21. A proof-theoretic version of this closure principle is common to all 'normal' modal logics: if the logic validates an inference from zero or more premises to a conclusion, then also it validates the inference obtained by prefixing the necessity operator to each premise and to the conclusion. Further, this rule is all we need to take us from classical sentential logic to the least normal modal logic. See Brian Chellas, *Modal Logic: An Introduction* (Cambridge: Cambridge University Press, 1980) p. 114.

23. See Stalnaker, *Inquiry*, pp. 79–99.

24. Worse still: by what right can I even say that we used to be in a position to say truly that we knew? Then, we were in a context where we properly ignored certain uneliminated possibilities of error. Now, we are in a context where we no longer ignore them. If *now* I comment retrospectively upon the truth of what was said *then*, which context governs: the context now or the context then? I doubt there is any general answer, apart from the usual principle that we should interpret what is said so as to make the message make sense.

✧ A NEO-MOOREAN RESPONSE ✧

29. INDISCERNABILITY SKEPTICISM[1]

Steven Luper

Ideally, our account of knowledge would help us to understand the appeal of (and flaws in) skepticism,[2] while remaining consistent with our 'intuitions,' and supporting epistemic principles that seem eminently plausible. Of course, we don't always get what we want; we may not be able to move from intuitions and principles to an account that fully squares with them. As a last resort, we may have to move in the other direction, and give up intuitions or principles that are undermined by an otherwise compelling account of knowledge, so as to achieve 'reflective equilibrium.'[3] But last resorts come last.

As is well known, Fred Dretske and Robert Nozick devised accounts of knowledge that perform well as measured by two of these three expectations. Their 'tracking' theory (to apply Nozick's term to both Dretske's and Nozick's analyses) seems intuitive and it allows us to offer an intriguing explanation of skepticism.[4] However, their view forces us to reject the principle of closure, even qualified extensively. As far as I know, no one accepts the following stark version of the closure principle:

If S knows p, and p entails q, then S knows q.

This principle implies—falsely—that S knows q even if S does not believe q or realize that q follows from p. Nevertheless, the closure principle, suitably restricted, seems too obvious to give up; because tracking theorists reject it even when thoroughly qualified, several writers have attempted to improve upon the tracking theorists' approach.

In particular, contextualists have offered a way of coming to terms with skepticism without giving up the principle of closure. However, in my view we should not accept their approach, for its disadvantages outweigh its advantages. First, according to contextualists, thinking about skepticism destroys our knowledge. Only people who ignore skepticism know anything, and even *they* lose their knowledge if skeptical possibilities are brought up. Second, while contextualism is consistent with some plausible epistemic principles, it forces us to reject others, such as this metalinguistic version of the closure principle:

If person S correctly attributes to herself knowledge that p, then if S *had* believed q by deducing q from p, S *would have been* correct to attribute to herself knowledge that q.

Fortunately, there is no need to say that thinking about its implications destroys our knowledge, and no need to give up closure, even on the metalinguistic level. There is an intuitively compelling account of knowledge that helps us to understand the problem with—and appeal of—leading forms of skepticism, *and* that squares with plausible epistemic principles: the *indicator* analysis.[5] We can meet our three expectations fully.

To defend these claims, I'll review the tracking and indicator analyses, and show that the latter handles skepticism at least as well as the former yet sustains closure. Then I'll consider the contextualist account, and suggest that it is inconsistent with plausible epistemic principles, and cannot handle skepticism as well as the indicator approach.

I: Tracking Versus The Indicator Account

Consider rough and somewhat oversimplified versions of the theories offered by Dretske and Nozick:

DRETSKE: A person S knows p if and only if there is a reason R such that: S's belief p is based on the fact that R holds, and *not-p* → not-(R holds).[6]

NOZICK: A person S knows p if and only if there is a method M such that: S believes p via M, and *not-p* → not-(S believes p via M).[7]

Simplifying even more, I am going to ignore the differences between these two approaches, and lay out a bare-bones version of the tracking account of knowledge. S knows p if and only if there is a reason R such that (using 'T' for 'tracking theory'):

> (T1) S's belief p is based on the fact that R holds
> (T2) $not\text{-}p \rightarrow not\text{-}(\text{R holds})$.

What I have set forth is the heart of the tracking view. But now consider a simple modification, in which we replace (T2). S knows p if and only if there is a reason R such that:

1. S's belief p is based on the fact that R holds
2. R holds $\rightarrow p$.[8]

Condition (2) is just the contrapositive of (T2). So (2) and (T2) must amount to the same thing, right?

Tracking Versus Indication

No; in fact, the contrapositives of subjunctive conditionals are not equivalent, and while (2) and (T2) work similarly in many cases, they differ in crucial ways. Consider a case in which they converge and a case in which they diverge.

Convergence first. In one of his examples, Dretske asks you to imagine that you are at a perfectly ordinary wildlife show, standing in front of a cage marked 'zebra'. There are no Cartesian demons lurking in the wings, no Gettieresque surprises waiting to spring themselves at you. You are looking right at the zebra inside, and you come to believe z: the animal in the cage is a zebra. The source of your belief is a familiar empirical test by which you examine a scene and see if you get zebra-in-a-cage-type experiences; you take having these experiences to indicate that z is true, and not having them to indicate that z is false. You meet (T2): in the close worlds in which z is false, you do not have zebra-in-a-cage-type experiences. You also meet (2): in the close worlds in which you have these experiences, z is true.

Now divergence. Suppose you use zebra-in-a-cage-type experiences as your basis for believing $not\text{-}m$: the animal in the cage in front of me is *not* a mule cleverly disguised to look just like a zebra. That is, you take getting zebra-type experiences to indicate that $not\text{-}m$ is true. You *fail* to meet (T2). (T2), applied to $not\text{-}m$, requires that

$m \rightarrow$ S does not get zebra-type experiences.

And in the close worlds in which the animal is a zebra-like mule, you still have zebra-type experiences, leading you to think that the animal is *not* a zebra-like mule. Yet you *will* meet (2). Applied to $not\text{-}m$, (2) requires that

S gets zebra-type experiences $\rightarrow not\text{-}m$.[9]

In the actual world we are imagining, you are in an ordinary wildlife show looking at a caged zebra. In such a world, and in close worlds where you get zebra-like percepts, you are led to think the animal is not a zebra-like mule, and, of course, in these worlds the animal isn't.

So (T2) is not equivalent to (2), even though both are met in many of the same cases.

Tracking, Indication, and Closure

Perhaps (T2) and (2) are distinct, but isn't (T2) *preferable* to (2)? Won't Dretske and Nozick insist that seeming to see a zebra does *not* position us to know that we are not looking at a zebra-like mule, and that it only positions us to know that we are looking at a zebra? But when they say these things we know what comes next: they deny the principle of closure of knowledge under entailment, and say you cannot know that the animal in the cage is a not a made-up mule even if you *deduce* it from something you admittedly know—namely, that it is a zebra. Why do they reject closure? Consider condition (T2). Let us say that when a true belief meets (T2), it *tracks the fact* that p via R. Here's the main problem: a belief can track the fact that p via some reason R without tracking p's logical consequences. So we can know a claim is true, believe things that follow, yet fail to know that those things are true.[10] Dretske's zebra case illustrates the point.[11]

I assume that incompatibility with the principle of closure counts heavily against an analysis of knowledge, while compatibility counts in its favor. Hence before we decide on the relative merits of (2) versus (T2), it is important to see that (2) *supports* closure. Let us say that when belief p meets (2), R is an *infallible indicator* that p is true (or, more fully, we might say that, *relative to S's situation*, R is an infallible indicator that p is true). If R is an infallible indicator that p is true, as (2) requires, then R is also an infallible indicator that p's logically consequences are true. If

R holds → p
p entails q

hold, then it *must* also be the case that

R holds → q

is true.[12] So if my belief p is based on a reason R that is an infallible indicator that p is true, and I come to believe q by deducing q from p, then my belief q is also based on a reason that is an infallible indicator that q is true—namely R, or R plus the fact that p entails q (we could even say that the reason q is based on is p itself). For example, my zebra experiences are situationally infallible indicators that the animal in the cage is a zebra: in the close worlds in which I have these experiences, I'm seeing a zebra. But all the worlds in which I'm seeing a zebra are worlds where what I'm seeing is not a disguised mule. The upshot is that while tracking is hostile to closure, infallible indication is not.[13]

Even when strengthened in various ways, the indicator analysis will sustain closure. This is fortunate, since our account does need to be refined and clarified in various ways. We cannot go into all of these, but one adjustment seems especially important, since conditions (1)–(2) can be met in cases in which our belief's source is (generally) unreliable. To make this point clear, let's tinker with one of Goldman's examples. We'll play a prank on Sue, a wacko who takes highly realistic barn appearances to indicate the presence of *papier-mâché copies* of barns. The prank is innocent enough: we bundle her off to a region of the world in which all the real barns have been replaced with papier-mâché duplicates. When she spots a papier-mâché barn in the distance, her visual impressions lead her to think that she's looking at a papier-mâché barn. Here's the point: the fact that she has barn-type percepts is, then and there, an infallible indicator that she sees a papier-mâché barn, so she meets our two conditions for knowledge. Given her peculiar circumstances, if she were to see barn appearances, a papier-mâché barn would be present. Yet she does *not* have knowledge. She takes highly realistic barn appearances to indicate the presence of papier-mâché barns, but barn appearances are not generally reliable indicators of papier-mâché barns (instead, realistic barn appearances are reliable indicators of

barns). Generally, in the situations in which we have barn appearances, we are not confronted with papier-mâché barns.

These considerations suggest the need to add the following to our list of conditions for knowledge (naturally, those who are not convinced by the example can get by without the addition):

(3) Generally, when an R-type situation holds, a p-type situation holds.

Let us say R is a *reliable indicator* that p is true if and only if this condition is met.
Requiring a reliable indicator does not stop us from accepting closure. If R is a reliable indicator that p is true, and p entails q, R is also a reliable indicator that q is true. (I'm assuming that to identify a p-type situation, we start with the situation described by p and abstract away the element of time, and that if p entails q, then when a p-type situation holds, a q-type situation must also hold.) Now,

generally, when an R-type situation holds, a p-type situation holds
p entails q

together entail

generally, when an R-type situation holds, a q-type situation holds.

So if S's belief p is based on a reason R that reliably indicates that p is true, and S believes q by deducing q from p, then S's belief q will be based on a reason that reliably indicates that q is true. By contrast, the tracking counterpart of (3), namely

(T3) Generally, when a p-type situation does not hold, an R-type situation does not hold,

will not support closure.[14]

The fact that conditions (1)-(3) endorse closure, while their tracking counterparts do not, is prima facie grounds for preferring the former. Nonetheless, Dretske and Nozick would probably argue that the tracking condition (T2) is preferable to the indication condition (2) precisely because the former positions us to acknowledge our ignorance of skeptical hypotheses, which gives us a way to account for skepticism. Skepticism seems correct because skeptical conclusions can be reached using the closure principle. As for where skepticism goes wrong, we can blame the closure principle itself: skeptics assume it, but it is false. Is this response plausible?

Tracking and Skepticism

It *is* plausible. Some versions of skepticism do rely on closure. An example is the following *skeptical argument from closure*:

1. If S knows *p*, and believes *q* by deducing *q* from *p*, then S knows *q*.
2. But S does not know that S is not a brain in a vat on a planet far from earth whose sensory experiences are completely misleading. (S does not know this because S does not track the fact that S is not a brain in a vat.)
3. So S does not know anything that entails that S is not in the vat scenario (including most of S's ordinary beliefs).

Of course, the skeptical argument from closure constitutes a form of indiscernability (Cartesian) skepticism, and has nothing to do with regress (Pyrrhonian) skepticism. By denying closure, tracking theorists leave regress skepticism untouched, and address only one form of indiscernability skepticism. A response to one skeptical argument is not necessarily a response to others. But progress is made if one prominent form of skepticism is defeated. And I think that this is a substantial virtue of tracking accounts.

As powerful as the above response is, we can reject it if we provide an account of knowledge that sustains closure yet explains the appeal of skepticism while pinning down the flaw in the argument from closure. And in fact we have such an account: knowledge as indication. We already know that (1)–(3) support closure. And, as I will explain later, we can locate the flaw in the skeptic's argument at step (ii): by the conditions of the indicator analysis, we know we are *not* brains in vats. We can even explain the appeal of skepticism—in much the same way as the tracking theorists do. Let me elaborate.

Why One Form of Skepticism Is Appealing

I begin with a concession. Dretske's and Nozick's story is basically the right explanation of the appeal of (one form of) skepticism. This is true even though the tracking account is wrong and the indication account is right. Skepticism is appealing because people often *think* of knowledge as tracking. They think of knowledge as tracking because knowledge closely *resembles* tracking.[15] It is easy to conflate (2) with its tracking counterpart (and (3) with *its* tracking counterpart), and if we do, we are likely to believe—falsely—that to know we are not brains in vats we must track the fact that we are not brains in vats. We will then disavow knowing we are not brains in vats. So even if (1)–(3) are the correct conditions for knowledge, and we do know we are not brains in vats, at least part of the explanation of why skepticism is tempting is surely that we do not track the fact that we are not in skeptical scenarios. We also see our way past the temptation: we can see through the skeptical argument from closure by familiarizing ourselves with the differences between tracking and indication, and carefully applying (1)–(3) rather than the tracking counterpart.

At this point Dretske and Nozick might well object. Perhaps (2) closely resembles (T2), and perhaps people run the two conditions together, but aren't these points grounds for concluding that the ordinary notion of knowledge can be captured only if we adopt *both* sets of conditions? If so, we are back to an analysis that undermines closure, and we seem forced to accept the tracking theorists' account of skepticism in its entirety.

This objection has substantial merit, but it can be overcome. True, in conflating indication with tracking, people might end up insisting on both. But it is more likely that people who conflate the two shift back and forth from one to the other, using the first on some occasions and the second on other occasions, oblivious, all the while, to the equivocation. There is plenty of evidence that people equivocate in this way. For example, consider the fact that we vehemently cling to the principle of closure. It is when we interpret knowledge as indication that we adopt this principle. We would not adopt it if we accepted all of the conditions or just the tracking conditions by themselves. Consider, too, how natural it is for people to claim to know a possibility does not hold on the grounds that the possibility is *remote*, and sometimes they stick to their guns even when we point out that they do not meet the tracking requirement. On the other hand, sometimes they will not stick to their guns: perhaps then they are worried about tracking.

I admit that it is difficult to pin down the ordinary concept of knowledge, and show that I have it right while Dretske and Nozick have it wrong. I do not have a knockdown case against the tracking theorists. We should not expect too much from 'intuitions' and appeals to the ordinary concept of knowledge; anyone familiar with post-Gettier attempts to analyze knowledge realizes that 'intuitions' and language analysis do not always provide the means to choose among competing accounts. When this happens, however, we can defend a view on the grounds that it *refines* the ordinary conception of knowledge.[16] And in that spirit I recommend the indicator analysis. Indication *improves upon* the commonsense concept of knowledge, for, unlike the ordinary notion, it unambiguously sustains the principle of closure.

Where Our Skeptical Argument Goes Wrong

Still another objection is available. On the view I have offered, we know we are not brains in vats. Surely, tracking theorists might insist, we can know no such thing—about *that*, at least, skeptics are correct. And anyone who disagrees needs to explain how such knowledge is possible. This challenge seems fair enough, and I think it can be met. At a minimum, I can make my position as plausible as Dretske's and Nozick's. That is, the combination,

(1) I know I am not a brain in a vat, and

(2) I know ordinary claims that are incompatible with being a brain in a vat,

my view, is at least as plausible as the combination,

1 is false, yet

2 is true,

which is their view.

Consider what, specifically, is involved in knowing that a skeptical possibility does not hold. I know that

h: I am sitting in my house typing out an essay

is true. My reason R^1 for believing *h* is my having certain familiar sensory experiences, relating to my house

and computer, and these are infallible (and reliable) indicators that *h* is true. Furthermore, *h* entails

> *not-biv*: I am not a brain in a vat on a far-off planet whose experiences are completely misleading.

Seeing this, I believe *not-biv*. And I have an infallible reason for believing *not-biv*, namely, R^1—my having the experiences on which I based belief *h*. Of course, if asked why I believe *not-biv*, I will likely answer that my belief is based on a compound reason: the fact that *h* is suggested by the experiences involved in R^1 together with the fact that *not-biv* follows from my belief *h*. (Alternatively, I might say that my reason for believing *not-biv* is *h* itself.) No matter: this complex reason (or *h* by itself) is itself an infallible (and reliable) indicator that I am not a brain in a vat on a far-off planet.

What might make us suspicious about knowing *not-biv* is the fact that normally our grounds for it (like our grounds for many other claims, as G. E. Moore (1959) pointed out) are indirect.[17] Just now, when I explained the typical way in which we know that *not-biv*, I mentioned one source (R^1—involving experiences of sitting at the keyboard and so on) for the commonsense belief *h*, and a compound source for *not-biv*. We base commonsense beliefs directly on experience; why can't we base beliefs about skeptical possibilities directly on experience? Why must the latter be based on the commonsense beliefs instead? Unless we can answer these questions, we will suspect that beliefs about skeptical possibilities are special—and perhaps that skeptics are right about them. Fortunately, there are answers.

As to why our grounds against skeptical possibilities typically are indirect, here is part of the story: suppose I am asked why I believe I am in my house typing right now. In crafting my answer, I must deal with the fact that I did not go through any explicit reasoning, or apply any explicit test. I rarely do when perception leads me to believe things. Nonetheless, I find that certain sorts of familiar experiences habitually trigger certain sorts of commonsense beliefs. So I can give an answer by laying out the sorts of experiences that typically trigger beliefs about typing, buildings, and so on. But the belief that I am not a brain in a vat is not one I ordinarily entertain, hence it is not possible to link it with experiences that habitually trigger it. It rarely comes up. But when it does, I find myself believing it because I see that it follows from my common-sense beliefs.

Here is another part of the story: suppose I clarify the ways I arrive at perceptual beliefs by explicitly crafting rules of the form, if I have experiences E, then *p* is true. For example: If I get zebra-in-a-cage-type experiences, then the statement, 'There is a zebra in the cage' is true. Such rules explicitly address a particular statement. But they need not explicitly address claims that *follow* from this statement. Clearly, my rules can say that a claim *p* is true without (explicitly) saying that *p*'s consequences are true.[18] In a fairly straightforward sense, a thermometer (made out on a Fahrenheit scale) that registers 70 degrees *says* it is 70 degrees Fahrenheit, but *not* that the temperature is not 0 degrees Celsius. Nonetheless, we can know the latter indirectly, since the one fact entails the other. The upshot is that my experiences can be infallible (and reliable) indicators that I am at home, and that I am not a brain in a vat on a distant planet, yet I might fail to have belief management rules which *prompt* me to believe I am not in a vat on the basis of my experiences.

Finally, let me address the claim that we *must* base beliefs about skeptical possibilities indirectly on commonsense beliefs, and not directly on experience. *This claim is false*. There is nothing to stop us from converting what is usually indirect knowledge into direct knowledge. I can simply take, as my reason for believing that it is not 0 Celsius, the fact that a Fahrenheit thermometer says that it is above 32. And I can know I am not a brain in a vat directly on the basis of the experiences that led me to believe that I am at home typing, rather than by inferring I am not in a vat from this belief.

One other potential criticism should be addressed. Lately, some philosophers apply the label 'Moorean,' disparagingly, to any attempt to say that we can know skeptical possibilities do not hold. The thought is that Moore merely turned the tables on the skeptic, without describing where the skeptic goes wrong. Such critics might try to dismiss my own efforts in the same way. I have two reactions.

First. Moore's demonstration that the tables can be turned on the skeptic is itself important. All of us who are not clinging to skepticism find Moore's antiskeptical argument[19] at *least* as powerful as the skeptic's argument from closure. Second. Unlike Moore, I have explained what is *involved* in knowing that skeptical possibilities do not hold. I have not just *asserted* that the skeptic's argument fails. Skepticism can be resisted even if we grant the closure principle, however qualified. The key is the Mooresque claim that we know skeptical scenarios do not hold.

II: Contextualism Versus the Indicator Account

Let's turn to the contextualists' explanation of skepticism, and begin by confronting a possible source of confusion: those of us who defend subjunctive accounts, whether we view knowledge as tracking or as indication or the like, have always thought that knowledge depends on the knower's context. Yet we are not contextualists—not, in any case, as that term is usually meant these days. In what ways do the two approaches overlap, and how do they differ?

Subjunctive Accounts and Contextual Variables

For the subjunctivist, it is a straightforward matter that our status as knowers depends on features of our situation. In some circumstances a belief source R must be especially versatile to generate knowledge. To be a reliable indicator, R must display a minimal level of reliability, but to be a situationally infallible indicator, R often must do still better, depending on the specific nature of the circumstances at hand. In optimal conditions I can know I see a barn by looking at it. If there are papier-mâché barns scattered through the area, however, I can look right at a barn, recognize it as a barn, and still not know that it is a barn. I will need to become (or employ) a better barn detector. I will need to walk inside the barn, or touch it, or the like. I will need a belief source that, even in the presence of fake barns, would indicate the presence of a barn only if there were one there, and the more undetectable the fakes in my vicinity, the abler my source must be at detecting the fakes.

The point holds for noninferential as well as inferential knowledge. If our belief is noninferential—if, for example, it is perceptual—then the more deceptive our circumstances, the more acute our perceptual process must be.[20] If inferential, then the more deceptive our circumstances, the better our evidence must be. It is easy to imagine circumstances in which I can know the butler did it on the basis of evidence involving an honest eyewitness. But this evidence will not suffice if it turns out that the butler has a twin brother with a grudge against the victim. The required discriminatory powers of our knowledge-producing belief sources varies on a *sliding scale*, starting with a minimal level in ordinary circumstances, and rising with the level of deceptiveness of our situation.[21]

The element of contextualism evident in subjunctivist accounts of knowledge allows us to explain and put aside a skeptical argument that is quite different from the skeptical argument from closure. The argument—from the situation principle—is this:

1. If, in some situation, E is the evidence we have about *p*, and we know *p* on the basis of E, then we know *p* in any situation in which E is our evidence and we believe *p* on the basis of E. (Call this the *situation principle*.[22])
2. For virtually any evidence E, there are circumstances in which we will not know *p* on the basis of E. (There are circumstances in which E is the evidence we have about *p*, and we believe *p* on the basis of E, yet fail to know *p*. That is, nearly all of our belief sources fail to produce knowledge in some circumstances.)
3. So our evidence rarely positions us to know anything.

Reflection about Gettier cases reveals what is wrong with the situation principle.[23] When I look at a caged zebra at an ordinary wildlife show, I know the animal is a zebra. Yet in the Gettierized version of this situation, where I stumble into the Hey Presto wildlife show, featuring zebra doppelgangers, I fail to know, even though my belief source is the same in both cases. But there is no mystery here. What is going on is that a belief source that is discriminatory enough in ordinary circumstances is not discriminatory enough in others. The situation principle has to go.

Agent-Centered Contextualism Versus Speaker-Centered Contextualism

According to the subjunctivist as well as the contextualist approach, it is harder to know things in some circumstances than in others—our epistemic apparatus must be more versatile in some circumstances in order to produce knowledge.[24] Both accept a view we might call *agent-centered* contextualism, which claims that whether it is correct to attribute knowledge to a given agent S depends on features of S's context. But subjunctivists and contextualists diverge when it comes to a further issue. The latter usually defend a position we might call *speaker-centered* contextualism,[25] which says that whether it is correct for a speaker to attribute knowledge to a given agent depends on features of the *speaker's* context. Whether I, the speaker, am right when I say that Mary, the agent I am discussing, knows *p*, depends on my context, as opposed to Mary's (it could also depend on Mary's context, too—this is not ruled out by definition). The truth conditions for knowledge attributions vary with speakers' contexts. Thus when I say Mary knows *p*, and you, referring to the same person, say Mary does not know *p*, we can both be correct—we are not contradicting each other. Subjunctivists acknowledge that all sorts of features of a speaker's context might affect whether she will *say* (or be *warranted* in saying) that an individual knows something. But subjunctivists typically deny that the *truth conditions* of knowledge attributions vary with speakers' contexts. Hereinafter, I'll use the term 'contextualism' to refer to speaker-centered contextualism.

The Contextualist Explanation of Skepticism

So how do contextualists deal with skepticism? Their approach has two parts: a diagnosis (accounting for the appeal of skepticism), and a cure.

Here's the diagnosis. When skeptics discuss their hypotheses with us, they put us into a special context; there, we may correctly attribute knowledge to an agent S only if S meets very demanding epistemic standards. These are so rigorous that it is almost always a mistake to attribute knowledge to anyone (whether ourselves or others). So there is an element of truth in skepticism, according to contextualists: when we discuss skeptical possibilities, we enter a context where heightened standards apply, forcing us to conclude that no one knows that skeptical possibilities do not hold. Because skepticism prevails in this special context, skeptics think their view must be accepted: Surely if we have to deny anyone knowledge when pressed by skeptics, then we have to deny anyone knowledge period—we have to deny it when we are not thinking about skepticism. Still, there is a suppressed assumption here: namely, that proper attributions of knowledge do not depend on the context of those who judge. The assumption is analogous to the situation principle:

> The context principle: if it is correct for judges in one context to attribute knowledge to an agent S, then it is correct for judges in any context to attribute knowledge to S. (If it is improper for judges in one context to attribute knowledge to S, then it is improper for judges in any context.)[26]

Fully spelled out, then, the skeptic's argument (from the context principle) is this:

a. The context principle is true.

b. People who raise skeptical doubts create a context in which they must say that no one knows very much.

c. So everyone, regardless of her context, must say that no one knows very much.

Now the contextualists' cure: the skeptic's argument is no good because the context principle on which it relies is false. What skeptics fail to see (what they deny?) is that the epistemic standards that are appropriate for knowledge attributions *vary* from context to context. In ordinary contexts, we may attribute knowledge to a given agent S when S meets quite low epistemic standards. So in ordinary contexts it is correct to say that people know ordinary knowledge claims. Skeptics think that by getting us to admit ignorance in the special context they create when they raise their doubts, they can show that everyone is ignorant regardless of context. But people who ignore skepticism and skeptical possibilities are in a context where lower

standards are in place, and it is correct for them to attribute knowledge to themselves and to others who ignore skepticism.

The upshot is that contextualists can say that skeptics are more right than they are wrong: anyone who discusses skepticism must end up embracing it, while those who ignore skepticism can escape it. An added bonus is that contextualists do not have to reject closure, so long as its application is confined to one context at a time. In all contexts, the principle of closure is correct, but if we shift from one context to another in the course of applying closure, "all bets are off," as Lewis (1996) says. This is the error involved in the skeptical argument from closure; it is also involved in the Moore-style inversion of the skeptic's argument.

To make the contextualist approach more concrete, let us outline a version offered by Keith DeRose (1995). Suppose we ask whether some agent S knows p. And suppose that sk is the most remote alternative to p that we are considering. Let us say that p's *DeRose zone* is the sphere of possible worlds centered on the actual world that includes the closest worlds in which p is false. For us to correctly say S knows p, two requirements must be met. First, S's belief as to whether p is true must match the fact of the matter throughout p's DeRose zone: that is, S must believe p throughout the p portion of p's DeRose zone, and *not-p* throughout the *not-p* portion of p's DeRose zone (DeRose 1995, reprinted in DeRose 1999, p. 206). Second, S's belief as to whether p is true must match the fact of the matter throughout *not-sk's* DeRose zone.

Using DeRose's account, let us see how the contextualist will deal with skepticism. DeRose's second condition will be hard to meet if sk is a very remote alternative to p: in a context where skeptical possibilities are raised, knowledge is difficult to attain. For example, we will not qualify as knowing there is a zebra before us in a context where the possibility of cleverly disguised mules arises, for there are *not-z* worlds in which we believe z within the *not-m* DeRose zone. So if the context principle were true, we would be judged to know little in any context. This is the diagnosis of skepticism. Now the cure: both of DeRose's conditions easy can be met when skeptical possibilities do not arise. In an ordinary context, we will count people as knowing there is a zebra in front of them. So the context principle is false; people can be credited with knowledge in ordinary contexts.

There you have the contextualists' story. I will argue that it should be rejected, since we have already offered a better diagnosis of skepticism as well as a better cure.

Problems with the Contextualists' Approach

This essay began with three requirements an account of knowledge ought to meet:

a. It should square with our intuitions about clear examples of knowledge and ignorance.

b. It should help us to diagnose and cure skepticism.

c. It should not be in tension with plausible epistemic principles.

Like subjunctivists, contextualists can defend their view on the basis of these requirements. Their approach to skepticism is superior (they might say) because tracking theorists reject the principle of closure, thus violating (c), while contextualists need not, and otherwise the two approaches are fairly evenly matched: both explain the appeal of skepticism by saying that people do not know that skeptical possibilities fail to hold, and both say we know about ordinary possibilities, such as that we have arms and legs, so both look good from the standpoint of (a) and (b).

As for the indicator theorist's diagnosis of and cure for skepticism, contextualists would reject it, too, even though it supports closure, as suggested by (c). They would argue that on our account we know that skeptical possibilities do not hold, and this stops us from explaining the appeal of skepticism, in violation of (b).

However, this argument is unconvincing. We need not accept skepticism to account for its appeal. In one form—the argument from the situation principle—skepticism's appeal is due to the (limited) charms of the situation principle. This form of skepticism will be especially irresistible if we confuse the situation principle (which is false) with the context principle (which is true even while it is denied by contextualists). In another, skepticism derives from the persistent impression that we must jump-start our justificatory efforts in a way that seems ruled out by the Pyrrhonian regress argument. And the skeptical argument from closure has its own source of appeal. As we have already explained, its attractiveness derives from an *error* that is very hard to detect and avoid—an error that results when we conflate tracking conditions and their non-tracking counterparts, and conclude that we cannot know that skeptical scenarios don't hold.[27]

Our explanation can be adapted to the metalinguistic level, too, so there is no need whatever to accept attribution conditions that support skepticism. The view we need is this: it is correct for a speaker to attribute knowledge that p to agent S if and only if S meets the indicator conditions for knowing p. On this view, it is easy to explain people's hesitation to attribute knowledge when a skeptical scenario sk arises, either for the speaker or the agent, since they confuse indication with tracking and notice that the tracking conditions are not met. They then reason: S would not know *not-sk*, so (by closure) S does not know ordinary things. Later, when the skeptical possibilities are ignored, people switch back to the indicator conditions, attribute knowledge accordingly, and refresh their confidence in the closure principle.

This reasoning shows that our way of dealing with skepticism is at least as plausible as the contextualists'. Now let's argue that it is superior.

The main concern is that the contextualists' approach forces us to reject very plausible epistemic principles, thus violating (c). All things being equal, we are entitled to resist a theory that forces us to abandon such principles, as contextualists themselves say in defense of their view against Nozick and Dretske. In fairness, we must note that contextualists (or at least David Lewis) have seen this sort of objection coming, but, as some of Nozick's critics said, a theorist cannot preclude criticism by being first to point out the troublesome consequences of his own view. Applying *modus ponens* does not stop others from applying *modus tollens*. Let me mention a couple of principles contextualists must reject.

The first we might call the *principle of stability:*

If at time 1 S is correct in saying, 'I know p at time 1,' and at time 2 S's situation remains the same (as far as possible) except that S thinks of one or more implications of p, then, at time 2, S will (still) be correct in saying, 'I knew p at time 1.'

To see why contextualists reject this principle, let's use Dretske's example again. You are at an ordinary wildlife show, looking at a caged zebra, believing that a zebra is there. Speaking at time 1, you are correct when you say, 'I know z', for you meet the low epistemic standards in place in this context. A moment later, at time 2, you continue to believe z on the same basis, but you start thinking through the implications of z; realizing that z entails not-m, you come to believe not-m thereby. Speaking at time 2, you have to say that you do not know not-m, and further that you do not know z, for you are now considering a skeptical possibility, which triggers high standards that are not met by either belief. Worse: judging at time 2, you have to say that you did not know z at time 1! For you-at-time-1 cannot meet the standards which you-at-time-2 are relying on to issue correct attributions of knowledge. Thinking through what is implied by your knowledge destroys your knowledge. More carefully, it destroys your knowledge as assessed while considering skeptical possibilities: judging at time 2, you will admit that *what you said* at time 1 when you uttered the words 'I know z' was *true* (since what you *said* was, in effect, that your belief z met the lower epistemic standards in place at time 1) but you will be forced to add that you did not know z at time 1 (since you did not meet the higher standards *now* in place)![28]

Another plausible principle contextualists must reject is a metalinguistic version of the closure principle:

If S correctly attributes to herself knowledge that p, then if S *had* believed q by deducing q from p, S *would have been* correct to attribute to herself knowledge that q.[29]

This principle is extremely plausible, since p *must* be true if S correctly attributes to herself knowledge

that p, so that if S were to believe q by deducing q from p, q must be true, too. Yet the contextualist will have to deny this principle. Why?—Back to Dretske's zebra case. I know z (the possibility that m not having occurred to me). But the close worlds in which I deduce not-m from z are worlds in which heightened standards apply; there, I cannot be said to know not-m. (I cannot be said to know z in such worlds either, but this does not stop me from knowing z in the actual world.) So the antecedent of the metalinguistic closure principle is true, while the consequent is false.

Does the contextualist give plausible grounds for denying the metalinguistic closure principle? I don't think so. According to the contextualist, S-in-the-actual-world does not meet the higher epistemic standards applied to S-in-the-hypothetical-world-where-S-believes-not-m. So what? The fact that actual-S meets the *lower* epistemic standards *entails* p! Even by the lowest plausible standards, knowing p entails p. So if, as the antecedent of the metalinguistic closure principle says, S's knowing z is certifiable (by weak standards), z must be true, and if S believed not-m by deducing it from z, S could not be wrong about not-m, even if neither the belief z nor the belief not-m meets the contextualist's higher epistemic standards. Truth is preserved from the one context to the other.

Once we notice that contextualists reject the metalinguistic closure principle, their solution to skepticism resembles that of the tracking theorists quite a bit. For the skeptic could draw on the metalinguistic closure principle to offer an argument against all commonsense knowledge attributions. As follows:

1. No matter what S's circumstances are, it is *never* proper for S to say she knows that she is not a brain in a vat (not-biv).
2. So if S were to believe not-biv by deducing it from a claim h that entails not-biv, she still could not properly say that she knows not-biv, no matter how well grounded her belief h happens to be.
3. The metalinguistic closure principle is true.
4. So S will always be incorrect in attributing to herself knowledge of anything that entails not-biv.

The contextualists' response will be that the principle at step 3 is false. But given this response, do we really want to say their solution to skepticism is better than the solution offered by the tracking theorists? Tracking theorists confront a skeptic who argues at the object level; they reject the object level version of the closure principle. Contextualists simply move up a level, and confront a skeptic who appeals to the metalinguistic closure principle. This is progress? Perhaps the metalinguistic closure principle is not quite as plausible as the principle Dretske and Nozick deny, but isn't it much too close for comfort? Both are plausible for similar reasons. Can't we at least say that we should avoid denying either if we can? And we *can*—by using the indicator account as a theory of both the truth conditions and attribution conditions for knowledge.

A final point: suppose the indicator account of attribution conditions did *not* square with our intuitions (if we have any!) about attribution conditions quite as well as the contextualist account. Suppose that the contest were very close, but lost by the former. There is a further important consideration against contextualist theories. In the spirit of revision, it would be much better to adopt the indicator account, for thereby we avoid the puzzling complications introduced when we say that truth conditions for knowledge claims vary with the speaker's context. In particular, our knowledge will not collapse in epistemic contexts. For the contextualist, knowledge can be correctly attributed only to people who have overlooked possibilities, and once those possibilities are looked at squarely, the knowledge attribution must be retracted. Not so on our account. We can boldly claim to know that skeptical possibilities do not hold, while still seeing the appeal of many sorts of skepticism. I endorse a remark Lewis[30] makes:

> It is a Moorean fact that we know a lot. It is one of those things that we know better than we know the premises of any philosophical argument to the contrary.

One of those flawed premises is the claim that I do not know I am not a brain in a vat.

III: Knowledge and Rational Belief

So far we have ignored the issue of how knowledge is related to justified, or rational, belief. There is not enough space for a full discussion of this matter, but a few comments are in order.

Knowledge and Nonjustified Belief

First, we ought not to rule out noninferential (hence non-justified yet rational, as opposed to unjustified and irrational) knowledge; nor does the indicator account do so. If perception produces noninferential beliefs, it sometimes generates noninferential knowledge about such things as tables and chairs. Here's why: In optimal circumstances, and circumstances that are close to optimal, perception causes me to believe there is a chair in front of me (or what have you) only if there *is* a chair. Moreover, generally, perception is accurate when it leads me to believe in the presence of chairs (and such).

Knowledge and Rational Belief

Second, we will want to specify that an inferentially known belief *p* be rational. From an internalist perspective, this entails that *p* be sufficiently justified, so that the preponderance of one's evidence counts in favor of believing *p*. Gettieresque concerns will be handled by (1)–(3), which are externalist conditions. In other words, we can say that S knows an inferential belief *p* if and only if S believes *p* on the basis of some fact R that provides sufficient justification for *p*, and R is both a reliable and infallible indicator that *p*.

So understood, inferential knowledge is closed under entailment, since we are justified in believing things that are entailed by individual things we justifiably believe. That is, the following principle of closure of justification is true:

> If S has sufficient justification for S's belief *p*, and S believes *q* because it follows individually from *p*, then S has sufficient justification for S's belief *q*.

Our principle is restricted to things that are entailed by *individual* things we justifiably believe in order to avoid the lottery paradox, which is generated if we say that we are justified in believing the *conjunctions* of things we are justified in believing.[31]

Many objections to the principle of closure of justification can be met once we notice two points. First, as Peter Klein (1981) pointed out, our evidence for *p* need not be the evidence for *p*'s consequences. The evidence for the latter might be *p* itself, which suffices since *p entails* its consequences.[32] The second point is that evidence against any of the consequences of *p* counts against *p*. So if we are justified in believing *p*, we will not have strong evidence against any of *p*'s consequences, and we will have powerful grounds *for* them—namely *p*.

Needless to say, many theorists will not be satisfied with the above analysis of knowledge, combining, as it does, internalist with externalist elements. For them, I can only sketch a few suggestions. The most promising way to clarify the idea of a rational belief involves developing the notion of belief management practices, which are the predictable patterns by which each of us adopt, maintain and revise our beliefs. These belief management practices can be described, at least roughly, in the form of rules. An example of such a rule might be: accept spontaneously occurring experiential beliefs, unless they contradict other, firmly accepted beliefs. Such rules need not be consciously applied, and it might be difficult indeed for anyone to fully articulate rules that accurately capture their practices. Furthermore, some rules may not function to steer us toward an accurate picture of the world: wishful thinking, for example, preserves assumptions that make for happiness. We must set these aside in assessing the *epistemic* status of our views, and focus on rules used to get us to an accurate picture. (Hereinafter, the term 'belief management rules' will refer to the latter.) With these points in mind, and drawing on the work of Alvin Goldman (1979, 1988), we can offer a characterization of rationality. Roughly speaking, a person S's belief *p* is *objectively* rational if and only if:

    a. S believes *p* in conformity with S's belief management rules.

    b. Generally, when S holds a *p*-type belief in conformity with S's rules, it is true.[33]

The reason: again roughly speaking, a belief is objectively rational if and only if it is held in conformity with belief management practices that are reliable when they endorse *p*-type beliefs. The contrast is with beliefs that are *subjectively* rational—i.e., held in conformity with management practices that one accepts for the purpose of arriving at an accurate picture of the world. (That my belief *p* is subjectively rational is ensured by (a).) Thus, a belief is objectively rational when and only when believing it in conformity with one's belief management practices is a *reliable indicator* that it is true.

Notes

1. I thank Curtis Brown and Peter Klein for helpful suggestions about an earlier draft.

2. Several people have emphasized this point or something like it. E.g., Robert Nozick (1981) writes, "an account of knowledge should illuminate skeptical arguments and show wherein lies their force" (p. 197).

3. Goodman 1955; Rawls 1971, p. 20.

4. Dretske 1970, Nozick 1981; cf. Goldman (1976), who develops a tracking account of perceptual knowledge.

5. Luper 1984, 1987; Sosa 1999.

6. Dretske (1971) puts his condition as follows: where R is the basis for S's belief that P, S knows that P is true if and only if "R would not be the case unless P were the case."

7. Nozick formulates his account on p. 179 of Nozick 1981; in the text, I simplified his third condition, and ignored the fourth.

8. Note that the truth condition would be redundant, since
    R holds
(which is implied by (1)), together with
    R holds → p
entail
    p.
We may need to define knowledge recursively, ensuring that inferential beliefs countas knowledge only if they rest ultimately on facts that are themselves known to hold noninferentially, but I leave this matter aside.

9. The point of condition (2) is to require that *p* be true in the *R-holds*-neighborhood of the actual world. But, as Peter Klein reminded me, if we require that this neighborhood be very extensive, the condition is too strong. To use an example Jonathan Vogel (1987) used against Nozick, suppose I left a tray of ice cubes

in the sun an hour ago, and believe, correctly, and for obvious reasons, that they have melted. Nonetheless, there is a world in which someone put the cubes back in the freezer without telling me; if we define the relevant neighborhood so that this world is in it, I fail to meet condition (2), for in that world I will still have my reasons for believing the cubes have melted, even though they are frozen. In my view, if there is someone standing by seriously considering putting the tray back into the freezer, or someone who just might do so, then I do not know the ice has melted. However, those who disagree can weaken (2), even to the point where it requires only that in S's situation as it was when R held, p is true.

10. Consider the following inference:
    a. $not\text{-}p \rightarrow not\text{-}(R \text{ holds})$
    b. p entails q
    c. So: $not\text{-}q \rightarrow not\text{-}(R \text{ holds})$.
    It is not valid, because the following is not a valid pattern of inference:
    1. $not\text{-}p \rightarrow not\text{-}q$
    2. p entails r
    3. So: $not\text{-}r \rightarrow not\text{-}q$
    Nor is the following, which commits the fallacy of contraposition twice:
    1. $not\text{-}p \rightarrow not\text{-}q$
    2. $q \rightarrow p$ (from 1—fallacy of contraposition)
    3. p entails r
    4. $q \rightarrow r$ (from 2,3 by strengthening the consequent)
    5. $not\text{-}r \rightarrow not\text{-}q$ (from 4—fallacy of contraposition).

11. Actually, it is not obvious that we should reject closure if we accept the tracking account. As I point out in footnote 32, if we track p via some fact, say R, and believe q by deducing it from p, then we track q via p. We track q if we take p itself as our basis for believing q. We will deny closure only if we insist that knowing q entails tracking q via R, the fact via which we track p. But why say that? For other doubts about Nozick's case against closure, see various essays in Luper (1987a).

12. The inference pattern here is strengthening the consequent, which is valid:
    1. $p \rightarrow q$
    2. q entails r
    3. So: $p \rightarrow r$

13. Our thesis applies directly to Nozick's tracking account, too. Consider the following revision of his view (contraposing his third condition, and leaving out the first, which is redundant): S knows p if and only if there is a method M such that
    S believes p via M, and
    S believes p via $M \rightarrow p$.
    Suppose S knows p via M^1, and believes q by deducing

q from p. Then there is a method M^2 via which S believes q such that
S believes q via $M^2 \rightarrow q$,
namely, *arriving at belief p via M^1 and believing q by deducing q from p.*

14. Apply it to Dretske's zebra case. z meets (T3): when we are not confronted with zebras, generally we do not get zebra-type experiences that might lead us to suspect the presence of zebras. Furthermore, z entails *not-m*. But *not-m* does not meet (T3): on those (rare) occasions when we are confronted with mules disguised as zebras, generally we get zebra-type experiences, indicating that *not-m* is true. (But recall the sort of reservation expressed in notes 11 and 32.)

15. Luper 1984; Sosa 1999.

16. Compare Quine's (and Carnap's) notion of explication in "Two Dogmas of Empiricism," p. 25 of Quine 1953.

17. Cf. Richard Feldman (1999, p. 105).

18. This does not threaten closure. Suppose our source R for believing p does not address one of p's consequences q. Suppose also that we know that p is true and we believe that q is true by deducing it from p. Then our source for believing q is: seeing that q follows from p which is itself indicated by R, and this compound source is a reliable and infallible indicator that q is true.

19. His antiskeptical argument is this:
    1. I know all sorts of commonsense claims: I am in my house typing an essay, and so on.
    2. If I know these things that are incompatible with being a brain in a vat, then I know I am not a brain in a vat.
    3. So I know I am not a brain in a vat.

20. Assuming for the sake of argument that perception is a noninferential process.

21. Luper 1986.

22. A weaker principle is also false: if, in some situation, the evidence we have about p is the *fact* that E holds, and we know p on the basis of E, then we know p in any situation in which E is our evidence and we base belief p on the fact that E holds. Goldman's papier-mâché barn case tells us how to construct a counterexample.

23. Luper 1987b. For more on aligning Gettier cases with skeptical scenarios, see Luper 1984.

24. In this sense subjectivists have always accepted a claim contextualists have been emphasizing lately: the standards knowers must meet vary with context.

25. For example, Unger 1984 and 1986, Cohen 1988, 1991 and 1999, DeRose 1995, and Lewis 1996.

26. If challenged about this principle, a skeptic might respond that those who deny it are probably confusing

it with a principle other skeptics adopt: the situation principle, used in the skeptical argument from the situation principle. One might defend the argument from the context principle without defending the argument from the situation principle. Alternatively, skeptics might claim that their critics are confusing the context principle with the following warranted assertability principle, which is also false: if a judge in one context is *warranted* in attributing knowledge to an agent S, then a judge in any context is warranted in attributing knowledge to S.

27. As we have said, the skeptical argument from closure is by no means the only defense of skepticism. Different errors are involved in some of the other defenses. For example, the argument from the situation principle is flawed because the situation principle is false.

28. As Curtis Brown pointed out to me, a bizarre consequence of contextualism is that the following reasoning is invalid:

> At time 1 S said 'I know *p*.'
> What S said was true.
> So S knew *p* at time 1.

29. Here is another metalinguistic closure principle contextualists must deny:

> If at time 1 S is correct in saying, 'I know that *p*, "and at time 2 S's situation remains the same (as far as possible) except that S comes to believe *q* by deducing *q* from *p*, then, at time 2, S will be correct in saying, 'I know that *q*.'

30. Lewis 1996, p. 220.

31. A particular lottery ticket has little probability of winning given that the game has many entries. So you are justified in believing that ticket 1 will lose. Similarly, you are justified in believing that ticket 2 will lose, and that 3 will lose, and so on. But you are not justified in believing the *conjunction* of these claims, which is tantamount to the claim that every ticket will lose.

32. Klein's point can also be pressed against the tracking theorists' denial of the closure of knowledge: if we track *p*, and believe *q* by deducing it from *p*, then we track *q* if we take *p* as our basis for believing *q*.

33. Certain sorts of objection can be forestalled by qualifying this condition (and the same goes for the tentative externalist account of inferential knowledge to follow):

> Generally, when S holds a *p*-type belief in conformity with (that subset of) S's rules, in the circumstances for which those rules were developed, *p* is true.
> We might also want to refer to S's community:
> Generally, when a member of S's community holds a *p*-type belief in conformity with (that subset of) S's

rules, in the circumstances for which those rules were developed, *p* is true.

References

Annis, David. 1978. "A Contextualist Theory of Epistemic Justification." *American Philosophical Quarterly* 15.

Armstrong, D. M. 1973. *Belief Truth and Knowledge.* Cambridge: Cambridge University Press.

BonJour, Laurence. 1980. "Externalist Theories of Empirical Knowledge." *Midwest Studies in Philosophy* V:53–71.

Cohen, Stewart. 1988. "How to be a Fallibilist." *Philosophical Perspectives* 2:91–123.

———. 1991. "Skepticism, Relevance, and Relativity." In McLaughlin 1991.

———. 1999. "Contextualism, Skepticism, and the Structure of Reasons." *Philosophical Perspectives* 13:57–89.

DeRose, Keith. 1995. "Solving the Skeptical Problem." *Philosophical Review* 104.1:1–15.

Dretske, Fred. 1970. "Epistemic Operators." *Journal of Philosophy* 67:1022.

———. 1971. "Conclusive Reasons." *Australasian Journal of Philosophy* 49:1–22.

Feldman, Richard. 1999. "Contextualism and Skepticism." *Philosophical Perspectives* 13:91–114.

Goldman, Alvin. 1976. "Discrimination and Perceptual Knowledge." *Journal of Philosophy* 73:771–91.

———. 1979. "What Is Justified Belief?" In *Justification and Knowledge* edited by George Pappas, 1–23. Dordrecht: Kluwer Academic Publishers.

———. 1988. "Strong and Weak Justification." In *Philosophical Perspectives* 2, 51–69.

Goodman, Nelson. 1955. "New Riddle of Induction." In *Fact, Fiction and Forecast.* Cambridge, MA: Harvard University Press.

Harman, Gilbert. 1986. *Change in View.* Cambridge, MA: MIT Press.

Klein, Peter. 1981. *Certainty: A Refutation of Scepticism.* Minneapolis: University of Minnesota Press.

Lewis, David. 1996. "Elusive Knowledge." *Australasian Journal of Philosophy* 74.4:549–67.

Luper(-Foy), Steven. 1984. "Knowledge, Nozickian Tracking, and Scepticism." *Australasian Journal of Philosophy* 62:26–50.

————. 1987a. *The Possibility of Knowledge*. Totowa, NJ: Rowman and Littlefield.

————. 1987b. "The Possibility of Skepticism." In Luper (1987a).

————. 1987c. "The Causal Indicator Indicator Analysis of Knowledge." *Philosophy and Phenomenological Research* 47:563–87.

McLaughlin, B. 1991. *Dretske and his Critics*. Oxford: Basil Blackwell.

Moore, G. E. 1959. "A Defense of Common Sense." In *Philosophical Papers*, pp. 32–59. George Allen & Unwin.

Nozick, Robert. 1981. *Philosophical Explanations*. Cambridge: Harvard University Press).

Quine, W. V. O. 1953. *From a Logical Point of View*. New-York: Harper & Row.

Rawls, John. 1971. *A Theory of Justice*. Cambridge: Harvard University Press.

Sosa, Ernest. 1999. "How to Defeat Opposition to Moore." *Philosophical Perspectives* 13:141–52.

Stine, Gail. 1976. "Skepticism, Relevant Alternatives, and Deductive Closure." *Philosophical Studies* 29:249–61.

Unger, Peter. 1986. "The Cone Model of Knowledge." *Philosophical Topics* 14:125–78.

————. 1984. *Philosophical Relativity*. Minneapolis: University of Minnesota Press.

Vogel, Jonathan. 1987. "Tracking, Closure, and Inductive Knowledge." In Luper(-Foy) 1987a.

◆ AN INFINITIST RESPONSE ◆

30. THERE IS NO GOOD REASON TO BE AN ACADEMIC SKEPTIC*

Peter Klein

Introduction

When most contemporary philosophers think of skepticism, they think of a form of Academic Skepticism. Roughly, Academic Skeptics claim that we cannot have knowledge in those areas that we ordinarily think are well within our ken. For example, we cannot know that the sun is now shining, that it shone yesterday, or that it will shine tomorrow. It is not merely that we do not have such knowledge, we *cannot* have such knowledge because there is nothing we can do to acquire it. The Academic Skeptics think that there are some good arguments for their view.

Now, of course, most contemporary philosophers are not Academic Skeptics. They do not think Academic Skepticism is at all plausible—intriguing maybe, but not plausible. They think that not only *can* we have ordinary knowledge, but that we *do* have such knowledge. Further, they think they can refute Academic Skepticism and produce some good arguments whose conclusion is that we do, or at least can, have such knowledge.

The purpose of this paper is to provide some reasons for thinking that another form of skepticism, namely, Pyrrhonian Skepticism, is the appropriate stance to take regarding the possibility that we can have such knowledge. The Pyrrhonians held that with regard to every proposition which requires an argument in order for it to be assented to (I will explain what I mean by "assent" later) there will be no better reasons for asserting it than for rejecting it and, hence, withholding judgment is always the appropriate attitude. I will be arguing for the claim that there are no good arguments for Academic Skepticism. If my argument is cogent, an important step towards a full vindication of Pyrrhonism will have taken. In order to provide that full vindication of the Pyrrhonian response to Academic Skepticism it would be necessary to show that there are no good arguments for the claim that we can have the very kind of knowledge the Academic Skeptics think is beyond our capacity. But that is beyond the scope of this paper.

Further, I cannot examine every argument for Academic Skepticism. What I can do is to examine the ones that most contemporary philosophers find most plausible—or at least most intriguing—and show, in so far as that is possible, that they are not at all compelling. Perhaps there are other arguments that are more compelling. But one can only respond to a discussion at the point where one enters it.

Philosophical Versus Ordinary Incredulity

Suppose Anne sees what she takes to be a crow flying in the distance. She thinks it is a crow and thinks she knows it is a crow. But as it approaches and lands, it looks too big to be a crow and its beak is too long. She begins to have doubts and no longer thinks she knows it is a crow. It might be a crow, but maybe it is a raven. Her reasons for the proposition that it is a crow are not sufficiently compelling in the face of the doubts.

This is a case of ordinary incredulity. What makes it a case of ordinary incredulity is that there are ways of resolving the doubts once they are raised. Anne could consult an expert or check *The Audubon Society Field Guide to North American Birds*, or look again to see how much larger these birds are than typical crows. Or perhaps she could remember that there are some large crows that live in the area and that those crows tend to have longer than usual beaks. The point is that in cases of ordinary incredulity there are accepted ways of resolving doubts once they arise. Even in cases where it is not immediately obvious how to resolve the doubts— for example whether a new element, say 116, has been detected—there are, at least in principle, methods of confirming or disconfirming a proposition. These ways need not lead to certainty. But they can make a proposition sufficiently likely to be true so that we would be justified in believing it. Perhaps revisions or even outright reversal of opinion will be the appropriate stance to take in the future if and when new evidence becomes available. Or, perhaps, withholding belief will be the appropriate stance if the reasons for and against a proposition are nearly balanced. The basic point is that in cases of ordinary doubt, propositions that once were justified can regain that status even in the presence of serious doubts because there are ways to answer the doubts.

Return to Anne's crow. She will answer the doubts by bringing up new evidence of roughly the same sort that prompted the doubt in the first place: evidence concerning the size of crows and relative beak length. More generally, to answer the doubts she can appeal to accepted sources of evidence: perceptual experience, memory, testimony of others, and reasoning. Those are the same sources that are taken to generate justifications. In ordinary cases of justification or doubt, it is a particular judgement that is at stake. The issue is how to weigh the strength of the evidence for and against the particular proposition.

Philosophical skeptics, on the other hand, seek to raise doubts in a way such that they *cannot* be answered. They will raise doubts about the trustworthiness of the very sources of evidence that are used to answer the doubts. Perceptual experience is not to be trusted. Reasoning is not to be trusted. Testimony is not to be trusted. Memory is not to be trusted. If there are legitimate doubts that can be raised about the sources of evidence, then they cannot be answered without begging the question—or so the philosophical skeptic will claim. In contemporary parlance, the skeptic will seek to raise doubts about the trustworthiness of our epistemic equipment and if we acknowledge the legitimacy of those doubts, the skeptic will think that we cannot answer them.

Two Forms of Philosophical Skepticism

With regard to any proposition, p, we can assent to it, we can assent to its negation (that is, deny it) or we can withhold assent to it and its negation. So it is with the proposition that we can have knowledge. Let us call a person who assents to the proposition that we can have knowledge an "Epistemist." (There is no accepted name for the anti-skeptics, so we are free to make one up.) The Academic Skeptic assents to the proposition that we cannot have knowledge. Finally, the Pyrrhonian Skeptic withholds assent to the proposition that we can have knowledge and to the proposition that we cannot have knowledge. Thus, there are two forms of philosophical skepticism. One form claims we cannot have knowledge of propositions we ordinarily think we know; the other form withholds judgment about whether we can have such knowledge.

Academic Skepticism

Let us begin our discussion of Academic Skepticism by citing a passage in Descartes' "First Mediation" in which, speaking on behalf of the Academic Skeptic, he presents the following basis for doubting all of our beliefs that arise from the ordinarily accepted sources of justification:

> . . . In whatever way [it is supposed] that I have arrived at the state of being that I have reached—whether [it is attributed] to fate or to accident, or [made] out that it is by a continual succession of antecedents, or by some other method—since to err and deceive oneself is a defect, it is clear that the greater will be the probability of my being so imperfect as to deceive myself ever, as is the Author of my being to whom [is assigned] my origin the less powerful.[1]

Descartes is claiming (at this point in the *Meditations*) that possibly his epistemic equipment is not able to produce sufficiently justified beliefs. That possibility is captured in the famous Evil Genius argument that is designed to show that our epistemic equipment is untrustworthy because it is unable to detect an extremely well constructed malicious deception. I think that most contemporary philosophers would put the argument for Academic Skepticism in one of two ways (where "S" designates any person and "p" designates any proposition thought to be well within our ken).[2]

Justification Version of the Argument for Academic Skepticism

J1. If S can be justified in believing that p, then S can be justified in believing that he/she is not in a skeptical scenario in which p is false but it appears just as though p were true.

J2. S cannot be justified in believing that he/she is not in a skeptical scenario in which p is false but it appears just as though p were true.

J3. Therefore, S cannot be justified in believing that p.

Knowledge Version of the Argument for Academic Skepticism

K1. If S can know that p, then S can know that he/she is not in a skeptical scenario in which p is false but it appears just as though p were true.

K2. S cannot know that he/she is not in a skeptical scenario in which p is false but it appears just as though p were true.

K3. Therefore, S cannot know that p.

The arguments have a similar structure. Both employ simple *modus tollens*. Further, both J1 and K1 are instantiations of some form of closure (that is, if x has *P* and x entails y, then y has *P*). J1 is the instantiation of this general principle:

> Closure of Justification Principle: (CJP) If S is justified in believing that x, and x entails y, then S is justified in believing that y.

K1 is the instantiation of this general principle:

> Closure of Knowledge Principle: (CKP) If S knows that x, and x entails y, then S knows that y.

The first question before us is this: Which version of the Argument for Academic Skepticism is the one we should consider?[3] The traditional account of knowledge was that knowledge was true, adequately justified belief.[4] Neither the truth of p nor our ability to believe that p is under challenge by the skeptic. In other words, the skeptic thought we could not know that p because we could not be adequately justified in believing that p.

So, if the traditional account of knowledge were the correct one, we should use the Justification Version of the Argument for Academic Skepticism since it focuses attention on the central issue, namely: Can we be justified in believing those things we normally take to be well within our ken? But what if the traditional account is wrong? What if justification is not a necessary condition of knowledge? For example, suppose that an account of knowledge currently in vogue, namely strong reliabilism, were correct and that S knows that p at some time, t, just in case at t, S's true belief that p arises or is causally sustained in some reliable fashion, i.e., a fashion such that beliefs arising or being sustained in that fashion are highly likely to be true or tend to be true.[5] Would the Justification Version still be the one most worthy of examining even if reliabilism were true?

I think that the answer is "yes." I say that for two reasons. *First*, again on the assumption that the Academic Skeptic is not challenging the possibility of S's truly believing p, an Academic Skeptic employing the reliabilist concept of knowledge in the Knowledge Version would be arguing for a lost cause. Recall that the Academic Skeptic is claiming that we *cannot* have knowledge, and since it is not the truth or belief condition that is at stake, such a "reliabilist" skeptic must argue that beliefs *cannot* be reliably caused. But why *can't* beliefs arise or be sustained in a reliable fashion? Consider an example: I think so-called fortune tellers arrive at their beliefs in a completely unreliable fashion (assuming they believe what they tell their customers), but I will grant that it is possible that their methods work. If there (merely) *could* be an Evil Genius who succeeds in deceiving us, it remains possible that my beliefs arose and are sustained in a reliable fashion. The Academic Skeptic would have to argue successfully that there actually is an Evil Genius who actually succeeds in causing me to employ unreliable methods if such a skeptic is to show that my beliefs *could not* be produced by a reliable process. Given that the Academic Skeptic's claim is that we cannot have even ordinary knowledge, this looks like a road best left untraveled by the Academic Skeptic.

Second, even if knowledge did not entail justification, it seems equally, if not more disturbing, to accede to the conclusion that we could not have justified beliefs than it is to acquiesce to the conclusion that we could never have knowledge—if knowledge were merely reliably produced true belief. If we could have no adequate reasons for any of our beliefs, rational investigation would be pointless and inevitably frustrating. In addition, merely having a

reliably produced true belief without any reason for thinking that it is reliably produced seems like having money in the bank without knowing that it is there. And, of course, if we have a reason for thinking a belief is reliably produced, we have a reason for thinking it is true.

So, we will focus on the Justification Version of the Argument for Academic Skepticism.

The Pyrrhonian Response to the Justification Version of the Argument for Academic Skepticism

The Academic Skeptic thinks that the Justification Version of the Argument for Academic Skepticism establishes that we cannot be justified in believing any of those propositions ordinarily thought to be known. How would a Pyrrhonian Skeptic respond to the Justification Version? Recall that the Pyrrhonians thought that the proper attitude toward any proposition that required an argument in order to be justified was to withhold belief. Of course, "belief" covers a wide variety of attitudes that one can have toward a proposition. One can believe it, but very hesitatingly. Or one could believe it very strongly; so strongly that one's attitude was that the matter had been settled by the reasoning. Let us call the strong form of believing "assenting" and refer to expressing assent by "asserting." In describing the three attitudes that distinguished the Pyrrhonian from the Epistemist and the Academic Skeptic, I used "assent," and it was assent that the Pyrrhonians withheld with regard to any proposition whose justification depended upon reasoning.[6]

The Pyrrhonians developed techniques—or "modes" as they put it—designed to help them to resist the temptation to assent to propositions arrived at through reasoning. The modes functioned like finger exercises for the piano that provide an almost automatic response to the printed notes in a recital piece. Here is an excerpt from what is probably the most famous passage in the Pyrrhonian corpus describing the modes that could be employed to help resist accepting a proposition whose justification was provided by reasoning ("Dogmatist" refers to anyone who assented to propositions):

The Mode based upon regress *ad infinitum* is that whereby we assert that the thing adduced as a proof of the matter proposed needs a further proof, and this again another, and so on *ad infinitum*, so that the consequence is suspension [of assent], as we possess no starting-point for our argument. . . . We have the Mode based upon hypothesis when the Dogmatists, being forced to recede *ad infinitum*, take as their starting-point something which they do not establish but claim to assume as granted simply and without demonstration. The Mode of circular reasoning is the form used when the proof itself which ought to establish the matter of inquiry requires confirmation derived from the matter; in this case, being unable to assume either in order to establish the other, we suspend judgement about both.[7]

There are two relevant, crucial insights in this passage. *First*, the stated premises in arguments should be seen as only partial fragments of the total set of reasons for believing the stated conclusion. If someone asserts some conclusion, c, and gives as reasons $\{r_1 - r_n\}$, the Pyrrhonians will ask for the reasons for $r_1 - r_n$. And, then, she will ask for the reasons for the reasons, etc. In other words, the Pyrrhonian will ask for the argument to be fully articulated and will not rest content with the stated argument. Only when the argument is fully articulated can it be determined whether it provides a good, reasonable basis for the conclusion, c. *Second*, once the process of tracing back the reasons begins, there are only three possible outcomes. (1) The more fully articulated argument could include as a reason the very conclusion, c, of the stated argument or something equivalent to c. In that case, the fully articulated argument begs the question because c is provided as a basis for c. The argument can provide no basis for believing c; and providing such a basis was the point of giving the argument in the first place. It begs the question because the very issue requiring support, or something equivalent to it, is offered as part of its own support. The Pyrrhonian need not ask for a further articulation of the argument since it would already have become apparent that the argument cannot provide a basis for increasing the degree of justification one has for c. Withholding assent to c would be appropriate.[8] (2) If c does not reappear in the set of reasons, then the process of giving reasons

could continue *ad infinitum*. In that case, the matter will not (yet) have been settled, and withholding assent to c is appropriate. (3) The process of giving reasons could end with a proposition for which no further reason is available. If that happens, then although the final "reason" might be accepted by all parties in the actual situation, if one party in the dispute were to demur, there is nothing the presenter of the argument can do to rationally convince that party to accept the "final" reason (because there is no further reason available) and, hence, the fully articulated argument would not be able to provide a new basis for accepting c to the demurring interlocutor, and withholding assent would be the appropriate response.

Now whether the Pyrrhonian is correct *in general* about the upshot of the three possible structures of the fully articulated argument is an important and complex matter. Is it true that once it is recognized that a proposition needs an argument in order to be assented to, withholding assent to it is bound to be the appropriate stance? I have argued elsewhere that the Pyrrhonian is correct.[9] But luckily for our purposes we need only see whether the Pyrrhonian modes work on the Justification Version of the Argument for Academic Skepticism. That argument has two premises, J1 and J2, and we will begin our Pyrrhonian-like response to the stated argument by asking what reasons the Academic Skeptic has for each of the premises given the possible criticisms of them. Then, I will try to show that the more fully articulated argument either begs the question or rests upon an arbitrary assumption—one the Epistemist will rightly not accept. In other words, I want to practice two of the modes, the mode of circular reasoning and the mode of hypothesis. In particular, I will argue that given the only possible defense of J1, either the arguments that can be given for J2 beg the question or the argument for J1 rests upon an assumption that the Epistemist can rightly reject.

But first, a few more words about how the Pyrrhonian modes work. Recall, that the Pyrrhonians thought that one could not tell whether an argument begged the question until it was fully articulated. Let me give an example to illustrate their point. Consider this argument:

1. Everything the bible says is true.
2. The bible says that God exists.

   Therefore, God exists.

Does the argument beg the question? The Pyrrhonians would say that we need to see a more fully articulated argument in order to determine the answer. Suppose the person giving the argument, Ms. Believer, says that there are no reasons for believing (1) and no reasons for believing (2). She says that there is no way to further articulate the argument. Surely, the correct response would be to withhold assent to the conclusion because those premises should not be assented to without some reasons being given.

But suppose that Ms. Believer gives the following as her reason for believing (1): *The bible was written by God and everything God writes is true.* She has begged the question because her reason implicitly includes the conclusion. The proposition "the bible was written by God" is equivalent to "there is a God and there is a bible and God wrote the bible."

On the other hand, suppose Ms. Believer gives the following as her reason for (1): *There are 3,100 claims in the bible. Five hundred (500) of them were chosen at random and they all were true.* Now, of course, her reason does not imply (1), but good reasoning is not limited to deductive reasoning. So far, she has not begged the question, but once again the Pyrrhonian could practice the modes and ask for her reasons for thinking that there are 3,100 claims and her reasons for thinking that the 500 were randomly chosen and her reasons for thinking that they were all true. She could assert that those propositions were such that no reasons are available. If she did, withholding would be appropriate. If she gave her reasons, the Pyrrhonian would look to see whether she begged the question. If she did, then withholding would be appropriate. If she didn't, the Pyrrhonian would continue asking for reasons.

Now, whether the modes will always work to induce suspense of assent is the issue we have set aside for another time. The point here is merely to illustrate the Pyrrhonian's claim that in order to tell whether a stated argument provides a basis for the stated conclusion the argument needs to be more fully articulated. So, let us apply the modes to the Justification Version of the Argument for Academic Skepticism and begin with J1. What reasons would the Academic Skeptics have for J1? Why should we think that if S is justified in believing x, and x entails y, then S is justified in believing that y?[10]

Let us suppose that S *is justified in believing that* x if and only if S has reasons that make x sufficiently likely to be true.[11] That is a supposition both the Epistemist and Academic Skeptic can agree to. Of course, they will differ on whether S ever has such reasons. Now, given that supposition, here is an argument for thinking that J1 is correct:

1. If S is justified in believing that x, then S has reasons that make x sufficiently likely to be true. [by the supposition]
2. If S has reasons that make x sufficiently likely to be true, then S has reasons that make y sufficiently likely to be true. [because x entails y, the likelihood of y will be at least as high as the likelihood of x]
3. If S is justified in believing that x, then S has reasons that make y sufficiently likely to be true. [from 1, 2]
4. If S has reasons that make y sufficiently likely to be true, then S is justified in believing that y. [by the supposition]
5. Therefore, if S is justified in believing that x, then S is justified in believing that y. [from 3, 4]

Premise 2 contains the crucial claim. Even though the probabilities (whether subjective or objective) transmit through entailment, the modes would require that we examine whether it is true. Indeed, Fred Dretske and others have produced purported counterexamples to premise 2.[12]

> Dretske writes:
> . . . something's being a zebra implies that it is not a mule . . . cleverly disguised by the zoo authorities to look like a zebra. Do you know that these animals are not mules cleverly disguised? If you are tempted to say "Yes" to this question, think a moment about what reasons you have, what evidence you can produce in favor of this claim. The evidence you *had* for thinking them zebras has been effectively neutralized, since it does not count toward their *not* being mules cleverly disguised to look like zebras.[13]

Dretske is speaking of "knowledge" rather than justification, but I think it is clear from the passage that he thinks whether you know that the animals are cleverly disguised mules depends upon whether your reasons are good enough. The claim essentially is this: You have good enough reasons for thinking that the animals are zebras but you do not have good enough reasons for thinking that the animals are not cleverly disguised mules. The evidence you have for thinking that they are zebras can't be used to justify the proposition that they are not cleverly disguised mules because it "has been effectively neutralized."

If Dretske were right that this is a counterexample to premise 2 in the argument for CJP, we could stop here because we would have established the main claim of the paper, namely that there is no good reason to be an Academic Skeptic. The argument based upon CJP would have been shown to be based upon a false premise.

But I think the Academic Skeptic has a convincing reply to this purported counterexample. She can point out that Dretske has assumed that the only reasons that one can have for thinking that the zebras are not cleverly disguised mules are the very reasons one has for thinking that they are zebras. Letting 'xRy' mean that x is an adequate reason for y, Dretske is supposing that the evidence path must look like this whenever x entails y:

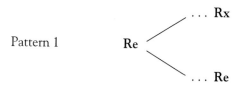

Pattern 1

Evidence paths specify what propositions serve as good enough reasons for believing other propositions and their depiction is intended to capture the supposition we began with, namely that S is justified in believing x just in case S has reasons that make x sufficiently likely to be true. The evidence paths depict acceptable patterns of those reasons.

Dretske is supposing that the very same reason, e, that I have for x must be adequate for y whenever x entails y. The Academic Skeptic can grant that Pattern 1 sometimes correctly portrays the relevant evidential relationships when some proposition, x, entails some other proposition, y. But she should point out that CJP merely says that if S is justified in believing x, and x entails y, then S is justified in believing that y. It does not require that the evidence for y is the very same evidence that is used for x. Indeed, the Academic Skeptic

could point out that there are two other possible evidence paths that satisfy or instantiate CJP:

Pattern 2   . . . **ReRx** . . . **Ry**

Pattern 3   . . . **Re** (where e includes y) **Rx**

In Pattern 2 cases, there is some adequate evidence, e, for x; and x, itself, is the adequate evidence for y, since x strictly implies y. For example, if I have adequate evidence for believing that Anne is in Paris, then I can use the very proposition that Anne is in Paris as my reason for thinking that Anne is in France, because the former entails the latter.

In Pattern 3 cases, the order of the evidence is reversed because y serves as part of the evidence for x. The entailing proposition is part of the evidence for the entailed one. Arguments by elimination often work that way. Suppose I know that the object hidden under a cloth is either a basketball or a football. If I were to find out that it is not a football, I could use that as part of my evidence for the claim that it is basketball. But its being a basket ball entails that it is not a football. More generally, often the negation of alternative hypotheses forms part of our evidence for a particular claim. For example, in Dretske's zebra-in-the-zoo case, if there were some reason to think that the animals might be cleverly disguised mules, then it could be argued that such an alternative hypothesis must be eliminated *before* I would be justified in believing that the animals are zebras.

What is crucial to note here is that the Academic Skeptic has ways of defending the argument for CJP that avoid Dretske's counterexample. But those ways require that she argue that there is more than one evidence path that instantiates CJP. For any pair of propositions {x,y}, CJP is satisfied just in case one of the three patterns correctly depicts the evidential relationship between x and y.

So far, the more fully articulated Justification Version of the Argument for Academic Skepticism has not begged the question. In addition, it does not seem to be based upon an assumption the Epistemist could not accept. Of course, it is possible that as we push back the reasoning for CJP, and its instantiation, J1, we would encounter a step that either begs the question or depends upon an assumption the Epistemist could not accept. Be that as it may, I think we are on the verge of being able to show that the Justification Version does fall prey to the modes.

Let us turn our attention to J2. The Pyrrhonian will ask the Academic Skeptic for her reasons for thinking that S cannot be justified in believing that he/she is not in a skeptical scenario in which p is false but it appears just as though p were true. Using the terminology developed in supporting J1, the Academic Skeptic will have to argue that there is no good evidence path of the appropriate sort that terminates in the proposition that S is not in such a skeptical scenario. We have seen that if CJP is to be defended adequately, the Academic Skeptic must argue that there are three possible evidence paths relating the entailing proposition to the entailed one. So, in arguing for J2, the Academic Skeptic must specify which path correctly depicts the relevant evidential relationships and show that there are no reasons of the appropriate sort available to S which terminate in the proposition that S is not in a skeptical scenario in which it merely appears that p.

Suppose the Academic Skeptic says that the appropriate pattern is Pattern 2. She will be claiming that J1 is true because the appropriate evidential relationship between "p" (the entailing proposition) and "S is not in a skeptical scenario in which it merely appears that p" (the entailed proposition) is that p is the reason to be given for the proposition that S is not in a skeptical scenario in which it merely appears that p. So, if one could move along the evidence path from e to p, one could arrive at "S is not in a skeptical scenario . . ." All well and good; but note that when she now argues for J2, she will have to show that S has no reason, e, which makes p sufficiently likely to be true. For if S had such a reason, then according to Pattern 2, S would have an adequate reason, namely p, for believing that she is not in a skeptical scenario. So, S could not have adequate reasons for thinking that p is true. But in arguing that there are no adequate reasons that make p sufficiently likely to be true, she will be arguing for something equivalent to the claim that S is not justified in believing that p because the supposition she used in the argument for CJP was that S is justified in believing that x if and

only if S has reasons that make x sufficiently likely to be true. But if that premise—the premise that S does not have adequate reasons for believing that p—is part of this version of the fully articulated argument, she will have begged the question since she will have claimed something equivalent to the proposition that S is not justified in believing p in her argument for J2 and that is the very conclusion of the Justification Version of the Argument for Academic Skepticism.[14]

Suppose that the Academic Skeptic says that the pattern which correctly depicts the evidential relationships is Pattern 1. She will be claiming that J1 is true because the appropriate evidential relationship between "p" and "S is not in a skeptical scenario in which it merely appears that p" is that there is some common reason, e, which (were it available) provides an adequate basis for both. Thus, in arguing for J2, she would have to show that there is no adequate reason that is available for each of the two propositions. In other words, a step in this version of the fully articulated argument would require showing that there is no adequate common evidence for p and the proposition that S is not in a skeptical scenario. The Academic Skeptic will, once again, have begged the question for she will have claimed as part of her argument for J2 that S is not justified in believing p.[15]

So, if the Academic Skeptic thinks J1 is true because the appropriate evidential relationship between "p" and "S is not in a skeptical scenario in which it merely appears that p" is either Pattern 1 or Pattern 2, in giving her reasons for J2 in the more fully articulated arguments, she will perforce beg the question.

Now, finally, suppose that the Academic Skeptic claims that the pattern which correctly depicts the evidential relationships is Pattern 3. She will be claiming that J1 is true because the appropriate evidential relationship between "p" and "S is not in a skeptical scenario in which it merely appears that p" is that the latter serves as evidence for p. S must be justified in believing that he/she is not in a skeptical scenario *prior* to being justified in believing that p. What should the Epistemist do in this case?

I think the answer is clear. The Epistemist is entitled to reject that requirement. The Academic Skeptic cannot require that in order to be justified in believing a proposition, all rival hypotheses must first be eliminated. If that requirement were accepted, there is an all too easy route to Academic Skepticism. Consider any proposition, p. Both (~p and x) and (~p & ~x) are rival hypotheses of p. So in order to be justified in believing that p, the evidence must include the denials of those rival hypotheses. But {~(~p &x) &~(~p&~x)} entails p. Thus, this requirement would be tantamount to requiring that in order to be justified in believing that p, the evidence must entail p. This is a too quick and dirty argument for Academic Skepticism because in so far as that form of skepticism remains an interesting philosophical position, the Academic Skeptic cannot impose such an outrageous departure from our ordinary epistemic practices. So, the issue is this: When does a rival hypothesis to a proposition have to be eliminated prior to that proposition being justified?"

The Epistemist could argue plausibly that contraries need to be eliminated just in case there is some evidence for them. Return to the zebra-in-the-zoo case. Suppose S claims to know that the animals in the pen are zebras. The Academic Skeptic could ask S whether he/she has eliminated the hypothesis that the animals are aliens from another galaxy. Or whether S has eliminated the alternative that they are robots. Or whether S has eliminated the hypothesis that they are members of the lost tribe of Israel who have perfected the zebra-disguise in their efforts to hide from Assyrians. (After all, they have had almost three millennia to perfect the disguise!) The Epistemist could respond on S's behalf by pointing out that one need eliminate a rival hypothesis only when there is some evidence, however slight, that the rival hypothesis is true and in this case there is no such evidence for any of the rival hypotheses, including the one that S is in a skeptical scenario in which the animals are not zebras but appear to be. Thus, if the Academic Skeptic chooses to argue for J2 by claiming that the appropriate evidential relationship between "p" and "S is not in a skeptical scenario in which it merely appears that p" is depicted in Pattern 3, she will have based her argument upon a premise that the Epistemist can rightly reject.[16]

The upshot is that the fully articulated Justification Version of the Argument for Academic Skepticism either begs the question or is based upon an assumption that the Epistemist can legitimately reject.

A Partial Vindication of Pyrrhonism

Pyrrhonists think the proper attitude toward the proposition that we can have knowledge is to withhold assent. If the argument in this paper is correct, I have shown that the fully articulated argument for the claim that we cannot have such knowledge falls prey to the modes. But that would not be enough to fully vindicate the Pyrrhonist's attitude. For perhaps there is an argument for the claim that we can have such knowledge that does not fall prey to the modes. Maybe the Epistemist has a way of showing—without begging the question, or without employing a premise that the Academic Skeptic could rightly reject, or without providing reasons *ad infinitum*—that we can have knowledge[17] What can be said at this point is that the Pyrrhonians seem to be correct that there is no good reason to be an Academic Skeptic.

Notes

* I wish to thank Anne Ashbaugh for her help with this paper. Also I should note that much of this paper repeats and revises some ideas about the various forms of skepticism discussed in other papers of mine. In particular, see "How a Pyrrhonian Skeptic Might Respond to Academic Skepticism" in *The Skeptics: Contemporary Essays*, Ashgate Press, ed. Steven Luper, forthcoming; "Skepticism," *Stanford Encyclopedia of Philosophy*, http://plato.stanford.edu/entries/skepticism/, "When Infinite Regresses Are *Not* Vicious," *Philosophy and Phenomenological Research*, forthcoming; "Skepticism," *The Oxford Handbook of Epistemology*. Oxford University Press, ed. Paul Moser, forthcoming; "What *IS* Wrong with Foundationalism is that it Cannot Solve the Epistemic Regress Problem," *Philosophy and Phenomenological Research*, forthcoming.

1. "Meditations on First Philosophy" in *Philosophical Works of Descartes*, eds. Elizabeth Haldane and G.R.T. Ross (Dover Publications, 1931), vol. I, p. 147.
2. See, for example, *Skepticism: A Contemporary Reader*, eds. Keith DeRose and Ted A. Warfield, (New York and Oxford: Oxford University Press, 1999). In that

volume most of the authors take one of these two forms of argument to be the primary one. There is an excellent discussion of Academic Skepticism in the "Introduction" to that volume.

3. It might be thought that the argument for Academic Skepticism explored by Descartes is not captured by either of the two versions I have presented. Instead of either CJP or KJP, it could be claimed that Descartes makes use of another principle we can call the "Eliminate All Doubt Principle" or simply "EAD."

EAD: (x,d)(if d provides a basis for genuine doubt that x, then if S is justified in believing that p to the degree necessary for knowledge, then S is justified in denying d.)

The proposition, d, provides a basis for genuine doubt that x for S just in case adding d to his/her beliefs and justified beliefs would make it the case that S is not justified in believing that x. In more contemporary terminology, EAD requires that if S is justified in believing that p, then S must be justified in rejecting every potential defeater of his/her justification of p. (See my essay, "Knowledge is True, Non-Defeated, Justified Belief" in this volume, pp 124–135.) Further, it could be claimed that there is an all-purpose, general defeater that S cannot be in a position to reject, namely:

U: My epistemic equipment is untrustworthy.

Thus, it could be thought that the actual *Cartesian-style argument for Academic Skepticism* should be put like this:

1. If S is justified in believing that p to the degree necessary for knowledge, then there are no genuine grounds for doubting p that S is not justified in denying.
2. U is a genuine ground for doubting p that S is not justified in denying.
   Therefore, S is not justified in believing that p to the degree necessary for knowledge.
   And, therefore, S does not know that p.

I chose not to put the argument that way for two reasons. *First*, EAD is an extremely strong requirement compared to CJP. Thus, the skeptic's burden is extremely heavy were she to employ EAD; and we are trying to give the skeptic the best possible chance of demonstrating that her position is reasonable. *Second*, EAD implies CJP. If x entails y, then EAD requires that if S is justified in believing that x (to the degree necessary for knowledge), then S is justified in denying that ~y (because ~y is a potential defeater). To be justified in denying ~y is equivalent to being justified in believing y. Hence, if EAD is true, and if x entails y,

and S is justified in believing that x (to the degree necessary for knowledge), then S is justified in believing that y. Since EAD implies CJP, if we locate objections to the argument employing CJP, those will redound to EAD.

4. Edmund Gettier accurately dubbed that notion the "traditional" account in his "Is Justified True Belief Knowledge?" *Analysis*, 23.6, 1963, 121–123.

5. This is a very unnuanced gloss of reliabilism. Some reliabilists would *add* a reliability condition to the traditional account rather than replace the justification condition with a reliability condition. I use the expression "strong reliabilism" to indicate the view that knowledge is to be understood as true, reliably produced belief. For a full discussion of reliabilism see Alvin Goldman, *Epistemology and Cognition* (Cambridge, MA: Harvard University Press, 1986); *Liaisons: Philosophy Meets the Cognitive and Social Sciences* (Cambridge, MA: MIT Press, 1992). Also see Fred Dretske, *Knowledge and the Flow of Information*, (Cambridge, MA: MIT Press, 1981).

6. In this passage, Sextus makes clear that it is the strong form of belief that the Pyrrhonians withheld:

... although both the Academics and the [Pyrrhonian] Skeptics say that they believe some things, yet here too the difference between the two philosophies is quite plain. For the word "believe" has different meanings; it means not to resist but simply to follow without any strong impulse or inclination, as the boy is said to believe his tutor; but sometimes it means to assent to a thing of deliberate choice and with a kind of sympathy due to strong desire, as when the incontinent man believes him who approves of an extravagant mode of life. Since, therefore, Carneades and Cleitomachus [two Academic Skeptics] declare that a strong inclination accompanies their credence ... While we say that our belief is a matter of simply yielding without any consent, here too there must be difference between us and them. [Sextus Empiricus, *Outlines of Pyrrhonism* (Cambridge, Massachusetts: Harvard University Press, 1967), I, 230, trans. R.G. Bury.]

7. Sextus Empiricus, *op. cit.*, I, 166–169.

8. The issue is a bit more complex than the text suggests. Consider this argument:

1. Sally says "p & q" [Premise]
2. Whatever Sally says is true. [Premise]
3. Therefore, p & q [from 1,2]
4. Therefore, p [from 3]

In this case, p does appear (in 3) as a reason for the conclusion, p. But I do not think this is a case of begging the question. The reason is that one could go directly from 1 and 2 to 4 without going through 3 if we had a disquotational rule of the following sort: If S truly says "x & y," then x. In other words, there is a way to articulate the stated argument without p occurring in a premise. So, a more precise but less immediately understandable way of stating a sufficient (but perhaps not necessary) condition for an argument begging the question is this: An argument, A, with conclusion, c, begs the question if, as A becomes more fully articulated, c or something equivalent to c occurs as a conjunct in one of the premises and there is no alternative way of articulating A without including c, or something equivalent to c, as a conjunct in one of the premises. [Note: Since c is equivalent to (c & c), the condition would be fulfilled whenever c occurs alone in a premise and there is no way to articulate the argument without c occurring as a conjunct in a premise.]

9. See, for example, the following: "Foundationalism and the Infinite Regress of Reasons," *Philosophy and Phenomenological Research*, 58.4, 1998, 919–925; "Human Knowledge and the Infinite Regress of Reasons," *Philosophical Perspectives*, 13, J. Tomberlin (ed.), 1999, 297–325; "Why Not Infinitism?" in *Epistemology: Proceedings of the Twentieth World Congress in Philosophy* Richard Cobb-Stevens (ed.), 2000, vol 5, 199–208.

10. Let me grant at this point that, as stated, both KJP and CJP are false. But they can easily be repaired in a way that the Academic Skeptic would be willing to grant. For example, every necessary truth is entailed by every proposition. Thus, if S knows or is justified in believing any proposition, S would know or be justified in believing every necessary truth. Also, if S were ever justified in believing a necessarily false proposition (which seems possible), the S would be justified in believing every proposition. In addition, the entailment might be a very difficult one for S to recognize. And finally, since S might believe x but not believe y (perhaps out of epistemic timidity or perversity), KJP is false; and if "S is justified in believing that y" entailed "S believes that y," CJP would be false as well. But both principles could easily be rectified. We could limit the domain to contingent truths, limit the entailments to ones that S recognizes, stipulate that to be justified in believing that p does not entail that one actually believes that p, and finally we could replace "S knows that p" with "S is in a position to know that p." There might be other minor difficulties that need to be repaired. But they are all distractions that need not concern us here.

11. By "S has reasons that make x sufficiently likely to be true" I mean that S's *overall* set of reasons is such it makes x sufficiently likely to be true. If a subset of S's reasons made it sufficiently likely that x is true but some other subset countervailed or counterbalanced, I take it that S's total set of reasons would not make x sufficiently likely to be true and S would not be justified in believing that x is true.

12. For another, similar, proposed counterexample, see Robert Audi, *Belief, Justification and Knowledge* (Belmont, California: Wadsworth, 1988), 77.

13. Fred Dretske, "Epistemic Operators," *Journal of Philosophy*, 67 (1970), 1015–16.

14. Given the qualification discussed in endnote 8, a minor amendment in the argument is required because, as we noted there, the conclusion of a stated argument could occur as a conjunct in a premise of the more fully articulated argument and the argument not beg the question if there is an alternative way of articulating the argument such that the conclusion does not occur. But since it is essential to this way of more fully articulating the argument that J1 is true because the evidential relationships are correctly depicted by Pattern 2, the argument for J2 would have to show that there is no good evidential path to p. Hence, there is no alternative way of articulating the argument along these lines without including the conclusion of the argument or something equivalent to it as a conjunct in a premise of the argument for J2.

15. A parallel amendment to that discussed in endnote 14 would be needed with regard to articulating the argument in this fashion.

16. There is a possible objection that needs to be considered here. The claim the Epistemist is making is that a contrary must be eliminated just in case there is some evidence that it is true. Now, suppose that c_1, c_2 and c_3 are contraries and that there is some evidence for c_2 but there is no evidence for c_3. The proposal is that in order for S to be justified in believing c_1, S needs to eliminate c_2 but that S need not eliminate c_3. Now, it could be objected that if there is some evidence for c_2, then there is some evidence for $(c_2 \lor c_3)$ namely the very evidence for c_2. If that were correct, then according to the suggestion S would have to eliminate $(c_2 \lor c_3)$ before being justified in believing c_1. That requires eliminating both c_2 and c_3 - contrary to the proposal that c_3 need not be eliminated. The Epistemist can respond that this objection is based upon a false assumption, namely that if there is evidence for c_2, then that very evidence is also evidence for $(c_2 \lor c_3)$. As we have seen in discussing the zebra-in-the-zoo case, just because x entails y, it does not follow that the evidence for x is also evidence for y. So, the Epistemist can resist this objection.

17. I have addressed two such attempts to show that we can have knowledge. See "Skepticism: Ascent and Assent?" in *Philosophers and Their Critics*, ed. John Greco, Blackwell Publishers, forthcoming; "Coherence, Knowledge and Skepticism," *The Epistemology of Keith Lehrer*, ed. Erik Olsson, Kluwer, forthcoming.

CHAPTER 6 EXTERNALISM VERSUS INTERNALISM ✦

INTRODUCTION

Traditionally, epistemologists understood the discriminatory powers we need to achieve knowledge or justified belief in terms of evidence that is directly accessible. They accepted *justification internalism,* which says the conditions that determine whether we are justified in believing something are accessible from within our cognitive perspective, and *knowledge internalism,* which says the factors that determine whether we know something are accessible from within our cognitive perspective. Contemporary theorists have tended to abandon one or both forms of internalism, in part because internalism seems to make traditional issues in knowledge intractable, and in part because a leading motivation behind internalism was incorrigibilist foundationalism (which says that basic beliefs are certain), a view that has been abandoned by nearly every epistemologist. Contemporary theorists frequently offer *externalist* accounts, according to which knowledge or justified belief or both depend on factors that are external to the epistemic agent's cognitive perspective. But while theorists have tended to drift toward externalism in recent years, the issue remains controversial.

In this chapter we offer one essay that raises problems for externalism, two that speak in favor of externalism, and one, by Ernest Sosa, that attempts to combine externalist and internalist elements.

Armstrong's Defense of Externalism

The term 'externalism' was popularized by D. M. Armstrong, author of *Belief, Truth, and Knowledge* (1973), who borrowed it from unpublished work by Gregory O'Hair. According to 'externalist' accounts

of noninferential knowledge, as Armstrong defines the term, "what makes a true noninferential belief a case of knowledge is some natural relation which holds between the belief state . . . and the situation which makes the belief true." Thus causal theories and reliabilist theories are externalist accounts. Armstrong argues that Gettier-style considerations force us to accept a reliabilist, externalist account of knowledge. He says that people who know things are like thermometers whose mercury levels indicate the temperature: they base their beliefs on something that reliably (indeed: infallibly, given their circumstances) indicates that their beliefs are true.

BonJour's Defense of Internalism

According to Laurence BonJour, author of "Can Empirical Knowledge Have a Foundation?", epistemic justification requires aiming at the goal of truth and accepting only beliefs we have good reason to think true. That is, it requires being epistemically responsible in our choice of beliefs. He defends internalism because "on the externalist view, a person may be ever so irrational and irresponsible in accepting a belief, when judged in light of his own subjective conception of the situation, and may still turn out to be epistemically justified."

Sosa's Mixed View

In "Reflective Knowledge in the Best Circles," Ernest Sosa offers a critical discussion of G. E. Moore's proof of the external world. Then Sosa distinguishes between two levels of knowledge. There is a low-grade of knowledge, called *animal* knowledge, for which it is correct to give an externalist reliabilist analysis. That is, when we arrive at our belief using reliable faculties, which Sosa calls virtues, we possess animal knowledge. By contrast, the high-grade of knowledge, called *reflective* knowledge, cannot be given an externalist analysis. To gain reflective knowledge, one must not only possess animal knowledge, but one must also have a perspective on one's manner of acquiring beliefs. One must be able to explain how it is that one comes to possess one's knowledge.

Goldman's Critique of Internalism

In "Internalism Exposed," Alvin Goldman suggests that internalism is motivated by the guidance-deontological conception of justification, according to which epistemology is to guide our intellectual conduct and we have a duty to guide our beliefs by our evidence. This conception supports the view that "the only facts that qualify as justifiers of an agent's believing *p* at time *t* are facts that the agent can readily know, at *t*, to obtain or not to obtain." However, Goldman says, this conception of justification is not really able to support internalism. To support internalism, we must make additional assumptions that are counterintuitive and not derivable from the guidance-deontological conception of justification.

QUESTIONS FOR REFLECTION

1. According to BonJour, externalist accounts of knowledge are unacceptable because they allow people to be epistemically irresponsible. Is he correct? How would Armstrong respond?

2. Is Goldman correct in saying that internalism is motivated by the guidance-deontological conception of justification? If so, are his criticisms decisive, or are there other grounds for accepting internalism?

3. How might BonJour respond to Goldman's critique of internalism?

4. Compare Sosa's view of knowledge to Susan Haack's "foundherentism." Is one account more plausible? Would Haack accept the combination of internalism and externalism offered by Sosa?

5. Does naturalism (discussed in the last chapter) commit us to externalism? Does externalism commit us to naturalism? What is the relationship between the two?

⋄ A DEFENSE OF EXTERNALISM ⋄

31. KNOWLEDGE

D. M. Armstrong

The Infinite Regress of Reasons

Knowledge entails true belief, but true belief does not entail knowledge. It is therefore suggested that knowledge is a true belief for which the believer has sufficient evidence, or some such formula. But the evidence will have to be some proposition, 'q', which is *known* to A. I think that this becomes evident if the 'method of subtraction' is applied, and we contemplate the situation where this condition *fails* to obtain. Let us suppose that it is not the case that A knows that q is true (~ Kaq). Surely this weakness in the foundations ensures that the belief founded upon it is not known either? If I claim to know that p solely on the basis of evidence 'q', but go on to admit that it is not the case that I know that q is true, you will laugh at my claim to know.

This simple consideration seems to make redundant the ingenious argument of Edmund L. Gettier's brief but influential article 'Is Justified True Belief Knowledge?' (Gettier 1963). Gettier produces counter-examples to the thesis that justified true belief is knowledge by producing true beliefs based on justifiably believed grounds, in the 'ordinary language' sense of 'justifiably believed', but where these grounds are in fact *false*. But because possession of such grounds could not constitute possession of *knowledge,* I should have thought it obvious that they are too weak to serve as suitable grounds. It is not surprising, therefore, that Gettier is able to construct examples where a true belief is justified in an ordinary sense of 'justified', but the true belief is clearly not a case of knowledge.

Gettier's paper has been commented upon, with a view to excluding his counter-example by judiciously chosen extra conditions, in a truly alarming and ever-increasing series of papers. For instance, it has been suggested that in order to count as proper grounds, the justifying beliefs must be not only 'justifiably believed' but also true. But whatever amendments have been proposed, counterexamples have still been constructed. It seems to me clear that it must always be possible to construct counter-examples until a condition is introduced that the justifying beliefs are *known* to be true.

Of course, it is easy to see why those who try to introduce extra conditions to exclude Gettier's counter-examples do not introduce *knowledge* of the justifying beliefs into their analyses. For then the very notion of knowledge which an analysis is being sought for crops up again in the analysis. Knowledge that p will be analysed in terms of knowledge that q, knowledge that q in terms of knowledge that r, and so, it would seem, *ad infinitum.*

Nevertheless, if we are going to have an Evidence-condition at all, then, as has been argued, it *must* involve *knowledge* of the evidence. And the threatened infinite regress — first noticed in the literature by Plato at the end of the *Theaetetus* (209E–210B) — does not leave the supporter of an Evidence-condition completely without resource. Knowledge that q is used in defining knowledge that p. This is not flat circularity. The term 'knowledge' crops up both in *definiendum* and *definiens.* But one piece of knowledge is defined in terms of *another* piece of knowledge. This gives a little space for manoeuvre and there have been all sorts of attempts to exploit this space.

Indeed, Gregory O'Hair has attempted, in unpublished work, to classify all the various philosophers' analyses or accounts of knowledge as *different reactions to the threatened regress.* The sketch which follows is greatly indebted to this idea of his, although I have not stuck to all his particular sub-divisions. I am not proposing to discuss exhaustively the alternatives to my own view, but will content myself simply with a brief indication of objections. My object is only to place the type of solution to the problem which I defend in a perspective of other attempted solutions. Gettier-type analyses must, of course, be excluded, because they do not allow the regress even to begin. But we have argued that they operate with too weak a form of the Evidence-condition.

Different Reactions to the Regress

1. The *'Sceptical' Reaction.* We may begin by distinguishing between 'sceptical' and 'non-sceptical' reactions to the regress. An extreme form of the sceptical reaction would be to say that the infinite regress showed that the concept of knowledge involves a contradiction. A moderate view would be that the word 'know', although it attributes true belief, attributes nothing further of an objective nature to the belief — no relation to the facts — except truth.

One straightforwardly sceptical account of knowledge is the view suggested in much of Karl Popper's work that the word 'know' is not theoretically useful, and that all our beliefs should be treated as 'hypotheses'. (To avoid possible misunderstanding, let me say now that it is not being claimed that all the views mentioned are actually formed under the stimulus of the threatened infinite regress. The claim is only that these views can usefully be classified *as if* they were reactions to the regress.)

In J. L. Austin's well-known article 'Other Minds' (Austin 1961) it is suggested that the special linguistic function of the phrase 'I know . . .' is to pledge the speaker's word, or give his authority, that the statement which follows is true. This suggests, although it may not actually entail, a 'sceptical' view of knowledge. (For what seems definitive criticism of this so-called 'performative' view of 'I know . . .' see Jonathan Harrison 1962, and W. H. F. Barnes 1963.)

The only comment which seems required about 'sceptical' views of knowledge is this. A non-sceptical solution to the problem posed by the infinite regress is to be preferred if it can be found. After all, there does appear to be a clear, objective, distinction between knowledge and mere true belief (*vide* the optimistic punter).

2. *The regress is infinite but virtuous.* The first non-sceptical solution which may be canvassed is that the regress exists, but is virtuous. Suppose that event A has a prior cause B, B has a prior cause C, and so, perhaps, *ad infinitum*. Few modern philosophers would consider this latter progression to infinity a vicious one. So perhaps A's knowledge that p rests upon knowledge that q which rests upon knowledge that r, and so on without stop. Such a view was held by C. S. Peirce. (See 'Some Consequences of Four Incapacities', Peirce 1940.)

This solution depends upon maintaining that, in order to know anything, we must know an infinite number of things. And so it might seem to be sufficiently refuted by pointing out that the mind of man is finite. However, this does not completely dispose of the suggestion. For instance, if we know a rule for generating an open set of formulae then, it can be argued, we have potential access to an infinite number of formulae, despite the fact that our minds are finite. In some similar way to this, it may be suggested, we could know the infinite number of things which serve as the infinite chain of good reasons standing behind everything we know.

It can hardly be pretended, however, that this reaction to the regress has much plausibility. Like the 'sceptical' solution, it is a *desperate* solution, to be considered only if all others are clearly seen to be unsatisfactory.

3. *The regress is finite, but has no end.* Suppose, then, that the regress is not virtuous. Then either the regress has no end, or it has an end. If it has no end, then at some point the reasons must come back upon their own tail, so that 'p' is supported by 'q', which is supported by 'r', which is supported by 's', . . . which is supported by . . . , which is supported by 'p'. This may seem to involve *vicious* circularity. But perhaps it need not. If we have a circle of true beliefs which mutually support each other in this way, then it might be suggested that, once the circle is sufficiently comprehensive and the mutual support sufficiently strong, we would not have mere true beliefs but pieces of knowledge. This may be called the *Coherence* analysis of the concept of knowledge. I do not know anywhere that it has been worked out in detail, but it is close in spirit to the Coherence theory of truth.

There are complications here, depending upon the theory of truth accepted. If one took the Coherence view of truth also, then the notions of knowledge and truth might come into close logical connection. But if one accepted the sort of view of truth already argued for in Part II, truth and knowledge would be quite independent. One would have an objective view of truth, but combine it with the idea that coherence of such true beliefs turned the cohering beliefs into knowledge. The traditional analysis of knowledge implicitly assumes that the Truth-condition and the Belief-condition are logically independent.

Clearly, there are many difficulties for this 'Coherence theory of knowledge'. For instance, what criterion can be given to show that a circle of true beliefs is 'sufficiently comprehensive'? It is not easy to say. And might there not be a sufficiently comprehensive circle of true beliefs which was arrived at so irregularly and luckily that we would not want to call it knowledge?

4. *The regress ends in self-evident truths.* If the Coherence analysis is rejected, then at some point in the regress of reasons (perhaps right at the beginning) we will reach knowledge which is *not* based on reasons. I will call such knowledge '*non-inferential*' *knowledge*. I oppose it to 'inferential' knowledge, which *is* based on reasons. Once it is granted that there is an objective notion of knowledge; that the infinite regress of reasons is in some way vicious; and that the regress cannot be stopped by judicious circularity; then it must be granted that, when A knows that p, then *either* this knowledge is non-inferential, or it is based on a finite set of reasons terminating in non-inferential knowledge.

The problem then comes to be that of giving an account of non-inferential knowledge. Suppose that A believes that p, but that A's belief does not rest upon any reason for believing that p. We have already (Chapter Six, Section One) called such a case 'non-inferential belief'. It is clear that non-inferential knowledge entails true non-inferential belief, but that the reverse entailment does not hold. So the question becomes: what further restriction must be placed on true non-inferential beliefs to yield non-inferential *knowledge*?

The classical answer is: non-inferential beliefs which are self-evident, indubitable or incorrigible. They will serve to stop the regress and act as the foundations of knowledge. This has been the *standard* solution from the time of Descartes until quite recently.

However, I reject the whole notion of beliefs that it is logically impossible to be wrong about. I think the logical possibility of error is always present in any belief about any subject matter whatsoever. In any case, it has been demonstrated again and again that, even if there is such self-evident knowledge, it is completely insufficient in *extent* to serve as a foundation for all the things we ordinarily claim to know, even when we have circumscribed that claim by careful reflection. In the past, defenders of this Cartesian solution have regularly had to cut down the scope of our supposed knowledge in a completely unacceptable manner. (For instance, it becomes difficult to claim that there is any empirical knowledge, non-inferential or inferential, beyond that of our own current states of mind.)

5. '*Initial credibility*'. The alternative is to attempt an account of non-inferential knowledge without appealing to such self-evident truths. O'Hair has distinguished two sorts of view here, which he calls 'Initial credibility' and 'Externalist' views.

First a word about 'Initial credibility' theories. It might be maintained that certain classes of our non-inferential beliefs have an intrinsic claim to credibility, even although error about them is a logical and even an empirical possibility. Instances might be beliefs based directly upon sense-perception, upon memory, upon intuition of the simpler logical necessities, or perhaps only upon suitable subclasses of these classes. Now suppose that a belief is non-inferential, is 'initially credible' and is also *true*. Might it not then be accounted a case of non-inferential *knowledge*?

This approach strikes me as more hopeful than the possible reactions to the infinite regress which have already been mentioned. But it involves certain difficulties. It is easy, for instance, to construct non-inferential memory beliefs which are true, but which we certainly would not call knowledge. Thus, a probe in my brain might produce the belief in me that I had an itch in my little finger three days ago. By sheer coincidence, the belief might be true. Or a veridical memory-trace might degenerate but, in the course of a multi-stage degeneration, the original encoding might be reinstated by a sheer fluke. Some way of excluding such cases would have to be found. I myself am convinced, although I will not try to demonstrate the point here, that the only way to achieve such exclusions satisfactorily is to pass over into an 'Externalist' theory.

6. '*Externalist*' *theories*. According to 'Externalist' accounts of non-inferential knowledge, what makes a true non-inferential belief a case of *knowledge* is some natural relation which holds between the belief-state, Bap, and the situation which makes the belief true. It is a matter of a certain relation holding between the believer and the world. It is important to notice that, unlike 'Cartesian' and 'Initial Credibility' theories, Externalist theories are regularly developed as theories, Externalist theories are regularly developed as theories of the nature of knowledge *generally* and not simply as theories of non-inferential knowledge. But they still have a peculiar importance in the case of non-inferential knowledge because they serve to solve the problem of the infinite regress.

Externalist theories may be further sub-divided into 'Causal' and 'Reliability' theories.

7. (i) *Causal theories*. The central notion in causal theories may be illustrated by the simplest case. The suggestion is that Bap is a case of Kap if 'p' is true and, furthermore, the situation that makes 'p' true is causally responsible for the existence of the belief-state Bap. I not only believe, but *know*, that the room is rather hot. Now it is certainly *the excessive heat of the room* which has caused me to have this belief. This causal relation, it may then be suggested, is what makes my belief a case of knowledge.

Ramsey's brief note on 'Knowledge', to be found among his 'Last Papers' in *The Foundations of Mathematics*, put forward a causal view. A sophisticated recent version of a causal theory is to be found in 'A Causal Theory of Knowing' by Alvin I. Goldman (Goldman 1967).

Causal theories face two main types of difficulty. In the first place, even if we restrict ourselves to knowledge of particular matters of fact, not every case of knowledge is a case where the situation known is causally responsible for the existence of the belief. For instance, we appear to have some knowledge of the future. And even if all such knowledge is in practice inferential, non-inferential knowledge of the future (for example, that I will be ill tomorrow) seems to be an intelligible possibility. Yet it could hardly be held that my illness tomorrow causes my belief today that I will be ill tomorrow. Such cases can perhaps be dealt with by sophisticating the Causal analysis. In such a case, one could say, both the illness tomorrow and today's belief that I will be ill tomorrow have a *common* cause, for instance some condition of my body today which not only leads to illness but casts its shadow before by giving rise to the belief. (An 'early-warning' system.)

In the second place, and much more seriously, cases can be envisaged where the situation that makes 'p' true gives rise to Bap, but we would not want to say that A *knew* that p. Suppose, for instance, that A is in a hypersensitive and deranged state, so that almost any considerable sensory stimulus causes him to believe that there is a sound of a certain sort in his immediate environment. Now suppose that, on a particular occasion, the considerable sensory stimulus which produces that belief is, in fact, *a sound of just that sort in his immediate environment*. Here the p-situation produces Bap, but we would not want to say that it was a case of knowledge.

I believe that such cases can be excluded only by filling out the Causal Analysis with a *Reliability* condition. But once this is done, I think it turns out that the Causal part of the analysis becomes redundant, and that the Reliability condition is sufficient by itself for giving an account of non-inferential (and inferential) knowledge.

(ii) *Reliability theories.* The second 'Externalist' approach is in terms of the *empirical reliability* of the belief involved. Knowledge is empirically reliable belief. Since the next chapter will be devoted to a defence of a form of the Reliability view, it will be only courteous to indicate the major precursors of this sort of view which I am acquainted with.

Once again, Ramsey is the pioneer. The paper 'Knowledge', already mentioned, combines elements of the Causal and the Reliability view. There followed John Watling's 'Inference from the Known to the Unknown' (Watling 1954), which first converted me to a Reliability view. Since then there has been Brian Skyrms' very difficult paper 'The Explication of "X knows that p"' (Skyrms 1967), and Peter Unger's 'An Analysis of Factual Knowledge' (Unger 1968), both of which appear to defend versions of the Reliability view. There is also my own first version in Chapter Nine of *A Materialist Theory of the Mind*. A still more recent paper, which I think can be said to put forward a Reliability view, and which in any case anticipates a number of the results I arrive at in this Part, is Fred Dretske's 'Conclusive Reasons' (Dretske 1971).

It is interesting to notice that a Reliability analysis is considered for a moment by Plato in the *Meno*, only to be dropped immediately. At 97b Socrates asserts that

'. . . true opinion is as good a guide as knowledge for the purpose of acting rightly', and goes on to ask whether we should not draw the conclusion that 'right opinion is something no less useful than knowledge'. Meno however objects:

> Except that the man with knowledge will always be successful, and the man with right opinion only sometimes.

Unfortunately, however, Socrates brushes aside this tentative development of a Reliability view, saying:

> What? Will he not always be successful so long as he has the right opinion?

Meno immediately concedes the point.

This concludes our brief survey. In philosophy, when one finds oneself in a difficult intellectual situation, it is often vitally important to be aware of the full range of response which is open to one. And in philosophy, if one practises it honestly, one invariably is in a more or less difficult intellectual situation. The survey just made was intended to create an awareness of the many different responses open to us in the difficult situation created by the threatened infinite regress involved in the classical analysis of knowledge. Against this background, I proceed to put forward a suggested solution of the problem.

The 'Thermometer' View of Non-Inferential Knowledge

Suppose that 'p' is true, and A believes that p, but his belief is not supported by any reasons. 'p' might be the proposition that there is a sound in A's environment. (The previous section indicates why this example is chosen.) What makes such a belief a case of knowledge? My suggestion is that there must be a *law-like connection* between the state of affairs Bap and the state of affairs that makes 'p' true such that, given Bap, it must be the case that p.

The quickest way to grasp the suggestion is to use a model. Let us compare non-inferential beliefs to the temperature-readings given by a thermometer. In some cases, the thermometer-reading will fail to correspond to the temperature of the environment. Such a reading may be compared to non-inferential false belief. In other cases, the reading will correspond to the actual temperature. Such a reading is like non-inferential true belief. The second case, where reading and actual environmental temperature coincide, is then sub-divided into two sorts of case. First, suppose that the thermometer is a bad one, but that, on a certain occasion, the thermometer-reading coincides with the actual temperature. (*Cf.* the stopped clock that shows the right time twice a day.) Such a reading is to be compared with non-inferential true belief which falls short of knowledge. Suppose finally that the thermometer is a good one, so that a reading of 'T° ' on the thermometer ensures that the environmental temperature is T° . Such a reading is to be compared with non-inferential *knowledge*. When a true belief unsupported by reasons stands to the situation truly believed to exist as a thermometer-reading in a good thermometer stands to the actual temperature, then we have non-inferential knowledge.

I think the picture given by the thermometer-model is intuitively clear. The problem is to give a formal account of the situation.

Here is one immediate difficulty. Laws of nature are connections between things (in the widest sense of 'things') of certain *sorts*. But the suggested connection between belief-state and situation which makes the belief true is a connection between particular states of affairs: between singulars.

The reply to this is that the belief-state is an *instance* of a certain sort of thing: a person believing a certain sort of proposition. Equally, the situation is an instance of a certain sort of thing: say, a certain sort of sound within earshot of the believer. So we can say that a law-like connection holds between the two singulars in virtue of the fact that the two are of certain sorts, and things of these sorts are connected by a law.

Here, however, we must be careful. What is the law that is involved? Take the example of knowing non-inferentially that there is a sound in one's environment. A believes that there is a sound in his environment now, and indeed there is. Do we want to say that A *knows* there is a sound in his environment only if the whole situation is covered by the following law-like generalization: 'If anybody believes that there is a sound in his environment, then there is indeed a sound in his environment'? Of course not. The proposed generalization is clearly false, because people have sometimes believed that there was a sound in their environment when there was none. Yet we are not led by this to say that nobody ever *knows* that such sounds are occurring.

The model of the thermometer gives us further assistance here. For a thermometer to be reliable on a certain occasion in registering a certain temperature as T° we do not demand that there be a true law-like generalization: 'If any thermometer registers "T° ", then the temperature is T° .' In the first place, we recognize that there can be good and bad thermometers. In the second place, we do not even demand that a good thermometer provide a reliable reading under every condition. We recognize that there may be special environmental conditions under which even a 'good' thermometer is unreliable.

What do we demand? Let us investigate a far less stringent condition. Suppose, on a certain occasion, a thermometer is reliably registering 'T° '. There must be some property of the instrument and/or its circumstances such that, if anything has this property, and registers 'T° ', it must be the case, as a matter of natural law, that the temperature *is* T°. We might find it extremely hard to specify this property (set of properties). The specification might have to be given in the form of a blank cheque to be filled in only after extensive investigation. But it may be relatively easy to recognize that a certain thermometer is operating reliably, and so that such specification is possible. (In general, the recognition of the existence of general connections in nature precedes their specification.)

Let us now try applying this to the case of non-inferential knowledge. A's non-inferential belief that p is non-inferential *knowledge* if, and only if:

1. p is the case
2. There is some specification of A such that, if any person is so specified, then, if they further believe that p, then p is the case.

References

Austin, J.L. (1961) "Other Minds," *Philosophical Papers* (Oxford: Oxford University Press).

Barnes, W.H.F. (1963) "Knowing," *Philosophical Review* 72.

Dretske, Fred (1971) "Conclusive Reasons," *Australasian Journal of Philosophy* 49: 1–22.

Goldman, Alvin (1967) "A Causal Theory of Knowing," Journal of Philosophy 64: 357–72.

Peirce, C.S. (1940) *The Philosophy of Peirce*, ed. J. Buchler (Cambridge: Routledge).

Skyrms, Brian (1967) "The Explication of 'X knows that p'", *Journal of Philosophy* 64.

Unger, Peter (1968) "An Analysis of Factual Knowledge," *Journal of Philosophy* 65.

◇ A DEFENSE OF INTERNALISM ◇

32. I. CAN EMPIRICAL KNOWLEDGE HAVE A FOUNDATION?

Laurence BonJour

The main reason for the impressive durability of foundationism is not any overwhelming plausibility attaching to the main foundationist thesis in itself, but rather the existence of one apparently decisive argument which seems to rule out all non-skeptical alternatives to foundationism, thereby showing that *some* version of foundationism must be true (on the assumption that skepticism is false). In a recent statement by Quinton, this argument runs as follows:

> If any beliefs are to be justified at all, . . . there must be some terminal beliefs that do not owe their . . . credibility to others. For a belief to be justified it is not enough for it to be accepted, let alone merely entertained: there must also be good reason for accepting it. Furthermore, for an inferential belief to be justified the beliefs that support it must be justified themselves. There must, therefore, be a kind of belief that does not owe its justification to the support provided by others. Unless this were so no belief would be justified at all, for to justify any belief would require the antecedent justification of an infinite series of beliefs. The terminal . . . beliefs that are needed to bring the regress of justification to a stop need not be strictly self-evident in the sense that they somehow justify themselves. All that is required is that they should not owe their justification to any other beliefs.[1]

I shall call this argument *the epistemic regress argument*, and the problem which generates it, *the epistemic regress problem*. Since it is this argument which provides the primary rationale and argumentative support for foundationism, a careful examination of it will also constitute an exploration of the foundationist position itself.

I

The epistemic regress problem arises directly out of the traditional conception of knowledge as *adequately justified true belief*[2]—whether this be taken as a fully adequate definition of knowledge or, in light of the apparent counter-examples discovered by Gettier,[3] as merely a necessary but not sufficient condition. (I shall assume throughout that the elements of the traditional conception are at least necessary for knowledge.) Now the most natural way to justify a belief is by producing a justificatory argument: belief A is justified by citing some other (perhaps conjunctive) belief B, from which A is inferable in some acceptable way and which is thus offered as a reason for accepting A.[4] Call this *inferential justification*. It is clear, as Quinton points out in the passage quoted above, that for A to be genuinely justified by virtue of such a justificatory argument, B must itself be justified in some fashion; merely being inferable from an unsupported guess or hunch, e.g., would confer no genuine justification upon A.

Suppose then that belief A is (putatively) justified via inference, thus raising the question of how the justifying premise-belief B is justified. Here again the answer may be in inferential terms: B may be (putatively) justified in virtue of being inferable from some further belief C. But then the same question arises about the justification of C, and so on, threatening an infinite and apparently vicious regress of epistemic justification. Each belief is justified only if an epistemically prior belief is justified, and that epistemically prior belief is justified only if a still prior belief is justified, etc., with the apparent result that justification can never get started—and hence that there is no justification and no knowledge. The foundationist claim is that only through the adoption of some version of foundationism can this skeptical consequence be avoided.

Prima facie, there seem to be only four basic possibilities with regard to the eventual outcome of this potential regress of epistemic justification: (i) the regress might terminate with beliefs for which no justification of any kind is available, even though they were earlier offered as justifying premises; (ii) the regress might proceed infinitely backwards with ever more new premise beliefs being introduced and then themselves requiring justification; (iii) the regress might circle back upon itself, so that at some point beliefs which appeared earlier in the sequence of justifying arguments are appealed to again as premises; (iv) the regress might terminate because beliefs are reached which are justified—unlike those in alternative (i)—but whose justification does not depend inferentially on other empirical beliefs and thus does not raise any further issue of justification with respect to such beliefs.[5] The foundationist opts for the last alternative. His argument is that the other three lead inexorably to the skeptical result, and that the second and third have additional fatal defects as well, so that some version of the fourth, foundationist alternative must be correct (assuming that skepticism is false).

As thus formulated, the epistemic regress argument makes an undeniably persuasive case for foundationism. Like any argument by elimination, however, it cannot be conclusive until the surviving alternative has itself been carefully examined. The foundationist position may turn out to be subject to equally serious objections, thus forcing a reexamination of the other alternatives, a search for a further non-skeptical alternative, or conceivably the reluctant acceptance of the skeptical conclusion.[6] In particular, it is not clear on the basis of the argument thus far whether and how foundationism can itself solve the regress problem; and thus the possibility exists that the epistemic regress argument will prove to be a two-edged sword, as lethal to the foundationist as it is to his opponents.

II

The most straightforward interpretation of alternative (iv) leads directly to a view which I will here call *strong foundationism*. According to strong foundationism, the foundational beliefs which terminate the regress of justification possess sufficient epistemic warrant, independently of any appeal to inference from (or coherence with) other empirical beliefs, to satisfy the justification condition of knowledge and qualify as acceptable justifying premises for further beliefs. Since the justification of these *basic beliefs*, as they have come to be called, is thus allegedly not dependent on that of any other empirical belief, they are uniquely able to provide secure starting-points for the justification of empirical knowledge and stopping-points for the regress of justification.

The position just outlined is in fact a fairly modest version of strong foundationism. Strong foundationists have typically made considerably stronger claims on behalf of basic beliefs. Basic beliefs have been claimed not only to have sufficient non-inferential justification to qualify as knowledge, but also to be *certain*, *infallible*, *indubitable*, or *incorrigible* (terms which are usually not very carefully distinguished).[7] And most of the major attacks on foundationism have focused on these stronger claims. Thus it is important to point out that nothing about the basic strong foundationist response to the regress problem demands that basic beliefs be more than adequately justified.

Indeed, many recent foundationists have felt that even the relatively modest version of strong foundationism outlined above is still too strong. Their alternative, still within the general aegis of the foundationist position, is a view which may be called *weak foundationism*. Weak foundationism accepts the central idea of foundationism—viz. that certain empirical beliefs possess a degree of independent epistemic justification or warrant which does not derive from inference or coherence relations. But the weak foundationist holds that these foundational beliefs have only a quite low degree of warrant, much lower than that attributed to them by even modest strong foundationism and insufficient by itself to satisfy the justification condition for knowledge or to qualify them as acceptable justifying premises for other beliefs. Thus this independent warrant must somehow be augmented if knowledge is to be achieved, and the usual appeal here is to coherence with other such minimally warranted beliefs.

Weak foundationism thus represents a kind of hybrid between strong foundationism and the coherence views discussed earlier, and it is often thought to embody the virtues of both and the vices of neither. Whether or not this is so in other respects, however, relative to the regress problem weak foundationism is finally open to the very same basic objection as strong foundationism, with essentially the same options available for meeting it. As we shall see, the key problem for any version of foundationism is whether it can itself solve the regress problem which motivates its very existence, without resorting to essentially *ad hoc* stipulation. The distinction between the two main ways of meeting this challenge both cuts across and is more basic than that between strong and weak foundationism. This being so, it will suffice to concentrate here on strong foundationism, leaving the application of the discussion to weak foundationism largely implicit.

The fundamental concept of strong foundationism is obviously the concept of a basic belief. It is by appeal to this concept that the threat of an infinite regress is to be avoided and empirical knowledge given a secure foundation. But how can there be any empirical beliefs which are thus basic? In fact, though this has not always been noticed, the very idea of an epistemically basic empirical belief is extremely paradoxical. For on what basis is such a belief to be justified, once appeal to further empirical beliefs is ruled out? Chisholm's theological analogy, cited earlier, is most appropriate: a basic belief is in effect an epistemological unmoved (or self-moved) mover. It is able to confer justification on other beliefs, but apparently has no need to have justification conferred on it. But is such a status any easier to understand in epistemology than it is in theology? How can a belief impart epistemic "motion" to other beliefs unless it is itself in "motion"? And, even more paradoxically, how can a belief epistemically "move" itself?

This intuitive difficulty with the concept of a basic empirical belief may be elaborated and clarified by reflecting a bit on the concept of epistemic justification. The idea of justification is a generic one, admitting in principle of many specific varieties. Thus the acceptance of an empirical belief might be morally justified, i.e. justified as morally obligatory by reference to moral principles and standards; or pragmatically justified, i.e. justified by reference to the desirable practical consequences which will result from such acceptance; or religiously justified, i.e. justified by reference to specified

religious texts or theological dogmas; etc. But none of these other varieties of justification can satisfy the justification condition for knowledge. Knowledge requires *epistemic* justification, and the distinguishing characteristic of this particular species of justification is, I submit, its essential or internal relationship to the cognitive goal of truth. Cognitive doings are epistemically justified, on this conception, only if and to the extent that they are aimed at this goal—which means roughly that one accepts all and only beliefs which one has good reason to think are true.[8] To accept a belief in the absence of such a reason, however appealing or even mandatory such acceptance might be from other standpoints, is to neglect the pursuit of truth; such acceptance is, one might say, *epistemically irresponsible*. My contention is that the idea of being epistemically responsible is the core of the concept of epistemic justification.[9]

A corollary of this conception of epistemic justification is that a satisfactory defense of a particular standard of epistemic justification must consist in showing it to be truth-conductive, i.e. in showing that accepting beliefs in accordance with its dictates is likely to lead to truth (and more likely than any proposed alternative). Without such a meta-justification, a proposed standard of epistemic justification lacks any underlying rationale. Why after all should an epistemically responsible inquirer prefer justified beliefs to unjustified ones, if not that the former are more likely to be true? To insist that a certain belief is epistemically justified, while confessing in the same breath that this fact about it provides no good reason to think that it is true, would be to render nugatory the whole concept of epistemic justification.

These general remarks about epistemic justification apply in full measure to any strong foundationist position and to its constituent account of basic beliefs. If basic beliefs are to provide a secure foundation for empirical knowledge, if inference from them is to be the sole basis for the justification of other empirical beliefs, then that feature, whatever it may be, in virtue of which a belief qualifies as basic must also constitute a good reason for thinking that the belief is true. If we let 'F' represent this feature, then for a belief B to qualify as basic in an acceptable foundationist account, the premises of the following justificatory argument must themselves be at least justified:[10]

1. Belief B has feature F.
2. Beliefs having feature F are highly likely to be true.

Therefore, B is highly likely to be true.

Notice further that while either premise taken separately might turn out to be justifiable on an a priori basis (depending on the particular choice of), it seems clear that they could not both be thus justifiable. For B is *ex hypothesi* an empirical belief, and it is hard to see how a particular empirical belief could be justified on a purely a priori basis.[11] And if we now assume, reasonably enough, that for B to be justified for a particular person (at a particular time) it is necessary, not merely that a justification for B exist in the abstract, but that the person in question be in cognitive possession of that justification, we get the result that B is not basic after all since its justification depends on that of at least one other empirical belief. If this is correct, strong foundationism is untenable as a solution to the regress problem (and an analogous argument will show weak foundationism to be similarly untenable).

The foregoing argument is, no doubt, exceedingly obvious. But how is the strong foundationist to answer it? *Prima facie*, there seem to be only two general sorts of answer which are even remotely plausible, so long as the strong foundationist remains within the confines of the traditional conception of knowledge, avoids tacitly embracing skepticism, and does not attempt the heroic task of arguing that an empirical belief could be justified on a purely a priori basis. First, he might argue that although it is indeed necessary for a belief to be justified and *a fortiori* for it to be basic that a justifying argument of the sort schematized above be in principle available in the situation, it is *not* always necessary that the person for whom the belief is basic (or anyone else) know or even justifiably believe that it is available; instead, in the case of basic beliefs at least, it is sufficient that the premises for an argument of that general sort (or for some favored particular variety of such argument) merely be *true*, whether or not that person (or anyone else) justifiably believes that they are true. Second, he might grant that it is necessary both that such justification exist and that the person for whom the belief is basic be in cognitive possession of it, but insist that his cognitive grasp of the premises required for

that justification does not involve further empirical beliefs which would then require justification, but instead involves cognitive states of a more rudimentary sort which do not themselves require justification: *intuitions* or *immediate apprehensions*. I will consider each of these alternatives in turn. [BonJour's discussion of the second alternative has been omitted—ed.]

III

The philosopher who has come the closest to an explicit advocacy of the view that basic beliefs may be justified even though the person for whom they are basic is not in any way in cognitive possession of the appropriate justifying argument is D. M. Armstrong. In his recent book, *Belief, Truth and Knowledge*,[12] Armstrong presents a version of the epistemic regress problem (though one couched in terms of knowledge rather than justification) and defends what he calls an "Externalist" solution:

> According to 'Externalist' accounts of non-inferential knowledge, what makes a true non-inferential belief a case of *knowledge* is some natural relation which holds between the belief-state . . . and the situation which makes the belief true. It is a matter of a certain relation holding between the believer and the world. [157].

Armstrong's own candidate for this "natural relation" is "that there must be a *law-like connection* between the state of affairs Bap [i.e. a's believing that p] and the state of affairs that makes 'p' true such that, given Bap, it must be the case that p." [166] A similar view seems to be implicit in Dretske's account of perceptual knowledge in *Seeing and Knowing*, with the variation that Dretske requires for knowledge not only that the relation in question obtain, but also that the putative knower *believe* that it obtains—though *not* that this belief be justified.[13] In addition, it seems likely that various views of an ordinary-language stripe which appeal to facts about how language is learned either to justify basic belief or to support the claim that no justification is required would, if pushed, turn out to be positions of this general sort. Here I shall mainly confine myself to Armstrong, who is the only one of these philosophers who is explicitly concerned with the regress problem.

There is, however, some uncertainty as to how views of this sort in general and Armstrong's view in particular are properly to be interpreted. On the one hand, Armstrong might be taken as offering an account of how basic beliefs (and perhaps others as well) satisfy the adequate-justification condition for knowledge; while on the other hand, he might be taken as simply repudiating the traditional conception of knowledge and the associated concept of epistemic justification, and offering a surrogate conception in its place—one which better accords with the "naturalistic" world-view which Armstrong prefers.[14] But it is only when understood in the former way that externalism (to adopt Armstrong's useful term) is of any immediate interest here, since it is only on that interpretation that it constitutes a version of foundationism and offers a direct response to the anti-foundationist argument set out above. Thus I shall mainly focus on this interpretation of externalism, remarking only briefly at the end of the present section on the alternative one.

Understood in this way, the externalist solution to the regress problem is quite simple: the person who has a basic belief need not be in possession of any justified reason for his belief and indeed, except in Dretske's version, need not even think that there is such a reason; the status of his belief as constituting knowledge (if true) depends solely on the external relation and not at all on his subjective view of the situation. Thus there are no further empirical beliefs in need of justification and no regress.

Now it is clear that such an externalist position succeeds in avoiding the regress problem and the anti-foundationist argument. What may well be doubted, however, is whether this avoidance deserves to be considered a *solution*, rather than an essentially *ad hoc* evasion, of the problem. Plainly the sort of "external" relation which Armstrong has in mind would, if known, provide a basis for a justifying argument along the lines sketched earlier, roughly as follows:

1. Belief B is an instance of kind K.
2. Beliefs of kind K are connected in a law-like way with the sorts of states of affairs which would make them true, and therefore are highly likely to be true.

Therefore, B is highly likely to be true.

But precisely what generates the regress problem in the first place is the requirement that for a belief B to be epistemically justified for a given person P, it is necessary, not just that there be justifiable or even true premises available in the situation which could in principle provide a basis for a justification of B, but that P himself know or at least justifiably believe some such set of premises and thus be in a position to employ the corresponding argument. The externalist position seems to amount merely to waiving this general requirement in cases where the justification takes a certain form, and the question is why this should be acceptable in these cases when it is not acceptable generally. (If it were acceptable generally, then it would seem that any true belief would be justified for any person, and the distinction between knowledge and true belief would collapse.) Such a move seems rather analogous to solving a regress of causes by simply stipulating that although most events must have a cause, events of a certain kind need not.

Whatever plausibility attaches to externalism seems to derive from the fact that if the external relation in question genuinely obtains, then P will not go wrong in accepting the belief, and it is, in a sense, not an accident that this is so. But it remains unclear how these facts are supposed to justify P's acceptance of B. It is clear, of course, that an external observer who knew both that P accepted B and that there was a law-like connection between such acceptance and the truth of B would be in a position to construct an argument to justify *his own* acceptance of B. P could thus serve as a useful epistemic instrument, a kind of cognitive thermometer, for such an external observer (and in fact the example of a thermometer is exactly the analogy which Armstrong employs to illustrate the relationship which is supposed to obtain between the person who has the belief and the external state of affairs [166ff.]). But P himself has no reason at all for thinking that B is likely to be true. From his perspective, it *is* an accident that the belief is true.[15] And thus his acceptance of B is no more rational or responsible from an epistemic standpoint than would be the acceptance of a subjectively similar belief for which the external relation in question failed to obtain.[16]

Nor does it seem to help matters to move from Armstrong's version of externalism, which requires only that the requisite relationship between the believer and the world obtain, to the superficially less radical version apparently held by Dretske, which requires that P also believe that the external relation obtains, but does not require that this latter belief be justified. This view may seem slightly less implausible, since it at least requires that the person have some idea, albeit unjustified, of why B is likely to be true. But this change is not enough to save externalism. One way to see this is to suppose that the person believes the requisite relation to obtain on some totally irrational and irrelevant basis, e.g. as a result of reading tea leaves or studying astrological charts. If B were an ordinary, non-basic belief, such a situation would surely preclude its being justified, and it is hard to see why the result should be any different for an allegedly basic belief.

Thus it finally seems possible to make sense of externalism only by construing the externalist as simply abandoning the traditional notion of epistemic justification and along with it anything resembling the traditional conception of knowledge. (As already remarked, this may be precisely what the proponents of externalism intend to be doing, though most of them are not very clear on this point.) Thus consider Armstrong's final summation of his conception of knowledge:

> *Knowledge of the truth of particular matters of fact* is a belief which must be true, where the 'must' is a matter of law-like necessity. Such knowledge is a reliable representation or 'mapping' of reality. [220].

Nothing is said here of reasons or justification or evidence or having the right to be sure. Indeed the whole idea, central to the western epistemological tradition, of knowledge as essentially the product of reflective, critical, and rational inquiry has seemingly vanished without a trace. It is possible of course that such an altered conception of knowledge may be inescapable or even in some way desirable, but it constitutes a solution to the regress problem or any problem arising out of the traditional conception of knowledge only in the radical and relatively uninteresting sense that to reject that conception is also to reject the problems arising out of it.

Notes

1. Anthony Quinton, *The Nature of Things* (London, 1973), p. 119. This is an extremely venerable argument, which has played a central role in epistemological discussion at least since Aristotle's statement of it in the *Posterior Analytics*, Book I, ch. 2–3. (Some have found an anticipation of the argument in the *Theaetetus* at 209E–210B, but Plato's worry in that passage appears to be that the proposed definition of knowledge is circular, not that it leads to an infinite regress of justification.)

2. "Adequately justified" because a belief could be justified to some degree without being sufficiently justified to qualify as knowledge (if true). But it is far from clear just how much justification is needed for adequacy. Virtually all recent epistemologists agree that certainty is not required. But the lottery paradox shows that adequacy cannot be understood merely in terms of some specified level of probability. (For a useful account of the lottery paradox, see Robert Ackermann, *Knowledge and Belief* (Garden City, N. Y., 1972), pp. 39–50.) Armstrong, in *Belief, Truth and Knowledge* (London, 1973), argues that what is required is that one's reasons for the belief be "conclusive," but the precise meaning of this is less than clear. Ultimately, it may be that the concept of knowledge is simply too crude for refined epistemological discussion, so that it may be necessary to speak instead of degrees of belief and corresponding degrees of justification. I shall assume (perhaps controversially) that the proper solution to this problem will not affect the issues to be discussed here, and speak merely of the reasons or justification making the belief *highly likely* to be true, without trying to say exactly what this means.

3. See Edmund Gettier, "Is Justified True Belief Knowledge?" *Analysis*, vol. 23 (1963), pp. 121–123. Also Ackermann, *op. cit.*, ch. V, and the corresponding references.

4. For simplicity, I will speak of inference relations as obtaining between beliefs rather than, more accurately, between the propositions which are believed. "Inference" is to be understood here in a very broad sense; any relation between two beliefs which allows one, if accepted, to serve as a good reason for accepting the other will count as inferential.

5. Obviously these views could be combined, with different instances of the regress being handled in different ways. I will not consider such combined views here. In general, they would simply inherit all of the objections pertaining to the simpler views.

6. The presumption against a skeptical outcome is strong, but I think it is a mistake to treat it as absolute. If no non-skeptical theory can be found which is at least reasonably plausible in its own right, skepticism might become the only rational alternative.

7. For some useful distinctions among these terms, see William Alston, "Varieties of Privileged Access," *American Philosophical Quarterly*, vol. 8 (1971), pp. 223–241.

8. How good a reason must one have? Presumably some justification accrues from any reason which makes the belief even minimally more likely to be true than not, but considerably more than this would be required to make the justification adequate for knowledge. (See note 3, above.) (The James-Clifford controversy concerning the "will to believe" is also relevant here. I am agreeing with Clifford to the extent of saying that epistemic justification requires some positive reason in favor of the belief and not just the absence of any reason against.)

9. For a similar use of the notion of epistemic irresponsibility, see Ernest Sosa, "How Do You Know?" *American Philosophical Quarterly*, vol. 11 (1974), p. 117.

10. In fact, the premises would probably have to be true as well, in order to avoid Gettier-type counterexamples. But I shall ignore this refinement here.

11. On a Carnap-style a priori theory of probability it could, of course, be the case that very general empirical propositions were more likely to be true than not, i.e. that the possible state-descriptions in which they are true outnumber those in which they are false. But clearly this would not make them likely to be true in a sense which would allow the detached assertion of the proposition in question (on pain of contradiction), and this fact seems to preclude such justification from being adequate for knowledge.

12. Armstrong, *op. cit.*, chapters 11–13. Bracketed page references in this section are to this book.

13. Fred I. Dretske, *Seeing and Knowing* (London, 1969), chapter III, especially pp. 126–139. It is difficult to be quite sure of Dretske's view, however, since he is not concerned in this book to offer a general account of knowledge. Views which are in some ways similar to those of Armstrong and Dretske have been offered by Goldman and by Unger. See Alvin Goldman, "A Causal Theory of Knowing," *The Journal of Philosophy*, vol. 64 (1967), pp. 357–372; and Peter Unger, "An Analysis of Factual Knowledge," *The Journal of Philosophy*, vol. 65 (1968), pp. 157–170. But both Goldman and Unger are explicitly concerned with the Gettier problem and not at all with the regress problem, so it is hard to be sure how their views relate to the sort of externalist view which is at issue here.

14. On the one hand, Armstrong seems to argue that it is not a requirement for knowledge that the believer have "sufficient evidence" for his belief, which sounds like a rejection of the adequate-justification condition. On the other hand, he seems to want to say that the presence of the external relation makes it rational for a person to accept a belief, and he seems (though this is not clear) to have *epistemic* rationality in mind; and there appears to be no substantial difference between saying that a belief is epistemically rational and saying that it is epistemically justified.

15. One way to put this point is to say that whether a belief is likely to be true or whether in contrast it is an accident that it is true depends significantly on how the belief is described. Thus it might be true of one and the same belief that it is "a belief connected in a law-like way with the state of affairs which it describes" and also that it is "a belief adopted on the basis of no apparent evidence"; and it might be likely to be true on the first description and unlikely to be true on the second. The claim here is that it is the believer's own conception which should be considered in deciding whether the belief is justified. (Something analogous seems to be true in ethics: the moral worth of a person's action is correctly to be judged only in terms of that person's subjective conception of what he is doing and not in light of what happens, willy-nilly, to result from it.)

16. Notice, however, that if beliefs standing in the proper external relation should happen to possess some subjectively distinctive feature (such as being spontaneous and highly compelling to the believer), and if the believer were to notice empirically that beliefs having this feature were true a high proportion of the time, he would then be in a position to construct a justification for a new belief of that sort along the lines sketched at the end of section II. But of course a belief justified in that way would no longer be basic.

33. REFLECTIVE KNOWLEDGE IN THE BEST CIRCLES*

Ernest Sosa

Is the existence of external things just an article of faith? Certainly not, says G. E. Moore,[1] who offers us a proof, thus aiming to remove Immanuel Kant's "scandal to philosophy."

> Moore's proof
> Here is a hand (a real, flesh and bone hand). Therefore, there is at least one external thing in existence.[2]

According to Moore, his argument meets three conditions for being a proof: first, the premise is different from the conclusion; second, he knows the premise to be the case; and, third, the conclusion follows deductively (*ibid.*, pp. 144-45). Further conditions may be required, but he evidently thinks his proof would satisfy these as well.

I: Moore's Proof

As Moore is well aware, many philosophers will feel he has not given "any satisfactory proof of the point in question" (*ibid.*, p. 147). Some, he believes, will want the premise itself proved. But he does not try to prove it, and does not believe it can be proved. Proving that here is a hand requires proving one is awake, and this cannot be done.

Does Moore adequately answer the skeptic?[3] Many have denied it for the reason that he fails to rule out a crucial possibility: that our faculties are leading us astray—for example, that we are dreaming. Aware of this objection, Moore grants, in "Certainty,"[4] that to know he is standing, he must know he is awake. The point "cuts both ways," however, and he would prefer to conclude that he does know he is awake since he does know he is standing. This has persuaded nearly nobody. On the contrary, some have thought him committed to an argument, M below, like the following:

Argument A
  A1. This map is a good guide to this desert.
  A2. According to the map, an oasis lies ahead.
  A3. Therefore, an oasis lies ahead.

Argument M
  M1. My present experience is a veridical guide to reality (and I am not dreaming).
  M2. My present experience is as if I have a hand before me.
  M3. Therefore, here (before me) is a hand.

When challenged on premise A1, our desert dullard responds: "I must know A1, since the only way I could know A3 is through argument A, and I do know A3." Is this a just comparison? Is Moore's response to the skeptic relevantly similar?[5]

If Moore depends on argument M for his knowledge of M3, his response seems like the dullard's. The dullard is wrong to respond as he does. He must say how he knows his premise without presupposing that he already knows the conclusion. And Moore would seem comparably wrong in the analogous response to the skeptic. In explaining how he knows M1, he must not presuppose that he already knows M3.

Does Moore depend on argument M for his knowledge of M3? There is reason to think that he does not, given his emphatic acknowledgment that he cannot *prove* M3. After all, M would seem a proof of M3 just as good as Moore's own "proof of an external world." Moore concedes, in effect, that, if he does not know that he is not dreaming, *then* he does not know of the hand before him. But that is not necessarily because he takes himself to know M3 only through M or any other such argument. In any case, even if he is relying on some such argument, which would require making that concession, the defender of common sense has other options.

One might, after all, make that concession only because of the following "principle of exclusion" (PE):

If one is to know that *h*, then one must exclude (rule out) every possibility that one knows to be incompatible with one's knowing that *h*.

As Moore grants explicitly, the possibility that he might be just dreaming is incompatible with his knowing (perceptually) that he has a hand before him. And this, in combination with PE, is quite sufficient to explain his concession above.

Suppose Moore is not depending on argument M for his knowledge of M3. Although he recognizes his need to know he is not dreaming, suppose that is only because he accepts PE, our principle of exclusion. Then the sort of ridicule cast on the dullard is misdirected against Moore. What is more, it is not even clear that Moore must know *how* he knows he is not dreaming if he is to know M3. That is not entailed by the application of the principle of exclusion. All that follows from such application is that Moore must know *that* he is not dreaming, not that he must know *how* he knows this.

In fact, however, the historical Moore did rely on something very much like argument M (more on this below). So is he not, after all, exposed to the damaging comparison with the desert dullard? Not at all. There seems to be no good reason why, in responding to the skeptic, Moore must *show how* he knows he is not dreaming. Of course, his response to the skeptic would be enhanced if he could show that. But it now seems not properly subject to ridicule even if he is not then in a position to show how he knows he is not dreaming. The question he is addressing is *whether* he knows that he is not dreaming, and, at most, by extension, what grounds he might have for his answer to that question, in answering which he does not, nor need he, also answer the question of *how* he knows himself to be awake and not dreaming.

It might be replied that one cannot know that here is a hand if one's belief rests on the unproved assumption that one is awake. According to Moore, however, things that cannot be proved might still be known. Besides, even though he cannot prove

that he is awake, he has "conclusive evidence" for it. Unfortunately, he cannot state his evidence, and the matter is left in this unsatisfactory state at the end of "Proof of an External World." But Moore has more to say in another paper of the period, "Four Forms of Scepticism."[6] There, he takes himself to know for sure about the hand before him, and takes this knowledge to be based on an inductive or analogical argument. We are told that introspective knowledge of one's own sensory experience, unlike perceptual knowledge of one's physical surroundings, can be immediate. While agreeing with Bertrand Russell that one cannot know *immediately* that one sees a hand, Moore thinks, contra Russell, that he can know it for certain. And he disagrees with Russell more specifically in allowing knowledge for certain about his hand through analogical or inductive reasoning from premises known introspectively.

It is doubtful, however, that any allowable form of inference—whether deductive, inductive, or analogical—will take us from the character of our experience to the sort of knowledge of our surroundings we ordinarily claim.

Familiar skeptical scenarios—dreaming, evil demon, brain in a vat, and the like—show that our experience prompts but does not logically entail its corresponding perceptual beliefs. Experience as if there is a fire before us does not entail that there is a fire there, experience as if here is a hand does not entail that here is a hand, and so on. Perhaps what is required for one's beliefs and experiences to have certain contents entails that these could not possibly be *entirely* false or misleading. Indeed, some such conclusion follows from certain externalist and epistemic requirements on one's justified attribution of familiar contents to one's own experiences or beliefs. But even if that much is right—which is still controversial—one's experience or belief that here is a hand, or yonder a fire, might still be wildly off the mark. We cannot deduce much of our supposed knowledge of the external world from unaided premises about our experience.

As for inductive or analogical reasoning, only abductive reasoning—inference to the best explanation—offers much promise, but it seems questionable as a solution to our problem.[7] Suppose (a) that we restrict ourselves to data just about the qualitative character of our own sensory experience, and (b) that we view belief in a commonsensical external world as a theory postulated to explain the course of our experience. What exactly is the proposal? Is it proposed that when ordinarily we accept the presence of a hand before us, we do know, and know on the basis of an abductive inference? Or is it proposed, rather, that in such circumstances we have resources that would enable us to know if only we used those resources to make effective abductive arguments? The second, more modest, proposal is too modest, since it leaves our ordinary perceptual beliefs in a position like that of a theorem accepted through a guess or a blunder, one which we do have the resources to prove after much hard thought, but one which we have not come close to proving at the time when we are just guessing or blundering.

Even the modest proposal, moreover, seems unlikely to succeed. Could we form a rich enough set of beliefs purely about the qualitative character of our sensory experience, one rich enough to permit abductive inferences yielding our common-sense view of external reality? This seems doubtful when we consider (a) that such pure data beliefs could not already presuppose the external reality to be inferred, and (b) that the postulated common-sense "theory" of external reality must presumably meet constraints on abductive inference: for example, that the postulated theory be empirically testable and also simpler and less ad hoc than alternatives (for example, George Berkeley's). These requirements plausibly imply that our data must go beyond detached observations, and include some acceptable correlations. Yet these correlations are unavailable if we restrict ourselves to beliefs about the character of our experience.[8] Most especially are they unavailable, and most especially is the postulated inference implausible, when our database is restricted, as it is by Moore, to introspectively known facts of one's own then-present subjective experience and to directly recalled facts of one's own earlier experience. (If deprived of the epistemic resources of testimony and of retentive memory—except insofar as such resources can be validated by reason-cum-introspection, which is not very far if at all—then there is

precious little we can any longer see ourselves as knowing, thus deprived.)

Accordingly, the skeptic has a powerful case against Moore's claim that our knowledge of the external world is based on an inductive or analogical inference from such information about our experience. It is not realistic to suppose that we consciously make such inferences in everyday life. It is less implausible to conceive of such inferences as implicit and/or dispositional, but even this strains belief. Besides, even granted that we make such inferences if only implicitly, do they yield simpler and less ad hoc hypotheses than alternatives? That is far from clear; nor do such hypotheses seem empirically testable and credible simply as explanations of the purely qualitative character of our then-present or directly recalled experience.

Having reached a dead end, let us have some second thoughts on Moore's view of perceptual beliefs as inferential, whereby he joined a venerable tradition, along with Russell himself. If perceptual knowledge is thus mediate and inferential, what knowledge can qualify as immediate and foundational? Modern philosophy begins with René Descartes's canonical answer to this question.[9] Descartes had two circles, not only the big famous one involving God as guarantor of our faculties, but also a smaller one found in the second paragraph of his third meditation, where he reasons like this:

> I am certain that I am a thinking being. Do I not therefore also know what is required for my being certain about anything? In this first item of knowledge there is simply a clear and distinct perception of what I am asserting; this would not be enough to make me certain of the truth of the matter if it could ever turn out that something which I perceived with such clarity and distinctness was false. So I now seem to be able to lay it down as a general rule that whatever I perceive very clearly and distinctly is true.[10]

Yet when he looks away from particular clear and distinct items, such as the proposition that he thinks, Descartes grants that a powerful enough being could deceive him even about what seems most manifest. Descartes grants that he could be astray in his beliefs as to what he perceives or remembers, and even in taking himself to intuit something as quite clear and distinct. This doubt must be blocked if one is to attain certainty by intuiting something as clear and distinct. Accordingly, Descartes launches the theological reflections that lead eventually to his nondeceiving God.

Even without the further boost of certainty provided by the proof of a nondeceiving God, however, Descartes takes himself to have attained some positive justification. Early in the third meditation, he takes himself to perceive clearly and distinctly that he thinks, which he takes to be what gives him the certainty that he thinks. He reasons that this clear and distinct perception would not give him such certainty if it were less than perfectly reliable, and apparently concludes from this that his clear and distinct perception is perfectly reliable. One could demand how he knows all these things: How can he be sure that he does clearly and distinctly perceive that he thinks, for one thing? How can he be sure that there is nothing else in his situation that could provide the degree of certainty involved? How can he be sure that the clarity and distinctness of his perception could not possibly provide that degree of certainty unless it were infallible? What could he say in response? Descartes might well have a uniform response to all such questions: in each case, he might appeal once again to clear and distinct perception, each of the things in question being something we are assured of by our clearly and distinctly perceiving it.

About the cogito, I wish to highlight not Descartes's answers to such questions, however, but the inference that he draws: "so I now seem to be able to lay it down as a general rule that whatever I perceive very clearly and distinctly is true." Just what is Descartes's argument in support of this general rule? Would his reasoning take the following form?

1. Datum: I know with a high degree of certainty that I think.
2. I clearly and distinctly perceive that I think, and that is the only, or anyhow the best account of the source of my knowledge that I think.

3. So my clear and distinct perception that I think is what explains why or how it is that I know I think.
4. But my clear and distinct perception could not serve as a source of that knowledge if it were not an infallibly reliable faculty.
5. So, finally, my clear and distinct perception must be an infallibly reliable faculty.

The move from 1 and 2 to 3 is an inference to an explanatory account that one might accept for the coherence it gives to one's view of things in the domain involved. Elsewhere, Descartes does appeal to coherence at important junctures.[11] So he may be doing so here as well, although questions do arise about how Descartes views coherence. Does he accept the power of coherence to add justified certainty, and, in particular, would he claim infallibility for (sufficiently comprehensive and binding) coherence as he does for clear and distinct intuition?[12] In any case, the comprehensive coherence of his world view would be enhanced by an explanation of how clear and distinct perception comes to be so highly reliable, even infallible. And this is just what Descartes attempts, through his theological and other reasoning. Descartes can see that reason might take him to a position that is sufficiently comprehensive and interlocking—and thereby defensible against any foreseeable attack, no holds barred, against any specific doubt actually pressed or in the offing, no matter how slight. Unaided reason might take him to that position. Need he go any further? What is more: Might one reach a similar position while dispensing with the trappings of Cartesian rationalism?

Circular Externalism

Compare now how Moore might have proceeded:

1. Datum: I know with a high degree of certainty that here is a hand.
2. I can see and feel that here is a hand, and that is the only, or anyhow the best account of the source of my knowledge that here is a hand.

3. So my perception that here is a hand is what explains why or how it is that I know (with certainty) that here is a hand.

4. But my perception could not serve as a source of that degree of justified certainty if it were not a reliable faculty.[13]

5. So, finally, my perception must be a reliable faculty.

Moore could, of course, go on to say more about the nature of the perception that assures him about the hand. He might still say that such perception involves an implicit inference from what is known immediately and introspectively, perhaps an inductive or analogical inference of some sort. That might make his view more comprehensively coherent, but we have already seen reasons why postulating such an inference is questionable. So we focus rather on a second alternative: Moore might well take perceiving to involve no inference at all, not even implicit inference, but only transfer of light, nerve impulses, and so on, in such a way that the character of one's surroundings has a distinctive impact on oneself and occasions corresponding and reliable beliefs. This might also amount eventually to a comprehensively coherent view of one's knowledge of the external world. Its epistemologically significant features would not distinguish it in any fundamental respect from the procedure followed by Descartes.

The theme of accidentally true belief has loomed large in the epistemology of recent decades. The Gettier problem, for example, is posed by a justified belief true for reasons far removed from whatever causes it to be held and justified. Externalist conceptions of propositional knowledge focus on this theme, as do one offered by Peter Unger (nonaccidentally true belief) and one offered by Alvin Goldman (belief caused by the truth of its content). Robert Nozick's tracking account is also a conception of this sort: S knows that p if and only if S believes correctly that p, and also (in the circumstances): *both* it would have been true that p only if S had believed it, *and* if it had not been true that p, then S would not have believed it.[14]

Why are these conceptions of knowledge of special interest to us here? Because each offers a way to explain how one can know that p without reasoning from prior knowledge. The key idea exploited is this: you can know something noninferentially so long as it is no accident or coincidence that you are right.

Both the tracking and the causal accounts defensibly require a special nonaccidental connection between the belief and the fact believed. Nevertheless, in each case other levels of accidentality remain. Suppose I fancy myself a connossieur of tomato ripeness, but suffer from a rare form of color blindness that precludes my discerning nearly any shade of red except that displayed by this particular tomato. Therefore, my judgments of tomato ripeness are in general apt to be right with no better than even chance. But when it is the particular (and rare) shade of red now displayed, then I am nearly infallible. Oblivious to my affliction, however, I issue judgments of tomato ripeness with abandon over a wide spectrum of shades of red. Assuming that, unknown to me, the variety of tomato involved always ripens with this shade of red, then my belief that this tomato is ripe is in step with the truth, and arguably satisfies the requirements of Unger, Goldman, and Nozick. But, again, it is nevertheless in some relevant sense or respect only an accident that I am right in my belief.[15] We need a clearer and more comprehensive view of the respects in which one's belief must be nonaccidentally true if it is to constitute knowledge.

Unaided, the tracking or causal requirements proposed suffer from a sort of tunnel vision. They permit too narrow a focus on the particular target belief and its causal or counterfactual relation to the truth of its content. Just widening our focus will not do, however, if we widen it only far enough to include the process that yields the belief involved. We need an even broader view.

Virtue Epistemology

[When] . . . thought is concerned with study, not with action or production, its good or bad state consists [simply] in being true or false. For truth is the function of whatever thinks. . . .

Hence the function of each of the understanding parts is truth; and so the virtue of each part will be the state that makes that part grasp the truth most of all.

—Aristotle[16]

Virtue epistemology is distinguished by its emphasis on the subject as seat of justification. In order to qualify as knowledge, a belief must be "apt," epistemically so, in a strong sense that goes beyond its being just a belief that coheres well within the subject's perspective. The "tracking account" (Nozick) sees here little more than a claim about that belief's counterfactual relation to the truth of what is believed. "Reliable-indicator" accounts require rather that the belief itself or the reasons for it have properties nomically sufficient for its truth (David Armstrong, Marshall Swain.[17]). "Reliable-process" accounts focus instead on the cognitive process, beneath the skin, that yields the belief, and on the truth ratio in the products of that process, actual and counterfactual (Goldman).

It is rather the subject and her cognitive virtues or aptitudes which hold primary interest for virtue epistemology. Consider the athletic virtues of a tennis champion. When we say that a shot is not just a winning shot but a skillful one, we imply a comment on the player as shotmaker. Suppose a tyro wields a racquet on a court and, unaware of the approaching ball, issues what amounts by luck to a stylish and effective backhand stroke. Such a shot might be an unreturnable winning shot, but it would manifest no real skill.

Why are we unwilling to admire a performance as "skillful" if it manifests only a fleeting, or even an instantaneous state of the agent's? Skills, abilities, competences, aptitudes, prowess—these come and go, true enough, but they do not flit by instantaneously. Why not? Why do we tend to define these concepts so as to require such stability? We might have defined similar concepts without requiring stability. Why do we define these concepts as we do? Why have we adopted

The fact that an atheist can be "clearly aware that the three angles or a triangle are equal to two right angles" is something I do not dispute. But I maintain that this awareness of his [*cognitionem*] is not true knowledge [*scientia*], since no act of awareness that can be rendered doubtful seems fit to be called knowledge [*scientia*]. Now since we are supposing that this individual is an atheist, he cannot be certain that he is not being deceived on matters which seem to him to be very evident (as I fully explained). And although this doubt may not occur to him, it can still crop up if someone else raises the point or if he looks into the matter himself. So he will never be free of this doubt until he acknowledges that God exists.[19]

Descartes considers reasons to doubt, not only one's faculties of perception, memory, and introspection, but even one's faculty of intuitive reason, by which one might know that $3 + 2 = 5$, that if one thinks one exists, and the like. He defends against such doubts by coherence-inducing theological reasoning that yields an epistemic perspective on himself and his world, in terms of which he can feel confident about the reliability of his faculties, including the very faculties employed in arriving, via a priori theological reasoning, at that perspective on himself and his world, the perspective that enables him to see his world as epistemically propitious.[20]

In structure, virtue perspectivism is thus Cartesian, though in content it is not. Radical rationalism admits only (rational) intuition and deduction (along with memory) as its faculties of choice (or anyhow of top choice) and wishes to validate all knowledge in terms of these faculties; thus the Cartesian grand project. Virtue perspectivism admits also perception and introspection, along with intuition and deduction, as well as inductive and abductive reasoning. Gladly using all such faculties, it also accepts through testimony the aid of one's epistemic community. Fortunately, the overview thus attained inspires confidence in the means used.

Rejected as viciously circular by Descarte's critics, and by many today, our procedure does present a troubling aspect of circularity. A closer look, however, may show this to be only an illusion.[21]

Epistemic Circularity: What Is the Problem?

"I think, therefore I am," says Descartes, adding: "Here at last is something I really know. But what is it about this knowledge that makes it knowledge? As far as I can see, it is knowledge because it is a clear and distinct intuition. But it would not be real knowledge unless such intuition were reliable. So I can already lay it down as a general rule that clear and distinct intuition *is* reliable."

"Here is a hand," says Moore, adding: "Here is something I really know. But what gives me this knowledge? As far as I can see, it is knowledge in virtue of being a deliverance of perceptual experience. But it would not be knowledge if I were dreaming. So I can already conclude that I am *not* dreaming."

Descartes goes on to buttress the reliability of his rational intuition by developing a theology through vigorous use of that very rational intuition. Moore can similarly appeal to what he knows about his reliable senses on the basis largely of those very senses.

But is not any such reasoning circular? Yes, circular it does seem to be, "*epistemically* circular," let us say. But it is *viciously* circular? Skeptics through the ages have attacked it as such. Sextus Empiricus already uses the tropes of Agrippa in order to develop the so-called *diallelus*, or "problem of the criterion." Many have followed his lead in a long tradition. Today, skepticism cum relativism has spread beyond epistemology and ethics, beyond philosophy, and even beyond the academy, and its champions often wield circularity as a weapon. But, again: Is such circularity vicious? To say that it is vicious, in the present context, is to say that it is somehow bad, intellectually bad, that it puts us in a situation that is somehow intellectually unsatisfactory. When we ask how the circularity is vicious, therefore, what we want to know is just how it puts us in an unsatisfactory state: When we reason in the way alleged to be viciously circular, wherein lies the defect in our reasoning or in the resulting state?

Largely through the use of rational intuition, Descartes supports the view that rational intuition is reliable and that through its exercise he knows that he thinks and exists. Largely through the use of perception, Moore could support the view that perception is reliable, that he is not misled by a dream, and that through the exercise of perception he knows of the hand before him. If a crystal ball claims itself to be reliable, then, largely through the crystal ball, a crystal-ball gazer could support the view that such gazing is reliable, that it is rarely misleading, and that through the crystal ball he can foretell the future.

Epistemic circularity is vicious, it might be said, because it would make the gazer as well justified as Descartes or Moore. *Since* there is no way to support adequately the view that intuition is reliable, or that perception is reliable, without employing those very faculties; and *since* the same goes for memory, deduction, abduction, and testimony; *therefore*, there is no way to arrive at an acceptable theory of our knowledge and its general sources.

Perhaps that shows only how defective is the attempt to develop such a general theory of one's knowledge and its sources. There is an easy way to avoid the intellectual discomfort of having to use a faculty in answering the question whether that faculty is reliable, namely, not to ask the question. Call this the *avoidance strategy*.

Of course, we shall hardly lack company if we avoid philosophy because we find it frustrating. But the avoidance strategy that I wish to consider is not just a rejection of what seems too difficult for one's own intelligence. The implication of the avoidance strategy is not that there is something lacking in one's intelligence but that there is something wrong with the questions avoided.

Much might indeed be wrong with our very general, philosophical questions. Many find them too abstract, too impractical, too useless, and so on. But these are not the concerns of my avoidance strategist. He is, after all, a philosopher. His concern is not that the questions are just too hard for his intelligence, nor is it their abstractness, impracticality, or uselessness. He would hardly have gone into philosophy with such concerns, nor are they his concerns now. Difficulty, abstractness, impracticality, and uselessness are not in his view disqualifying drawbacks.

Why then should one as philosopher avoid questions of epistemology, such as those about the reliability of one's faculties? These questions become pressing with the realization that only if they reliably yield truth can our faculties yield knowledge. This is not just a commitment peculiar to contemporary reliabilism. Indeed, it is found already in Descartes, who, as we have seen, also stresses that intuition (and clear and distinct perception) yields knowledge only if reliable.

Consider again our principle of exclusion:

If one is to know that p, then one must exclude (rule out) every possibility that one knows to be incompatible with one's knowing that p.[22] (By 'excluding' here I mean 'knowing not to be the case'.)

On the basis of PE, we can see that in order to know that p, one must know that the faculties employed in arriving at one's belief that p are reliable faculties. After all, just consider the possibility that one's operative faculties were unreliable. That is surely a possibility generally known to be incompatible with attaining knowledge through them. Unreliable mechanisms of belief acquisition will not yield knowledge.

If the principle of exclusion is right, therefore, one cannot possibly know that p unless one knows that the faculties involved are reliable. But this is just the sort of knowledge that we seem able to attain only through epistemically circular reasoning.

One might, of course, question the principle of exclusion.[23] One might hold that in order to know that p, one's pertinent faculties need only *be* reliable; one need not *know* them to be reliable.

One might, for example, appeal to a conception of knowledge as mere tracking. One might grant Richard Rorty that causation should not be confused with justification, while joining Nozick in taking tracking as the essence of knowledge. "To know is just to mirror (or to track) nature. Justification is quite another matter. Justification of some sort may well require the principle of exclusion. Thus, it may be that in order to be justified in believing that p, one must exclude every possibility

one knows to be incompatible with one's knowing that p. But such justification is *not* required for simple knowledge."

That response seems essentially right. What is more, even Descartes would agree. For Descartes, you will recall, our knowledge that our faculties are reliable, even our faculty of reason, depends on our knowledge of God's epistemic good will. Yet, as we have seen, Descartes grants explicitly that the atheist mathematician can know some mathematics.

The knowledge of an atheist is said to be *cognitio*, however, a second-class accomplishment by comparison with *scientia*. *Scientia* by contrast, does require relevant knowledge of one's reliability. Only thus can one repel doubts about the possible unreliability of one's faculties. Only thus can one exclude a possibility evidently incompatible with one's knowing that p, namely, the possibility that only unreliable faculties yield one's belief.

By analogy, we can more generally distinguish *animal* knowledge, which requires only that one track reality, on one hand, and *reflective* knowledge, on the other, which in addition requires awareness of how one knows, in a way that precludes the unreliability of one's faculties. Unlike Descartes's *cognitio* and *scientia*, our more general animal and reflective knowledge do not require infallible reliability, but only a high level of reliability.[24] The avoidance strategy now has not only the cost of suppressing philosophical curiosity about knowledge. We can now see how it also precludes first-level reflective knowledge, and of course *scientia*.

Given these costs, what again counts in favor of avoidance? So far we have been told that we must avoid epistemic circularity because it entails arriving at a generally positive view of one's faculties only by use of those very faculties. But why should that be frustrating when it is the inevitable consequence of its generality? So far the answer is only that the superstitious crystal gazer could reason analogously and with equal justification in defense of his own perspective. How damaging is this?

Suppose we grant the gazer epistemic justification and internal coherence equal to our own. Still, internal coherence is clearly insufficient. Is that not obvious in view of paranoia, hypochondria, and similar psychoses? Logical brilliance permits logical coherence but does not even ensure sanity, much less general epistemic aptitude. There are faculties other than reason whose apt functioning is also crucial to the subject's epistemic welfare.

In light of that result, why not distinguish between the gazers and the perceivers in that, though both reason properly and attain thereby coherence and justification, only the perceivers' beliefs are epistemically apt and constitute knowledge?

On this view, the crystal gazers differ from the perceivers in that gazing is not reliable while perceiving is. So the theory of knowledge of the perceivers is right, that of the gazers wrong. Moreover, the perceivers can know their theory to be right when they know it in large part through perception, since their theory is right and perception can thus serve as a source of knowledge. The gazers are, by hypothesis, in a very different position. Gazing, being unreliable, cannot serve as a source of knowledge. So the perceivers have a good source or basis for their knowledge, but the gazers, lacking any such source or basis, lack knowledge.

Still one might insist that the perceivers should not be so smug. They should still feel acute discomfort and intellectual frustration. This I find a very widely shared view, in epistemology and, mutatis mutandis, far beyond. According to Barry Stroud,[25] the perceivers can at best reach a position where they can affirm the conditional proposition that if their perception is reliable, then they know. And he has recently reemphasized what is essentially the same thesis as follows:

> . . . Sosa's "externalist" could say at most: "If the theory I hold is true, I do know or have good reason to believe that I know or have good reason to believe it, and I do understand how I know the things I do." I think. . . we can see a way in which the satisfaction the theorist seeks in understanding his knowledge still eludes him. Given that all of his knowledge of the world is in question, he will still find himself able to say only "I might understand my knowledge, I

might not. Whether I do or not all depends on how things in fact are in the world I think I've got knowledge of."[26]

It is not easy to understand this position, however. If our perceivers believe (a) that their perception, if reliable, yields them knowledge, and (b) that their perception is reliable, then why are they restricted to affirming only the conditional, a, and not its antecedent, b? Why must they wonder whether they understand their relevant knowledge? Indeed, to the extent that they are really convinced of both a and b, it would seem that, far from being logically constrained to wondering whether they know, they are, on the contrary, logically constrained from so wondering. After all, first, if you are really certain that p, then you cannot well consider whether you know it without thinking that you do. Moreover, second, is it not incoherent to be convinced that p and yet wonder whether p?

In sum, I see no sufficient reason to settle either for irresoluble frustration or for the avoidance strategy. The main argument we have seen for that depends on the claim that, if we allow the circular defense offered for externalist epistemology, then the gazers turn out no less epistemically justified than the perceivers. In a sense that is true: but then in a sense they are equally internally justified, equally coherent. Nevertheless, their beliefs are *not* equally apt in all epistemically relevant respects. Perception is, of course, reliable while gazing is not. Therefore, the perceivers are right and apt both in their particular perceptual beliefs, at least generally, and in their theory of knowledge—for it all rests in large measure on their reliable perception. By contrast, the gazers are wrong and inapt both in their particular gaze-derived beliefs and in their theory of knowledge—for it all rests on their unreliable gazing. Moreover, I see no reason why the perceivers must be restricted to affirming only the conditional that, if perception is reliable, then they know. I see no reason why they cannot also affirm the antecedent, why they cannot believe, both rationally and aptly, that perception is reliable and does enable them to know.

Circles Beyond Belief

Why require the appeal to comprehensive enough coherence for justification, an appeal that I have attributed, tentatively, to Descartes, as part of what justifies his recourse to theology in accounting for true knowledge (*scientia*)? Why not say that what justifies is that one's beliefs be caused by the gods? If the question arises—why not add that *this* belief itself is justified because it is itself caused by the gods?—we could, of course, proceed in this simplified way without worrying about coherence or about the source of these beliefs beyond attributing them to divine agency. But that is not the way we are built, most of us: we just do not acquire such beliefs the way we do acquire beliefs willy-nilly when we open our eyes in good light. But what if we were built that way? Would we then be justified in having such beliefs, and in explaining our justification for having them, by their origin in divine agency? Would we then be justified to the degree and in the way in which Descartes is justified or in the way in which our imagined Moore would be justified through his appeal to a more ordinary reliabilism than that of Descartes? Internally regarded, the structure of beliefs would share prominent features in all three cases. Of course, from our Moorean, common-sense position we can object both to Cartesianism and to the invocation of the gods. These views are internally coherent, but we might still reject them as wrong. And we might be able to explain what is wrong with them, from our point of view, especially if our point of view rules out their leading ideas. But they can, for their part, return the favor. Besides, we can anyhow imagine someone brilliant but insane, who weaves a system of immense interlocking complexity, but one wholly detached from reality as we know it commonsensically. Such a madman could object to our common-sense beliefs in a way that would seem relevantly analogous to the way in which we would object to his mad beliefs.

What all of that shows, it seems to me, is nothing more than that knowledge does not live by coherence and truth alone. Knowledge requires truth and coherence, true enough, but it often requires more: for example, that one be adequately related, causally or counterfactually, to the objects of one's knowledge, which is not necessarily ensured by the mere truth-*cum*-coherence of one's beliefs, no matter how comprehensive the coherence. Madmen can be richly, brilliantly coherent; not just imaginary madmen, but real ones, some of them locked up in asylums. Knowledge requires not only internal justification or coherence or rationality, but also external warrant or aptness. We must be both in good internal order and in appropriate relation to the external world.

Notes

* I am pleased to acknowledge helpful discussion, first here at Brown University; at the University of California/Santa Barbara; at the Oxford Philosophical Society; at Cambridge University; and at the University of Granada.

1. "Proof of an External World," in his *Philosophical Papers* (New York: Collier, 1962), pp. 144–45. Originally in the *Proceedings of the British Academy*, xxv (1939): 273–300.

2. This is, of course, a simplified version of Moore's proof.

3. Henceforth 'knowledge' here will be short for 'plain knowledge', leaving aside Cartesian superknowledge.

4. In his *Philosophical Papers*, pp. 226–51.

5. Compare Barry Stroud, *The Significance of Philosophical Scepticism* (New York: Oxford, 1984), chapters 1 and 3.

6. In his *Philosophical Papers*, pp. 193–223.

7. For Russell the "common-sense hypothesis" of independent physical objects is "simpler" than the supposition that life is but a dream (as he explains in *The Problems of Philosophy* (New York: Oxford, 1959), chapter 2). For W.V. Quine, the "hypothesis of ordinary physical objects" is "posited" or "projected" from the data provided by sensory stimulations: "Subtracting his cues from his world view, we get man's net contribution as the difference"—*Word and Object* (Cambridge: MIT, 1960), p. 5. That Quine's position is deeply problematic is shown by Stroud, chapter 6.

8. This is argued by Wilfrid Sellars in "Phenomenalism," in his *Science, Perception, and Reality* (New York: Routledge, 1963), pp. 60–105.

9. The shift to discussion of Descartes may seem abrupt; however, what we find about the nature of immediate knowledge in that discussion has important implications for a position that Moore failed to explore. Skeptics who are willing to grant Descartes his immediate knowledge through introspection or rational intuition would need to explain exactly why perception could never yield such knowledge. (And what of memory?) The discussion of Descartes to follow is meant to highlight this issue.

10. *The Philosophical Writings of Descartes*, J. Cottingham, R. Stoothoff, and D. Murdoch, eds. (New York: Cambridge, 1975), Volume II, p. 24.

11. In his *Principles of Philosophy* (part IV, art. 205), for example, he notes that, if we can interpret a long stretch of otherwise undecipherable writing by supposing that it is written in "one-off natural language," where the alphabet has all been switched forward by one letter, and so on, then this is good reason for that interpretation. There, he also argues for his scientific account of reality in terms of certain principles by claiming that "it would hardly have been possible for so many items to fall into a coherent pattern if the original principles had been false"—*The Philosophical Writings of Descartes*, Volume I, p. 290.

12. My attribution to Descartes is tentative because of the enormous bibliography on the "Cartesian Circle." In deference to that important tradition of scholarship, I do no more than suggest that there is logical space for an interpretation of Descartes that is perhaps more complex than many already tried, but that seems coherent and interesting. (I am myself convinced that this is Descarte's actual position, and defend this more fully in "How to Resolve the Pyrrhonian Problematic: A Lesson from Descartes," *Philosophical Studies*, LXXXV (1997): 229–49. In "Mythology of the Given," in *The History of philosophy Quarterly* (forthcoming), I argue for the relevance of this Cartesian strategy to issues of empirical foundations that have divided philosophers since the Vienna Circle, and have pitted, for example, Wilfrid Sellars, Richard Rorty, and Donald Davidson, on one side, against C. I. Lewis, Carl Hempel, and Roderick Chisholm, on the other. My warm thanks to Lex Newman and James Van Cleve for helpful discussion of, and further references relevant to, this way of viewing Descartes.)

13. Here, one would reduce Descartes's requirement of infallible certainty.

14. Unger, "An Analysis of Factual Knowledge," this *journal*, LXV, 6 (March 21, 1968): 157–70; Goldman, "A Causal Theory of Knowing," this *journal*, LXIV, 12 (June 22, 1967): 357–72; Nozick, *Philosophical Explanations* (Cambridge: Harvard, 1981), chapter 3.

15. For an early statement of this sort of problem, urged against Nozickian tracking, see Colin McGinn's "The Concept of Knowledge," *Midwest Studies in Philosophy*, IX (1984): 529–54.

16. *Nichomachean Ethics*, T. Irwin, trans. (Indianapolis: Hackett, 1985), 1139a27–30.

17. Armstrong, *Belief, Truth, and Knowledge* (New York: Cambridge, 1973); Swain, *Reasons and Knowledge* (Ithaca: Cornell, 1981).

19. This passage is from the Second Set of Replies as it appears in *The Philosophical Writings of Descartes*, Volume II, p. 101. I must add, however, that where this translation says that an atheist can be "clearly aware," Descartes's Latin is *clare cognoscere*.

20. Although unremarked by Descartes, the role of dreams in his perception skepticism is analogous to a role assignable to paradoxes and aporias in a parallel skepticism vis-à-vis rational intuition.

21. See my "Philosophical Skepticism and Epistemic Circularity," *Proceedings of the Aristotelian Society*, Supplementary Volume LXIV (1994): 263–90; and compare Stroud's response, "Scepticism, 'Externalism', and the Goal of Epistemology," pp. 291–307.

22. Chapter 1 of Stroud's *The Significance of Philosophical Scepticism* is an illuminating discussion of this principle and its importance for understanding philosophical skepticism. In "How to Resolve the Pyrrhonian Problematic: A Lesson from Descartes," I suggest how to derive it from other principles with independent plausibility.

23. For one thing, as it stands it leads, apparently, to a vicious regress. But that is an illusion. After all, what PE requires one to rule out is, not every possibility incompatible with one's knowing that *p*, but rather every possibility known to be thus incompatible. Since, for one thing, knowledge requires belief, the regress is hence not infinite, nor does it seem vicious.

24. This distinction figures in my *Knowledge in Perspective* (New York: Cambridge, 1991), pp. 240, 282.

25. "Understanding Human Knowledge in General," in M. Clay and K. Lehrer, eds., *Knowledge and Scepticism* (Boulder: Westview, 1989), pp. 31–50, here p. 47.

26. "Scepticism, 'Externalism', and the Goal of Epistemology," pp. 303–04.

◈ A CRITIQUE OF INTERNALISM ◈

34. INTERNALISM EXPOSED*

Alvin Goldman

In recent decades, epistemology has witnessed the development and growth of externalist theories of knowledge and justification.[1] Critics of externalism have focused a bright spotlight on this approach and judged it unsuitable for realizing the true and original goals of epistemology. Their own favored approach, internalism, is defended as a preferable approach to the traditional concept of epistemic justification.[2] I shall turn the spotlight toward internalism and its most prominent rationale, revealing fundamental problems at the core of internalism and challenging the viability of its most popular rationale. Although particular internalist theories such as (internalist) foundationalism and coherentism will occasionally be discussed, those specific theories are not my primary concern. The principal concern is rather the general architecture of internalism, and the attempt to justify this architecture by appeal to a certain conception of what justification consists in.

I: Deontology, Access, and Internalism

I begin with a certain rationale for internalism that has widespread support. It can be reconstructed in three steps:

1. The *guidance-deontological* (GD) *conception of justification* is posited.
2. A certain constraint on the determiners of justification is derived from the GD conception, that is, the constraint that all justification determiners must be *accessible to*, or *knowable by*, the epistemic agent.
3. The accessibility or knowability constraint is taken to imply that only internal conditions qualify as legitimate determiners of justification. So justification must be a purely internal affair.[3]

What motivates or underlies this rationale for internalism? Historically, one central aim of epistemology is to guide or direct our intellectual conduct, an aim expressed in René Descartes's title, "Rules for the Direction of the Mind."[4] Among contemporary writers, John Pollock expresses the idea this way:

> I have taken the fundamental problem of epistemology to be that of deciding what to believe. Epistemic justification, as I use the term, is concerned with this problem. Considerations of epistemic justification guide us in determining what to believe. We might call this the "belief guiding" or "reason-guiding" sense of 'justification' (*op. cit.*, p. 10).

The guidance conception of justification is commonly paired with the deontological conception of justification. John Locke[5] wrote of a person's "duty as a rational creature" (*ibid.*, p. 413), and the theme of epistemic duty or responsibility has been echoed by many contemporary epistemologists, including Laurence BonJour (*op. cit.*), Roderick Chisholm (*op. cit.*), Carl Ginet, Paul Moser, Matthias Steup, Richard Feldman, and Hilary Kornblith.[6] Chisholm defines cousins of the concept of justification in terms of the relation 'more reasonable than', and he re-expresses the relation 'p is more reasonable than q for S at t' by saying: "S is so situated at t that his intellectual *requirement*, his *responsibility as* an intellectual being, is better fulfilled by p than by q."[7] Similarly, Feldman says that one's epistemic duty is to "believe what is supported or justified by one's evidence and to avoid believing what is not supported by one's evidence" (*op. cit.*, p. 254).

The guidance and deontological conceptions of justification are intimately related, because the deontological conception, at least when paired with the guidance conception, considers it a person's epistemic duty to guide his doxastic attitudes by his evidence, or by whatever factors determine the justificational status of a proposition at a given time. Epistemic deontologists commonly maintain that being justified in believing a proposition *p* consists in being (intellectually) required or permitted to believe *p*; and being unjustified in believing *p* consists in not being permitted, or being forbidden, to believe *p*. When a person is unjustified in believing a proposition, it is his duty not to believe it.

It is possible to separate the deontological conception from the guidance idea. In ethical theory, a distinction has been drawn between accounts of moral duty that aim to specify what makes actions right and accounts of moral duty that aim to provide practical decision procedures for what to do.[8] If an account simply aims at the first desideratum, it need not aspire to be usable as a decision guide. Similarly accounts of epistemic duty need not necessarily be intended as decision guides. When the deontological conception is used as a rationale for epistemic internalism of the sort I am sketching, however, it do incorporate the guidance conception. Only if the guidance conception is incorporated can the argument proceed along the intended lines to the accessibility constraint, and from there to internalism. This is why I shall henceforth speak of the GD conception of justification.

I turn now to the second step of the argument for internalism. Following William Alston,[9] I shall use the term *justifiers* for facts or states of affairs that determine the justificational status of a belief, or the epistemic status a proposition has for an epistemic agent. In other words, justifiers determine whether or not a proposition is justified for an epistemic agent at a given time. It seems to follow naturally from the GD conception of justification that a certain constraint must be placed on the sorts of facts or states of affairs that qualify as justifiers. If a person is going to avoid violating his epistemic duty, he must know, or be able to find out, what his duty requires. By *know*, in this context, I mean only: have an *accurate*, or *true*, belief. I do not mean: have a *justified* true belief (or whatever else is entailed by the richer concept of knowledge). Admittedly, it might be possible to avoid violating one's duties by chance, without knowing (having true

beliefs about) what one's duties are. As a practical matter, however, it is not feasible to conform to duty on a regular and consistent basis without knowing what items of conduct constitute those duties. Thus, if you are going to choose your beliefs and abstentions from belief in accordance with your justificational requirements, the facts that make you justified or unjustified in believing a certain proposition at a given time must be facts that you are capable of knowing, at that time, to hold or not to hold. There is an intimate connection, then, between the GD conception of justification and the requirement that justifiers must be accessible to, or knowable by, the agent at the time of belief. If you cannot accurately ascertain your epistemic duty at a given time, how can you be expected to execute that duty, and how can you reasonably be held responsible for executing that duty."[10]

The *knowability constraint* on justifiers which flows from the GD conception may be formulated as follows:

> KJ: The only facts that qualify as justifiers of an agent's believing *p* at time *t* are facts that the agent can readily know, at *t*, to obtain or not to obtain.

How can an agent readily know whether candidate justifiers obtain or do not obtain? Presumably, the agent must have a way of determining, for any candidate class of justifiers, whether or not they obtain. Such a way of knowing must be reliable, that is, it must generate beliefs about the presence or absence of justifiers that are usually (invariably?) correct. Otherwise, the agent will often be mistaken about what his epistemic duty requires. The way of knowing must also be "powerful," in the sense that when justifiers obtain it is likely (certain?) that the agent will believe that they obtain; at least he will believe this if he reflects on the matter or otherwise inquires into it.[11] As we shall soon see, internalists typically impose additional restrictions on how justifiers may be known. But the minimal, generic version of KJ simply requires justifiers to be the sorts of facts that agents have *some* way of knowing. In other words, justification-conferring facts must be the sorts of facts whose presence or absence is "accessible" to agents.[12]

Given the KJ constraint on justifiers, it becomes fairly obvious why internalism about justification is so attractive. Whereas external facts are facts that a cognitive agent might not be in a position to know about, internal facts are presumably the sorts of conditions that a cognitive agent can readily determine. So internal facts seem to be the right sorts of candidates for justifiers. This consideration leads to the third step of our rationale for internalism. Only internal facts qualify as justifiers because they are the only ones that satisfy the KJ constraint; at least so internalists suppose.

One possible way to criticize this rationale for internalism is to challenge the GD conception directly. This could be done, for example, by arguing that the GD conception of justification presupposes the dubious thesis of doxastic voluntarism, the thesis that doxastic attitudes can be "guided" by deliberate choices or acts of will. This criticism is developed by Alston,[13] and I have sympathy with many of his points. But the voluntarism argument against the GD conception is disputed by Feldman (*op. cit*, and John Heil, [14] among others. Feldman, for example, argues that epistemic deontologism is not wedded to the assumption of doxastic voluntarism. Many obligations remain in force, he points out, even when an agent lacks the ability to discharge them. A person is still legally obligated to repay a debt even when his financial situation makes him unable to repay it. Perhaps epistemic obligations have analogous properties.[15] Since the complex topic of doxastic voluntarism would require article-length treatment in its own right, I set this issue aside and confine my attention to other issues. Although I do not accept the GD conception of justification, I take it as given for purposes of the present discussion and explore where it leads. In any case, what is ultimately crucial for internalism is the accessibility requirement that the GD conception hopes to rationalize. Even if the GD conception fails to provide a good rationale, internalism would be viable if some other rationale could be provided for a suitable accessibility requirement.

II: Direct Knowability and Strong Internalism

The initial KJ constraint was formulated in terms of knowability plain and simple, but proponents of

internalism often add the further qualification that determinants of justification must be *directly* knowable by the cognitive agent. Ginet, for example, writes as follows:

> Every one of every set of facts about S's position that minimally suffices to make S, at a given time, justified in being confident that p must be *directly recognizable* to S at that time (*op. cit.*, p. 34).

Similarly, Chisholm writes:

> [T]he concept of epistemic justification is. . . internal and immediate in that one can *find out directly*, by reflection, what one is justified in believing at any time.[16]

Thus, Ginet and Chisholm do not endorse just the minimal KJ constraint as earlier formulated, but a more restrictive version, which might be written as follows:

> KJ_{dir}: The only facts that qualify as justifiers of an agent's believing p at time t are facts that the agent can readily know *directly*, at t, to obtain or not to obtain.

An initial problem arising from KJ_{dir} is this: What warrants the imposition of KJ_{dir} as opposed to the looser constraint, KJ? KJ was derived from GD conception on the grounds that one cannot reasonably be expected to comply with epistemic duties unless one knows what those duties are. How does such an argument warrant the further conclusion that *direct* knowledge of justification must be available? Even indirect knowledge (whatever that is) would enable an agent to comply with his epistemic duties. So the second step of the argument for internalism cannot properly be revised to feature KJ_{dir} in place of KJ. Proponents of KJ_{dir} might reply that direct forms of knowledge are more powerful than indirect knowledge, but this reply is unconvincing. The power requirement was already built into the original version of KJ, and it is unclear how directness adds anything of significance on that score. Whether KJ_{dir} can be derived from GD is a serious problem, because the argument for internalism rests on something like the directness qualification. I shall say more about this later, for now I set this point aside in order to explore where KJ$_{dir}$ leads.

What modes of knowledge count as direct? At least one form of direct knowledge is introspection. A reason for thinking that introspection is what Chisholm means by direct knowledge is that he restricts all determiners of justification to conscious states:

> A consequence of our "internalistic" theory of knowledge is that, if one is subject to an epistemic requirement at any time, then this requirement is imposed by the *conscious state* in which one happens to find one-self at that time (*ibid*, pp. 59–60).

Since he restricts justifiers to conscious states, it is plausible to assume that direct knowledge, for Chisholm, means introspective knowledge, and knowledge by "reflection" coincides with knowledge by introspection.[17] At least in the case of Chisholm, then, KJ$_{dir}$ might be replaced by:

> KJ$_{int}$: The only facts that qualify as justifiers of an agent's believing *p* at time *t* are facts that the agent can readily know *by introspection*, at *t*, to obtain or not to obtain.

Now, the only facts that an agent can know by introspection are facts concerning what conscious states he is (or is not) currently in, so these are the only sorts of facts that qualify as justifiers under KJ$_{int}$. This form of internalism may be called *strong internalism*:

> SI: Only facts concerning what conscious states an agent is in at time *t* are justifiers of the agent's beliefs at *t*.

Strong internalism, however, is an unacceptable approach to justification, for it has serious, skepticism-breeding, consequences. This is demonstrated by the *problem of stored beliefs*. At any given time, the vast majority of one's beliefs are stored in memory rather than occurrent or active. Beliefs about personal data (for example, one's social security number), about world history, about geography, or about the institutional affiliations of one's professional colleagues, are almost all stored rather than occurrent at a given moment. Furthermore, for almost any of these beliefs, one's conscious state at the time includes nothing that justifies it. No perceptual experience, no conscious memory event, and no premises consciously entertained at the selected moment will be justificationally sufficient for such a belief. According to strong internalism, then, none of these beliefs is justified at that moment. Strong internalism threatens a drastic diminution in the stock of beliefs ordinarily deemed justified, and hence in the stock of knowledge, assuming that justification is necessary for knowledge. This is a major count against this type of theory.

Feldman anticipates this problem because his own account of having evidence also implies that only consciously entertained factors have evidential force (*op. cit.*, pp. 98–99). Feldman tries to meet the threat by distinguishing between occurrent and dispositional senses of epistemic terms. (He actually discusses knowledge rather than justification, but I shall address the issue in terms of justification because that is the target of our investigation.) Feldman is not simply restating the familiar point that 'belief' has occurrent and dispositional senses. He is proposing that the term 'justified' is ambiguous between an occurrent and a dispositional sense. Feldman apparently claims that in the case of stored beliefs, people at most have dispositional justification, not occurrent justification.

There are two problems with this proposal. First, if having a disposition to generate conscious evidential states qualifies as a justifier of a belief, why would this not extend from memorial to perceptual dispositions? Suppose a train passenger awakes from a nap but has not yet opened his eyes. Is he justified in believing propositions about the details of the neighboring landscape? Surely not. Yet he is *disposed*, merely by opening his eyes, to generate conscious evidential states that would occurrently justify such beliefs. So the dispositional approach is far too permissive to yield an acceptable sense of 'justified'.[18] Second, can an internalist, especially a strong internalist, live with the idea that certain dispositions count as justifiers? Having or not having a disposition (of the requisite type) is not the sort of fact or condition that can be known by introspection. Thus, the proposal to supplement the occurrent sense of 'justified' with a dispositional sense of 'justified' is simply the abandonment of strong internalism.

III: Indirect Knowability and Weak Internalism

The obvious solution to the problem of stored beliefs is to relax the KJ constraint: allow justifiers to be merely indirectly knowable. This yields:

> KJ_{ind}: The only facts that qualify as justifiers of an agent's believing p at time t are facts that the agent can readily know at t, either directly or indirectly, to obtain or not to obtain.

The danger here is that indirect knowledge might let in too much from an internalist perspective. How are externalist forms of knowledge—for example, perceptual knowledge—to be excluded? Clearly, internalism must propose specific forms of knowledge that conform with its spirit. It is fairly clear how internalism should deal with the problem of stored beliefs: simply allow knowledge of justifiers to include memory retrieval. Stored evidence beliefs can qualify as justifiers because the agent can know that they obtain by the compound route of first retrieving them from memory and then introspecting their conscious contents. This yields the following variant of the KJ constraint:

> $KJ_{int+ret}$: The only facts that qualify as justifiers of an agent's believing p at time t are facts that the agent can readily know, at t, to obtain or not to obtain, *by introspection and/or memory retrieval.*

This KJ constraint allows for a more viable form of internalism than strong internalism. We may call it *weak internalism*, and initially articulate it through the following principle:

> WI: Only facts concerning what conscious and/or stored mental states an agent is in at time t are justifiers of the agent's beliefs at t.

WI will certify the justification of many stored beliefs, because agents often have other stored beliefs that evidentially support them. A person who believes that Washington, D. C. is the capital of the United States may have a stored belief to the effect that a map of the U.S. he recently consulted showed Washington as the capital. The latter stored belief is what justifies the former one. So weak internalism is not plagued with the problem of stored justified beliefs. Weak internalism seems to be a legitimate form of internalism because even stored beliefs qualify, intuitively, as internal states.

Although weak internalism is better than strong internalism, it too faces severe problems. First is the *problem of forgotten evidence*[19] Many justified beliefs are ones for which an agent once had adequate evidence that she subsequently forgot. At the time of epistemic appraisal, she no longer possesses adequate evidence that is retrievable from memory. Last year, Sally read a story about the health benefits of broccoli in the "Science" section of the *New York Times*. She then justifiably formed a belief in broccoli's beneficial effects. She still retains this belief but no longer recalls her original evidential source (and has never encountered either corroborating or undermining sources). Nonetheless, her broccoli belief is still justified, and, if true, qualifies as a case of knowledge. Presumably, this is because her past acquisition of the belief was epistemically proper. But past acquisition is irrelevant by the lights of internalism (including weak internalism), because only her current mental states are justifiers relevant to her current belief. All past events are "external" and therefore irrelevant according to internalism.

It might be replied that Sally does currently possess evidence in support of her broccoli belief. One of her background beliefs, we may suppose, is that most of what she remembers was learned in an epistemically proper manner. So does she not, after all, now have grounds for the target belief? Admittedly, she has *some* evidence, but is this evidence sufficient for justification? Surely not. In a variant case, suppose that Sally still has the same background belief—namely, that most of what she remembers was learned in an epistemically proper manner—but she in fact acquired her broccoli belief from the *National Inquirer* rather than the *New York Times*. So her broccoli belief was never acquired, or corroborated, in an epistemically sound manner. Then even with the indicated current background belief, Sally cannot be credited with justifiably believing that broccoli is healthful. Her past acquisition is still relevant, and decisive. At least it is relevant so long as we are considering the "epistemizing" sense of justification, in which justification carries a true belief a good distance toward knowledge. Sally's belief in the healthfulness of broccoli is not justified in that sense, for surely she does not know that broccoli is healthful given that the *National Inquirer* was her sole source of information.

The category of forgotten evidence is a problem for weak internalism because, like the problem of stored beliefs facing strong internalism, it threatens skeptical outcomes. A large sector of what is ordinarily counted as knowledge are beliefs for which people have forgotten their original evidence.

In reply to the problem of forgotten evidence, Steup[20] offers the following solution. An additional requirement for memorial states to justify a belief that p, says Steup, is that the agent have adequate evidence for believing the following counterfactual: "If she had encountered p in a questionable source, she would not have formed the belief that p." Steup's suggestion is that in the *National Inquirer* variant, Sally fails to have adequate evidence for this counterfactual, and that is why her broccoli belief is not justified. My response to this proposal is twofold. First, the proposed requirement is too strong to impose on memorially justified belief. It is quite difficult to get adequate evidence for the indicated counterfactual. Second, the proposed requirement seems too weak as well. Sally might have adequate evidence for the counterfactual but still be unjustified in holding her broccoli belief. She might have adequate evidence for the counterfactual without its being true; but if it is not true and the rest of the story is as I told it, her broccoli belief is not justified. So Steup's internalist-style solution does not work.

A second problem confronting weak internalism is what I call the *problem of concurrent retrieval*. Principle WI says that *only* conscious and stored mental states are justifiers, but it does not say that *all* sets or conjunctions of such states qualify as justifiers.[21] Presumably, which sets of such states qualify is a matter to be decided by reference to $KJ_{int+ret}$. If a certain set of stored beliefs

can all be concurrently retrieved at time t and concurrently introspected, then they would pass the test of $KJ_{int+ret}$, and could qualify as justifiers under the principle of indirect knowability. But if they cannot all be concurrently retrieved and introspected at t, they would fail the test. Now it is clear that the totality of an agent's stored credal corpus at a time cannot be concurrently retrieved from memory. So that set of stored beliefs does not qualify as a justifier for purposes of weak internalism. Unfortunately, this sort of belief set is precisely what certain types of internalist theories require by way of a justifier. Consider holistic coherentism, which says that a proposition p is justified for person S at time t if and only if p coheres with S's entire corpus of beliefs at t (including, of course, the stored beliefs). A cognitive agent could as certain, at t, whether p coheres with her entire corpus only by concurrently retrieving all of her stored beliefs. But such concurrent retrieval is psychologically impossible.[22] Thus, the critically relevant justificational fact under holistic coherentism does not meet even the indirect knowability constraint, much less the direct knowability constraint. Here is a clash, then, between a standard internalist theory of justification and the knowability rationale under scrutiny. Either that rationale is indefensible, or a familiar type of internalism must be abandoned at the outset. Nor is the problem confined to coherentism. Internalist foundationalism might also require concurrent retrieval of more basic (or low-level) beliefs than it is psychologically feasible to retrieve.

IV: Logical and Probabilistic Relations

As these last examples remind us, every traditional form of internalism involves some appeal to logical relations, probabilistic relations, or their ilk. Foundationalism requires that nonbasically justified beliefs stand in suitable logical or probabilistic relations to basic beliefs, coherentism requires that one's system of beliefs be logically consistent, probabilistically coherent, or the like. None of these logical or probabilistic relations is itself a mental state, either a conscious state or a stored state. So these relations do not qualify as justifiers according to either SI or WI. The point may be illustrated more concretely within a foundationalist perspective. Suppose that

Jones possesses a set of basic beliefs at t whose contents logically or probabilistically support proposition p. This property of Jones's basic beliefs—the property of supporting proposition p—is not a justifier under WI, for the property itself is neither a conscious nor a stored mental state. Nor is the possession of this property by these mental states another mental state. So WI has no way of authorizing or permitting Jones to believe p. Unless WI is liberalized, no nonbasic belief will be justified, which would again threaten a serious form of skepticism.

Can this problem be remedied by simply adding the proviso that all properties of conscious or stored mental states also qualify as justifiers?[23] This proviso is unacceptably permissive for internalism. One property of many conscious and stored mental states is the property of *being caused by a reliable process*, yet surely internalism cannot admit this archetypically externalist type of property into the class of justifiers. How should the class of properties be restricted? An obvious suggestion is to include only formal properties of mental states, that is, logical and mathematical properties of their contents. But should *all* formal properties be admitted? This approach would fly in the face of the knowability or accessibility constraint, which is the guiding theme of internalism. Only formal properties that are knowable by the agent at the time of doxastic decision should be countenanced as legitimate justifiers under internalism. Such properties, however, cannot be detected by introspection and/or memory retrieval. So some knowing operations suitable for formal properties must be added, yielding a liberalized version of the KJ constraint.

How should a liberalized KJ constraint be designed? The natural move is to add some selected computational operations or algorithms, procedures that would enable an agent to ascertain whether a targeted proposition p has appropriate logical or probabilistic relations to the contents of other belief states he is in. Precisely which computational operations are admissible? Again, problems arise. The first is the *problem of the doxastic decision interval*.

The traditional idea behind internalism is that an agent is justified in believing p *at time t* if the evidential beliefs (and perhaps other, nondoxastic states) possessed *at t* have an appropriate logical or probabilistic relation to p. In short, justification is conferred simultaneously with evidence possession. Feldman makes this explicit: "For any person S and proposition p and time t, S epistemically ought to believe p at t if and only if p is supported by the evidence S has at t" (*op. cit.*, p. 254). Once the knowability constraint is introduced, however, simultaneous justification looks problematic. If justification is contingent on the agent's ability to know what justifiers obtain, the agent should not be permitted to believe a proposition p *at t* unless she can know *by t* whether the relevant justifiers obtain. Since it necessarily takes some time to compute logical or probabilistic relations, the simultaneity model of justification needs to be revised so that an agent's mental states at t justify her in believing only p at $t + E$, for some suitable E. The value of E cannot be too large, of course, lest the agent's mental states change so as to affect the justificational status of p. But E must be large enough to allow the agent time to determine the relevant formal relations.

These two conditions—(1) avoid mental change, but (2) allow enough time to compute formal relations—may well be jointly unsatisfiable, which would pose a severe problem for internalism. Mental states, including perceptual states that generate new evidence, change very rapidly and they could easily change before required computations could be executed. On the other hand, although mental states do change rapidly, the agent's belief system might not be epistemically required to reflect or respond to each change until interval E has elapsed. Some doxastic decision interval, then, might be feasible.

Is there a short enough decision interval during which justificationally pertinent formal properties can be computed? Coherentism says that S is justified in believing proposition p only if p coheres with the rest of S's belief system held at the time. Assume that coherence implies logical consistency. Then coherentism requires that the logical consistency or inconsistency of any proposition p with S's belief system must qualify as a justifier. But how quickly can consistency or inconsistency be ascertained by mental computation? As Christopher Cherniak[24] points out, determination of even tautological consistency is a computationally complex task in the general case. Using the truth-table method to check for the consistency of a belief system with 138 independent atomic propositions, even an ideal computer working at "top speed" (checking each row of a truth table in the time it takes a light ray to traverse the diameter of a proton) would take twenty billion years, the estimated time from the "big-bang" dawn of the universe to the present. Presumably, twenty billion years is not an acceptable doxastic decision intervall

Any reasonable interval, then, is too constraining for garden-variety coherentism. The knowability constraint again clashes with one of the stock brands of internalism.[25] Dyed-in-the-wool internalists might be prepared to live with this result. "So much the worse for traditional coherentism," they might say, "we can live with its demise." But this does not get internalism entirely off the hook. There threaten to be many logical and probabilistic facts that do not qualify as justifiers because they require too long a doxastic interval to compute. Furthermore, it is unclear what is a principled basis for deciding what is too long. This quandary confronting internalism has apparently escaped its proponents' attention.

A second problem for logical and probabilistic justifiers is the *availability problem* Suppose that a particular set of *computational operations*—call it COMP—is provisionally selected for inclusion alongside introspection and memory retrieval. COMP might include, for example, a restricted (and hence noneffective) use of the truth-table method, restricted so as to keep its use within the chosen doxastic decision interval.[26] This yields a new version of the KJ constraint:

> $KJ_{int+ret+COMP}$: The only facts that qualify as justifiers of an agent's believing p at time t are facts that the agent can readily know within a suitable doxastic decision interval *via introspection, memory retrieval, and/or COMP.*

Now, the KJ constraint is presumably intended to apply not only to the cleverest or best-trained epistemic agents but to all epistemic agents, including the most naive and uneducated persons on the street. After all, the point of the knowability constraint is

that justifiers should be facts within the purview of every epistemic agent. Under the GD conception, compliance with epistemic duty or responsibility is not intended to be the private preserve of the logical or mathematical elite. It is something that ought to be attained—and should therefore be attainable—by any human agent. The truth-table method, however, does not seem to be in the intellectual repertoire of naive agents, so it is illegitimate to include COMP operations within a KJ constraint. Unlike introspection and memory retrieval, it is not available to all cognitive agents.

It may be replied that computational operations of the contemplated sort would be within the *capacity* of normal human agents. No super-human computational powers are required. Computing power, however, is not the issue. A relevant sequence of operations must also be *available* in the agent's intellectual repertoire; that is, she must know which operations are appropriate to obtain an answer to the relevant. (formal) question.[27] Since truth-table methods and other such algorithms are probably not in the repertoire of ordinary cognitive agents, they cannot properly be included in a KJ constraint.

A third problem concerns the proper methodology that should be used in selecting a KJ constraint that incorporates computational operations. As we see from the first two problems, a KJ constraint that conforms to the spirit of the GD rationale must reflect the basic cognitive skills or repertories of actual human beings. What these basic repertories consist in, however, cannot be determined a priori. It can only be determined with the help of empirical science. This fact fundamentally undermines the methodological posture of internalism, a subject to which I shall return in section VII.

Until now, I have assumed a *universal* accessibility constraint, one that holds for all cognitive agents. But perhaps potential justifiers for one agent need not be potential justifiers for another. Justifiers might be allowed to vary from agent to agent, depending on what is knowable by the particular agent. If two agents have different logical or probabilistic skills, then some properties that do not qualify as justifiers for one might yet qualify as justifiers for the other. Indeed, the constraint $KJ_{int+ret+COMP}$

might be read in precisely this agent-relativized way. The subscripts may be interpreted as indicating knowledge routes that are available *to the agent in question*, not necessarily to all agents.

If KJ constraints are agent relativized as a function of differences in knowledge skills, this means that two people in precisely the same evidential state (in terms of perceptual situation, background beliefs, and so on) might have different epistemic entitlements. But if the two agents are to comply with their respective epistemic duties, each must *know* which knowledge skills she has. This simply parallels the second step of the internalist's original three-step argument. If one's epistemic duties or entitlements depend on one's knowledge skills (for example, on one's computational skills), then compliance with one's duties requires knowledge of which skills one possesses. There are two problems with this approach. First, it is unlikely that many people—especially ordinary people on the street—have this sort of knowledge, and this again threatens large-scale skepticism. Second, what is now required to be known by the agent is something about the *truth-getting* power of her cognitive skills—that is, the power of her skills in detecting justifiers. This seems to be precisely the sort of *external* property that internalists regard as anathema. How can they accept this solution while remaining faithful to the spirit of internalism.[28]

V: Epistemic Principles

When the KJ constraint speaks of justifiers, it is not clear exactly what these comprehend. Specifically, do justifiers include epistemic principles themselves? I believe that principles should be included, because epistemic principles are among the items that determine whether or not an agent is justified in believing a proposition, which is just how 'justifiers' was defined. Furthermore, true epistemic principles are items an agent must know if she is going to determine her epistemic duties correctly. Knowledge of her current states of mind and their properties will not instruct her about her epistemic duties and entitlements unless she also knows true epistemic principles.

How are epistemic principles to be known, according to internalism? Chisholm[29] says that central epistemic principles are normative supervenience principles, which (when true) are necessarily true. Since they are necessary truths, they can be known a priori—in particular, they can be known "by reflection."

> The internalist assumes that, merely by reflecting upon his own conscious state, he can formulate a set of epistemic principles that will enable him to find out, with respect to any possible belief he has, whether he is justified in having that belief.[30]

This passage is ambiguous as to whether (correct) epistemic principles are accessible on reflection just to epistemologists, or accessible to naive epistemic agents as well. The latter, however, must be required by internalism, because justifiers are supposed to be determinable by all epistemic agents.

Are ordinary or naive agents really capable of formulating and recognizing correct epistemic principles? This seems highly dubious. Even many career-long epistemologists have failed to articulate and appreciate correct epistemic principles. Since different epistemologists offer disparate and mutually conflicting candidates for epistemic principles, at most a fraction of these epistemologists can be right. Perhaps none of the principles thus far tendered by epistemologists is correct! In light of this shaky and possibly dismal record by professional epistemologists, how can we expect ordinary people, who are entirely ignorant of epistemology and its multiple pitfalls, to succeed at this task?[31] Nor is it plausible that they should succeed at this task purely "by reflection" on their conscious states, since among the matters epistemic principles must resolve is what computational skills are within the competence of ordinary cognizers. I do not see how this can be answered a priori, "by reflection."

A crippling problem emerges for internalism. If epistemic principles are not knowable by all naive agents, no such principles can qualify as justifiers under the KJ constraint. If no epistemic principles so qualify, no proposition can be justifiably believed by any agent Wholesale skepticism follows.

VI: The Core Dilemma for the Three-Step Argument

I raise doubts here about whether there is any cogent inferential route from the GD conception to internalism via an acceptable KJ constraint. Here is the core dilemma. The minimal, unvarnished version of the KJ constraint does not rationalize internalism. That simple constraint merely says that justifiers must be readily knowable and some readily knowable facts might be external rather than internal. If *all* routes to knowledge of justifiers are allowed, then knowledge by perception must be allowed. If knowledge by perception is allowed, then facts of an external sort could qualify for the status of justifiers. Of course, no epistemologist claims that purely external facts should serve as justifiers. But partly external facts are nominated by externalists for the rank of justifiers. Consider properties of the form: being a reliable perceptual indicator of a certain environmental fact. This sort of property is at least partly external because reliability involves truth, and truth (on the usual assumption) is external. Now suppose that a certain auditory perceptual state has the property of being a reliable indicator of the presence of a mourning dove in one's environment. Might the possession of this reliable indicatorship property qualify as a justifier on the grounds that it is indeed readily knowable? If every route to knowledge is legitimate, I do not see how this possibility can be excluded. After all, one could use past perceptions of mourning doves and their songs to determine that the designated auditory state is a reliable indicator of a mourning dove's presence. So if unrestricted knowledge is allowed, the (partly) external fact in question might be perfectly knowable. Thus, the unvarnished version of the KJ constraint does not exclude external facts from the ranks of the justifiers.

The simple version of the KJ constraint, then, does not support internalism. Tacit recognition of this is what undoubtedly leads internalists to favor a "direct" knowability constraint. Unfortunately, this extra rider is not rationalized by the GD conception. The GD conception at best implies that cognitive agents must know what justifiers are present or absent. No particular *types* of knowledge, or *paths* to

knowledge, are intimated. So the GD conception cannot rationalize a restrictive version of the KJ constraint that unambiguously yields internalism.

Let me put the point another way. The GD conception implies that justifiers must be readily knowable, but are internal facts always *more readily* knowable than external facts? As discussed earlier, probabilistic relations presumably qualify as internal, but they do not seem to be readily knowable by human beings. An entire tradition of psychological research on "biases and heuristics" suggests that naive agents commonly commit probabilistic fallacies, such as the "conjunction fallacy," and use formally incorrect judgmental heuristics, such as the representativeness heuristic and the anchoring-and-adjustment heuristic.[32] If this is right, people's abilities at detecting probabilistic relationships are actually rather weak. People's perceptual capacities to detect external facts seem, by contrast, far superior. The unqualified version of the KJ constraint, therefore, holds little promise for restricting all justifiers to internal conditions in preference to external conditions, as internalism requires.[33]

VII: The Methodology of Epistemology: Empirical or A priori?

Internalism standardly incorporates the doctrine that epistemology is a purely a priori or armchair enterprise rather than one that needs help from empirical science. Chisholm puts the point this way:

The epistemic principles that [the epistemologist] formulates are principles that one may come upon and apply merely by sitting in one's armchair, so to speak, and without calling for any outside assistance. In a word, one need only consider one's own state of mind.[34]

Previous sections already raised doubts about the merits of apriorism in epistemology, even in the context of the theoretical architecture presented here. I now want to challenge the viability of apriorism in greater depth.

Assume that, despite my earlier reservations, an internalist restriction on justifiers has somehow been derived, one that allows only conscious states and certain of their nonexternal properties to serve as justifiers. How should the epistemologist identify particular conscious states and properties as justifiers for specific propositions (or types of propositions)? In other words, how should specific epistemic principles be crafted? Should the task be executed purely a priori, or can scientific psychology help?

For concreteness, consider justifiers for memory beliefs. Suppose an adult consciously remembers seeing, as a teenager, a certain matinee idol. This ostensible memory could have arisen from imagination, since he frequently fantasized about this matinee idol and imagined seeing her in person. What clues are present in the current memory impression by which he can tell whether or not the recollection is veridical? This is precisely the kind of issue which internalist epistemic principles should address. If there are no differences in features of memory states that stem from perceptions of real occurrences versus features of states that stem from mere imagination, does this not raise a specter of skepticism over the domain of memory? If there are no indications by which to distinguish veridical from nonveridical memory impressions, can we be justified in trusting our memory impressions? Skepticism aside, epistemologists should surely be interested in identifying the features of conscious memory impressions by which people are made more or less justified (or prima facie justified) in believing things about the past.

Epistemologists have said very little on this subject. Their discussions tend to be exhausted by characterizations of memory impressions as "vivid" or "nonvivid." There is, I suspect, a straightforward reason for the paucity of detail. It is extremely difficult, using purely armchair methods, to dissect the microfeatures of memory experiences so as to identify telltale differences between trustworthy and questionable memories. On the other hand, empirical methods have produced some interesting findings, which might properly be infused into epistemic principles in a way entirely congenial to internalism. Important research in this area has been done by Marcia Johnson and her colleagues.[35] I shall illustrate my points by brief reference to their research.

Johnson calls the subject of some of her research *reality monitoring*. She tries to characterize the detectable differences between (conscious) memory traces derived from veridical perception of events versus memory traces generated by mere imaginations of events.[36] Johnson and Raye (*op. cit*) propose four dimensions along which memory cues will typically differ depending on whether their origin was perceptual or imaginative. As compared with memories that originate from imagination, memories originating from perception tend to have (1) more perceptual information (for example, color and sound), (2) more contextual information about time and place, and (3) more meaningful detail. When a memory trace is rich along these three dimensions, this is evidence of its having originated through perception. Memories originating from imagination or thought, by contrast, tend to be rich on another dimension: they contain more information about the cognitive operations involved in the original thinkings or imaginings (for example, effortful attention, image creation, or search). Perception is more automatic than imagination, so a memory trace that originates from perception will tend to lack attributes concerning effortful operations. Johnson and Raye therefore suggest that differences in average value along these types of dimensions can form the basis for deciding whether the origin of a memory is perceptual or nonperceptual. A memory with a great deal of visual and spatial detail, and without records of intentional constructive and organizational processes, should be judged to have been perceptually derived.[37]

Epistemologists would be well-advised to borrow these sorts of ideas and incorporate them into their epistemic principles. A person is (prima facie) justified in believing in the real occurrence of an ostensibly recalled event if the memory trace is strong on the first three dimensions and weak on the fourth dimension. Conversely, an agent is unjustified in believing in the real occurrence of the recalled event if the memory trace is strong on the fourth dimension but weak on the first three dimensions. All of these dimensions, of course, concern features of conscious experience. For this reason, internalist epistemologists should be happy to incorporate these kinds of features into their epistemic principles.

Let me distinguish two categories of epistemologically significant facts about memory experience which empirical psychology might provide. First, as we have seen, it might identify types of representational materials which are generally available in people's memory experiences. Second, it might indicate which of these representational materials are either reliable or counter-reliable indicators of the veridicality of the ostensibly recalled events. Is the reliability of a memory cue a legitimate issue from an internalist perspective? It might be thought not, since reliability is usually classed as an external property. But epistemologists might use reliability considerations to decide which memory characteristics should be featured in epistemic principles. They need not insert reliability per se into the principles. There is nothing in our present formulation of internalism, at any rate, which bars the latter approach. Any KJ constraint provides only a necessary condition for being a justifier; it leaves open the possibility that additional necessary conditions, such as reliable indication, must also be met. Indeed, many internalists do use reliability as a (partial) basis for their choice of justifiers. BonJour (op. cit., p. 7) says that the basic role of justification is that of a *means* to truth and he defends coherence as a justifier on the ground that a coherent system of beliefs is likely to correspond to reality. This point need not be settled definitively, however. There are already adequate grounds for claiming that internalism cannot be optimally pursued without help from empirical psychology, whether or not reliability is a relevant consideration.

VIII: Conclusion

Let us review the parade of problems infecting internalism which we have witnessed, though not all in their order of presentation. (1) The argument from the GD conception of justification to internalism does not work. Internalism can be derived only from a suitably qualified version of the KJ constraint because the unqualified version threatens to allow external facts to count as justifiers. No suitably qualified version of the KJ constraint is derivable from the GD conception. (2) A variety of qualified KJ constraints are possible, each leading to a different version of internalism. None of these versions is intuitively acceptable. Strong internalism, which restricts justifiers to conscious states, is stuck with the problem of stored beliefs. Weak internalism, which allows stored as well as conscious beliefs to count as justifiers, faces the problem of forgotten evidence and the problem of concurrent retrieval. (3) The question of how logical and probabilistic facts are to be included in the class of justifiers is plagued by puzzles, especially the puzzle of the doxastic decision interval and the issue of availability. (4) Epistemic principles must be among the class of justifiers, but such principles fail internalism's knowability requirement. (5) The favored methodology of internalism—the armchair method—cannot be sustained even if we grant the assumption that justifiers must be conscious states.

Internalism is rife with problems. Are they all traceable to the GD rationale? Could internalism be salvaged by switching to a different rationale? A different rationale might help, but most of the problems raised here arise from the knowability constraint. It is unclear exactly which knowability constraint should be associated with internalism, and all of the available candidates generate problematic theories. So I see no hope for internalism; it does not survive the glare of the spotlight.

Notes

* An earlier version of this paper was presented in Pittsburgh, at the Central Division meeting of the American Philosophical Association, April 25, 1997. My commentator on that occasion was Matthias Steup, and I am much indebted to him for valuable correspondence on this topic. I am also grateful to Tim Bayne and Holly Smith for very useful suggestions.

1. Prominent statements of externalism include D. M. Armstrong, *Belief, Truth and Knowledge* (New York: Cambridge, 1973); Fred Dretske, *Knowledge and the Flow of Information* (Cambridge: MIT, 1981); Robert Nozick, *Philosophical Explanations* (Cambridge: Harvard, 1981); my *Epistemology and Cognition* (Cambridge: Harvard, 1986); and Alvin Plantinga, *Warrant and Proper Function* (New York: Oxford, 1993).

2. Major statements of internalism include Roderick Chisholm, *Theory of Knowledge* (Englewood Cliffs, NJ: Prentice-Hall, 1966, 1st edition; 1977, 2nd edition; 1989, 3rd edition); Laurence BonJour, *The Structure of Empirical Knowledge* (Cambridge: Harvard, 1985); John Pollock, *Contemporary Theories of Knowledge* (Totowa, NJ Rowman and Littlefield, 1986); Richard Foley, *The Theory of Epistemic Rationality* (Cambridge: Harvard, 1987); and Keith Lehrer, *Theory of Knowledge* (Boulder: West view, 1990). In addition to relatively pure versions of externalism and internalism, there are also mixtures of the two approaches, as found in William Alston, *Epistemic Justification* (Ithaca: Cornell, 1989); Ernest Sosa, *Knowledge in Perspective* (New York: Cambridge, 1991); and Robert Audi, *The Structure of Justification* (New York: Cambridge, 1993).

3. Plantinga also traces internalism to the deontological conception: "If we go back to the source of the internalist tradition . . . we can see that internalism arises out of deontology; a deontological conception of warrant. . . leads directly to internalism" (*op. cit.*, pp. 24–25). Alston proposes a slightly different rationale for internalism, although his rationale also proceeds via the knowability constraint *op. cit.*, p. 236). He suggests that the concept of justification derives from the interpersonal practice of criticizing one another's beliefs and asking for their credentials. A person can appropriately respond to other people's demands for credentials only if he knows what those credentials are. So it is quite understandable, says Alston, that justifiers must meet the requirement of being accessible to the agent. Clearly, this is one way to derive the accessibility constraint without appeal to the deontological conception. But Alston is the only one I know of who advances this ground for the accessibility constraint. In any case, most of the problems I shall identify pertain to the accessibility constraint itself, which Alston's rationale shares with the deontological rationale.

4. *Philosophical Works of Descartes, Volume I*, Elizabeth Haldane and G. R. T. Ross, trans. (New York: Dover, 1955).

5. *An Essay Concerning Human Understanding, Volume II*, A. C. Fraser, ed. (New York: Dover. 1955)

6. Ginet, *Knowledge, Perception, and Memory* (Dordrecht: Reidel, 1975); Moser, *Empirical Justification* (Dordrecht: Reidel, 1985); Steup, "The Deontic Conception of Epistemic Justification," *Philosophical Studies*, LIII (1988): 65–84; Feldman, "Epistemic Obligations," in J. Tomberlin, ed., *Philosophical Perspectives*, Volume II (Atascadero, CA: Ridgeview, 1988), pp. 235–56; and Kornblith, "Justified Belief and Epistemically Responsible Action," *Philosophical Review*, XCII (1983): 33–48.

7. *Theory of Knowledge*, 2nd edition, p. 14 (emphasis added).

8. For example, R. Eugene Bales distinguishes between two possible aims of act utilitarianism: as a specifier of a right-making characteristic or as a decision-making procedure. See "Act-utilitarianism: Account of Right-making Characteristics or Decision-making Procedure," *American Philosophical Quarterly*, VIII (1971): 257–65. He defends utilitarianism against certain critics by saying that it does not *have* to perform the latter function

9. "Internalism and Externalism in Epistemology," reprinted in his *op. cit.*, pp. 185–226, here p. 189.

10. Some internalists explicitly reject externalism on the grounds that it cannot be used as a decision guide. For example, Pollock says: "[I]t is in principle impossible for us to actually employ externalist norms. I take this to be a conclusive refutation of belief externalism" (*op. cit.*, p. 134). He would not subscribe to the full argument for internalism I am discussing, however, because it is committed to the "intellectualist model" of epistemology, which he disparages.

11. For the distinction between reliability and power (phrased slightly differently), see my *op. cit*, chapter 6.

12. Jack Lyons points out that to comply with one's epistemic duty it suffices to know *that one has* (undefeated) justifiers for proposition *p*; one does not have to know *which* justifiers these are. So the argument is not entitled to conclude that knowledge of particular justifiers is required by epistemic duty. Practically speaking, however, it is difficult to see how a cognitive agent could know that relevant justifiers exist without knowing which particular ones exist. So I shall pass over this objection to the internalist line of argument.

13. "The Deontological Conception of Justification," reprinted in his *op. cit.*, pp. 115–152

14. "Doxastic Agency," *Philosophical Studies*, XL (1983): 355–64.

15. Feldman's response, however, undercuts the step from the GD conception of justification to the knowability constraint. If epistemic duty does not require that the agent be *able* to discharge this duty, there is no longer a rationale for the knowability constraint. A different line of response to the voluntarism worry is taken by Lehrer, who suggests that epistemological analysis should focus not on belief but on *acceptance*, where acceptance is some sort of action that is subject to the will—"A Self-Profile," in R. Bogdan, ed., *Keith Lehrer* (Dordrecht: Reidel, 1981), pp. 3-104.

16. *Theory of Knowledge*, 3rd edition, p. 7; emphasis added and original emphasis deleted.

17. Other epistemologists who restrict justifiers to conscious states or discuss access in terms of introspection include Moser, p. 174; Feldman, "Having Evidence,"

in D. Austin, ed., *Philosophical Analysis* (Dordrecht: Kluwer, 1988), pp. 83–104; and Audi, "Causalist Internalism," *American Philosophical Quarterly*, XXVI, 4 (1989): 309–320

18. Feldman might reply that there is an important distinction between memorial and perceptual dispositions; but it is not clear on what basis a principled distinction can be drawn.

19. This sort of problem is discussed by Gilbert Harman, *Change in View* (Cambridge: MIT, 1986); Thomas Senor, "Internalist Foundationalism and the Justification of Memory Belief," *Synthese*, XCIV (1993): 453–76; and Audi, "Memorial Justification," *Philosophical Topics*, XXIII (1995): 31–45.

20. His proposal was part of his commentary (see acknowledgment note above).

21. Obviously, one would need to reject the principle that the knowability of fact A and the knowability of fact B entail the knowability of the conjunction fact A & B.

22. The "doxastic presumption" invoked by BonJour (*op, cit.*, pp. 101–06) seems to assume that this is possible, but this is simply an undefended assumption. Pollock (*op. cit.*, p. 136) also raises the problem identified here, though in slightly different terms.

23. More precisely, the contemplated proviso should say that the possession of any property by a mental state (or set of mental states) qualifies as a justifier. This reading will be understood wherever the the text talks loosely of "properties."

24. "Computational Complexity and the Universal Acceptance of Logic," this JOURNAL, LXXXI, 12 (December 1984): 739-58.

25. This computational difficulty for coherentism is identified by Kornblith, "The Unattainability of Coherence," in J. Bender, ed., *The Current State of the Coherence Theory* (Dordrecht: Kluwer, 1989). pp. 207–14.

26. Because of the contemplated restriction, there will be many questions about formal facts to which COMP cannot deliver answers. Thus, formal facts that might otherwise qualify as justifiers will not so qualify under the version of the KJ constraint that incorporates COMP.

27. Propositional (or "declarative") knowledge of the appropriate sequence of operations is, perhaps an unduly restrictive requirement. It would suffice for the agent to

have "procedural" skills of the Right sort. But even such skills will be lacking in naive cognitive agents.

28. It might be argued that internalism's spirit leads to a similar requirement even for universal versions of a KJ constraint, not just for agent-relativized versions. Perhaps so; but so much the worse for the general form of internalism.

29. "The Status of Epistemic Principles," *Noûs* XXIV (1990): 209–15.

30. *Theory of Knowledge*, 3rd edition, p. 76; emphasis omitted.

31. A similar worry is expressed by Alston in "Internalism and Externalism in Epistemology," pp. 221-22.

32. See Amos Tversky and Daniel Kahneman, "Judgment under Uncertainty: Heuristics and Biases," in Kahneman, P. Slovic, and Tversky, eds., *Judgment under Uncertainty* (New York: Cambridge, 1982), pp. 3–20; and Tversky and Kahneman, "Extensional versus Intuitive Reasoning: The Conjunction Fallacy in Probability Judgment," *Psychological Review*, XCI (1983): 293–315.

33. It is not really clear, moreover, why logical or probabilistic facts intuitively count as "internal" facts. They certainly are not internal in the same sense in which mental states are internal. This is an additional problem about the contours of internalism.

34. *Theory of Knowledge*, 3rd edition, p.76.

35. See Johnson and Carol Raye, "Reality Monitoring," *Psychological Review*, LXXXVIII (1981): 67–85; and Johnson, Mary Foley, Aurora Suengas, and Raye, "Phenomenal Characteristics of Memories for Perceived and Imagined Autobiographical Events," *Journal of Experimental Psychology: General*, CXVII (1988): 371–76.

36. Memory errors are not confined, of course, to confusions of actual with imagined events. There are also errors that arise from confusing, or blending, two actual events. But this research of Johnson's focuses on the actual/nonactual (or perceived versus imagined) problem.

37. They also recognize that people can compare a target memory with memories of contextually related events to assess the target's veridicality. This kind of "coherence" factor is a stock-in-trade of epistemology, however, and hence not a good example of the distinctive contributions (I) three fore pass over it.

CHAPTER 7 NATURALIZED EPISTEMOLOGY

INTRODUCTION

In his 1969 publication bearing the same name, W.V.O. Quine (1908–2000) introduced the term 'naturalized epistemology'. He claims that the traditional project of epistemology—the project of reformulating our empirical beliefs into an edifice resting on a firm foundation—should be abandoned, and replaced with a far more modest task—the project of explaining scientifically how some beliefs come to count as knowledge. Naturalistic epistemology is to become a component of empirical psychology. Like other scientific projects, naturalistic epistemology is to be neither indefeasible nor aprioristic, and it will take for granted the apparatus, techniques and assumptions of natural science. Skeptical issues are to be considered only insofar as they arise in the course of scientific inquiry, and resolved using the resources of science (1975).

The externalist turn among contemporary theorists has helped make them receptive to the strategy of treating knowledge as a natural phenomenon, and the reverse is true as well: naturalism fosters externalism. Theorists writing under the banner of externalism more and more resemble those writing under the banner of naturalism. Nonetheless, the defining boundaries of both projects are in flux, and the naturalist project is not fully described in Quine's essay, as critics such as Hilary Putnam and Jaegwon Kim have pointed out. Quine's criticisms of traditional epistemology are standard fare, and are familiar enough, but the project that is to replace traditional epistemology needs clarification. One central difficulty is that Quine does not make it clear whether the new epistemology is to be a merely descriptive enterprise, and if so what is to happen to the normative questions central to traditional epistemology. If we merely describe how we arrive at the beliefs that normally count as knowledge, how are we to decide how we *ought* to arrive at our views, and which views we ought to accept?

In later writings (1992) Quine suggests that "insofar as theoretical epistemology gets naturalized into a chapter of theoretical science, so normative epistemology gets naturalized into a chapter of engineering: the technology of anticipating sensory stimulation." This suggests that normative epistemology is naturalistic because naturalized epistemology embraces engineering science which, in turn, settles the normative issues in epistemology. But it is far from clear that the issue of how epistemic agents ought to behave is an engineering issue.

Putnam (b.1926) on Naturalism

In "Why Reason Can't Be Naturalized," Hilary Putnam argues that we cannot give up traditional epistemic notions such as justification and reason, as Quine's project seems to suggest. To do so we would have to avoid the notion of truth, but unless we construe our statements as true in a substantive sense we must view them as mere noise. Nonetheless, Putnam is critical of the "metaphysically realist", or correspondence, theory of truth. According to Putnam, we must understand truth in terms of rational acceptability, in terms of what is justifiably believed, and not the other way around—not justified belief in terms of truth. Primarily, this is because we have no way of picking out claims as true except by picking them out as rationally acceptable. Putnam is also critical of evolutionary epistemologists whose attempt to naturalize reason involves explaining it as a truth-detecting mechanism with survival value. The problem with this strategy is that it is committed to metaphysical realism. He rejects Goldman's reliabilist account of justification on the same grounds, as well as on the grounds that circular justifications can be reliable but aren't rationally acceptable. Finally, he rejects cultural relativism on the grounds that it is self-refuting: the statement, everyone's claims are true only relative to her culture, is an exception to itself.

Kim (b.1934) on Naturalism

In "What is 'Naturalized Epistemology?'", Jaegwon Kim is critical of Quine's project for reasons that overlap with Putnam's. The concept of justification is essential to our epistemological activities, and this notion is inescapably normative. Hence when Quine urges us to abandon normative epistemology, the project of identifying how we should select our beliefs, and which beliefs to accept, he is, in effect, telling us to drop the notion of justification, which is tantamount to abandoning epistemology itself.

Kornblith on Naturalism

Hilary Kornblith is perhaps the leading twenty-first century advocate of naturalism. He defends the naturalistic project in "Naturalistic Epistemology and Its Critics." With Quine, he says that we should explore the natural phenomenon called knowledge, not people's concept of knowledge, which is confused and misinformed, much like their concepts of other natural phenomena, such as aluminum. Against Quine's critics, Kornblith claims that naturalistic epistemology can be thoroughly empirical without losing its normative force.

QUESTIONS FOR REFLECTION

1. In (1985) Quine appears to think that the naturalist can answer the skeptic. Is he correct? Does he mean that all forms of skepticism can be answered by the naturalist? What should we make of his admission in "Epistemology Naturalized" that "the Humean Predicament is the human predicament"?

2. Can the normative questions of epistemology—questions like, What beliefs should we acquire?—be answered by treating them as engineering issues? How will that go?

3. Does Kornblith provide a convincing argument for the claim that naturalistic epistemology can be thoroughly empirical without losing its normative force? Does "thoroughly empirical" mean "*entirely empirical*"? How might Putnam and Kim respond to Kornblith?

4. Many of Putnam's criticisms of naturalistic strategies depend on our understanding truth in terms of rational acceptability. Is Putnam correct about truth? Can we analyze justification without doing so in terms of truth? Can we then turn around and analyze truth in terms of justification? Which concept, if either, is more primitive?

5. Suppose that psychologists discover that scientists do not employ wishful thinking, but most people do. Would it follow that beliefs arrived at via wishful thinking counts as knowledge for most people but not for scientists? Can the naturalist argue that wishful thinking does not generate knowledge? If so, would the argument succeed?

6. Suppose that we accept the idea that epistemology does not handle normative issues. It follows that these issues have to be part of some other area of inquiry (or set aside entirely). What would it be? Should it be politicians or humanists who answer questions like, What beliefs should I accept?

◇ A DEFENSE ◇

35. EPISTEMOLOGY NATURALIZED

W. V. O. Quine

Epistemology is concerned with the foundations of science. Conceived thus broadly, epistemology includes the study of the foundations of mathematics as one of its departments. Specialists at the turn of the century thought that their efforts in this particular department were achieving notable success:

mathematics seemed to reduce altogether to logic. In a more recent perspective this reduction is seen to be better describable as a reduction to logic and set theory. This correction is a disappointment epistemologically, since the firmness and obviousness that we associate with logic cannot be claimed for set theory. But still the success achieved in the foundations of mathematics remains exemplary by comparative standards, and we can illuminate the rest of epistemology somewhat by drawing parallels to this department.

Studies in the foundations of mathematics divide symmetrically into two sorts, conceptual and doctrinal. The conceptual studies are concerned with meaning, the doctrinal with truth. The conceptual studies are concerned with clarifying concepts by defining them, some in terms of others. The doctrinal studies are concerned with establishing laws by proving them, some on the basis of others. Ideally the obscurer concepts would be defined in terms of the clearer ones so as to maximize clarity, and the less obvious laws would be proved from the more obvious ones so as to maximize certainty. Ideally the definitions would generate all the concepts from clear and distinct ideas, and the proofs would generate all the theorems from self-evident truths.

The two ideals are linked. For, if you define all the concepts by use of some favored subset of them, you thereby show how to translate all theorems into these favored terms. The clearer these terms are, the likelier it is that the truths couched in them will be obviously true, or derivable from obvious truths. If in particular the concepts of mathematics were all reducible to the clear terms of logic, then all the truths of mathematics would go over into truths of logic; and surely the truths of logic are all obvious or at least potentially obvious, i.e., derivable from obvious truths by individually obvious steps.

This particular outcome is in fact denied us, however, since mathematics reduces only to set theory and not to logic proper. Such reduction still enhances clarity, but only because of the interrelations that emerge and not because the end terms of the analysis are clearer than others. As for the end truths, the axioms of set theory, these have less obviousness and certainty to recommend them than do most of the mathematical theorems that we would derive from them. Moreover, we know from Gödel's work that no consistent axiom system can cover mathematics even when we renounce

self-evidence. Reduction in the foundations of mathematics remains mathematically and philosophically fascinating, but it does not do what the epistemologist would like of it: it does not reveal the ground of mathematical knowledge, it does not show how mathematical certainty is possible.

Still there remains a helpful thought, regarding epistemology generally, in that duality of structure which was especially conspicuous in the foundations of mathematics. I refer to the bifurcation into a theory of concepts, or meaning, and a theory of doctrine, or truth; for this applies to the epistemology of natural knowledge no less than to the foundations of mathematics. The parallel is as follows. Just as mathematics is to be reduced to logic, or logic and set theory, so natural knowledge is to be based somehow on sense experience. This means explaining the notion of body in sensory terms; here is the conceptual side. And it means justifying our knowledge of truths of nature in sensory terms; here is the doctrinal side of the bifurcation.

Hume pondered the epistemology of natural knowledge on both sides of the bifurcation, the conceptual and the doctrinal. His handling of the conceptual side of the problem, the explanation of body in sensory terms, was bold and simple: he identified bodies outright with the sense impressions. If common sense distinguishes between the material apple and our sense impressions of it on the ground that the apple is one and enduring while the impressions are many and fleeting, then, Hume held, so much the worse for common sense; the notion of its being the same apple on one occasion and another is a vulgar confusion.

Nearly a century after Hume's *Treatise*, the same view of bodies was espoused by the early American philosopher Alexander Bryan Johnson.[1] "The word iron names an associated sight and feel," Johnson wrote.

What then of the doctrinal side, the justification of our knowledge of truths about nature? Here, Hume despaired. By his identification of bodies with impressions he did succeed in construing some singular statements about bodies as indubitable truths, yes; as truths about impressions, directly known. But general statements, also singular statements about the future, gained no increment of certainty by being construed as about impressions.

On the doctrinal side, I do not see that we are farther along today than where Hume left us. The Humean predicament is the human predicament. But on the conceptual side there has been progress. There the crucial step forward was made already before Alexander Bryan Johnson's day, although Johnson did not emulate it. It was made by Bentham in his theory of fictions. Bentham's step was the recognition of contextual definition, or what he called paraphrasis. He recognized that to explain a term we do not need to specify an object for it to refer to, nor even specify a synonymous word or phrase; we need only show, by whatever means, how to translate all the whole sentences in which the term is to be used. Hume's and Johnson's desperate measure of identifying bodies with impressions ceased to be the only conceivable way of making sense of talk of bodies, even granted that impressions were the only reality. One could undertake to explain talk of bodies in terms of talk of impressions by translating one's whole sentences about bodies into whole sentences about impressions, without equating the bodies themselves to anything at all.

This idea of contextual definition, or recognition of the sentence as the primary vehicle of meaning, was indispensable to the ensuing developments in the foundations of mathematics. It was explicit in Frege, and it attained its full flower in Russell's doctrine of singular descriptions as incomplete symbols.

Contextual definition was one of two resorts that could be expected to have a liberating effect upon the conceptual side of the epistemology of natural knowledge. The other is resort to the resources of set theory as auxiliary concepts. The epistemologist who is willing to eke out his austere ontology of sense impressions with these set-theoretic auxiliaries is suddenly rich: he has not just his impressions to play with, but sets of them, and sets of sets, and so on up. Constructions in the foundations of mathematics have shown that such settheoretic aids are a powerful addition; after all, the entire glossary of concepts of classical mathematics is constructible from them. Thus equipped, our epistemologist may not need either to identify bodies with impressions or to settle for contextual definition; he may hope to find in some subtle construction of sets upon sets of sense impressions a category of objects enjoying just the formula properties that he wants for bodies.

The two resorts are very unequal in epistemological status. Contextual definition is unassailable. Sentences that have been given meaning as wholes are undeniably meaningful, and the use they make of their component terms is therefore meaningful, regardless of whether any translations are offered for those terms in isolation. Surely Hume and A. B. Johnson would have used contextual definition with pleasure if they had thought of it. Recourse to sets, on the other hand, is a drastic ontological move, a retreat from the austere ontology of impressions. There are philosophers who would rather settle for bodies outright than accept all these sets, which amount, after all, to the whole abstract ontology of mathematics.

This issue has not always been clear, however, owing to deceptive hints of continuity between elementary logic and set theory. This is why mathematics was once believed to reduce to logic, that is, to an innocent and unquestionable logic, and to inherit these qualities. And this is probably why Russell was content to resort to sets as well as to contextual definition when in *Our Knowledge of the External World* and elsewhere he addressed himself to the epistemology of natural knowledge, on its conceptual side.

To account for the external world as a logical construct of sense data—such, in Russell's terms, was the program. It was Carnap, in his *Der logische Aufbau der Welt* of 1928, who came nearest to executing it.

This was the conceptual side of epistemology; what of the doctrinal? There the Humean predicament remained unaltered. Carnap's constructions, if carried successfully to completion, would have enabled us to translate all sentences about the world into terms of sense data, or observation, plus logic and set theory. But the mere fact that a sentence is *couched* in terms of observation, logic, and set theory does not mean that it can be *proved* from observation sentences by logic and set theory. The most modest of generalizations about observable traits will cover more cases than its utterer can have had occasion actually to observe. The hopelessness of grounding natural science upon immediate experience in a firmly logical way was acknowledged. The Cartesian quest for certainty had been the remote motivation of epistemology, both on its conceptual and its doctrinal side; but that quest was seen as a lost cause. To endow the truths of nature with the full authority of immediate experience was as forlorn a hope as hoping to endow the truths of mathematics with the potential obviousness of elementary logic.

What then could have motivated Carnap's heroic efforts on the conceptual side of epistemology, when hope of certainty on the doctrinal side was abandoned? There were two good reasons still. One was that such constructions could be expected to elicit and clarify the sensory evidence for science, even if the inferential steps between sensory evidence and scientific doctrine must fall short of certainty. The other reason was that such constructions would deepen our understanding of our discourse about the world, even apart from questions of evidence; it would make all cognitive discourse as clear as observation terms and logic and, I must regretfully add, set theory.

It was sad for epistemologists, Hume and others, to have to acquiesce in the impossibility of strictly deriving the science of the external world from sensory evidence. Two cardinal tenets of empiricism remained unassailable, however, and so remain to this day. One is that whatever evidence there *is* for science *is* sensory evidence. The other, to which I shall recur, is that all inculcation of meanings of words must rest ultimately on sensory evidence. Hence the continuing attractiveness of the idea of a *logischer Aufbau* in which the sensory content of discourse would stand forth explicitly.

If Carnap had successfully carried such a construction through, how could he have told whether it was the right one? The question would have had no point. He was seeking what he called a *rational reconstruction*. Any construction of physicalistic discourse in terms of sense experience, logic, and set theory would have been seen as satisfactory if it made the physicalistic discourse come out right. If there is one way there are many, but any would be a great achievement.

But why all this creative reconstruction, all this make-believe? The stimulation of his sensory receptors is all the evidence anybody has had to go on, ultimately, in arriving at his picture of the world. Why not just see how this construction really proceeds? Why not settle for psychology? Such a surrender of the epistemological burden to psychology is a move that was disallowed in earlier times as circular reasoning. If the epistemologist's goal is validation of the grounds of empirical science, he defeats his purpose by using psychology or other empirical science in the validation. However, such scruples against circularity have little point once we have stopped

dreaming of deducing science from observations. If we are out simply to understand the link between observation and science, we are well advised to use any available information, including that provided by the very science whose link with observation we are seeking to understand.

But there remains a different reason, unconnected with fears of circularity, for still favoring creative reconstruction. We should like to be able to *translate* science into logic and observation terms and set theory. This would be a great epistemological achievement, for it would show all the rest of the concepts of science to be theoretically superfluous. It would legitimize them—to whatever degree the concepts of set theory, logic, and observation are themselves legitimate—by showing that everything done with the one apparatus could in principle be done with the other. If psychology itself could deliver a truly translational reduction of this kind, we should welcome it; but certainly it cannot, for certainly we did not grow up learning definitions of physicalistic language in terms of a prior language of set theory, logic, and observation. Here, then, would be good reason for persisting in a rational reconstruction: we want to establish the essential innocence of physical concepts, by showing them to be theoretically dispensable.

The fact is, though, that the construction which Carnap outlined in *Der logische Aufbau der Welt* does not give translational reduction either. It would not even if the outline were filled in. The crucial point comes where Carnap is explaining how to assign sense qualities to positions in physical space and time. These assignments are to be made in such a way as to fulfill, as well as possible, certain desiderata which he states, and with growth of experience the assignments are to be revised to suit. This plan, however illuminating, does not offer any key to *translating* the sentences of science into terms of observation, logic, and set theory.

We must despair of any such reduction. Carnap had despaired of it by 1936, when, in "Testability and meaning,"[2] he introduced so-called *reduction forms* of a type weaker than definition. Definitions had shown always how to translate sentences into equivalent sentences. Contextual definition of a term showed how to translate sentences containing the term into equivalent sentences lacking the term. Reduction forms of Carnap's liberalized kind, on the other hand, do not in general give equivalences; they give implications. They explain a new term, if only partially, by specifying some sentences which are implied by sentences containing the term, and other sentences which imply sentences containing the term.

It is tempting to suppose that the countenancing of reduction forms in this liberal sense is just one further step of liberalization comparable to the earlier one, taken by Bentham, of countenancing contextual definition. The former and sterner kind of rational reconstruction might have been represented as a fictitious history in which we imagined our ancestors introducing the terms of physicalistic discourse on a phenomenalistic and set-theoretic basis by a succession of contextual definitions. The new and more liberal kind of rational reconstruction is a fictitious history in which we imagine our ancestors introducing those terms by a succession rather of reduction forms of the weaker sort.

This, however, is a wrong comparison. The fact is rather that the former and sterner kind of rational reconstruction, where definition reigned, embodied no fictitious history at all. It was nothing more nor less than a set of directions—or would have been, if successful—for accomplishing everything in terms of phenomena and set theory that we now accomplish in terms of bodies. It would have been a true reduction by translation, a legitimation by elimination. *Definire est eliminare*. Rational reconstruction by Carnap's later and looser reduction forms does none of this.

To relax the demand for definition, and settle for a kind of reduction that does not eliminate, is to renounce the last remaining advantage that we supposed rational reconstruction to have over straight psychology; namely, the advantage of translational reduction. If all we hope for is a reconstruction that links science to experience in explicit ways short of translation, then it would seem more sensible to settle for psychology. Better to discover how science is in fact developed and learned than to fabricate a fictitious structure to a similar effect.

The empiricist made one major concession when he despaired of deducing the truths of nature from sensory evidence. In despairing now even of translating those truths into terms of observation and logico-mathematical auxiliaries, he makes another major concession. For suppose we hold, with the old empiricist Peirce, that the very meaning of a statement consists in the difference its truth would make to possible experience. Might we not formulate, in a chapter-length sentence in observational language, all the difference that the truth of a given statement might make to experience, and might we not then take all this as the translation? Even if the difference that the truth of the statement would make to experience ramifies indefinitely, we might still hope to embrace it all in the logical implications of our chapter-length formulation, just as we can axiomatize an infinity of theorems. In giving up hope of such translation, then, the empiricist is conceding that the empirical meanings of typical statements about the external world are inaccessible and ineffable.

How is this inaccessibility to be explained? Simply on the ground that the experiential implications of a typical statement about bodies are too complex for finite axiomatization, however lengthy? No; I have a different explanation. It is that the typical statement about bodies has no fund of experiential implications it can call its own. A substantial mass of theory, taken together, will commonly have experiential implications; this is how we make verifiable predictions. We may not be able to explain why we arrive at theories which make successful predictions, but we do arrive at such theories.

Sometimes also an experience implied by a theory fails to come off; and then, ideally, we declare the theory false. But the failure falsifies only a block of theory as a whole, a conjunction of many statements. The failure shows that one or more of those statements is false, but it does not show which. The predicted experiences, true and false, are not implied by any one of the component statements of the theory rather than another. The component statements simply do not have empirical meanings, by Peirce's standard; but a sufficiently inclusive portion of theory does. If we can aspire to a sort of *logischer Aufbau der Welt* at all, it must be to one in which the texts slated for translation into observational and logico-mathematical terms are mostly broad theories taken as wholes, rather than just terms or short sentences. The translation of a theory would be a ponderous axiomatization of all the experiential difference that the truth of the theory would make. It would be a queer translation, for it would translate the whole but none of the parts. We might better speak in such a case not of translation but simply of observational evidence for theories; and we may, following Peirce, still fairly call this the empirical meaning of the theories.

These considerations raise a philosophical question even about ordinary unphilosophical translation, such as from English into Arunta or Chinese. For, if the English sentences of a theory have their meaning only together as a body, then we can justify their translation into Arunta only together as a body. There will be no justification for pairing off the component English sentences with component Arunta sentences, except as these correlations make the translation of the theory as a whole come out right. Any translations of the English sentences into Arunta sentences will be as correct as any other, so long as the net empirical implications of the theory as a whole are preserved in translation. But it is to be expected that many different ways of translating the component sentences, essentially different individually, would deliver the same empirical implications for the theory as a whole; deviations in the translation of one component sentence could be compensated for in the translation of another component sentence. Insofar, there can be no ground for saying which of two glaringly unlike translations of individual sentences is right.[3]

For an uncritical mentalist, no such indeterminacy threatens. Every term and every sentence is a label attached to an idea, simple or complex, which is stored in the mind. When on the other hand we take a verification theory of meaning seriously, the indeterminacy would appear to be inescapable. The Vienna Circle espoused a verification theory of meaning but did not take it seriously enough. If we recognize with Peirce that the meaning of a sentence turns purely on what would count as evidence for its truth, and if we recognize with Duhem that theoretical sentences have their evidence not as single sentences but only as larger blocks of theory, then the indeterminacy of translation of theoretical sentences is the natural conclusion. And most sentences, apart from observation sentences, are *theoretical*. This conclusion, conversely, once it is embraced, seals the fate of any general notion of propositional meaning or, for that matter, state of affairs.

Should the unwelcomeness of the conclusion persuade us to abandon the verification theory of meaning? Certainly not. The sort of meaning that is basic to translation, and to the learning of one's own language, is necessarily empirical meaning and nothing more. A child learns his first words and sentences by hearing and using them in the presence of appropriate stimuli. These must be external stimuli, for they must

act both on the child and on the speaker from whom he is learning.[4] Language is socially inculcated and controlled; the inculcation and control turn strictly on the keying of sentences to shared stimulation. Internal factors may vary *ad libitum* without prejudice to communication as long as the keying of language to external stimuli is undisturbed. Surely one has no choice but to be an empiricist so far as one's theory of linguistic meaning is concerned.

What I have said of infant learning applies equally to the linguist's learning of a new language in the field. If the linguist does not lean on related languages for which there are previously accepted translation practices, then obviously he has no data but the concomitances of native utterance and observable stimulus situation. No wonder there is indeterminacy of translation—for of course only a small fraction of our utterances report concurrent external stimulation. Granted, the linguist will end up with unequivocal translations of everything; but only by making many arbitrary choices—arbitrary even though unconscious—along the way. Arbitrary? By this I mean that different choices could still have made everything come out right that is susceptible in principle to any kind of check.

Let me link up, in a different order, some of the points I have made. The crucial consideration behind my argument for the indeterminacy of translation was that a statement about the world does not always or usually have a separable fund of empirical consequences that it can call its own. That consideration served also to account for the impossibility of an epistemological reduction of the sort where every sentence is equated to a sentence in observational and logico-mathematical terms. And the impossibility of that sort of epistemological reduction dissipated the last advantage that rational reconstruction seemed to have over psychology.

Philosophers have rightly despaired of translating everything into observational and logico-mathematical terms. They have despaired of this even when they have not recognized, as the reason for this irreducibility, that the statements largely do not have their private bundles of empirical consequences. And some philosophers have seen in this irreducibility the bankruptcy of epistemology. Carnap and the other logical positivists of the Vienna Circle had already pressed the term "metaphysics" into pejorative use, as connoting meaninglessness; and the term "epistemology" was next. Wittgenstein and his followers, mainly at Oxford, found a residual philosophical vocation in therapy: in curing philosophers of the delusion that there were epistemological problems.

But I think that at this point it may be more useful to say rather that epistemology still goes on, though in a new setting and a clarified status. Epistemology, or something like it, simply falls into place as a chapter of psychology and hence of natural science. It studies a natural phenomenon, viz., a physical human subject. This human subject is accorded a certain experimentally controlled input—certain patterns of irradiation in assorted frequencies, for instance—and in the fullness of time the subject delivers as output a description of the three-dimensional external world and its history. The relation between the meager input and the torrential output is a relation that we are prompted to study for somewhat the same reasons that always prompted epistemology; namely, in order to see how evidence relates to theory, and in what ways one's theory of nature transcends any available evidence.

Such a study could still include, even, something like the old rational reconstruction, to whatever degree such reconstruction is practicable; for imaginative constructions can afford hints of actual psychological processes, in much the way that mechanical simulations can. But a conspicuous difference between old epistemology and the epistemological enterprise in this new psychological setting is that we can now make free use of empirical psychology.

The old epistemology aspired to contain, in a sense, natural science; it would construct it somehow from sense data. Epistemology in its new setting, conversely, is contained in natural science, as a chapter of psychology. But the old containment remains valid too, in its way. We are studying how the human subject of our study posits bodies and projects his physics from his data, and we appreciate that our position in the world is just like his. Our very epistemological enterprise, therefore, and the psychology wherein it is a component chapter, and the whole of natural science wherein psychology is a component book—all this is our own construction or projection from stimulations like those we were meting out to our epistemological subject. There is thus reciprocal containment, though containment in different senses: epistemology in natural science and natural science in epistemology.

This interplay is reminiscent again of the old threat of circularity, but it is all right now that we have stopped dreaming deducing science from sense data. We are after an understanding of science as an institution or process in the world, and we do not intend that understanding to be any better than the science which is its object. This attitude is indeed one that Neurath was already urging in Vienna Circle days, with his parable of the mariner who has to rebuild his boat while staying afloat in it.

One effect of seeing epistemology in a psychological setting is that it resolves a stubborn old enigma of epistemological priority. Our retinas are irradiated in two dimensions, yet we see things as three-dimensional without conscious inference Which is to count as observation—the unconscious two-dimensional reception or the conscious three-dimensional apprehension? In the old epistemological context the conscious form had priority, for we were out to justify our knowledge of the external world by rational reconstruction, and that demands awareness. Awareness ceased to be demanded when we gave up trying to justify our knowledge of the external world by rational reconstruction. What to count as observation now can be settled in terms of the stimulation of sensory receptors, let consciousness fall where it may.

The Gestalt psychologists' challenge to sensory atomism which seemed so relevant to epistemology forty years ago, is likewise deactivated. Regardless of whether sensory atoms or Gestalten are what favor the forefront of our consciousness, it is simply the stimulations of our sensory receptors that are best looked upon as the input to our cognitive mechanism. Old paradoxes about unconscious data and inference, old problems about chains of inference that would have to be completed too quickly—these no longer matter.

In the old anti-psychologistic days the question of epistemological priority was moot. What is epistemologically prior to what? Are Gestalten prior to sensory atoms because they are noticed, or should we favor sensory atoms on some more subtle ground? Now that we are permitted to appeal to physical stimulation, the problem dissolves; A is epistemologically prior to B if A is causally nearer than B to the sensory receptors. Or, what is in some ways better, just talk explicitly in terms of causal proximity to sensory receptors and drop the talk of epistemological priority.

Around 1932 there was debate in the Vienna Circle over what to count as observation sentences, or *Protokollsätze*.[5] One position was that they had the form of reports of sense impressions. Another was that they were statements of an elementary sort about the external world, e.g., "A red cube is standing on the table." Another, Neurath's, was that they had the form of reports of relations between percipients and external things: "Otto now sees a red cube on the table." The worst of it was that there seemed to be no objective way of settling the matter: no way of making real sense of the question.

Let us now try to view the matter unreservedly in the context of the external world. Vaguely speaking, what we want of observation sentences is that they be the ones in closest causal proximity to the sensory receptors. But how is such proximity to be gauged? The idea may be rephrased this way: observation sentences are sentences which, as we learn language, are *most strongly conditioned* to concurrent sensory stimulation rather than to stored collateral information. Thus let us imagine a sentence queried for our verdict as to whether it is true or false; queried for our assent or dissent. Then the sentence is an *observation sentence* if our verdict depends only on the sensory stimulation present at the time.

But a verdict cannot depend on present stimulation to the exclusion of stored information. The very fact of our having learned the language evinces much storing of information, of information without which we should be in no position give verdicts on sentences however observational. Evidently then we must relax our definition of observation sentence to read thus: a sentence is an observation sentence if all verdicts on it depend on present sensory stimulation and on no stored information beyond what goes into understanding the sentence.

This formulation raises another problem: how are we to distinguish between information that goes into understanding a sentence and information that goes beyond? This is the problem of distinguishing between analytic truth, which issues from the mere meanings of words, and synthetic truth, which depends on more than meanings. Now I have long maintained that this distinction is illusory. There is one step toward such a distinction, however, which does make sense: a sentence that is true by mere meanings of words should be expected, at least if it is simple, to be subscribed to by all fluent speakers in the community. Perhaps the controversial notion of analyticity can be dispensed with, in our definition of observation sentence, in favor of this straightforward attribute of community-wide acceptance.

This attribute is of course no explication of analyticity. The community would agree that there have been black dogs, yet none who talk of analyticity would call this analytic. My rejection of the analyticity notion just means drawing no line between what goes into the mere understanding of the sentences of a language and what else the community sees eye-to-eye on. I doubt that an objective distinction can be made between meaning and such collateral information as is community-wide.

Turning back then to our task of defining observation sentences, we get this: an observation sentence is one on which all speakers of the language give the same verdict when given the same concurrent stimulation. To put the point negatively, an observation sentence is one that is not sensitive to differences in past experience within the speech community.

This formulation accords perfectly with the traditional role of the observation sentence as the court of appeal of scientific theories. For by our definition the observation sentences are the sentences on which all members of the community will agree under uniform stimulation. And what is the criterion of membership in the same community? Simply general fluency of dialogue. This criterion admits of degrees, and indeed we may usefully take the community more narrowly for some studies than for others. What count as observation sentences for a community of specialists would not always so count for a larger community.

There is generally no subjectivity in the phrasing of observation sentences, as we are now conceiving them; they will usually be about bodies. Since the distinguishing trait of an observation sentence is intersubjective agreement under agreeing stimulation, a corporeal subject matter is likelier than not.

The old tendency to associate observation sentences with a subjective sensory subject matter is rather an irony when we reflect that observation sentences are also meant to be the intersubjective tribunal of scientific hypotheses. The old tendency was due to the drive to base science on something firmer and prior in the subject's experience; but we dropped that project.

The dislodging of epistemology from its old status of first philosophy loosed a wave, we saw, of epistemological nihilism. This mood is reflected somewhat in the tendency of Polányi, Kuhn, and the late Russell Hanson to belittle the role of evidence and to accentuate cultural relativism. Hanson ventured even to discredit the idea of observation, arguing that so-called observations vary from observer to observer with the amount of knowledge that the observers bring with them. The veteran physicist looks at some apparatus and sees an x-ray tube. The neophyte, looking at the same place, observes rather "a glass and metal instrument replete with wires, reflectors, screws, lamps, and pushbuttons."[6] One man's observation is another man's closed book or flight of fancy. The notion of observation as the impartial and objective source of evidence for science is bankrupt. Now my answer to the x-ray example was already hinted a little while back: what counts as an observation sentence varies with the width of community considered. But we can also always get an absolute standard by taking in all speakers of the language, or most.[7] It is ironical that philosophers, finding the old epistemology untenable as a whole, should react by repudiating a part which has only now moved into clear focus.

Clarification of the notion of observation sentence is a good thing, for the notion is fundamental in two connections. These two correspond to the duality that I remarked upon early in this lecture: the duality between concept and doctrine, between knowing what a sentence means and knowing whether it is true. The observation sentence is basic to both enterprises. Its relation to doctrine, to our knowledge of what is true, is very much the traditional one: observation sentences are the repository of evidence for scientific hypotheses. Its relation to meaning is fundamental too, since observation sentences are the ones we are in a position to learn to understand first, both as children and as field linguists. For observation sentences are precisely the ones that we can correlate with observable circumstances of the occasion of utterance or assent, independently of variations in the past histories of individual informants. They afford the only entry to a language.

The observation sentence is the cornerstone of semantics. For it is, as we just saw, fundamental to the learning of meaning. Also, it is where meaning is firmest. Sentences higher up in theories have no empirical consequences they can call their own; they confront the tribunal of sensory evidence only in more or less inclusive aggregates. The observation sentence, situated at the sensory periphery of the body scientific, is the minimal verifiable aggregate; it has an empirical content all its own and wears it on its sleeve.

The predicament of the indeterminacy of translation has little bearing on observation sentences. The equating of an observation sentence of our language to an observation sentence of another language is mostly a matter of empirical generalization; it is a matter of identity between the range of stimulations that would prompt assent to the one sentence and the range of stimulations that would prompt assent to the other.[8]

It is no shock to the preconceptions of old Vienna to say that *epistemology now becomes semantics.* For epistemology remains centered as always on evidence, and meaning remains centered as always on verification; and evidence is verification. What is likelier to shock preconceptions is that meaning, once we get beyond observation sentences, ceases in general to have any clear applicability to single sentences; also that epistemology merges with psychology, as well as with linguistics.

This rubbing out of boundaries could contribute to progress, it seems to me, in philosophically interesting inquiries of a scientific nature. One possible area is perceptual norms. Consider, to begin with, the linguistic phenomenon of phonemes. We form the habit, in hearing the myriad variations of spoken sounds, of treating each as an approximation to one or another of a limited number of norms—around thirty altogether—constituting so to speak a spoken alphabet. All speech in our language can be treated in practice as sequences of just those thirty elements, thus rectifying small deviations. Now outside the realm of language also there is probably only a rather limited alphabet of perceptual norms altogether, toward which we tend unconsciously to rectify all perceptions. These, if experimentally identified, could be taken as epistemological building blocks, the working elements of experience. They might prove in part to be culturally variable, as phonemes are, and in part universal.

Again there is the area that the psychologist Donald T. Campbell calls evolutionary epistemology.[9] In this area there is work by Hüseyin Yilmaz, who shows how some structural traits of color perception could have been predicted from survival value.[10] And a more emphatically epistemological topic that evolution helps to clarify is induction, now that we are allowing epistemology the resources of natural science.[11]

Notes

1. A. B. Johnson, *A Treatise on Language* (New York, 1836; Berkeley, 1947).
2. *Philosophy of Science* 3 (1936), 419–471; 4 (1937), 1–40.
3. See above, p. 2 ff.
4. See above, p. 28.
5. Carnap and Neurath in *Erkenntnis* 3 (1932), 204–228.
6. N. R. Hanson, "Observation and interpretation," in S. Morgenbesser ed., *Philosophy of Science Today* (New York: Basic Books, 1966).
7. This qualification allows for occasional deviants such as the insane or the blind. Alternatively, such cases might be excluded by adjusting the level of fluency of dialogue whereby we define sameness of language. (For prompting this note and influencing the development of this paper also in more substantial ways I am indebted to Burton Dreben.)
8. Cf. Quine, *Word and Object*, pp. 31–46, 68.
9. D. T. Campbell, "Methodological suggestions from a comparative psychology of knowledge processes," *Inquiry* 2 (1959), 152–182.
10. Hüseyin Yilmaz, "On color vision and a new approach to general perception," in E. E. Bernard and M. R. Kare, eds., *Biological Prototypes and Synthetic Systems* (New York: Plenum, 1962); "Perceptual invariance and the psychophysical law," *Perception and Psychophysics* 2 (1967), 533–538.
11. See "Natural Kinds," Chapter 5 in this volume.

✧ RESERVATIONS ✧

36. WHAT IS "NATURALIZED EPISTEMOLOGY?"

Jaegwon Kim

Epistemology As a Normative Inquiry

Descartes' epistemological inquiry in the *Meditations* begins with this question: What propositions are worthy of belief? In the *First Meditation* Descartes canvasses beliefs of various kinds he had formerly held as true and finds himself forced to conclude that he ought to reject them, that he ought not to accept them as true. We can view Cartesian epistemology as consisting of the following two projects: to identify the criteria by which we ought to regulate acceptance and rejection of beliefs, and to determine what we may be said to know according to those criteria. Descartes' epistemological agenda has been the agenda of Western epistemology to this day. The twin problems of identifying criteria of justified belief and coming to terms with the skeptical challenge to the possibility of knowledge have defined the central tasks of theory of knowledge since Descartes. This was as true of the empiricists, of Locke and Hume and Mill, as of those who more closely followed Descartes in the rationalist path.[1]

It is no wonder then that modern epistemology has been dominated by a single concept, that of *justification*, and two fundamental questions involving it: What conditions must a belief meet if we are justified in accepting it as true? and What beliefs are we in fact justified in accepting? Note that the first question does not ask for an "analysis" or "meaning" of the term "justified belief". And it is generally assumed, even if not always explicitly stated, that not just any statement of a necessary and sufficient condition for a belief to be justified will do. The implicit requirement has been that the stated conditions must constitute "criteria" of justified belief, and for this it is necessary that the conditions be stated *without the use of epistemic terms*. Thus, formulating conditions of justified belief in such terms as "adequate evidence", "sufficient ground", "good reason", "beyond a reasonable doubt", and so on, would be merely to issue a promissory note redeemable only when these epistemic terms are themselves explained in a way that accords with the requirement.[2]

This requirement, while it points in the right direction, does not go far enough. What is crucial is this: *the criteria of justified belief must be formulated on the basis of descriptive or naturalistic terms alone, without the use of any evaluative or normative ones, whether epistemic or of another kind.*[3] Thus, an analysis of justified belief that makes use of such terms as "intellectual requirement"[4] and "having a right to be sure"[5] would not satisfy this generalized condition; although such an analysis can be informative and enlightening about the inter-relationships of these normative concepts, it will not, on the present conception, count as a statement of *criteria* of justified belief, unless of course these terms are themselves provided with nonnormative criteria. What is problematic, therefore, about the use of epistemic terms in stating criteria of justified belief is not its possible circularity in the usual sense; rather it is the fact that these epistemic terms are themselves essentially normative. We shall later discuss the rationale of this strengthened requirement.

As many philosophers have observed,[6] the two questions we have set forth, one about the criteria of justified belief and the other about what we can be said to know according to those criteria, constrain

each other. Although some philosophers have been willing to swallow skepticism just because what we regard as correct criteria of justified belief are seen to lead inexorably to the conclusion that none, or very few, of our beliefs are justified, the usual presumption is that our answer to the first question should leave our epistemic situation largely unchanged. That is to say, it is expected to turn out that according to the criteria of justified belief we come to accept, we know, or are justified in believing, pretty much what we reflectively think we know or are entitled to believe.

Whatever the exact history, it is evident that the concept of justification has come to take center stage in our reflections on the nature our preoccupation with justification: it is the only specifically epistemic component in the classic tripartite conception of knowledge. Neither belief nor truth is a specifically epistemic notion: belief is a psychological concept and truth a semantical-metaphysical one. These concepts may have an implicit epistemological dimension, but if they do, it is likely to be through their involvement with essentially normative epistemic notions like justification, evidence, and rationality. Moreover, justification is what makes knowledge itself a normative concept. On surface at least, neither truth nor belief is normative or evaluative (I shall argue below, though, that belief does have an essential normative dimension). But justification manifestly is normative. If a belief is justified for us, then it is *permissible* and *reasonable*, from the epistemic point of view, for us to hold it, and it would be *epistemically irresponsible* to hold beliefs that contradict it. If we consider believing or accepting a proposition to be an "action" in an appropriate sense, belief justification would then be a special case of justification of action, which in its broadest terms is the central concern of normative ethics. Just as it is the business of normative ethics to delineate the conditions under which acts and decisions are justified from the moral point of view, so it is the business of epistemology to identify and analyze the conditions under which beliefs, and perhaps other propositional attitudes, are justified from the epistemological point of view. It probably is only an historical accident that we standardly speak of "normative ethics" but not of "normative epistemology". Epistemology is a normative discipline as much as, and in the same sense as, normative ethics.

We can summarize our discussion thus far in the following points: that justification is a central concept of our epistemological tradition, that justification, as it is understood in this tradition, is a normative concept, and in consequence that epistemology itself is a normative inquiry whose principal aim is a systematic study of the conditions of justified belief. I take it that these points are uncontroversial, although of course there could be disagreement about the details—for example, about what it means to say a concept or theory is "normative" or "evaluative".

The Foundationalist Strategy

In order to identify the target of the naturalistic critique—in particular, Quine's—it will be useful to take a brief look at the classic response to the epistemological program set forth by Descartes. Descartes' approach to the problem of justification is a familiar story, at least as the textbook tells it: it takes the form of what is now commonly called "foundationalism". The foundationalist strategy is to divide the task of explaining justification into two stages: first, to identify a set of beliefs that are "directly" justified in that they are justified without deriving their justified status from that of any other belief and then to explain how other beliefs may be "indirectly" or "inferentially" justified by standing in an appropriate relation to those already justified. Directly justified beliefs, or "basic beliefs", are to constitute the foundation upon which the superstructure of "nonbasic" or "derived" beliefs is to rest. What beliefs then are directly justified, according to Descartes? Subtleties aside, he claimed that beliefs about our own present conscious states are among them. In what does their justification consist? What is it about these beliefs that make them directly justified? Somewhat simplistically again, Descartes' answer is that they are justified because they are *indubitable*, that the attentive and reflective mind *cannot but assent to them*. How are nonbasic beliefs justified? By "deduction"—that is, by a series of inferential steps, or "intuitions", each of which is indubitable. If, therefore, we take Cartesian indubitability as a psychological notion, Descartes' epistemological theory can be said to meet the desideratum of providing nonepistemic, naturalistic criteria of justified belief.

Descartes' foundationalist program was inherited, in its essential outlines, by the empiricists. In particular, his "mentalism", that beliefs about one's own current mental state are epistemologically basic, went essentially unchallenged by the empiricists and positivists, until this century. Epistemologists have differed from one another chiefly in regard to two questions: first, what else belonged in our corpus of basic beliefs, and second, how the derivation of the nonbasic part of our knowledge was to proceed. Even the Logical Positivists were, by and large, foundationalists, although some of them came to renounce Cartesian mentalism in favor of a "physicalistic basis".[7] In fact, the Positivists were foundationalists twice over: for them "observation", whether phenomenological or physical, served not only as the foundation of knowledge but as the foundation of all "cognitive meaning"—that is, as both an epistemological and a semantic foundation.

Quine's Arguments

It has become customary for epistemologists who profess allegiance to a "naturalistic" conception of knowledge to pay homage to Quine as the chief contemporary provenance of their inspiration—especially to his influential paper "Epistemology Naturalized".[8] Quine's principal argument in this paper against traditional epistemology is based on the claim that the Cartesian foundationalist program has failed—that the Cartesian "quest for certainty" is "a lost cause". While this claim about the hopelessness of the Cartesian "quest for certainty" is nothing new, using it to discredit the very conception of normative epistemology is new, something that any serious student of epistemology must contend with.

Quine divides the classic epistemological program into two parts: *conceptual reduction* whereby physical terms, including those of theoretical science, are reduced, via definition, to terms referring to phenomenal features of sensory experience, and *doctrinal reduction* whereby truths about the physical world are appropriately obtained from truths about sensory experience. The "appropriateness" just alluded to refers to the requirement that the favored epistemic status ("certainty" for classic epistemologists, according to Quine) of our basic beliefs be transferred, essentially undiminished, to derived beliefs, a necessary requirement if the derivational process is to yield knowledge from knowledge. What derivational methods have this property of preserving epistemic status? Perhaps there are none, given our proneness to err in framing derivations as in anything else, not to mention the possibility of lapses of attention and memory in following lengthy proofs. But logical deduction comes as close to being one as any; it can at least be relied on to transmit truth, if not epistemic status. It could perhaps be argued that no method can preserve certainty unless it preserves (or is known to preserve) truth; and if this is so, logical deduction is the only method worth considering. I do not know whether this was the attitude of most classic epistemologists; but Quine assumes that if deduction doesn't fill their bill, nothing will.

Quine sees the project of conceptual reduction as culminating in Carnap's *Der Logische Aufbau der Welt*. As Quine sees it, Carnap "came nearest to executing" the conceptual half of the classic epistemological project. But coming close is not good enough. Because of the holistic manner in which empirical meaning is generated by experience, no reduction of the sort Carnap and others so eagerly sought could in principle be completed. For definitional reduction requires point-to-point meaning relations[9] between physical terms and phenomenal terms, something that Quine's holism tells us cannot be had. The second half of the program, doctrinal reduction, is in no better shape; in fact, it was the one to stumble first, for, according to Quine, its impossibility was decisively demonstrated long before the *Aufbau*, by Hume in his celebrated discussion of induction. The "Humean predicament" shows that theory cannot be logically deduced from observation; there simply is no way of deriving theory from observation that will transmit the latter's epistemic status intact to the former.

I don't think anyone wants to disagree with Quine in these claims. It is not possible to "validate" science on the basis of sensory experience, if "validation" means justification through logical deduction. Quine of course does not deny that our theories depend on observation for evidential support; he has said that sensory evidence is the only evidence there is. To be sure, Quine's argument against the possibility of conceptual reduction has a new twist: the application of his "holism". But his conclusion is no surprise; "translational phenomenalism" has been moribund for many

years.[10] And, as Quine himself notes, his argument against the doctrinal reduction, the "quest for certainty", is only a restatement of Hume's "skeptical" conclusions concerning induction: induction after all is not deduction. Most of us are inclined, I think, to view the situation Quine describes with no great alarm, and I rather doubt that these conclusions of Quine's came as news to most epistemologists when "Epistemology Naturalized" was first published. We are tempted to respond: of course we can't define physical concepts in terms of sense-data; of course observation "underdetermines" theory. That is why observation is observation and not theory.

So it is agreed on all hands that the classical epistemological project, conceived as one of deductively validating physical knowledge from indubitable sensory data, cannot succeed. But what is the moral of this failure? What should be its philosophical lesson to us? Having noted the failure of the Cartesian program, Quine goes on:[11]

> The stimulation of his sensory receptors is all the evidence anybody has had to go on, ultimately in arriving at his picture of the world. Why not Just see how this construction really proceeds? Why not settle for psychology? Such a surrender of the epistemological burden to psychology is a move that was disallowed in earlier times as circular reasoning. If the epistemologist's goal is validation of the grounds of empirical science, he defeats his purpose by using psychology or other empirical science in the validation. However, such scruples against circularity have little point once we have stopped dreaming of deducing science from observation. If we are out simply to understand the link between observation and science, we are well advised to use any available information, including that provided by the very science whose link with observation we are seeking to understand.

And Quine has the following to say about the failure of Carnap's reductive program in the *Aufbau*.[12]

> To relax the demand for definition, and settle for a kind of reduction that does not eliminate, is to renounce the last remaining advantage that we

supposed rational reconstruction to have over straight psychology; namely, the advantage of translational reduction. If all we hope for is a reconstruction that links science to experience in explicit ways short of translation, then it would seem more sensible to settle for psychology. Better to discover how science is in fact developed and learned than to fabricate a fictitious structure to a similar effect.

If a task is entirely hopeless, if we know it cannot be executed, no doubt it is rational to abandon it; we would be better off doing something else that has some hope of success. We can agree with Quine that the "validation"—that is, logical deduction—of science on the basis of observation cannot be had; so it is rational to abandon this particular epistemological program, if indeed it ever was a program that anyone seriously undertook. But Quine's recommendations go further. In particular, there are two aspects of Quine's proposals that are of special interest to us: first, he is not only advising us to quit the program of "validating science", but urging us to take up another specific project, an empirical psychological study of our cognitive processes; second, he is also claiming that this new program replaces the old, that both programs are part of something appropriately called "epistemology". Naturalized epistemology is to be a kind of epistemology after all, a "successor subject"[13] to classical epistemology.

How should we react to Quine's urgings? What should be our response? The Cartesian project of validating science starting from the indubitable foundation of first-person psychological reports (perhaps with the help of certain indubitable first principles) is not the whole of classical epistemology—or so it would seem at first blush. In our characterization of classical epistemology, the Cartesian program was seen as one possible response to the problem of epistemic justification, the two-part project of identifying the criteria of epistemic justification and determining what beliefs are in fact justified according to those criteria. In urging "naturalized epistemology" on us, Quine is not suggesting that we give up the Cartesian foundationalist solution and explore others within the same framework[14]—perhaps, to adopt some sort of "coherentist" strategy, or to require of our basic beliefs only some degree of "initial credibility" rather

than Cartesian certainty, or to permit some sort of probabilistic derivation in addition to deductive derivation of nonbasic knowledge, or to consider the use of special rules of evidence, like Chisholm's "principles of evidence",[15] or to give up the search for a derivational process that transmits undiminished certainty in favor of one that can transmit diminished but still useful degrees of justification. Quine's proposal is more radical than that. He is asking us to set aside the entire framework of justification-centered epistemology. That is what is new in Quine's proposals. Quine is asking us to put in its place a purely descriptive, causal-nomological science of human cognition.[16]

How should we characterize in general terms the difference between traditional epistemological programs, such as foundationalism and coherence theory, on the one hand and Quine's program of naturalized epistemology on the other? Quine's stress is on the *factual* and *descriptive* character of his program; he says. "Why not see how [the construction of theory from observation *actually proceeds*? Why not settle for psychology?";[17] again, "Better to *discover how science is in fact developed and learned than.*][18] We are given to understand that in contrast traditional epistemology is not a descriptive, factual inquiry. Rather, it is an attempt at a "validation" or "rational reconstruction" of science. Validation, according to Quine, proceeds via deduction, and rational reconstruction via definition. However, their *point* is justificatory—that is, to rationalize our sundry knowledge claims. So Quine is asking us to set aside what is "rational" in rational reconstruction.

Thus, it is normativity that Quine is asking us to repudiate. Although Quine does not explicitly characterize traditional epistemology as "normative" or "prescriptive", his meaning is unmistakable. Epistemology is to be "a chapter of psychology", a law-based predictive-explanatory theory, like any other theory within empirical science; its principal job is to see how human cognizers develop theories (their "picture of the world") from observation ("the stimulation of their sensory receptors"). Epistemology is to go out of the business of justification. We earlier characterized traditional epistemology as essentially normative; we see why Quine wants us to reject it. Quine is urging us to replace a normative theory of cognition with a descriptive science.

Losing Knowledge from Epistemology

If justification drops out of epistemology, knowledge itself drops out of epistemology. For our concept of knowledge is inseparably tied to that of justification. As earlier noted, knowledge itself is a normative notion. Quine's nonnormative, naturalized epistemology has no room for our concept of knowledge. It is not surprising that, in describing naturalized epistemology. Quine seldom talks about knowledge; instead, he talks about "science" and "theories" and "representations". Quine would have us investigate how sensory stimulation "leads" to "theories" and "representation" of the world. I take it that within the traditional scheme these "theories" and "representations" correspond to beliefs, or systems of beliefs; thus, what Quine would have us do is to investigate how sensory stimulation leads to the formation of beliefs about the world.

But in what sense of "lead"? I take it that Quine has in mind a causal or nomological sense. He is urging us to develop a theory, an empirical theory, that uncovers lawful regularities governing the processes through which organisms come to develop beliefs about their environment as a causal result of having their sensory receptors stimulated in certain ways. Quine says:[19]

> [Naturalized epistemology] studies a natural phenomenon, viz., a physical human subject. This human subject is accorded experimentally controlled input—certain patterns of irradiation in assorted frequencies, for instance—and in the fullness of time the subject delivers as output a description of the three-dimensional external world and its history. *The relation between the meager input and torrential output* is a relation that we are prompted to study for somewhat the same reasons that always prompted epistemology; namely, in order to see *how evidence relates to theory*, and in what ways one's theory of nature transcends any available evidence.

The relation Quine speaks of between "meager input" and "torrential output" is a causal relation; at least it is qua causal relation that the naturalized epistemologist investigates it. It is none of the naturalized epistemologist's business to assess whether, and to what degree, the input "justifies" the output, how a given irradiation of the subject's retinas makes it "reasonable" or "rational" for the subject to emit certain representational output. His interest is strictly causal and nomological: he wants us to look for patterns of lawlike dependencies characterizing the input-output relations for this particular organism and others of a like physical structure.

If this is right, it makes Quine's attempt to relate his naturalized epistemology to traditional epistemology look at best lame. For in what sense is the study of causal relationships between physical stimulation of sensory receptors and the resulting cognitive output a way of "seeing how evidence relates to theory" in an epistemologically relevant sense? The causal relation between sensory input and cognitive output is a relation between "evidence" and "theory"; however, it is not an *evidential relation*. This can be seen from the following consideration: the nomological patterns that Quine urges us to look for are certain to vary from species to species, depending on the particular way each biological (and possibly nonbiological) species processes information, but the evidential relation in its proper normative sense must abstract from such factors and concern itself only with the degree to which evidence supports hypothesis.

In any event, the concept of evidence is inseparable from that of justification. When we talk of "evidence" in an epistemological sense we are talking about justification: one thing is "evidence" for another just in case the first tends to enhance the reasonableness or justification of the second. And such evidential relations hold in part because of the "contents" of the items involved, not merely because of the causal or nomological connections between them. A strictly nonnormative concept of evidence is not our concept of evidence; it is something that we do not understand.[20]

None of us, I think, would want to quarrel with Quine about the interest or importance of the psychological study of how our sensory input causes our epistemic output. This is only to say that the study of human (or other kinds of) cognition is of interest. That isn't our difficulty; our difficulty is whether, and in what sense pursuing Quine's "epistemology" is a way of doing epistemology—that is, a way of studying "how evidence relates to theory". Perhaps, Quine's recommendation that we discard justification-centered epistemology is worth pondering; and his exhortation to take up the study of psychology perhaps deserves to be heeded also. What is mysterious is why this recommendation has to be coupled with the rejection of normative epistemology (if normative epistemology is not a possible inquiry, why shouldn't the would-be epistemologist turn to, say, hydrodynamics or ornithology rather than psychology?). But of course Quine is saying more; he is saying that an understandable, it misguided, motivation (that is, seeing "how evidence relates to theory") does underlie our proclivities for indulgence in normative epistemology, but that we would be better served by a scientific study of human cognition than normative epistemology.

But it is difficult to see how an "epistemology" that has been purged of normativity, one that lacks an appropriate normative concept of justification or evidence, can have anything to do with the concerns of traditional epistemology. And unless naturalized epistemology and classical epistemology share some of their central concerns, it's difficult to see how one could *replace* the other, or be a way (a better way) of doing the other.[21] To be sure, they both investigate "how evidence relates to theory". But putting the matter this way can be misleading, and has perhaps misled Quine: the two disciplines do not investigate the same relation. As lately noted, normative epistemology is concerned with the evidential relation properly so-called—that is, the relation of justification—and Quine's naturalized epistemology is meant to study the causal-nomological relation. For epistemology to go out of the business of justification is for it to go out of business.

Belief Attribution and Rationality

Perhaps we have said enough to persuade ourselves that Quine's naturalized epistemology, while it may be a legitimate scientific inquiry, is not a kind of epistemology, and, therefore, that the question whether it is a better kind of epistemology cannot arise. In reply, however, it might be said that there was a sense in which Quine's epistemology and traditional epistemology could be viewed as sharing a common subject matter, namely this: they both concern beliefs or "representations". The only difference is that the former investigates their causal histories

and connections whereas the latter is concerned with their evidential or justificatory properties and relations. This difference, if Quine is right, leads to another (so continues the reply): the former is a feasible inquiry, the latter is not.

I now want to take my argument a step further: I shall argue that the concept of belief is itself an essentially normative one, and in consequence that if normativity is wholly excluded from naturalized epistemology it cannot even be though of as being about beliefs. That is, if naturalized epistemology is to be a science of beliefs properly so called, it must presuppose a normative concept of belief.

Briefly, the argument is this. In order to implement Quine's program of naturalized epistemology, we shall need to identify, and individuate, the input and output of cognizers. The input, for Quine, consists of physical events ("the stimulation of sensory receptors") and the output is said to be a "theory" or "picture of the world"—that is, a set of "representations" of the cognizer's environment. Let us focus on the output. In order to study the sensory input-cognitive output relations for the given cognizer, therefore, we must find out what "representations" he has formed as a result of the particular stimulations that have been applied to his sensory transducers. Setting aside the jargon, what we need to be able to do is to attribute *beliefs*, and other contentful intentional states, to the cognizer. But belief attribution ultimately requires a "radical interpretation" of the cognizer, of his speech and intentional states; that is, we must construct an "interpretive theory" that simultaneously assigns meanings to his utterances and attributes to him beliefs and other propositional attitudes.[22]

Even a cursory consideration indicates that such an interpretation cannot begin—we cannot get a foothold in our subject's realm of meanings and intentional states—unless we assume his total system of beliefs and other propositional attitudes to be largely and essentially rational and coherent. As Davidson has emphasized, a given belief has the content it has in part because of its location in a network of other beliefs and propositional attitudes; and what at bottom grounds this network is the evidential relation, a relation that regulates what is reasonable to believe given other beliefs one holds. That is, unless our cognizer is a "rational being", a being whose cognitive "output" is regulated and constrained by norms of rationality—typically, these norms holistically constrain his propositional attitudes in virtue of their contents—we cannot intelligibly interpret his "output" as consisting of beliefs. Conversely, if we are unable to interpret our subject's meanings and propositional attitudes in a way that satisfies a minimal standard of rationality, there is little reason to regard him as a "cognizer", a being that forms representations and constructs theories. This means that there is a sense of "rational" in which the expression "rational belief" is redundant; every belief must be rational in certain minimal ways. It is not important for the purposes of the present argument what these minimal standards of rationality are; the only point that matters is that unless the output of our cognizer is subject to evaluation in accordance with norms of rationality, that output cannot be considered as consisting of beliefs and hence cannot be the object of an epistemological inquiry, whether plain or naturalized.

We can separate the core of these considerations from controversial issues involving the so-called "principle of charity", minimal rationality, and other matters in the theory of radical interpretation. What is crucial is this: for the interpretation and attribution of beliefs to be possible, not only must we assume the overall rationality of cognizers, but also we must continually evaluate and re-evaluate the putative beliefs of a cognizer in their evidential relationship to one another and other propositional attitudes. It is not merely that belief attribution requires the umbrella assumption about the overall rationality of cognizers. Rather, the point is that *belief attribution requires belief evaluation*, in accordance with normative standards of evidence and justification. If this is correct, rationality in its broad and fundamental sense is not an optional property of beliefs, a virtue that some beliefs may enjoy and others lack; it is a precondition of the attribution and individuation of belief—that is, a property without which the concept of belief would be unintelligible and pointless.

Two objections might be raised to counter these considerations. First, one might argue that at best they show only that the normativity of belief is an epistemological assumption—that we need to assume the rationality and coherence of belief systems when we are

trying to *find out* what beliefs to attribute to a cognizer. It does not follow from this epistemological point, the objection continues, that the concept of belief is itself normative.[23] In replying to this objection, we can bypass the entire issue of whether the rationality assumption concerns only the epistemology of belief attribution. Even if this premise (which I think is incorrect) is granted, the point has already been made. For it is an essential part of the business of naturalized epistemology, as a theory of how beliefs are formed as a result of sensory stimulation, to *find out* what particular beliefs the given cognizers have formed. But this is precisely what cannot be done, if our considerations show anything at all, unless the would-be naturalized epistemologist continually evaluates the putative beliefs of his subjects in regard to their rationality and coherence, subject to the overall constraint of the assumption that the cognizers are largely rational. The naturalized epistemologist cannot dispense with normative concepts or disengage himself from valuational activities.

Second, it might be thought that we could simply avoid these considerations stemming from belief attribution by refusing to think of cognitive output as consisting of "beliefs", namely as states having propositional contents. The "representations" Quine speaks of should be taken as appropriate neural states, and this means that all we need is to be able to discern neural states of organisms. This requires only neurophysiology and the like, not the normative theory of rational belief. My reply takes the form of a dilemma: either the "appropriate" neural states are identified by seeing how they correlate with beliefs[24] in which case we still need to contend with the problem of radical interpretation, or beliefs are entirely by-passed. In the latter case, belief, along with justification, drops out of Quinean epistemology, and it is unclear in what sense we are left with an inquiry that has anything to do with knowledge.[25]

The "Psychologistic" Approach to Epistemology

Many philosophers now working in theory of knowledge have stressed the importance of systematic psychology to philosophical epistemology. Reasons proffered for this are various, and so are the conceptions of the proper relationship between psychology and epistemology.[26] But they are virtually unanimous in their rejection of what they take to be the epistemological tradition of Descartes and its modern embodiments in philosophers like Russell, C. I. Lewis, Roderick Chisholm, and A. J. Ayer; and they are united in their endorsement the naturalistic approach of Quine we have been considering. Traditional epistemology is often condemned as "aprioristic", and as having lost sight of human knowledge as a product of natural causal processes and its function in the survival of the organism and the species. Sometimes, the adherents of the traditional approach are taken to task for their implicit antiscientific bias or indifference to the new developments in psychology and related disciplines. Their own approach in contrast is hailed as "naturalistic" and "scientific", better attuned to significant advances in the relevant scientific fields such as "cognitive science" and "neuroscience", promising philosophical returns far richer than what the aprioristic method of traditional epistemology has been able to deliver. We shall here briefly consider how this new naturalism in epistemology is to be understood in relation to the classic epistemological program and Quine's naturalized epistemology.

Let us see how one articulate proponent of the new approach explains the distinctiveness of his position vis-à-vis that of the traditional epistemologists. According to Philip Kitcher, the approach he rejects is characterized by an "apsychologistic" attitude that takes the difference between knowledge and true belief—that is, justification—to consist in "ways which are independent of the causal antecedents of a subject's states".[27] Kitcher writes:[28]

> . . . we can present the heart of [the apsychologistic approach] by considering the way in which it would tackle the question of whether a person's true belief that p counts as knowledge that p. The idea would be to disregard the psychological life of the subject, looking just at the various propositions she believes. If p is 'connected in the right way' to other propositions which are believed, then we count the subject as knowing that p. Of course, apsychologisitc epistemology

will have to supply a criterion for propositions to be 'connected in the right way' . . . but proponents of this view of knowledge will emphasize that the criterion is to be given in *logical* terms. We are concerned with logical relations among propositions, not with psychological relations among mental states.

On the other hand, the psychologistic approach considers the crucial difference between knowledge and true belief—that is, epistemic justification—to turn on "the factors which produced the belief", focusing on "processes which produce belief, processes which will always contain, at their latter end, psychological events."[29]

It is not entirely clear from this characterization whether a psychologistic theory of justification is to be *prohibited* from making *any* reference to logical relations among belief contents (It is difficult to believe how a theory of justification respecting such a blanket prohibition could succeed); nor is it clear whether, conversely, an apsychologistic theory will be permitted to refer at all to beliefs qua psychological states, or exactly what it is for a theory to do so. But such points of detail are unimportant here; it is clear enough, for example, that Goldman's proposal to explicate justified belief as belief generated by a reliable belief-forming process[30] nicely fits Kitcher's characterization of the psychologistic approach. This account, one form of the so-called "reliability theory" of justification, probably was what Kitcher had in mind when he was formulating his general characterization of epistemological naturalism. However, another influential form of the reliability theory does not qualify under Kitcher's characterization. This is Armstrong's proposal to explain the difference between knowledge and true belief, at least for noninferential knowledge, in terms of "*a law-like connection* between the state of affairs [of a subject's believing that p] and the state of affairs that makes 'p' true such that, given the state of affairs [of the subject's believing that p], it must be the case that p.[31] There is here no reference to the causal *antecedents* of beliefs, something that Kitcher requires of apsychologistic theories.

Perhaps, Kitcher's preliminary characterization needs to be broadened and sharpened. However, a salient characteristic of the naturalistic approach has already emerged, which we can put as follows: justification is to be characterized in terms of *causal* or *nomological* connections involving beliefs as *psychological states* or *processes*, and not in terms of the *logical* properties or relations pertaining to the *contents* of these beliefs.[32]

If we understand current epistemological naturalism in this way, how closely is it related to Quine's conception of naturalized epistemology? The answer, I think, is obvious: not very closely at all. In fact, it seems a good deal closer to the Cartesian tradition than to Quine. For, as we saw, the difference that matters between Quine's epistemological program and the traditional program is the former's total renouncement of the latter's normativity, its rejection of epistemology as a normative inquiry. The talk of "replacing" epistemology with psychology is irrelevant and at best misleading, though it could give us a momentary relief from a sense of deprivation. When one abandons justification and other valuational concepts, one abandons the entire framework of normative epistemology. What remains is a descriptive empirical theory of human cognition which, if Quine has his way, will be entirely devoid of the notion of justification or any other evaluative concept.

As I take it, this is not what most advocates of epistemological naturalism are aiming at. By and large they are not Quinean eliminativists in regard to justification, and justification in its full-fledged normative sense continues to play a central role in their epistemological reflections. Where they differ from their nonnaturalist adversaries is the specific way in which criteria of justification are to be formulated. Naturalists and nonnaturalists ("apsychologists") can agree that these criteria must be stated in descriptive terms—that is, without the use of epistemic or any other kind of normative terms. According to Kitcher, an apsychologistic theory of justification would state them primarily in terms of *logical* properties and relations holding for propositional contents of beliefs, whereas the psychologistic approach advocates the exclusive use of *causal* properties and relations holding for beliefs as events or states. Many traditional epistemologists may prefer criteria that confer upon a cognizer a position of special privilege and responsibility with regard to the epistemic status of his beliefs, whereas most self-avowed

naturalists prefer "objective" or "externalist" criteria with no such special privileges for the cognizer. But these differences are among those that arise within the familiar normative framework, and are consistent with the exclusion of normative terms in the statement of the criteria of justification.

Normative ethics can serve as a useful model here. To claim that basic ethical terms, like "good" and "right", are *definable* on the basis of descriptive or naturalistic terms is one thing; to insist that it is the business of normative ethics to provide *conditions* or *criteria* for "good" and "right" in descriptive or naturalistic terms is another. One may properly reject the former, the so-called "ethical naturalism", as many moral philosophers have done, and hold the latter; there is no obvious inconsistency here. G. E. Moore is a philosopher who did just that. As is well known, he was a powerful critic of ethical naturalism, holding that goodness is a "simple" and "nonnatural" property. At the same time, he held that a thing's being good "follows" from its possessing certain naturalistic properties. He wrote:[33]

> I should never have thought of suggesting that goodness was 'non-natural', unless I had supposed that it was 'derivative' in the sense that, whenever a thing is good (in the sense in question) its goodness. . . 'depends on the presence of certain non-ethical characteristics' possessed by the thing in question: I have always supposed that it did so 'depend', in the sense that, if a thing is good (in my sense), then that it is so *follows* from the fact that it possesses certain natural intrinsic properties. . .

It makes sense to think of these "natural intrinsic properties" from which a thing's being good is thought to follow as constituting naturalistic criteria of goodness, or at least pointing to the existence of such criteria. One can reject ethical naturalism, the doctrine that ethical concepts are definitionally eliminable in favor of naturalistic terms, and at the same time hold that ethical properties, or the ascription of ethical terms, must be governed by naturalistic criteria. It is clear, then, that we are here using "naturalism" ambiguously in "epistemological naturalism" and "ethical naturalism". In our present usage, epistemological naturalism does not include (nor does it necessarily exclude) the claim that epistemic terms are definitionally reducible to naturalistic terms. (Quine's naturalism is eliminative, though it is not a definitional eliminativism.)

If, therefore, we locate the split between Quine and traditional epistemology at the descriptive vs. normative divide, then currently influential naturalism in epistemology is not likely to fall on Quine's side. On this descriptive vs. normative issue, one can side with Quine in one of two ways: first, one rejects, with Quine, the entire justification-based epistemological program; or second, like ethical naturalists but unlike Quine, one believes that epistemic concepts are naturalistically definable. I doubt that very many epistemological naturalists will embrace either of these alternatives.[34]

Epistemic Supervenience—Or Why Normative Epistemology Is Possible

But why should we think that there *must* be naturalistic criteria of justified belief and other terms of epistemic appraisal? If we take the discovery and systematization of such criteria to be the central task of normative epistemology, is there any reason to think that this task can be fruitfully pursued, that normative epistemology is a possible field of inquiry? Quine's point is that it is not. We have already noted the limitation of Quine's negative arguments in "Epistemology Naturalized", but is there a positive reason for thinking that normative epistemology is a viable program? One could consider a similar question about the possibility of normative ethics.

I think there is a short and plausible initial answer, although a detailed defense of it would involve complex general issues about norms and values. The short answer is this: we believe in the supervenience of epistemic properties on naturalistic ones, and more generally, in the supervenience of all valuational and normative properties on naturalistic conditions. This comes out in various ways. We think, with R.M. Hare,[35] that if two persons or acts coincide in all descriptive or naturalistic details, they cannot differ in respect of being good or right, or any other valuational aspects. We also think that if something is "good"—a "good car", "good drop shot", "good argument"—then that must be

so "in virtue of" its being a "certain way", that is, its having certain "factual properties". Being a good car, say, cannot be a brute and ultimate fact: a car is good *because* it has a certain contextually indicated set of properties having to do with performance, reliability, comfort, styling, economy, etc. The same goes for justified belief: if a belief is justified, that must be so *because* it has certain factual, nonepistemic properties, such as perhaps that it is "indubitable", that it is seen to be entailed by another belief that is independently justified, that it is appropriately caused by perceptual experience, or whatever. That it is a justified belief cannot be a brute fundamental fact unrelated to the kind of belief it is. There must be a *reason* for it, and this reason must be grounded in the factual descriptive properties of that particular belief. Something like this, I think, is what we believe.

Two important themes underlie these convictions: first, values, though perhaps not reducible to facts, must be "consistent" with them in that objects that are indiscernible in regard to fact must be indiscernible in regard to value; second, there must be nonvaluational "reasons" or "grounds" for the attribution of values, and these "reasons" or "grounds" must be *generalizable*—that is, they are covered by *rules* or *norms*. These two ideas correspond to "weak supervenience" and "strong supervenience" that I have discussed elsewhere.[36] Belief in the supervenience of value upon fact, arguably, is fundamental to the very concepts of value and valuation.[37] Any valuational concept, to be significant, must be governed by a set of criteria, and these criteria must ultimately rest on factual characteristics and relationships of objects and events being evaluated. There is something deeply incoherent about the idea of an infinitely descending series of valuational concepts, each depending on the one below it as its criterion of application.[38]

It seems to me, therefore, that epistemological supervenience is what underlies our belief in the possibility of normative epistemology, and that we do not need new inspirations from the sciences to acknowledge the existence of naturalistic criteria for epistemic and other valuational concepts. The case of normative ethics is entirely parallel: belief in the possibility of normative ethics is rooted in the belief that moral properties and relations are supervenient upon nonmoral ones. Unless we are prepared to disown normative ethics as a viable philosophical inquiry, we had better recognize normative epistemology as one, too.[39] We should note, too, that epistemology is likely to parallel normative ethics in regard to the degree to which scientific results are relevant or useful to its development.[40] Saying this of course leaves large room for disagreement concerning how relevant and useful, if at all, empirical psychology of human motivation and action can be to the development and confirmation of normative ethical theories.[41] In any event, once the normativity of epistemology is clearly taken note of, it is no surprise that epistemology and normative ethics share the same metaphilosophical fate. Naturalized epistemology makes no more, and no less, sense than naturalized normative ethics.[42]

Notes

1. In making these remarks I am only repeating the familiar textbook history of philosophy; however, what *our* textbooks say about the history of a philosophical concept has much to do with *our* understanding of that concept.

2. Alvin Goldman explicitly states this requirement as a desideratum of his own analysis of justified belief in "What is Justified Belief?", in George S. Pappas (ed.), *Justification and Knowledge* (Dordrecht: Reidel, 1979), p. 1. Roderick M. Chisholm's definition of "being evident" in his *Theory of Knowledge*, 2nd ed. (Englewood Cliffs, N.J.: Prentice-Hall, 1977) does not satisfy this requirement as it rests ultimately on an unanalyzed epistemic concept of one belief being *more reasonable than another*. What does the real "criteriological" work for Chisholm is his "principles of evidence". See especially (A) on p. 73 of *Theory of Knowledge*, which can usefully be regarded as an attempt to provide nonnormative, descriptive conditions for certain types of justified beliefs.

3. The basic idea of this stronger requirement seems implicit in Roderick Firth's notion of "warrant-increasing property" in his "Coherence, Certainty, and Epistemic Priority", *Journal of Philosophy* 61 (1964): 545–57. It seems that William P. Alston has something similar in mind when he says,"... like any evaluative property, epistemic justification is a supervenient property, the application of which is based on more fundamental properties" (at this point Alston refers to Firth's paper cited above), in "Two Types of Foundationalism". *Journal of Philosophy* 73 (1976): 165–85 (the quoted remark occurs on p. 170). Although Alston doesn't further explain what he means by "more fundamental properties", the context makes it plausible to suppose that he has in mind nonnormative, descriptive properties. See Section 7 below for further discussion.

4. See Chisholm, ibid., p. 14. Here Chisholm refers to a "person's responsibility or duty *qua* intellectual being".

5. This term was used by A.J. Ayer to characterize the difference between lucky guessing and knowing; see *The Problem of Knowledge* (New York & London: Penguin Books, 1956), p. 33.

6. Notably by Chisholm in *Theory of Knowledge*, 1st ed., ch. 4.

7. See Rudolf Carnap, "Testability and Meaning", *Philosophy of Science* 3 (1936), and 4 (1937). We should also note the presence of a strong coherentist streak among some positivists; see, e.g., Carl G. Hempel, "On the Logical Positivists' Theory of Truth", *Analysis* 2 (1935): 49–59, and "Some Remarks on 'Facts' and Propositions", *Analysis* 2 (1935): 93–96.

8. In W.V. Quine, *Ontological Relativity and Other Essays* (New York: Columbia University Press, 1969). Also see his *Word and Object* (Cambridge: MIT Press, 1960); *The Roots of Reference* (La Salle, Ill.: Open Court, 1973); (with Joseph Ullian) *The Web of Belief* (New York: Random House, 1970); and especially "The Nature of Natural Knowledge" in Samuel Guttenplan (ed.). *Mind and Language* (Oxford: Clarendon Press, 1975). See Frederick F. Schmitt's excellent bibliography on naturalistic epistemology in Hilary Kornblith (ed.), *Naturalizing Epistemology* (Cambridge: MIT/Bradford, 1985).

9. Or confirmational relations, given the Positivists' verificationist theory of meaning.

10. I know of no serious defense of it since Ayer's *The Foundations of Empirical Knowledge* (London: Macmillan, 1940).

11. "Epistemology Naturalized", pp. 75–76.

12. Ibid., p. 78.

13. To use an expression of Richard Rorty's in *Philosophy and the Mirror of Nature* (Princeton: Princeton University Press, 1979), p. 11.

14. Elliott Sober makes a similar point: "And on the question of whether the failure of a foundationalist programme shows that questions of justification cannot be answered, it is worth nothing that Quine's advice 'Since Carnap's foundationalism failed, why not settle for psychology' carries weight only to the degree that Carnapian epistemology exhausts the possibilities of epistemology", in "Psychologism", *Journal of Theory of Social Behaviour* 8 (1978): 165–191.

15. See Chisholm, *Theory of Knowledge*, 2nd ed., ch. 4.

16. "If we are seeking only the causal mechanism of our knowledge of the external world, and not a justification of that knowledge in terms prior to science...', Quine, "Grades of Theoreticity", in L. Foster and J.W. Swanson (eds.). *Experience and Theory* (Amherst: University of Massachusetts Press, 1970), p. 2.

17. Ibid., p. 75. Emphasis added.

18. Ibid., p. 78. Emphasis added.

19. Ibid., p. 83. Emphasis added.

20. But aren't there those who advocate a "causal theory" of evidence or justification? I want to make two brief points about this. First, the nomological or causal input/output relations are not in themselves evidential relations, whether these latter are understood causally or otherwise. Second, a causal theory of evidence attempts to state *criteria* for "e is evidence for h" in causal terms; even if this is successful, it does not necessarily give us a causal "definition" or "reduction" of the concept of evidence. For more details see section 6 below.

21. I am not saying that Quine is under any illusion on this point. My remarks are directed rather at those who endorse Quine without, it seems, a clear appreciation of what is involved.

22. Here I am drawing chiefly on Donald Davidson's writings on radical interpretation. See Essays 9, 10, and 11 in his *Inquiries into Truth and Interpretation* (Oxford: Clarendon Press, 1984). See also David Lewis, "Radical Interpretation", *Synthese* 27 (1974): 331–44.

23. Robert Audi suggested this as a possible objection.

24. For some considerations tending to show that these correlations cannot be lawlike see my "Psychophysical Laws", in Ernest LePore and Brian McLaughlin (eds.), *Actions and Events: Perspectives on the Philosophy of Donald Davidson* (Oxford: Blackwell, 1985).

25. For a more sympathetic account of Quine than mine, see Hilary Kornblith's introductory essay, "What is Naturalistic Epistemology?", in Kornblith (ed.). *Naturalizing Epistemology.*

26. See for more details Alvin I. Goldman, *Epistemology and Cognition* (Cambridge: Harvard University Press, 1986).

27. *The Nature of Mathematical Knowledge* (New York: Oxford University Press, 1983), p. 14.

28. Ibid.

29. Ibid., p. 13. I should note that Kitcher considers the apsychologistic approach to be an aberration of the twentieth century epistemology, as represented by philosophers like Russell, Moore, C.I. Lewis, and Chisholm, rather than an historical characteristic of the Cartesian tradition. In "The Psychological Turn". *Australasian Journal of Philosophy* 60 (1982): 238–253, Hilary Kornblith gives an analogous characterization of the two approaches to justification; he associates "justification-conferring processes" with the psychologistic approach and "epistemic rules" with the apsychologistic approach.

30. See Goldman, "What is Justified Belief?"

31. David M. Armstrong, *Truth, Belief and Knowledge* (London: Cambridge University Press, 1973), p. 166.

32. The aptness of this characterization of the "apsychologistic" approach for philosophers like Russell, Chisholm, Keith Lehrer, John Pollock, etc. can be debated. Also, there is the issue of "internalism" vs. "externalism" concerning justification, which I believe must be distinguished from the psychologistic vs. apsychologistic division.

33. Moore, "A Reply to My Critics", in P.A. Schilpp (ed.), *The Philosophy of G.E. Moore* (Chicago & Evanston: Open Court, 1942). p. 588.

34. Richard Rorty's claim, which plays a prominent role in his arguments against traditional epistemology in *Philosophy and the Mirror of Nature*, that Locke and other modern epistemologists conflated the normative concept of justification with causal-mechanical concepts is itself based. I believe, on a conflation of just the kind I am describing here. See Rorty, ibid., pp. 139ff. Again, the critical conflation consists in not seeing that the view, which I believe is correct, that epistemic justification, like any other normative concept, must have factual, naturalistic criteria, is entirely consistent with the rejection of the doctrine, which I think is incorrect, that justification itself *is*, or *is reducible* to, a naturalistic-nonnormative concept.

35. *The Language of Morals* (London: Oxford University Press, 1952), p. 145.

36. See "Concepts of Supervenience", *Philosophy and Phenomenological Research* 65 (1984): 153–176.

37. Ernest Sosa, too, considers epistemological supervenience as a special case of the supervenience of valuational properties on naturalistic conditions, in "The Foundation of Foundationalism", *Nous* 14 (1980): 547–64; especially p. 551. See also James Van Cleve's instructive discussion in his "Epistemic Supervenience and the Circle of Belief", The *Monist* 68 (1985): 90–104; especially, pp. 97–99.

38. Perhaps one could avoid this kind of criteriological regress by embracing directly apprehended valuational properties (as in ethical intuitionism) on the basis of which criteria for other valuational properties could be formulated. The denial of the supervenience of valuational concepts on factual characteristics, however, would sever the essential connection between value and fact on which, it seems, the whole point of our valuational activities depends. In the absence of such supervenience, the very notion of valuation would lose its significance and relevance. The elaboration of these points, however, would have to wait for another occasion: but see Van Cleve's paper cited in the preceding note for more details.

39. Quine will not disagree with this: he will "naturalize" them both. For his views on values see "The Nature of Moral Values" in Alvin I. Goldman and Jaegwon Kim (eds.), *Values and Morals* (Dordrecht: Reidel, 1978). For a discussion of the relationship between epistemic

and ethical concepts see Roderick Firth, "Are Epistemic Concepts Reducible to Ethical Concepts?" in the same volume.

40. For discussions of this and related issues see Goldman, *Epistemology and Cognition.*

41. For a detailed development of a normative ethical theory that exemplifies the view that it is crucially relevant, see Richard B. Brandt, *A Theory of the Good and the Right* (Oxford: The Clarendon Press, 1979).

42. An early version of this paper was read at a meeting of the Korean Society for Analytic Philosophy in 1984 in Seoul. An expanded version was presented at a symposium at the Western Division meetings of the American Philosophical Association in April, 1985, and at the epistemology conference at Brown University in honor of Roderick Chisholm in 1986. I am grateful to Richard Foley and Robert Audi who presented helpful comments at the APA session and the Chisholm Conference respectively. I am also indebted to Terence Horgan and Robert Meyers for helpful comments and suggestions.

References

Alston, William P., "Two Types of Foundationalism," *Journal of Philosophy* 73 (1976): 165–85.

Armstrong, David M., *Truth, Belief and Knowledge* (London: Cambridge University Press, 1973).

Ayer, A.J., *The Foundations of Empirical Knowledge* (London: Macmillan, 1940).

Ayer, A.J., *The Problem of Knowledge* (New York & London: Penguin Books, 1956).

Brandt, Richard B., *A Theory of the Good and the Right* (Oxford: The Clarendon Press, 1979).

Carnap, Rudolf, "Testability and Meaning", *Philosophy of Science* 3 (1936), and 4 (1937).

Chisholm, Roderick M., *Theory of Knowledge*, 2nd ed. (Englewood Cliffs, N.J.: Prentice-Hall, 1977).

Davidson, Donald, *Inquiries into Truth and Interpretation* (Oxford: Clarendon Press, 1984).

Firth, Roderick, "Coherehce, Certainty, and Epistemic Priority", *Journal of Philosophy* 61 (1964): 545–57.

Firth, Roderick, "Are Epistemic Concepts Reducible to Ethical Concepts?" in Goldman, Alvin I. and Jaegwon Kim (eds.), *Values and Morals* (Dordrecht: Reidel, 1978).

Goldman, Alvin I., "What is Justified Belief?", in George S. Pappas (ed.), *Justification and Knowledge* (Dordrecht: Reidel, 1979).

Goldman, Alvin I., *Epistemology and Cognition* (Cambridge: Harvard University Press, 1986).

Hare, R.M., *The Language of Morals* (London: Oxford University Press, 1952).

Hempel, Carl G., "On the Logical Positivists' Theory of Truth", *Analysis* 2 (1935): 49–59.

Hempel, Carl G., "Some Remarks on 'Facts' and Propositions", *Analysis* 2 (1935): 93–96.

Kim, Jaegwon, "Concepts of Supervenience", *Philosophy and Phenomenological Research* 65 (1984): 153–176.

Kim, Jaegwon, "Psychophysical Laws", In Ernest LePore and Brian McLaughlin (eds.). *Actions and Events: Perspecties on the Philosophy of Donald Davidson* (Oxford: Blackwell, 1985).

Kitcher, Phillip, *The Nature of Mathematical Knowledge* (New York: Oxford University Press, 1983).

Kornblith, Hilary, "The Psychological Turn", *Australasian Journal of Philosophy* 60 (1982): 238–253.

Kornblith, Hilary, (ed.), *Naturalizing Epistemology* (Cambridge: MIT/ Bradford, 1985).

Kornblith, Hilary, "What is Naturalistic Epistemology?", in Kornblith (ed.), *Naturalizing Epistemology.*

Lewis, David, "Radical Interpretation", *Synthese* 27 (1974): 331–44.

Moore, G.E., "A Reply to My Critics", in P.A. Schilpp (ed.), *The Philosophy of G. E. Moore* (Chicago & Evanston: Open Court, 1942).

Quine, W.V., *Word and Object* (Cambridge: MIT Press, 1960).

Quine, W.V., *Ontological Relativity and Other Essays* (New York: Columbia University Press, 1969).

Quine, W.V., (with Joseph Ullian), *The Web of Belief* (New York: Random House, 1970).

Quine, W.V., "Grades of Theoreticity", in L. Foster and J. W. Swanson (eds.), *Experience and Theory* (Amherst: University of Massachusetts Press, 1970).

Quine, W.V., *The Roots of Reference* (La Salle, IL.: Open Court, 1973); Quine, W.V., "The Nature of Natural Knowledge" in Samuel Guttenplan (ed.), *Mind and Language* (Oxford: Clarendon Press, 1975).

Quine, W.V., "The Nature of Moral Values" in Alvin I. Goldman and Jaegwon Kim (eds.), *Values and Morals* (Dordrecht: Reidel, 1978).

Rorty, Richard, *Philosophy and the Mirror of Nature* (Princeton: Princeton University Press, 1979).

Sober, Elliott, "Psychologism", *Journal of Theory of Social Behavior* 8 (1978): 165–191.

Sosa, Ernest, "The Foundation of Foundationalism", *Nous* 14 (1980): 547–64.

Van Cleve, James, "Epistemic Supervenience and the Circle of Belief", *The Monist* 68 (1985)" 90–104.

⬦ RESERVATIONS ⬦

37. WHY REASON CAN'T BE NATURALIZED[*]
Hilary Putnam

The preceding chapter described the failure of contemporary attempts to 'naturalize' metaphysics; in the present chapter I shall examine attempts to naturalize the fundamental notions of the theory of knowledge, for example the notion of a belief's being *justified* or *rationally acceptable*.

While the two sorts of attempts are alike in that they both seek to reduce 'intentional' or mentalistic notions to materialistic ones, and thus are both manifestations of what Peter Strawson (1979) has described as a permanent tension in philosophy, in other ways they are quite different. The materialist metaphysician often uses such traditional metaphysical notions as *causal power,* and *nature* quite uncritically. (I have even read papers in which one finds the locution 'realist truth', as if everyone understood this notion except a few fuzzy anti-realists.) The 'physicalist' generally doesn't seek to *clarify* these traditional metaphysical notions, but just to show that science is progressively verifying the *true* metaphysics. That is why it seems just to describe *his* enterprise as 'natural metaphysics', in strict analogy to the 'natural theology' of the eighteenth and nineteenth centuries. Those who raise the slogan 'epistemology naturalized', on the other hand, generally *disparage* the traditional enterprises of epistemology. In this respect, moreover, they do not differ from philosophers of a less reductionist kind; the criticism they voice of traditional epistemology—that it was in the grip of a 'quest for certainty', that it was unrealistic in seeking a 'foundation' for knowledge as a whole, that the 'foundation' it claimed to provide was by no means indubitable in the way it claimed, to provide was by no means indubitable in the way it claimed, that the whole 'Cartesian enterprise' was a mistake, etc., — are precisely the criticisms one hears from philosophers of all countries and types. Hegel already denounced the idea of an 'Archimedean point' from which epistemology could judge all of our scientific, legal, moral, religious, etc. beliefs (and set up standards for all of the special subjects). It is true that Russell and Moore ignored these strictures of Hegel (as they ignored Kant), and revived 'foundationalist epistemology'; but today

that enterprise has few defenders. The fact that the naturalized epistemologist is trying to reconstruct what he can of an enterprise that few philosophers of any persuasion regard as unflawed is perhaps the explanation of the fact that the naturalistic tendency in epistemology expresses itself in so many incompatible and mutually divergent ways, while the naturalistic tendency in metaphysics appears to be, and regards itself as, a unified movement.

Evolutionary Epistemology

The simplest approach to the problem of giving a naturalistic account of reason is to appeal to Darwinian evolution. In its crudest form, the story is familiar: reason is a capacity we have for discovering truths. Such a capacity has survival value; it evolved in just the way that any of our physical organs or capacities evolved. A belief is rational if it is arrived at by the exercise of this capacity.

This approach assumes, at bottom, a metaphysically 'realist' notion of truth: truth as 'correspondence to the facts' or something of that kind. And this notion, as I have argued in the papers in this volume, is incoherent. We don't have notions of the 'existence' of things or of the 'truth' of statements that are independent of the versions we construct and of the procedures and practices that give sense to talk of 'existence' and 'truth' within those versions. Do *fields* 'exist' as physically real things? Yes, fields really exist: relative to one scheme for describing and explaining physical phenomena; relative to another there are particles, plus 'virtual' particles, plus 'ghost' particles, plus. . . Is it true that *brown* objects exist? Yes, relative to a common-sense version of the world: although one cannot give a necessary and sufficient condition for an object to be brown,[1] (one that applies to all objects, under all conditions) in the form of a finite closed formula in the language of physics. Do *dispositions* exist? Yes, in our ordinary way of talking (although disposition talk is just as recalcitrant to translation into physicalistic language as counterfactual talk, and for similar reasons). We have many irreducibly different but legitimate ways of talking, and true 'existence' statements in all of them.

To postulate a set of 'ultimate' objects, the furniture of the world, or what you will, whose 'existence' is *absolute*, not relative to our discourse at all, and a notion of truth as 'correspondence' to these ultimate objects is simply to revive the whole failed enterprise of traditional metaphysics. We saw *how* unsuccessful attempts to revive *that* enterprise have been in the last chapter.

Truth, in the only sense in which we have a vital and working notion of it, *is rational acceptability* (or, rather, rational acceptability under sufficiently good epistemic conditions; and which conditions are epistemically better or worse is relative to the type of discourse in just the way rational acceptability itself is). But to substitute this characterization of truth into the formula 'reason is a capacity for discovering truths' is to see the emptiness of that formula at once: 'reason is a capacity for discovering what is (or would be) rationally acceptable' is *not* the most informative statement a philosopher might utter. The evolutionary epistemologist must either presuppose a 'realist' (i.e., a metaphysical) notion of truth or see his formula collapse into vacuity.

Roderick Firth[2] has argued that, in fact, it collapses into a kind of epistemic vacuity on *any* theory of rational acceptability (*or* truth). For, he points out, whatever we take the correct epistemology (or the correct theory of truth) to be, we have no way of *identifying* truths except to posit that the statements that are currently rationally acceptable (by our lights) are true. Even if these beliefs are false, even if our rational beliefs contribute to our survival for some reason *other* than truth, the way 'truths' are identified *guarantees* that reason will seem to be a 'capacity for discovering truths'. This characterization of reason has thus no real empirical content.

The evolutionary epistemologist could, I suppose, try using some notion *other* than the notion of 'discovering truths'. For example, he might try saying that 'reason is a capacity for arriving at beliefs which *promote our survival*' (or our 'inclusive genetic fitness'). But this would be a loser! Science itself, and the methodology which we have developed since the seventeenth century for constructing and evaluating theories, has *mixed* effects on inclusive genetic fitness and all too uncertain effects on survival. If the human race perishes in a nuclear war, it may well be (although there will be no one alive to say it) that scientific beliefs did *not*, in a sufficiently long time scale, promote 'survival'. Yet that will not have been because the scientific theories were not rationally acceptable, but because our *use* of them was irrational. In fact, if rationality were measured by survival value, then the proto-beliefs of the cockroach, who has been around for tens of millions of years longer than we, would have a far higher claim to rationality than the sum total of human knowledge. But such a measure would be cockeyed; there is no contradiction in imagining a world in which people have utterly irrational beliefs which for some reason enable them to survive, or a world in which the most rational beliefs quickly lead to extinction.

If the notion of 'truth' in the characterization of rationality as a 'capacity for discovering truths' is problematic, so, almost equally, is the notion of a 'capacity'. In one sense of the term, *learning* is a 'capacity' (even, a 'capacity for discovering truths'), and *all* our beliefs are the product of *that* capacity. Yet, for better or worse, not all our beliefs are rational.

The problem here is that there are no sharp lines in the brain between one 'capacity' and another (Chomskians to the contrary). Even seeing includes not just the visual organs, the eyes, but the whole brain; and what is true of seeing is certainly true of *thinking* and *inferring*. We draw lines between one 'capacity' and another (or build them into the various versions we construct); but a sharp line at one level does not usually correspond to a sharp line at a lower level. The table at which I write, for example, is a natural unit at the level of everyday talk; I am aware that the little particle of food sticking to its surface (I must do something about that!) is not a 'part' of the table; but at the physicist's level, the decision to consider that bit of food to be outside the boundary of the table is not natural at all. Similarly, 'believing' and 'seeing' are quite different at the level of ordinary language psychology (and usefully so); but the corresponding brain-processes interpenetrate in complex ways which can only be separated by looking outside the brain, at the environment and at the output behavior *as structured by our interests and saliencies*. 'Reason is a capacity' is what Wittgenstein called a 'grammatical remark'; by which he meant (I think) not an analytic truth, but simply the sort of remark that philosophers often *take* to be informative when in fact it tells us nothing useful.

None of this is intended to deny the obvious scientific facts: that we would not be able to reason if we did not have brains, and that those *brains* are the product of evolution by natural selection. What is wrong with evolutionary epistemology is not that the scientific facts are wrong, but that they don't answer any of the philosophical questions.

The Reliability Theory of Rationality

A more sophisticated recent approach to these matters, proposed by Professor Alvin Goldman (1978), runs as follows: let us call a *method* (as opposed to a single belief) *reliable* if the method leads to a high frequency (say, 95%) of *true* beliefs in a long run series of representative applications (or *would* lead to such a high truth-frequency in such a series of applications). Then (the proposal goes) we can define a *rational* belief to be one which is *arrived at by using a reliable method*.

This proposal does not avoid the first objection we raised against evolutionary epistemology: it too presupposes a metaphysical notion of truth. Forgetting that rational acceptability does the lion's share of the work in fixing the notion of 'truth', the reliability theorist only pretends to be giving an analysis of rationality in terms that do not presuppose it. The second objection we raised against evolutionary epistemology, namely that the notion of a 'capacity' is hopelessly vague and general, is met, however, by replacing that notion with the notion of an arbitrary method for generating true or false statements, and then restricting the class to those methods (in this sense) whose reliability (as defined) is high. 'Learning' may be a method for generating statements, but its *reliability* is not high enough for every statement we 'learn' to count as rationally acceptable, on this theory. Finally, *no* hypothesis is made as to whether the reliable methods we employ are the result of biological evolution, cultural evolution, or what: this is regarded as no part of the theory of what rationality *is*, in this account.

This account is vulnerable to many counterexamples, however. *One* is the following: suppose that Tibetan Buddhism is, in fact, *true*, and that the Dalai Lama is, in fact, *infallible* on matters of faith and morals. Anyone who believes in the Dalai Lama, and who invariably believes any statement the Dalai Lama makes on a matter of faith or morals, follows a method which is 100% reliable; thus, if the reliability theory of rationality were correct, such a person's beliefs on faith and morals would all be rational *even if his argument for his belief that the Dalai Lama is never wrong is 'the Dalai Lama says so'*.

Cultural Relativism

I have already said that, in my view, truth and rational acceptability—a claim's being right and someone's being in a position to make it—are relative to the sort of language we are using and the sort of context we are in. 'That weighs one pound' may be true in a butcher shop, but the same sentence would be understood very differently (as demanding four decimal places of precision, perhaps) if the same object were being weighed in a laboratory. This does not mean that a claim is right *whenever* those who employ the language in question would accept it as right in its context, however. There are two points that must be *balanced*, both points that have been made by philosophers of many different kinds: (1) talk of what is 'right' and 'wrong' in any area only makes sense against the background of an *inherited tradition*; but (2) traditions themselves can be *criticized*. As Austin (1961) says, remarking on a special case of this, 'superstition and error and fantasy of all kinds do become incorporated in ordinary language and even sometimes stand up to the survival test (only, when they do, why should we not detect it?)'.

What I am saying is that the 'standards' accepted by a culture or a subculture, either explicitly or implicitly, cannot *define* what reason is, even in context, because they *presuppose* reason (reasonableness) for their interpretation. On the one hand, there is no notion of reasonableness at all *without* cultures, practices, procedures; on the other hand, the cultures, practices, procedures we inherit are not an algorithm to be slavishly followed. As Mill said, commenting on his own inductive logic, there is no rule book which will not lead to terrible results 'if supposed to be conjoined with universal idiocy'. Reason is, in this sense, both immanent (not to be found outside of concrete language games and institutions) and transcendent (a regulative idea that we use to criticize the conduct of *all* activities and institutions).

Philosophers who lose sight of the immanence of reason, of the fact that reason is always relative to context and institution, become lost in characteristic philosophical fantasies. 'The ideal language', 'inductive logic', 'the empiricist criterion of significance'— these are the fantasies of the positivist, who would replace the vast complexity of human reason with a kind of intellectual Walden II. 'The absolute idea': this is the fantasy of Hegel, who, without ignoring that complexity, would have us (or, rather, 'spirit') reach an endstage at which we (it) could comprehend it all. Philosophers who lose sight of the transcendence of reason become cultural (or historical) relativists.

I want to talk about cultural relativism, because it is one of the most influential—perhaps the most influential—forms of naturalized epistemology extant, although not usually recognized as such.

The situation is complicated, because cultural relativists usually *deny* that they are cultural relativists. I shall count a philosopher as a cultural relativist for our purposes if I have not been able to find anyone who can explain to me why he *isn't* a cultural relativist. Thus I count Richard Rorty as a cultural relativist, because his explicit formulations are relativist ones (he identifies truth with right assertibility by the standards of one's cultural peers, for example), and because his entire attack on traditional philosophy is mounted on the basis that the nature of reason and representation are non-problems, because the only kind of truth it makes sense to seek is to convince one's cultural peers. Yet he himself *tells* us that relativism is self-refuting (Rorty, 1980*b*). And I count Michel Foucault as a relativist because his insistence on the determination of beliefs by language is so overwhelming that it is an incoherence on his part not to apply his doctrine to his *own* language and thought. Whether Heidegger ultimately escaped something very much like cultural, or rather historical, relativism is an interesting question.

Cultural relativists are not, in their own eyes, scientistic or 'physicalistic'. They are likely to view materialism and scientism as just the hang-ups of one particular cultural epoch. If I count them as 'naturalized epistemologists' it is because their doctrine is, none the less, a product of the same deference to the claims of nature, the same desire for harmony with the world version of some science, as physicalism. The difference in style and tone is thus explained: the physicalist's paradigm of science is a *hard* science,

physics (as the term 'physicalism' suggests); the cultural relativist's paradigm is a *soft* science: anthropology, or linguistics, or psychology, or history, as the case may be. That reason is whatever the norms of the local culture determine it to be is a naturalist view inspired by the *social* sciences, including history.

There is something which makes cultural relativism a far more dangerous cultural tendency than materialism. At bottom, there is a deep irrationalism to cultural relativism, a denial of the possibility of *thinking* (as opposed to making noises in counterpoint or in chorus). An aspect of this which is of special concern to philosophy is the suggestion, already mentioned, that the deep questions of philosophy are not deep at all. A corollary to this suggestion is that philosophy, as traditionally understood, is a *silly* enterprise. But the questions *are* deep, and it is the easy answers that are silly. Even seeing that relativism is inconsistent is, if the knowledge is taken seriously, seeing something important about a deep question. Philosophers *are* beginning to talk about the great issues again, and to feel that something can be *said* about them, even if there are no grand or ultimate solutions. There is an excitement in the air. And if I react to Professor Rorty's book (1980*a*) with a certain sharpness, it is because one more 'deflationary' book, one more book telling us that the deep questions aren't deep and the whole enterprise was a mistake, is just what we *don't* need right now. Yet I am grateful to Rorty all the same, for his work has the merit of addressing profound questions head-on.

So, although we all know that cultural relativism is inconsistent (or say we do) I want to take the time to say again that it is inconsistent. I want to point out one reason that it is: not one of the quick, logic-chopping refutations (although every refutation of relativism teaches us something about reason) but a somewhat messy, somewhat 'intuitive', reason.

I shall develop my argument in analogy with a well-known argument against 'methodological solipsism'. The 'methodological solipsist'—one thinks of Carnap's *Logische Aufbau* or of Mach's *Analyse der Empfindungen*—holds that *all* our talk can be reduced to talk about experiences and logical constructions out of experiences. More precisely, he holds that everything he can conceive of is identical (in the ultimate logical analyses of his language) with one or another complex of his *own* experiences. What makes him a *methodological* solipsist as opposed to a real solipsist is that he kindly adds that *you*, dear reader, are the 'I' of this construction when *you* perform it: he says *everybody* is a (methodological) solipsist.

The trouble, which should be obvious, is that his two stances are ludicrously incompatible. His solipsist stance implies an enormous asymmetry between persons: my body is a construction out of my experiences, in the system, but *your* body isn't a construction out of *your* experiences. It's a construction out of *my* experiences. And your experiences—viewed from within the system—are a construction out of your bodily behavior, which, as just said, is a construction out of *my* experiences. My experiences are different from everyone else's (within the system) in that they are what *everything* is constructed from. But his transcendental stance is that it's all symmetrical: the 'you' he addresses his higher-order remark to cannot be the *empirical* 'you' of the system. But if it's really true that the 'you' of the system is the only 'you' he can *understand*, then the transcendental remark is *unintelligible*. Moral: don't be a methodological solipsist unless you are a *real* solipsist!

Consider now the position of the cultural relativist who says, 'When I say something is *true*, I mean that it is correct according to the norms of *my* culture.' If he adds, 'When a member of a different culture says that something is true, what he means (whether he knows it or not) is that it is in conformity with the norms of *his* culture', then he is in exactly the same plight as the methodological solipsist.

To spell this out, suppose R. R., a cultural relativist, says

When Karl says 'Schnee ist weiss', what Karl means (whether he knows it or not) is that snow is white *as determined* by the norms of Karl's culture

(which we take to be German culture).

Now the sentence 'Snow is white as determined by the norms of German culture' is itself one which R.R. has to *use*, not just mention, to say what Karl says. On his own account, what R.R. means by *this* sentence is

'Snow is white as determined by the norms of German culture' is true by the norms of R. R.'s culture

(which we take to be American culture).

Substituting this back into the first displayed utterance, (and changing to indirect quotation) yields:

When Karl says 'Schnee ist weiss', what he means (whether he knows it or not) is that it is true as determined by the norms of *American* culture that it is true as determined by the norms of German culture that snow is white.

In general, if R. R. understands *every* utterance *p* that *he* uses as meaning 'it is true by the norms of American culture that *p*', then he must understand his own hemeneutical utterances, the utterances he uses to interpret others, the same way, no matter how many qualifiers of the 'according to the norms of German culture' type or however many footnotes, glosses, commentaries on the cultural differences, or whatever, he accompanies them by. Other cultures become, so to speak, logical constructions out of the procedures and practices of American culture. If he now attempts to add 'the situation is reversed from the point of view of the *other* culture' he lands in the predicament the methodological solipsist found himself in: the transcendental claim of a *symmetrical* situation cannot be *understood* if the relativist doctrine is right. And to say, as relativists often do, that the other culture has 'incommensurable' concepts is no better. This is just the transcendental claim in a special jargon.

Stanley Cavell (1979, part IV) has written that skepticism about other minds can be a significant problem because we don't, in fact, always fully acknowledge the reality of others, their equal *validity* so to speak. One might say that the methodological solipsist is led to his transcendental observation that everyone is equally the 'I' of the construction by his praiseworthy desire to *acknowledge* others in this sense. But you *can't* acknowledge others in this sense, which involves recognizing that the situation *really is* symmetrical, if you think they are really constructions out of *your* sense data. Nor can you acknowledge others in this sense if you think that the *only* notion of truth there is for *you* to understand is 'truth-as-determined-by-the-norms-of-*this*-culture'.

For simplicity, I have discussed relativism with respect to truth, but the same discussion applies to relativism about rational acceptability, justification, etc; indeed, a relativist is unlikely to be a relativist about one of these notions and not about the others.

Cultural Imperialism

Just as the methodological solipsist can become a *real* solipsist, the cultural relativist can become a cultural imperialist. He can say, 'Well then, truth—the only notion of truth I understand—is defined by the norms of *my* culture.' ('After all', he can add, 'which norms should I rely on? The norms of *somebody else's* culture?') Such a view is no longer relativist at all. It postulates an *objective* notion of truth, although one that is said to be a product of our culture, and to be defined by our culture's criteria (I assume the culture imperialist is one of *us*). In this sense, just as consistent solipsism becomes indistinguishable from realism (as Wittgenstein said in the *Tractatus*), consistent cultural relativism also becomes indistinguishable from realism. But cultural imperialist realism is a special *kind* of realism.

It is realist in that it accepts an objective difference between what is true and what is merely thought to be true. (Whether it can consistently *account for* this difference is another question.)

It is not a *metaphysical* or transcendental realism, in that truth cannot go beyond right assertibility, as it does in metaphysical realism. But the notion of right assertibility is fixed by 'criteria', in a positivistic sense: something is rightly assertible only if the norms of the culture specify that it is; these norms are, as it were, an *operational definition* of right assertibility, in this view.

I don't know if any philosopher holds such a view, although several philosophers have let themselves fall into talking at certain times as if they did. (A philosopher in this mood is likely to say, '*X* is *our* notion', with a certain petulance, where X may be *reason, truth, justification, evidence* or what have you.)

This view is, however, self-refuting, in our culture. I have discussed this elsewhere (Putnam, 1981); the argument turns on the fact that our culture, unlike totalitarian or theocratic cultures, does not have 'norms' which decide *philosophical* questions. (Some philosophers have thought it does; but they had to postulate a 'depth grammar' accessible only to *them*, and not describable by ordinary linguistic or anthropological investigation.) Thus the philosophical statement:

A statement is true (rightly assertible) only if it is assertible according to the norms of modern European and American culture

is itself neither assertible nor refutable in a way that requires assent by everyone who does not deviate from the norms of modern European and American culture. So, if this statement is true, it follows that it is not true (not rightly assertible). Hence it is not true QED. (I believe that *all* theories which identify truth or right assertibility with what people agree with, or with what they would agree with in the long run, or with what educated and intelligent people agree with, or with what educated and intelligent people would agree with in the long run, are contingently self-refuting in this same way.)

Cultural imperialism would not be contingently self-refuting in this way if, as a matter of contingent fact, our culture were a totalitarian culture which erected its own cultural imperialism into a required dogma, a culturally normative belief. But it would still be wrong. For every culture has norms which are vague, norms which are unreasonable, norms which dictate inconsistent beliefs. We have all become aware how many inconsistent beliefs about *women* were culturally normative until recently, and are still strongly operative, not only in subcultures, but in all of us to some extent; and examples of inconsistent but culturally normative beliefs could easily be multiplied. Our task is not to mechanically *apply* cultural norms, as if they were a computer program and we were the computer, but to interpret them, to criticize them, to bring them and the ideals which inform them into reflective equilibrium. Cavell has aptly described this as 'confronting the culture with itself, along the lines in which it meets in me'. And he adds (Cavell, 1979, p. 125), 'This seems to me a task that warrants the name of Philosophy.' In this sense, we are all called to be philosophers, to a greater or lesser extent.

The culturalist, relativist or imperialist, like the historicist, has been caught up in the fascination of something really fascinating; but caught up in a sophomorish way. Traditions, cultures, history, deserve to be emphasized, as they are not by those who seek Archimedian points in metaphysics or epistemology. It is true that we speak a public language, that we inherit versions, that talk of truth and falsity only make sense against the background of an 'inherited tradition', as Wittgenstein says. But it is also true that we constantly remake our language, that we make new versions out of old ones, and that we have to use reason to do all this, and, for that matter, even to understand and apply the norms we do not alter or criticize. Consensus definitions of reason do not work, because consensus among grown-ups *presupposes* reason rather than defining it.

Quinian Positivism

The slogan 'epistemology naturalized' is the title of a famous paper by Quine (1969). If I have not discussed that paper up to now, it is because Quine's views are much more subtle and much more elaborate than the disastrously simple views we have just reviewed, and it seemed desirable to get the simpler views out of the way first.

Quine's philosophy is a large continent, with mountain ranges, deserts, and even a few Okefenokee Swamps. I do not know how all of the pieces of it can be reconciled, if they can be; what I shall do is discuss two different strains that are to be discerned in Quine's epistemology. In the present section I discuss the positivistic strain; the next section will discuss 'epistemology naturalized'.

The positivist strain, which occurs early and late, turns on the notion of an *observation sentence*. In his earliest writings, Quine gave this a phenomenalistic interpretation but, since the 1950s at least, he has preferred a definition in neurological and cultural terms. First, a preliminary notion: The *stimulus meaning* of a sentence is defined to be the set of stimulations (of 'surface neurons') that would 'prompt assent' to the sentence. It is thus supposed to be a *neurological* correlate of the sentence. A sentence may be called 'stimulus-true' for a speaker if the speaker is actually experiencing a pattern of stimulation of his surface neurons that lie in its stimulus meaning; but one should be careful to remember that a stimulus-true sentence is not necessarily true *simpliciter*. If you show me a life-like replica of a duck, the sentence, 'That's a duck', may be stimulus-true for me, but it isn't true. A sentence is defined to be an *observation* sentence for a community if it is an occasioned sentence (one whose truth value is regarded as varying with time and place, although this is not the Quinian definition) and it has the *same* stimulus meaning for all speakers. Thus 'He is a bachelor' is not an observation sentence, since different stimulations will prompt

you to assent to it than will prompt me (we know different people); but 'That's a duck' is (nearly enough) an observation sentence. Observe that the criterion is supposed to be entirely physicalistic. The key idea is that observation sentences are distinguished among occasioned sentences by being keyed to the same stimulations *intersubjectively*.

Mach held that talk of unobservables, including (for him) material objects, is justified only for reasons of 'economy of thought'. The business of science is *predicting regularities in our sensations*; we introduce 'objects' other than sensations only as needed to get theories which neatly predict such regularities.

Quine (1975) comes close to a 'physicalized' version of Mach's view. Discussing the question, whether there is more than one correct 'system of the world', he gives his criteria for such a system: (1) it must predict a certain number of stimulus-true observation sentences;[3] (2) it must be finitely axiomatized; (3) it must contain nothing unnecessary to the purpose of predicting stimulus-true observation sentences and conditionals. In the terminology Quine introduces in this paper, the theory formulation must be a 'tight fit'[4] over the relevant set of stimulus-true observation conditionals. (This is a formalized version of Mach's 'economy of thought'.)

If this were all of Quine's doctrine, there would be no problem. It is reconciling what Quine says here with what Quine says elsewhere that is difficult and confusing. I am *not* claiming that it is impossible however; a lot, if not all, of what Quine says *can* be reconciled. What I claim is that Quine's position is much more complicated than is generally realized.

For example, what is the *status* of Quine's ideal 'systems of the world'? It is tempting to characterize the sentences in one of Quine's ideal 'theory formulations' as *truths* (relative to that language and that choice of a formulation from among the equivalent-but-incompatible-at-face-value formulations of what Quine would regard as the *same* theory) and as *all* the truths (relative to the same choice of language and formulation), but this would conflict with *bivalence*, the principle that *every* sentence, in the ideal scientific language Quine envisages, is true or false.

To spell this out: Quine's ideal systems of the world are *finitely axiomatizable theories*, and contain standard mathematics. Thus Gödel's celebrated result applies to them: there are sentences in them which are neither provable nor refutable on the basis of the system. If being *true* were just being a theorem in the system, such sentences would be neither true nor false, since neither they nor their negations are theorems. But Quine (1981) holds to bivalence.

If Quine were a metaphysical realist there would again be no problem: the ideal system would contain everything that could be *justified* (from a very idealized point of view, assuming knowledge of all observations that *could* be made, and logical omniscience); but, Quine could say, the undecidable sentences are still determinately true or false–only we can't tell which. But the rejection of metaphysical realism, of the whole picture of a determinate 'copying' relation between words and a noumenal world, is at the heart of Quine's philosophy. And, as we shall see in the next section, 'justification' is a notion Quine is leery of. So what *is* he up to?[5]

I hazard the following interpretation: bivalence has *two* meanings for Quine: a 'first-order' meaning, a meaning as viewed *within* the system of science (including its Tarskian metalanguage) and a 'second-order' meaning, a meaning as viewed by the philosopher. In effect, I am claiming that Quine too allows himself a 'transcendental' standpoint which is different from the 'naive' standpoint that we get by just taking the system at face value. (I am not claiming that this is *inconsistent* however; some philosophers feel that such a move is *always* an inconsistency, but taking this line would preclude using *any* notion in science which one would explain away as a useful fiction in one's commentary on one's first-order practice. There was an inconsistency in the case of the methodological solipsist, because he claimed his first-order system reconstructed the *only* way he could understand the notion of another mind; if he withdraws that claim, then his position becomes perfectly consistent; it merely loses all philosophical interest.)

From *within* the first-order system, '*p* is true or *p* is false' is simply true; a derivable consequence of the Tarskian truth definition, given standard propositional calculus. From *outside,* from the metametalinguistic point of view Quine occupies, there is no unique 'world', no unique 'intended model'. Only *structure* matters; every model of the ideal system (I assume there is just one ideal theory, and we have fixed a formulation) is an intended model. Statements that are provable are true in *all* intended models; undecidable statements are true or false in each intended model, but not *stably* true or false. Their truth value varies from model to model.

If *this* is Quine's view, however, then there is still a problem. For Quine, what the philosopher says from the 'transcendental' standpoint is subject to the same methodological rules that govern ordinary first-order scientific work. Even mathematics is subject to the same rules. Mathematical truths, too, are to be certified as such by showing they are theorems in a system which we need to predict sensations (or rather, stimulus-true observation conditionals), given the physics which we are constructing as we construct the mathematics. More precisely, the *whole system of knowledge* is justified *as a whole* by its utility in predicting observations. Quine emphasizes that there is no room in this view for a special status for philosophical utterances. There is no 'first philosophy' above or apart from science, as he puts it.

Consider, now, the statement:

A statement is *rightly assertible* (true in all models) just in case it is a theorem of the relevant 'finite formulation', and that formulation is a 'tight fit' over the appropriate set of stimulus-true observation conditionals.

This statement, like most philosophical statements, does not imply *any* observation conditionals, either by itself or in conjunction with physics, chemistry, biology, etc. Whether we say that some statements which are undecidable in the system are really rightly assertible or deny it does not have any effects (that one can foresee) on prediction. Thus, *this* statement *cannot* itself be rightly assertible. In short, *this* reconstruction of Quine's positivism makes it *self-refuting.*

The difficulty, which is faced by all versions of positivism, is that positivist exclusion principles are always self-referentially inconsistent. In short, *positivism produced a conception of rationality so narrow as to exclude the very activity of producing that conception.* (Of course, it also excluded a great many other kinds of rational activity.) The problem is especially sharp for Quine, because of his explicit rejection of the analytic/synthetic distinction, his rejection of a special status for philosophy, etc.

It may be, also, that I have just got Quine wrong. Quine would perhaps reject the notions of 'right assertibility', 'intended model', and so on. But then I just don't know *what* to make of this strain in Quine's thought.

'Epistemology Naturalized'

Quine's paper 'Epistemology naturalized' takes a very different tack. 'Justification' has failed. (Quine considers the notion only in its strong 'Cartesian' setting, which is one of the things that makes his paper puzzling.) Hume taught us that we *can't* justify our knowledge claims (in a foundational way). Conceptual reduction has also failed (Quine reviews the failure of phenomenalism as represented by Carnap's attempt in the *Logische Aufbau*.) So, Quine urges, let us give up epistemology and 'settle for psychology'.

Taken at face value, Quine's position is sheer epistemological eliminationism: we should just *abandon* the notions of justification, good reason, warranted assertion, etc., and *reconstrue* the notion of 'evidence' (so that the 'evidence' becomes the sensory stimulations that *cause us* to have the scientific beliefs we have). In conversation, however, Quine has repeatedly said that he didn't mean to 'rule out the normative'; and this is consistent with his recent interest in such notions as the notion of a 'tight fit' (an economical finitely axiomatized system for predicting observations).

Moreover, the expression 'naturalized epistemology' is being used today by a number of philosophers who explicitly consider themselves to *be* doing normative epistemology, or at least methodology. But the paper 'Epistemology naturalized' really does rule all that out. So it's all *extremely* puzzling.

One way to reconcile the conflicting impulses that one sees at work here might be to replace justification theory by reliability theory in the sense of Goldman; instead of saying that a belief is justified if it is arrived at by a reliable method, one might say that the notion of justification should be *replaced* by the notion of a verdict's being the product of a reliable method. This is an *eliminationist* line in that it does not try to reconstruct or analyze the traditional notion; that was an intuitive notion that we now perceive to have been defective from the start, such a philosopher might say. Instead, he proposes a *better* notion (by his lights).

While some philosophers would, perhaps, move in this direction, Quine would not for a reason already given: Quine rejects metaphysical realism, and the notion of reliability presupposes the notion of *truth*. Truth is, to be sure, an acceptable notion for Quine, if defined à la Tarski, but so defined, it cannot serve as the primitive notion of epistemology or of methodology. For Tarski simply defines 'true' so that '*p* is true' will come out equivalent to '*p*'; so that, to cite the famous example, '*Snow is white*' *is true* will come out equivalent to 'Snow is white'. What the procedure does is to define 'true' so that saying that a statement is true is equivalent to assenting to the statement; truth, as defined by Tarski, is not a *property* of statements at all, but a syncategorematic notion which enables us to 'ascend semantically', i.e., to talk about sentences instead of about objects.[6]

I will assent to '*p* is true' whenever I assent to *p*; therefore, I will accept a method as reliable whenever it *yields verdicts I would accept*. I believe that, in fact, this is what the 'normative' becomes for Quine: the search for methods that yield verdicts that one oneself would accept.

Why We Can't Eliminate the Normative

I shall have to leave Quine's views with these unsatisfactory remarks. But why not take a full blown eliminationist line? Why *not* eliminate the normative from our conceptual vocabulary? Could it be a superstition that there is such a thing as reason?

If one abandons the notions of justification, rational acceptability, warranted assertibility, right assertibility, and the like, completely, then 'true' goes as well, except as a mere device for 'semantic ascent', that is, a mere mechanism for switching from one level of language to another. The mere introduction of a Tarskian truth predicate cannot define for a language any notion of *rightness* that was not already defined. To reject the notions of justification and right assertibility while *keeping* a *metaphysical realist notion of truth* would, on the other hand, not only be peculiar (what ground could there be for regarding truth, in the 'correspondence' sense, as *clearer* than right assertibility?), but incoherent; for the notions the naturalistic metaphysician uses to explain truth and reference, for example the notion of causality (explanation), and the notion of the *appropriate type* of causal chain depend on notions which presuppose the notion of reasonableness.

But if *all* notions of rightness, both epistemic and (metaphysically) realist are eliminated, then what are our statements but noise-makings? What are our thoughts but *mere* subvocalizations? The elimination of the normative is attempted mental suicide.

The notions, 'verdict I accept' and 'method that leads to verdicts I accept' are of little help. If the *only* kind of rightness any statement has that I can understand is 'being arrived at by a method which yields verdicts *I* accept', then I am committed to a solipsism of the present moment. To solipsism, because this *is* a methodologically solipsist substitute for assertibility ('verdicts *I* accept'), and we saw before that the methodological solipsist is only consistent if he is a real solipsist. And to solipsism of the present moment because this is a *tensed* notion (a substitute for warranted assertibility at *a time,* not for assertibility in the best conditions); and if the *only* kind of rightness my present 'subvocalizations' have is *present* assertibility (however defined); if there is no notion of a *limit* verdict, however fuzzy; then there is no sense in which my 'subvocalizations' are *about* anything that goes beyond the present moment. (Even the thought 'there is a future' is 'right' only in the sense of being *assertible at the present moment,* in such a view.)

One could try to overcome this last defect by introducing the notion of 'a verdict I would accept *in the long run*', but this would at once involve one with the use of counterfactuals, and with such notions as 'similarity of possible worlds'. But it is pointless to make further efforts in this direction. Why should we expend our mental energy in convincing ourselves that we aren't thinkers, that our thoughts aren't really *about* anything, noumenal *or* phenomenal, that there is *no* sense in which any thought is *right* or *wrong* (including the thought that no thought is right or wrong) beyond being the verdict of the moment, and so on? This is a self-refuting enterprise if there ever was one! Let us recognize that one of our fundamental self-conceptualizations, one of our fundamental 'self-descriptions', in Rorty's phrase, is that we are *thinkers,* and that *as* thinkers we are committed to there being *some* kind of truth, some kind of correctness which is substantial and not merely 'disquotational'. That means that there is no eliminating the normative.

If there is no eliminating the normative, and no possibility of reducing the normative to our favorite science, be it biology, anthropology, neurology, physics, or whatever, then where are we? We might try for a grand theory of the normative in its *own* terms, a formal epistemology, but that project seems decidedly overambitious. In the meantime, there is a great deal of philosophical work to be done, and it will be done with fewer errors if we free ourselves of the reductionist and historicist hang-ups that have marred so much recent philosophy. If reason is both transcendent and immanent, then philosophy, as culture-bound reflection and argument about eternal questions, is both in time and eternity. We don't have an Archimedean point; we always speak the language of a time and place; but the rightness and wrongness of what we say is not *just* for a time and a place.

Notes

* This was delivered as the second Howison Lecture at the University of California on 30 April 1981.

1. I chose brown because brown is not a spectral color. But the point also applies to spectral colors: if being a color were purely a matter of reflecting light of a certain wavelength, then the objects we see would change color a number of times a day (and would all be black in total darkness). Color depends on background conditions, edge effects, reflectancy, relations to amount of light etc. Giving a description of all of these would only define *perceived* color; to define the 'real' color of an object one also needs a notion of 'standard conditions': traditional philosophers would have said that the color of a red object is a power (a disposition) to look red to normal observers under normal conditions. This, however, requires a counterfactual conditional (whenever the object is *not* in normal conditions) and we saw in the previous chapter that the attempt to define counterfactuals in 'physical' terms has failed. What makes color terms physically undefinable is not that color is subjective but that it is *subjunctive.* The common idea that there is some one molecular structure (or whatever) common to all objects which look red 'under normal conditions' has no foundation: consider the difference between the physical structure of a red star and a red book (and the difference in what we count as 'normal conditions' in the two cases).

2. This argument appears in Firth's Presidential Address to the Eastern Division of the American Philosophical Association (29 December 1981), titled 'Epistemic merit, intrinsic and instrumental'. Firth does not specifically refer to evolutionary epistemology, but rather to 'epistemic utilitarianism'; however, his argument applies as well to evolutionary epistemology of the kind I describe.

3. Quine actually requires that a 'system of the world' predict that certain 'pegged observation sentences' be true. I have oversimplified in the text by writing 'observation sentence' for 'pegged observation sentence'. Also the 'stimulus meaning' of an observation sentence includes a specification of conditions under which the speaker *dissents*, as well as the conditions under which he assents. The details are in Quine (1975).

4. A theory is a 'tight fit' if it is interpretable in *every* axiomatizable theory which implies the observation conditionals (conditionals whose antecedent and consequent are pegged observation sentences) in question in a way that holds the pegged observation sentences fixed. To my knowledge, no proof exists that a 'tight fit' even exists, apart from the trivial case in which the observation conditionals can be axiomatized *without* going outside of the observation vocabulary.

5. Quine *rejected* the interpretation I offer below (discussion at Heidelberg in 1981), and opted for saying that our situation is 'asymmetrical': he is a 'realist' with respect to his *own* language but not with respect to other languages below for my rejoinder.

6. Quine himself puts this succinctly. 'Whatever we affirm, after all, we affirm as a statement within our aggregate theory of nature as we now see it; and to call a statement true is just to reaffirm it.' (Quine, 1975, p. 327)

References

Austin, J.L. (1961) "A Plea for Excluses," in his *Philosophical Papers* (Oxford: Oxford University Press), 175-204.

Cavell, Stanley (1979) *The Claim of Reason* (Oxford: Oxford University Press), 175-204.

Goldman, Alvin (1978) *"What is Justified Belief,"* in G.S. Pappas and M. Swain, ed.s, *Justification and Knowledge* (Ithaca: Cornell Univeristy Press).

Putnam, Hilary (1981) *Reason, Truth and History* (Cambridge: Cambridge University Press).

Quine, W.V.O. (1975) "On Empirically Equivalent Systems of the World," *Erkenntis* 9: 313-28.

Rorty, Richard (1980a) *Philosophy and the Mirror of Nature* (Oxford: Oxford University Press).

—— (1980b) "Pragmatism, Relativism and Irrationalism," *Proceedings and Addresses of the American Philosophy Association* 53.

Strawson, Peter (1979) "Universals," *Midwest Studies in Philosophy* 4: 3-10.

✧ A RESPONSE TO CRITICS ✧

38. NATURALISTIC EPISTEMOLOGY AND ITS CRITICS

Hilary Kornblith

The naturalistic approach to epistemology has undergone substantial development in the last several years. Here I present the state of the art, as well as an account of the most important criticisms to date.

I

Let me begin with a few socio-historical remarks. One of the proximate causes of current interest in naturalistic epistemology traces to W. V. Quine's 1969 paper, "Epistemology Naturalized."[1] Quine there argued for a new approach to epistemological questions. Traditional epistemology, as Quine viewed it, was a failed research program. Philosophers from Descartes to the present day have sought to put knowledge on its "proper foundation." Showing that

knowledge has a proper foundation would require a set of beliefs which enjoy a special epistemological status: Depending on one's preferred foundational view, these beliefs are certain, infallible, incorrigible, indubitable, prima facie justified, or the like. They are justified but not in virtue of their relations to other beliefs. For many philosophers, beliefs about one's own sense experience were said to enjoy this special status. Other beliefs, if they are to be justified at all, must somehow derive their justification from foundational beliefs. A proper epistemological theory would give an account of the special property which foundational beliefs enjoy; it would demonstrate that an important class of beliefs actually have the preferred property; a set of epistemic principles, themselves enjoying a special epistemic status, would then be shown to be justification-transmitting; and these principles, when applied to the foundational beliefs, would generate the remainder of the class of justified beliefs. We could thereby show the extent of our knowledge, as well as, simultaneously, display its epistemic credentials.

The foundationalist program is undeniably attractive. As practiced by Descartes, for example, it serves to unify a number of distinct epistemological projects. First, it gives us an account of what knowledge and justification are. Second, by showing that a large number of beliefs meet the appropriate epistemic standards, it demonstrates the extent of our knowledge and thereby provides a response to the skeptic. Third, it provides us with epistemic advice, i.e., a set of instructions to follow if we wish to be more accurate in arriving at our beliefs. Each of these projects seems, on its face, well worth pursuing. Foundationalism seems to provide a method for simultaneously addressing all three.

Now Quine, as I've said, sees the history of epistemology up to 1969 as the history of a failed research program: Foundationalism has simply failed to deliver the goods.2 The years since 1969 have not, to my mind, provided reasons for reversing Quine's verdict. Foundationalism has faced serious difficulties at every turn. The class of foundational beliefs has proven to be extremely elusive. Those who favor extremely strong requirements on foundations, such as incorrigibility or infallibility, have not clearly demonstrated that *any* beliefs at all meet the favored standard. At best, the class of beliefs meeting such requirements is so slight as to provide insufficient support for the vast majority of beliefs which, pretheoretically, seem to be justified. Those who favor very strong requirements on the foundations thus find themselves in a difficult situation: They must severely narrow the class of beliefs which are claimed to enjoy the special epistemological status; but in so doing, they thereby make far more difficult any attempt to respond to the skeptic on that basis. One might, at this point, simply embrace skepticism, but this is a very high price for holding on to the foundationalist account of knowledge and justification.

The obvious solution here is to weaken one's requirements on foundational belief. This makes far easier the project of deriving a substantial edifice of knowledge from the favored foundation, but the weaker the foundation, the less impressive the edifice. If foundational beliefs have very little going for them epistemically, the fact that we can derive lots of other beliefs from them tells us little of interest. Moreover, even foundational accounts placing weak requirements on the privileged class of beliefs have run into substantial difficulties in deriving an interesting superstructure of knowledge. So long as substantial constraints are placed on the principles by which the superstructure is derived, the task of providing a foundationalist reconstruction of knowledge proves extraordinarily difficult.

Now one might also loosen up the requirements on the epistemic principles by which the superstructure is derived. Once again, the looser these requirements, the less impressive is the fact that one can generate a large body of beliefs answering to them. But long before one starts loosening up on these requirements, it should start dawning on one that one's commitment to foundationalism is no longer doing a great deal of epistemological work. All of this loosening up of standards is driven by one's pretheoretical commitments—the view that, in the end, we do have a great deal of knowledge. But so long as we hold on to this pretheoretical commitment, foundationalism itself is not really addressing any of the three epistemological projects with which we began. The first project, saying what constitutes knowledge, is addressed only formally by foundationalism; all the content in one's account is now being driven by the desire to make our ordinary commitments meet whatever criteria we eventually endorse. The second project, answering the skeptic, has now been trivialized, because we are endorsing an account of knowledge in virtue of the very fact that it permits a response to skepticism. The ability to reject skepticism is not so much an interesting result—as it would have been for Descartes, had his project worked out—it is instead something which we built in from the beginning, a constraint on what we would even count as an adequate account of knowledge. Finally, the desire for substantive epistemic advice is shortchanged as well.[3] When our pretheoretical ideas about what we are justified in believing are put in the driver's seat, the only epistemic advice which results is to keep believing what we pretheoretically believed. The idea that epistemology might give us some instruction about how better to get at the truth is thereby abandoned.

If foundationalism is an idea which simply failed to work out, what should we put in its place? Quine's suggestion is enigmatic:

> [E]pistemology still goes on, though in a new setting and a clarified status. Epistemology, or something like it, simply falls into place as a chapter of psychology and hence of natural science.[4]

This suggestion of Quine's has seemed to many to amount to nothing more than changing the subject.[5] Epistemology has historically been interested in normative questions: What should we believe? Under what conditions are we justified in believing something? Psychology, on the other hand, seems to have no interest in such questions. Instead, it attempts to provide an accurate description of the mechanisms by which beliefs are produced, retained, and modified. But the descriptive enterprise, it seems, is no more a substitute for the normative one than an account of how people act is a substitute for a study of the right and the good. After all, people sometimes arrive at beliefs in ways which are just crazy. While it is perfectly appropriate for psychology to describe these and other ways of arriving at beliefs, without editorial comment, a proper epistemological theory must do more. Some have thus seen Quine's argument for naturalizing epistemology as little more than a non sequitur: Foundationalism was a bad solution to the normative questions epistemology traditionally asked; so we should stop asking those questions and do psychology instead.[6]

I do not wish to get involved here in the details of Quine exegesis, but this much, I believe, is quite safe to say. There are ways of interpreting Quine which do not have him offering obviously dreadful arguments; both good sense and charity, therefore, suggest that we should explore such interpretations. In particular, there are two aspects of Quine's program of naturalizing epistemology which we will need to examine: First, there is the rejection of the a priori and, along with it, the conception of epistemology as first philosophy; second, there is the idea that skeptical questions arise from within science. Let me say a bit about each of these.

Famously, Quine has argued for the rejection of the analytic-synthetic distinction and, with it, the very idea of a priori truth. One source of Quine's rejection of apriority is his holism: No statement is immune to rational revision; sufficiently large changes in our body of beliefs can force changes even in beliefs which appeared to be held independently of any empirical evidence. The notion of a priori truth is thus empty. But once we reject the idea of a priori truth, Descartes' conception of epistemology as first philosophy must be rejected as well. On Descartes' view, epistemology is logically prior to science. First, we must figure out how properly to arrive at our beliefs; this is the business of epistemology. It must be investigated independently of any of our empirical beliefs, for until we figure out how properly to arrive at such beliefs, the empirical beliefs we currently have, and upon which we might be tempted to rely in forming our epistemological theory, are nothing more than a potential source of misinformation. Once we have our epistemological theory in place, we may then put it to use in arriving at empirical beliefs. Epistemology thus precedes science; it tells us how science is properly done.

But if there are no a priori truths, then this conception of epistemology is misguided. Epistemology cannot precede science; it must, instead, be viewed as continuous with science. Moreover, as Quine argues, the very idea of responding to skepticism in the way Descartes envisioned misunderstands the skeptical problematic. Skeptical problems arise from within science. It is because science shows us how various aspects of our common-sense view of the world may be mistaken that we come to raise the question of whether we might be entirely mistaken in the way we view the world. But because this question arises from within science, it is perfectly appropriate to draw on the resources of science to answer it.

There are many ways in which this approach to epistemology might be filled out. What I want to do here is describe a project which flows naturally from the suggestions Quine made in "Epistemology Naturalized," a project which fits well with much of the research going on today under that heading. But before I turn to an account of a viable naturalistic project for epistemology, I will need to discuss another important influence on the development of naturalism: the work of Alvin Goldman.

II

Alvin Goldman's first paper in epistemology, "A Causal Theory of Knowing,"[7] appeared in 1967, and if one were to read it side by side with Quine's "Epistemology Naturalized," one might easily get the impression that Goldman's approach to epistemology and Quine's approach have nothing to do with one another. Goldman is engaged in a project of giving an analysis of the concept of knowledge; Quine rejects the very idea of conceptual analysis. Goldman, as he announces in his first paragraph, is moved by a desire to solve the Gettier problem; Quine has shown little interest in this problem.[8] Nevertheless, the project which Goldman inaugurated with "A Causal Theory of Knowing," while different from Quine's in nontrivial ways, also has deep affinities with Quinean naturalism.

Goldman proposed that knowledge that *p* is properly analyzed as belief that *p* caused by the fact that *p*. Thus, on this account, when I know that there is a table in front of me, my belief that there is such a table is caused by the fact that there is a table. Goldman revised and developed this account in "Discrimination and Perceptual Knowledge,"[9] identifying perceptual knowledge with true belief which is the product of a discriminatory capacity. To know that there is a table before one, one must be able to discriminate between situations in which there is a table and those in which no table is present. This account was then further developed to provide an account of justified belief.[10] A belief is justified just in case it is reliably produced, that is, just in case it is the product of a psychological process which tends to produce true beliefs.

Although Goldman was engaging in conceptual analysis, and in that respect was very much in tune with epistemologists of the sixties and seventies who had no sympathy whatsoever with naturalism, his proposed analyses of knowledge and justification nevertheless marked a radical break with tradition. On traditional accounts, a person is justified in holding a belief just in case a good argument for the belief is, in some suitable sense, available to that person.[11] Theorists disagreed

about precisely what was to count as a good argument. On Goldman's view, however, a person is justified in holding a belief just in case the belief is produced in the right sort of way; the person in question need have no idea at all about how the belief is produced, nor need any sort of argument for the belief be available to the person. Being justified is a property some beliefs have in virtue of their causal history, not in virtue of the believer's grasp of some kind of justificatory argument.

It is this feature of Goldman's account which led many philosophers to suggest that Goldman was, not so much addressing traditional epistemological questions in a distinctive way, but rather changing the topic and ignoring the traditional questions. It is no coincidence that Goldman's account, like Quine's, tended to evoke this kind of response. But the similarity between the two is far deeper than that. If Goldman was changing the topic—and I will want to say something about that—then the direction in which Goldman was moving the focus of epistemological discussion was very similar to the direction in which Quine was also moving the focus of epistemological discussion.

Remember that on Quine's view, a proper naturalistic epistemology becomes "a chapter of psychology." Similarly, on Goldman's account, if we are to investigate the features of our beliefs in virtue of which they are justified, what is required is a detailed understanding of the psychological mechanisms by which our beliefs are produced.[12] Justified beliefs are ones which are produced by mechanisms which are well-adapted to the kinds of environments in which human beings tend to be found. The good-making features of these psychological mechanisms need not be such that they would tend to produce true beliefs in every possible world; rather, they need only be well-adapted to this world. Thus, for example, just as our perceptual mechanisms tend to provide us with a rich and accurate understanding of many features of the world around us, without being well-adapted to every possible environment, the appropriate approach to understanding human inference would have us examine the kinds of inferences which would allow for an accurate understanding of our world, not those inferences which could not help but provide an accurate understanding of any possible world. Carrying out Goldman's program would thus have us investigate the kinds of psychological mechanisms which are found in human beings and would have us examine the extent to which they operate well in human environments, providing an accurate understanding of the world.[13] This is, of course, a thoroughly empirical study.

Now this is not to say that Goldman and Quine would entirely agree on the proper conduct of epistemology. They would not. Goldman's epistemology still retains substantial connections with the tradition of conceptual analysis, a tradition which Quine entirely repudiates. On Goldman's view, conceptual analysis is the vehicle by which we are provided with an account of knowledge and justification. An understanding of which beliefs are justified, however, and an account of the ways in which our epistemic practice may be improved require careful empirical investigation. In addition, the kinds of psychology to which Goldman and Quine would assign a good deal of epistemological work are importantly different. On Goldman's view, it is cognitive science which will do the lion's share of the work here. Quine's deep skepticism about intentional notions, however, has him defer to a behaviorally oriented psychology.

In the end, however, what Goldman and Quine have in common is, to my mind at least, far more important than their differences. If they are even roughly right, then at least much of epistemology becomes an empirical discipline, continuous with the sciences. This marks a substantial change in how epistemology is done.

I will now turn to providing a sketch of how such an empirical epistemology might be carried out, together with an account of the relationship between this approach to epistemology and the kinds of concerns which, traditionally, have motivated epistemologists.

III

The kind of approach to epistemological questions I favor shares with Quine a skepticism about the very idea of conceptual analysis, but shares with Goldman a commitment to the research program of cognitive psychology. I see a proper naturalistic epistemology as empirical all the way down, and yet, at the same time, I believe that there is a great deal of continuity between any such epistemology and the traditional projects which have motivated epistemologists for centuries.

On my view, knowledge is a natural phenomenon, and it is this natural phenomenon that is the subject matter of epistemology—not the concept of knowledge, but knowledge itself. Analyzing our concept of knowledge, to the extent that we can make sense of such a project, is no more useful than analyzing the ordinary concept of, say, aluminum. The ordinary concept of aluminum is of little interest for two reasons. First, most people are largely ignorant of what makes aluminum the kind of stuff it is, and so their concept of aluminum will tell us little about the stuff itself. Second, most people have many misconceptions about aluminum, and so their concepts of aluminum will reflect this misinformation as well. There are interesting anthropological questions about the ordinary concept of aluminum, but precisely because this concept is as much a reflection of ignorance and misinformation as it is a reflection of anything about aluminum, those who have an interest in aluminum are ill-advised to study our concept of it.

Now the same may be said, I believe, of knowledge. Epistemologists ought to be interested in the study of knowledge itself. If we substitute a study of the ordinary concept of knowledge, we are getting at knowledge only indirectly; knowledge is thereby filtered through a good deal of ignorance about the phenomenon, as well as a good deal of misinformation. Better to examine the phenomenon of human knowledge in its natural setting and leave an examination of ordinary concepts to cognitive anthropology. The same may of course be said about justification and related epistemological notions.

The phenomenon of knowledge is ubiquitous. It may be found in simple perceptual situations, where an epistemic agent confronts a table in good light and in clear viewing conditions, as well as in the more complex interactions between agent and environment found in the scientific laboratory. I am assuming that there is a single phenomenon here to be studied, that these clear-cut cases of knowledge constitute a natural kind and not some grue-like hodgepodge or, like the class of individuals thought to be witches, a largely heterogeneous group whose few commonalities are entirely different from what they are ordinarily taken to be. If this assumption is mistaken, then the very idea of knowledge is based on a mistake, and it requires either elimination or radical revision. But the defeasibility of this project—its assumption that knowledge and justification and other allied epistemic notions constitute natural kinds—is not just a feature of a naturalistic epistemology; it is a feature of any epistemology whatsoever. If epistemic kinds are merely gerrymandered and grue-like, or if they presuppose a radically false theory and are witch-like, they thereby lose their interest. I see no reason to think, at the present time, that epistemic notions have this undesirable feature.

I will thus assume that, at least pretheoretically, there is a robust phenomenon of human knowing and that this phenomenon is susceptible to investigation. We may try to figure out what the phenomenon consists in; what it is that makes these cases instances of a single kind. We may ask about the extent of the phenomenon and the conditions that make it possible. And we may ask how to improve human performance; how we might go about gaining more knowledge. Let us examine each of these projects in turn.

Just as Plato was interested in what knowledge is, the naturalistic epistemologist is also concerned with the phenomenon of human knowledge and what it is which makes the various instances of it instances of a single kind. There is a sociological and deflationary answer which might be given to this question: What instances of knowledge have in common is that they play a certain social role; they provide assurance which is backed by socially recognized experts. It seems to me clear enough that instances of knowledge do answer to some such characterization, but what makes the sociological account deflationary is the suggestion that this is all that instances of knowledge have in common, that there is nothing more to knowledge than the social role it plays. If something along these lines is correct, then knowledge turns out to be a far more shallow and less interesting kind than philosophers have traditionally thought it to be.

The account of knowledge which Goldman offers makes knowledge a more interesting and deeper kind. On Goldman's account, knowledge is reliably produced true belief. Such an account does not conflict with the suggestion that knowledge plays a certain social role; instead, by offering a deeper account of what makes something an item of knowledge, Goldman's account seeks to explain how it is that items of knowledge are well suited to play the social role they in fact play. At the same time, Goldman is

committed to the view that the social forces which play a role in the production of belief genuinely are, by and large, conducive to truth. Our social institutions, and in particular, our scientific institutions, are so structured as to produce true belief; they are not merely vehicles for the dissemination of belief of whatever sort or vehicles for the concentration and perpetuation of political power, as some would have it. An account such as Goldman's must therefore show how the social arrangement of scientific institutions lends itself to playing this truth-connected role. In particular, it must be shown that various features of our social institutions which seem to conflict with getting at the truth nevertheless play a role, by and large, in producing true belief. Accordingly, Goldman—and others of a like turn of mind, such as Philip Kitcher—have devoted considerable attention to this project.[14]

It might be thought that these claims about our social institutions are really detachable from the view that knowledge is reliably produced true belief.[15] Couldn't one hold that knowledge has some such essential connection with truth and yet remain neutral on the claim about the connection between our social institutions and truth? In the end, I do not think that these two views are so neatly detachable, at least not for a naturalist. If one insists on insulating claims about the nature of knowledge from claims about the social practices and institutions in which knowledge is embodied, then one is giving up the view of knowledge as a natural phenomenon susceptible to empirical investigation, which, to my mind, is a crucial constituent of the naturalistic approach. It is the investigation of knowledge as a phenomenon in the world which distinguishes naturalism from other approaches to knowledge. It is this feature as well which lends substance to the various claims made about knowledge; without tying knowledge to the world in this way, we would leave nothing for our account to answer to.

By the same token, the naturalist who favors a Goldman-style account of knowledge and justification is committed to explaining how it is that the psychological mechanisms by which beliefs are produced, modified, and retained are, on the whole, conducive to the production of true belief. This empirical investigation of the reliability of belief production is not in any way trivial. While it is certainly true that this investigation is itself carried out by using the very mechanisms of belief production whose reliability is in question, this does not assure that the investigation will confirm the overall reliability of our mechanisms of belief production.[16] Indeed, this kind of investigation typically results in a better understanding of the ways in which such mechanisms may go wrong. In addition, there is no reason to think that every mechanism of belief production must be reliable; there may well be mechanisms which, by and large, tend to produce false beliefs. There is, indeed, a good deal of evidence that some mechanisms of belief production are like this.

This empirical investigation of the mechanisms of belief production at both the level of the individual and at the level of the group allows us to begin to answer the question of how knowledge is possible. The possibility of human knowledge is examined from two different perspectives. On the one hand, we wish to know what it is about us that allows us to understand the world. On the other hand, we wish to know what it is about the world that allows it to be known. What is required, in the end, is an account of how the various presuppositions of our mechanisms of belief acquisition, both individual and social, dovetail with various features of the world so that the resulting beliefs tend to get things right. I will provide two brief illustrations of how such an account proceeds.[17]

First, consider the familiar visual illusion in which a series of lights are turned on and off in succession so as to give the impression of motion. Highway signs frequently trade on this illusion. One of the interesting facts about this phenomenon, and about visual illusions of motion generally, is that even when we know how the illusion is produced, and, in this case, that there is no motion at all, we are still presented with an impression of motion. What seems to be going on in this case is the following. The visual system is so constructed as to assume a world populated, for the most part, by three-dimensional objects with more or less stable boundaries. Given a series of impressions of a sort which might be caused by such objects, the visual system automatically imposes an interpretation on them consistent with that assumption. Because the assumption is in fact true of our world, that is, because our world is largely made up of three-dimensional objects with more or less stable

boundaries, the visual system works quite quickly and, for the most part, accurately. The assumption built into the system, however, is not true of every possible world, and, were we placed in an environment largely populated by objects violating the assumption, the beliefs produced by the visual system would tend to be mistaken. The presuppositions of our visual system match, or roughly match, certain pervasive features of the world, and it is in virtue of that approximate match that we are able reliably to gain information about the world. We should not expect our epistemology to discover techniques of belief acquisition which would work in any world whatsoever. Instead, we should expect to discover processes like the one embodied in the visual system which are tailored to contingent though pervasive features of the actual world.

We may examine our native inferential tendencies in the same way. As Tversky and Kahneman[18] have illustrated in great detail, human beings have a natural tendency to draw conclusions about a population of objects on the basis of extremely small samples, indeed, often on the basis of a single case. This is a dramatic violation of the law of large numbers. As Tversky and Kahneman argue, we ought to draw conclusions about a population only when we have a fairly large sample on which to base a conclusion; to do otherwise is simply irrational. Tversky and Kahneman draw the obvious conclusion. Human beings are built to reason badly.

This inferential tendency, however, must be evaluated in light of the environments in which it is operative. We ought to be asking, not whether it would work well in any possible environment, but whether it works well in the environments in which human beings tend to be found. I have argued, in fact, that this tendency serves us well and that it does so precisely because, on the whole, it tends to produce true beliefs.

Drawing conclusions about a population on the basis of a single sample will work well when the populations are largely uniform with respect to the traits which are projected. Thus, for example, if I conclude that all copper conducts electricity after noting that a single sample of copper conducts electricity, I will not go wrong. In general, if we tend to project essential features of natural kinds, the tendency to generalize quickly will be a reliable one. What is needed here in order to evaluate our inferential tendency is an examination of the structure of human concepts and an understanding of the features of kinds which tend to be projected. Work in conceptual development indicates that from the beginning, children assume that the observable properties of objects do not determine kind membership and that, instead, there are unobservable features of objects which are essential to the kinds of which they are members. In short, it is a feature of human conceptual structure that we take for granted that natural kinds have Lockean real essences. If natural kinds do have Lockean real essences, as I have argued they do, and if we are even roughly attuned to the essential properties of kinds, as I have argued we are, then the tendency to make inferences about a population on the basis of small samples is broadly reliable. Once again, we see the respects in which features of our psychology track pervasive though contingent features of the world. It is this sort of fit which makes knowledge possible.

The search for principles of reasoning which would work well in any possible world was, to my mind, a mistake. A proper explanation of the possibility of human knowledge will not appeal to such principles of reasoning but rather to principles like the ones just illustrated, ones whose reliability is deeply contingent and whose success can only be explained by demonstrating the fit between features of the world and features of the principles themselves. It is for this reason that epistemology becomes an empirical discipline, continuous with the sciences, and it is for this reason that epistemology must draw so heavily on work in psychology.

This project of explaining how human knowledge is possible also provides the basis for empirically informed epistemic advice. If we wish to give advice to agents on how to improve their belief acquisition, we need to know where agents are most liable to err and what kinds of psychological processes may in fact be realized. It is of little use to tell human agents, for example, to make all of their beliefs consistent, given that checking our entire body of beliefs for consistency is not within our power. Even attempting to gain as much consistency in our beliefs as we can is not good advice, for our efforts are far better spent in other kinds of cognitive management. The empirical examination of processes of belief acquisition will thus give us the information which is needed to advise agents on where

their efforts are best employed. Those who are interested in cognitive improvement should thus be interested in this project.

The naturalistic project thus provides a way of unifying the three epistemological projects undertaken by Descartes: giving an account of what knowledge is; explaining how knowledge is possible; and providing useful epistemic advice. The way in which these projects are unified is, of course, quite different from the way in which Descartes attempted to unify them. Indeed, the project of explaining how knowledge is possible is interpreted in such a different way by naturalists and Cartesians that many will want to claim that the subject here has simply been changed. Descartes wished to answer the total skeptic; the naturalistic account of how knowledge is possible does not even attempt to address that kind of challenge. As naturalists see it, however, what was legitimate in the skeptical challenge is, in fact, addressed by the naturalistic project. What remains unanswered has proven to be a fruitless research project and is thus best abandoned. Naturalists may be proven wrong here by being shown that a response to the Cartesian skeptic would in some way be illuminating.

Whatever one thinks of the challenge presented by the Cartesian skeptic, there is something powerful in the unifying vision presented by epistemological naturalists, just as there was something powerful in the unifying vision presented by Descartes. The three epistemological projects which have been described are surely worthy of pursuit. The fact that empirical work is required in order to pursue them hardly makes them less worthy of our attention, although I recognize that many will think that this makes them appear less philosophical. It is interesting to note, however, that more traditional and a priori approaches to epistemological questions have not been able to provide such a unifying account, at least once one rejects some of Descartes' more implausible claims. The project of providing constructive epistemic advice, so central to Descartes' conception of epistemology, has been largely abandoned by traditional epistemologists, for they recognize that a priori means alone are insufficient to the task.[19] But the remaining projects, when divorced from their connection with epistemic advice, arguably lose much of their interest.[20] Why should we care about having justified beliefs, for example, when justification is so understood that making our beliefs justified will not make it more likely that they be true? Much of what motivated Descartes' epistemological work is now pursued in a different manner by epistemological naturalists. Much of the more traditional epistemology, which is so much influenced by Descartes' methods, has abandoned his concerns.

I am not arguing that we should pursue the naturalistic approach because, in the end, it is more nearly continuous with the history of epistemological endeavors than a priori work in epistemology. By my lights, being continuous with the history of epistemological endeavors is not automatically a good thing. Rather, I am arguing that many of the concerns which were central to Descartes' project are still rightly viewed as legitimate ones, and the fact that a priori work in epistemology does not properly address them counts against that project. The real issue here should not be, "Which kind of work is more nearly continuous with what actually concerned Descartes and the other late, great epistemologists?" Instead, we need to ask, "What kind of questions about knowledge are worthy of our pursuit?" The naturalistic approach has, I believe, clearly identified a set of such questions and has shown us how they may be productively addressed. That is, to my mind, a real achievement.

IV

Naturalistic epistemologists do not claim merely to be addressing some of the legitimate questions in the field; rather, it is claimed that the naturalistic approach addresses all of the legitimate questions and that there is nothing left for more traditional approaches to deal with. It will come as no surprise then that naturalism has met with more than a few challenges. Indeed, as the naturalistic approach has become better established, more epistemologists have registered their doubts about the project. I will briefly summarize the main lines of criticism and sketch the sorts of reply which are available to the naturalist.

One objection which has arisen repeatedly is that a naturalistic epistemology cannot be both "a chapter of psychology" and, simultaneously, a normative enterprise. Insofar as epistemology is absorbed by empirical science, it thereby becomes merely descriptive. But a central project of epistemology involves developing

epistemic advice; and this normative dimension of epistemology must therefore be bypassed. Epistemology without normativity, it is argued, is just *Hamlet* without the Prince of Denmark.[21]

I myself am quite sympathetic with the suggestion that the normative dimension of epistemological inquiry is essential to it. The idea that a naturalistic epistemology is thoroughly empirical, however, does not in any way rob it of its normative force. As I have already indicated, the project of providing useful epistemic advice must be empirically informed, for we need to know what kinds of errors human beings are most liable to make if we are to give advice where it is most needed, and we must know what kinds of advice are humanly followable if we are to provide advice which can address our shortcomings. That empirical information is essential to the task of providing epistemic advice in this way is undeniable.

The disagreement, however, does not end here. Some will see the empirical project I have described as merely applied epistemology; on some accounts, it is no part of philosophy at all. Rather, the project I have described cannot get going, it will be urged, without a prior account of how we ought, ideally, to arrive at our beliefs. This is the proper business of epistemology. The empirical work only comes in when we try to figure out how far human beings tend to be from the ideal and when we try to figure out the best strategies for remedial work, that is, for getting individuals as close to the ideal as is humanly possible. Some a priori work having to do with ideals of reasoning, however, is required before any of the empirical work can be done.[22] Whatever one may want to call the empirical work, surely the a priori project just described is part of epistemology.

Now obviously those, such as Quine, who reject the very idea of apriority are not going to be moved by this kind of argument, nor should they. But important as I believe the issue of apriority to be in the debate between naturalists and their critics, we need not raise that issue here. I will suppose, for the sake of argument, that there is such a thing as a priori knowledge. What I want to suggest on behalf of naturalism is that even if there were such knowledge, it could not play the role just described in launching the project of devising useful epistemic advice.

The objection just considered supposes that we have available some useful notion of ideal reasoning which can be arrived at a priori. Such an account will abstract away from various human limitations, including limits on memory, attention, life span, and so on. Now this account cannot abstract from all human limitations. After all, if we allow superhuman intellectual abilities, then reasoning itself becomes entirely unnecessary: A creature with no intellectual limitations would be able to intuit truths directly. The very necessity of reasoning is itself a sign of our intellectual limits. So suppose that we hold fixed a certain class of beliefs which can be arrived at without reasoning—say, perceptual beliefs as well as some others—and we then ask what further beliefs might be inferred from them by way of ideal reasoning. What is to constrain this notion of the ideal? What is to give it content?

The problem with appealing to the notion of a priori principles of good reasoning in order to constrain this conception of an ideal is that such principles—assuming there to be such—may make no contact at all with the project of providing useful epistemic advice. Human beings are innately disposed to reason in certain ways, and these innate dispositions may be extremely reliable in the actual world even without being identical to, or even close approximations to, any principles which are a priori reasonable. When we reason reliably, the only epistemic advice which is called for is to keep doing what we are already doing, however the principles that we are innately disposed to apply may compare with a priori principles. Similarly, when we reason badly, when principles of reasoning which we are innately disposed to apply are unreliable, what we wish to replace these principles with are ones which we can act in accord with in such a way as to regularly arrive at true beliefs *in the actual world*. We needn't be concerned about whether such principles are a priori knowable. Even if it should turn out that the way in which such principles achieve their reliability can only be understood a posteriori, perhaps because they trade on some contingent though pervasive feature of the world, these would still be the kind of principles which we would want to recommend. More than this, principles which we know a priori to be reliable when we abstract away from human limitations may turn out to be very bad principles to reason in accord with once those limitations

are factored back in. Empirical work on human reasoning has shown these concerns to be more than merely imaginary. The apriorist notion of the ideal, naturalists will want to argue, turns out, as a matter of empirical fact, to be irrelevant to the project of offering epistemic advice. Indeed, it thus seems a misnomer to call it any kind of ideal at all.[23]

I thus conclude that the objection against naturalism we have been considering—that in making epistemology thoroughly empirical, it loses all normative force—is entirely without merit. First, there is a clear respect in which an empirical theory of reasoning may have normative force; the mere fact that it is empirical does not, by itself, rob the theory of normative consequences. And second, there is reason to think that if any account is robbed of normative force here, it is, not the empirical theory, but the theory which deprives itself of empirical input. It is the antinaturalist, I believe, who must be concerned that his theory is irrelevant to normative concerns.[24]

Let me turn then to a different objection to naturalism, an objection which Laurence BonJour has presented quite forcefully.[25] BonJour presents an argument against naturalism which, he says, "seems . . . as obvious and compelling as any in the whole of philosophy . . . [26] Let me quote BonJour at length:

> I will assume here, without worrying about the details, that the fact that a belief is a report of direct observation or experience constitutes an adequate reason for thinking it to be true. But what about the non-observational or non-experiential beliefs? If we are to have any reason for thinking these latter beliefs to be true, such a reason must apparently either (i) depend on an inference of some sort from some of the directly observational beliefs or (ii) be entirely independent of direct observation. A reason of sort (ii) is plainly *a priori*. And a reason of sort (i) can only be cogent if its corresponding conditional, a conditional statement having the conjunction of the directly observational premises as antecedent and the proposition that is the content of the nonobservational belief as a consequent, is something that we in turn have a reason to think to be true. But the reason for thinking that this latter, conditional statement is true can again only be a priori:

if, as we may assume, all relevant observations are already included in the antecedent, they can offer no support to the claim that *if* that antecedent is true, then something further is true. Thus if, as the naturalist claims, there are no *a priori* reasons for thinking anything to be true ... the inevitable result is that we have no reason for thinking that any of our beliefs whose content transcends direct observation are true.

This is epistemological disaster in itself, but a further consequence is that the vast majority of claims about the nature of the world, the nature and reliability of human psychological processes, etc., upon which naturalized epistemology so lovingly focuses, are things that we have no reason at all for thinking to be true—as, indeed, are the very theses that epistemology must be naturalized or that traditional epistemology is untenable .... In this way, naturalized epistemology is *self-referentially inconsistent*: its own epistemological claims exclude the possibility of there being any cogent reason for thinking that those claims are true.[27]

But this argument is not conclusive.

Let us put aside, for the sake of argument, as BonJour does, worries about the notion of direct observation. BonJour explicitly assumes that if an observation statement O is to provide good reason for believing some further claim T, then the conditional 'If O, then T' must itself be a claim which the agent has good reason to believe. But naturalists would deny this premise. Naturalists believe that human beings are so provided by nature that they are inclined to make certain kinds of inferences which are in fact reliable, long before they have evidence that those inferences are reliable. On the naturalistic account, such inferences constitute cases of good reasoning. Thus, for example, children and animals may reason quite well without having the evidence or in some cases even the conceptual repertoire, which would license those inferences. This is not to say that such evidence is inevitably and for all time out of their reach. Nonhuman animals are unlikely to be able to assess the reliability of their own inferences. But children do grow up, and when they are in a position to raise the question of the reliability of their own inferences,

they are also in a position to gather evidence on the issue and, in some cases, resolve it. This project of evaluating one's own inferences by means of the inferential machinery under evaluation, as I earlier argued, is not an idle exercise. There are circumstances under which such an investigation would reveal deep problems in the inferential machinery. Passing this kind of test, then, although it is not a guarantee against all conceivable challenges, is informative.

What could BonJour's complaint here be? It cannot be that *a priori* assurances, if we had them, would quiet the total skeptic, for, on BonJour's own account, a priori reasoning gives us no such definitive refutation; rather what it does, at best, is make it reasonable to believe that the skeptic is mistaken. But in this respect, it is not all clear that the naturalist is worse off. BonJour is simply taking for granted certain constraints on good reasoning which the naturalist rejects.[28] So there is a substantive dispute here as to what good reasoning consists in, not, as BonJour portrays things, a simple case of self-referential inconsistency. Contrary to what BonJour suggests, naturalism is not self-refuting.

These are, to my mind, the two most important objections to naturalism available in the literature. At this point, the dispute between naturalists and antinaturalists will turn on the fruits of their theories. What each side needs to show is that it has a productive research program available, a program of research which will be genuinely illuminating. It is in this that the future of epistemology will be determined.[29]

Notes

1. W. V. O. Quine, "Epistemology Naturalized," in his *Ontological Relativity and Other Essays* (New York: Columbia University Press, 1969).
2. While Quine focuses exclusively on foundationalism, there is reason to think that the naturalist critique applies equally well to coherentism, at least as traditionally conceived. See my "Beyond Foundationalism and the Coherence Theory," *Journal of Philosophy* 77 (1980): 597–612.
3. This last point is made especially forcefully in Stephen Stich, *The Fragmentation of Reason* (Cambridge, Mass.: MIT Press, 1990), and in Mark Kaplan, "Epistemology Denatured," *Midwest Studies in Philosophy* 19 (1994): 350–365.
4. Quine, op. cit., 82.

5. See especially Barry Stroud, *The Significance of Philosophical Skepticism* (Oxford: Oxford University Press, 1984), and Jaegwon Kim, "What Is 'Naturalized Epistemology'?" *Philosophical Perspectives* 2 (1988): 381–405.

6. See Kim, op. cit., Stroud, op. cit., and Elliott Sober, "Psychologism," *Journal for the Theory of Social Behavior* 8 (1978): 165–191.

7. Alvin Goldman, "A Causal Theory of Knowing," *Journal of Philosophy* 64 (1967): 357–72.

8. The only mention of the Gettier problem in the Quinean corpus with which I am familiar is to be found in *Quiddities* (Cambridge, Mass.: Harvard University Press, 1987). Quine there suggests that "the best we can do is give up the notion of knowledge as a bad job and make do rather with its separate ingredients" (ibid., 109).

9. Alvin Goldman, "Discrimination and Perceptual Knowledge," *Journal of Philosophy* 73 (1976): 771–91.

10. In Alvin Goldman, "What Is Justified Belief?" in George Pappas, ed. *Justification and Knowledge* (Dordrecht: Reidel, 1979), 1–23. The account is further developed in great detail in his *Epistemology and Cognition* (Cambridge, Mass.: Harvard University Press, 1986).

11. I argue that this is the proper way to view the central difference between reliabilism, on the one hand, and foundationalism and the coherence theory, on the other, in Kornblith, op. cit.

12. This empirical investigation takes the place of the search for epistemic principles connecting the foundation of knowledge with its superstructure. While the foundationalist account requires that these connecting epistemic principles enjoy a privileged epistemological status, the investigation of these psychological mechanisms is simply a part of empirical science.

13. This is one, though only one, of the defining features of James Gibson's approach to psychology. See especially his *The Senses Considered as Perceptual Systems* (Boston: Houghton Mifflin Co., 1966) and *The Ecological Approach to Visual Perception* (Boston: Houghton Mifflin Co., 1979).

14. For Goldman's work here, see the papers in part 3 of his *Liaisons: Philosophy Meets the Cognitive and Social Sciences* (Cambridge, Mass.: MIT Press, 1993). For Kitcher's work, see "The Division of Cognitive Labor," *Journal of Philosophy* 87 (1990): 5–22; "Socializing Knowledge," *Journal of Philosophy* 88 (1991): 675–676; "Authority, Deference and the Role of Individual Reason," in Ernan McMullin, ed., *The Social Dimension of Scientific Knowledge* (South Bend, Ind.: Notre Dame University Press, 1992); and *The Advancement of Science* (Oxford: Oxford University Press, 1993). My own view on this matter is further developed in "A Conservative Approach to Social Epistemology," in Frederick Schmitt, ed., *Socializing Epistemology: The Social Dimensions of Knowledge* (Lanham, Md.: Rowman and Littlefield, 1994), 93–110.

15. Miriam Solomon argues that they are in "Is There an Invisible Hand of Reason?" (forthcoming).

16. This point is nicely defended in Michael Friedman, "Truth and Confirmation," *Journal of Philosophy* 76 (1979): 361–382, and in Philip Kitcher, "The Naturalists Return," *Philosophical Review* 101 (1992): 53–114.

17. This approach, and the two illustrations, are developed in detail in my *Inductive Inference and Its Natural Ground* (Cambridge, Mass.: MIT Press, 1993).

18. Tversky and Kahneman, "Belief in the Law of Small Numbers," *Psychological Bulletin* 2 (1971): 105–110.

19. Thus, see, for example, BonJour's remarks about the meliorative project in epistemology in his "Against Naturalized Epistemology," *Midwest Studies in Philosophy* 19 (1994): 283–300.

20. Here I am echoing Kaplan, op. cit., and Stich, op. cit., although Kaplan attempts to use this perspective to argue against naturalism.

21. See especially Kim, op. cit., and Stroud, op. cit.

22. BonJour, op. cit., defends this approach.

23. I believe that this kind of response can be developed to answer the challenge to naturalism presented in Kaplan, op. cit., but a full reply to Kaplan must await another occasion. See my "Cogent Arguments for Naturalism: A Reply to Kaplan" (in preparation).

24. There is another way of construing the worry about normativity, and this has to do with the alleged fact-value gap. I address this challenge to naturalism in my "Epistemic Normativity," *Synthese* 94 (1993): 357–376. For a different attempt to defend naturalism on this score, see James Maffie, "Naturalism and the Normativity of Epistemology," *Philosophical Studies* 59 (1990): 87–103.

25. See BonJour, op. cit.

26. Ibid., 24.

27. Ibid., 22–23.

28. BonJour does argue for these constraints elsewhere (see his *The Structure of Empirical Knowledge* [Cambridge, Mass.: Harvard University Press, 1985]), but this argument too is open to challenge. Indeed, BonJour himself acknowledges that his account of what counts as good reason forces him to total skepticism. So he can hardly complain that the naturalist is worse off in this respect. Indeed, it seems clear that the naturalist is far better off here, for the naturalist does not endorse the account of good reasoning which leads to the skeptical conclusion.

29. Earlier versions of this paper were presented at a symposium on naturalism at the Eastern Division Meeting of the American Philosophical Association in December 1994, where Sandra Rosenthal commented, and at Brigham Young University. I am indebted to audiences at both of these presentations. I am also indebted to David Christensen, Derk Pereboom, Miriam Solomon, and Bill Talbott for very helpful comments on a previous draft of this paper.

INTRODUCTION

While the details about how we acquire knowledge through experience are controversial, the basic picture is that information about the world is carried to our brains via channels that include sensory experience. But a priori knowledge, as opposed to a posteriori knowledge, is supposed to be a kind of knowledge that does not involve information channeled to us through the senses. To understand it, we must therefore clarify the sorts of propositions that are knowable a priori, and the devices through which nonexperiential knowledge is produced.

What sorts of propositions might be knowable a priori? The most obvious candidates are analytic truths, which are of two sorts. First, there are *semantically true* propositions such as "all bachelors are unmarried males"; these are true by virtue of the meanings of constituent terms. Second, there are *logically true* propositions such as "all bachelors are bachelors"; these are true by virtue of their logical form. It seems possible to know semantically and logically true propositions a priori because they can be verified by anyone who can grasp meaning and logical form, and these are operations of reason.

Kant thought some synthetic truths were also knowable a priori. Among these he numbered the propositions of mathematics. Some synthetic propositions are knowable a priori, he said, because they are made true by virtue of the ways the mind structures experience, and we have access to that structure. They are necessarily true in the sense that they hold across all possible experience.

Analytic truths and, perhaps, the synthetic truths Kant singled out, are all necessary in some sense. The position of Western philosophers up to, and including, Kant was that necessary truths are the only candidates for a priori knowledge, that necessary truths cannot be known a posteriori, and that a priori knowledge is possible only because we can grasp the concepts that constitute the meanings of our words or that we impose on experience. But in recent years the traditional picture of a priori knowledge has been challenged. C.I. Lewis argued that elements of our conceptual scheme are genuinely a priori, but are not part of a fixed and unchanging order that is imposed by 'mind.' They are changed over time on pragmatic grounds. W.V.O. Quine has questioned the idea that individual statements have their own meaning; thereby he challenged the idea that a statement can be seen true by virtue of its meaning. Saul Kripke has argued that some contingent (non-necessary) propositions can be known a priori, and some propositions that are necessarily true are knowable a posteriori.

C. I. Lewis (1883–1965) and the Pragmatic Approach to the A priori

In "A Pragmatic Conception of the A priori," Clarence Irving Lewis carves out a place for the a priori while rejecting the Kantian idea that the mind is familiar with "principles that are legislative for experience" and the rationalist idea that there is a "natural light or any innate ideas." Lewis maintains that inquiry must take place against the backdrop of a conceptual scheme that includes the fundamental laws and definitive concepts of science. This scheme is a priori in the sense that the activity of justifying various claims on the basis of experience cannot proceed until the scheme is in place, partly since it provides our criteria for what is real, so that the scheme itself is not based on experience in any straightforward way. Instead, we choose, and revise, our fundamental scheme on the basis of pragmatic considerations.

Quine (1908–2000) and Reservations About the Analytic

Willard Van Orman Quine claims that a sharp line cannot be drawn between analytic and synthetic sentences. His attack is prompted by his holistic view of meaning, according to which sentences never have meanings individually (unless they are observation sentences), but only collectively. As he puts the point, "the unit of empirical significance is the whole of science." The meanings of sentences are bound up with the truth of other sentences, which blurs the line between analytic and synthetic truth. Quine bases his semantic holism on his pragmatist/positivist assumption that "the meaning of a sentence turns purely on what would count as evidence for its truth," (in 1969, p. 80) and the Duhem-Quine thesis, so-called because Quine borrowed it from Pierre Duhem (1861–1916): "theoretical sentences have their evidence not as single sentences but only as larger blocks of theory" (pp. 80–81); that is, it is the whole of science that faces experience, and the whole that has experiential evidence.

In "Two Dogmas of Empiricism," Quine tries to blur the analytic-synthetic distinction by arguing that it can be made sharp only if we can provide a clear idea of synonymy, but we cannot.

Kripke (b.1940) and A priori Knowledge of the Contingent

Saul Kripke argues that some statements are both contingent and a priori, while others are both necessary and a posteriori. To confirm the former, he provides examples such as the following: suppose that I fix the units of the metric system by reference to a particular stick, S, at a given time *t*. Then I know a priori that stick S is one meter long at time *t*. But this statement is also contingent. To explain why, Kripke coins the term *rigid designator*. A rigid designator is a term that refers, in other possible worlds, to the same thing it refers to in the actual world. I fix the reference of the term *meter* by stipulating that *meter* is a *rigid designator* of the length which is in fact the length of S at a given time *t*. Since *meter* is a rigid designator of the length S actually had at *t*, it refers to that length in all possible worlds. And in some possible worlds the stick did not have that length at *t*.

To show that some propositions are both necessary and a posteriori, Kripke offers the example, *Hesperus is Phosphorus*. According to a view inspired by Gottlob Frege (1892) and Bertrand Russell (1956), the referent of a name is determined by a description associated with it. In the case of *Hesperus*, this description might be *the morning star*. Since the description associated with *Hesperus* might be distinct from that associated with *Phosphorus*, and since these descriptions might pick out different things in the actual world or in other possible worlds, the Frege-Russell view suggests that the proposition *Hesperus is Phosphorus* is contingent. But Kripke rejects this view, saying that, like all proper names, *Hesperus* and *Phosphorus* are rigid designators whose referents are determined by a chain of usage. And so if it is true that Hesperus is Phosphorus, it is true necessarily, just because *Hesperus* and *Phosphorus* will refer to precisely the same objects in all possible worlds. It is a necessary truth that a thing is identical to itself. There is no world in which they are distinct. And in fact, Hesperus *is* Phosphorus; *Hesperus* and *Phosphorus* refer to the planet Venus. So it is necessarily true that Hesperus is Phosphorus. But it does not follow that a person can know this a priori, for it might require experience to know that *Hesperus* and *Phosphorus* refer to the same planet.

BonJour's Rationalist Account of the A priori

"Toward a Moderate Rationalism," by Laurence Bon-Jour, is the precursor to the central chapters of his book *In Defense of Pure Reason: A Rationalist Account of A Priori Justification* (1997). In his essay BonJour offers what he alludes to in the subtitle of his book: a rationalist account of a priori justification. His rationalism is moderate in that he portrays a priori justification as fallible. BonJour's strategy is to establish a prima facie case for apriorism using examples of what looks to be genuine a priori justification. One such example concerns the proposition that nothing can be red all over and green all over at the same time, which we are justified in accepting when we grasp its elements and see that it cannot fail to be true. Then he defends his position against objections.

1. Lewis claims our conceptual scheme provides our criteria for what is real. How, then, can we revise it on the basis of pragmatic considerations? What sorts of considerations would support our changing our scheme?

2. Some maintain that the meanings of words are mental entities. On this view, we could say that two words are synonymous if and only if the mental entities that constitute their meaning are the same. How would Quine criticize this account of meaning? Would he be correct?

3. Does Quine commit himself to the view that all knowable claims are empirical? Is the thesis that all propositions can be given up consistent with the claim that some propositions are necessarily true?

4. Suppose you gave the name *Twinkie* to the particular copy of *Essential Knowledge* which you are reading. Twinkie is, in fact, made of paper. But is 'Twinkie is made of paper' knowable a posteriori? Is it a necessary truth?

5. Does Kripke's claims about aprioricity commit him to rationalism? If so, what precisely is the form of rationalism he must accept?

6. Is BonJour's case for rationalism successful? How might Quine respond?

7. Is BonJour-style rationalism consistent with Kornblith-style naturalism? If not, in what ways do these views clash? Which is most adequate?

◇ A PRAGMATIC VIEW ◇

39. A PRAGMATIC CONCEPTION OF THE A PRIORI[1]

C. I. Lewis

The conception of the a priori points two problems which are perennial in philosophy; the part played in knowledge by the mind itself, and the possibility of "necessary truth" or of knowledge "independent of experience." But traditional conceptions of the a priori have proved untenable. That the mind approaches the flux of immediacy with some godlike foreknowledge of principles which are legislative for experience, that there is any natural light or any innate ideas, it is no longer possible to believe.

Nor shall we find the clue to the a priori in any compulsion of the mind to incontrovertible truth or any peculiar kind of demonstration which establishes first principles. All truth lays upon the rational mind the same compulsion to belief; as Mr. Bosanquet has pointed out, this character belongs to all propositions or judgments once their truth is established.

The difficulties of the conception are due, I believe, to two mistakes: whatever is a priori is necessary, but we have misconstrued the relation of necessary truth to mind. And the a priori is independent of experience, but in so taking it, we have misunderstood its relation to empirical fact. What is a priori is necessary truth not because it compels the mind's acceptance, but precisely because it does not. It is given experience, brute fact, the *a posteriori* element in knowledge which the mind must accept willy-nilly. The a priori represents an attitude in some sense freely taken, a stipulation of the mind itself, and a stipulation which might be made in some other way if it suited our bent or need. Such truth is necessary as opposed to contingent, not as opposed to voluntary. And the a priori is independent of experience not because it prescribes a form which the data of sense must fit, or anticipates some preëstablished harmony of experience with the mind, but precisely because it prescribes nothing to experience. That is a priori which is true, *no matter what*. What it anticipates is not the given, but our attitude toward it: it concerns the uncompelled initiative of mind or, as Josiah Royce would say, our categorical ways of acting.

The traditional example of the a priori *par excellence* is the laws of logic. These can not be derived from experience since they must first be taken for granted in order to prove them. They make explicit our general modes of classification. And they impose upon experience no real limitation. Sometimes we are asked to tremble before the spectre of the "a logical," in order that we may thereafter rejoice that we are saved from this by the dependence of reality upon mind. But the "a logical" is pure bogey, a word without a meaning. What kind of experience could defy the principle that everything must either be or not be, that nothing can both be and not be, or that if x is y and y is z, then x is z? If anything imaginable or unimaginable could violate such laws, then the ever-present fact of change would do it every day. The laws of logic are purely formal; they forbid nothing but what concerns the use of terms and the corresponding modes of classification and analysis. The law of contradiction tells us that nothing can be both white and not-white, but it does not and can not tell us whether black is not-white, or soft or square is not-white. To discover *what contradicts what* we must always consult the character of experience. Similarly the law of the excluded middle formulates our decision that whatever is not designated by a certain term shall be designated by its negative. It declares our purpose to make, for every term, a complete dichotomy of experience, instead—as we might choose—of classifying on the basis of a tripartite division into opposites (as black and white) and the middle ground between the two. Our rejection of such tripartite division represents only our penchant for simplicity.

Further laws of logic are of similar significance. They are principles of procedure, the parliamentary rules of intelligent thought and speech. Such laws are independent of experience be cause they impose no limitations whatever upon it. They are legislative because they are addressed to ourselves—because definition classification, and inference represent no operations of the objective world, but only our own categorical attitudes of mind.

And further, the ultimate criteria of the laws of logic are pragmatic. Those who suppose that there is, for example, *a* logic which everyone would agree to if he understood it and understood him self, are more optimistic than those versed in the history of logical discussion have a right to be. The fact is that there are several logics, markedly different, each self-consistent in its own terms and such that whoever, using it, avoids false premises, will never reach a false conclusion. Mr. Russell, for example, bases *his* logic on an implication relation such that if twenty sentences be cut from a newspaper and put in a hat, and then two of these be drawn at random, one of them will certainly imply the other, and it is an even bet that the implication will be mutual. Yet upon a foundation so remote from ordinary modes of inference the whole structure of *Principia Mathematica* is built. This logic—and there are others even more strange—is utterly consistent and the results of it entirely valid. Over and above all questions of consistency, there are issues of logic which can not be determined—nay, can not even be argued—except on pragmatic grounds of conformity to human bent and intellectual convenience. That we have been blind to this fact, itself reflects traditional errors in the conception of the a priori.

We may note in passing one less important illustration of the a priori—the proposition "true by definition." Definitions and their immediate consequences, analytic propositions generally, are necessarily true, true under all possible circumstances. Definition is legislative because it is in some sense arbitrary. Not only is the meaning assigned to words more or less a matter of choice—that consideration is relatively trivial—but the manner in which the precise classifications which definition embodies shall be effected, is something not dictated by experience. If experience were other than it is, the definition and its corresponding classification might be inconvenient, fantastic, or useless, but it could not be false. Mind makes classifications and determines meanings; in so doing it creates the a priori truth of analytic judgments. But that the manner of this creation responds to pragmatic considerations, is so obvious that it hardly needs pointing out.

If the illustrations so far given seem trivial or verbal, that impression may be corrected by turning to the place which the a priori has in mathematics and in natural science. Arithmetic, for example, depends *en toto* upon the operation of counting or correlating, a procedure which can be carried out at will in any world containing identifiable things—even identifiable ideas—regardless of the further characters of experience. Mill challenged this a priori character of arithmetic. He asked us to suppose a demon sufficiently powerful and maleficent so that every time two things were brought together with two other things, this demon should always introduce a fifth. The implication which he supposed to follow is that under such circumstances 2 + 2 = 5 would be a universal law of arithmetic. But Mill was quite mistaken. In such a world we should be obliged to become a little clearer than is usual about the distinction between arithmetic and physics, that is all. If two black marbles were put in the same urn with two white ones, the demon could take his choice of colors, but it would be evident that there were more black marbles or more white ones than were put in. The same would be true of all objects in any wise identifiable. We should simply find ourselves in the presence of an extraordinary physical law, which we should recognize as universal in our world, that whenever two things were brought into proximity with two others, an additional and similar thing was always created by the process. Mill's world would be physically most extraordinary. The world's work would be enormously facilitated if hats or locomotives or tons of coal could be thus multiplied by anyone possessed originally of two pairs. But the laws of mathematics would remain unaltered. It is because this is true that arithmetic is a priori. Its laws prevent *nothing*; they are compatible with anything which happens or could conceivably happen in nature. They would be true in any possible world. Mathematical addition is not a physical transformation. Physical changes which result in an increase or decrease of the countable things involved are matters of everyday occurrence. Such physical processes present us with phenomena in which the purely mathematical has to be separated out by abstraction. Those laws and those laws only have necessary truth which we are prepared to maintain, no matter what. It is because we shall always separate out that part of the phenomenon not in conformity with arithmetic and designate it by some other category—physical change, chemical reaction, optical illusion—that arithmetic is a priori.

The a priori element in science and in natural law is greater than might be supposed. In the first place, all science is based upon definitive concepts. The formulation of these concepts is, indeed, a matter determined by the commerce between our intellectual or our pragmatic interests and the nature of experience. Definition is classification. The scientific search is for such classification as will make it possible to correlate appearance and behavior, to discover law, to penetrate to the "essential nature" of things in order that behavior may become predictable. In other words, if definition is unsuccessful, as early scientific definitions mostly have been, it is because the classification thus set up corresponds with no natural cleavage and does not correlate with any important uniformity of behavior. A name itself must represent *some* uniformity in experience or it names nothing. What does not repeat itself or recur in intelligible fashion is not a thing. Where the definitive uniformity is a clue to other uniformities, we have successful scientific definition. Other definitions can not be said to be false; they are merely useless. In scientific classification the search is, thus, for *things worth naming*. But the naming, classifying, defining activity is essentially prior to investigation. We can not interrogate experience in general. Until our meaning is definite and our classification correspondingly exact, experience can not conceivably answer our questions.

In the second place, the fundamental laws of any science—or those treated as fundamental—are a priori because they formulate just such definitive concepts or categorical tests by which alone investigation becomes possible. If the lightning strikes the railroad track at two places, A *and* B, how shall we tell whether these events are simultaneous? "We . . . require a definition of simultaneity such that this definition supplies us with the method by means of which . . . we can decide whether or not both the lightning strokes occurred simultaneously. As long as this requirement is not satisfied, I allow myself to be deceived as a physicist (and of course the same applies if I am not a physicist), when I imagine that I am able to attach a meaning to the statement of simultaneity. . . .

"After thinking the matter over for some time you then offer the following suggestion with which to test simultaneity. By measuring along the rails, the connecting line AB should be measured up and an observer placed at the mid-point M of the distance AB. This observer should be supplied with an arrangement (*e.g.*, two mirrors inclined at 90°) which allows him visually to observe both places A and B at the same time. If the observer perceives the two flashes at the same time, then they are simultaneous.

"I am very pleased with this suggestion, but for all that I can not regard the matter as quite settled, because I feel constrained to raise the following objection: 'Your definition would certainly be right, if I only knew that the light by means of which the observer at M perceives the lightning flashes travels along the length A—M with the same velocity as along the length B—M. But an examination of this supposition would only be possible if we already had at our disposal the means of measuring time. It would thus appear as though we were moving here in a logical circle.'

"After further consideration you cast a somewhat disdainful glance at me—and rightly so—and you declare: 'I maintain my previous definition nevertheless, because in reality it assumes absolutely nothing about light. There is only *one* demand to be made of the definition of simultaneity, namely, that in every real case it must supply us with an empirical decision as to whether or not the conception which has to be defined is fulfilled. That light requires the same time to traverse the path A—M as for the path B—M is in reality *neither a supposition nor a hypothesis* about the physical nature of light, but a *stipulation* which I can make of my own free-will in order to arrive at a definition of simultaneity.' . . . We are thus led also to a definition of 'time' in physics."[2]

As this example from the theory of relatively well illustrates we can not even ask the questions which discovered law would answer until we have first by a priori stipulation formulated definitive criteria. Such concepts are not verbal definitions, nor classifications merely; they are themselves laws which prescribe a certain uniformity of behavior to whatever is thus named. Such definitive laws are a priori; only so can we enter upon the investigation by which further laws are sought. Yet it should also be pointed out that such a priori laws are subject to abandonment if the structure which is built upon them does not succeed in simplifying our interpretation of phenomena. If, in the illustration given, the relation "simultaneous with," as defined, should not prove transitive—if event A should prove simultaneous with B, and B with C, but not A with C—this definition would certainly be rejected.

And thirdly, there is that a priori element in science— as in other human affairs—which constitutes the criteria of the real as opposed to the unreal in experience. An object itself is a uniformity. Failure to behave in certain categorical ways marks it as unreal. Uniformities of the type called "natural law" are the clues to reality and unreality. A mouse which disappears where no hole is, is no real mouse; a landscape which recedes as we approach is but illusion. As the queen remarked in the episode of the wishing carpet; "If this were real, then it would be a miracle. But miracles do not happen. Therefore I shall wake presently." That the uniformities of natural law are the only reliable criteria of the real, is inescapable. But such a criterion is *ipso facto a priori*. No conceivable experience could dictate the alteration of a law so long as failure to obey that law marked the content of experience as unreal.

This is one of the puzzles of empiricism. We deal with experience: what any reality may be which underlies experience, we have to learn. What we desire to discover is natural law, the formulation of those uniformities which obtain amongst the real. But experience as it comes to us contains not only the real but all the content of illusion, dream, hallucination, and mistake. The *given* contains both real and unreal, confusingly intermingled. If we ask for uniformities of this unsorted experience, we shall not find them. Laws which characterize all experience, of real and unreal both, are non-existent and would in any case be worthless. What we seek are the uniformities of the *real*; but *until we have such laws, we can not sift experience and segregate the real.*

The obvious solution is that the enrichment of experience, the separation of the real from the illusory or meaningless, and the formulation of natural law, all grow up together. If the criteria of the real are a priori, that is not to say that no conceivable character of experience would lead to alteration of them. For example, spirits can not be photographed. But if photographs of spiritistic phenomena, taken under properly guarded conditions, should become sufficiently frequent, this a priori dictum would be called in question. What we should do would be to redefine our terms. Whether "spook" was spirit or matter, whether the definition of "spirit" or of "matter" should be changed; all this would constitute one interrelated problem. We should reopen together the question of definition or classifiation, of criteria for this sort of real, and of natural law. And the solution of one of these would mean the solution of all. Nothing could *force* a redefinition of spirit or of matter. A sufficiently fundamental relation to human bent, to human interests, would guarantee continuance unaltered even in the face of unintelligible and baffling experiences. In such problems, the mind finds itself uncompelled save by its own purposes and needs. I *may* categorize experience as I will; but *what* categorical distinctions will best serve my interests and objectify my own intelligence? What the mixed and troubled experience shall be—that is beyond me. But what I shall do with it—that is my own question, when the character of experience is sufficiently before me. I am coerced only by my own need to understand.

It would indeed be inappropriate to characterize as a priori a law which we are wholly prepared to alter in the light of further experience, even though in an isolated case we should discard as illusory any experience which failed to conform. But the crux of the situation lies in this; beyond such principles as those of logic, which we seem fully prepared to maintain no matter what, there must be further and more particular criteria of the real prior to any investigation of nature whatever. We can not even interrogate experience without a network of categories and definitive concepts. And we must further be prepared to say what experimental findings will answer what questions, and how. Without tests which represent anterior principle, there is no question which experience could answer at all. Thus the most fundamental laws in any category—or those which we regard as most fundamental—are a priori, even though continued failure to render experience intelligible in such terms might result eventually in the abandonment of that category altogether. Matters so comparatively small as the behavior of Mercury and of starlight passing the sun's limb may, if there be persistent failure to bring them within the field of previously accepted modes of explanation, result in the abandonment of the independent categories of space and time. But without the definitions, fundamental principles, and tests, of the type which constitute such categories, no experience whatever could prove or disprove anything. And to that mind which should find independent space and time absolutely necessary conceptions, no possible experiment could prove the principles of relativity. "There must be some error in the experimental findings or some law not yet discovered," represents an attitude which can never be rendered impossible. And the only sense in which it could be proved unreasonable would be the pragmatic one of comparison with another method of categorical analysis which more

successfully reduced all such experience to order and law.

At the bottom of all science and all knowledge are categories and definitive concepts which represent fundamental habits of thought and deep-lying attitudes which the human mind has taken in the light of its total experience. But a new and wider experience may bring about some alteration of these attitudes, even though by them selves they dictate nothing as to the content of experience, and no experience can conceivably prove them invalid.

Perhaps some will object to this conception on the ground that only such principles should be designated a priori as the human mind *must* maintain, no matter what; that if, for example, it is shown possible to arrive at a consistent doctrine of physics in terms of relativity, even by the most arduous reconstruction of our funds mental notions, then the present conceptions are by that fact shown not to be a priori. Such objection is especially likely from those who would conceive the a priori in terms of an absolute mind or an absolutely universal human nature. We should readily agree that a decision by popular approval or a congress of scientists or anything short of such a test as would bring to bear the full weight of human capacity and interest, would be ill-considered as having to do with the a priori. But we wish to emphasize two facts: first that in the field of those conceptions and principles which have altered in human history, there are those which could neither be proved nor disproved by any experience, but represent the uncompelled initiative of human thought—that without this uncompelled initiative no growth of science, nor any science at all, would be conceivable. And second, that the difference between such conceptions as are, for example, concerned in the decision of relativity versus absolute space and time, and those more permanent attitudes such as are vested in the laws of logic, there is only a difference of degree. The dividing line between the a priori and the *a posteriori* is that between principles and definitive concepts which *can* be maintained in the face of all experience and those genuinely empirical generalizations which *might* be proven flatly false. The thought which both rationalism and empiricism have missed is that there are principles, representing the initiative of mind, which impose upon experience no limitations whatever, but that such conceptions are still subject to alteration on pragmatic grounds when the expanding boundaries of experience reveal their infelicity as intellectual instruments.

Neither human experience nor the human mind has a character which is universal, fixed, and absolute. "The human mind" does not exist at all save in the sense that all humans are very much alike in fundamental respects, and that the language habit and the enormously important exchange of ideas has greatly increased our likeness in those respects which are here in question. Our categories and definitions are peculiarly social products, reached in the light of experiences which have much in common, and beaten out, like other pathways, by the coincidence of human purposes and the exigencies of human coöperation. Concerning the a priori there need be neither universal agreement nor complete historical continuity. Conceptions, such as those of logic, which are least likely to be affected by the opening of new ranges of experience, represent the most stable of our categories; but none of them is beyond the possibility of alteration.

Mind contributes to experience the element of order, of classification, categories, and definition. Without such, experience would be unintelligible. Our knowledge of the validity of these is simply conscious-ness of our own fundamental ways of acting and our own intellectual intent. Without this element, knowledge is impossible, and it is here that whatever truths are necessary and independent of experience must be found. But the commerce between our categorical ways of acting, our pragmatic interests, and the particular character of experience, is closer than we have realized. No explanation of any one of these can be complete without consideration of the other two.

Pragmatism has sometimes been charged with oscillating between two contrary notions; the one, that experience is "through and through malleable to our purpose," the other, that facts are "hard" and uncreated by the mind. We here offer a mediating conception: through all our knowledge runs the element of the a priori, which is indeed malleable to our purpose and responsive to our need. But throughout, there is also that other element of experience which is "hard," "independent," and unalterable to our will.

Notes

1. Read at the meeting of the American Philosophical Association, Dec. 27, 1923.
2. Einstein, *Relativity*, pp. 26–28: italics are the author's.

❖ A RATIONALIST VIEW ❖

40. TOWARD A MODERATE RATIONALISM

Laurence BonJour

Introduction

In a previous paper,[1] I argued that empiricist positions on a priori justification and knowledge, despite their apparent dominance throughout most of the twentieth century, are epistemological dead ends: the moderate empiricist attempt to reconcile a priori justification with empiricism by invoking the concept of analyticity does not succeed, indeed does not really even get off the ground; and the radical empiricist attempt to dispense entirely with such justification ends in a nearly total skepticism. My conclusion there was that a viable nonskeptical epistemology, rather than downgrading or rejecting a priori insight, must accept it more or less at face value as a genuine and autonomous source of epistemic justification and knowledge. This, of course, is the main thesis of epistemological rationalism. And the fundamental reason advanced for this conclusion was that only a priori insight can justify the transition from the relatively small body of claims that are matters of direct observation to the vastly greater body of claims that are not.

Obviously, however, such a result can at best be only tentative until the rationalist view has been explored more fully and shown to be defensible. For even if the objections to empiricist views are indeed decisive, the possibility remains that the negative empiricist claim is correct: that a priori justification as understood by the rationalist simply does not exist. If this were correct, then skepticism would be the correct conclusion with respect to a priori justification, even if, as argued in that paper, such a skepticism would inevitably encompass most (or perhaps even all) putative empirical knowledge as well. A thoroughgoing skepticism of this sort is obviously massively implausible from a common-sense or intuitive standpoint, but this cannot, in my judgment, be taken as a conclusive philosophical objection to it, so long as no alternative epistemological view has been successfully explicated and defended.

It is important to be clear at the outset, however, as to what can reasonably be demanded of a defense of rationalism. It is obvious at once that there can be no general a priori argument in favor of the rationalist view and against skepticism concerning the a priori that is not intrinsically question-begging. Nor does any straightforwardly empirical consideration appear to be relevant here: the truth or falsity of rationalism is obviously not a matter of direct observation; and any sort of inductive or explanatory inference from observational data, as argued in the paper previously referred to,[2] would have to be justified a priori if it is to be justified at all, thereby rendering the argument circular.

Thus, in a way that parallels many other philosophical issues, the case in favor of rationalism must ultimately depend on intuitive and dialectical considerations rather than direct argument. Such a case will, I suggest, involve three main components: first, the arguments against competing views already alluded to; second, an exhibition of the basic intuitive or phenomenological plausibility of rationalism in relation to particular examples, which will lead to a fuller statement of the rationalist position; and, third, responses to the leading and allegedly decisive objections.

Having dealt previously with the first of these components, my aim in the present paper is to present an initial and fairly tentative outline of the other two. I begin in the next section by considering a modest selection from the wide variety of examples that illustrate, and indeed at an intuitive level virtually demand, a rationalist construal. My basic claim is that the prima facie case for rationalism that is provided by examples of the kinds to be considered is extremely obvious and compelling, enough, when taken together with the failure of the alternative positive views, to put the burden of proof heavily upon the opponents of rationalism. Succeeding sections will then be devoted to stating, refining, and clarifying the basic rationalist position and to a consideration of some of the main objections. What emerges is what may reasonably be described as a moderate version of rationalism, one that rejects the traditional claim that a priori insight is infallible while nevertheless preserving its status as a fundamental source of epistemic justification.

As already noted, rationalism has been generally repudiated in recent times, indeed has often not been regarded as even a significant epistemological option. My own suspicion is that much of the explanation for this repudiation is relatively superficial in character, that it is due more to arbitrary winds of philosophical fashion and a certain philosophical failure of nerve than to serious argument. Indeed, I think it is very plausible to think that many of those who claim to reject rationalism are in fact, though unbeknownst to themselves, committed to rationalism by their own philosophical practice. But be that as it may, it is clear that there are also objections to rationalism that need to be examined and assessed—objections which, though widely regarded as more or less conclusive, are seldom very fully articulated. The rest of the paper will be devoted to a consideration of three of the most important and influential of these objections.

A priori Justification: Some Intuitive Examples[3]

I begin with what is perhaps the most familiar and hackneyed example of all: the proposition that nothing can be red all over and green all over at the same time. Suppose that this proposition is presented for my consideration (or perhaps that I am invited to consider the cogency of the inference from the premise that a certain object is red all over at a particular time to the conclusion that it is not green all over at that same time). After extremely brief consideration, I accept the proposition (or inference) and moreover am strongly inclined at the intuitive level to regard such an acceptance as more than adequately justified from an epistemic standpoint. But what is the basis, if any, for that (apparent) justification?

The overwhelmingly natural and obvious response to this question would go roughly as follows. First, I *understand* the proposition in question. This means that I comprehend or grasp the property indicated by the word 'red' and also that indicated by the word 'green': I have an adequate conception of redness and greenness (which is not, of course, to say that I know everything about even their intrinsic natures, let alone their relational properties). Similarly, I understand the relation of incompatibility or exclusion that is conveyed by the rest of the words in the verbal formulation of the proposition, together with the way in which this relation is predicated of the two properties by the syntax of the sentence. Second, given this understanding of the ingredients of the proposition, I am able to see or grasp or apprehend in a seemingly direct and unmediated way that the claim in question cannot fail to be true—that the natures of redness and greenness are such as to preclude their being jointly realized.[4] It is this direct insight into the necessity of the claim in question that seems, at least prima facie, to justify my accepting it as true.

It may be helpful to relate this account to one of the familiar conceptions of analyticity. It is natural enough in a case of this kind to characterize the sentence that formulates the proposition in question as being "true by virtue of meaning," where this means simply that it must be true by virtue of the configuration of properties and relations that its words mean or stand for or convey (and also, perhaps, that this fact can be self-evidently grasped). Such a characterization is unobjectionable in itself. The mistake would arise in thinking that it conveys any epistemological insight into *how* the truth of the proposition in question is seen or grasped or apprehended which differs from that offered by the rationalist, especially any insight of the reductive sort that at least seems to be offered by other conceptions of analyticity; or that it shows the justification or knowledge that results to be in any significant way

dependent on language. The sentence in question is necessarily true because it expresses a necessary relation between certain properties, and it is in virtue of its meaning that it does this; but the status of that relational fact as necessary and its cognitive accessibility are in no obvious way dependent on how it happens to be linguistically formulated or even, so far as I can see, on whether it is linguistically formulated or formulable at all.[5]

It is common to refer to the intellectual act in which the necessity of such a proposition is seen or grasped or apprehended as an act of *rational insight or rational intuition* (or, sometimes, a priori insight or intuition), where these phrases are mainly a way of stressing that such an act is seemingly (*a*) direct or immediate, nondiscursive, and yet also (*b*) intellectual or reason governed, anything but arbitrary or brute in character. Here I shall mostly prefer the former term, in order to avoid potential confusion stemming from other meanings of the term "intuition."[6] Since this justification or evidence apparently depends on nothing beyond an understanding of the propositional content itself, a proposition whose necessity is apprehended in this way (or, sometimes, whose necessity is capable of being apprehended in this way) may be correlatively characterized as *rationally self-evident*: its very content provides, for one who grasps it properly, an immediately accessible reason for thinking that it is true.

As a second example, consider the proposition that if a certain person A is taller than a second person B and person B is taller than a third person C, then person A is taller than person C. Here again the natural view from an intuitive or phenomenological standpoint is that one who understands the elements of this proposition and the way in which they are combined, including most centrally the relational property of one thing being taller than another, will on that basis be able to see or grasp or apprehend directly and immediately that the proposition in question must be true: that there is no possible way in which both of the propositions conjoined in the antecedent or the conditional could be true without the consequent proposition being true as well. In this case it is easier than in the previous one to offer an abstract logical characterization of the basic rationale, namely that the relational property of x being taller than y is *transitive* and that it is upon that transitivity alone that the necessary truth of the proposition in question depends. And this might tempt someone to attempt a reductive account of the a priori insight at issue.[7] I have considered the general deficiencies of this sort of approach elsewhere.[8] Here it is enough to point out that from a purely intuitive standpoint, it is clearly my grasp or understanding of the relational property of one thing being taller than another that justifies the claim of transitivity, not the other way around.

As a third example, consider the proposition that there are no round squares, i.e., that no surface (or demarcated part of a surface) that is round can also be square. My justification for accepting this proposition appears to be entirely parallel to that in the red-green case. I understand the properties of roundness and squareness and on the basis of that understanding am able to see or grasp or apprehend directly and immediately that nothing can simultaneously satisfy them both, that anything which possesses the property of roundness must fail to possess the property of squareness and vice versa. To be sure, in this case at least a partial discursive account is potentially available. There are obvious definitions of roundness and squareness from which, together with some simple axioms of geometry, it is possible to demonstrate the truth of the proposition in question by showing that its denial leads to a formal contradiction. Moreover, in this case, unlike some others, it is at least somewhat plausible to suppose that the requisite definitions and other apparatus are at least implicitly familiar to anyone who understands the proposition in question. All this notwithstanding, however, it also seems abundantly clear at the intuitive level at which we are so far operating that my justification for accepting the original proposition need not and in general will not appeal to such a discursive demonstration, but will instead be just as direct and immediate as in the red-green case. And once it is realized that any such reduction to discursive reasoning will inevitably be only partial, appealing ultimately to axioms and inferences for which such an account is not in turn available,[9] there seems to be no particular reason to deny that this more immediate justification can be entirely adequate by itself from a purely epistemic standpoint, even though the partially discursive one is potentially available.

Something very similar can also be said about simple propositions of arithmetic, e.g., the proposition that two plus three equals five. Here again, though a claim of general familiarity would be much more dubious, it is clear that a partial discursive account is available. But here again too, there is no apparent reason for thinking that an appeal to such an account is in any way essential from an epistemic standpoint. On the contrary, it once again seems abundantly clear at the intuitive level that one who understands the various ingredients of this proposition and the way in which they are structurally combined will be able to see or grasp or apprehend directly that the proposition has to be true: that any collection of exactly two entities (of whatever kind) together with exactly three more distinct entities must contain five entities altogether. (This is not to deny, of course, that the deductive systematization and unification of claims of this kind in an axiomatic system of arithmetic may have considerable epistemic significance and indeed may enhance the justification of the various propositions involved;[10] the point is merely that there is no reason to think that appeal to such an account is required in order for the acceptance of propositions like the one originally in question to be epistemically justified.)

Consider, finally, a logical example, which it will be more perspicuous to put in the explicit form of an inference. I am invited to assess the cogency of inferring the conclusion that David ate the last piece of cake from the premises, first, that either David ate the last piece of cake or else Jennifer ate it and, second, that Jennifer did not eat it (perhaps because she was at work for the entire time in question). In a way that is parallel to the earlier examples, the obvious construal of this case from an intuitive standpoint is that if I understand the three propositions involved, I will be able to directly and immediately see or grasp or apprehend that the indicated conclusion follows from the indicated premises, i.e., that there is no way for the premises to be true without the conclusion being true as well. It is obvious, of course, that I might appeal in this case to a formal rule of inference, viz., the rule of disjunctive syllogism. But there is no reason to think that any such appeal is required in order for my acceptance of the inference as valid to be epistemically justified. Nor is there any reason to think that such a rule would not itself have to be justified either by appeal to the same sort of apparent a priori insight at a more abstract level or else to other rules or propositions for which an analogous sort of justification would be required.

Examples of these and similar kinds could obviously be multiplied more or less without limit, but the foregoing will suffice for the moment. My claim for the moment is that it is overwhelmingly obvious on an intuitive level (*a*) that the claims and inferences involved are justified a priori and (*b*) that this justification is direct or intuitive, involving no appeal to the reductive apparatus of definitions, linguistic conventions, and the like, which has in any case been shown elsewhere to be of no avail.[11] Since only a rationalist position can account for these apparent facts, we have a strong intuitive reason for thinking that some form of rationalism is correct.

It is worth mentioning, however, that I am not at all concerned here with the important issue of the *scope* of a priori justification. It is obvious that the examples considered so far are relatively unexciting from a philosophical standpoint: if our capacity for a priori knowledge was limited to examples of these specific kinds, it would arguably have little philosophical importance outside of the philosophy of mathematics and of logic. But it is abundantly clear that the central issue from a historical and dialectical standpoint is not how widely a priori justification extends but whether such justification as understood by the rationalist, genuinely exists at all. Thus it is appropriate to focus initially on the thesis that such justification genuinely exists in at least some cases, without worrying about how widely it extends.

Rationalism: An Initial Formulation

At this point, we are in a position to give a more general, though initially still quite intuitive statement of the rationalist view, drawing on the examples just discussed. From an intuitive standpoint, as we have seen, what happens in cases of the kinds in question is this: when I carefully and reflectively consider the proposition (or inference) in question, I simply see or grasp or apprehend that the proposition is *necessary*, that it must be true in any possible world or situation (or alternatively that the conclusion of the inference must be true if the premises are true). Such a rational insight, as I have chosen to call it, does not seem in

general to depend on any sort of criterion or on any further discursive or ratiocinative process, but is instead direct and immediate (though in some cases, as we have seen, there are possible discursive processes of reasoning, beginning from other insights of essentially the same kind, that could have yielded that claim as a conclusion).

The occurrence of such an insight does obviously depend on a correct understanding of the claim in question, which requires in turn an adequate grasp or comprehension of the various properties and relations involved and how they are connected. Such a comprehension may itself depend on having had experiences of some specific sort—e.g., comprehending the properties of redness and greenness involved in our initial example may well involve having had experiences involving these two colors. But once the requisite understanding is achieved, the insight in question does not seem to depend on experience in any further way, thus allowing it to be the basis for a priori justification and a priori knowledge.

From an intuitive standpoint, such an apparent rational insight purports to be nothing less than a direct insight into the necessary character of reality, albeit, in the cases discussed so far, a relatively restricted aspect of reality. When I see or grasp or apprehend the necessary truth of the claim, e.g., that nothing can be red and green all over at the same time, I am seemingly apprehending the way that reality *must* be in this respect, as contrasted with other ways that it could not be. If taken at face value, as the rationalist claims that it in general should be, such a rational or a priori insight seems to provide an entirely adequate epistemic justification for believing or accepting the proposition in question. What, after all, could be a better reason for thinking that a particular proposition is true than that one sees clearly and after careful reflection that it reflects a necessary feature that reality could not fail to possess?

As already observed above, the idea of such insight has been widely rejected in recent epistemology. It will strike many, perhaps most, contemporary philosophers as unreasonably extravagant, a kind of epistemological hubris that should be eschewed by any sober and hardheaded philosophy. Once it is accepted that this sort of insight cannot be accounted for in any epistemologically useful way by appeal to the allegedly unproblematic apparatus of definitions or linguistic conventions, a standard reaction is to disparage it as objectionably mysterious, perhaps even somehow occult, in character and hence as incapable of being accepted at face value—no matter how compelling the intuitive or phenomenological appearances or how unavailing the search for an alternative epistemological account may be.

This sort of reaction is not entirely unrelated to some of the more articulated objections that will be considered later on, especially the first. Taken in itself on an intuitive level, however, it seems very hard to take seriously. There is, to be sure, one reasonably clear sense in which many alleged rational or a priori insights are, if not necessarily *mysterious*, at least *inexplicable* in the sense of being apparently *irreducible*: they are apparently incapable of being reduced to or constituted out of some constellation of discursive steps or simpler elements of some other kind. But once it is realized that any such reduction would have to appeal to other apparent insights of a similar sort and thus ultimately, if an infinite regress is ruled out, to irreducible ones, it is hard to see why this admitted irreducibility should be thought to bring with it mysteriousness or lack of intelligibility.

Moreover, if the implicit demand for reducibility is set aside as unwarranted and the alleged rational or a priori insight is examined for intelligibility on its own merits, it is extremely difficult, I submit, to see any serious basis for the charge of mysteriousness. Returning to our initial example, it is not as though I somehow just find myself thinking willy-nilly, for no apparent reason, that nothing can be red all over and green all over at the same time, not as though this conviction were somehow a product of something analogous to revelation or oracular prophecy.[12] On the contrary, I at least seem to myself to see with perfect clarity just *why* this proposition holds and even to be able to articulate this insight to some extent, though not in a way that lends itself to discursive reduction: it is in the nature of both redness and greenness to completely occupy the surface or area that instantiates them, so that once one of these qualities is in place, there is no room for the other; since there is no way for the two qualities to coexist in the same part of a surface or area, a red item can become green only if the green replaces the red. And analogous, though often more complicated accounts could be given for the other examples. Contrary to the claim

of mysteriousness, it is hard to see that there is anything in our cognitive experience that is, at first glance at least, any more transparently and pellucidly intelligible, any *less* mysterious than this.[13]

As will emerge more fully later but is probably obvious enough even now, there is no way to *prove* that such apparent insights are ever, let alone always, what they purport to be. But there are two further things that can be said at this point. First, if current philosophical fashions are set aside, and pending the consideration of more developed objections, there is nothing obviously unreasonable about the idea of such insight. If the proposition in question is, sheerly in virtue of its content, necessarily true, true in all possible worlds, why should this fact not be at least sometimes apparent to an intelligence that understands that content? Second, it is at least arguable that some such capacity of insight is in fact required for any sort of rational intelligence: if one never in fact grasps any necessary connections between anything, it is difficult to see what reasoning could possibly amount to. There is thus a way in which our very ability to dispute issues of this kind, if it genuinely has the rational character that it seems to have, shows that we do possess such a capacity.

The foregoing account is, however, still too simple in one crucial respect. It assumes or at least strongly suggests that rational insight is always genuine, i.e., that the claim that is apprehended to be necessary is always in fact necessary, so that an apparent insight of this kind would guarantee truth. But such a thesis turns out to be extremely difficult, indeed impossible, to defend. And this, as we shall see in the next section, forces a major revision of the rationalist view.

The Fallibility of Rational Insight

It is a familiar fact that an overwhelming majority of the historical proponents of rationalist conceptions of a priori justification and knowledge regarded such knowledge as *certain*—where the primary import of the notion of certainty was that a proposition that is justified a priori, via rational insight, cannot fail to be true, that a priori justification is *infallible*.[14]

Despite this almost exceptionless historical consensus, however, there is no immediately obvious way in which infallibility is a consequence of the minimal conception of a priori justification: that of having a reason for thinking something to be true that does not derive from sensory or introspective or analogous kinds of experience, but rather from reason or pure thought alone. Indeed, once the question is explicitly raised, it is by no means obvious what the rationale for the historical belief in infallibility might have been. The most obvious suggestion is that it was the perceived *necessity* of the claims that are the objects of rational insight which led to the conviction that such insights could not be mistaken. The fallacy that this would involve is rather gross: a necessary proposition cannot, of course, be mistaken, but one *perceived* to be necessary could still be neither necessary nor true—unless the perception of necessity is itself taken to be infallible. Such an explanation of a deeply entrenched historical claim is unsatisfying, but I have no better account to offer.

In any case, the immediate issue is whether such a view of rational insight is correct, and here the answer is much more straightforward and indisputable. It is as clear as anything philosophical could be that the claim of infallibility, if not trivialized in a way to be noted shortly, is false and completely indefensible. There are simply too many compelling examples of propositions and inferences that were claimed to be objects of rational insight, and hence to be justified a priori, but that subsequently turned out to be false. And while some of these examples were not available to most of the proponents of the infallibility thesis, many of them were. (It should also be stressed, however, that while identifiable mistakes of these kinds are clear enough and frequent enough to undeniably refute the thesis of infallibility, they are at the same time extremely rare in relation to the overall body of claims that are, if the rationalist is correct, accepted on an a priori basis.)

At least three classes of counterexamples to the infallibility thesis suggest themselves. In the first place, there are claims in mathematics and logic which though universally regarded as self-evident by the leading minds in the field in question at a particular time have subsequently proved to be false. The most historically salient example here is Euclidean geometry, regarded for centuries as describing the necessary character of space, but apparently refuted under that interpretation, indeed apparently refuted *empirically*, by the use of non-Euclidean geometry in the theory of General Relativity.[15] A

further, somewhat more esoteric example is provided by the fate of naive set theory in light of the Russell paradox and other similar paradoxes. And there are other examples of the same general kind, though their number should not be exaggerated.

Secondly, there are the various allegedly a priori claims of rationalist metaphysicians, from Plato and Aristotle through Spinoza and Leibniz down to philosophers of the present century such as McTaggart and Whitehead. Without pausing to list specific cases, it is obvious that all such claims cannot be true, and thus cannot be infallible, if only because of the high degree to which they conflict with each other. For example, reality cannot consist both of a system of timeless, windowless monads and also of pure process.

As contrasted with the mathematicians and scientists whose views provided the first set of counterexamples, it is rather more reasonable to doubt whether all of the philosophers in question genuinely found their claims self-evident after careful reflection, but it would be unduly optimistic to assume that all such conflicts can be dealt with in this way.

Thirdly, and perhaps most obviously, there are the routine errors in calculation, proof, and reasoning that are familiar to anyone who has ever engaged in such processes. Notoriously, even the most powerful minds are susceptible to such slips. As we will see more fully below, the exercise of a high degree of care in the consideration of a claim is a requirement for the resulting judgment to even count as an apparent rational insight, so some errors of this kind, those produced by sheer sloppiness, can be dismissed as irrelevant. But there is no reason to think that a degree of care that would ordinarily be taken to be adequate will make mistake impossible. And even if there is a degree of care (and length of attention) that would avoid all such mistakes, there is obviously no way to be sure that such a degree of care has been exercised in a particular case and thus no reason to regard any particular case of alleged rational insight as infallible.

What these kinds of examples seem to show is that it is quite possible for a proposition (or inference) that *seems* necessary and self-evident to a particular person, even after careful reflection, and thus that *seems* to be the object of a rational insight, to nonetheless turn out to be false. Neither does there appear in general to be any further, subjectively accessible criterion that would serve to weed out the cases where mistake is possible, leaving only the genuinely infallible ones. Since the existence of such cases must be admitted, the only possible defense of the thesis of the infallibility of rational insight would be to deny that *genuine* rational insights are involved in cases of these kinds, insisting that a genuine rational insight must involve an insight into necessity that is not capable of being mistaken. In the absence of a workable criterion of genuineness, however, this response safeguards the infallibility of rational insight only by refusing to call a state of mind a genuine rational insight if it turns out to be mistaken, no matter how subjectively or intuitively compelling it may have been. It is thus best regarded as a mere terminological or conceptual stipulation: an apparent rational insight will count as genuine only if it actually involves the sort of authentic grasp of the necessary character of reality that would guarantee truth. When understood in this way, such a stipulation is useful for clarification and will indeed be adopted here. But it does nothing at all to establish that any particular case of apparent intuition that we may be interested in is genuine and thus fails to secure infallibility in any epistemologically interesting sense. (This is the trivialization of the claim of infallibility noted earlier.)

The implication of all this is that the rationalist view considered so far must be modified in a major way. To insist that a priori epistemic justification requires a *genuine* rational insight, in the sense just specified, would make it impossible to tell whether a given claim was justified in this way or not without at least knowing independently whether or not the claim of necessity was correct—thus making the appeal to rational insight entirely useless as an independent and self-contained basis for justification. Thus, I suggest, a moderate rationalism that abandons the indefensible claim of infallibility should hold instead that it is *apparent* rational insight (and, correlatively, apparent self-evidence) that provides the basis for a priori epistemic justification. Such justification will thus, in common with all or virtually all other kinds of justification, be fallible, since it will be possible that the apparent insight that justifies a particular claim is not genuine. The moderate rationalist's main

thesis is that such an apparent insight still yields a reason, albeit a fallible one, for thinking that the proposition in question is true.

It is crucially important, however, to stress that the idea of an apparent rational insight must not be construed too weakly. Even an apparent rational insight (*i*) must be considered with a reasonable degree of care[16] (which obviously includes a clear and careful understanding of precisely which claim is at issue) and also (*ii*) must involve a genuine comprehension by the person of the concept of rational insight itself, i.e., of what it is to find a proposition necessary on an immediate or intuitive basis in the strong logical or metaphysical sense. Thus the person in question must, upon careful consideration and reflection, genuinely find the claim to be necessary in this quite demanding way. An instance that fails to satisfy these requirements will not even count as an apparent rational insight in the sense that is of interest to the rationalist—however the person in question might describe it.

Pending a consideration of objections, such an intellectual conviction still seems at an intuitive level a more than adequate reason, ceteris paribus, for accepting the claim in question as true. The ceteris paribus clause reflects at least two possibilities: a person's apparent rational insights might conflict internally in a way that would force him to give at least some of them up, with something like coherence determining the choice (see the next section for further discussion); or it might be clear on simple inductive grounds that apparent insights of a particular sort were frequently mistaken and hence not to be trusted. But both of these bases for doubt about particular apparent insights would rely essentially on other such insights[17] and hence could not constitute a reason for being skeptical about apparent rational insight in general.

None of this shows, of course, that there may not be other, more compelling grounds for skepticism about the a priori, and we will examine the most important possibilities later on. The point for the moment is that the fallibility of a priori insight is in no obvious way an adequate justification for such skepticism, however frequently it may have provided a motive for the skeptic. Fallibility appears indeed to be an unavoidable aspect of the human condition in all or virtually all areas of cognition. But no one seriously proposes to give up reliance on sense perception because of its fallibility, and such a course seems equally extreme, unnecessary, and quixotic in the area of a priori cognition. The simple fact is that fallible a priori insight, while perhaps not all that we might have hoped for, is vastly better than no insight at all.

The Corrigibility of A priori Insight

If rational insight is indeed fallible, then it is natural to think that some further, epistemically prior criterion or standard is needed in order to distinguish genuine rational insights from merely apparent ones. But such an approach is inherently futile: any such criterion or standard would itself have to be somehow justified; and only a little reflection will show that there is no possible way in which it could be justified without either impugning the a priori status of the claims that are justified by appeal to it (if it is justified empirically) or else being guilty of obvious circularity (if it is justified a priori). This point will be elaborated below (in section 9), in a somewhat more general context. For now, however, I want to consider in this section two complementary ways in which it is possible to correct mistakes in apparent rational insight without appealing to any general criterion of this sort.

First. In thinking about this issue, it is useful to distinguish two significantly different sorts of mistakes that a cognitive process may be vulnerable to. On the one hand, there is the sort of mistake, typical of at least many kinds of sensory illusions, hallucinations, and misperceptions, in which there is nothing internal to the cognitive state or process that provides any clue as to its erroneous character. If, e.g., I am the victim of sufficiently complete and detailed hallucinations, it is futile for me to try to decide whether a given perceptual state is hallucinatory or veridical by reflecting, however carefully, on that perceptual state alone, no matter how long it may persist and how clear its content may be; instead I will have to identify such a hallucination, if at all, by appealing to some kind of criterion or standard that is external to the state itself (which may, of course, involve a comparison of many such states). We may say that a mistake of this sort is only *externally correctable*.

Other sorts of cognitive mistakes, in contrast, are *internally correctable*: further reflection on the very state or process that led to the mistaken result is capable of

revealing that it was a mistake and of replacing it with the correct result. At least some perceptual mistakes, those due to carelessness or inattention, seem to fall into this latter category. Thus, for example, my snap judgment that a certain tree is a pine may, upon focusing more carefully on its sharp, unbundled needles, be corrected to the judgment that it is a spruce.

It seems apparent that many at least of the mistakes that are involved in states of apparent rational insight are of the internally correctable kind. This is obviously true, for example, of at least most routine mistakes of reasoning or calculation, which yield to equally routine corrections. For catching and correcting mistakes of this sort, no external criterion is required (however helpful one might be), since it is always possible to avoid error by further consideration of the initial judgment itself.[18] There is, of course, no way to guarantee that this process of internal correction will succeed in any specified length of time, but it nonetheless provides a way in which any particular mistake of this kind can eventually be rectified.

The important question is whether *all* mistakes of apparent rational insight, all cases in which something seems necessary that is not really necessary, are mistakes that are internally correctable in this sense. Such a thesis seems plausible enough on an intuitive basis, though there is no apparent way to argue for it. There is also, however, no compelling argument, so far as I can see, for an opposing view, such as that of Kant's, according to which certain kinds of a priori illusion are so essentially built into the nature of human reason that we can never escape them, at least not via internal reflection.[19]

Thus one solution to the problem of how to distinguish genuine rational insights from mistaken ones is to appeal to the fact that many such errors, and perhaps all of them, are correctable "from the inside" via further reflection. There is still obviously room here for skepticism as to just how widespread this possibility of internal correction actually is, but we have so far seen no particular reason that supports such skepticism.

Second. A further, complementary approach to the problem of eliminating errors in apparent rational insight is to appeal to *coherence*: to the ways in which such apparent insights may fit together or fail to fit together with each other. Thus, for example, errors in calculation or argument are often uncovered via various kinds of checking procedures that lead to contradictions or conflicts when an error has been committed.

Such an appeal to coherence has limitations that must be clearly understood. There are various conceptions of coherence, ranging from simple logical consistency to more elaborate appeals to mutual inferability or to relations of explanation. But any conception of coherence, however restricted, will presuppose certain fundamental premises or principles that define the conception in question and thus cannot be assessed by appeal to it. Thus in the case of simple logical consistency, at least the principle of noncontradiction (the principle that contradictions are false) and enough logical machinery to make implicit contradictions explicit must be treated as in effect immune to challenge in order to apply the test to other claims. And if the application of the coherence test is to yield genuinely a priori justification, then these presupposed fundamental premises or principles must themselves be justified a priori.

It is for this reason that a thoroughgoing coherence theory of a priori justification and knowledge is impossible, so that a theory of a priori justification must be essentially foundationalist in character. But an appeal to coherence can still play the derivative role already suggested of providing one means for catching and correcting mistakes in apparent rational insight. For this to work, two conditions must be satisfied: (i) The prima facie a priori justification of the fundamental premises or principles that underlie the conception of coherence in question must be stronger than that of the other claims whose justification is being assessed, so that there is a priori justification for thinking that in a case of incoherence, it is some among those other claims, rather than the fundamental premises or principles of coherence themselves, that are mistaken. (ii) There must be some epistemically relevant, a priori basis for choosing one of the various ways in which some prima facie claims can be rejected and coherence restored as epistemically preferable to the others; this might again involve relative strengths of prima facie a priori justification, but it might perhaps also involve something like preserving the greater number of claims whose justificatory

strength is equal. While a full account of all these matters would be very complicated, it seems highly plausible from an intuitive standpoint that these two conditions are frequently satisfied.

Thus even without an external criterion to distinguish genuine from mistaken rational insights, there is no reason to think that such mistakes are somehow impossible or in general even especially difficult to correct. One further important possibility that appears to be frequently realized is that these two methods of error correction in effect work together and reinforce each other: a likely candidate for a mistake is initially identified via coherence considerations, following which an internal reassessment of the apparent insight reveals the mistake. (Having devoted this much space to ways in which mistakes in rational insights might be corrected, it is worthwhile to reiterate once more that even though it cannot be denied that such mistakes are possible and do occur, the cases in which we have reason to think that mistakes have actually occurred represent a tiny fraction of the cases in which, according to the rationalist view, apparent rational insights are involved.)

One ingredient of the foregoing account was the idea that a priori justification can vary in degree, an idea that is sufficiently at odds with the historical tradition to require some further discussion. Both proponents and opponents of the a priori often write as though all claims justified in this way would automatically have equal degrees of justification, perhaps because all are found to be (apparently) necessary. Only a little reflection, however, will make clear that this is not so. For example, when I consider the claim that $2 + 2 = 4$, I have an apparent rational insight that this claim is necessarily true, that there is no possible world in which it fails to hold. Similarly, when I consider the claim that $2^5 - 5 = 3^3$, I have a second rational insight that this claim too is necessary. Thus, I do not understand how either claim could fail to be true in any possible situation. But all this is quite compatible with saying that if I were somehow convinced that one of these two claims had to be false, I would have no hesitation about choosing the latter claim as the one that is more likely to be mistaken. Though mistake in either case appears impossible, the intuitive justification, though surely strong enough in either case to yield strong prima facie justification, is slightly weaker in the latter case than in the former, due to the greater complexity of the latter claim. And this in turn seems to provide an epistemically rational basis for preferring the former claim, should it somehow become necessary to choose between them (which, of course, itself appears impossible).[20]

In this case, the difference in the two degrees of a priori justification results from the relative complexity of the two claims. But it is also possible, as mentioned earlier, that such a difference might be produced by a factor of some other sort, e.g., the relative degree of time and care that the person has devoted to the two issues in question. Here I do not mean to suggest that the empirical fact that less time or care was employed in one case as compared to the other would play a direct epistemic role; the suggestion is instead that the two insights might, as a causal result of this empirical fact, possess different degrees of internal clarity and firmness, and that different degrees of justification might result directly from this internal difference.

Can A priori Justification Be Refuted by Experience?

The recognition of the fallibility of rational insight, together with the appreciation that a priori justification can come in degrees, also lends increased urgency to a further issue about a priori justification: the issue of whether such justification, though not requiring the positive support of favorable experience, is nonetheless capable of being negatively undermined or overridden by unfavorable experience. We may approach this issue—in a somewhat oblique, but still useful way—by considering a line of argument, rather freely extrapolated from Philip Kitcher's discussion of apriorism in the philosophy of mathematics,[21] that challenges the compatibility of a priori justification and fallibility. In effect, Kitcher claims that infallibility is a necessary condition for a priori justification,[22] so that one who abandons the thesis of infallibility as indefensible must abandon the idea of a priori justification as well. If this were correct, the moderate rationalism advocated here would of course be untenable.

Kitcher's initial rationale for this view is that only an infallible basis for selecting which beliefs to accept, i.e., an infallible mode of justification, can be allowed to override experience:

> [I]f a person is entitled to ignore empirical information about the type of world she inhabits, then that must be because she has at her disposal a method that guarantees *true* belief.[23]

There are, however, two difficulties with this argument. The first and more obvious is that it is in no obvious way a requirement for a significant conception of a priori justification that such justification be allowed to override experience. Rather it is enough that such justification be capable of warranting belief where experience is silent. Such a moderate conception of a priori justification may not measure up to the more grandiose historical claims made on behalf of the a priori, but it would still arguably have enormous epistemological importance—in particular, by providing a possible answer to the otherwise completely intractable problem of how both inference beyond direct experience and reasoning generally are to be justified.[24]

Though it is hard to be sure, I suspect that Kitcher's response to this first difficulty might be to concede the tenability of the moderate conception of a priori justification, but to insist that its applicability is so limited, because of the pervasiveness of potential empirical challenges, as to render it epistemologically insignificant.[25] To evaluate this point and to get a better idea of the problems that experience might pose for a priori justification, we need to consider his catalog of the different kinds of experiential challenges that a claim that is allegedly justified a priori might face.

Kitcher recognizes three sorts of experiential challenges, which he does not claim to be sharply distinguished from each other.[26] First, there are *direct challenges*, in which perceptual experience directly contradicts the allegedly a priori statement or claim. Second, there are *theoretical challenges*, e.g., involving "a sequence of experiences which suggest that a physics-cum-geometry which does not include this statement will provide a simpler total description of the phenomena than a physics-cum-geometry which does." Third, there are *social challenges*, consisting in "a sequence of experiences in which apparently reliable experts deny the statement, offer hypotheses about errors we have made in coming to believe it, and so forth."

Do direct challenges to serious a priori claims ever in fact occur? Is a claim that seems rationally self-evident ever flatly and unambiguously contradicted by experience? No examples spring readily to mind, though the question is admittedly rendered somewhat vague by some uncertainty, which there is plainly no space to resolve here, over just how the direct upshot of perceptual experience should be construed. But it seems clear that such direct challenges, if they occur at all, are very rare indeed, much too rare to lend any significant support to the present line of objection. Indeed, while he does not speak directly to the issue, it may well be that Kitcher himself would also concede this point, for his main emphasis in discussing the vulnerability of a priori claims to experiential challenge is on challenges of the other two kinds, i.e., on theoretical and social challenges.[27]

In assessing the threat to a priori justification and to rationalism posed by the possibility of these latter sorts of challenges, however, it is crucial to make clearer than Kitcher ever does exactly how the experiences in each case are supposed to pose a challenge to the a priori claim in question, given that they do not contradict it directly. The only available answer seems to be this: in each case, though the experiences do not contradict the a priori claim, it is possible to *infer* from those experiences to a contradictory claim in a way that yields a suitably strong reason for thinking that the contradictory claim is true. Only if such an inference exists will the experiences in question genuinely provide a reason for thinking that the a priori claim is false and hence that the a priori justification in question is mistaken. But any such inference would have to rely, tacitly if not explicitly, on some background premise or principle of inference connecting the experiences in question with this further result: premises or principles having to do, roughly, with the likely truth of an account possessing theoretical virtues such as simplicity or with the likely truth of the testimony of experts of the kinds in question. And the obvious question that leaps to mind on the basis of this formulation is: What sort of reason do we have or

could we have for thinking that such connecting premises are true or at least reasonably likely to be true? That is, what form might the epistemic justification of such premises or principles take?

Since direct experience cannot justify an inference that goes beyond direct experience and since background premises or principles of the sorts in question are plainly not themselves matters of direct experience, there seem to be only three possible answers to the foregoing question. Either (*i*) such premises or principles are themselves justified a priori, or (*ii*) they are justified by appeal to an a priori justified inference from some further set of empirical claims (perhaps via several stages of inference), or (*iii*) they are not justified at all, so that the supposed challenge collapses. Taken as the basis for a general objection to a priori justification, therefore, the appeal to theoretical and social challenges is self-defeating, because such challenges can be cogent only if they are themselves justified, directly or indirectly, in the very way that they are supposed to call into question.

It is this point that constitutes the second and more important difficulty for Kitcher's original argument. If a significant challenge to an a priori claim requires, in virtually all cases, appeal to one or more further a priori claims, then the whole issue of whether a priori justification can be refuted by experience or whether, on the contrary, it warrants ignoring conflicting experience simply does not arise in any straightforward way. The upshot of all this is not, of course, that the appeal to theoretical or social considerations of the sorts indicated cannot generate a challenge to a particular a priori claim. But in such a case, the situation is not that experience by itself conflicts with an a priori claim but rather that, assuming (as we shall) that the experiences in question are themselves epistemologically unproblematic, two or more a priori claims in effect conflict with each other.

How such conflicts are to be resolved is an issue yet to be fully considered, though the discussion of the preceding section is relevant (see section 8, below). Thus the possibility still exists that our inability to resolve them in a rationally acceptable way might by itself impugn the whole idea of a priori justification. But however that may turn out, the objection we have extrapolated from Kitcher—i.e., that once a priori justification is recognized as fallible, instances of such justification will be virtually nonexistent unless pervasive experiential challenges are illegitimately ignored—turns out to have little force in itself. And the indicated response to the issue posed in the title of this section is that a priori justification, if we set aside the rare or nonexistent case of direct experiential challenge, is incapable of being undermined or overridden by experience alone.

Admittedly, the foregoing argument is at a very high level of abstraction and ignores the more specific features of the kinds of cases in question. Thus, for all that has been said, it remains possible that there are cases where an experiential challenge to a particular a priori claim requires only the support of other a priori premises that are entirely unproblematic and that may be, for many purposes, taken for granted. In such a case, the occurrence of the right sort of experience would in effect refute the original a priori claim, simply because there would be no question of abandoning the supporting a priori premises instead. But while there would be a point to putting things in this way, this does not alter the fact that ultimate resolution of such a case depends primarily on a choice between two competing a priori claims, in relation to which experience plays only a subsidiary role.

Our initial account of the moderate rationalist view is now largely complete. On this conception, such justification derives from direct or immediate rational insights or apparent insights, insights that purport to be direct apprehensions of the necessary character of reality. It is clear, in light of the undeniable (albeit rare) mistakes that do occur, that not all apparent rational insights are genuine apprehensions of this kind and that there is accordingly no justification for regarding apparent rational insight as infallible and indeed much reason to the contrary. The claim of the moderate rationalist is that such fallibility does not prevent such an apparent rational insight from being an adequate, albeit defeasible, reason for thinking that the proposition in question is true. In addition, while there are plausible ways in which mistaken apparent rational insights can be corrected, such insights do not appear to be vulnerable to strictly empirical refutation.

Such a conception of a priori justification seems to me to possess enormous initial plausibility in light of examples such as those considered above. But, as already noted, rationalism has been supposed by many to be afflicted by many compelling objections. A consideration of some of those objections will also help to refine the view and develop it further.

The Very Idea of Rational Insight

In the rest of this paper, I will consider three familiar epistemological objections to the moderate rationalism just outlined, focusing here on those that seem to me to bear most directly on the tenability of the view. There can be little doubt that an apparent rational insight provides *some* sort of reason for believing the proposition in question. A belief arrived at in this way is certainly not merely arbitrary or capricious and may indeed be psychologically compelling to the point of being inescapable. But none of this shows that the believer in question possesses a genuinely *epistemic* reason for his belief, and it is this that the objections to be considered attempt to call into question.[28]

The central focus of the first objection to be discussed is the *directness* or *immediacy*, the essentially nondiscursive character, of rational insight as contrasted with other sorts of intellectual operations or processes. The basic suggestion, often left fairly implicit, is that while intellectual processes that appeal to criteria or rules or to articulated steps of some kind are thereby rendered intellectually transparent and hence capable of possessing rational force in a comprehensible and plausibly objective way, allegedly direct intellectual insights that involve no such appeal are fundamentally opaque and unacceptably subjective in character. How, it may be asked, can a supposed insight count as rational when it is arrived at on the basis of no intelligible process or objective criterion, no *reason*, but amounts merely to a brute subjective conviction? Is not the appeal to such an immediate and not further articulable insight essentially foreign to the very idea of rationality? Such seeming insights may no doubt be subjectively compelling, but, precisely because of their unarticulated character, there can be no genuine basis for ascribing rational cogency to them—and in particular no reason to think that beliefs adopted in accordance with them are likely to be true.

What the proponents of the objection do not seem to have noticed, however, is that the application of any sort of criterion or the employment of any discursive, stepwise process must ultimately rely on immediate insights of the very same kind that the objection is designed to impugn. In the first place, any criterion or rule itself requires justification, and an eventual appeal to immediate insight is the only alternative to an infinite and vicious regress. Secondly, less obviously but more fundamentally, criteria or rules do not, after all, somehow apply themselves. They must be judged or intellectually seen to apply or not to apply, and this judging or seeing can only involve the very same sort of rational insight or intuition that the rationalist is advocating. This is true of the application of even the most severely formal rule of inference. Even to apply as straightforward and seemingly unproblematic a rule as modus ponens, I must see or grasp in an immediate, not further reducible way that the three propositions comprising the premises and conclusion are of the right form and are related in the right way: for example, that the two simpler propositions in question are in fact identical with the antecedent and consequent of the conditional proposition is as much a necessary, a priori knowable truth as anything else. Contrary to the view that seems to be assumed in many discussions, perhaps most commonly in elementary logic books, there is no way to replace this act of insight with a purely mechanical appeal to linguistic forms and linguistic templates without utterly destroying the claim of the inference in question to be genuinely cogent. In many cases, of course, the requisite insight is extremely simple and obvious, making it all too easy to fail to notice that it is required. But the objection that we are presently considering makes no exception for simple and obvious insights, and could not do so without abandoning its central thrust.

The same is even more obviously true for the appeal to discursive, stepwise processes of inference. While it is frequently possible to replace a simple propositional insight with a more extended inference involving a number of steps, or similarly to interpose a series of steps between the premise and conclusion of a previously direct or immediate inference, the cogency of each of the steps must in the end still be recognized or apprehended by immediate insight—as must the new premise or premises in the case where a discursive inference replaces a previous propositional insight. In many such cases, still further steps can be interposed; but while this may be of value in

relation to some more specific problem or interest, it clearly does not avoid the general need for rational or intellectual insight to certify each newly added step or premise.

In this way it may be seen that the demand that is implicit in the present objection—viz., to somehow find a mode of intellectual process that is entirely a function of criteria, rules, or steps, that is somehow purely discursive in character, requiring no immediate insight or judgment of any kind—is futile in principle. As even some moderate empiricists, e.g., Quinton,[29] have recognized, this would be true even if the thesis that all a priori justified claims are analytic could be defended. Indeed, it would be true even if the appeal to a priori justification in the sense advocated here were abandoned, so long as any theses going beyond direct observation or any kind of inference or reasoning or allegedly rational transition from one claim or proposition (or set of claims or propositions) to another continue to be accepted. Renouncing the idea of a priori justification makes the credentials of such theses or inferences obscure, but as long as some are regarded as acceptable and others not, there will ultimately have to be an appeal to immediate, nondiscursive acts of intellectual insight or judgment to distinguish between the two categories.

What emerges from the discussion of this initial objection is that there is no apparent alternative to the reliance on immediate, nondiscursive insights of some sort as long as any sort of reasoning or thinking that goes beyond the bounds of direct observation is to be countenanced. This being the case, the immediate and nondiscursive character of rational insight cannot by itself provide the basis for a cogent objection to moderate rationalism. But the indispensability of rational insight does not by itself show, of course, that such insights are genuinely cogent or truth-conducive. This underlying skeptical concern is taken up, in somewhat different ways, by the other two objections.

Disparities of Insight

The second objection begins from the seemingly undeniable fact that disparities of rational insight, or at least of apparent rational insight, occur: situations in which a proposition (or inference) *P* that seems rationally self-evident to one person either *(a)* fails to seem rationally self-evident to a second person or else (*b*) is in clear conflict with something that does seem rationally self-evident to the second person—where the conflicting claim that seems rationally self-evident to the second person might be either *not-P*, the denial or contradictory of the original proposition, or else merely the weaker thesis that *not-P* is possible.[30] How, the objection asks, are such conflicts to be resolved, given the immediate and nondiscursive nature of the alleged insight, except via essentially irrational or arational processes like coercion or nonrational persuasion? And if only such nonrational means of persuasion are available to the parties in such a disparity, is this not a further reason for thinking that the appeal to rational insight is fundamentally contrary to the demands of reason? In this way, it is argued, the moderate rationalist view, far from being the embodiment of reason, threatens to lead to intellectual chaos.

Though some historical proponents of rationalism may have been tempted to deny that conflicts of this sort genuinely occur, it seems clear that this is not an adequate response to the problem. Given our earlier terminological stipulation that a genuine rational insight must be a grasp of the necessity of a proposition that really is necessary, it indeed follows (together with the principle of contradiction) that at least one of any conflicting pair of alleged rational insights must automatically fail to be genuine. But this sort of terminological legislation obviously provides no way to distinguish genuine insights from merely apparent ones and in any case says nothing about the case where one person has an apparent insight that the other fails to share. Thus it does not really speak to the main problem raised by the objection, viz., that of how to resolve such conflicts in a rational way and what to say about cases where they cannot be thus resolved.

In some cases, of course, it may be possible to resolve an apparent disparity of insight by appeal to an argument whose premises and inferential steps are certified by shared rational insights, or perhaps by appeal to a version of coherence that is grounded in such shared insights. But there is no very apparent reason for thinking that such a resolution will always be available in the sort of case in question, and still less for thinking that it somehow *must* be available. The moderate rationalist must thus concede that disparities of the sort needed to pose the problem may and very likely do occur: cases where each of two (or more) people sincerely and reflectively differ, in one of the ways we have distinguished, on an issue of rational insight, and where the conflict is ultimate in the sense of not being resolvable by appeal to further rational insights that are shared.[31]

To say that the disparity is in this sense ultimate, however, is not yet to say that rational means of resolving it have been exhausted, so that only flattery, threats of violence, and the like remain available as means of persuasion. One obvious possibility in such a case is that the individuals in question have failed to adequately understand the claim or claims in question and that there is some way of clarifying or refining the contents of their insights that will remove the appearance of disparity or conflict. This familiar possibility is often spoken of as "clarification of meaning." But while the elimination of strictly linguistic ambiguity or vagueness may occasionally be involved, it is unlikely to be central. The main sort of clarification at issue will instead involve refining and distinguishing subtleties and nuances of content that have little essential relation to language, though language must of course be involved in conveying them. There can be little doubt that apparent disparities of insight are often eliminated in this way.

A further possibility in the same general vicinity is what might be called "talking around" the issue: attempting through rephrasing, examples, analogies, contrasting cases, and similar devices to display the alleged insight or insights more fully, present problems for a competing insight, etc. Such discussion may of course lead to the discovery of a relevant discursive argument, but its helpfulness in resolving the disparity is not confined to the cases where this occurs. What may happen instead is that as the parties to the dispute are led in this way to think further and in different ways about the issue, the original apparent insight or insights that were the basis of the disparity either dissolve entirely or come to have a significantly different content, so that the disparity is resolved. Here we have what amounts to a multiperson version of the sort of rational reexamination that was discussed earlier as a means of eliminating errors of apparent rational insight.

There is obviously once again no guarantee that such a solution will emerge. But reflection on actual cases seems to suggest strongly that if both parties enter into this process seriously and in good faith, it is quite unlikely that the apparent insight or insights in question will emerge sufficiently unscathed to preserve the conflict. Thus it is simply not true that the absence of discursive procedures must result in either stalemate or the employment of nonrational means of persuasion.

Suppose, however, at least for the sake of the argument, that despite the best efforts of both parties, none of these possible ways of eliminating a given disparity of insight actually succeeds. Suppose, that is, that after all reasonable efforts towards such a resolution have been made, the two parties still find themselves either (a) with a clear and unshaken apparent insight on the part of one that the other does not share or (b) with two clear and unshaken apparent insights into the necessity of seemingly incompatible claims. Cases of the former sort seem relatively rare, and those of the latter sort, rarer still. But I can see no way to rule them out entirely, and thus we need to consider how the rationalist might deal with them.

Consider first cases of sort (a), which we may refer to as cases of *mere disparity*: cases where one person has an apparent insight that the second person fails to share but without the second person having a conflicting apparent insight. Is the person who has the apparent insight still justified a priori in accepting the claim (or inference) in question?

It is a familiar, albeit perhaps not entirely satisfactorily explained fact that rational insights are not easily arrived at and are often easy to miss. Especially with regard to claims or inferences of great complexity, it seems intuitively to be often the case that one person grasps or apprehends a necessary connection that eludes others, at least for a time. This is less common where serious efforts of the sorts discussed earlier in this section to elucidate the claim in question have been made, but still seemingly common enough. For this reason, the fact that another person fails to share my apparent insight is not in itself a very strong reason for thinking that the insight is not genuine. Such a situation is surely a reason for reexamination, but if the insight in question continues to

seem clear and solid, the failure of another person to share it does not seem in general sufficient to defeat it. (One obviously relevant factor here is the extent to which a plausible explanation for the other person's failure to agree is available.)

On the other hand, the longer the situation persists (given continued effort and examination by the dissenting person) or the more people that are involved (given adequate understanding and effort on their part), the more serious the challenge to the apparent rational insight becomes. Also, the simpler the apparent insight, the harder to understand how it could be missed, and again the more serious the challenge. Thus the point may be reached at which the presence of dissenting opinions meeting these various conditions makes it empirically more likely than not that the original apparent insight is mistaken, thus defeating the justification that it would otherwise have provided. But such a situation is inherently problematic and unstable so long as the original insight continues to appear clear and unshaken: how can one reject a claim that continues to seem clearly and plainly self-evident without thereby impugning rational insights generally—including those that, as we have seen, are inevitably needed to undergird the empirical counterargument? About the only thing one can do is to "bracket" the issue and hope for some further development. Fortunately, such situations are very rare.

Something analogous should also be said about cases of sort (b), cases of *actual conflict*, the difference being that the presence of a conflicting insight presents a much more serious challenge, since the possibility that the second person has simply failed to notice the point is no longer available. In such a case, each of the two knows: (i) that at least one of them is mistaken (assuming that the rational insights according to which the competing claims are incompatible are not themselves in doubt); and (ii) that each of them has what seems to him a compelling reason for thinking that it is the other person that is mistaken. This surely constitutes a significant empirical reason for each of them to believe that he himself may well be the mistaken one, thus tending to defeat the justificatory force of his own insight. Where the situation is as described above, i.e., where all possible efforts at clarification, elucidation, and reexamination have been made, the correct result seems to be that neither of the competing claims is justified. Again, the situation is inherently unstable and problematic until some further resolution is reached. And again, such situations are extremely rare.

Such situations of unresolved disparity or conflict are thus quite unsatisfactory from an epistemological standpoint, and it is fortunate that they are rare. It is hard to see, however, why the possibility or even the actuality of such cases should be taken to destroy the justificatory force of apparent rational insight in general, even in cases where no such conflict is present, especially since, as we have already seen, the empirical challenge that they present must inevitably depend on other apparent rational insights. (Here it is worth noting again that sensory observation is itself by no means immune to conflicts of an analogous sort, but no one presumably takes this as a reason to deny any epistemic force to sensory observation in general.)

The Demand for Metajustification

The final objection is also the most straightforward and can be seen to be in effect lurking behind the other two. It challenges the moderate rationalist to offer a second-order reason or justification for thinking that accepting beliefs on the basis of apparent rational insight or apparent self-evidence is likely at least to lead to believing the truth. Without such a reason, it is argued, the supposed a priori justification that results from rational insight will simply not count as justification in the relevant epistemic sense, and accepting beliefs on that basis will accordingly be quite irrational from an epistemic standpoint. To adopt a term that I have employed elsewhere,[32] what is wanted is a *metajustification* for accepting a priori insight as a source of epistemic justification.

The demand for a metajustification is in effect a demand for a justifiable overarching premise or principle saying that beliefs that are the contents of apparent a priori insights—and perhaps that also meet some specifiable set of further criteria intended to distinguish genuine rational insights from merely apparent ones—are likely to be true. The implicit

suggestion is that one who accepts a claim on the basis of such insight must be taken to be appealing, at least tacitly, to a premise of this sort if the resulting justification is to be construed as genuinely epistemic in character. And the obvious problem, already briefly noticed earlier, is that there is clearly no way in which the rationalist can hope to provide justification for such a premise itself. To construe it as justified empirically, e.g., by finding that claims that are the contents of apparent rational insights are mostly true and generalizing inductively, is to abandon any claim to a priori justification: being essentially dependent on such an empirical justification, the justification of the original claim would become empirical as well. But to argue that the metajustificatory premise is justified a priori results in obvious circularity, since that premise would then in effect have to be appealed to for its own justification. Thus, if such a premise is indeed necessary in the way alleged, the rationalist view collapses.

But is such a demand for metajustification dialectically legitimate? The picture that it in effect assumes is one in which apparent rational insight has no epistemic value in itself, but instead functions merely as a kind of earmark or symptom for picking out a class of believed propositions that the supposedly required metajustificatory premise would then tell us are, on some independent ground, likely to be true. That the earmark in question consists, in whole or in part, in the believed proposition seeming, after careful consideration, to be logically or metaphysically necessary would play no essential role in the justification. The ultimate reason for accepting such a proposition, on this view, would be not that it seems to be necessary, but just that it has a feature (any subjectively identifiable feature would do) that there is some independent metajustificatory ground for regarding as a reliable index of truth.

But from the intuitive standpoint depicted earlier in this paper, this is obviously the wrong picture and amounts simply and obviously to a refusal to take rational insight seriously as a basis for justification: a refusal for which the present objection offers no further rationale, and which is thus question begging. As discussed above, when I consider, e.g., the proposition that nothing can be red and green all over at the same time, my intuitively apparent reason for accepting this proposition as true is that I see or grasp or apprehend, or at least seem to myself to see or grasp or apprehend, that it must be true in any possible world or situation—or, equivalently, that I am unable to understand how it could be false, unable to make intelligible sense of a falsifying situation. As remarked earlier, this seems intuitively to be in itself an excellent reason for accepting such a claim, one that does not in any obvious way need to be supplemented by an overarching metajustificatory premise of the sort being considered in the present section. This intuitive assessment may, of course, be mistaken. But this must be shown rather than simply being assumed, which is what in effect occurs when it is claimed without further defense that a metajustification is required.

This amounts to saying that according to the moderate rationalist position, each instance of apparent rational intuition or apparent self-evidence, each alleged case of a priori justification, should be construed as *epistemically autonomous*, as dependent on nothing beyond itself for its justification. We have already conceded that such justification is fallible. In addition, we have seen that it may be only initial or prima facie in the sense that it is capable of being overturned by further a priori reflection, by considerations of coherence, or by (partly) empirical considerations. But this does not alter the fact that apparent rational insight is, according to the moderate rationalist, sufficient by itself to justify the claim so long as these sorts of countervailing considerations do not arise. Such a view of the epistemic status of rational insight is at least prima facie plausible in light of examples like those discussed earlier, and we have so far seen no compelling reason for giving it up. And if such a thesis of epistemic autonomy is correct, then there is no legitimacy to the demand for a metajustification.

The Epistemological Case for Rationalism: Overview and Summary

I conclude with some further reflections on both the nature and inherent limitations of the epistemological case for rationalism. Each of the objections discussed here questions whether the existence of an apparent rational insight really provides a good reason, as claimed by the moderate rationalist, for thinking that the proposition that is its content is true. Several reasons were offered for doubting that this is so: the immediate, nondiscursive character of the alleged reason; the absence of an independent standard for resolving conflicts; and, most fundamentally, the absence and indeed impossibility of a non-question-begging metajustificatory argument. My response to these objections has been essentially defensive and dialectical in character, with the core point being that the demand, explicit in the final objection but implicit to some degree in each of the others, for an independent criterion or standard or metajustificatory premise for determining when and why an apparent rational intuition should be accepted is itself unjustified and ultimately question-begging against the rationalist.

But though this response and the more detailed discussions that embody it seem to me correct as far as they go, they may appear unsatisfying in a way that still needs to be addressed. Even if there is no conceivable alternative to reasons of an immediate nondiscursive sort, and even if it is both futile and illegitimate to demand a further independent standard or criterion for resolving conflicts or for providing a metajustification, it still seems possible to simply question or doubt whether accepting apparent rational insights is indeed conducive to arriving at the truth and to point out that no clear reason, over and above appeal to intuitions about particular cases, has yet been offered for an affirmative answer. Even if the demand for a further criterion or standard is dialectically illegitimate, this essentially negative point does not constitute a positive reason.

What the foregoing considerations may be taken to show, in first approximation, is that the appeal to apparent rational insight is epistemologically so basic and fundamental as not to admit of any sort of independent justification. I believe that there is a correct and fundamental point to be made here, but one that needs to be carefully focused and clarified if it is not to be misleading. It seems obvious that some mode of justification (perhaps more than one) must have this status, that it is impossible for each mode to be justified by appeal to others. It also seems clear that the appeal to apparent rational insight is a plausible candidate for such a role, both intuitively and dialectically, and indeed that it has no apparent rival for this status.[33]

The foregoing is not intended as an argument (which would of course be question-begging) to show that conferring this foundational status on apparent rational intuition is likely to lead to believing the truth. What it does show, I believe, is something like this: apart from direct observation, narrowly construed, we have no conception at all of what a standard of epistemic justification that did not appeal to apparent rational insight would even look like. This is also not intended to be an instance of the long-discredited paradigm-case argument. A skepticism that holds that the only standard of epistemic justification that we can understand is nonetheless incorrect, not conducive to finding the truth, remains dialectically tenable. But a fundamental standard of justification that is intuitively plausible, dialectically defensible, and to which there is no apparent alternative, though it may not be all that we could ask for, is almost certainly all that we can ever hope to have. My claim is that the moderate rationalist view has this status.

My tentative conclusion is that a moderate rationalism of the sort described here does not face any insuperable objections of an epistemological kind. It is, to be sure, unfortunate that our apparent rational insights are not infallible (as it is similarly unfortunate that our capacities are limited in numerous other respects). But the fact that our powers of rational thought are imperfect and do not guarantee success is hardly a reason for giving up rational thought altogether, which is what the rejection of rationalism, if consistently carried through (even in the absence of any reason to be consistent!) would amount to.[34]

Notes

1. Laurence BonJour, "A Rationalist Manifesto," *Canadian Journal of Philosophy* 18 (1992): 53–88.
2. Ibid., 54–55.
3. All of the examples in this section are putative examples of immediate or intuitive a priori justification. There is also, of course, justification that depends on a series of a priori inferential steps, each step being itself a matter of immediate intuition.
4. Many attempts have been made to argue that this sort of example is either not genuinely a priori or even not genuinely true—usually by moderate empiricists attempting to avoid what would otherwise be

a clear example of synthetic a priori justification. The most recent such attempt, by C. L. Hardin in his book *Color for Philosophers* (Indianapolis: Hackett, 1986), construes the claim in question as empirical, but in doing so is forced to treat many analogous claims, e.g., the claim that nothing can be red and blue all over at the same time, as false. According to Hardin, this latter claim is falsified by the existence of purple objects. But while there may be a sense in which a purple object is red and blue all over at the same time, and in which it is then an empirical fact that nothing can be red and green all over at the same time, there is a clear and much more obvious sense in which a purple object is neither red nor blue–in which I would simply be lying if I told someone that a particular object that I know to be purple in color is red. And nothing in Hardin discussion seems to me to provide any reason for rejecting the view that in this latter sense both the proposition that nothing can be red all over and green all over at the same time and the analogous proposition involving red and blue are justified a priori. I have no space here to consider other such attempts, but can only report that none of them seem to me to possess any serious degree of plausibility.
5. For much more on the vicissitudes of the concept of analyticity, see BonJour, op. cit.
6. A second sense of the term "intuition" is that involved in saying that the discussion of this section is being conducted on an *intuitive* level. By this, I intend only the vague but useful sense of "intuition" that is philosophically current, that which pertains to judgments and convictions which, though considered and reflective, are not arrived at via an explicit discursive process and thus are (hopefully) uncontaminated by theoretical or dialectical considerations. Yet a third use of "intuition" is that employed by Kant.
7. Thus Quinton, for example, would presumably argue that an explicit statement of the transitivity of the taller-than relation constitutes a partial "implicit definition" of the term "tall." See Anthony Quinton, "The A Priori and the Analytic," in R. C. Sleigh, ed., *Necessary Truth* (Englewood Cliffs, N.J.: Prentice-Hall, 1972), 105, for such a discussion of a parallel example.
8. BonJour, op. cit., 68–69.
9. See ibid. and section 7 below.
10. This assumes of course that it is possible for the justification of a proposition that is justified a priori to be enhanced, that a priori justification does not automatically confer the highest possible degree of justification. This point will be considered further below.
11. See BonJour, op. cit.
12. Nor is it, as Plantinga seems to suggest, a matter of a conviction of necessity accompanied by some peculiar,

indescribable phenomenology. See Alvin Plantinga, *Warrant and Proper Function* (New York: Oxford University Press, 1993), 105–6.

13. In one of the best recent discussions of a priori knowledge, Butchvarov suggests that what really happens in such a case is that the subject finds it *unthinkable* (or inconceivable or unintelligible) that a judgment whose content is the proposition in question could be mistaken. See Panayot Butchvarov, *The Concept of Knowledge* (Evanston, Ill.: Northwestern University Press, 1970), 76–88. But while this way of putting the matter has the virtue of emphasizing that a priori justification is of course a product of the individual person's psychological processes, it is misleading in that it could be taken to suggest that the unthinkability in question is just a brute fact: I try to entertain falsehood of the proposition in question and simply find that I cannot do so. On the contrary, as Butchvarov himself acknowledges, for me to find mistake unthinkable is not for it to be the case that I literally cannot understand the supposition that the proposition in question is false; rather I do understand what is claimed by such a supposition, but am unable to *think* it (ibid., 81). What this seems to mean is that I cannot think this supposition to be *true,* that I find it *impossible,* not merely unthinkable, which is of course equivalent to finding the original proposition to be necessary. This is not to deny that what *seems* impossible or necessary may not really be impossible or necessary (see the discussion of fallibility in the next section), but only to insist that the semblance in question is one of impossibility or necessity, not merely of unthinkability.

14. This, at least, is what their most explicit statements on the subject seem to convey. At the same time, it must be noted that such a claim of infallibility is pretty obviously not compatible with much of their actual practice—most obviously with the fact that views of competing philosophers, put forward on allegedly a priori grounds, were obviously often rejected as mistaken. (As discussed further below, to resolve this conflict by saying that the mistaken claims did not reflect *genuine* instances of rational insight threatens to trivialize the concept of rational insight.)

15. I believe that the standard understanding of the situation with regard to geometry and relativity, as described in the text, is at the very least much too simple. But there is no room here for a consideration of this issue.

16. As discussed more fully below, and contrary to what has often been assumed, an adequate conception of a priori justification will admit, indeed insist, that it comes in degrees. A recognition of this fact will make it possible to say, what in any case seems obvious, that more sustained or careful consideration may result in a greater degree of justification. But there will still be something like a minimum threshold in this respect, beneath which no justification results.

17. For the argument that induction must be justified a priori if it is to be justified at all, see my paper "A

Reconsideration of the Problem of Induction," *Philosophical Topics* 14 (1986): 93–124.

18. There is obviously an issue here as to when a situation of this kind involves further reflection on the same cognitive state or process and when it involves replacing the original state or process with a different one. I doubt that there is any one obviously correct way of drawing this distinction. But what matters for present purposes is that the later state be closely enough related to the original one that it is capable of illuminating and correcting the mistake involved, as opposed to simply juxtaposing a contrary judgment.

19. See the "Transcendental Dialectic," in the *Critique of Pure Reason.* Notice that any argument for a view like Kant's that did not have specific exceptions built into it would be self-defeating, in that there would be no way to exclude the possibility that the apparent cogency of the argument was itself an illusion of the sort in question.

20. For a good discussion of this point and some further examples, see Plantinga, op. cit., 109–10.

21. Kitcher's presentation of this objection, in *The Nature of Mathematical Knowledge* (Oxford: Oxford University Press, 1983), is explicitly directed only at mathematical claims, but there is no reason to think that he regards its force as limited to that context. It is also formulated in a way that is not immediately applicable to the version of rationalism offered here, because Kitcher, for reasons that seem to me quite uncompelling, eschews the concept of justification in favor of what amounts to a process reliabilism. For present purposes, I will simply reconstruct the objection so that it applies to a conception of a priori justification like that developed here and also extends beyond mathematics.

22. Ibid., 24.

23. Ibid., 30.

24. See "A Rationalist Manifesto."

25. It is worth noting that Kitcher himself, though without much in the way of explanation, seems to accept the idea of "nonempirical processes which actually warrant belief" (Kitcher, op. cit., 59). This suggests that the issue between him and the moderate rationalist may be partly terminological.

26. Ibid., 55.

27. Ibid., 55–56.

28. There are other epistemological objections to rationalism that I have no space in this paper to consider. And there are also, of course, objections of a more metaphysical sort. For a discussion of these additional objections, see my forthcoming book on a priori knowledge, on which the present paper is based.

29. See Quinton, op. cit., 90.

30. The tenability of the distinction between case (*a*) and case (*b*) obviously depends on not construing every case in which a person fails to find a claim necessary

as one in which he has a conflicting apparent rational insight into the *possibility* of its denial, for on this construal any case where one person has an insight that another fails to share would be a case of conflicting insights. It seems clear enough from an intuitive standpoint, however, that the distinction is genuine, that there are cases of sort (*a*) that are not cases of sort (*b*).

31. It is of course also possible, though perhaps less common, for one person to have conflicting apparent insights, either at the same time or at different times, or to have an insight at one time and fail to have it at a later time (the opposite case is obviously less troubling). But these sorts of cases are similar enough to the multiperson cases not to require separate consideration.

32. See my *The Structure of Empirical Knowledge* (Cambridge, Mass.: Harvard University Press, 1985), ch. 8.

33. Even if a foundationalist view of observation were acceptable, it would still be too narrow in its application and too incapable of lending justification to other modes of justification to plausibly constitute this epistemological bedrock on its own.

34. Much of the work leading to this paper was done during my tenure of a fellowship from the National Endowment for the Humanities during the 1991–92 academic year, support for which I am very grateful. Ann Baker was an invaluable source of comments and criticism.

✧ RESERVATIONS ABOUT THE ANALYTIC ✧

41. TWO DOGMAS OF EMPIRICISM

W. V. O. *Quine*

Modern empiricism has been conditioned in large part by two dogmas. One is a belief in some fundamental cleavage between truths which are *analytic*, or grounded in meanings independently of matters of fact, and truths which are *synthetic*, or grounded in fact. The other dogma is *reductionism*: the belief that each meaningful statement is equivalent to some logical construct upon terms which refer to immediate experience. Both dogmas, I shall argue, are ill-founded. One effect of abandoning them is, as we shall see, a blurring of the supposed boundary between speculative metaphysics and natural science. Another effect is a shift toward pragmatism.

Background for Analyticity

Kant's cleavage between analytic and synthetic truths was foreshadowed in Hume's distinction between relations of ideas and matters of fact, and in Leibniz's distinction between truths of reason and truths of fact. Leibniz spoke of the truths of reason as true in all possible worlds. Picturesqueness aside, this is to say that the truths of reason are those which could not possibly be false. In the same vein we hear analytic statements defined as statements whose denials are self-contradictory. But this definition has small explanatory value; for the notion of self-contradictoriness, in the quite broad sense needed for this definition of analyticity, stands in exactly the same need of clarification as does the notion of analyticity itself. The two notions are the two sides of a single dubious coin.

Kant conceived of an analytic statement as one that attributes to its subject no more than is already conceptually contained in the subject. This formulation has two shortcomings: it limits itself to statements of subject-predicate form, and it appeals to a notion of containment which is left at a metaphorical level. But Kant's intent, evident more from the use he makes of the notion of analyticity than from his definition of it, can be restated thus: a statement is analytic when it is true by virtue of meanings and independently of fact. Pursuing this line, let us examine the concept of *meaning* which is presupposed.

Meaning, let us remember, is not to be identified with naming.[1] Frege's example of 'Evening Star' and 'Morning Star', and Russell's of 'Scott' and 'the author of *Waverley*', illustrate that terms can name the same thing but differ in meaning. The distinction between meaning and naming is no less important at the level of abstract terms. The terms '9' and 'the number of the planets' name one and the same abstract entity but presumably must be regarded as unlike in meaning; for astronomical observation was needed, and not mere reflection on meanings, to determine the sameness of the entity in question.

The above examples consist of singular terms, concrete and abstract. With general terms, or predicates, the situation is somewhat different but parallel. Whereas a singular term purports to name an entity, abstract or concrete, a general term does not; but a general term is *true* of an entity, or of each of many, or of none.[2] The class of all entities of which a general term is true is called the *extension* of the term. Now paralleling the contrast between the meaning of a singular term and the entity named, we must distinguish equally between the meaning of a general term and its extension. The general terms 'creature with a heart' and 'creature with kidneys', for example, are perhaps alike in extension but unlike in meaning.

Confusion of meaning with extension, in the case of general terms, is *less* common than confusion of meaning with naming in the case of singular terms. It is indeed a commonplace in philosophy to oppose intension (or meaning) to extension, or, in a variant vocabulary, connotation to denotation.

The Aristotelian notion of essence was the forerunner, no doubt, of the modern notion of intension or meaning. For Aristotle it was essential in men to be rational, accidental to be two-legged. But there is an important difference between this attitude and the doctrine of meaning. From the latter point of view it may indeed be conceded (if only for the sake of argument) that rationality is involved in the meaning of the word 'man' while two-leggedness is not; but two-leggedness may at the same time be viewed as involved in the meaning of 'biped' while rationality is not. Thus from the point of view of the doctrine of meaning it makes no sense to say of the actual individual, who is at once a man and biped, that his rationality is essential and his two-leggedness accidental or vice versa. Things had essences, for Aristotle, but only linguistic forms have meanings. Meaning is what essence becomes when it is divorced from the object of reference and wedded to the word.

For the theory of meaning a conspicuous question is the nature of its objects: what sort of things are meanings? A felt need for meant entities may derive from an earlier failure to appreciate that meaning and reference are distinct. Once the theory of meaning is sharply separated from the theory of reference, it is a short step to recognizing as the primary business of the theory of meaning simply the synonymy of linguistic forms and the analyticity of statements; meanings themselves, as obscure intermediary entities, may well be abandoned.[3]

The problem of analyticity then confronts us anew. Statements which are analytic by general philosophical acclaim are not, indeed, far to seek. They fall into two classes. Those of the first class, which may be called *logically true*, are typified by:

1. No unmarried man is married.

The relevant feature of this example is that it not merely is true as it stands, but remains true under any and all reinterpretations of 'man' and 'married'. If we suppose a prior inventory of *logical* particles, comprising 'no', 'un-', 'not', 'if', 'then', 'and', etc., then in general a logical truth is a statement which is true and remains true under all reinterpretations of its components other than the logical particles.

But there is also a second class of analytic statements, typified by:

2. No bachelor is married.

The characteristic of such a statement is that it can be turned into a logical truth by putting synonyms for synonyms; thus (2) can be turned into (1) by putting 'unmarried man' for its synonym 'bachelor'. We still lack a proper characterization of this second class of analytic statements, and therewith of analyticity generally, inasmuch as we have had in the above description to lean on a notion of "synonymy" which is no less in need of clarification than analyticity itself.

In recent years Carnap has tended to explain analyticity by appeal to what he calls state-descriptions.[4] A state-description is any exhaustive assignment of truth values to the atomic, or noncompound, statements of the language. All other statements of the language are, Carnap assumes, built up of their component clauses by means of the familiar logical devices, in such a way that the truth value of any complex statement is fixed for each state-description by specifiable logical laws. A statement is then explained as analytic when it comes out true under every state description. This account is an adaptation of Leibniz's "true in all possible worlds." But note that this version of analyticity serves its purpose only if the atomic statements of the language are, unlike 'John is a bachelor' and 'John is married', mutually independent. Otherwise there would be a state-description which assigned truth to 'John is a bachelor' and to 'John is married', and consequently 'No bachelors are married' would turn out synthetic rather than analytic under the proposed criterion. Thus the criterion of analyticity in terms of state-descriptions serves only for languages devoid of extralogical synonym-pairs, such as 'bachelor' and 'unmarried man'—synonym-pairs of the type which give rise to the "second class" of analytic statements. The criterion in terms of state-descriptions is a reconstruction at best of logical truth, not of analyticity.

I do not mean to suggest that Carnap is under any illusions on this point. His simplified model language with its state-descriptions is aimed primarily not at the general problem of analyticity but at another purpose, the clarification of probability and induction. Our problem, however, is analyticity; and here the major difficulty lies not in the first class of analytic statements, the logical truths, but rather in the second class, which depends on the notion of synonymy.

Definition

There are those who find it soothing to say that the analytic statements of the second class reduce to those of the first class, the logical truths, by

definition; 'bachelor', for example, is *defined* as 'unmarried man'. But how do we find that 'bachelor' is defined as 'unmarried man'? Who defined it thus, and when? Are we to appeal to the nearest dictionary, and accept the lexicographer's formulation as law? Clearly this would be to put the cart before the horse. The lexicographer is an empirical scientist, whose business is the recording of antecedent facts; and if he glosses 'bachelor' as 'unmarried man' it is because of his belief that there is a relation of synonymy between those forms, implicit in general or preferred usage prior to his own work. The notion of synonymy presupposed here has still to be clarified, presumably in terms relating to linguistic behavior. Certainly the "definition" which is the lexicographer's report of an observed synonymy cannot be taken as the ground of the synonymy.

Definition is not, indeed, an activity exclusively of philologists. Philosophers and scientists frequently have occasion to "define" a recondite term by paraphrasing it into terms of a more familiar vocabulary. But ordinarily such a definition, like the philologist's, is pure lexicography, affirming a relation of synonymy antecedent to the exposition in hand.

Just what it means to affirm synonymy, just what the inter-connections may be which are necessary and sufficient in order that two linguistic forms be properly describable as synonymous, is far from clear; but, whatever these interconnections may be, ordinarily they are grounded in usage. Definitions reporting selected instances of synonymy come then as reports upon usage.

There is also, however, a variant type of definitional activity which does not limit itself to the reporting of preexisting synonymies. I have in mind what Carnap calls *explication*—an activity to which philosophers are given, and scientists also in their more philosophical moments. In explication the purpose is not merely to paraphrase the definiendum into an outright synonym, but actually to improve upon the definiendum by refining or supplementing its meaning. But even explication, though not merely reporting a preexisting synonymy between definiendum and definiens, does rest nevertheless on *other* preexisting synonymies. The matter may be viewed as follows. Any word worth explicating has some contexts which, as wholes, are clear and precise enough to be useful; and the purpose of explication is to preserve the usage of these favored contexts while sharpening the usage of other contexts. In order that a given definition be suitable for purposes of explication, therefore, what is required is not that the definiendum in its antecedent usage be synonymous with the definiens, but just that each of these favored contexts of the definiendum, taken as a whole in its antecedent usage, be synonymous with the corresponding context of the definiens.

Two alternative definientia may be equally appropriate for the purposes of a given task of explication and yet not be synonymous with each other; for they may serve interchangeably within the favored contexts but diverge elsewhere. By cleaving to one of these definientia rather than the other, a definition of explicative kind generates, by fiat, a relation of synonymy between definiendum and definiens which did not hold before. But such a definition still owes its explicative function, as seen, to preexisting synonymies.

There does, however, remain still an extreme sort of definition which does not hark back to prior synonymies at all: namely, the explicitly conventional introduction of novel notations for purposes of sheer abbreviation. Here the definiendum becomes synonymous with the definiens simply because it has been created expressly for the purpose of being synonymous with the definiens. Here we have a really transparent case of synonymy created by definition; would that all species of synonymy were as intelligible. For the rest, definition rests on synonymy rather than explaining it.

The word 'definition' has come to have a dangerously reassuring sound, owing no doubt to its frequent occurrence in logical and mathematical writings. We shall do well to digress now into a brief appraisal of the role of definition in formal work.

In logical and mathematical systems either of two mutually antagonistic types of economy may be striven for, and each has its peculiar practical utility. On the one hand we may seek economy of practical expression—ease and brevity in the statement of multifarious relations. This sort of economy calls usually for distinctive concise notations for a wealth of concepts. Second, however, and oppositely, we may seek economy in grammar and vocabulary; we may try to find a minimum of basic concepts such that, once a distinctive notation has been appropriated to each of them, it becomes possible to express any desired further concept by mere combination and iteration of our basic notations. This second sort of economy is impractical in one way, since a poverty in basic idioms tends to a necessary lengthening of discourse. But it is practical in another way: it greatly simplifies theoretical discourse *about* the language, through minimizing the terms and the forms of construction wherein the language consists.

Both sorts of economy, though prima facie incompatible, are valuable in their separate ways. The custom has consequently arisen of combining both sorts of economy by forging in effect two languages, the one a part of the other. The inclusive language, though redundant in grammar and vocabulary, is economical in message lengths, while the part, called primitive notation, is economical in grammar and vocabulary. Whole and part are correlated by rules of translation whereby each idiom not in primitive notation is equated to some complex built up of primitive notation. These rules of translation are the so-called *definitions* which appear in formalized systems. They are best viewed not as adjuncts to one language but as correlations between two languages, the one a part of the other.

But these correlations are not arbitrary. They are supposed to show how the primitive notations can accomplish all purposes, save brevity and convenience, of the redundant language. Hence the definiendum and its definiens may be expected, in each case, to be related in one or another of the three ways lately noted. The definiens may be a faithful paraphrase of the definiendum into the narrower notation, preserving a direct synonymy[5] as of antecedent usage; or the definiens may, in the spirit of explication, improve upon the antecedent usage of the definiendum; or finally, the definiendum may be a newly created notation, newly endowed with meaning here and now.

In formal and informal work alike, thus, we find that definition—except in the extreme case of the explicitly conventional introduction of new notations—hinges on prior relations of synonymy. Recognizing then that the notion of definition does not hold the key to synonymy and analyticity, let us look further into synonymy and say no more of definition.

Interchangeability

A natural suggestion, deserving close examination, is that the synonymy of two linguistic forms consists simply in their interchangeability in all contexts without change of truth value—interchangeability, in Leibniz's phrase, *salva veritate*.[6] Note that synonyms so conceived need not even be free from vagueness, as long as the vaguenesses match.

But it is not quite true that the synonyms 'bachelor' and 'unmarried man' are everywhere interchangeable *salva veritate*. Truths which become false under substitution of 'unmarried man' for 'bachelor' are easily constructed with the help of 'bachelor of arts' or 'bachelor's buttons'; also with the help of quotation, thus:

'Bachelor' has less than ten letters.

Such counterinstances can, however, perhaps be set aside by treating the phrases 'bachelor of arts' and 'bachelor's buttons' and the quotation "bachelor" each as a single indivisible word and then stipulating that the interchangeability *salva veritate* which is to be the touchstone of synonymy is not supposed to apply to fragmentary occurrences inside of a word. This account of synonymy, supposing it acceptable on other counts, has indeed the drawback of appealing to a prior conception of "word" which can be counted on to present difficulties of formulation in its turn. Nevertheless some progress might be claimed in having reduced the problem of synonymy to a problem of wordhood. Let us pursue this line a bit, taking "word" for granted.

The question remains whether interchangeability *salva veritate* (apart from occurrences within words) is a strong enough condition for synonymy, or whether, on the contrary, some heteronymous expressions might be thus interchangeable. Now let us be clear that we are not concerned here with synonymy in the sense of complete identity in psychological associations or poetic quality; indeed no two expressions are synonymous in such a sense. We are concerned only with what may be called *cognitive* synonymy. Just what this is cannot be said without successfully finishing the present study; but we know something about it from the need which arose for it in connection with analyticity in §1. The sort of synonymy needed there was merely such that any analytic statement could be turned into a logical truth by putting synonyms for synonyms. Turning the tables and assuming analyticity, indeed, we could explain cognitive synonymy of terms as follows (keeping to the familiar example): to say that 'bachelor' and 'unmarried man' are cognitively synonymous is to say no more nor less than that the statement:

3. All and only bachelors are unmarried men is analytic.[7]

What we need is an account of cognitive synonymy not presupposing analyticity—if we are to explain analyticity conversely with help of cognitive synonymy as undertaken in §1. And indeed such an independent account of cognitive synonymy is at present up for consideration, namely, interchangeability *salva veritate* everywhere except within words. The question before us, to resume the thread at last, is whether such interchangeability is a sufficient condition for cognitive synonymy. We can quickly assure ourselves that it is, by examples of the following sort. The statement:

4. Necessarily all and only bachelors are bachelors

is evidently true, even supposing 'necessarily' so narrowly construed as to be truly applicable only to analytic statements. Then, if 'bachelor' and 'unmarried man' are interchangeable *salva veritate*, the result:

5. Necessarily all and only bachelors are unmarried men

of putting 'unmarried man' for an occurrence of 'bachelor' in (4) must, like (4), be true. But to say that (5) is true is to say that (3) is analytic, and hence that 'bachelor' and 'unmarried man' are cognitively synonymous.

Let us see what there is about the above argument that gives it its air of hocus-pocus. The condition of interchangeability *salva veritate* varies in its force with variations in the richness of the language at hand. The above argument supposes we are working with a language rich enough to contain the adverb 'necessarily', this adverb being so construed as to yield truth when and only when applied to an analytic statement. But can we condone a language which contains such an adverb? Does the adverb really make sense? To suppose that it does is to suppose that we have already made satisfactory sense of 'analytic'. Then what are we so hard at work on right now?

Our argument is not flatly circular, but something like it. It has the form, figuratively speaking, of a closed curve in space.

Interchangeability *salva veritate* is meaningless until relativized to a language whose extent is specified in relevant respects. Suppose now we consider a language containing just the following materials. There is an indefinitely large stock of one-place predicates (for example, 'F' where 'Fx' means that x is a man) and many-place predicates (for example, 'G' where 'Gxy' means that x loves y), mostly having to do with extralogical subject matter. The rest of the language is logical. The atomic sentences consist each of a predicate followed by one or more variables 'x', 'y', etc.; and the complex sentences are built up of the atomic ones by truth functions ('not', 'and', 'or', etc.) and quantification.[8] In effect such a language enjoys the benefits also of descriptions and indeed singular terms generally, these being contextually definable in known ways.[9] Even abstract singular terms naming classes, classes of classes, etc., are contextually definable in case the assumed stock of predicates includes the two-place predicate of class membership.[10] Such a language can be adequate to classical mathematics and indeed to scientific discourse generally, except in so far as the latter involves debatable devices such as contrary-to-fact conditionals or modal adverbs like 'necessarily'.[11] Now a language of this type is extensional, in this sense: any two predicates which agree extensionally (that is, are true of the same objects) are interchangeable *salva veritate*.[12]

In an extensional language, therefore, interchangeability *salva veritate* is no assurance of cognitive synonymy of the desired type. That 'bachelor' and 'unmarried man' are interchangeable *salva veritate* in an extensional language assures us of no more than that (3) is true. There is no assurance here that the extensional agreement of 'bachelor' and 'unmarried man' rests on meaning rather than merely on accidental matters of fact, as does the extensional agreement of 'creature with a heart' and 'creature with kidneys'.

For most purposes extensional agreement is the nearest approximation to synonymy we need care about. But the fact remains that extensional agreement falls far short of cognitive synonymy of the type required for explaining analyticity in the manner of §1. The type of cognitive synonymy required there is such as to equate the synonymy of 'bachelor' and 'unmarried man' with the analyticity of (3), not merely with the truth of (3).

So we must recognize that interchangeability *salva veritate*, if construed in relation to an extensional language, is not a sufficient condition of cognitive synonymy in the sense needed for deriving analyticity in the manner of §1. If a language contains an intensional adverb 'necessarily' in the sense lately noted, or other particles to the same effect, then interchangeability *salva veritate* in such a language does afford a sufficient condition of cognitive synonymy; but such a language is intelligible only in so far as the notion of analyticity is already understood in advance.

The effort to explain cognitive synonymy first, for the sake of deriving analyticity from it afterward as in §1, is perhaps the wrong approach. Instead we might try explaining analyticity somehow without appeal to cognitive synonymy. Afterward we could doubtless derive cognitive synonymy from analyticity satisfactorily enough if desired. We have seen that cognitive synonymy of 'bachelor' and 'unmarried man' can be explained as analyticity of (3). The same explanation works for any pair of one-place predicates, of course, and it can be extended in obvious fashion to many-place predicates. Other syntactical categories can also be accommodated in fairly parallel fashion. Singular terms may be said to be cognitively synonymous when the statement of identity formed by putting '=' between them is analytic. Statements may be said simply to be cognitively synonymous when their biconditional (the result of joining them by 'if and only if') is analytic.[13] If we care to lump all categories into a single formulation, at the expense of assuming again the notion of "word" which was appealed to early in this section, we can describe any two linguistic forms as cognitively synonymous when the two forms are interchangeable (apart from occurrences within "words") *salva* (no longer *veritate* but) *analyticitate*. Certain technical questions arise, indeed, over cases of ambiguity or homonymy; let us not pause for them, however, for we are already digressing. Let us rather turn our backs on the problem of synonymy and address ourselves anew to that of analyticity.

Semantical Rules

Analyticity at first seemed most naturally definable by appeal to a realm of meanings. On refinement, the appeal to meanings gave way to an appeal to synonymy or definition. But definition turned out to be a will-o'-the-wisp, and synonymy turned out to be best understood only by dint of a prior appeal to analyticity itself. So we are back at the problem of analyticity.

I do not know whether the statement 'Everything green is extended' is analytic. Now does my indecision over this example really betray an incomplete understanding, an incomplete grasp of the "meanings", of 'green' and 'extended'? I think not. The trouble is not with 'green' or 'extended', but with 'analytic'.

It is often hinted that the difficulty in separating analytic statements from synthetic ones in ordinary language is due to the vagueness of ordinary language and that the distinction is clear when we have a precise artificial language with explicit "semantical rules." This, however, as I shall now attempt to show, is a confusion.

The notion of analyticity about which we are worrying is a purported relation between statements and languages: a statement S is said to be *analytic for* a language L, and the problem is to make sense of this relation generally, that is, for variable 'S' and 'L'. The gravity of this problem is not perceptibly less for artificial languages than for natural ones. The problem of making sense of the idiom 'S is analytic for L', with variable 'S' and 'L', retains its stubbornness even if we limit the range of the variable 'L' to artificial languages. Let me now try to make this point evident.

For artificial languages and semantical rules we look naturally to the writings of Carnap. His semantical rules take various forms, and to make my point I shall have to distinguish certain of the forms. Let us suppose, to begin with, an artificial language L_0 whose semantical rules have the form explicitly of a specification, by recursion or otherwise, of all the analytic statements of L_0. The rules tell us that such and such statements, and only those, are the analytic statements of L_0. Now here the difficulty is simply that the rules contain the word 'analytic', which we do not understand! We understand what expressions the rules attribute analyticity to, but we do not understand what the rules attribute to those expressions. In short, before we can understand a rule which begins 'A statement S is analytic for language L_0 if and only if . . .', we must understand the general relative term 'analytic for'; we must understand 'S is analytic for L' where 'S' and 'L' are variables.

Alternatively we may, indeed, view the so-called rule as a conventional definition of a new simple symbol 'analytic-for-L_0', which might better be written untendentiously as 'K' so as not to seem to throw light on the interesting word 'analytic'. Obviously any number of classes K, M, N, etc. of statements of L_0 can be specified for various purposes or for no purpose; what does it mean to say that K, as against M, N, etc., is the class of the "analytic" statements of L_0?

By saying what statements are analytic for L_0 we explain 'analytic-for-L_0' but not 'analytic', not 'analytic for'. We do not begin to explain the idiom 'S is analytic for L' with variable 'S' and 'L', even if we are content to limit the range of 'L' to the realm of artificial languages.

Actually we do know enough about the intended significance of 'analytic' to know that analytic statements are supposed to be true. Let us then turn to a second form of semantical rule, which says not that such and such statements are analytic but simply that such and such statements are included among the truths. Such a rule is not subject to the criticism of containing the un-understood word 'analytic'; and we may grant for the sake of argument that there is no difficulty over the broader term 'true'. A semantical rule of this second type, a rule of truth, is not supposed to specify all the truths of the language; it merely stipulates, recursively or otherwise, a certain multitude of statements which, along with others unspecified, are to count as true. Such a rule may be conceded to be quite clear. Derivatively, afterward, analyticity can be demarcated thus: a statement is analytic if it is (not merely true but) true according to the semantical rule.

Still there is really no progress. Instead of appealing to an unexplained word 'analytic', we are now appealing to an unexplained phrase 'semantical rule'. Not every true statement which says that the statements of some class are true can count as a semantical rule—otherwise *all* truths would be "analytic" in the sense of being true according to semantical rules. Semantical rules are distinguishable, apparently, only by the fact of appearing on a page under the heading 'Semantical Rules'; and this heading is itself then meaningless.

We can say indeed that a statement is *analytic-for-L_0* if and only if it is true according to such and such specifically appended "semantical rules," but then we find ourselves back at essentially the same case which was originally discussed:'*S* is analytic-for-L_0 if and only if . . . .' Once we seek to explain '*S* is analytic for *L*' generally for variable '*L*' (even allowing limitation of '*L*' to artificial languages), the explanation 'true according to the semantical rules of *L*' is unavailing; for the relative term 'semantical rule of' is as much in need of clarification, at least, as 'analytic for'.

It may be instructive to compare the notion of semantical rule with that of postulate. Relative to a given set of postulates, it is easy to say what a postulate is: it is a member of the set. Relative to a given set of semantical rules, it is equally easy to say what a semantical rule is. But given simply a notation, mathematical or otherwise, and indeed as thoroughly understood a notation as you please in point of the translations or truth conditions of its statements, who can say which of its true statements rank as postulates? Obviously the question is meaningless—as meaningless as asking which points in Ohio are starting points. Any finite (or effectively specifiable infinite) selection of statements (preferably true ones, perhaps) is as much *a* set of postulates as any other. The word 'postulate' is significant only relative to an act of inquiry; we apply the word

to a set of statements just in so far as we happen, for the year or the moment, to be thinking of those statements in relation to the statements which can be reached from them by some set of transformations to which we have seen fit to direct our attention. Now the notion of semantical rule is as sensible and meaningful as that of postulate, if conceived in a similarly relative spirit—relative, this time, to one or another particular enterprise of schooling unconversant persons in sufficient conditions for truth of statements of some natural or artificial language *L*. But from this point of view no one signalization of a subclass of the truths of *L* is intrinsically more a semantical rule than another; and, if 'analytic' means 'true by semantical rules', no one truth of *L* is analytic to the exclusion of another.[14]

It might conceivably be protested that an artificial language *L* (unlike a natural one) is a language in the ordinary sense *plus* a set of explicit semantical rules—the whole constituting, let us say, an ordered pair; and that the semantical rules of *L* then are specifiable simply as the second component of the pair *L*. But, by the same token and more simply, we might construe an artificial language *L* outright as an ordered pair whose second component is the class of its analytic statements; and then the analytic statements of *L* become specifiable simply as the statements in the second component of *L*. Or better still, we might just stop tugging at our bootstraps altogether.

Not all the explanations of analyticity known to Carnap and his readers have been covered explicitly in the above considerations, but the extension to other forms is not hard to see. Just one additional factor should be mentioned which sometimes enters: sometimes the semantical rules are in effect rules of translation into ordinary language, in which case the analytic statements of the artificial language are in effect recognized as such from the analyticity of their specified translations in ordinary language. Here certainly there can be no thought of an illumination of the problem of analyticity from the side of the artificial language.

From the point of view of the problem of analyticity the notion of an artificial language with semantical rules is a *feu follet par excellence*. Semantical rules determining the analytic statements of an artificial language are of interest only in so far as we already understand the notion of analyticity; they are of no help in gaining this understanding.

Appeal to hypothetical languages of an artificially simple kind could conceivably be useful in clarifying analyticity, if the mental or behavioral or cultural factors relevant to analyticity—whatever they may be—were somehow sketched into the simplified model. But a model which takes analyticity merely as an irreducible character is unlikely to throw light on the problem of explicating analyticity.

It is obvious that truth in general depends on both language and extralinguistic fact. The statement 'Brutus killed Caesar' would be false if the world had been different in certain ways, but it would also be false if the word 'killed' happened rather to have the sense of 'begat'. Thus one is tempted to suppose in general that the truth of a statement is somehow analyzable into a linguistic component and a factual component. Given this supposition, it next seems reasonable that in some statements the factual component should be null; and these are the analytic statements. But, for all its a priori reasonableness, a boundary between analytic and synthetic statements simply has not been drawn. That there is such a distinction to be drawn at all is an unempirical dogma of empiricists, a metaphysical article of faith.

The Verification Theory and Reductionism

In the course of these somber reflections we have taken a dim view first of the notion of meaning, then of the notion of cognitive synonymy, and finally of the notion of analyticity. But what, it may be asked, of the verification theory of meaning? This phrase has established itself so firmly as a catchword of empiricism that we should be very unscientific indeed not to look beneath it for a possible key to the problem of meaning and the associated problems.

The verification theory of meaning, which has been conspicuous in the literature from Peirce onward, is that the meaning of a statement is the method of empirically confirming or infirming it. An analytic statement is that limiting case which is confirmed no matter what.

As urged in §1, we can as well pass over the question of meanings as entities and move straight to sameness of meaning, or synonymy. Then what the verification theory says is that statements are synonymous if and only if they are alike in point of method of empirical confirmation or infirmation.

This is an account of cognitive synonymy not of linguistic forms generally, but of statements.[15] However, from the concept of synonymy of statements we could derive the concept of synonymy for other linguistic forms, by considerations somewhat similar to those at the end of 3. Assuming the notion of "word," indeed, we could explain any two forms as synonymous when the putting of the one form for an occurrence of the other in any statement (apart from occurrences within "words") yields a synonymous statement. Finally, given the concept of synonymy thus for linguistic forms generally, we could define analyticity in terms of synonymy and logical truth as in §1. For that matter, we could define analyticity more simply in terms of just synonymy of statements together with logical truth; it is not necessary to appeal to synonymy of linguistic forms other than statements. For a statement may be described as analytic simply when it is synonymous with a logically true statement.

So, if the verification theory can be accepted as an adequate account of statement synonymy, the notion of analyticity is saved after all. However, let us reflect. Statement synonymy is said to be likeness of method of empirical confirmation or infirmation. Just what are these methods which are to be compared for likeness? What, in other words, is the nature of the relation between a statement and the experiences which contribute to or detract from its confirmation?

The most naïve view of the relation is that it is one of direct report. This is *radical reductionism*. Every meaningful statement is held to be translatable into a statement (true or false) about immediate experience. Radical reductionism, in one form or another, well antedates the verification theory of meaning explicitly so called. Thus Locke and Hume held that every idea must either originate directly in sense experience or else be compounded of ideas thus originating; and taking a hint from Tooke we might rephrase this doctrine in semantical jargon by saying that a term, to be significant at all, must be either a name of a sense datum or a compound of such names or an abbreviation of such a compound. So stated, the doctrine remains ambiguous as between sense data as sensory events and sense data as sensory qualities; and it remains vague as to the admissible ways of compounding. Moreover, the doctrine is unnecessarily and intolerably restrictive in the term-by-term critique which it imposes. More reasonably, and without yet exceeding the limits of what I have called radical reductionism, we may take full statements as our significant units—thus demanding that our statements as wholes be translatable into sense-datum language, but not that they be translatable term by term.

This emendation would unquestionably have been welcome to Locke and Hume and Tooke, but historically it had to await an important reorientation in semantics—the reorientation whereby the primary vehicle of meaning came to be seen no longer in the term but in the statement. This reorientation, seen in Bentham and Frege, underlies Russell's concept of incomplete symbols defined in use;[16] also it is implicit in the verification theory of meaning, since the objects of verification are statements.

Radical reductionism, conceived now with statements as units, set itself the task of specifying a sense-datum language and showing how to translate the rest of significant discourse, statement by statement, into it. Carnap embarked on this project in the *Aufbau*.

The language which Carnap adopted as his starting point was not a sense-datum language in the narrowest conceivable sense, for it included also the notations of logic, up through higher set theory. In effect it included the whole language of pure mathematics. The ontology implicit in it (that is, the range of values of its variables) embraced not only sensory events but classes, classes of classes, and so on. Empiricists there are who would boggle at such prodigality. Carnap's starting point is very parsimonious, however, in its extralogical or sensory part. In a series of constructions in which he exploits the resources of modern logic with much ingenuity, Carnap succeeds in defining a wide array of important additional sensory concepts which, but for his constructions, one would not have dreamed were definable on so slender a basis. He was the first empiricist who, not content with asserting the reducibility of science to terms of immediate experience, took serious steps toward carrying out the reduction.

If Carnap's starting point is satisfactory, still his constructions were, as he himself stressed, only a fragment of the full program. The construction of even the simplest statements about the physical world was left in a sketchy state. Carnap's suggestions on this subject were, despite their sketchiness, very suggestive. He explained spatio-temporal point-instants as quadruples of real numbers and envisaged assignment of sense qualities to point-instants according to certain canons. Roughly summarized, the plan was that qualities should be assigned to point-instants in such a way as to achieve the laziest world compatible with our experience. The principle of least action was to be our guide in constructing a world from experience.

Carnap did not seem to recognize, however, that his treatment of physical objects fell short of reduction not merely through sketchiness, but in principle. Statements of the form 'Quality q is at point-instant $x;y;z;t$' were, according to his canons, to be apportioned truth values in such a way as to maximize and minimize certain over-all features, and with growth of experience the truth values were to be progressively revised in the same spirit. I think this is a good schematization (deliberately oversimplified, to be sure) of what science really does; but it provides no indication, not even the sketchiest, of how a statement of the form 'Quality q is at $x;y;z;t$' could ever be translated into Carnap's initial language of sense data and logic. The connective 'is at' remains an added undefined connective; the canons counsel us in its use but not in its elimination.

Carnap seems to have appreciated this point afterward; for in his later writings he abandoned all notion of the translatability of statements about the physical world into statements about immediate experience. Reductionism in its radical form has long since ceased to figure in Carnap's philosophy.

But the dogma of reductionism has, in a subtler and more tenuous form, continued to influence the thought of empiricists. The notion lingers that to each statement, or each synthetic statement, there is associated a unique range of possible sensory events such that the occurrence of any of them would add to the likelihood of truth of the statement, and that there is associated also another unique range of possible sensory events whose occurrence would detract from that likelihood. This notion is of course implicit in the verification theory of meaning.

The dogma of reductionism survives in the supposition that each statement, taken in isolation from its fellows, can admit of confirmation or infirmation at all. My countersuggestion, issuing essentially from Carnap's doctrine of the physical world in the *Aufbau*, is that our statements about the external world face the tribunal of sense experience not individually but only as a corporate body.[17]

The dogma of reductionism, even in its attenuated form, is intimately connected with the other dogma—that there is a cleavage between the analytic and the synthetic. We have found ourselves led, indeed, from the latter problem to the former through the verification theory of meaning. More directly, the one dogma clearly supports the other in this way: as long as it is taken to be significant in general to speak of the confirmation and infirmation of a statement, it seems significant to speak also of a limiting kind of statement which is vacuously confirmed, *ipso facto*, come what may; and such a statement is analytic.

The two dogmas are, indeed, at root identical. We lately reflected that in general the truth of statements does obviously depend both upon language and upon extralinguistic fact; and we noted that this obvious circumstance carries in its train, not logically but all too naturally, a feeling that the truth of a statement is somehow analyzable into a linguistic component and a factual component. The factual component must, if we are empiricists, boil down to a range of confirmatory experiences. In the extreme case where the linguistic component is all that matters, a true statement is analytic. But I hope we are now impressed with how stubbornly the distinction between analytic and synthetic has resisted any straightforward drawing. I am impressed also, apart from prefabricated examples of black and white balls in an urn, with how baffling the problem has always been of arriving at any explicit theory of the empirical confirmation of a synthetic statement. My present suggestion is that it is nonsense, and the root of much nonsense, to speak of a linguistic component and a factual component in the truth of any individual statement. Taken collectively, science has its double dependence upon language and experience; but this duality is not significantly traceable into the statements of science taken one by one.

The idea of defining a symbol in use was, as remarked, an advance over the impossible term-by-term empiricism of Locke and Hume. The statement, rather than the term, came with Bentham to be recognized as the unit accountable to an empiricist critique. But what I am now urging is that even in taking the statement as unit we have drawn our grid too finely. The unit of empirical significance is the whole of science.

Empiricism Without the Dogmas

The totality of our so-called knowledge or beliefs, from the most casual matters of geography and history to the profoundest laws of atomic physics or even of pure mathematics and logic, is a man-made fabric which impinges on experience only along the edges. Or, to change the figure, total science is like a field of force whose boundary conditions are experience. A conflict with experience at the periphery occasions readjustments in the interior of the field. Truth values have to be redistributed over some of our statements. Reevaluation of some statements entails reevaluation of others, because of their logical interconnections —the logical laws being in turn simply certain further statements of the system, certain further elements of the field. Having reëvaluated one statement we must reëvaluate some others, which may be statements logically connected with the first or may be the statements of logical connections themselves. But the total field is so underdetermined by its boundary conditions, experience, that there is much latitude of choice as to what statements to reëvaluate in the light of any single contrary experience. No particular experiences are linked with any particular statements in the interior of the field, except indirectly through considerations of equilibrium affecting the field as a whole.

If this view is right, it is misleading to speak of the empirical content of an individual statement—especially if it is a statement at all remote from the experiential periphery of the field. Furthermore it becomes folly to seek a boundary between synthetic statements, which hold contingently on experience, and analytic statements, which hold come what may. Any statement can be held true come what may, if we make drastic enough adjustments elsewhere in the system. Even a statement very close to the periphery can be held true in the face of recalcitrant experience by pleading hallucination or by amending certain statements of the kind called logical laws. Conversely, by the same token, no statement is immune to revision. Revision even of the logical law of the excluded middle has been proposed as a means of simplifying quantum mechanics; and what difference is there in principle between such a shift and the shift whereby Kepler superseded Ptolemy, or Einstein Newton, or Darwin Aristotle?

For vividness I have been speaking in terms of varying distances from a sensory periphery. Let me try now to clarify this notion without metaphor. Certain statements, though *about* physical objects and not sense experience, seem peculiarly germane to sense experience—and in a selective way: some statements to some experiences, others to others. Such statements, especially germane to particular experiences, I picture as near the periphery. But in this relation of "germaneness" I envisage nothing more than a loose association reflecting the relative likelihood, in practice, of our choosing one statement rather than another for revision in the event of recalcitrant experience. For example, we can imagine recalcitrant experiences to which we would surely be inclined to accommodate our system by reëvaluating just the statement that there are brick houses on Elm Street, together with related statements on the same topic. We can imagine other recalcitrant experiences to which we would be inclined to accommodate our system by reevaluating just the statement that there are no centaurs, along with kindred statements. A recalcitrant experience can, I have urged, be accommodated by any of various alternative reëvaluations in various alternative quarters of the total system; but, in the cases which we are now imagining, our natural tendency to disturb the total system as little as possible would lead us to focus our revisions upon these specific statements concerning brick houses or centaurs. These statements are felt, therefore, to have a sharper empirical reference than highly theoretical statements of physics or logic or ontology. The latter statements may be thought of as relatively centrally located within the total network, meaning merely that little preferential connection with any particular sense data obtrudes itself.

As an empiricist I continue to think of the conceptual scheme of science as a tool, ultimately, for predicting future experience in the light of past experience. Physical objects are conceptually imported into the situation as convenient intermediaries—not by definition in terms of experience, but simply as irreducible posits[18] comparable, epistemologically, to the gods of Homer. For my part I do, qua lay physicist, believe in physical objects and not in Homer's gods; and I consider it a scientific error to believe otherwise. But in point of epistemological footing the physical objects and the gods differ only in degree and not in kind. Both sorts of entities enter our conception only as cultural posits. The myth of physical objects is epistemologically superior to most in that it has proved more efficacious than other myths as a device for working a manageable structure into the flux of experience.

Positing does not stop with macroscopic physical objects. Objects at the atomic level are posited to make the laws of macroscopic objects, and ultimately the laws of experience, simpler and more manageable; and we need not expect or demand full definition of atomic and subatomic entities in terms of macroscopic ones, any more than definition of macroscopic things in terms of sense data. Science is a continuation of common sense, and it continues the common-sense expedient of swelling ontology to simplify theory.

Physical objects, small and large, are not the only posits. Forces are another example; and indeed we are told nowadays that the boundary between energy and matter is obsolete. Moreover, the abstract entities which are the substance of mathematics—ultimately classes and classes of classes and so on up—are another posit in the same spirit. Epistemologically these are myths on the same footing with physical objects and gods, neither better nor worse except for differences in the degree to which they expedite our dealings with sense experiences.

The over-all algebra of rational and irrational numbers is underdetermined by the algebra of rational numbers, but is smoother and more convenient; and it includes the algebra of rational numbers as a jagged or gerrymandered part.[19] Total science, mathematical and natural and human, is similarly but more extremely underdetermined by experience. The edge of the system must be kept squared with experience; the rest, with all its elaborate myths or fictions, has as its objective the simplicity of laws.

Ontological questions, under this view, are on a par with questions of natural science.[20] Consider the question whether to countenance classes as entities. This, as I have argued elsewhere,[21] is the question whether to quantify with respect to variables which take classes as values. Now Carnap [6] has maintained that this is a question not of matters of fact but of choosing a convenient language form, a convenient conceptual scheme or framework for science. With this I agree, but only on the proviso that the same be conceded regarding scientific hypotheses generally. Carnap ([6], p. 32n) has recognized that he is able to preserve a double standard for ontological questions and scientific hypotheses only by assuming an absolute distinction between the analytic and the synthetic; and I need not say again that this is a distinction which I reject.[22]

The issue over there being classes seems more a question of convenient conceptual scheme; the issue over there being centaurs, or brick houses on Elm Street, seems more a question of fact. But I have been urging that this difference is only one of degree, and that it turns upon our vaguely pragmatic inclination to adjust one strand of the fabric of science rather than another in accommodating some particular recalcitrant experience. Conservatism figures in such choices, and so does the quest for simplicity.

Carnap, Lewis, and others take a pragmatic stand on the question of choosing between language forms, scientific frameworks; but their pragmatism leaves off at the imagined boundary between the analytic and the synthetic. In repudiating such a boundary I espouse a more thorough pragmatism. Each man is given a scientific heritage plus a continuing barrage of sensory stimulation; and the considerations which guide him in warping his scientific heritage to fit his continuing sensory promptings are, where rational, pragmatic.

Notes

1. See above, p. 9.
2. See above, p. 10, and below, pp. 107–115.
3. See above, pp. 11f, and below, pp. 48f.
4. Carnap [3], pp. 9ff; [4], pp. 70ff.
5. According to an important variant sense of 'definition', the relation preserved may be the weaker relation of mere agreement in reference; see below, p. 132. But definition in this sense is better ignored in the present connection, being irrelevant to the question of synonymy.
7. This is cognitive synonymy in a primary, broad sense. Carnap ([3], pp. 56ff) and Lewis ([2], pp. 83ff) have suggested how, once this notion is at hand, a

narrower sense of cognitive synonymy which is preferable for some purposes can in turn be derived. But this special ramification of concept-building lies aside from the present purposes and must not be confused with the broad sort of cognitive synonymy here concerned.

8. Pp. 81ff, below, contain a description of just such a language, except that there happens there to be just one predicate, the two-place predicate '*e*'
9. See above, pp. 5–8; also below, pp. 85f, 166f.
10. See below, p. 87.
11. On such devices see also Essay VIII.
12. This is the substance of Quine [1], *121.
13. The 'if and only if' itself is intended in the truth functional sense. See Carnap [3], p. 14.
14. The foregoing paragraph was not part of the present essay as originally published. It was prompted by Martin (see Bibliography), as was the end of Essay VII.
15. The doctrine can indeed be formulated with terms rather than statements as the units. Thus Lewis describes the meaning of a term as "*a criterion in mind, by reference to which one is able to apply or refuse to apply the expression in question in the case of presented, or imagined, things or situations*" ([2], p. 133).—For an instructive account of the vicissitudes of the verification theory of meaning, centered however on the question of meaning*fulness* rather than synonymy and analyticity, see Hempel.
16. See above, p. 6.
17. This doctrine was well argued by Duhem, pp. 303–328. Or see Lowinger, pp. 132–140.
18. Cf. pp. 17f above.
19. Cf. p. 18 above.
20. "L'ontologie fait corps avec la science elle-même et ne peut en être separée." Meyerson, p. 439.
21. Above, pp. 12f; below, pp. 102ff.
22. For an effective expression of further misgivings over this distinction, see White [2].

References

Carnap, Rudolf [3], *Meaning and Necessity* (Chicago: University of Chicago Press, 1947).

—— [4], *Logical Foundations of Proability* (Chicago: University of Chicago Press, 1950).

Duhem, Pierre, *La Theorie physique* (Paris, 1906).

Lewis, C. I. [1], *A Survey of Symbolic Logic* (Berkeley, 1918).

—— [2], *An Analysis of Knowledge and Valuation* (La Salle, Ill.: Open Court, 1946).

Lowinger, Armand, *The Methodolgy of Pierre Duhem* (New York: Columbia University Press, 1941).

Meyerson, Emile, *Identite et realite*. (Paris 1908; 4th ed., 1932).

Quine, W.V. [1], *Mathematical Logic* (New York: Norton, 1940).

—— [2], *Methods of Logic* (New York: Holt, 1950).

White, Morton [2], "The analytic and the synthetic: an untenable dualism," in Sidney Hood (ed.,), John Dewey: *Philosopher of Science and Freedom* (New York: Dial Press, 1950), pp. 316-330.

⬦ A PRIORI KNOWLEDGE OF ⬦
THE CONTINGENT

42. NAMING AND NECESSITY
Saul A. Kripke

Lecture I

The first topic in the pair of topics [in the title] is naming. By a name here I will mean a proper name, i.e., the name of a person, a city, a country, etc. It is well known that modern logicians also are very interested in definite descriptions: phrases of the form 'the x such that φx', such as 'the man who corrupted Hadleyburg'. Now, if one and only one man ever corrupted Hadleyburg, then that man is the referent, in the logician's sense, of that description. We will use the term 'name' so that it does *not* include definite descriptions of that sort, but only those things which in ordinary language would be called 'proper names'. If we want a common term to cover names and descriptions, we may use the term 'designator'.

Frege and Russell both thought, and seemed to arrive at these conclusions independently of each other, that . . . a proper name, properly used, simply was a definite description abbreviated or disguised. Frege specifically said that such a description gave the sense of the name.

Many people have said that the theory of Frege and Russell is false, but, in my opinion, they have abandoned its letter while retaining its spirit, namely, they have used the notion of a cluster concept. Well, what is this? The obvious problem for Frege and Russell, the one which comes immediately to mind, is already mentioned by Frege himself . . .

According to Frege, there is some sort of looseness or weakness in our language. Some people may give one sense to the name 'Aristotle', others may give another. But of course it is not only that; even a single speaker when asked 'What description are you willing to substitute for the name?' may be quite at a loss. In fact, he may know many things about him; but any particular thing that he knows he may feel clearly expresses a contingent property of the object. If 'Aristotle' meant *the man who taught Alexander the Great*, then saying 'Aristotle was a teacher of Alexander the Great' would be a mere tautology. But surely it isn't; it expresses the fact that Aristotle taught Alexander the Great, something we could discover to be false. So, *being the teacher of Alexander the Great* cannot be part of [the sense of] the name.

The most common way out of this difficulty is to say 'really it is not a weakness in ordinary language that we can't substitute a *particular* description for the name; that's all right. What we really associate with the name is a *family* of descriptions'. . . . According to this view, and a *locus classicus* of it is Searle's article on proper names,[1] the referent of a name is determined not by a single description but by some cluster or family. Whatever in some sense satisfies enough or most of the family is the referent of the name. I shall return to this view later.

Let me say (and this will introduce us to another new topic before I really consider this theory of naming) that there are two ways in which the cluster concept theory, or even the theory which requires a single description, can be viewed. One way of regarding it says that the cluster or the single description actually gives the meaning of the name; and when someone says 'Walter Scott', he means *the man such that such and such and such and such*.

Now another view might be that even though the description in some sense doesn't give the *meaning* of the name, it is what *determines its reference* and although the phrase 'Walter Scott' isn't *synonymous* with 'the man such that such and such and such and such', or even maybe with the family (if something can be synonymous with a family), the family or the single description is what is used to determine to whom someone is referring when he says 'Walter Scott'. . . .

Before I go any further into this problem, I want to talk about another distinction which will be important in the methodology of these talks. Philosophers have talked (and, of course, there has been considerable controversy in recent years over the meaningfulness of these notions) [about] various categories of truth, which are called 'a priori', 'analytic', 'necessary'—and sometimes even 'certain' is thrown into this batch. . . .

Consider what the traditional characterizations of such terms as 'a priori' and 'necessary' are. First the notion of a prioricity is a concept of epistemology. I guess the traditional characterization from Kant goes something like: a priori truths are those which can be known independently of any experience. This introduces another problem before we get off the ground, because there's another modality in the characterization of 'a priori', namely, it is supposed to be something which *can* be known independently of any experience. That means that in some sense it's *possible* (whether we do or do not in fact know it independently of any experience) to know this independently of any experience. And possible for whom? For God? For the Martians? Or just for people with minds like ours? To make this all clear might [involve] a host of problems all of its own about what sort of possibility is in question here. It might be best therefore, instead of using the phrase 'a priori truth', to the extent that one uses it at all, to stick to the question of whether a particular person or

knower knows something a priori or believes it true on the basis of a priori evidence.

I won't go further too much into the problems that might arise with the notion of a prioricity here. I will say that some philosophers somehow change the modality in this characterization from *can* to *must*. They think that if something belongs to the realm of a priori knowledge, it couldn't possibly be known empirically. This is just a mistake. Something may belong in the realm of such statements that *can* be known a priori but still may be known by particular people on the basis of experience. To give a really common sense example: anyone who has worked with a computing machine knows that the computing machine may give an answer to whether such and such a number is prime. No one has calculated or proved that the number is prime; but the machine has given the answer: this number is prime. We, then, if we believe that the number is prime, believe it on the basis of our knowledge of the laws of physics, the construction of the machine, and so on. We therefore do not believe this on the basis of purely a priori evidence. We believe it (if anything is *a posteriori* at all) on the basis of *a posteriori* evidence. Nevertheless, maybe this could be known a priori by someone who made the requisite calculations. So 'can be known a priori' doesn't mean '*must* be known a priori'.

The second concept which is in question is that of necessity. Sometimes this is used in an epistemological way and might then just mean a priori. And of course, sometimes it is used in a physical way when people distinguish between physical and logical necessity. But what I am concerned with here is a notion which is not a notion of epistemology but of metaphysics, in some (I hope) nonpejorative sense. We ask whether something might have been true, or might have been false. Well, if something is false, it's obviously not necessarily true. If it is true, might it have been otherwise? Is it possible that, in this respect, the world should have been different from the way it is? If the answer is 'no', then this fact about the world is a necessary one. If the answer is 'yes', then this fact about the world is a contingent one. This in and of itself has nothing to do with anyone's knowledge of anything. It's certainly a philosophical thesis, and not a matter of obvious definitional equivalence, either that everything a priori is necessary or that everything necessary is a priori. Both concepts may be vague. That may be another problem. But at any rate they are dealing with two different domains, two different areas, the epistemological and the metaphysical. Consider, say, Fermat's last theorem—or the Goldbach conjecture. The Goldbach conjecture says that an even number greater than 2 must be the sum of two prime numbers. If this is true, it is presumably necessary, and, if it is false, presumably necessarily false. We are taking the classical view of mathematics here and assume that in mathematical reality it is either true or false.

If the Goldbach conjecture is false, then there is an even number, n, greater than 2, such that for no primes p_1 and p_2, both $< n$, does $n = p_1 + p_2$. This fact about n, if true, is verifiable by direct computation, and thus is necessary if the results of arithmetical computations are necessary. On the other hand, if the conjecture is true, then every even number exceeding 2 is the sum of two primes. Could it then be the case that, although in fact every such even number is the sum of two primes, there might have been such an even number which was not the sum of two primes? What would that mean? Such a number would have to be one of 4, 6, 8, 10, . . . ; and, by hypothesis, since we are assuming Goldbach's conjecture to be true, each of these can be shown, again by direct computation, to be the sum of two primes. Goldbach's conjecture, then, cannot be contingently true or false; whatever truth-value it has belongs to it by necessity.

But what we can say, of course, is that right now, as far as we know, the question can come out either way. So, in the absence of a mathematical proof deciding this question, none of us has any a priori knowledge about this question in either direction. We don't know whether Goldbach's conjecture is true or false. So right now we certainly don't know anything a priori about it.

Perhaps it will be alleged that we *can* in principle know a priori whether it is true. Well, maybe we can. Of course an infinite mind which can search through all the numbers can or could. But I don't know whether a finite mind can or could. Maybe there just is no mathematical proof whatsoever which decides the conjecture. At any rate this might or might not be the case. Maybe there is a mathematical proof deciding this question;

maybe every mathematical question is decidable by an intuitive proof or disproof. Hilbert thought so; others have thought not; still others have thought the question unintelligible unless the notion of intuitive proof is replaced by that of formal proof in a single system. Certainly no one formal system decides all mathematical questions, as we know from Gödel. At any rate, and this is the important thing, the question is not trivial; even though someone said that it's necessary, if true at all, that every even number is the sum of two primes, it doesn't follow that anyone knows anything a priori about it. It doesn't even seem to me to follow without some further philosophical argument (it is an interesting philosophical question) that anyone *could* know anything a priori about it. The 'could', as I said, involves some other modality. We mean that even if no one, perhaps even in the future, knows or will know a priori whether Goldbach's conjecture is right, in principle there is a way, which *could* have been used, of answering the question a priori. This assertion is not trivial.

The terms 'necessary' and 'a priori', then, as applied to statements, are *not* obvious synonyms. . . .

Another term used in philosophy is 'analytic'. Here it won't be too important to get any clearer about this in this talk. The common examples of analytic statements, nowadays, are like 'bachelors are unmarried'. Kant (someone just pointed out to me) gives as an example 'gold is a yellow metal', which seems to me an extraordinary one, because it's something I think that can turn out to be false. At any rate, let's just make it a matter of stipulation that an analytic statement is, in some sense, true by virtue of its meaning and true in all possible worlds by virtue of its meaning. Then something which is analytically true will be both necessary and a priori. (That's sort of stipulative.)

Another category I mentioned was that of certainty. Whatever certainty is, it's clearly not obviously the case that everything which is necessary is certain. Certainty is another epistemological notion. Something can be known, or at least rationally believed, a priori, without being quite certain. You've read a proof in the math book; and, though you think it's correct, maybe you've made a mistake. You often do make mistakes of this kind. You've made a computation, perhaps with an error. . . .

Let's use some terms quasi-technically. Let's call something a *rigid designator* if in every possible world it designates the same object, a *nonrigid* or *accidental designator* if that is not the case. Of course we don't require that the objects exist in all possible worlds. Certainly Nixon might not have existed if his parents had not gotten married, in the normal course of things. When we think of a property as essential to an object we usually mean that it is true of that object in any case where it would have existed. A rigid designator of a necessary existent can be called *strongly rigid*. . . . For example, the President of the U.S. in 1970 designates a certain man, Nixon; but someone else (e.g., Humphrey) might have been the President in 1970, and Nixon might not have; so this designator is not rigid.

In these lectures, I will argue, intuitively, that proper names are rigid designators, for although the man (Nixon) might not have been the President, it is not the case that he might not have been Nixon (though he might not have been *called* 'Nixon').

Above I said that the Frege-Russell view that names are introduced by description could be taken either as a theory of the meaning of names (Frege and Russell seemed to take it this way) or merely as a theory of their reference. Let me give an example, not involving what would usually be called a 'proper name,' to illustrate this. Suppose someone stipulates that 100 degrees centigrade is to be the temperature at which water boils at sea level. Another sort of example in the literature is that one meter is to be the length of S where S is a certain stick or bar in Paris.

Wittgenstein says something very puzzling about this. He says: 'There is one thing of which one can say neither that it is one meter long nor that it is not one meter long, and that is the standard meter in Paris. But this is, of course, not to ascribe any extraordinary property to it, but only to mark its peculiar role in the language game of measuring with a meter rule.'[2] This seems to be a very 'extraordinary property', actually, for any stick to have. I think he must be wrong. If the stick is a stick, for example, 39.37 inches long (I assume we have some different standard for inches), why isn't it one meter long? Anyway, let's suppose that he is wrong and that the stick is one meter long. Part of the problem which is bothering Wittgenstein is, of course, that this stick

serves as a standard of length and so we can't attribute length to it. Be this as it may (well, it may not be), is the statement 'stick S is one meter long', a necessary truth? Of course its length might vary in time. We could make the definition more precise by stipulating that one meter is to be the length of S at a fixed time t_0. Is it then a necessary truth that stick S is one meter long at time t_0? Someone who thinks that everything one knows a priori is necessary might think: 'This is the *definition* of a meter. By definition, stick S is one meter long at t_0. That's a necessary truth.' But there seems to me to be no reason so to conclude, even for a man who uses the stated definition of 'one meter'. For he's using this definition not to *give the meaning* of what he called the 'meter', but to *fix the reference*. (For such an abstract thing as a unit of length, the notion of reference may be unclear. But let's suppose it's clear enough for the present purposes.) He uses it to fix a reference. There is a certain length which he wants to mark out. He marks it out by an accidental property, namely that there is a stick of that length. Someone else might mark out the same reference by another accidental property. But in any case, even though he uses this to fix the reference of his standard of length, a meter, he can still say, 'if heat had been applied to this stick S at t_0, then at t_0 stick S would not have been one meter long.'

Well, why can he do this? Part of the reason may lie in some people's minds in the philosophy of science, which I don't want to go into here. But a simple answer to the question is this: Even if this is the *only* standard of length that he uses,[3] there is an intuitive difference between the phrase 'one meter' and the phrase 'the length of S at t_0'. The first phrase is meant to designate rigidly a certain length in all possible worlds, which in the actual world happens to be the length of the stick S at t_0. On the other hand 'the length of S at t_0' does not designate anything rigidly. In some counterfactual situations the stick might have been longer and in some shorter, if various stresses and strains had been applied to it. So we can say of this stick, the same way as we would of any other of the same substance and length, that if heat of a given quantity had been applied to it, it would have expanded to such and such a length. Such a counterfactual statement, being true of other sticks with identical physical properties, will also be true of this stick. There is no conflict between that counterfactual statement and the definition of 'one meter' as 'the length of S at t_0', because the 'definition', properly interpreted, does *not* say that the phrase 'one meter' is to be *synonymous* (even when talking about counterfactual situations) with the phrase 'the length of S at t_0', but rather that we have *determined the reference* of the phrase 'one meter' by stipulating that 'one meter' is to be a *rigid* designator of the length which is in fact the length of S at t_0. So this does *not* make it a necessary truth that S is one meter long at t_0. In fact, under certain circumstances, S would not have been one meter long. The reason is that one designator ('one meter') is rigid and the other designator ('the length of S at t_0') is not.

What then, is the *epistemological* status of the statement 'Stick S is one meter long at t_0', for someone who has fixed the metric system by reference to stick S? It would seem that he knows it a priori. For if he used stick S to fix the reference of the term 'one meter', then as a result of this kind of 'definition' (which is not an abbreviative or synonymous definition), he knows automatically, without further investigation, that S is one meter long.[4] On the other hand, even if S is used as the standard of a meter, the *metaphysical* status of 'S is one meter long' will be that of a contingent statement, provided that 'one meter' is regarded as a rigid designator: under appropriate stresses and strains, heatings or coolings. S would have had a length other than one meter even at t_0. (Such statements as 'Water boils at 100° C at sea level' can have a similar status.) So in this sense, there are contingent a priori truths. More important for present purposes, though, than accepting this example as an instance of the contingent a priori, is its illustration of the distinction between 'definitions' which fix a reference and those which give a synonym.

In the case of names one might make this distinction too. Suppose the reference of a name is given by a description or a cluster of descriptions. If the name *means the same* as that description or cluster of descriptions, it will not be a rigid designator. It will not necessarily designate the same object in all possible worlds, since other objects might have had the given properties in other possible worlds, unless (of course) we happened to use essential properties in our description. So suppose we say, 'Aristotle is the greatest man who studied with Plato'. If we used that as a *definition*, the name 'Aristotle' is to mean 'the greatest man who studied with Plato'. Then of course in some other possible world that man might not have studied with Plato and some other man would have been Aristotle. If, on the other hand, we merely use the description to *fix the referent* then that man will be the referent of 'Aristotle' in all possible worlds. The only use of the description will have been to pick out to which man we mean to refer. But then, when we say counterfactually 'suppose Aristotle had never gone into philosophy at all', we need not mean 'suppose a man who studied with Plato, and taught Alexander the Great, and wrote this and that, and so on, had never gone into philosophy at all', which might seem like a contradiction. We need only mean, 'suppose that *that man* had never gone into philosophy at all'.

It seems plausible to suppose that, in some cases, the reference of a name is indeed fixed *via* a description in the same way that the metric system was fixed. When the mythical agent first saw Hesperus, he may well have fixed his reference by saying, 'I shall use "Hesperus" as a name of the heavenly body appearing in yonder position in the sky.' He then fixed the reference of 'Hesperus' by its apparent celestial position. Does it follow that it is part of the *meaning* of the name that Hesperus has such and such position at the time in question? Surely not: if Hesperus had been hit earlier by a comet, it might have been visible at a different position at that time. In such a counterfactual situation we would say that Hesperus would not have occupied that position, but not that Hesperus would not have been Hesperus. The reason is that 'Hesperus' rigidly designates a certain heavenly body and 'the body in yonder position' does not—a different body, or no body might have been in that position, but no other body might have been Hesperus (though another body, not Hesperus, might have been *called* 'Hesperus'). Indeed, as I have said, I will hold that names are always rigid designators.

Frege and Russell certainly seem to have the full blown theory according to which a proper name is not a rigid designator and is synonymous with the description which replaced it. But another theory might be that this description is used to determine a rigid reference. . . .

Lecture II

I think the next topic I shall want to talk about is that of statements of identity. Are these necessary or contingent? The matter has been in some dispute in recent philosophy. First, everyone agrees that descriptions can be used to make contingent identity statements. If it is true that the man who invented bifocals was the first Postmaster General of the United States—that these were one and the same—it's contingently true. That is, it might have been the case that one man invented bifocals and another was the first Postmaster General of the United States. So certainly when you make identity statements using descriptions—when you say 'the x such that φx and the x such that ψx are one and the same'—that can be a contingent fact. But philosophers have been interested also in the question of identity statements between names. When we say 'Hesperus is Phosphorus' or 'Cicero is Tully', is what we are saying necessary or contingent?

What should we think about this? First, it's true that someone can use the name 'Cicero' to refer to Cicero and the name 'Tully' to refer to Cicero also, and not know that Cicero is Tully. So it seems that we do not necessarily know a priori that an identity statement between names is true. It doesn't follow from this that the statement so expressed is a contingent one if true. This is what I've emphasized in my first lecture. There is a very strong feeling that leads one to think that, if you can't know something by a priori ratiocination, then it's got to be contingent: it might have turned out otherwise; but nevertheless I think this feeling is wrong.

Let's suppose we refer to the same heavenly body twice, as 'Hesperus' and 'Phosphorus'. We say: Hesperus is that star over there in the evening; Phosphorus is that star over there in the morning. Actually, Hesperus is Phosphorus. Are there really circumstances under which Hesperus wouldn't have been Phosphorus? Supposing that Hesperus is Phosphorus, let's try to describe a possible situation in which it would not have been. Well, it's easy. Someone goes by and he calls two *different* stars 'Hesperus' and 'Phosphorus'. It may even be under the same conditions as prevailed when we introduced the names 'Hesperus' and 'Phosphorus'. But are those circumstances in which Hesperus is not Phosphorus or would not have been Phosphorus? It seems to me that they are not.

Now, of course I'm committed to saying that they're not, by saying that such terms as 'Hesperus' and 'Phosphorus', when used as names, are rigid designators. They refer in every possible world to the planet Venus. Therefore, in that possible world too, the planet Venus is the planet Venus and it doesn't matter what any other person has said in this other possible world. How should *we* describe this situation? He can't have pointed to Venus twice, and in the one case called it 'Hesperus' and in the other 'Phosphorus', as we did. If he did so, then 'Hesperus is Phosphorus' would have been true in that situation too. He pointed maybe neither time to the planet Venus—at least one time he didn't point to the planet Venus, let's say when he pointed to the body he called 'Phosphorus'. Then in that case we can certainly say that the name 'Phosphorus' might not have referred to Phosphorus. We can even say that in the very position when viewed in the morning that we found Phosphorus, it might have been the case that Phosphorus was not there—that something else was there, and that even, under certain circumstances it would have been *called* 'Phosphorus'. But that still is not a case in which Phosphorus was not Hesperus. There might be a possible world in which, a possible counterfactual situation in which, 'Hesperus' and 'Phosphorus' weren't names of the things they in fact are names of. Someone, if he did determine their reference by identifying descriptions, might even have used the very identifying descriptions we used. But still that's not a case in which Hesperus wasn't Phosphorus. For there couldn't have been such a case, given that Hesperus is Phosphorus.

Now this seems very strange because in advance, we are inclined to say, the answer to the question whether Hesperus is Phosphorus might have turned out either way. So aren't there really two possible worlds—one in which Hesperus was Phosphorus, the other in which Hesperus wasn't Phosphorus—in advance of our discovering that these were the same? First, there's one sense in which things might turn out either way, in which it's clear that that doesn't imply that the way it finally turns out isn't necessary. For example, the four color theorem might turn out to be true and might turn out to be false. It might turn out either way. It still doesn't mean that the way it turns out is not necessary. Obviously, the 'might' here is purely 'epistemic'—it merely expresses our present state of ignorance, or uncertainty.

But it seems that in the Hesperus-Phosphorus case, something even stronger is true. The evidence I have before I know that Hesperus is Phosphorus is that I see a certain star or a certain heavenly body in the evening and call it 'Hesperus', and in the morning and call it 'Phosphorus'. I know these things. There certainly is a possible world in which a man should have seen a certain star at a certain position in the evening and called it 'Hesperus' and a certain star in the morning and called it 'Phosphorus'; and should have concluded—should have found out by empirical investigation—that he names two different stars, or two different heavenly bodies. At least one of these stars or heavenly bodies was not Phosphorus, otherwise it couldn't have come out that way. But that's true. And so it's true that given the evidence that someone has antecedent to his empirical investigation, he can be placed in a sense in exactly the same situation, that is a qualitatively identical epistemic situation, and call two heavenly bodies 'Hesperus' and 'Phosphorus', without their being identical. So in that sense we can say that it might have turned out either way. Not that it might have turned out either way as to Hesperus's being Phosphorus. Though for all we knew in advance, Hesperus wasn't Phosphorus, that couldn't have turned out any other way, in a sense. But being put in a situation where we have exactly the same evidence, qualitatively speaking, it could have turned out that Hesperus was not Phosphorus; that is, in a counterfactual world in which 'Hesperus' and 'Phosphorus' were not used in the way that we use them, as names of this planet, but as names of some other objects, one could have had qualitatively identical evidence and concluded that 'Hesperus' and 'Phosphorus' named two different objects. But we, using the names as we do right now,

can say in advance, that if Hesperus and Phosphorus are one and the same, then in no other possible world can they be different. We use 'Hesperus' as the name of a certain body and 'Phosphorus' as the name of a certain body. We use them as names of those bodies in all possible worlds. If, in fact, they are the *same* body, then in any other possible world we have to use them as a name of that object. And so in any other possible world it will be true that Hesperus is Phosphorus. So two things are true: first, that we do not know a priori that Hesperus is Phosphorus, and are in no position to find out the answer except empirically. Second, this is so because we could have evidence qualitatively indistinguishable from the evidence we have and determine the reference of the two names by the positions of two planets in the sky, without the planets being the same.

Of course, it is only a contingent truth (not true in every other possible world) that the star seen over there in the evening is the star seen over there in the morning, because there are possible worlds in which Phosphorus was not visible in the morning. But that contingent truth shouldn't be identified with the statement that Hesperus is Phosphorus. It could only be so identified if you thought that it was a necessary truth that Hesperus is visible over there in the evening or that Phosphorus is visible over there in the morning. But neither of those are necessary truths even if that's the way we pick out the planet. These are the contingent marks by which we identify a certain planet and give it a name.

Notes

1. John R. Searle, 'Proper Names', *Mind* 67 (1958), 166–73.
2. *Philosophical Investigations*, § 50.
3. Philosophers of science may see the key to the problem in a view that 'one meter' is a 'cluster concept'. I am asking the reader hypothetically to suppose that the 'definition' given is the *only* standard used to determine the metric system. I think the problem would still arise.
4. Since the truth he knows is contingent, I choose *not* to call it 'analytic', stipulatively requiring analytic truths to be both necessary and a priori.

CHAPTER 9   RELATIVISM AND SUBJECTIVISM

INTRODUCTION

In this chapter we consider some challenges to the absolutist, objectivist presuppositions of mainstream epistemologists. Such challenges are increasingly made by theorists whose approaches are more relativist and subjective. We can begin by discussing the term 'relative,' which is defined in opposition to 'absolute' (or 'universal'), and the term 'subjective,' defined in contrast with 'objective,' starting with the latter.

The contrast between subjective and objective is made out in terms of items found in individual subjects (as opposed to mere objects). Examples of these items include perceptions, beliefs, desires, emotions, and so forth. These mental phenomena are the clearest cases of entities that are classified as subjective. Other items, such as stars and trees, whose features do not depend on the minds of individuals, are classified as objective.

In derivative ways, views (beliefs, theories, and so forth) and standards (by which we assess value—epistemic merit, moral merit, and so on) can be classified as either objective or subjective. A *standard* is subjective to the extent that its authoritativeness or claim to acceptability is contingent upon the features of an individual subject, and objective to the extent that its authoritativeness is independent of such features. Thus standards of taste are highly subjective since they have no claim to authoritativeness beyond their actual acceptance, while standards of epistemic justifiability are quite objective since presumably their authoritativeness is not contingent upon personal idiosyncrasies; in particular, they are authoritative whether an individual accepts them or not. As for *views*, there are two main approaches to their classification as subjective or objective. According to the first, or *subject-based* approach, a view may be considered subjective to the extent that it concerns or expresses only the features of an individual's mind or its contents, and objective to the extent that it does not. The second approach appeals to the notion of an objective epistemic standard, defined independently. According to this *standard-based* approach, a view is objective if its acceptance is warranted according to an objective epistemic standard; otherwise it is subjective. Either approach suggests that claims of taste ('Chocolate is tasty', 'The best TV program is *CSI*,' and so forth) are highly subjective while claims of physics are highly objective since only the latter concern the nature of the world and are endorsed by generally applicable standards. Note finally that objectivity and subjectivity come in degrees. One of two highly subjective views might be less subjective than the other, for example, because one concerns the mental life of a single individual ('Fred is in pain') while the other concerns the mental life of all ('Everyone hates pain').

Consider now the contrast between absolutism and relativism. Absolutism comes in two forms. The first, which might be termed *ontological absolutism*, says that there is a single, objectively true characterization of reality (although this true account is enormously complex), at least in its broadest outlines. Of course, different parts of reality must be described differently; blind people feeling different parts of an elephant will describe what they sense differently because they are feeling distinct things. And different aspects of reality will have to receive different accounts: describing the color of an elephant is one thing, while describing its shape is quite another. But at least one of two substantially distinct accounts of the whole elephant or the whole of reality must be false. The second form of absolutism, called *epistemic absolutism*, says that there is a single, objectively correct set of standards for assessing the epistemic credentials of competing views of reality. Let us add that epistemic absolutism addresses *fundamental* cognitive standards only—that is, standards for assessing the fundamental shape of reality—not standards at all levels of abstraction. These standards need not be capable of adjudicating all issues; quite possibly, two competing claims (even two claims about the broad outlines of reality) will be equally justified, or equally unjustified, according to the objectively correct epistemic standards, leaving us unable to settle some disputes on a rational basis.

As long as there have been absolutists, there have also been relativists. Relativism is the denial of absolutism. In one form, it denies ontological absolutism; in another, it denies epistemic absolutism. Thus *ontological relativism* denies that there is but one objectively correct characterization of reality. And *epistemic relativism* denies that there is only one objectively correct set of epistemic standards. (Ontological relativism is not the claim that any account of reality is made using, or relative to, the concepts involved in that account, which is a mere truism that everyone, including absolutists, grants. Similarly, epistemic relativism should be distinguished from the truism that assessments of the epistemic merit of claims must be made relative to some standard or another.)

Epistemic relativism can take either of two forms, since there are two ways to deny the absolutist claim that there is one objectively correct set of fundamental epistemic standards. First, we might say that there are *no* objectively correct fundamental epistemic standards. This view might be called *subjectivist* epistemic relativism, and says that epistemic merit is always assessed relative to standards that are entirely subjective. Second, we might say that there is *more than one* objectively correct set of fundamental epistemic standards. This view, which we can call *pluralist* epistemic relativism, says that the assessment of epistemic merit at every level of abstraction is relative to a range of competing epistemic standards each of which is objectively correct, perhaps because, from the standpoint of rationality,

each of several competing sets of fundamental standards is as defensible as the next.

Traditionally, epistemologists have said that justification, or rational acceptability, is in its very nature truth-conducive: views that are justified are more likely to be true than those that are unjustified. Hence the notion of truth is more primitive than the notion of justification: justification must be defined in terms of truth, so that the latter cannot be defined in terms of the former. In fact, many theorists believe that truth is some sort of correspondence between reality on the one hand and a depiction of reality on the other, and justification is something that assists us in reaching the truth. These philosophers are ontological absolutists, and while ontological absolutism is logically consistent with epistemic relativism (even if we say that there is only one correct account of reality we might insist that epistemic standards are subjective), people who adopt ontological absolutism are often drawn to epistemic absolutism as well.

Nonetheless, in recent years theorists have defended ontological relativism on the basis of epistemic relativism. They claim that the notion of truth must be cashed out in terms of rational acceptability, or justification, while the proper account of rational acceptability is that given by the subjectivist version of epistemic relativism, so that 'truth' is itself acceptability relative to varying subjective epistemic standards (subjective standards of rationality). This argument from subjectivist epistemic relativism can seem to support ontological relativism, but which form of ontological relativism does it support? On the one hand, one might opt for a *pluralist* form of ontological relativism, according to which there are as many 'true' versions of the world as there are competing epistemic standards. But if we say that truth is nothing more than truth-relative-to-a-subjective-standard, aren't we denying that there is any such thing as objective truth? If so, then those who accept the argument from subjectivist epistemic relativism might prefer to say that it supports the *subjectivist* form of ontological relativism, according to which there is no objective truth at all.

Theorists as early as Plato have criticized relativism on the grounds that it is self-refuting. The thought is that, to defend their view, relativists must assume the truth of absolutism. In particular, epistemic relativists can support their view only by arguing that it is supported by the objectively correct epistemic standards. Yet no such standards exist if epistemic relativism is correct. However, its supporters generally see this criticism coming, and try to avoid it using one or both of two strategies. First, they might develop a negative defense of their view. They can criticize epistemic absolutism, and argue that the available defenses of absolutism are disappointing, primarily because absolutists must assume the truth of their view in order to defend it, which is circular reasoning, then offer relativism as the best alternative. However, even if available defenses of absolutism are weak, we are not forced to adopt relativism. We can retain absolutism and acknowledge that its justification is not as powerful as one might hope for. Second, relativists might try to develop a relativist defense of relativism. Perhaps by arguing on the basis of their own epistemic standards they can conclude that there is no such thing as the one correct set of standards. However, this strategy seems to give nonrelativists no reason to accept relativism. For the relativist is unable to give the nonrelativist any reason to accept the relativist standards that purportedly support relativism.

Relativism is related to, but distinct from, skepticism, for skeptics need not deny absolutism. In fact, skeptics will presuppose the truth of absolutism if they mean to say that, by the objectively correct epistemic standards, things are not known (or justifiably believed).

In this chapter we include one essay that defends epistemic relativism, two that attack it, and one that attacks both relativism and absolutism. Richard Foley defends the subjectivist form of epistemic relativism, according to which epistemic merit is assessed relative to subjective standards. Harvey Siegel defends epistemic absolutism as against epistemic relativism. Richard Rorty argues that both absolutism and relativism should be rejected: instead of relativist accounts of truth and justification, which are self-refuting, or absolutist accounts of truth and justification, which apply, at best, only to natural science, Rorty recommends the view that ideal inquiry is aimed at "solidarity," or a consensus reached by people who respect each other's views and freedom of thought, and who are interested in new ideas. Finally, Louise

Antony defends absolutism and the notion of objective truth against theorists who think that relativism facilitates the goals of feminism.

Antony's essay has another virtue: it surveys some of the views contemporary feminist epistemologists have defended. Generalizations about what feminists do and do not claim are hazardous, for the term 'feminism' covers a diverse group of people with a wide range of views. (There is liberal feminism, deriving, at least in part, from Wollstonecraft (1792) and J. S. Mill (1869), which emphasizes the importance of overcoming legal and social barriers that place women at a disadvantage as compared to men; Marxist feminism, which sees economic disparities created by capitalism as inevitable causes of the subordination of women; radical feminism, which traces oppression of women to social structures such as family and church as well as to the biological differences between the sexes; and so on.) But one claim that is frequently defended in the feminist literature is that mainstream epistemic views are products of, and biased towards, males as against females. According to some feminists, such as Genevieve Lloyd (1979), the notions of reason, rationality and objectivity have come to be defined in ways that promote male interests at the expense of female interests, and that tie together being male and being rational. Epistemologists may think they are identifying the one set of objectively correct epistemic standards, but they are actually promoting standards that benefit males and harm females. But other feminists disagree. Louise Antony, in particular, says that feminists need such epistemic notions as rationality and objective truth in order to make clear sense of the view that the subordination of women is objectionable.

Siegel: Absolutism Rather Than Relativism

In "The Incoherence Argument and the Notion of Relative Truth," which is the first chapter of his book *Relativism Refuted* (1987), Harvey Siegel attacks ontological and epistemic relativism, claiming that both are self-refuting. Thus ontological relativists must defend their view on the basis of absolutist assumptions, and epistemic relativists must make absolutist assumptions in order to defend their view. He then considers various attempts to fend off the charge of incoherence, including work by Harold Brown (1977) and

Jack Meiland (1977, 1979). Siegel also criticizes an attempt by Hartry Field (1982) to combine epistemic relativism with ontological absolutism.

Foley: Subjectivist Relativism Rather Than Absolutism

In "Epistemically Rational Belief as Invulnerability to Self-Criticism," Richard Foley defends an account of rational belief that is predominately subjectivist. His view is that an individual's beliefs are epistemically rational if they are in accord with the individual's own deepest epistemic standards, which has the effect of making the individual's beliefs invulnerable to self-criticism on reflection. For one's beliefs and belief-formation methods to be rational is for them to be capable of standing up to one's own most severe criticism, which, in the final analysis, is based on critical standards rooted in one's own deep psychology.

Rorty: Solidarity Rather Than Relativism or Absolutism

In "Science and Solidarity," which is reproduced in his book *Objectivity, Relativism, and Truth* (1991), Richard Rorty suggests that we reject both sides of the bifurcation between "relativism" and "absolutism." Relativist accounts of truth and justification are self-refuting, and absolutist, objectivist accounts are unacceptable because they apply, at best, only to natural science, and not to the humanities. A better view, which sees ideal inquiry (in all areas of the sciences and humanities) as an attempt to achieve "solidarity," is arrived at in two main steps. First, we understand truth roughly as Putnam, and perhaps pragmatists, did: as rational acceptability, as justified belief. Second, we say that a view is rationally acceptable when it would be adopted by people who embody certain moral virtues characteristic of Western liberal democracies: "the habits of relying on persuasion rather than force, of respect for opinions of colleagues, of curiosity and eagerness for new data and ideas."

Antony: A Feminist Critique of Relativism

In "Quine as Feminist: The Radical Import of Naturalized Epistemology," Louise Antony argues that mainstream epistemology is not biased towards males, not antipathetic to the ends of feminism, and that epistemology naturalized in particular is useful from the standpoint of feminism. She focuses on two charges associated with feminism: that mainstream epistemology is skewed by male bias, and that the ideal of objectivity or impartiality is misguided because that ideal itself is the product of male bias. According to Antony, feminists cannot criticize "the partiality of the concept of objectivity without presupposing the very value under attack. Put baldly: If we don't think it's good to be impartial, then how can we object to men's being partial?"

Some feminists, such as Lorraine Code (1988, 1989), claim that mainstream epistemology puts on a mask of objectivity and value-neutrality. However, Antony claims, for decades contemporary analytic epistemology has been attacking a particular picture of epistemology with criticisms that are even more radical than those of the feminists. Analytic epistemologists argue that bias is not eliminable and that it has positive value. She says that once we acknowledge this, we need a way to distinguish good from bad bias, and the solution is to embrace the notion of truth, so that we can distinguish the "grounds of a statement's truth from the explanation of a statement's acceptance." That way we can say that "what makes the good bias good is that it facilitates the search for truth, and what makes the bad bias bad is that it impedes it."

QUESTIONS FOR REFLECTION

1. Is epistemic relativism self-refuting? If so, is there a version of epistemic relativism that is not self-refuting? Do any of Siegel's criticisms of epistemic relativism apply to that (non-self-refuting) version of relativism?

2. What is the relationship between epistemic relativism and skepticism? Should the Pyrrhonians be considered skeptics or relativists (or both)?

3. How might Foley respond to Siegel's criticisms of epistemic relativism?

4. Rorty says that as a pragmatist he accepts an ethnocentric view that is sometimes considered to be a form of relativism. He also says that ethnocentricism should not be viewed as a form of relativism. Is he correct, or is Rorty's ethnocentricism actually

a form of relativism? (How might he defend the view that truth and rational acceptability is to be defined in terms of values embraced by his culture rather than some other culture?)

5. Imagine that you are part of a community that comes to regard standard ideas about gravity as stale; in the interest of novelty, you adopt the view that gravity is generated because matter loves, and is therefore attracted to, other matter. Your community reaches a consensus about the love theory of gravity. Does it follow that the love theory is true, and rationally acceptable, according to Rorty? If so, is he correct?

6. Suppose that accepted epistemic concepts, including the notion of truth and objectivity, were invented by males, and that they serve male interests. Suppose, too, that females invented alternative concepts that served female interests, or that, at least, were neutral as concerns the interests of males versus females. Which concepts should males and females adopt? On what grounds should they make their selection?

7. Is it true that epistemic concepts are biased towards males? How would Antony respond? Would her response be correct?

8. Suppose I can succeed in making myself accept, even in my heart of hearts, that I should believe only what makes me happy. (Or imagine a country in which people are brainwashed into accepting, wholeheartedly, that whatever the current propaganda says is always true.) According to Foley's subjectivism, are beliefs that meet this 'standard' justified for me? If so, is this result acceptable?

9. Is Harman's account of rational belief (see Chapter 4) subjectivist in the way Foley's is? (In 2003 Harman argues that any accepted method of belief formation is intrinsically justified. Does this claim commit him to subjectivism?)

10. Is structural contextualism a form of relativism? If so, what sort of relativism is it?

✧ ABSOLUTISM RATHER THAN RELATIVISM ✧

43. THE INCOHERENCE ARGUMENT AND THE NOTION OF RELATIVE TRUTH

Harvey Siegel

Epistemological relativism has been defended by a variety of thinkers stretching back at least as far as Protagoras. For just as long, however, others have thought the doctrine to be incoherent because self-refuting. This is perhaps the most fundamental challenge faced by the relativist. The present investigation begins, therefore, by considering the status of the incoherence charge.

In this chapter I review the debate between Plato and Protagoras regarding relativism and incoherence, and consider a series of more recent defenses of epistemological relativism. A central focus will be the role that the notion of relative truth plays in the various arguments for relativism, both ancient and contemporary; though a defense of relativism that eschews that notion, developed by Hartry Field, will also be examined. I shall argue that, like Protagoras, the recent defenders fail to meet the challenge posed by the incoherence charge, and that the doctrine of epistemological relativism remains untenable because incoherent.

Protagorean Relativism and the Socratic Arguments for Incoherence

In the *Theaetetus*, Protagoras is portrayed as holding that "man is the measure of all things," and that any given thing "is to me such as it appears to me, and is to you such as it appears to you."[1] In considering Theaetetus' suggestion that knowledge is perception, Socrates concludes that it is equivalent to Protagoras' view: "Then my perception is true for me, for its object at any moment is my reality, and I am, as Protagoras says, a judge of what is for me, that it is, and of what is not, that it is not."[2] Protagoras holds, according to Socrates, that "Each one of us is a measure of what is and of what is not. . . . To the sick man his food appears sour and is so; to the healthy man it is and appears the opposite. Now there is no call to represent either of the two as wiser—that cannot be—nor is the sick man to be pronounced unwise because he thinks as he does, or the healthy man wise because he thinks differently. . . . In this way it is true . . . that no one thinks falsely."[3] Socrates encapsulates Protagoras' relativism as consisting in the view that "what seems true to anyone is true for him to whom it seems so."[4]

Protagoras' view is an extreme version of relativism: knowledge and truth are relative to the person contemplating the proposition in question. p is true (for me) if it so seems; false (for me) if it so seems. Since the final arbiter of truth and knowledge is the individual, Protagoras' view denies the existence of any standard or criterion higher than the individual by which claims to truth and knowledge can be adjudicated.

Socrates offers several arguments against the Protagorean view. Two in particular will be of interest here. The first questions the justifiability of Protagoras' sophistical activity, given his doctrine:

> If what every man believes as a result of perception is indeed to be true for him; if, just as no one is to be a better judge of what another experiences, so no one is better entitled to consider whether what another thinks is true or false, and . . . every man is to have his own beliefs for himself alone and they are all right and true—then . . . where is the wisdom of Protagoras, to justify his setting up to teach others and to be handsomely paid for it, and where is our comparative ignorance or the need for us to go and sit at his feet, when each of us is himself the measure of his own wisdom? . . . to set about overhauling and testing one another's notions and opinions when those of each and every one are right, is a tedious and monstrous display of folly, if the Truth of Protagoras is really truthful . . . [5]

Here Socrates levels the first version of the incoherence charge: Protagoras is involved in the project of "overhauling and testing one another's notions and opinions"—that is, he is engaged in the epistemological task of assessing the warrant and justification of knowledgeclaims—but his thesis undermines that very project, since if his thesis is right, then there is no chance of any thesis failing a test of adequacy, or being judged unjustified or unwarranted, because the rival theses "of each and every one are right." If knowledge is relative, then the task of judging claims to knowledge is pointless. If Protagoras' thesis is right, it cannot be right, for it undermines the very notion of rightness. Protagorean relativism is thus self-defeating—if it is right, it cannot be right—and so is incoherent. Let us call this first argument for the incoherence charge the 'undermines the very notion of rightness' (henceforth *UVNR*) argument: relativism is incoherent because, if it is right, the very notion of rightness is undermined, in which case relativism cannot be right.

The second argument for the incoherence charge focuses on the Protagorean view that all opinions are true for those who believe them, and concomitantly that no sincerely held opinion is false ("that no one thinks falsely"). Socrates argues that this thesis cannot be correct, and in fact is self-defeating, for if true, some beliefs will be false—contrary to the thesis. Socrates' argument[6] centers on the phenomenon of conflicting opinion. Suppose A believes p, and B believes not-p. p is true for A, according to Protagoras, yet false for B. Then p is true for some, and false for others. Now, suppose that p is a statement expressing Protagorean relativism. Then Protagorean relativism is false for all those who do not believe it: it is false for all if no one believes it; and true only to the extent that some number of people (perhaps only Protagoras himself) believe it:

> Supposing that not even he [i.e. Protagoras] believed in man being the measure and the world in general did not believe it either—as in fact it doesn't—then this *Truth* which he wrote would not be true for anyone. If, on the other hand, he did believe it, but the mass of mankind does not agree with him, then, you see, it is more false than true by just so much as the unbelievers outnumber the believers.[7]

In fact, Socrates argues, the situation is even worse for Protagoras than that. For Protagoras seems to have to acknowledge, given his doctrine, that his opponents' view that he is wrong is itself right:

> [Moreover,] Protagoras, for his part, admitting as he does that everybody's opinion is true, must acknowledge the truth of his opponents' belief about his own belief, where they think he is wrong.[8]

Protagoras would be forced, Socrates argues, to:

> acknowledge his own belief to be false, if he admits that the belief of those who think him wrong is true . . . [for he] admits that this opinion of theirs is as true as any other.[9]

So, Socrates argues, Protagoras is bound by his own lights to grant the truth of his opponents' beliefs, even in the case where their belief is that Protagorean relativism is false. And since their opinion is true, according to the Protagorean doctrine, and their opinion is that that doctrine is false, then that doctrine is false—even for Protagoras himself.[10] Thus Protagorean relativism is self-defeating in a second way. If opinions conflict, and the doctrine holds that all opinions are true, then some opinions cannot be true. In particular, if opinions conflict about the truth of Protagorean relativism, then the Protagorean relativist must acknowledge the truth of the opinion that that doctrine is false. Thus, if it is true, then (as long as there is one who holds that it is false) it is false. Hence the doctrine is self-defeating, and so incoherent. Let us call this second argument for the incoherence charge the 'necessarily some beliefs are false' (henceforth *NSBF*) argument: relativism is incoherent because it holds that all beliefs and opinions are true, yet, given conflicting beliefs, some beliefs must necessarily be false—in which case relativism cannot be true.

We have seen thus far two independent arguments for the incoherence of Protagorean relativism. The *UVNR* argument concludes that such relativism is incoherent because, if right, its rightness cannot be established, because the very notion of rightness is undermined—so that, if right, it cannot be right. The *NSBF* argument concludes that Protagorean relativism is incoherent because, if true, then it is false

(so long as at least one person is of the opinion that it is false), because the Protagorean relativist is bound by her doctrine to regard all opinions as true, including the opinion that that doctrine is false. Our question is: Are these arguments conclusive? Is Protagorean relativism incoherent? Several recent writers have argued that it is not; their defenses of the doctrine, or of some related version of epistemological relativism, will be the focus of attention during most of the remainder of this chapter. First, however, it will be helpful to consider more contemporary, and more generalized, versions of the Protagorean doctrine and the Socratic arguments for its incoherence.

Epistemological Relativism and the Incoherence Charge in Their Modern Dresses

Epistemological relativism may, without violence to Protagoras or more recent defenders, be characterized as follows:

> *ER*: For any knowledge-claim *p*, *p* can be evaluated (assessed, established, etc.) only according to (with reference to) one or another set of background principles and standards of evaluation s_1, . . . s_n; and, given a different set (or sets) of background principles and standards s'_1, . . . s'_n, there is no neutral (that is, neutral with respect to the two (or more) alternative sets of principles and standards) way of choosing between the two (or more) alternative sets in evaluating *p* with respect to truth or rational justification. *p*'s truth and rational justifiability are relative to the standards used in evaluating *p*.

***

The Protagorean relativist will assent to *ER*, since it captures the intuition that knowledge and truth are relative to each individual thinker: if *p* is true (or a genuine item of knowledge) according to my standards, then it is true (for me), and there is no other standard by which my individual judgments and standards may themselves be neutrally evaluated. *ER* is more general than Protagorean relativism, however, for it places the source of relativism at the level of standards rather than the level of personal opinion or perception, and as such aptly characterizes more recent relativisms such as those of Kuhn, Young, Bloor, Barnes, Winch, Wittgenstein, and others.

It immediately follows from *ER* that if *p* is evaluated differently according to two different sets of principles and standards—that is, for example, if *p* is true (probably true, highly confirmed, etc.) according to $s_1, \ldots s_n$, but false (probably false, poorly confirmed, etc.) according to $s'_1, \ldots s'_n$, there is no way to evaluate these conflicting evaluations. *p* is true relative to $s_1, \ldots s_n$, and false relative to $s'_1, \ldots s'_n$. Since there is no neutral way of evaluating the rival sets of standards, there is no neutral way of evaluating conflicting evaluations of *p*. Such evaluations can only be carried out relative to one or another set of principles and criteria of evaluation. Given my set of standards, opinions, and convictions, *p*'s epistemic status is as I judge it to be.

If *ER* effectively characterizes epistemological relativism, how can we reformulate, with respect to *ER*, Socrates' arguments against Protagorean relativism? The second (*NSBF*) argument is easily recast. Instantiating *ER* in the original formulation yields:

ER': *ER* can be evaluated (assessed, established, etc.) only according to (with reference to) one or another set of background principles and standards of evaluation $s_1, \ldots s_n$; and, given a different set (or sets) of background principles and standards of evaluation $s'_1, \ldots s'_n$, there is no neutral (that is, neutral with respect to the two (or more) alternative sets of principles and standards) way of choosing between the two (or more) alternative sets in evaluating *ER* with respect to truth or rational justification. *ER*'s truth and rational justifiability are relative to the standards utilized in evaluating *ER*.

If *ER* is true, then, as *ER*' states, *ER* is itself relative to alternative, and equally legitimate, sets of background principles and standards of evaluation. Since these alternative sets will suggest differing evaluations of *ER*, and since there is no way neutrally to pick one evaluation over and against any others, it follows that, if *ER* is true, then *ER*'s truth will vary according to the principles and criteria by which *ER* is evaluated. In particular, it follows that, if according to some set of standards $s_1, \ldots s_n$ *ER* is judged to be false, then, if *ER* is true, (at

least according to that set of standards $s_1, \ldots s_n$) *ER* is false. (This neatly mirrors the Socratic argument according to which Protagoras is bound by his own principles to recognize the falsity of Protagorean relativism, so long as someone is of the opinion that it is false.) In this way, *ER* is self-refuting, and so incoherent.

Socrates' first (*UVNR*) argument has it that Protagorean relativism is self-refuting in that, if it is right, it undermines the very idea of rightness, and so cannot be right. Another way to put this point is that the notion of rightness is intelligible only when understood nonrelativistically. "Relative rightness' is not rightness at all. For the relativist wants to argue that relativism is right (or true, or cognitively superior) and that non-relativism is wrong (or false, or cognitively inferior), or less adequate philosophically, than relativism. To make this claim non-relativistically, however, is to give up relativism; conversely, to make the claim only relatively is not to make it at all.

Put in terms of *ER*, the *UVNR* argument can be cast as follows. Assume *ER* to be a rationally justifiable position. Then there are good reasons for holding *ER*. But good reasons cannot be biased or non-neutral or arbitrary or idiosyncratic (by definition of 'good reason'—this point will be pursued further below). Therefore, if *ER* is rationally justifiable, there must be some non-relative, neutral (with respect to the presuppositions of relativists and non-relativists) framework or ground from which we can make that judgment. Thus *ER*, which denies the possibility of such a framework, is incorrect. In short, if relativism is rationally justifiable, it must have a non-relativistic ground, which possibility it denies. Thus *ER*, if true, is not rationally justifiable, since if *ER* is true there can be no neutral ground from which to assess the rational justifiability of any claim, including *ER* itself. Moreover, if *ER* is (true and) rationally justifiable, then it is false, for the rational defense of *ER* requires the sort of non-relativistic ground which *ER* itself denies. Thus *ER* is either not rationally justifiable, or false. The assertion and defense of *ER* is thus self-refuting, and so incoherent.

This argument points out what Socrates' first argument points out: namely, that the relativist must appeal to non-relativistic criteria, and assert relativism non-relativistically, in order to make the case for relativism. This is self-defeating for the relativist. But to fail to assert and defend relativism in this (non-relativistic) way is to fail to join the issue with the non-relativist who asserts that relativism is false (or incoherent). So the relativist can defend relativism only by rendering it incoherent. Conversely, to defend relativism relativistically is to fail to defend it at all. For if relativism is right, the very notion of rightness, and indeed that of rational defense, is given up, and so it cannot coherently be claimed that relativism is right or rationally defensible. In short: to defend relativism is to defend it non-relativistically, which is to give it up; to 'defend' it relativistically is not to *defend* it at all. And this is precisely the lesson of Socrates' first argument.

Do the Incoherence Arguments Beg the Question? A Relativist Conception of Truth

Several recent writers have sought to defend relativism from the charge of incoherence. The first major line of defense to be considered is that which holds that the incoherence arguments beg the question by assuming an absolutist conception of knowledge or truth.

Harold I. Brown, for example, writes, with respect to the *NSBF* argument, that

> . . . this argument has no force against any consistent relativism, even the extreme relativism of Protagoras. Its apparent cogency derives from a tacit acc eptance of the absolutist assumption that we are justified in making a knowledge claim only if it is based on an unquestionable foundation. Given this assumption, once we admit the possibility of knowledge claims contrary to but as well founded as our own, our own knowledge claims become illegitimate. But the acceptability of this thesis is the central issue in dispute between relativism and absolutism.[11]

Thus, Brown concludes, the absolutist begs the question against the relativist by assuming absolutism.

The problem with Brown's argument against the absolutist is that it confuses absolutism with foundationalism. If relativism is the view that knowledge and truth are relative to framework, conceptual scheme, paradigm, cultures, personal predilection, etc., and there are no criteria or standards by which claims put forth by rival positions can be fairly, neutrally, or objectively judged, then absolutism should be understood as the (contrary) view that such claims can be evaluated in a non-question-begging way, and that objective comparison of rival claims is possible. But absolutism so construed is not at all tantamount to foundationalism, that is, to the epistemological thesis that "knowledge requires an indubitable foundation and that knowledge is developed by building on that foundation."[12] One can hold that knowledge is absolute in the sense that claims to knowledge can be fairly, non-question-beggingly assessed without holding further that knowledge "requires an indubitable foundation." Brown here confuses absolutism with foundationalism; he similarly confuses relativism with *fallibilism*:

> The main thesis of relativist epistemology is that knowledge can be constructed on a fallible foundation. Relativism affirms my right to hold my own presuppositions in spite of their fallibility, to proceed on the basis of these presuppositions, and to reject competing sets of presuppositions as false.[13]

But these rights are affirmed, not by relativism, but by fallibilism. One needn't be a relativist to affirm the first two rights Brown mentions; moreover, it is not clear (as we shall see below,) that the relativist can consistently affirm the third right. Relativism's commitment to the non-existence of neutral standards aligns it, not with fallibilism, but with *arbitrariness*. It is this arbitrariness which makes relativism the radical and potentially destructive doctrine that it is perceived by its critics to be. In any case, one can consistently espouse a fallibilist absolutism—that is, one can consistently hold that knowledge is fallible, and not certain or indubitable, and also that claims to knowledge can be neutrally and objectively evaluated and assessed.

A more systematic attempt to discredit the incoherence arguments and to develop a positive case for epistemological relativism is that of Jack W. Meiland. In a series of articles, Meiland denies that relativism is self-refuting, and he has developed an analysis of relative truth which, he argues, stands as a legitimate alternative to an absolutist conception of truth. In fact, these two efforts are connected in Meiland's work, for it is by establishing a viable conception of relative truth, according to Meiland, that relativism escapes the self-refutation problem:

> That relativism is self-refuting ... is a myth which must be laid to rest. It *would* be inconsistent for the relativist to say both that all doctrines are relatively true and that relativism is not relatively true but instead is absolutely true. However, the careful relativist would not and need not say this. He would either say that all doctrines except relativism (and perhaps its competitors on the meta-level) are relatively true or false, or else he would say that his own doctrine of relativism is relatively true too. And saying that relativism is only relatively true does not produce inconsistency.[14]

The first alternative Meiland mentions is unhelpful for the relativist, in the absence of an argument which reasonably distinguishes between relativism (and perhaps its competitors on the meta-level) and all other doctrines and claims with respect to truth such that the former, but not the latter, can properly be regarded as either true or false absolutely. Meiland has furnished no such argument; nor is it easy to see on what consideration such an argument might be based.[15] It is Meiland's second alternative—that the self-refutation charge can be avoided by holding that the doctrine of relativism is itself only relatively true—that is worth scrutiny here. And this alternative clearly rests on the coherence of the notion of relative truth. It is no surprise, therefore, that Meiland seeks to establish the tenability of that notion.

Meiland's discussion of relative truth hinges on his claim that relative truth can be understood independently of the concept of absolute truth—for, as he rightly acknowledges, relativism would not escape the self-refutation problem if it denied the legitimacy of absolute truth by affirming a concept of relative truth which itself depended on or appealed to the absolute conception.[16] Meiland offers an analysis of absolute and relative truth which he suggests is such that the latter does not depend on the former. On this analysis, absolute truth is a two-term relation, while relative truth is a three-term relation:

1. The concept of absolute truth seems to be a concept of a *two*-term relation between statements (or perhaps propositions) on the one hand and facts (or states of affairs) on the other. But the concept of relative truth, as used by some relativists, seems to be a concept of a *three*-term relation between statements, the world, and a third term which is either persons, world views, or historical and cultural situations.
2. The relation denoted by the expression 'absolute truth' is often said to be that of correspondence. The relativist can make use of this type of notion and say that "P is true relative to W" means something like "P corresponds to the facts from the point of view of W" (Where W is a person, a set of leading principles, a world view, or a situation).[17]

Meiland acknowledges that the analysis of the concept of relative truth here offered "is very incomplete and raises more questions than it answers."[18] He puts it forward, nonetheless, for the following purpose:

> My point in putting this suggestion forward is to begin to show that ... absolutists are making a great mistake by assuming that relative truth must be either nothing at all or else a variety of absolute truth.[19]

And Meiland summarizes what he takes to be the significance of his analysis as follows:

> When we use expressions of the form 'Ø is true for W', it seems legitimate to ask the question "What does 'true' mean in this expression?" ... The correct relativist answer to this question is: "It means that Ø is true-for-W." The hyphens in this answer are extremely important. For they show that the relativist is not talking about truth but instead about truth-for-W. Thus, one can no more reasonably ask what 'true' means in the expression 'true-for-W' than one can ask what 'cat' means in the word 'cattle'. 'True-for-W' denotes a special three-term relation which does not include the two-term relation of absolute truth as a distinct part.[20]

Meiland offers his analysis for two (related) purposes: he wants to establish the concept of relative truth as a viable, coherent concept which the relativist

452 ◇ PART II CONTEMPORARY READINGS

can appeal to as an alternative to the concept of absolute truth; and he wants to show that relative truth, once shown to be viable, enables the relativist to escape the problem of self-refutation. Unfortunately, neither of these ends are achieved by the analysis offered. I consider them in turn.

The Viability of the Concept of Relative Truth

Consider first Meiland's analysis of relative truth as a "three-term relation between statements, the world, and a third term which is either persons, world views, or historical and cultural situations." To be a genuine three-term relation, it must be possible to individuate each relatum and to distinguish each from the other two. On a conception of absolute truth, this condition (as Meiland recognizes) is easily met: the world, however difficult to apprehend directly, is clearly distinguishable from statements about it. What, however, is the status of the world on the three-term conception? Is it clearly distinguishable from the other two relata? Unfortunately, the answer is no. On the relativist conception, the world is not distinguishable from the third relatum (either persons, world views, or historical and cultural situations). What are related by the alleged three-term relation are statements and the-world-relative-to-W (where W is a person, a set of leading principles, a world view, or a situation—in short, where W is the third relatum). On the relativist conception, the world cannot be conceived as independent of W; if it is so conceived, the relativist conception collapses into an absolutist one, for it is granted that there is a way the world is, independent of statements and of W's. This is precisely what the relativist must deny, however.[21] So Meiland's three-term relation collapses into a two-term relation, between statements and the-world-relative-to-W, or, in a Goodman's terminology, between statements and world-versions.[22] This point can be seen in Meiland's remarks about the relativist's ability to utilize the notion of relations of correspondence. Meiland writes that the relativist "can make use of this type of notion and say that 'P is true relative to W' means something like 'P corresponds to the facts from the point of view of W'."[23] Grant Meiland the

use of relations of correspondence: what corresponds is not statements, independent facts, and some W; but rather statements and facts-from-the-point-of-view-of-W. Thus Meiland's three-term relation turns out upon inspection to be a two-term relation.

Now this point by itself is not very damaging to Meiland's position. He can still argue that the two-term relativist conception of truth is distinct from the two-term absolutist conception—the former relates statements and facts-relative-to-W, while the latter relates statements and facts (which are not relative to any W)—and that the relativist conception does not appeal to, incorporate, or rely upon the absolutist conception. And this last point is the point Meiland is most concerned to make: "'True-for-W' denotes a special . . . relation which does not include the . . . relation of absolute truth as a distinct part."[24] This point is important for Meiland because, if it can be sustained, it rescues the relativist from the charge that she relies on the notion of absolute truth in holding a concept of relative truth, thereby refuting her own position by relying on a concept she expressly rejects. Is it the case, however, that the relativist conception does avoid reliance on the absolute conception? It is not clear that it does. Consider Meiland's reasoning here. He writes that the hyphens in 'true-for-W'

> are extremely important. For they show that the relativist is not talking about truth but instead about truth-for-W. Thus, one can no more reasonably ask what 'true' means in the expression 'true-for-W' than one can ask what 'cat' means in the word 'cattle'.[25]

There are two points to make here. The first is that Meiland's conclusion does not follow, for 'true' is not related to 'true-for-W' as 'cat' is related to 'cattle'. 'Cattle' is made up of the concatenation of the letters 'c', 'a', 't', 't', 'l', and 'e'; 'cat' is no more a meaningful part of 'cattle' than is 'ca', 'catt', 'cattl', etc. 'True-for-W', on the other hand, is made up of the hyphenization of distinct concepts which are independently meaningful.[26] The occurrence of 'true' in 'true-for-W' is *not* like the occurrence of 'tru' or 'ru' in 'true-for-W'. In fact, if the role of 'true' if 'true-for-W' is analogous to that of 'cat' in 'cattle', it is difficult to understand why Meiland would bother with his discussion. For it is after all, a conception of relative *truth* he is concerned to articulate. The hyphens in 'true-for-W' show that on the relativist conception truth is always to be regarded as relative to some W; that it is never to be conceived of as independent of every W. But it does not follow that the hyphenated phrase "does not include the concept of absolute truth as a distinct part."[27] If this did follow, it would be difficult to see why the hyphenated phrase constituted a conception of relative *truth* at all. Adding the hyphens does not eliminate the concept of truth from the hyphenated phrase—as well it shouldn't, if the aim of the relativist's project is to articulate a conception of truth. 'True' in 'true-for-W' is not analogous to 'cat' in 'cattle'; a better analogy is with 'action' in 'action-at-a-distance'. The latter phrase is to be distinguished from contiguous, mechanically connected action; it is still a conception, nonetheless, of *action*. Similarly, 'true-for-W' is to be distinguished from absolute truth, i.e. truth that is not relative to any W; it is still a conception, nonetheless, of *truth*.[28]

The immediate upshot of the above discussion is that Meiland has not shown that his conception of relative truth avoids reliance on the absolute conception, and so he has not shown that his analysis avoids the self-refutation problem it is designed to avoid. . . .

Relative Truth and Self-Refutation

As noted earlier, one of the classical objections to epistemological relativism is that the concept of relative truth, on which the doctrine of relativism seems to depend, is incoherent (or trivial). Meiland's analysis has given us no reason to doubt the cogency of the classical objection. However, there is still a deeper problem. For even if it could be shown that the concept of relative truth is coherent, that by itself would not establish the cogency of epistemological relativism. I now want to argue that, even if some conception of relative truth were to be shown to be coherent, the doctrine of epistemological relativism would nevertheless remain unworthy of our embrace, for it would still fail to avoid the problem of self-refutation. Specifically, a coherent conception of relative truth fails to enable the relativist to avoid the perils of the *UVNR* argument for the incoherence of relativism discussed above.

Recall that the *UVNR* argument has it that relativism is self-refuting in that, if relativism is right, it undermines the very idea of rightness. For to say that relativism is *right* is to presuppose the existence of nonrelative criteria of rightness by which the judgment that relativism is right can be made. But relativism denies the existence of any such criteria. Thus, if relativism is right, it undermines the very notion of rightness, by denying the very criteria necessary for the judgment of its rightness to have cognitive or epistemic force.

Now, if the relativist embraces the concept of relative truth, she embraces the thesis that any claim is true for those who believe it. (Meiland says, recall, that while 'Ø is true-for-X' does not *mean* 'X believes that Ø', nevertheless such belief is the *criterion* for relative truth.) To embrace this thesis, however, is to accept that the establishment of a claim or proposition or belief p as relatively true is not in any way an establishment of the epistemic worthiness of p. If p is relatively true, according to the relativist, then p is believed by the person it is true for; it corresponds with that person's conception of reality. The relative truth of p thus renders p no more worthy of belief than the equally (relatively) true not-p or arbitrary belief q. The relativist conception of truth commits one to the view that relative truths are not in any way cognitively superior or preferable to their contradictories, to relative falsehoods, or to alternative relative truths. It is not much of an accomplishment, in short, for a statement to achieve the status of relative truth; the cognitive preferability the absolutist claims for truths over falsehoods is lost for the relativist. To label p relatively true is not in any way to praise it or to acknowledge it to be cognitively preferable to rival propositions; it is only to register that someone believes it.

What then of relativism? Meiland seeks to develop a tenable conception of relative truth, and to defend relativism as itself relatively true. But, granting for the moment the tenability of the concept, Meiland's thesis comes simply to the claim that he believes it; that relativism corresponds-to-reality-for-Meiland. Let us grant this thesis as well. Does it follow that relativism is enhanced in cognitive status, or that absolutism suffers? Not in the least. If relativism is only relatively true, then by its own lights it is no better than its alternatives. Meiland is seeking to defend relativism, but the very notion of rational defense is given up by the relativist, for the relativist has rejected the possibility of nonrelative criteria by which rival claims or hypotheses can be evaluated. Thus to hold that relativism is relatively true is not in any way to suggest that there is good reason for being a relativist, nor is it to discredit absolutism. Defending relativism as relatively true is not *defending* it at all; nor is it asserting anything about the *rightness* of relativism. Even if we grant the relativist the coherence of the concept of relative truth, then, a relativism based upon this concept does not avoid the self-refutation problem. The *UVNR* argument remains a powerful argument for the incoherence of relativism: one cannot embrace relativism as right without giving up the very notion of rightness; to defend relativism as relatively true or right is not to defend it at all. The problem here is not with the *formulation* of the concept of relative truth, but rather, with the impossibility of the *defense* of a relativism which depends upon that concept.

The Impotence of Relativism

These considerations show, I think, the inability of relativism to sanction significant judgments, to recognize or do justice to the notions of warrant and justification with respect to beliefs and knowledge-claims, or to offer direction with respect to action. This inability may be thought of as the *impotence* of relativism. Since to say of p that it is relatively true is not to praise p or claim it to be more worthy of belief than rival claims not-p or q, and since the relativist recognizes this feature of relativism—it is true for her, since, being a relativist, she believes that truth is relative—then the relativist must realize, from her own relativistic point of view, that p's being true-for-her in no way warrants belief in p or establishes p as in any way more worthy of belief than not-p or q. For the relativist must realize that not-p and q are also relatively true, and so p has no claim to cognitive superiority or worthiness of belief on grounds of *its* relative truth. Moreover, the relativist

must realize the thrust of the *UVNR* argument, which (in this context) comes to the view that the very notion of cognitive worthiness or superiority is given up with the adoption of relative truth.

Consequently, the relativist cannot say "I should adopt the belief p," or "p is justified for me, because p is true for me," because p's relative truth in no way—from the relativist's own point of view—sanctions p or affords p epistemic warrant of any sort. Thus the relativist cannot regard her beliefs, or her relative truths, as warranted or worthy of belief. Similarly for action. The relativist is thus left in the position of being unable to recognize relative merits of propositions, knowledge-claims, or actions—all are as worthy as the rest, and the very notion of worthiness has been jettisoned—and therefore cannot rationally prefer any relative truth to any other. Warranted adoption of belief and of courses of action is impossible for the relativist. Here is relativism's impotence.

Of course the relativist can respond by claiming that p's being true-for-*her* makes it, though only relatively true, more worthy of belief for her than a rival proposition q, which, while relatively true, is true-for-*someone-else*. But unless the relativist can say why a relative truth which is true-for-her is superior to or more worthy of belief than a relative truth which is true-for-someone-else—which she can't, since, in embracing relativism, she has given up the very notion of worthiness of belief—then adoption of one relative truth over another on the grounds that the adopted truth is true for the person doing the adopting is arbitrary. p's truth-for-Jones is not in any way superior to not-p's truth-for-Smith—even for Jones. Thus the relativist can adopt beliefs (and act) only arbitrarily. Either arbitrariness or impotence—these are the sole options of the relativist. . . .

Did Socrates Beg the Question?

If the points made thus far are correct, the relativist has failed to secure for the concept of relative truth a modicum of intelligibility, and has failed to meet the challenge of the arguments for the incoherence of relativism. Because these arguments trace their lineage to Socrates' discussion of Protagoras in the *Theaetetus*, it is important to consider the charge, put forward by several defenders of relativism, that Socrates' arguments beg the question against the relativist and so fail to demonstrate the untenability of relativism. We must consider both whether Socrates' arguments so beg the question, and also whether more recent formulations of the arguments for self-refutation do so.

It has long been recognized in the literature that Socrates' arguments seem to beg the question, by dropping the relativizing phrase 'for ... when discussing truth, thus collapsing the Protagorean notion of relative truth into the standard absolutist one. Thus Meiland writes that

> Plato's own attempt, in the *Theaetetus* to show Protagorean relativism to be self-refuting appears to be radically defective due to Plato's dropping of the relativistic qualifier (the "for me" in "true for me") at crucial points.[29]

Chris Swoyer similarly concludes that

> such criticisms beg the question against relativism in their implicit reliance upon an absolute theory of truth.[30]

James N. Jordan also argues that, in response to Socrates' arguments,

> Protagoras would doubtless reply, and rightly, that this leaves him untouched, that in fact it begs the question.... "For ... " is an addendum whose power Socrates has misjudged, if, indeed, he has not entirely overlooked it.[31]

M.F. Burnyeat similarly recognizes a problem for Socrates here.[32]

It is undeniable that Socrates does drop the qualifier 'for ... ' in several passages in his response to Protagoras. The crucial question is, to what extent does this deletion vitiate his criticisms of Protagorean relativism? The answer, I think, is that the deletions do not in the end limit the force of his critique, or of the present reconstruction of it.

First, it must be noted that the Socratic argument can itself be analyzed in such a way that a portion of the argument includes a demonstration of Protagoras' commitment to and reliance upon the notion of absolute truth and consequently of the incoherence of his concept of relative truth. If Socrates' argument shows

this, then it does not beg the question against Protagoras by deleting the qualifier 'for ... ', but rather deletes it for the very good reason that the expression 'true for' is only intelligible when taken to be equivalent to 'true (simpliciter)'.

But whether the arguments in the *Theaetetus* can be shown to be compelling, the reconstructions of them offered here clearly can. The *UVNR* argument has not been satisfactorily fended off, either by Protagoras or by the contemporary relativists considered thus far; similarly, the *NSBF* argument stands as a powerful refutation of relativism. For, as we have seen above, the relativist cannot coherently assert relativism only relatively: to argue that relativism is only correct for the relativist is to fail to join the issue with the opponent of relativism; it is to fail to assert the correctness or cognitive superiority of relativism. But to defend or assert relativism non-relativistically is to acknowledge the cognitive force of criteria or principles of reasoning by which the relativistic thesis can itself be assessed, and this acknowledgement constitutes a rejection of the relativistic thesis (which rejects the force of such criteria or principles) which is purportedly being defended. Thus the relativist cannot coherently defend or assert relativism either relatively or non-relatively. And, as the *NSBF* argument illustrates this dilemma for the relativist, if the relativist defends relativism relativistically, she recognizes the equal cognitive legitimacy of absolutism (and the standards by which absolutism is (relatively) established as superior to relativism) and thus the non-superiority of relativism and the arbitrariness of her commitment to it; while if she defends relativism non-relativistically she gives up the very doctrine she is attempting to defend.[33] Both the *UVNR* and *NSBF* arguments proceed without a commitment to absolute truth, but rather portend trouble for the relativist whatever conception of truth she adopts, and so these arguments do not beg the question against the relativist. . . .

Relativism Without Relative Truth

Up to this point we have been concerned mainly with the difficulties attending versions of epistemological relativism which incorporate or rely upon the concept of relative truth. A very different sort of relativism is that which eschews that concept. In this section I want briefly to consider a recent defense of relativism which explicitly rejects relative truth, that of Hartry Field.

Field's discussion of relativism takes place in the context of his critique of Hilary Putnam's recent work.[34] As is well known, Putnam has recently given up his earlier embrace of 'metaphysical' realism, and has embraced what he calls 'internal' realism. In the course of his discussion of realism, Putnam forcefully rejects epistemological relativism as incoherent.[35] Field seeks to defend metaphysical realism from Putnam's critique; in addition he offers a conception of epistemological relativism which he believes shows relativism to be "a coherent and palatable doctrine."[36] The relativism Field defends "is a relativism as to values only, not to facts."[37] Being a physicalist and a metaphysical realist, Field regards truth as factual and thus non-relative; there is therefore no sanction of relative truth in Field's relativism. There is, however, relativism about values, including especially *epistemic* values: "to say that a belief is justified is to evaluate it."[38] Field articulates his view further as follows:

> I understand it [epistemological relativism] as the doctrine that the basic epistemological properties are not such properties as that of belief B *being justified,* but rather such relativized properties as that of belief B *being justified relative to* evidential system E. (An *evidential system* is, roughly, a bunch of rules for determining under what conditions one is to believe various things; a belief is justified relative to an evidential system in certain circumstances if the rules license the belief under those circumstances.)[39]

Field is quick to point out that, while relativism so conceived allows the relativist to say that B is justified relative to E_1, or not-B relative to E_2, she cannot say that B is justified *simpliciter* or to *the true* evidential system, for these notions of justification are unrelativized and so are not available to the relativist. Field's relativist can say that B is true 'absolutely', but that B is justified only relatively to some E.

The obvious question to be put to Field's brand of relativism is: can rival, incompatible evidential systems themselves be non-relatively or objectively or rationally evaluated? For if they can, so that we can say that E_1 is a better or superior or more justified evidential system than E_2 absolutely or non-relatively, then the relativism Field offers is not very relativistic—for while two relativists who hold different E's can claim that their incompatible beliefs B and non-B are justified relative to their respective E's, we can nevertheless judge (say) that B should not be believed since it is justified only relative to E_1, which we can argue is inferior to, or less adequate than, E_2. This would reduce Field's relativism to a species of absolutism, and seems in any case to be incompatible with Field's view that epistemic values are relative—for in judging E's we are, after all, *evaluating* E's, and such evaluating, no less than evaluating beliefs, is epistemic evaluating and so should be relativized (to 'meta-E's') on Field's view. On the other hand, if rival, incompatible E's cannot be non-relatively evaluated, then it is difficult to see how any belief, no matter how bizarre, can be ruled out or evaluated negatively, for some E which will sanction it could always be constructed. Consequently, the relative evaluation of beliefs will be empty—*all* beliefs will be justified relative to some E's, unjustified relative to others, and the notion of epistemic justification will be not simply relativized, but trivialized; to say that a belief is justified will be not to praise it at all. The impotence noted earlier with respect to relative truth resurfaces in full force with respect to relative epistemic evaluation. . . .

Conclusion

I conclude that the defenses of relativism considered thus far have been successfully undercut. More specifically, the arguments for the incoherence of relativism are as compelling as ever, and have manifestly not been laid to rest by contemporary relativists. The basic Socratic insight that relativism is self-refuting, and so incoherent, remains a fundamental difficulty for those who would resuscitate and defend the ancient Protagorean doctrine or a modern variant of it.

But, of course, there are many other avenues to relativism yet to be considered.

Notes

1. Plato, *Theaetetus*, 152a.
2. Ibid., 160c.
3. Ibid., 166d–167d.
4. Ibid., 170a.
5. *Theaetetus*, 162a.
6. Ibid., 169d–171c.
7. Ibid., 170e–171a.
8. Ibid., 171a. Here begins a famous difficulty for the Socratic argument. Socrates deletes the relativizing phrase 'for . . .' after 'true', thus unfairly characterizing Protagoras' position. This opens the door to the charge that Socrates has begged the question against Protagoras by assuming an 'absolute' conception of truth, according to which a claim's truth is independent of a person's belief in its truth, which the relativist rejects.
9. Ibid., 171b. Cf. also 179b.
10. Ibid., 171c.
11. Harold I. Brown, "For a Modest Historicism", pp. 549–550.
12. Ibid., p. 541.
13. Ibid., p. 550.
  Jack W. Meiland, 'Is Protagorean Relativism Self-Refuting?'; Meiland, 'Concepts of Relative Truth'; Meiland, 'On the Paradox of Cognitive Relativism'; and Meiland, 'Cognitive Relativism: Popper and the Argument From Language'. Cf. also Jack W. Meiland and Michael Krausz, eds., *Relativism: Cognitive and Moral*.
14. Meiland, 'On the Paradox of Cognitive Relativism', p. 121, emphasis in original. Cf. in this regard James N. Jordan, 'Protagoras and Relativism: Criticisms Bad and Good'.
15. And in any case this is a move which is contrary to the spirit of relativism, and makes that doctrine less challenging and interesting—as Meiland notes, "On the Paradox of Cognitive Relativism", p. 119.
16. 'Concepts of Relative Truth', p. 571.
17. Meiland, 'Concepts of Relative Truth', p. 571, emphasis in original.
18. Ibid., p. 571.
19. Ibid., pp. 571–572.
20. Ibid., p. 574.
21. Actually this is not quite right. The *metaphysical* relativist must deny that there is a way the world is, independent of statements and W's; the *epistemological* relativist must deny only that one can *know* the way the world is, independent of statements and of W's.
22. Cf. Nelson Goodman, *Ways of Worldmaking*. Goodman's unique brand of relativism is considered in Chapter 7, below.
23. Meiland, "Concepts of Relative Truth", p. 571.
24. Ibid., p. 574.
25. Ibid.
26. Recall that W is not just a letter here; it is a place-holder for persons, world-views, situations, etc.
27. To paraphrase Meiland, Ibid., p. 574.
28. Meiland recognizes this point is another context when he writes: " 'Relative truth' is a form of truth; the expression 'relative truth' is not a name for something bearing little relation to our ordinary conception of truth." 'Introduction', in Meiland and Krausz, eds., *Relativism*, p. 4.
29. 'Is Protagorean Relativism Self-Refuting?', p. 54.
30. Swoyer, 'True For', p. 95.
31. Jordan, 'Protagoras and Relativism: Criticisms Bad and Good', pp. 10–11. Cf. also pp. 14 and 15. It should be noted that Jordan ultimately argues for relativism's incoherence, but on grounds he regards as different from Socrates'.
32. Burnyeat, "Protagoras and Self-Refutation in Plato's Theaetetus", pp. 174–175 and throughout.
33. Thus the *NSBF* argument, as well as the *UVNR* argument, gives rise to the difficulty the relativist faces regarding the defense of relativism.
34. Hartry Field, 'Realism and Relativism'.
35. Hilary Putnam, *Reason, Truth and History*. Putnam's discussion of relativism occurs at pp. 119–124; cf. also pp. 157 and 161–162. Putnam also criticizes relativism in his second Howison Lecture, "Why Reason Can't be Naturalized", pp. 3–23. Cf. pp. 7–14.
  As several writers have pointed out, it is not clear that the positive view of internal realism Putnam defends is not itself relativistic, and thus inconsistent with his rejection of relativism. (Cf. in this regard Field, 'Realism and Relativism', p. 563, note 12; also Eric Matthews' review of *Reason, Truth and History*, esp. pp. 115–116). I believe that this is indeed a serious difficulty for Putnam, but space forbids detailed consideration of the point here.
36. Field, 'Realism and Relativism', p. 562.
37. Ibid., p. 562. Field argues that this distinguishes his version of relativism from Protagoras', which Field agrees is incoherent.
38. Ibid., p. 563.
39. Ibid., emphasis in original. Note that this version of epistemological relativism neatly matches the characterization, *ER*, given earlier in this chapter, at least with respect to justification.

44. EPISTEMICALLY RATIONAL BELIEF AS INVULNERABILITY TO SELF-CRITICISM[1]

Richard Foley

Part of the appeal of classical foundationalism was that it purported to provide a definitive refutation of skepticism. With the fall of foundationalism, we can no longer pretend that such a refutation is possible. We must instead acknowledge that skeptical worries cannot be completely banished and that, thus, inquiry always involves an element of risk which cannot be eliminated by further inquiry, whether it be scientific or philosophical. The flip side of this point is that inquiry always involves some element of unargued-for trust in one's faculties and the opinions they generate.

The trust need not be and should not be unrestricted, however. Unquestioning faith in our faculties and opinions is not only naïve but also risky, given what we know about our own fallibility. Thus, among the most pressing questions for epistemology are ones concerning the limits of intellectual self-trust. What degree of trust is it appropriate to have in one's opinions and faculties? An approximate answer to this question is that trust ought to be proportionate to the degree of confidence one has in one's opinions and to what I shall call the "depth" of this confidence. Similarly, trust in one's intellectual faculties, methods, and practices ought be proportionate to the confidence one has in these faculties, methods, and practices and the depth of this confidence.

Sheer confidence is never a guarantee of truth or reliability, of course, but for the first-person questions that are my principal concern, namely, questions about how intellectual issues look from one's own perspective, it is the appropriate place to begin. One begins with what one feels most sure of. Not just any kind of confidence will do, however. It is epistemic confidence that matters, that is, confidence in the accuracy of one's opinions and the reliability of one's faculties, methods and practices. Epistemic confidence is to be distinguished from confidence that one can successfully defend an opinion against attacks by others. With enough information and dialectical skills, one may be able to defend even that which one disbelieves. Similarly, it is to be distinguished from confidence that an opinion will serve one well economically, socially, or psychologically.

Even epistemic confidence counts for little in and of itself, however. What does count is deep confidence. Some opinions are confidently held but not deeply held. They are the belief counterparts of whims, impulses, and urges, which in practical reasoning should not be treated with the same seriousness as full-blooded, less fleeting, and more deeply seated drives, preferences, and needs. The analogous point holds for theoretical reasoning. Hunches, inklings, and other such shallow opinions are not to be treated with the same seriousness as deeply held ones.

What distinguishes a deeply held from a shallowly held opinion is not mere revisability. Virtually all of our opinions are revisable over time. There are conceivable turns of events and evidence that would cause us to abandon or modify them. On the other hand, for some opinions, even some that are confidently held, new evidence is not needed to undermine them. All that is required is a little reflection. Other opinions are not so shallow, however. Some are the products of careful deliberation and, hence, are unlikely to be affected by further deliberation. Others are acquired with little thought but are nonetheless deeply held. For example, most perceptual beliefs are not the products of deliberation. We acquire them automatically, and yet many are such that reflection would not prompt us to revise them. They are reflectively stable, in the sense that we would continue to endorse them even if we were to reflect deeply on them.

Like confidence, depth is a matter of degree, varying inversely with how vulnerable the opinion is to criticism on reflection. Some opinions are such that even superficial reflection would be enough to undermine our trust in them. Others are such that only lengthy or difficult reflection would undermine them. Still others are such that we would continue to endorse them even if we were to be ideally reflective.

So, to repeat, not every opinion is equally credible, or equally appropriate to trust, or equally suitable for deliberating and theorizing about what else to believe. The rough rule is that the more confidently and deeply held an opinion is, the more one is entitled to rely on it, at least until some new consideration or evidence arises that interferes with its credibility.

An account of rational belief lies behind the above claims, or more precisely, an account of a specific type of rational belief. "Rational belief" is used by epistemologists in a variety of senses, but with some oversimplification, the senses can divided into two broad categories. One sense tends to be externalist and closely connected with knowledge, that is, with what is required to turn true belief into a good candidate for knowledge. The other tends to be internalist and closely connected with responsible believing, that is, with what is required to put one's own intellectual house in order and have intellectual integrity. It is this second sense that principally concerns me here.

Being rational in this sense involves making oneself invulnerable to intellectual self-criticism to the extent possible. It is a matter of having opinions and using faculties, methods, and practices capable of standing up to one's own, most severe scrutiny. For an opinion to pass this test, it must not be the case that one's other opinions can be used to mount what one on reflection would regard as a convincing critique of it. Nor can it be the case that one has, or would have on reflection, criticisms about the ways one has acquired the opinion. Thus, not only must the opinion be in accord with one's other reflective first-order opinions, it must also be in accord with one's reflective second-order opinions about the kinds of faculties, methods, and practices that can be used to generate and revise opinions reliably.

Even opinions that are currently invulnerable to self-criticism are revisable over time. Additional evidence can undermine even the most confidently and deeply held opinion. Thus, being rational in the above sense does not entitle one to be complacent. Neither this nor any other sense of rationality is capable of providing one with a final intellectual resting place, with immunity from the need for future revisions. Getting one's opinions to fit together so well that one is invulnerable to self-criticism does achieve, in Robert Frost's memorable phrase, a momentary stay against confusion, but there is always room for the acquisition of further evidence and for the re-evaluation and further monitoring of one's opinions, methods, and faculties in light of this evidence.

Opinions are not the only phenomena that can be assessed for their rationality. Actions, decisions, intentions, strategies, methods, and plans can also be judged as rational or irrational. There is a common way of understanding all these assessments; they are claims from a given perspective about how effectively the belief, action, decision, etc. promotes a goal or set of goals. More precisely, this is so for what might be called a "strong" sense of rationality. In a weak sense, one is rational provided that one's cognitive states are sufficiently rich and complex to warrant being assessed as either rational or irrational in the strong sense. To say that something is rational in this weak sense contrasts with saying that it is arational. Mountains, rivers, rocks, buildings, and acorns are not capable of being either rational or irrational in the strong sense. They are arational. It is strong senses of rationality that are to be understood in terms of goals and perspectives.

A perspective is a set of beliefs, but a convenient way of identifying these beliefs is by reference to the individual whose beliefs they are. My perspective is constituted by my beliefs, your perspective by your beliefs, and so on for other individuals. Groups of individuals can also have perspectives. The perspective of a religious group or a political group, for example, is constituted by the beliefs widely shared by the individuals making up the group. By extension, we can also talk of the perspectives of hypothetical individuals. The perspective of an omniscient observer, for example, is constituted by the beliefs that a being with fully comprehensive and fully accurate opinions would have. Likewise, we can speak of the perspective that an individual would have on reflection.

We can and do assess each other's actions, beliefs, decisions, etc. from various perspectives, depending on our interests and the situation. For example, we sometimes evaluate decisions from the perspective of what an omniscient observer would have done in the decision-maker's situation if the observer were pursuing the same goals as the decision-maker, and we then use the language of rationality to express these evaluations. The decision was rational in this fully objective sense if it accords with the decision that would have been made by an omniscient observer, that is, by one who knows what the consequences would be of each of the alternatives open to the decision-maker. More precisely, a decision is rational in this sense if from the perspective of this hypothetical omniscient observer, its desirability is sufficiently high to make it a satisfactory option given the context, where desirability is a function of both the effectiveness of the decision in promoting the goals in question and the relative values of these goals,[2] and where the context is defined by the relative desirability of the alternatives and their relative accessibility to the decision-maker. The fewer the alternatives there are with greater desirability and the less readily accessible they are, the more likely it is that the decision in question is rational. It is rational not necessarily because it is the single best option, but rather because it is good enough given the context.

However, if from our external vantage point we are aware that no ordinary individual could be expected to foresee the consequences of the decision at issue, we may be more interested in evaluating the decision not from the perspective of an omniscient observer but rather from the perspective of a reasonably well informed, normal person. And again, often enough, in both legal and everyday contexts, we use the language of rationality to express this evaluation. The decision in question was reasonable if it accords with what a normal, reasonable person could be expected to do in that kind of situation, where this hypothetical, normal individual is not to be thought of as someone who knows with certainty the consequences of each of the options available to the decision-maker, but rather as one who is well-informed and, as such, is in possession of widely available information about the probabilities of various options yielding various outcomes.

Sometimes, however, we are interested in evaluating a decision not from the perspective of an omniscient observer nor even from the perspective of someone who is reasonably well informed but rather from the perspective of the very individual who is making the decision. We want to project ourselves to the extent possible into the decision-maker's skin and see the decision from her personal viewpoint. One kind of situation in which we are especially likely to be interested in doing this is when the decision has turned out badly. In retrospect, it may even be obvious to us why it turned out badly and, accordingly, we are perplexed by it. Simply dismissing the decision as irrational does not remove our bewilderment. Besides, we may be inclined to be charitable, assuming that there may have been something in her situation, not immediately apparent to us, that resulted in her not recognizing what seems so apparent to us. So, we try to enter into her situation and see the decision from her perspective. We bracket to the extent possible information that is available to us but was not available to her, and we try to locate grounds for the decision that might have seemed appropriate to her, given her information and situation. The grounds might strike us as unacceptably risky or unreliable, but we might nonetheless grant that they were convincing and even natural for her. If we succeed in discovering grounds that identify the decision as a satisfactory one relative to her information, circumstances, and outlook, we can express this finding by saying that we have shown why, in at least one sense of reason, she had reasons for her decision and hence, why, in at least one sense of rational, the decision was a rational, albeit mistaken, one for her to have made. By contrast, if we judge that even given her limited information, she would have seen the decision's shortcomings had she been more reflective, we will have shown in an especially convincing way why her decision was irrational. It was irrational not so much because it was at odds with what an omniscient observer would have regarded as a satisfactory way of achieving her goals, and not so much because it was at odds with what reasonably well-informed person would have regarded as a satisfactory way of achieving her goals, but rather because it was at odds with what she herself would have regarded as satisfactory had she been more careful, more reflective, and more vigilant.

This notion of rational (and irrational) decision is the practical counterpart of the notion of epistemically rational belief that is my principal concern, a notion which is to be understood in terms of a distinctively epistemic goal, that of now having an accurate and comprehensive belief system, and the individual's own perspective on reflection. An individual's belief is rational in this sense if on reflection she would think that her belief effectively promotes the goal of her now having accurate and comprehensive beliefs. On the other hand, if on reflection she herself would be critical of the belief, insofar as her goal is now to have accurate and comprehensive beliefs, her belief is irrational.

How lengthy are we to conceive this reflection as being? Is it enough that the individual would not be critical of her belief were she to reflect for a few moments, or is it necessary that she would not be critical of it even if she were to engage in lengthy reflection? The brief answer is that for her belief to be epistemically rational, there must be a point of reflective stability. If one imagines a continuum from no reflection at all to increasingly lengthy reflection, there must be a point along this continuum which is such that she would endorse the belief, and which is also such that there is no point further along the continuum at which she would be critical of it (insofar as her goal is to have accurate and comprehensive beliefs). For some beliefs, the point of reflective stability is the current state. These beliefs are reflectively stable as they are; no amount of additional reflection would undermine them. Other beliefs are such that the point of reflective stability would be reached with brief reflection. With still others, it would be reached only with lengthy reflection, and with yet others, it would not be reached at all, in which case the beliefs are not epistemically rational.[3]

For an opinion to be rational in this sense, the individual need not actually deliberate in arriving at the opinion. It is enough that were she to be sufficiently reflective, she would endorse the opinion and further reflection would not prompt her to change her mind. Indeed, it may be positively unreasonable for her to spend time deliberating about the opinion. All of us have goals that place constraints on how much effort we should devote to intellectual pursuits. The amount of time and effort that it is reasonable for an individual to

spend in investigating and reflecting on an topic is a function of the topic's importance, given the individual's total constellation of goals, both intellectual and practical. If a topic is insignificant, it is irrational to devote time or effort to it.

Considerations such as these illustrate that there is an important distinction between epistemically rational belief and what can be termed "responsible belief." Assume that a topic T has little intellectual or practical importance. Then it is not reasonable, given the total constellation of an individual's goals, for her to devote much time to thinking about it. Nevertheless, suppose it is the case that were she to reflect thoroughly, she would be critical of her current beliefs about T, insofar as her goal is to have accurate and comprehensive beliefs. Under these conditions, her beliefs about T are not epistemically rational, because she herself on reflection would be critical of them, insofar as her goal is to have accurate and comprehensive beliefs. Nonetheless, they may be responsible beliefs for her to have, given that it was reasonable, relative to all of her goals, for her not to engage in this reflection.[4]

In characterizing epistemic rationality in terms of a present-tense epistemic goal, that of now having an accurate and comprehensive belief system, I am assuming that goals can be concerned with current states of affairs as well as future states of affairs and, correspondingly, that there can be constitutive means as well as causally effective means to goals. If someone has the goal of being in good health and if good health is a state in which one not only lacks disease but also is not prone to disease, then not having high blood pressure is not so much a causal means to the goal of good health but rather part of what constitutes good health. Similarly, if being wise is incompatible with being rash, then not being rash is not so much a causal means to the goal of being wise as part of what constitutes being wise. Moreover, insofar as it is valuable for one not merely to be wise and in good health in the future but also to be wise and in good health now, then now not being rash and now not having high blood pressure is part of what is involved in achieving the goal of now being wise and healthy. In an analogous manner, believing P can be a part of what is involved in achieving the goal of now having accurate and comprehensive beliefs.

Nevertheless, if anyone thinks that this is stretching the standard meanings of "goal" and "means" too far, it is easy enough to devise alternative terminology. "Goal" can be replaced with "desideratum" or "value" and "means" with a locution about what is appropriate or fitting given this desideratum. The overall schema for understanding the epistemic rationality of a belief P thus becomes: Insofar as it is a desideratum (that is, a valuable state of affairs) for one now to have accurate and comprehensive beliefs, it is appropriate (that is, fitting) for one now to believe P, if on reflection one would regard believing P as part of what is involved in one's now having accurate and comprehensive beliefs.

To understand the rationale for characterizing epistemic rationality in terms of a present tense, intellectual goal, imagine that one's prospects for having accurate and comprehensive beliefs in a year's time would be enhanced by believing something for which one now lacks adequate evidence. For example, suppose a proposition P involves a more favorable assessment of my intellectual talents than my evidence warrants, but suppose also that believing P would make me more intellectually confident than I would be otherwise, which would make me a more dedicated inquirer, which in turn would enhance my long-term prospects of having an accurate and comprehensive belief system. Despite these long-term benefits, there is an important sense of rational belief, indeed the very sense that traditionally has been of the most interest to epistemologists, in which it is not rational for me to believe P. Moreover, the point of this example is not affected by shortening the time period in which the benefits are forthcoming. It would not be rational, in this sense, for me to believe P if we were instead to imagine that believing P would somehow improve my prospects for having accurate and comprehensive beliefs in the next few weeks, or in the next few hours, or even in the next few seconds. The precise way of making this point, in light of the above distinctions, is to say that in such a situation, it is not rational in a purely epistemic sense for me to believe P, where this purely epistemic sense is to be understood in terms of the present tense goal of now having accurate and comprehensive beliefs.

This notion of epistemic rationality can be loosely characterized in terms of what one would continue to believe were one to be reflective, but it is more exact to say that a belief is rational in this sense if it is capable of standing up to one's own critical scrutiny. Beliefs that would survive reflection are usually such that one would not be critical of them on reflection, and vice versa, but occasionally the distinction is important. Some beliefs are automatic and, as such, tend to be unaffected by deliberation, for instance, beliefs about what one is directly perceiving. Suppose I believe that I see a red ball in front of me, but suppose also that if I were to reflect, I would recall that I have been taking a drug that often causes highly realistic hallucinations. Nevertheless, it might still be psychologically difficult for me not to believe that I am seeing a red ball. Even so, my belief need not be epistemically rational, because what makes a belief epistemically rational is not that it would survive reflection but rather that it would be immune to criticism on reflection, insofar as one's goal is to have accurate and comprehensive beliefs.

Automatic beliefs provide one illustration of the distinction between beliefs that would survive reflection and those that one would not critical of were one to be reflective, but there are other examples as well. Let P be the proposition that banana quits resemble goldfinches, and let notP* be the proposition that I am not currently thinking about P. Assume that notP* is true and that I believe notP*. Like most of my beliefs at any moment, this belief is latent; by hypothesis I am not thinking about banana quits or gold finches. So far, there is nothing especially unusual about this case. It is simply an instance of the familiar distinction between activated and latent beliefs. Notice, however, that if I were to reflect on notP*, I would also be reflecting on P, since the proposition notP* involves the proposition P, and accordingly I would presumably come to believe P*. Moreover, it would be appropriate for me to do so, because I would now be thinking about banana quits and goldfinches. Nevertheless, this does not mean that it is now rational for me to believe P* rather than notP*. All it indicates is that the nature of the proposition not P* is such that were I reflect upon it, the reflection itself would alter what it is reasonable for me to believe about P* and notP*. Reflecting on notP* creates a reason, which currently does not exist, to believe P*. So, in this case, even though my opinions about P* and notP* on reflection would be different from my current opinions, and even though on reflection it would be appropriate for me to have these different opinions, these are not grounds for me to be critical of my current opinions.

I have said that if one's opinions are invulnerable to self-criticism insofar as one's goal is to have accurate and comprehensive beliefs, they are rational in an important sense, but to accommodate such cases, as well as cases of automatic belief, invulnerability to intellectual self-criticism must be understood in terms of reflection on one's current opinions and not merely reflection on the propositional content of these opinions. In particular, one's current opinion about a proposition can be invulnerable to self-criticism in the relevant sense and, hence, be rational, even if one would appropriately have a different opinion about the proposition on reflection. The key issue is not whether on reflection one would believe what one currently believes but rather whether one's current attitude can withstand reflective scrutiny. Ordinarily these amount to the same thing, but as the above cases illustrate, this is not always so.

A variety of other useful epistemological distinctions can be spelled out in terms of this general conception of epistemic rationality. According to the conception, a proposition P is epistemically rational for me if on reflection I would not be critical of my believing P, insofar as my goal is now to have accurate and comprehensive beliefs. If the proposition P is epistemically rational for me and I believe P, my belief is rational in one important sense, a propositional sense, but it need not be "doxastically" rational. For the belief to be doxastically rational, it must also be the case that I have acquired it and am sustaining it in an appropriate way. More precisely, the way I acquired and am sustaining the belief must not be such that on reflection I would be critical of it, insofar as my goal is to have accurate and comprehensive beliefs. For example, if I am in possession of information that on reflection I would regard as convincing evidence that Jones is guilty, but, unbeknownst to me, it is my dislike of Jones rather than this evidence which causes me to believe that Jones is guilty, then my belief is propositionally rational but it need not be doxastically rational.[5]

Concepts of *prima facie* (epistemic) reason and *prima facie* (epistemic) rationality can also be developed out of the above conception. To say that a set of considerations constitutes a *prima facie* reason for me to believe P is to say that (1) I believe that this set of considerations obtains, (2) this belief is propositionally rational for me, and (3) on reflection I would think that

when these considerations obtain, P is sufficiently likely to be true to make believing P appropriate, all else being equal, insofar as my goal is now to have accurate and comprehensive beliefs. My belief P is *prima facie* rational, then, just in case there is a *prima facie* reason for me to believe P.

In addition, the concept of one belief being more reasonable than another can be explicated in terms of the above concepts. To say that in my current circumstances believing P is more reasonable for me than believing Q is to say that on reflection I would think that given such circumstances, believing P is more appropriate than believing Q, insofar as my goal is now to have accurate and comprehensive beliefs. Similarly, to say that in my current circumstances withholding on P is more reasonable than either believing or disbelieving P is to say that on reflection I would think that given such circumstances, withholding on P is more appropriate than either believing or disbelieving P, insofar as my goal is now to have accurate and comprehensive beliefs.

Two thought experiments, each focusing on an extreme situation, place in sharp relief some of the most important features of this notion of epistemic rationality. First, consider skeptical thought experiments, for instance, the so-called "brain-in-a-vat" hypothesis, which imagines a world in which, unbeknownst to you, your brain is in a vat hooked up to equipment programmed to provide it with precisely the same visual, auditory, tactile, and other sensory inputs that you have in this world. As a result, your opinions about your immediate environment are the same as they are in this world. You have the same beliefs about your recent activities, your physical appearance, your present job, your current surroundings, and so on, but in fact you are a brain in a vat tucked away in a corner of a laboratory. So, in the brain-in-a-vat world, all these beliefs are mistaken, and mistaken not just in detail but massively mistaken. Even so, nothing in this scenario implies that you are irrational. On the contrary, in at least one important sense, your beliefs in the brain-in-a-vat world are as rational as they are in this world. After all, from your point of view, there is nothing to distinguish the two worlds.

Such scenarios are possible even on so-called "externalist" accounts of belief, which imply that the contents of beliefs are shaped by external as well as internal factors.[6] According to these accounts, even if from the

skin in there is no difference between you in the imagined brain-in-a-vat world and you in this world, what
you believe in the vat world might nonetheless be different from what you believe in this world. Externalist
accounts of belief are themselves controversial, but for
purposes here, it is a narrower point that needs making,
namely, the above thought experiment is compatible
with all but the most extreme versions of belief externalism. All versions of belief externalism imply that external as well as internal factors play a role in determining the contents of one's beliefs, but only the most
extreme allow the former to dominate the latter to such
an extent that extensive error becomes impossible. Indeed, a plausibility constraint on any proposed account
of belief is that it not a priori rule out the possibility of
extensive error. Any account of belief that meets this
plausibility constraint will be compatible with thought
experiments of the above sort, which imagine two situations, indistinguishable from your viewpoint, in which
you have very similar beliefs but in which these beliefs
differ markedly in accuracy.[7]

Being a brain-in-a-vat, or for that matter being in
any situation where you are thoroughly deceived, deprives you of knowledge of your environment, but it
does not also automatically prevent you from being rational in at least one important sense, a sense that is
closely associated with how things look from your perspective. Accuracy of opinion is the goal of this kind of
rationality, but not a prerequisite of it. Even in a bub-
bling vat, it is possible for you to have rational opinions. You may be a brain-in-a-vat, but you can
nonetheless be a rational brain-in-a-vat.

The second thought experiment concerns intellectual rebels who consciously reject the prevailing opinions of their communities and the intellectual practices
and assumptions of their traditions. The history of ideas
is filled with examples of iconoclasts and mavericks. Indeed, according to one influential reading of the history
of science, scientific progress is largely the result of
those who foment scientific revolutions by replacing
one paradigm with another. Of course, there will always
be questions as to just how extensively the rebels were
rejecting prevailing opinions and practices as opposed
to making novel applications of opinions and practices
that were already in the air, but these historical questions do not affect the key conceptual point of the
thought experiment, which is that in one important

sense, being rational is not a matter of adhering to the
opinions, rules, practices, or presuppositions of one's
community or tradition. Even if, historically, most intellectual revolutionaries draw heavily upon assumptions and standards implicit in their intellectual traditions, there are possible scenarios in which this is not
the case, that is, scenarios in which the revolutionaries
reject in a wholesale manner the prevailing intellectual
assumptions and practices. However, the radical nature
of their intellectual revolutions does not necessarily
preclude their opinions from being rational in at least
one important sense.

These two thought experiments help mark off the
conceptual boundaries of a notion of rationality that
cannot be understood in terms of reliability or in terms
of social practices. Being rational in this sense is instead
a matter of making oneself invulnerable to intellectual
self-criticism to the extent possible, of living up one's
own deepest intellectual convictions and standards. It
requires one to have opinions and to use faculties,
methods, and practices that are capable of withstanding one's own, most severe critical scrutiny. One can be
rational in this sense even if one is a brain-in-a-vat
whose opinions are massively unreliable. Likewise, one
can be rational in this sense even if one's opinions,
methods, and assumptions are massively at odds with
those of one's community, era, and tradition.

The thought experiments also help illustrate
other key characteristics of this notion of rational
belief, as well as forestall some possible objections
against it. For example, they help make clear various respects in which this is an internalist notion of
rational belief. It is internalist, first, because the
conditions that make a belief rational are internal
psychological conditions, which involve no significant, direct reference to conditions external to the
individual. In particular, it is not a prerequisite that
the faculties or procedures generating the belief be
ones that are reliable in the individual's environment. Second, the notion is internalist because it
emphasizes the perspectives of individual believers,
as opposed to the perspective of the individual's
community or some other perspective external to
the individual. What any given individual believes
is almost always deeply influenced by what other
people believe. Nevertheless, the conditions that
make an individual's beliefs rational in the above

sense involve no significant, direct reference to the beliefs of other people. Third, when one's opinions are irrational, one is capable of generating on one's own a critique of those opinions. One need not rely on anything or anyone external to oneself to generate the criticism; all that is needed is thorough enough reflection. Thus, one always has access to the conditions that make an opinion irrational, in the sense that with enough thought one can oneself generate a criticism of the opinion. By contrast, when an opinion is rational, there is no such criticism of it available to one on reflection.

One can be rational in this sense despite having various intellectual flaws. Just as having opinions that are invulnerable to self-criticism does not necessarily inoculate one against error, so too it does not necessarily inoculate one against other intellectual failings. For example, some people are invulnerable to intellectual self-criticism only because they are dogmatically fixed on their opinions. They have views and employ methods that effectively shield these opinions against all potential challenges. Such dogmatists are intellectual flawed, but they are not necessarily irrational. Even if their opinions are bizarre, these opinions may be capable of standing up to their own toughest critical scrutiny. Their first-order opinions and second-order opinions about the faculties, methods, and practices used to generate and revise their first-order opinions may fit together in a way that satisfies even their own deepest intellectual dispositions. So, in one important sense, their beliefs may be rational despite being seriously mistaken, perhaps even delusional. Michel Foucault was fond of pointing out that the insane often reason impeccably from their delusional premises.[8] In a similar spirit, G.K. Chesterton once observed that madness is not always the absence of reason; sometimes it is the absence of everything else.

So, being fixed on an opinion is not necessarily a mark of irrationality. This is the case even in scientific contexts. As Duhem and Quine both emphasized,[9] there are always ways of immunizing a favored scientific hypothesis against revision when faced with recalcitrant data. Background assumptions, auxiliary hypotheses, and even observational reports can be revised in order to shield the hypothesis against revision. To be sure, such protective maneuvers may result in theories that are needlessly complex and inelegant,

and these are defects that are to be avoided, all else being equal. Be this as it may, one's theoretical opinions can display such defects and nonetheless be rational in one important sense.

The more general lesson here is that not every intellectual defect is a defect of rationality. Being dogmatic is an intellectual failing but not necessarily a failure of rationality, and the same is true of other intellectual failings. Imagine individuals who think that simple direct observation is a less reliable way of getting information about the environment than, say, relying on dreams. Most of us are convinced that we can rely on perception to provide us with generally reliable information about the world. Our beliefs, of course, typically extend beyond what we can directly perceive, but direct observational beliefs, we think, provide a kind of tether even for these beliefs. They constrain our other beliefs and, we trust, prevent them from being utter fabrications. By contrast, these hypothetical individuals are convinced, and not just superficially convinced but deeply and thoroughly convinced, that perception is a less reliable way of getting information about the world than dreams. Such individuals will be continually faced with data that appear to conflict with this conviction, but suppose that we stipulate that in good Duhemian fashion, they somehow find ways, albeit perhaps complex and inelegant, to explain away the apparently recalcitrant data. As a result, their beliefs are invulnerable to intellectual self-criticism. Their opinions and the faculties, methods, and practices that they use to generate these opinions are capable of standing up to their own, most severe scrutiny.

Because the convictions of such people strike us as bizarre, it can be tempting to insist that an adequate account of epistemic rationality should include conditions that altogether preclude the possibility of their being epistemically rational. Building such conditions into the account of epistemically rationality would have the effect of making it necessarily the case that people who regulate their opinions in accordance with such convictions are being irrational. Tempting as this may seem, it is a temptation to be avoided. Serious intellectual error is not necessarily a mark of irrationality. These people may have deeply flawed ways of obtaining information about the world but they are not necessarily being irrational.

On the other hand, it is irrational for you and I to organize our opinions about the world in accordance with our dreams as opposed to our observations, but not because doing so is inherently and necessarily irrational but rather because it is sharply at odds with our deepest convictions about how to obtain information about the external world. Among these convictions is that relying on perception is a more effective way of having accurate and comprehensive beliefs than relying on dreams. For example, I believe, and presumably reflection would not cause me to change my mind, that when I seem to see a cat in front of me, then all else being equal it is reliable for me to believe that there is in fact a cat in front of me. I have analogous convictions about ostensible memories. For example, I believe, and on reflection would continue to believe, that when I seem to remember seeing to see a cat in front of me yesterday, then all else being equal it is reliable for me to believe that I in fact did seem to see a cat in front of me yesterday.[10] By contrast, I do not think that dreams are a straightforward, reliable way to get information about the external world. For example, I do not think that my dreaming that I had a conversation with my grandfather when I was an adult and he was a child is a reliable indication that this conversation in fact took place.

Because the above notion of epistemic rationality emphasizes the perspectives of individual believers, it leaves room for the possibility that one can be epistemically rational and yet distant from the truth, and so too it leaves room for the possibility that one can be epistemically rational and yet distant from the opinions of other people. Nevertheless, every human is a social being, and not just behaviorally but also intellectually. My opinions and intellectual standards are constantly and thoroughly influenced by the people, culture and tradition surrounding me, and the same is true of you and every other human. But insofar as culture, tradition and other people shape the perspectives of individual believers, these factors also shape what it is epistemically rational for these individuals to believe. According to the above account, an individual's opinions are rational in an important sense if they are invulnerable to self-criticism, but whether opinions are invulnerable to self-criticism is a function of the individual's deepest convictions, which are typically absorbed from one's

social environment. Thus, the above account allows social factors to sculpt what it rational for an individual to believe, but it does so in a contingent way. It is at least possible for opinions that are capable of withstanding one's own most severe critical scrutiny to be seriously at odds with the opinions of one's contemporaries and tradition. Accordingly, it is possible for one's opinions to be seriously at odds with one's contemporaries and tradition and yet still be rational, as the thought experiment involving intellectual iconoclasts illustrates.

This conclusion stands in tension with the views of philosophers as otherwise diverse as Peirce, Wittgenstein, Rorty, Latour, Vygotsky, and Foucault, each of whom understands rationality as being constituted by social practices.[11] On such accounts, there is a necessary connection between what is rational and what the community or tradition would approve or at least tolerate. Accounts of this kind have also been embraced, in stronger or weaker forms, by a number of sociologists and historians of science.[12] One of the characteristic drawbacks of such accounts is that they are inherently conservative. They risk canonizing the intellectual *status quo* as intrinsically rational, and hence also risk demonizing intellectual revolutions as intrinsically irrational. Even moderate social approaches to epistemic rationality run these risks. For example, Catherine Elgin proposes an account of epistemic rationality that in many ways resembles the account I have given, but she also inserts a strong social requirement. She maintains that "an acceptable cognitive system must answer not just to my initially tenable commitments but to ours."[13] Such a requirement flirts with definitionally prohibiting intellectual revolutionaries from being epistemically rational.

By contrast, the account I have been defending, by emphasizing opinions that are invulnerable to criticism from one's own perspective, leaves room not only for the possibility of one's opinions being seriously unreliable and yet still being rational, but also for the possibility of their being seriously at odds with one's tradition or community and still being rational.

Even so, it is not an easy thing to be epistemically rational in this sense. On the contrary, there can be sharp divergence between one's current opinions and one's own deep epistemic convictions. Nothing in the above account precludes the possibility that one would be radically dissatisfied with one's current opinions, given deep enough and thorough enough reflection. This is so even though reflection on one's current opinions must begin with these very opinions.

Consider an analogy with a reading of the history of science that views this history not as a series of successive revolutions but rather as one in which past theories are largely incorporated into successor theories. On this view of science, there are rarely wholesale rejections of immediately preceding theories, but nevertheless the changes over time made by successive theories can be momentous, with both deep and broad implications. An analogous point is true of the critiques one can mount on reflection against one's own current opinions. Given that the critiques must originate with one's current opinions, it may be relatively rare for them to result in a wholesale rejection of one's current opinions, but it nonetheless would be incorrect to say that what epistemic rationality requires on the above account is nothing more than a tidying up of one's belief system. This way of putting the matter under appreciates how extensive and significant self-critiques can be, and hence how extensive the current irrationality can be. Any homeowner knows how a little light dusting can sometimes turn into an extensive spring cleaning and can occasionally even result in major renovations.

Moreover, it is all the more difficult to meet one's own deepest epistemic standards, given the "quick and dirty" ways we have to acquire most of our beliefs. Epistemic evaluations assess opinions against a single goal, that of having accurate and comprehensive opinions, but we have numerous other goals and needs, which impose constraints on how much time and effort it is reasonable to devote to intellectual concerns. It is not feasible, given the total set of our goals and needs, to devote all one's time and energy to having accurate and comprehensive opinions. Indeed, many topics are neither intellectually nor pragmatically important. Accordingly, it would be foolish to spend much time on them. Thus, the small amount of time I have devoted to investigating and reflecting on a topic may have been reasonable, given the relative unimportance of the topic and the pressing nature of my other goals and needs, and yet my resulting opinions may very well be ones that on

deeper reflection I would not endorse as effectively satisfying the epistemic goal of having accurate and comprehensive beliefs. In other words, even if I have been a responsible believer with respect to a topic, devoting as much time and effort to it as is warranted, it need not be the case my beliefs about the topic are epistemically rational, illustrating yet again why it is often not a simple or easy matter to be epistemically rational in the above sense.[14]

This isn't surprising. One of life's most difficult pieces of business is that of fully and completely living up to one's own deepest standards of correct behavior, that is, of acting not just in accordance with what one superficially regards as defensible standards but rather in accordance with standards that one could and would endorse on the deepest, most thorough reflection. It is no easy matter to behave in a way that does not leave oneself vulnerable to self-criticism and regret. The press of our daily lives makes it all too easy to dwell in established patterns of behavior even when they have outlived their usefulness; our constitution as social animals makes all too easy to bow to other people's expectations of our behavior even when those expectations are not well grounded; and to make matters even more complicated, our own deepest standards can change over time, improving (we hope) with additional experience and insight.

No one should expect things to be any different with respect to our intellectual lives. It is every bit as difficult to have opinions that are invulnerable to self-criticism, and for precisely analogous reasons. The press of our daily lives makes it all too easy to dwell in established patterns of beliefs even when new information suggests that they have outlived their appropriateness; our constitution as social animals makes all too easy to bow to other people's opinions even when those opinions are not well grounded; and our own deepest intellectual standards and can change over time, improving and becoming more rigorous (we again hope) with additional experience and insight.

Notes

1. Adapted from Chapter Two of *Intellectual Trust in Oneself and Others* (Cambridge: Cambridge University Press, 2001).

2. Compare with Richard Jeffrey, *The Logic of Decision*, 2nd ed (Chicago: University of Chicago Press, 1983).

3. For more details, see Richard Foley, *Working Without a Net* (Oxford: Oxford University Press, 1993), pp. 98–100.

4. For a discussion of the distinction between epistemically rational belief and responsible belief, see Richard Foley, "The Foundational Role of Epistemology in a General Theory of Rationality," in *Virtue Epistemology*, eds. L. Zagzebski and A. Fairweather (Oxford: Oxford University Press, 2001).

5. For a more detailed discussion of the distinction between propositionally rational beliefs and doxastically rational beliefs, see Richard Foley, *The Theory of Epistemic Rationality* (Cambridge: Harvard University Press, 1987), 175–186.

6. See, for example, Donald Davidson, "On the Very Idea of a Conceptual Scheme," in *Proceedings and Addresses of the American Philosophical Association* 17 (1973–74), 5–20.

7. See Peter Klein, "Radical Interpretation and Global Skepticism," in E. LePore, ed., *Truth and Interpretation* (Oxford: Basil Blackwell, 1986), 369–386; Colin McGinn, 'Radical Interpretation and Epistemology," in Lepore, op. cit., 356–368; and Richard Foley, *Working Without a Net*, 70–75.

8. Foucault, *Madness and Civilization*, trans., R. Howard (New York: Pantheon, 1965).

9. Pierre Duhem, *The Aims and Structure of Physical Theory*, trans. P. Wiener (Princeton: Princeton University Press, 1951); W.V. Quine, "Two Dogmas of Empiricism," in *From a Logical Point of View*, 2nd ed. (New York: Harper, 1961), 20–46.

10. It is convictions such as these that provide the epistemic principles of Roderick Chisholm with an aura of plausibility. *See Chisholm, Theory of Knowledge*, editions in 1966, 1977, and 1989 (Engelwood Cliffs, NJ: Prentice-Hall).

11. C.S. Peirce, *Collected Works* (Cambridge: Harvard University Press, 1958); Ludwig Wittgenstein, *On Certainty*, trans. G.E.M. Anscombe and G.H. Von Wright (New York: Harper, 1969); Richard Rorty, *Philosophy and the Mirror of Nature* (Princeton: Princeton University Press, 1979): Bruno Latour, *Science in Action* (Cambridge; Harvard University Press, 1987); L.S. Vygotsky, *Mind in Society*, eds. Michael Cole et al. (Cambridge: Harvard University Press, 1978); Michel Foucault, *Discipline and Punish*, trans. A. Sheridan (New York: Vintage Books).

12. For example, see B. Barnes, *Scientific Knowledge and Sociological Theory* (London: Routledge, 1974); and D. Bloor, *Knowledge and Social Imagery*, 2nd ed. (Chicago: University of Chicago Press, 1991).

13. Catherine Elgin, *Considered Judgement* (Princeton: Princeton University Press, 1996), especially 115–145.

14. See Richard Foley, "The Foundational Role of Epistemology in a General Theory of Rationality."

◆ SOLIDARITY RATHER THAN RELATIVISM OR ABSOLUTISM ◆

45. SCIENCE AS SOLIDARITY

Richard Rorty

In our culture, the notions of "science," "rationality," "objectivity," and "truth" are bound up with one another. Science is thought of as offering "hard," "objective" truth: truth as correspondence to reality, the only sort of truth worthy of the name. Humanists like philosophers, theologians, historians, and literary critics have to worry about whether they are being "scientific"—whether they are entitled to think of their conclusions, no matter how carefully argued, as worthy of the term "true." We tend to identify seeking "objective truth" with "using reason," and so we think of the natural sciences as paradigms of rationality. We also think of rationality as a matter of following procedures laid down in advance, of being "methodical." So we tend to use "methodical," "rational," "scientific," and "objective" as synonyms.

Worries about "cognitive status" and "objectivity" are characteristic of a secularized culture in which the scientist replaces the priest. The scientist is now seen as the person who keeps humanity in touch with something beyond itself. As the universe was depersonalized, beauty (and, in time, even moral goodness) came to be thought of as "subjective." So truth is now thought of as the only point at which human beings are responsible to something nonhuman. A commitment to "rationality" and to "method" is thought to be a recognition of this responsibility. The scientist becomes a moral exemplar, one who selflessly exposes himself again and again to the hardness of fact.

One result of this way of thinking is that any academic discipline which wants a place at the trough, but is unable to offer the predictions and the technology provided by the natural sciences, must either pretend to imitate science or find some way of obtaining "cognitive status" without the necessity of discovering facts. Practitioners of these disciplines must either affiliate themselves with this quasi-priestly order by using terms like "behavioral sciences" or else find something other than "fact" to be concerned with. People in the humanities typically choose the latter strategy. They either describe themselves as concerned with value as opposed to facts or as developing and inculating habits of "critical reflection."

Neither sort of rhetoric is very satisfactory. No matter how much humanists talk about "objective values," the phrase always sounds vaguely confused. It gives with one hand what it takes back with the other. The distinction between the objective and the subjective was designed to parallel that between fact and value, so an objective value sounds as vaguely mythological as a winged horse. Talk about the humanists' special skill at critical reflection fares no better. Nobody really believes that philosophers or literary critics are better at critical thinking, or at taking big broad views of things, than theoretical physicists or microbiologists. So society tends to ignore both these kinds of rhetoric. It treats humanities as on a par with the arts, and thinks of both as providing pleasure rather than truth. Both are, to be sure, thought of as providing "high" rather than "low" pleasures. But an elevated and spiritual sort of pleasure is still a long way from the grasp of a truth.

These distinctions between hard facts and soft values, truth and pleasure, and objectivity and subjectivity are awkward and clumsy instruments. They are not suited to dividing up culture; they create more difficulties than they resolve. It would be best to find another vocabulary, to start afresh. But in order to do so, we first have to find a new way of describing the natural sciences. It is not a question of debunking or downgrading the natural scientist, but simply of ceasing to see him as a priest. We need to stop thinking of science

as the place where the human mind confronts the world, and of the scientist as exhibiting proper humility in the face of superhuman forces. We need a way of explaining why scientists are, and deserve to be, moral exemplars which does not depend on a distinction between objective fact and something softer, squishier, and more dubious.

To get such a way of thinking, we can start by distinguishing two senses of the term "rationality." In one sense, the one I have already discussed, to be rational is to be methodical: that is, to have criteria for success laid down in advance. We think of poets and painters as using some faculty other than "reason" in their work because, by their own confession, they are not sure of what they want to do before they have done it. They make up new standards of achievement as they go along. By contrast, we think of judges as knowing in advance what criteria a brief will have to satisfy in order to invoke a favorable decision, and of business people as setting well-defined goals and being judged by their success in achieving them. Law and business are good examples of rationality, but the scientist, knowing in advance what would count as disconfirming his hypothesis and prepared to abandon that hypothesis as a result of the unfavorable outcome of a single experiment, seems a truly heroic example. Further, we seem to have a clear criterion for the success of a scientific theory—namely, its ability to predict, and thereby to enable us to control some portion of the world. If to be rational means to be able to lay down criteria in advance, then it is plausible to take natural science as the paradigm of rationality.

The trouble is that in this sense of "rational" the humanities are never going to qualify as rational activities. If the humanities are concerned with ends rather than means, then there is no way to evaluate their success in terms of antecedently specified criteria. If we already knew what criteria we wanted to satisfy, we would not worry about whether we were pursuing the right ends. If we thought we knew the goals of culture and society in advance, we would have no use for the humanities—as totalitarian societies in fact do not. It is characteristic of democratic and pluralistic societies to continually redefine their goals. But if to be rational means to satisfy criteria, then this process of redefinition is bound to be nonrational. So if the humanities are to be viewed as rational activities, rationality will have to be thought of as something other than the satisfaction of criteria which are stabile in advance.

Another meaning for "rational" is, in fact, available. In this sense, the word means something like "sane" or "reasonable" rather than "methodical." It names a set of moral virtues: tolerance, respect for the opinions of those around one, willingness to listen, reliance on persuasion rather than force. These are the virtues which members of a civilized society must possess if the society is to endure. In this sense of "rational," the word means something more like "civilized" than like "methodical." When so construed, the distinction between the rational and the irrational has nothing in particular to do with the difference between the arts and the sciences. On this construction, to be rational is simply to discuss any topic—religious, literary, or scientific—in a way which eschews dogmatism, defensiveness, and righteous indignation.

There is no problem about whether, in this latter, weaker, sense, the humanities are "rational disciplines." Usually humanists display the moral virtues in question. Sometimes they don't, but then sometimes scientists don't either. Yet these moral virtues are felt to be not enough. Both humanists and the public hanker after rationality in the first, stronger sense of the term: a sense which is associated with objective truth, correspondence to reality, and method, and criteria.

We should not try to satisfy this hankering, but rather try to eradicate it. No matter what one's opinion of the secularization of culture, it was a mistake to try to make the natural scientist into a new sort of priest, a link between the human and the nonhuman. So was the idea that some sorts of truths are "objective" whereas others are merely "subjective" or "relative"— the attempt to divide up the set of true sentences into "genuine knowledge" and "mere opinion," or into the "factual" and "judgmental." So was the idea that the scientist has a special method which, if only the humanists would apply it to ultimate values, would give us the same kind of self-confidence about the moral ends as we now have about technological means. I think that we should content ourselves with the second, "weaker" conception of rationality, and avoid the first, "stronger" conception. We should avoid the idea that

there is some special virtue in knowing in advance what criteria you are going to satisfy, in having standards by which to measure progress.

One can make these issues somewhat more concrete by taking up the current controversy among philosophers about the "rationality of science." For some twenty years, ever since the publication of Thomas Kuhn's book *The Structure of Scientific Revolutions*, philosophers have been debating whether science is rational. Attacks on Kuhn for being an "irrationalist" are now as frequent and as urgent as were, in the thirties and forties, attacks on the logical positivists for saying that moral judgments were "meaningless." We are constantly being warned of the danger of "relativism," which will beset us if we give up our attachment to objectivity, and to the idea of rationality as obedience to criteria.

Whereas Kuhn's enemies routinely accuse him of reducing science to "mob psychology," and pride themselves on having (by a new theory of meaning, or reference, or verisimilitude) vindicated the "rationality of science," his pragmatist friends (such as myself) routinely congratulate him on having softened the distinction between science and non-science. It is fairly easy for Kuhn to show that the enemies are attacking a straw man. But it is harder for him to save himself from his friends. For he has said that "there is no theory-independent way to reconstruct phrases like 'really there.' "[1] He has asked whether it really helps "to imagine that there is some one full, objective, true account of nature and that the proper measure of scientific achievement is the extent to which it brings us closer to that ultimate goal."[2] We pragmatists quote these passages incessantly in the course of our effort to enlist Kuhn in our campaign to drop the objective-subjective distinction altogether.

What I am calling "pragmatism" might also be called "left-wing Kuhnianism." It has been also rather endearingly called (by one of its critics, Clark Glymour) the "new fuzziness," because it is an attempt to blur just those distinctions between the objective and the subjective and between fact and value which the criterial conception of rationality has developed. We fuzzies would like to substitute the idea of "unforced agreement" for that of "objectivity." We should like to put all of culture on an epistemological level—or, to put it another way, we would like to get rid of the idea of "epistemological level" or "cognitive status." We would like to disabuse social scientists and humanists of the idea that there is something called "scientific status" which is a desirable goal. On our view, "truth" is a univocal term. It applies equally to the judgments of lawyers, anthropologists, physicists, philologists and literary critics. There is no point in assigning degrees of "objectivity" or "hardness" to such disciplines. For the presence of unforced agreement in all of them gives us everything in the way of "objective truth" which one could possibly want: namely, intersubjective agreement.

As soon as one says that objectivity is intersubjectivity, one is likely to be accused of being a relativist. That is the epithet traditionally applied to pragmatists. But this epithet is ambiguous. It can name any of three different views. The first is the silly and self-refuting view that every belief is as good as every other. The second is the wrong-headed view that "true" is an equivocal term, having as many meanings as there are contexts of justification. The third is the ethnocentric view that there is nothing to be said about either truth or rationality apart from descriptions of the familiar procedures of justification which a given society—*ours*—uses in one or another area of inquiry. The pragmatist does hold this third, ethnocentric, view. But he does not hold the first or the second.

But "relativism" is not an appropriate term to decribe this sort of ethnocentrism. For we pragmatists are not holding a positive theory which says that something is relative to something else. Instead, we are making the purely *negative* point that we would be better off without the traditional distinctions between knowledge and opinion, construed as the distinction between truth as correspondence to reality and truth as a commendatory term for well-justified belief. Our opponents call this negative claim "relativistic" because they cannot imagine that anybody would seriously deny that truth has an intrinsic nature. So when we say that there is nothing to be said about truth save that each of us will commend as true those beliefs which he or she finds good to believe, the realist is inclined to interpret this as one more positive theory about the nature of truth: a theory according to which

truth is simply the contemporary opinion of a chosen individual or group. Such a theory would, of course, be self-refuting. But we pragmatists do not have a theory of truth, much less a relativistic one. As partisans of solidarity, our account of the value of cooperative human inquiry has only an ethical base, not an epistemological or metaphysical one.

To say that we must be ethnocentric may sound suspicious, but this will only happen if we identify ethnocentrism with pig-headed refusal to talk to representatives of other communities. In my sense of ethnocentrism, to be ethnocentric is simply to work by our own lights. The defense of ethnocentrism is simply that there are no other lights to work by. Beliefs suggested by another individual or another culture must be tested by trying to weave them together with beliefs which we already have. We *can* so test them, because everything which we can identify as a human being or as a culture will be something which shares an enormous number of beliefs with us. (If it did not, we would simply not be able to recognize that it was speaking a language, and thus that it had any beliefs at all.)

This way of thinking runs counter to the attempt, familiar since the eighteenth century, to think of political liberalism as based on a conception of the nature of man. To most thinkers of the Enlightenment, it seemed clear that the access to Nature which physical science had provided should now be followed by the establishment of social, political, and economic institutions which were "in accordance with Nature." Ever since, liberal social thought has centered on social reform as made possible by objective knowledge of what human beings are like—not knowledge of what Greeks or Frenchmen or Chinese are like, but of humanity as such. This tradition dreams of a universal human community which will exhibit a nonparochial solidarity because it is the expression of an ahistorical human nature.

Philosophers who belong to this tradition, who wish to ground solidarity in objectivity, have to construe truth as correspondence to reality. So they must construct an epistemology which had room for a kind of justification which is not merely social but natural, springing from human nature itself, and made possible by a link between that part of nature and the rest of nature. By contrast, we pragmatists, who wish to reduce objectivity to solidarity, do not require either a meta-physics or an epistemology. We do not need an account of a relation between beliefs and objects called "correspondence," nor an account of human cognitive abilities which ensures that our species is capable of entering into that relation. We see the gap between truth and justification not as something to be bridged by isolating a natural and transcultural sort of rationality which can be used to criticize certain cultures and praise others, but simply as the gap between the actual good and the possible better. From a pragmatist point of view, to say that what is rational for us now to believe may not be *true* is simply to say that somebody may come up with a better idea.

On this pragmatist view of rationality as civility, inquiry is a matter of continually reweaving a web of beliefs rather than the application of criteria to cases. Criteria change in just the way other beliefs change, and there is no touchstone which can preserve any criterion from possible revision. That is why the pragmatist is not frightened by the specter of "cultural relativism." Our interchange with other communities and cultures is not to be thought of as a clash between irreconcilable systems of thought, deductively inferred from incompatible first premises. Alternative cultures should not be thought of on the model of alternative geometries—as irreconcilable because they have axiomatic structures and contradictory axioms. Such geometries are *designed* to be irreconcilable. Individual and cultural webs of belief are not so designed, and do not have axiomatic structures.

Cultures can, indeed, protect themselves by institutionalizing knowledge-claims and making people suffer who do not hold certain beliefs. But such institutional backups take the form of bureaucrats and policemen, not of "rules of language" or "criteria of rationality." The criterial conception of rationality has suggested that every distinct culture comes equipped with certain unchallengeable axioms, "necessary truths," and that these form barriers to communication between cultures. So it has seemed as if there could be no conversation between cultures but only subjugation by force. On the pragmatic conception of rationality, there are no such barriers. The distinction between different cultures differs only in degree from the distinction between theories held by members of a single culture. The Tasmanian aborigines and the British colonies, for example, had trouble in communicating, but this trouble was different only in extent from the difficulties in communication experienced by Gladstone and Disraeli. The trouble in all such cases is just the difficulty of explaining why other people disagree with us, and of reweaving our beliefs so as to fit the fact of disagreement together with the other beliefs we hold. The same pragmatist (and, more specifically, Quinean) arguments which dispose of the positivist's distinction between analytic and synthetic truths dispose of the anthropologists' distinction between the intercultural and the intracultural.

Another reason for describing us as "relativistic" is that we pragmatists drop the idea that inquiry is destined to converge to a single point—that Truth is "out there" waiting for human beings to arrive at it. This idea seems to us an unfortunate attempt to carry a religious conception over into a culture. All that is worth preserving of the claim that rational inquiry will converge to a single point is the claim that we must be able to explain why past false views were held in the past, and thus explain how we go about reeducating our benighted ancestors. To say that we think we are heading in the right direction is just to say, with Kuhn, that we can, by hindsight, tell the story of the past as a story of progress.

But the fact that we can trace such a direction and tell such a story does not mean that we have gotten closer to a goal which is out there waiting for us. We cannot, I think, imagine a moment at which the human race could settle back and say, "Well, now that we've finally arrived at the Truth we can relax." Paul Feyerabend is right in suggesting that we should discard the metaphor of inquiry, and human activity generally, as converging rather than proliferating, becoming more unified rather than more diverse. On the contrary, we should relish the thought that the sciences as well as the arts will *always* provide a spectacle of fierce competition between alternative theories, movements, and schools. The end of human activity is not rest, but rather richer and better human activity. We should think of human progress as making it possible for human beings to do more interesting things and be more interesting people, not as heading toward a place which has somehow been prepared for us in advance. To drop the criterial conception of rationality in favor of the pragmatist conception would be to give up the idea of Truth as something to which we were responsible. Instead we should think of "true" as a word which applies to those beliefs upon which we are able to agree, as roughly synonymous with "justified." To say that beliefs can be agreed upon without being true is, once again, merely to say that somebody might come up with a better idea.

Another way of characterizing this line of thought is to say that pragmatists would like to drop the idea that human beings are responsible to a nonhuman power. We hope for a culture in which questions about the "objectivity of value" or the "rationality of science" would seem equally unintelligible. Pragmatists would like to replace the desire for objectivity—the desire to be in touch with a reality which is more than some community with which we identify ourselves—with the desire for solidarity with that community. They think that the habits of relying on persuasion rather than force, of respect for the opinions of colleagues, of curiosity and eagerness for new data and ideas, are the *only* virtues which scientists have. They do not think that there is an intellectual virtue called "rationality" over and above these moral virtues.

On this view there is no reason to praise scientists for being more "objective" or "logical" or "methodical" or "devoted to truth" than other people. But there is plenty of reason to praise the institutions they have developed and within which they work, and to use these as models for the rest of culture. For these institutions give concreteness and detail to the idea of "unforced agreement." Reference to such institutions fleshes out the idea of "a free and open encounter"—the sort of encounter in which truth cannot fail to win. On this view, to say that truth will win in such an encounter is not to make a metaphysical claim about the connection between human reason and the nature of things. It is merely to say that the best way to find out what to believe is to listen to as many suggestions and arguments as you can.

My rejection of traditional notions of rationality can be summed up by saying that the only sense in which science is exemplary is that it is a model of human solidarity. We should think of the institutions

and practices which make up various scientific communities as providing suggestions about the way in which the rest of culture might organize itself. When we say that our legislatures are "unrepresentative" or "dominated by special interests," or that the art world is dominated by "fashion," we are contrasting these areas of culture with areas which seem to be in better order. The natural sciences strike us as being such areas. But, on this view, we shall not explain this better order by thinking of the scientists as having a "method" which the rest of us would do well to imitate, nor as benefiting from the desirable hardness of their subjects compared with the undesirable softness of other subjects. If we say that sociology or literary criticism "is not a science," we shall mean merely that the amount of agreement among sociologists or literary critics on what counts as significant work, work which needs following up, is less than among, say, microbiologists.

Pragmatists will not attempt to explain this latter phenomenon by saying that societies or literary texts are squishier than molecules, or than the human sciences cannot be as "value-free" as the natural sciences, or that the sociologists and critics have not yet found their paradigms. Nor will they assume that "a science" is necessarily something which we want sociology to be. One consequence of their view is the suggestion that perhaps "the human sciences" *should* look quite different from the natural sciences. This suggestion is not based on epistemological or metaphysical considerations which show that inquiry into societies must be different from inquiry into things. Instead, it is based on the observation that natural scientists are interested primarily in predicting and controlling the behavior of things, and that prediction and control may not be what we want from our sociologists and our literary critics.

Despite the encouragement he has given it, however, Kuhn draws back from this pragmatist position. He does so when he asks for an explanation of "why science works." The request for such an explanation binds him together with his opponents and separates him from his left-wing friends. Anti-Kuhnians tend to unite in support of the claim that "merely psychological or sociological reasons" will not explain why natural science is so good at predicting. Kuhn joins them when he says that he shares "Hume's itch"—the desire for "an explanation of the viability of the whole language game that involves 'induction' and underpins the form of life we live."[3]

Pragmatists think that one will suffer from Hume's itch only if one has been scratching oneself with what has sometimes been called "Hume's fork"—the distinction between "relations of ideas" and "matters of fact." This distinction survives in contemporary philosophy as the distinction between "questions of language" and "questions of fact." We pragmatists think that philosophers of language such as Wittgenstein, Quine, Goodman, Davidson, and others have shown us how to get along without these distinctions. Once one has lived without them for a while, one learns to live without those between knowledge and opinion, or between subjective and objective, as well. The purposes served by the latter distinctions come to be served by the unproblematic sociological distinction between areas in which unforced agreement is relatively infrequent and areas in which it is relatively frequent. So we do not itch for an explanation of the success of recent Western science any more than for the success of recent Western politics. That is why we fuzzies applaud Kuhn when he says that "one does not know what a person who denies the rationality of learning from experience is trying to say," but are aghast when he goes on to ask *why* "we have no rational alternatives to learning from experience."[4]

On the pragmatist view, the contrast between "relations of ideas" and "matters of fact" is a special case of the bad seventeenth-century contrasts between being "in us" and being "out there," between subject and object, between our beliefs and what those beliefs (moral, scientific, theological, etc.) are trying to get right. Pragmatists avoid this latter contrast by instead contrasting our beliefs with proposed alternative beliefs. They recommend that we worry only about the choice between two hypotheses, rather than about whether there is something which "makes" either true. To take this stance would rid us of questions about the objectivity of value, the rationality of science, and the causes of the viability of our language games. All such theoretical questions would be replaced with practical questions about whether we ought to keep our present values, theories, and practices or try to replace them with others. Given such a replacement, there would be nothing to be responsible to except ourselves.

This may sound like solipsistic fantasy, but the pragmatist regards it as an alternative account of the nature of intellectual and moral responsibility. He is suggesting that instead of invoking anything like the idea-fact, or language-fact, or mind-world, or subject-object distinctions to explicate our intuition that there is something out there to be responsible to, we just drop that intuition. We should drop it in favor of the thought that we might be better than we presently are—in the sense of being better scientific theorists, or citizens, or friends. The backup for this intuition would be the actual or imagined existence of other human beings who were already better (utopian fantasies, or actual experience, of superior individuals or societies). On this account, to be responsible is a matter of what Peirce called "contrite fallibilism" rather than of respect for something beyond. The desire for "objectivity" boils down to a desire to acquire beliefs which will eventually receive unforced agreement in the course of a free and open encounter with people holding other beliefs.

Pragmatists interpret the goal of inquiry (in any sphere of culture) as the attainment of an appropriate mixture of unforced agreement with tolerant disagreement (where what counts as appropriate is determined, within that sphere, by trial and error). Such a reinterpretation of our sense of responsibility would, if carried through, gradually make unintelligible the subject-object model of inquiry, the child-parent model of moral obligation, and the correspondence theory of truth. A world in which those models, and that theory, no longer had any intuitive appeal would be a pragmatist's paradise.

When Dewey urged that we try to create such a paradise, he was said to be irresponsible. For, it was said, he left us bereft of weapons to use against our enemies; he gave us nothing with which to "answer the Nazis." When we new fuzzies try to revive Dewey's repudiation of criteriology, we are said to be "relativistic." We must, people say, believe that every coherent view is as good as every other, since we have no "outside" touchstone for choice among such views. We are said to leave the general public defenseless against the witch doctor, the defender of creationism, or anyone else who is clever and patient enough to deduce a consistent and wide-ranging set of theorems from his "alternative first principles."

Nobody is convinced when we fuzzies say that we can be just as morally indignant as the next philosopher. We are suspected of being contritely fallibilist when righteous fury is called for. Even when we actually display appropriate emotions we get nowhere, for we are told that we have no *right* to these emotions. When we suggest that one of the few things we know (or need to know) about truth is that it is what wins in a free and open encounter, we are told that we have defined "true" as "satisfies the standards of our community." But we pragmatists do not hold this relativist view. We do not infer from "there is no way to step outside communities to a neutral standpoint" that "there is no rational way to justify liberal communities over totalitarian communities." For that inference involves just the notion of "rationality" as a set of ahistorical principles which pragmatists abjure. What we in fact infer is that there is no way to beat totalitarians in argument by appealing to shared common premises, and no point in pretending that a common human nature makes the totalitarians unconsciously hold such premises.

The claim that we fuzzies have no right to be furious at moral evil, no right to commend our views as true unless we simultaneously refute ourselves by claiming that there are objects out there which *make* those views true, begs all the theoretical questions. But it gets to the practical and moral heart of the matter. This is the question of whether notions like "unforced agreement" and "free and open encounter"—descriptions of social situations—can take the place in our moral lives of notions like "the world," "the will of God," "the moral law," "what our beliefs are trying to represent accurately," and "what makes our beliefs true." All the philosophical presuppositions which make Hume's fork seem inevitable are ways of suggesting that human communities must justify their existence by striving to attain a nonhuman goal. To suggest that we can forget about Hume's fork, forget about being responsible to what is "out there," is to suggest that human communities can only justify their existence by comparisons with other actual and possible human communities.

I can make this contrast a bit more concrete by asking whether free and open encounters, and the kind of community which permits and encourages such encounters, are for the sake of truth and goodness, or whether "the quest for truth and goodness" is simply the quest for that kind of community. Is the sort of community which is exemplified by groups of scientific inquirers and by democratic political institutions a means to an end, or is the formation of such communities the only goal we need? Dewey thought that it was the only goal we needed, and I think he was right. But whether he was or not, this question is the one to which the debates about Kuhn's "irrationalism" and the new fuzzies' "relativism" will eventually boil down.

Dewey was accused of blowing up the optimism and flexibility of a parochial and jejune way of life (the American) into a philosophical system. So he did, but his reply was that *any* philosophical system is going-to be an attempt to express the ideals of *some* community's way of life. He was quite ready to admit that the virtue of his philosophy was, indeed, nothing more than the virtue of the way of life which it commended. On his view, philosophy does not justify affiliation with a community in the light of something ahistorical called "reason" or "transcultural principles." It simply expatiates on the special advantages of that community over other communities. Dewey's best argument for doing philosophy this way is also the best argument we partisans of solidarity have against partisans of objectivity: it is Nietzsche's argument that the traditional Western metaphysico-epistemological way of firming up our habits is not working anymore.

What would it be like to be less fuzzy and parochial than this? I suggest that it would be to become less genial, tolerant, open-minded, and fallibilist than we are now. In the nontrivial, pejorative, sense of "ethnocentric," the sense in which we congratulate ourselves on being less ethnocentric now than our ancestors were three hundred years ago, the way to avoid ethnocentrism is precisely to abandon the sort of thing we fuzzies are blamed for abandoning. It is to have only the most tenuous and cursory formulations of criteria for changing our beliefs, only the loosest and most flexible standards. Suppose that for the last three hundred years we had been using an explicit algorithm for determining how just a society was, and how good a physical theory was. Would we have developed either parliamentary democracy or relativity physics? Suppose that we had the sort of "weapons" against the fascists of which Dewey was said to deprive us—firm, unrevisable, moral principles which were not merely "ours" but "universal" and "objective." How could we avoid having these weapons turn in our hands and bash all the genial tolerance out of our own heads?

Imagine, to use another example, that a few years from now you open your copy of the *New York Times* and read that the philosophers, in convention assembled, have unanimously agreed that values are objective, science rational, truth a matter of correspondence to reality, and so on. Recent breakthroughs in semantics and meta-ethics, the report goes on, have caused the last remaining noncognitivists in ethics to recant. Similar breakthroughs in philosophy of science have led Kuhn formally to abjure his claim that there is no theory-independent way to reconstruct statements about what is "really there." All the new fuzzies have repudiated all their former views. By way of making amends for the intellectual confusion which the philosophical profession has recently caused, the philosophers have adopted a short, crisp, set of standards of rationality and morality. Next year the convention is expected to adopt the report of the committee charged with formulating a standard of aesthetic taste.

Surely the public reaction to this would not be "Saved!" but rather "Who on earth do these philosophers think they *are?*" It is one of the best things about the form of intellectal life we Western liberals lead that this *would* be our reaction. No matter how much we moan about the disorder and confusion of the current philosophical scene, about the treason of the clerks, we do not really want things any other way. What prevents us from relaxing and enjoying the new fuzziness is perhaps no more than cultural lag, the fact that the rhetoric of the Enlightenment praised the emerging natural sciences in a vocabulary which was left over from a less liberal and tolerant era. This rhetoric enshrined all the old philosophical oppositions between mind and world, appearance and reality, subject and object, truth and pleasure. Dewey thought that it was the continued prevalence of such oppositions which prevented us from seeing that modern science was a new and promising invention, a way of life which had not existed before and which ought to be encouraged and imitated, something which required a new rhetoric rather than justification by an old one.

Suppose that Dewey was right about this, and that eventually we learn to find the fuzziness which results from breaking down such oppositions spiritually comforting rather than morally offensive. What would the rhetoric of the culture, and in particular of the humanities, sound like? Presumably it would be more Kuhnian, in the sense that it would mention particular concrete achievements—paradigms—more, and "method" less. There would be less talk about rigor and more about originality. The image of the great scientist would not be of somebody who got it right but of somebody who made it new. The new rhetoric would draw more on the vocabulary of Romantic poetry and socialist politics, and less on that of Greek metaphysics, religious morality, or Enlightenment scientism. A scientist would rely on a sense of solidarity with the rest of her profession, rather than a picture of herself as battling through the veils of illusion, guided by the light of reason.

If all this happened, the term "science," and thus the oppositions between the humanities, the arts, and the sciences, might gradually fade away. Once "science" was deprived of an honorific sense, we might not need it for taxonomy. We might feel no more need for a term which groups together paleontology, physics, anthropology, and psychology than we do for one which groups together engineering, law, social work, and medicine. The people now called "scientists" would no longer think of themselves as a member of a quasi-priestly order, nor would the public think of themselves as in the care of such an order.

In this situation, "the humanities" would no longer think of themselves as such, nor would they share a common rhetoric. Each of the disciplines which now fall under that rubric would worry as little about its method or cognitive status as do mathematics, civil engineering, and sculpture. It would worry as little about its philosophical foundations. For terms which denoted disciplines would not be thought to divide "subject-matters," chunks of the world which had "interfaces" with each other. Rather, they would be thought to denote communities whose boundaries were as fluid as the interests of their members. In this heyday of the fuzzy, there would be as little reason to be self-conscious about the nature and status of one's discipline as, in the ideal democratic community, about the nature and status of one's race or sex. For one's ultimate loyalty would be to the larger community which permitted and encouraged this kind of freedom and insouciance. This community would serve no higher end than its own preservation and self-improvement, the preservation and enhancement of civilization. It would identify rationality with that effort, rather than with the desire for objectivity. So it would feel no need for a foundation more solid than reciprocal loyalty.

Notes

1. Thomas S. Kuhn, *The Structure of Scientific Revolutions*, 2d ed. (Chicago: University of Chicago Press, 1970), p. 206.
2. Ibid., p. 171.
3. Thomas S. Kuhn, "Rationality and Theory Choice," *Journal of Philosophy*, 80 (1983): 570.
4. Ibid., pp. 569–70.

✧ A FEMINISM CRITIQUE OF RELATIVISM ✧

46. QUINE AS FEMINIST: THE RADICAL IMPORT OF NATURALIZED EPISTEMOLOGY

Louise Antony

The truth is always revolutionary.
Antonio Gramsci

Introduction

Do we need a feminist epistemology? This is a very complicated question. Nonetheless it has a very simple answer: yes and no.

If we focus on the existence of what might be called a "feminist agenda" in epistemology—that is, if the question, "Do we need a feminist epistemology?" is taken to mean, "Are there specific questions or problems that arise as a result of feminist analysis awareness, or experience that any adequate epistemology must accommodate?"—then I think the answer is clearly yes. But if, taking for granted the existence of such an agenda, the question is taken to be, "Do we need, in order to accommodate these questions, insights, and projects, a specifically feminist alternative to currently available epistemological frameworks?" then the answer, to my mind, is no.

Now it is on this point that I find myself in disagreement with many feminist philosophers. For despite the diversity of views within contemporary feminist thought, and despite the disagreements about even the desiderata for a genuinely feminist epistemology, one theoretical conclusion shared by almost all those feminists who explicitly advocate the development of a feminist epistemology is that existing epistemological paradigms—particularly those available within the framework of contemporary analytic philosophy—are fundamentally unsuited to the needs of feminist theorizing.

It is this virtual unanimity about the inadequacy of contemporary analytic epistemology that I want to challenge. There is an approach to the study of knowledge that promises enormous aid and comfort to feminists attempting to expose and dismantle the oppressive intellectual ideology of a patriarchal, racist, class-stratified society, and it is an approach that lies squarely within the analytic tradition. The theory I have in mind is Quine's "naturalized epistemology"—the view that the study of knowledge should be treated as the empirical investigation of knowers.

My primary aim in this essay is to highlight the virtues, from a feminist point of view, of naturalized epistemology. But—as is no doubt quite clear—I have a secondary, polemical aim as well. I want to confront head-on the charges that mainstream epistemology is irremediably phallocentric, and to counter the impression, widespread among progressives both within and outside of the academy, that there is some kind of natural antipathy between radicalism on the one hand and the methods and aims of analytic philosophy on the other. I believe that this impression is quite false, and its promulgation is damaging not only to individual feminists—especially women—working within the analytic tradition, but also to the prospects for an adequate feminist philosophy.

The "Bias" Paradox

I think the best way to achieve both these aims—defending the analytic framework in general and showcasing naturalized epistemology in particular—is to put the latter to work on a problem that is becoming increasingly important within feminist theory. The issue I have in mind is the problem of how properly to conceptualize *bias*.

But what is the problem? Within certain theoretical frameworks, the analysis of the notion of "bias" is quite straightforward. In particular, strict empiricist epistemology concurs with liberal political theory in analyzing bias as the mere possession of belief or interest prior to investigation. But for anyone who wishes to criticize the liberal/empiricist ideal of an "open mind," the notion of bias is enormously problematic and threatens to become downright paradoxical.

Consider feminist theory: On the one hand, it is one of the central aims of feminist scholarship to expose the male-centered assumptions and interests—the male *biases*, in other words—underlying so much of received "wisdom." But on the other hand, there's an equally important strain of feminist theory that seeks to challenge the ideal of pure objectivity by emphasizing both the ubiquity and the value of certain kinds of partiality and interestedness. Clearly, there's a tension between those feminist critiques that accuse science or philosophy of displaying male bias and those that reject the ideal of impartiality.

The tension blossoms into paradox when critiques of the first sort are applied to the concepts of objectivity and impartiality themselves. According to many feminist philosophers, the flaw in the ideal of impartiality is supposed to be that the ideal itself is biased: Critics charge either that the concept of "objectivity" serves to articulate a masculine or patriarchal viewpoint (and possibly a pathological one),[1] or that it has the ideological function of protecting the rights of those in power, especially men.[2] But how is it possible to criticize the partiality of the concept of objectivity without presupposing the very value under attack? Put baldly: If we don't think it's good to be *im* partial, then how can we object to men's being *partial?*

The critiques of "objectivity" and "impartiality" that give rise to this paradox represent the main source of feminist dissatisfaction with existing epistemological theories. It's charged that mainstream epistemology will be forever unable to either acknowledge or account for the partiality and locatedness of knowledge, because it is wedded to precisely those ideals of objective or value-neutral inquiry that ultimately and inevitably subserve the interests of the powerful. The valorization of impartiality within mainstream epistemology is held to perform for the ruling elite the critical ideological function of *denying the existence of partiality itself.*[3]

Thus Lorraine Code, writing in the *APA Newsletter on Feminism and Philosophy,*[4] charges that mainstream epistemology (or what she has elsewhere dubbed "malestream" epistemology[5]) has "defined 'the epistemological project' so as to make it illegitimate to ask questions about the identities and specific circumstances of these knowers." It has accomplished this, she contends, by promulgating a view of knowers as essentially featureless and interchangeable, and by donning a "mask of objectivity and value-neutrality." The transformative potential of a feminist—as opposed to a malestream—epistemology lies in its ability to tear off this mask, exposing the "complex power structure of vested interest, dominance, and subjugation" that lurks behind it.

But not only is it not the case that contemporary analytic epistemology is committed to such a conception of objectivity, it was analytic epistemology that was largely responsible for initiating the critique of the empiricistic notions Code is attacking. Quine, Goodman,

Hempel, Putnam, Boyd, and others within the analytic tradition have all argued that a certain received conception of objectivity is untenable as an ideal of epistemic practice. The detailed critique of orthodox empiricism that has developed within the analytic tradition is in many ways more pointed and radical that the charges that have been leveled from without.

Furthermore, these philosophers, like many feminist theorists, have emphasized not only the *ineliminability* of bias but also the *positive value* of certain forms of it. As a result, the problems that arise for a naturalized epistemology are strikingly similar to those that beset the feminist theories mentioned above: Once we've acknowledged the necessity and legitimacy of partiality, *how do we tell the good bias from the bad bias?*

What kind of epistemology is going to be able to solve a problem like this? Code asserts that the specific impact of feminism on epistemology has been "to move the question '*Whose* knowledge are we talking about?' to a central place in epistemological discussion,"[6] suggesting that the hope lies in finding an epistemological theory that assigns central importance to consideration of the nature of the subjects who actually do the knowing. I totally agree: No theory that abjures empirical study of the cognizer, or of the actual processes by which knowledge develops, is ever going to yield insight on this question.

But more is required than this. If we as feminist critics are to have any basis for distinguishing the salutary from the pernicious forms of bias, we can't rest content with a *description* of the various ways in which the identity and social location of a subject make a difference to her beliefs. We need, in addition, to be able to make *normative* distinctions among various processes of belief-fixation as well. Otherwise, we'll never escape the dilemma posed by the bias paradox: either endorse pure impartiality or give up criticizing bias.[7]

It is here that I think feminist philosophy stands to lose the most by rejecting the analytic tradition. The dilemma will be impossible to escape, I contend, for any theory that eschews the notion of *truth*—for any theory, that is, that tries to steer some kind of middle course between absolutism and relativism. Such theories inevitably leave themselves without resources for making the needed normative

distinctions, because they deprive themselves of any conceptual tools for distinguishing the grounds of a statement's truth from the explanation of a statement's acceptance.

Naturalized epistemology has the great advantage over epistemological frameworks outside the analytic tradition (I have in mind specifically standpoint and postmodern epistemologies) in that it permits an appropriately realist conception of truth, viz., one that allows a conceptual gap between epistemology and metaphysics, between the world as we see it and the world as it is.[8] Without appealing to at least this minimally realist notion of truth, I see no way to even state the distinction we ultimately must articulate and defend. Quite simply, an adequate solution to the paradox must enable us to say the following: What makes the *good* bias good is that it facilitates the search for truth, and what makes the *bad* bias bad is that it impedes it.

Getting at the truth is complicated, and one of the things that complicates it considerably is that powerful people frequently have strong motives for keeping less powerful people from getting at the truth. It's one job of a critical epistemology, in my view, to expose this fact, to make the mechanisms of such distortions transparent. But if we, as critical epistemologists, lose sight of what we're after, if we concede that there's nothing at stake other than the matter of whose "version" is going to prevail, then our projects become as morally bankrupt and baldly self-interested as Theirs.

This brings me to the nature of the current discussion. I would like to be clear that in endorsing the project of finding a "feminist epistemology," I do not mean to be advocating the construction of a serviceable epistemological ideology "for our side." And when I say that I think naturalized epistemology makes a good feminist epistemology, I don't mean to be suggesting that the justification for the theory is instrumental. A good *feminist* epistemology must be, in the first place, a good epistemology, and that means being a theory that is likely to be *true*. But of course I would not think that naturalized epistemology was likely to be true unless I also thought it explained the facts. And among the facts I take to be central are the long-ignored experiences and wisdom of women.

In the next section, I will explain in more detail the nature of the charges that have been raised by feminist critics against contemporary analytic epistemology. I'll argue that the most serious of these charges are basically misguided—that they depend on a misreading of the canonical figures of the Enlightenment as well as of contemporary epistemology. In the last section, I'll return to the bias paradox and try to show why a naturalized approach to the study of knowledge offers some chance of a solution.

What Is Mainstream Epistemology and Why Is It Bad?

One difficulty that confronts anyone who wishes to assess the need for a "feminist alternative" in epistemology is the problem of finding out exactly what such an epistemology would be an alternative to. What is "mainstream" epistemology anyway? Lorraine Code is more forthright than many in her willingness to name the enemy. According to her, "mainstream epistemology," the proper object of feminist critique, is "post-positivist empiricist epistemology: the epistemology that still dominates in Anglo-American philosophy, despite the best efforts of socialist, structuralist, hermeneuticist, and other theorists of knowledge to deconstruct or discredit it."[9]

By the "epistemology that still dominates in Anglo-American philosophy," Code would have to be referring to the set of epistemological theories that have developed within the analytic paradigm, for analytic philosophy has been, in fact, the dominant philosophical paradigm in the English-speaking academic world since the early twentieth century.[10] This means, at the very least, that the agents of sexism within academic philosophy—the individuals who have in fact been the ones to discriminate against women as students, job applicants, and colleagues—have been, for the most part, analytic philosophers, a fact that on its own makes the analytic paradigm an appropriate object for feminist scrutiny.

But this is not the main reason that Code and others seek to "deconstruct or discredit" analytic epistemology. The fact that the analytic paradigm has enjoyed such an untroubled hegemony within this country during the twentieth century—the period of

the most rapid growth of American imperial power—suggests to many radical social critics that analytic philosophy fills an ideological niche. Many feminist critics see mainstream analytic philosophy as the natural metaphysical and epistemological complement to liberal political theory, which, by obscuring real power relations within the society, makes citizens acquiescent or even complicit in the growth of oppression, here and abroad.

What is it about analytic philosophy that would enable it to play this role? Some have argued that analytic or "linguistic" philosophy, together with its cognate fields (such as formal linguistics and computationalist psychology), is inherently male, "phallogocentric."[11] Others have argued that the analytic paradigm, because of its emphasis on abstraction and formalization and its valorization of elite skills, may be an instrument of cognitive control, serving to discredit the perspectives of members of nonprivileged groups.[12]

But most of the radical feminist critiques of "mainstream" epistemology (which, as I said, must denote the whole of analytic epistemology) are motivated by its presumed allegiance to the conceptual structures and theoretical commitments of the Enlightenment, which provided the general philosophical background to the development of modern industrialized "democracies."[13] By this means, "mainstream" epistemology becomes identified with "traditional" epistemology, and this traditional epistemology becomes associated with political liberalism. Feminist theorists like Alison Jaggar and Sandra Harding, who have both written extensively about the connection between feminist political analysis and theories of knowledge, have encouraged the idea that acceptance of mainstream epistemological paradigms is tantamount to endorsing liberal feminism. Jaggar contends that the connection lies in the radically individualistic conception of human nature common to both liberal political theory and Enlightenment epistemology. In a chapter entitled "Feminist Politics and Epistemology: Justifying Feminist Theory," she writes:

> Just as the individualistic conception of human nature sets the basic problems for the liberal political tradition, so it also generates the problems for

the tradition in epistemology that is associated historically and conceptually with liberalism. This tradition begins in the 17th century with Descartes, and it emerges in the 20th century as the analytic tradition. Because it conceives humans as essentially separate individuals, this epistemological tradition views the attainment of knowledge as a project for each individual on her or his own. The task of epistemology, then, is to formulate rules to enable individuals to undertake this project with success[14]

Harding, in a section of her book called "A Guide to Feminist Epistemologies," surveys what she sees as the full range of epistemological options open to feminists. She imports the essentially conservative political agenda of liberal feminism, which is focused on the elimination of formal barriers to gender equality, into mainstream epistemology, which she labels "feminist empiricism": "*Feminist empiricism* argues that sexism and androcentrism are social biases correctable by stricter adherence to the existing methodological norms of scientific inquiry."[15] Harding takes the hallmark of feminist empiricism (which on her taxonomy is the only alternative to feminist standpoint and postmodernist epistemologies) to be commitment to a particular conception of objectivity, which, again, is held to be part of the legacy of the Enlightenment. In her view, acceptance of this ideal brings with it faith in the efficacy of "existing methodological norms of science" in correcting biases and irrationalities within science, in the same way that acceptance of the liberal ideal of impartiality brings with it faith in the system to eliminate political and social injustice.

In Harding's mind, as in Jaggar's, this politically limiting conception of objectivity is one that can be traced to traditional conceptions of the knowing subject, specifically to Enlightenment conceptions of "rational man." The message, then, is that mainstream epistemology, because it still operates with this traditional conception of the self, functions to limit our understanding of the real operations of power, and of our place as women within oppressive structures. A genuine feminist transformation in our thinking therefore requires massive overhaul, if not outright repudiation, of central aspects of the tradition.

This is clearly the message that political scientist Jane Flax gleans from her reading of feminist philosophy; she argues that feminist theory ought properly to be viewed as a version of postmodern thought, since postmodern theorists and feminist theorists are so obviously engaged in a common project:

> Postmodern philosophers seek to throw into radical doubt beliefs still prevalent in (especially American) culture but derived from the Enlightenment . . . ;[16] feminist notions of the self, knowledge and truth are too contradictory to those of the Enlightenment to be contained within its categories. The way to feminist future(s) cannot lie in reviving or appropriating Enlightenment concepts of the person or knowledge.[17]

But there are at least two serious problems with this argument. The first is that the "tradition" that emerges from these critiques is a gross distortion and oversimplification of the early modern period. The critics' conglomeration of all classical and Enlightenment views into a uniform "traditional" epistemology obscures the enormous amount of controversy surrounding such notions as knowledge and the self during the seventeenth and eighteenth centuries, and encourages crude misunderstandings of some of the central theoretical claims.

The second problem is that the picture of analytic epistemology that we get once it's allied with this oversimplified "traditional" epistemology is downright cartoonish. When we look at the actual content of the particular conceptions of objectivity and scientific method that the feminist critics have culled from the modern period, and which they subsequently attach to contemporary epistemology, it turns out that these conceptions are precisely the ones that have been the focus of *criticism* among American analytic philosophers from the 1950s onward.

The misreading of contemporary epistemology is partly a matter of the critics' failure to realize the extent to which analytic philosophy represents a *break* with tradition. I do not mean to deny that there were *any* important theoretical commitments common to philosophers of the early modern period. One such commitment, shared at least by classical rationalists and empiricists, and arguably by Kant, was an episte-mological meta-hypothesis called "externalism." This is the view that the proper goal of epistemological theory is the rational *vindication* of human epistemic practice. But if externalism is regarded as the hallmark of "traditional epistemology," then the identification of analytic epistemology with traditional epistemology becomes all the more spurious.

In what follows, I'll discuss in turn these two problems: first, the mischaracterization of the tradition, and then the caricature of contemporary analytic epistemology.

Rationalism Versus Empiricism: The Importance of Being Partial

What I want to show first is that the "traditional epistemology" offered us by Jaggar and Flax grafts what is essentially a rationalist (and in some respects, specifically Cartesian) theory of *mind* onto what is essentially an empiricist conception of *knowledge*. This is a serious error. Although Jaggar and Flax claim that there are deep connections between the one and the other, the fact of the matter is that they are solidly opposed. The conception of objectivity that is ultimately the object of radical critique—perfect impartiality—is only supportable as an epistemic ideal on an empiricist conception of *mind*. Thus, I'll argue, the rationalistic conception of the self attacked by Jaggar and Flax as unsuitable or hostile to a feminist point of view actually provides the basis for a critique of the view of knowledge they want ultimately to discredit.

Much of what is held to be objectionable in "traditional epistemology" is supposed to derive from the tradition's emphasis on *reason*. But different traditional figures emphasized reason in different ways. Only the rationalists and Kant were committed to what I'll call "cognitive essentialism," a feature of the "traditional" conception of mind that comes in for some of the heaviest criticism. I take cognitive essentialism to be the view (1) that there are certain specific properties the possession of which is both distinctive of and universal among human beings, (2) that these properties are cognitive in nature, (3) that our possession of these properties amounts to a kind of innate knowledge, and (4) that our status as moral agents is connected to the possession of these properties. Empiricists denied all these claims—in particular,

they denied that reason had anything but a purely instrumental role to play in either normative or nonnormative activity, and tended to be opposed to any form of essentialism, cognitive or otherwise.

Although the purely instrumental conception of reason is also criticized by feminist scholars, cognitive essentialism is the focus of one specific set of feminist concerns. It is held to be suspect on the grounds that such a doctrine could easily serve to legitimate the arrogant impulses of privileged Western white men: first to canonize their own culture- and time-bound speculations as revelatory of the very norms of human existence, and then simultaneously to deny the very properties deemed "universal" to the majority of human beings on the planet.

Here's how it is supposed to work: Cognitive essentialism is supposed to engender a kind of fantasy concerning actual human existence and the actual prerequisites of knowledge. Because of its emphasis on *cognitive* characteristics, it's argued, the view permits privileged individuals to ignore the fact of their embodiment, and with that, the considerable material advantages they enjoy in virtue of their class, gender, and race.[18] To the extent that the characteristics they find in themselves are the result of their particular privileges instead of a transcendent humanity, the fantasy provides a basis for viewing less-privileged people—who well may lack such characteristics—as inherently less human. But since these characteristics have been lionized as forming the essence of moral personhood, the fantasy offers a rationale for viewing any differences between themselves and others as negative deviations from a moral norm.

Recall, for example, that the particular elements of Enlightenment thought that Flax finds inimical to feminist theory and praxis are the alleged universality, transcendence, and abstractness assigned to the faculty of reason:

> The notion that reason is divorced from "merely contingent" existence still predominates in contemporary Western thought and now appears to mask the embeddedness and dependence of the self upon social relations, as well as the partiality and historical specificity of this self's existence. . . .

In fact, feminists, like other postmodernists, have begun to suspect that all such transcendental claims reflect and reify the experience of a few persons—mostly White, Western males[19]

But moreover, cognitive essentialism is supposed to lead to what Jaggar calls "individualism,"[20] the view that individual human beings are epistemically self-sufficient, that human society is unnecessary or unimportant for the development of knowledge. If the ideal "man of reason" is utterly without material, differentiating features, then the ideal knower would appear to be *pure* rationality, a mere calculating mechanism, a person who has been stripped of all those particular aspects of self that are of overwhelming human significance. Correlatively, as it is precisely the features "stripped off" the self by the Cartesian method that "traditional" epistemology denigrates as distorting influences, the ideally objective cognizer is also the man of reason. Knowledge is then achieved, it appears, not by active engagement with one's world and with the people in it, but by a pristine transcendence of the messy contingencies of the human condition.[21]

Lending support to Lorraine Code's grievance against "traditional" epistemology, Jaggar thus insists that it is this abstract and detached individualism that underwrites a solipsistic view of the construction of knowledge and precludes assigning any epistemological significance to the situation of the knower.

> Because it conceives humans as essentially separate individuals, this epistemological tradition views the attainment of knowledge as a project for each individual on his or her own. The task of epistemology, then, is to formulate rules to enable individuals to undertake this project with success.[22]

It is here that the link is supposed to be forged between the Cartesian/Kantian conception of the self and the particular conception of objectivity—objectivity as pure neutrality—that is thought to be pernicious.

But the individualism Jaggar takes to unite rationalists and empiricists is not in fact a view that *anyone* held. She derives it from a fairly common—indeed, almost canonical—misreading of the innate ideas debate. Significantly, Jaggar acknowledges the existence of disagreements within the early modern period, but avers that such issues as divided rationalists from empiricists are differences that make no difference. Both were foundationalists, she points out, and though the foundation for rationalists was self-evident truths of reason and the foundation for empiricists was reports of sensory experience, "in either case, . . . the attainment of knowledge is conceived as essentially a solitary occupation that has no necessary social preconditions."[23]

The reading, in other words, is that whereas the empiricists thought all knowledge came from experience, the rationalists thought *all knowledge came from reason*. But the second element of this interpretation is simply wrong. It was no part of *Descartes's* project (much less Kant's) to assert the self-sufficiency of reason. Note that a large part of the goal of the exercise of hyperbolic doubt in the *Meditations* was to establish the reliability of sensory experience, which Descartes took to be essential to the development of adequate knowledge of the world. And although he maintained the innateness of many ideas, including sensory ideas, he carefully and repeatedly explained that he meant by this only that human beings were built in such a way that certain experiences would trigger these ideas and no others.[24]

The bottom line is that rationalists, Descartes especially, did not hold the view that experience was inessential or even that it was unimportant; nor did they hold the view that the best epistemic practice is to discount one's own interests. The misreading that saddles Descartes with such views stems from a popular misconception about the innate ideas debate.

The disagreement between rationalists and empiricists was not simply about the existence of innate ideas. Both schools were agreed that the mind was natively structured and that that structure partially determined the shape of human knowledge. What they disagreed about was the *specificity* of the constraints imposed by innate mental structure. The rationalists believed that native structure placed quite specific limitations on the kinds of concepts and hypotheses the mind could form in response to experience, so that human beings were, in effect, natively *biased* toward certain ways of conceiving the world. Empiricists, on the other hand, held that there were relatively few native constraints on how the mind could organize sensory experience, and that such constraints as did exist were *domain-general* and *content-neutral*.

According to the empiricists, the human mind was essentially a mechanism for the manipulation of sensory data. The architecture of the mechanism was supposed to ensure that the concepts and judgments constructed out of raw sense experience accorded with the rules of logic. This did amount to a minimal constraint on the possible contents of human thought—they had to be logical transforms of sensory primitives—but it was a highly general one, applying to every subject domain in precisely the same way. Thus, on this model, any one hypothesis should be as good as any other as far as the mind is concerned, as long as both hypotheses are logically consistent with the sensory evidence.[25] This strict empiricist model of mind, as it turns out, supports many of the elements of epistemology criticized by Code, Jaggar, and others (e.g., a sharp observation/theory distinction, unmediated access to a sensory "given," and an algorithmic view of justification). I'll spell this out in detail in the next section. For present purposes, however, the thing to note is that the model provides clear warrant for the particular conception of the ideal of objectivity—perfect neutrality—that is the main concern of Jaggar and the others and that is supposed to follow from cognitive essentialism. Here's how.

Because the mind itself, on the empiricist model, makes no substantive contribution to the contents of thought, knowledge on this model is *entirely* experience-driven: All concepts and judgments are held to reflect regularities in an individual's sensory experience. But one individual cannot see everything there is to see—one's experience is necessarily limited, and there's always the danger that the regularities that form the basis of one's own judgments are not general regularities, but only artifacts of one's limited sample. (There is, in other words, a massive restriction-of-range problem for empiricists.) The question then arises how one can tell whether the patterns one perceives are present in nature generally, or are just artifacts of one's idiosyncratic perspective.

The empiricists' answer to this question is that one can gauge the general validity of one's judgments by the degree to which they engender reliable expectations about sensory experience. But although this answer addresses the problem of how to tell whether one's judgments are good or bad, it doesn't address the problem of how to get good judgments in the first place. Getting good judgments means getting good data—that is, exposing oneself to patterns of sensations that are representative of the objective distribution of sensory qualities throughout nature.

This idea immediately gives rise to a certain ideal (some would say fantasy) of epistemic location—the best spot from which to make judgments would be that spot which is *least particular*. Sound epistemic practice then becomes a matter of constantly trying to maneuver oneself into such a location—trying to find a place (or at least come as close as one can) where the regularities in one's own personal experience match the regularities in the world at large. A knower who could be somehow stripped of all particularities and idiosyncrasies would be the best possible knower there is.

This is not, however, a fantasy that would hold any particular appeal for a rationalist, despite the image of detachment evoked by a cursory reading of the *Meditations*. The rationalists had contended all along that sensory experience *by itself* was insufficient to account for the richly detailed body of knowledge that human beings manifestly possessed, and thus that certain elements of human knowledge—what classical rationalists called *innate ideas*—must be natively present, a part of the human essence.

Because the rationalists denied that human knowledge was a pure function of the contingencies of experience, they didn't need to worry nearly as much as the empiricists did about epistemic location. If it is the structure of mind, rather than the accidents of experience, that largely determines the contours of human concepts, then we can relax about at least the broad parameters of our knowledge. We don't have to worry that idiosyncratic features of our epistemic positions will seriously distort our worldviews, because the development of our knowledge is not dependent upon the patterns that happen to be displayed in our particular experiential histories. The regularities we "perceive" are, in large measure, regularities that we're *built* to perceive.

"Pure" objectivity—if that means giving equal weight to every hypothesis consistent with the data, or if it means drawing no conclusions beyond what can be supported by the data—is thus a nonstarter as an epistemic norm from a rationalist's point of view. The rationalists were in effect calling attention to the *value* of a certain kind of partiality: if the mind were not natively biased—i.e., disposed to take seriously certain kinds of hypotheses and to disregard or fail to even consider others—then knowledge of the sort that human beings possess would itself be impossible. There are simply too many ways of combining ideas, too many different abstractions that could be performed, too many distinct extrapolations from the same set of facts, for a pure induction machine to make much progress in figuring out the world.

The realization that perfect neutrality was not necessarily a good thing, and that bias and partiality are potentially salutary, is thus a point that was strongly present in the early modern period, *pace* Jaggar and Flax. There was no single "traditional" model of mind; the model that can properly be said to underwrite the conceptions of rationality and objectivity that Jaggar brings under feminist attack is precisely a model to which Descartes and the other rationalists were *opposed*, and, ironically, the one that, on the face of it, assigns the most significance to experience. And although it is the cognitive essentialists who are charged with deflecting attention away from epistemically significant characteristics of the knower, it was in fact these same essentialists, in explicit opposition to the empiricists, who championed the idea that human knowledge was necessarily "partial."

Hume, Quine, and the Break with Tradition

Let me turn now to the second serious problem with the feminist criticisms of "mainstream" epistemology: To the extent that there really is a "tradition" in epistemology, it is a tradition that has been explicitly rejected by contemporary analytic philosophy.

If the rationalists solved one problem by positing innate ideas, it was at the cost of raising another. Suppose that there are, as the rationalists maintained, innate ideas that perform the salutary function of narrowing down to a manageable set the hypotheses that

human minds have to consider when confronted with sensory data. That eliminates the problem faced by the empiricists of filtering out idiosyncratic "distortions." But now the question is, How can we be sure that these biases—so helpful in getting us to *a* theory of the world—are getting us to the *right* theory of the world? What guarantees that our minds are inclining us in the right direction? Innate ideas lead us somewhere, but do they take us where we want to go?

The rationalists took this problem very seriously. A large part of their project was aimed at validating the innate constraints, at showing that these mental biases did not lead us astray. Descartes's quest for "certainty" needs to be understood in this context: The method of hyperbolic doubt should be viewed not as the efforts of a paranoid to free himself forever from the insecurity of doubt, but as a theoretical exercise designed to show that the contours imposed on our theories by our own minds were proper reflections of the topography of reality itself.

It is at this point that we're in a position to see what rationalists and empiricists actually had in common—not a conception of mind, not a theory of how knowledge is constructed, but a theory of *theories* of knowledge. If there is a common thread running through Enlightenment epistemologies, it is this: a belief in the possibility of providing a *rational* justification of the processes by which human beings arrive at theories of the world. For the empiricists, the trick was to show how the content of all knowledge could be reduced to pure reports of sensory experience; for the rationalists, it was showing the indubitability of the innate notions that guided and facilitated the development of knowledge. Philosophers in neither group were really on a quest for certainty—all they wanted was a reliable map of its boundaries.

But if one of the defining themes of the modern period was the search for an externalist justification of epistemic practice, then *Hume* must be acknowledged to be the first postmodernist. Hume, an empiricist's empiricist, discovered a fatal flaw in his particular proposal for justifying human epistemic practice. He realized that belief in the principle of induction—the principle that says that the future will resemble the past or that similar things will behave similarly—could not be rationally justified. It was clearly not a truth of reason, since its denial was not self-contradictory. But neither could it be justified by experience: Any attempt to do so would be circular, because the practice of using past experience as evidence about the future is itself only warranted if one accepts the principle of induction.

Hume's "skeptical solution" to his own problem amounted to an abandonment of the externalist hopes of his time. Belief in induction, he concluded, was a *custom*, a tendency of mind ingrained by nature, one of "a species of natural instincts, which no reasoning or process of the thought and understanding is able, either to produce or to prevent."[26] For better or worse, Hume contended, we're stuck with belief in induction—we are constitutionally incapable of doubting it and conceptually barred from justifying it. The best we can do is to *explain* it.

Hume's idea was thus to offer as a replacement for the failed externalist project of rational justification of epistemic practice, the *empirical* project of characterizing the cognitive nature of creatures like ourselves, and then figuring out how such creatures, built to seek knowledge in the ways we do, could manage to survive and flourish. In this way, he anticipated to a significant degree the "postmodernist" turn taken by analytic philosophy in the twentieth century as the result of Quine's and others' critiques of externalism's last gasp—logical positivism.

Epistemology, according to Quine, had to be "naturalized," transformed into the empirical study of the actual processes—not "rational reconstructions" of those processes—by which human cognizers achieve knowledge.[27] If we accept this approach, several consequences follow for our understanding of knowledge and of the norms that properly govern its pursuit.

The first lesson is one that I believe may be part of what the feminist critics are themselves pointing to in their emphasis on the essential locatedness of all knowledge claims. The lesson is that all theorizing *takes some knowledge for granted*. Theorizing about theorizing is no exception. The decision to treat epistemology as the empirical study of the knower requires us to presume that we can, at least for a class of clear cases, distinguish epistemic success from epistemic failure. The impossibility of the externalist project shows us that we cannot expect to learn *from our philosophy* what counts as knowledge and how much of it we have; rather, we must begin with the assumption that we know certain things and figure out how that happened.

This immediately entails a second lesson. A naturalized approach to knowledge requires us to give up the idea that our own epistemic practice is transparent to us—that we can come to understand how knowledge is obtained either by a priori philosophizing or by casual introspection. It requires us to be open to the possibility that the processes that we actually rely on to obtain and process information about the world are significantly different from the ones our philosophy told us had to be the right ones.

Let me digress to point out a tremendous irony here, much remarked upon in the literature on Quine's epistemology and philosophy of mind. Despite his being the chief evangelist of the gospel that everything is empirical, Quine's own philosophy is distorted by his a prioristic commitment to a radically empiricistic, instrumentalist theory of psychology, namely psychological behaviorism. Quine's commitment to this theory—which holds that human behavior can be adequately explained without any reference to mental states or processes intervening between environmental stimuli and the organism's response—is largely the result of his philosophical antipathy to intentional objects, together with a residual sympathy for the foundationalist empiricism that he himself was largely responsible for dismantling.

Chomsky, of course, was the person most responsible for pointing out the in-principle limitations of behaviorism, by showing in compelling detail the empirical inadequacies of behaviorist accounts of the acquisition of language.[28] Chomsky also emphasized the indefensibility of the a prioristic methodological constraints that defined empiricistic accounts of the mind, appealing to considerations that Quine himself marshaled in his own attacks on instrumentalism in nonpsychological domains.[29]

Chomsky's own theory of language acquisition did not differ from the behaviorist account only, or even primarily, in its mentalism. It was also rationalistic: Chomsky quite self-consciously appealed to classical rationalistic forms of argument about the necessity of mental partiality in establishing the empirical case for his strong nativism. Looking at the actual circumstances of language acquisition, and then at the character of the knowledge obtained in those circumstances, Chomsky argued that the best explanation of the whole process is one that attributes to human beings a set of innate biases limiting the kinds of linguistic hypotheses available for their consideration as they respond to the welter of data confronting them.[30]

Chomsky can thus be viewed, and is viewed by many, as a naturalized epistemologist *par excellence*. What his work shows is that a naturalized approach to epistemology—in this case, the epistemology of language—yields an *empirical* vindication of rationalism. Since Chomsky's pathbreaking critique of psychological behaviorism, and the empiricist conception of mind that underlies it, nativism in psychology has flourished, and a significant degree of rationalism has been imported into contemporary epistemology.

A casual student of the analytic scene who has read only Quine could, of course, be forgiven for failing to notice this, given Quine's adamant commitment to an empiricist conception of mind; this may explain why so many of the feminist critics of contemporary epistemology seem to identify analytic epistemology with empiricism and to ignore the more rationalistic alternatives that have developed out of the naturalized approach. But I think, too, that the original insensitivity to the details of the original rationalist/empiricist controversy plays a role. Anyone who properly appreciates the import of the rationalist defense of the value of partiality will, I think, see where Quine's rejection of externalism is bound to lead.

So let's do it. I turn now to the feminist critique of objectivity and the bias paradox.

Quine as Feminist: What Naturalized Epistemology Can Tell Us About Bias

I've argued that much of the feminist criticism of "mainstream" epistemology depends on a misreading of both contemporary analytic philosophy, and of the tradition from which it derives. But it's one thing to show that contemporary analytic philosophy is not what the feminist critics think it is, and quite another to show that the contemporary analytic scene contains an epistemology that can serve as an adequate

feminist epistemology. To do this, we must return to the epistemological issues presented to us by feminist theory and see how naturalized epistemology fares with respect to them. I want eventually to show how a commitment to a naturalized epistemology provides some purchase on the problem of conceptualizing bias, but in order to do that, we must look in some detail at those feminist arguments directed against the notion of objectivity.

Capitalist Science and the Ideal of Objectivity

The "traditional" epistemology pictured in the work of Flax, Code, and Jaggar, I've argued, is an unvigorous hybrid of rationalist and empiricist elements, but the features that are supposed to limit it from the point of view of feminist critique of science all derive from the empiricist strain. Specifically, the view of knowledge in question contains roughly the following elements:

1. it is strongly foundationalist: It is committed to the view that there is a set of epistemically privileged beliefs, from which all knowledge is in principle derivable.
2. it takes the foundational level to be constituted by reports of sensory experience, and views the mind as a mere calculating device, containing no substantive contents other than what results from experience.
3. as a result of its foundationalism and its empiricism, it is committed to a variety of sharp distinctions: observation/theory, fact/value, context of discovery/context of justification.

This epistemological theory comes very close to what Hempel has termed "narrow inductivism,"[31] but I'm just going to call it the "Dragnet" theory of knowledge. To assess the "ideological potential" of the Dragnet theory, let's look first at some of the epistemic values and attitudes the theory supports.

To begin with, because of its empiricistic foundationalism, the view stigmatizes both inference and theory. On this view, beliefs whose confirmation depends upon logical relations to other beliefs bear a less direct, less "objective" connection to the world than reports of observations, which are supposed to provide us transparent access to the world.

To "actually see" or "directly observe" is better, on this conception, than to infer, and an invidious distinction is drawn between the "data" or "facts" (which are incontrovertible) on the one hand and "theories" and "hypotheses" (unproven conjectures) on the other.

Second, the view supports the idea that any sound system of beliefs can, in principle, be rationally reconstructed. That is, a belief worth having is either itself a fact or can be assigned a position within a clearly articulated confirmational hierarchy erected on fact. With this view comes a denigration of the epistemic role of hunches and intuitions. Such acts of cognitive impulse can be difficult to defend "rationally" if the standards of defense are set by a foundationalist ideal. When a hunch can't be defended, but the individual persists in believing it anyway, that's *ipso facto* evidence of irresponsibility or incompetence. Hunches that happen to pay off are relegated to the context of discovery and are viewed as inessential to the justification of the ensuing belief. The distinction between context of discovery and context of justification itself follows from foundationalism: As long as it's possible to provide a rational defense of a belief *ex post facto* by demonstrating that it bears the proper inferential relation to established facts, we needn't give any thought to the circumstances that actually gave rise to that belief. Epistemic location becomes, to that extent, evidentially irrelevant.

Finally, the Dragnet theory is going to lead to a certain conception of how systematic inquiry ought to work. It suggests that good scientific practice is relatively mechanical: that data gathering is more or less passive and random, that theory construction emerges from the data in a relatively automatic way, and that theory testing is a matter of mechanically deriving predictions and then subjecting them to decisive experimental tests. Science (and knowledge-seeking generally) will be good *to the extent that* its practitioners can conform to the ideal of objectivity.

This ideal of objective method requires a good researcher, therefore, to put aside all prior beliefs about the outcome of the investigation, and to develop a willingness to be carried wherever the facts may lead. But other kinds of discipline are necessary, too. Values are different in kind from facts, on this view, and so are not part of the confirmational hierarchy. Values (together with the emotions and desires connected with them) become, at best, epistemically irrelevant and, at worst, disturbances or distortions. Best to put them aside, and try to go about one's epistemic business in as calm and disinterested a way as possible.

In sum, the conception of ideal epistemic practice yielded by the Dragnet theory is precisely the conception that the feminist critics disdain. Objectivity, on this view (I'll refer to it from now on as "Dragnet objectivity"), is the result of complete divestiture—divestiture of theoretical commitments, of personal goals, of moral values, of hunches and intuitions. We'll get to the truth, sure as taxes, provided everyone's willing to be rational and to play by the (epistemically relevant) rules. Got an especially knotty problem to solve? Just the facts, ma'am.

Now let's see how the Dragnet theory of knowledge, together with the ideal of objectivity it supports, might play a role in the preservation of oppressive structures.

Suppose for the sake of argument that the empirical claims of the radical critics are largely correct. Suppose, that is, that in contemporary U.S. society institutionalized inquiry does function to serve the specialized needs of a powerful ruling elite (with trickle-down social goods permitted insofar as they generate profits or at least don't impede the fulfillment of ruling-class objectives). Imagine also that such inquiry is very costly, and that the ruling elite strives to socialize those costs as much as possible.

In such a society, there will be a great need to obscure this arrangement. The successful pursuit of the agendas of the ruling elite will require a quiescent—or, as it's usually termed, "stable"—society, which would surely be threatened if the facts were known. Also required is the acquiescence of the scientists and scholars, who would like to view themselves as autonomous investigators serving no masters but the truth and who would deeply resent the suggestion (as anyone with any self-respect would) that their honest intellectual efforts subserve any baser purpose.

How can the obfuscation be accomplished? One possibility would be to promote the idea that science is organized for the sake of *public* rather than *private* interests. But the noble lie that science is meant to make the world a better place is a risky one. It makes the public's support for science contingent upon science's producing tangible and visible public benefits (which may not be forthcoming) and generates expectations of publicity and accountability that might lead to embarrassing questions down the road.

An altogether more satisfactory strategy is to promote the idea that science is *value-neutral*—that it's organized for the sake of *no* particular interests at all! Telling people that science serves only the truth is safer than telling people that science serves *them*, because it not only hides the truth about who benefits, but deflects public attention away from the whole question. Belief in the value-neutrality of science can thus serve the conservative function of securing *unconditional* public support for what are in fact ruling-class initiatives. Any research agenda whatsoever—no matter how pernicious—can be readily legitimated on the grounds that it is the natural result of the self-justifying pursuit of truth, the more or less inevitable upshot of a careful look at the facts.

Now in such a society, the widespread acceptance of a theory of knowledge like the Dragnet theory would clearly be a good thing from the point of view of the ruling elite. By fostering the epistemic attitudes it fosters, the Dragnet theory helps confer special authority and status on science and its practitioners and deflects critical attention away from the material conditions in which science is conducted. Furthermore, by supporting Dragnet objectivity as an epistemic ideal, the theory prepares the ground for reception of the ideology of the objectivity of science.

We can conclude from all this that the Dragnet theory, along with the ideal of objectivity it sanctions, has clear ideological value, in the sense that their acceptance may play a causal role in people's acceptance of the ideology of scientific objectivity.

But we cannot infer from this fact either that the Dragnet theory is false or that its ideals are flawed. Such an inference depends on conflating what are essentially *prescriptive* claims (claims about how science ought to be conducted) with *descriptive* claims (claims about how science is in fact conducted). It's one thing to embrace some particular ideal of scientific method and quite another to accept ideologically useful assumptions about the satisfaction of that ideal within existing institutions.[32]

Note that in a society such as the one I've described, the ideological value of the Dragnet theory depends crucially on how successfully it can be promulgated *as a factual characterization* of the workings of the intellectual establishment. It's no use to get everyone to believe simply that it would be a good thing if scientists *could* put aside their prior beliefs and their personal interests; people must be brought to believe that scientists largely *succeed* in such divestitures. The ideological cloud of Dragnet objectivity thus comes not so much from the belief that science *ought* to be value-free, as from the belief that it *is* value-free. And of course it's precisely the fact that science is *not* value-free in the way it's proclaimed to be that makes the ideological ploy necessary in the first place.

If science as an institution fails to live up to its own ideal of objectivity, then the character of existing science entails nothing about the value of the ideal, nor about the character of some imagined science which *did* live up to it. In fact, notice that the more we can show that compromised science is *bad* science (in the sense of leading to false results), the less necessary we make it to challenge the Dragnet theory itself. A good part of the radical case, after all, is made by demonstrating the ways in which scientific research has been *distorted* by some of the very factors a Dragnet epistemologist would cite as inhibitors of epistemic progress: prejudiced beliefs, undefended hunches, material desires, ideological commitments.

There's no reason, in short, why a Dragnet theorist couldn't come to be convinced of the radical analysis of the material basis of science.

Naturalized Epistemology and the Bias Paradox

What I think I've shown so far is that if our only desideratum on an adequate critical epistemology is that it permits us to expose the real workings of capitalist patriarchy, then the Dragnet theory will do just fine, *pace* its feminist critics. But I certainly do not want to defend that theory; nor do I want to defend as an epistemic ideal the conception of objectivity as neutrality. In fact, I want to join feminist critics in rejecting this ideal. But I want to be clear about the proper basis for criticizing it.

There are, in general, two strategies that one can find in the epistemological literature for challenging the ideal of objectivity as impartiality. (I leave aside for the moment the question of why one might want to challenge an epistemic ideal, though this question will figure importantly in what follows.) The first strategy is to prove the *impossibility* of satisfying the ideal—this involves pointing to the *ubiquity* of bias. The second strategy is to try to demonstrate the *undesirability* of satisfying the ideal—this involves showing the *utility* of bias. The second strategy is employed by some feminist critics, but often the first strategy is thought to be sufficient, particularly when it's pursued together with the kind of radical critique of institutionalized science discussed above. Thus Jaggar, Code, and others emphasize the essential locatedness of every individual knower, arguing that if all knowledge proceeds from some particular perspective, then the transcendent standpoint suggested by the ideology of objectivity is unattainable. All knowledge is conditioned by the knower's location, it is claimed; if we acknowledge that, then we cannot possibly believe that anyone is "objective" in the requisite sense.

But the appeal to the *de facto* partiality of all knowledge is simply not going to justify rejecting the ideal of objectivity, for three reasons. In the first place, the wanted intermediate conclusion—that Dragnet objectivity is impossible—does not follow from the truism that all knowers are located. The Dragnet conception of impartiality is perfectly compatible with the fact that all knowers start from some particular place. The Dragnet theory, like all empiricist theories, holds that knowledge is a strict function of the contingencies of experience. It therefore entails that differences in empirical situation will lead to differences in belief, and to that extent validates the intuition that all knowledge is partial.[33] Thus the neutrality recommended by the Dragnet theory does not enjoin cognizers to abjure the particularities of their own experience, only to honor certain strictures in drawing conclusions from that experience. Impartiality is not a matter of where you are, but rather how well you do from where you sit.

In the second place, even if it could be shown to be impossible for human beings to achieve perfect impartiality, that fact in itself would not speak against Dragnet objectivity *as an ideal*. Many ideals—particularly moral ones—are unattainable, but that does not make them useless, or reveal them to be inadequate as ideals.[34] The fact—and I have no doubt that it is a fact—that no one can fully rid oneself of prejudices, neurotic impulses, selfish desires, and other psychological detritus, does not impugn the moral or the cognitive value of attempting to do so. Similarly, the fact that no one can fully abide by the cognitive strictures imposed by the standards of strict impartiality doesn't entail that one oughtn't to try. The real test of the adequacy of a norm is not whether it can be realized, but (arguably) whether we get closer to what we want if we try to realize it.

But the third and most serious problem with this tack is that it is precisely the one that is going to engender the bias paradox. Notice that the feminist goal of exposing the structures of interestedness that constitute patriarchy and other forms of oppression requires doing more than just demonstrating that particular interests are being served. It requires criticizing that fact, showing that there's something wrong with a society in which science selectively serves the interests of one dominant group. And it's awfully hard to see how such a critical stand can be sustained without some appeal to the value of impartiality.

The question that must be confronted by anyone pursuing this strategy is basically this: If bias is ubiquitous and ineliminable, then what's the good of exposing it? It seems to me that the whole thrust of feminist scholarship in this area has been to demonstrate that androcentric biases have distorted science and, indeed, distorted the search for knowledge generally. But if biases are distorting, and if we're all biased in one way or another, then it seems there could be no such thing as an *undistorted* search for knowledge. So what are we complaining about? Is it just that we want it to be distorted in *our* favor, rather than in theirs? We must say something about the badness of the biases we expose or our critique will carry no normative import at all.

We still have to look at the second of the two strategies for criticizing the ideal of objectivity, but this is a good place to pick up the question I bracketed earlier on: *Why* might one want to challenge an epistemic ideal? If my arguments have been correct up to this point, then I have shown that many of the arguments made against objectivity are not only unsound but ultimately self-defeating. But by now the reader must surely be wondering why we need *any* critique of the notion of objectivity as neutrality. If radical critiques of the ideology of scientific objectivity are consistent with respect for this ideal, and if we need some notion of objectivity anyway, why not this one?

The short answer is this: because the best empirical theories of knowledge and mind do not sanction pure neutrality as sound epistemic policy.

The fact is that the Dragnet theory is *wrong*. We know this for two reasons: First, the failure of externalism tells us that its foundationalist underpinnings are rotten and second, current work in empirical psychology tells us that its empiricist conception of the mind is radically incorrect. But if the Dragnet theory is wrong about the structure of knowledge and the nature of the mind, then the main source of warrant for the ideal of epistemic neutrality is removed. It becomes an open question whether divestiture of emotions, prior beliefs, and moral commitments hinders, or aids, the development of knowledge.

Naturalized epistemology tells us that there is no presuppositionless position from which to assess epistemic practice, that we must take some knowledge for granted. The only thing to do, then, is to begin with whatever it is we think we know, and try to figure out how we came to know it: Study knowledge by studying the knower. Now if, in the course of such study, we discover that much of human knowledge is possible only because our knowledge seeking does not conform to the Dragnet model, then we will have good empirical grounds for rejecting perfect objectivity as an epistemic ideal. And so we come back to the second of the two strategies I outlined for challenging the ideal of objectivity. Is there a case to be made against the desirability of epistemic neutrality? Indeed there is, on the grounds that a genuinely open mind, far from leading us closer to the truth, would lead to epistemic chaos.

Far from being the streamlined, uncluttered logic machine of classical empiricism, the mind now appears to be much more like a bundle of highly specialized modules, each natively fitted for the analysis and manipulation of a particular body of sensory data. General learning strategies of the sort imagined by classical empiricists, if they are employed by the mind at all, can apply to but a small portion of the cognitive tasks that confront us. Rationalism vindicated.

But if the rationalists have turned out to be right about the structure of the mind, it is because they appreciated something that the empiricists missed—the value of partiality for human knowers. Whatever might work for an ideal mind, operating without constraints of time or space, it's clear by now that complete neutrality of the sort empiricists envisioned would not suit human minds in human environments. A completely "open mind," confronting the sensory evidence we confront, could never manage to construct the rich systems of knowledge we construct in the short time we take to construct them. From the point of view of an *unbiased* mind, the human sensory flow contains both too much information and too little: too much for the mind to generate *all* the logical possibilities, and too little for it to decide among even the relatively few that *are* generated.

The problem of paring down the alternatives is the defining feature of the human epistemic condition. The problem is partly solved, I've been arguing, by one form of "bias"—native conceptual structure. But it's important to realize that this problem is absolutely endemic to human knowledge seeking, whether we're talking about the subconscious processes by which we acquire language and compute sensory information, or the more consciously accessible processes by which we explicitly decide what to believe. The everyday process of forming an opinion would be grossly hampered if we were really to consider matters with anything even close to an "open mind."

What all this means is that a naturalized approach to knowledge provides us with *empirical* grounds for rejecting pure neutrality as an epistemic ideal, and for valuing those kinds of "biases" that serve to trim our epistemic jobs to manageable proportions. But it also seems to mean that we have a new route to the bias paradox—if biases are now not simply ineliminable, but downright *good*, how is it that *some* biases are *bad*?

I'm going to answer this question, honest, but first let me show how bad things really are. It's possible to see significant analogies between the function of a paradigm within a scientific community, and what is sometimes called a "worldview" within other sorts of human communities. Worldviews confer some of the same cognitive benefits as paradigms, simplifying routine epistemic tasks, establishing an informal methodology of inquiry, etc., and they also offer significant social benefits, providing a common sense of reality and fostering a functional sense of normalcy among members of the community.

But what about those outside the community? A shared language, a set of traditions and mores, a common sense of what's valuable and why—the very things that bind some human beings together in morally valuable ways—function simultaneously to exclude those who do not share them. Moreover, human communities are not homogeneous. In a stratified community, where one group of people dominates others, the worldview of the dominant group can become a powerful tool for keeping those in the subordinate groups in their places.

The real problem with the liberal conceptions of objectivity and neutrality begins with the fact that while they are unrealizable, it's possible for those resting comfortably in the center of a consensus to find that fact invisible. Members of the dominant group are given no reason to question their own assumptions: Their worldview acquires, in their minds, the status of established fact. Their opinions are transformed into what "everybody" knows.[35] Furthermore, these privileged individuals have the power to promote and elaborate their own worldview in public forums while excluding all others, tacitly setting limits to the range of "reasonable" opinion.[36]

Because of the familiarity of its content, the "objectivity" of such reportage is never challenged. If it were, it would be found woefully lacking *by liberal standards*. That's because the liberal ideal of objectivity is an *unreasonable* one; it is not just unattainable, but unattainable by a long measure. But because the challenge is *only* mounted against views that are aberrant, it is *only* such views that will ever be demonstrated to be "non-objective," and thus *only* marginal figures that will ever be charged with bias.[37]

Lorraine Code makes a similar point about the unrealistic stringency of announced standards for knowledge.[38] She rightly points out that most of what we ordinarily count as knowledge wouldn't qualify as such by many proposed criteria. I would go further and say that as with all unrealistically high standards, they tend to support the status quo—in this case, received

opinion—by virtue of the fact that they will only be invoked in "controversial" cases, i.e., in case of challenge to familiar or received or "expert" opinion. Since the standards are unreasonably high, the views tested against them will invariably be found wanting; since the only views so tested will be unpopular ones, their failure to pass muster serves to add additional warrant to prevailing prejudices, as well as a patina of moral vindication to the holders of those prejudices, who can self-righteously claim to have given "due consideration" to the "other side."

But what are we anti-externalist, naturalized epistemologists to say about this? We can't simply condemn the members of the dominant class for their "bias," for their lack of "open-mindedness" about our point of view. To object to the hegemony of ruling-class opinion on this basis would be to tacitly endorse the discredited norm of neutral objectivity. "Biased" they are, but then, in a very deep sense, so are we. The problem with ruling-class "prejudices" cannot be the fact that they are deeply-held beliefs, or beliefs acquired "in advance" of the facts—for the necessity of such *kinds* of belief is part of the human epistemic condition.

The real problem with the ruling-class worldview is not that it is biased; it's that it is false. The epistemic problem with ruling-class people is not that they are closed-minded; it's that they hold too much power. The recipe for radical epistemological action then becomes simple: Tell the truth and get enough power so that people have to listen. Part of telling the truth, remember, is telling the truth about how knowledge is actually constructed—advocates of feminist epistemology are absolutely correct about that. We do need to dislodge those attitudes about knowledge that give unearned credibility to elements of the ruling-class worldview, and this means dislodging the hold of the Dragnet theory of knowledge. But we must be clear: The Dragnet theory is not false because it's pernicious; it's pernicious because it is false.

A naturalized approach to knowledge, because it requires us to give up *neutrality* as an epistemic ideal, also requires us to take a different attitude toward bias. We know that human knowledge requires biases; we also know that we have no possibility of getting a priori guarantees that our biases incline us in the right direction. What all this means is that the "biasedness" of biases drops out as a parameter of epistemic evaluation. There's only one thing to do, and it's the course always counseled by a naturalized approach: *We must treat the goodness or badness of particular biases as an empirical question.*

A naturalistic study of knowledge tells us biases are good when and to the extent that they facilitate the gathering of *knowledge*—that is, when they lead us to the truth. Biases are bad when they lead us *away* from the truth. One important strategy for telling the difference between good and bad biases is thus to evaluate the overall theories in which the biases figure. This one point has important implications for feminist theory in general and for feminist attitudes about universalist or essentialist theories of human nature in particular.

As we saw in section II, much of the feminist criticism raised against cognitive essentialism focused on the fact that rationalist and Kantian theories of the human essence were all devised by men, and based, allegedly, on exclusively male experience. Be that so—it would still follow from a naturalized approach to the theory of knowledge that it is an *empirical* question whether or not 'androcentrism' of that sort leads to bad theories. Partiality does not in general compromise theories; as we feminists ourselves have been insisting, all theorizing proceeds from *some* location or other. We must therefore learn to be cautious of claims to the effect that particular forms of partiality will inevitably and systematically influence the outcome of an investigation. Such claims must be treated as empirical hypotheses, subject to investigation and challenge, rather than as enshrined first principles.

The End

I began this essay by asking whether we need a "feminist" epistemology, and I answered that we did, as long as we understood that need to be the need for an epistemology informed by feminist insight, and responsive to the moral imperatives entailed by feminist commitments. But I've argued that we do not necessarily need a conceptual transformation of epistemological theory in order to get a feminist epistemology in this sense. We need, in the first instance, a *political* transformation of the

society in which theorizing about knowledge takes place. We've got to stop the oppression of women, eliminate racism, redistribute wealth, and *then* see what happens to our collective understanding of knowledge.

My bet? That some of the very same questions that are stimulating inquiry among privileged white men, right now in these sexist, racist, capitalist-imperialist times, are *still* going to be exercising the intellects and challenging the imaginations of women of color, gay men, physically handicapped high school students, etc.

I'm not saying that we should stop doing epistemology until after the revolution. That would of course be stupid, life being short. What I am saying is that those of us who think we know what feminism is, must guard constantly against the presumptuousness we condemn in others, of claiming as Feminist the particular bit of ground upon which we happen to be standing. We need to remember that part of what unites philosophers who choose to characterize their own work as "feminist" is the conviction that philosophy ought to matter—that it should make a positive contribution to the construction of a more just, humane, and nurturing world than the one we currently inhabit.

I have argued that contemporary analytic philosophy is capable of making such a contribution and that it is thus undeserving of the stigma "malestream" philosophy. But there's more at stake here than the abstract issue of mischaracterization. Attacks on the analytic tradition as "androcentric," "phallogocentric," or "male-identified" are simultaneously attacks on the feminist credentials of those who work within the analytic tradition. And the stereotyping of contemporary analytic philosophy—the tendency to link it with views (like the Dragnet theory) to which it is in fact antipathetic—has turned feminists away from fruitful philosophical work, limiting our collective capacity to imagine genuinely novel and transformative philosophical strategies.

I acknowledge both the difficulty and the necessity of clarifying the implications of feminist theory for other kinds of endeavors. It's important, therefore, for feminist theorists to continue to raise critical challenges to particular theories and concepts. But surely this can be done without the caricature, without the throwaway refutations, in a way that is more respectful of philosophical differences.

Let's continue to argue with each other by all means. But let's stop arguing about which view is more feminist, and argue instead about which view is more likely to be true. Surely we can trust the dialectical process of feminists discussing these things with other feminists to yield whatever "feminist epistemology" we need.[39]

Notes

1. See Naomi Scheman, "Othello's Doubt/Desdemona's Death: The Engendering of Skepticism," in *Power, Gender, Values*, ed. Judith Genova (Edmonton, Alberta: Academic Printing and Publishing, 1987); and also Scheman's essay in this volume. See also Evelyn Fox Keller, "Cognitive Repression in Physics," *American Journal of Physics* 47 (1979): 718–721; and "Feminism and Science," in *Sex and Scientific Inquiry*, ed. S. Harding and J. O'Barr (Chicago: University of Chicago Press, 1987), pp. 233–246, reprinted in *The Philosophy of Science*, ed. by Richard Boyd, Philip Gaspar, and John Trout (Cambridge, Mass.: MIT Press, 1991).

2. For example, see Catharine A. MacKinnon, *Towards a Feminist Theory of the State* (Cambridge, Mass.: Harvard University Press, 1989).

3. This is not quite right—the ideology of 'objectivity' is perfectly capable of charging those *outside* the inner circle with partiality, and indeed, such charges are also crucial to the preservation of the status quo. More on this below.

4. Lorraine Code, "The Impact of Feminism on Epistemology," *APA Newsletter on Feminism and Philosophy* 88, 2 (March 1989): 25–29.

5. Lorraine Code, "Experience, Knowledge, and Responsibility," in *Feminist Perspectives in Philosophy*, ed. by Morwenna Griffiths and Margaret Whitford (Bloomington: Indiana University Press, 1988), pp. 189ff.

6. Code, "Impact of Feminism on Epistemology," p. 25.

7. It might be objected that there is a third option—that we could criticize those biases that are biases against our interests and valorize those that promote our interests. But if we are in fact left with only this option, then we are giving up on the possibility of any medium of social change other than power politics. This is bad for two reasons: (1) As moral and political theory, egoism should be repugnant to any person ostensibly concerned with justice and human well-being; and (2) as tactics, given current distributions of power, it's really stupid.

8. I have defended a kind of non-realist conception of truth, but one which maintains this gap. See my "Can Verificationists Make Mistakes?" *American Philosophical Quarterly* 24, 3 (July 1987): 225–236. For a defense of a more robustly realist conception of truth, see Michael Devitt, *Realism and Truth* (Princeton, N.J.: Princeton University Press, 1984). (A new edition is in press.)

9. Code, "Impact of Feminism on Epistemology," p. 25.

10. Significantly, these theories are not all empiricist, and the theories that are most "post-positivist" are the least empiricist of all. I'll have much more to say about this in what follows.

11. See, e.g., Helene Cixous, "The Laugh of the Medusa," tr. by Keith Cohen and Paula Cohen, *Signs* 1, 4 (1976): 875–893; Luce Irigaray, "Is the Subject of Science Sexed?" tr. by Carol Mastrangelo Bove, *Hypatia* 2, 3 (Fall 1987): 65–87; and Andrea Nye, "The Inequalities of Semantic Structure: Linguistics and Feminist Philosophy," *Metaphilosophy* 18, 3–4 (July/October 1987): 222–240. I must say that for the sweepingness of Nye's claims regarding "linguistics" and "semantic theory," her survey of work in these fields is, to say the least, narrow and out-of-date.

12. See, e.g., Ruth Ginzberg, "Feminism, Rationality, and Logic" and "Teaching Feminist Logic," *APA Newsletter on Feminism and Philosophy* 88, 2 (March 1989): 34–42 and 58–65.

13. Note that the term "Enlightenment" itself does not have any single, precise meaning, referring in some contexts to only the philosophers (and *philosophes*) of eighteenth-century France, in other contexts to any philosopher lying on the trajectory of natural-rights theory in politics, from Hobbes and Locke through Rousseau, and in still other contexts to all the canonical philosophical works of the seventeenth and eighteen centuries, up to and including Kant. I shall try to use the term "early modern philosophy" to denote seventeenth-century rationalism and empiricism, but I may slip up.

14. In Alison Jaggar, *Feminist Politics and Human Nature* (Totowa, N.J.: Rowman and Allenheld, 1983), p. 355.

15. In Harding, *Science Question in Feminism*, p. 24.

16. Jane Flax, "Postmodernism and Gender Relations in Feminist Theory," *Signs* 12, 4 (Summer 1987): 624.

17. Ibid., p. 627.

18. Cognitive essentialism generally gets associated with another thesis singled out for criticism—namely, dualism, the view that the mind is separate from the body and that the self is to be identified with the mind. Although dualism is not exclusively a rationalist view (Locke is standardly classified as a dualist), it is most closely associated with Descartes, and it is Descartes's a priori argument for dualism in the *Meditations* that seems to draw the most fire. Cartesian dualism is seen as providing a metaphysical rationale for dismissing the relevance of material contingencies to the assessment of knowledge claims, because

it separates the knowing subject from the physical body, and because it seems to assert the sufficiency of disembodied reason for the attainment of knowledge. In fact, dualism is a red herring. It's an uncommon view in the history of philosophy. Many people classically characterized as dualists, like Plato, were surely not Cartesian dualists. And on top of that, the dualism does no work. Being a dualist is neither necessary nor sufficient for believing that the human essence is composed of cognitive properties.

19. Flax, "Postmodernism," p. 626.

20. "Individualism" as Jaggar uses it is rather a term of art. It has a variety of meanings within philosophical discourse, but I don't know of any standard use within epistemology that matches Jaggar's. In the philosophy of mind, the term denotes the view that psychological states can be individuated for purposes of scientific psychology, without reference to objects or states outside the individual. This use of the term has *nothing* to do with debates in political theory about such issues as individual rights or individual autonomy. A liberal view of the moral/political individual can work just as well (or as poorly) on an anti-individualist psychology (such as Hilary Putnam's or Tyler Burge's) as on an individualist view like Jerry Fodor's.

21. See also Naomi Scheman's essay in this volume.

22. Jaggar, "Postmodernism," p. 355.

23. Ibid.

24. See, for example, the excerpts from *Notes Directed against a Certain Program*, in Margaret Wilson, ed., *The Essential Descartes* (New York: Mentor Press, 1969).

25. A little qualification is necessary here: The empiricist's requirement that all concepts be reducible to sensory simples does count as a substantive restriction on the possible contents of thought, but it's one which is vitiated by the reductionist semantic theory favored by empiricists, which denies the meaningfulness of any term which cannot be defined in terms of sensory primitives. See the discussion of this point in Jerry Fodor, *Modularity of Mind: An Essay on Faculty Psychology* (Cambridge, Mass.: MIT Press, 1983).
Also, the empiricists did allow a kind of "bias" in the form of innate standards of similarity, which would permit the mind to see certain ideas as inherently resembling certain others. This innate similarity metric was needed to facilitate the operation of *association*, which was the mechanism for generating more complex and more abstract ideas out of the sensory simples. But the effects of a bias such as this were vitiated by the fact that associations could also be forged by the contiguity of ideas in experience, with the result once more that no effective, substantive limits were placed on the ways in which human beings could analyze the data presented them by sensory experience.

26. David Hume, *An Enquiry Concerning Human Understanding* (Indianapolis: Hackett, 1977), p. 30. For a different assessment of Hume's potential contributions to a feminist epistemology, see Annette Baier's essay in this volume.

27. W.v.O. Quine, "Epistemology Naturalized," in Quine, *Ontological Relativity and Other Essays* (New York: Columbia University Press, 1969), pp. 69–90.

28. See Noam Chomsky, "Review of B. F. Skinner's *Verbal Behavior*," *Language* 35, 1 (1959): 53–68.

29. See Noam Chomsky, "Quine's Empirical Assumptions," in *Words and Objections: Essays on the Work of W. V. Quine*, ed. by D. Davidson and J. Hintikka (Dordrecht: D. Reidel, 1969). See also Quine's response to Chomsky in the same volume.
I discuss the inconsistency between Quine's commitment to naturalism and his *a prioristic* rejection of mentalism and nativism in linguistics in "Naturalized Epistemology and the Study of Language," in *Naturalistic Epistemology: A Symposium of Two Decades*, ed. by Abner Shimony and Debra Nails (Dordrecht: D. Reidel, 1987), pp. 235–257.

30. For an extremely helpful account of the Chomskian approach to the study of language, see David Lightfoot's *The Language Lottery: Toward a Biology of Grammars* (Cambridge, Mass.: MIT Press, 1984).

31. Carl R. Hempel, *Philosophy of Natural Science* (Englewood Cliffs, N.J.: Prentice-Hall, 1966). See especially pp. 10–18.

32. This follows from a general point emphasized by Georges Rey in personal conversation: It's important in general to distinguish people's theories of human institutions from the actual character of those institutions.

33. This despite the fact that the Dragnet theory supports a strong context of discovery/context of justification distinction. On empiricist theories, the justification of an individual's belief is ultimately a relation between the belief and the sensory experience of that individual. Location matters, then, because the same belief could be justified for one individual and unjustified for another, precisely because of the differences in their experiences.

34. This is not to say that there are no puzzling issues about moral ideals that are in some sense humanly unattainable. One such issue arises with respect to the ideals of altruism and supererogation, ideals which it would be, arguably, *unhealthy* for human beings to fully realize. See Larry Blum, Marcia Homiak, Judy Housman, and Naomi Scheman, "Altruism and Women's Oppression," in *Women and Philosophy*, ed. by Carol C. Gould and Marx W. Wartofsky (New York: G. P. Putnam, 1980), pp 222–247. On the question of whether it would be good for human beings to fully realize *any* moral ideal, see Susan Wolf, "Moral Saints," *The Journal of Philosophy* 79, 8 (August 1982): 419–439.

35. Notice that we don't have to assume here that anyone is knowingly telling lies. Clearly, in the real world, members of the ruling elite *do* consciously lie, and they do it a lot. But here I'm trying to point out that some of the mechanisms that can perpetuate oppressive structures are epistemically legitimate.

36. See Edward Herman and Noam Chomsky, *Manufacturing Consent* (New York: Pantheon, 1988); Noam Chomsky, *Necessary Illusions: Thought Control in Democratic Society* (Boston: South End Press, 1989), esp. ch. 3 ("The Bounds of the Expressible"); and Martin A. Lee and Norman Solomon, *Unreliable Sources: A Guide to Detecting Bias in News Media* (New York: Carol Publishing Group, 1990).

37. This explains some of what's going on in the so-called "debate" about so-called "political correctness." Most of what's going on involves pure dishonesty and malice, but to the extent that there are some intelligent and relatively fair-minded people who find themselves worrying about such issues as the "politicization" of the classroom, or about "ideological biases" among college professors, these people are reacting to the *unfamiliarity* of progressive perspectives. Those foundational beliefs that are very common within the academy—belief in a (Christian) god, in the benignity of American institutions, in the viability of capitalism—generally go without saying and are thus invisible. *Our* worldviews are unfamiliar, and so must be articulated and acknowledged. Precisely because we are willing and able to do that, while our National Academy of Scholars colleagues are not, we become open to the charge of being "ideological."

It's the very fact that there are so *few* leftist, African-American, Hispanic, openly gay, feminist, female persons in positions of academic authority that accounts for all this slavish nonsense about our "taking over."

38. Lorraine Code, "Credibility: A Double Standard," in *Feminist Perspectives*, ed. Code, Mullett, and Overall, pp. 65–66.

39. Much of the preliminary work for this essay was done during a fellowship year at the National Humanities Center, and I wish to thank both the center and the Andrew J. Mellon Foundation for their support. The essay is based on a presentation I gave at the Scripps College Humanities Institute Conference, "Thinking Women: Feminist Scholarship in the Humanities," in March 1990. I want to thank the institute, especially Norton Batkin, for the invitation to think about these issues. I also want to thank my co-participants at the conference, especially Naomi Scheman, to whom I owe a special debt. I have enjoyed an enormous amount of stimulating and challenging conversation and correspondence with Naomi about all the issues in this essay. It's a tribute to her sense of intellectual fairness and her commitment to feminist praxis that she and I have managed to conduct such an extended dialogue about these issues, given the intensity of our disagreements. I also want to make it clear that while I had the benefit of reading Naomi's essay before completing my own, I did not finish mine in time for her to react to any of the points I raise here.

Many other people have helped me with this essay. I want to thank Judith Ferster, Suzanne Graver, Charlotte Gross, Sally Haslanger, Barbara Metcalf, and Andy Reath for hours of valuable conversation. Marcia Homiak, Alice Kaplan, and Georges Rey supplied extremely useful comments on earlier drafts; David Auerbach did all that *and* extricated me from an eleventh-hour computer crisis, and I thank them heartily. Very special thanks to my co-editor, Charlotte Witt, for her excellent philosophical and editorial advice and for her abundant patience and good sense. I cannot fully express my thanks to Joe Levine for all he's done, intellectually and personally, to help me complete this project. Thanks as well to my children, Paul and Rachel, for their patience during all the times I was out consorting with my muse.

⬩ FURTHER READINGS ⬩

General Introduction

The Truth Condition

Armstrong, D. M. 1973. *Belief, Truth, and Knowledge.* Cambridge: Cambridge University Press.

Austin, J. L. 1961a. "Truth." In *Philosophical Papers.* Oxford: Clarendon Press.

Blandshard. 1939. *The Nature of Thought.* London: Allen and Unwin.

Fisch, M., ed. 1951. *Classic American Philosophers.* New York: Appleton-Century-Crofts, Inc.

James, W. 1896. "The Will to Believe." *The New World* 5, no. 18: 327–347. Also in Fisch 1951.

Moore, G. E. 1953. *Some Main Problems in Philosophy.* London: Allen and Unwin.

Peirce, C. 1877b. "How to Make Our Ideas Clear." In *Popular Science Monthly.* D. Appleton and Company, 1877. Also in Fisch 1951.

Russell, B. 1910. Chap. 7 in *Philosophical Essays.* New York: Simon and Schuster.

Tarski, A. 1944. "The Semantic Conception of Truth and the Foundations of Semantics." *Philosophy and Phenomenological Research* 4: 341–375.

The Belief Condition

Ayer, A. J. 1956. *The Problem of Knowledge.* Harmondsworth: Penguin Books, Ltd.

Duncan-Jones, A. 1938. "Further Questions about 'Know' and 'Think'." *Analysis* 5, no. 5.

Lehrer, K. 1974. *Knowledge.* Oxford: Oxford University Press.

———. 1989. "Knowledge Reconsidered." In *Knowledge and Skepticism,* edited by M. Clay and K. Lehrer. Boulder: Westview Press.

Radford, C. 1966. "Knowledge—By Examples." *Analysis* 27, no. 1: 1–11.

Luper, S. 1998. "Belief and Knowledge." *Routledge Encyclopedia of Philosophy.* London: Routledge.

Justification

Alston, W. 1971. "Varieties of Privileged Access." *American Philosophical Quarterly* 9: 223–41.

———. 1976. "Has Foundationalism Been Refuted?" *Philosophical Studies* 29: 287–305.

———. 1985. "Concepts of Epistemic Justification." *Monist.*

Annis, D. 1978. "A Contextualist Theory of Epistemic Justification." *American Philosophical Quarterly* 15: 213–19.

Audi, R. 1993. *The Structure of Justification.* Cambridge: Cambridge University Press.

BonJour, L. 1985. *The Structure of Empirical Knowledge.* Cambridge, Mass. Harvard University Press.

Bosanquet, B. 1920. *Implication and Linear Inference.* London: Macmillan.

Chisholm, R.M. 1966. *Theory of Knowledge.* Englewood Cliffs, N.J.: Prentice-Hall.

———, and R.J. Swartz, eds. 1973. *Empirical Knowledge.* Englewood Cliffs, N.J.: Prentice-Hall.

———. 1982. *The Foundations of Knowing.* Minneapolis: University of Minnesota Press.

Cohen, S. (1988) "How to be a Fallibilist." *Philosophical Perspectives* 2: 581–605.

———. 1998. "Contextualist Solutions to Epistemological Problems: Scepticism, Gettier, and the Lottery." *Australasian Journal of Philosophy* 76: 289–306.

——— "Contextualism." In this volume.

DeRose, K. 1995. "Solving the Skeptical Problem." *The Philosophical Review* 104: 1–52.

Descartes, R. 1641. *Meditations.* In *The Philosophical Writings of Descartes,* trans. J. Cottingham et al. Cambridge: Cambridge University Press, 1984.

Feldman, R., and E. Conee. 1985. "Evidentialism." *Philosophical Studies* 48: 15–34.

———. 2003. "Evidentialism." In this volume.

Foley, R. 2003. "Epistemically Rational Belief as Invulnerability to Self-Criticism." In this volume.

Goldman, A. 1976b. "What Is Justified Belief?" In *Justification and Knowledge,* edited by G.S. Pappas, 1–23. Dordrecht: D. Reidel.

Haack, S. 1997. "A Theory of Empirical Justification. This volume.

Harman, G. 1986. *Change In View.* Cambridge, Mass. MIT Press.

Quine, W.V.O., and J. S. Ullian. 1970. *The Web of Belief.* New York: Random House.

Quinton, A.M. 1973. *The Nature of Things.* London: Routledge & Kegan Paul.

Lewis, D. 1979. "Scorekeeping in a Language Game."*Journal of Philosophical Logic* 8: 339–59.

———. 1996. "Elusive Knowledge." *Australasian Journal of Philosophy* 74: 549–67.

Peirce, C. 1877. "The Fixation of Belief." *Popular Science Monthly* (November). D. Appleton and Company.

Wittgenstein, L. 1969. *On Certainty,* trans. G. E. M. Anscombe and G. H. von Wright. New York: Harper Torchbooks.

Analysis of Knowledge

Austin, J. L. 1961b. "Other Minds." In *Philosophical Papers.* Oxford: Clarendon Press.

Carrier, L. S. 1971. "An Analysis of Empirical Knowledge." *Southern Journal of Philosophy* 9: 3–11.

Clark, M. 1963. "Knowledge and Grounds: A Comment on Mr. Gettier's Paper." *Analysis* 24, no. 2: 46–48.

Dretske, F. 1970. "Epistemic Operators." *Journal of Philosophy* 67: 1007–23.

———. 1971. "Conclusive Reasons." *Australasian Journal of Philosophy* 49: 1–22.

Gettier, E. 1963. "Is Justified True Belief Knowledge?" *Analysis* 23: 121–23.

Goldman, A. 1967. "A Causal Theory of Knowing." *Journal of Philosophy* 64: 355–72.

———. 1976a. "Discrimination and Perceptual Knowledge." *Journal of Philosophy* 78: 771–91.

Grice, H. P. 1961. "The Causal Theory of Perception." *Proceedings of the Aristotelian Society,* Supp. Vol. 35: 121–52.

Harman, G. 1968. "Knowledge, Inference, and Explanation." *American Philosophical Quarterly* 5: 164–73.

Klein, P. 1971. "A Proposed Definition of Propositional Knowledge." *Journal of Philosophy* 68: 471–82.

Lehrer, K. 1965. "Knowledge, Truth, and Evidence." *Analysis* 25: 168–75.

———, and Paxson, T. 1969. "Knowledge: Undefeated Justified True Belief." *Journal of Philosophy* 64: 225–37.

Lewis, D. 1973. *Counterfactuals.* Oxford: Blackwell.

Luper, S. 1984. "The Epistemic Predicament." *Australasian Journal of Philosophy* 62: 26–48.

Nozick, R. 1981. *Philosophical Explanations.* Cambridge, MA: Harvard University Press.

Prichard, H. A. 1950. *Knowledge and Perception.* Oxford: The Clarendon Press.

Ryle, G. 1949. *The Concept of Mind.* London: Hutchinson.

Russell, B. 1912. *Problems of Philosophy.* New York: Henry Holt and Co.

Sellars, W. 1973. "Givenness and Explanatory Coherence." *Journal of Philosophy* 70: 612–24.

Shope, R. K. 1983. *The Analysis of Knowing.* Princeton: Princeton University Press.

Sosa, E. 1969. "Propositional Knowledge." *Philosophical Studies* 20: 33–43.

———. 1999. "How to Defeat Opposition to Moore." *Philosophical Perspectives* 13: 141–52.

———. 2003. "Neither Contextualism Nor Skepticism." In *The Skeptics,* edited by S. Luper. Aldershot: Ashgate Publishing, 2003. Also in this volume.

Stine, G. 1976. "Skepticism, Relevant Alternatives, and Deductive Closure." *Philosophical Studies* 29: 249–61. Also in this volume.

Unger, P. 1968. "The Analysis of Factual Knowledge." *Journal of Philosophy* 65: 157–70.

Skepticism

Stroud, B. 1984. *The Significance of Philosophical Skepticism.* Oxford: Clarendon Press.

Unger, P. 1975. *Ignorance: A Case for Scepticism.* Oxford: Clarendon Press.

Klein, P. 2002. "Skepticism." *Stanford Encyclopedia of Philosophy,* http://plato.stanford.edu/entries/skepticism/.

Chapter 1
Plato

Gulley, N. 1962. *Plato's Theory of Knowledge.* London: Methuen; New York: Barnes & Noble.

Kraut, R., ed. 1992. *The Cambridge Companion to Plato.* Cambridge, N.Y.: Cambridge University Press.

Plato 1953. *Theaetetus.* In *The Dialogues of Plato,* trans. B. Jowett. Oxford: Clarendon Press.

———. 1953. *Republic.* In *The Dialogues of Plato,* trans. B. Jowett. Oxford: Clarendon Press.

———. 1953. *Meno.* In *The Dialogues of Plato,* trans. B. Jowett. Oxford: Clarendon Press.

———. 1953. *Phaedo.* In *The Dialogues of Plato,* trans. B. Jowett. Oxford: Clarendon Press.

Ross, W.D. 1952. *Plato's Theory of Ideas.* Oxford: Oxford University Press.

Vlastos, G., ed. 1971. *Metaphysics and Epistemology.* New York.

Pyrrhonism

Annas, J. and J. Barnes. 1985. *The Modes of Scepticism.* Cambridge: Cambridge University Press.

Barnes, J. 1990. *The Toils of Scepticism.* Cambridge: Cambridge University Press.

Bett, R. 2000. *Pyrrho, his Antecedents, and his Legacy.* Oxford: Oxford University Press.

Burnyeat, M. ed. 1983. *The Skeptical Tradition.* Berkeley: University of California Press.

Stough, C. 1969. *Greek Scepticism*. Berkeley: University of California Press.

Chapter 2

Descartes

Atherton, M. 1993. "Cartesian Reason and Gendered Reason." In *A Mind of One's Own: Feminist Essays on Reason and Objectivity*, edited by L. Antony and C. Witt. Boulder: Westview Press.

Descartes, R. 1955. *The Philosophical Works of Descartes*, 2 vols., trans. E. S. Haldane and G. R. T. Ross. Cambridge: Cambridge University Press.

Doney, W., ed. 1968. *Descartes: A Collection of Critical Essays*. Notre Dame: University of Notre Dame Press.

Frankfurt, H. G. 1970. *Demons, Dreamers, and Madmen: The Defense of Reason in Descartes's Meditations*. Indianapolis: The Bobbs-Merrill Company, Inc.

Kenny, A. 1968. *Descartes: A Study of His Philosophy*. New York: Random House.

Williams, B. 1978. *Descartes: The Project of Pure Inquiry*. Harmondsworth: Penguin Books.

Wilson, M. D. 1978. *Descartes*. London: Routledge and Kegan Paul.

Locke

Armstrong, D. M. and C. B. Martin, eds. 1968. *Locke and Berkeley: A Collection of Critical Essays*. Notre Dame: University of Notre Dame Press.

Bennett, J. 1971. *Locke, Berkeley, Hume: Central Themes*. Oxford: Clarendon Press.

Locke, J. 1690. *An Essay Concerning Human Understanding*, edited by J. Yolton. London: Everyman's Library, 1961.

Mackie, J. L. 1976. *Problems From Locke*. Oxford: Clarendon Press.

Berkeley

Berkeley, G. 1710. *Principles of Human Knowledge*. In *A Treatise Concerning the Principles of Human Knowledge*, edited by J. Dancy. Oxford: Oxford University Press, 1998.

———. 1713. *Three Dialogues Between Hylas and Philonous*. In *Three Dialogues Between Hylas and Philonous*, edited by J. Dancy. Oxford: Oxford University Press, 1998.

Dancy, J. 1987. *Berkeley: An Introduction*. Oxford: Blackwell.

Grayling, A. C. 1986. *Berkeley: The Central Arguments*. London: Duckworth.

Pitcher, G. 1977. *Berkeley*. London: Routledge.

Turbayne, C., ed. 1982. *Berkeley: Critical and Interpretative Essays*. Minnesota: Minnesota University Press.

Urmson, J. O. 1982. *Berkeley*. Oxford: Oxford University Press.

Hume

Atherton, M., ed. 1999. *The Empiricists: Critical Essays on Locke, Berkeley, and Hume*. Lanham, Md.: Rowman & Littlefield Publishers.

Ayer, A. J. 1980. *Hume*. New York: Hill and Wang.

Baier, A. 1993. "Hume: The Reflective Women's Epistemologist?" In *A Mind of One's Own: Feminist Essays on Reason and Objectivity*, edited by L. Antony and C. Witt. Boulder: Westview Press.

Hume, D. 1739. *A Treatise of Human Nature*, edited by L. A. Selby-Bigge. Oxford: Clarendon Press.

———. 1748. Hendel, C. W., ed. *An Inquiry Concerning Human Understandings*. New York: Bobbs-Merrill, 1955.

Norton, D. F., ed. 1994. *The Cambridge Companion to Hume*. Cambridge: Cambridge University Press.

Strawson, G. 1989. *The Secret Connexion: Causation, Realism, and David Hume*. Oxford: Clarendon Press.

Stroud, B. 1977. *Hume*. London: Routledge and Kegan Paul.

Kant

Bennett, J. 1966. *Kant's Analytic*. Cambridge: Cambridge University Press.

Broad, C. D. 1978. *Kant: An Introduction*. Cambridge: Cambridge University Press.

Guyer, P. 1992. *The Cambridge Companion to Kant*. Cambridge: Cambridge University Press.

Henrich, D. 1994. *The Unity of Reason: Essays on Kant's Philosophy*. Cambridge, Mass.: Harvard University Press.

Kant, I. 1781. *Critique of Pure Reason*, trans. N. Kemp Smith. London: Macmillan.

———. 1783. *Prolegomena to Any Future Metaphysics*, trans. L. W. Beck. Indianapolis: The Bobbs-Merrill Company, Inc.

Scruton, R. 2001. *Kant: A Very Short Introduction*. Oxford: Oxford University Press.

Strawson, P. F. 1966. *The Bounds of Sense: An Essay on Kant's Critique of Pure Reason*. London: Methuen & Co., Ltd.

Peirce and James

Aune, B. 1970. *Rationalism, Empiricism, and Pragmatism*. New York: Random House.

Ayer, A. J. 1968. *The Origins of Pragmatism*. San Francisco: Freeman.

Fisch, M., ed. 1951. *Classic American Philosophers*. New York: Appleton-Century-Crofts, Inc.

James, W. 1897. *Pragmatism*. New York: Longmans, 1907.

———. 1896. "The Will to Believe." *The New World* 5, no. 18: 327–47. Also in Fisch 1951.

Peirce, C. 1877. "The Fixation of Belief." *Popular Science Monthly*. D. Appleton and Company, November, 1877. Also in Fisch 1951 and Wiener 1966.

———. 1877b. "How to Make Our Ideas Clear." *Popular Science Monthly*. D. Appleton and Company, 1877. Also in Fisch 1951 and Wiener 1966.

Perry, R. B. 1948. *The Thought and Character of William James*. Cambridge, Mass.: Harvard University Press.

Murphy, J. 1990. *Pragmatism: From Peirce to Davidson*. Boulder: Westview Press.

Rorty, R. 1982. *Consequences of Pragmatism*. Minneapolis: University of Minnesota Press.

Scheffler, I. 1974. *Four Pragmatists*. London: Routledge and Kegan Paul.

Wiener, P., ed. 1966. *C.S. Peirce: Selected Writings*. New York: Dover.

Chapter 3

Armstrong, D. M. 1973. *Belief, Truth and Knowledge*. Cambridge: Cambridge University Press.

Austin, J. L. 1961. "Other Minds." In *Philosophical Papers*. Oxford: Clarendon Press.

Clark, M. 1963. "Knowledge and Grounds: A Comment on Mr. Gettier's Paper." *Analysis* 24, no. 2: 46–48.

Dretske, F. 1970. "Epistemic Operators." *Journal of Philosophy* 67: 1007–23.

———. 1971. "Conclusive Reasons." *Australasian Journal of Philosophy* 49: 1–22.

Gettier, E. 1963. "Is Justified True Belief Knowledge?" *Analysis* 23: 121–23.

Goldman, A. 1976. "Discrimination and Perceptual Knowledge." *Journal of Philosophy* 78: 771–91.

———. 1986. *Change in View*. Cambridge, Mass.: MIT Press.

Harman, G. 1973. *Thought*. Princeton: Princeton University Press.

———. 1968. "Knowledge, Inference, and Explanation." *American Philosophical Quarterly* 5: 164–73.

Klein, P. 1971. "A Proposed Definition of Propositional Knowledge." *Journal of Philosophy* 68: 471–82.

Lehrer, K., and T. Paxson. 1969. "Knowledge: Undefeated Justified True Belief." *Journal of Philosophy* 64: 225–37.

———. 1974. *Knowledge*. Oxford: Oxford University Press.

———. 1989. "Knowledge Reconsidered," edited by M. Clay and K. Lehrer. *Knowledge and Skepticism*. Boulder: Westview Press.

Luper(-Foy), S., ed. 1987. *The Possibility of Knowledge: Nozick and His Critics*. Totowa: Rowman & Littlefield.

Nozick, R. 1981. *Philosophical Explanations*. Cambridge, Mass.: Harvard University Press.

Pappas, G., and M. Swain. 1978. *Essays on Knowledge and Justification*. Ithaca: Cornell University Press.

———. 1979. *Justification and Knowledge*. Dordrecht: D. Reidel Publishing Company.

Pollock, J. 1986. *Contemporary Theories of Knowledge*. Totowa, N.J.: Rowman and Littlefield.

Roth, M. D., and L. Galis. 1970. *Knowing: Essays in the Analysis of Knowledge*. New York: Random House.

Shope, R. K. 1983. *The Analysis of Knowing*. Princeton: Princeton University Press.

Sosa, E. 1969. "Propositional Knowledge." *Philosophical Studies* 20: 33–43

Stine, G. 1976. "Skepticism, Relevant Alternatives, and Deductive Closure." *Philosophical Studies* 29: 249–61, and this volume.

Chapter 4

Alston, W. 1976. "Has Foundationalism Been Refuted?" *Philosophical Studies* 29:287–305.

———. 1989. *Epistemic Justification*. Ithaca: Cornell University Press.

Annis, D. 1978. *American Philosophical Quarterly* 15:213–19.

Audi, R. 1993. *The Structure of Justification*. Cambridge: Cambridge University Press.

Bender, J., ed. 1989. *The Current State of the Coherence Theory*. Boston: Kluwer.

BonJour, L. 1985. *The Structure of Empirical Knowledge*. Cambridge, Mass.: Harvard University Press.

———. 1999. "The Dialectic of Foundationalism and Coherentism." In edited by J. Greco and E. Sosa, 117–42. *The Blackwell Guide to Epistemology*, Oxford: Blackwell Publishers Inc.

Bosanquet, B. 1920. *Implication and Linear Inference*. London: Macmillan.

Chisholm, R. 1966. *Theory of Knowledge*. Englewood Cliffs, N.J.: Prentice-Hall.

———. 1982. *The Foundations of Knowing*. Minneapolis: University of Minnesota Press.

Cohen, S. 1988. "How to be a Fallibilist." *Philosophical Perspectives* 2:581–605.

———. 1998. "Contextualist Solutions to Epistemological Problems: Scepticism, Gettier, and the Lottery." *Australasian Journal of Philosophy* 76:289–306.

DeRose, K. 1995. "Solving the Skeptical Problem." *The Philosophical Review* 104:1–52.

Descartes, R. 1641. *Meditations*. In., *The Philosophical Writings of Descartes*, trans. J. Cottingham et al. Cambridge: Cambridge University Press, 1984.

Feldman, R. and E. Conee. 1985. "Evidentialism." *Philosophical Studies* 48:15–34.

———. 1985. "Evidentialism." *Philosophical Studies* 48:15–34. Revised version in this volume.

Foley, R. 1987. *The Theory of Epistemic Rationality*. Cambridge: Harvard University Press.

———2003. "Epistemic Rationality as Invulnerability to Self-Criticism." This volume. Haack, S. 1993. *Evidence and Inquiry*. Oxford: Blackwell.

———1999. "Evidentialism." In *The Theory of Knowledge*, edited by L. Pojman, 283–93. Belmont, Calif. Wadsworth.

Goldman, A. (1976) "What Is Justified Belief?" In *Justification and Knowledge*, edited by G. S. Pappas, 1–23 Dordrecht: D. Reidel.

Greco, J. 1993. "Virtues and Vices of Virtue Epistemology." *Canadian Journal of Philosophy* 23.

———2003. "Virtues in Epistemology." This volume.

Harman, G. 1986 *Change In View*. Cambridge, Mass. MIT Press.

———2003. "Skepticism and Foundations." In *The Skeptics*, edited by S. Luper. Ashgate Press.

Lewis, D. 1979. "Scorekeeping in a Language Game." *Journal of Philosophical Logic* 8: 339–59.

———1996. "Elusive Knowledge." *Australasian Journal of Philosophy* 74:549–67.

Luper(-Foy), S. 1990. "Arbitrary Reasons." In *Doubting*, edited by M. Roth and G. Ross Dordrecht: Kluwer Academic Publishers.

Pappas, G, ed. 1979. *Justification and Knowledge*. Dordrecht: Kluwer Academic Publishers.

Peirce, C. 1877. "The Fixation of Belief." *Popular Science Monthly*. D. Appleton and Company, November, 1877.

Plantinga, A. 1993. *Warrant and Proper Function*. Oxford: Oxford University Press.

Quinton, A.M. 1973. *The Nature of Things*. London: Routledge & Kegan Paul.

Sellars, W. 1963. *Science, Perception and Reality*. London: Routledge & Kegan Paul.

———1973. "Givenness and Explanatory Coherence." *Journal of Philosophy* 70:612–24.

Sosa, E. 1991. "Intellectual Virtue in Perspective." In *Knowledge in Perspective: Collected Essays in Epistemology*. Cambridge: Cambridge University Press.

Wittgenstein, L. 1969. *On Certainty*, trans. G.E.M. Anscombe and G.H. von Wright, New York: Harper Torchbooks.

Zagzebski, L. 1996. *Virtues of the Mind*. Cambridge: Cambridge University Press.

Chapter 5

Block, I., ed. 1981. *Perspectives on the Philosophy of Wittgenstein*. Oxford: Blackwell.

Carnap, R. 1950. "Empiricism, Semantics, and Ontology." *Revue Internationale de Philosophie* 4: 20–40.

Clay, M. and Lehrer, K. eds. 1989. *Knowledge and Skepticism*. Boulder: Westview Press.

Coffa, J.A. 1991. *The Semantic Tradition from Kant to Carnap: To the Vienna Station*. Cambridge: Cambridge University Press.

DeRose, K. and Warfield, T., eds. 1999. *Skepticism: A Contemporary Reader*. Oxford: Oxford University Press.

Frege, G. 1879. "Begriffschrift." In *Translations from the Philosophical Writings of Gotlob Frege*, eds. P. Geach and M. Black. Oxford: Oxford University Press, 1952.

———. 1884. Austin, J. L. trans. *The Foundations of Mathematics*, trans. J. L. Austin. Oxford: Blackwell, 1950.

Fumerton, R. 1995. *Metaepistemology and Skepticism*. Lanham, Mass. Rowman & Littlefield.

Klein, P. 1981. *Certainty: A Refutation of Scepticism*. Minneapolis: University of Minnesota Press.

———. 2000. "Why Not Infinitism?" In *Epistemology: Proceedings of the Twentieth World Congress in Philosophy* 5, ed. R. Cobb-Stevens: 199–208.

———. 2003. "How a Pyrrhonian Skeptic Might Respond to Academic Skepticism." In *The Skeptics: Contemporary Essays*, ed. S. Luper. Aldershot: Ashgate Press.

Lewis, D. 1979. "Scorekeeping in a Language Game." *Journal of Philosophical Logic* 8: 339–59.

Luper(-Foy), S. 1984. "The Epistemic Predicament." *Australasian Journal of Philosophy* 62: 26–48.

———. 1987a. The Causal Indicator Analysis of Knowledge." *Philosophy and Phenomenological Research* 47: 563–587.

———, ed. 1987b. *The Possibility of Knowledge: Nozick and His Critics*. Totowa, N.J.: Rowman and Littlefield.

———. 2003. "Indiscernability Skepticism." In *The Skeptics*, ed. S. Luper. Aldershot: Ashgate Press, and this volume.

Malcolm, N. 1949. "Defending Common Sense." *The Philosophical Review*.

———. 1963. *Knowledge and Certainty*. Englewood Cliffs, N.J.: Prentice-Hall.

———. 1977. *Thought and Knowledge*. Ithaca, N.Y.: Cornell University Press.

Nozick, R. 1981. *Philosophical Explanations*. Cambridge, Mass.: Harvard University Press.

Moore, G. E. 1958. *Philosophical Studies*. London: Kegan Paul.

———. 1959. *Philosophical Papers*. London: George Allen & Unwin, Ltd.

Pitcher, G., ed. 1967. *Wittgenstein*. London: Macmillan.

Putnam, H. 1981. *Reason, Truth and History*. Cambridge: Cambridge University Press.

Roth, M. D., and Ross, G, eds. 1990. *Doubting*. Dordrecht: Kluwer Academic Publishers.

Russell, B. 1910–13, with Whitehead, A. N. *Principia Mathematica*. 3 Volumes. Cambridge: Cambridge University Press.

———. 1919. *Introduction to Mathematical Philosophy*. London: G. Allen & Unwin, Ltd.

Schilpp, P.A., ed. 1942. *The Philosophy of G.E. Moore*. La Salle, Ill: Open Court Press.

———. 1963. *The Philosophy of Rudolf Carnap*. La Salle, Ill: Open Court Press.

Sosa, E. 1999. "How to Defeat Opposition to Moore." *Philosophical Perspectives* 13: 141–152.

———. 2003. "Neither Contextualism Nor Skepticism." In *The Skeptics*, ed. S. Luper. Aldershot: Ashgate Publishing, 2003.

Stine, G. 1976. "Skepticism, Relevant Alternatives, and Deductive Closure." *Philosophical Studies* 29: 249–61, and this volume.

Strawson, P.F. 1985. *Skepticism and Naturalism: Some Varieties*. London: Methuen.

Stroud, B. 1984. *The Significance of Philosophical Skepticism*. Oxford: Clarendon Press.

Unger, P. 1974. "An Argument for Skepticism." In *Philosophical Exchange* 1.

———. 1975. *Ignorance: A Case for Scepticism*. Oxford: Clarendon Press.

Williams, M. 1991. *Unnatural Doubts*. Oxford: Blackwell Publishers.

———. 1999. "Skepticism." In *The Blackwell Guide to Epistemology*, eds. J. Greco E. Sosa, 35–70. Oxford: Blackwell Publishers Ltd.

Wittgenstein, L. 1921. *Tractatus Logico-Philosophicus* trans. D.F. Pears and B.F. MacGuinness. London: Routledge & Kegan Paul, 1961.

———. 1969. *On Certainty*. Oxford: Oxford University Press.

Chapter 6

Alston, W. 1989. *Epistemic Justification*. Ithaca, N.Y.: Cornell University.

Armstrong, D. M. 1973. *Belief, Truth, and Knowledge*. Cambridge: Cambridge University Press.

BonJour, L. 2002. "Internalism and Externalism." In *Epistemology: Classic Problems and Contemporary Responses*, pgs. 221–38. Lanham: Rowman & Littlefield Publishers, Inc.

Conee, E., and Feldman, R. 1998. "The Generality Problem for Reliabilism." *Philosophical Studies* 89.

——— 2001. "Internalism Defended." H. Kornblith, ed. *Epistemology Internalism and Externalism*. Blackwell: 231–260.

Feldman, R. 1985. "Reliability and Justification." *Monist* 68: 235–56.

Fumerton, R. 1990. "The Internalism/Externalism Controversy." In *Philosophical Perspectives* 2: 43–60.

Kornblith, H. 1988. "How Internal Can You Get?" *Synthese* 74:313–27.

Lehrer, K. 1990. *Theory of Knowledge*. Boulder, CO: Westview Press.

McDowell, J. 1995. "Knowledge and the Internal." *Philosophy and Phenomenological Research* 55: 877–93.

Sosa, E. 1991. *Knowledge in Perspective*. Cambridge: Cambridge University Press.

Chapter 7

Barrett, R. and R. Gibson, eds. 1990. *Perspectives on Quine*. Oxford: Blackwell Publishers.

Goldman, A. 1985. *Epistemology and Cognition*. Cambridge, Mass.: Harvard University Press.

———. 1992. *Liaisons: Philosophy Meets the Cognitive and Social Sciences*. Cambridge, Mass.: MIT Press.

Hookway, C. 1988. *Quine*. Cambridge: Polity Press.

Kitcher, P. 1992. "The Naturalists Return." *Philosophical Review* 101: 53–114.

Kim, I. 1988 "What Is Naturalized Epistemology?" *Philosophical Perspectives* 2: 381–405. Reprinted in this volume.

Kornblith, H. 1985. *Naturalizing Epistemology*. Cambridge, Mass.: MIT Press.

———. 1993. *Inductive Inference and its Natural Ground: An Essay in Naturalized Epistemology*. Cambridge, Mass.: MIT Press.

Kornblith, H. 1995, "Naturalistic Epistemology and its critics "*Philosophical Topics* 23: 237–255. Reprinted in this volume.

Quine, W.V.O. 1969. "Epistemology Naturalized." *Ontological Relativity and Other* Essays. New York: Columbia University Press. Also reprinted in this volume.

Quine, W.V.O. 1975. "The Nature of Natural Knowledge." In *Mind and Language*, ed. S. Guttenplan. Oxford: The Clarendon Press.

———. 1992. *Pursuit of Truth*. Cambridge, Mass.: Harvard University Press.

Romanos, G. 1983. *Quine and Analytic Philosophy*. Cambridge, Mass.: MIT Press.

Siegel, H. 1984. "Empirical Psychology, Naturalized Epistemology, and First Philosophy." *Philosophy of Science* 51: 667–76.

Sosa, E. 1991. "Nature Unmirrored, Epistemology Naturalized." In *Knowledge in Perspective*, 86–107. Cambridge: Cambridge University Press.

Stroud, B. 1981. "The Significance of Naturalized Epistemology." *Midwest Studies in Philosophy* 6: 455–71.

Chapter 8

Bealer, G. 1999. "The A Priori." In *The Blackwell Guide to Epistemology*. ed. J. Greco and E. Sosa, 243–70. Oxford: Blackwell Publishers Ltd.

Benacerraf, P., and H. Putnam. 1983. *Philosophy of Mathematics: Selected Readings*. Cambridge: Cambridge University Apress.

Boghossian, P., and C. Peacocke. 2000. *New Essays on the A Priori*. Oxford: Oxford University Press.

BonJour, L. 1997. *In Defense of Pure Reason: A Rationalist Account of A Priori Justification*. Cambridge: Cambridge University Press.

Chisholm, R.M. 1977. "The Truths of Reason." In *Theory of Knowledge*, 34–61. Englewood Cliffs, N.J.: Prentice-Hall.

Carruthers, P. 1992. *Human Knowledge and Human Nature*. Oxford: Oxford University Press.

Ewing, A.C. 1939. "The Linguistic Theory of A Priori Propositions." *Proceedings of the Aristotelian Society* 40:221–30.

Frege, G. (1892). "On Sense and Reference." *Zeitschrift fur Philosophie und Philosophische Kritik* 100:25–50. Reprinted in *Translations from the Philosophical Writings of Gottlob Frege*, P. Geach and M. Black, trans., 56–78. Oxford: Basil Blackwell, 1977.

Hanson, P., and B. Hunter. 1992. *Return of the A Priori*. Calgary: University of Calgary Press.

Kant, I. 1781. *Critique of Pure Reason*, trans. N. Kemp Smith. London: Macmillan, 1963.

Kitcher, P. 1983. *The Nature of Mathematical Knowledge*. Oxford: Oxford University Press.

Kripke, S. 1972. "Naming and Necessity." In *Semantics of Natural Language*, ed. D. Davidson and G. Harman. Dordrecht: Reidel. Reprinted as *Naming and Necessity*. Cambridge, Mass.: Harvard University Press, 1980.

Moser, P., ed. 1987. *A Priori Knowledge*. Oxford: Oxford University Press.

Pap, A. 1958. *Semantics and Necessary Truth*. New Haven: Yale University Press.

Russell, B. 1956. "On Denoting." In *Logic and Knowledge*, ed. R. C. Marsh, 41–56. London: Allen & Unwin.

Quine, W.V.O. 1969. "Epistemology Naturalized." In *Ontological Relativity and Other Essays*, 69–90. New York: Columbia University Press.

———. 1976. "Truth by Convention." In *The Ways of Paradox and Other Essays*. Cambridge, Mass.: Harvard University Press.

Sleigh, R.C., ed. 1972. *Necessary Truth*. Englewood Cliffs, N.J.: Prentice-Hall.

Chapter 9

Antony, L., and C. Witt. C 1993. *A Mind of One's Own: Feminist Essays on Reason and Objectivity*. Boulder: Westview Press.

Bloor, D. 1976. *Knowledge and Social Imagery*. Boston: Routledge Direct Editions.

Brown, H. 1977. "For a Modest Historian." *The Monist* 60:540–555.

Burnyeat, M.F. 1976. "Protagoras and Self-Refutation in Later Greek Philosophy." *Philosophical Review* 85:44–69.

Code, L. 1988. "Experience, Knowledge, and Responsibility." In *Feminist Perspectives in Philosophy*, Griffiths eds M.,

and M. Whitford, 187–204. Bloomington,: Indiana University Press,

———. 1989. "The Impact of Feminism on Epistemology." *APA Newsletter on Feminism and Philosophy* 88: 25–29.

Elgin, C. 1996. *Considered Judgment*. Princeton: Princeton University Press.

Field, H. 1982. "Realism and Relativism." *Journal of Philosophy* 79:553–67.

Garry, A., and M. Pearsall, eds. 1989. *Women, Knowledge, and Reality: Explorations in Feminist Philosophy*. Boston: Unwin Hyman.

Goodman, N. 1978. *Ways of Worldmaking*. Indianapolis: Hackett Publishing Co.

Griffiths, M., and M. Whitford. 1988. *Feminist Perspectives in Philosophy*. Bloomington, IN: Indiana University Press.

Krausz, M., and J. Meiland, eds. 1982. *Relativism: Cognitive and Moral*. Notre Dame: University of Notre Dame Press.

Kuhn, T. 1970. *The Structure of Scientific Revolutions*. Chicago: University of Chicago Press.

Lloyd, G. 1979. "The Man of Reason." *Metaphilosophy* 10: 18–37.

Longino, H. 1987. "Can There be a Feminist Science?" *Hypatia* 2:51–64.

———. 1999. "Feminist Epistemology." In *The Blackwell Guide to Epistemology* Greco eds. J. and E. Sosa, 327–53. Oxford: Blackwell Publishers Ltd.

Mandelbaum, M. 1979. "Subjective, Objective, and Conceptual Relativisms." *The Monist* 62:403–28.

Meiland, J. 1977. "Concepts of Relative Truth." *The Monist* 60:568–82.

———. 1979. "Is Protagorean Relativism Self-Refuting?" *Grazer Philosophische Studien* 9:51–68.

Mill, J. S. 1869. *The Subjection of Women*. In *Three Essays*. Oxford: Oxford University Press, 1975.

Moser, P. 1993. *Philosophy After Objectivity*. Oxford: Oxford University Press.

Putnam, H. 1979. "Reflections of Goodman's *Ways of Worldmaking*." *Journal of Philosophy* 76:603–18.

Rorty, R. 1989. *Contingency, Irony, and Solidarity*. Cambridge: Cambridge University Press.

———. 1990. "Putnam and the Relativist Menace." *Journal of Philosophy* 90:443–61.

———. 1991. *Objectivity, Relativism, and Truth*. Cambridge: Cambridge University Press.

Scheffler, I. 1967. *Science and Subjectivity*. New York: Bobbs-Merrill.

Siegel, H. 1980. "Epistemological Relativism in Its Latest Form." *Inquiry* 23:107–17.

———. 1987. *Relativism Refuted: A Critique of Contemporary Epistemological Relativism*. Dordrecht: Reidel.

Williams, M. 1991. *Unnatural Doubts*. Oxford: Blackwell Publishers.

Wollstonecraft. 1792. *A Vindication of the Rights of Woman*.

✦ CREDITS ✦

Selection Credits (by selection number): **1.** From Plato, "Meno" in Jowett, B., trans., *The Dialogues of Plato* 1 (1900): 254–262. **2.** From Plato, "On Knowledge" in Davies, John and Vaughan, David, trans., *The Republic of Plato*. (1900). **3.** From Plato, "Theaetetus." In Edith Hamilton and Huntington Cairns, eds., *The Collected Dialogues of Plato, Including the Letters* copyright © 1961 renewed 1989 by Princeton University Press. Reprinted by permission of the Princeton University Press. **4.** From *Scepticism, Man, and God: Selections from the Major Writings of Sextus Empiricus*, © 1964 by Philip P. Hallie and reprinted by permission of Wesleyan University Press. **5.** From Rene Descartes, "Meditations on the First Philosophy." In Veitch, John trans., *The Meditations and Selections from the Principles of Rene Descartes*. (1950): 21–74. **6.** From John Locke, *An Essay Concerning Human Understanding*. (1690). **7.** From George Berkeley, *A Treatise Concerning the Principles of Human Knowledge*. (1710). **8.** *Inquiry Concerning Human Understanding: With a Supplement and Abstract of a Treatise of Human Nature* by Hendel, © 1955: 26–77. Reprinted by permission of Pearson Education, Inc., Upper Saddle River, NJ. **9.** From Immanuel Kant, *Prolegomena and Metaphysical Foundations of Natural Science*. Bax, Ernest trans., (1883): 1–36. **10.** From Charles Peirce, "The Fixation of Belief." And "How to Make Our Ideas Clear." In *The Popular Science Monthly* (November 1877): © 1878 D. Appleton and Co. **11.** Edmund Gettier, "Is Justified True Belief Knowledge?" *Analysis* 23.6 (June 1963): 121–127. **12.** Gilbert Harman, "Knowledge, Inference, and Explanation." *American Philosophical Quarterly* 5.3 (1968): 164–173. **13.** Alvin Goldman, "A Causal Theory of Knowing." *Journal of Philosophy* LXIV 12 (1967): 357–372. Reprinted with permission of the author and the *Journal of Philosophy*. **14.** Peter Klein, "Knowledge is True, Non-Defeated, Justified Belief." (2003, Essay written for this volume). **15.** Reprinted by permission of the publisher from "Philosophical Explanations" by Robert Nozick, pp. 172–178, Cambridge, Mass.: The Belknap Press of Harvard University Press, copyright © 1981 by Robert Nozick. **16.** Laurence BonJour, "Foundationalism and Coherentism." *Epistemology* (2002): 193–219. Laurence BonJour is Professor of Philosophy at the University of Washington. **17.** © 1997 Susan Haack. This paper first appeared in *Theory of Knowledge: Classic and Contemporary Sources*, ed. Pojman, Louis, Wadsworth, Belmont, CA, second edition, 1998, 283–93; reprinted in *Epistemology: An Anthology*, eds. Sosa, Ernest, and Jaegwon Kim, Blackwell, Oxford, 2000, 226–36, and in *The Epistemology Reader*, ed. Huemer, Michael, ed., Routledge, New York, 2002; translated into Spanish in *Agora*, 18.1, 1999, 35–53, and into French in Carrefour, October 2001. **18.** From Gilbert Harmon, "Positive vs. Negative Undermining" and "Implicit Commitments." In *Change in View: Principles of Reasoning*. © 1968 by The Massachusetts Institute of Technology Press: pps. 29–48. Reprinted with the permission of the publisher. **19.** Alvin Goldman, "What Is Justified Belief?" in *Justification and Knowledge* by George S. Pappas (Kluwer Academic Publishers 1979); 1–23. With kind permission from Kluwer Academic Publishers. **20.** Richard Feldman and Earl Conee, "Evidentialism." *Philosophical Studies* 89 (1998): 1–29. **21.** Stewart Cohen, "Contextualism." (2003, Essay written for this volume). **22.** From *Handbook of Epistemology*, edited by Paul Moser, copyright by Oxford University Press. Used by permission of Oxford University Press, Inc. **23.** From George Edward Moore, "Proof of an External World." In *Philosophical Papers* © 1959: 127–150. Reprinted with the permission of the Oxford University Press. **24.** Rudolph Carnap, "Empiricism, Semantics, and Ontology." *Revue Internationale de philosophie* (1950): 20–40. **25.** Wittgenstein, Ludwig *On Certainty* (1969) G.E.M. Anscombe and G.H. Von Wright., eds., Denis, Paul and G.E.M. Anscombe, trans., Harper & Row. **26.** Fred Dretske, "Skepticism: What Perception Teaches." *The Skeptics*, (Ashgate Publishing, October 2002). **27.** G.C. Stine, "Skepticism, Relevant Alternatives, and Deductive Closure." *Philosophical Studies* 29 (Kluwer Academic Publishers 1976): 249–261. Reprinted with kind permission from Kluwer Academic Publishers. **28.** Lewis, David "Elusive Knowledge," from the *Australian Journal of Philosophy* 47.4 (1996): 549–567. Reprinted with the permission of the Oxford University Press. **29.** From Steven Luper, "Indiscernability Skepticism." *The Skeptics* (2003) Luper, S. ed. Aldershot, UK: Ashgate Publishing. Reprinted with permission from the author. **30.** Peter Klein, "There is No Good Reason to be An Academic Skeptic." (2003, Essay written for this volume). **31.** D.M. Armstrong, "The Infinite Regress of Reasons." from *Belief Truth and Knowledge* (1973): 152–161. Reprinted with the permission of Cambridge University Press. **32.** Laurence BonJour, "Can Empirical Knowledge Have a Foundation?" *American Philosophical Quarterly* 15.1 (January 1978): 1–8. Laurence BonJour is Professor of Philosophy at the University of Washington. **33.** Ernest Sosa, "Reflective Knowledge in the Best Circles." *Journal of Philosophy* XCIV .8 (August 1997): 410–430. This paper is reprinted with the permission of the author and the *Journal of Philosophy*. **34.** Alvin I. Goldman, "Internalism Exposed." *Journal of Philosophy* XCVI .6 (June 1999): 271–293. **35.** From *Ontological Relativity & Other Essays* by/ed. W.V.O. Quine © 1982 Columbia University Press. Reprinted with the permission of the publisher. **36.** "What is "Naturalized Epistemology"?" by Jaegwon Kim appeared in *Philosophical Perspectives, 2, Epistemology, 1988* edited by James E. Tomberlin (copyright by Ridgeview Publishing Co., Atascadero, CA). Reprinted by permission of Ridgeview Publishing Company. **37.** Hilary Putnam, "Why Reason Can't Be Naturalized." *Philosophical Papers, Realism and Reason* 3 (1983): 229–247. Reprinted with the permission of Cambridge University Press. **38.** Hilary Kornblith, "Naturalistic Epistemology & Its Critics." *Philosophical Topics* 232.1 (1995): 237–255. **39.** Clarence I. Lewis, "A Pragmatic Conception of the A Priori." *Journal of Philosophy* XX .7 (March 29, 1923): 169–77. **40.** Laurence BonJour, "Toward a Moderate Rationalism." *Philosophical Topics* 23.1 (Spring 1995): 47–78. Laurence BonJour is Professor of Philosophy at the University of Washington. **41.** Reprinted by permission of the publisher from "Two Dogmas of Empiricism." In *From a Logical Point of View: Nine Logico-Philosophical Essays* by Willard V. Quine, pp. 20–46, Cambridge, Mass.: Harvard University Press, Copyright © 1953, 1961, 1980 by the President and Fellows of Harvard College, renewed 1989 by W.V. Quine. **42.** Reprinted by permission of the publisher from *Naming and Necessity* by Saul A. Kripke, Cambridge, Mass.: Harvard University Press, Copyright © 1972, 1980 by Saul A. Kripke. **43.** Harvey Siegel, "The Incoherence Argument and the Notion of Relative Truth." *Relativism Refuted* (Kluwer Academic Publishers, August 1987): 3–28. Reprinted with the kind permission of Kluwer Academic Publishers. **44.** Richard Foley, "Epistemically Rational Belief as Invulnerability to Self-Criticism." (2003, Essay written for this volume). **45.** Richard Rorty, "Science and Solidarity." In Nelson, John S. et al., eds. *The Rhetoric of the Human Sciences* © 1987: 38–52. Reprinted by permission of The University of Wisconsin Press. **46.** From *A Mind of One's Own: Feminist Essays on Reason and Objectivity* by Louise Antony and Charlotte Witt. Copyright © 1992 by Westview Press. Reprinted by permission of Westview Press, a member of Perseus Books, L.L.C.